D1598722

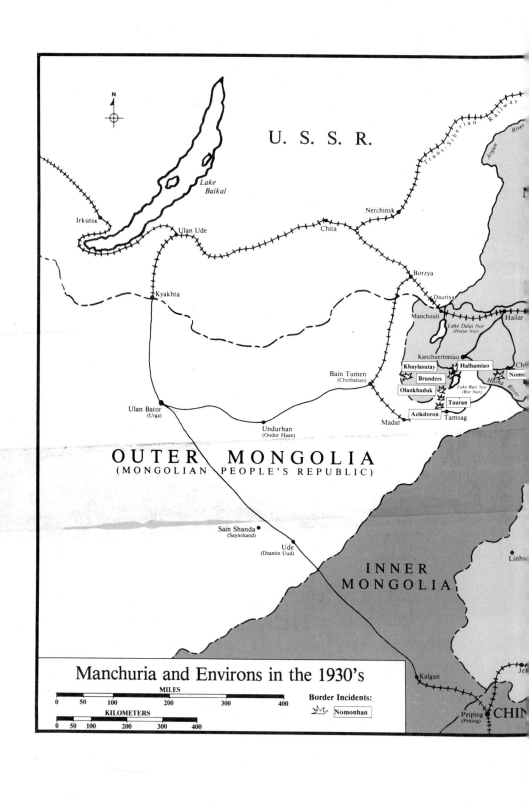

Manchuria and Environs in the 1930's

Nomonhan

Alvin D. Coox

NOMONHAN
Japan Against Russia, 1939

Stanford University Press, Stanford, California

Stanford University Press, Stanford, California
© 1985 by the Board of Trustees of the Leland Stanford Junior University
Printed in the United States of America
First paperback printing, two volumes combined, 1990
Last figure below indicates year of this printing:
99   98

CIP data appear at the end of the book

The epigraph to Chapter 37 is taken from "Spain 1937" by W. H. Auden, in *The English Auden: Poems, Essays and Dramatic Writings, 1927-1939*, edited by Edward Mendelson (New York: Random House, 1977), and appears by permission of the publisher.

Published with the assistance of The Japan Foundation

Cartography by Dana Lombardy, with graphic assistance from Bruce Weigle and Judy Tart

Contents

Tables, Maps, and Appendixes

Appendixes

Preface

I have been studying the Kwantung Army and working with its survivors for so long—almost 35 years—that I sometimes feel as if I served in Manchuria and fought at Nomonhan. I well remember how, in the spring and summer of 1939, my curiosity was gripped by short newspaper accounts of an undeclared war that was raging between the Japanese and Soviet armies on a desolate stretch of disputed frontier lying between the client states of Manchukuo and Outer Mongolia. It was impossible, however, to trace the origins of the clash at Nomonhan, to follow its course, or to pick winners or losers, for, as Professor Buss wryly noted soon aferwards, "neither Russian nor Japanese dispatches had any except perhaps an accidental relation with the truth."[1] And nothing constructive was contributed by the few Western observers who tried to make sense of the scant information available. One ostensible expert on the Far East wove a particularly confusing account. The Nomonhan Incident, he said, "began as the 'insincere cavalry practice' on the part of the Russian Army. A group of twenty Mongolian ponies came across the border. They were repulsed by two divisions of Japanese troops. The Russians had been hiding something in the Urals. They brought out a few more troops and it was a real massacre. That is why the Japs have to keep half a million men up there."[2]

After the outbreak of hostilities in Europe in September 1939, the affair at Nomonhan was overshadowed by the events of the Second World War. One wondered whether the true story would ever be uncovered. Whatever basis for optimism existed after the capitulation of Japan in 1945 and the creation of the International Military Tribunal for the Far East in Tokyo was soon dissipated. The Soviet prosecutors concentrated on charges of Japanese conspiracy and aggression and mainly wrangled over the cartography of the Halha River sector.[3] Defense counsel retorted that Nomonhan was simply a frontier affray; "it was not aggression, not a war," and it was "settled and closed" by bilateral agreement. "Despite the size of the forces involved on both sides, [Nomonhan] was typical of the border incidents which have occurred not only along the Soviet-Mongolian and Manchukuoan borders but along the borders of any two states suspicious of each other when the troops of two nations are brought too close together. Such clashes have occurred along disputed borders or borders along which armed troops of adjacent countries are stationed since time immemorial on every continent."[4]

The proceedings of the trial and conviction of Japanese "A" class defendants for complicity in the events of 1939 did little to enlarge our historical knowledge of the Nomonhan Incident.[5] When I went to Japan during the postwar Occupation, I retained my interest in the Kwantung Army and Nomonhan. So, even before the Japan Defense Agency's Office of Military History (Senshi Shitsu) was formally established in 1955 and started collecting materials on the Pacific War, I had already commenced my own researches on the Kwantung Army. My initial monograph, centering on the end of the war in Manchuria and based upon Japanese sources, was written in 1951.[6] In 1954, I conducted my first important private interview with a former IJA general officer.[7]

I hoped for a breakthrough in 1955 when I joined the Japanese Research Division (JRD), the Tokyo agency of the U.S. Army's Office of the Chief of Military History. From the Historical Records Branch of the Japanese Repatriation Relief Bureau, I received for editing a number of original manuscripts authored after the war and dealing briefly with Soviet-Japanese border problems and clashes of the 1930's and 1940's. Drawing on collateral data, by 1956 I prepared five anonymous, unclassified monographs in English, subsequently distributed by the U.S. Department of the Army in Washington. The expanded portion on Nomonhan alone grew to such proportions that it become necessary to issue two separate volumes.[8] Although these monographs represented the largest, most authoritative treatment in English and came to be relied upon by many historians in the years that followed, I realized that they contained errors and gaps. Therefore, I determined to prepare my own definitive study of Nomonhan one day.

Thanks to postdoctoral research grants from the Rockefeller Foundation, I traversed Japan between 1960 and 1964, tracking down veterans. Approximately 175 Japanese granted me interviews or corresponded with me, then and afterwards, and another 50 individuals assisted me in other ways. During my field work, I was able to collect unpublished primary materials, including diaries, letters, journals, albums, photographs, sketches, maps, and notes, as well as memoirs and official records only recently made available.[9]

My long journey into the annals of the Kwantung Army closely parallels developments in postwar Japanese history. Until the repatriation of the last IJA survivors of Siberian prison camps around 1956, Japanese were disinclined, with few exceptions, to speak openly about the Soviet Union in general and the Nomonhan Incident in particular. Even in literature, allusions to Nomonhan were fleeting, as in Tsuboi Sakae's widely read *Nijūshi no hitomi* (*Twenty-four Eyes*) of 1952.[10] Gradually, interest began to stir openly in Japan. For example, in 1966 a notice appeared in the *Tokyo Asahi* appealing to survivors and families of a heavy artillery brigade's transport unit that served at Nomonhan to contact a certain veteran in Tokyo; "we are going to conduct worship services and hold a reunion."[11] In 1969, the same national daily newspaper carried word that the Nomonhan-kai (Nomonhan Society) had been formed and that the old soldiers were meeting regularly. The coordinator in Yokohama wanted to hear from "comrades and the families of those who took part in the severe fighting at Nomonhan; comrades of the 64th Infantry Regiment stationed in Hailar who participated in the battles; families; and anybody who knows about them."[12] Former Col. Sumi Shin'ichirō was especially vigorous in rallying survivors and commemorating his 26th Regiment from Asahigawa.[13]

As word of my far-flung researches spread in Japan, on four occasions the Nomonhan-kai's journal notified its readership of my work and my interest, starting with an acknowledgment by Lt. Gen. Koga Takeshi.[14] Recently, Tamada Yoshio, the colonel commanding the 4th Tank Regiment at Nomonhan, recalled in his published memoirs that I once traveled to far-off Itoigawa to interview him.[15]

Meanwhile, during the period that the present book was reaching fruition, the subject of Nomonhan had been attracting wider attention in Japan, betokened by the publication of many new and interesting works,[16] and by the reprinting of several classics.[17] The year 1969 was particularly memorable, for it was then that Senshi Shitsu finally brought out the official history, written by Nishihara Yukio, treating the Nomonhan Incident in authentic detail.[18] The discovery in 1979 of an unpublished diary by an IJA second lieutenant from the 71st Regiment who died at Nomonhan received national publicity in the Japanese press and on television.[19]

The new interest in Nomonhan has even extended to America, where the U.S. Army's Command and General Staff College, expressing interest in small-unit tactical combat wherever encountered, around 1980 commissioned a detailed historical study of one IJA infantry battalion's battle experience—Kajikawa's 2nd Battalion of the 28th Infantry Regiment, whose after-action report of 1939 was available in Japanese.[20] Regrettably, however, a certain amount of flawed history infests the literature on Nomonhan. For instance, Prof. Ienaga Saburō, long at the center of controversy for his legal suits against the Japanese Education Ministry because of alleged censorship of his textbooks, claims that until two years before the appearance of one of his books in 1968, the Japanese government continued to hush up the data on total IJA battle deaths at Nomonhan. This misstatement, which is refuted in Chapter 39 of the present study, has received more than usual dissemination by appearing in the 1978 English translation of Ienaga's volume.[21]

In my book, after sketching the early history of the Kwantung Army and the South Manchuria Railway conglomerate through the assassination of Marshal Chang Tso-lin in 1928, I examine the coming of the Manchurian Incident, the skulduggery of the IJA officers in Mukden, and the creation of the fiction of Manchukuo. Next, I discuss Japan's "Northern problem" and the occurrence of border affrays along the extensive Manchurian and North Korean borders until the eruption of the Changkufeng Incident in 1938. The core of the book deals with the most dangerous interwar Japanese-Soviet confrontation of all—the Nomonhan Incident—and starts with the reasons for the outbreak of trouble on the west Manchurian frontier in 1939, the political and military dynamics of Choibalsan's Mongolian People's Republic and the nature of its relationship with its Soviet Russian protectors, the Kwantung Army's issuance of tough and controversial border guidelines in April 1939, the deployment of a green and untried IJA division—Komatsubara's 23rd—to the Hailar sector, and the first skirmishing along the disputed Halha River in May 1939. Once the Azuma reconnaissance unit was ambushed and destroyed at the end of May, by a force made up mainly of Russians, escalation ensued on land and in the air. The Kwantung Army first unleashed the air force to conduct strikes (unauthorized by the High Command in Tokyo) against bases inside Outer Mongolia. Then the Japanese threw a puny bridge across the Halha and launched an infantry offensive into Mongolia at the beginning of July. Quickly driven back to the right shore by superior firepower and armor, the Japanese tried to clear the area of the Halha-Holsten confluence by committing a few undergunned tank formations and, after they were mauled fatally, by launching a series of night attacks based on foot soldiers. The IJA infantry made very costly progress but were pulled back in favor of a new offensive drawing primarily on reinforcements of heavy artillery and designed to neutralize the powerful enemy batteries emplaced on higher ground on the other side of the Halha. Jumping off on 23 July, this offensive failed too, whereupon the Kwantung Army drafted plans to last through the winter and resume operations after the spring thaw in 1940.

Zhukov and the Soviet command gave the Japanese no such leeway. Synchronizing their actions with fast-breaking developments in Europe, where the Second World War was about to explode, the Russians unleashed a powerful offensive on the Halha-Holsten front on 20 August, crushed counterattacks, and, by month's end, shattered the 23rd Division and its attached units and cleared the whole disputed border zone in their favor. Kwantung Army hopes of wreaking revenge or at least of retrieving the thousands of abandoned IJA corpses were thwarted by the worried authorities in Tokyo, who retired or reshuffled the command structure in Manchuria and, to a certain degree, at the AGS level. I close this portion of the book with an examination of the price and the punishment, the subsequent bilateral settlement of the boundary issue, and the military lessons and applications learned by both sides. A final chapter surveys the history of the Kwantung Army after Nomonhan, past the period of grand maneuvers and an unfought war against Russia in 1941–42, to the disintegration of the field army under Soviet hammer blows and the collapse of the empire of Manchukuo in August 1945. In my epilogue, I discuss the myth and the reality of the Kwantung Army, the fate of Manchukuo, and Nomonhan as a turning point in history in terms of the approaching Pacific War with the Western powers. I also offer a glimpse into the Soviet way of war, and caveats and lessons of relevance today. A comprehensive bibliography details my interviews and correspondence, and primary and secondary materials, unpublished and published, drawn from Japanese, Manchukuoan, Russian, Outer Mongolian, and Western sources.

Acknowledgments

I am grateful to the Rockefeller Foundation for postdoctoral research fellowships in the humanities that allowed me to initiate this project; to the San Diego State University Foundation for faculty research grants in aid that supported the cartography and facilitated currency in the literature; and to the Japan Foundation for professional fellowships that enabled me to complete my researches in the field.

It is both a responsibility and a pleasure to record my indebtedness to Japanese individuals and agencies that assisted and encouraged me through the years. Special thanks go to the recent Presidents of the National Defense College, Miyoshi Fumio and Itō Shingo, and to the four Directors of Military History since 1955: Nishiura Susumu and Shimanuki Takeharu in the era of Senshi Shitsu (the Office of Military History), and Toga Hiroshi and Koiwai Chisato since the formation of Senshibu (the Department of Military History) in 1976. Among their professional staff, I would particularly like to single out Nishihara Yukio, Iwashima Hisao, Kano Nobuyuki, Hatano Sumio, and Takahashi Hisashi; and from the archives and library corps, Baba Takashi, Matwatari Mitsuru, Koyama Kenji, and Saitō Teruo.

Other facilities at which I examined materials in Japan included the Foreign Ministry Diplomatic Archives (Gaikō Shiryōkan), where Kurihara Ken and Usui Katsumi were most helpful; the Japan Defense Agency Historical Office; the Ground Self-Defense Force Medical School; the National Diet Library; the National Film Center of Japan; the International House of Japan; and the research organizations once directed by Hattori Takushirō, Tomioka Sadatoshi, and Doi Akio. I also received the full cooperation of veterans' organizations and military alumni groups, including Nomonhankai, Gōyū Renmei, and Kaikōsha, the association of IJA military academy graduates, which honored me by enrollment as an associate member in 1984.

My military consultant since 1960 has been Imaoka Yutaka, ex-colonel, IJA; my closest academic colleague, Dr. Hata Ikuhiko. To the master list of respondents and associates, gratefully acknowledged in the Bibliography, section II, I want to add the names of others who were unusually helpful: Fujii Makoto, Hidaka Tsunetoshi, Kanō Sadahiko, Kōno Ichirō, Mitsui Shunji, and Tanibayashi Hiroshi.

In the United States, I received particular assistance with my researches from the National Archives and Records Service, and from the U.S. Army Military History Institute. The following individuals in Great Britain, Australia, Japan, and Finland, as well as the United States, provided valuable substantive information through interviews, correspondence, or consultations: Ben Bruce Blakeney, Paochin Chu, Lord and Lady Cobbold, Harry I. T. Creswell, John Erickson, George A. Furness, Owen Lattimore, Markku Melkko, Richard Storry, Michael Underdown, and Wu Ko-tei. Close friends and professional associates who contributed to my project in important ways included Charles Burton Fahs, Robert W. Hiatt, Chalmers Johnson, Arthur Marder, Maurice Schneps, Laurence H. Snyder, and Billie K. Walsh. Michael Parrish, who prepared the portion of the Bibliography dealing with Russian-language sources (section V), joins me in thanking those experts who provided historiographical and technical help. At the Word Graphics Center of San Diego State University, Gwendolyn Sayers began the typing, Dorothy Woodyard continued it, and Luis A. Molina conscientiously retyped the entire manuscript.

No author could ask for a more patient, compassionate, and empathetic publisher than J. G. Bell of Stanford University Press. Peter J. Kahn edited the manuscript with rare fortitude and good humor.

Lastly, I must record my special gratitude to my wife, Hisako, who held out like a samurai of old, without thought of defeat or surrender; and to my son, Roy, who says that the word "Nomonhan" was engraved in his memory ever since he was repeatedly called upon to vacate our Tokyo premises so that interviewing could proceed without juvenile interruption.

To each preceding person and organization, as well as to others unnamed, the present book owes whatever merits it may possess. Needless to say, responsibility for the opinions expressed and for sins of omission or commission is entirely my own.

San Diego   A. D. C.

A Note to the Reader

Japanese names follow the Japanese style, family name first. The system of transcription of Japanese is based on the fourth edition of *Kenkyūsha's New Japanese-English Dictionary*, ed. Masuda Koh (Tokyo: 1974). Macrons are provided throughout the text, notes, and bibliography except in well-known Japanese place names. Manchurian and Korean place names are generally rendered with traditional Chinese readings, which are more familiar in Western literature than Japanese readings or the new Chinese transliteration. Alternative readings, in parentheses, will be found in the case of Mongolian and certain Manchurian place names. All translations from the Japanese are by the author unless otherwise stated. Only initials are usually provided for Russian given names, in accordance with common usage. IJA weapon calibers are given in centimeters, and Russian references to their own calibers are given in millimeters, conforming to the practice in the two armies.

The list that follows gives the most frequently used abbreviations in the book. Only one requires a word of explanation, and that is my use of OSS for the IJA secret intelligence organization Tokumukikan. I have adopted OSS from the IJA service's resemblance to the U.S. wartime Office of Strategic Services.

AAA	Antiaircraft artillery	IMTFE	Int'l Military Tribunal for the Far East
AGS	Army General Staff		
AP	Armor-piercing (shells)	KIA	Killed in action
AT	Antitank	LMG	Light machine gun
BGU	Border garrison unit	MG	Machine gun
CG	Commanding general	MIA	Missing in action
CP	Command post	NCO	Noncommissioned officer
GPU	Secret police (USSR)	NGS	Navy General Staff
HE	High explosive (shells)	NKVD	People's Commissariat for Internal Affairs (USSR)
HFA	Heavy field artillery		
HMG	Heavy machine gun	OP	Observation post
HQ	Headquarters	OSS	IJA secret intelligence agency (Tokumukikan)
IG	Inspectorate general		
IGHQ	Imperial General HQ	S/O	Staff Officer
IGU	Independent garrison unit	WIA	Wounded in action
IJA	Imperial Japanese Army	WO	Warrant officer
IJN	Imperial Japanese Navy		

Nomonhan

VOLUME ONE

1

The Genesis of the Kwantung Army, 1905-29

Here in the hinterland of far Manchuria,
Hundreds of leagues from the homeland,
The setting sun reddens the stones
Beneath which our comrades lie.

—"Senyū" [Comrades], a military song
composed after the Russo-Japanese War

Manchuria is known in China as the Three Eastern Provinces: Heilung-kiang to the north, Kirin to the east, and Fengtien or Liaoning to the south. With an area estimated at 985,000 square kilometers, Manchuria is as large as all of Germany and France combined. To the southwest stands the Great Wall of China; to the west, Inner and Outer Mongolia; to the north and east, Russian Siberia; to the southeast, Korea (annexed by Japan in 1910); to the south, the Liaotung Peninsula and two arms of the Yellow Sea.

During the Russo-Japanese War of 1904-5, the Japanese army pushed as far north as Changchun and conquered all of South Manchuria, which had been occupied by Russian troops in force at the time of the Boxer Uprising of 1900 and had not been relinquished afterward. By the terms of the Treaty of Portsmouth, which ended the war in September 1905, the victorious Japanese ousted the Russians from South Manchuria and took from them the balance of the 25-year lease of the Liaotung area that the Chinese had yielded in 1898. Renamed the Kwantung Leased Territory, this Japanese-occupied strategic zone of 3,400 square kilometers at the southern tip of the peninsula commanded the seaward approaches to Tientsin and Peking and contained the great port of Dairen (Dalny or Talien) and the major fortress and ice-free naval base of Port Arthur (Lushun or Ryojun).[1]

Japan also acquired, by the Portsmouth settlement, the right to the Changchun–to–Port Arthur main portion of the rail network that the Russians had built to the south of the Chinese Eastern Railway (CER), their shortcut across Manchuria from Manchouli in the west to Vladivostok in the east. After obtaining the Chinese government's nominal consent to the new arrangements in December 1905 by the Treaty of Peking, the Japanese cabinet in June 1906 authorized the formation of a single corporate enterprise to be known as the South Manchuria Railway Joint Stock Company (Minami Manshū Tetsudō Kabushiki Kaisha, or Mantetsu). The organizing committee was headed by Gen. Kodama Gentarō, the chief of staff of the Japanese army during the Russo-Japanese War. When Kodama died soon afterward, Gen. Terauchi Masatake (Masakata), the war minister, replaced him. By April 1907 the quasigovernmental South Manchuria Railway (SMR) began full operation, taking over from the army's field railway corps. Count Gotō Shinpei, most recently governor of Formosa, became the first president of the SMR, now headquartered in Dairen. At the end of 1907 the railway company employed 9,000 Japanese and 4,000 Chinese.

The core of the SMR was the 700-km. trunk railroad extending south from Changchun to Dairen. Coal mines, warehouses, and electrical facilities along the right-of-way were also included, as were the 260-km. Mukden-to-Antung rail connection and four other spurs, bringing the total trackage to more than 1,100 kilometers. The extraterritorial strip encompassed by the SMR zone itself was no wider than 62 meters and only 250 square kilometers in area, but the main trunk and branch rail lines connected 25 towns.[2]

As a counterweight to Russian and Japanese encroachment in China's Northeast, in the late nineteenth century the authorities in Peking belatedly encouraged Chinese migration to Manchuria—a migration that was further stimulated by the railway-building projects which drew Chinese laborers and merchants. From an estimated three million in 1870, Manchuria's Chinese or assimilated Manchu population grew to nine million in 1906. The soil was some of the richest in the world, and soy and cereal crops dominated agricultural output. Unlike the rest of China, Manchuria consistently exported far more than it imported. Manchuria also possessed huge coal and iron deposits, supplemented by magnesite, gold, oil shale, and lumber, all of which could be exploited by cheap indigenous labor and hauled easily by rail to good ports.[3]

The role of the South Manchuria Railway Company in spearheading Japan's aggressive continental policy, at the expense of China and Russia, was apparent from the outset. In the words of the diplomat Matsuoka Yōsuke, later president of the SMR, the railroad was "a bulwark in the first line of national defense" and represented "the sum total of the special rights that Japan had won as a result of the wars on which she had staked her existence." By securing control of the transportation system, the Japanese could exert strategic domination over all of South Manchuria. Among the first tasks that the SMR set for itself were the double-tracking of the rail line between Dairen and the Mukden area, and the conversion of the Russian broad-gauge to standard-gauge track.[4]

The new Japanese sphere of influence in South Manchuria, however, needed to be consolidated and protected, especially since according to the peace terms the combat forces of both the Japanese and the Russians were to be withdrawn from Manchuria within 18 months, by the spring of 1907. Already in 1907 there was a considerable Japanese civilian population in Manchuria: about 25,000 in the Kwantung Leased Territory, and another 13,000 in the SMR zone. Three years later, in 1910, those numbers had increased to nearly 37,000 and 25,000, respectively. Chinese mounted bandits, demobilized soldiers, vagrants, and other lawless elements posed a familiar threat in Manchuria, especially in the rural sectors. But the major concern of the Japanese High Command was the possibility that the Russians would seek revenge for their recent defeat. Consequently, the traditional defensive or reactive emphasis of the Japanese army was transformed in the annual operations plans drafted after the Russo-Japanese War, and a clear-cut offensive strategy was designed. Japan's primary hypothetical enemy was identified as Russia in the first Imperial National Defense Policy enunciated in 1907. This crystallization of Japanese thinking is attributable to the elimination of Russian naval power in Asiatic waters and to the acquisition by Japan of extensive footholds in Manchuria and Korea. As early as 1906, the Japanese army's contingency planning called for a decisive offensive to be launched against the Russian main body in Manchuria, with the rapid capture of Harbin and the severing of the enemy's main line of communications between the Ussuri and the rest of Siberia.[5]

The Japanese army's new strategy demanded a sizable military presence in South Manchuria, even in peacetime—the genesis of the force known later as the Kwantung Army. During the Russo-Japanese War the Japanese field forces in Manchuria had served under the commander in chief of the Manchuria Army (*Manshūgun sōshireikan*). In October 1905, shortly after the Portsmouth settlement, a Kwantung Military Government (*Kantō sōtokufu*), headed by Gen. Ōshima Yoshimasa, was established at Liaoyang under the Manchuria Army. There was soon no need for a combat staff organization, however, and the Manchuria Army headquarters was returned to Japan. Thereupon, in November 1905, national responsibility for the security of South Manchuria was assumed by Imperial General Headquarters (IGHQ) in Tokyo, to whom General Ōshima and his command were subordinated. The mission of the Kwantung Military Government was to administer the leasehold, handle army affairs, and defend the region. The number of regular troops Japan might station in the Kwantung Territory was not stipulated by treaty, but the initial strength of the Kwantung Garrison amounted to two regular army divisions and fortress units stationed at Port Arthur and Dairen.[6]

To defend the tracks and concessions in the SMR zone, Japan had insisted at Portsmouth on its right—and indeed duty—to station railway guard soldiers along the right-of-way. Subject to Chinese ratification, it was agreed by the Russian and Japanese negotiators that no more than 15 such guards might be detailed per kilometer of track. In practice, the number of men was to be held to a minimum, "having in view the actual requirements." During the subsequent discussions at Peking, the Chinese side particularly resisted the idea of allowing foreign guards and other evidence of foreign authority in Chinese territory on a permanent basis. If, for example, the Japanese demanded the right to deploy the maximum railway guard strength, the working distance between Changchun, Dairen, and Port Arthur (755 kilometers) would alone justify more than 11,000 men. From the arguments of Foreign Minister Komura Jutarō, chief delegate at Portsmouth and Peking, it is apparent that the Japanese government viewed the defense of Manchuria from two angles. First, Komura predicted another Russo-Japanese War. Second, he insisted that a Japanese guard force was imperative until such time as "tranquillity" was restored to Manchuria and China itself became fully able to protect the lives and property of foreigners. By an additional agreement appended to the treaty of December 1905, the Chinese reluctantly assented to the stationing of the Japanese railway guards in the hope that this provision might prove temporary.[7]

In 1906, over the objections of the Japanese army, the cabinet in Tokyo agreed to replace the Kwantung Military Government (which had been relocated to Port Arthur) by a peacetime Kwantung government-general (*Kantō totokufu*). The most significant feature of the reorganization was the transfer of the Japanese administration in Manchuria from the control of IGHQ to the foreign ministry, so far as civil affairs were concerned. Nevertheless, the government-general was by no means freed from a strong military coloration. By imperial ordinance, the Kwantung governor-general—a lieutenant general or full general on active duty—was to "take charge of the defense of the territory within the limits of his jurisdiction" and, whenever he found an emergency to exist, was authorized to employ military force. Apart from the regular units in the leasehold, that force included the railway guards, since the government-general was also responsible for the protection and operation of the South Manchuria Railway. General Ōshima, the former military governor, was retained as governor-general from September 1906 until April 1912.

To handle military matters in Manchuria, an army bureau was set up under the governor-general. His military superiors in Tokyo were the chief of the Army General Staff (AGS) for the categories of operations and mobilization, the war minister for personnel, and the inspector general for training and education. By the time the Japanese army of occupation was removed and the South Manchuria Railway Company became operational in 1907, the governor-general could call upon the following military forces: six new independent garrison battalions, which were made up of regular soldiers serving as railway guards and which were deployed at important stations such as Kaiyuan and Mukden (Shenyang or Fengtien), with central headquarters in Kungchuling; a regular army garrison of one division stationed in the Kwantung Leased Territory; and a heavy siege artillery battalion for the fortress at Port Arthur.[8] (See Table 1.1 for a list of Kwantung Leased Territory governors and Kwantung Army commanders and units, 1906-32.)

The outbreak of the First World War in the summer of 1914 gave Japan a great opportunity to strengthen its control of Manchuria and acquire other parts of China, such as Shantung, the site of a German leasehold. The overthrow of the Manchu dynasty in 1912 had left China rent by civil unrest and the rivalry of cliques, warlords, and opportunists. No support for China could be expected now from the European powers, and the Japanese cemented their existing diplomatic links with the British and French by entering the war on the Allied side in late August. After crushing German resistance in Shantung by early November, Japan turned immediately against China and sought to impose the harsh and self-serving Twenty-one Demands upon the weak regime in Peking. Under tremendous Japanese pressure, which extended to the threat of force in the event of noncompliance, President Yüan Shih-kai was finally compelled in May 1915 to accept the bulk of Japan's terms. Insofar as Manchuria was concerned, the most important feature was the extension of the Kwantung lease and of the SMR and Antung-to-Mukden railroad accords to a term of 99 years—that is, from the approaching expiration date of 1923 to far-off 1997.[9]

With their grip on Manchuria tightened as a result of the Chinese concessions of 1915, Kwantung Governor-General Fukushima Yasumasa and the South Manchuria Railway Company pressed the Japanese government to untangle the snarled lines of authority and competitive relationships that had evolved between the civilians and the military, and especially to strengthen the hand of the governor-general vis-à-vis the consuls dispatched to Manchuria by the foreign ministry. General Terauchi, who as war minister had headed the organizing committee of the SMR, became prime minister in October 1916 and soon endorsed the recommendations of those who agreed with his own tough policy of continental expansion. As a result, in 1917 the Kwantung governor-general was made responsible to the prime minister instead of the foreign minister and was, in addition, assigned to oversee the managing director of the SMR. Under this arrangement Lt. Gen. Nakamura Yūjirō, the railway president since 1914, was appointed governor-general in July 1917. From Tokyo a Department of Colonial Affairs was to coordinate matters (other than diplomacy) affecting the leasehold and the South Manchuria Railway Company, to which the management of the Chōsen (Korea) Railway Company was added. Within the government-general, a Military

TABLE 1.1

Governors of the Kwantung Leased Territory (1906-34),
Garrison Divisions (1905-32), and Kwantung Army Commanders (1919-45)

Kwantung Leased Territory governors		Garrison divisions, Port Arthur		Kwantung Army commanding generals	
Kantō totoku (governor-general)		*Divisions*	*Date of assignment*	Tachibana Koichirō	April 1919
Ōshima Yoshimasa	Sept. 1906	14th, 16th	1905-7	Kawai Misao	Jan. 1921
Fukushima Yasumasa	Apr. 1912	10th	1907-9	Ono Minobu	May 1922
Nakamura Satoru	Sept. 1914	11th	1909-11	Shirakawa Yoshinori	Oct. 1923
Nakamura Yūjirō	July 1917	5th	1911-13	Mutō Nobuyoshi	June 1926
		2nd	1913-15	Muraoka Chōtarō	Aug. 1927
Kantō chōkan (governor)		17th	1915-17	Hata Eitarō	June 1929
Hayashi Gonsuke	Apr. 1919	7th	1917-19	Hishikari Takashi	Sept. 1930
Yamagata Isaburō	May 1920	16th	1919-21	Honjō Shigeru	Aug. 1931
Ijūin Hikokichi	Sept. 1922	15th	1921-23	Mutō Nobuyoshi	Aug. 1932
Kodama Hideo	Sept. 1923	6th	1923-25	Hishikari Takashi	July 1933
Kinoshita Kenjirō	Dec. 1927	10th	1925-27	Minami Jirō	Dec. 1934
Ōta Masahiro	Aug. 1929	14th	1927-29	Ueda Kenkichi	March 1936
Tsukamoto Seiji	Jan. 1931	16th	1929-May 1931	Umezu Yoshijirō	Sept. 1939
Yamaoka Mannosuke[a]	Jan. 1932	2nd	Apr. 1931-1932	Yamada Otozō	July 1944

[a] Yamaoka served as *chōkan* until Aug. 1932, when the military, in the person of the Kwantung Army commander, General Mutō, took over the function concurrently. In Dec. 1934, during General Minami's tenure, the post of *chōkan* was abolished.

Police Command was created to handle not only the police forces in the lease-hold but also the consular police. The authority of the Kwantung governor-general thus reached its peak during the First World War, a period when the Japanese military and their associates were in the ascendancy. It is no coincidence that Gotō Shinpei, the first president of the SMR, served in General Terauchi's cabinet, as home minister from 1916 until April 1918 and then as foreign minister until the resignation of the government in September of that year.[10]

Terauchi's replacement was Hara Takashi (Kei), Japan's first "commoner premier." (For a list of Japanese prime ministers, foreign ministers, and war ministers from 1901 through 1945, see Appendix A.) The world scene in the fall of 1918 was characterized by currents of liberalism, disarmament, collective security, and self-determination. In Japan the military supremacy of the wartime years was supplanted by "Taishō democracy," Taishō being the era name of the Meiji Emperor's successor. Korea took the dream of self-determination seriously, and demonstrations in March 1919 led to bloody rioting throughout the peninsula. Although the Japanese military soon put down the Korean independence movement with ferocity, Hara and the foreign ministry were determined to reform Japan's entire colonial administration in favor of civilian leadership as a rule. In South Manchuria the centralized structure of the Kwantung government-general was ended in April 1919, and the military and political spheres were separated for the first time. Replacing the military governor-general of the Kwantung Leased Territory was a civilian governor (*chōkan*) appointed by the Throne. Guidance on external affairs would be provided by the foreign ministry, and advice on transportation matters by the president of the South Manchuria Railway. The initial governor under the new system was Hayashi Gonsuke, a senior diplomat with extensive experience concerning China.[11]

The old army bureau at Port Arthur was removed from the governor's direction and reorganized as Kwantung Army headquarters. The first commander of the Kwantung Army was Lt. Gen. Tachibana Koichirō, 58, whose record included membership in the Portsmouth delegation in 1905. Tachibana was responsible not to the civil governor but directly to the war minister and the AGS chief in Tokyo. Though the civil governor might ask the Kwantung Army commanding general for military assistance to "preserve peace and order," he could not assume control of either the regular forces or the railway guards. Since the Kwantung Army commander (always a lieutenant general or full general) was appointed by the High Command in Tokyo and was only responsible to it, he could operate in the name of the "supreme command prerogative" (*tōsuiken dokuritsu*) and take independent action if desired, without interference in practice. Even before the Manchurian Incident of 1931, an American expert on South Manchuria discerned that the Japanese railway guards had become "an instrument of a military clique in Tokyo, acting through" the commander of the Kwantung Army.[12]

At the time of its creation in 1919, the Kwantung Army was more an administrative than a tactical grouping. Although it retained the previous mission of defending the Kwantung leasehold and the rail lines in South Manchuria, it still disposed of only one division (rotated from the homeland every two years) and the six independent garrison battalions of railway guards. As for the latter, War Minister Yamanashi Hanzō considered abolishing them unilaterally during the general phase of international disarmament in 1922. The strength remained at six battalions, however, until War Minister Ugaki Kazushige (Kazunari, or Issei), in a budget-cutting move, "streamlined" the Japanese army in 1925 and lopped off two of the guard battalions in the process. With the resurgence of Russian strength in Siberia and the return of military men as premiers of Japan (e.g., Gen. Tanaka Giichi, 1927-29), the two railway guard battalions were restored in 1929.[13]

New opportunities for Japanese expansion in Northeast Asia had occurred after the collapse of tsardom in 1917, at a time when Russia was distracted by war, revolution, civil war, and early Bolshevism. By 1918 Japan hoped to extend its influence into North Manchuria, eliminate the northern or Russian problem once and for all, and save the Far East from Communism. Therefore the Japanese were the prime movers behind the Siberian Expedition, the campaign by the Allied Powers ostensibly to extricate Czech forces trapped in Russia but in fact to support White Russian elements and overthrow the Soviet regime.

Even before the establishment of the Kwantung Army, the need for military assistance in the operations against the Soviets caused the Japanese High Command to draw upon the Kwantung Garrison. Although Japanese and other Allied units (American, British, French, Italian, and Chinese) had succeeded in overrunning the Maritime Province and the Amur region, White Russian troops had been driven back from the Trans-Baikal area into Manchuria. In August 1918 the Kwantung governor-general, Lieutenant General Nakamura, was directed by Tokyo to dispatch a reinforced brigade from Lieutenant General Fujii's 7th Division in the leasehold to the Manchouli area, and a regiment to the sector between Harbin and Hailar. Supported by White Russian and Czech troops, the main Fujii detachment crossed into Siberia from Manchouli and advanced along the railroad about 450 km. to Chita in September 1918. Within a month and a half of the first landings at Vladivostok, almost the whole area of Siberia east of Lake Baikal, most particularly the Trans-Siberian Railway, had been occupied by mainly Japanese forces. In concert with the headquarters of the Japanese expeditionary army in Vladivostok and a reinforcement division sent from

Japan to North Manchuria in September, the Kwantung governor-general was instructed to expand his zone of responsibility by garrisoning and maintaining security in North Manchuria and the Trans-Baikal region.

Starting in 1919, all of the Allied powers except Japan began pulling out of Siberia. The Kwantung Army, created in 1919, participated in the expanded Japanese effort to go it alone and knock out the Bolshevik regime in the Far East. It was a losing proposition. The Japanese intervention incurred the hatred of most Russians and the distrust of all of the powers. At home the Hara government came under attack not only for the fecklessness of the expedition but also for its expense in money (¥700 million) and in manpower (a total of 240,000 troops saw service in Siberia, of whom 12,000 officers and men became casualties). Slowly the Japanese abandoned their hold on the Trans-Baikal and Amur provinces, clinging only to the southern Maritime Province and the Kwantung Army's zone in North Manchuria. After the Washington Conference of 1921-22, Japanese troops finally evacuated these last footholds outside South Manchuria in October 1922, over four years after the campaign had begun. Twice, Soviet and Japanese negotiators had met in Manchuria to try to restore diplomatic relations: at Dairen in the Kwantung leasehold in 1921 and at Changchun in 1922. These parleys failed because Japanese troops had not evacuated Sakhalin Island after a "punitive" landing there in 1920.[14]

EARLY JAPANESE OPERATIONAL PLANNING

With the end of the First World War, Japanese national defense policy was reexamined in 1918, and the concept of protracted war was introduced into strategic thinking. For planning purposes, Russia remained the army's main hypothetical enemy, the United States the navy's. China was the third hypothetical foe, to be dealt with by both armed services in the event of all-out hostilities. With respect to Russia, the mission of the Japanese army was clouded because of the uncertain stability of the Soviet regime. Contingency plans called for the destruction of Russian forces in the Far East and the seizure of key areas east of Lake Baikal, with the main offensive launched against Harbin and North Manchuria, and ancillary operations directed against the Maritime Province and northern Sakhalin Island. There are similarities between this hypothetical concept and actual operations during the Siberian Expedition, but the differences from the scenario of a "real war" with the Soviet Union were numerous: Russian forces were not deployed in North Manchuria; the Kwantung Army was not reinforced to a wartime level; a grand total of only 11 Japanese divisions and 70,000 men went to Siberia at one time; and the Americans dispatched two supporting regiments, and the other Allies five and a half battalions. As a matter of fact, the Japanese army ceased drafting operational plans against Russia during the Siberian Expedition and instead relied on ad hoc tactical movements.[15]

After the Washington Conference (which dealt with naval reduction and Asian-Pacific problems) and the Japanese withdrawal from Siberia, Japanese defense policy was revised once more in 1923, reflecting the great enhancement of American influence in the Far East as well as the virtual disappearance of any immediate military danger from Russia during the early years of the Soviet state. The Japanese army, which believed that a flash point in troubled China could also bring war against the United States and/or Russia, yielded to the navy's contention that the threat from America was overriding, and accepted a ranking of hypothetical national enemies which placed the United States ahead of the Soviet Union and China. As for operational details, since the Kwantung Army was so small, IJA planners in the 1920's expected that, if there were a war with Russia, the preponderance of the Japanese army would be transferred quickly to Manchuria in two increments (five divisions from Japan and Korea at first) for decisive action. In 1918 the north of Sakhalin Island and the Trans-Baikal had been added to the objectives of offensive operations, the former specifically, the latter in vague terms. In 1923 Petropavlovsk on Kamchatka was appended as a secondary objective.

Drawing on the experience of 1904-5 but lacking comprehensive planning data such as tactical maps, the AGS grappled with problems of troop mobilization, transport, and concentration. Without the pressure of a de facto Russian threat, the planners did not produce concrete tactical details; indeed, the precise locale of the decisive engagement in North Manchuria was not stipulated originally, although advance concentration was to take place near Changchun, the CER terminus, and the main body was to mass to the rear near Mukden. The 1923 revision in operational planning took account of the extension of the rail network inside Manchuria from Ssupingchieh (Szepingkai) to Taoan (Paichengtzu) and called for an engagement on the Tsitsihar Plain. Concentration of the Kwantung Army and the first five reinforcing divisions would be conducted as before, but the advance force would mass near the end of Japanese rail control in the Taonan-Taoan sector to the north.

Despite the decision in 1923 to draft contingency plans against three hypothetical enemies, in practice the Japanese army found it difficult to avoid focusing on one foe, namely the Russians. By 1926, however, the AGS Operations staff began to formulate plans for utilizing a wartime mobilized strength of 32 divisions against the three national enemies. To engage the Americans in the Philippines and Guam, three divisions and one detachment would be employed. Against China, 16 divisions would be committed, including five from a strengthened Kwantung Army front. It is noteworthy that the strength to be deployed against Russia was now less than that to be used against China: one army (three divisions) on the Maritime Province–Amur sector; one area army made up of two armies (a total of 10 divisions) in North Manchuria; and a detachment in North Sakhalin Island. The apportionment of strength against the hypothetical enemies remained constant in IJA plans until 1932. In the case of hostilities against Russia, the AGS envisaged the formation of a command structure in the homeland to be sent quickly to Manchuria as a field headquarters to direct all operations, including those of the Kwantung Army and the reinforcements. During this period, however, overall war plans for the Manchurian theater were not revealed to Kwantung Army headquarters, which was only advised of initial steps it should take if war broke out with the USSR.[16]

JAPANESE MILITARY INVOLVEMENT IN CHINA AND THE ASSASSINATION OF CHANG TSO-LIN

Meddling in Chinese affairs by the Japanese authorities in South Manchuria was apparent even in the era of the *totokufu* or Kwantung government-general, especially after the outbreak of revolutionary disturbances in China late in 1911. Only about a week before the child Emperor Pu Yi abdicated in February 1912, a bridge was blown up north of Shanhaikwan, on the Manchurian side of the Great Wall, causing a train from Peking to overturn with heavy casualties. Since IJA troops were on guard along the rail line, it is probable that the Japanese army was involved in a plot to sever Manchuria and Mongolia from China during the chaotic winter of 1911-12. Army activists, including Kwantung Governor-General Ōshima, wanted two divisions to be rushed to Manchuria, but Premier Saionji Kinmochi and his foreign minister, Uchida Yasuya, were able to prevent escalation of the crisis.[17]

There were sporadic collisions with local Chinese forces after the overthrow of the Manchu dynasty, amid the crossplay of regional separatism, rebellion, and banditry involving eastern Inner Mongolia, North China, Jehol Province, and North Manchuria. After one shooting affray known as the Chengchiatun (Teikaton) incident, which involved Japanese troops and Chinese police in August 1914, Kwantung Governor-General Fukushima Yasumasa made a number of recommendations to the foreign ministry calling for stern action against China. Although not accepted immediately, some of Fukushima's ideas can be discerned in the Twenty-one Demands. At the same time that those conditions were forced on China in May 1915, the new Kwantung governor-general, Nakamura Satoru, advised the war ministry that *totokufu* administration and the garrison division headquarters should be moved north from remote Port Arthur to Mukden, a far better strategic location vis-à-vis the Russians in terms of South Manchuria and eastern Mongolia. Lieutenant General Nakamura had various other practical suggestions, including realignment of the fuzzy boundaries between South and North Manchuria to include in the Japanese sphere all of Fengtien and Kirin provinces, and deployment of the troops at Kungchuling northward to Changchun. Having so recently extorted major concessions from China, however, the Japanese foreign ministry was not particularly sympathetic to Nakamura's proposals.[18]

A new and more ambitious Japanese plan to separate Manchuria and Mongolia from China by force materialized in early 1916 during the last stage of Yüan Shih-kai's stormy career. The driving force behind the plan was the AGS deputy chief, Tanaka Giichi, abetted by Kwantung Governor-General Nakamura. In this instance, however, the commander of the 17th Division garrisoned in Manchuria, Lt. Gen. Hongō Fusatarō, and the commander of the IGU battalions, Major General Fujii, did not concur. Particularly critical were two Japanese consuls—Yada Shichitarō at Mukden and Yoshida Shigeru at Antung. A more practical approach, the consuls urged Foreign Minister Ishii Kikujirō, would be to support the pretensions of a certain Chinese division commander, Chang Tso-lin, a former bandit chieftain who was known to crave the post of governor of Mukden. Ishii agreed with the idea, as did General Tanaka, surprisingly. Tanaka, in fact, ordered the Kwantung governor-general to confer with Chang and encourage him to rise. However, the death of Yüan Shih-kai in June 1916 led the Japanese to reverse their China policy and accept the new national president, Li Yuan-hung, and abandon the separatist movement for the time being.[19]

The decade following the death of Yüan Shih-kai was a period of war-lordism and cliques, generally regarded as the bleakest years in the history of the tormented Chinese republic. Chang Tso-lin's Fengtien Army helped the Chihli Clique to overcome the Anhwei Clique, but by 1922 the forces of Fengtien and Chihli were at each other's throats. The Kwantung Army's encouragement of Chang Tso-lin did not save him from defeat, although the Japanese military presence in South Manchuria helped him to hold on to the Northeast Provinces, independent of the government in Peking. Foreign Minister Uchida's policy of nonintervention in the Chinese civil war over-came the adventurist intentions of the Kwantung Army.[20]

In the autumn of 1924 Chang Tso-lin's Fengtien Army waged a war of revenge against the Chihli forces. The Kwantung Army, the consuls in Manchuria, and almost all of the members of the Katō Takaaki cabinet argued that assistance to Chang would favor Japan's best interests. But as Uchida had done in 1922, Foreign Minister Shidehara Kijūrō vigorously espoused nonintervention. Shidehara's policy of restraint seemed to bear fruit when the Chihli Army's defense of Peking collapsed as the result of a mutiny by Feng Yu-hsiang, known as "the Christian general." What Shidehara did not realize was that the Kwantung Army, under Gen. Shirakawa Yoshinori, had been extremely active behind the scenes, apparently with the connivance of high-ranking military officials in Tokyo such as War Minister Ugaki. IJA officers serving as advisers to Chinese warlords—the shadowy "China hands" (*Shinaya*)—played an important role in the outcome of the second Fengtien-Chihli war. Working with Chang were Teranishi Hidetake, a retired colonel, and Matsui Shichio, a colonel on active duty. A famous AGS officer, Lt. Col. Dohihara Kenji, was operating in Feng's camp, together with Maj. Matsumuro Takayoshi, Feng's military adviser. It is known that a million yen passed from Chang to Feng through the Japanese officers.[21] By engineering the defeat of the Chihli Clique, without the sanction or the knowledge of the civil government in Tokyo, the Kwantung Army was gaining confidence in its ability to do as it liked in fragmented China.

In October 1925 a coalition of warlords renewed the civil war against Fengtien. At this juncture, it was Chang Tso-lin who was betrayed by a subordinate, Kuo Sung-ling, who proceeded to march on Mukden itself. Once again the leading Japanese officials in Manchuria, including Chang's adviser, Matsui,[22] recommended that Chang be saved. The Kwantung Army commander, General Shirakawa, sought authority to block Kuo's advance by inserting Japanese troops at the Liao River line. This time War Minister Ugaki concurred with Foreign Minister Shidehara that Japan should not "pull [Chang's] chestnuts from the fire." For the moment, the Kwantung Army was to limit itself to safeguarding public order by concentrating elements of the 10th Division at Mukden.

By late November 1925 the Fengtien Army had been beaten and Chang Tso-lin was near elimination. The High Command in Tokyo merely instructed the Kwantung Army to warn both sides to respect Japan's interests. Nevertheless, when about 2,000 of Kuo's men tried to cross the Liao River and head toward the town of Yingkow, at the northwestern base of the Liaotung Peninsula, General Shirakawa on his own initiative ordered his local unit commander on the rail line to block Kuo. On the pretext of maintaining law and order, the Japanese would not allow Kuo to advance to Yingkow. Indeed, Shirakawa proceeded to draw an arbitrary 30-kilometer buffer strip on each side of the South Manchuria Railway, which Kuo's troops in particular must not enter. War Minister Ugaki reduced the extent of Shirakawa's buffer zone by more than half, and Foreign Minister Shidehara sent Consul Yoshida instructions that in effect lifted the prohibition on Kuo's entry into Yingkow if public safety was not endangered.

Shirakawa, however, was determined to disarm Kuo's men if they still attempted to occupy Yingkow, and he sent a token company to the town. A dozen IJA artillerymen were even attached to the Fengtien Army to help operate the Chinese heavy cannon. The seriousness of Shirakawa's intentions is also discernible from the fact that he borrowed (with the government's permission) two infantry battalions and two field artillery battalions from the Japanese Korea Army, and was even able to wheedle a composite brigade from the homeland for deployment at Mukden. Thanks to the Kwantung Army's favor, the fortunes of Chang Tso-lin were restored by the end of December 1925. Kuo Sung-ling tried to flee but was caught by Chang's men and executed; Feng Yu-hsiang (who had backed Kuo this time) escaped to Russia. Chang entered Peking in triumph in April 1926. The following year he assumed the grandiose rank of marshal.[23]

IJA military advisers had again played a significant part in the warlords' machinations and rivalries: Matsui Shichio with Chang, Matsumuro Takayoshi with Feng, and Sasaki Tōitsu with the unfortunate Kuo. More importantly, in 1924 and particularly in 1925, by acting so zealously Shirakawa had set a dangerous example for the Kwantung Army of "going off on its own hook" (*dokusō*) in Manchuria. That his reputation was not at all damaged in military circles in Tokyo, however, is demonstrated by his appointment soon afterward as war minister in the cabinet formed in 1927 by Gen. Tanaka Giichi, three years his senior.

While the strife of the warlords was ravaging the north of China, the chance of unifying the country progressed in the south. After the establishment of a Nationalist (Kuomintang or KMT) government in Canton in July 1925 and the elimination of regional opposition by the summer of 1926, the commandant of the Whampoa Military Academy, Chiang Kai-shek, led the National Revolutionary Army in the Northern Expedition, which despite many vicissitudes was ultimately successful in breaking the power of the warlords. Although deflected by Japanese units protecting Tsinan in Shantung, Chiang was able to maintain his momentum and advance on Peking in the spring of 1928.[24]

Clinging to Peking, Chang Tso-lin found himself caught between Nationalist Chinese and Japanese military and political pressures. If, as expected, Chang's forces were defeated by the Nationalists and retreated to Manchuria, the Kwantung Army, pleading neutrality, intended to disarm them—and any KMT troops that came in pursuit—near Shanhaikwan. Even more significantly, the Kwantung Army, having moved from Port Arthur to Mukden, planned to take forceful action to maintain security in Manchuria by radiating from the Mukden area to Chinchow, with SMR support. At the last minute, the Tanaka Giichi government, vacillating in its attitude toward Chang, recoiled from endorsing the military plan, to the surprise of the jingoes at Kwantung Army headquarters. Instead, a reluctant Chang was prevailed upon by his Japanese advisers to leave Peking "voluntarily" for his domain in Manchuria, there to rebuild his forces under Japanese protection.

Since Tokyo was not authorizing decisive military action, and since Chang might make progress in other directions, the senior Kwantung Army staff officer, Col. Kōmoto Daisaku, now took matters into his own hands. Apparently he had had the idea for some six months of eliminating the bothersome Chang Tso-lin once and for all. To test the feasibility of fomenting a train "accident," Kōmoto had organized the blowing up of two Chinese Eastern Railway bridges a month apart in early 1928. From the success of his efforts, as measured by press reaction (which never suspected the Japanese), Kōmoto became convinced that he could inculpate Chinese warlord rivals of Chang. A Japanese demolition expert was brought from Seoul and drew about 150 kilograms of explosive charges from Kwantung Army ordnance supplies, and other tasks were carefully assigned to cohorts of Kōmoto. On the morning of 4 June, the destruction of Chang's railway car on the outskirts of Mukden was accomplished with murderous perfection, although the death of the marshal was not revealed immediately by the Chinese authorities. Kōmoto's scenario even included the killing of three Chinese vagrants dressed as guerrillas, the finding of bombs made in Russia, and the discovery of secret papers on one corpse.[25]

Premier Tanaka, it is said, wept when news of Chang's death reached him. "What fools! They [the Kwantung Army] behave like children," he lamented to General Ugaki. "They have no idea what the parent has to go through."[26] Kwantung Army headquarters had denied complicity even in classified messages sent to the vice minister of war, and Kōmoto himself brazened it out when called to Tokyo. Unfortunately for the plotters, however, one of the Chinese vagrants had escaped his intended murderers, and there were also some payoff problems. Thus details of the murder began to leak out, although censorship prevented the Japanese press from alluding to more than "a certain serious incident in Manchuria." In the end, Premier Tanaka, who served concurrently as foreign minister, incurred the Emperor's stern displeasure and resigned, to die several months later in despair. Kōmoto was retired from the army for having "committed a mistake in guarding the railway," but the suspicion could never be laid to rest that at least Kwantung Army commander Muraoka Chōtarō and perhaps his chief of staff, Saitō Hisashi, were indirectly involved, and that Kōmoto was acting at the behest of his superiors. After all, the Japanese consul general in Mukden, Hayashi Kyūjirō, had sniffed out the plot before its execution and had protested to the army commander beforehand.

The Kwantung Army chiefs had certainly wanted Chang out of the way, but did this go so far as to mean the marshal's murder—something not advocated by either the government or the general staff? According to a Japanese revelation published only in 1961, Kōmoto admitted privately to a political leader in 1930 that General Muraoka had put him up to the idea of the assassination, to which he was at first opposed.[27] Sasaki Tōitsu, however, a lieutenant colonel when reassigned to Chiang Kai-shek in 1928, has said that it was he who first suggested the assassination scheme to Kōmoto.[28]

Kōmoto had evidently hoped that the murder would lead to major disturbances, the immediate seizure of Mukden and the eventual control of all of Manchuria, and the installation of a puppet leader in the detached provinces. However, the local Chinese authorities kept calm, Chinese troops backed away, and the Kwantung Army chief of staff had second thoughts about allowing the alerted Japanese units to sortie from their barracks into Mukden "prematurely." We know that three days after the killing of Chang Tso-lin, War Minister Shirakawa proposed, for reasons of "security," to give the Kwantung Army, poised at Mukden, two additional missions: to move out along the rail lines and disarm "confused" Chinese troops; and to concentrate and protect Japanese residents even at such places as Harbin and Kirin. Shirakawa called for reinforcements to be authorized in support of what might amount to a preventive takeover of Manchuria—in other words, a realization of the Manchurian Incident of 1931 three years earlier. The cabinet rejected the Shirakawa proposal, and the Kwantung Army, which was standing by to exploit the situation, was disappointed for the second time in two weeks.[29] It would profit from this "bitter lesson" of the fruits of docility.

Although Chang Tso-lin was dead, Manchuria had been neither occupied by the Nationalists nor detached from China by the Kwantung Army. The accession of the old warlord's unexpectedly vigorous son, Chang Hsüeh-liang (called the Young Marshal), did not sit well with all Japanese. But in one respect the Japanese were in agreement, regardless of complicated individual preferences for a successor: KMT influence—and Chinese unity—must be thwarted in the Northeast Provinces. Such hopes were undone fairly soon, for the Young Marshal, although beset by stiff Japanese pressure, announced adherence to the Nationalist government by the end of 1928, and got Jehol added to the three Northeast Provinces. And at home Shidehara Kijūrō, who replaced Tanaka as foreign minister in the new Hamaguchi Osachi cabinet of July 1929, pursued a milder policy stressing economic rather than military approaches to diplomacy.

2

To the Kwantung Army's Provocation of September 1931

"Our soldiers . . . stand outside the pale of contemptible politics. They are responsible directly to the Emperor, in no sense obligated to heed the barkings of the Diet or the snobberies of the Administration."

—Akimoto Shunkichi, *The Manchuria Scene* (1933), p. 25

On the international scene after the First World War, the Japanese suffered a number of indignities. They were humiliated by their fellow-victors at Versailles, who refused to allow their retention of Shantung and rejected their plea for a general statement of racial equality; by the failure of the costly Siberian Expedition; by the demeaning naval ratio established at the Washington Conference in 1922 and confirmed at London in 1930; by worsening tariff exclusions; and by blockage of emigration abroad. At home, the "Liberal Decade" of the 1920's was permeated by ideas stimulated by the recent War to End All Wars: socialism, communism, unionism, religious idealism, and democracy. The pacifism generated by the worldwide revulsion at the butchery of the First World War gave rise to antimilitarism, exemplified in Japan by lack of interest in and disrespect for the army in particular. The high prestige the army had acquired in the wars against China in 1894-95 and Russia in 1904-5 was dissipated in Siberia. In the cities, military men dreaded wearing their uniforms on the streets. Officers who lived outside the barracks put on a kimono or a business suit when they were in public. In rural areas, regimental and brigade commanders who were invited to official functions attended in formal cutaway attire. Even common soldiers were often not immune from laborers' jeers as "tax robbers" (*zeikin dorobō*). There were relatively more dropouts from the service academies than ever before. Veterans recall the early 1920's as an era of crucifixion for the army.[1]

At the very time that scientific and technological advances in firepower, armor, and aviation demanded an upgrading of the Japanese ground forces, the army's financial needs had to compete with those of the popular navy, which was engaged in an enormously expensive building race with the United States that consumed about 30 percent of the Japanese national budget until 1922. Amid the postwar economic recession, Japan's limited assets were being devoured, and the populace demanded a reduction of the "useless" army in terms of funding and the number of standing divisions. In the Diet, hostile members disconcerted the war ministry by pointing out that the number of full generals had doubled to 29 since the supposed peak years of the Russo-Japanese War. In a famous two-hour speech in 1922, a distinguished old liberal, Ozaki Yukio, asked the Diet why arrows were needed when there were no targets. In peacetime, he asserted, healthy men were more necessary than healthy soldiers.

Under Premier Katō Tomosaburō (1922-23), War Minister Yamanashi Hanzō was able to trim the army by 2,000 officers and more than 56,000 soldiers. That the cutback did not go further derived in part from the rather unexpected objections of the people who lived in regimental towns, and from the counterattacks launched by rightist elements. But although the equivalent of five divisions had been eliminated and the Military Academy had already reduced its annual graduating class by 50 percent since 1919, the public and the political opposition did not miss the fact that the period of military service had been reduced by only 40 days and that the previous 21 divisions, though pared back, were still on the books. Ozaki called it illogical and dangerous to maintain so many divisions when they had no practical function in terms of the international situation of the time. In 1925 a new war minister, Gen. Ugaki Kazushige, bravely wielded a heavier axe, dismissing 34,000 personnel and abolishing four divisions, thereby reducing the standing army to 17 divisions—the level of 1906. The ¥60 million saved, Ugaki argued, could be applied to modernization and mechanization, supplanting quantity by quality. But many in the army never forgave him for "selling out" to politicians and the media, damaging his chance of becoming prime minister a dozen years later when he tried to form a cabinet.[2]

So far as Japan was concerned, unprecedented prosperity and a surge of industrial growth had marked the era of the First World War. Then came a series of domestic setbacks throughout the 1920's: sensational financial scandals associated with the Siberian Expedition; the cataclysmal Kantō Earthquake of 1923; bank failures in 1927; industrial overproduction and a worsening balance of payments; financial panic; and ultimately the catastrophe of the Great Depression following the American collapse of 1929-30. Unemployment soared and small and medium-sized enterprises foundered. Hardest hit were the demoralized agrarian communities, where the prices of agricultural products, fruit, and raw silk had been plummeting from 1926. Many peasants had to sell their daughters into prostitution. Since the mainstay soldiery came from the impoverished, generally overpopulated rural areas, junior officers—who dealt most directly with the conscripts—were driven to distraction by the heartrending problems of the lads from farming, mountain, and fishing villages. "Burning with feelings of righteousness, endowed with sensitivity, unsophisticated and pure," the young officers tended to be agitated and infected by cloudy renovationist and reformist views that smacked of Italian fascism and German National Socialism. Lt. Gen. Araki Sadao, soon to become war minister, in December 1930 spoke of breaking the "deadlock in the national situation" by means of the Yamato Spirit—the soul of Japan.[3]

The army, of course, could not be insulated from the rest of society in the heyday of the Liberal Decade of the 1920's. Even in the strict Military Academy, a brass band and baseball and tennis teams were formed, a canteen was opened where cadets might smoke, and passes were made more readily available. In the mid-1920's, lectures on social thought were introduced at the academy, and the education program for serving officers included instruction on the theories of socialism, anarchism, and communism. The traditional military dictum of absolute obedience gave way to "thinking obedience." A degree of sensitivity to personal rights entered the army, and individuals were authorized to submit formal recommendations (*iken gushin*) and to report grievances to superiors.[4]

Yet even after the army began to recover its self-respect, it was always the bourgeois politicians ("exhausted, used up, and corrupt"), the diplomats ("effete and unpatriotic"), and big business ("bloodsucking profiteers") who bore the brunt of accumulated resentments and frustrations. Steadily the military encroached upon the political arena. Impressionable and passionate, the highly motivated younger officers exuded the features of their spiritual training (*seishin kyōiku*): monomaniacal obsession with country and race, the habit of making clear-cut, black-or-white decisions, and self-sacrifice tinted with feudalistic excess.[5]

Thus was spawned *gekokujō*—a term meaning domination of seniors by juniors, rule of the higher by the lower—a complex, highly Japanese, and baneful phenomenon. The social, economic, and political origins of *gekokujō* can be traced to the bloody disturbances of the Ōnin-Bunmei era in the last part of the fifteenth century, when farmers, small merchants, and militant Buddhists resorted to violence to cope with money-grubbing warlords and other oppressors who had usurped the authority of the Muromachi Shōgunate. As a consequence of the Ōnin War (1467-75), which ravaged Kyoto and brought down the Shōgun, there was "approval of disorder and acceptance of the inferior rising above his superior."[6]

In the modern manifestation of *gekokujō*, junior officers—cocky and conceited because of their youth and supposed powers of execution, though still untested—reproached the prudence of older officers, mistaking deliberation for hesitation. Logic and persuasion yielded to the fait accompli; matters could always be worked out if only something were done. Important affairs were handled increasingly by young and forceful officers, for the seniors were often seen as lacking judgment, ability, and moral courage.

Headquarters staff officers, who by definition should have been laboring in the background, began to act like high commanders or even prime ministers. Private cynicism could belie all the talk of justice and morality. A war ministry officer is once said to have remarked, "There's a stiff penalty for outright robbery. Let's see if we can't manage it by fraud this time."[7] The locus of *gekokujō* was generally to be found among the *chūken shōkō*— mid-range officers, generally captains, majors, and lieutenant colonels. Satō Kenryō, a captain in the war ministry in 1928 who rose to prominence during the Pacific War and attained the rank of lieutenant general, had his own explanation for the emergence of military *gekokujō*: the permissiveness in vogue since the Liberal Decade. The army had modified its training program on the basis of self-awareness. "This had something in common with democracy," Satō felt, "but the indigestion experienced during the period of excess caused the later cramps of insubordination."[8]

Manchuria became the theater for the Kwantung Army's brand of *gekokujō* in the late 1920's and early 1930's for a variety of reasons. Psychologically, the Northeast Provinces beckoned like El Dorado to the Japanese, crammed into their craggy home islands ampler in scenery than in arable land. Officers who served in Manchuria never forgot the open space there. Some were reminded of a story from the *Arabian Nights*, where one could have all the land that could be traversed in a day. Army cantonments were so huge that the soup was usually cold by the time it reached the far-off billets. Even the blueprints for the layout of buildings differed from those in Japan, since so much more space was available. Illustrative of the romantic outlook toward Manchuria were the stanzas of a stirring military song, composed soon after the Russo-Japanese War and highly popular in Japan for decades afterward, which eulogized slain comrades reposing beneath the earth of Manchuria, far from home, under the big red setting sun.[9]

By 1930 about 230,000 Japanese, mainly employees of the SMR and their families, lived in Manchuria; half were in the Kwantung Leased Territory and half in the railway zone. Japanese farmers numbered hardly more than 1,000; a similarly small proportion of the Japanese newcomers came as adventurers, fortune hunters, and outlaws, some young men even joining bandit cavalry gangs. As for Chinese Manchuria as a whole, the population had more than doubled since the Russo-Japanese War, reaching 30 million by 1930. Since 1926 alone, the net gain in settlers from North China amounted to two and a half million.[10]

Economically, Manchuria proved especially alluring to Japan. Manchuria benefited in particular from the fact that it was on a silver standard, which afforded temporary protection from the catastrophic fall in world prices of agricultural commodities. In Manchuria, in fact, the land under cultivation had increased by approximately 70 percent in 20 years. From this "granary of Asia," Japan was importing huge amounts of soy (beans, cake, and oil), kaoliang (sorghum), millet, maize, and wheat, as well as substantial supplies of bran, buckwheat, flour, seeds, ground nuts, ginseng, and salt. Manchuria also furnished Japan with coal, iron ore, and timber in increasing quantity, together with hides, furs, wool, and cotton yarn.

Dominating the commerce and transportation was the South Manchuria Railway Company, which was capitalized at ¥440 million until 1932, and whose gains were very substantial. By the company's own admission, the profit on the rail lines was 43 percent in 1926. But when the figure dropped to 39 percent in 1929 and in 1930, hardliners among the Japanese residents sent a lobbying group to the homeland to try to convince the populace that the SMR was in crisis and that the Japanese government must pursue a tougher policy in Manchuria. Actually, the SMR was not at all in trouble; even in the crisis year of 1931, the company earned a profit of 44 percent. Meanwhile, the lucrative network of feeder lines in Manchuria had been extended markedly—the so-called "loan railways" outside the SMR zone, subsidized by Japanese capital. The SMR had also improved the harbors and port facilities at Dairen, Yingkow, Antung, and Port Arthur, greatly facilitating the foreign trade of Manchuria. Of Dairen it was said that 60 percent of the world crop of soy passed across its wharves.[11]

Japanese publicists and diplomats provided sophisticated and pious explanations of the lust for Manchuria. Some argued that the Northeast differed from other parts of China in its geographical, economic, and historical ties to Japan. Although enjoying sovereignty, China, they claimed, regarded Manchuria as a sort of white elephant and did nothing for the inhabitants, who were oppressed by warlords and extortionists. The Japanese brought peace and prosperity, and asked nothing in return. Peace and order—"justice and paradise"—were indispensable not only for the safeguarding of Japan's interests but also for the benefit of the Chinese themselves. Japan had fostered trade and new industry, railways and mining enterprises, agricultural and experimental stations and laboratories, scientific farming, animal husbandry, hospitals, schools, model dwellings, and reforestation. As for Japanese motives, wrote one apologist, they "are those of all powers with colonial interests; neither better nor worse, especially when the peculiar character is considered of the people with whom Japan has to deal."[12] This racist note appears in more grotesque fashion in the assertion of a Japanese correspondent that, before "the Japanese system" arrived, "the Manchurians barely eked out a living by taking in each other's washing."[13] Twice Japan had risked its own national existence to save Korea and Manchuria from imminent peril; surely the Japanese had the right to take legitimate defensive actions "to ward off, at any price, the imminent danger menacing the very existence of our position in Manchuria." [14]

Whereas by these accounts the Japanese were bringing blessings to Manchuria, the Chinese were indulging in ungrateful xenophobia. Antiforeignism, in fact, had become the guiding principle in Chinese national policy. The anti-Japanese movement had progressed from simple local unfriendliness to outright contempt, protest, and (by the late 1920's) organized national provocation. Concessions only encouraged insolence; it was impossible not to detect a Communist taint in KMT anti-Japanese activity. Worst of all, the movement had spread from Central and South China to the hitherto quiet Northeast. The Chinese instigated boycotts of Japanese goods; built competitive rail lines; harassed Japanese merchants, manufacturers, lessees, travelers, and shipping; assaulted individuals and wrecked shops; insulted the national flag; posted inflammatory placards; imposed discriminatory taxes and tariffs; and persecuted the 800,000 Koreans, Japan's wards, residing in Manchuria. Between mid-1925 and mid-September 1931, Japanese authorities recorded 667 separate instances of illegal Chinese actions perpetrated against Japanese in Manchuria and China as a whole. [15]

One of the more famous episodes centered on the killing and incineration in June 1931 of a party of four led by a captain in civilian clothes, Nakamura Shintarō, operating covertly as an "agricultural team" on the Inner Mongolian borders. Chinese military authorities were accused of official complicity in the killings. The aggressive atmosphere permeating the incensed Kwantung Army headquarters is typified by a recommendation to Tokyo that a search by force be conducted, using an armored train and railway artillery. [16] In the homeland, army aircraft dropped propaganda leaflets on various cities, calling for a more forceful policy vis-à-vis Manchuria. [17]

Anti-Japanese propaganda was rife in Chinese elementary schools; Japanese primary pupils en route to their own schools were stoned by Chinese. Obstructions were placed on railway tracks, rocks were thrown at passing trains, and Japanese residents in Mukden noticed anti-Japanese posters demanding "liberation" of the South Manchuria Railway. Japanese railroad garrisons were buzzed by Chinese aircraft, but no warplanes had been assigned to the Kwantung Army as of 1931, despite repeated requests. Sensing their danger, Japanese residents pressed for a stronger government stand. As early as 1928, a Manchurian Youth League was formed, with Kwantung Army encouragement, to promote an autonomous state in Manchuria and Mongolia. [18] Like the French in Algeria decades later, the *colons* in Manchuria were developing an indentity as "Manchurian Japanese."

By 1931, the officers at Kwantung Army headquarters, like many of those in the homeland, had become exasperated by the social, political, and economic reverses afflicting Japan domestically and internationally. They felt that Japanese interests in Manchuria were being slighted, despite Japan's investments in blood and treasure there since 1904. Too often, it was alleged, high-level diplomats and military chiefs avoided posting to China or to Manchuria—the abode of "carpetbaggers." The greatest prestige came from assignment to European posts, especially to Germany or France. Yet to the Kwantung Army, the expansion of Communist influence from China proper and from the USSR by means of the latter's Chinese Eastern Railway rights was very real. The retention of Japanese interests in Manchuria was regarded as a matter of national security, for the Northeast constituted a buffer against threats from Russia or China, and a springboard for possible operations against those countries or Mongolia. The only choice, it began to be thought, was between disengaging totally from Manchuria and compelling China to abandon the so-called policy of recapturing national rights. Kwantung Army headquarters, in particular, clamored for the latter course.[19] Force, not diplomacy, seemed to be the only alternative.

Militarily, several factors affected Kwantung Army thinking by 1931. First, the Japanese despised and made light of Chinese military capabilities, especially leadership, and conversely were themselves high-spirited and convinced of their own invincibility.[20] Second, the Japanese army was secretly impressed and alarmed by the ease, speed, and ability with which the reconstituted Soviet army had overrun Manchouli in a campaign against Chang Hsüeh-liang in 1929-30.[21] Third, a sizable proportion of Chinese forces in Manchuria were redeployed to North China on at least two occasions to save Chiang Kai-shek from resurgent warlords, and this left the Northeast even more vulnerable than usual.[22] Fourth, international attention was diverted from Far Eastern matters by economic and naval problems, and the League of Nations was no stronger than its distracted members. Fifth, Chinese unification posed a potentially fatal threat to the Japanese hold on Manchuria, but at the moment Chiang Kai-shek had by no means eliminated powerful KMT rivals or the Communists, and China had recently suffered serious natural disasters.[23] Disaffected rivals of the late Chang Tso-lin could easily be found to cooperate with the Japanese in separating Manchuria from China.[24] Sixth, a crisis in Manchuria could be expected to stall disarmament sentiment in the homeland, improve the prospects for army budgets, and restore Japanese morale.

Still, it would not be excessive to say that the plot prepared at Kwantung Army headquarters in 1931 to conquer Manchuria reflected a larger military movement designed to renovate Japan itself. Anonymous pamphlets and broadsides, distributed within the military, alleged frequently that the political parties were corrupt and addicted to the spoils system, and that the indecisive High Command was riddled with politics and was as degenerate as the parties. The arrival of two new officers at Kwantung Army headquarters in late 1928 and 1929, both with important associates in Tokyo, sharpened the tenor of the command. The first to arrive was Lt. Col. Ishiwara Kanji, a staff officer, in October 1928. Ishiwara was an intellectual officer with a predilection for arbitrary action (*dokudan senkō*), by which was meant decisive initiative rather than insubordination for its own sake. He was followed in June of 1929 by Col. Itagaki Seishirō, a senior staff officer with a reputation for methodical organization. What distinguished these men from their predecessors was the fact that "both had breathed the air of reform in Japan" and that they had a broader vision than mere seizure of Manchuria.[25] Itagaki originally did not seem to agree with the notion of arbitrary settlement of the Manchurian problem by the Kwantung Army alone. In fact, Maj. Hanaya Tadashi of the Mukden Office of Special Services (OSS) teamed up with Ishiwara first. Eventually Itagaki was won over by Ishiwara's eloquence, logic, and enthusiasm. To these three main activists was added Capt. Imada Shintarō, an adviser to Chang Hsüeh-liang.[26]

Determined not to repeat the mistakes of the Chang Tso-lin affair of 1928, in which Colonel Kōmoto had acted prematurely and without coordination, the core of conspirators saw to it that by early 1931 all the necessary links had been set up with trusted officers in Manchuria, in the High Command, and in the neighboring Korea Army.[27] The scenario of provocation would be tighter, too, involving only Japanese military experts inside the SMR zone, without excessive dynamiting that could implicate IJA demolition crews. But whereas sympathetic officers in the homeland might speak of spring 1932 or even 1936 as the optimum target date, the plotters at Kwantung Army headquarters, working themselves with little effort into a frenzy of desperation, argued for prompt action. Certainly they had ruled out any early peaceful resolution of pending Sino-Japanese problems.[28]

In the meantime, matters in the homeland were heading toward a crisis. Premier Hamaguchi was shot by a rightist in November 1930 after the signing of the London Naval Treaty, and that same autumn the *Sakura-kai* or Cherry Society was formed secretly under Lt. Col. Hashimoto Kingorō and Capt. Chō Isamu. Although by no means homogeneous, this group envisaged political reform through the elimination of party government by coup d'état and the establishment of a new reformist cabinet based on state socialism. Active-duty adherents included many staff officers from the war ministry and the General Staff, as well as civilian ideologues such as Kita Ikki and Ōkawa Shūmei. The extremist wing's plans for 1931 called for the instigation of massive riots in Tokyo, the call-up of troops, the proclamation of martial law, and the execution of a coup. A cabinet would then be formed under the premiership of Hamaguchi's war minister, General Ugaki, whose renovationist views and political ambition were well known to the plotters.

A commotion was indeed fomented outside the Diet Building late in February 1931, but the disturbance failed of its purpose and the whole affair disintegrated before the end of March. Although Ugaki had already been approached, he recoiled and hushed up the episode. As usual, punishments were far too mild to nip the extremists' ambitions in the bud. Lieutenant Colonel Hashimoto, for example, remained in place as AGS Russia Subsection chief.[29]

High-ranking officers traveled constantly between the Kwantung Army and Tokyo during the period from June to September 1931, including the Kwantung Army commander, the chief of staff, the senior staff officer, and the Mukden OSS intelligence chief. Traffic at the AGS Operations Section became so distracting that a sign was put up saying "Authorized Personnel Only." Maintaining liaison between the Cherry Society and the conspirators in Manchuria was retired Col. Kōmoto Daisaku, the killer of Chang Tso-lin.[30]

The routine personnel shuffles of August brought in many new officers, both in Tokyo and in the field, who could be expected to sympathize with forceful handling of the Manchurian problem. For example, the incoming AGS Operations Bureau chief was Maj. Gen. Tatekawa Yoshitsugu, the hardline author of a document calling for a military solution. The new commander of the Korea Army was Gen. Hayashi Senjūrō, who impressed his staff as far more understanding of the need to deal with the Manchurian crisis by force than his predecessor had been.[31] At Kwantung Army headquarters itself, Gen. Hishikari Takashi was replaced as commander by Gen. Honjō Shigeru, 55. A China expert and linguist who had once served as adviser to Chang Tso-lin and who had even been considered for the post of AGS deputy chief, Honjō had been very carefully selected to command the Kwantung Army. Lord Lytton later recorded his impressions of Honjō in his private diary: "I found the General much more human and pleasant than I had expected. He has a very kind face and is, I am sure, honest and sincere according to his own lights. His attitude, however, is quite medieval, and he has very little regard for the political conditions of the world to-day."[32]

Meanwhile, at Kwantung Army headquarters, conspirators Ishiwara and Itagaki were so careful about disseminating details of their operational plans that the full particulars will never be known. Certainly the headquarters as a whole was by no means involved. The new commander, Honjō, was not told of the plot beforehand, but from day-to-day observations it was judged that he could be depended upon in an emergency. In late August Itagaki sounded him out about what action he would take in the event of a major incident. The general replied, "Since my mission as Kwantung Army commander is clear, I would take decisive action accordingly. But of course Tokyo is very worried about the situation in Manchuria, so kindly act carefully, as I won't trouble Tokyo constantly for instructions and will act within the purview of my mission." This reaction was markedly different from the line followed by General Hishikari, who had been the type to ask the High Command for all kinds of directions.[33] The plotters were consequently pleased. On 17 September, when Honjō had completed his first inspection tour of Japanese forces, he assembled most of his officers at Liaoyang for a critique and said: "In case of riots and the like, don't be timid. You may act positively to a certain extent."[34] The attitude of the new commander was clearly going to make matters easier for the conspirators.

Prior information about the plot was similarly withheld from the new Kwantung Army chief of staff, Maj. Gen. Miyake Mitsuharu, a weak but congenial officer who had been told in Tokyo to localize and minimize any crisis that might erupt.[35] Also ignorant of the exact plans were the new Mukden OSS chief, Col. Dohihara Kenji, and the headquarters staff officers in charge of organization and mobilization; logistics, guard, and transport; intelligence and espionage; and general affairs.[36] Many of the most important officers in the field were left out of the plot too, including the commander and chief of staff of the garrison division, the general in command of the railway guard battalions, and the senior IJA adviser to Chang Hsüeh-liang.[37]

On the eve of the operation in Manchuria, there was a shortage of men and a paucity of equipment in the Kwantung Army—as in the rest of the Japanese army until well after the nadir of the Depression was past, despite the promises of modernization following the retrenchment of the 1920's. The chief Japanese unit in Manchuria was the 2nd Division, which had arrived in April 1931 and was commanded by Lt. Gen. Tamon Jirō. Since a third of the division had been left in Japan, Tamon had only about 4,500 men available in practice, and his units were divided among Changchun, Mukden, and Port Arthur as well as Liaoyang, the site of division headquarters. Lt. Gen. Mori Muraji commanded the Independent Garrison Unit, consisting of the six railway guard battalions (a total of approximately 4,000 men) dispersed in 24 component companies throughout the SMR zone. The Kwantung Army Military Police Unit disposed of 500 gendarmes, similarly scattered. Artillery support for the field forces was scanty. Apart from the sixteen 75-mm. pieces in the two batteries belonging to the 2nd Division's own field artillery regiment, there were merely eight 15-cm. howitzers in the 279-man Port Arthur Heavy Artillery Battalion, five mountain guns aboard armored trains, and two 24-cm. howitzers in a special battery (which will be described later). In all, the military manpower under the control of the Kwantung Army did not exceed 10,400.[38] (See Table 2.1.) There was no extra matériel, and trucks and engineers were in especially

TABLE 2.1

The Kwantung Army on the Eve of the Manchurian Incident

Organization	Location	Officers	NCO's and Men	Total
2nd Infantry Division				
Division headquarters	Liaoyang	19	35	54
3rd Brigade headquarters	Changchun	3	16	19
4th Regiment	Changchun	40	816	856
29th Regiment	Mukden	43	888	931
15th Brigade headquarters	Liaoyang	4	13	17
16th Regiment	Liaoyang	41	878	919
30th Regiment	Port Arthur	36	748	784
2nd Cavalry Regiment	Kungchuling	11	106	117
2nd Field Artillery Regt.	Haicheng	42	500	542
2nd Co., 2nd Engineer Bn.	Tiehling	2	53	55
Signal Unit	Liaoyang	2?	54?	56
TOTAL		243	4,107	4,350

SOURCE: BBSS, *SS* [180], vol. 27, pp. 14-15.

NOTE: Another 2,000 men were included in the Port Arthur Heavy Artillery Battalion, the Kwantung Army Military Police Unit, the special battery, and the armored trains. Approximately 4,000 additional men were available in the six battalions of the Independent Garrison Unit, headquartered at Kungchuling and stationed as follows: 1st Battalion, Kungchuling; 2nd Battalion, Mukden; 3rd Battalion, Tashihchiao; 4th Battalion, Lienshankuan; 5th Battalion, Ssupingchieh and Tiehling; 6th Battalion, Liaoyang and Anshan. The only breakdown we have is for the 2nd Battalion at Mukden: 25 officers, 674 NCO's and men, for a total of 699.

short supply. Logistical backup was lacking for a force designed merely to garrison the Leased Territory and the railway zone.

In terms of manpower, the Kwantung Army was outnumbered by Chinese troops by perhaps 15 or 20 to one. Estimates of Chang Hsüeh-liang's total force varied, but the figure in common use at Kwantung Army headquarters was 80,000 irregulars and 250,000 regulars, the latter including 33 infantry and 10 cavalry brigades, nine artillery regiments, and 100 warplanes (among which there were new French aircraft), apart from an untabulated inventory of armored cars and tanks. Of the regular troops, perhaps 110,000 were deployed in North China between Peking and Tientsin, leaving the remainder, 140,000 or so, supported by 216 guns, inside Manchuria. The best Chinese regulars were stationed in the Mukden area; the usual 3,000-man garrison had been reinforced to 14,000-20,000 soldiers, with some 40 guns.[39]

The disparity in numbers between the Japanese and the Chinese in Manchuria is illustrated by the fact that, in the crucial Mukden region, the Kwantung Army had only about 1,500 infantrymen and railway guards at the outset of operations in 1931. But the Chinese forces as a whole were regarded as very weak, whereas the Japanese were elite and more mobile. To compensate for its numerical inferiority, the Kwantung Army stressed very careful operational planning and rigorous exercises. The training of the IGU battalions, stationed permanently in Manchuria, must have produced fiercer or less restrained soldiers than those of the army division rotated periodically from Japan, for there was reportedly a saying among Chinese bandits that they should flee railway guards but halt when division regulars were encountered.[40]

The basic strategic plan of the Kwantung Army in the event of hostilities with the Chinese called for a defensive posture after the lightning destruction of the strongest enemy formation at the outset—the Mukden Army, at the center of Chinese politics in Manchuria. Given the presumed Chinese tendency to collapse when the core was shattered, the Japanese expected that a hammer blow at Mukden would cause early negotiations and a solution favorable to themselves. Although the South Manchuria Railway Company was not involved in the plot of 1931, the Kwantung Army's transport plans were based on immediate use of the SMR, which the military had wide latitude to direct in emergencies. Under the plan to strike at Mukden "in an instant" with all the Japanese forces dispersed in the vicinity, the railway guards would be concentrated in twenty minutes and the 2nd Division in an hour.[41]

It is important to differentiate between general operational preparations and preparations specific to the military conspiracy headed by Colonels Itagaki and Ishiwara. Even Japanese confuse the two matters, sometimes to avoid responsibility. For example, two 24-cm. siege howitzers were secretly sent to Mukden before the incident, yet this was simply an operational preparation—they had been requested of Tokyo at the end of 1930 in case of emergency at Mukden, since available explosives would be unable to breach the old city's walls and it was felt that long-range howitzer fire would have great psychological effect on the Chinese. Moreover, the howitzers could be used to bombard the military airfield near Mukden. The Japanese plotters merely exploited Kwantung Army capabilities; the transfer of the howitzers was known by the commander and was sanctioned well in advance by the High Command, neither of whom approved of the conspiracy itself. Even if Chinese forces had concocted a plot and started the troubles, the Kwantung Army would have taken precisely the same military measures it did in September 1931, in accordance with contingency planning.[42]

One of the core conspirators, Major Hanaya, says that the incident was to be provoked by the Kwantung Army on 28 September, a date that has been retailed widely. The latest scholarship suggests that the plotters had vaguer timing in mind at the outset—"late September," after the fields of ten-foot-high kaoliang had been harvested.[43] In any case, Foreign Minister Shidehara Kijūrō, known for his devotion to a policy of nonintervention and international cooperation, got wind of trouble in mid-September and pressed War Minister Minami Jirō, recently the Korea Army commander, for restraining action, although it was Minami who had denounced Shidehara's policy in a widely publicized speech to division commanders and the most senior military leaders at a conference in Tokyo on 4 August.[44] The Emperor, too, had warned Minami as recently as 11 September to take extra precautions and to restore army discipline.[45] Yet the High Command decided to send Maj. Gen. Tatekawa Yoshitsugu, well-known for his advocacy of a military solution, to cool off the Kwantung Army. Several officers at Port Arthur thought it odd that a telegram from Tokyo specifically designated Colonels Itagaki or Ishiwara to meet General Tatekawa at Mukden on the 17th.[46]

Duly alerted, and fearful of an imperial order directing suspension of their activities, the conspirators stepped up their planning. They were also anxious to strike before Chinese conciliation could lead to a settlement of the crises caused in June and July by the killing of Nakamura and his party of "agricultural experts" and by the rioting at Wanpaoshan (north of Changchun) between hundreds of Korean and Chinese farmers.[47] Itagaki arranged to distract and delay Tatekawa at a geisha inn. Captain Imada, adviser to Chang Hsüeh-liang, pushed even harder than Ishiwara and Itagaki for lightning action; if they hesitated, he intimated, he would go it alone.[48] Because of the sudden increase of pace in Manchuria, Lieutenant Colonel Hashimoto of the Cherry Society could not synchronize an uprising in Japan as he had hoped. The homeland terrorist plot, which proved abortive, was not unfurled until October.[49]

3

The Mukden Incident

The Mukden provocation proceeded with ridiculous ease. Sometime between 9 and 10 P.M. on 18 September 1931, suspicious and unscheduled Japanese movements on the South Manchuria Railway took place: three or four handcars pulled into the village of Wenkuantun, three miles north of Mukden station and a short distance from the Chinese barracks at Peitaying, and a "considerable number" of Japanese soldiers jumped off. Shortly after 10 P.M. an explosion was heard, followed by rifle fire. The Chinese believed that the blast was only a signal for a Japanese assault. By 11 P.M. Japanese troops, supported by artillery, were attacking the Chinese cantonment at Peitaying, where no blackout was in effect. The Chinese sentries possessed only dummy rifles, and no ammunition had been issued to the troops, so there was little or no resistance. Because conditions had grown tense and in recent months Japanese troops had been conducting constant night maneuvers, Chang Hsüeh-liang (who was in North China at the time) had directed his men to be "extremely patient and never resort to force . . . no matter how [the Japanese] may challenge us." Thus, insisted the Chinese, the Japanese offensive at Peitaying was "entirely unprovoked and came as a complete surprise." [1]

The Japanese claimed, by contrast, that Chinese troops, under the direction of an officer, dynamited a short section of main SMR track before 10:30 P.M. A seven-man Japanese patrol from the 3rd Company of the 2nd IGU Battalion, which happened to be in the vicinity, rushed to the scene, found the point where the explosion occurred, and was fired on by a small force of Chinese soldiers. Returning the fire, the Japanese pursued their attackers until they ran into the main body of some 300-400 enemy troops (two or three companies). At that point 1st Lt. Kawamoto Suemori, the patrol leader, called the 3rd Company for reinforcements.

Meanwhile, since a southbound express train from Changchun was approaching the damaged track, Lieutenant Kawamoto ordered detonators placed before the gap in the tracks in an attempt to warn the engineer. But the detonators failed of their purpose, and the train roaring on at full speed, was supposedly "seen to sway and heel over to one side" when it reached the site of the explosion; still, "it recovered, . . . passed on without stopping," and arrived at Mukden station on time at 10:30 P.M. [2]

Now Kawamoto's superior, Capt. Kawashima Tadashi, the 3rd Company commander, brought up 120 reinforcements and fighting resumed. According to the Japanese official account, when the 2nd IGU Battalion commander, Lt. Col. Shimamoto Masaichi (Shōichi), had 500 men in hand, he ordered an attack against the barracks at Peitaying, into which the Chinese troops had been driven. Although between 7,000 and 10,000 Chinese were in the cantonment, Shimamoto adhered to the old maxim that "a good offense is the best defense." By dawn the barracks had been overrun, at a cost of two Japanese privates killed and 22 wounded. The Japanese claimed to have buried 320 Chinese and found approximately 20 wounded, and to have discovered in the barracks large numbers of grenades and cartridges strewn about, ammunition the Chinese army customarily did not issue except in wartime. Even more importantly, according to a Japanese news agency dispatch from Mukden on 22 September, Japanese troops salvaged from the debris of the barracks a filing cabinet belonging to the Chinese 7th Brigade commander in which was found a copy of a wire addressed to all regimental commanders by the chief of staff, "apparently having reference to the explosion." The wire reportedly stated that "commanders are expected to discharge their respective duties completely by making an urgent call on troops at 2 [A.M.?] on 19 September, and by executing the prearranged action in absolute secrecy in the promptest possible manner."[3]

The Japanese also claimed to have recovered a 400-page secret Chinese document containing plans for a general drive and a provision that, once a Chinese offensive was launched, "we shall proclaim, both at home and abroad, that the conflict originated in Japanese aggression."[4] Lastly, the corpses of three Chinese soldiers were found in the mud at the foot of the railway embankment. Shot in the back, and having dripped blood along the tracks, they had fallen in the direction of the Peitaying barracks. This demonstrated, said the Japanese, that that was where they had been fleeing from the rail line when Japanese gunfire cut them down.[5]

After the Pacific War, a very different version of events began to come out. According to Captain Kawashima, the commander of the first reinforcements, the Kwantung Army plotters had originally considered blowing up the express train and blaming the resulting tragedy on the Chinese. But Major Hanaya, one of the ringleaders, has revealed that Japanese army engineers selected a stretch of SMR right-of-way where the rails could be broken—a sufficient outrage to ascribe to the Chinese—but a passing train would not be derailed. Instructed by Captain Imada, another main conspirator, Lieutenant Kawamoto took a sergeant and several soldiers to a point on the railway about half a mile south of the Chinese barracks and himself set yellow explosive, the type used by Japanese cavalry, on the rails and detonated it.[6] Who commenced the rifle fire? Hanaya subsequently disclosed that he had been "saving a Chinese officer" for the provocation and got him to fire into the air.[7]

As for the allegedly captured Chinese wire ordering prearranged action, Capt. Katakura Tadashi, the Kwantung Army general affairs staff officer but not a participant in the plot, admitted to me that the document was a forgery. Just before General Honjō was to arrive in Mukden from Port Arthur, Captain Imada brought to Katakura a copy of a Chinese maneuver order by Gen. Wang I-cheh purporting to show premeditation on the Chinese part. The document had been found in the Peitaying barracks, said Imada. Katakura read the order, detected mention of the date 19 September, and "caught on" immediately. "Shouldn't it have been the 18th?," he asked Imada. Since the paper was supposed to have been found in burned-out barracks, the two Japanese officers agreed to light a match and singe that portion of the order which showed the date. It was this scorched version that was shown to Honjō, and later to the League of Nations' Lytton Commission.[8]

One other item of evidence published by the Japanese at the time contributes nothing to the accusation of Chinese responsibility for touching off the incident: a photo of an "inspired poster" plastered on a wall in the Peitaying cantonment, reading "Keep a watch at the railway to the west of our barracks."[9] As for the Chinese soldiers reportedly found shot to death at the foot of the embankment after fleeing from the explosion, Katakura thinks the corpses were not really soldiers and may even have been brought to the scene later. The victims could have been vagrants dressed in Chinese uniforms (like Colonel Kōmoto's "guerrillas" of 1928), recruited by Japanese outlaws working with the Kwantung Army. Even if they were soldiers, they may simply have been casualties from the plentiful number around the Peitaying barracks. When he inspected the site with Honjō, Katakura remembers being bothered about the unconvincing way the Chinese corpses were lying; but this he kept to himself.[10] Even the Japanese consul general at Mukden smelled a rat when the Kwantung Army prevented SMR repair workers from approaching the allegedly wrecked right-of-way.[11]

After the hectic night of 18 September, on the 19th the walled city of Mukden, the arsenal, the East Barracks, and the airfield (with 60 planes) were occupied by the 2nd Division's 29th Regiment between dawn and 1 P.M. Chinese troops put up no resistance, although about 75 Chinese policemen were killed in the streets of Mukden.

The SMR terminus city of Changchun, defended by a garrison of 10,000 Chinese soldiers (with 40 artillery pieces) who refused to be disarmed peaceably, was attacked early on the 19th by a task force made up of elements of the 2nd Division and the 1st IGU Battalion, under Maj. Gen. Hasebe Shōgo. Against some resistance, and with losses of 67 killed and 88 wounded, the Japanese seized their objectives by 3 P.M. on the 19th. The northern approach to the SMR was thus secured.

Several questions have never been answered fully. First, how did the unin-itiated Kwantung Army staff officers fit into the workings of the plot once it was unleashed? Katakura, at Port Arthur with Kwantung Army headquar-ters when the first information about the SMR explosion arrived around 11 P.M., phoned all other officers concerned, and a conference was held at Chief of Staff Miyake's residence. Katakura had sensed that something was afoot; now he thought, "They've done it." Personally, he felt an "only hu-man resentment" that he had been excluded, especially since he had been handling the sensitive Nakamura affair. Except for Ishiwara, all the officers were in civilian attire. From Miyake's house a call was placed to General Honjō, but since he was taking a bath after returning, past 10 P.M., from a six-day tour of inspection of the 2nd Division, the staff officers decided to return to headquarters. Under a willow near Miyake's residence, Katakura and three other "outsiders" chatted. Should they cooperate with the con-spirators? Although the details were not known to them, all four agreed that it was a golden opportunity for the Kwantung Army to implement its opera-tional preparations and settle the Manchurian problem once and for all. If they did not cooperate, the Kwantung Army staff would have been badly split at a crucial moment. Once the officers agreed to throw their lot in with the plotters, they kept their reservations to themselves.[12]

Other unanswered questions center on the Kwantung Army commander's role in the early operations. Were Ishiwara and Itagaki really in control of events throughout? Honjō did not leave Port Arthur for Mukden with the 30th Regiment reserves until about 3:30 A.M. on the 19th, and he only reached the city at noon that day, setting up a combat headquarters at the station. Significantly, as we saw, Honjō was so unprepared for a crisis on the night of the 18th that he was in the bath when word reached him of the Chinese provocation. He told the Lytton Commission that this first news came by telephone from a news agency at about 11:00 P.M. and that he did not react for a while. Official details reached Chief of Staff Miyake from the Mukden OSS at 11:46 P.M.—perhaps an hour and a half after the explosion on the SMR.

Ishiwara's initial message to the general recommended that offensive or-ders, based on the standing operational plan, be issued immediately to the 2nd Division and the IGU elements. An important fact is often ignored at this point: Honjō did *not* approve Ishiwara's first proposal. Instead the gen-eral, near midnight, ordered only that Japanese forces be concentrated in the Mukden area and that the situation be examined. Second Division com-mander Tamon was notified by 1 A.M. When further reports arrived, how-ever, stating that the 29th Regiment and IGU elements had exchanged fire with Chinese troops at Mukden, Honjō concluded that he had no choice, in view of his assigned mission, and he reached his second decision: the 2nd

Division and the IGU troops should attack the enemy at Mukden, and a brigade of infantry and cavalry should neutralize the strong Chinese forces in the Changchun area to the north.

In addition to deciding to move Kwantung Army headquarters to Mukden, Honjō took three further actions. First, after much mulling, he reported to Tokyo.[13] Second, he asked the Japanese Navy's 2nd Squadron at Port Arthur to send units to Yingkow to block the escape of Chang's forces. (This request, officially designed to protect Japanese residents at Yingkow, was rejected.) Third, he wired the Korea Army commander, Gen. Hayashi Senjūrō, for reinforcements. On the 19th, too, at 5:40 P.M. from Mukden, Honjō asked Tokyo for three divisions to be sent from the homeland to provide security for "all of Manchuria" (*zen Manshū*).[14]

At 6 P.M. on the 19th, wires arrived from War Minister Minami Jirō and AGS chief Kanaya Hanzō approving Kwantung Army activities to that point but requesting nonexpansion of the affair. The staff officers got together at the Shinyōkan, the biggest hotel in Mukden, to discuss their further course of action. Characteristically, Ishiwara said he was "guilty," but Katakura retorted that such talk was irresponsible and suggested that General Tatekawa be brought into the discussion. Itagaki agreed. While Katakura went to get Tatekawa (whose whereabouts he did not even know at first) late on the evening of the 19th, a vigorous and emotional discussion ensued at the Shinyōkan. By 2 A.M. on the 20th, all the staff officers had agreed that Tatekawa should be told, "You have been writing about these matters of settling the Manchurian troubles. Whether 'good' or 'bad,' now is the best time to carry it out—all or nothing. It is a fait accompli."

Itagaki and Ishiwara, who did the actual talking when Katakura and Tatekawa got to the Shinyōkan, argued that the best chance was indeed at hand to solve the Manchurian problem, now that a clash had occurred and the enemy was being wiped out. The Japanese must be truly aggressive or there would simply be another abortive Chang Tso-lin episode. "So let's make a rush." The Young Marshal's government was unsatisfactory and should be ignored in favor of a new regime that would solve the accumulated problems. No intervention by force need be feared from the USSR, the United States, Britain, or the League. And to eliminate Soviet influence in the north, the best method would be to control all of Manchuria. This would be beneficial not only for Japan but also for Korea and China, against the threat of Communism. Now was the ideal time.

General Tatekawa had had the wool pulled over his eyes by Itagaki on the 18th. It had been a skillful case of *haragei* (playacting) on Itagaki's part— "his best scene," says Katakura, "the climax of the drama." Like Honjō and others on the "outside," Tatekawa did not expect an outburst by the Kwantung Army so soon, and of course the plotters had hastened the crisis. Taken by surprise on the night of 18 September, the hung-over Tatekawa had tried to stay calm, to think things out. Now, on the night of the 19th, he argued that if the Kwantung Army operated all over Manchuria, even penetrating into the Russians' railway sphere in the north, the Soviet Union might be provoked into war, something Tokyo feared. Instead, Japanese operations should focus on securing the southern approach to Manchuria at Shanhai-kwan against the possibility of Chinese action. As for a new, pro-Japanese regime in Manchuria, it might be all right to set up a separate, "improved," and moderate government in the second stage, but not a completely new administration—and not yet.

No meeting of minds was possible on these most controversial points. It was decided to "sleep on it" and to confer again next day. The Kwantung Army officers were particularly disturbed by Tatekawa's fear of hostilities with Russia, a fear they did not share. Ishiwara castigated the High Command as *koshinuke*, "paralyzed by dread." He was convinced that Soviet industrial, supply, and transport capabilities were very poor, especially in the Far East. If the Japanese advanced, the Russians would abandon the whole region east of Baikal. As for the Americans, their fleet lacked balance, they had no base of operations in the Far East, and the actual ratio of naval strength in the Western Pacific was not unfavorable to Japan. Without concomitant force, any American threats of economic blockade were mere talk.[15] This difference in estimating the international situation would prove to be the most important complication between the Japanese field and higher commands, in this instance and throughout the 1930's.

On the morning of 20 September, Tatekawa bypassed the staff and went straight to see General Honjō. Tatekawa admitted the necessity of a new government in Manchuria; this much he had agreed to the night before. He was still uncertain whether Manchuria should be an independent country and what its relationship should be vis-à-vis the Chinese Nationalist regime. Kirin and Taonan ought to be taken, but on one point Tatekawa was adamant: there should be no military actions in North Manchuria. Honjō agreed with this "minimum" program, and a wire was dispatched accordingly to Tokyo. Then Honjō left to inspect the battleground in Mukden and the site of the SMR explosion.

Now the Kwantung Army activists, secretly thinking about operations against Kirin and Harbin, prevailed upon General Honjō to order General Tamon and the 2nd Division to concentrate by train at Changchun on the 20th as a "defensive measure." This was done without encountering resistance en route. Meanwhile, stimulated by Japanese provocateurs and orchestrated by Ishiwara, message after message began arriving from the OSS chief and civilian representatives at Kirin from the morning of the 20th pleading for Japanese troop protection. The Kwantung Army staff officers were united in their desire to escalate matters. With the latest message (received at 6 P.M.) in hand as an excuse, on the evening of the 20th Ishiwara went to press Honjō to rush forces to Kirin. The city, however, lay well outside the SMR zone, and the general, despite his earlier agreement with Tatekawa, said no.

Ishiwara returned disgusted, announced again that he was "quitting," and told Katakura to carry on. The latter suggested that all the staff officers go to see the commander at his quarters in the Shinyōkan hotel and proffer their unanimous recommendation to him. At 10:30 P.M. Miyake and seven staff officers paid their visit. Honjō, who had retired for the night, got up to hear them out. Intelligence officer Arai Tadao (Masao) explained the situation and Ishiwara very strongly urged the dispatch of Japanese forces. Following them up, Itagaki employed rather harsh language toward Honjō, implying that the general was backing away from tough decision-making. Honjō flushed; tension and embarrassment gripped the room. Miyake told everybody except Itagaki to leave. They all went to Ishiwara's billet and waited impatiently, from 11 P.M. until after 2 A.M.[16]

Without Ishiwara's hot presence, Miyake and Itagaki reasoned soberly with Honjō. To cover the South Manchuria Railway was imperative. If Kirin were ignored, defense of North Korea, by way of the Chientao region, would be endangered. But if Kwantung Army forces were moved to Kirin, this would have the added benefit of obliging the Korea Army to send reinforcements to screen the east. There were also political advantages to the move from the Japanese point of view, since it might strengthen the hand of a Chinese faction at Kirin known to be wavering in its allegiance to Chang Hsüeh-liang. In sum, from various standpoints the occupation of Kirin made sense, and Honjō eventually came around. The decision was announced at 3 A.M. to send the 2nd Division to Kirin. When Itagaki told the waiting staff officers, they all shouted *Banzai!* Messages were sent to the Korea Army and, after a deliberate delay of three hours, to War Minister Minami and AGS chief Kanaya.

Tokyo approved the action but requested that the troops be pulled back as soon as feasible. The 2nd Division forces still in Mukden were so keen to be in the first wave of the advance to Kirin that a 40- or 50-car train had to be strung together with three locomotives to accommodate them all. Kirin, which had been evacuated by its Chinese garrison, was occupied by the 22nd, "not with a view to military occupation but only for the purpose of removing a menace to the SMR on its flank," as the official announcement put it. Supposedly the Japanese "pacification"campaign was over. From the High Command's point of view, the main objectives had been achieved by the Kwantung Army in Manchuria, and stabilization and retrenchment were now in order.[17]

In Harbin, however, the situation grew tense. Not only the local Chinese but also Japanese agents and bomb-throwers were agitating the populace. Consul General Ōhashi Chūichi and the OSS chief, Col. Komatsubara Michitarō, asked Kwantung Army headquarters for protection for the city's 4,000 Japanese and 1,000 Korean residents. The delighted Kwantung Army staff, eager for a pretext to expand operations, discerned another great opportunity at Harbin and began preparations. While negotiations went on with the Chinese Eastern Railway authorities, Kwantung Army headquarters asked Tokyo repeatedly for authorization to send troops to Harbin. By the 24th the main body of the 2nd Division was free to return from Kirin to Changchun for a possible drive against Harbin.

On 23 September, Kwantung Army headquarters heard from Ōhashi that he had advised the foreign ministry to support the Harbin operation. Katakura says that Ōhashi was "a positive type," sympathetic to the Kwantung Army's way of thinking; in other words, Katakura adds, "Not all Japanese diplomats were uncooperative with the military." On the 23rd, however, came a wire from the AGS chief instructing Honjō not to send forces to Harbin. The same day, War Minister Minami sent Honjō a telegram stating that the AGS chief's wire had already been approved by the Emperor. The community in Harbin might even be repatriated. To the intemperate Kwantung Army staff, which saw this as a betrayal of Japanese *colons* and Japanese interests, it was typical of the home government's weak-kneed policy, built on needless fears of the USSR and the Western powers. Yet even Itagaki had to admit that matters had progressed remarkably well to date; the Harbin operation need not be jettisoned permanently, if recent events were a guide.[18]

By the end of September, the Kwantung Army had assigned elements to guard the rail lines and to cover the main body in South Manchuria, occupied areas had been consolidated, and a pro-Japanese regime had been established in Yingkow. There were problems, however; at Mukden all the Chinese officials fled, and the Japanese OSS chief, Colonel Dohihara, was obliged to become mayor and staff the municipal government with Japanese personnel only—an embarrassing matter for the Kwantung Army, countermanded by the home government. Not until 20 October could a Chinese mayor be recruited.[19]

From the actions on and after 18 September it can be seen that the Kwantung Army lost no opportunity to attempt to enlarge the incident, to "solve" the Manchurian problem by force, and to drag along the High Command and the home government by presenting them with faits accomplis. Nevertheless, except for the original conspiracy and fighting in Mukden, no Japanese troops were moved without General Honjō's approval. Opinions about the role of the Kwantung Army chief have varied, with some alleging he was merely a pliable robot in the hands of the conspirators and others crediting him with much of the success of the operation. Certainly Ishiwara, though he considered the general a political "minus," gave him high marks from an operational standpoint. And Katakura called Honjō a very strong man, a man of firm convictions. While en route to Mukden on 19 September, Honjō told Katakura: "Maybe we cannot settle matters unless we advance as far as Harbin." Not even Ishiwara and Itagaki were talking about a Harbin operation this early.[20]

Crucial to victory in South Manchuria was the assistance of the neighboring Korea Army. The new commander of that army, Gen. Hayashi Senjūrō, cooperated wholeheartedly with the Kwantung Army, at great personal risk. As early as 10 A.M. on the 19th, Maj. Gen. Kamura Tatsujirō's 39th Mixed Brigade of the 20th Division (2,900 men at first, later built up to 4,000 men and artillery) was alerted on Hayashi's initiative to leave duty stations for Sinuiju (Shingishū) on the Korean border opposite Antung. Yet the transfer of troops outside of imperial territory (in this case across the Yalu River into Manchuria) required cabinet approval and imperial sanction, which were not promptly forthcoming. Restrained by the High Command, Hayashi and Kamura held the brigade south of Sinuiju, although early in the morning of the 19th Hayashi did authorize the immediate dispatch of two air squadrons to Mukden, on the basis of existing contingency plans.[21]

On the night of 19 September, Hayashi pressed Tokyo for leeway to move ground units pending issuance of the imperial order. Still no word came. At length, with the news from Manchuria that Kwantung Army troops, already spread dangerously thin, were being rushed to Kirin on the 21st, the Korea Army chief decided to take action to assist. He wired the High Command that he could no longer ignore the Kwantung Army's pleas for help, that he had ordered the Kamura brigade to cross into Manchuria, and that he was very sorry that this action had become imperative prior to receipt of an imperial order. Between 1:20 and 4:30 P.M. on the 21st, successive units from the Korea Army entered the jurisdiction of the Kwantung Army; they reached Mukden by midnight and fanned out to Liaoyuan and Sinmin the next day.[22] Well might Hayashi dread the consequences of the arbitrary crossing of the border (*dokudan ekkyō*), for self-destruction might be the penalty for defiance of the Throne, however well-intentioned and patriotic.

In Tokyo, tremendous difficulties faced the Wakatsuki Reijirō cabinet, the High Command, and ultimately the Emperor. AGS chief Kanaya was thinking of resigning with War Minister Minami, thus bringing down the government, if cabinet endorsement could not be obtained. After seven hours of debate on 21 September, the crisis petered out the next morning when the cabinet neither disapproved nor approved the Korea Army's action, accepted the fait accompli, and agreed to provide the necessary fiscal credits.

General Kanaya could therefore be received in audience by the Emperor in the afternoon, although His Majesty was disgusted with the army's actions and said as much, to the chief of staff's mortification.[23]

Thus was the Korea Army's operation finally upheld by rare sanction after the fact. The crossing of the Yalu became known as the "suicidal troop movement" (*hara-kiri shuppei*), and General Hayashi earned the title of "border-jumping general" (*ekkyō shōgun*). Although Hayashi managed to survive the emergency his actions had brought on, the question whether he had formally agreed beforehand to send troops in the event of a crisis in Manchuria has never been resolved. But certainly the success of the Manchurian Incident is in good measure attributable to the strength of purpose at headquarters in Seoul.[24]

4

The Creation of
the Empire of Manchukuo

The period after the 18 September incident is almost anticlimactic, in the sense that within five months the Kwantung Army had inexorably dragged the Japanese High Command and government into the conquest of all Manchuria and the establishment of a puppet regime at Changchun. Chiang Kaishek's 22 September call for "dignified calm," and Chinese protests to Japan and appeals to the League, to the Kellogg-Briand Pact, and to the terms of the Nine-Power Treaty, could simply not match what one Chinese writer has called "the glamour of aggression."[1] Gen. Wang I-cheh extricated the last of his Chinese regular troops from South Manchuria by 4 October, and into the vacuum poured the eager Kwantung Army, alleging provocations, banditry, and misbehavior by disbanded Chinese soldiers. Yet all the while the Japanese High Command in Tokyo was struggling to apply the brakes.

On 8 October the Treaty Port of Chinchow, outside the SMR zone, was bombed by a dozen Japanese aircraft on loan from the Korea Army—indiscriminately, said foreign observers; with accuracy and only in retaliation, claimed the Kwantung Army. Next came the problem of repairing and reopening three long wooden railroad bridges burned by Chinese forces in mid-October along the Taonan-Angangchi feeder line leading to Tsitsihar. Lieutenant Colonel Ishiwara saw immediately the opportunity presented to the Japanese: the SMR, faced with losing the revenues from shipping the huge new soybean harvest, would complain to the Japanese government and demand military assistance in restoring and protecting the line. Even the "timorous" High Command would have to authorize Kwantung Army troop movement—a splendid excuse to enter North Manchuria. Soon enough this came to pass, and the Kwantung Army was asked to protect a repair operation.

Amid declarations of strict neutrality in the local Chinese civil strife, a detachment of 800 infantrymen, artillerymen, and engineers under Col. Hamamoto Kisaburō left Kirin on the night of 1 November. When the Japanese reached the marsh country around the Nonni River where the burned bridges were, they encountered heavy artillery fire from Chinese forces under Gen. Ma Chan-shan and, badly outnumbered, bogged down. Despite kidney trouble, Ishiwara rushed to the front under fire and prevailed on Hamamoto not to conduct a final charge of desperation but to await the strong relief columns that had been requested. A hastily assembled advance force of one infantry battalion, supported by aircraft, was followed on the 5th by infantry and artillery reinforcements under the 3rd Brigade commander, Maj. Gen. Hasebe Shōgo, who saved the situation and drove back Ma's troops by 6 November. There was now no need for the 2nd Division commander, Lt. Gen. Tamon Jirō, to bring up more troops, but Ishiwara was disgusted by High Command restraints, which prevented pursuit of the retiring Chinese cavalry and infantry and only enhanced Ma's reputation as a national hero. In this action the Japanese lost 36 killed and 144 wounded—23 percent casualties on the 5th alone. About 200 Chinese were killed, as well as two men said to be Russians.[2]

It is true that the High Command was striving to control matters. Thus when Tokyo surmised that the Kwantung Army would cross the Nonni, the AGS on 5 November obtained delegated authority from the Throne to issue direct orders to the field forces in an effort to curtail the scope of operations.[3] Central pressure and restrictions were so great that General Honjō was thinking of resigning. Frustrated and irritated younger officers such as Katakura visited Ishiwara to complain of the spiritlessness and limited vision of superiors who knuckled under to intrusions upon the traditional prerogatives of command. Ishiwara was reassuring. AGS orders were private communications only, not really imperial orders; no matter how many such messages arrived, the Kwantung Army would carry out its missions.[4] In fact, by 1932 the practice of delegating certain command responsibilities to the AGS chief had to be abandoned once and for all; the chief of staff was again required to petition the Throne for orders in each situation, which meant that the field army no longer had to undergo direct ordering by the AGS.[5]

New considerations of alleged self-defense against the "prevaricating maneuvers" of Ma Chan-shan soon justified a Kwantung Army assault upon and "temporary" seizure of Tsitsihar.[6] Two air squadrons, the 2nd Division, and an infantry regiment from the Korea Army, a total of 5,900 men, launched the attack on 17 November in high wind and temperatures of −20°F., against an estimated 20,000 to 30,000 Chinese. The heart of Tsitsihar was seized by the afternoon of the 19th, in the hardest fighting of the campaign. According to secret records, 400 Japanese were killed, 278 were wounded, and 996 suffered frostbite, for the 2nd Division lacked winter clothing and Ma Chan-shan saw to it that heating systems were wrecked in the barracks before he retired to Hailun. Chinese casualties were estimated publicly at 300-600 killed and 1,000-3,000 wounded. Of course, the Kwantung Army was not eager to relinquish any of its gains, despite the reassurances it gave, and there was now talk in Tokyo of relieving General Honjō, especially since on 13 November he was quoted openly as contemptuously dismissing a League Council prescription for withdrawal of

Kwantung Army forces into the old railway zone.[7] The month of November also saw the outbreak of rioting in Tientsin, which attracted Kwantung Army attention to North China itself.[8]

General Ma was still very popular in Manchuria, his men were relatively the best Chinese in the field, and he boasted at various times that twenty, thirty, or even fifty thousand Soviet troops were behind him. The Japanese, for their part, had had the misfortune of backing only losers against him. Colonel Itagaki therefore made the daring move of going with merely four other Japanese volunteers to Ma's own headquarters at Hailun in early December. Ma admitted to the Japanese that his resistance to date had been "meaningless," and Itagaki insisted that the Kwantung Army entertained no territorial ambitions in Manchuria, that it only wanted to replace Chang Hsüeh-liang's regime with a new one separate from Nationalist China and to create a "paradise for 30 millions" in the Northeast. Ma's forces should cease hostilities and the warlord himself should cooperate in securing Heilungkiang Province. Ma agreed, although no written agreement was possible since he was illiterate and his staff was unenthusiastic. The strange secret interview of 7-8 December brought about temporary amicable relations between the Kwantung Army and the ablest Chinese chieftain in Manchuria.[9]

Meanwhile, in Geneva the League Council unanimously accepted a Japanese invitation to dispatch a commission of inquiry to Manchuria. The Japanese representative, however, made the weakening reservation that the investigation was not to preclude Japanese action "necessary to provide directly for the protection of the lives and property of Japanese subjects against the activities of bandits and lawless elements rampant in various parts of Manchuria."[10] The Kwantung Army, comprehending the implications of this reservation, proceeded apace.

On 13 December the government of liberal Prime Minister Wakatsuki fell, and Inukai Tsuyoshi (Ki) took over the premiership. With him came Yoshizawa Kenkichi as foreign minister, and the fire-eating Araki Sadao as war minister. In the military reshuffle, Prince Kan'in Kotohito relieved General Kanaya as AGS chief. On 17 December the new cabinet revealed publicly that an additional brigade was being sent to the Kwantung Army—a decision that had actually been taken during Wakatsuki's incumbency.[11] But now regular reinforcements of men and equipment, which had been ignored until recently by Tokyo, began to be authorized for the Kwantung Army from the homeland. Field inspections by senior AGS staff officers in late October had led to recommendations for the first reinforcements, and on 11 November the AGS deputy chief had advised the Kwantung Army that a mixed brigade, an air unit headquarters, a radio unit, and a motor vehicle unit would be forthcoming. On 17 December transfer orders went out to a further mixed brigade, a tank unit, a 15-cm. howitzer battalion, and a 10-cm. cannon battery. Ten days later the Korea Army commander, General Hayashi, was directed to rush the 20th Division and one mixed brigade from the 19th Division to Manchuria, plus a heavy bomber squadron. War Minister Araki said openly on 21 February 1932 that 11,600 reinforcements had been sent to the Kwantung Army.[12]

In late November, at the time of the Tientsin riots, the High Command managed, by repeated efforts involving some strong language and four orders in one day, to prevent a Kwantung Army attack on Chinchow, an important city on the road to Tientsin in southwest Manchuria, to which Chang Hsüeh-liang had transferred his headquarters in early October.[13] But after some fruitless negotiations between Chang and the Japanese in Peking in December concerning a neutral zone, the overworked 2nd Division set out to seize the city late in the month, in the depth of winter. Once the fresh 20th Division arrived from Korea, Chinchow fell speedily to the "punitive" army on 3 January. The new Japanese troops had a fairly easy time against the so-called bandits, pushing them to the Great Wall at Shanhaikwan, the "gate between the mountains and the sea." As a result of "incidental" fighting west of Suichung, the last Chinese regular forces withdrew entirely inside the Great Wall by 5 January. In the words of the Kwantung Army, "This was [the] pitiable ending of the rather grandiose attempt which Chang Hsüeh-liang had made for the recovery of Mukden."[14] What the Kwantung Army leadership was losing sight of, however, was the fact that, from the bombing of Chinchow in October to the seizure of the "Far Eastern Thermopylae" (Shanhaikwan) in January, world opposition to Japan's stance in Manchuria had stiffened, as the discomfited foreign ministry well knew.[15]

Now a dénouement to the north was being prepared, for as Itagaki had predicted, the Kwantung Army would not be denied Harbin permanently. Conveniently for the Japanese, rival Chinese forces clashed south of the city in late January. Urgent appeals went out to the Kwantung Army, with Chinese merchants even joining in from fear that their property might be looted, according to the Japanese. Several Japanese and Koreans were killed, and several Korean women were kidnapped. Colonel Dohihara of the OSS urged prompt counteraction, as did the Japanese residents and Consul General Ōhashi. This time the AGS easily approved, on 28 January, General Honjō's request for permission to move two infantry battalions north from Changchun. Although cautioning the Kwantung Army to beware of provoking the USSR, the AGS had clearly lost some of its dread of Soviet intervention. A military spokesman expressed Japanese pleasure that Soviet Russia, and particularly its representatives on the management of the Chinese Eastern Railway, "properly appreciating the rightful policy of Japan, adopted a fair-minded attitude toward our military operations in and around Harbin." [16] War Minister Araki publicly stated that as long as the USSR refrained from interference and showed "full regard for our actions, we shall never encroach upon the rights of the [CER] or break in upon Russian territory. As for the allegation of instigating the White Russians [the émigré community in Manchuria], about which Soviet Russia seems most seriously concerned, it is nothing but a wild fantasy." [17]

Arguing that their sole objective was to protect Japanese residents at Harbin, the Kwantung Army, through Consul General Ōhashi, prevailed upon the Chinese and Soviet administrators of the broad-gauge Chinese Eastern Railway to allow 2nd Division troops to use the line at the end of January. The fares of the troops, it was said, were paid in cash. The last part of the journey had to be conducted on foot, in subzero cold, since the rail line was broken. After some sharp fighting, on 5 February the Japanese occupied vital Harbin, home of at least 100,000 White Russian émigrés. Japanese losses were given as 31 killed and 65 wounded. [18] The Soviet threat had proved to be only hypothetical, as Ishiwara insisted it was. For the time being, all of the Kwantung Army's military objectives had been achieved. World attention had shifted to Shanghai, where a Sino-Japanese clash seemed inevitable; and Japanese domestic opinion was growing belligerent, stimulated by the policies of the new Inukai government.

To distract attention from Manchuria, Japanese undercover agents working for Maj. Tanaka Ryūkichi had fomented a serious incident in January at the "dominant magnetic point" of Shanghai. Over 25,000 Japanese subjects resided there, and anti-Japanese sentiment had already been exacerbated by the troubles in Manchuria. Major Tanaka, the assistant military attaché at Shanghai, received an urgent wire in early October from his friend Major Hanaya, one of the Kwantung Army plotters, asking him to come quickly to Mukden. Tanaka set off without notifying his superior, a gentle major general who hardly ever interfered with his activities. At Mukden, Tanaka was informed by Hanaya and Colonel Itagaki that the Japanese government, out of fear of the League of Nations, had been behaving timidly and hampering Kwantung Army plans, which called for the occupation of Harbin and the establishment of an independent Manchukuo by the spring of 1932. Colonel Dohihara had already been sent to Tientsin to enlist the new head of state, the former Manchu Emperor. But if all this succeeded, Tanaka was told, the League was bound to embarrass the Japanese government and complicate the Kwantung Army's secret plans. Tanaka was therefore asked to create a disturbance in Shanghai as soon as possible in order to divert international attention while Manchuria was being detached from China.

Tanaka was happy to oblige. He was given ¥20,000 as capital, borrowed another ¥100,000 from a Japanese mill manager in Shanghai, and sought a further disbursement from the clandestine funds of the China intelligence staff in Tokyo. Friends on the General Staff were enthusiastic and encouraging but proved tightfisted. Working with a major of military police in Shanghai, Tanaka carried on as best he could and produced in January 1932 exactly what the activists in the Kwantung Army had desired: an eruption at already tense Shanghai, entailing assaults, arson, and riots. Developments followed fast. Representatives of the Japanese residents clamored for military protection and the suppression of the anti-Japanese movement. Ignorant of the premeditated nature of the affair, even the local Japanese diplomats felt compelled to request troop reinforcements from the homeland after severe fighting broke out on 28 January between the vastly outnumbered Japanese naval infantry and the Chinese Communist 19th Route Army, soon reinforced by the elite Nationalist 87th and 88th Divisions. The fierce six-week resistance obliged the Japanese to rush three divisions and a mixed brigade to Shanghai and to install Gen. Shirakawa Yoshinori as commander. Unrelenting Japanese air and naval bombardments, coupled with ground assaults, crumbled the last Chinese defenses at Woosung by 3 March, whereupon General Shirakawa, a cautious commander, ordered a cease-fire. The Japanese admitted losing 718 killed and 1,788 wounded; Chinese casualties were estimated at 40,000.[19]

Tanaka was not preoccupied with the military aspects; his objective was to keep the eyes of the world focused on Shanghai while the Kwantung Army was triumphing in Manchuria. In that sense, Tanaka concluded that the plot had succeeded. The Navy was unhappy with him, berated him in Shanghai, and complained in Tokyo. Although Tanaka was reprimanded, War Minister Araki was "magnanimous" and matters ended at that. "If there was any scolding to be done," argues Tanaka, "it should have been directed against the Kwantung Army. They were the real instigators of the Shanghai plan, as well as of the Manchurian Incident."[20]

Despite the apparent Japanese success, the heroic Chinese defense of Shanghai hardened Chinese opinion, inflamed the spirit of resistance, and brought about a temporary reconciliation among the warring Chinese factions. In Manchuria the news from Shanghai put fresh heart into the scattered forces still combating the Kwantung Army.[21] Western opinion increasingly turned against Japan, resulting in greater support for U.S. Secretary of State Stimson's doctrine of nonrecognition of the Japanese takeover of Manchuria.[22] Soon, too, there would be a rapprochement between Nationalist China and the USSR.

But posting of even more Japanese troops to Manchuria—such as the full 10th Division to Kirin in mid-April 1932 and the 14th Division from Shanghai to Heilungkiang in May—enabled the Kwantung Army to send expedition after expedition east and north. After months of sporadic fighting against irregulars, the Japanese zone of occupation had been extended to Hailun in the north and to Fangcheng and Hailin in the east. By August, fighting along a branch of the Peking-Mukden rail line in the southwest, involving Japanese armored trains and aircraft, suggested to observers that the Kwantung Army intended to move on into Jehol Province.[23]

First, though, the Kwantung Army was determined to create an independent regime in Manchuria. Since the League of Nations had organized the Lytton Commission in mid-January to investigate Japan's activities, the staff officers in Mukden hastened to present another fait accompli, on a grand geopolitical scale, before the Commission could arrive. Already at the time of the disturbances in Tientsin in November 1931, the 25-year-old former Manchu Emperor, now known as Henry Pu Yi, was induced by OSS Major General Dohihara to relocate from the Japanese concession there to a "safer refuge." Dohihara, Pu Yi wrote after the war, claimed that "the Kwantung Army had no territorial ambitions in Manchuria and 'sincerely wants to help the Manchurian people to set up their own independent state.'" That the views of the Kwantung Army did not reflect those of the Japanese government seemed impossible to Pu Yi. Dohihara, who struck him as a very important personage, stated unequivocally and specifically that the Japanese Emperor trusted the Kwantung Army.[24] The "safer refuge" proved to be Port Arthur, to which the hopeful Pu Yi was whisked secretly on 18 November, after a short stay in Yingkow.

Now, throughout the provinces of Manchuria in succession, the Kwantung Army established local self-governing administrations centering on peace-and-order-maintenance committees, debating societies, boards of finance and industry, communications committees, supreme advisory boards, and self-government guiding boards—with Chinese "front men" in all cases. For technical matters such as law and finances, the Kwantung Army invited the collaboration of a dozen Japanese academic consultants. After some false starts, the Mukden Conference of 16-17 February 1932, including the Chinese governors of Manchuria, announced the immediate formation of a new state—to be called Manchukuo, "Manchuland." A supreme administrative council, established at once with Inner Mongolian representation, agreed that the infant state would be a republic, with a regent as chief executive. A declaration of independence was published on the 18th.[25]

With the breakoff from the Kuomintang regime at Nanking, good government was promised the people of Manchuria. Pu Yi would be invited to serve as chief executive, the capital would be established at Changchun, the era would be termed Ta-tung (Great Harmony), and a national flag would be designed. Throughout Manchuria the supreme administrative council set up Societies for the Acceleration of the Foundation of the New State. After the various provinces and districts had tendered their formal support, an All-Manchuria Convention was held in Mukden on 29 February. The previous regime was denounced, and the new state welcomed unanimously.[26]

Pu Yi, however, was still languishing in South Manchuria, unhappy at not being allowed to proceed to Mukden (which he had thought was his destination in November), and shocked at not being recognized as the restored Manchu Emperor. Told that he should regard himself as the "guest" of the Kwantung Army until he ascended the throne, Pu Yi was appalled when he learned in late February that the Kwantung Army now wanted him to be "President of the Republic of Manchuria and Mongolia." In reply to his questions he was told that the Japanese had not really settled the form of the new government, though the Kwantung Army did support his restoration; it was just that the Manchurians had to be consulted about Manchurian matters. What Pu Yi did not realize in his own confusion was how desperately confused the Japanese were at the time as well, so that the Kwantung Army could not yet allow him to take the stage.[27] For as the Lytton Commission later wryly observed, "the Independence Movement, which had never been heard of in Manchuria before September 1931, was only made possible by the presence of the Japanese troops."[28]

From the first weeks of the Manchurian Incident, the Japanese government and the High Command had tried to keep the Kwantung Army from becoming involved in the politics of state-building. Nevertheless, the authorities in Tokyo continued to be disconcerted by what they called unauthorized statements emanating from Kwantung Army headquarters in Mukden. Thus, on 4 October, General Honjō issued a proclamation to the people of Manchuria that spoke of "our hearty wish to realize an era of happy coexistence and mutual prosperity for the population of 30 millions inhabiting Manchuria and Mongolia," and that called such a development "the only means to establish permanent peace in the Orient." The war ministry in Tokyo admitted that this proclamation led to considerable misapprehension abroad and asked Kwantung Army headquarters for the full text. The foreign ministry asserted that General Honjō had not been authorized to announce that Chang Hsüeh-liang's regime would no longer be recognized by the Japanese government. Privately, however, the war minister, General Minami, was saying that if there were no new regime in Manchuria, Japan might as well consider withdrawing from the League.[29]

The field army was convinced that Tokyo did not understand the local situation; the only real question in the Mukden staff's minds was whether the ideal form of government in Manchuria would be a "democratic" republic of five harmonious races (Dohihara's idea, supported by Ishiwara, Hanaya, and Katakura) or a patriarchal empire (Itagaki's idea). All agreed that Chang Hsüeh-liang could not be brought back and that Pu Yi was the best candidate to head the new state, so eventually a compromise was worked out adopting Itagaki's proposal on a trial basis and establishing a regency under Pu Yi, with the understanding that if the experiment did not work out, the country would become a republic.

Early in October, Kwantung Army headquarters had been plunged into despair when messages arrived from the vice minister and minister of war instructing the field army to stay away from Pu Yi. There was some wild talk at the time of a Kwantung Army secession, of resignations from the army, and of building a revolutionary new Manchu-Mongol nation single-handed. Ishiwara suggested that the High Command be advised of the Kwantung Army's minimum program: independence for Manchuria; equality of races, under Japanese protection; elimination of Communist influence; and direction of national defense, railways, and communications by the Japanese. If these aspirations were not accepted, the staff of the Kwantung Army should consider relinquishing Japanese nationality, exclaimed Ishiwara, although he recoiled from putting this sentiment into writing.[30]

Whatever its doubts about the seriousness of reports reaching it about Kwantung Army separatism, the High Command could not afford to ignore such sentiments. After high-level conferences in Tokyo, it was decided that Gen. Shirakawa Yoshinori, then a military councillor (adviser to the Throne), and Col. Imamura Hitoshi, AGS Operations Section chief, should look into the matter during an inspection tour of Manchuria, for which they left on 17 October. In Mukden, Shirakawa spoke with Honjō, who replied that he would "never deviate from the path of righteousness." In discussions with Imamura, both Itagaki and Ishiwara appeared unperturbed, although Ishiwara cast aspersions on the "weak-kneed" central authorities in general. Katakura, who was known for his sincerity, privately assured Imamura that the separatist rumors had been spread only by ex-Colonel Kōmoto, who had even prepared printed matter and seemed to be in touch with somebody in Tokyo; Itagaki and Ishiwara had not been moved by Kōmoto's ideas and were paying them no heed. Imamura conveyed this information to Shirakawa, who compared it with the impression he had derived from Honjō and dispatched a telegram of reassurance to the war minister and the AGS chief.[31] In the clash of attitudes, what saved face for the authorities in both Tokyo and Mukden, of course, was the "discretion" of the Kwantung Army manipulators, Ishiwara's personal ties with the High Command and the government, and the alleged spontaneity of the Manchurian populace's desire for an independent new state.

Brought out of Tientsin by Dohihara and ensconced in Port Arthur since November, Pu Yi was horrified by the recommendation of the supreme administrative council in Mukden that the form of the new regime be republican. Pathetically and unrealistically, he thought of returning to Tientsin.

Itagaki came to reason with him on 23 February. After a national assembly was formed, said Itagaki, the new constitution would undoubtedly restore the imperial system; the position of chief executive was only temporary. No agreement was reached in three hours of discussion, and Itagaki was unsmiling when he departed. The Chinese were thinking of the fate of Chang Tso-lin when Pu Yi gave a formal dinner for Itagaki that night.

Next day Itagaki told Pu Yi's advisers that the demands of the Kwantung Army were final and unalterable. Rejection would be regarded as evidence of a hostile attitude, and appropriate countermeasures would be taken. Pu Yi's retinue advised compliance. The most that was suggested was that a time limit of one year be set for restoration of the imperial system; if it were not achieved by then, Pu Yi could resign. Itagaki agreed, for the Kwantung Army itself, as we have seen, was thinking of ousting Pu Yi in a year if the regency–chief executive concept did not work. Japan's "Emperor Maximilian" attended Itagaki's return banquet that night "trembling with fear and dreaming of [his] future restoration."[32]

A Manchurian delegation proceeded to Port Arthur to proffer to Pu Yi an invitation to become provisional president of the new state. He declined, as planned. Thereupon, on 4 March, a second, larger delegation "prevailed" on him, by set speeches, to serve for only a year. Pu Yi was inaugurated as Regent of Manchukuo, in the new capital of Changchun, on 9 March. Three days later, telegrams were sent to 50 foreign powers advising them of the establishment of Manchukuo and inviting recognition. The Lytton Commission was in Kyoto, en route to Shanghai, when word of this development was received. Significantly, the declaration of the founding of Manchukuo was prepared in concert between Japanese foreign ministry representatives and the Kwantung Army. The consul at Mukden, Morishima Morito, wrote the diplomatic portions—the principles of equal opportunity and of the Open Door, etc.—and the Kwantung Army staff then worked up a full declaration for submission to the diplomatic bureau chief of Manchukuo, another Japanese.[33]

The Lytton Commission spent over six weeks in Manchuria, from 20 April to 4 June, and completed its final report in Peking on 4 September. Though recognizing the great importance of Manchuria in Japanese economic development and the advisability of a stable regime to maintain order in the Northeast, as Japan demanded, the team concluded that the Kwantung Army's actions of 18 September could not "be regarded as measures of legitimate self-defense," although it was possible that the local officers "may have *thought* they were acting in self-defense." Admittedly, restoration to the status quo ante was out of the question, for Sino-Japanese relations now amounted to "those of war in disguise" and the future was dangerous, but the economic interests of both countries in Manchuria were not irreconcilable.[34]

Pu Yi had had some very private idea of escaping to London by means of the good offices of the Lytton Commission, but even if he had possessed the courage to speak out, he had only 15 minutes of conversation with the team and was hemmed in by Kwantung Army officers. For his docile remarks, Pu Yi was congratulated by Itagaki. The most that Pu Yi could hope for Manchuria was international control, perhaps a League mandate, although this too would be difficult for him. In the event, he found the Lytton report pro-Japanese and anti-Soviet, and chiefly concerned with fair pickings for all the imperialist powers by way of the Open Door and equality of opportunity. Pu Yi was given to understand that the adviser assigned to him by the Kwantung Army, Komai Tokuzō, had been told by the commissioners that they comprehended fully the position of Manchukuo and were completely satisfied; Lytton had personally shaken hands with Komai and said, "I wish the new state of Manchukuo a healthy development." [35]

Not surprisingly, the reactions of the Japanese government and of the Kwantung Army were diametrically opposed to those of Pu Yi and of the Chinese. One Kwantung Army officer felt that Lytton himself was a Japanophobe who disliked inspecting the Manchurian countryside because it was unsafe. But, although the commissioners entertained diverse views of conditions in Manchuria, the Japanese detected friendly attitudes on the part of the French representative, Gen. Henri Claudel, who had once been stationed at Tientsin and knew something of Far Eastern matters, and of the American member, Maj. Gen. Frank R. McCoy, who admitted privately, "I took the same measures of self-defense in Cuba." [36]

Private comments by George H. Blakeslee, General McCoy's adviser, tend to bear out the preceding Kwantung Army evaluations. The reservation that Japanese officers on the spot on 18 September may have believed they were acting in self-defense was added to satisfy the French representative. General Claudel, "while intellectually forced to condemn the Japanese . . . was sympathetic with them and wished to drape the naked truth regarding their actions with the flowing phraseology of a pleasing and somewhat illusive literary style. He was opposed to any expression which appeared to be an indictment of them. The whole problem he seemed to view sympathetically from the Japanese point of view." As for the chairman, Lytton had come "to the conviction that the Japanese were completely unjustified in their actions in Manchuria. . . . He was inclined to present an indictment of Japan upon every count." But the American member, McCoy, although "convinced that the Japanese were wrong on the Manchurian issues . . . understood their point of view and wished the conclusions of the Commission, necessarily critical of the Japanese, to be as little offensive to them as possible. He had many friends among the Japanese leaders, and showed his own breadth of sympathy by the comment, which he often made: 'The best people in every country are much alike.'" [37]

According to Kwantung Army sources, the Japanese and the Manchukuoan governments finally decided to oppose the Lytton Commission's stern findings because, among other things, they refused to take into consideration the question of the USSR, the most serious threat to Manchukuo and to Japan, and because foreign missionaries in Manchuria pleaded with the Kwantung Army for the protection afforded by the Japanese presence in Manchukuo against Communists and bandits.[38] Members of the League lacked comprehension of the extent of Communist encroachment in Manchuria and in China, and of the depth of Japan's special interests in the Northeast Provinces.[39]

French diplomatic archives reveal that in early July 1932 a military adviser to the Japanese delegation at Geneva, Colonel Kobayashi, privately approached the French delegation (in the person of René Massigli) to stress the community of interests and the military friendship between his country and France. If only a rapprochement could be arranged now, and if only France would refuse to subscribe to any League report that was injurious to Japan's vital stake in Manchuria, then stability and respect for treaties would be assured in the Far East, and Japan would not have to consider withdrawing from the League. Furthermore, France would be guaranteed against the Soviet Union in Europe and against Communism in Indochina, and Japan would be able to reestablish a European alliance, which she had not enjoyed since the Washington Conference of 1921-22. In response to Massigli's diplomatic assurance of France's friendly attitude, Kobayashi asked whether General Claudel might not be given confidential instructions for his guidance. Massigli replied that Claudel was acting as an agent of the League, not of France, and he declined even to ask the French government for its views in writing concerning the Japanese proposal for rapprochement. Kobayashi's superior, Gen. Matsui Iwane, apparently wished to broach the subject with Joseph Paul-Boncour, the French head of delegation. The foreign ministry in Paris, however, called Kobayashi's feeler "unacceptable" and directed that no response be made.

Meanwhile in Tokyo, French Ambassador Damien de Martel was visited by Vice Minister of War Koiso Kuniaki for a discussion along the same lines, with an added request for French financial assistance. De Martel advised Paris that, in view of Koiso's importance, his proposal had great merit. As in the case of Massigli, though, de Martel was obliged to decline courteously the Japanese proposal (citing, among other reasons, an alleged shortness of financial reserves); nonetheless, Koiso assured him that the IJA chiefs thought very favorably of France. Indeed, the fact that the Kobayashi-Matsui demarche in Geneva had been undertaken outside official war ministry channels only proved the Francophile outlook of the Japanese Army.[40]

Largely because of international considerations the Japanese government delayed public action on the formal recognition of the state of Manchukuo for about six months after Pu Yi's inauguration as regent. When foreign correspondents queried Shiratori Toshio, the foreign ministry information bureau chief, he replied sarcastically that Japan was in no hurry since there was no canal to be built in Manchukuo.[41] It took little imagination to realize that Shiratori was needling the United States about the circumstances of its acquisition of the Panama Canal Zone. Count Uchida Yasuya, the forceful president of the SMR, told Lord Lytton as well as the American and British ambassadors that recognition was imminent, regardless of the words or actions of the League and the great powers. Finally, in September 1932 the formal decision was announced. By now there was a new cabinet, Adm. Saitō Makoto having replaced Premier Inukai, who had been assassinated in May. Of particular importance was the fact that Count Uchida had become foreign minister in July, and that Araki had remained as war minister. Pressed by the Kwantung Army and by a frenzied public opinion stimulated by impassioned lobbyists from Manchuria, the government "defiantly recognized Manchukuo and knowingly invited world opposition."[42] Half-expecting the League to impose economic sanctions, some hotheaded Japanese foresaw a need to wage open war against the whole world.[43]

With General Honjō due for routine replacement as Kwantung Army commander in August, Gen. Mutō Nobuyoshi was designated special ambassador to Manchukuo, commander of the Kwantung Army, and governor of the Kwantung Leased Territory. These titles suggest the vast civil, military, and diplomatic powers to be vested in the Kwantung Army. Although the negotiation of a Japan-Manchukuo mutual-defense accord was essentially a formality, the document did call for Japanese recognition of Manchukuo. Even before Honjō left, Pu Yi countersigned a secret summary of conditions that served as the basis for the short public protocol signed in Hsinking (as Changchun was now known) by Mutō and the prime minister of Manchukuo on 15 September.[44] Japan specifically recognized Manchukuo as an independent state, and Manchukuo agreed to abide by applicable Chinese international engagements, to confirm and respect all public and private rights and interests possessed by Japan through agreements with China, and to collaborate with Japan in matters of joint defense. Under this last heading, Japan reserved the right to station such forces as deemed necessary in Manchukuo.[45] A supplementary joint military pact, spelling out the details, was signed the same day.[46]

Japan's recognition of Manchukuo antedated publication of the Lytton Commission's report by about two weeks, and the League's censure by nearly six months. The Japanese advised the League that, although the Lytton Commission's report possessed "many admirable qualities, it is not a document one can possibly look upon as containing all the facts of the case or upon which alone final judgment should be based." Particularly distressing was the League's visible failure to realize "the actual situation in the Far East, the difficulties of Japan's position in the midst of unparalleled and appalling circumstances, and the ultimate aim that is impelling Japan in her action."[47] To prepare public opinion for the expected condemnation or even expulsion of Japan, it is said that Shiratori even tampered with the Japanese text of the report for the benefit of inflammatory foreign ministry news releases. In Geneva, special delegate Matsuoka Yōsuke, a former SMR vice president who would become the railway's head in 1935, provided the press with good copy through his pugnacious analyses.[48] Especially objectionable to some Westerners were Matsuoka's impassioned extemporaneous remarks of 8 December 1932, in which he seemed to liken Japan's ordeal to that of the crucifixion of Jesus and predicted that, in only a few years, Japan would be understood by the world in the same way Jesus had been.[49]

As the Japanese saw it, the Europe-centered League's adherence to inapplicable formulas and false hopes with regard to China was demonstrated by the vote of 24 February 1933, in a special session of the Assembly. By a vote of 42-1, with Siam abstaining and 12 members absenting themselves, the body adopted the draft report of the commission of inquiry incorporating the recommendations of a 19-member Assembly committee that Manchuria should be made autonomous under Chinese sovereignty, that the Kwantung Army should pull back inside the railway zone, and that Japan and China should begin direct negotiations. Most importantly, members of the League should pursue a policy of nonrecognition of Manchukuo. After expressing the "profound regret and disappointment" of the Japanese, Matsuoka led his delegation in a walkout from the chamber.

Resentful, frustrated, and isolated internationally, the Japanese government on 27 March gave formal notice of its intention to resign from the League of Nations.[50] On the same day an imperial rescript was issued concerning the withdrawal; according to the official explanation, it stemmed from the "difference of opinion with other powers concerning the policy of maintaining peace in East Asia."[51] In other words, as one historian has put it, Japan may have been "willing to let the League withhold endorsement of the new order in Manchuria, but she was not going to accept any League condemnation labeling Japan an aggressor or violator of the Covenant, nor any resolution that would control the effects of the relationship which Japan and Manchukuo had established through the protocol."[52] Thus did the Kwantung Army's actions of 18 September 1931 in Mukden reverberate in the halls of Geneva seventeen months after China's appeal. Ironically, Colonel Ishiwara, a principal architect of the Manchurian Incident, was sent to assist the Matsuoka delegation in Geneva. He attended none of the League sessions and spent his days browsing through Swiss bookstores and galleries for memorabilia of his favorite captains, Napoleon and Frederick the Great.[53]

In his capital of Hsinking, Pu Yi complained that he never elicited more than smiles, bows, and polite talk from the Kwantung Army commander. But in due course, the Japanese did decide to recognize Pu Yi as Emperor of Manchukuo; he first heard the news in October 1933 from Gen. Hishikari Takashi, who had assumed command of the Kwantung Army for the second time, most recently from the late Mutō Nobuyoshi.[54] Spokesmen for Manchukuo attributed the decision to the adoration of the people for the benevolent rule of Pu Yi, who was following the will of Heaven in founding the Empire of Manchukuo. The title of chief executive had clearly been of a transitional nature only; a republican form of government did not suit the Orient. A more pragmatic explanation was that the Kwantung Army desired to reassure the populace and the world that the new regime was secure and well-established, and that Japan would neither annex Manchukuo nor abandon it to dissolution in favor of China or Russia. The formal enthronement rites of Pu Yi took place on 1 March 1934. Three months later, the Japanese Emperor's brother, Prince Chichibu, came to Hsinking as imperial proxy to congratulate Pu Yi and to bestow the highest imperial award upon him.[55] Only a journalist as irreverent as John Gunther would have dared to write of the gilded new monarch of Manchukuo, "It can be said with complete assurance that he is the least consequential ruler on earth."[56]

5

The Manchurian Incident
in Retrospect

The Machiavellian actions of the Kwantung Army before, during, and after September 1931 stunned China and the world by their brazenness, celerity, success, and inexpensiveness in men. Even including the hard-fought operations at Shanghai in 1932, the Japanese lost only 3,000 killed and 7,500 wounded, with another 2,500 frostbitten in Manchuria. The grand total of 150,000 IJA troops involved represented a mere 0.4 percent of Japan's male population of 33.8 million.[1]

Only for a matter of about an hour on the night of 18/19 September had Colonel Itagaki taken actions on his own, but it was a crucial hour, and General Honjō never doubted then or in the autumn of 1945, on the verge of suicide, that the operations of the local units and his own orders were entirely justified measures of self-defense stemming from the need to protect the SMR zone and the lives and property of Japanese and Korean residents. Honjō was not in on the plot, and he never spoke or wrote of any conspiracy. Katakura has illustrated the general's outlook by recounting an event that took place on 8 September 1932, when the recently rotated Honjō went with his staff to report to the Throne on the completion of his tenure as Kwantung Army commander. After luncheon with the Emperor, all joined the monarch for an informal tea-reception in another room. There the Emperor asked Honjō about rumors that the 18 September 1931 affair had been a Kwantung Army conspiracy. Tension gripped the room as Honjō rose to reply. "Your Majesty," he said, "I have heard that elements of the military and some civilians did carry out a plot. But I myself as well as the Kwantung Army did not conduct any plot whatsoever." The staff officers relaxed; they thought Honjō's reply was superb.[2] Long after the Second World War, Katakura was still insisting that it was inaccurate to say the Kwantung Army had fomented the Manchurian Incident. The times fed the eruption, and the Kwantung Army was only the instrument.[3] A Japanese publicist has gone so far as to call the Mukden affair the Manchurian counterpart to the blowing up of the American battleship *Maine* in 1898.[4]

Such views have led to the charge that commanders of Honjō's type were only rubber stamps, or more precisely *mekuraban*, which means the blind affixing of one's seal to a document. Maruyama Masao has argued that the men who held supreme power were mere robots manipulated by subordinates, who in turn were in league with right-wing *rōnin* (freelance desperadoes) and ruffians associated with the army. "In fact the nominal leaders were always panting along in a desperate effort to keep up with the faits accomplis created by anonymous, extra-legal forces."[5] It has also been suggested that the noncommittal attitude of general officers played a significant role in obscuring their goals and intentions, and in fostering the practice of *gekokujō*. The Olympian, "general-like" outlook was supposed to derive from Chinese tradition, where silence was valued as truly golden. Such an attitude tended to imply at least superficial encouragement of subordinates' opinions, but without commitment. The "gallant mien" did indeed go back to Oriental military ways of old. It was the technique of grasping only the broad features and not bothering with trifles, the details of which should be entrusted to subordinates. This was a fine practice, Satō Kenryō has suggested, if it was in fact only the details that were handled by staff officers. Instead, the staff was inclined to do everything, from preparing drafts to planning to implementation, and this created a tendency for superiors to become automatons.[6]

Others deny that Honjō or his chief of staff, Miyake, were robots at the time of the Manchurian Incident. In this view, the general simply recognized the unusual talents of Ishiwara, 42, and Itagaki, 46, and gave them full play. The key to the success of the small Kwantung Army was Honjō's unfailing expression of gratitude to his subordinates. The commander, according to Katakura, always reflected carefully about matters, worried a lot, and consulted his staff. Although it might be too much to say that such a mild person exercised strong control over developments, Honjō was certainly no puppet. The smooth interworking of his headquarters has in fact been likened to the teamwork of Ōyama-Kodama and Kodama-Nogi in the Russo-Japanese War, and of Hindenburg-Ludendorff in the First World War.[7]

That the High Command regarded Ishiwara highly is shown by the fact that when he submitted his resignation in order to assume personal responsibility after the Manchurian Incident, it was not accepted. Instead, Ishiwara was promoted to full colonel at the head of his classmates and was brought back to Tokyo in the August rotation of 1932. Itagaki, for his part, was routinely promoted to major general at the same time.[8] Indeed, all four of the main conspirators of 1931 eventually became generals: Itagaki, full general; Ishiwara and Hanaya, lieutenant generals; and Imada, major general. And, despite the Emperor's annoyance with the Kwantung Army on occasion, His Majesty so esteemed Honjō personally that the general served as senior imperial aide-de-camp from April 1933 to March 1936. Gen. Hayashi Senjūrō, the border-crossing Korea Army commander, even became prime minister between February and June of 1937.

In this connection it must be stressed that the Emperor was being told essentially what the Japanese people were reading in the censored press, as is apparent from the text of the secret briefing given the monarch by Honjō himself in Tokyo in September 1932.[9] This presentation, in turn, was almost identical with the propagandistic, pro-Japanese situation report delivered secretly in Mukden to the imperial ADC, Maj. Gen. Kawagishi Bunzaburō, for transmission to the Emperor on 18 October 1931.[10] It is small wonder that, on the basis of what he was told, the Emperor should send messages of sympathy to the far-flung Kwantung Army forces in October through Kawagishi,[11] or that he should issue a rescript of appreciation on Army Day, 8 January 1932. Itagaki, who had been sent to Tokyo for liaison in connection with the recent drive against Chinchow, was received by the Emperor and given the text of the rescript. He wired word to Kwantung Army headquarters, where the deeply moved staff officers wept at receipt of the gracious imperial message. "We have triumphed after all!," they cheered. A week later, Itagaki hand-carried the full imperial rescript to Mukden. It lauded all of the actions—from the Nonni to Tsitsihar and Chinchow—that the High Command had been trying to thwart. Thus the jubilant Kwantung Army staff officers concluded that they had *not* been out of line, for their actions seemed in accord with the imperial will. A celebration party was held by Kwantung Army headquarters staff at a Japanese restaurant, at which even Ishiwara, a teetotaler, and Honjō, no partygoer, showed up.[12]

Of course the Kwantung Army often chose to interpret matters to its own advantage. For example, after a high-level conference in Tokyo on 19 September 1931, at the outset of the Manchurian Incident, the AGS chief wired Honjō that the Kwantung Army commander's decisions and handling of affairs since the night of the 18th had been appropriate and had added luster to the Japanese army, but that since the cabinet had decided upon nonexpansion, the Kwantung Army would want to proceed within that context. Inasmuch as the first portion seemed to approve their actions, the Kwantung Army staff officers were exultant, and their morale soared. But the General Staff's intentions were, of course, to be found in the second, neglected part of the wire.[13]

Despite the bad name the Kwantung Army was earning abroad, public opinion in Japan underwent a great change soon after the outbreak of the Manchurian Incident. There was now a tendency to cheer on the mighty struggle against restrictions imposed upon Japan by foreign countries. Significantly, disgruntled politicians began to seek a rapprochement with the military. According to the memoirs of Kawabe Torashirō (a major in the AGS Operations Section in 1931-32), staff officers were accorded the highest esteem and were encouraged directly and indirectly. Kawabe experienced this treatment himself on a number of occasions, although he was personally disturbed by such a trend in society.[14] It is true, as Satō Kenryō has pointed out, that by arbitrarily and unilaterally causing the Manchurian affair the Kwantung Army dragged the nation into a revolutionary situation from which retreat was inconceivable. But according to Satō, cruel facts had outstripped theory and chains of command; there was no other way out for Japan. Given the circumstances prior to September 1931, he added, the timing was good and the method appropriate.[15]

A number of very important Japanese began to share these views early in the course of the Manchurian Incident. Ugaki, then Governor-General of Korea, was enthusiastic about the objectives of the Kwantung Army from the outset. After an exchange of telegrams with Honjō, he left Seoul in late September 1931 for Tokyo, where he spoke with Minami and Premier Wakatsuki, who was not overjoyed to see him. Later Ugaki reported to Honjō that matters were taking what from the Kwantung Army's point of view could be considered a turn for the better at the High Command and cabinet level; his own visit to the capital may have helped to influence the situation there.[16]

SMR President Uchida, supposedly a partisan of Foreign Minister Shidehara's pacific beliefs, visited Kwantung Army headquarters and then Ugaki in Seoul before going to Tokyo in early October 1931, where it became clear that he had come around to the Kwantung Army's way of thinking.[17] Similarly, Mukden Consul General Hayashi Kyūjirō, who had been identified as an opponent of the Kwantung Army before the September affair and who had deduced the army's complicity in it, also eased his resistance afterward.[18]

For its part, the Kwantung Army set out deliberately to foster a favorable image of itself at home and abroad, for it was convinced that antimilitary elements, such as retainers surrounding the Throne, were disseminating lies and half-truths. Honjō made himself available to correspondents and attachés, as his diary attests; his subordinates remember seeing his antechambers crowded with visitors, even lowly farmers and craftsmen coming to report on local conditions. Honjō treated all with respect and courtesy. Awards and gifts were given correspondents who were especially cooperative.

Military censorship was lenient; for example, only one English-speaking noncom was assigned to the post and telegraph office that handled news dispatches. Kwantung Army staff officers were of the opinion that nothing could really stop the swift and daring movement of their elite troops, so why antagonize the press needlessly? Working in their favor, too, was the fact that the field forces were made up of regulars, who were much better disciplined than the masses of overnight soldiers committed during the China Incident and the Pacific War. A public information office was set up at Kwantung Army headquarters, with displays, frequent briefings, and free handouts of translated texts and photographs. In Japan as well as Manchuria, propaganda was disseminated willingly by numerous organizations—reservists' groups, women's patriotic associations, White Russian émigré groups, school training centers, religious bodies, martial arts associations, patriotic students' leagues, and the army itself. Even a Japanese Boy Scout delegation offered to be of assistance to Kwantung Army headquarters. The SMR was highly cooperative in terms of technical assistance, services, and manpower, and turned out fine film documentaries. Radio was put to particularly good use, with broadcasts beamed at Manchuria, Japan, China, the USSR, the United States, and Europe. General Honjō himself went on the air with an American correspondent.[19]

The Japanese propaganda emanating from Mukden reached an especially receptive audience in Japan, where the populace was well aware of the sacrifices made in the Russo-Japanese War; monuments to fallen soldiers abounded in such places as Dairen, Mukden, and Port Arthur, which were household words in the homeland. The Kwantung Army even broadcast music of the 1905 era to engender not only nostalgia but also enthusiasm for the labors of the army in Manchuria. General Honjō and SMR President Uchida saw to it that there were jobs for the children and grandchildren of Japanese who had participated in the Russo-Japanese War, and for Manchurians who collaborated with the Japanese.

Also facilitating the work of the Kwantung Army propagandists was the fact that the headquarters was very small and that staff officers held concurrent positions or had easy access to other offices. Thus the propaganda officer could visit the operations and the intelligence sections, examine domestic and foreign dispatches, and meet local residents and foreigners before preparing fact-crammed releases. When the Kwantung Army was about to conduct a certain operation or the Manchukuoan authorities were going to institute a particular policy, releases containing accounts of local conditions, statements of local residents, or comments by anonymous individuals would be issued to justify the actions and win public support. The press responded so enthusiastically in the early phases of the Manchurian affair that when its news value diminished and smaller type and headlines were used, a number of operations officers in the Kwantung Army grumbled openly, calling the tendency harmful to IJA prestige.

The Japanese remark generally that Chinese propaganda, especially on the international scene, was better financed and more effective than their own.[20] According to a foreign observer, China "played the Geneva game with such superb skill that she quickly established herself as the 'good boy' of the League; China was obviously much cleverer at this game than Japan."[21] Nevertheless, a number of propaganda points were scored by the Kwantung Army. For instance, European officers who remembered General Honjō from the days of the Siberian Expedition sent him personal letters of encouragement, and it is said that some who had fought in Siberia even asked to serve in the Kwantung Army as volunteers. German and Italian visitors to Mukden were predictably friendly, but the Japanese were surprised to find the British army attachés who came up to Mukden from Peking quite sympathetic.[22] The picture in Britain, on whom the burden of League "enforcement" would have fallen, underwent a change after the elections of October 1931, when "appeasing" Sir John Simon entered the foreign office, and when the specter of Nazism began to disquiet Europe.[23] At Geneva even the Americans began to waver in their resistance to Japanese actions in Manchuria. After Matsuoka delivered his impassioned farewell speech in 1933, the American minister to Switzerland, Hugh Wilson, wrote that "for the first time the gravest doubts arose as to the wisdom of the course which the Assembly and my country were pursuing. I began to have a conception of the rancor and resentment that public condemnation could bring upon a proud and powerful people, and I began to question, and still do question, whether such treatment is wise."[24] Although the French member of the Lytton Commission, General Claudel, admitted privately that Manchukuo was "an illegitimate child," he was opposed to "idealistic and largely impractical" recommendations. "We have it [Manchukuo] on our hands. What are we going to do with it?"[25]

Meanwhile, Kwantung Army efforts were stimulating patriotism and renovation in the homeland. The bravery of Japanese soldiers was even surpassing the glorious record of the Russo-Japanese War, and the Japanese people's enthusiastic support of the army was no less impressive. As Araki was saying, "the true spirit of our nation has been quickened to life through the Manchurian crisis."[26] If the Japanese had put the same percentage of troops into Manchuria to defend the one million Japanese and Korean residents there as the United States had landed in Nicaragua to protect 600 or 700 Americans, the Kwantung Army would have had to number over 10,000,000 soldiers. Other comparisons, similarly unflattering, were made to the United States in Cuba and Panama, and to Great Britain in Egypt and China (most recently in 1927); yet would America or England willingly abandon what they too called special interests? New independent countries such as Manchukuo must undergo growing pains, as had Cuba, Panama, and the many countries spawned in Europe after the First World War. The world should deal with the Japanese on their terms and show confidence in them. Earthly paradises were worth it. On the larger scene, since the autumn of 1931 Japan had "made great strides in the vanguard of the forces struggling for world renovation."[27]

Despite its self-congratulation, the Kwantung Army had not only damaged Japan's power and prestige abroad but established dangerous precedents at home. As Ōtani Keijirō has put it, unbridled staff officers flouted Tokyo, attained huge successes, but failed to conduct the self-reflection imperative among disciplined military men. Conspirators ended up as commanders at the highest levels. Great triumphs came to outweigh so-called negligible wrongdoing: if you believed that what you attempted was for the sake of the nation and that you were without selfish motives, you could oppose even the highest authorities. The latter might worry temporarily, but later they would be pleased, and you might even end up in Tokyo itself. Such thinking was decisive. Since the Manchurian Incident had succeeded, it was regarded as a brilliant exploit; but when the 26 February ("2–26") Mutiny of 1936 failed, the ringleaders were executed. In other words, as the saying had gone since the days of Saigō Takamori's ill-fated insurrection in the nineteenth century, "If you win, you're the loyal army; if you lose, you're a rebel army." Supreme direction became inordinately difficult and dangerous, although the High Command deserved even greater censure for its flabby attitude than did the fire-eating young staff officers in the field army. Central leaders could not or would not pull in the reins ruthlessly.[28]

A senior Japanese colonel has interpreted the phenomenon as follows.[29] The Manchurian Incident, no handiwork of the central authorities, proved unexpectedly successful; the Kwantung Army staff responsible for it might be compared with the son who buys stock against his parents' wishes but makes a huge killing in the market. Instead of cracking down regardless, the High Command botched matters. It praised the troublemakers, promoted them and brought them to Tokyo, bestowed the highest awards on them, and sent the scamps off on European junkets—all of which was a decadent racket. Inside the army the feeling grew that the end justified the means. An atmosphere was created in which Tokyo's wishes could be defied by local staff officers. The ideal of the time became the goddess Success. Having neglected to enforce obedience upon the son, the father (the central authorities) failed to teach what was wrong. "To be crude," continues the colonel, "if you committed a robbery and got away with it, that was all right."

> The comparison with families and generations is apt. When a man is bringing up a household he has to be capable enough himself, and work hard. This is true in business or any other activity. Whereas the father starts from scratch, the second generation doesn't have to work so hard or have to face such travails. Still the son knows how hard the father struggled, and is able to carry on with the business. Then comes the third-generation boy, with no recollection of the difficult life of his grandfather or father. The grandson is very well educated, extremely cultured and sophisticated. He is superb in calligraphy and uses it to paint a sign: "House for rent." I submit that this story could be superimposed correctly on the history of the Japanese Army. The creators of that army, from the Emperor Meiji downward, were top-notch, able people. Those who fought the Sino-Japanese and Russo-Japanese Wars—the second generation—handled matters quite well. But by the time of the Manchurian Incident and the China [1937] and Nomonhan [1939] Incidents, we had the third generation. Maybe very cultured and accomplished in foreign languages and bridge playing, they lacked the brilliance of their grand-

fathers and fathers, and favored only those who were quiescent and docile. This was the generation that brought destruction and ultimate disaster to Japan.

In other words, bravado, patriotism, courage, and fantasy were no true substitute for pragmatism, levelheadedness, responsibility, and statesmanship.[30] Ironically, the practitioners of *gekokujō* suffered from the effects when they themselves attained high office, a case of sowing the wind and reaping the whirlwind. Thus in 1936 when Ishiwara, now an AGS colonel, hastened from Tokyo to Hsinking to attempt to dissuade Kwantung Army headquarters from carrying out the abortive Suiyuan affair, the Operations Section chief of the field army, Mutō Akira, is said to have retorted: "Ishiwara-san, we are just doing what you did at the time of the Manchurian Incident, you know." The remark elicited raucous laughter among the other Kwantung Army staff officers.[31] What thoughts must have crossed the mind of the mortified Ishiwara!

As Satō has pointed out, the machinations of Kōmoto, Itagaki, and Ishiwara were staff officers' initiative and arbitrariness, pure and simple. The 18 September episode was such a splendid success that it inspired emulation.[32] After the Manchurian Incident, the nickname "Kwantung Army" came to be applied in IJA circles to any expeditionary force that ignored and disrespected the High Command's dictates. The fact that such a nickname could now be heard in public, says Hayashi Saburō, gave evidence of the great transformation that was overtaking the Japanese army.[33] At the core of the problem was the equation of national interest with policies of imperialism, and the solution of crises on an individual military basis—what has aptly been termed the anatomy of overreaction.[34]

6

The "Marvel"
of Manchukuo, 1932-37

"'The Heavens declare the Advent of Manchukuo!' said one blood-red poster [in Dairen, 1932]. *Another: 'Birds Sing and Flowers Smile in Welcome for the New Manchukuo!' Yet another: 'A New Era of Freedom and Prosperity Is Here!'"*
—Akimoto Shunkichi, *The Manchuria Scene* (1933), p. 32

The history of the Kwantung Army after 1931 encompasses the history of Manchukuo and the policies of the Japanese toward the client regime.[1] Kwantung Army staff officers saw themselves as the best kind of civilizers and empire builders, with a heaven-sent opportunity to demonstrate "ability in the handling of men of diverse breeds and the development of virgin territory that in history has been the privilege of the new and the best."[2] As a contemporary Japanese writer put it, for the first time "a nonwhite race has undertaken to carry the white man's burden, and the white man, long accustomed to think the burden exclusively his own, is reluctant to commit it to the young shoulders of Japan, yellow and an upstart at that."[3] To the journalist John Gunther, the Kwantung Army was making of Manchukuo a type of "proving ground, a testing station for social and economic theory . . . the great guinea pig of Asia."[4]

Lt. Gen. Koiso Kuniaki in 1933 described Japan's policy as the unification and rationalization of the economic systems of Japan and Manchukuo, and the utilization of the resources of the two countries in order to improve their economic positions in the world. Though paying lip service to the encouragement of foreign investment and the principles of the Open Door and equal opportunity, Koiso publicly called for the consolidation of Japan's economic situation in Manchukuo before any of the world powers started economic activities there. The authoritarian military thrust of the economic policy fostered by the Kwantung Army is reflected in the stipulation that national considerations must take precedence over those of individuals, and that the economic structures of Japan and Manchukuo must be so meshed as to meet wartime necessity. The public interest of the two countries must govern the establishment of industries in Manchukuo.[5]

Old *zaibatsu* conglomerates had long pursued a vigorous role in Manchuria. Mitsui Bussan, first into the region in 1908, made enormous profits from the soybean trade, and Ōkura had gained a powerful foothold in the coal and iron sectors. After Russian firms withdrew from North Manchuria during the Bolshevik Revolution, the semigovernmental SMR more than doubled its capitalization; by the early 1920's it also doubled its passenger and freight loads, especially in soybeans. From the profits of its transportation monopoly, and working closely with Japanese banks such as Yokohama Specie and later Bank of Chōsen, the SMR invested deeply in Manchurian heavy industry, which it accorded preferential freight rates. SMR geologists were active in discovering mineral deposits. Yet though the SMR possessed immense military value, the Kwantung Army sought "reforms" where the private capital sector was concerned. According to an official pronouncement, the SMR was an "anachronism, intent on maintaining its kingdom and not understanding the post-Incident outlook." One of the so-called reformist measures was to organize the Japan-Manchuria Trading Company to replace SMR sales and supplies activities. SMR subsidiaries—chemical, steel, and electric power—were reorganized.[6]

The Kwantung Army was often said to have warned that capitalists would not be allowed into Manchukuo. Katakura calls the charge exaggerated. What the Kwantung Army staff officers really meant, he has argued, was that they did not want greedy capitalist tycoons to exploit the outcome of the Manchurian Incident for unfair profits.[7] A more precise rendering of the Kwantung Army staff's original economic reservations would be opposition to the expansion of the old-line monopolies in Manchuria. Though commerce, industry, and finance were important to Japanese interests, the main investments had continued to emphasize railroads, harbors, mining, forestry, and agriculture. As a foreign economist put it, the Japanese investors in Manchuria had been furthering the underdevelopment of the traditional economy while engendering the modern one.[8]

In addition to castigating traditional big business and special interests, the Kwantung Army wanted to exclude "degenerate and grasping" Japanese political parties from Manchukuo. Formation of a single, authoritarian-style Concordia Association (Kyōwa Kai) was the Kwantung Army's preference in the matter of creating grass-roots politics in the new state. Drawing upon the ideologues of *minzoku kyōwa* (racial harmony), Ishiwara and Katakura—who were instrumental in the establishment of the association in July 1932 as a substitute for traditional parties—spoke of warding off Communism, constructing a moral nation through ethnic harmony, and preventing the growth of an overweening bureaucracy. Although Pu Yi was named honorary president of the association and General Honjō honorary adviser, and although the Manchukuo premier was president, the key officials were three Japanese directors: Colonel Itagaki, Komai Tokuzō (Pu Yi's "consultant"), and Maj. Gen. Hashimoto Toranosuke, who had replaced Miyake as Kwantung Army chief of staff. Behind the scenes, the 4th Section (civil affairs) of Kwantung Army headquarters influenced Concordia Association policy, which was designed to achieve domestic pacification and to suggest a program of unity rather than Japanese domination. By the organization's own admission, the spur to its success was the Kwantung Army, its "inner supreme guiding force." By 1934 the association numbered 300,000 members organized into 900 local branches.[9]

The ambitious enterprise known as Manchukuo required new sophistication in government. Idealists on the Kwantung Army staff wanted an administration based on merit, "absolutely free from the irregularities, corruption, and peculation that had characterized the old regime under the warlords, and that marked all governments in China proper."[10] By all accounts the most difficult period for Manchukuo in administrative terms occurred between the time the embryonic government was formed in Hsinking (February-March 1932) and Kwantung Army headquarters followed from Mukden (June 1932). Without constant military guidance at the outset, the Manchukuo bureaucrats "wasted time" with Japanese officials at restaurants until all hours and slept till noon. Concerned over the unstable situation, the IJA chief of staff hastened from Tokyo to Hsinking to discipline as well as to encourage the Japanese and Manchukuoan officials.[11] Trained and efficient Chinese administrators were certainly unavailable in sufficient numbers, so that "Japanese organizational ability and executive efficiency seem to have been availed of wherever necessary," although some observers noted that the quality of the Japanese bureaucrats was not consistently good. Of 27 bureau chiefs, seventeen were Japanese. Two Japanese served on the privy council. The Board of General Affairs, all-important in the formative year of 1932, was headed by Komai Tokuzō. Of 135 central officials, 100 were Japanese, and Japanese were especially numerous in the areas of finance and supply. In all, over 200 Japanese served as officials of the new state in 1932—exclusive of local authorities, government enterprises, and the armed forces. Japanese officials exerted greater influence than even these statistics suggest, because they occupied the preponderance of vital posts involving the most responsible and important duties. Vice ministers, for example—the key men—were regularly Japanese.[12]

Still, even enemies of Manchukuo had to admit that the Japanese were able to recruit a goodly number of generals and high officials of the former Chang Hsüeh-liang regime. Though some called the higher Manchukuoan officials "leftover old literati" and figureheads, others observed that Manchu emphasis upon a Confucian basis for government and education served the needs of the Japanese, who could now use it to counter Kuomintang and Communist espousal of nationalism.[13] As a British observer noted, if the Chinese had opposed the new state with passive resistance the way the Germans had sabotaged the French in the Ruhr crisis of 1923, "the Japanese would have had either to abandon the attempt [to create a puppet state] altogether or else annex Manchuria outright."[14]

In the view of the Kwantung Army staff, nation-building would be impossible unless Manchukuo's security were assured. Actual or potential threats to that security were (1) domestic "bandits," (2) Nationalist China, and (3) Soviet Russia. The first were a motley and dispersed collection of professional brigands, opium smugglers, patriotic or ideological adherents of the Kuomintang or the Communists, warlord followers, unemployed ex-soldiers, vagrants, displaced railway workers, and distressed farmers (the last called "bandits of despair"). As one foreigner saw it, "In a repressive society demoralized by foreign imperialism and warlord-inflicted misery, banditry remained one of the few roads open for human beings to assert themselves."[15] Arnold Toynbee, who traveled in South Manchuria shortly before the Mukden Incident, discerned conditions peculiar to a frontier territory undergoing rapid settlement and development, comparable to the situation in the Australian hinterland and American West in the nineteenth century. Since a greater degree of insecurity was observable in Manchuria close to the fringes of settlement, Toynbee questioned the Kwantung Army's claim of a recrudescence of brigandage in the built-up areas.[16]

The Japanese explanation was that bandit forces, which had approximated a total of 130,000 men in early 1932, swelled to 200,000 in summer and to a peak of 360,000 by autumn as the result of major accretions from the remnants of the army of Chang Hsüeh-liang.[17] The "bandit menace" led the Kwantung Army to clear away kaoliang fields for hundreds of meters along both sides of railroad right-of-way, to spread apart double-tracked rail lines across rivers, and to store ammunition near military camp guardrooms, unlike the practice in Japan.[18]

To buttress its own pacification capability, the Kwantung Army in March 1932 sponsored the creation of a Manchukuoan army, whose expenses were footed entirely by the Japanese war ministry until fiscal year 1934-35. By 1935 the Manchukuoan army consisted of 26 infantry brigades and eight cavalry brigades, all mainly engaged in quelling banditry. During the period 1932-35, its operations cost the Manchukuoan forces 1,470 dead and 1,261 wounded. Although the Kwantung Army admitted ridiculously few of its own casualties in bandit-suppression operations during the same period, it is noteworthy that the Japanese losses were mainly in officers: 37 of 41 slain, five of seven wounded. Presumably the high ratio of officer losses is attributable to the Japanese need to fight in the forefront of the Manchukuoan army, to which many Kwantung Army officers were attached in key positions. Significantly, IJA generals were publicly revealed to have commanded a few of the pacification efforts: Maj. Gen. Hino Takeo (Chientao,

July-September 1934) and Maj. Gen. Fujii Jūzaburō (Chientao, January 1935). The Kwantung Army admitted much higher casualties in bandit-suppression operations in 1937 (289 killed and 471 wounded), but claimed to have killed 6,351 and captured 1,229 bandits.[19]

Drawn at first mainly from elements of Chang Hsüeh-liang's forces and ex-brigands, Manchukuoan army soldiers were of dubious reliability; they often deserted or rebelled, and they suffered many a reverse in combat. Indeed, the Japanese were chary about providing heavy weapons and ammunition to their protégés, who, as the bandits exulted, were their best source of supply for military stores. Still, under Kwantung Army tutelage the Manchukuoan army troops, especially when rotated from desolate garrisons, began to give a creditable account of themselves.[20] Undoubtedly the puppet forces, by their numbers alone, helped to ease the combat burden of the Kwantung Army. As early as the spring of 1932, 7,000 Manchukuoan troops were in action in a campaign against bandits. Eight thousand fought in the Tungpientao area in the autumn, and forces as large as 15,000-20,000, and even 35,000, were reported in the field in 1933 and 1934. For the subjugation of Jehol Province in early 1933, a large portion of the Manchukuoan army—42,000 men—operated in support of the Kwantung Army.

Better quality was infused into the Manchukuoan army by the introduction of native conscripts untainted by a questionable past. According to Kwantung Army advisers, the Manchukuoan forces performed particularly well against guerrilla elements in eastern Manchuria and, in fact, endured hardships better than the Japanese. Plotting data on banditry like a "fever chart," the Kwantung Army claimed that, despite many ups and downs, dissident forces had been reduced to a total of 20,000-25,000 men by 1935, and to 7,300 by the end of 1938, operating mainly in the northeast. Whereas in 1932 some bandit forces had numbered 30,000 armed men, the groups in 1938 were said to average fewer than 30 horsemen.[21]

Of larger moment for the Kwantung Army than the domestic pacification of Manchukuo was the relationship of the new protectorate to China. To consolidate the approaches from Inner Mongolia, Kwantung Army forces in the first months of 1933 penetrated "disaffected" Jehol Province and seized their main objectives against an estimated 235,000-245,000 Chinese troops. By the 4th of March all of Jehol was cleared; the Great Wall was reached by the 10th. In April, in the face of Chinese "provocation," the Kwantung Army extended its operations across the wall into North China. By the terms of the Tangku Truce, signed by the local commanders at the end of May 1933, eastern Hopeh Province—some 13,000 sq. km. between Manchuria and Peking—was demilitarized. Chinese forces were to be withdrawn from this zone, subject to verification by the Kwantung Army, which would then fall back north to the Great Wall. A police force friendly to Japan would be responsible for security in the buffer region. The net result of the Kwantung Army's actions of 1933, from the Chinese standpoint, was the loss by default of the defenses of Peking and Tientsin. From the Japanese point of view, the Manchurian Incident was officially over.[22]

Intensified efforts to solidify and enlarge the Japanese position were undertaken by the Japanese army in 1935, especially after the Okada Keisuke government implemented a conciliatory policy of exchanging ambassadors with China in May. In January, Kwantung Army staff officers had already met in Dairen to devise a strategy for the penetration of North China. OSS Maj. Gen. Dohihara Kenji, an old China hand, traveled at various times to the Peking region from his headquarters in Mukden to explore the possibilities of creating a nominally autonomous regional administration in North China. Chahar Province was the first objective, but ultimately Shantung, Hopeh, Shansi, and Suiyuan provinces were to be severed from Nationalist China politically and economically. Once such a new regional regime was established, the Kwantung Army hoped to force or cajole it (preferably without recourse to invasion) into giving Japanese interests the untrammeled chance of exploiting the markets and resources of all North China.[23]

In June 1935, Lt. Gen. Umezu Yoshijirō, the commander of the Tientsin Garrison in North China,[24] extracted major concessions from Gen. Ho Ying-chin, the Nationalist minister of war and head of the Peking branch of the National Military Council. According to the terms of the Ho-Umezu agreement of 10 June, Chinese government troops and KMT organs were to be withdrawn immediately from Hopeh, officials unacceptable to the Japanese dismissed, and anti-Japanese agitation discontinued.[25] Encouraged by Umezu's easy success, the Kwantung Army staff met to consider ways of dominating Chahar Province. Boxed in between the Kwantung Army and the Tientsin Garrison, Gen. Ching Teh-chin (the acting governor of Chahar) on 27 June yielded to the demands pressed upon him by Major General Dohihara. The Ching-Dohihara accord called for the Chinese Nationalist presence in Chahar to be purged as thoroughly as in Hopeh.[26]

Dohihara next worked strenuously in the autumn of 1935 to bring about the Kwantung Army's larger scheme of regional autonomy, dealing only with opportunistic local Chinese leaders and bypassing the KMT government at Nanking as well as the Japanese foreign ministry. Behind him stood 15,000 Kwantung Army troops massed at Shanhaikwan, with air support. Learning of these unauthorized developments, the central authorities in Tokyo advised against arbitrary action. Unexpectedly foiled in his grandiose ambitions, Dohihara instead arranged the formation in Tientsin, in late November, of the East Hopeh Anti-Communist Autonomous Council, under Japanese military control. Since this contravened the terms of the Tangku Truce of May 1933, Chinese reaction was vehement. The Nanking regime struggled to limit such Japanese political schemes while not provoking Kwantung Army military retaliation.

In December, at Peking, Dohihara orchestrated the formation of the Hopeh-Chahar Political Council. The council, however, was subordinate to the Executive Yuan, the Nationalist government's highest administrative organ, contrary to Dohihara's original intention to merge the Hopeh-Chahar and East Hopeh councils and to insure their control by the Japanese army. Transferred to Japan in March 1936 after about six months of activity in North China, Dohihara told Japanese reporters in Peking: "Japan does not aim at making North China a second 'Manchukuo,' completely separated from Nanking, but is seeking to make the region an experimental ground for actual Sino-Japanese rapprochement by means of economic and military cooperation." [27] When Tōjō Hideki was war minister in 1941, however, he confided to a subordinate that the whole North China separatist movement had been amateurish, and that the establishment of the buffer zone between Manchukuo and China led to abuse by smugglers—"a horrible kind of filth attached to the military"—which only served to provoke anti-Japanese feelings on the part of the Chinese. [28]

The Nanking government, engaged in unification efforts and a long series of campaigns against the Chinese Communists, was still unready to challenge the Japanese military. In addition, pro-Japanese elements remained fairly influential in KMT foreign policy matters. As for the Japanese themselves, although only partially successful in their stratagems in North China, until mid-1936 they were distracted by various problems in the homeland, such as the serious 2–26 Mutiny in Tokyo. Calm prevailed in Manchukuo where Itagaki, now Kwantung Army chief of staff, and Tōjō, military police commander, swiftly arrested army and civilian suspects before they could foment disturbances, and strongly urged the High Command to suppress the Imperial Way insurgents mercilessly. [29]

Tanaka Ryūkichi, who had touched off the 1932 Shanghai Incident, was now a lieutenant colonel and intelligence staff officer at Kwantung Army headquarters. As a Mongolian expert of long standing, he had been concentrating on building up Inner Mongol forces friendly to the Japanese. The Kwantung Army viewed Inner Mongolia as a buffer against Communist inroads from the Mongolian People's Republic (MPR) and as a springboard against the Chinese Nationalists. Playing upon the dream of the Mongol Prince Teh for a Greater Mongolia, Tanaka diverted funds amassed from "special trade" (a euphemism for smuggling activities) to support the prince's "autonomous" regime. The Kwantung Army also allocated a total of some ¥6,000,000 to what was labeled the Mongol independence movement, and lump sums of ¥500,000 and ¥600,000 went through Tanaka's hands.

By the fall of 1936, Lieutenant Colonel Tanaka was more or less ready for another military adventure as dangerous as the Shanghai Incident: a campaign, using Mongol puppet forces, against Suiyuan in Inner Mongolia. The Japanese had been building an army of sorts, which they planned to supplement with Japanese OSS agents. According to reliable Japanese sources, only 300 horsemen and 200 artillerymen were available for the first element, which was described as "bandit-like in quality"; 3,000 men, including many ex-Nationalist Chinese, made up the second element; and another 3,000, mainly from Chahar, made up the third. Fairly new weapons and ammunition came from the old northeastern armies. Tanaka felt that the Mongol units would not really be ready for field use until the spring of 1937 and blamed Prince Teh for pressing for early action, past "poor" Chahar into "rich" eastern Suiyuan. Some of the Japanese OSS officers who worked most closely with the Inner Mongolians strongly opposed the projected campaign in the summer of 1936 as reckless under the circumstances. One such officer was ousted in mid-July. Prince Teh was not the only one eager for action; Col. Mutō Akira, Kwantung Army intelligence director, supported aggressive policies and overruled Tanaka's efforts at relative caution. Thus, assisted by a Kwantung Army major and captain, Tanaka drafted plans in September for operations to commence in mid-November. He envisioned guerrilla raids that would exhaust KMT forces in Suiyuan and bring about a negotiated cession of territory. Japanese OSS units would undertake behind-the-lines sabotage, such as the blowing-up of fuel dumps, and would be ready to guide the invaders. Earlier, Tanaka had privately contacted the Chinese chieftain in Suiyuan, Fu Tso-i, and others. But because Prince Teh was speaking of independence for all of Inner Mongolia and Tanaka had called for the overthrow of Chiang Kai-shek, no progress was made in the discussions. An ultimatum was finally sent to Fu, who rejected the anti-KMT conditions and concentrated his forces to meet the incursion in the middle of November.

The invading vanguard amounted to a mere 2,000 soldiers, ten artillery pieces, and eight planes. Japanese air support—by an independent volunteer air battalion consisting of 80 men headed by a retired Japanese air force major on loan from the Manchukuo Airways Company—may eventually have numbered 23 "volunteer" aircraft, including four fighters and two scout planes. Radio and wire communications were supplied by the Manchukuo Telephone and Telegraph Services, and the SMR provided 150 vehicles. The Inner Mongolian troops, however, were still poor in quality and lacking in fighting spirit. At the first real Chinese counterattack on 18 November, they fell back rapidly, some without even firing. Despite this initial reverse, the Inner Mongol losses were not heavy; but the Chinese side made great propaganda capital out of the so-called victory. Deliberately or not, the Chinese called the invaders Kwantung Army regulars wearing Mongol insignia. Fu Tso-i became a hero overnight.[30] Many Japanese sources agree that the setback to the Inner Mongolians provided an important psychological reinforcement to sagging KMT morale.

When Foreign Minister Hirota Kōki denied on 21 November that the Japanese government had any connection with the Suiyuan affair, he was telling the truth. Not only were the foreign ministry and the navy in the dark, but even the Kwantung Army was so out of touch with Tanaka's close handling of the adventure that it originally thought there had been a Japanese victory. Chiang Kai-shek was now moving large forces, estimated to number over 200,000 men, toward the north, threatening the whole Japanese position in North China. KMT troops seized vital Pailingmiao on 24 November; an Inner Mongolian "division" fled precipitously when armored vehicles were seen. There was some controversy between the Inner Mongol command and the OSS advisers—the latter having barely escaped from Pailingmiao—concerning the feasibility of recapturing the town. At an emergency conference, a flustered Tanaka is said to have encouraged or goaded Prince Teh into deciding upon a counteroffensive.

Some 4,000 Inner Mongols under a Japanese major launched the foolhardy counterattack in the snow on the night of 2/3 December, were smashed the next day, and fell back again, afflicted by frostbite and pursuers. A revolt now occurred among a portion of the Inner Mongolian forces; the insurgents murdered their IJA military adviser, a retired colonel, and others, before defecting to the KMT forces. Despite Tanaka's contention that the Chinese pursuit would not be conducted relentlessly, the facts appeared to contradict him. The Kwantung Army, fearing that the annihilation of their outnumbered Mongolian allies was near, sent the deputy chief of staff, Maj. Gen. Imamura Hitoshi, to Tokyo about 10 December. He was to obtain authorization for Kwantung Army forces to be committed in an emergency, and to secure an additional ¥3,000,000 to support the Inner Mongolian activities.

In Tokyo, however, the central authorities were in a bad mood. Even before Major General Imamura's arrival, the Japanese government had reached a decision to prevent enlargement of the incident, and the AGS was to issue the necessary orders. Thus when Imamura appeared in Tokyo, not only was his request turned down but he was also reprimanded sternly by Lt. Gen. Umezu Yoshijirō, now vice minister of war. The Kwantung Army, growled Umezu, had been conducting actions "off the track of the High

Command's intentions on every occasion," and had rendered an "impolite reception" to the new AGS war guidance section chief, Colonel Ishiwara, when that old principal from the Mukden Incident went to Hsinking in late November to try to convince the staff to suspend the "premature and excessive" Suiyuan operation. Umezu pointedly reminded Imamura that he had been sent to Manchukuo in the first place to prevent this very type of subversion. Imamura said nothing.

In the field, the lack of cooperation by the Japanese garrison forces in North China, who felt that the Kwantung Army had been intruding into their bailiwick since the days of Dohihara's "meddling" in matters affecting northern Chinese autonomy, made it difficult even to get ammunition to Jehol via Tientsin and Peking. Now the question was how to end the Suiyuan operation. Fortunately for the Japanese, Chang Hsüeh-liang arrested Chiang Kai-shek at Sian on 12 December; and though Kwantung Army headquarters may originally have considered renewing the Suiyuan offensive, it was decided eventually to pursue a wait-and-see policy, probably because of Tokyo's displeasure as well as the dim prospects of military success. An armistice soon became inevitable, and Prince Teh made the best of a difficult situation by announcing on 15 December that he would not take mean advantage of China's current misfortune by prolonging the struggle. By the end of January 1937, the Inner Mongolian forces had generally fallen back to their starting locations. Tanaka returned to Hsinking in a state of uncharacteristic depression.

Thus had the Kwantung Army bungled the Suiyuan campaign. Looking back, Tanaka wondered what would have happened without a Sian Incident to provide a deus ex machina. In a classic understatement, he judged that "matters were bound to have become much worse." In China, the story that the Chinese had routed Japanese military forces in Suiyuan was widely disseminated, with the desired effect of stimulating anti-Japanese feeling. Not only had the progress of the Inner Mongolian independence movement suffered, but the Japanese lost ground vis-à-vis China. Even Tanaka had to confess that the Suiyuan episode would have to be called a failure.

Recent Japanese scholarship confirms this candid view. The Suiyuan affair aroused suspicion abroad regarding Japan's motives and enhanced Chinese nationalism and confidence, leading to an unexpectedly fierce reaction after the Sino-Japanese clash at the Marco Polo Bridge in July 1937. Some go so far as to suggest that the so-called China Incident might have started at the time of Tanaka's invasion of Suiyuan if there had been no Sian Incident, for the Inner Mongolians might have felt obliged to press matters excessively for reasons of "face." Tsuji Masanobu, an exemplar of *gekokujō* himself, provides an acerbic appraisal of the fiasco in Suiyuan: "Staff officer Tanaka

Ryūkichi had wanted to equal the achievements of Generals Itagaki and Ishiwara by establishing a second Manchukuo, through an attempt to bestow independence on Inner Mongolia under Prince Teh. After Fu Tso-i's army had routed his thrown-together Mongol cavalry, Tanaka was feeling disconsolate. Then, while he was consoling himself with the news that Chiang Kai-shek had been incarcerated at Sian, the Nationalists and the Communists worked to build a combined anti-Japanese front." [31]

7

Facing North: The Problem and the "Solutions"

Other than China and Japan, the only major state directly concerned with developments in Manchuria was the Soviet Union. Inasmuch as the part of Manchuria south of a line along the upper Sungari River and stretching to Angangchi had long been considered a sphere of Japanese influence, the Kwantung Army was convinced that operations limited to that zone would cause no change in Russia's essentially passive policy. By Foreign Commissar Maxim Litvinov's own admission, good Soviet-Japanese relations had characterized the period after 1925. Nevertheless, a clash with the Russians could complicate a delicate situation, so the Japanese High Command sought to avoid direct infringement on Soviet interests. As the Manchurian Incident unfolded in 1931, the AGS, though eventually authorizing the campaign begun without its command, directed the Kwantung Army to avoid the southern portion of the Chinese Eastern Railway between Harbin and Changchun, and to be careful not to damage the CER trunk line when crossing it.[1]

As soon as Kwantung Army operations began in 1931, the Russians reacted by transferring their rolling stock from the southern to the eastern and western branches of the CER, and by concentrating troops near the Siberian borders. IJA intelligence picked up disturbing information that the Russians had offered troops to the Chinese Nationalists to help maintain law and order on the CER, causing some Japanese military analysts to deduce that the Soviets were trying to get China to create an opportunity for armed confrontation between the USSR and Japan. That Russian troops did not appear was attributed by Japanese intelligence to the presumed fact that the Nanking government had declined the Soviet proposal, but it may have been Stalin and Litvinov who curbed any hawkish ideas on the part of Gen. V. K. Blyukher, commander of the Special Far Eastern Army (created in 1929), and of War Commissar K. E. Voroshilov.[2]

The Kwantung Army soon reassured itself that the Russians would indeed not intervene in Manchuria. Undoubtedly damping the USSR's ardor in the Far East were such factors as its diplomatic isolation, domestic problems, and preoccupation with the First Five-Year Plan, which foresaw an immense buildup of economic and military strength east of the Urals, where strength was seriously lacking in 1931. For example, at the time of the Mukden Incident, the Kwantung Army estimated that east of Krasnoyarsk the Russians had only six rifle divisions, two cavalry brigades, perhaps 150 planes, and a few tanks. Troop strength may have totaled fifty or sixty thousand men. Blyukher's soldiers might be good, but there were obvious weaknesses in Soviet reserves and in the command structure.[3]

By late 1931 the Kwantung Army was reporting to Tokyo that military considerations dictated operations beyond South Manchuria "in pursuit of enemy stragglers." Such euphemistic language, of course, scarcely disguised the Kwantung Army's conviction that the Japanese could and should expand their control to the "natural boundaries" of Manchuria. Although the AGS continued to try to lay down strict lines of maneuver, some of the anxiety dissipated when it was observed that local Russian officials of the CER seemed willing to cooperate with the Kwantung Army, and when the Soviet government in December and January not only proposed a nonaggression pact but also offered to sell the Chinese Eastern Railway, which had become an indefensible pawn at a time when the Politburo must have decided to avoid international complications at almost any cost.[4]

In response to the Soviet proposals, the Japanese High Command advised the government that it was premature to discuss a nonaggression treaty while many issues remained unsettled. There was much less agreement with respect to the purchase of the CER. At first the Japanese army did not show much interest, expecting the price to be too high and the acquisition of the railway to be likely to incite the Russians to strengthen their border defenses even more. A number of staff officers, particularly in the AGS Operations Section and the Transport and Communications Bureau, felt that the purchase was not really necessary, since the isolated CER would automatically fall into Japanese hands once a new state was established in Manchuria under Kwantung Army tutelage. To these contentions, powerful counterarguments were presented by such officers as Maj. Gen. Nagata Tetsuzan, the AGS Intelligence Bureau chief, and by Maj. Ayabe Kitsuju, in charge of the war ministry's important budget subsection. Not only was it irrational, they believed, to have a foreign-dominated railroad running through the heart of Manchukuo—especially when the owner was Communist Russia—but it was also imperative to acquire the CER if Japan's operational preparations were to match those of the Soviets in the Far East. After much argument, the idea of buying the railroad carried the day, and the army recommended that for strategic reasons the matter be given early consideration.[5]

When Kwantung Army troops first penetrated the Russian sphere of influence by crossing the CER and moving on Tsitsihar in November 1931, the possibility of Soviet counteraction exercised the Japanese High Command to the point that it devised contingency plans for war and espionage. Tension mounted again in February 1932, even at Kwantung Army headquar-

ters, at the time of the Harbin operation. Yet despite the fact that the apparently fearful Russians launched sabotage activities in North Manchuria
during the spring and gave sanctuary to the beaten Ma Chan-shan and the
remnants of his forces in the summer, Soviet troops remained north of the
Amur, allowing the Kwantung Army to secure the river boundaries, as on
the Sungari between March and June. By the close of 1932, the Japanese
had swept northwest to the Hulun Buir plains past Hailar and had reached
Manchouli near the Outer Mongolian frontier.[6]

Toward the end of 1932, the Russians commenced the eastward transportation of reinforcements in earnest. Thus, less than a year and a half after
the Mukden Incident, Soviet strength in the Far East was judged to have
been built up to eight or nine rifle divisions (from six), a full cavalry division
as well as a cavalry brigade (from two brigades), 200 combat planes, and
250 armored vehicles. On the eastern Manchurian border, along the vital
axis toward Vladivostok, the Russians had already begun building fortifications near Tungning and Suifenhō, where the CER entered the Maritime
Province. After the spring thaw in 1933, the OSS branch at Heihō, on the
Amur River opposite Blagoveshchensk, reported observing a wooden barri-
cade under construction on the Soviet side. From a Manchurian agent sent
to spy across the river, the Kwantung Army learned that the Russians were
erecting ferroconcrete *tochkas* (pillboxes) as part of a fortified zone similar
to the one Polish intelligence had reported the Russians were building along
the Soviet-Polish border. Japanese OSS agents from Manchouli and Hailar
also brought word of a third fortification belt under construction along the
northwest shore of the Borzya River, guarding the approaches to Chita and
the main line of the Trans-Siberian Railway. Although this belt was far from
the frontier and its northeastern anchor could not be determined, the general shape of the zone was discernible, as was its great frontage.[7]

By the autumn of 1933, IJA intelligence believed that the Soviets had five
of their eight or nine rifle divisions stationed in the Maritime Province, and
had increased their cavalry to perhaps two full divisions, their tanks to 300
or 350, and their planes to 350 in the Far East. Construction units had appeared in notable numbers in all areas; work on roads, bridges, and airfields
had gradually assumed major proportions in the fortified zones; and the
building of strong ferroconcrete defenses was under way at every border
point of strategic importance. From systematic aerial reconnaissance of the
frontiers, conducted in July and August at an altitude of about 3,500 meters, it was apparent that Soviet *tochka* construction was also being pressed
forward in a fourth main district: the area near the confluence of the Amur
and the Sungari rivers. The overall layout of Soviet defenses was now becoming clear. The first zone in the southeast would cover the air bases and
lines of communications toward Voroshilov (Ussuriysk) and Vladivostok. (It

was probably intended to be capable of autonomous operations.) The second zone was designed to obstruct Japanese forces pushing down the Sungari and toward Khabarovsk along the Amur. The third zone, stretching from northwest of Blagoveshchensk toward the bend in the Amur across from Heihō, would serve to cover the Trans-Siberian Railway and the grain lands of the lower Zeya River valley. The fourth zone would not only protect the Trans-Siberian line but also block any Japanese invasion of the Trans-Baikal region by way of Manchouli and Chita.[8] As General Blyukher announced publicly, the Soviet Union was investing more in the Far East during the First Five-Year Plan than the tsarist regime had invested there during its entire history. And the Second Five-Year Plan called for allocating 25 percent of capital investments to the industrialization of the region. Moreover, special concessions were being made to settlers and to the armed forces in eastern Siberia.[9]

Soviet military preparations were still judged to be in the defensive stage, and the Russians were not expected to interfere openly with the development of Manchukuo as a state. Still, IJA intelligence thought it was possible that the USSR would adopt an aggressive policy a year or two after the First Five-Year Plan was completed, and also would harass Manchukuo by waging psychological warfare and by supporting guerrillas. The time of crisis, from the Japanese military point of view, would occur around 1936.[10] Accordingly, during the whole period between 1932 and 1934 there was much talk among Japanese hawks of a preventive war against Russia. Very belligerent public statements were made, especially by mystics and ultranationalists such as War Minister Araki, who spoke not only from anti-Communist ideological conviction but also from concern about the remarkable success of Soviet state planning. Araki once told an American: "If the Soviet does not cease to annoy us, I shall have to purge Siberia as one cleans a room of flies." At the end of 1933, the American ambassador in Berlin received diplomatic information that the Japanese would attack Vladivostok in the spring of 1934.[11]

The combination of Japanese words and actions in the Far East was not ignored by the Soviet authorities. At the close of 1933, Foreign Commissar Litvinov told the Central Executive Committee that important Japanese were openly calling for the conquest of the Soviet Maritime Province and indeed of all Siberia, while at the same time the Kwantung Army was massing troops, building up munitions, and developing a railway and road network aimed toward the USSR. Japan, Litvinov commented, posed "the darkest thundercloud on the international horizon."[12] Kawabe Torashirō, who was military attaché in Moscow as a lieutenant colonel between 1932 and 1934, has insisted that the bellicose pronouncements emanating from military circles in Japan were harmful to Russo-Japanese relations.[13]

The years 1934 and 1935 saw the continuation of Soviet military preparations in the Far East, with a surprising new emphasis on air power. By mid-1934 the Russians had deployed about 500 planes, including 170 TB-5 "superbombers," in the southern Maritime Province. Clearly this heavy bomber force was intended to strike at political and economic objectives in Manchukuo, Korea, and Japan itself (Tokyo, Osaka, and northern Kyushu). Publicly there might be talk in Japan that the Russian long-range aircraft were "mostly antiquated models," but it could not be denied that transoceanic bombers were less than six hours away from Japan's "paper and matchwood cities," for it is only 1,200 km. from Vladivostok to Tokyo. In the Japanese capital, Soviet Ambassador Yurenev told foreign correspondents undiplomatically that he thought Tokyo and other Japanese industrial centers could be destroyed easily, perhaps in one night's raid. According to secret IJA estimates, the total number of Soviet planes was almost doubled, to 950 (including trainers), by the end of 1935.[14]

Much the same pattern of Soviet buildup was visible with respect to ground forces. Rifle divisions were increased in 1934 to a total of eleven (seven of which were stationed in the Maritime Province), and in 1935 to fourteen. These figures were particularly impressive to the Japanese, who had counted on two years to establish each new combat division in view of the severity of the winter months in the Far East, which made training difficult, and the need to supplement local manpower resources from western Russia.

Two Soviet mechanized brigades were identified in 1934, and the total of 650 tanks deployed that year was reinforced to 800 or 900 by the end of 1935. The two cavalry divisions of 1934 were increased to three the next year. IJA intelligence, which first carried numerical estimates of Soviet troop strength in 1934, gave a figure of 230,000 men in the middle of that year, and 240,000 at the end of 1935. The data included the border guards of the People's Commissariat for Internal Affairs (GPU; later NKVD) as well as regular personnel. Lastly, 14 submarines were initially identified in 1934; the figure for 1935 was 20. It was thought that individual submersibles were assembled at Vladivostok after having been sent east by rail. The naval estimate is in keeping with the Russians' own announcement in the spring of 1932 that a Soviet Pacific Fleet was being formed, operating from new bases at Vladivostok, Nikolayevsk, and Kamchatka. Admiral N. G. Kuznetsov later admitted that the Pacific Fleet began its existence with only one warship, a submarine.[15]

At last in March 1935, after considerable haggling over price and some serious war scares, the Russians finally sold their rights in the 1,732 kilometers of the Chinese Eastern Railway for Manchukuoan ¥170 million. The ostensible buyer was Manchukuo, which by fronting for Japan temporarily eased Soviet-Japanese friction. A Japanese OSS officer in Harbin remembers asking several Russian railway workers whether they were not sad or sorry about leaving Manchuria after so many years of labor, and whether they did not regard the sale of the CER as an "utter defeat" for the Soviet Union. "No! no!" the Russians replied. "We'll get the railroad back sooner or later—and free of charge too!" [16] March 1935 was also the month when Hitler announced that Germany intended to rearm in defiance of the Versailles Treaty, and the effect of these simultaneous events was to lead the Japanese AGS to conclude that Russia's attention would increasingly be turned westward, preventing aggressive action in the Far East for the time being. Although it was true that the USSR had greatly enhanced its defensive posture as the result of the First Five-Year Plan, completed a year ahead of schedule in 1932, it would be quite some time before the USSR could contemplate simultaneous independent strategic operations against both Germany in the west and Japan in the east. The overall Soviet troop balance was probably two-thirds in European Russia, one-third in the Far East. In due course, the Second Five-Year Plan would provide a major improvement in Russia's total position and allow the more positive world policy called for by the Comintern, but the major crisis envisaged by the Japanese for 1936 was now expected to take place one or two years after the Second Five-Year Plan was completed—i.e., around 1940. [17]

With the revival of Russian power in the Far East in the early 1930's, it became imperative to strengthen IJA intelligence potential in this area. The Russia desk of the AGS 2nd Bureau (Intelligence) had long had the reputation of being the "easiest" of the intelligence subsections. With little to do, owing to the military impotence of the USSR during much of the 1920's, the Japanese officers used to while away many of their hours playing chess. The situation changed after General Blyukher came from China (where he was known as Galen) and created the Special Far Eastern Army, with which he smashed Chang Hsüeh-liang in a lightning campaign in 1929—the first serious manifestation of Soviet military strength since the Bolshevik Revolution. As one Japanese officer put it, the Russia subsection now "awakened a bit." Whereas it had been IJA practice to let new army war college graduates posted to intelligence "take it easy" for a year or so, after the Manchurian Incident there was no break-in period—the new man received an immediate assignment. Until then, too, the Russia subsection customarily received about one new officer every year or every other year; in 1932, by contrast, three war college graduates were assigned to it. Belated attention was accorded to Siberia, which had been essentially ignored since the Japanese withdrawal a decade earlier, and Russia subsection staff officers were now sent on frequent trips to Moscow. By the mid-1930's the subsection was elevated to a full-fledged 5th Section. [18]

Until the Manchurian Incident, IJA field intelligence capabilities were modest with respect to the USSR. Military attachés were assigned to three neighbors of Russia: Poland, Latvia, and Turkey. In Manchuria, the Harbin OSS headquarters oversaw some regional branches. After 1931, however, attachés were sent to Finland, Rumania, Bulgaria, Hungary, Persia (Iran), and Afghanistan, and specialists on Soviet affairs were stationed in Berlin and Paris. The various activities of these attachés and specialists were coordinated by the Japanese military attaché in Warsaw, now upgraded to a general officer. Particularly good relations existed with the armies and "Moscow-watchers" of Poland and the Baltic states of Latvia, Lithuania, and Estonia, which regarded distant Japan and the United States as their best friends. The Polish AGS was especially helpful, loaning officers and providing accurate and precise intelligence on the USSR. As early as 1933-34, IJA cryptographic experts were sent to Warsaw to learn advanced techniques from Polish army officers, who were regarded as the best codebreakers in the world. From the nucleus of returned Japanese officers, a small unit was formed and assigned to the Kwantung Army to intercept and break Soviet wireless codes.[19]

Although intelligence from within the USSR was generally scanty and uncertain, Japanese and Manchukuoan consulates supported IJA espionage missions, especially at those locations near enough the Trans-Siberian Railway to facilitate visual observation of train movements. At the Manchukuoan posts, including Blagoveshchensk and vital Chita, the consul was always a Manchurian but his staff would include a number of Japanese OSS captains and majors in diplomatic guise. Japanese consulates were situated at Khabarovsk, Blagoveshchensk, Novosibirsk, and Vladivostok, as well as at Petropavlovsk on the Kamchatka Peninsula and at Aleksandrovsk on Sakhalin. Ill-disguised army couriers traveling in civilian clothes took the Trans-Siberian Railway west monthly, delivering new secret codes to the Japanese embassies in Russia and Europe and seeing what they could: air bases, ammunition dumps, defensive works, transport facilities, movements east of the Urals, training activities, and armaments.[20]

Within the Kwantung Army's domain, IJA intelligence activities against the Soviet Union, especially after 1934, included border observation, aerial reconnaissance flights, radio monitoring, and analyses conducted by the research sections of the SMR and the Manchukuo Telegraph and Telephone system. The OSS also directed espionage (originally under AGS control) using White Russians and Chinese. At the time of the Manchurian Incident, the OSS agencies at Heihō and Manchouli were closed, but once the Kwantung Army reached the borders and its 2nd Section assumed general supervision of the OSS in Manchukuo, old branches were reopened and new ones set up. By 1934, the Harbin OSS agency had more than 100 military and civilian personnel on its staff, and smaller units were at Manchouli, Hailar, Heihō, Chiamussu (Kiamusze), and Suifenhō. Payment for OSS activities came from the Kwantung Army's secret funds, and the 2nd Section saw its mission as extending beyond information collection and analysis into the realms of propaganda, sabotage, counterespionage, and countersabotage.[21]

Clandestine operations were of course two-way. The USSR had 70,000 potential spies in the White Russians living inside Manchuria, mainly at Harbin. When the CER was acquired and all Soviet nationals lost their jobs, some 1,500 White Russians were hired to replace them. IJA officers estimated that no fewer than 200 of these workers were really Soviet spies. One officer remembered the assistance in selecting personnel that he received from an able White Russian with whom he worked most amiably for at least ten years; after the war, his assistant turned out to have been a deep-cover Soviet agent all the time. In addition to the tens of thousands of émigrés, about 4,000 Soviet nationals resided at Harbin and along the Manchouli rail line and could move fairly freely within Manchuria. Subversion and espionage were known to be handled by the Soviet consulate in Harbin.

On balance, Kwantung Army intelligence experts judged that, in the delicate contest for the White Russians' assistance, the Japanese derived much benefit but suffered at least equally. Operations officers have been less charitable; the Soviet effort, they are convinced, was larger, better equipped, better funded, and far more effective than the Japanese. Terrain and the Soviet canine corps interfered particularly with Japanese-sponsored agent activity and led to the detection of most of the operatives.[22]

While the Soviets were striving to develop their power in Siberia and covert actions were proliferating on both sides, the Kwantung Army was busying itself mainly with consolidating the approaches to North China and Mongolia and with suppressing the large bandit forces inside Manchukuo. The bandit campaigns were used to justify the Kwantung Army's advance to the eastern, northern, and western borders of Manchukuo, but they also served to disperse the limited strength of the Japanese. By mid-1934, as Soviet strength grew, the Kwantung Army began to concentrate its own scattered units and to turn over certain counterinsurgency functions to the Manchukuoan army and police.

In order to allow it to concentrate on anti-Soviet operational preparations, the Kwantung Army drew up a three-year general security plan, to start in 1936. Working closely with the Manchukuoan authorities, the Japanese sought to tighten relations among the armed forces, the police, the government, and the populace, with a view not only to "constructing" security but also to developing industry and enforcing administrative measures. Official records indicate that the security plan encompassed such features as (1) legislation calling for the recruitment of neighborhood informers and the imposition of collective responsibility; (2) increases in regional police and railway guards, regular and volunteer; (3) the creation of hamlets defended by colonists; (4) the formation of a Korean farmers' "cooperative assistance society" in Chientao to encourage bandit submission; and (5) the establishment of a labor society in Hsinking to rehabilitate captured bandits. By the third year of the security plan, 1938-39, it finally became possible for the Kwantung Army to focus on training matters.[23]

Despite its dreams for the prosperity of Manchukuo, the Kwantung Army began its operations in 1931 from a position of relative fiscal weakness. When the Japanese government provided only a limited amount of funds during the Manchurian Incident in an effort to prevent its escalation, the Kwantung Army asked the war ministry for an increase in secret funding, but was told to borrow the money from the SMR. The sum was not repaid by the war ministry until the following year.[24] Once the Red Army began to build *tochka* defenses in 1932, the Kwantung Army could no longer overlook border forts of its own. After conducting the Japanese army's first field studies of anti-Soviet operations, the AGS Operations Section chief, Col. Suzuki Yorimichi (Ritsudō), conferred with Col. Harada Kumakichi of the Kwantung Army staff in the autumn of 1933 and the two decided that the Manchukuoan government should undertake construction from its own budget. But the building of defenses did not progress well, due to financial and jurisdictional problems, until in the summer of 1935 Lt. Col. Ayabe Kitsuju joined the Kwantung Army's operations staff, studied the borders, and advised Tokyo that it was imperative to expedite construction of fortifications on all fronts. Following a series of inspections by AGS and war ministry officers, the High Command agreed that the Manchukuoan government should provide the necessary funds on a regular annual basis. Construction of defenses thereupon began in earnest at more than a dozen sites on every border sector; artillery and other ordnance were installed and garrison units were assigned. As for the fiscal aspects, however, Manchukuo ended up never paying more than 10 percent of the bill.[25]

Supporting the logistical needs of the fortification system, the Kwantung Army embarked upon the development of roads and railways on the various fronts. By the end of 1935, trackage in Manchukuo and Jehol had been increased to 8,700 km. (up 2,600 km. from 1931), with the greatest growth occurring in North Manchuria.[26] Another 1,300 km. were added by early 1939, completing the Kwantung Army's program for a basic rail network.[27] Between 1932 and 1938, too, more than 13,000 km. of national and local roads were built in Manchukuo. Ambitious original plans called for another 60,000 km.—including 20 percent in first-class highways—to be added by 1941, but this was scaled down to a more realistic 23,000 km. and 57 bridges. Next on the Kwantung Army's agenda was the construction of military industries and warehouses. These tasks took the most money and the most time. In 1936, the industrialist Ayukawa Gisuke became an economic consultant to the Kwantung Army, for whom he prepared a plan whereby his huge Nippon Sangyō interests in Japan (20 companies with ¥200 million in capital and ¥900 million in investments, 80 percent of which was military-production-oriented) would be transformed into a Manchuria Industrial Development Corporation (Mangyō). With Ayukawa as president, and greatly subsidized and underwritten by the Manchukuoan government, the new conglomerate started operations in March 1938, absorbing many existing firms and then concentrating on the development of enterprises favored by the Kwantung Army—iron- and steelworks; cement, chemical, and machinery plants; shipyards; and automobile and airplane factories. Melding natural resources with investment opportunities, gradually the Japanese built up a yen-denominated area binding Japan, Manchukuo, and occupied North China into a largely self-sufficient bloc.[28]

Despite its success in nurturing the economic infrastructure of Manchukuo, and despite its knowledge of the continuing Soviet military buildup in the Far East, the Kwantung Army was not able to enlarge its own power sufficiently in the years after the Manchurian Incident to meet its perceived needs. Table 7.1 shows the strength of the Kwantung Army from 1931 to 1939, in terms of manpower, divisions, aircraft, and tanks, and contrasts the Japanese military growth with that of the Soviet forces in the Far East during the same period.[29] Regarding Soviet air capabilities, the Kwantung Army estimated that the Russians could dispatch the first air reinforcements to the Chita area within two weeks of the outbreak of a war against Japan, that approximately 1,500 planes could arrive in the Far East within the next month or so, and that by the outset of the third month more than 2,000 additional aircraft could be available. Of course, the number of such reinforcements would depend upon the degree of pressure on the Russians elsewhere, especially by the Germans. According to Kwantung Army estimates, the maximum number of Soviet planes that could be deployed in Siberia at any one time did not exceed 4,000, but it was possible that Russian air strength could outnumber its Kwantung Army counterpart by as much as 10:1.[30]

The Russians were clearly proud of their progress in the Far East under the five-year plans. Lt. Gen. Hata Hikosaburō, an expert on Soviet affairs, said General V. K. Putna told him on a train in 1936 that during Putna's three years as deputy commander of the Special Far Eastern Army, just after the Manchurian Incident, he had accomplished things that would have taken eighteen years in the tsarist period, and that he was not worried about a Japanese invasion.[31] The Soviet forces in the Far East were reported to have succeeded in stockpiling weapons and military stores adequate to support

TABLE 7.1
Buildup of Japanese and Soviet Far Eastern Forces, 1931-39

	Kwantung Army				Soviet Far Eastern Army					
Year	Military manpower	Infantry divisions	Aircraft[a]	Tanks[a]	Military manpower	Rifle divisions	Cavalry divisions	Aircraft	Tanks	Submarines
1931	64,900	1	100	50		6				
1932	94,100	4	130	100		8		200	250	
1933	114,100	3	130	100		8		350	300	
1934	144,100	3	130	120	230,000	11		500	650	
1935	164,100	3	220	150	240,000	14		950	850	
1936	194,100	3	230	150	300,000	16[b]	3	1,200	1,200	30
1937	200,000	5	250	150	370,000	20	3	1,560[c]	1,500	64-67[d]
1938	220,000	7	340	170	450,000	24	2-3	2,000	1,900	70-75[d]
1939	270,000	9	560	200	570,000	30	2-3	2,500	2,200	90[d]

NOTE: Soviet data are based on Japanese AGS estimates. Two caveats should be mentioned. First, the U.S. military attaché in Moscow, who heard about the Japanese estimates of Soviet rifle division and manpower strength via Chinese diplomatic sources in February 1938, considered them "excessive." FRUS [974], 1938, vol. 3, p. 71 (5 Feb. 1938). Second, according to Erickson's authoritative figures, the Soviet Far East fleet had 45 submarines as of Dec. 1935/Jan. 1936, 69 in 1937. Soviet [722], p. 804.
[a]Estimates are based upon calculations from tables of organization and equipment.
[b]Includes four mechanized divisions.
[c]Includes naval aircraft. Air squadron numbers are as follows: heavy bomber, 95; light bomber, 59; assault, 29; fighter, 112; reconnaissance, 109. Imaoka, "Tai-so handan" [12], pp. 14-15.
[d]Also 10 destroyers, 32 river gunboats, about 100 other small craft.

two years of fighting against Japan. In Moscow, Japanese Ambassador Shigemitsu Mamoru told U.S. Ambassador Joseph Davies that it was the fixed policy of the USSR constantly to maintain in Siberia "two Soviet soldiers for every one Japanese soldier in Manchukuo." [32]

Privately, senior Japanese military officials entertained serious misgivings about their own nation's power. When Maj. Gen. Ishiwara Kanji took over the post of AGS Operations Section chief in August 1935, he was distressed by the inadequacy of Japanese strength, especially in Manchuria, where the three ground divisions available to the Kwantung Army since 1933 were obviously insufficient for wartime responsibilities. Gen. Itagaki Seishirō, who became war minister in 1938, later said that Soviet national strength had increased enormously and that the Russians' armaments in Siberia were "overwhelmingly superior, threatening the Japanese rear gate." One AGS intelligence expert noted that the Russians devoted themselves preponderantly to the buildup of military industry, thereby depressing living standards to a level so appalling that it would have provoked revolution in Japan. But the result was a profusion of tanks and planes "beyond the conception" of the Japanese. As early as 1936 General Honjō, now senior imperial aide-de-camp, volunteered to Marquis Kido Kōichi the information that Japanese aircraft and other modern weapons were inferior to those available to the USSR. Undoubtedly the Japanese, said Honjō, would encounter a "tough opponent" in the Russians; "equipped with the present poor armaments, the junior officers fighting in the front line will inevitably enter the jaws of death, one after another." The Japanese army's main immediate concern was armaments. An AGS operations expert, Lt. Gen. Hashimoto Gun, added that Soviet military power in the Far East had become a great menace, "against which our supreme command exhausted its wits in thinking out countermeasures." [33]

In a sense, says Col. Inada Masazumi—AGS Operations Section chief in 1939—the Kwantung Army of the 1930's was confronting the Russians with a bluff since Japanese strength was "clearly inferior," particularly insofar as matériel and equipment were concerned. To live with the knowledge of rising Soviet power in the Far East, and of its own unimpressive capability in Manchuria, the Japanese military had to reassure itself by trying to underestimate the potential adversary. The most important source of negative reassurance derived from the bloody Stalinist purges, which were decimating Red Army leadership. When Maj. Gen. Honma Masaharu, about to become chief of the AGS Intelligence Bureau, returned to Japan from a visit to Moscow in mid-1937, he told the press on several occasions that he shared the opinion of those who felt that the executions of Marshal M. N. Tukhachevsky and other Soviet High Command officers had so weakened the Russian army that it was faced with disintegration and destruction. His trip to the USSR had convinced him, said Honma, that the Japanese "had no need to fear the Soviet Army." Wrote one Japanese analyst in 1938: "Despite the national despotism, the Russian armed forces are uncontrolled, in a state of confusion, and corrupt in morale. This holds as true for the Red Army as for the tsarist army; they have almost the same characteristics and they always will, as long as the essence of the Russian people does not change."[34]

Japanese contempt for Russian military abilities dated back to the Russo-Japanese War; the tsarist defeat was regarded as not at all atypical. Observers on the Eastern Front in the First World War, such as Gen. Hayashi Senjūrō, brought back adverse professional impressions after the final debacles of 1916-17. The experience of the Japanese during the Siberian Expedition seemed to provide little reason to believe the maxim that armies generally emerge stronger from the travails of revolution. Japanese soldiers tended to equate the Soviet army with the poorly trained, poorly equipped, and poorly led Chinese forces that were all they had encountered in combat since the First World War. The Soviet armed forces of the 1930's were judged to be weak in nearly every respect except manpower and the number of long-range bombers. The best that could be said by one AGS officer who visited the USSR in 1934 was that he could not rate the Russians as weak but that he could not call them very strong either. The Japanese military attaché in Moscow in 1938-39 says that his observations of the Soviet Far Eastern Army "showed him nothing": he had once been an exchange officer to the Red Army and had seen their best units in Europe, yet despite their undoubted quantitative superiority, he derived no particular fear of Soviet qualitative strength in Siberia vis-à-vis the Kwantung Army.[35]

Gen. Giga Tetsuji, however, a famous combat veteran, asserts that the Japanese army did *not* underestimate the Russians. "We were always careful, where Soviet troops were concerned," he insists, "and we did not at all accord them the low respect we had for the Chinese forces, who were weak-spirited despite their numerical superiority in men and arms."[36] Even at the time, a few Japanese military observers deemed it necessary to warn against the common practice of comparing all field experience with the lessons of the China theater. Lt. Gen. Kawamura Kyōsuke, returning to Japan in 1938 after more than two years with the Kwantung Army in North Manchuria, told reporters that there were "great differences between the Soviet army and the regular Chinese forces, with respect to training, organization, and materiel. Soviet deserters tell us that even though they detest Stalin, they love their country. It stands to reason that the USSR is stronger than China, even if only for the reason of ardent patriotism."[37] Maj. Gen. Tanaka Ryūkichi remembered publishing an article in an IJA officers' journal before the Pacific War decrying the "irrelevance" of the Japanese army's experience against the Chinese, in terms of tactics and equipment, so far as fighting the

Russians was concerned. Response to his article, according to Tanaka, was trifling.[38]

In the inner sanctums of the Japanese AGS, however, it seems that the planners were far more hardheaded in evaluating the Soviet armed forces than were their colleagues speaking among themselves or for the public. It was not that the Japanese army, despite its emphasis on the intangible factors of high morale and offensive élan, undervalued or ignored matériel; even in the 1920's military leaders such as Ugaki had consistently stressed the need for mechanization. But Japan was simply too poor to afford the "infinite" amounts of artillery and armor employed in Europe in the First World War. Against an enemy as numerous and well-equipped as the Red Army, the Japanese expected always to have to fight—and win—with inferior numbers. "It was Japan's fate," numerous interviewees have commented, often adding that the problem of Japan and of Germany was identical strategically.

Countervailing IJA tactics entailed envelopment, mobility, detouring, and hand-to-hand combat, all requiring aggressive, superior esprit. Whether the Japanese liked it or not, they could not help thinking in terms of smashing hordes with relatively small forces (*ika gekishū*). One important initial advantage of the Japanese was the ability to concentrate more easily than the Russians, who were limited by the capacity of the Trans-Siberian Railway. Locally, in limited sectors, the Japanese army might attain numerical superiority, but it could never hope for that at the theater or national level. Thus, other sectors might have to be weakened to achieve local success, with the process repeated elsewhere. The enemy must be encircled and destroyed piecemeal (*kakko gekiha*). Not only IJA intelligence experts but the whole army were working on ways of coping with Soviet masses that were expected to outnumber them by a factor of 3:1. That the Japanese planned to win despite such numerical odds suggests that they greatly underrated the USSR.[39] But it is not true, former AGS planners insist, that they ever thought one Japanese division could successfully engage two or three Soviet divisions. In their in-house calculations, Japanese strategists assigned a weight of 0.8 to a Russian division against an IJA division, which suggests that the Japanese army secretly regarded itself as only slightly stronger than the Red Army.[40]

In dispassionate terms, however, the Japanese High Command believed that the Kwantung Army's movement to every Manchurian border represented a basic improvement in Japan's strategic position. Now in the heart of Manchuria in force, the Kwantung Army had become the advance guard in all IJA thinking about the USSR, and Manchuria was the base of any operations against the Russians. By its decisive conduct of operations in 1931-32, the Kwantung Army had demonstrated to the military authorities in Tokyo that there was no need for a provisional expeditionary headquarters to be rushed to the field from Japan to direct the overall campaign, as had been envisaged before the Mukden affair. Consequently Kwantung Army headquarters gradually assumed the functions of a supreme field command of its own, with a direct chain of command to the Throne.

The field army's general mission was laid down in September 1932, when the Kwantung Army commander, Gen. Mutō Nobuyoshi, happily undertook to defend the new state of Manchukuo. By the terms of the so-called mutual defense protocol, it will be recalled, he was authorized to station Japanese forces anywhere he saw fit within the client country. The day after the protocol was signed, the Japanese AGS promulgated special orders directing the Kwantung Army commander to assume the mission of defending vital strategic areas in Manchukuo and of protecting Japanese nationals in those locations. Later in 1932, the Kwantung Army's own regulations called for the army commander to defend Manchukuo, including the Kwantung Leased Territory. On the basis of this strategic mission, the Kwantung Army commander allocated defensive areas of responsibility to each of his tactical units.[41]

The numbers of men and the quantity of matériel allotted to the Kwantung Army always represented a large proportion of IJA assets, because the fundamental combat orientation of the ground army remained anti-Soviet until the Pacific War. Although the military typically exploited the Soviet bogey in order to justify increased national appropriations, near-parity with the Russians was the theme of IJA news or publicity releases. According to a pamphlet put out by the war ministry in November 1935, "To consolidate our defenses on the Asiatic continent and to assure full protection of our first line in case of war with the USSR, it is essential to increase the strength of the Japanese garrison [the Kwantung Army] in proportion to the strength of the Soviets. Even if the efficiency of the Japanese army is taken into account, it is [hardly necessary] to reiterate the need for achieving approximate equilibrium with the peacetime strength of the Soviets in the Far East."[42]

While he was chief of the AGS Operations Section, Major General Ishiwara was convinced that the Japanese army should retain at least 80 percent of its strength in Manchukuo and Korea. Even when armed conflict with China erupted unexpectedly in July 1937, the Japanese High Command still secretly expected that 60 of Japan's envisaged total of 90 wartime divisions would be reserved for hypothetical operations against the USSR, only 20 against China, and 10 against other targets such as Southeast Asia. The same approximate percentages applied to planes and tanks, but here Japan was beset by an inability to produce sufficient amounts of equipment in each category.[43]

After Manchukuo had been established, the Japanese High Command drafted revolutionary operational plans whereby, in case of hostilities with the USSR, the Kwantung Army would use its new bases in North Manchuria to preempt any Russian advance and to seek to force the enemy to wage most of the war on Soviet soil. The plans for 1934-36 called for the Kwantung Army initially to fight holding actions against Russian offensives on the western and northern fronts, while the main Japanese body struck eastward, along interior lines, engaging the Russians in the Maritime Province—the Ussuri front in Japanese AGS parlance. Among the reasons for attacking to the east first were the Japanese inability to conduct more than a one-front operation at a time; the prompt need to knock out Soviet air power, especially the heavy bombers, deployed around Voroshilov (Ussuriysk); the desire to eliminate the Russian submarine threat to Japanese maritime lines of communication; the relative ease of launching enveloping assaults against the Voroshilov district by land and sea; and the advisability of smashing enemy defenses in the Maritime Province before massive Soviet reinforcements arrived from Europe. After enemy forces in the east had been destroyed in two months, the main body of the Kwantung Army would proceed in the fourth and fifth months to the Greater Hsingan Mountains in the west, defeat the Russians decisively in that region, and then push north toward Lake Baikal.

At first it was thought that the decisive battle might be fought east of the Hsingan range, but by 1935-36 the Kwantung Army expected to engage the Russians on the west side of the mountains. Japanese aerial operations, in the face of expected Soviet numerical superiority, were to be predominantly of a ground-support nature. Long-range missions were not planned, as the most attractive strategic target—the Trans-Siberian Railway—was within easy range on the Voroshilov front. The railroad bridge at Iman, for example, stood only four kilometers from the border.[44]

Japanese intelligence judged that the Red Air Force would seek to destroy individual Kwantung Army ground units, from all three directions, by employing superior air strength from the outset of hostilities. If they could obtain control of the air, Russian warplanes would support land operations. Even in peacetime, the Soviet Far Eastern Army would strive to maintain its ground forces east of Baikal at a level more than twice that of the Kwantung Army. The Russians would make every effort to prevent isolation of their armies on the three Manchurian fronts, would hasten the concentration of units and equipment from the European theater, and would use planes and submarines to disrupt concentration of IJA forces from the homeland. Since it was clear that the Japanese were planning offensive action on the eastern front, the Russians would increase their defenses there and would retain about half of their Far Eastern strength to check a Kwantung Army attack. The Soviet reinforcements from Europe would be committed mainly in support of large-scale thrusts from the west—and from the north until about 1935, when the Russians apparently decided to emphasize their western offensive. Soviet armored and cavalry concentrations were pronounced between the Trans-Baikal and Outer Mongolia; by the same token, Russian defensive fortifications were generally poor on the western front, and Japanese intelligence discerned nothing noteworthy there, other than some concentrated covering positions in the Borzya sector northwest of Manchouli.[45]

The Japanese were especially mindful of the Russians' improvement of the permanent *tochka* zones in the east. One Kwantung Army staff officer was astounded at what he saw when he secretly overflew the southern Maritime Province for two hours in the spring of 1938: splendid motor routes from Iman that did not appear on maps; defensive belts—not just *tochkas*—as much as 30 km. inside the border past Tungning and 10-20 km. east of Voroshilov; and a very modern, paved air base at Voroshilov, far better than the fields in Manchuria.[46] Two IJA officers who traveled the length of the Trans-Siberian Railway round-trip in the summer of 1937 were surprised to see the large number of Soviet military warehouses in such areas as Voroshilov, Khabarovsk, and Irkutsk.[47]

The Soviet buildup of defenses on the Maritime Province borders caused the Kwantung Army constantly to adjust its target sectors for an offensive breakthrough during first-phase hostilities. In addition, the new rail lines behind the Manchurian frontiers facilitated an invasion farther south of the Lake Khanka district. Thus the 1933 plans called for a breakthrough opposite Grodekovo on the Suifenhō front; the 1934-35 plans specified the Tungning sector above Poltavka; and the 1936-39 plans envisioned an attack below Tungning in the general direction of Voroshilov and Razdolnoye. After 1938, the vulnerable Iman district was added as a penetration point for Kwantung Army forces operating across the Ussuri from Hulin; the main Japanese body could be used on this front when the river was frozen. Meanwhile, in the western zone, the area for Japanese holding actions was moved steadily, from the line of the Greater Hsingans and Tsitsihar in 1933-34, to the region west of the mountains, on the Hailar or Hulun Buir Plain, from 1939.[48]

The ultimate military objectives of the Kwantung Army had to be adjusted to strategic and logistical considerations. After the hypothetical defeat of the Russians on the eastern front, the Japanese planned until 1936 to seize the region east of Lake Baikal. From 1937, however, problems of national strength compelled the Japanese army to think in terms of "endurance," entailing a final operational objective along a line between Rukhlovo (Skovorodino) and the Greater Hsingans. The Hailar Plain was now regarded as a strategic buffer zone, and previously contemplated amphibious operations to capture the Vladivostok fortress region were abandoned on the eastern front. Achievement of Japanese air supremacy assumed great importance.[49]

In 1938 and 1939, the Japanese High Command and the Kwantung Army examined two concepts for the new, long-range Operations Plan No. 8, the Hachi-gō plan targeted for completion in five years. One alternative considered simultaneous Japanese offensives on the Ussuri and Amur fronts, involving a 20-15-15 divisional apportionment among the eastern-northern-western fronts in three months, against an anticipated Soviet 20-15-25 divisional deployment in the same time. The second alternative boldly called for an initial Kwantung Army offensive on the western front, the Trans-Baikal; the Japanese deployment would be 10-10-25 against Soviet forces estimated at 18-12-30. Beset by apprehensions concerning the feasibility of breaking through the powerful Russian defenses on the eastern front, the military authorities in both Tokyo and Hsinking preferred the second alternative, but it was soon realized that an immense railroad construction program would be indispensable, as would the amassing of great numbers of motor vehicles and the stockpiling of huge stores of matériel on the Hailar Plain.

The events of 1939, as we shall see, spelled the doom of any plan calling for a Japanese western offensive. Even the first alternative became unrealistic for Japan as world war with the Western powers approached. The Hachi-gō plan thus became academic, and the contingency plan of 1937 remained essentially in effect.[50]

8

Rumblings on the Borders

Despite an agreement reached as recently as 1924 (the Soviet-Chinese Mukden Accord) for a joint commission to achieve definitive delimitation of the unclear international frontiers, at the time of the creation of Manchukuo the borders were generally characterized by ambiguity. Along the land frontiers the few or dilapidated markers were ordinarily not complemented by wire, fences, ditches, or other boundary indicators. On the 632 km. of eastern Manchurian frontier, for example, there were only 35 markers at best; the distance between markers was two km. at the shortest, 49 km. at the longest, 18.7 km. on average. Only seventeen of the markers were at their original location; twelve had disappeared; and the remaining six were obscure or had been moved to new sites. It is said that one missing marker turned up in a display in Khabarovsk. An IJA intelligence officer has observed that portions of the border were as difficult to demarcate as the South Pole.[1]

Although the Kwantung Army possessed the strategic advantage of interior lines, the extent of Manchurian frontier to be manned was immense: almost 7,600 km. Of this, almost 4,800 km. were controversial—4,000 km. facing Soviet territory and 740 adjoining the Mongolian People's Republic. The remaining 2,800 km. lay essentially within the Japanese orbit: 1,100 km. abutting North Korea, and 1,700 km. delimiting the boundary with Inner Mongolia and China. (See endpaper map.) That the larger portion of the borders was not delineated clearly—either on the spot or on earlier maps— is attributed by Japanese sources to indifference on the part of the Chinese authorities in Peking and in Manchuria prior to the establishment of Manchukuo. Much of the frontier zone, especially in the complicated terrain of the east, was adjudged to possess only minor political, economic, or cultural value because it was densely forested and uninhabited. Both tsarist Russia and the USSR evinced greater interest in the matter of borders, however, and the result had been a certain degree of encroachment at the expense of feeble China—until the Kwantung Army arrived on the scene. In the Japanese view, the Russians tended to distort ambiguous demarcation provisions in their favor.[2]

The historical seesaw meant little to the border residents, whose interests centered on survival, not patriotic loyalties. Even for a certain period after the Japanese took over Manchuria matters were not brought to a head. Not only were there considerations of the initial balance of power, but it is also said that the Japanese, being island people, cannot easily visualize land border lines. In the "good old days" in the east, the natives could chase straying cattle or pets across perfunctorily marked or unmarked borders, or snag driftwood floating downriver, without fear of snipers or patrols. Wrote a Japanese former army officer:[3]

> Up north on the Ussuri River, poppies were grown on both banks, and the production from the Manchurian side was simply transported across to the Russian side, from which the derived opium was shipped to Shanghai via Vladivostok. Movement along the rivers was free and easy. There was little notion of national sovereignty, state frontiers, or border towns. Public security was actually handled by the regional bandits. During the days of opium harvest, there were opium bandits to guard the farmers against intruders. When woodcutters went to work, logger bandits protected them. Only the districts along railway lines were developed; the rest of the area remained highly primitive.

As its operations brought the Kwantung Army to the outer reaches of Manchuria, and as first the Russians and then the Japanese began to gird the borders with fortifications, there ensued tension and controversies regarding national boundaries. Between 1932 and 1934, according to Japanese sources, 152 small-scale border disputes occurred, largely because the Russians now found it necessary to initiate an intensive program of collecting intelligence inside Manchuria and of countering espionage operations emanating from there. Soviet border guard units sought information, and small parties of Russians crossed into Manchurian territory at least twenty times during the period to abduct natives or White Russians and to interfere with the mails. The Kwantung Army also noted several airspace violations; over fifty cases of firing affrays, ground trespassing, and tampering with border markers; and six blatant instances of interference with or attack upon river shipping.[4] For their part, the Russians alleged fifteen cases of border violation by the Japanese, six air intrusions, and twenty episodes of "spy smuggling" in 1933 alone.[5]

Though Russo-Japanese relations improved temporarily after the Soviet sale of the Chinese Eastern Railway in early 1935, German pressures not only drew Russian attention to Europe but hardened the Soviet attitude against both the Nazis and the Japanese. An IJA military attaché in the USSR detected the sterner outlook quickly. When he set off to visit the Ukraine in April 1935, the Soviet attitude toward the Japanese was very good; but by the time he got back to Moscow at the close of the month the situation had deteriorated, his female interpreter was arrested, and anti-Japanese propaganda intensified greatly. At the Seventh Comintern Congress in July, the Japanese and Germans were openly called "fascist enemies" and a resolution demanded opposition to them by the Soviet Union and the "popular fronts." At the same time, the Soviet diplomatic position was improved by entry into the League of Nations and consummation of a major pact with France.[6]

The Japanese called the years 1935-36 a period of medium-scale border disputes characterized by a doubling of Russian violations, which were "more systematic and more flagrant" than before. Soviet reconnaissance efforts seem to have been accelerated at the same time that the Russians sought to secure strategic locations on the frontier. Since Kwantung Army and Manchukuoan border guard forces had also been reinforced, the confrontations became increasingly violent. The Kwantung Army reported 176 frontier disputes in 1935 and 152 in 1936 (94 in the east). Foreign ministry figures for the two years were 136 and 203.[7]

Two of these incidents deserve mention because of their seriousness. In June 1935, Kwantung Army and Russian patrols exchanged fire directly for the first time and inflicted casualties on each other. West of Lake Khanka, an eleven-man Japanese patrol claimed to have been ambushed by six NKVD horsemen inside Manchukuoan territory. In the ensuing affray, one Russian soldier was killed and two horses were seized. An effort was made, through diplomacy, to induce the Soviet side to join in an investigation of the affair, but the Russians rejected the Japanese-Manchukuoan note of protest.[8] In October 1935, nine Japanese and 32 Manchukuoan troops and border guards were engaged in setting up a post at the scene of an incident that had occurred a week before, about 20 km. north of Suifenhō, when a force of some fifty Soviet soldiers opened fire on them with small arms and four or five heavy machine guns. In the ensuing firefight, two Japanese and four Manchurians were killed, and five more frontier guards were wounded. The Manchukuoan foreign affairs representative at Suifenhō lodged a verbal protest with the Soviet consul there, and the Kwantung Army sent an OSS captain to investigate the scene of the clash.[9]

The Japanese were convinced (and they made no effort to conceal the fact) that the Russians were seeking deliberately to keep the frontiers in an uproar, to disrupt local security and subvert Manchukuoan military and police agencies, to frighten the natives and undermine their confidence in the protectors of Manchukuo, and ultimately to bolshevize the area. Soviet agents and native collaborators continued to form cells and establish zones of Communist control. According to the Manchukuoan authorities, in December 1935 six Communist bandit commanders addressed a manifesto to the Manchurian people, advising them that a half-dozen confederated groups, numbering tens of thousands of partisans, were operating under the direction of an anti-Japanese allied committee. One of the bandit chiefs reportedly had obtained 10,000 rounds of small-arms ammunition from Soviet agents on eight occasions in 1935. Security forces often took Russian-made ammunition from captured guerrillas. In one instance, when a Soviet plane crash-landed 100 km. inside the eastern Manchukuoan frontier, the Russian fliers distributed thousands of rounds of ammunition to bandits before burning their aircraft and returning to Soviet territory under guerrilla escort.[10]

Such was the disturbed security situation when, at the end of January 1936, a mutiny by over 100 men occurred at a Manchukuoan army border observation post at Chingchangkou, southwest of Lake Khanka in eastern Manchuria. After slaying three of their officers and setting fire to their barracks, the men fled eastward. A Kwantung Army punitive force, assisted by loyal Manchukuoan troops, engaged in hot pursuit north of Suifenhō and caught up with the mutineers, who returned the fire and escaped across the border into the USSR. At first the Soviet government was reported ready to extradite the rebels; then it was announced that they would be disarmed and granted political asylum. But the Japanese contended that these same Manchurian deserters—rearmed, allegedly accompanied by Russian soldiers, and led by Russian officers—reentered Manchukuo, over 100 strong, and engaged defense forces for a day or two. During the heaviest combat, "three men of a commanding rank in the Soviet army were unmistakably observed to be directing the deserters with whips." When the fighting ended, the mutineers retired again to Soviet territory, leaving behind not only some of their own dead but also a number of Russian corpses, as well as Soviet-manufactured weapons. Japanese casualties amounted to ten killed and ten wounded; the loyal Manchukuoan forces lost two killed and two wounded.

Manchukuo's protests were prompt and blunt. They demanded that the Soviet authorities extradite the Manchukuo army deserters, punish the Russians who were at fault, pay an indemnity, and guarantee tranquillity on the frontier. Rejection of the complaints, it was asserted, would only serve to substantiate the contention that the Soviet government had ties with and incited the mutineers, and had scattered "cat's paws" along the borders to upset domestic law and order. Inflammatory Soviet propaganda leaflets had, in fact, been found among the deserters' effects. The protests concluded with a new call for demarcation of the disputed frontiers to eliminate causes of tension, for the Russians erred when they said the lines were definite and did not require demarcation; the frontier was defined neither by pact nor by practice. Far from accepting the Manchukuoan complaints, the Soviets responded with strong protests of their own.[11]

The diplomatic din occasioned by the Chingchangkou mutiny was still echoing when another border clash occurred in late March 1936 near the Korean frontier with the USSR. Reports of Soviet violations of the border and kidnappings of natives led the Korea Army to send ten men by truck to investigate, but this party was itself ambushed by some twenty NKVD soldiers deployed at a point about 300 meters inside territory claimed by the Japanese. After incurring several casualties the IJA patrol withdrew, and both sides quickly brought up reinforcements. Within hours, 100 Japanese troops drove back the Soviet force, but new fighting erupted later in the day after the Russians had obtained further reinforcements. An IJA captain and his interpreter, advancing to negotiate under a white flag, drew fire. In all, a dozen Japanese and Manchukuoan soldiers were wounded, and two slain men were removed by the Russians, who later claimed that the corpses were picked up 250 meters inside Soviet territory. By nightfall the fighting had stopped and both sides had pulled back. Protests to local Soviet diplomatic representatives having foundered as usual over the question of conflicting border claims, matters were transferred to Moscow, where Ambassador Ōta Tamekichi visited Vice Foreign Commissar Stomonyakov. The Russians were conciliatory and promised to arrange the return of the fallen IJA soldiers. A week after the affray, the two corpses, deep-frozen, were repatriated in all solemnity in the presence of two dozen armed witnesses on each side.[12]

These were by no means the sole incidents that kept the borders in turmoil. Contemporary records indicate continuing firefights, abductions, raids, and violations of airspace by reconnaissance planes. Apparently, however, the Japanese government was encouraged by the fact that the Russians were at least willing to return corpses of IJA soldiers that fell into their hands, as they did again with a Japanese lieutenant and two enlisted men killed near Suifenhō early in April 1936.[13]

Mention has been made of unsuccessful efforts to discuss border demarcation problems. After the birth of Manchukuo the Japanese-Manchukuoan side made some overtures, but the Soviet reaction seemed to indicate a reluctance that must have stemmed from a feeling there was nothing to be gained. Before the Soviet sale of the CER, there had been a number of fruitless conversations envisaging the establishment of mixed demarcation committees, possibly to precede a nonaggression pact. In June and July of 1935, while Soviet-Japanese relations were still satisfactory, Foreign Minister Hirota Kōki discussed with Ambassador Yurenev the possibility that the two countries might revive the joint-commission approach, which the Soviet side had accepted in principle. Yurenev concurred, whereupon procedural and organizational problems began to be thrashed out. In all, seventeen different types of potential incident were to be addressed by the border committees.[14]

The discussions were still in progress when the summer clashes of 1935 broke out along the east Manchurian frontier, followed by the customary diplomatic jousting. Soviet preconditions on 1 August for the establishment of a dispute-settlement commission proved offensive, and no agreement could be reached. The authorities in Tokyo were particularly incensed by what they considered extraordinarily strong if not slanderous language used by the Soviet government in support of its "groundless" protests. Kwantung Army headquarters, in a long statement, contended that the Russians lacked "sincerity" and "self-reflection." If the joint committees were to deal with national border demarcation, that would be commendable; but case by case adjudications would not eliminate the series of meaningless incidents provoked by unilateral (Soviet) interpretation of the boundaries. The Manchukuoan government added that committees did not appear to be the solution to the recurring clashes; what was needed was intergovernmental negotiation of the state frontiers. The Japanese foreign minister conveyed these views to Yurenev.[15]

In 1936, in view of Ambassador Ōta's minor success in getting the Russians to repatriate corpses, the Japanese government again proposed that mixed boundary commissions, working in tandem, might prove most effective: one would handle border disputes; the other would investigate demarcation of the controversial eastern frontier between Lake Khanka and the Tumen River. In April 1936 the Soviet government dropped its opposition and agreed to consider these proposals. In July the Japanese-Manchukuoan side advanced concrete drafts of agreements to implement the concept of working committees, and in October the Soviet authorities submitted counterproposals concerning organization, agenda, and working materials. It was the main Russian contention that, pending definitive demarcation, the Japanese-Manchukuoan side should provisionally observe the line put forward by the Russians on the basis of nineteenth-century maps. Japan argued that disputed sectors ought to be converted into neutral zones until final agreement was reached. There was also a difference in views on the composition of the border-dispute-settlement committees, the problem centering on the Russian argument that there should be only two equally represented delegations: one Soviet, the other Japanese-Manchukuoan. Since the Japanese argued for three parties of equal representation—the USSR, Japan, and Manchukuo—an impasse ensued in November.[16]

In the spring of 1937, the Soviet government indicated that it was willing to reexamine the matter of border committees. The Japanese in turn proposed a face-saving formula concerning their composition, by which three parties would be represented but the total of Japanese and Manchukuoan members would equal the total of Russian members. Not only was this feature unattractive to the Soviets, but they also reiterated matters that had been mentioned by them in the early 1930's: frontier-demarcation questions should not be limited to the Khanka-Tumen sector. Nevertheless, when the subject was in the forefront of debate early in 1937, Foreign Minister Arita Hachirō told the Diet that "an agreement of views has been reached on all basic questions involved, excepting one or two points. And our government hopes to see this question settled as soon as possible." Despite the optimistic tone of the foreign minister's remarks, no further progress was made, that year or the next. Underlying the consistent Soviet position was Litvinov's later assertion: "We consider the boundary fixed. One can only demarcate it or redemarcate it."[17]

The Japanese authorities were not of one mind concerning full-scale delimitation of the frontiers of Manchukuo. From the time of the purchase of the CER in 1935, the foreign ministry sought to convince the High Command of the importance of demarcating the borders in order to better relations with the Soviet Union. Although the central military authorities comprehended the wisdom of this course, elements of the Kwantung Army thwarted its implementation, arguing that the time was not ripe. Early in 1936, Col. Kawabe Torashirō, who had been military attaché in Moscow from 1932 to 1934 and was now on the Kwantung Army staff, convinced the war ministry that the time *was* ripe, and that joint local committees ought indeed to be formed to survey the borders on the basis of existing agreements. The war ministry suggested coordination with the foreign ministry and invited Kawabe to Tokyo to represent Kwantung Army interests. Arriving in the capital at the very moment the 26 February Mutiny undid whatever progress had been made, he was shortly escorting to Manchuria the new Kwantung Army commander, Gen. Ueda Kenkichi, who was replacing banished Gen. Minami Jirō in the wake of the mutiny.[18]

The matter of border committees arose once more when Katakura Tadashi, who had been at Kwantung Army headquarters at the time of the Mukden Incident, was again sent there from the AGS in March 1937 to be the staff officer charged with guiding Manchukuoan political policy in the 3rd Section. Katakura's examination of the border situation revealed treaty interpretation disagreements in the east, shifting river courses on the north and east, and unknown boundaries in the west. Even with the best of intentions, it was impossible for the Manchukuo-Japan side to draw one universally accepted frontier line. The Kwantung Army's 3rd Section therefore felt it was imperative to establish a border-demarcation commission. The all-important Operations Section, however, was convinced that the army's defensive mission required demarcation on its own initiative, by force if necessary. Although neither the Russians nor the Japanese possessed the power yet to wage major hostilities, the Kwantung Army Operations Section's aggressive attitude stimulated many a border incident.[19]

The annual incidence of frontier disputes after 1936 remained under 200. In 1937 Japanese sources reported 113 episodes, of which 82 took place in the east.[20] The figure for 1938 was 166 (110 in the east); for 1939, incidents numbered 195. Of the 110 disputes on the eastern frontier in 1938, 85 were illegal intrusions, shootings, or kidnappings; 23 were aerial violations; one involved interference with river navigation; and one was listed as "miscellaneous." Among the total of 431 alleged incidents on all fronts in the years 1936 through 1938, only 47 were termed "half-solved" and two "solved fully." During the entire history of Manchukuo (1932-45), the Japanese asserted that over 1,600 reportable border disputes took place. The Russians were particularly displeased with the Japanese for cataloging lumber-detention cases as "incidents."[21]

The Soviets, of course, kept their own records of border troubles. Violations blamed on the Japanese side were said to have totaled 1,850 between 1932 and 1945: 321 through 1937, and 1,529 between 1938 and the end of the Pacific War. Japanese intrusions into Soviet territorial waters occurred 1,350 times during the entire period; airspace trespasses 789 times; and cases of spy smuggling 3,666 times. From a mere fifteen instances of alleged Japanese border violation, six air intrusions, and twenty episodes of spy smuggling in 1933, the Russians have charged that Japanese frontier violations rose to 387 and air trespasses to 83 by 1939, in addition to 1,754 instances of spy smuggling in 1938.[22] According to the postwar testimony of a Soviet border guard officer, "life there in the Far East and guarding the frontier was really a very troublesome matter. It was very difficult. There were . . . provocations on the part of the Japanese-Manchurian troops almost daily; very often frontier guards were killed and those . . . who worked in the fields could not feel safe—worked under the defense of frontier guards. . . . Some really big detachments of Japanese and Manchurian troops tried to violate the border."[23]

After touring the Manchukuoan frontiers around 1938, a Japanese foreign ministry official submitted an internal report on the explosive situation: "It was a matter of strictly de facto boundaries. Both sides were pressing against each other, and the trigger-happy attitude seemed to be summed up in the phrase, 'Take another step forward and we'll "let you have it."'"[24] Though this was certainly the feeling along the borders, it is illuminating to learn of Soviet subjective reactions at the highest levels of the Russians' military command, as experienced by Japanese army officers serving in Moscow. At one particularly tense time in 1936, Ambassador Ōta gave a farewell party for Col. Hata Hikosaburō, his senior military attaché, who was leaving for Tokyo on reassignment to the war ministry. A dozen Soviet marshals and senior generals attended the ambassador's dinner party on 22 April. It was, by all accounts, not only a large but a very successful affair, with the most important conversation occurring after dinner in the salon, over cognac. Around one table, in convivial fashion, were seated Ōta and his assistant military attaché, Capt. Kōtani Etsuo; Marshal Voroshilov, commissar for defense; Marshal S. M. Budennyi, cavalry inspector general; Marshal A. I. Yegorov, army chief of staff; and Corps Commander Ya. I. Alksnis, air force chief. The guest of honor, Hata, now somewhat in his cups, came over to join the group. The ensuing conversation went something as follows.[25]

> *Hata*: Marshal Voroshilov, recently many border incidents have occurred between our countries. This bothers me. When I get back to Tokyo, I am going to give War Minister Terauchi this advice: "All Japanese soldiers on border duty should be ordered to carry a flask of sake in their pockets." Now, Marshal, please order all of your troops also to carry a small bottle of vodka with them. When Japanese and Russian soldiers run into each other on the frontier, all they will have to do is take out their bottles and share a couple of drinks. Then there will be no more troubles.
>
> *Voroshilov* (sober, speaking calmly, without anger): No, Colonel, borders don't mean this. We do not want a bit of others' soil, but we don't want to yield a bit of our own either. This is what we instruct our soldiers. So if anybody violates the borders, it is only natural that they will be shot. It cannot be otherwise, and that applies to both sides.

At this point Budennyi got excited; his mustachios bristled, his nostrils flared, and he leaned forward tensely in his chair. A chill fell over the group. None of the Russian officers was intoxicated; Yegorov sat listening, a smile on his face. The Japanese assistant attaché plunged into the breach in the conversation.

> *Kōtani*: Marshal Voroshilov, I believe that you misunderstood the colonel. He was using sake merely as an example. He really meant to convey the idea of "softening the atmosphere" along the borders to avert incidents.

This broke the ice. Voroshilov laughed: "If that is so, I get it." Thereupon Budennyi sat back, relaxed, and smiled a bit. The party resumed where it had left off.[26]

According to a Tass release several days later, the most significant exchange at the ambassador's party took place between Ōta and Voroshilov. The Japanese diplomat had said that there were no grounds for mistrust between the Soviet Union and Japan, and no question that could not be settled peacefully; to which Voroshilov was reported to have replied that Russia "does not fear war, but does not desire it; and so it is with the Japanese government." When the economic problems that existed between the two countries were solved, matters would improve. That was why the USSR had offered a nonaggression pact to Japan, and why the Soviet Union wanted all border incidents to be solved peaceably, as Ōta had indicated too. It was unfortunate that, in recent months, the border disputes—through no fault of the Russians—had grown worse. The Soviet authorities expected that the Japanese regime, if it really wanted peace, would control "irresponsible elements" and put an end to the troubles. Soviet policy meant peace. Colonel Hata, upon his return to Tokyo, should work to transmit the true intention of the USSR.[27]

In conveying to Berlin the text of the Tass communiqué on the Ōta-Voroshilov conversation, German Ambassador Schulenburg observed that it was clear the Soviet government was not willing to have the "threads of the negotiations over frontier incidents snap, but rather wished to go on taking them up." In this connection it was interesting, noted Schulenburg, that on the day of the Tass release, Ambassador Yurenev was meeting with the new Japanese foreign minister, Arita, for the first time about the serious interest of the Russian government in border commissions to settle trouble zones on east and west.[28]

Foreign ministry officials in Tokyo were of the private opinion that (despite Manchukuo's irredentism) more stood to be lost than gained, in the long run, by the formation of dispute-settlement and border-marking committees. Fundamental international or domestic changes were the prerequisite to eradication of the constant boundary controversies: a basic improvement in Soviet-Japanese relations, a remarkable enhancement of the relative strength of the Japanese-Manchukuoan side, or a weakening of Soviet power. The timing for redemarcation seemed to be awkward; the realities were complicated and difficult; and the results appeared to be incommensurate with the frustration and the effort. Why abandon key terrain features in de facto possession? IJA forces on the scene were apparently convinced that, on balance, definitive redemarcation of the borders was entirely unnecessary, and that failure to agree might only serve to exacerbate the situation.[29]

9

Year of Crisis: 1937

Sino-Japanese relations, which had been deteriorating at the same time that a Popular Front uniting the previously warring Kuomintang and Communist factions was emerging in China, collapsed in the summer of 1937. Early in July, a clash at the Marco Polo Bridge near Peking escalated into what would prove to be an eight-year war. Lt. Gen. Tōjō Hideki, Kwantung Army chief of staff since March, had for some time been extremely hawkish toward China, advising the AGS on 9 June, for example, that the Nationalist regime should be eliminated before attending to the northern problem, in order to remove any threat to Japan's rear. Typically and shortsightedly, he believed in "solutions" by force while stressing Japan's need for self-defense. To those who were still nervous, he retorted that there was nothing to fear from the Soviet Union, the only great power that could realistically intervene. Since Stalin's bloody purges of the Soviet government and of the Red Army were in full swing, the Russians would not dare to do more than scuffle along the borders with Manchukuo. On the Asian continent, hostilities would end in a quick Japanese victory, for the Chinese armed forces were inconsequential except in number.

As soon as the Marco Polo Bridge affray occurred on 7 July, the Kwantung Army rushed a message to the IJA chief of staff, in the name of its commander, Gen. Ueda Kenkichi, to the effect that two mixed brigades and six air force squadrons were being readied for action against North China. Next day Kwantung Army headquarters issued an unusual statement—strictly on its own initiative, since affairs outside Manchukuo lay beyond its official purview—asserting that Chinese actions had been outrageous and that the authorities in Hsinking were watching events very closely and resolutely. At the same time, Tōjō's deputy chief, Maj. Gen. Imamura Hitoshi, and a number of staff officers were sent to Tokyo to urge decisive action against China by the High Command. In these activities the Kwantung Army was supported eagerly by the Korea Army, whose commander, Lt. Gen. Koiso Kuniaki, was a former Kwantung Army chief of staff.[1]

In Tokyo, however, the AGS Operations Bureau chief, Maj. Gen. Ishiwara Kanji, the fire-eater of the Kwantung Army at the time of the Mukden Incident, was reacting like a dove to the crisis in China. He insisted that readiness for operations against the USSR must take precedence over anything else in IJA planning, especially since unforeseeable and uncontrollable expansion might face the Japanese on the boundless China continent. Col. Kawabe Torashirō of the Operations Bureau's War Guidance desk supported Ishiwara's policy, arguing that the Kwantung Army was underestimating China, was intruding into High Command affairs, and was behaving impru- dently. But the jingoists won—if that is the proper word for a dénouement that would spell ultimate doom for Japan. On 11 July the High Command approved sending to North China the forces recommended by the Kwan- tung and Korea armies, plus three divisions from the homeland.[2]

Uncompromising Ishiwara, though his career would be ruined by his irreconcilable conflict with Tōjō (whom he despised as the "uneducated Corporal Tōjō"), always blamed the plight of Japan on Tōjō and his short- sighted, grasping, and petty cronies who were dominating policies in Man- chukuo. The protégé state, claimed Ishiwara when he was sent to the Kwan- tung Army as Tōjō's deputy chief of staff in the autumn of 1937, had lost the character of unselfishness and idealism that he and his associates had fos- tered, and was now the nest of opportunists and vested interests. From plush, kingly headquarters in Hsinking the Kwantung Army and its bloated Man- churian Affairs Section were "bossing thieves" despoiling a betrayed popu- lace.[3] During an interview in 1938, Ishiwara turned on a reporter and roared, "What do *you* think of Manchukuo? That mental defective [*teinōji*] Tōjō has made a mess of it."[4] As for China, Ishiwara snorted after the war, "Tōjō and I didn't differ on the . . . policy. We couldn't, for Tōjō is not the kind of man who could have a plan of any sort. He was a smart person in small office details but he was useless in such major problems as the China policy."[5]

If Tōjō did have a plan while he was in Manchukuo as Kwantung Army chief of staff, it was to clean up Chahar Province, not only to team up with the hard-pressed IJA forces in the Tientsin area and thus eliminate Chinese resistance in North China, but also to carry out the Kwantung Army's old scheme of controlling adjacent Inner Mongolia through a separatist regime confronting the Mongolian People's Republic and the USSR. In Tokyo, however, the High Command was recommending caution and was dragging its feet despite Tōjō's frequent badgering and his obvious enthusiasm to sor- tie into Inner Mongolia from Manchuria. As we have seen, Major General Ishiwara felt that the Kwantung Army should not be distracted from its main operational problem—the Soviet Union. But to the surprise of many, in mid-August 1937—a mere month after the Marco Polo Bridge clash— Tōjō created a combat headquarters, flew out of Hsinking, and personally conducted a blitzkrieg by three brigades against a huge force supposedly numbering 100,000 Chinese. Tōjō's handling of the lightning campaign re- vealed qualities that might have been expected of him—deep raids, addic- tion to the fait accompli, relentless pursuit, and insensitivity to his subordi- nate officers but concern for his enlisted men. The "Tōjō corps" achieved extensive military successes in Chahar and Inner Mongolia within two weeks: Kalgan (Changchiakow) fell on 29 August, Tatung on 13 September. Tōjō felt free to fly back to Kwantung Army headquarters, leaving final details in the hands of the deputy chief of staff, Maj. Gen. Kasahara Yukio. As Tōjō had hoped and expected, Tokyo approved his actions after the fact.[6]

In thinking that the main hostilities against China would be mercifully short, however, Tōjō and the other hawks miscalculated grievously. Although Peking, Shanghai, and Nanking fell into Japanese hands by the end of 1937, the end was nowhere in sight; indeed, the commandship of the widening war required the activation of Imperial General Headquarters (IGHQ) in November. In only one important respect had Tōjō been correct about recent events: the USSR would not yet interfere directly with the Japanese on the Asian mainland. At Kwantung Army headquarters there was full agreement with this conclusion, especially after the worst border crisis of the year passed; namely the Amur River or Kanchatzu Island Incident, which took place just before fighting broke out at the Marco Polo Bridge.

There had been a history of Soviet incursions onto the more fertile or important Amur River islets since 1929. Questions of river passage and of boundaries had long been in dispute, for 1,300 large and small sandbanks dot the broad and navigable Amur and Ussuri rivers, the nineteenth-century agreements were vague, and the river channels vary considerably from season to season.[7] After a Soviet-Manchukuoan basic accord on navigational facilities was reached at Heihō (Kokka) in 1934, dozens of hydrographic conferences were held until 1937, all without success. One of Manchukuo's complaints was that the Russians refused to allow surveyors to approach their half of the Amur River and blocked the northern channel, thereby forcing shipping to traverse the southern passage nearest Manchukuo.[8] The status of many important islets in the Amur thus continued to be unresolved, claimed by both the USSR and Manchukuo.

In mid-May 1937, the Russians notified the Manchukuoan consulate in Blagoveshchensk that they were renouncing the waterway accord of 1934. The authorities in Hsinking condemned this unilateral abrogation and proceeded to publish the records of all waterway conferences with the Russians since 1934. In the meantime, Soviet military and naval activity intensified along the Amur and its shores after the spring thaw of 1937, according to Kwantung Army intelligence. Control of the islets, now no longer subject to negotiation, seemed likely to be resolved by force, and two in particular looked like potential sites for armed confrontation: Kanchatzu (also called Sennufa or Sennukha), and Chinamho (known also as Bolshoi or Kinamur). Kanchatzu Island, about eight by six km. in size, dominates a bend in the Amur some 100 km. downstream from Blagoveshchensk. Chinamho, by contrast, is a longer narrow island opposite the Soviet town of Konstan-tinovka (now Konstantinovskoye) about 85 km. below Blagoveshchensk. Both islands are on the Manchukuo side of the main current of the Amur, but on the Soviet side of the deepest channel of the river. By abrogating the 1934 accord, the Soviets were understood to be asserting that the border should run through the middle of the deepest channel, not the main current as stipulated by long-standing international law.[9]

On 19 June, according to word reaching Kwantung Army headquarters from Manchukuo army lookouts and from the nearest Japanese formation, the 49th Regiment of the 1st Division, Soviet troops crossed the river border claimed by Manchukuo and occupied or raised havoc on the two islands in the Amur. At Kanchatzu, 20 Russian soldiers landed from two motorboats in the early morning, removed or destroyed the buoy marker, and chased off some "trespassing" Manchurians who were panning for gold. The process was repeated at another beacon island eight km. downstream. Opposite Konstantinovka, some 30 Soviet soldiers entered Chinamho Island at night, evicted about 40 Manchurians, and abducted several more.

The next day, 20 June, 17 Manchukuoan police and soldiers tried to come ashore on Kanchatzu to investigate but were driven back by fire from a gun-boat and a cutter on the river and from newly landed machine gunners. On 21 June, 40 Russian soldiers were reported to be digging positions on Kan-chatzu. Further incidents were reported from the Amur islets between the 22nd and 24th; the Soviet forces involved at this point were estimated at 80 to 100 men. Protests by the government of Manchukuo, lodged with the So-viet consul general at Harbin, were of no avail. According to some sources, Manchukuoan patrol boats fired on the Russian-occupied islands.[10]

IJA 1st Division headquarters at Tsitsihar reported the developments on the Amur promptly to the Kwantung Army and awaited reports from recon-naissance units at the river. Having learned from scouts that the Soviet sol-diers had apparently come to stay, the Heihō sector commander, Lt. Col. Mihara Kanae, telephoned division headquarters for permission to evict the Russians. One of Mihara's reconnaissance lieutenants was sent to Tsitsihar by plane to report directly to Lt. Gen. Kawamura Kyōsuke, the 1st Division commander. According to additional intelligence from the OSS branch at Heihō, most of the two Soviet divisions deployed in the sector that included the stretch of river facing Kanchatzu had been transferred 50 km. inland for field exercises. Furthermore, Marshal Tukhachevsky and other capable se-nior Red Army associates had been executed this very month, around 12 June. On the basis of this information, and in view of the basic defensive mission assigned him, Kawamura decided to approve the ouster of the Rus-sians from the Amur islands they had seized. The 1st Division chief of staff,

Col. Teshima Fusatarō, accordingly set off to brief the Kwantung Army operations staff in Hsinking about the Amur situation and the intentions of Kawamura.[11]

Deliberately excluding the "loose-lipped" political-policy officers of the 3rd Section, the Kwantung Army's operations staff now "clenched their fists" and prepared the draft of a vigorous operational plan to recapture the islands in the Amur. Katakura is of the opinion that the Operations Section wanted to deal the Russians a blow in order to settle the riverine border problem once and for all. Operations officer Maj. Tsuji Masanobu, who admits to having been one of the hawks, says that the time was ripe to get even with the Russians for seizing the Amur islands. And, of course, the Kwantung Army had as its basic responsibility the defense of Manchukuo, entailing the policy "not to be invaded, not to invade."

Maj. Nakayama Takesada of the Operations Section went to Dairen to brief Kwantung Army Chief of Staff Tōjō, who was returning on 21 June from a trip to Tokyo. Once back in Hsinking, Tōjō and the Kwantung Army commander, General Ueda, approved the staff's offensive plan, which required the completion of preparations by 26 June for a surprise night attack to recapture the islands on the 27th. Assisting the 1st Division would be mountain artillery from Jehol, an air unit from Kungchuling, signal troops from Hsinking, and Manchukuoan land and riverine forces.[12]

Kawamura had relatively few troops up front in the Kanchatzu area; most of the one available infantry battalion of the 49th Regiment was stationed to the north around Heihō.[13] The other two battalions, rapid-fire guns, and an engineer company to handle the river crossing would have to be rushed by train and truck from 1st Brigade headquarters at Peian, 300 km. away. The division's three additional infantry regiments stationed at Tsitsihar and northeast of that city at Taian would have to be placed on full alert too. Because of the difficult terrain and long distances involved, and the fact that the 1st Division had to conduct its movements, concentration, and deployment by night for reasons of security, General Kawamura asked Kwantung Army headquarters for permission to postpone the night attack until the 28th or 29th of June. Meanwhile word was spread, for the benefit of the natives as well as Soviet spies, that any IJA units seen arriving in the north were going to engage resurgent bandit forces in the Sunwu region. The Japanese troops thought they were bound for maneuvers, although they began to have doubts when they were issued live ammunition and fuzes and actually embarked with their weapons and horses aboard freight cars.[14]

Tōjō had informed Tokyo on 22 June about conditions on the Amur. Two days later the AGS deputy chief, Lt. Gen. Imai Kiyoshi, cabled word that the High Command regarded the Soviet occupation of territory clearly belonging to Manchukuo as illicit and dangerous, and therefore wanted the Kwantung Army to "endeavor to maintain the previous situation by appropriate measures." Encouraged by this strong language, Kwantung Army headquarters authorized the 1st Division to move out and, in the greatest secrecy, deployed one light bomber and four fighter squadrons in Peian, preparing for "sudden developments." All border garrison units were alerted to the fact that trouble was expected with the Russians, so preparedness was imperative.[15]

Unknown to the high-spirited Japanese 49th Regiment, which had proceeded to the Amur with its colors, the AGS in Tokyo was having second thoughts about the proposed offensive. A dozen Russian gunboats and cutters appeared from Blagoveshchensk on 23 June and took up stations blocking the Konstantinovka channel north of Chinamho Island. Soviet planes were sighted flying over the eastern front of Manchukuo on 26 June, and a Japanese provincial government employee was killed by NKVD soldiers on the Ussuri next day. More ominously, it was now reported that the Russians had canceled their annual maneuvers and were reinforcing the Kanchatzu sector by returning their border garrison units and regular divisions from field bivouac. IJA intelligence detected evidence of the possible mobilization of as many as three rifle divisions in the Blagoveshchensk area. The AGS Operations Bureau chief, Major General Ishiwara, therefore pressed Deputy Chief of Staff Imai to limit the scope of the Amur crisis, lest a full-scale war ensue. A couple of trifling isles located in such a remote and distant region were not worth staking the country's power on and risking attrition during a period of national buildup. Diplomacy ought to be employed, accompanied by the threat of force. In short, the thinking among AGS officers, including Col. Mutō Akira in Operations and Col. Kawabe Torashirō and Lt. Col. Inada Masazumi in War Guidance, was that caution should be used toward Russia, although there were mixed views about policy toward China. The important Russia Intelligence Section agreed entirely with this cautious proposed handling of the Amur Incident. As an operations officer noted, the General Staff's attitude now became one of "absolute and unanimous nonexpansionism."[16]

Conferences were held in Tokyo between the army, the navy, and the foreign ministry; on the morning of 28 June the full cabinet adopted a policy of nonenlargement of the Amur affair. Diplomatic negotiations would now take precedence, and the Kwantung Army was directed to suspend any attack on the Amur islands for the time being. The new approach was explained to the Kwantung Army deputy chief of staff when he came to Tokyo on the 28th. According to the telegram transmitted by the navy High Command to its bureau chief in Manchukuo the same day,

Since the solution of the incident lies in a persistent policy of nonexpansion, even if force is used by local elements of the army it is imperative not to allow matters to spread to the riverine and air units; this is the opinion held jointly by the navy and army. . . . Although there were varying ideas in the army High Command about the timing and method of recapture by force, we have deferred the problem, as the result of careful deliberations, even if there should be a recapture by force. The decision was taken to develop diplomatic negotiation as an immediate measure.[17]

Directly upon receipt of the unexpected message from Tokyo, the Kwantung Army operations staff prepared an order to suspend the attack temporarily but to remain on the alert against any new Soviet intrusion. Tōjō approved the draft, and General Ueda agreed in turn. Copies of the order were rushed to the front by plane. Maj. Gen. Koizumi Kyōji had already completed concentrating his brigade at the front, and Lieutenant Colonel Mihara had ordered a landing at Kanchatzu on the night of 28 June, when the courier arrived from Hsinking in the nick of time with the countermanding instructions. Apparently unbeknown to higher headquarters, however, Mihara prevailed upon the courier, a Kwantung Army staff officer, to allow one infantry company to land on Kanchatzu, with the understanding that the Japanese troops would not open fire if the Russians did not. Luckily for all concerned, the Japanese amphibious force encountered no enemy near the landing points. Before the situation could deteriorate, the 1st Division commander ordered Mihara to recall his forces, and the Japanese pulled out on the morning of 29 June.[18]

Mihara's eager troops were disgusted by what they called the timidity of Kwantung Army headquarters in backing down although intelligence had just been received that 50 Soviet tanks were heading south along the Amur from Blagoveshchensk. But the chance for a scrap seemed to have been lost: Japanese lookouts discerned no special movement on the Russian side of the Amur, and divisional signal officers reported the interception of a message "not to fight" transmitted by Defense Commissar Voroshilov to Soviet forces in the Kanchatzu sector.

The Japanese had reluctantly fallen back from the river when Russian gunboats were reported in the southern channel, west of Kanchatzu, in the early afternoon of 30 June. According to Japanese propaganda, the Soviet warships precipitated the action that followed by repeatedly firing in battle formation against the Japanese positions ashore. Even General Kawamura was assured by his subordinates that the Russians had started the episode and that the Japanese had only responded "automatically" in self-defense. Still, the 49th Regiment's official history admits that the gunboats first bombarded Kanchatzu Island, which the Japanese had already evacuated but where a dummy position was visible. Only after Japanese machine guns and infantry cannon, displaced to the riverbank, opened fire on the vessels did the latter turn their Maxim guns against the south shore. The Japanese, firing two horse-drawn 37-mm. guns from hastily improvised sites and using high-explosive as well as armor-piercing shells, proceeded to sink the lead gunboat, cripple the second, and drive off a third, all within ten minutes.[19] Whereas Tass admitted two crewmen killed and three wounded, the Japanese believed that only a few Russians survived from the complement of 50 or 60 aboard the sunken ship, a number of whom, while swimming naked toward the north shore, were picked off by machine gunners and riflemen. Total Soviet casualties were estimated at 37. The Japanese suffered no losses, although one gunner remembers Russian machine-gun bullets crashing against the shield of his rapid-fire piece.[20]

The IJA regimental history claims that an additional 20 Soviet vessels of the Amur flotilla appeared off Kanchatzu, and that this time Japanese gunners took the initiative and drove them off.[21] Japanese historians are still not sure whether the bombardments against the Russian gunboats were authorized beforehand by Kwantung Army headquarters; nor is the level of the combat decision authenticated.[22] The regimental history suggests that Lieutenant Colonel Mihara acted on his own and then obtained 1st Division commander Kawamura's sanction.[23] But a junior colleague of Mihara's asserts that the lieutenant colonel was a mild and quiet officer—no fire-eater like Col. Hashimoto Kingorō, whose batteries shelled other gunboats, the USS *Panay* and HMS *Ladybird*, on the Yangtze River in December of 1937. In fact, Mihara's front-line battalion had been the only one in the regiment that did not participate in the 2–26 Mutiny of 1936 brought on by the reassignment of the 1st Division from Tokyo to northern Manchuria. Thus Mihara was not the kind of army officer who would have taken unilateral action, unless provoked by overt enemy action.[24]

This interpretation tends to jibe with the remarks of an enlisted gunner to the effect that, because of the unexpected appearance of the Soviet gunboats in the south channel, the decision to shift the artillery to the shoreline had to be made on the spot by the front-line commander, who ordered bombardment only after the gunboats directed machine-gun fire against the Japanese-occupied riverbank.[25] A Kwantung Army news release on 6 July implied that the firing was begun by subordinate troops even before Mihara arrived on the scene, and that he cautiously suspended the bombardment for a while:[26]

> After the Soviet crewmen had gone inside the gunboats, the commander of the first ship appeared on the bridge, observing us through binoculars. As soon as he went below, the same gunboat illegally opened fire with its machine guns first and then with cannon against our lookouts and against one of our units. . . . Thereupon the Yoshioka [infantry?] unit immediately returned the fire. . . . Upon re-

ceiving this report, Force Commander Mihara came to the spot and ordered the Yoshioka unit to hold its fire temporarily, while observing the combat intentions of the Soviet gunboats. But the Russian crewmen continued to shoot fiercely, so . . . Mihara was obliged to respond, and he had the rapid-fire gun unit advance to the river bank and commence shooting at the gunboats.

Despite his alleged circumspection on this occasion, though, Mihara seems to have acted very aggressively in sending an infantry company to Kanchatzu even after word was received from Hsinking to suspend offensive action on 28 June. There can be no doubt that the Japanese infantry went to the island in full expectation of having to fight the Russians. Before boarding their landing craft, the men of the 7th Company exchanged ceremonial sips of water, a traditional prelude to combat. Once ashore on Kanchatzu, a seven-man patrol probed as far as an abandoned, squad-size Russian campsite. Still, Mihara did not move the main part of the company past the center of the island, "lest he break the promise to the Kwantung Army staff officer." [27]

On the evening of 30 June, Major Nakayama of the Kwantung Army's Operations Section was ordered to proceed from Hsinking next day to direct activities in the Sunwu area, south of Heihō, and to collect intelligence. He was told that no further actions were planned along the Amur, except for a landing on an unnamed islet. As recently ordered, Japanese forces would not adopt an offensive attitude; but all units would remain at their forward positions at present. In case of emergency, forces on the spot were to cooperate promptly with arriving reinforcements. [28] That same night of 30 June, in Tokyo, the AGS Operations staff recapitulated its fundamental approach to the Kanchatzu crisis: "The Operations Bureau has adhered to the principle of nonenlargement of the dispute ever since the outbreak of the Amur Incident. . . . This is not yet a good opportunity to punish the enemy. . . . We believe that it is not suitable for our Empire alone to embark on war before 1939 against a Soviet army that has completed the framework of its modern military preparations a step ahead of our own national forces, which are now in the process of striving to assume a position of invincibility." [29]

In the meantime, the foreign ministry, acting on the government's decision of 28 June, instructed Ambassador Shigemitsu Mamoru in Moscow to lodge a strong protest and try to settle the controversy through diplomacy. The ambassador promptly saw Vice Foreign Commissar Stomonyakov, and met with Commissar Litvinov on the 29th. The Soviet side insisted that an agreement of 1860, and more particularly a map made the following year, indicated that the Amur islands belonged to Russia. Shigemitsu not only denied this on the basis of Japanese evidence but also insisted that the sole way to solve the current crisis was for Soviet troops and warships to withdraw immediately from the contested area. Litvinov finally agreed, asserting that the problem was strictly local and did not concern the central authorities. Though the USSR had no objection to a withdrawal from the disputed points, he requested that the Japanese side clear its forces from the region too, and he reserved the problem of jurisdiction over the islands to further negotiations, separate from the current dispute. Definition of the boundaries was necessary, as the controversy stemmed from the uncertain border.

Russian sources indicate that Shigemitsu agreed to convey the request for Japanese-Manchukuoan withdrawal to the Japanese government and the Kwantung Army. Japanese materials agree that a mutual accord on the point was reached at this meeting. As the American ambassador, Davies, saw matters in Moscow, Shigemitsu "had, in practical effect, issued an ultimatum to Litvinov," and the Japanese "had stood pat" in their firm position.

From the Japanese standpoint, however, the Russians showed bad faith by continuing to operate gunboats in the crisis area, which led to the fight on 30 June. Premier Konoe Fumimaro conferred with the army, navy, and foreign ministers on 1 July, at which time it was decided to wire Shigemitsu strong instructions calling for prior withdrawal of Soviet forces in the Kanchatzu area. The gunboat affray briefly stiffened the Russians' attitude, and on 1 July Litvinov spoke of a possible Soviet demand for an indemnity. Shigemitsu was adamant about restoration of the status quo ante, without any simultaneous pullback by the Japanese side from what was considered Manchukuoan territory. Litvinov responded that if Manchukuo gave evidence of withdrawal, the Russians might pull out by the next day. Upon learning the details of this conference, the foreign ministry informed Shigemitsu that "simultaneous" evacuation was impossible because there were no Japanese or Manchukuoan soldiers on the Amur islands and no Manchukuoan gunboats nearby. When Shigemitsu went back to see Litvinov on 2 July with this assurance, the foreign commissar promised orally that his government would order the Soviet soldiers on the Amur islands and the gunboats operating in the vicinity to be withdrawn immediately. The matter of borders and of ownership of the islands was left for further negotiation.[30]

On the afternoon of 3 July, the Russians began to evacuate the Amur islands. The process of dismantling defenses and withdrawing the soldiers and patrol boats was completed in a day or two. Most of the advanced forces of the Japanese 1st Division returned to their duty stations on 17 July, although some strong reinforcements were left in the Kanchatzu area. Almost immediately after the diplomatic settlement, however, the Manchukuoan authorities took steps to occupy the islands themselves, it being their contention that there had never been any real question of jurisdiction and that the Russians had only tried to suspend the matter in order to save face during the Moscow negotiations. Although the Russian representatives in Manchukuo raised no formal objection, the Soviet foreign ministry protested to the Japanese embassy in Moscow on 6 July that a Japanese army company had landed on Chinamho Island and was digging in, thereby violating the Shigemitsu-Litvinov agreement. The Japanese side brushed off the Soviet complaint and the Russians chose not to press matters, especially since there were graver developments in North China. The IJA regimental history notes, however, that on an unstated day after the diplomatic settlement, seven Soviet patrol boats appeared once more in the contested waterway south of Kanchatzu Island. Heated discussions ensued among the Japanese border defense officers concerning the steps to take. Since it was prohibited to open fire without specific Kwantung Army authority, and since it was higher headquarters' policy not to irritate the Soviet Union in view of the latest warfare in China, the Japanese forces on the Amur made no new attack upon the Russian gunboats.[31]

Though Litvinov did not again mention reparations, he did tell Shigemitsu that the Soviet government would like to refloat the gunboat sunk off Kanchatzu Island. The matter of salvage operations was transferred to Soviet and Manchukuoan representatives at Harbin, although Japanese diplomatic good offices had to be requested twice in September by the Soviet embassy in Tokyo. The refloating of the gunboat was eventually agreed upon, and the task was accomplished between the 22nd and 29th of October. An accord was also reached at Harbin in October to effect the exchange of one Russian steamer for four Manchukuoan vessels that had been seized on the Amur; two of the Manchukuoan ships had been in Soviet hands since 1936.[32]

To this day, Japanese sources do not agree on the reasons for such vigorous behavior by Soviet front-line forces in the area of the Amur islands during June 1937. Some maintain that the Russians, having recently decided to denounce the 1934 navigational accord, may have wanted to clarify the borders, counter Manchukuoan irredentism, tighten their control along the waterway, and keep the Japanese and Manchukuoan side from steaming too close to the shore defenses they were building. They may also have believed that the undefended islands were theirs legally or that they must occupy them for strategic reasons regardless of technical details of ownership. Others argue that at a time of severe domestic troubles inside the Soviet Union, the Russian authorities may have opted to divert shaken public attention outward; or, more likely, that the local Soviet border commander in Siberia, all too aware of the dangers posed by the great purges which by now had reached the Far East, may have been seeking to prove his personal loyalty to the Stalin regime by aggressively defending the Amur frontier on his own initiative. The region was perhaps regarded on the one hand as too remote for the Japanese to bother about, or on the other just remote enough for testing Japanese reactions to the abrogated waterway accord. One extreme theory suggests that domestic foes of the Soviet regime fomented the trouble locally as a prologue to insurrection.

According to secret intelligence intercepted by the Kwantung Army, however, the Russian division commander on the scene had ordered subordinate units not to enlarge the incident; all actions were to be taken only on direct instructions from Moscow. But whereas the Kwantung Army judged that the whole episode was merely a "demonstration" by the Soviet Far Eastern forces designed to cheer up the Russian people, at the end of June the Japanese AGS drew up the following précis concerning the Amur affair: (1) the present action was not premeditated by the Soviet government; (2) it represented an arbitrary action by local authorities; (3) the Soviet Far Eastern Army was obliged to provide guidance after the incident broke out; and (4) therefore there was almost no Soviet press coverage—by contrast to the handling of earlier incidents.[33]

Japanese diplomatic analysts agreed that the Russians played down the Amur Incident, perhaps because they dared not disturb the populace so soon after such Red military heroes as Marshal Tukhachevsky had been exterminated and while the Soviet High Command was in a state of confusion and shock. The Russian authorities must have had to balance the need to restrain events with the need to keep the USSR alert to the Japanese "threat." At the show trial of Karl Radek and others in January 1937, several of the accused men confessed to sabotage at Japanese direction. In the first half of the year, 200-300 Soviet officials were arrested in Siberia. A month before the Amur affair, over 40 railway officials in the Soviet Far East were shot on charges of involvement with Japanese intelligence in cases of espionage and "wrecking." About 200 more executions of officials ensued in the summer, undoubtedly further affecting the already limited capability of the Siberian railway system. The Russians were distracted, too, by developments in Europe, where Hitler had remilitarized the Rhineland, Mussolini had attacked Abyssinia, and a civil war with dangerous international ramifications had broken out in Spain. According to unauthenticated Japanese sources, some Soviet forces had had to be transferred from Siberia to the west. Female Russian soldiers were seen in increasing numbers in the Soviet Far East from early 1936.[34]

Thus, when the dispute occurred on the Amur, the length, intensity, and frequency of the diplomatic parleys in Moscow—crammed into a tense period of only five days—betokened the concern of both parties. Ambassador Davies called the conferences "of an unusually serious character" and later testified that, despite the strong defense of their respective diplomatic positions, both Litvinov and Shigemitsu impressed him with their devotion to localizing the clash. Dangerous as the Kwantung Army's challenge to the

Russians on 30 June had been, the local attack on the gunboats seems to have shocked the Soviet authorities into settling an affair that was fast getting out of hand. Retired Major General Hasebe, who was in the employ of the South Manchuria Railway and had been traveling in the Irkutsk district at the time of the Amur Incident, discerned no evidence of warlike tension in Siberia and, in fact, believed that the crisis must have been manufactured by the Japanese side.[35]

For its part, the Japanese government was well aware of the danger of war inherent in an uncontrolled dispute like the confrontation on the Amur. Foreign Minister Hirota told the Diet on 27 July that the Russians' "illicit invasion and occupation" of the Manchukuo-claimed islands was the most serious border episode to date, causing a situation that "threatened for a time to develop into one of extreme gravity."[36] Rumors were rife, even within Kwantung Army units far from the Amur, that war was at hand. On the eastern Manchurian front the OSS branch chief at Suifenhō (Pogranichnaya) remembers that some Japanese were evacuating their families already. Yet if he sent his own wife and children away, that would seem only to confirm the wild rumors. Therefore, he resolved to kill his whole family in case his exposed post were overrun by the Russians.[37]

The naval aspect of the affray off Kanchatzu particularly excited the Japanese public; the media's use of the word for sinking an enemy warship (*gekichin*) had not been heard, so far as the Japanese navy was concerned, since the days of Tsushima and the Russo-Japanese War. When an AGS intelligence officer went to Osaka to give a lecture, he was surrounded by reporters asking about the sinking of a Russian warship—wouldn't this action lead to war? Knowing secretly that the 1st Division's offensive plan had been countermanded, the Japanese officer replied that the "warship" was merely a small river gunboat,[38] that all border incidents should be settled by diplomacy, and that there would be no war. Newspaper extras carried the news of the interview; next day, when the AGS officer went to Kobe to speak to the chamber of commerce, he was thanked for having helped to calm the gyrations of the Osaka Kitahama stock exchange. In this connection, Ambassador Davies had already heard in Moscow around 1 July that the stock exchange in Tokyo would probably be closed because of the grave crisis on the Siberian border.[39]

As for the Japanese navy, one officer who was serving at Sasebo when the Amur affair broke out remembers that for two or three days his squadron of light cruisers and destroyers was on two hours' alert to sortie against the Soviet Far Eastern Fleet, which was regarded so lightly that the men at Sasebo felt they could handle it with only their squadron. But when the navy High Command officers in Tokyo learned of the gunboat affray on 30 June, they were apprehensive that the Kwantung Army was starting a war on its own. Orders went out to the IJN officers directing Manchukuoan naval forces not to cooperate with the Kwantung Army and to stay away from the area of the incident.[40]

There is no evidence that the Kwantung Army had deliberately set out to provoke a crisis on the distant Amur River. Still, the field army's operations officers were undoubtedly more than pleased to exploit the situation once the opportunity presented itself. Katakura, whose Manchukuo Affairs Section was excluded from operational planning, surmises that the operations staff may have had the idea of probing the Russians by *iryoku sōsaku*, "reconnaissance in force." Others think that the benefits of a 1st Division offensive were incidental to more important tasks of clearing the river islets, upholding Kwantung Army prestige, protecting Manchukuo, and the like.[41]

Regarding the USSR's capabilities in the Far East in 1937, the AGS deduced that Soviet military preparations had not been completed substantially, and that the international situation militated against Russian engagement in serious hostilities. Certainly the Soviet government had made all the diplomatic concessions in the Litvinov-Shigemitsu discussions, by a "simple surrender." The Amur affair convinced the Kwantung Army that the Russians were too distracted and too weak to cross swords with the imperial armed forces. Not one of my Kwantung Army interviewees believed that the Red Army might have intervened in 1937. Intelligence experts found the Soviet chain of command to be snarled, uncoordinated, and confused; three separate control channels emanated from Moscow, and they were all involved inefficiently in practice—the NKVD security units, the naval flotilla forces, and the army regulars to the rear.[42]

Japanese intelligence experts especially ridiculed what they considered to be hysteria and turmoil detected in Soviet military communications. Kwantung Army cryptanalysts had recently broken the toughest local Russian military codes, for which they had earned a letter of commendation from the army commander. Yet when the gunboat affray occurred, the Russians "went wild," and the bewildered Amur flotilla mainly used an easy two-digit code. The most important message monitored by the Kwantung Army was a transmission from General Blyukher in Khabarovsk directing the Amur flotilla commander to pull out all his vessels immediately. Blyukher's order suggested that the problem on the river had been arbitrarily caused locally. Still, the Japanese found it ludicrous that such a message, although conveyed in four-digit code, was not even scrambled, thus enabling relatively easy statistical breaking by Japanese radio intelligence. As noted above, the 1st Division signal section reported, even before the gunboats appeared on 30 June, that Defense Commissar Voroshilov had ordered Russian forces on the Kanchatzu front not to fight. According to other accounts circulating among Japanese OSS officers, the flustered Soviet authorities were transmitting messages *en clair* to the effect that Japanese attacks should be resisted, but that otherwise Russian forces should not fire.[43]

If, as the Kwantung Army concluded, merely a few artillery rounds and the sinking of one small gunboat could so terrorize the Soviet Union, there was indeed nothing to fear from the Red Army. After all, the ratio of forces on the Amur was 3:1 in the Soviets' favor, and the Manchukuoan river units were no match for the Russians in quantity or quality. Since IJA intelligence on Soviet military capabilities had been chronically weak, the Amur affair— an instance of overt and direct confrontation in a brink-of-war situation— struck the Japanese army as a particularly insightful "revelation." The effects on Kwantung Army thinking were very important, ranging from relaxation of border defense to across-the-board underestimations (nurtured far too long) of Soviet military organization, logistics, leadership, morale, tactics, and equipment. Having "poked" the Red Army, the Japanese were reassured to find a "sleeping hog," not a "sleeping lion." In an AGS officer's words recorded at the time, "I think it was a really good 'reconnaissance in force.'"[44]

That the Kwantung Army seized upon a minor dispute on a far-off river to try to check upon Russian military strength, that the probe was not only successful but also took place a week before the Marco Polo Bridge Incident at Peking, and that Kwantung Army Chief of Staff Tōjō felt free to invade Chahar so soon afterward—this sequence of events has led to inevitable suppositions of IJA collusion and conspiracy. In other words, by writing off the power of the Soviet Union, the Kwantung Army was clearing the way for IJA aggression in North China. Naturally, Chinese observers are convinced of the connections. The troubles at Peking, so soon after the test by Japanese "militarists" on the Amur, struck Aitchen Wu as "obviously part of a prearranged plan." Henry Wei judged that the Russians' "feigned or real weakness" at Kanchatzu, coupled with mounting anti-Japanese incitement by the Chinese Communists, may have induced the Japanese to increase their aggressive actions against China. Many Western analysts agree with the hypothesis that the exact date of the opening of hostilities in China was determined by the Amur "feint" conducted by the Kwantung Army.[45]

It is undeniable that the Japanese army, at the outset of the China Incident, was thinking in terms of "chastising" the Nationalists by dealing them a grievous blow but without becoming involved too deeply. In the subsequent words of an AGS operations officer, "This complacency derived partially from an 'easy feeling' learned in the Kanchatzu affair—that Moscow was weak-kneed." Nevertheless, no Japanese source supports the allegation that the two episodes were directly interconnected. AGS intelligence expert Kōtani asserts that, on the basis of his intimate acquaintance with all the incidents of 1937, the General Staff had no such thinking, either with respect to Kanchatzu and the Marco Polo Bridge, or with respect to Kanchatzu as one of a series of probes of great power reactions to Japanese activities on the Asian mainland (the other similar probes supposedly being the attacks against the American and British river gunboats near Nanking in December 1937). The connections, Kōtani insists, are plausible but unfounded.

Colonel Inada, serving in AGS War Guidance at the time, agrees with Kōtani, as does Col. Sumi Shin'ichiro, an OSS expert on Soviet affairs assigned to the Kwantung Army in the period of the Amur Incident. Military thinking at the High Command level, states Sumi, was not unified or coordinated. The Kwantung Army and the China Garrison Army were two autonomous and individual armies looking in fundamentally opposite directions. Theoretically, the AGS should have been the coordinator, and thus the reputed manager of any concerted "conspiracy." Yet in practice, the General Staff's power to control subordinate commands was rather weak, and the AGS tended to be dragged by the separate field armies. The experience of the forces in Manchukuo and in North China may have been mutually reinforcing in the psychological sense, but the armies were not acting in unison according to a master plan. Several Japanese sources remark upon the fact that the very closeness in point of time between the Amur Incident and the clash at the Marco Polo Bridge militated against, rather than corroborated, theories of conspiracy. Might not the Kanchatzu Incident, in fact, have stimulated hawkish Chinese elements to adopt a stiff attitude toward the Japanese forces in North China?[46]

The Amur episode exerted three major effects on the Japanese army itself. First, the front-line combat units of the Kwantung Army were unhappy with the alleged timidity of higher headquarters. Second, hawks serving on the Kwantung Army staff were displeased with the doves in their midst. Third, the field army was resentful of the vacillation and interference on the part of the General Staff in Tokyo.

The first problem centered on the 1st Division, which had had to restore discipline in its ranks after the great 2–26 Mutiny of 1936, and which had largely rebuilt its morale and professionalism by dint of hard training in northern Manchuria. Because of geographical, logistical, and other difficulties, however, the division had been obliged to request a delay in the date of launching the offensive to recapture the Amur islands. When it was ready, for incomprehensible reasons Kwantung Army headquarters seemed to reverse its decision cravenly. IJA experts believe that, if the Amur River had not interposed such a major natural obstacle, the 1st Division units at the front may well have dared an offensive against the Russians entirely on their own initiative. As it was, the more aggressive officers at Kwantung Army headquarters were openly delighted by the front-line forces' successful bombardment against the Russian gunboats on 30 June. Even though this arbitrary action represented disobedience of High Command instructions, says Tsuji, the younger Kwantung Army staff officers (such as he) agreed that positive handling of affairs was the natural duty of the army "in the tradition of the Manchurian Incident."[47] One wonders whether Tsuji and others may have covertly "egged on" the 1st Division even after arrival of the unpopular AGS order suspending the offensive. Did the courier officer, for example, somewhat incite Mihara, instead of the other way around?

The second IJA difficulty occurred within Kwantung Army headquarters, where Tōjō had seemed to be very enthusiastic about the offensive plan at first. After being briefed by Major Nakayama about the Soviet "intrusion" and after examining the maps, the chief of staff concluded that the Russians were indeed inside Manchukuoan territory, and he rushed plans to evict them. Yet when the High Command reversed itself at the last minute, Tōjō— who was usually a "bull"—cooperated meekly with the AGS and supervised the Operations Section's prompt drafting of the order of suspension, neither uttering any objections nor insisting upon the matter of the Kwantung Army's lost "face." In fact, when operations officers Nakayama and Lt. Col. Ayabe Kitsuju, the desk chief, brought the draft to Tōjō, he asked them why the whole plan should not be called off, once and for all, in view of the latest developments in Tokyo.

The atmosphere in Hsinking was explosive. Officers in the Intelligence and the Manchukuo Affairs sections were particularly incensed at the secrecy surrounding the Operations Section. Katakura remembers the fury of intelligence officers Col. Tominaga Kyōji and Lt. Col. Tanaka Ryūkichi, who railed against Ueda and Tōjō and bellowed that Operations chief Ayabe should commit suicide and Tōjō should resign. It was General Ueda's responsibility, as Kwantung Army commander and ambassador to Manchukuo, to defend the Manchurian frontiers, even if it meant violating the orders of the High Command. The Amur dispute was a trifling matter that could be handled easily by the field army itself, whose business it was. By interfering, the AGS would cause the line units to lose confidence in their own army headquarters, which had issued the attack order in the first instance. Tsuji, in Manchukuo Affairs, asked rhetorical and inflammatory questions centering on the point whether the Kwantung Army should "counter the illegal actions of the enemy by bravely and positively attacking" or should "remain silent and endure humiliation passively and prudently." Even Ayabe admits that he had had no fear that the incident would escalate into war. Katakura and Tsuji were heard to deplore the "spinelessness" and "weak wills" of the Kwantung Army leaders, by comparison with the "heroes" of 1931, and to lament the effect of recent developments upon the minds of the Manchurian natives. These opinions were expressed not only to the Operations Section but also to General Tōjō himself.

In the event, the hawks could not reverse the basic decision, for Ueda had already approved it. Katakura says that the Kwantung Army leaders, like sumō wrestlers, "sort of pushed [the militants] out of the ring." When Katakura happened to be going to Tokyo at the end of June, General Ueda told him to assure the IJA chief of staff and war minister that the Kwantung Army was *not* going to attack.[48]

The third and most baleful effect of the Amur Incident concerned long-term relations between the Kwantung Army and the High Command. Putting it mildly, one AGS officer admitted that there had been "some lack of understanding about intentions" between the two headquarters. Certainly the AGS cancellation of its sanction for the offensive plan placed the Kwantung Army in a very awkward spot. Although his hawkish subordinates may not have known it, General Ueda tried to resign as commander at least twice. Of course, the field army had its border defense mission, which ordinarily invited no interference; but when a border incident might grow to major proportions it would inevitably exert a great effect on the whole Japanese army. Thus the Kwantung Army had to ask for the High Command's approval of a projected major operation, as in the case of the Amur offensive. Since the directions to cancel the attack were entirely legal, the Kwantung Army had no choice but to obey. Nevertheless, the episode seriously affected the Kwantung Army's own chain of command.[49]

The result was that the more aggressive Kwantung Army staff officers swore that they would never again allow their proud field army to be hamstrung by the High Command in handling future border disputes with the Soviet "paper tiger," or to be humiliated in directing their own subordinate units. In the words of one Japanese writer, the Kwantung Army, compelled to abandon its offensive against the Russians in 1937, was left sulking (*fukuretsura*).[50] It is true that when the next, larger crises erupted in 1938 and 1939, the sole Kwantung Army staff holdover from the Kanchatzu period was Tsuji, but he had been among the most militant and unforgiving officers, and his personality had only grown more acerbic with the passage of time. Thus, although minor strategically, the Amur affair—publicized widely outside Russia—sowed bitter seeds at many levels for the Japanese, politically and militarily, both inside and outside the Kwantung Army.

10

A Neighboring Small War: Changkufeng, 1938

Despite the Russian setback on the Amur River in June 1937, Soviet authorities still claimed to be able to wage a successful two-front war against Germany in the west and Japan in the east, and to provide total protection for the state frontiers. At the end of July 1937, Soviet President M. I. Kalinin told the American ambassador in Moscow that he and his associates "had every confidence in their army and felt secure against attack, even though it were simultaneous on both sides."[1] IJA intelligence secretly accepted the fact that the USSR had changed its defense policy and had achieved a two-front operational capability by 1936.[2] As for the security of the Soviet frontiers, Foreign Commissar Litvinov, speaking in Leningrad in late June 1938, asserted that the USSR was directly interested "in the growth of Japanese aggression, which is not confined to the boundaries of China [but] also threatens the borders of the Soviet Union." Aggressors, Litvinov continued, "will always seek new prey in those territories whose masters have shown their flabbiness and their inability to defend their positions. [Aggressors] need short distances and weakly defended territories—and neither the one nor the other will they find in our country. . . . We will remind these States that every inch of Soviet soil is protected—and thus keep them from our frontiers."[3]

Within two weeks of Litvinov's speech, the most serious and much the largest Soviet-Japanese border controversy to date commenced several kilometers northwest of the juncture of the frontiers of northeast Korea, southeast Manchukuo, and the Soviet Maritime Province near Posyet Bay. The Japanese called it the Changkufeng (Chōkohō) Incident, after the obscure but valuable hillock lying across the Tumen River within the Manchurian appendix jutting southeast from Hunchun. To the Russians it was the Lake Khasan affair, named after the small body of water situated east of the disputed high ground. The Japanese assigned responsibility for military defense of the poorly demarcated tongue of land, mainly populated by Koreans, to the Hunchun garrison and elements of the 19th Division of the Korea Army. This confusing fact—the defense of a salient of Manchukuo by the Korea Army instead of the Kwantung Army—has long vexed Japanese, Western, and especially Soviet historians and commentators. Since the Changkufeng Incident was not fought from Hsinking so far as the Japanese were concerned, the combat aspects of this dangerous small war will not be examined in detail, and attention will be focused mainly upon the connections with the Kwantung Army.[4]

On 6 July, Kwantung Army signal monitors, covering the Changkufeng sector from Manchurian facilities, intercepted a very significant message from the new Soviet front-line commander in the Posyet region, addressed to headquarters in Khabarovsk. Decoded and translated, the item revealed a recommendation to higher headquarters that Russian military elements secure certain previously unoccupied high ground west of Lake Khasan. Justifying the proposed action, the Soviet commander reportedly commented on the envisaged terrain advantages: the construction of emplacements would serve to command the Korean port of Najin and the vital Korean railway extending from Manchuria. As a start, at least one Russian platoon should be authorized to dig in on the highest ground, presumably Changkufeng, and to employ four tons of barbed wire for entanglements staking out the Soviet claim. Years later, at least one Kwantung Army intelligence officer was no longer so sure that the message was not a plant by the Russians designed to entrap the Japanese at meaningless Changkufeng. The fact of IJA interception of Soviet border guard messages was apparently suppressed at the postwar Tokyo trials.[5]

Immediately upon deciphering the Soviet message, Kwantung Army intelligence wired the Korea Army garrison and OSS branch at Hunchun as well as Korea Army headquarters in Seoul. The same information was transmitted by the Kwantung Army to the High Command at a lower priority. On the same day as the interception, three or four Soviet horsemen were observed reconnoitering in the vicinity of Changkufeng Heights, in what seemed to be the first stage of the local Russian authorities' implementation of higher headquarters' assent. At Seoul the Korea Army staff recommended that, in the absence of more comprehensive intelligence, the Soviet stirrings ought to be ignored or disregarded at this stage, though strict guarding and reconnaissance measures should be conducted on the scene. The Korea Army commander, Gen. Koiso Kuniaki, accepted his staff's counsel, probably because he agreed on the relative unimportance of the border problem so far, realized the overriding importance of concentrating Japanese military efforts in China, and was reluctant to reach any definitive decisions since he was about to be replaced routinely, about 15 July, by Gen. Nakamura Kōtarō. For the time being, Koiso alerted the 19th Division and the units at Hunchun.[6]

Some time between 9 and 14 July, Soviet soldiers atop Changkufeng were reinforced from a dozen to 40 men with 30 horses. Construction of emplacements, observation trenches, entanglements, and communications facilities had begun, supported logistically by several boats operating across

Lake Khasan.[7] There could no longer be any doubt in the minds of local IJA military commanders that the Russians were preparing for a stay of indefinite duration. The fierce 19th Division commander, Lt. Gen. Suetaka Kamezō, sent staff officers to the front and prepared to reinforce the weak border guard elements. When he went to Seoul on 13 or 14 July to pay his respects to the departing General Koiso, Suetaka indicated that he wanted to concentrate powerful forces in Korean territory on the right shore of the Tumen River opposite the Changkufeng appendix. Koiso replied that he would immediately ask the High Command.[8]

At this early juncture of the brewing crisis, the Kwantung Army inserted itself into the picture. Ever dynamic and aggressive in their thinking, the staff officers in Hsinking did not enjoy what they felt was timidity on the part of the Korea Army. A composite of interviewee recollections suggests the following reactions at Kwantung Army headquarters.

> We are an operational field army with great experience against the Russians, unlike the mere garrison force in Korea. Last summer, during the Amur affair, we showed the world how to deal with the Soviets. We had to smash some gunboats and move up an infantry division, but the Russians backed off in panic. That is the way to handle their outrageous actions around Changkufeng; they are always probing for weak spots where they can acquire something on the cheap. The Changkufeng locale happens to belong to Manchukuo, our administrative zone, although the Korea Army is unfortunately responsible for its defense. Hence we are very concerned to see that our interests and honor are upheld. The Russians are clearly trying to upset the Korean natives at the expense of their Japanese protectors. Already the people in Manchuria are jibing that the Kwantung Army is a tiger in the south [China] but a pussycat in the north [Russia]. We cannot let the Russians get away with this at Changkufeng.

Against this background, a field-grade officer in Kwantung Army intelligence, an expert on Soviet affairs, suddenly dispatched a "personal and unofficial" telegram to Seoul. It was in effect an indirect warning to the Korea Army that, if the latter were too hesitant and ignored Changkufeng, the Kwantung Army would be obliged to handle matters itself and oust the Russians.[9]

To this point, the staff officers at Seoul had been pondering matters quietly, in full realization that defensive responsibility was theirs but with the feeling that unilateral field action was not warranted. "We still were not particularly enthusiastic about acting," recalls one Korea Army headquarters officer, "but now the Kwantung Army came along and booted us in the ass. Although we felt that we had to do something, we greatly resented the butting-in by the Kwantung Army." General Koiso therefore approved the dispatch of a message, early on 14 July, to AGS Deputy Chief Tada Hayao (Shun), Vice Minister of War Tōjō, and Kwantung Army Chief of

Staff Isogai Rensuke, bringing them up to date on the situation at Changku-feng. Though the Korea Army was not going to counterattack immediately and was thinking of reasoning with the Russians on the spot in an effort to get them to withdraw peaceably, in case the other side did not accede "we have the intention of endeavoring to drive the Soviet soldiers out to the area east of Khasan, firmly, by the use of force." Meanwhile, a formal protest should be lodged with the USSR on behalf of Manchukuo and Japan, and matters should be guided by the central authorities so that the Russians withdrew quickly to their original locations.[10]

In the Operations Bureau of the General Staff, Section Chief Inada Masa-zumi had been wrestling with the army's problems in China. After Hsuchow fell in May, Colonel Inada and his subordinates were drafting plans to se-cure the Wuhan complex—Wuchang, Hanyang, and most importantly Hankow—the target for the largest Japanese effort ever deployed for a single operation in China. The High Command never doubted that Japanese forces could continue to defeat the Chinese, but what if the Soviet Union chose this particular time to intervene? Already the Japanese had had to commit to China a portion of the precious troop strength hitherto reserved against the contingency of a war against Russia. In February 1938, for ex-ample, certain offensive operations in China were rejected because of AGS preoccupation with the USSR. General Tada was eager to suspend hostilities in China and to shift the main emphasis northward. The highest-level IJA sources agree that Japanese military success in China depended on maintain-ing tranquillity on the Soviet-Manchukuoan frontiers.[11]

Inada was of an aggressive temperament, further colored by forceful young subordinates and by influences emanating from the Kwantung Army. The colonel visited Tada frequently while the plans for the Wuhan operation were being drafted and tried to convince the deputy chief of the validity of his deep-seated conviction that Japan had nothing to fear from Russia at this time. Among many reasons, Inada argued that Japanese experience on the Amur in 1937 demonstrated that the USSR was in no condition to engage the Kwantung Army. Tada finally began to "come around" in April, but Inada had long been thinking of some way to prove to the still-apprehensive High Command that his contentions were sound. Of particular interest to him was the intelligence provided daily by Kwantung Army OSS units. The most important news, until now, had been the sensational defection in June of the Siberian NKVD commissar, G. S. Lyushkov. Since Lyushkov had been such an important security officer of Stalin in the Far East, Inada surmised that the USSR was being jolted to its roots and that something was bound to ensue.[12] Inada's innermost hopes were borne out by the Soviet garrison unit messages intercepted by the Kwantung Army only a few weeks after

Lyushkov's flight, and from the same sector. When word came that Russian troops had begun to dig in atop Changkufeng, Inada was delighted. "My thoughts were jelling now," he says. "We were to conduct *iryoku teisatsu*, 'reconnaissance in force,' in the strategic sense."[13] Thus, whereas in the Amur Incident a year earlier the idea of a probe arose at the Kwantung Army level and was squelched by the High Command, the situation was very different in 1938. Inada explains it as follows.

> At the tactical textbook level *iryoku teisatsu* might mean the dispatch of small forces into enemy territory to seek local combat intelligence. At the IGHQ level it meant something far more sweeping: to test or fish for (really to prove in overall terms, so far as I was concerned) the seriousness of Soviet intentions toward the China Incident. Changkufeng, to me, was just a welcome coincidence, something that had been started by the Russians but that we could exploit. We had no thought whatsoever of seizing real estate or provoking a war. If that had been our intention, all we needed to do was to detour that narrow neck of land, cut behind the Russian rear from the direction of the high ground near Hunchun, block the lines of communication, and trap all the Soviet forces in the forward zone. We would have hurled in the Kwantung Army divisions too. Such an idea would have been quite easy, and we were not so deeply involved at Wuhan that we could not have altered our strategic dispositions. The Russians clearly understood the nature of the problem; their reactions, if any, elsewhere along the Manchurian borders were the things to observe. The little hill of Changkufeng thus possessed a far deeper meaning from the broad standpoint of both sides. If the Russians did cause major trouble—something I refused to believe—they could have the damn hillock. But just how would they react? That was the answer I sought. Victory in China depended on it.

As Inada saw it, the local terrain favored an operation with strictly limited objectives. Enlargement on the part of the Russians could only occur farther north. The Japanese would fight their way to Changkufeng peak, ostensibly to secure the border line, but would not cross into accepted Soviet territory. There would be no pursuit operations. Japanese forces would be limited to no more than one division, the 19th Division of the Korea Army, without tank or air support. IGHQ alone would direct the probe, carried out by the local forces through the Korea Army operational chain of command. The Kwantung Army would not be allowed to lay a finger on the affair. Parallel with the military actions, the Japanese government might seek a settlement through diplomacy. As soon as the High Command's reconnaissance objectives had been achieved, local forces would be withdrawn immediately from the hill. By seizing Changkufeng, the Japanese would have taught the high-handed Russians a lesson. If a mere show of force sufficed, so much the better; the affair would be over, and Inada's point proved. But in case the 19th Division were forced by the Russians to withdraw from the battlefield, it could be done without great difficulty. Evacuation would be handled, if it proved necessary, voluntarily and resolutely, on IGHQ's responsibility without considerations of "face." At worst, Inada claims, the Japanese might lose one division; but the affair could be brought to a halt at the Tumen River barrier without fail, since behind the scenes IGHQ possessed armor, heavy artillery, fighter planes, and bombers, held in check in Manchukuo and Korea, as well as strategic reserves in Japan.

Although Inada admits that some of his staff officers believed the Japanese should not play with fire at such a time, "they all eventually agreed with my plan of their own volition." Even today, however, those Japanese who were most closely connected with the handling of the Changkufeng Incident are not in agreement that everybody at the central level became an ardent proponent of *iryoku teisatsu*. Some believe that most if not all of Inada's subordinates were in favor of a swift and effective deterrent strike against the Russians, whereas others deny the very existence of the Inada concept.[14] The self-proclaimed author insists that, after coordination at the various levels, his scheme was approved all the way up through the General Staff and the war ministry with unexpected ease. The only serious opposition came from the navy, which was eventually won over reluctantly after demanding that the Japanese air force be leashed.[15]

When the new Korea Army commander, General Nakamura, arrived in Seoul on 17 July, he found waiting for him an IGHQ army order, dated the 16th, authorizing him to concentrate units under his command in Korea near the border against the alleged violation by the Russians in the Changkufeng area. Resort to force, however, was dependent upon further orders from Tokyo. Supplementary directives explained that the concentration was designed as a demonstration to support diplomatic negotiations in Moscow and Harbin by assuring IJA readiness to respond immediately in case the situation deteriorated. Implementation of the order should be handled with discretion, from the broad viewpoint. Although air actions were prohibited, Inada agrees that the IGHQ order left room for action preparatory to an attack. Since the Korea Army lacked an Operations staff, Inada arranged to send two AGS field-grade liaison officers to study the situation and to be of assistance. Unlike the Kwantung Army staff, the headquarters officers in Seoul were said to be gentle in nature, generally speaking; there were no "wild boars" under the rather passive new army commander. By all accounts, the Korea Army did its best to localize matters, loyally obeying the intentions of the High Command. In the more picturesque language of an AGS officer, Korea Army headquarters functioned "like a record player."[16]

Despite Inada's desire to keep the Kwantung Army away from the Changkufeng locale, intelligence officer Ōgoshi Kenji and probably operations officer Tsuji Masanobu, the *enfant terrible*, were sent from Hsinking to observe the Changkufeng sector. According to officers who served in the 19th Division, when General Koiso (still in Korea) heard that the Kwantung

Army had dispatched observers such as Tsuji, who were denouncing the Korea Army's alleged inability to defend Changkufeng, he ordered the "spies" to be ousted. Ōgoshi asserts that the Korea Army staff officers were not disturbed by the visit, but that Koiso became furious and ordered Ōgoshi to be arrested for trespassing into the Korea Army's jurisdiction. Koiso may have felt that outsiders arriving from the Kwantung Army would only cause trouble, if not war. Some think that the "arrest" talk must have been a joke, if uttered at all. Tsuji says it was only natural that the Korea Army garrison unit did not welcome the visitors; Ōgoshi adds that the local outpost commander was caused some embarrassment by his stay overnight. Ōgoshi insists that the Kwantung Army was merely trying to be helpful to the Korea Army. The Changkufeng sector was poorly known in Hsinking; Ōgoshi had originally thought that all Manchurian territory lay within the Kwantung Army's defensive responsibility. He climbed up the slopes of Changkufeng, observed the Russian shovelers, and confirmed to his own satisfaction that they were operating on the Manchukuoan side of the crest.[17]

In Hsinking, Katakura (now a lieutenant colonel in charge of the Manchukuo Affairs Section at Kwantung Army headquarters) had obtained authorization at last to attend meetings of the Operations Section and to view classified maps. Tsuji and Ōgoshi told him that, on the basis of on-the-spot observations at Changkufeng, an enemy intrusion had been verified, and that the Operations and Intelligence sections were now studying ways and means of evicting the Russians. Katakura went to the army commander's residence, where he found Major General Ishiwara, who was acting as chief of staff pending the arrival of Tōjō's replacement (Tōjō had been called to Tokyo as vice minister of war in May). Ishiwara, according to Katakura, was already in possession of the draft of a Kwantung Army operations order calling for offensive preparations against the Russians at Changkufeng. Katakura says he remonstrated in the following vein.

> This is not a problem to be handled by the Operations Section. Since borders—international matters—are involved, the Manchukuo Affairs Section as well as the foreign ministry are concerned directly. The forward observers are merely expressing their personal opinions on the basis of having seen some Soviet sentries on a hilltop. We ought not to raise a fuss. The operations people are imagining too much. From the operational standpoint, this is strictly a Korea Army matter. Investigations are fine, but if it is a question of the Korea Army's defensive prerogative, they ought to handle the matter. And since Manchurian territory is involved, the diplomatic aspects should be taken care of by the government of Manchukuo. There are many preliminaries that ought to be explored before operational offensive orders can be invoked by this headquarters.

The acting chief of staff apparently concurred with this line of reasoning, for the draft order was not approved.[18]

In the view of one source, the Kwantung Army was essentially un-enthusiastic about pulling the Korea Army's chestnuts out of the fire, since the neighboring garrison army was unduly cooperative with IGHQ. The latest displeasure with the High Command stemmed from the fact that the defector Lyushkov had been whisked to Tokyo from Seoul in June "right from under the nose" of the Kwantung Army. It is said that the chief of staff in Hsinking even took vexed countermeasures to disconcert higher head-quarters at that time. Later, according to a Japanese correspondent's ac-count, General Ishiwara went so far as to refuse to budge in support of the Korea Army after the Changkufeng affair broke out. "The Korea Army claims jurisdiction over Hunchun prefecture," Ishiwara supposedly snorted, "so the incident belongs to them. Anyhow, no large-scale hostilities are pos-sible in such a cramped area." Some think that Ishiwara's ire was prompted in this instance, as always, by his hostility toward Tōjō.[19]

The records state, however, that on 15 July the Korea Army was advised that the Kwantung Army would gladly cooperate in matters such as opera-tional movement and matériel. Nevertheless, a number of interviewees dis-tinctly recall seeing or hearing about Kwantung Army messages that cast grave doubts on the wisdom of the High Command's having accepted the Korea Army's mild recommendations. Inada's superior, Operations Bureau chief Hashimoto Gun, remembers that the Kwantung Army staff officers seemed to think the Korea Army's actions were excessively timid and that they did make a number of recommendations of their own to the General Staff concerning a more positive policy. "This was not official advice to us," states General Hashimoto, "or criticism of the Korea Army, but represented messages transmitted from staff officer to individual staff officer." A Kwan-tung Army infantry regiment commander, whose unit was deployed along the eastern Manchurian front as part of the army's demonstration, de-scribed the mood: "The Korea Army is too obedient to Papa. If only this case were left to us, it would be over in a flash: just one wallop and the Rus-sians would be gone."[20]

Further insight into contemporary military appraisals is found in IJN Capt. Takagi Sōkichi's notes prepared in late July 1938. The Kwantung Army had judged that it was imperative to compel the Russians to withdraw from Changkufeng; for this purpose, force was necessary. Under no circum-stances would the incident be expanded by the Russians, because aggrava-tion of the situation, such as preparations for combat or troop reinforce-ment, had not been detected on the Soviet side, and because the relationship between the Red Army and the NKVD was extremely tense. On the basis of these observations, the Kwantung Army was incessantly urging the General Staff to use force.[21]

Staff officers in Tokyo felt that the Kwantung Army could not see the forest for the trees. Recommendations to exacerbate a negligible frontier incident must stem from a failure to comprehend the strategic requirements of national defense—prosecution of the campaign in China, nurturing of the state of Manchukuo, and buildup of operational readiness for the ultimate solution of the northern problem. The High Command cautioned the Kwantung Army in mid-July that it was the imperial will that utmost prudence be exercised and that trouble with the Russians be avoided. The Kwantung Army commander accordingly issued stern cautionary instructions to his units, especially the forces on the eastern borders. Still, one can be sure that the injunctions neither ended the grumbling and recriminations at the lower levels of Kwantung Army headquarters nor stilled the concern felt in high circles in Tokyo. A former war minister, Gen. Kawashima Yoshiyuki, told Baron Harada Kumao repeatedly in late July that the Kwantung Army was no good, and Police Superintendent Abe Genki added that the Kwantung Army was making things very difficult for Foreign Minister Ugaki.[22]

In the Changkufeng sector the situation was deteriorating. On 15 July a small Japanese MP patrol reconnoitering across the Tumen, southeast of the hilltop, came under fire. A Corporal Matsushima was killed, and his body was retrieved by Soviet troops, who found a camera and notebook among his effects. Japanese protests to the USSR concerning the Matsushima affair were added to the general conversations about the disputed border, and encountered a Soviet counterprotest against the Japanese patrol's alleged violation of the Russian boundary. The Japanese correspondent who first learned of the death of the corporal wrote that his sixth sense told him the incident might become worse now. The killing of Matsushima infuriated the Japanese border defense authorities and, compounded with the Russians' illegal occupation of the crest, proved to be the immediate cause of the Changkufeng Incident.[23]

On 18 July, the Korea Army dispatched two emissaries, under a white flag, to the Changlingtzu area (the site of Lyushkov's defection) to deliver a message to the Russians that there would be grave consequences unless the Soviet troops ended their illicit occupation of Changkufeng Heights forthwith. Nothing came of this effort at low-level summitry. According to a Soviet source, after receipt of the message from the Japanese side the 59th Khasan Border Guard Detachment prepared against an attack and intensified its observation of the Tumen region. At Changkufeng, by 20 July, the Russians were said by the Japanese to have built up their force to 250 men equipped with heavy weapons.[24]

The Korea Army had finally set offensive plans in motion on 16 July, while at the same time the Kwantung Army was drawing up its own "Outline for the Remedial Conduct of the Changkufeng Incident." The commander of the 19th Division, Lieutenant General Suetaka, issued his implementing order on the 17th, alerting an infantry regiment, a mountain artillery regiment, elements of a heavy artillery regiment, and various other divisional units. Preparations were to be made in great secrecy for a possible attack against enemy intruders in the Khasan area. Utmost care was to be taken not to irritate the Soviets, and action beyond clearing the region on the Japanese side of the claimed frontier was expressly forbidden. The Korea Army notified Suetaka that further orders would govern unit advance east of the Tumen, as well as the use of force.[25]

The first-phase alert of the 19th Division was completed on 19 July, a day behind schedule; approximately 3,200 Japanese troops had moved to the Korean shore of the Tumen. Reconnaissance revealed at least modest amounts of Soviet entrenchment on Changkufeng Hill. Two AGS consultants at the front intimated to Tokyo that the authorities in Seoul were merely toying with unimaginative and ponderous concepts involving a frontal attack. Inada therefore sent a message to Korea suggesting that Changkufeng be retaken by a surprise night attack of limited scope, employing small ground units. General Suetaka advised Seoul that his forces would be ready for such an assault by 20 or 21 July.[26]

As reports reached Tokyo, some of the younger officers on the General Staff concluded that the Korea Army was still dragging its feet; it would be nice if somebody did something on his own in Korea before the chance was lost. Influencing this view was an important message received from Kwantung Army intelligence on 19 July that, according to agents in Khabarovsk, the USSR would not let the Changkufeng affair develop into war; the Russians were also of the opinion that there would be no large-scale entry into Soviet territory by Japanese forces. The AGS Operations Section therefore prepared the draft of an IGHQ order, which would require imperial sanction, instructing the Korea Army to evict the Russian troops from Changkufeng in the way the Kwantung Army would have done. Other than the core of several battalions, at most, assigned to the attack force, the Korea Army should concentrate units on the Hunchun front to pose a strategic threat to the Russians from the north of Changkufeng. The wording of the draft was mild, says Inada, but it meant unleashing the energetic front-line forces. On 20 July he notified his representatives in Korea that a third AGS consultant was being sent from the Operations Section to convey details of the "general atmosphere" in Tokyo. By now the matter of using force seemed practically fixed.[27]

Suddenly, for reasons as inexplicable to the front-line forces as the order countermanding the 1st Division's planned offensive on the Amur in June

1937, Inada dispatched an urgent message to Korea on the evening of 20 July: "We have not been able to obtain imperial sanction for the order authorizing use of force. . . . Be prudent in your guidance so as not to provoke [incidents]."[28] A reconstruction of events indicates why the reversal of the High Command's decision had taken place: On the afternoon of 20 July, first Foreign Minister Ugaki and then Army Chief of Staff Kan'in had been received by the Emperor in separate audiences. In reporting on the petition for the use of force, the aged Prince Kan'in apparently bungled the sovereign's astute question about what measures the army had in mind in the distressing event that serious hostilities with the Soviet Union ensued. Kan'in was ushered out of the audience chamber after a remarkably short stay of about ten minutes.

It had been expected that once the chief of staff's petition was sanctioned, War Minister Itagaki would report to the Throne concerning proposed mobilization matters, which the operations staff had considered to be inseparable from the use-of-force question. But since the reports appeared to be uncoordinated, it seemed unadvisable to admit Itagaki to an audience, and he did not get to see the Emperor for about an hour and a half after he had come to the palace. It might have been better if the war minister never did report to the Throne that day; his presentation seemed to contain slipshod or perfunctory points reflecting contradictions in thinking or errors in detail between the General Staff and the war ministry. Upon hearing about the proposed mobilization against the USSR, the monarch apparently gathered that Itagaki meant to challenge the Russians to war. The Emperor therefore asked whether the war minister had already achieved full understanding with his cabinet colleagues. Clearly the sovereign had discerned a difference in views between Itagaki and Ugaki, who had essentially disagreed with the idea of using force prematurely. When Itagaki waffled in his reply, the Emperor rather agitatedly rebuked him in the following sensational terms, according to Harada's diary.

"From the outset the army's methods have been outrageous. In the case of . . . the Manchurian Incident, and again in the early stage of the present [China] Incident, the army frequently acted basely and only in accordance with judgments made locally, without obeying the central authorities' orders. These are measures unbecoming to our army. It is our feeling that these matters are truly outrageous in the extreme. This time there must not be anything resembling those other incidents." The Emperor added emphatically: "Not even one man may be moved without our order."

When Itagaki emerged from the audience, he said he dared not face His Majesty ever again, and wanted to resign. Similarly humiliated, Prince Kan'in indicated that he wished to quit too. Although neither did step down, bitterness welled up among certain AGS officers against Ugaki, who was blamed for undercutting and making a fool of Itagaki; undoubtedly it was lack of understanding rather than malice that had caused the problem. Ugaki's diary reveals his own skepticism: "Although the army was trying to use force, this was rectified as the result of my remonstrations. [The army] attempted to obtain imperial sanction for the manipulation of troops and simultaneously for preparations to take the field. Is this some sort of trickery?"

Others who deserve to be blamed for the mishandling of affairs on 20 July must include Prince Kan'in and, to a lesser extent, his deputy Tada, who ought to have overseen the details. But it is the prudent action of the Emperor that deserves special attention, for it was shown that the sovereign could occasionally thwart underlings' actions when ill-conceived or poorly coordinated. Knowing the monarch's profound dislike for hostilities, the High Command should have gone out of its way to reassure him, and should not have expected automatic sanction for any petition.[29]

Just as the 1st Division and Kwantung Army headquarters had been infuriated by Tokyo's curbs a year before, so the 19th Division was chagrined, frustrated, and resentful when the red light was flashed in 1938. Since offensive preparations in Korea were nearly completed, the third AGS consultant still seemed to be pressing for early permission to use force. This induced Inada to send him telegrams on 21 July and again on 24 July, stressing that there was no further prospect of obtaining imperial sanction for the project, because of various internal and external circumstances mentioned earlier. The situation had extended beyond the limits of AGS responsibility or initiative, and the previous offensive outlook must be renovated. Present policy emphasized negotiations at the diplomatic level. The Korea Army chief of staff requested the 19th Division commander to "be patient about an attack . . . for a while." On 24 July the Korea Army notified Inada that the division commander understood the injunctions to act cautiously, "so please rest assured."[30]

Suetaka, however, did wheedle approval from the Korea Army, after the fact, for the secret occupation by one company of a hill 800 meters west of Changkufeng. Nonetheless, most of the Japanese forces that had been deployed to the Tumen were ordered back to cantonments on 26 July. The pullback began in all seriousness on the 28th, and the AGS consultants returned to Tokyo. Suetaka remained at the front, perhaps in the hope that some golden opportunity to smite the Russians might yet arise. After all, according to a communication received from Tokyo on 23 July, the AGS was of the opinion that the use of force would not be authorized "unless some new developments occur, such as a great deterioration in the situation entailing sheer necessity."[31]

Suetaka's heaven-sent opportunity occurred on 29 July, when a small Soviet patrol was observed on an unnamed hill south of Shachaofeng (Bezy-myannaya), about two km. north of Changkufeng. As the 19th Division commander and other hawks saw it, the imperial order suspending the use of force was not a blanket prohibition, especially in the case of a new and incontrovertible border incident other than at Changkufeng. This time the Russians had intruded beyond doubt, according to Japanese maps; defense of the frontier would not contravene the imperial will. After consultation with Suetaka, a 20-man platoon was promptly ordered by the local IJA border garrison unit commander to cross the Tumen and destroy the Soviet patrol, while another 25 Japanese were deployed on the crestline north of Changkufeng. According to Soviet sources, eleven Russian border guards were attacked by somewhere between 100 and 150 Japanese in as many as two companies. The Japanese say they annihilated eight mounted enemy trespassers.[32]

From these modest beginnings, the Changkufeng crisis escalated to major proportions. Suetaka not only allowed more Japanese troops to cross the Tumen than the authorities in either Seoul or Tokyo knew about or desired, but he also played down the numbers of Japanese involved in the Shachao-feng affray. At the same time, he suspended the pullback of his forces and began concentrating more and more troops in the frontier area on both sides of the river. Some of the units that had already left the scene were ordered to return. Several hours after the clash at Shachaofeng, Suetaka's engineer commander already knew about "preparations for a future offensive." Soon afterward, the engineers were told by the forwardmost infantry officers from Col. Satō Kōtoku's 75th Regiment that a night attack was going to be launched by them against Changkufeng on the night of 30/31 July.[33]

On 30 July, Korea Army commander Nakamura advised Suetaka to limit his counteraction to the eviction of Soviet troops, if necessary, from the heights south of Shachaofeng. Prudence and localization of the affair were enjoined; Changkufeng Heights was not mentioned. Unless there was an attack by the enemy, resort to force must depend upon separate orders. The Korea Army chief of staff was being sent to the scene to insure careful action. Considering the fundamental limitations imposed by higher headquarters in Seoul and Tokyo upon Suetaka's freedom of action, one cannot avoid being impressed by the fact that the general's actions stressed the loopholes, not the substance. A queer logic had to be invoked, sometimes separating but sometimes linking events at Changkufeng. As the 75th Regiment's records state: "In order to annihilate the enemy on the heights southwest of Shachaofeng, we had to smash the foe on Changkufeng first, from the standpoint of terrain. However, since it was said that it had been decided not to use force against Changkufeng because of imperial will, we felt truly awestruck."[34]

By noon of 30 July, Suetaka had issued orders to Colonel Satō promptly to evict from Manchurian territory the intruding and advancing enemy, although pursuit must not be pressed too far lest the border be crossed. Several hours later, Satō dictated attack instructions to all of his subordinate officers. In ordering his 1st Battalion to assault Changkufeng by night from the southwest, he stated the exact time of jump-off: 2:00 A.M. on 31 July. One company would simultaneously attack on the north side of the hill to cut off enemy retreat. At dawn, after Changkufeng crest had been seized, a second infantry battalion would clear the Shachaofeng area. Support fire would be rendered at dawn too by a heavy artillery battery located on the Korean side of the Tumen.[35]

The operational orders said nothing about prerequisites for either the night or dawn attacks; Suetaka was justifying the offensive only on the basis of reports of a Soviet buildup of infantry and armor in the area. When the general came to visit Satō's command post in the late afternoon of 30 July, the regimental commander asserted that the front-line enemy forces had been reinforced steadily and that their actions had become offensive. The Russians, Satō claimed, were deliberately provoking the Japanese side, and the affair had grown serious. It was necessary to assume the initiative and deal the enemy a crushing blow. Suetaka agreed to give Satō something in writing. On a calling card he wrote: "You are to mete out a firm and thorough counterattack, without fail, once you gather that the enemy is advancing even in the slightest."[36]

As planned, the Satō force stormed Changkufeng in the early hours of 31 July and cleared the hill by dawn, after very fierce fighting that eliminated the garrison of about 300 Russian soldiers and knocked out ten tanks. Another 300 Russians were defeated in the Shachaofeng sector at dawn and seven more tanks were immobilized. Japanese casualties were severe: 34 killed and 99 wounded, of 1,114 engaged at Changkufeng; 11 killed and 34 wounded, of another 379 committed at Shachaofeng. In the assault battalion at Changkufeng, seven of nine officers were killed or wounded. Overall IJA officer losses were about 25 percent; enlisted casualties, almost 10 percent. Three platoons were so lacerated that they lacked leaders; two others were taken over by corporals. The 1st Battalion came under the temporary command of a lieutenant.[37] The Russians admitted casualties of 13 killed and 55 wounded, and the loss of only one tank and one gun. They put Japanese casualties at 400, although the figure for captured rifles, 157, more closely approximates the real losses of the IJA attackers.[38]

In Tokyo, when Inada learned of the 19th Division's arbitrary attack at

Changkufeng, his first reaction was to say, "Well, well, they have gone and done it!" This had been exactly Inada's original hope, but now he felt that the best thing to do was to "stop where we were, firmly." He had had no inkling of the attack and was neither pleased nor displeased with it. But merely to occupy Changkufeng was meaningless. To Inada the front-line actions, however well done in practice, came as something of an anticlimax. The only question now would be the Emperor's attitude. What if His Majesty surmised that the High Command was in clandestine collusion with the forces in Korea, so soon after the fiasco of the audiences on 20 July? Since it was out of the question to send old Prince Kan'in to report, the "terrified" AGS deputy, Tada, went to the imperial villa on 31 July. Assured that the Japanese front-line forces had been acting only in self-defense to protect the border and that they had not crossed the international boundary, the monarch reacted favorably, to General Tada's relief.[39] Suetaka, too, was delighted when he received an IGHQ order via the Korea Army on 1 August, indicating that the High Command had obtained post factum sanction for the use of force, although prudence must now be the keynote and there must be no provocations. "This order," Suetaka exulted, "is worth a million reinforcements!"[40]

If Suetaka thought that the preemptive clearing of the Changkufeng-Shachaofeng hill complex would promptly end the affair, he and his fellow hawks were soon to be disabused. Not only had the Russians put up surprising resistance at Changkufeng, but they also must have reached the decision to allow no repetition of their backdown on the Amur in 1937. On 1 August, new Soviet ground forces were deployed to the front and the Red Air Force roared into action. The 75th Regiment reported eight attacks by Soviet light bombers and fighters, estimated at between 120 and 150 in all, operating in waves of two dozen or three dozen that bombed and strafed the forward ground defenses. AGS records show that Soviet light and heavy bombers, in flights of 26, 35, 55, and 35, also attacked a railhead, a bridge, and towns on the Korean side of the river. The Russians had obviously concluded that support points in northern Korea just behind the Japanese front need not be granted sanctuary. Eventually, according to IJA intelligence, the Russians committed two air brigades consisting of 100-220 aircraft operating in formations of as many as 80, including four-engine heavy bombers never before seen in action. During six flying days, a total of 700 Soviet combat sorties were reported.[41]

To avoid escalation, as Inada had promised the navy, IGHQ allowed no Japanese planes to enter action. Only once, on 2 August, did a few Japanese aircraft fly a covering patrol, an unauthorized mission to protect a train movement inside Korea. As soon as the AGS heard about this, it sternly warned the guiltless Korea Army that such action was entirely improper.

The staff officer responsible was reprimanded speedily.[42] No further Japanese flights were ever conducted, although the Japanese air crews wept in frustration and the Japanese foot soldiers indulged in recrimination as they scanned the cloudless skies in vain for the *hinomaru* red-ball insignia.

During ten days of bloody fighting in the Changkufeng area, IJA intelligence correctly identified the Soviet front-line divisions as the 40th and 32nd Rifle Divisions. These two units were judged to have lost their power to continue the offensive in the period just before the cease-fire on 11 August. Interviewees are not sure about the combat entry of the 39th Rifle Division, but the AGS identified it as a participant. We know from Russian sources that the 39th Rifle Corps, which directed the fighting, contained this division too. G. M. Shtern, chief of staff of the Far Eastern Military District, had taken command of the corps from KomBrig (brigade commander) V. N. Sergeev in the midst of the fighting on 3 August. Possibly committed in addition, the Japanese thought, was a fourth Soviet division, the 92nd Rifle, based in pillbox positions in the Barabash sector.[43]

Until almost the end of the fighting, Suetaka was not allowed to bring up the last of the four infantry regiments belonging to his already understrength division; the reserve regiment saw almost no combat action. General Nakamura estimated that the infantry forces at the front numbered merely 3,000 men. In all, Suetaka possessed only 12 infantry battalions against an estimated 27 battalions available to the Russians by 8 August. Japanese estimates of committed Soviet troop strength range from 14,000 or 15,000 to 20,000 or 30,000. If, as the AGS records assert, Japanese ground forces were outnumbered by about 3:1, the Russians must have sent 21,000 men into action, for the 19th Division and attached units numbered 10,000 soldiers at most, of whom 7,000-7,300 were engaged in the fighting.[44]

At the beginning of August, the Russians were judged to have 150 tanks in the Khasan area, built up to perhaps two brigades numbering 200 tanks from 3 August. After the affair, AGS analysts spoke only of one, the 2nd Armored Brigade from Voroshilov, which was believed to have been compelled to withdraw its main forces from the battlefield about 8 August as the result of severe losses. Col. A. P. Panfilov, say Soviet sources, commanded the 2nd Mechanized Brigade of the 39th Corps.[45] The Russians used 100 to 120 artillery pieces, including long-range cannon and howitzers, by the end of the incident. Even with artillery reinforcements provided by the Kwantung Army on request, the 19th Division never had the support of more than 37 pieces, and these only on the last two days, apart from antiaircraft guns increased to 16 by the 11th of August. The IJA artillery force commander later observed that the Soviet guns fired as many rounds in one day as did the Japanese side throughout the two-week affray.[46]

On 3 August, Suetaka recommended an outflanking offensive to counter the buildup of Soviet forces across the Tumen. The High Command forbade such action and again warned against committing air units. Consequently the Japanese ground forces merely defended the disputed, exposed crestline; they were forbidden to attack and of course they would not retreat. "Sitting ducks," the foot soldiers called themselves. By 11 August some of the Japanese line companies had only 20 or 30 men left. In one regiment, two battalion commanders and seven company commanders had already been killed, and the third battalion commander was wounded. A corporal was commanding one infantry company; a sergeant, another. One depleted battalion was led by a 2nd lieutenant. Division casualties were averaging 200 killed and wounded per day. One regiment had lost 51 percent of its effectives; another, 31 percent. Of all the Japanese soldiers who fought at Changkufeng and Shachaofeng, one out of five had fallen in action by 11 August.[47]

Nevertheless, Japanese higher headquarters never weakened in their consistent resolve not to be entrapped into major escalation at Changkufeng. A clandestine scheme was even devised in High Command circles to withdraw the Japanese forces unilaterally at an opportune time if the bloodletting continued much longer. This highly unusual evacuation might well have occurred if Shigemitsu had not succeeded in hammering out a cease-fire accord in Moscow with Litvinov, effective 11 August.[48]

By that date, secret AGS statistics reveal, 526 Japanese soldiers had been killed and 913 wounded, for a total of 1,439 casualties. The foreign ministry used an approximate figure of 1,350—450 killed and 900 wounded. Russian military authorities put Japanese casualties at 600 dead and 2,500 wounded. The Japanese war ministry officially admitted 158 killed and 644 wounded.[49]

IJA sources, though admitting publicly that Japanese losses were comparatively heavy, claimed that Soviet casualties were even greater because of the number of times the Russians had attempted to storm the Japanese defenses. Suetaka was more specific when he told an American correspondent that Soviet losses amounted to perhaps 3,000: the Russians' outflanking tactics had cost them dearly because the northern end of Lake Khasan was swampy and well-protected by Shachaofeng, and the southern anchor at Heights 52 was held firmly by the Japanese. Tass stated on 15 August that, on the basis of calculations by the Soviet High Command, 236 Russians had been killed in action and 611 wounded. At the time, Japanese estimates of Soviet casualties varied from 4,000 to 5,500. The foreign ministry privately judged Russian losses at the upper range—1,200 killed, 2,100 wounded seriously, and 2,200 wounded slightly. After the fighting, Suetaka prepared an increased estimate of at least 8,000 Russians killed or wounded; his line regiment commander, Satō, gave a figure of 7,000. AGS and Korea Army records show 96 Russian tanks destroyed or immobilized on the battlefield, including two captured; 28 or 29 artillery pieces knocked out; three to seven planes shot down behind Japanese lines and four or five probably forced to crash-land on the Soviet side. The 75th Regiment claimed to have knocked out or captured 39 heavy and 26 light machine guns and two 45-mm. antitank guns.[50]

Having presumably made their point about the legal ownership of the hill complex by clawing to their side of Changkufeng crest despite the counter-attacks, the Japanese arbitrarily and unexpectedly abandoned the whole controversial area east of the Tumen. The main body came back across the river promptly by 13 August; the last patrol, next day. Soviet forces thereupon occupied all of the high ground in the Manchurian appendix, including cratered Changkufeng, where the Red flag now flew. The pullback was conducted by the Japanese veterans with considerable emotion and frustration. It had ended up, in one officer's words, as "40 percent of a victory."[51]

Justifying the withdrawal in strategic and logistical terms, Suetaka nevertheless confessed that the reappearance of Russian forces in the Changkufeng sector "nullified our accomplishments" and could be viewed as a criticism of him. "Still, when I reflect on various matters, I believe that the effects will suffice," insisted the division commander. Inada is explicit about the "various matters" mentioned by Suetaka: "The results of this struggle were exploited fully by our High Command, and we could proceed rapidly with what we expected to be the decisive Hankow and Canton operations, freed from apprehension about the Russians, which was what I had sought in the first place. My only sorrow was that we had lost too many men in achieving the purposes of strategic reconnaissance, since the cease-fire negotiations had dragged on and the brave, hard-fighting 19th Division could not be withdrawn dishonorably before a truce was signed."[52]

Through the close cooperation of Korea Army headquarters and the High Command, the dangerous situation at Changkufeng was ended by diplomatic agreement, without the much-feared arbitrary intervention of the Kwantung Army. Nevertheless, the weak Korea Army was obliged to ask for the assistance of the neighboring field army on several occasions. Long-range artillery was particularly lacking; on 5 August the Korea Army asked the General Staff for the loan of two batteries of 75-mm. field artillery and a 15-cm. cannon unit from the Kwantung Army. The request was approved immediately, as were further requests for antiaircraft artillery, engineers, an armored train, and a hospital train. In practice, the various reinforcements from the Kwantung Army (and some from North China and Inner Mongolia) were not put under the 19th Division but were retained under the direct control of the Korea Army.[53]

Though consciously striving to keep off the escalator, IGHQ took a further measure designed to anticipate an emergency at Changkufeng. Held at Dairen in South Manchuria and earmarked for use in the Canton operation had been the 104th Infantry Division, under direct IGHQ control. Inada, who had become worried privately about the dangerous aspects of the situation at Changkufeng, took steps on 9 August to have this strategic-reserve division diverted to the Hunchun sector adjacent to northeast Korea. Still, Inada stresses, the 104th Division never left IGHQ's direct control, and the Kwantung Army was never permitted to touch it. Only the logistical and transport requirements of the division were handled by the staff in Hsinking.[54]

Within its own area of jurisdiction, the Kwantung Army closely watched developments along the frontiers. Except for a small action on 7 August in the Suifenhō-Grodekovo district, where elements of the Kwantung Army's 8th Division drove out a dozen Soviet "intruders" from a hilltop position, the borders remained generally quiet and Russian forward movements were deemed negligible. The Kwantung Army tightened frontier security measures and scouted the movement of Soviet troops facing them, and the civil authorities sent border police reinforcements to local areas to suppress rumor-mongering and to calm Korean refugees who had fled to the Hunchun district to escape the Russian aerial bombings along the North Korean frontier. Pacification squads were also sent out to protect, propagandize, and control the populace. The Kwantung Army maintained "loose ties" with the Korea Army, but the staff officers in Hsinking were convinced that the only effective way of lifting the pressure on the desperately fighting 19th Division was to menace and restrain the flank of the Maritime Province, where the main body of the Soviet Far Eastern Army was concentrated. Despite the danger of provoking all-out war, a Japanese plunge against the Posyet region from the high ground in the Wuchiatzu neck would have trapped the Soviet forces around Changkufeng "like a rat in a sack," as Inada once put it, and as the Russians certainly knew.[55]

Not only to help the 19th Division but also to strengthen its own military posture in case of a crisis with the USSR, the Kwantung Army took what it considered to be necessary steps. By 9 August, General Ueda reached the decision to order the first-stage alert of his own units on the east Manchurian sector. The 12th Division on the Tungning-Suifenhō front was to be reinforced by two of the Kwantung Army's five other divisions: the 7th from Tsitsihar and the 2nd from Harbin. In North Manchuria, too, one infantry regiment was moved closer to the Amur border. IGHQ promptly approved the Kwantung Army's troop concentrations. Greatly cheered by the news, General Suetaka expected the Kwantung Army units to be ready for use by 13 August. A brigade commander in the 7th Division remembers making offensive preparations near the frontier for about a month until ordered back to duty stations at the end of August. From the sister brigade, an infantry regiment commander took things very seriously at first, in the belief that war was at hand. Soon he realized that the movements only represented a demonstration, since the government was pursuing a policy of localizing the affair at Changkufeng. His regiment received no operational preparation orders and no instructions to conduct reconnaissance.[56]

Though the Japanese High Command remained convinced that the commitment of the Japanese air force at Changkufeng would only aggravate the situation, the Kwantung Army alerted its bomber units at the same time as the first-stage alert of its ground units on 9 August. A Kwantung Army air group commander felt that his headquarters acted with great caution in 1938, by comparison with the situation next year at Nomonhan. When this senior colonel's 12th Heavy Bomber Group at Kungchuling was suddenly ordered to stand by for combat, he was given no specific targets, but the alerted planes were fully fueled and loaded with bombs.

> Other Japanese army units at Kungchuling, such as the tanks, had been deployed to the eastern border too, and naturally we all knew about the events at Changkufeng; therefore we had a rather good idea of the general direction we might be ordered to hit. We never did receive operational orders—only readiness orders. So we stood there on the ramps, under the broiling sun, waiting and waiting. To be loaded like this in the terrific heat was very dangerous for us; the tires, for example, might have blown out. After I went up to Kwantung Army headquarters to explain the situation, we were allowed to unload the bombs, but they were to be stored nearby and we were to remain constantly ready to take off if ordered. I remember waiting the whole day afterward [10-11 August], but then the alert was rescinded.[57]

It is the consensus of Japanese sources that the effects of the joint demonstration achieved by IGHQ and the Kwantung Army were excellent from their point of view. Pinned at Changkufeng, the Russians did not or could not choose to react elsewhere as well. By shifting its main strength to the eastern frontier, the Kwantung Army was exerting a powerful but silent threat, an invisible pressure, as intended. IJA intelligence judged that the Russians must be particularly nervous about threats to their flank from the direction of Tungning and Hunchun. Though they were reported to have shifted forces from the Maritime Province corps to cope with the danger, the strategic disadvantages were thought to constitute a very severe weakness. According to Japanese intelligence, the Soviet headquarters at Khabarovsk had apparently detected the movements of Kwantung Army forces about 10 August and had been compelled to take countermeasures: to reinforce frontier positions along the borders adjoining eastern and northern Manchuria, to concentrate the air force, to order move-out preparations by elements in the Blagoveshchensk district, and to commandeer most of the motor vehicles in the Amur Province.[58]

Although the covert intention of the Kwantung Army was to press, restrain, and divert the Russians, an American correspondent who visited the Changkufeng area around 13 August reported privately that the army was massing large forces near the frontier and was expecting further trouble. The Kwantung Army might be claiming for public consumption that only annual summer maneuvers were involved, but there was no denial that "the troops would be ready if a new outbreak occurred."[59] A high-ranking AGS interviewee admits that, although the Kwantung Army was claiming to have moved forces eastward only for reasons of security, it was actually looking for trouble—language similar to that employed by the above-mentioned Associated Press correspondent.

Despite earlier evidence that it wanted to interfere with the Korea Army's handling of the Changkufeng crisis, the Kwantung Army cooperated effectively after the 19th Division had cleared the hills and Soviet air and ground forces went into major action. Kwantung Army staff visits were now of a strictly observer, consultant, or student nature. Being intimately involved in anti-Soviet military preparations, the Kwantung Army understandably desired the latest and most authentic information on Red Army theory and practice. The Changkufeng Incident furnished such a firsthand opportunity and the highly professional observers sent from Hsinking were well-received at the front. Military academy classmate ties contributed to the excellent working relationships; as one division staff officer put it, the teams from the Kwantung Army came as friends now. On 30 July the Kwantung Army had formed a technical team to observe the fighting on the spot and to collect data and research materials regarding intelligence and propaganda. In all, 26 officers and men were sent, under Lt. Col. Kawame Tarō, an artillery expert. Though many reservations have been expressed concerning the effectiveness of the Kawame team in comprehending the nature of ground and air warfare as witnessed at Changkufeng, and particularly the level of Soviet technical and tactical capabilities, AGS sources were very pleased with the intelligence materials that were collected. A division staff officer feels that the Kwantung Army's assistance was increasingly helpful to the 19th Division in settling the incident.[60]

As for the original border dispute which had contributed to the outbreak of the fierce fighting for the possession of Changkufeng Hill, the armistice agreement signed in Moscow provided for the establishment of a commission for redemarcation. The Soviet government's adherence to the cartographic engagements of tsarist Russia and imperial China was in part responsible for the eventual failure to implement this feature of the cease-fire.

For a while matters seemed to be progressing toward creation of the envisaged commission, but the two sides could not agree on the necessary preliminary accords, such as the admissibility of "other materials" to be submitted by the Japanese. In addition, once the appeal to arms had ended in August 1938, both sides tended to lose interest in the subject of redemarcation.

The small war at Changkufeng had been a close thing. For a time it had seemed to Hoshino Naoki, a high official in Manchukuo, that the crisis could not be limited to the Chientao region. Only by some very conscious efforts at restraint by the authorities in Tokyo, Seoul, and latterly Hsinking had the fighting been kept from spilling over into neighboring areas. Even Inada admits that, during the period of the Changkufeng Incident, the attitude of the Kwantung Army was "very reasonable and in accord with common sense."[61] Yet if, as Hoshino says, the affair of 1938 rang the tocsin for the Japanese army, the alarm accomplished nothing in practice, for a similar case, many times larger in scale, flared up the next year at Nomonhan. And the fact that civil and military observers in Japan essentially learned only what they wanted to learn from the experience at Changkufeng was one of the reasons for the stunning success of Zhukov over the Kwantung Army in 1939 on the steppes at Khalkhin Gol.[62]

11

Of Cairns and Flatlands:
The Western Frontier

"Such a wasteland! I wouldn't give five dollars for it."
—A foreign correspondent at 23rd Division
headquarters, 1939; contributed by
Col. Sumi Shin'ichiro

The affrays that occurred on Manchukuo's northern and eastern borders involved distinctive, although disputed, physical features, such as a broad river and islands in the Amur in 1937 and a hill and lake at Changkufeng in 1938. Troubles in the west, however, took place on the sparsely populated Hulun Buir Plateau southwest of Hailar town, a zone of flatland pasture and desert much like a trackless sea. This 700-km. portion of the Manchukuoan frontier adjoined the Mongolian People's Republic (MPR), in the salient looping westward from Arshaan and Handagai around Lake Buir (Buir Nor or Buyr Nuur) to Manchouli on the north.[1] (See Map 1.)

In the common meaning of the term, there were no visible borders between Manchukuo and Outer Mongolia, with the possible exceptions of the Halha River (Khalkhin Gol) and Lake Buir, about which, too, no mutual agreement existed. During the early part of the eighteenth century, the Ching dynasty had vaguely delineated "outer" and "inner" Mongolia for convenience of administration. Akin in blood, language, and customs, the Mongolian nomads sought grazing land for their herds of sheep; trading was unhampered and borders were immaterial. The water of the Halha area was precious, and the grass grew profusely. The land by the river is low and the wind does not blow too hard; snow does not accumulate heavily there, and thus the nomads could stake out pastures and stay through the winter, which was not possible elsewhere. (Winter begins around the end of September or early October, when the temperature may drop to −10° C. at night.) Mongolian nomads were on the move once the grass at a site had been consumed, and since there is little grass on the Outer Mongol side of the Halha, nomads from the west always came to the frozen river to spend the winter with their brethren from the east.[2]

In the 1920's, after the creation of the MPR, there was some tightening of border security. When the Kwantung Army overran Manchuria, the Outer Mongol and Soviet authorities naturally showed great concern, although the

MPR reacted meekly. Nevertheless, political and strategic considerations underlay the need to control sources of water such as the Halha and the mouth of Lake Buir, with their additional assets of salt deposits and fisheries. The Manchukuoan government became particularly exercised by reports that the Outer Mongolians were trespassing on the eastern shores of Lake Buir and establishing a cannery there.³

As a political entity claiming sovereignty, Manchukuo sought to substantiate its western border contentions by calling upon protocols, documents, and local traditions, but the frontiers claimed by the MPR often bit into Manchuria. When an AGS staff member visited Hsinking in 1933 or 1934, he was told privately by a senior Kwantung Army officer that, whereas Manchukuo's borders were fairly clear in the east and north, they were indistinct in the west. For Manchukuo's sake it would be better not to try to clarify the western sector yet. After Manchukuo became strong, the boundaries could be established there; but if this were attempted prematurely, Manchukuo would lose territory.⁴

During the Manchurian Incident, Japanese troops had seized Soviet-made maps of a 1:100,000 scale used by Chang Hsüeh-liang's forces, but these materials were old and incomplete. Since the Japanese army's own maps dated back to the Siberian Expedition, the Kwantung Army commenced land surveying in 1933. One engineer specialist was dispatched next year from the Land Survey Bureau in Tokyo to Hailar, where he collaborated with a large staff for eight months, charting the southern half of the Greater Hsingan range. On occasion, this officer's party even crossed the Halha River into MPR territory to study the topography and the boundaries. A couple of Outer Mongol horsemen, probably border guards, approached with guns slung over their backs, barrels pointed downward. The Japanese gave cigarettes and caramels to the Mongolians, who departed soon, without any evidence of hostility. On the basis of this experience as well as study of the natives' grazing, trading, and religious patterns, the IJA officer concluded that, indeed, neither the Outer nor the Inner Mongols were boundary-conscious or liked the idea of fixed frontiers.

The field surveys of 1934 revealed that, on the Manchurian side of the Halha, *obos* or cairns⁵ could be found, 10 to 15 km. apart; across the river there were only piles of stones. None of the *obos* postdated the establishment of the MPR. Nevertheless, with respect to the location of the border, the IJA engineering expert found that Soviet railway economic bureau maps showed a line inside Manchukuo from the Halha and that natives in the region also pointed to a similar boundary linked to *obos* and local religious beliefs. Upon his return to Tokyo, the Japanese officer reported his findings and asked where the border line was to be drawn on IJA maps. The General Staff responded that the survey results were unsuitable; on the basis of what

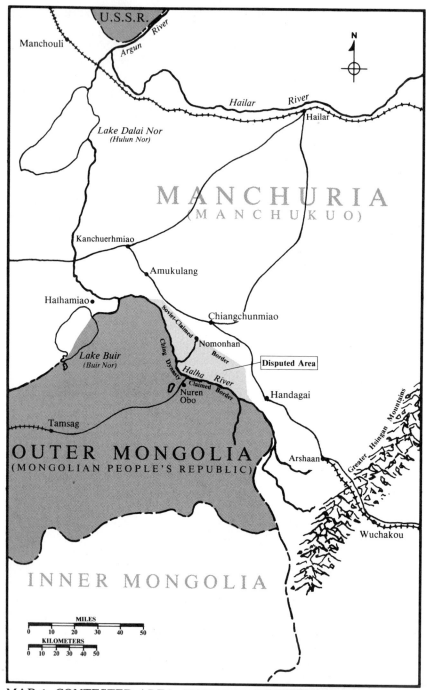

MAP 1: CONTESTED AREA, NORTHWEST MANCHURIA

it called its own studies, the AGS drew the boundary along the Halha. Probably these studies originated within the China Intelligence Section, which had cartographic functions and whose recommendations undoubtedly supported the preconceived AGS contentions. One basis for the General Staff's deduction, surmises the engineer officer, is the fact that in Mongolian the word "Halha" can mean border or defense of country.[6]

The outbreak of the China Incident brought new attention to the Outer Mongolian region, especially the so-called "Red military route" conveying aid to Nationalist China via Ulan Ude–Ulan Bator–Kalgan. In December 1937 and again in late September and early October 1938, the Japanese army's main authority on Mongolia, Maj. Yano Mitsuji, set off on long reconnaissance trips through Inner Mongolia and western Manchukuo.[7] During the second journey, in company with two friendly Mongol guides, he proceeded westward on horseback to the Holsten River (Hailastyn Gol), a tributary of the Halha southwest of Nomonhan, through a deserted area of sparse grass and sand dunes without outposts. Midway to the Holsten, he discerned a Manchukuo border police checkpoint, on the river about two km. north of the Halha junction. Yano cut across the triangle to this "Nomonhan branch" post, manned by six Manchukuoan border guards under a Japanese chief. After a visit to the confluence, the Yano party traveled on, now watched closely but never bothered by two Outer Mongolian horsemen with a sentry dog.

The Mongolian side of the Halha was much higher—50-60 meters higher—than the Japanese side, but no MPRA posts were sighted. Heading north for Amukulang, Yano and his men were intercepted by a mounted scout from a Manchukuoan cavalry company, who suspected infiltrators. On the basis of his experience along the Halha, Yano reported to the AGS that that river was the boundary, a decision for which the major still feels a certain responsibility.[8] Some months after the second Yano reconnaissance, the chief of the OSS branch at Hailar, Maj. Gen. Yokoi Tadamichi, inspected western Manchukuo, by car, to a point several kilometers away from the Halha. He and his party observed no Outer Mongolian frontier guards on either shore of the Halha.[9]

Further efforts were made by the Japanese army to establish the precise location of the western frontier. During the Nomonhan Incident in 1939, an officer in the Military Geography Section of the General Staff examined the Sino-Russian Treaty of Aigun (1858) and then proceeded to the locale to study the problem just before the great Soviet ground offensive of August. From his observations, the officer concluded that he could not verify the Halha line but that it would be best for the Japanese to maintain their claim to it. Upon receiving this report, the AGS Russia Section chief, Col. Yamaoka

Michitake, replied that he remembered having seen some source that identified the river as the line. Thereupon the subordinate restudied the matter and found that, when an IJA surveying party had once been captured by the Outer Mongolians and when the Manchukuoan side had protested that the river was the boundary, the MPR authorities replied to the effect that they would accede to the claim if documentary proof could be provided. No definitive documentation had ever materialized, but at least the Outer Mongolian statement furnished some kind of basis, the Japanese believed, for claiming the river line.

Still, it proved embarrassing when, on one occasion, Prince Chichibu (then a staff officer with the 2nd Section) came to the AGS military geographer and asked to be given sources demonstrating that the Halha was truly the boundary. Upon being told that no concrete evidence was at hand, the prince asked, "Is this all there is, then?" The pointed query left the geographer with the feeling that there ought to be more on the subject of the Halha border; he felt responsibility for this gap but could not produce anything substantial.[10]

Even if portions of the border looked clear on maps, recognition on the spot was extremely difficult, even in the best of times. A map might call for a line from one hilltop to another, but there would be a region of crude or nonexistent markings and immense distances. If the atmosphere on the scene were amicable, problems could be overlooked—but not if lateral delineations were demanded. A Kwantung Army map expert says: "Even I, a military geography specialist and chief of the mapping subsection, could not corroborate the so-called 'real' lines, although I used to fly slowly over the area with my maps in hand. Of course a common soldier, on foot and on the spot, could not tell where the boundaries were at all." Hence a border along the Halha River should have made sense to both sides.[11]

A present-day Japanese historian of note, Hata Ikuhiko, concludes from his own studies that "from the objective point of view it would seem that the Soviet side's contention was sounder." The claims of Japan and Manchukuo to a Halha line were based arbitrarily on the local Mongols' assertions. A number of maps showed a boundary east of the Halha: the Chinese postal bureau (Peking, 1919); Tōa Dōbun Kai (East Asia Common-Script Society, 1932); the Kwantung government-general (1919, 1926, 1934); the Kwantung Army (1937 or 1938). Hata thinks that the Tokyo trials proved that the Kwantung government-general changed the border to the Halha River around 1935, as the Russians charged.[12] A semiofficial Japanese publication of 1935 admits that a certain map published in Shanghai includes the river entirely inside MPR territory. The present author has seen a Japanese AGS map, prepared in 1928, that does indicate a boundary line east of the Halha.[13]

Yano Mitsuji, however, the IJA specialist on Mongolian affairs who was called as a witness at the postwar Tokyo trials, remembers studying several Japanese maps that the Soviet prosecutors submitted in support of their own claim to the MPR boundary.[14] Though the maps were authentic, the Russians had irresponsibly drawn a line across the Halha on the Manchukuoan side of the river in order to show the boundary more clearly than a line drawn on the river. Nevertheless, the original Japanese-language notes on the cartography revealed that the border did run "along the Halha." The effort to rebut the Soviet presentation was fruitless.[15]

Although interpretations of the western boundaries differed, the antagonists were not necessarily insincere or scheming in their contentions. As stated earlier, the Russians have charged that the Japanese deliberately moved their claims to the Halha in the mid-1930's, but a Kwantung Army intelligence expert never heard of such a thing at the time. Some Japanese documents claimed the Halha as the border, others did not; the line was unclear, not faked. Naturally, the Japanese preferred the river boundary, but that did not mean that they transferred the frontier to suit their convenience.[16] The intelligence officer of the Japanese 23rd Division stationed in Hailar in 1938 was told by Kwantung Army headquarters that the Halha was the boundary, and "everybody honestly believed this in our division."[17]

The Japanese were never at a loss to locate cartographic evidence supporting their own claim. A 1935 study supported by the foreign ministry cited a map drawn up by the old Tōzan (Tangshan) authorities in Hopeh Province, various maps compiled in Russia, a map put out in England, and another plotted by the Japanese Land Survey Bureau—all issued before the Manchurian Incident. At the Chita conferences held after the Nomonhan fighting of 1939, the Japanese side offered 18 kinds of maps indicating the Halha as the boundary, based upon Chinese AGS maps of 1918.[18] When Major Yano studied all available map data in 1937-38, he located only one of six old Russian and Chinese documents that showed Lake Buir inside Mongolia, and that item was dated 1884. In agreements and treaties going back to 1734, Yano found evidence that the Chinese Empire considered the Halha to be the boundary. Yano's notes of 1938 admitted that the western border markings were "just on paper," and he concluded wryly that MPR-Manchukuo relations were so complicated "it will take a hundred years if matters are to be ironed out peaceably."[19]

Although the Kwantung Army never seriously considered assigning operational precedence to the western front until 1938-39, when Operations Plan No. 8, the Hachi-gō plan, was developed, all parties were aware of the geostrategic importance of Outer Mongolia. Japanese pronouncements were replete with allegations that the Soviet Union intended to use the MPR as a springboard to bolshevize Inner Mongolia, Manchukuo, and China. By checking or eliminating the threat, Japan would be taking the first step toward accomplishing its own continental policy. This thinking, according to foreign ministry documents, underlay the creation of buffer zones in North China and Inner Mongolia. In March 1936 General Itagaki, then Kwantung Army chief of staff, told Arita Hachirō, the ambassador to China, that the Kwantung Army planned an expansion of Japanese-Manchukuoan strength against the MPR and had already been attempting to conciliate the Outer Mongols by means of the movement in Inner Mongolia. Prince Teh, the Inner Mongol client leader, was quoted as saying that the birth of Manchukuo signaled the rejuvenation of all Mongolians. The Outer Mongols' disillusionment with communism would lead to eventual cooperation with Inner Mongolia and Japan in the "rehabilitation" of East Asia.[20] Outer Mongolia was thus part of the concept of Asia for the Asiatics and of a huge pan-Mongolia.

It was the Kwantung Army's optimistic judgment that if Outer Mongolia were brought into the Japanese-Manchukuoan sphere, the security of Soviet Far Eastern territories would be undercut. It might even be possible, in case of war, to force a Soviet pullback from Siberia with almost no fighting.[21] The Russians were certainly conversant with the value of the Mongolian People's Republic, their first foreign satellite, in the larger scheme of Soviet national security considerations. The MPR buffered the crucial Trans-Siberian Railway on one flank, and served as a base for activity in North China. Many times Outer Mongolia was termed the key to the whole Far East. By the same token, Japan's aggressive designs were castigated widely. According to one ridiculous tale—which received considerable currency—the Japanese militarists intended to move the capital of their country to the Asiatic mainland, first to Korea, then to Manchuria, and finally to Mongolia.[22]

The period of the early 1930's inside the MPR was marked by harsh but unsuccessful efforts to collectivize the Mongol economy. Although the authorities in Ulan Bator were able to put down five important domestic uprisings in 1930-33, they were obliged to retreat from the sternest policies of bolshevization in the economic and antireligious spheres, the latter being of special importance to the traditional lama class. Even after Outer Mongolia's Great Retreat, when the *kolkhoz* catastrophe had to be condemned by its own authors as a left-wing deviation, two more serious rebellions broke out in 1934 and 1935. In the latter year, IJA intelligence heard, 850 dissidents killed a number of Russian Jews and Communists, leading the Soviet Union to send three warplanes and 600 motor vehicles to help the MPR government put down the troubles.[23]

According to MPR-Soviet accounts, remnants of the feudal nobility and reactionary "parasitic" higher-ranking lamas sought particularly after 1935 to create within Outer Mongolia a situation favorable to a Japanese invasion. The threat to the regime was not inconsiderable, for there were more than 700 monasteries and 120,000 monks, exclusive of those who resided outside the "hornets' nests of counterrevolution." In 1935 and 1936, MPR counterintelligence claimed to have uncovered a counterrevolutionary organization of more than 100 senior lamas based in 20 monasteries situated near the southeastern frontier. The dissidents intended to foment a rebellion and, with Japanese assistance, restore the ancient feudal order under a Japanese protectorate. In January 1937 the MPR supreme court tried leaders of a monastery where arms had been found; the group was accused of links with Japanese agents and of preparations for an armed uprising.[24]

During the early 1930's, when neighboring Manchukuo was new, the borders on the west Manchurian front were quiet.[25] To shield the satellite regime in Outer Mongolia against the possibility of external interference, especially by Japan, the Soviet Union in November 1934 signed a so-called gentleman's agreement with MPR representatives in Moscow, providing for reciprocal assistance in case of attack on either party—though in practice this meant on Mongolia. The pact was not published openly, inasmuch as the USSR still ostensibly recognized China's traditional sovereignty in Mongolia.[26]

As a result of the Kwantung Army's continuing pressures on Inner Mongolia, the MPR began to reinforce the sectors facing Manchukuo. Inevitably, in such a broad and ill-defined region, small-scale collisions began to occur. The Kwantung Army had lightly garrisoned the western region of Manchukuo since early 1933. Diplomatic protests and counterprotests obscure the fact that, in practice, the Outer Mongolians seem to have roamed the border area almost by default. Throughout 1934, reports reached Hsinking concerning MPRA pressure on Manchukuoan army outposts and cases of abductions of natives on the Manchukuo-claimed side of the border. Finally, in early 1935, shooting affrays took place, the first of 108 incidents recorded by the Japanese between then and April 1939.[27]

On 8 January 1935, in an episode known as the Halhamiao (Khalkhin-sume) affair, a dozen Outer Mongolian soldiers reportedly invaded Manchukuo at the complicated estuary of the downstream Halha on northeastern Lake Buir, for the presumed purpose of occupying good fishing grounds. Thereupon the Manchukuoan army's Hsingan garrison unit on 14 January dispatched a patrol to reconnoiter. Local efforts to negotiate the dispute failed, and a clash resulted on the 24th near Halhamiao between several dozen Outer Mongolians and an 11-man Manchukuoan unit under Japanese command. A Japanese first lieutenant and a Manchurian soldier were killed, and six men were wounded.

The Kwantung Army promptly ordered elements of Lt. Gen. Hasunuma Shigeru's cavalry group in Hailar to clear the area, since the Mongolians had refused further requests to withdraw and the government in Ulan Bator was charging Manchukuo itself with aggressive trespassing. Though a relatively strong Japanese force appeared necessary to chastise the Outer Mongolian soldiers, General Hasunuma was cautious about escalating the incident. After a short delay to obtain definitive Kwantung Army approval, the cavalry headquarters sent out the punitive expedition on 27 January. Bringing the 13th Cavalry's precious regimental colors with him, Col. Wada Yoshio covered the 200 km. to the Halhamiao sector with his battle-ready task force of two motorized cavalry companies, a machine gun company, cavalry guns, and a platoon of tankettes in one day. Halhamiao was occupied without a fight,[28] the Mongolians having chosen to leave quickly when they learned of the Japanese arrival in force. Wada's men retained the disputed point without challenge for about three weeks, in temperatures that sank as low as $-40°$ C., before returning to their duty station. No new casualties had been incurred, with the exception of a few minor cases of frostbite.[29]

Although much propaganda regarding the Halhamiao case emanated from Ulan Bator–Moscow and Hsinking-Tokyo, there was an apparent conviction on all sides that serious bilateral discussions were warranted. After some haggling about a site, representatives of Manchukuo (including an IJA officer) and of the MPR finally assembled in Manchouli on 1 June 1935. The Manchukuoan side was interested not only in settling the Halhamiao dispute but also in normalizing relations with Outer Mongolia as a precondition to the removal of border differences; the MPR delegates disagreed on the agenda, however, and the meeting almost collapsed before it began.[30] The Manchouli conference did get started, but while it was limping along, a new frontier incident erupted in the west.

The Kwantung Army's cavalry brigade in the Hulun Buir sector had long been troubled by the poorness of IJA cartographic coverage of the western side of the Greater Hsingans. In the face of repeated requests, Hsinking had authorized new surveys, the first of which were conducted without incident in 1934. After the spring thaw of 1935, a five-man surveying party set out again, under a civilian expert by the name of Inukai, who had been assigned to the Kwantung Army from Tokyo. On 23 June at Khaylasutay, south of the Halha-Holsten confluence, Outer Mongolian troops surprised and seized Inukai, a White Russian assistant, the rest of the survey group, and their instruments. (For the location of Khaylasutay, and the other sites mentioned in the discussion of border incidents in this chapter, see the endpaper map "Manchuria and Environs in the 1930's.") Two of the prisoners managed to escape to Kanchuerhmiao and telephone the cavalry group headquarters in Hailar. As in the case of the Halhamiao affair, the Kwantung Army decided to form a punitive force. The 1st Cavalry Brigade commander, Maj. Gen. Nakayama Shigeru, dispatched a cavalry company, a machine gun company, and a signal squad, under the command of Maj. Yamazaki Takeshi. It took this mounted task force four days to reach the spot where the Inukai party had been seized. No trace of MPRA forces or the captured men was found. Yamazaki patrolled the area for about a month before returning to Hailar. Although there had been no combat, the men suffered from the shortage of water and the rigors of tent living on the arid plains.

At the Manchouli conference, the Manchukuoan side protested the seizure of the survey party and again asked that diplomatic representatives be exchanged and border committees be established or, at worst, that MPRA forces be withdrawn from the disputed region east of Tamsag. The Outer Mongolians responded that the survey party not only had violated the frontier but had opened fire first. (In about two months, however, Inukai was released after supposedly signing a confession that he had intruded into Outer Mongolian territory.[31]) On the larger questions, the Mongolian delegation at Manchouli finally relented, to the point of asserting that they had been authorized by the home government to accept the idea of setting up machinery to deal with frontier disputes, and to establish a joint body to handle the Halhamiao and Inukai cases specifically. Regarding the exact locations of the proposed representation, however, the Mongolians stated that they needed to consult the authorities in Ulan Bator and asked for a recess, which was agreed upon.

After considerable time, Manchukuo asked that the Manchouli talks be resumed; a new round commenced on 2 October. The Manchukuoan delegation now proposed that the central commissions be stationed at the respective capitals, Hsinking and Ulan Bator, and that the local organs be set up at Manchouli and Hailar in Manchuria, and at Tamsag and Bain Tumen in the MPR. Though the Mongolians seemed to favor the idea of one minor local post, they were unwilling to approve a central mission in Ulan Bator. Despite four more meetings in Manchouli, the impasse could not be broken.

The Manchukuoan delegates argued that it was ridiculous to limit their representation inside the MPR to one "lonely hamlet in the most desolate corner of Outer Mongolia"; if the few hundred Mongol tents were removed, the Manchukuoan representative would be left "shivering in the wilderness" more than 2,000 km. from Ulan Bator and several hundred from Hailar. For their part, the Mongolians intimated that the Manchukuoan proposal had been motivated by an "intrigue to send a military mission in disguise for the purpose of disturbing their country from the inside." Soviet-Mongolian sources assert that the demands of the Japanese "military clique" were "barefaced and obviously unacceptable," invoking as they did the threat of armed force in the event of rejection. Despite Manchukuoan protestations of sincerity and honest intentions, the Manchouli conference broke down with some acrimony on 25 November. The Manchukuoan delegation was convinced that the Mongolian "slander" and the ultimate rupture in negotiations were attributable to a decision by the Soviet Union, which not only feared to "expose the satellite nature of the so-called People's Republic" but also was genuinely concerned about the injection of Japanese-Manchukuoan influence into Outer Mongolia.[32]

A short time after the breakdown of the Manchouli discussions, new frontier troubles flared up in the area of Olankhuduk-Brunders (Adag Dulan–Bulan Ders). Kwantung Army and Manchukuoan forces had been engaged in reconnoitering projected border outposts southwest of Lake Buir when, on 19 December 1935, a Manchukuoan army unit clashed for several hours with an MPRA garrison party and reportedly captured ten Mongol soldiers. Five days later, about 60 truck-borne Outer Mongolian reinforcements came to dislodge the Manchukuoan unit from Olankhuduk but were repulsed at a cost of three Manchurian dead. The same day, at Brunders, MPRA troops attempted to drive out the Manchukuoan force three times. An unsuccessful night attack followed on the 27th.

With Olankhuduk and Brunders in Manchukuoan hands, all was quiet until a Mongolian light bomber reconnoitered the border watch posts on 7 January 1936. Thereafter between the 8th and 16th of January a number of ground actions occurred in which MPRA motorized and cavalry elements attacked Manchukuoan outposts, laid land mines, and disseminated propaganda leaflets. On 22 January, a new force of Japanese and Manchukuoan troops, aboard three trucks, cleared the disputed sector, with a few casualties incurred on both sides. Kwantung Army observers noted that the scale of MPRA ground activity had escalated from an initial level of 5- to 10-man patrols to 100-man units. Outer Mongol tactics had also become more sophisticated, extending to aerial reconnaissance preceding dawn operations involving armored cars.

Responding to the deteriorating conditions on the Mongolian border, Lt. Gen. Kasai Heijūrō, successor to Hasunuma Shigeru as commander of the Kwantung Army's cavalry group stationed at Hailar,[33] ordered Lt. Col. Sugimoto Yasuo to form a detachment from the 14th Cavalry Regiment, set out on 8 February, and oust the Outer Mongol "intruders" from the Olankhuduk region. Entirely motorized and carrying two days' supply of emergency rations, the Sugimoto detachment included Japanese cavalry, heavy machine guns, cavalry guns, and tankettes, and Manchukuoan cavalry and guard forces. According to his secret orders, Sugimoto was not authorized to cross the MPR frontier "unless unavoidable tactically." Japanese intelligence reported that Mongolian forces in the Olankhuduk sector numbered 140 horsemen equipped with light artillery, machine guns, and three vehicles; no defensive works were visible.

The Sugimoto force reached its jump-off location by 12 February, in pre-dawn temperature of −20° C. After a sharp exchange of fire, the enemy artillery fell back; but when the Japanese tankette platoon began to attack, the Mongolian cannon reversed course and opened fire, setting one armored care aflame and damaging a second. Mongol automatic weapons and small arms fire frustrated the Japanese advance until a flank attack by reserves gradually broke the resistance after two hours of hard fighting. The cost to Sugimoto was one officer and seven men killed, and four soldiers wounded. Soviet sources assert that the Japanese committed aircraft and armor in the course of the fierce battle.

Having achieved its mission by driving the enemy south, the Japanese task force began its withdrawal. At this point five or six Mongolian armored cars appeared and conducted pursuit operations against stragglers, especially among the Manchukuoan force, which was encountering problems with its vehicles. The Japanese rearguard cavalry platoon had trouble coping with the MPRA armored cars until Japanese artillery support could be obtained. Several Mongolian aircraft also bombed the Japanese column in the Brunders area, without inflicting any losses. On the morning of 13 February, the Kwantung Army deputy chief of staff, Major General Itagaki, accompanied by a senior staff officer from the cavalry group, flew to the front to inspect the situation and cheer on the task force. That evening Sugimoto was ordered to return to Hailar, after detaching Manchukuoan units to keep watch. The main force reached the garrison town on the afternoon of the 15th.[34]

On 25 February the Manchukuoan government addressed a document to the Outer Mongolian prime minister, requesting efforts toward improvement of relations and urging "introspection." The Mongolian authorities replied by blaming Manchukuo for having provoked the clash. Undoubtedly the tough Mongol stance was influenced by the gratifying combat performance of MPRA cavalrymen, artillerymen, and armored soldiers. According to Mongolian historians: "When one [Mongol] armored car was destroyed and fell into the hands of the surrounding enemy, the crew fired at oncoming soldiers till the very last minute, and not one Mongol fell prisoner. Artillerymen, though badly wounded by the enemy and surrounded, did not abandon their weapons but continued firing with rifles." Concluded the Mongolian historians, "People who saw our soldiers fight, commented upon their attitude on the battlefield in these terms: 'The soldiers never tire during combat, and their strength of bearing was worthy of admiration.'"[35]

Irked by the unexpectedly strong attitude of the Outer Mongolians, the Kwantung Army decided to mete out a powerful blow, "to match force with force." The main instrument would be a provisional unit that had been formed in February 1936 to reinforce the Hailar cavalry group as well as to reconnoiter the western Manchurian border area. Named after its chief, Col. Shibuya Yasuaki, who had most recently served as 4th Tank Regiment commander at Kungchuling in South Manchuria, the Shibuya detachment was one of the initial mechanized units in the entire Japanese army (the parent 1st Independent Mixed Brigade, the first such mechanized force, was organized in 1934). To form his task force, Shibuya took elements of an infantry battalion, including a machine gun company; signal, supply, and engineer troops; separate platoons of mountain and battalion guns; and the nine machines belonging to his tankette company. The latter were designed strictly for reconnaissance, not combat; they were to rely upon their speed and not their firepower, which amounted originally only to a light machine gun.[36] The Matsumura Kōjirō fighter unit of the Kwantung Army air force was also made available at Hailar.

In early March, the Shibuya detachment advanced from Hailar to Assuirmiao. The border area had thus far been screened merely by small Manchukuoan sentry and police posts, and during a series of trifling recent affrays, three or four border policemen had been captured by Outer Mongolian troops. Among his objectives, Shibuya was to liberate the prisoners if possible. After some minor sparring, about which the accounts of the opposing sides are in conflict,[37] more serious fighting occurred on the afternoon of 29 March. According to MPR sources, Japanese-Manchukuoan units aboard seven trucks and one car attacked the border observation post at Azikdoron, about 50 km. inside Mongolia, while another invading force aboard two trucks hit the Brunders post, eight km. inside the boundary and 80 km. northeast of Azikdoron. Mongolian reinforcements enabled the border guards to repulse the attacks after two hours' fighting.

Although discrepancies exist in the several Japanese accounts,[38] especially with respect to casualties—if any—there is general agreement that small Japanese motorized reconnaissance elements under a company commander, with some Manchukuoan soldiers attached, were found and attacked on 29 March on the road to Olankhuduk by a flight of two Outer Mongolian aircraft. The strafing planes shot out tires on the wheeled vehicles, and one truck broke down and was subsequently seized by the Mongolians, who apparently captured the personnel aboard. Japanese sources denied that Japanese-Manchukuoan forces had attacked MPRA units at Brunders.[39]

On 31 March the Shibuya detachment moved forward a motorized infantry company, some Manchukuoan guards, two heavy machine guns, a 37-mm. battalion gun, and several tankettes. Reconnoitering in the Tauran sector, the force was observed by two Mongolian scout planes, followed soon after by a dozen aircraft (L-16 or L-18) that dropped two bombs each coming and going, from a very low altitude. In all, 70 bombs were said to have been released, although 20 or 30 were duds. The tankettes dispersed and were not hit. When the Mongolian light bombers swooped down to strafe five or six times, the Japanese responded with heavy machine guns and other weapons. The shooting was easy, for the planes were crisscrossing very slowly, at only about 80 km. per hour. Eight aircraft were hit quickly, three being downed "for sure" and another three being forced to land somewhere on Manchurian soil. The defenders were exultant: "It was Japan's first combat against Russians!" cried one survivor, who claimed to have seen the blue eyes of the Soviet light-bomber pilots. Whether the aviators were Russian or Mongolian caused minor disagreement among interviewees. It was thought that the flight leader was certainly Mongolian; he was the one Red ace and the chief of the entire air force in the region, estimated to number no more than the dozen planes committed on 31 March.[40]

After the air-ground phase had ended, the Shibuya detachment observed the strength of the MPRA forces: about 300 horsemen, one company of motorized infantry, a motorized artillery battery, and about ten Soviet-type BT tanks or armored cars, which far outclassed the little Japanese tankettes. The Mongolians, however, did not come too close—which was fortunate, since the outranged Japanese possessed only the 37-mm. artillery (which could not penetrate enemy armor) against the 47-mm. cannon of the BT.[41] Second Lieutenant Hiramoto, the platoon leader, took forward some tankettes, one of which broke down in a bog and had to be towed back at low speed. The other Japanese tankettes moved away, leaving behind lame ducks, which entered a dip out of sight of their fellows. Here the Mongol machines closed in and destroyed the tankettes with gunfire. In one Japanese vehicle, whose hatch was shut, both crewmen were burned to death. In the second, the platoon leader's, Hiramoto may have leaped out and been killed; his enlisted driver was wounded and captured.[42]

OSS Master Sgt. Ochiai, Superior Pvt. Sano, and others from the Japanese supply unit had been striving to cover Lieutenant Hiramoto's retreat, but their light machine guns were ineffective against enemy armored plate, and ten of Ochiai's men were cut down by Mongol fire. During the close fighting, a Mongolian armored car, attacking from the rear, ran over one Japanese soldier and stalled on his corpse. The three Japanese survivors saw what had happened and leaped atop the vehicle. When a Mongol crewman opened the hatch and brandished his pistol, Sano knocked the weapon down with his rifle, bayoneted the enemy soldier, disarmed and killed the second crewman, and dragged out the body.[43] The Japanese soldiers were not sure how to start the Mongolian vehicle but, being associated with an armored unit of their own, they tinkered with it and got it under way. Meanwhile, the main Shibuya detachment, which had pulled back to observe after the hard fighting, suddenly detected the lone Mongolian armored car approaching. A Japanese major ordered a mountain gun to open fire at about 1,500 meters; the vehicle stopped without being hit, and through binoculars Japanese soldiers could be seen clambering out, with five or six enemy armored cars in hot pursuit. Japanese mountain artillery drove off the pursuers; thereupon the IJA major set off in a six-wheel vehicle and towed back the prize, which later was displayed in Hailar.[44]

According to Outer Mongolian sources, the Japanese detachment numbered 86 trucks loaded with Japanese-Manchukuoan troops, supported by 12 tanks and three planes. Although outnumbered, MPRA border forces resisted for four hours. An Outer Mongol armored car company attacked five times and inflicted severe losses. Several MPRA cars were shot up like a beehive by IJA tank cannon, but the Japanese defense line was taken eventually, and the invaders fled, leaving behind ten corpses, two inoperable tankettes,[45] and many rifles and machine guns—all well inside Mongolian territory. One MPRA armored car suffered a puncture while in the rear of the foe; the crew dragged the machine gun from the vehicle, hid by the side of the car, and expended all of the ammunition before charging against the enemy platoon that was surrounding them.

Colonel Shibuya may have wanted to counterattack to retrieve his losses, but night had fallen and the enemy seemed to have retired. The cavalry group commander in Hailar was asked to provide aerial reconnaissance of Mongolian ground activities and the status of the enemy planes downed on 31 March. Accordingly, on 1 April two squadrons, one of fighters and another of scout planes, were sent out, and an artillery platoon was dispatched to reinforce Shibuya. According to the aerial reconnaissance, 50-60 MPRA vehicles, including 20 tanks, were observed moving toward Tauran.[46] The Shibuya detachment hoped to ambush the enemy force, but the Mongols changed course, probably in order to salvage the planes that had been shot down. The Japanese air force unit reported breaking up and inflicting considerable losses on the Mongolian ground force; "it was perceived from the planes that the snow around the enemy was turned bright red by blood."[47]

If the Tauran fighting was a great test for Japanese mechanized forces, it cannot have been viewed as a tactical success, although it supposedly achieved the reconnaissance mission. Manchukuoan or Japanese prisoners lost before the affair were not liberated, and neither were those captured on 29 or 31 March. Colonel Shibuya, a tank officer who had had limited experience reconnoitering the frontier area, was not overly familiar with joint-force operations. Having incurred the disgrace of losing military personnel and equipment to the despised Mongolians, Shibuya was subsequently placed into retirement.[48]

In late May 1936, the Japanese-Manchukuoan authorities proposed an exchange of prisoners, and on 30 June the Outer Mongolians returned the wounded Japanese crewman who had been taken from Lieutenant

Hiramoto's tankette, plus three Japanese officers serving in the Manchukuoan Army[49] and five or six Inner Mongolian soldiers whose capture predated the Tauran Incident. For their part, the Japanese returned a dozen MPRA soldiers seized before Tauran. As for corpses from the Tauran affair, all eleven missing Japanese bodies (including that of Lieutenant Hiramoto) were eventually returned on 30 September south of Olankhuduk; there were no Outer Mongol corpses to repatriate. An IJA officer remembers that the Mongolians were "rough" in their exchange of prisoners but respectful and gracious in their treatment of the dead.[50]

Though the clash at Tauran was the Kwantung Army's first serious combat experience against modern armor and aircraft, the Japanese tankettes, as noted, had been designed to scout at high speed, not to fight. The defensive success against the Mongolian warplanes on 31 March, however, led to an underestimation of the effectiveness of airpower against ground formations—although even a Japanese publicist admitted at the time that the Japanese side had been given something to think about after encountering the Soviet progress in the field of military aircraft.[51]

On the basis of IJA news releases, the Tauran Incident was reported very widely in the press, "creating a sensation among the populace as well as among world opinion." Despite their scale and mechanization, the Outer Mongolian ground forces, it was stressed, had been crippled and driven back after a short fight by the "splendid" Shibuya detachment. No longer could MPRA forces cross the borders with impunity, exploiting the numerical weakness of defensive outposts and causing "a certain uneasiness" among the Japanese people. Though the Ulan Bator authorities were as usual shifting the blame for affrays by means of propaganda and deceit, Mongolian border forces had grown passive since the fighting on 31 March; no planes were observed and no soldiers violated the frontier: "All that could be seen were enemy patrol forces watching nervously from within their own territory."[52]

In Moscow, however, the Japanese assistant military attaché remembers another fact of the Tauran fighting. According to an item in *Pravda* soon after the outbreak of the affair, the senior IJA attaché had recommended to the Japanese High Command that, since the Soviet Union lacked strength now, it would be best for the Japanese army to secure all necessary strategic points along the frontiers; this counsel had ostensibly contributed to the Tauran clash. The attaché in question, Col. Hata Hikosaburō, had been offended greatly by the news item and had privately told his assistants to get ready to leave Moscow within 12 hours. Thinking that this outburst derived only from overimbibing, the aides did nothing, but they were reminded sharply of the seriousness of the orders by a phone call from Hata in the middle of the night. The aides then went to the attaché's office and spent the rest of the night burning classified materials, except code books, causing black smoke to billow from the chimney in clear view of watching Russian plainclothesmen. When Hata came to the office in the morning, he commended his assistants, who were haggard from fatigue and had bloodshot eyes from the heat of the incineration. It seems that the two aides, both of whom were taken in, had participated in a dramatic demonstration to impress the Russian authorities with the presumed Japanese seriousness of purpose toward the Tauran Incident. To some degree the demonstration may have contributed to the restrained Soviet handling of the crisis, although the *Pravda* item had reflected the burgeoning Russian political hostility toward Japan (and Germany).[53]

Outer Mongolian writers claim that, between 24 January 1935 and 31 March 1936, Japanese forces penetrated MPR-claimed territory in eight instances, with elements from platoon to battalion in size, exclusive of numerous assaults by patrols of 10-15 men each. In particular, the Russians were lauded for military assistance rendered against Japanese "capitalist aggression and invasions" between December 1935 and March 1936. Although the pro-Soviet MPR leader Choibalsan admitted that the Mongols lost 233 men in 1935-36, apart from civilian casualties, he claimed that the Japanese were routed with "tremendous losses" thanks to powerful Soviet army counterattacks. The role of Russian troops, advisers, and matériel is not further delineated. A search of Soviet sources reveals specific reference only to the Olankhuduk affair of February 1936; Tauran is not mentioned. Japanese historians have therefore begun to wonder whether the clash of March 1936 was really so large and so important as suggested by Japanese documentation at the time.[54]

There was speculation in Japanese public sources that the Outer Mongolians and Russians may have been probing Kwantung Army frontier defenses in the wake of the great 26 February 1936 army mutiny in Tokyo. According to IJA intelligence, however, shortly before the Tauran affair there had been evidence of subversive contact between disloyal Inner Mongol elements within Manchukuo and the authorities in Outer Mongolia.[55] In this view, the outbreak of the clash at Tauran interfered with the MPR's disruptive plans. Interviewee testimony suggests, on the other hand, that hawkish circles in Kwantung Army headquarters consistently played up border disputes and sought to solve differences by violence, despite the more restrained preferences of the area command at Hailar.[56]

Mongolian-Soviet sources speak of intensified Kwantung Army efforts around 1936 to infiltrate secret agents into Outer Mongolia to "consolidate the forces of reaction inside the MPR and organize counterrevolutionary plots, subversive activities, and espionage."[57] Japanese OSS interviewees admit that Manchukuoan Mongols were employed to "investigate beyond the borders" in the Handagai-Arshaan sector. Smugglers and double agents abounded at Apaka and elsewhere. Even known agents were allowed to operate because they were of some use to both sides. For their part, the Russians and Outer Mongolians easily obtained information on the Kwantung Army. According to a Soviet army officer who defected from the MPR in 1938, the Russian military adviser to the Mongolian border garrison unit at Zamin Ude told him in the autumn of 1937 that intelligence concerning Japanese forces deployed near the frontiers was always accurate because it was very easy for spies to enter the region.[58]

12

The Coming of the Nomonhan War: The Mongolian Connection

"I am tempted to call [Nomonhan] the battle of no-man's land. The wonderful pasturage talked about might just as well have been so much camel pasturage in the Sahara desert. The country resembles certain portions [of the United States] such as Iowa and parts of Idaho."

—Maurice D'Alton, Reuter News Agency, June 1939

Insignificant in military terms, the Tauran affray of 1936 could have possessed major importance in one sense: it might have warned the Japanese-Manchukuoan side of the extent of Soviet-Mongol cooperation. Instead, the Kwantung Army ignored the open Russian signals and rushed to secure the western borders by force. Mongolian-Russian sources call the gentleman's agreement of 1934 "immensely important for safeguarding the independence of the MPR." There is a particularly striking chronological link between forceful Mongolian reactions in the Tauran sector and two actions taken by the Soviet government. On 1 March 1936 (four weeks before the Tauran Incident), Stalin announced publicly, through his widely disseminated interview with Roy Howard of the Scripps-Howard newspapers, that "if Japan should venture to attack the MPR and encroach upon its independence, we will have to help [it]. . . . We will help the MPR just as we [did] in 1921." Less than two weeks later, on 12 March, a ten-year Soviet-Mongolian pact of friendship was announced, including a vital mutual defense protocol but making no mention of Chinese claims to sovereignty. MPR and Russian writers stressed that the protocol "enlarged upon and put into legal form" the accord of 1934; the new agreement, too, was termed "exceptionally important."[1]

Although the Japanese authorities may have felt some silent geopolitical pressure, the Kwantung Army essentially defied Mao Tse-tung's future dictum of "strategically despising the enemy but tactically taking him seriously."[2] Few besides IJA intelligence specialists detected the significance of recent changes in Russian military doctrine. For example, the Soviet field regulations of 1929 said the Red Army must constitute "the backbone of the battles for attaining the freedom of the oppressed laboring classes of the world." This stipulation could mean that the Red Army would fight whether the USSR was invaded or not; i.e., Russian forces might even have to cross borders on occasion. Nine months after the Tauran affair the Red Army field regulations were revised, under date of 30 December 1936, to indicate that Soviet military forces had the mission not only of defending the homeland but also of serving as the backbone for the development of fellow socialist countries. Certainly the Mongolian People's Republic was a potential recipient of such "backbone" assistance.[3]

The low level of Japanese army interest in the western Manchurian front derived partly from distractions elsewhere. From the summer of 1937 the China theater, of course, devoured Japanese military energies; and as we have already seen, a serious clash in the north on the Amur just before the China Incident and a small war on the eastern frontier at Changkufeng a year later drew the attention of the IJA in those directions. Then, too, since the Kwantung Army thought so little of Outer Mongolian capabilities, relatively little heed was paid to developments within the Soviet satellite republic. Until the time of the China Incident, the IJA General Staff possessed no intelligence section dealing separately with Outer Mongolia. Even Inner Mongolia was a concurrent function of the China desk; consequently, there were no military specialists on the MPR. Only after the Chinese began to employ Outer Mongolian supply routes did the MPR come to the fore in AGS thinking. One officer in Mongol-language training was assigned in September 1937 to be in charge of a new Outer Mongol desk[4] within the Russia Intelligence (5th) Section of the AGS. While on duty with the section this officer produced the army's first "definitive" study of the MPR. But when he was transferred to the staff of (Inner) Mongolia Garrison Army headquarters at Kalgan in January 1939, there was no designated successor at the Mongolia desk in Tokyo. The Russia Intelligence Section handled Mongolian affairs thereafter and merely revised the basic study; it was regarded as unnecessary to have an Outer Mongolian specialist as officer in charge. Once a year, in May, a new estimate of the situation would be prepared in Tokyo for submission to the Throne, on the basis of information acquired in reply to a questionnaire mailed to the officer at Kalgan in Inner Mongolia.[5]

Given the feebleness of IJA practical attention to Outer Mongolian affairs, it is not surprising that the expert Walter Kolarz believes the Japanese authorities in Manchukuo "mismanaged the Mongol problem completely. They showed as little understanding of the mentality and the point of view of the Mongols as the German Nazis [were to show] to the peoples of the western borderlands of Soviet Russia . . . during the Second World War." Not only did the Japanese fail to win the allegiance of the indigenous Mongols residing inside Manchukuo, but they also "forfeited such sympathies as they might have had in the MPR. . . ."[6] According to a British correspondent in early 1938, "about eighty percent of Inner Mongols would prefer unity with Outer Mongolia to continuing under Japanese military rule."[7]

Still, there is evidence of disaffection within the Outer Mongolian army and of a preference for fellow-Asian Japanese over Slavic Russian "protectors"—at least from what that rare and knowledgeable MPRA defector Captain Bimba told the Kwantung Army when he fled to Manchukuo in 1938.[8] According to Bimba, the greatest influence upon the Mongol anti-Soviet faction emanated from the Manchukuoan-Japanese direction at the end of 1935, when MPRA General Damba returned to Mongolia from the Manchouli meetings via Siberia.

> Although the conference with Manchukuo could not be termed a success [Bimba said], it did provide us with some sort of pleasure. Corps commander Damba convened us [in Bain Tumen] upon his return and told us covertly: "My determination regarding the anti-Soviet movement has been intensified. We must get out from under Moscow's pressure. . . . The time spent at the Manchouli meetings was no waste. I met Mongols [from Manchuria] as well as Japanese. In particular, I studied the Japanese thoroughly, through Japanese delegate Kanki [Shōichi]. We tried to get close to Kanki, but eyes were watching, and we could not do so, to my regret. But I certainly believe that rescue will be effected, once my group and I begin the anti-Soviet movement."

Bimba is the main source for authentication of charges that Marshal Demid, war minister and commander of the Mongol armed forces, was involved in an anticommunist or at least anti-Russian conspiracy centering on the slogan "Outer Mongolia for the Outer Mongolians."[9] In the spring of 1937, at a secret meeting of plotters, it was asserted that 60 to 80 percent of the populace favored an anti-Soviet policy. The proposal was made that ex-Premier Gendun should be the leader of Free Outer Mongolia, that all Russian forces should be obliged to evacuate the republic, and that the borders adjoining Manchukuo and Inner Mongolia should be opened. With regard to the prospects, General Damba remarked:

> Comrades inside the government are expecting our eastern area, Dornot Aimak [province], to rise. It is very favorable for this movement that our corps [at Bain Tumen] is located the closest to both Japan and Manchukuo, and that this locale happens to be the soil of the Halhas. Once we raise the banner of the anti-Russian campaign, Japan and our compatriots in neighboring [Manchukuo] are bound to help.
>   We can expect two good opportunities: First, there is the situation today, when relations between Japan and the USSR are tense. This scheme of ours could be realized at the very same time a war broke out between Japan and the Soviet Union. This is one excellent possibility. Another one would arise if hostilities occur between Japan and China. We could seize the chance of Japan's entering Inner

Mongolia and thus accomplish what we have in mind. One or the other of these opportunities will develop soon. We must be ready and make preparations quietly and secretly.

In proof of his dedication, General Damba left his wife and children soon after the conference of 1937, and many other MPRA officers similarly divorced their wives. Married only in 1936, Bimba followed the general's example.

The plotters' chance seemed to come when the China Incident broke out in July 1937. At the news, "for which we had been yearning," said Bimba, "great tremors occurred inside Outer Mongolia. How we were hoping that the Japanese forces would advance northward from Inner Mongolia!" A fellow plotter, General Marj, the army chief of staff, issued secret orders calling for the four divisions in Dornot Province, a little over 10,000 men, to rise in concert with the cavalry division in the capital, under Damba's command; for Chinese forces to be checked; and for the Japanese to be invited north. These remarkable orders were intercepted by the Mongolian security police. Under the direction of the staunchly pro-Russian leader Choibalsan, a fierce purge was conducted. "When I think back to August 1937," groaned Captain Bimba, "I feel like going mad: the continuing gunfire in the suburbs of the capital, . . . the greatest leaders of Outer Mongolia being shot down one after another." The seizures and the killings were at their peak between August and October. By Bimba's enumeration the following officials were liquidated: former Premier Gendun; Foreign Minister Sambuu; War Minister Marshal Demid, poisoned 21 August 1937 at Taiga station en route to Moscow on the Trans-Siberian Railway;[10] Vice Minister of War General Damba, lured to Ulan Bator by a faked order, ostensibly issued by Marj; Army Chief of Staff Marj; the army political section chief and his staff; two corps commanders; six division commanders, including one who died with Demid; the army air force chief; the army medical section chief; three general staff officers and one army air force staff officer; the ministers of commerce, health, justice, and education; the commandant of the Ulan Bator military academy and three instructors; and the governor of Dornot Province.

Several hundred officers of regimental command rank and government officials were seized. Japanese civilian analyst Ishida Kiyoshi speaks of 14 important victims in the armed forces and government, 23 powerful lamas in the east, and several hundred members of cooperatives, governmental organizations, local political bodies, and military and party organs.[11] According to authentic intelligence, 10 MPRA division-level officers were purged in the autumn of 1937;[12] unconfirmed reports reaching Hailar in 1938 indicated that 11 of 12 provincial governors had been arrested.[13] On the night of 18 September 1937, about 60 MPRA officers and provincial chiefs in eastern

Mongolia were seized in Bain Tumen and whisked to Ulan Bator.[14] Prisons in the capital were crammed with political offenders. The numbers of those arrested in the purges, as of early September 1937, were estimated reliably at more than 10,000; by 1938, some 2,000 monks and abbots had been shot.[15] The security services completed their expansion by January 1938. Choibalsan, 42, the new war minister, deputy premier, army commander in chief, and security boss, had triumphed.[16]

The Soviet Russian authorities, however, seem not to have been entirely satisfied with the Mongolian situation. In Manchukuo the Japanese had established a Department of Mongolian Affairs, whose nominal head was a prince of Mongolian extraction, and whose central administrative offices were staffed by an unusually high proportion of native Mongol administrators—almost 75 percent. Hsingan Province had been transformed into an autonomous Mongol territory within Manchukuo, and the Teh regime had been created in Inner Mongolia.[17] According to an Inner Mongol interviewee, the Kwantung Army's actions did have some effects—both psychological and actual—on Outer Mongolia, especially after 1936 and the attempted conquest of Suiyuan.[18] The Russians apparently feared the emergence of a pro-Japanese faction in Outer Mongolia; most MPR leaders seemed to be distrusted deeply. Even Choibalsan, the "real power" in Ulan Bator, derived his strength from the Russians, whose "robot" he was, and who allowed him to handle mainly internal affairs.[19]

Although the Mongolian soldiery were under the de facto control of Soviet agents and military advisers, the Russians clearly did not ascribe much importance to the Outer Mongolian armed forces.[20] According to a Russian army officer who defected from Mongolia to Manchukuo in 1938, even the most capable MPRA general, Vice Minister of War Damba, was only the equivalent of a Soviet cavalry regiment commander. The Soviet defector provided illuminating information regarding the true state of relations between Mongolian and Russian forces.[21]

> Although there is a bit of fraternization among high-ranking officers, the two armies are isolated from each other. The NKVD is always watching, and when associations are too frequent the NKVD always intervenes. The isolation and the vigilance are for security purposes, which shows that the Russians do not fully trust the MPRA. Hence the Mongolian army is rather dissatisfied with the Soviet attitude and with the irrational actions of Russian military advisers. The Soviet military assistance advisory bureau [MAAG] has powers of life or death over the MPRA, and Sovietization is handled by the Russian minister to Mongolia and by the MAAG chief, Major General Litvinov, and the approximately 100 officers stationed with units. It is said that relations between the advisers and commanders at the local-unit level are quite bad, which constitutes a source of anti-Soviet feeling in the Mongolian army. The MPRA officers are ostensibly loyal to the USSR, for self-protection, but covertly most of them seem to nurture different feelings. Gen-

eral Damba, who was my classmate at the Frunze Military Academy and to whom I was closer than to the Soviet officers, wielded the real strength in the army, yet there is no doubt that he harbored anti-Soviet feelings. Because Damba knew that I was of non-Russian [i.e., Finnish] extraction, I believe that he talked more openly with me. When I came from Chita, he provided better quarters in Ulan Bator for me and my wife. This caused troubles with the other Soviet military advisers, whose houses were not as good. But the fact that my good treatment was regarded as quite exceptional must illustrate MPRA officers' feelings toward Soviet army officers in general.

Captain Bimba, himself a 1935 graduate of the Soviet cavalry school in Leningrad, has recorded at length his own denunciations of the attitudes and actions of the Russian occupiers and Russified Mongolians. To him, "hateful Choibalsan looked as if he were only proud to become like a Russian." Just as the Outer Mongolians had never been assimilated by the Chinese, no matter the sufferings they endured as a result, "so they did not like to become Russianized. Although our people knew the strength of the USSR, they were beginning to think, 'This is exactly the way the Russians took over from the Chinese in Outer Mongolia.'" Why did Bimba take no Russian wife, as had so many other MPRA officers? "Because," he snorted, "I don't want my son to have a big hooked nose and red hair. I'm a Halha."

Against the preceding backdrop of dissidence and unrest among important civil and military circles inside the MPR, a Kwantung Army intelligence specialist feels that the Russians prodded the Outer Mongols into purging the do-nothings and thus leaving only those loyal to the USSR. In this sense, the purges in Mongolia represented the deferred backlash of the earlier Tukhachevsky affair, which had become a nationwide operation in Russia.[22] Furthermore, at a time when Japanese military actions were spilling from North to Central China and encouraging Outer Mongol separatists, the Soviet government decided to shore up the shaky power of the MPR Communists with Red Army bayonets. The public version stated that the authorities in Ulan Bator appealed for Soviet troops to be brought into Mongolia because, after the unmasking of the Demid-Gendun plot of 1937 involving Japanese agents, "the Japanese imperialists [had] speeded up preparations for a direct invasion of the MPR and intensified their provocative attacks on frontier posts." In conformity with the mutual assistance protocol of 1936, the Soviet government dispatched units of the Red Army into Outer Mongolia in early September 1937. They "stood shoulder to shoulder with the soldiers of the Mongolian People's Revolutionary Army to protect the MPR's independence against Japanese imperialist aggression."[23]

The historian Gerard Friters has warned that after 1934 "fantastic reports were spread about the strength of Soviet Russian forces stationed in Outer Mongolia, most of these reports coming either from Japanese sources or from sensational journalists who received their impressions while traveling on the Trans-Siberian Railway." In the latter category, Friters includes the American correspondents H. R. Knickerbocker and Karl H. von Wiegand. In practice, Friters believes, "Soviet Russia probably sent such officers and troops to Outer Mongolia as she thought necessary in order to supplement the forces of the Mongolian People's Republic trained by her, and to be ready for the emergency foreseen" in the mutual assistance protocol of 1936.[24]

The Japanese press reported in mid-1938 that two or three infantry divisions and another two or three mechanized brigades made up of Soviet personnel had been definitely identified in Outer Mongolia.[25] Writing in 1941, the Japanese author of a work on the Nomonhan Incident (a work that ran quickly through 270 impressions) asserted that in the Nomonhan district, until just before the fighting, the Russians had deployed four armored brigades. In the southeast there was a cavalry division, and in the south a motorized (truck-borne) division. By the time of the fighting, the front-line Russians were said to possess two cavalry units built around a rifle regiment from the Berm area. Heavy and field artillery accompanied the 36th Regiment from Ulan Bator. In the category of armor there were six brigades totaling 2,500 armored vehicles. The air force centered on one air brigade consisting of two air regiments (the "Tartar" and the "Dabriya"), equipped with Soviet SB and TB heavy bombers and the latest I-15 and I-16 fighters.[26] Though the intervention of sizable Soviet military forces in the Nomonhan sector in 1939 took a large number of Japanese army personnel by surprise, the intelligence officer of the 23rd Division recalls that the Kwantung Army reported on Soviet order of battle within Outer Mongolia, and he specifically remembers mention of the Tamsag and Sanbeise areas.[27] IJA intelligence experts recollect that, after the Changkufeng Incident of mid-1938, the USSR poured considerable numbers of reinforcements into the MPR. The 57th Special Corps, formed in early 1938, was built around the 36th Rifle Division, an old division from Chita; it had now been introduced gradually into the Ulan Bator region, and it was motorized during late 1938.[28] Another AGS intelligence officer is certain that Soviet troops began entering Outer Mongolia after the mutual defense accord of 1936, but believes that the largest numbers appeared only after the Nomonhan crisis erupted in 1939.[29]

An authentic IJA intelligence document dating from the spring of 1939 shows the motorized 36th Rifle Division confirmed at Sainshanda, a rifle battalion near Zatakaid, elements of I Corps at Ulan Bator, and two other concentrations at Yukujur and Pelot to the east. Armor is found at Ulan Bator, and an armored car brigade at Undurhan. Madat, Tamsag, and Sanbeise house air force units.[30] According to Japanese intelligence summaries, the Russians possessed, apart from 57th Corps headquarters, one motorized division in southern Mongolia, one cavalry division in the southeast, a mechanized brigade and an air brigade in the east, and three more armored car brigades in various places. Aircraft numbered 200-300, as did tanks and armored cars. Soviet military manpower was judged to total 30,000 to 40,000.[31]

The Outer Mongolian authorities had been endeavoring to build up the size and quality of their own small armed forces, especially in view of Japanese activities in China, Manchukuo, and Inner Mongolia. In 1934 the national military budget amounted to 13 million tugriks, or 34.6 percent of the announced total outlays. In the year before the Nomonhan affair, 1938, the figure had risen to 46.8 million tugriks, or 52.7 percent of the national budget.[32] The term of military service was raised from two to three years in 1937, and the ages of liability to service were changed from 18-22 to 18-25.[33] According to an authoritative survey prepared in Japan in the summer of 1938, the numerical strength of the MPRA increased from less than 12,000 men before the China Incident to more than 20,000 afterward.[34] General Damba was reported to have said that in the winter of 1937 the MPRA numbered 15,000 men and that by the end of 1938 it would increase to 25,000.[35] Even this figure would be extremely difficult to attain, from a national population of little more than 800,000. Certainly the MPRA could not have exceeded 50,000 men by 1939.[36]

The preponderance of the MPRA was stationed at Ulan Bator (II Corps), Bain Tumen (I Corps), Tamsag, and Yukujur. By 1939, cavalry divisions totaled seven in fact and one on paper, though they were believed to have as few as 1,000 to 2,000 troops each. Facing Manchukuo were three cavalry divisions and an air brigade; on the Inner Mongolian front, three more cavalry divisions; around Ulan Bator, one or two cavalry divisions and some aircraft. Training for all branches of service except air and armor was provided at the Ulan Bator Military Academy; mechanized and aerial training was conducted at the Sukhe Bator Army Air Force School.[37]

IJA interviewees speak of the Mongol forces as about comparable in quality to the Japanese-commanded Manchukuoan military forces. Cavalry was the Mongolians' forte. They were most capable of small-unit actions—not large-scale, highly organized, combined operations. At least by the time of the Nomonhan campaign, the individual Mongol, though strong and durable, was not yet skilled in the use of complicated weapons and vehicles. According to the Soviet officer defector, MPRA quality around 1938 was generally unsatisfactory. Although in organization and equipment the Mongolians aped the Russians, they suffered from organizational deficiencies, insufficient matériel, shortages of firepower, lack of enthusiasm in training under Soviet advisers, and lack of time—the average training day amounted to only two or three hours. As IJA intelligence viewed matters, MPRA con-

tradictions stemmed from the rapid buildup and modernization under Soviet guidance.[38] Mongolian officer quality and capability did not improve,
nor did esprit, especially after the great purges.[39]

Beset by domestic distractions and by external pressures, the MPR government and its Soviet mentors were obliged to devote greater attention to the
border sectors fronting on Manchukuo and Inner Mongolia. According to
Japanese open sources, the frontier regions were cleared between 10 and 30
km. behind the boundaries.[40] Especially after the outbreak of the China Incident, the Outer Mongolians set up new border defense units and independent station units along the frontiers on a small scale. In the Dariganga sector, for example, observation posts were established about 50-60 km. apart,
with 20 or 30 men per post.[41] By the Mongols' own admission, the interior
ministry organized the border forces; moreover, signal units were moved to
the jurisdiction of that ministry in early 1938.[42] One of the five organs under
Choibalsan in his capacity as security chief consisted of the provincial internal security bureaus. Every bureau in turn had three branches, one of which
was the *atoryat* (zone) border-observation battalion made up of about 200
men under a commander equivalent in rank to a lieutenant colonel. Each
battalion had three observation-post platoons, consisting of 30 men each.[43]

The Kwantung Army, of course, played its part in continuing to stir up
troubles, ethnically and religiously especially in the complicated district of
Kobut, adjoining Inner Mongolia. The many Moslems on the MPR side of
the border proved difficult for the Ulan Bator regime to rule, so special treatment had to be accorded them; yet at the same time the government sought
to communize them. Fear bred resistance and local troubles, which spread
to compatriots not only in Inner and Outer Mongolia but in northern Sinkiang as well, and as far away as Soviet territory. Kwantung Army intelligence may have exaggerated the scale of the uprisings when it spoke of several thousand, but there is no doubt that the authorities in Hsinking hoped
to affect the MPR through their protégés under Prince Teh.[44] One Kwantung
Army staff officer is of the opinion that the Soviet troop buildup in Outer
Mongolia in 1938 may have stemmed from the formation of the IJA field
force known as the Inner Mongolia Army in the spring of 1938 at Kalgan, in
accordance with IGHQ orders to the Kwantung Army.[45] A Tokyo-level staff
officer sees no necessarily direct connection between the activations of the
Inner Mongolia Army and of the Russian 57th Special Corps, but he discerns an indirect relationship: the consistent buildup by both sides in the
general area was leading to a situation wherein neither party could or would
overlook border violations.[46]

The increased Russian military presence in the MPR was a mixed blessing
for the Mongolians. Though Choibalsan needed all the help he could get,
the USSR began to convert the country into something like a Soviet colony,

which shocked the patriotic feelings of a number of Mongolian officials and officers who had survived the purges of 1937-38. A severe struggle raged for leadership between the pro-Russian clique of Choibalsan and the extreme xenophobes and nationalists who opposed Soviet influence.[47] We know that the eastern border regions of the MPR, adjacent to Manchukuo, were the scene of revolutionary disturbances in November and December 1938, shortly before the outbreak of the Nomonhan crisis. About 400 MPRA officers and men were arrested in Frontier Zone 24 (the important Nomonhan/Khalkhin Gol zone *) by the end of December. Another 200 MPRA personnel were charged with being anti-Soviet elements and taken to Ulan Bator from Zone 27, which included Tamsag and Kerulen. The allegedly dissident forces were replaced by Outer Mongol troops who had crushed Moslem incursions from Sinkiang into the Kobut and Altai zones at the end of June 1938.[48] Captain Bimba spoke of massive transfers of units by the MPRA, at Choibalsan's order, "to prevent tremors among the soldiery." For example, troops were shifted from Dzabkhan Aimak in the west to the troubled Dornot Aimak in the east; all easterners were transferred to the Tsupan Kotob area.[49]

Japanese publicists have often contended that the Mongolian People's Republic became increasingly hostile toward Manchukuo around 1939 because the MPRA, under Soviet military tutelage, had been greatly strengthened; after all, the MPR was "completely communized and was in reality part of the Soviet Union." [50] Such an interpretation overlooks the more profound connection between the coming of the border war and the convulsions inside the Mongolian People's Republic. From discussions in 1939 with an MPRA colonel who had recently defected [51] and from analysis of all available documentation, a Japanese General Staff expert on Communist affairs concluded that the power struggle within the MPR lay behind the Nomonhan Incident: [52]

> I think that the whole affair was fomented by Choibalsan's group, heeding Soviet intentions, in order to curry favor with the USSR. Ordinarily the Mongolians' interest in boundaries or real estate is very weak; on the contrary, the people who evince greatest interest in such matters are the Russians. . . . However, in the particular case of the Nomonhan border dispute, I think it has to be said that the Choibalsan faction, for the purpose of enlarging its own power, exploited the frontier affray (about which the Russians, not the Mongolians, were highly sensitive) as a pretext to borrow Soviet strength.

Ishida has propounded the convincing theory that there were intimate connections between a final purge in Outer Mongolia in early 1939 and the subsequent outbreak of major hostilities at Nomonhan. In particular, Ishida

---

*This area, which will be the focus of the remainder of the book, was called Nomonhan by the Japanese and Manchukuoans and Khalkhin Gol by the Soviets and Outer Mongols.

pinpoints a fateful clash between Choibalsan and Prime Minister Anandyn Amar, a little-known but important principal during that dark period of MPR history when the regime was "shaky and suspicion-ridden."[53] In mid-January 1939, as we shall see, the commander of a tiny MPRA border unit operating near the Nomonhan observation post fell into Manchukuoan hands. This trifling frontier skirmish and others like it were adduced as a justification for the denunciation of Amar. The Soviet army's entry into Outer Mongolia in force needed to be rationalized, and Choibalsan's main surviving political rival had to be liquidated. Choibalsan gave these reasons for Amar's execution: "Amar helped antigovernment plotters, opposed their arrest, and *neglected the defense of the borders.* He betrayed his own country and was a traitor to the Revolution."[54] Soviet Col. S. N. Shishkin agrees that the MPR's frontier defense system east of the Halha was poorly organized at the time; the Mongolian forces were ill-acquainted with the region and even lacked maps. Shishkin unintentionally provides an additional fact that may have contributed to Amar's doom: two weeks after the Mongolian border outpost commander had been captured, 21 leaflets fabricated by the Japanese were found. Over the alleged signature of the Mongol prisoner, the leaflets called for the rupture of relations between the MPR and the Soviet Union. Significantly, Amar was killed in March 1939, and the first serious fighting flared at Nomonhan two months later, with Soviet army regulars now backing the Mongolian border guards.[55]

Since the autumn of 1938, one Kwantung Army staff officer remembers, the Outer Mongolians had given signs of fomenting trouble in the general area of Nomonhan. The Mongols would set fire to grass in the west, and the prevailing wind pattern spread the flames to the Manchurian grasslands. Rendered uneasy, the natives complained to the Manchukuoan authorities.[56] On 4 October 1938, a 24-man Japanese survey team that was examining the Halha River border line drew fire from five MPRA horsemen on a hill on the Mongolian side of the river.[57]

The smallness, confusion, and color of a typical border affray, in this case a defeat from the IJA standpoint, are depicted in a secret report located among the sparse surviving records of the Kwantung Army.[58] In mid-morning on 1 November 1938, an element of the 11th Company of the 72nd Infantry Regiment, on observation post duty at Tsagan-ora in the Man-chouli sector under 2nd Lt. Sunahara Masatsugu, detected an enemy soldier advancing toward Manchukuoan territory. The lieutenant set forth with a corporal and a superior private. When the patrol approached, the Mongolian soldier fled. Then Sunahara observed another two or three MPRA troopers. In order to prevent the enemy soldiers from crossing the Japanese-claimed border, the lieutenant proceeded to "menace" them by advancing, without first contacting his own post.

Although the enemy quickly disappeared, the Japanese decided to continue their advance with the new intention of verifying the boundary line. After they came to a point 50 meters from the border marker, still on the Manchurian side, they were suddenly fired on by five horsemen. Although the Japanese returned the fire, the corporal and the private were shot down. Gathering that the Mongols intended to capture rather than kill him like the others, Sunahara managed to fall back gradually and to signal his observation post. After his return to safety, he encountered three Japanese outpost soldiers, whom he reprimanded for not having reported developments to the garrison unit commander. He then returned to the observation post, where he phoned a report to his chief. While preparing an operation to recover the two fallen soldiers, he received a message from the intelligence officer of the Manchouli Garrison Unit to the effect that further action should be suspended. Soon afterward an MPRA truck was seen approaching the place where the two Japanese lay. The vehicle stopped before returning in the direction of the Mongolian cantonment, which was about five kilometers from the Japanese outpost. The two slain IJA soldiers must have been picked up by the Mongols.

When the Japanese garrison commander at Manchouli received the report that two corpses had been lost to the enemy, he dispatched two platoons—one of IJA and one of Manchukuoan troops—under the battalion commander, a major. After reaching the incident site around 1 P.M., the major decided merely to secure the observation post area—a cautious judgment that was supported by the garrison commander, who decided that the matter of the dead soldiers ought to be transferred to diplomatic negotiation. Meanwhile, the 23rd Division sent a staff officer to the scene to investigate. Lt. Gen. Komatsubara Michitarō, commander of the 23rd Division, summoned the Manchouli Garrison Unit commander to division headquarters at Hailar on 4 November, and in the light of his account warned him "not to be taken advantage of by the enemy but to tighten defense and bolster the troops' alertness." The official report by Komatsubara to War Minister Itagaki admitted candidly that the cause of the Japanese setback was a lack of vigilance and a nonchalant approach to the enemy.[59]

According to Japanese sources, the Outer Mongolians intensified their activities and increased their forces operating in the Nomonhan region from January 1939 on. IJA intelligence judged that the MPRA border units and the corps deployed to the rear were made up of excellent forces trained in the Ulan Bator district under Soviet army chiefs.[60] To some, the Mongols' border actions seemed planned: crossings of the frozen Halha followed by attacks at short range against small Manchurian outposts, inside Manchukuoan-claimed territory around Nomonhan.[61] A Kwantung Army officer recalls flying to the scene to investigate during the intense cold of January. He could discern hoofprints and a few positions on what was claimed to be the Manchurian bank of the Halha River.[62]

Each side kept its own tally of the minor border affrays that took place in the early months of 1939. The MPR authorities charged that between January and May, "before the start of the Japanese offensive against Mongolia," the Kwantung Army launched attacks on 17 occasions in the Khalkhin Gol region; an official Russian military source speaks of about 30 systematic Japanese violations of the MPR border from January.[63] Referring to the period dating back to January 1935, Japanese records spoke of MPR-fomented episodes of border trespassing, kidnappings, shootings, demands to remove observation posts, occupation of disputed sites, and overflights. Specifically in 1939, the Kwantung Army reported ten incidents in January, starting on the 12th; two in February; and one in March. Until 2 February the MPRA patrols generally numbered from three to 15 soldiers, sometimes equipped with one or two light machine guns; but the episodes of 8 February and 17 March involved larger forces of about 40 men. The defending units were mainly Manchukuoan border police or army elements; usually the clashes took place at distances of six to 20 km. southwest of the Nomonhan outpost.[64]

Embedded in the preceding enumeration of border clashes taking place in early 1939 must have been the escalating troubles that would cost MPR Prime Minister Amar his life. As Ishida, the civilian expert on Mongolian affairs, recalls events, the crisis really began when a very small Outer Mongol reconnaissance party was captured by a Manchukuoan observation post unit. The account by Soviet Colonel Shishkin approximates Ishida's version: on 14 January large enemy forces surrounded a Mongolian outpost near Nomonhan, wounded one cavalryman, and seized the commander. Ishida claims that Mongolian efforts to recapture the prisoner or prisoners led to fighting on a larger scale, and that the Manchukuoan army then sent reinforcements from the Chiangchunmiao sector headquarters. When an MPRA 1st lieutenant and a dozen men approached the Manchukuoan outpost, all of the Mongolians were captured and sent to Hailar for interrogation by OSS agents. This development led to the Outer Mongolians' dispatch of further reinforcements, who retaliated by destroying the Manchukuoan post. Both sides sent up even more troops, and the incident mushroomed.[65]

Even if the authorities in Hsinking heard about the series of border disturbances in the Nomonhan region during early 1939, they were not particularly exercised by the reports. While visiting Shengwutun about 14 January, a Kwantung Army intelligence officer learned of clashes between Outer Mongolian reconnaissance parties and Manchukuoan police, but he never expected that the trifling skirmishes would escalate.[66] Officially, the Japanese insisted that there were frequent border violations in the vicinity of Nomonhan by the Outer Mongols from 12 January on, but that every one was driven off by Manchukuoan guards until May.[67] The intelligence officer of the Japanese 23rd Infantry Division stationed at Hailar is of the opinion that the early affrays must have been the exclusive problem of the Manchukuoan forces, not the Japanese.[68] At the Tokyo level, according to an intelligence staff officer, the minor incidents on the Mongolian boundary were too trifling to reach the ears of the AGS. After all, he contends, these were not clashes as such, but trespasses. Details were the Kwantung Army's concern, for the very name of Nomonhan was as unknown in Tokyo as it was to many in Hsinking.[69]

Whereas the Japanese had been reacting without sizable commitment to recent events on the MPR border, Soviet testimony reveals that the Russians began to transfer important troop elements in Outer Mongolia eastward toward the Manchurian frontier just before the spring of 1939. Maj. A. E. Bykov, a mechanized rifle battalion commander of the 11th Tank Brigade stationed at Undurhan, would eventually lead the first Russian troops to participate in the fighting at Nomonhan. According to Bykov, on 1 March the brigade commander, Maj. Gen. M. P. Yakovlev, put him in charge of a mixed detachment and ordered him to proceed to the area of Tamsag, 120-30 km. west of the Halha River. His mission was to prevent Japanese actions directed against the 7th Mongolian Border Guards. Bykov's detachment reached the area of Tamsag on 5 March; east of the town, Bykov has asserted, there were only Mongolian border guard outposts, not Soviet or Mongolian regular troops.[70]

At about the same time that Bykov's unit moved toward the Manchurian frontier, Stalin was telling the 18th Communist Party Congress in Moscow on 10 March 1939 that any invasion of the USSR would be met by double strength.[71] So far as the Mongolian People's Republic was concerned, Stalin's earlier pronouncement of 1936 to Roy Howard in parallel with the mutual defense protocol of the same year could now be interpreted as a warning that any serious Japanese violation of MPR-claimed borders would be regarded by the Kremlin authorities as tantamount to an invasion of the Soviet Union itself. Although Stalin's latest assertion of 10 March could be viewed as public propaganda on behalf of the Mongolian client state, it was also true that the USSR remained very sensitive about contiguous or nearby frontiers anywhere, in Asia as well as in Europe.[72]

13

Japanese Principals and
a Green Division

With the close of the Wuhan and Canton operations in 1938, the Japanese army prepared for prolonged warfare on the continent while keeping an eye on the Russians. The hostilities in China continued to swallow the preponderance of the Japanese ground forces, 27 of 37 divisions. To give IJA horse units a last chance to prove themselves in modern war, the unique division-size cavalry group of two brigades stationed in Hailar was transferred to the China theater in July 1938. For a while IGHQ considered sending the existing 8th Division to Hailar and motorizing it. Since the men of this division came from Hirosaki in Aomori prefecture on northern Honshu, they were presumably well suited to operate in the dreadful winters of northwest Manchuria. Opposition to this posting arose, however, because natives of Aomori are said to lack mechanical aptitude and to be weak in educational background. In addition, the 8th Division was needed in China too.[1]

Meanwhile the Japanese High Command had been obliged to form new infantry divisions quickly. Many weak special divisions (*tokusetsu shidan*) were activated in succession.[2] The old regular divisions were not themselves reinforced but were reserved, first in Japan and then in Manchuria, for the main contingency, a hypothetical war against the Soviet Union. New divisions differed from their predecessors in the number of active-duty soldiers; they were made up mainly of recalled reservists and older personnel. During the first stages of hostilities in China, the new divisions were still organized along "square" or four-regiment lines, but from early 1938 the "triangular" or three-regiment division was instituted.[3] The 23rd Division, ordered in April 1938 to be activated at Kumamoto on semitropical Kyushu Island instead of at wintry Hirosaki, was among the new triangular formations.[4] Its men were called up from Kyushu and, to a lesser extent, from western Honshu—that is, from Kurume, Hiroshima, and Kokura.[5]

The division's three organic infantry regimental headquarters, all from Kyushu, were the 64th, 71st, and 72nd. In addition, there was a single brigade or group setup (the 23rd *Dan*) and the following other elements: a cavalry reconnaissance or search regiment (the 23rd), with one troop of horsemen and a tankette company; a field artillery regiment (the 13th), with nine batteries; an engineer regiment (the 23rd) of two companies; and a transport regiment (the 23rd) composed of two motor companies.[6] Total personnel strength of the 23rd Division approximated 13,000 officers and men. From the outset, the force was at full strength quantitatively, but opinions regarding quality are mixed. The officer corps seems to have been relatively poorer in quality, as a whole, than the men. Although generally young and inexperienced, the latter were aggressive, vigorous, and dependable; soldiers from Kyushu were particularly good, famous for their physical strength and stamina. The core of the divisional officers, including most of the platoon leaders, consisted mainly of cadets and one-year volunteers; graduates of the military academy were few. Most of the junior officers, in fact, were recalled reservists commissioned on graduation from a university. Among the line officers, only about a half were graduates of the service academy. While the regiment commanders were generally regarded as satisfactory, the company and battalion commanders were less highly esteemed.

Of the Japanese principals in the warfare at Nomonhan, none is more important and none suffered more cruelly than Lt. Gen. Komatsubara Michitarō, 53, who became commander of the 23rd Division on its creation in July 1938. An infantry graduate of the 18th military academy class of 1906 and a Russian-speaker, Komatsubara was regarded as one of the Japanese army's experts on the Soviet Union. Between 1919 and 1921 he served as assistant military attaché in Russia. During the final phase of the Siberian Expedition, in the summer of 1922, he visited Siberia. In 1927-30, Komatsubara was again assigned to the Soviet capital, this time as military attaché, in the rank of colonel from August 1929. From 1932 to 1935 he was once more in contact with Russian affairs as chief of the OSS branch at Harbin in Manchuria, where the Lytton Commission interviewed him. In August 1934 he became a major general. Preceding his takeover of the 23rd Division, he commanded an independent garrison unit at Kirin (1937-38), being promoted to lieutenant general in November 1937. Although he possessed great confidence in case of operations against the Russians, he was also cautious and conservative where the USSR was concerned.

For a Japanese, Komatsubara was rather tall at 5'7" or a little more, and husky at about 145 pounds. He wore glasses, had a small moustache, and spoke in a somewhat high voice. Neatness always concerned him; even in his combat tent he tried to keep his clothing pressed and his face smooth-shaven, and to wash daily. In Europe he had acquired a taste for cheese and pastries, delicacies he would never savor at Nomonhan. The general partook of the foods enjoyed by his juniors, such as canned mandarin oranges and pineapple. From attaché days he had developed an educated taste in liquors, and there was some sake and whiskey at the front, but the general gave up smoking at Nomonhan. Komatsubara was quite a literary type; he kept minute diaries and wrote many detailed letters. After the hostilities in

1939, he wrote poems then in fashion; for example, one to be sung to the tune of the popular "Hakutōzan." Slightly nervous and a worrier, the general was rather short-tempered. Emotions showed readily on his face, although he was never heard to shout. His likes and dislikes among officers were pronounced, to the point that some feel he did not truly gain the "love" of his division. Getting along with him professionally, however, seems to have posed no particular problem for his immediate staff and subordinates. Several sources remark that Komatsubara always gave his staff officers a full hearing; there was no railroading of command views.

Though Komatsubara lacked combat and command experience, he did participate as a battalion aide in the brief expedition against the Germans in Shantung during October-November 1914. Personally warm and paternal, the general nonetheless administered many a scolding and was very strict in seeing that orders were carried out. Concrete evidence of Komatsubara's stern professional outlook may be found in the border episode of 1 November 1938, described in the last chapter, in which a second lieutenant acted with more nonchalance than discretion during a clash with Outer Mongolian troops and suffered the disgrace of losing two Japanese corpses to the enemy. After investigation, Komatsubara ordered the Manchouli garrison unit commander, a lieutenant colonel, to enter into a "state of apology," involving confinement to quarters for five days, because his program of training and education had proved unsatisfactory in terms of the defensive mission. The garrison commander administered the same punishment to his battalion commander, a major, for alleged inappropriateness of measures to cope with a sudden enemy attack. From the battalion commander, the unfortunate second lieutenant received ten days of heavy punishment—disciplinary confinement plus forfeiture of certain pay and allowances—because of unsuitable actions in sustaining attack and abandonment of two subordinates to the foe. Thereupon the garrison unit commander tacked on another 20 days of heavy punishment, for a total of 30 assessed against the lieutenant. But General Komatsubara went further and recommended to the war minister in Tokyo that the lieutenant be deprived of his army commission.[7]

Associates and subordinates employ the following terms in describing Komatsubara: severe but considerate and personally gentle; meticulous and honest; very intelligent, indeed brilliant and first-rate, although not razor-sharp (the appellation given to Tōjō Hideki); theoretical, studious, rational, deeply contemplative; noble and brave; personally refined, sensitive, and dignified; quiet and steady, neither reckless nor excitable. Critics call Komatsubara cold and egotistical, disliked and unpopular. Some suggest that he lacked the power of decision.[8]

The 23rd Division chief of staff, Col. Ōuchi Tsutomu (Atsushi), 46, was another Soviet intelligence expert, but with a background in cavalry. A graduate of the 26th military academy class of 1914, he had served as military attaché in Latvia (1933-35) before becoming chief of staff of the Cavalry Group in Manchuria (1936-37). In August 1937 Ōuchi was promoted to colonel. He possessed a keen, clear mind and a well-rounded personality that rendered him a fine choice to assist a general such as Komatsubara. Associates say that Ōuchi did much to pull together the division headquarters and that, had it not been for him, the organization might have come apart at the seams. Relied upon fully by Komatsubara, the colonel made full and effective use of personal relationships. Gentle and not particularly strong-willed, Ōuchi was magnanimous and adopted the broad view without being obsessed by small details; in this respect he was rather different from the commander. An intellectual and more of a thinker than a doer, the colonel was sensitive, sympathetic, humane, and loyal.

Senior operations officer on the 23rd Division staff was Lt. Col. Murata Masao, 40, an artillery graduate of the 33rd military academy class of 1921. Although he had had little or no previous staff experience, he had a valuable familiarity with special weapons such as gas from a period at the Narashino school. Calm, deliberate, and very greatly influenced by Chief of Staff Ōuchi, Murata was not markedly aggressive in drafting operational plans. He was neither short-tempered nor excitable, and he maintained excellent relationships with subordinate unit commanders.

The number-two staff member and intelligence officer of the division was Maj. Suzuki Yoshiyasu, 39, a cavalryman from the same military academy class as Lieutenant Colonel Murata. Suzuki had had no intelligence experience before assignment to the 23rd Division, but he had studied Russian in military prep school and had fought as a company commander during the Manchurian Incident.

Capt. Itō Noboru, 30, a native of Oita on Kyushu and a graduate of the 42nd military academy class of 1930, was the division's logistics staff officer.

Although it is the opinion of Tokyo-level observers that the quality and training of the 23rd Division were not very good in practice, there is consensus that the division commander and the chief of staff were hand-picked Soviet specialists who could be expected to develop an excellent training program designed to cope with possible hostilities against the USSR. When an IJA officer heard at the war ministry in Tokyo that one of the four brand-new triangular divisions was being sent to Hailar, he guessed from the choice of Komatsubara and Ōuchi that it must be the 23rd Division which had been earmarked for West Manchuria.[9] Kwantung Army staff officers agree that the higher command level of the 23rd Division had been well selected and possessed its share of experts on the Soviet Union, and that the commander was especially well qualified. Nevertheless, examination of the career data of every division staff officer, from the commanding general down, reveals a universal lack of significant combat experience.

The division's tactical units were commanded as follows: 23rd Infantry Group, Maj. Gen. Kobayashi Kōichi; 64th Infantry Regiment, Col. Yamagata Takemitsu; 71st Infantry Regiment, Col.. Okamoto Tokuzō; 72nd Infantry Regiment, Col. Sakai Mikio; 23rd Reconnaissance Regiment, Lt. Col. Azuma Yaozō; 13th Field Artillery Regiment, Col. Ise Takahide. Rounding out the main organization were the 23rd Engineer Regiment under Lt. Col. Saitō Isamu and the 23rd Transport Regiment under Lt. Col. Midorikawa Chūji. Asked to comment on the quality of the original line regiment commanders, a divisional staff officer replied that he felt at the time that the colonels were excellent, could survive on the same basis as their tough soldiers, and were well cut out for the type of combat they were to face at Nomonhan. Veterans of combat service with the 23rd Division at Nomonhan look back at the unit with fondness and nostalgia. General Komatsubara's aide reminisces that it was a "very good, well trained, strong, and pure" division. Compared to other units with which he served, the 23rd Division struck the aide as well disciplined. For this there may have been a very practical explanation: "There were no evil districts in the neighborhood upon which to waste yen!" [10]

The division commander took official command of his unit on 7 July 1938, in Japan. His intelligence-officer-designate, Major Suzuki, received orders on 1 July to proceed from Tokyo to Kumamoto, where division headquarters was in process of assembly. The major was received in audience, with ten civilians, by the Emperor and Empress on 6 July; [11] he left for Kumamoto the next day. Formation of the division was to be accomplished by the 10th, and was apparently done on schedule. On 16 July Suzuki left with an advance party for Kwantung Army headquarters at Hsinking; he proceeded from there to Harbin and Hailar to direct the setting up of division headquarters. After a series of flights back and forth between Hailar, Harbin, and Hsinking, the major went down to Dairen at the end of July or beginning of August to meet the division commander and the main body of the formation, who were bound for Hailar. Then he drew up Division Operations Order No. 1 directing move-out as a division.

Division staff officers agree that the organization and equipment of the 23rd Division were not suitable for mobile operations on the wide-open steppes of Hulun Buir. It was true that there was some degree of motorization: the reconnaissance regiment had a tankette company, and the division had a transport unit equipped with motor vehicles. Yet except for some cavalry, the 23rd Division had about the same degree of mobility as divisions stationed in the East Manchurian border areas, where a much lower degree of mobility was necessary. Numbers of weapons and equipment were up to authorized strength, but the quality was not satisfactory for desert operations; military evaluations varied from "not at all excellent" to "worst in the Japanese army." Apart from weaknesses in mechanized strength, the division was cursed with "classic" old artillery, such as the unimproved Type 38 short-range 75-mm. field piece of 1907, oldest in the entire army and in use by no other division. One 23rd Division staff officer remembers "weeping mentally" when he saw these antiques. Unit artillery commanders often visited division headquarters to ask the staff officers what they were supposed to do with the "old junk" that had been issued to them.

The 23rd Division was particularly deficient in antitank capabilities, although armored warfare was to be expected on the plains of western Manchuria. The reconnaissance regiment possessed no specific antitank weapons; the Kwantung Army expected this unit to be able to cope with only Outer Mongolian cavalry rushes. Even the Japanese engineer companies merely had explosive charges. Each divisional combat unit was issued a few antitank demolition charges, but in combat the infantry had to improvise close-quarter antitank measures: "hardtack" mines (small, round charges set on long poles) and incendiary firebombs (gasoline-filled bottles). By way of antitank guns, each infantry regiment was allotted one rapid-fire gun battery of four Type 94 37-mm. weapons and one regimental gun battery of four 75-mm. mountain guns—the old Type 41 of 1908. The artillery regiment itself included three battalions totaling 24 of the ancient 75-mm. field guns plus twelve 12-cm. howitzers. In all, the division thus could muster only 60 artillery pieces. As for light and heavy machine guns, the 23rd Division was provided with less than other IJA divisions, too.

As soon as the division reached Hailar, Colonel Ōuchi sent higher headquarters a bulky communication expressing his recommendations about the need for immediate improvements in organization and equipment, especially with respect to mechanization. Ōuchi had been a cavalry staff officer at Hailar for two years, and even the cavalry group stationed there had had much better armored forces than the 23rd Division. Yet whenever Ōuchi went to Kwantung Army headquarters to ask for changes, he would always be told that the western front was subsidiary and had bottom priority, after east and north. The division was left really alone and "independent" in the west. Kwantung Army staff officers would say, "You people are the boss of Hulun Buir." Consequently Ōuchi's recommendations were not acted upon.

Adversely affecting the cohesiveness and skill level of the 23rd Division was the fact that the divisional units had to be stationed separately at first because of a shortage of quarters at Hailar. Until facilities were completed in November 1938 and the division could be concentrated, there were only two regiments in the Hailar area—about half the division, and even these regiments were not together. Other organic units had to be temporarily located as far away as Harbin. Divisional training and control suffered accordingly; the division commander could not convene staff conferences quickly, in view of the dispersion. In addition, at the beginning there was no direct telephone or radio connection between 23rd Division and Kwantung Army headquarters. Thus even in ordinary times the poor communications imposed a severe hardship upon the division.

Until the division could be combined at Hailar, there was only individual-unit training up to the platoon level—not even to the company level. After the concentration of the division, some further individual training in cold-weather operations was conducted, but large-scale exercises were impossible in the biting cold, which sometimes dipped as low as −55° C. Since the soldiery came from a hot clime, they were unfamiliar with severe winter and were untrained to cope with it. Throughout the winter of 1938-39 there were many small exercises, and in March or April there were map maneuvers involving all officers from platoon leaders up (*kanbu enshū*). Apart from the tactical exercises, the division conducted division-level mobility maneuvers (*kidō enshū*) in the depth of winter. The headquarters staff did its best to hold as many combined-arms exercises as possible, involving infantry, cavalry, and engineers, and designed to foster unity. The fact that the 23rd Division was so new, and that the unit commanders did not know each other well, troubled General Komatsubara. Accordingly, he twice called all of his commanders to headquarters and conducted on-the-spot exercises for them only (*genchi enshū*). Afterward the officers dined and drank together, getting to know each other and their division commander. After the Nomonhan Incident, Komatsubara told one of his staff officers that these exercises had been very successful; all subordinates who had attended the maneuvers fought well in accordance with the commander's wishes, and all fell in combat facing the enemy. The only "disgrace," involving flight from the front, was incurred by a regiment commander who had not attended the exercises.

A division staff officer feels that relations between division headquarters and the subordinate units were "a little lacking." Among the units themselves there was a definite absence of cohesion and fraternity. This was natural, perhaps, since the organization was so new and the units had only come to Hailar recently. Among the divisional headquarters personnel, however, there did not seem to be any real trouble involving unity. On the basis of the 23rd Division's maneuvers in 1938-39, a critique was prepared, centering on four main points. First, the division lacked sufficient mobility. Second, there was a dearth of the flat-trajectory, long-range artillery necessary for fighting on level plains. Instead, the division was using mountain guns and howitzers suitable for mountainous terrain. Third, supply was based on animal power, not on motorization, and this was a grave error. And fourth, the water supply for men and horses was deficient. Since there were no water purification units yet, the question of supplying water posed a huge problem for the division staff. Consideration was even given to the formation of camel units, and some were in fact assembled; but this expedient was out of the question in the case of combat units. Since the division could not solve matters by itself, the problem was of course referred to the Kwantung Army.

Japanese army experts rated the combat capability of the 23rd Division as "below medium"; Inada compares it qualitatively to a mere garrison division on occupation duty in China. Newness of structure, lack of experience, quartering problems, unfamiliarity with rigorous winter conditions for soldiers hailing from southern Japan, obsolescent equipment, and qualitative weaknesses—these were some of the factors that prevented the division from becoming an elite force.[12]

In extenuation, officers stress that there were plans but no equipment, that the setup of the division was strictly temporary, and that the division was eventually to be motorized. Much of the problem stemmed from the relatively overnight buildup of the whole Imperial Japanese Army: from 1930 to 1937 the total number of divisions had remained fixed at 17, but as a result of the China conflict seven new divisions were added in 1938 and nine in 1939. The demands of the China theater prevented the first-rate equipping of all divisions simultaneously, and the 23rd Division, of course, was one of the newest.

As a rule of thumb, a minimum of one and a half years was required to whip a brand-new division into fighting shape. On this basis, the 23rd Division still needed another year's grace when the Nomonhan Incident broke out unexpectedly. General Komatsubara later told one of his staff that training was progressing but that he wished he had had one more year before the test came. Entering into the Kwantung Army's decision to assign the 23rd Division an exclusively defensive mission on the least important strategic front in Manchuria was the fact that the green division was deemed to be lacking in training and esprit de corps. In Tsuji's quaint words, the 23rd Division resembled newlyweds who do not know each other well and have to start out in life with only a kettle and a pan.[13]

Higher headquarters was fearful that the 23rd Division would prove incapable of fulfilling a vital mission in wartime. Although consideration of Japanese offensive operations in the west had been set aside, powerful Soviet thrusts were expected in this region shortly after the onset of hostilities, and the Japanese anticipated being surrounded strategically. An overall shortage of strength, however, precluded assigning more than one Japanese division and a border garrison unit to the northwestern front. Could the Hailar-Arshaan sector be held against an enemy offensive launched with far greater relative strength along a vulnerable invasion route radiating from feebly fortified Hailar? The Kwantung Army senior operations officer, Lt. Col. Hattori Takushirō, felt that "to allot sufficient manpower to this district would have meant the sacrifice of manpower in the main field of battle—operations in the interior. So, from a consideration of the general situation, we limited [the commitment] to the smallest possible number. We were perhaps risking even less than the minimum; [hence] instructions for operations were entirely defensive." [14] In 1939 the 23rd Division was engaged solely in training for holding operations, encompassing only tactical counterattacks at most.

14

Testing the Border Guidelines, May 1939

It has often been said that the troubles which erupted at Nomonhan in 1939 stemmed at best from a thoughtless collision, at worst from a conspiracy by Japanese militarists. A typical Soviet-Mongolian interpretation follows: "The aggressive plans of the Japanese imperialists were aimed at seizing and enslaving the Mongolian Republic and turning its territory into a military bridgehead for a 'great war' against the USSR. . . . Having convinced themselves [at Changkufeng in 1938] of the strength of the Far Eastern frontiers of the USSR, the Japanese aggressors reinforced troop concentrations on the frontiers of the MPR, reckoning they could attack the USSR through the territory of the MPR." [1] Carrying these charges even further, detractors of the Japanese Emperor have invented the theory that the Kwantung Army had the monarch's "mandate to take Outer Mongolia and so control the Trans-Siberian Railway." [2]

Such missions would have been remarkable for a thrown-together infantry division whose commander had only taken over in July 1938. But we need not rely only upon journalists for imaginative theorizing: in February 1939 an IJN staff officer reported to the naval chief of staff, after a trip to Manchuria, that the Kwantung Army had deployed almost 25 divisions along the frontiers with Russia and gave every impression of getting ready for aggressive action against the USSR. The whole Kwantung Army, as we know, possessed merely a third of the alleged number of divisions, but in view of the "very dangerous situation," the Emperor was advised. The alarmed sovereign gave strict orders to his chief aide de camp to find out the truth. Why was the army concentrating troops in Manchuria? "Are they going to do something, deliberately keeping it quiet?" According to the gossipy source for this account, Baron Harada, nothing came of the Emperor's inquiry; the embarrassed chief aide feared "a gap between His Majesty's will and the army's opinion," for the situation in the army was "deplorable." [3] (For the actual deployment of IJA forces in Manchukuo in 1939, see Map 2, "Opposing Orders of Battle, May 1939.")

On the west Manchurian front, however, all was quiet after the flurry of trifling affrays in early 1939. Spring had come to the Hulun Buir district, the ice clogging the Halha had melted, and the waters rose. Outer Mongolian troops had fallen back to the left side of the river; incidents ceased. Accord-

MAP 2: OPPOSING ORDERS OF BATTLE, MAY 1939

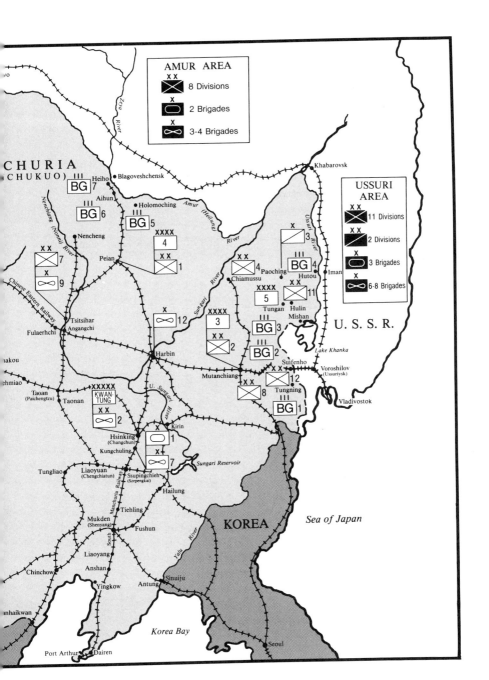

AMUR AREA

XX	8 Divisions
X	2 Brigades
X	3-4 Brigades

USSURI AREA

XX	11 Divisions
XX	2 Divisions
X	3 Brigades
X	6-8 Brigades

CHURIA
(CHUKUO)

Heiho ● Blagoveshchensk
BG 7

Aihun
BG 6

● Holomoching
BG 5

XXXX
4

XX
1

Nencheng

Peian

Khabarovsk

Amur (Heilung) River

Ussuri River

XX
3

Paoching
BG 4
Hutou

XX
4
Chiamussu
Iman

XXXX
5
Tungan ● Hulin
Mishan

XX
11

XX
7

X
9

Chinese Eastern Railway

Tsitsihar
Angangchi

Fulaerhchi

X
12

XXXX
3

BG 3

XX
2

BG 2

U.S.S.R.

Lake Khanka

Harbin

Sungari River

Suifenho
Voroshilov
(Ussuriysk)

Mutanchiang

XX
12

XX
8

Tungning
BG 1

Vladivostok

Taoan
(Paichengtzu)
Taonan

XXXXX
KWAN-
TUNG

XX
2

U. Sungari River

Hsinking
(Changchun)

Kirin

X
1

Kungchuling

X+
7

Sungari Reservoir

Tungliao

Liaoyuan
(Chengchiatun)
Ssupingchieh
(Szepengkai)

Hailung

Mukden
(Shenyang)

Tiehling

Fushun

KOREA

Sea of Japan

Liaoyang

Anshan

Chinchow

Yingkow
Antung
Sinuiju

Yalu River

Port Arthur Dairen

Korea Bay

Seoul

ing to the 23rd Division intelligence officer, General Komatsubara may have begun to pay attention to the frontier situation only from about April.[4] This supposition is supported by the fact that in Hsinking, on the 25th of that month, Kwantung Army commander Ueda Kenkichi personally issued to all his corps commanders "Principles for the Settlement of Soviet-Manchurian Border Disputes," a document actually drafted by hawkish operations officer Tsuji Masanobu.

The Kwantung Army command seems to have been dissatisfied with front-line units' handling of border problems; often Japanese forces "acted too passively to sustain their prestige," whereas on other occasions they overreacted and enlarged disputes. Specific guidelines appeared necessary. Tsuji's draft for General Ueda's signature was designed mainly to deal with border incidents within the Kwantung Army commander's responsibility for Manchukuo's defense. According to the text of Operations Section Order No. 1488, the Kwantung Army was guided by "the basic policy of neither committing nor allowing others to commit violations of the border." Experience with Soviet and Outer Mongolian units on the Manchurian frontiers indicated that "only resolute and thoroughgoing punitive action against their transgressions can prevent the aggravation or recurrence" of incidents. In cases of confrontation, the Kwantung Army would "nip [Soviet-MPR] ambitions in the bud by completely destroying them." Japanese troops, particularly those assigned to forward elements, must become conversant with the boundaries and be trained in the type of small-scale tactics that characterized border fighting. Where the frontier was delineated clearly, it must not be violated; but where demarcation was unclear, area defense commanders at the army and independent divisional level must establish boundaries on their own initiative, identify them for advanced units, and report their action promptly to the Kwantung Army.

Operations Order No. 1488 further required Japanese units to fight till victory, regardless of the site of the boundaries or of relative combat strengths. Action must be taken swiftly, employing forces built up carefully beforehand. Noteworthy stipulations were added:

> To accomplish our missions, or to trap or lure Soviet troops into Manchurian territory, it is permissible to enter Soviet territory temporarily. In such an event, however, never abandon friendly dead or wounded on Soviet soil. Endeavor to capture prisoners and to bear away enemy corpses. . . . Unnecessary ground movements are forbidden in frontier zones, however. Only unavoidable action will be taken, under strict security measures and with careful deployment of forces. Patrols and reconnaissance will be conducted in strength, under the command of an officer where possible. To maximize effectiveness, definite missions must be assigned.

Border clashes were to be reported immediately and information regarding developments conveyed in timely fashion, to facilitate early and effective countermeasures. Though every effort should be made to avoid trouble, friendly forces must keep a constant eye on the other side. When a hostile incursion occurred, Japanese troops "must challenge the enemy courageously and endeavor to triumph in their zone of action without concerning themselves about the consequences, which will be the responsibility of higher headquarters."[5]

By clarifying the Kwantung Army's border policy, Ueda was seeking to lighten the burden of front-line forces, who now "would not have to bear full responsibility for local disputes." Staff officer Hattori explains the rationale behind Order No. 1488 more fully:[6]

> It is obviously not within the Kwantung Army's purview to define borders, but diplomatic negotiations often consume considerable time, and in the past a considerable number of frontier disputes have arisen at poorly delimited border localities. Lines demarcated by the area defense commanders will be strictly provisional, and not arbitrary delimitations drawn in favor of our side. The greatest dilemma that confronts border defense units derives from a twofold problem: if passive action is taken, the unit will be regarded as timid and cowardly; but if overly aggressive measures are adopted, the unit is liable to be held responsible for aggravating a dispute. The clarification of responsibility is intended to correct the situation.

Not all Japanese historians are so laudatory of the Kwantung Army's stated intentions. Hayashi Katsuya, for example, charges that the guidelines really meant "Ignore the borders, go ahead and invade the other side and call it our territory. If anybody complains, use force, in the expectation of certain victory." To Hayashi and other postwar critics, the operations order represented not crisis management but justification for provoking disputes. In this view, the document "encouraged burglars"; in case of trouble the superiors promised to "look after their remains."[7] But Hata Ikuhiko reminds us that the Kwantung Army regarded the High Command's policy of not invading even if invaded as a weak and unrealistic injunction in the face of illicit Soviet-MPR actions on the border. Therefore the Kwantung Army devised its own provisos that completely ignored not only the Japanese civil government but also the central military authorities, who were preoccupied with the strategic problem in China. Tsunoda Jun refers to a Kwantung Army "border defense neurosis."[8]

There can be no doubt, however, that Ueda, as commander of the field army defending the client state of Manchukuo, possessed authority to implement the broad imperial mission assigned to him as he saw fit—a situation entirely different from that confronting the commander of the Korea Army, which had only garrison responsibilities in peacetime. Nevertheless, border problems always contained an important political coloration; therefore the High Command in Tokyo ought to have provided overall guidance for the Kwantung Army in the event not of minor commitments of force but of large-scale troop involvements. There is no evidence of coordination between headquarters in Hsinking and in Tokyo concerning the promulgation of a document so important as the new defense guidelines; no representative was present from Tokyo. Tsuji, however, asserts that the contents of the order were routinely communicated to the chief of the AGS, who said nothing at the time and only awoke to the document's significance after serious warfare broke out at Nomonhan months later. Tsunoda agrees that the General Staff did not react officially in April, and adds that officers in the AGS Operations Section endorsed the guidelines privately.[9]

As for the particular reasons why the Kwantung Army guidelines were drafted in the spring of 1939, it has been suggested that the war in China had quieted down and approximated a de facto truce, with large-scale operations to be suspended and hostilities settled politically, so that the military emphasis could again be shifted to Manchuria and the Soviet problem. The preceding year had been especially marked by Manchurian border disputes, of which the Changkufeng affair had been the most serious and, from the Kwantung Army's point of view, the worst handled. Aggressive operations staff officers—Col. Terada Masao, the new chief, Lt. Col. Hattori Takushirō, and Maj. Shimanuki Takeharu (Takeji)—had arrived at Kwantung Army headquarters to reinforce the hawkish Major Tsuji already in place.[10] Sometime in early 1939, probably in March, the Kwantung Army's civil affairs officer happened to visit General Komatsubara and the OSS branch chief in Hailar, where he learned of signs of a possible incident involving Outer Mongolian and Manchukuoan forces. Apparently the latter were being egged on by operations officers from Kwantung Army headquarters to "cause trouble." Feeling that danger did exist, the staff officer conveyed the information to the Kwantung Army chief of staff, Lt. Gen. Isogai Rensuke, and to the commanding general.[11]

There would soon be ample opportunity, however, to put the new border guidelines to the test. Soviet-MPR sources agree that Japanese detachments conducted systematic provocations along the Outer Mongolian frontier. As early as mid-March 1939 the new Soviet Far East commander, Gen. G. M. Shtern, stated publicly that the Japanese were preparing an attack against the MPR.[12] The 23rd Division intelligence officer may have the best explanation for the alleged provocations. After the division was concentrated at Hailar, says Major Suzuki, it was necessary, from the intelligence point of view, to study the northern and southern sectors of frontier defense responsibility. Two or three IJA reconnaissance parties were sent out for periods of two or three weeks, each team numbering ten or twenty men under an officer. Since the Kwantung Army had ordered field units not to provoke the other side, Suzuki told the intelligence parties not to proceed as far as the

Halha River, which "everybody" at division headquarters and in Hsinking "knew" was the boundary with the Mongolian People's Republic. Apparently one Japanese team did go to the Halha, however, since it was not acquainted with the region. The team almost "sank into the river" but made its way back safely.[13]

By all Japanese accounts, it was the Mongolians who became aggressive again in early May when the waters of the Halha had receded. The frequency and strength of opposing patrols increased, the Manchukuoans sending out 15 or more horsemen at a time now. As for the Mongolians, the Japanese heard of a young and ambitious MPRA second lieutenant, newly commissioned from the military academy, who was famous for conducting particularly aggressive actions.[14]

The first reportable large episode on the border, in the new series of affrays, occurred on 4 May when a party of more than 50 Mongolian horsemen rode as far as Balshagal Heights, southwest of the Nomonhan cairn and north of the Holsten, and began to set up positions. Manchukuoan troops and 16 policemen engaged the enemy in a firefight lasting ten hours. After incurring some 15 casualties, the Mongols were driven back across the Halha; the Japanese admitted losing one noncom killed.[15] Thereafter, Mongolian trespasses were said to be constant. The Mongols built positions at both Balshagal and Noro heights, south of the Holsten and less than 10 km. east of the Halha. Yurts (tents) could be seen, as well as trucks and armored vehicles. Large units from the Tamsag area were reported to be operating in the frontier district, and Soviet-built planes were also active. If we are to believe the Japanese sources, the tempo of confrontation was building inexorably by land and air along the indistinct border.

As is usually the case when frontier incidents erupt, accounts by the opposing sides are radically dissimilar. The experience of Nomonhan is no exception. According to Japanese materials, before dawn on 11 May the Manchukuoan guards encountered about 30 Mongolian horsemen who had crossed the Halha and penetrated near Balshagal Heights; meanwhile, another 60 Mongols armed with heavy machine guns were observed occupying positions on the northern edge of Noro Heights. A seven-hour battle ensued, after which the Mongolians retreated to or across the Halha, leaving behind five corpses, two horses, and much military matériel. Next day, 12 May, the affair was said to have become more serious. Presumably reinforced from Tamsag or a neighboring outpost, the Mongolians again invaded near Balshagal, committing 100 to 200 horsemen equipped with heavy and light machine guns. The intruders were driven back, and the Manchukuoan government wired a stern protest to the Outer Mongolian authorities.[16]

The sequences are inverted by the MPRA second lieutenant[17] who commanded the 200-man 7th Border Guard post. On the night of 10/11 May, he recalls, he sent a patrol numbering 20 men under the outpost's political commissar to an area six km. southwest of the Nomonhan cairn (known as Nomangan Burd Obo by the Mongolians). Around 8 A.M. on 11 May, a Japanese cavalry detachment of about 300 Barguts (as the Soviet-MPR side called Mongols living in Manchukuo), armed with machine guns, submachine guns, rifles, and grenades, and accompanied by four trucks, crossed the MPR-claimed border in the vicinity of Nomonhan and attacked the Outer Mongolian guard post. While engaging reconnaissance elements of the Manchukuoan unit, two MPRA soldiers were killed and one was wounded. Under pressure of superior enemy forces, the Outer Mongolian border guards were forced to retreat, whereupon the Bargut unit advanced 20 km. inside the Mongolian-claimed boundary. A reserve frontier guard force, which arrived at this time, stopped the invaders 18 km. south of Nomonhan. Toward evening on 12 May, the Outer Mongols were able to push the trespassers back onto their own soil.[18] The Russian account parallels the Mongolian version.[19]

The major points of difference between the Japanese and MPR-Soviet accounts of the initial troubles around Nomonhan in May 1939 center on the following five questions: (1) Whose border was "violated"? (2) Who attacked whom? (3) How many troops were involved in the first clashes? (4) Exactly when did the fighting commence? (5) How unexpected was the clash near Nomonhan?

1. *Whose border was "violated"?* If the boundary lay on the Halha or Khalkhin Gol, as the Japanese side claimed, it was the Mongolians who were trespassers. If the line extended 20 to 25 km. east of the river, according to the MPR contention, then it was the Manchukuoan-Japanese forces that intruded. Soviet–Outer Mongolian sources insist that the 7th Mongolian Border Guards' defensive responsibility extended in depth east of the Halha toward the cairn site of Nomangan Burd Obo. Although the main force of the Outer Mongol outpost was deployed west of the river, it was asserted that patrols were sent daily to the east, where posts were set up. Referring at least to the period from January 1939, Major Bykov states that "the eastern bank of the river was very carefully guarded by Mongolian border guards." The Japanese side, however, contends that Manchukuoan units operated on the eastern (right) shore of the Halha. Maj. Gen. Yokoi Tadamichi, chief of the OSS branch at Hailar, adds that during an inspection of the border region to a point several kilometers east of the Halha in early May 1939, his team encountered no Outer Mongolian frontier guards on the eastern (right) shore: "No one molested us or attempted to prevent us from traveling in the area." Lt. Gen. Ogisu Ryūhei (Tatsuhei or Rippei), who commanded the Sixth Army when it was formed in August 1939, agreed

that the Outer Mongolian side customarily deployed its pickets on the west or left bank. Nevertheless, the 23rd Division intelligence officer admits the probability of varying interpretations of the frontier. All Soviet army prisoners taken during the Nomonhan Incident, for example, told Major Suzuki that Russian officers and men had been instructed not to advance beyond a certain line drawn east of the Halha.[20]

2. *Who attacked whom?* The Japanese claimed that Manchukuoan elements were fired upon by MPRA soldiers first, whereas the other side asserted that its horses were merely grazing on the eastern shores of the Halha when attacked by the Japanese and Manchurians, who penetrated as far as the river.

3. *How many troops were involved in the first clashes?* Intelligence reaching Kwantung Army headquarters indicated that at least 700 Outer Mongolian horsemen had come across the Halha on 12 May and engaged smaller Manchukuoan forces. This figure exceeds all other estimates. By 17 May, Komatsubara already termed "erroneous" (*kyohō*) the report of 700 Outer Mongolian trespassers; he added that even Japanese air scouting estimates of 100 to 150 Mongols were excessive. Local evidence, wrote the general, suggested a figure closer to 30-50 horsemen.[21] Critics claim that the military authorities in Hsinking exaggerated the size of the MPRA forces in order to justify powerful counteraction.

4. *Exactly when did the fighting commence?* Here, too, discrepancies exist. Kwantung Army records state that the first telegram was received from General Komatsubara on the afternoon of 13 May concerning the major MPRA irruption from the morning of the 12th. Since the Kwantung Army deployed no installation of its own in the Nomonhan region, it was necessary to rely on the notoriously inefficient communications of the Manchukuoan army to connect Hailar with the site of the incident, some 160 km. away. Operations officer Hattori contends that it took approximately a day and a half for the information to reach Kwantung Army headquarters from the time the clash broke out. Critics again suggest that, since the generally accepted starting point for the affair is 11 May, Japanese higher headquarters must have tampered with the dates for reasons bearing upon the 23rd Division's or the Kwantung Army's justification for a counteroffensive. Still, one wonders why nefarious motives must be ascribed only to the Japanese side, in view of Soviet Major Bykov's testimony that even the headquarters of the MPRA 6th Cavalry Division did not learn from the Mongolians' 7th Border Guard outpost until the night of 14/15 May that there had been a clash on 11 May. Is it not probable that communications were equally poor in the Nomonhan area for the MPR-Soviet and Japanese-Manchukuoan forces?

5. *How unexpected was the clash near Nomonhan?* According to the offi-

cial Japanese version, expressed by Hattori and echoed by his associate Tsuji, when Komatsubara's telegram arrived at Kwantung Army headquarters the staff's reaction was, "Has it happened again? We felt unpleasant." Since Nomonhan was a remote and unimportant location, not one of the Kwantung Army headquarters officers knew where it was. After reporting to the commander, General Ueda, the officers returned to headquarters. "Although we requested the intelligence section of the staff to bring a map of the Hailar district, and ordered investigations by the chief of topography," says Hattori, "it was not easy to locate the place. At last, after several hours, we found a place called 'Nomonhan Buru' [Burd]. Deciding that this must be the place, we began to study countermeasures." None can deny that the defensive element stationed at Nomonhan itself was trifling in number: an observation post of seven Inner Mongolian guards from a Manchukuoan border unit. But those who believe that the Kwantung Army was directly or indirectly behind the frontier troubles scoff at the Hattori-Tsuji story, especially the reference to hours of map scrutiny with magnifying glasses.[22]

Komatsubara's initial report indicated only that Mongolian forces had violated the Manchukuo-claimed frontier south of Nomonhan, but offered no speculation regarding MPR motives. The Kwantung Army staff could not judge whether the Mongolian troops had crossed the Halha to conduct combat reconnaissance at the bidding of the Russians or merely to water their horses, toying with Manchukuoan guard units in the process. Possibly the Outer Mongolians had been emboldened by the feeble response they had elicited earlier from the Manchurian defenders of the Halhamiao district. Still, it was not originally believed in Hsinking that the border incident would expand. Nomonhan itself was unimportant in the larger strategic context. Movement of major ground forces seemed almost impossible in the area, by either side, because of highly adverse logistical factors. Certainly the 23rd Division could cope with marauding Mongolian horsemen. As Hattori put it, nobody at Kwantung Army headquarters believed that such an "insignificant little mound of sand would become the site of raging battles that made world headlines."[23]

Foreign diplomats and news gatherers knew very little about the origins of the border trouble. In Hsinking on 31 May, a Manchukuo foreign ministry official told an American diplomat that Outer Mongolian forces had come to the aid of herdsmen who had been evicted by Manchukuoan frontier guards. At the same time, the American correspondent Hugh Byas heard from Japanese authorities in Tokyo that the MPR government must have expected that the weapons acquired from the Soviet Union could open the "Nomonhan pastures" to Mongolian flocks and herds. Months later, the American military attaché's office in Tokyo concluded that the "proximate" cause for the fighting was the movement of Outer Mongolian nomads heading for their "traditional spring trading" near the shrine at Chiangchunmiao, and their interception by Manchukuoan troops on the east side of the Halha. The "Soviet" escorts were supposedly forced back across the river by the end of May.[24]

For his part, General Komatsubara was reacting strongly to the border flare-up. As the area defense commander defined by the April guidelines, he intended to destroy the intruders in the Nomonhan sector on his own initiative by committing the main body of his reconnaissance regiment under Lt. Col. Azuma Yaozō, two infantry companies under a battalion commander, and all available Manchukuoan army troops.[25] For the offensive operation, Komatsubara would use every military vehicle in Hailar, as well as commandeered transportation. At least 100 more trucks were needed now from Kwantung Army resources, since further reinforcements would have to be moved; the dispatch of additional motor vehicles should also be contemplated. The less than ten light tanks stationed in Hailar by the Kwantung Army for field testing should also be assigned to the division.

Komatsubara also asked higher headquarters to send him reconnaissance planes immediately and to attach the air force fighters at Hailar to him temporarily. This request stemmed from a problem he had encountered when he asked the 24th Air Group commander at Hailar, Lt. Col. Matsumura Kōjirō, to cooperate directly with the Azuma force by providing reconnaissance and liaison support. Murata and Suzuki remember that such assistance was rejected. Matsumura says that he had good reasons: apart from displeasure with chain-of-command relationships (since his unit was directly subordinate to 2nd Air Division headquarters in Hsinking), he felt that his men were trained to fight other aircraft, not to scout or to coordinate with ground troops. Changing his planes' customary mission might enlarge the incident, for interceptors are always instructed to shoot down any air trespassers, and the Russian fighters could be expected to do the same. Matsumura therefore declined to accept Komatsubara's request, arguing that he lacked reconnaissance capability, that such usage would be dangerous, and that an affray involving Mongolian horsemen did not strike him as particularly critical. The Kwantung Army air staff officer, Lt. Col. Miyoshi Yasuyuki, provides further insight into air force thinking:

> The Japanese army ground forces were ignoramuses in those days; they knew nothing about air force matters. At the outset, the 23rd Division commander was unacquainted with fighters' capabilities—for example, that they could remain airborne for only an hour and 20 minutes. Yet he wanted reconnaissance flights as far as Tamsag, which would have taken the fighters two hours. The general also requested aerial photography, which fighters could not handle. When Murata asked me for scouts, I had to instruct him about the illogicality of his demands.

Aerial reconnaissance as far as the Halha was feasible, entailing only visual observation. In all of Manchuria we had only one squadron of fast reconnaissance aircraft, and we were saving those precious planes to keep the eastern and northern fronts under surveillance; the western sector was out of the question.

Komatsubara was clearly dissatisfied. Shortly afterward, Matsumura received a telegram from his own headquarters, directing him to cooperate with the 23rd Division immediately; reconnaissance was not mentioned. Matsumura thinks that Komatsubara prevailed upon the Kwantung Army to reassign him, and so does the Air Division commander Lt. Gen. Giga Tetsuji.[26]

By 14 May, in fact, after conferring with General Ueda, the Kwantung Army staff was honoring all of Komatsubara's requests. The 2nd Air Division immediately placed under his control one light bomber squadron (nine planes) of the 10th Air Group, the two fighter squadrons (19 planes) of the 24th Air Group, and most of two airfield battalions. Also assigned to Komatsubara by the Kwantung Army were two truck companies under a major from the 1st Transport Regiment. The division commander was advised that although Ueda agreed with the decision to chastise the Mongolian intruders, settlement of the affair demanded that friendly forces should not be permitted to cross the frontier and that he should be extremely careful not to expand matters.[27] Although not much is known about the intelligence available to Komatsubara when he decided to send out Azuma, he seems to have believed that rather large hostile forces had entered the zone of Nomonhan. Apparently he was acquainted only with the actions of enemy elements that had clashed with the Manchurians. The general probably did not expect matters to escalate, but since the terrain of the incident was a boundless plain situated at a considerable distance from the divisional base at Hailar, he felt the need for immediate support by aircraft and trucks from the Kwantung Army. It is significant, however, that whereas Komatsubara had mainly asked for scout planes, he was assigned fighters and light bombers.[28]

As soon as it was learned that Komatsubara was dispatching the Azuma task force, the Kwantung Army attached one of its own logistics captains, Hara Seiroku (Zenshirō), to the 23rd Division. As Hara understood his instructions, he was to "look things over." It was true that some portion of Kwantung Army headquarters did already entertain the idea of smashing the Outer Mongolians and "teaching them a lesson," but Hara, from his logistics knowledge, comprehended the larger picture of opposing strengths and was no hawk.[29]

Always eager to be at the scene of action, another Kwantung Army officer, Major Tsuji, hand-carried Ueda's orders on 14 May to the 23rd Division at Hailar town, which was bustling with commandeered trucks. The Azuma detachment had already set off for Nomonhan the night before.

Tsuji arranged to be flown to the Halha sector in a scout plane, which circled low several times, enabling him to discern about 20 military horses grazing on open ground near the confluence of the Halha and Holsten rivers. Copses of small willows, capable of hiding 300 to 500 men, dotted the dunes, but not one enemy soldier could be spotted. After the reconnaissance plane returned to Hailar, a bullet hole was found in the fuel tank. Mongolian troops must indeed be operating on the eastern side of the Halha, Tsuji reported to Komatsubara and the division staff, and later to Ueda and his colleagues. He was convinced, Tsuji stressed, that the affair would be settled soon.[30]

In view of the Kwantung Army's unusual moderation in handling the first stage of the Nomonhan Incident, one wonders why Komatsubara, a studious and cautious type of general officer, was behaving so forcefully about Mongolian horsemen. The main explanation is to be found in the fact that, on the day the radio message concerning trouble was received from the Manchukuoan observation post in the Nomonhan area, the division commander was briefing his regimental commanders. Ironically, Komatsubara had convened them in Hailar to explain the operational details of the Kwantung Army's border regulations of April, which the general himself had learned of directly from Ueda in Hsinking only recently. The intelligence from the frontier ended the academic aspects of the Hailar meeting; it was time to apply the package of guidelines in practice, unexpectedly soon. As would be the case at Hsinking and Tokyo, the 23rd Division staff had difficulty locating Nomonhan; only Kanchuerhmiao, with a population of 3,000, appeared on most IJA maps of the general region. None of the division staff officers doubted, however, that the strict new border guidelines required prompt and effective action to smash the Mongolians. As the operations officer says, "A border division such as the 23rd had to pay utmost attention to the army guidelines, its 'bible.'" The document, in fact, seemed tailor-made for the problem of Nomonhan.[31]

Less known is the fact that, at the moment the Azuma task force was preparing to leave for the frontier on 13 May, the chief of the AGS Operations Section, Col. Inada Masazumi, arrived in Hailar after a routine ten-day inspection tour of Manchukuo. Inada remembers that the atmosphere in the garrison town was cheerful and animated, and that he sensed "something was up." At the division chief of staff's office, Inada was told by Colonel Ōuchi that a regiment was being rushed to Nomonhan to punish the Mongol tribesmen and cool them off. Inada's first question was, "Where's Nomonhan?" Although the decision to thrash the Mongolians had already been taken, undoubtedly the presence of a General Staff colonel from Tokyo affected the thinking of the division officers and subtly encouraged them to prove themselves to higher headquarters. Inada's brief encounter with

Azuma is illustrative. The lieutenant colonel, who greeted Inada in battle dress, struck him as a splendid officer, enthusiastic, full of pep, honest, and certainly no show-off. Indeed, Azuma appeared to be so solid and steady, Inada was convinced nothing rash was about to be undertaken by the division. Even so, Inada admits, Azuma must have deemed himself "lucky" to be seen off for the front and wished success by the Operations Section chief of the entire Japanese army.

Inada, of course, could not voice everything that was on his mind to a new division about to test itself under fire, and most particularly not to the fine commander of the sally force. After Azuma had departed, however, Inada remembers suggesting to Ōuchi that "things like this"—the offensive operation against the Mongolian raiders—ought not to be undertaken in such a region and at such a time. "I could not say, 'Don't send the regiment,'" Inada comments, "but I meant, 'Use your brain and not your heart' in attending to such a trifling episode." During further discussions with Ōuchi and Komatsubara, Inada stressed that while efforts were being made to settle the war in China no serious trouble must be caused in the north. It was senseless for a second-line division that was not "operational" to become involved in large-scale combat in a meaningless locale. At this very time, the High Command was quietly studying the possibility of shifting operational emphasis, in the event of hostilities against the Soviet Union, from the eastern and northern fronts of Manchukuo to the long-neglected west. To achieve wartime success, however, required a level of mechanization, equipment, and transport far beyond the Kwantung Army's present capabilities. Hence officers Terada, Hattori, and Shimanuki had been transferred from Tokyo to Hsinking, and the 23rd Division had been posted to the quiet Hailar sector; these moves would permit study of westward operations in wartime and the collection of data for a possible Kwantung Army campaign against the Trans-Baikal. Ōuchi seemed very pleased; to a Soviet expert, Inada's emphasis was welcome. Since Komatsubara, too, voiced no objection to the presentation by Inada, the latter left for Hsinking reassured for the time being.

At Kwantung Army headquarters, Inada conveyed his essentially favorable impressions of the situation at Hailar, including the reasonableness of Komatsubara and Ōuchi and the dependability of Azuma. Though it was imperative, Inada admitted, that those responsible for defense of the frontiers should uphold their dignity in the eyes of the natives, it was not too disturbing if the boundaries were moved a bit in such a vast, undeveloped plain as Hulun Buir. Terada agreed that IJA priority should be devoted to the solution of the war in China, and he promised Inada that the Kwantung Army would do nothing to interfere. When Inada visited Ueda, the army commander confirmed the AGS concept of training emphasis on eventual operations on the western front and of the consequent need to restrain the affair at Nomonhan. Despite Ueda's strong assurances, Inada came away with a gnawing suspicion that the commander did not fully comprehend the seriousness of the international situation, of Japan's peculiar problems involving national strength, and of the full rationale underlying the General Staff's cautious policy. Nonetheless, Inada returned to Tokyo and made his recommendation to leave matters to the Kwantung Army.[32] A summary of Komatsubara's actions and of the Kwantung Army's follow-up decisions regarding reinforcements had already been telegraphed to the AGS by Chief of Staff Isogai in Hsinking, and the AGS deputy chief had replied promptly: "We are counting on appropriate handling by the [Kwantung] army."[33] So far, relations between the two headquarters were of the best—a situation that was not to endure long, unfortunately for all concerned on the Japanese side.

To those who saw Azuma off from Hailar, the mission seemed too easy for such an able cavalry commander and such a strong task force: the shooing-away of a few hundred horsemen from the east bank of the Halha. Indeed, when Azuma reached Nomonhan on 15 May, he learned from the Manchukuoan guard post that most of the Mongolians had pulled back across the river during the preceding night. Although some elements remained on the east shore, they too seemed to be in the process of withdrawing before noon on the 15th. Thereupon Azuma ordered vigorous pursuit operations toward the river. Apparently little or no contact was made with the enemy. Japanese light bombers, however, caught sight of Mongolian troops and attacked a concentration, killing 30 or 40 soldiers.

Judging that Azuma had achieved his objective of clearing the eastern shore, 23rd Division headquarters ordered him to return to Hailar. A Manchukuoan cavalry regiment of 300 men was left behind to cover the Nomonhan sector. Most of the Azuma detachment got back to headquarters on the night of 16 May; the commander and the armor arrived the next day. It was thought, incorrectly, that the affair was over and that the stipulations of the border guidelines had been met.[34] Komatsubara's own reflections on the incident to date, recorded at the time in his private diary, centered on such matters as the advantage of surprise lost through enemy detection of Japanese trucks and scout planes, the need for across-the-border reconnaissance at high altitude, the difficulty of establishing ground-to-plane communications, and the initiative and dependability of the Manchukuoan troops but the problem of distinguishing them from Outer Mongolian soldiers.[35]

The Mongolian version of the events of 14-16 May differs from Soviet army descriptions only in detail; both suggest a continuity in the clashes starting on 11 May and tend to blend Manchukuoan-Mongolian (Bargut) and Japanese participation. According to a composite of accounts, up to two squadrons of Japanese Bargut cavalry, somewhere between 300 and 600 horsemen with ten trucks, had advanced from the Nomonhan sector between 5 and 6 A.M. on 14 May and had proceeded along the right shore of the Holsten River. Japanese planes constantly violated MPR airspace. Learning of these developments, Soviet Battalion Commander Bykov and the commander of the 6th Mongolian Cavalry Division set out from Tamsag to inspect the situation. Meanwhile the Mongolian lieutenant commanding the 7th Border Guard outpost on the west side of the Halha took 40 men, apparently crossed to the east bank to a point 15 km. southwest of Nomonhan, and engaged forward elements of the Japanese Bargut unit. By dint of "stubborn mobile defense" the Mongols slowed the enemy forces, who were eventually checked by 200 Mongolian border guards and reserves of 100 men.

Next day, 15 May, three Japanese planes were seen reconnoitering the Mongolians' 7th Border Guard post west of Lake Samburin/Tsagan Nur, on the left (western) side of the Halha. Then, at about 10 A.M. by the Mongolian version or at 12:45 P.M. according to the Russians, five single-engine Japanese light bombers dropped between 52 and 65 bombs from an altitude of 800 meters during two runs, and strafed at low level during another two passes. Mongolian casualties were three killed and 25 wounded (or, according to a Russian source, two killed and 19 wounded). The Bykov party learned this news from two Mongol horsemen, 30 or 40 km. from the outpost, to which they proceeded at once. After verifying the damage and the casualties, Bykov and his colleagues drove back to Tamsag the same day, phoned corps headquarters at Ulan Bator, and reported their observations.

Later on 15 May, at 5 P.M., the MPRA lieutenant has testified, Mongolian patrols reported the appearance on the right side of the Halha of two Japanese Bargut cavalry regiments accompanied by one tank and seven armored cars. Behind came 90 trucks carrying Japanese infantrymen. (Soviet military sources say Mongolian border guards observed 700 enemy horsemen and three trucks bearing Japanese foot soldiers.) The Japanese reinforcements joined the Bargut unit that had been occupying defensive positions since the morning of the 14th. "Under the pressure of superior enemy forces," the Mongol border guard reserves were forced to retreat to the left bank of the Halha.[36]

The discrepancies in time make it difficult to correlate the Mongolian-Soviet and Japanese accounts. From the Mongol version it would seem that on 15 May the Japanese light bombers hit the outpost on the west side of the Halha at least seven hours before the Azuma detachment pushed the Mongolian border forces back across the river. The Soviet description intimates that the Mongol ground elements may have retreated from the east bank on the morning of the 15th prior to the Japanese bomber strike, which occurred after noon. The latter version resembles the timing given by Japanese sources for Azuma's decision to pursue the last of the Mongolians to the river. Japanese estimates of enemy casualties (30-40) resemble the MPRA-Soviet figures (21-28). From Japanese materials it is not possible to pinpoint the site of the bomber raid, but Mongolian and Soviet accounts agree that the target outpost was located on the west side of the Halha, inside Outer Mongolian territory even by Japanese claims. Some postwar Japanese historians have suspected as much, although there is no documentary corroboration from Japanese sources, and no Japanese air force veterans of the raid can be located.[37] Given Azuma's mission to clear the east bank, one wonders about the Japanese air force's rationale for striking on the west side. During border affrays, even minor tactical actions can complicate matters; the small Japanese air raid on Samburin/Tsagan Nur surely contributed to the escalation of the Nomonhan Incident, especially from the standpoint of the MPRA-Soviet defense authorities.

15

The Trap on the Halha, May 1939

On 17 May 1939, the day that Azuma and his last elements got back to Hailar, enemy troops reappeared on the right (eastern) side of the Halha River, according to a report transmitted to the Kwantung Army by the 23rd Division. Even if it had been intended that the Azuma detachment be withdrawn, a portion of the Japanese force probably should have been left behind for a while, since the Manchukuoan defenses were not strong enough to cope with the renewed incursion. Inasmuch as the Outer Mongolians had been operating repeatedly on the right bank, it should have come as no surprise that any "zone of emptiness" would be occupied by them. The best military explanation for the pullback of the entire Azuma unit is that, with the long Manchurian winter at an end, Komatsubara considered full-scale training of his green division more important than tying up men in duty on a remote and unimportant front.[1]

When hostile soldiers recrossed the Halha, however, Komatsubara deemed it to be a provocation, especially in view of the explicit provisions of the same border guidelines that had fostered his organization of the Azuma detachment. On 21 May the division commander therefore decided to form a much stronger task force to be sent to the Nomonhan region. Led by Col. Yamagata Takemitsu, commander of the 64th Infantry Regiment, the new detachment would include the following main components: Azuma's small reconnaissance unit (officially called a regiment) made up of mounted cavalry and light armor (about 220 men, a tankette, two sedans, and a dozen trucks); the four companies of Maj. Fukumura Yasuhide's full-strength 3rd Infantry Battalion of 800 men from the 64th Regiment; the three mountain guns of the regimental gun battery and four guns of the rapid-fire battery; and three truck companies. The grand total of Japanese fighting men numbered perhaps 1,600. In addition to his IJA forces, Yamagata was to maintain contact with approximately 450 Manchukuoan troops in the area.[2]

Although Komatsubara's overall intention may have been clear—to oust the enemy from the region east of the Halha permanently—it was imperative that his operational concept be made known fully to his subordinates. Overconfidence, however, seems to have permeated the Yamagata detachment, especially since Azuma's smaller unit had had such an easy time. It should have been realized that evicting invaders from the plains by merely sending out a task force was entirely different from the usual type of experience of the Japanese army in combat against Chinese troops since 1937. Yet there is little evidence that the division commander was better acquainted with the larger picture of the forces opposing him than when he had sent out the Azuma expedition. He seems to have been mainly exercised by low-level reports received on 17 May concerning three armored cars, two artillery pieces, and 70 horsemen on the left (western) side of the Halha at Sambur Obo, and an MPRA cavalry troop at Noro Heights south of the Holsten.

But what were the presumable objectives of the foe, and what was the involvement of the Russian corps known to be stationed in Outer Mongolia? On 17 May it had been learned that some 30 Soviet soldiers were operating at Noro Heights; on the 19th, three hangars, 10 armored cars, and 20 trucks were sighted by IJA scout planes flying over Tamsag in eastern Outer Mongolia; and, on the 20th, not only was a Russian noncommissioned officer captured by Manchukuoan horsemen but the existence of a Soviet mechanized battalion was also confirmed in the Tamsag sector—500 men, 70 or 80 trucks, five tanks, and a dozen antitank guns.[3] After the Azuma unit had returned to Hailar, regimental commander Yamagata mentioned to subordinates that Soviet army regulars had definitely come across the border claimed by Manchukuo.[4] But Komatsubara apparently did not regard these Russian elements as the core of a rapid-deployment force that could endanger the success of the newly formed Yamagata detachment.

At this stage, the Kwantung Army staff officers—of all people—were trying to calm down Komatsubara. On 21 May the chief of staff sent Colonel Ōuchi an urgent message asking for reconsideration of the 23rd Division's proposed action. It did not seem wise to move out and launch a sudden attack so soon, without preparation, even though Soviet-MPRA forces had "crossed a step" into Manchukuoan territory. The division ought to wait until the opportunity presented itself and the "arrogant" enemy was "relaxed," at which time it would be advantageous to strike him at once.[5] Ōuchi, however, had already left to attend a Kwantung Army chiefs of staff conference; to his surprise, he learned in Hsinking that the division had decided to send out the Yamagata force immediately. Since Ōuchi agreed with the go-slow policy, he sent a message to Komatsubara reiterating in his own words what had already been suggested by the Kwantung Army. He added that it should be left for Manchukuoan troops to observe the enemy soldiers and try to lure them into friendly territory. Nevertheless, if Yamagata had already set out, he ought to complete his assignment as soon as possible and return to Hailar. Ōuchi apologized to Komatsubara for apparently contradicting the general's decision, but he assured his commander that the recommendations derived from "exhaustive deliberations" at army headquarters.[6]

Despite the cautions from Hsinking, Komatsubara went ahead with the dispatch of the Yamagata detachment. General officers were not given orders as such in the Japanese army; they received recommendations, for reference only, which they were free to accept or not. Hence Komatsubara was not ignoring any order but only reacting, at his own professional discretion, to suggestions transmitted by the Kwantung Army. Komatsubara's ultimate decision was based on his sense of responsibility as area defense commander within the meaning of the border guidelines.[7] After all, suggests Tsuji, "except for what the air force got, the Azuma unit had not been able to catch even a rat; maybe this was what irritated the division commander." Komatsubara gave as his reason the steady reinforcement of enemy strength in the Nomonhan district after the withdrawal of Azuma. The Kwantung Army said no more. "Leadership is not scientific," Tsuji wrote; "on the battlefield . . . sentiment overrules reason. Higher headquarters should not irritate the front-line forces but induce them to obey cheerfully."[8]

By way of demonstrating its philosophy in practice, Kwantung Army headquarters voluntarily began devoting attention to the air force dimension, which lay beyond the 23rd Division's purview but was exerting an important influence on the festering border incident. According to official Japanese releases, hostile aircraft first flew over Handagai as early as 18 May. Soon afterward, while new clashes flared on the ground, aerial fighting between Japanese and Soviet warplanes broke out in the skies above Nomonhan, costing the enemy one escorted LZ scout plane on 20 May, another on the 21st, and three out of four to six I-16 fighters on 22 May, without loss to the Japanese.[9] Outer Mongolian testimony indicates that Japanese planes frequently raided the 7th Border Guard outpost, still on the left side of the Halha, between 15 and 28 May. On the 22nd the Mongol post's political deputy was killed and six men were wounded.[10]

In his cautious message to Komatsubara on the 21st, Ōuchi paid tribute to the Japanese aviators' bravery but, in view of the IJAF bombing activities of early May, alluded in roundabout fashion to the "aggressive state of mind" of the air units at Hailar. From the broader standpoint, Ōuchi recommended that "a certain degree of restraint" be imposed.[11] Nevertheless, learning that Soviet air units had been assigned to Tamsag and that hostile reconnaissance planes were violating Manchurian airspace, the Kwantung Army decided to prepare for the worst. On 23 May it sent the 23rd Division two more fighter squadrons, from the 11th Air Group; 12th Air Wing headquarters; the main body of an airfield battalion; and elements of a radio intelligence unit. By now there were nine light bombers, 48 fighters, and nine scout planes in Hailar.[12]

Although Komatsubara privately resented higher headquarters' "meddling" with his local command authority, on 22 May he did instruct Yamagata not to launch a hurried attack but instead to assemble his detachment at Kanchuerhmiao and wait for a "good opportunity"; that is, to await a deep enemy inroad into Manchukuo before retaliating and destroying the intruders.[13] In reporting on steps taken to date, the Kwantung Army advised the AGS on 23 May that it was desirous of "thwarting the ambitions of the Outer Mongolian forces" but was quick to assure Tokyo that it was "making doubly certain not to expand the incident unnecessarily."[14] A follow-up message of 24 May explained that the IJA task force was being held at Kanchuerhmiao, and only small-scale reconnaissance was being conducted in concert with the Manchukuoan army near the border post at Nomonhan.[15] On the same day, the High Command responded that it continued to depend on the Kwantung Army to pursue appropriate measures and that the Throne would be so advised.[16]

New intelligence from the Nomonhan sector revealed that hostile elements had built military bridges north of the Halha-Holsten confluence (*kawamata* in Japanese), had gradually established a foothold on the right bank of the Halha, and were constructing a semicircle of defenses on the dunes about eight kilometers northeast of the junction, southwest of Nomonhan. Specifically, a Mongolian-Russian force numbering approximately 200 men was reported on the western Balshagal plateau above the Holsten, and another 200 were on Noro Heights to the southeast. Atop the high ground west of the Halha, at least two artillery pieces and two or three armored cars had been sighted.[17]

Hostile overflights of the region on the right side of the Halha became frequent. Between 25 and 27 May the air combat intensified, and the enemy was reported to have lost one of three LZ scout planes on the first of the three days, one of nine I-16 and one of six I-15 fighters on the second day, and nine of 18 I-16's on the third day.[18]

In the afternoon of 26 May, Komatsubara visited Yamagata's headquarters at Kanchuerhmiao, at which time he listened to the scouting reports and inspected the local situation. Deciding that the time was ripe to chastise the foe, the division commander sketched the gist of an operations order finally authorizing Yamagata to launch his offensive. Leaving operations officer Murata and logistics officer Itō to assist Yamagata, Komatsubara returned to Hailar that night.[19]

By 9 A.M. on the 27th, the detachment's operational order was ready, calling for an attack designed to trap and destroy enemy forces on the right bank of the Halha. Since surprise was impossible on the steppes in daylight, the assault forces were to move forward stealthily during the night and jump off at dawn (5 A.M.) on the 28th. Though typical of IJA tactical thinking, the plan for encirclement devised by Yamagata and his colleagues was complex. Azuma's reconnaissance unit was to seize the Halha-Holsten confluence quickly and cut off the retreating foe from the rear while Fukumura's infantry battalion, supported by the regimental and rapid-fire guns, assaulted hostile positions from the direction of Lake Manzute. One infantry platoon from 1st Lt. Someya Hatsuo's 4th Company—32 men under 2nd Lt. Asada Tadayoshi—was to advance on the far right, parallel to the main strike force, seize the Kita-watashi crossing six kilometers north of the river junction, and sever the enemy's line of retreat. Between Asada and the main force, Capt. Gotō Chikashi's 10th Infantry Company—1,000 meters in the lead—was to attack toward a crossing above the confluence and help to cut off the foe's escape route. Another unit was formed under Capt. Tachikawa Tsuneki, the regimental gun battery commander, assigned a platoon from the 4th Infantry Company, and given the mission of proceeding from Nomonhan along the north shore of the Holsten and, in conjunction with Manchukuoan elements, attacking any enemy forces encountered en route to the confluence. Moving in parallel with the Tachikawa unit but across the Holsten, other Manchukuoan troops were to sweep the southern shore. To the far left, 1st Lt. Kawabata Genkichi's 11th Infantry Company was to complete the envelopment of the foe by seizing three crossings in the Higashi-watashi sector and blocking an enemy retreat. (See Map 3.) The air force was to lend assistance.[20]

One important stipulation of Yamagata's order is omitted from most Japanese sources: that after the enemy was smashed on the right bank of the Halha, hostile forces remaining near the left shore were to be mopped up as fast as possible. Once these missions had been achieved, the whole Yamagata detachment should pull back to the right bank promptly and assemble in the vicinity of Nomonhan after cleaning up the battlefield.[21]

Yamagata must have expected an easy operation. Neither he nor Azuma nor Komatsubara had ever met Mongolian or Soviet forces in combat; like most IJA soldiers, they looked down on the Mongols and did not think too much of the purge-ridden Russians. On paper, the Japanese plan looked beautiful: separate advance and joint attack (*bunshin gōgeki*), thereby catching the fleeing enemy in a sack by double envelopment. The regiment commander had only to strike with a battalion of IJA regulars and the foe would flee. The main concern was how to prevent the enemy from escaping; there was no anticipation that he would stand or counterattack. Azuma exuded particular confidence because he had reached the Halha without effort, in the face of motley Mongolian horsemen, less than two weeks earlier. When Maj. Tsuji Masanobu arrived at division headquarters for liaison duty on 28 May, he found Komatsubara waiting for good news from the front. No one seemed at all worried in Hailar.[22]

It is true that Yamagata possessed a slight numerical advantage over the enemy: about 2,000 men (including the Manchukuoan soldiers) versus

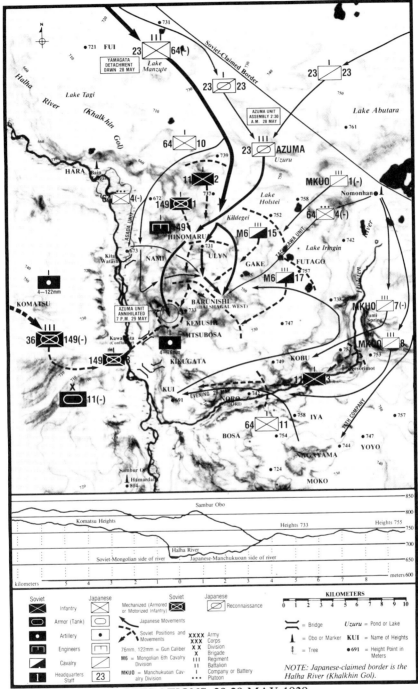

MAP 3: COMBAT OPERATIONS, 28-29 MAY 1939

some 1,450 Soviet-Mongolian troops, of whom 250 were MPRA cavalry. But whereas the Russians and Mongolians were largely concentrated in the area of the confluence and had constructed defenses in depth, Yamagata's detachment had sacrificed local superiority in favor of encirclement operations converging from six directions north and south of the Holsten. Though split-second timing was required to orchestrate a jumpoff at 5 A.M. on 28 May by all the units involved, the movements did not even originate from a central location. As of 27 May, Yamagata's headquarters and the main force of his infantry were stationed at Kanchuerhmiao. Azuma's headquarters and motorized company were based at Amukulang, but his cavalry company was at Chiangchunmiao, as was the 11th Infantry Company under Lieutenant Kawabata. The detachment's intelligence team and the Manchukuoan garrison's headquarters were located near Nomonhan. Even if the units were able to concert their arrival times, there were only five infantry companies, two reconnaissance companies, and the ill-equipped Manchukuoan horsemen to strike along a front of 26 or 27 kilometers between the Kita-watashi and Higashi-watashi crossings. The men had never operated together on such a scale, and not one artillery piece was available to them.[23]

Despite the problems imposed by blacked-out night movement across difficult and unfamiliar terrain, the Japanese columns made fairly good progress in their advance toward the confluence.[24] At about 2:30 A.M. on the 28th, Azuma was able to combine his two companies at a point 11 kilometers west of Nomonhan. Determined to catch the foe this time, he led his odd mixture of horses, trucks, and light armor in a fierce drive through the left side of the enemy defenses without encountering resistance at this stage. By 5:40 A.M. Azuma reached the dunes only 1.7 kilometers east of the enemy's bridge at the river junction. Here he ran into unexpectedly powerful resistance; he was never seen alive again.

Only after the battle could the fate of the commander and his reconnaissance unit be reconstructed.[25] Even as the force was digging in, before 6 A.M., enemy armored vehicles blundered in from the east, unaware of the arrival of the Japanese. Two tanks and a truck were seized. From a captured map and from visual observation and reports by patrols, Azuma soon understood that hostile armor and troops were ensconced in the Heights 733 sector behind him and to his northeast and that a considerable number of artillery, armored vehicles, and horses were on the high ground on the left side of the Halha. With his small unit, Azuma tried to accomplish several tasks: to retain positions generally facing west, to guard his rear and flanks, and to block the retreat route of enemy elements presumably being driven toward the confluence by Yamagata's infantry. While waiting for the main detachment to advance momentarily, Azuma sought to report to Yamagata by radio, but contact could not be made. It was a source of encouragement that friendly troops (elements of the 10th Infantry Company) could be discerned at about 8 A.M. behind a rise at a distance of two or three kilometers north of the reconnaissance unit. Nevertheless, the hostile strength facing Azuma had been built up steadily, and four 12-cm. howitzers began firing at the rate of seven or eight rounds per minute from the somewhat higher western shore. Enemy counterattacks struck Azuma's front all morning without letup, involving as many as 100 to 150 infantry and horsemen plus ten armored vehicles per group. The defenders took a heavy toll on the foe, one success occurring after 7 A.M. when Azuma's men stopped a Soviet tankette, killing the crew, hoisted a Japanese flag on the vehicle, and drove it back to the IJA lines, to the cheers of the troops.

Shortly before 10 A.M., sharp fighting broke out to the rear and the flanks of the Azuma unit as well-armed enemy infantry and cavalry pressed to the southwest before Yamagata's obvious pressure. Although Azuma beat off every attack, he was obliged to split his meager strength and seek cover behind the slope. In effect, the Japanese were surrounded by noon, under continuous bombardment by artillery from across the Halha and by mortars and a half-dozen antitank guns that sprayed fire blindly but effectively from the east shore against the remaining IJA heavy weapons. The Japanese horsemen had to fight dismounted, crawling and clawing out holes in the sand. Two junior officers and a dozen men were killed during the midday combat. There was a brief scare when enemy smoke shells masked IJA infantry positions to the right of the Azuma unit, evoking the fear of poison gas.

While the enemy kept feeding in reinforcements from the left side of the Halha, Azuma and his men were still hoping that Yamagata's detachment would relieve them soon. Even truck drivers, horse attendants, and the wounded had to fight as infantry or struggle to maintain the dwindling number of machine guns. Around noon, after six hours of hard fighting, Azuma assessed the situation with several of his officers. It was apparent that the friendly infantry who had earlier been observed to the right, numbering somewhat more than one company, had pulled behind the crestline, leaving less than one platoon on a rise 800 meters from the Azuma unit. Another two squads of Japanese infantry who had appeared on the northwestern edge of the Balshagal plateau were raked by enemy artillery fire. To the rear of the Azuma force, a platoon-size IJA infantry element had not advanced beyond the crestline. Some enemy shelling had been heard at a distance of two or three kilometers to the south but no further progress by friendly infantry could be observed, and the regimental and rapid-fire guns did not seem to have fired a round against hostile positions near the confluence. One of Azuma's officers wondered whether the Yamagata detachment had crossed the Holsten to the south side, in which case the reconnaissance unit ought to consider moving there too. Azuma, however, remained convinced that the center of gravity of the battle had not shifted southward and that he was still confronting the main force on his front. Therefore, for the moment, he decided to fight where he stood, in the hope that Yamagata would still break through.

Short of water, lacking time to eat or to tend to their horses since the preceding night, pounded by artillery, low on ammunition, and plagued by sandstorms that clogged their weapons, Azuma's men continued to repulse attacks and to make tactical adjustments in their thin lines. Since messengers had not returned and radio contact had still not been established with Yamagata's headquarters by 1 p.m., Azuma grew more apprehensive about the future of his own unit and the possible crisis confronting the detachment betokened by the inordinate delay, the silence, and the lack of forward movement by the infantry. Capt. Kanetake Mitsushige, Azuma's aide, was ordered to take a horse and try to get through to Yamagata and convey the following information. The reconnaissance unit was still clinging to its positions. If friendly forces were in difficulty, Azuma had the ability to repulse the foe on his front and destroy the bridge at the confluence if only one infantry company, or even a platoon, could be sent quickly to his left wing. The reconnaissance unit planned to launch an attack that night. If the detachment had crossed the Holsten and was having a tough time there, Yamagata should kindly advise Azuma of his intention.

Fired on by snipers and artillery all the way, Captain Kanetake managed to reach the crestline to the north, from which he detected Japanese infantry (1st Lt. Nishimura Shinzō's 9th Company) "resting" on western Balshagal with a couple of rapid-fire guns, the 64th Regiment's colors, and 3rd Battalion headquarters. The location was not more than two kilometers from the reconnaissance unit, and Kanetake felt that the infantry had only to ascend the crestline to observe both the enemy and the three red-ball flags of the beleaguered Azuma force below. Conferring with an officer whom he took to be the battalion commander, Kanetake was told that the whereabouts of Yamagata was unknown ever since the actions began at dawn, though the infantry had been looking for the colonel for hours. Kanetake graphically described the plight of the reconnaissance unit and implored the infantry to advance and help to clear the confluence sector, even with a platoon, but he could not get his auditors to budge, ostensibly because Yamagata's direct order was necessary. Frustrated and depressed, Kanetake ordered a noncom to carry a message to detachment headquarters; then he himself set out again to find Yamagata, wandering four or five kilometers in the process. The infantry's records suggest that both Kanetake and a runner who followed him were mistaken in thinking they were talking to the 3rd Battalion commander, that they actually met the "powerless" battalion aide, and that Major Fukumura was on his way to Yamagata's headquarters at the time.[26]

The only infantry reinforcements Azuma received on 28 May were of trifling size and not directly sent to him by Yamagata. After a morning of very severe fighting, 1st Lt. Kajima Yutaka, a platoon leader assigned to spearhead the 9th Company, had become separated from his parent unit and, quite by accident, joined the Azuma force in the early afternoon with four of his surviving soldiers. Another platoon leader, Second Lieutenant Asada from the 4th Company, who had been ordered to secure the Kita-watashi crossing, encountered no enemy troops there and rejoined the 3rd Battalion at Heights 733. As soon as he learned of Azuma's crisis, Asada took his 31 men and, on his own initiative, set forth to help Azuma. Proceeding downhill under murderous fire, Asada lost about one-third of his platoon en route, but at 7 P.M. broke through the encirclement and reached the reconnaissance unit. There were tears in Azuma's eyes as he thanked Asada and his survivors for having voluntarily braved such danger in broad daylight.[27]

Small-scale efforts to convey ammunition to Azuma ended in disaster, late on 28 May, as we shall see. After the sun set (around 9:30 P.M. in these latitudes) the battlefield fell still. While Azuma's men were preparing to launch a night attack on their own toward the confluence, the Russians preempted them. Armored vehicles could be heard rumbling up from the south-southeast, and at 10:10 P.M. three Soviet searchlights lit up the Japanese trenches while 45-mm. rapid-fire guns and mortars laid down a barrage paving the way for 500 or 600 infantry and the tanks that were approaching. Leaving only sentries on his right, Azuma collected all available soldiers in a dip near the vehicle assembly area on the endangered left flank. At 10:30 P.M., when the Russians were 50 meters away, the Japanese—led by their company and platoon commanders—stormed out "like fierce lions and tigers" (in the words of the after-action report) and drove off the grenade-throwing enemy, who left behind four armored vehicles and several trucks. It was heartening to see the foe "scream and run," but the price to the Japanese was high; among the dead were both of Azuma's company commanders—Capt. Aoyama Takashi of the 1st Company and Capt. Kōno Iwao of the 2nd. By now, the reconnaissance unit's casualties amounted to 19 killed and 72 wounded. Thirty Manchukuoan horsemen were also reported missing.

Reoccupying their positions, the IJA soldiers dug in for the next combat. At 2 A.M. on the 29th, sensing imminent destruction, Okamoto Kōichi, the major attached to the reconnaissance unit, recommended to Azuma that the force withdraw toward the main detachment on higher ground to the rear. Okamoto's reasoning was that the location of Yamagata was unknown, communication was impossible, and retention of the exposed defenses would become "difficult" after daylight on the 29th. Azuma replied that his mission was to secure the area of the river junction and that he would not fall back without orders. He then made a stirring speech, exhorting his troops not to yield an inch and beseeching them to hold out till the last man fell. They would all meet again at Yasukuni (the great Shintō shrine in Tokyo dedicated to the spirits of the nation's dead warriors).[28]

But since Azuma was still in the dark, literally and figuratively, about the situation of the infantry detachment, at 2:30 A.M. he sent Major Okamoto and a noncom to find Yamagata's command post, describe the latest developments, and reiterate the advisability of promptly moving up even a portion of the main force. Soon afterward, near 3 A.M., scouts brought word of a new Soviet advance by 300 or 400 soldiers. Once more, the Japanese troops counterattacked at close range and repulsed the Russians by daybreak, after a fierce melee that cost both sides dear, including the severe wounding of IJA infantry platoon leader Asada. As one Japanese survivor put it, many casualties were incurred because, contrary to their expectations from training, the men were not prepared for the short nights and "instant" daybreaks that characterized the locality of Nomonhan.[29]

With the coming of first light on 29 May, near 4 A.M., the Soviet artillery—12-cm. howitzers, field pieces, mortars, and antitank guns—which had been quiescent through the night, unleashed even more intensive fire than on the 28th, striking Azuma's isolated front, left, and rear. Scooped from the sandy soil, portions of the Japanese trenches caved in, threatening the defenders with burial alive. In the face of the pounding by incendiary, high-explosive, and smoke shells, the men in the dip at Azuma's command post tried to disperse and protect their last trucks and 140 horses, but cover was nearly impossible, the highest dune on Azuma's left jutting a mere two or three meters above the surface of the plain. At 6 A.M. the gasoline tank of Azuma's sedan was pierced by gunfire, and the resulting fire spread to all the trucks, including those containing the wounded, and blew up the dwindling stock of ammunition. The pyrotechnics, to one Japanese witness, were a hundred times more numerous than the great fireworks display that lights up the Sumida River each year at Ryōgoku in Tokyo. A dense pall of smoke blanketed the area, impeding visibility and conveying a sense of gloom. Reduced to about one-third of its original strength, Azuma's unit was too spread out and dislocated to conduct even the usual morning roll call of squads.[30]

Closing in for the kill, some 650 Soviet infantry—covered by mortars and

45-mm. guns and supported by several tanks—took up enveloping positions 500 meters from the IJA left-flank sector. Thirty more Japanese were killed and 20 wounded by noon, leaving Azuma with fewer than 100 able-bodied men and only two heavy machine guns in action. Second lieutenants were in command of what was left of the two reconnaissance companies. At 2:30 P.M. Azuma tried to extricate the more grievously wounded by sending them to the rear astride horses. Then he issued a formal order calling for the unit to proceed with its current mission, "covering the actions of the main detachment," and to strengthen its defenses, enabling the force "to hold out at the present positions in general." Specifically, Azuma instructed Lieutenant Asada to rejoin Yamagata when the situation allowed—an obvious effort to save an officer and a platoon who had had the rare courage to offer their lives to the doomed reconnaissance unit.[31]

By 3 P.M. the Soviet troops had come within 50 meters of the Japanese on both flanks and in the front, and three tanks had penetrated the rear. Four IJA soldiers, endeavoring to check the armor with hand-held explosive charges and jerricans filled with gasoline, died in a vain human-bullet charge. Azuma's precious little tankette was hit by artillery and set ablaze. Bereft of grenades of their own, Japanese soldiers grabbed the handles of Soviet grenades that hurtled in and threw them back at the attackers. Apparently the Russian tanks pulled out only because the collapse of the IJA trenches endangered their advance.[32]

Only about 25 Japanese soldiers were still on their feet. At the command post itself were Azuma, a wounded medical lieutenant (Ikeda Hisamitsu), a quartermaster lieutenant (Ōsaki Tetsuji), and a clerk (Sgt. Onizuka Hatsu-yoshi). Azuma decided that the time had come to transmit his last report to Yamagata by sending out Onizuka as a runner, bringing the colonel up to date and advising him that the reconnaissance unit had been intending to attack, once the main detachment advanced, but that there were now too few men to accomplish anything alone, and the unit was "helpless." Onizuka expected to leave after dusk, but Azuma said that he could not hold out that long; so the sergeant set forth, without escort, at 3:30 P.M.[33]

Between 4 and 6 P.M., the Russian vise closed to 20 meters from the Japanese at some points, crushing the left wing in particular. From that flank, spunky 2nd Lt. Iijima Teruo reported to Azuma that he and three men were still alive and would go down fighting. Iijima kept his word. He leaped aboard a Soviet tank, was cut down by enemy fire, and killed himself rather than risk being taken prisoner.[34] Sometime before 7 P.M., after apparently burning his vehicles and his dead, Azuma called on the last 19 survivors to charge ahead with him and, shouting loudly, jumped out of the trench. Gunfire hit him in the chest and elsewhere, and he died soon afterward. Falling near him were Ōsaki, the quartermaster lieutenant, and a medical noncom who was armed only with a bayonet. Lieutenant Asada, who had declined to save himself, shared Azuma's fate.[35]

The only officer left in the Azuma unit, the wounded medical lieutenant, Ikeda, took the initiative of ordering any survivors to retreat from the positions. With nothing to eat or drink for two days and nights, one badly wounded sergeant staggered back to friendly positions in the darkness, following tread marks leading away from the Halha and licking the blood from three wounds to slake his thirst.[36]

Haunting our account of the debacle that befell Azuma are the questions of the whereabouts and intentions of the main detachment, Yamagata's infantry. On the afternoon of 28 May, it will be recalled, Captain Kanetake had made it from the Azuma unit to the high ground about two kilometers to the rear and had found elements of the infantry "reposing" there with the regimental colors. We now know that Kanetake was referring to "Group 1" of the Yamagata detachment and that, after 5 A.M. on the 28th, the rear of the 3rd Infantry Battalion, centering mainly on 1st Lt. Tashiro Masanao's 12th Company and a machine gun unit, had strayed into a dune complex that prevented it from keeping up with the forward elements of the battalion. This mixup threw the rest of the main detachment ("Group 2") out of kilter: Yamagata's headquarters, the 4th Infantry Company, the regimental guns, part of the rapid-fire gun battery, the rearmost ammunition trucks, and the medical team.[37]

Major Fukumura supposedly commanded all of Group 1, built around his 3rd Infantry Battalion. But he was out of touch with First Lieutenant Kajima and his 17-man spearhead platoon from the 9th Company, which proceeded alone along the Holsten valley toward the Halha, ran into tanks, turned back to a point four kilometers east of the confluence, and was trying to bolt down some rations at noon when it was surrounded by 100 enemy horsemen. Kajima broke out with four soldiers, got lost, but blundered into Azuma's positions, as mentioned earlier. One of Kajima's noncoms made it back to the 9th Company that night with five men. The rest of the platoon was killed or disappeared.[38]

Fukumura had also lost touch with First Lieutenant Tashiro's 12th Company, Capt. Yamaguchi Seiichi's 3rd Machine Gun Company, and the rapid-fire gun unit. This left the major only First Lieutenant Nishimura's 9th Company, with whom he advanced by truck toward western Balshagal until they were stopped by difficult terrain—a mixture of dry and wet soil.[39] Disembarking from their trucks, the Japanese ran into the first hostile outposts north of Heights 731. Taken by surprise while eating breakfast, the enemy fled, leaving utensils strewn across the positions, as well as the corpses of 60 or 70 men, thought to be mainly Outer Mongolians.[40] This action drew

Lt. Gen. Honjō Shigeru (author's collection)

Ishiwara Kanji as a colonel commanding an infantry regiment, 1933 (author's collection)

Gen. Itagaki Seishirō (author's collection)

Maj. Gen. Hashimoto Gun (author's collection)

Manchukuo is proclaimed and Henry Pu Yi becomes Chief Executive,
9 Mar. 1932 (author's collection)

Site of the Mukden Incident, Sept. 1931 (author's collection)

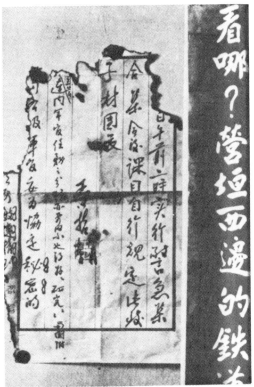

Portion of anti-Japanese poster and singed Chinese order purportedly calling for attack on Japanese forces, Sept. 1931 (author's collection)

Kanchatzu, June 1937: Soviet gunboat on Amur River under fire by IJA battery (courtesy of BBSS)

Type 94 tankette in which Lieutenant Hiromoto was killed: Tauran, 31 Mar. 1936 (courtesy of U. Masuda)

Gen. Ueda Kenkichi (painting by Wakita Kazu)

Inada Masazumi as a major (author's collection)

Col. Sakai Mikio at the time of 72nd Inf. Regt. organization, July 1938 (courtesy of T. Hamada)

Lt. Gen. Komatsubara Michitarō (left) with Maj. Gen. Yano Otosaburō, 4 July 1939 (author's collection)

Maj. Gen. Uchiyama Eitarō (left) with 1st Lt. Prince
Higashikuni Moriatsu, 22 July 1939 (author's collection)

Col. Okamoto Tokuzō
(courtesy of K. Onozuka)

Lt. Col. Ioki Eiichi (author's
collection)

Lt. Col. Higashi
Muneharu at Hailar
(courtesy of K. Onozuka)

Col. Ise Takahide (left)
(author's collection)

Maj. Gen. Morita Norimasa
(courtesy of S. Sumi)

Col. Sumi Shin'ichirō
(courtesy of S. Sumi)

Lt. Col. Kanaizuka Yukichi (courtesy of
Y. Kanaizuka)

Second lieutenant carrying 26th Inf. Regt. cased colors on the march to Chiangchunmiao, June 1939 (courtesy of N. Tsunashima)

IJA infantry marching from Hailar to Chiangchunmiao, June 1939 (author's collection)

IJA motorized unit, July 1939 (author's collection)

IJA motorized infantry debarking (courtesy of BBSS)

Aerial view of Halha River (courtesy of T. Hamada)

Preparing to enter Outer Mongolia, 1 July 1939; Halha River ahead,
Holsten to the left (Nomonhan-kai)

Lt. Gen. Yasuoka Masaomi (left), Lt. Gen. Isogai Rensuke (center), and Lt. Gen. Komatsubara Michitarō (right), at 23rd Div. Hq., July 1939 (courtesy of U. Masuda)

Maj. Gen. Kobayashi Kōichi (right), July 1939.
(courtesy of T. Hamada)

Crossing the Halha River bridge, 3 July 1939 (courtesy of BBSS)

The IJA bridge over the Halha, 3 July 1939 (Nomonhan-kai)

A Soviet tank crew surrendering, July 1939 (courtesy of N. Tsunashima)

A Soviet flamethrowing tank knocked out across the Halha; a dead crewman lies in the left foreground (courtesy of I. Saitō)

IJA infantry advancing in the open (courtesy of BBSS)

A 72nd Inf. Regt. close-quarter antitank team boarding trucks; explosives are attached to bamboo poles (courtesy of T. Hamada)

The 72nd Inf. Regt. in a dip, ca. 11 July 1939 (author's collection)

Carrying water for the 64th Inf. Regt. near Hgts. 733, 12 July 1939 (courtesy of BBSS)

down the fire of Soviet batteries emplaced across the Halha. Fukumura's men also heard gunfire to their left rear and sighted seven armored vehicles 1,000 meters north of Heights 733. Close-quarter attacks failed because of the lack of firepower and the ineffectiveness of bamboo-prodded explosive charges on the sandy soil. Near noon, the 12th Company, the rapid-fire gun platoon, and the heavy machine guns caught up, whereupon the combined IJA force knocked out two armored cars and captured one; the rest of the enemy armor pulled out. Fukumura headed south, under increasingly severe artillery fire, and by 1:30 P.M. reached the zone south of Heights 733, where he conducted reconnaissance and tried to raise detachment headquarters. Once more, contact was lost with Tashiro's 12th Company.

Tashiro's unit had changed course and sought a path closer to the riverbank, but its trucks were no more successful than those of other units in negotiating the treacherous soil. Once more the force changed direction, heading southeast until, at a point 1,000 meters north of Heights 731, it came under artillery fire after 6 A.M. To avoid being struck from two sides, the 12th Company took shelter in a hollow, left the trucks, and tried to catch up with Group 1 on foot. Hours had been lost, however; it was nearly 7 A.M. Efforts were made, without success, to establish radio contact with Azuma or other friendly units. During a lull in the bombardment, the company reboarded the trucks and soon was fired on again, this time from high ground to the southeast. IJA rapid-fire and regimental guns knocked out two of five armored cars that were approaching from the northeast. Someya's reserve 4th Infantry Company moved up, drove off 100 horsemen, and then outflanked 50 or 60 infantry who had been clinging to an elevation 2,000 meters to the southeast. In the process, the Japanese captured one prisoner and found 20 corpses, a water-purification vehicle, sedans, supply trucks, field telephones, uniforms, and rations. Next the 4th Company cleared a heights 400 meters farther to the southeast by 10:30 A.M., providing a new site for the detachment's command post. Regimental and rapid-fire gun crews assisted the infantry by knocking out six more armored vehicles on the 28th.[41]

Not until 5 P.M. on 28 May could Fukumura restore communications with detachment headquarters, which promptly ordered the battalion to reboard the trucks and come back to the main force. It was at this chaotic time that a horseman arrived from the Azuma unit and apparently mistook the "powerless" and unhelpful aide for the battalion commander. Lieutenant Asada thereupon told the aide to report to headquarters that he had decided to take his infantry platoon to help Azuma—an action approved by Yamagata when he was advised of it.[42] Rare radio contact was briefly made with the Azuma unit, which reported capturing two tanks and some prisoners after hard fighting. As for the shadowy 12th Company, it remained out of touch with its battalion headquarters all afternoon, but was finally able to rejoin the detachment by day's end.

In the early morning of the 28th, the detachment's spearhead unit—Gotō's 10th Company—had become separated from the main body, and its trucks—like the others—had bogged down in the dunes. The troops alighted and proceeded south along the Halha in pursuit of 80 horsemen. At 8 A.M. the Japanese sighted and brought under fire a column of trucks, armored vehicles, and 150 foot soldiers on the move along the Holsten valley toward the confluence; Gotō's men knocked out a tank, two armored cars, and three trucks. Soviet batteries in position on the high ground across the Halha opened fire on the 10th Company and forced it to seek cover, and enemy infantry counterattacked twice in formations of 100. Both assaults were repulsed, costing the foe 30-40 dead, and a tank and three armored cars were immobilized.[43]

Group 2 had a strange experience around 2 P.M., according to Captain Itō, who was with detachment headquarters. Between 140 and 150 Soviet Mongol (not MPRA) soldiers were sighted marching blithely forward from the southeast, singing their military songs. The Japanese waited until the range was point-blank and the aim perfect, laid down all available firepower, and smashed the formation. The Russians abandoned 80 bodies; two soldiers were taken prisoner. Itō says that the survivors fell back toward the Halha and combined with other Soviet elements to spring the reverse trap on Azuma.[44]

Enemy armored cars and troops, compressed in the gap between Azuma and the Japanese infantry, continued to clash with Group 2. Realizing that resistance was far from quashed and that his own forces were widely scattered, Yamagata issued an operations order at 5:30 P.M. on the 28th, identifying his location as five kilometers northeast of the confluence—the farthest advance of his headquarters. In typically optimistic prefatory remarks, he asserted that the main enemy forces had "collapsed" and retreated across the Halha, but admitted that hostile elements were still "popping up" on the right shore. The detachment would consolidate its strength, mop up the remaining foe, and clean up the battlefield that night. Azuma was explicitly directed to carry out his assigned mission. To remedy the wretched communication problem, the signal team should string lines from detachment headquarters to the 3rd Battalion and the Azuma unit.[45]

Fighting flared up after dusk. Major Fukumura took the 10th Company, occupied positions two kilometers northwest of Heights 733 by sunset, reconnoitered the area, and beat off assaults by armor and by "defeated" infantry. Tashiro's 12th Company and a platoon led by 2nd Lt. Satō Kōnosuke from the 4th Company did well against enemy cavalry and armored cars and returned to the detachment with a considerable amount of captured matériel. Nishimura's 9th Company tried to recover the remains of the squad lost with Lieutenant Kajima (who was thought to be dead), but the foe had overrun the region and forced Nishimura to turn back by dawn. Another IJA party, operating in the direction of Heights 755, could not locate the site of the Tachikawa unit. By midnight, the signal team completed laying wires to 3rd Battalion headquarters, but the lines could not be extended to the Azuma unit, partly because of enemy interference and partly because the signalmen went astray and could not find the reconnaissance unit.[46]

Near 8 P.M., the detachment received an urgent request from the Azuma force for replenishment of ammunition. Second Lt. Yuya Kyūhachirō, a regimental aide, was ordered to take four messengers from detachment headquarters, load a truck with five boxes of machine-gun ammunition, and head for the location of the reconnaissance troops, guided by Azuma's courier. One thousand meters southeast of the detachment command post, Yuya's team was circled by enemy cavalry and armor. Only the guide and one runner survived to report to headquarters.

Yamagata thereupon dispatched his code officer, 2nd Lt. Takahashi Kazuo, and 20 more messengers to look for Yuya. Again guided by Azuma's courier, Takahashi discovered neither the enemy nor the fate of Yuya. On the way back, the Japanese used grenades to knock out four of 10 parked enemy trucks, got lost, but ran into the 12th Company and made it back to detachment headquarters.

With dawn at hand, Yamagata knew that it was now or never if Azuma was to be resupplied. Second Lt. Nakano Toshiharu and his infantry platoon from the 4th Company were pulled out of the combat lines and ordered to march to Azuma's site with seven crates of machine-gun and rifle ammunition. Nakano had advanced to a point 700 or 800 meters behind Azuma's lines when, like Yuya's team, his platoon was encircled by cavalry and armor. Unable to break through to Azuma, the lieutenant had his men bury the ammunition, sent a runner back to report to the 4th Company, and then stormed the enemy ring until the last man fell. It was later reported that Nakano's party "took 50 of the foe with them."[47]

The actions of the other Japanese infantry strike forces, so carefully sketched in the basic operations plan of the Yamagata detachment, exerted little effect on the main fighting of 28-29 May. On the morning of the 28th, north of the Holsten, the Tachikawa unit overran the enemy's right-flank positions around Heights 755 by 1 P.M., but then slowed down in the face of stubborn resistance. A machine gun platoon leader, 2nd Lt. Toyoda Minoru, was never seen again, and Tachikawa lost touch with detachment headquarters.

South of the Holsten on the 28th, Kawabata's 11th Company encountered no enemy forces en route to the Higashi-watashi crossing at 5 A.M. as scheduled, proceeded another seven kilometers downstream by 7 A.M., but still met nothing more serious than lookouts. Ordered to join the detachment, the company was moving in the direction of the confluence at 11:30 A.M. when the trucks bogged down. Veering east, the unit teamed up with Manchukuoan troops to drive hostile elements from the Noro Heights sector by 5 P.M.—an artillery site and a command post. The Japanese took some prisoners and seized signal apparatus and ammunition. In a series of further actions, the company fought off two counterattacks by armor and cavalry, killing 30 or 40 men, and continued its pursuit to Heights 691 (Kui Heights). There, it surprised an enemy assembly area and accounted for 50 or 60 dead and found 50 or 60 untethered horses, two tanks, and three armored cars. Next the unit intended to cross to the north side of the Holsten, but was checked by artillery and machine guns and was ordered to shift, that night, to the Nomonhan sector, which it reached at 2 A.M. on the 29th. Efforts to ascertain the whereabouts of the main body of the detachment proved unavailing. As the company was about to set off for the confluence area near dawn to seek the detachment, an officer arrived from Azuma with a request for assistance. Adhering to its orders, however, the company headed south, under artillery fire, still looking for Yamagata's command post.[48]

Despite the local success of the 11th Company below the Holsten, the battle for the Halha junction was essentially decided, against the Japanese, as soon as the Azuma unit was trapped on 28 May and the main detachment proved permanently unable to break through. At the time that Yamagata needed every available man to regain the initiative, unit after unit was absent on grand outflanking maneuvers spanning both shores of the Holsten.

The separation of the core of the Yamagata detachment into two groups accounted for part of the Japanese troubles. Another complication stemmed from Yamagata's decision—presumably abetted by staff officers Murata and Itō, just as soon as the detachment reached the Heights 737 area in the early morning of the 28th—to shift the force's primary objective that day from the confluence to Heights 733, where the enemy was dug in.[49] Orders continued to be transmitted to Azuma by Morse code on the 28th, however, directing him to proceed with his previous tasks. In view of the problem with communications, it appears likely that the orders never reached Azuma; but the matter is academic, for Yamagata neither told him about nor directed him to share the main detachment's important change of mission. Three times on 28 May, Azuma urged the detachment to reinforce him; in the absence of a reply, he continued to fight exactly as instructed originally.[50]

Though situated far to the rear at division headquarters in Hailar, General Komatsubara ought to have realized by the end of 28 May that enemy forces east of the Halha had not been eliminated. Nevertheless, he convinced himself that everything was going according to plan: that Azuma had made it to the crossing north of the confluence, that Yamagata had occupied key terrain to the northeast, that the enemy's retreat route had been severed, and that heavy losses had been inflicted on the foe who, on the first day of the offensive, was said to have suffered 110 dead and lost four armored cars. Inasmuch as only mopping-up operations seemed to remain necessary, the Yamagata detachment was directed at 12:30 A.M. on 29 May to concentrate promptly near Kanchuerhmiao and return to Hailar as soon as possible. The air force would provide cover and reassemble gradually at the base in Hailar.[51]

Yamagata, however, had concluded that his detachment was in no condition to disengage yet. The Azuma unit was beyond his reach, and in practice only part of one machine gun platoon and two rifle squads were immediately available to him; moreover, his reserves numbered a mere 20 men, survivors of the battered signal team. Almost no messengers were left, and only a few clerks and color guards were at the command post, the rest of the troops being detailed to supply work, liaison, cleanup of the field, and combat. Indeed, there was concern that, if the enemy were to attack on the night of 28/29 May, the detachment's command post would collapse and the regimental colors would be endangered. As it was, hostile armor and soldiers were "wandering around the area of the detachment headquarters, opening fire here and there, and it was very noisy." Under the circumstances, Yamagata reported to Komatsubara that he first intended to deal the enemy one more blow on the night of 29/30 May.[52]

Presumably apprehensive about the possibility of a Japanese night attack on 28/29 May, the foe had withdrawn his main force to the high ground on the left side of the Halha since dusk on the 28th. Daybreak on 29 May brought intensified Soviet artillery barrages, particularly heavy in Azuma's area, and the gradual descent of armored vehicles, cavalry, and infantry to the river bank. Since Yamagata required maximum strength, he tried very hard, but without success, to make contact with the 11th Company and the Tachikawa unit, unavailable to him since the 28th. At 6 A.M. the 3rd Battalion transmitted information received from one of Azuma's officers that the reconnaissance unit had been nearly annihilated during the previous night's fighting and that Azuma and both company commanders had fallen. Since the recovery of friendly dead, especially officers, was always important to the Japanese army, Yamagata would dearly have liked to retrieve the corpses of Azuma and his subordinates immediately, but this was impossible in daylight, so the colonel deferred action till nightfall.

A bit of good news followed. The Tachikawa unit was heard from, and came back by noon. At 8 A.M. the 11th Company also turned up and was assigned to defend the Halha approaches. The arrival of these reinforcements allowed Yamagata to form a unit under First Lieutenant Someya to recover the bodies of the two young officers, Yuya and Nakano, lost during the disastrous efforts to convey ammunition to Azuma the previous night. Enemy artillery fire, however, had increased in severity and accuracy, converting the whole area northeast of the confluence into a zone of death. Someya's men were only able to bring back the corpse of one soldier from Nakano's team.[53]

At 11 A.M. a runner from the reconnaissance unit reached the 3rd Battalion with welcome word that Azuma and a considerable number of his soldiers were still alive and that, in spite of fierce combat, they were clinging to their positions. Eager to reestablish liaison with Azuma, Yamagata pressed his signalmen to try to get through via the two-way, insecure radio apparatus, but hostile fire foiled this attempt too.[54] The enemy launched battalion-size counterattacks, supported by artillery and armor, although Soviet tanks preferred to stay just beyond the range of IJA heavy machine guns and rely on their longer-reach primary armament to pound the Japanese positions.[55]

The intelligence reaching Japanese higher headquarters during the daylight hours of 29 May was mixed. After the second day of fighting, 200 enemy soldiers were reported killed, ten tanks and five machine guns knocked out, and code books and other matériel seized.[56] But since it was evident that the Yamagata detachment lacked the capacity to deliver a knockout punch and had been stopped in its tracks, the 23rd Division reconsidered its thinking of the 28th. Between 6:30 and 7 P.M. on 29 May (by which time Azuma was dead), Komatsubara sent a message lauding Yamagata for his detachment's good fighting and advising him that the 23rd Division and the Kwantung Army were sending reinforcements, especially artillery and heavy weapons. Therefore the colonel was to disregard the previous instructions about disengagement and go ahead with his original plan to destroy the foe.[57]

Yamagata had still been thinking of attacking on the night of 29/30 May, retrieving the corpses, and then leaving the battlefront. After having received another report from a reconnaissance unit courier, in the afternoon, that Azuma had fallen, the colonel took Kawabata's 11th Company at 6 P.M. and went to battalion commander Fukumura's position, where he studied the situation. As soon as Yamagata heard that Komatsubara's new order had been received, he gave up his idea of attacking that night and went back to detachment headquarters by 10 P.M. A little earlier, Lieutenant Kajima had "returned from the dead," reaching the battalion command post with wounded medical lieutenant Ikeda and about 10 injured soldiers, the last survivors of the reconnaissance unit. The death of Azuma was confirmed.[58]

The preceding account is based mainly on IJA infantry records and reflects a post factum recreation by the annalists that glosses over or omits certain events. Azuma's few survivors find the infantry's rationale offensive. On 29 May, for example, the reconnaissance unit sent messengers to detachment headquarters four times with word of its worsening plight, yet not a crate of ammunition was sent that day. Even an infantry platoon leader remembers that Azuma asked only for ammunition, never for relief.[59] Why did runners make it from the isolated reconnaissance force to the battalion command post and not the other way around? Admittedly, it took Sergeant Onizuka two and a half hours to wriggle two kilometers under fire to Fukumura's site, but he did get through by 6 P.M. on the 29th. A disturbing incident ensued. After submitting Azuma's last report and preparing to head back, Onizuka was asked by Yamagata "where he thought he was going." "Through our artillery periscopes," the colonel told him, "we have just witnessed the reconnaissance unit's final charge." Onizuka was stunned to learn that the detachment commander was near enough to observe the destruction of the sergeant's commander and comrades, but too far to try to help them.[60]

Yamagata, nevertheless, had decided to reschedule the infantry's attack for the next night, 30/31 May, by which time the promised reinforcements would have arrived from Hailar. At this stage, he would concentrate on evacuating the wounded, attending to resupply matters, conducting reconnaissance, reinforcing the positions, and cleaning up the battlefield—the last referring as before to the recovery of Japanese corpses and wounded men, as well as of enemy dead, plus weapons, equipment, clothing, and the like belonging to both sides. The medical team was instructed to take patients by truck to Amukulang, guarded by an infantry platoon. The rest of the trucks assigned by the division were to be used to haul water and obtain supplies from Hailar. With regard to the retrieval of bodies, Yamagata dispatched platoon leader Satō to look for Nakano's team, and battalion commander Fukumura to scour the area of Azuma's last stand.[61]

There is much more to be said, according to Tsuji Masanobu, the fiery Kwantung Army staff officer around whom controversy swirled whenever and wherever he put in an appearance on a battlefield. Eager as always to become involved in combat at firsthand, Major Tsuji arrived on the scene at this juncture, coming by car from Hailar on 29 May and reaching the Nomonhan sector around 5 P.M. In a tent in a hollow near the Holsten, he stumbled upon a wounded officer (undoubtedly medical lieutenant Ikeda) and three other crippled survivors of the Azuma force who had escaped the massacre and whom he sought to buck up with his usual aggressive language. Having no idea where to find Yamagata, Tsuji backtracked, spotted an IJA truck, and hitched a ride on it to the detachment's command post, observing evidence of battle and evading slowly moving enemy armor en route. Yamagata and his staff were "sitting around" in ignorance, still awaiting news from the front. To Tsuji, the officers appeared "strained and anxious." Another officer who arrived from Hailar remembers the exhaustion on the Japanese soldiers' faces; morale seemed not at all high.[62]

Yamagata, Tsuji says, told him that nothing could be done for Azuma; after dark, patrols would try to reach the locale of the battle. In view of what he had learned from the four survivors, Tsuji pressed for a night attack by all of the main force to rescue any remnants or at least to recover corpses. Pleading depleted strength, the colonel seems to have been willing to commit up to one infantry company. Infuriated, Tsuji asked how only 50 men or so could haul back as many as 200 bodies. He conferred separately with division staff officers Murata and Itō, and they in turn reasoned with Yamagata. Finally, the colonel agreed to have the whole 3rd Battalion attack in the direction of the confluence that night, leaving only the colors and heavy weapons at the command post.[63]

An IJA signalman who was present contributes an even more pungent account. Tsuji, he recalls, berated Yamagata for not raising a finger to save the colonel's own classmate Azuma. The wretched result of the combat was attributable to Yamagata's "lack of skill." When the colonel tried to explain, Tsuji employed a more conciliatory tack. Since the battle was over by now for the reconnaissance unit, it would be best to conduct a night assault using the entire detachment to recover Azuma's corpse in particular and all bodies that could be found on the field, even those of the enemy. Tsuji told Yamagata not to worry; after he got back to Hsinking, he would notify Kwantung Army headquarters and the media that the detachment had launched a big night attack and driven the foe beyond the border by dawn on 30 May. Then, "as if talking to a child," Tsuji cajoled Yamagata into assembling his force to the rear as soon as the bodies had been picked up, and quickly returning to Hailar without letting the enemy know.[64]

Understandably, the Yamagata detachment's after-action report does not even mention Tsuji's presence and certainly not his carrot-and-stick tactics vis-à-vis the colonel. As Komatsubara understood matters, however, Tsuji "could not remain an idle spectator, and therefore intervened, offering to launch a night attack and also take charge of the recovery of bodies."[65] Tsuji, of course, claims that he played a very important part in the infantry detachment's nocturnal expedition.

After discarding their canteens and ammunition, the Japanese infantry companies proceeded silently on foot toward the Halha by starlight, starting around 9 P.M. on the 29th. Encountering no trace of enemy soldiers or the Azuma force, the men were about to abandon the search when, near 3 A.M.

on the 30th, the "unique smell of a battlefield" was detected—the stench of dead men and dead horses. With one platoon from each company standing guard, each of the other two platoons began the grim process of picking up the corpses which lay in heaps on the dunes. Living horses stood with heads lowered, refusing to leave the spot where their masters had fallen. The sound of strange birds could be heard, as well as the moans of some terribly wounded soldiers, including one who was gasping for his platoon leader. More than half of the dead looked burned and blackened, immolated by surviving comrades or, some supposed, by enemy flamethrowers. Tsuji says that he did his best to encourage the shaken infantry. Though it was difficult to identify individuals, Azuma's corpse was recovered behind a rise. The bodies of both company commanders and most of the other officers were also found. A number of survivors believe that enemy corpses lay in the area; others, that the foe had vacated the site of the battle and left behind no dead.

In the hour before dawn, the troops extricated as many slain Japanese as they could. The dead officers were strapped to the backs of surviving horses; the corpses of noncoms and enlisted men were carried by the infantry or placed on litters. There was need for haste, as the roar of enemy armor could be heard before dawn. On the way back, the troops ran into a burned-out IJA medical (?) truck containing another 20 scorched remains. The men of the expedition returned to detachment headquarters by 5 A.M. with their doleful loads. Incoming enemy shells exploded nearby during simple rites for the dead.[66]

Whereas Tsuji's version of the events suggests that on 29/30 May many dead Japanese were picked up, as well as weapons that littered the killing ground, the infantry's records note only that elements of the 3rd Battalion reached the lines of the reconnaissance unit, without encountering much resistance, and made it back with the corpses of most of the officers, among whom were Azuma and both company commanders. The Satō platoon managed to locate the bodies of Lieutenant Nakano and one soldier and returned with them by 12:30 A.M. on the 30th.[67] The limited extent of the retrieval activities of 29/30 May is borne out by Komatsubara's diary, which states that the recovery of corpses was incomplete; apparently only a few bodies, including that of Azuma, were actually picked up that first night.[68] Indeed, the process of retrieving the slain continued for two more nights, on 30/31 May and 31 May/1 June.

Before daylight on the 30th of May, Fukumura's advanced lines were pulled back to the site of the detachment headquarters. Soviet artillery, which seemed to have run low on ammunition, fired only sporadically from the left side of the Halha that day. On the right shore, the enemy merely sent out small patrols; the Japanese therefore were able to attend to their trench-work and scouting assignments. For the first time in days, supplies of rice and water arrived at the front.[69] In addition, the 23rd Division notified Yamagata, in a message received early on 30 May, not only that two companies of trucks were coming to Hailar but also that the Kwantung Army was redeploying bombers, artillery, and more trucks, as well as considering the release of tanks "if necessary"—the first mention of the possible employment of Japanese armor (other than Azuma's inconsequential tankette) at Nomonhan.[70]

By the evening of 30 May, columns of trucks assigned to the 71st Infantry Regiment's 2nd Battalion commander, Maj. Baba Susumu, pulled into Yamagata detachment headquarters with 366 reinforcements and a moderate amount of firepower: one rifle company, one machine gun company with four weapons, a four-piece rapid-fire gun battery, and two mountain artillery batteries consisting of six guns. Yamagata's resulting operations order of 5 P.M. on 30 May, permeated by defensive thinking and realistic in scope when compared with the aggressive and far-reaching stipulations of the 26th, called only for defeating hostile forces that approached the IJA positions and using firepower, especially the mountain guns, to suppress the enemy on the riverbanks and on the high ground across the Halha.[71] Even the last provision, calling for light mountain pieces to conduct elevated fire at or beyond their maximum range of 6,000 meters with a limited number of shells, was overly ambitious—like trying to eat the painting of a rice cake (*e ni kaita mochi*), in the words of one critic.[72]

The enemy responded to Baba's arrival with limited exploratory actions: a resumption of artillery shelling and probes by armored cars on the IJA right flank. Baba's men drove off the armor, and the Soviet bombardment ceased after 30 or 40 minutes. After nightfall on 30 May, the 3rd Battalion of Fukumura, assisted by Yamagata and a portion of his headquarters personnel, moved down to the reconnaissance regiment's old positions again in an effort to finish the task of recovering the slain. Without interference by the enemy, the troops reached the site by 3 A.M. and completed their mission, returning to headquarters with 103 corpses by 6 A.M. on the 31st. The 4th Company was particularly relieved to have found the bodies of its 17 men, including Lieutenant Asada, who had opted to stay with Azuma to the end. The detachment's quartermaster major was ordered to take 10 trucks and convey the corpses to Kanchuerhmiao, where cremation took place on the same day. Captain Tachikawa's party, however, never could find the bodies of Lieutenant Toyoda and his attached machine gun platoon, although the search went on from dusk on the 30th until the early hours of the 31st.[73]

At 9:40 A.M. on 31 May, the 23rd Division directed Yamagata to finish the cleanup of the battleground, to disengage covertly that night, and to return to Hailar forthwith, via Kanchuerhmiao.[74] The highlight of the day, from the Japanese infantry's standpoint, was the sight of IJAF planes repeatedly raiding hostile artillery and armor across the Halha. According to the detachment's records, the enemy's "limited intentions" on the right side of the Halha were smashed and the foe's fighting spirit was eroded, causing him to remain on the left bank now—a rationale for the impending Japanese withdrawal from the disputed sector.[75]

In his final combat instructions at 3 P.M., Yamagata ordered his regimental guns and Baba's attached artillery to undertake neutralization fire (originally scheduled for 7 P.M.) against gun batteries and vehicles on both sides of the confluence. Teaming up with the artillery at sunset, a portion of the 3rd Battalion was to launch an attack designed to clear out enemy forces remaining on the right shore of the Halha, while other elements retrieved the last IJA corpses plus abandoned enemy bodies and matériel—weapons, armor, and trucks in particular. Motor vehicles should be used to haul away the heavier items.[76]

The bombardment by the Japanese guns began at 5 P.M. Though official sources extol the results, others say the fire proved ineffective because of the weapons' limited range, as might have been expected. Again, the more objective Japanese sources admit that no IJA infantry attack materialized, for the reason that "the aggressive spirit of all the units was dampened" after the detachment issued an order at 4 P.M. to prepare to leave the front, the target time for departure being set at 2 A.M. on 1 June.[77] Elements of the 3rd Battalion, however, did proceed once more to Azuma's positions in the afternoon, under shrapnel fire, and were able to retrieve more Japanese corpses and some enemy matériel, which they brought back at 6 P.M. The 4th Company managed to locate and pick up eight bodies belonging to the missing Nakano resupply platoon. A fierce sandstorm made the recovery work very difficult.[78]

According to participants, the departure of the Yamagata detachment was delayed a bit because only the few survivors of the Azuma unit plus some 40 infantrymen had been assigned to recover the very last corpses. Finally, around 2:30 A.M. on 1 June, the detachment left Balshagal. It assembled near Nomonhan by 5 A.M., though some of the trucks got lost on the way. The marching infantry finally caught up and, some time after 8 A.M., all the troops boarded trucks bound for Hailar via Kanchuerhmiao—the overdue "lateral advance" or "change of direction" (*tenshin* in Japanese, the term used by the armed forces during the Pacific War as a euphemism for the forbidden "retreat"). Even after the main force departed, the medical team had to camp overnight on the battlefield on 1/2 June, tending to the more helpless of the wounded.[79]

On 2 June, Komatsubara flew up to Amukulang and Kanchuerhmiao, prayed for the war dead, and addressed the troops. In addition to laudatory remarks, the general enjoined vigilance and warned that the incident was not settled yet; Soviet activities were increasing and the future was unpredictable. Afterward Komatsubara drove out to meet the survivors of the reconnaissance force, prayed over Azuma's ashes, and made another speech, stressing the lost unit's brilliant contribution to the success of the entire task force. Yamagata then brought his detachment back to Hailar, where other funeral rites followed for days.[80]

The High Command's understanding of events since 27 May was based on the Kwantung Army's version of them. Yamagata's detachment, it was reported, had launched a surprise attack, raced to the area of the Halha-Holsten river junction by mid-morning on the 28th, enveloped the enemy, and inflicted heavy losses on him. Komatsubara had hoped to withdraw the whole task force by the night of 28 May but, since confused fighting raged across a broad front and friendly troops were scattered, disengagement proved "difficult." First dispatches indicated that Japanese casualties approximated 30 killed and 70 wounded on the first day. When the 29th came, friendly positions were dominated by more than ten artillery pieces emplaced on much higher ground across the Halha, supporting 30 armored cars that came to the right bank. IJA casualties apparently exceeded 200—from the bombardments and from the desperate counterattacks of the enemy who, having lost his escape route, was "biting back like a cornered rat." The fighting abated by nightfall on the 29th. Although Japanese losses seemed high, morale remained very good and all ranks fought well. On the 30th the main hostile forces were located on the left shore, but elements were also deployed on the Japanese-claimed side of the bridge, at a distance of some 1,000 meters from friendly forces. Four mountain guns were no match for the hostile artillery; the 23rd Division planned to send up reinforcements of firepower as well as another infantry company at dawn on the 31st. Friendly forces would strike the enemy once more, making possible a withdrawal the same night and reassembly at Kanchuerhmiao to keep an eye on the situation. Though severe losses had been inflicted upon the enemy by ground and air, the Kwantung Army added, nothing unusual had been reported from the Soviet Far East region. Therefore the Kwantung Army would adhere to its policy of meting out heavy blows to any forces that invaded friendly territory, but of not thrusting across the border.[81]

Undoubtedly influenced by the exuberance of the first reports from the field detailing Azuma's plunge toward the confluence, Kwantung Army commander Ueda conveyed a commendation on 29 May, expressing delight that the 23rd Division had "chastised the foe by careful and appropriate measures and by swift and gallant action." Following this "victory," however, prudence was in order.[82] The High Command, in turn, congratulated the Kwantung Army on 30 May for the "splendid success" at Nomonhan and spontaneously offered to consider requests for more men and equipment in case Soviet-MPRA forces increased their strength in the border area and threatened to violate Manchurian soil again.[83] Significantly, from the Kwantung Army's point of view, nothing was said about the border defense guidelines.[84]

The reply of the Kwantung Army to the High Command's solicitation was low-key. Its operational thinking in the event of larger trouble, the headquarters in Hsinking reported, centered on the powerful use of air and ground mobility and the avoidance of prolonged attrition. But there was no expectation that the Soviet side would commit large forces on the west Manchurian frontier, in view of the geographical realities, i.e., logistical constraints. Therefore the defensive mission of the Japanese could be safely entrusted to the 23rd Division plus air and ground elements under the Kwantung Army's direct control. As for reinforcements from the homeland, the field army's want list mentioned only river-crossing matériel and a half-dozen mobile repair teams for the air force. It has been suggested that the modesty of this proposal reflected the Kwantung Army's view that merely emergency requirements had to be addressed at the time, that the Nomonhan affair itself was under control, that escalation was not foreseen, that IJA needs in the China theater took precedence, and that the long-range buildup of military capabilities was the main consideration insofar as Manchuria was concerned.[85]

The Kwantung Army's mention of mobile repair support, however, points to the increasing importance of the air dimension. Indeed, one of the bright spots of the recent fighting, from the Japanese point of view, was the successful performance of the friendly air force all day on 28 May. Not only were light bombers in action, but fighters waged a series of major battles with hostile aircraft that outnumbered them by three or four to one and reported 42 confirmed kills, eight of which fell on Manchurian soil. The Japanese met three Soviet twin-engine DB-3 bombers for the first time and shot one down. A Dōmei News Agency reporter likened the enemy pilots to "sheep attacked by wolves"; other correspondents said that Red aircraft went crashing to earth every three or four minutes, until the plains seemed on fire. The Japanese reported losing one aircraft, whose pilot parachuted to safety. According to the strange Tass version, Japanese fighters and bombers struck two MPRA field airdromes, surprising the Mongolian-Soviet fighter planes, which were late taking off. In a rare admission of an unfavorable ratio, Tass said nine Red planes were lost to three for the Japanese.[86]

IJA records indicate that one Soviet heavy bomber flew over Hailar from the direction of Manchouli on 28 May, but that hostile planes were not active on the 29th or 30th. A single enemy aircraft was shot down on 31 May and another on 2 June, bringing total Japanese claims to 62, including five unconfirmed, for the period since 20 May—still at the cost of only one plane.[87] Japanese fighter pilots were unimpressed by the enemy air force, judging that it lacked offensive spirit, was insufficiently trained, and relied excessively on group tactics. Inept Mongolian aviators, who were mixed in liberally with the Russians at first and saw action in the old I-15's, did not seem to reappear in combat afterward. Regarding the Soviet planes, Japanese veterans believed that the Russians needed at least one or two more years to improve and consolidate their types and quality.[88] As a precautionary measure, however, the Kwantung Army alerted three of its heavy bomber squadrons and an airfield battalion at Tsitsihar on 30 May and assigned them to the 23rd Division.[89] On the 30th, too, without being asked, the AGS attached the 1st Fighter Group to the Kwantung Army.[90]

Soon afterward, Japanese higher headquarters assembled the final data on the human and material costs and claims resulting from the fight for the Halha-Holsten junction. According to the 23rd Division's figures on IJA casualties, dated 2 June, the Azuma unit had lost 139 killed or wounded, out of 220 officers and men; Yamagata's infantry, 118 (including 12 missing) out of 1,058; and other elements, 33 out of 804. In all, the task force had lost 159 killed, 119 wounded,[91] and the dozen missing (who included Second Lieutenants Yuya and Toyoda), from a total authorized strength of 2,082. (See Table 15.1.) Komatsubara drew a certain consolation from the fact that Yamagata had suffered but 11 percent casualties and even Azuma "only" 63 percent. In fact, the general changed his diary wording of "annihilation" describing Azuma's fate to "reduced by a half," penned in red ink. Still, when Komatsubara heard that four or five more Japanese corpses might yet be lying on the desolate battlefield, he ordered a patrol to scout the area immediately on 8 June.[92] Consolidated AGS statistics as of 6 June showed the following IJA equipment and ordnance losses, incurred mainly at the hands of enemy artillery: one rapid-fire gun, 19 machine guns of various types, six heavy grenade launchers, eight trucks, two sedans, and two tankettes.[93]

As for enemy losses, AGS materials of 2 June showed approximately 300 dead, 15 tanks and armored cars and 12 machine guns knocked out, and a considerable amount of rifles and communication matériel seized. The figures were increased on 6 June to about 170 enemy slain in the Yamagata sector (including 130 Russians) and over 270 in the Azuma area. Most of the bodies were retrieved by the foe; the Japanese picked up 40 Soviet dead. Enemy losses of matériel were now put at 19 armored cars, two tanks, and nine mountain guns.[94]

Despite the good face put on matters and the many public compliments

TABLE 15.1

Initial Strength and Casualties of the Yamagata Detachment,
28-29 May 1939

	64th Infantry Regiment	Azuma Recon-naissance Unit	Transport Unit	Other units	Total
INITIAL STRENGTH					
Officers	53	13	14	20	100
Men	1,005	207	326	444	1,982
Total	1,058	220	340	464	2,082
TOTAL CASUALTIES					
Officers	8	9	1	1	19
Men	110	130	23	8	271
Total	118	139	24	9	290
Killed					
Officers	2	8	1	0	11
Men	49	97	1	1	148
Total	51	105	2	1	159
Wounded seriously					
Officers	4	1	0	1	6
Men	51	33	22	7	113
Total	55	34	22	8	119
Missing, presumed dead					
Officers	2	0	0	0	2
Men	10	0	0	0	10
Total	12	0	0	0	12

SOURCE: Combat reports of the 64th Infantry Regiment and its 1st Battalion, 2 June 1939; in BBSS, SS [180], vol. 27, p. 462.

NOTE: "Men" includes NCO's and below.

paid to the men of the Yamagata task force, the word "victory" was not bandied about within division headquarters itself. One visiting officer derived the impression that Yamagata had been compelled to return to Hailar because his task force lost its fighting power. As Major Suzuki put it, "Since the Yamagata detachment was so easily *beaten*, the general and his chief of staff, in particular, were very worried."[95] What if the Nomonhan crisis escalated and the entire division, with its visible weaknesses and defects, had to be committed? The abandonment of Azuma to defeat was particularly painful, and some of the survivors of the reconnaissance unit were known to be reviling the Yamagata regiment.

Komatsubara asked himself many questions. Had reconnaissance been at fault? Azuma, however, had penetrated the region of the confluence in early May and Yamagata had had several days to inspect the front before the attack on the 28th. In fact, Yamagata reportedly did scout the forward area by car while the detachment was waiting at Kanchuerhmiao.[96] Why did the two forces not act in closer harmony in such broad and exposed terrain?

From the strategic standpoint, a partial or unsustained breakthrough is always unsatisfactory. By the infantry detachment's own admission, the enemy concentrated not against Yamagata on the 29th, but entirely against Azuma. Why was the colonel out of touch with Azuma during the latter's fatal crisis?

Among the possible answers to the preceding questions was the fact that Yamagata was a foot soldier pure and simple—one who had no experience commanding a motorized unit in combat. His trucks moved far and wide on the flatlands, bogging down repeatedly and dispersing to the point that he did not know the location of all his elements. A transport company commander attests to the many difficulties encountered: establishing optimum truck loads, training men in boarding and jumping off vehicles, carrying out road reconnaissance and liaison, negotiating complicated soil conditions, and moving across the steppes by night under blackout restrictions. Moreover, he was hampered by insufficient firepower to cope with enemy armor and fieldworks, and by the divided command of motorized infantry forces in action.[97] Complicating Yamagata's command and control problems were the lack of landmarks on the plains and the need to rely almost entirely on runners for communication with subordinates, the radio and wire connections being notoriously undependable. Fighter aircraft were swift but untrained to coordinate with ground troops.

The personalities and styles of Azuma and Yamagata played their part in the debacle. Everyone agreed that Azuma was a dignified, very serious, and fine cavalry officer, an extremely brave "classic warrior." Infantry officers admitted that he could have saved his life, either by restraining the depth of his advance toward the river junction or by breaking out of the trap by night, but that he was too responsible a soldier to relax his interpretation of the explicit orders given to the reconnaissance unit by Yamagata.[98] The only possible criticism is that if Yamagata's estimate of the situation was unrealistic in its optimism, Azuma's undoubted courage verged on recklessness; but this is no derogation by IJA standards. After all, once his superiors had conducted a typically rigorous scrutiny of the combat actions of 28-29 May, they easily awarded Azuma a posthumous promotion to the rank of full colonel, effective from the date of his death.[99]

As for Yamagata, he had not at all been forced to set forth with the detachment. In the 64th Infantry, it was said by some of the officers that Yamagata—who had once been the proud bearer of the unit colors when he was a young lieutenant—now was seeking glory for the regiment as a colonel, and that in fact he had asked to be given the mission to the Halha.[100] By all accounts, Yamagata was relatively easygoing and not very impressive as a commander; some called him cautious, others foolhardy. Tsuji, as we saw, excoriated the colonel's behavior at the time that the Azuma unit was destroyed. Having discerned the various weaknesses in Yamagata's command capability, Komatsubara would weigh these factors in any further employment of the 64th Regiment. Meanwhile, according to one mild version, the general proffered comments and personal advice to Yamagata; others suggest that the critique went as far as admonishing every subordinate commander.[101]

Of course Komatsubara also felt a deep sense of personal responsibility for the Azuma disaster, and he conducted what the Japanese call "self-reflection." If, as is often said, the battle is the payoff for training in peacetime, then the 23rd Division's program had failed, and this was the commanding general's direct charge. One of the major lessons was the lack of cohesion, teamwork, and "spiritual inculcation"—apart from combat training. Additionally, immediate changes in organization and equipment were imperative; the amalgam of cavalry, tankette, truck, and infantry units was weirdly unsynchronized and ineffective. No thought had been given to the possibility that armor and artillery would be employed by the enemy in support of his horsemen. Many IJA observers felt that the unanticipated bombardment from the higher ground across the Halha proved decisive. As for defense against mechanized elements, the Azuma force lacked antitank weapons and unit training in their use. Yet Tsuji reported to his headquarters that, judging from track marks and other evidence, Azuma's formation must have been destroyed by 30 or 40 armored vehicles. The Kwantung Army called it "negligence on the part of the division commander not to have dispatched sufficient artillery and antitank strength."[102]

An AGS team that visited Hsinking in early June learned about the 64th Regiment's many logistical problems during the recent combat. Yamagata himself had reported difficulties with supply, hygiene, and communications —the last being so poor that he could not even maintain contact with division headquarters. The visiting officers identified water for men and horses as the greatest single supply problem, related also to difficulties concerning food, since the IJA staples of rice and hardtack required considerable water. Other problems included a lack of preparations to evacuate the wounded and the sick, a shortage of motor transportation, and the unsuitability of horse-drawn artillery in desert warfare. It was concluded that, although the Japanese air force enjoyed complete supremacy, the capabilities of the ground forces were inferior to the enemy by an overall ratio of 2:3. Nevertheless, almost none of the lessons from the fighting in May had been mastered by the time the next stage of the Nomonhan Incident broke out in the following month.[103]

Surprisingly, Japanese records say little about the decisive factor—the intervention of Russian ground and air forces in May. Inadequate intelligence, and faulty dissemination of what information was collected, played a big part here. Whenever the 23rd Division drew up operational orders, Major Suzuki suffered from a lack of military intelligence. The Kwantung Army conveyed data concerning the Soviet 57th Corps in Outer Mongolia, but the 23rd Division lacked details. Earlier mention was made of Komatsubara's acquaintance with rather low-level intelligence reports of local enemy strength before authorizing Yamagata's offensive on 26 May. The general knew a little more about hostile front-line troops by 28 May; he was aware that the 300 MPRA horsemen in the Halha area were part of a force that included one Soviet mechanized battalion, more than ten tanks and ten artillery pieces, and approximately 100 aircraft. By 30 May, from prisoner interrogation, the general learned the organization of the Russian "mechanized rifle/machine gun battalion"; its commander was Bykov, it had about 500 men and five armored cars, 26 machine guns of various types, and 14 45-mm. antitank guns. Even the preceding information, of course, was not available to Komatsubara when the operational plans for the Azuma and Yamagata sorties were drafted. Although a number of Japanese officers (including Komatsubara and Yamagata) knew that the opposing forces were partly Soviet, no one expected the Russians to become heavily involved in the Nomonhan fighting. Itō Noboru suggests that Kwantung Army assistance to the Manchukuoan border forces compelled the Soviet army to come to the help of the Mongolians for reasons of "face." [104] It is undeniable that Japanese underestimation of the Red Army aggravated the shortage of hard facts.

Soviet sources reveal that on 18 May, just after the Azuma force got back to Hailar from its first expedition, 57th Corps headquarters in Ulan Bator ordered Bykov's mixed detachment to begin advancing to the Halha sector from Tamsag. Major Bykov's own mechanized rifle battalion from the 11th Tank Brigade, made up of three motorized infantry companies, was reinforced by an armored car company of 16 BA-6 vehicles, a battery of four SU-76 (76-mm.) self-propelled guns, an engineer company, and a reconnaissance platoon of five armored cars. [105] Operating with the 6th Mongolian Cavalry Division, Bykov's reconnaissance platoon proceeded to Hamardaba Heights on the left shore of the Halha, crossed the river to conduct scouting in force, and advanced seven or eight kilometers eastward without difficulty. Fired upon and surrounded at this point on 22 or 23 May, the Russian platoon fought its way back to the left side of the Halha.

On 24 May, Bykov's 1,200-man main detachment arrived at the river. Next day the Mongol cavalry crossed the stream and deployed on the right shore. On the 26th the Soviet commander sent across two of his motorized infantry companies with supporting elements, including armored cars. Bykov shifted his own command post to the right bank on the 27th. His 2nd

Company held the left flank of the perimeter; forming the center were the 15th and 17th regiments of the MPRA 6th Cavalry Division. Below the Holsten, eight or nine kilometers away, Bykov deployed his 3rd Company to defend the right flank of the perimeter. Near the river crossing, on the left shore of the Halha, he placed his 1st Company, the engineers, the 76-mm. self-propelled guns, and a Mongolian artillery battalion. Since there were no combat actions on either 26 or 27 May, the frontier incident seemed to be over.

At 3 A.M. on 28 May, however, the Yamagata task force commenced its offensive, assisted by as many as 40 planes that attacked the river crossing, troop positions, and rear areas. It did not take the Russians long to comprehend what Yamagata and Azuma were trying to accomplish on the right shore. As the Japanese thrusts developed, Bykov's 2nd Company had to pull back, especially since the Mongolian 15th Cavalry in the left-center exposed the Soviet company by retreating to defend the MPRA command post. Consequently the Soviet-Mongolian left flank withdrew to a line of dunes two or three kilometers from the confluence. The Mongolian 17th Cavalry in the right-center was also dislodged to the shore of the Holsten, to which Bykov's 3rd Company repaired from the south.

Whatever success the Yamagata main force had achieved against the defenders was soon nullified. When the Russian 76-mm. battery commander, a lieutenant, observed the approach of Azuma's columns, he displaced his unit to the right shore on his own initiative and unleashed intense fire against the Japanese detachment which was moving toward the crossing point. In concert with Bykov's excellent 1st Company and stubborn engineers, who counterattacked a half-dozen times, the Soviet gunners virtually destroyed the Azuma force. The self-propelled battery knocked out two armored vehicles guarding detachment headquarters, as well as Azuma's staff car, from which a Russian platoon leader salvaged an IJA map said to confirm the border claimed by the Soviet-MPR side. Among other documents captured in three destroyed command posts was Komatsubara's order of 21 May stating that the 23rd Division was to wipe out the Mongolian army in the vicinity of the Halha.

On the evening of 28 May, elements of the Soviet 36th Infantry Division's 149th Regiment, under Maj. I. M. Remizov, boarded trucks in Tamsag and headed for the battlefield. Going into combat straight from the march, in piecemeal fashion and insufficiently coordinated with friendly artillery, the reinforcements made little impact on operations that day. Although fighting continued through the night and the artillery punished the Japanese, no decision had yet been reached. On the morning of the 29th, supported by two artillery battalions, the Soviet-MPRA forces mounted a successful counter-

TABLE 15.2

Soviet Data on Opposing Forces, Nomonhan Sector, May 1939

	Infantry	Cavalry	Machine guns	75-mm. or heavier guns	Antitank guns	Armored cars	Tanks
Soviet-MPRA forces	668	260	58	14	6	39	0
Japanese forces	1,676	900	75	8	10	6-8	1

SOURCE: JRD [965], JSM 11, part 3/B, p. 239; based on Shishkin [920].

offensive. By 4 P.M. the Japanese had been driven back some two kilometers; Mongolian armored elements fought particularly well. Apart from an unknown number of wounded, the Japanese were judged to have lost 400 men in the two days of fighting. Bykov's detachment suffered 65 or 70 casualties; Tass put total losses at 40 killed and 70 wounded. According to Colonel Shishkin, the Japanese outnumbered the Russian-Mongol forces in cavalry, infantry, machine guns, and antitank weapons. Soviet-MPRA troops excelled the Japanese greatly in armored cars and in the small category of regimental and divisional artillery. (See Table 15.2.)

Soviet military critiques after the fighting on 28-29 May commented on the bravery of Russian-MPRA forces but noted several weaknesses. Stationed 125-30 kilometers behind the front, the reserves of the 149th Infantry Regiment were too far away to support the fighting units rapidly. Soviet-Mongolian troops east of the Halha were deployed thinly on a 15-20 kilometer frontage. The Japanese were able to encircle the left wing and approach the crossing point because the Mongolian cavalry units were deployed in the center between the Russian infantry companies instead of providing flank protection or reconnoitering in depth.

In early June 1939, IJA intelligence heard that Choibalsan had bestowed 23 awards on Mongolian participants in the border fighting.[106] But, despite their local success at the Halha, the Russians maintained a strange silence publicly until 25 June, when Tass finally issued its first press release, noted but not reprinted fully in Japan. From May on, foreign military attachés in Moscow complained of receiving no reliable information on the Nomonhan Incident and of having to rely on newspaper reports. Soviet reticence was in marked contrast to the handling of the Changkufeng affair the year before, when full-page articles, pictures, and letters from all over Russia appeared in the press.[107] The American military attaché in Moscow believed that, at the outset of the Nomonhan hostilities, there was "a definite reluctance upon the part of the Soviet Government to give any publicity whatsoever to the present border fighting, and it was only after these incidents had been widely reported in the foreign press that any official acknowledgment of them was made. Apparently the Soviet Government either expected an early termination of the hostilities and did not care to advertise the fact that Soviet troops were in the Mongolian People's Republic or, after the fighting assumed somewhat more serious proportions, they were not confident of what its final outcome would be." [108]

The Soviet publicists were apparently stimulated by what they termed false information emanating from the Kwantung Army and by "lying assertions" that appeared in the Japanese press. For their part, the authorities in Hsinking were uncharacteristically quiet until 29 May when, as the American consul in Harbin saw it, the Kwantung Army "apparently considered that the situation had got out of hand" and issued its initial communiqué on the Nomonhan fighting. [109] But whereas in 1938 four foreign correspondents were permitted by the Korea Army to observe the Changkufeng sector, the Kwantung Army was allowing only one to visit Nomonhan at this stage—Maurice D'Alton of Reuter, "a paid propagandist of the Kwantung Army" who made "a highly colored broadcast of the Nomonhan battles" for retransmission to the United States. A few samples of D'Alton's fanciful "eyewitness" reporting will suggest why foreign diplomats and news media were so confused about developments at the Halha. For the "decisive battle" on 31 May [*sic*] the Japanese massed "three full divisions" to confront no less than "80,000 Mongol troops (officered by Russians), with complements of planes, tanks, and artillery." After cutting the "ford" across which Mongolian infantrymen and amphibian tanks had advanced, and "until cut to pieces by the desperate Mongols, [Azuma's detachment] formed the anvil upon which the main [Japanese] forces attacking from the front and both flanks broke the [Soviet-MPRA] invaders' resistance." D'Alton estimated that during the three-day engagement 2,000 Japanese and 4,000–6,000 Mongols were killed. His best story was that "a very famous Russian woman pilot" may have been the leader of the Soviet-Mongolian combat aircraft. [110]

More conversant with the facts, knowledgeable IJA survivors generally believe that liaison between Japanese higher headquarters went relatively smoothly and that Komatsubara handled matters as well as could be expected, within the border-defense responsibility assigned to his new and untried division, and not independent of Kwantung Army guidance. In this view, the actions of May could not be helped; Azuma and Yamagata carried out their missions satisfactorily; and there was no feeling of finishing with the Soviet Union once and for all, since the Kwantung Army knew that its condition was not good enough in terms of manpower and equipment. Katakura, however, feels that it was reckless for the Japanese to fight on the unclear frontier except in self-defense—if at all—lest "another Changkufeng Incident ensue." [111] At Kwantung Army headquarters, Tsuji and his colleagues called the 23rd Division's operations of May "one victory and one defeat." The "victory" referred to Azuma's sortie of the 15th; the "defeat" to the fate of the Azuma-Yamagata forces on 28-29 May. This dubious characterization has survived to the present day in the thinking of Japanese army veterans. [112]

16

The Two Faces of Escalation, June 1939

Addressing the Supreme Soviet on 31 May 1939, the new foreign affairs commissar, V. M. Molotov, warned the Japanese-Manchurian authorities that "in virtue of our treaty with Mongolia, we shall defend its frontiers as energetically as our own[;] . . . patience has its limits."[1] In Minsk next day, the deputy commander of the Byelorussian Military District, Georgi K. Zhukov, was analyzing the results of recent command and field exercises when a phone call from Moscow directed him to report promptly to Defense Commissar Voroshilov. In the Soviet capital on 2 June, Voroshilov's assistant hinted to Zhukov that he was going on "a long journey." From Voroshilov, Zhukov learned that Japanese forces from the Hailar garrison had launched a surprise attack and invaded Outer Mongolian territory, after having conducted many provocations against Mongol frontier guards defending the zone east of the Halha River. "I think," said Voroshilov, "that the Japanese have started a major military adventure. At any rate it is only the beginning." With a small team of experts Zhukov was to fly to Mongolia immediately, "see what is going on," and possibly take over as commander in chief. Maps shown Zhukov by the defense commissar and later by the deputy chief of staff indicated the situation in the Nomonhan area as of 30 May. "Please," the deputy told Zhukov, "the moment you arrive, see what's going on there and report to us, without pulling any punches." Shortly afterward Zhukov left for Mongolia, stopping en route at Chita, where he learned that Japanese aircraft were penetrating deeply into the MPR in pursuit of Soviet-Mongol planes.

On 5 June the Russian party arrived at Tamsag. It soon became clear to Zhukov that 57th Corps headquarters knew little about the situation at the front. None of the main staff except the commissar had inspected the battle zone; the corps chief of staff confessed that "things were not yet clear." To Zhukov's tart question whether operations could be directed 120 km. behind the lines, Corps commander N. V. Feklenko admitted that it was "a bit too far," but added that the forward zone lacked facilities such as telephone or telegraph lines and landing strips. Construction of a command post was about to begin. Zhukov told Feklenko to proceed to the front immediately and report, but the corps commander begged off, saying that he was expecting an urgent telephone call from Moscow momentarily. Zhukov therefore set off with Corps commissar M. S. Nikishev, who briefed him thoroughly about the weaknesses and strengths of the corps and who made a very good impression on him. By conducting a careful study of the front-line terrain and conferring with Russian and Mongolian commanders, operational staff, and commissars, Zhukov derived "a more or less clear picture of the nature and scope of military action and the battle capacity of the Japanese troops" and was able to point out "errors and shortcomings" on the part of Soviet-MPRA forces.[2]

Zhukov was particularly disturbed by the very serious "lack of thorough reconnaissance." Shishkin explains that the operations officer of the 57th Corps, who had been directing the actions of late May, had crossed to the eastern (right) shore of the Halha at the time the Azuma-Yamagata forces were beaten. Observers reported the movement of large numbers of trucks toward the Japanese positions. The 57th Corps staff officer, wrongly concluding that the enemy was rushing up reserves, decided to pull back Soviet-MPRA units from the right bank. For four days, because of poor scouting, it was not discovered that the trucks had been used to withdraw the Japanese troops, not to reinforce them. The blunder was rectified after 3 June, when the Soviet-MPRA formations reoccupied positions between the Halha and Nomonhan, "thereby assuring reconnaissance security [in] the immediate vicinity of the frontiers."[3]

Zhukov concluded that the troubles in the Halha region were no simple frontier incident and that military activities were going to escalate since the Japanese still nurtured plans of aggression against the MPR and the Soviet Far East. After reviewing the situation with the 57th Corps staff, Zhukov recommended to Voroshilov that Soviet-MPRA forces retain the bridgehead on the right shore of the Halha while getting ready to launch a counteroffensive from Mongol territory. The defense commissar replied next day that he was in full accord with the estimate and the proposed plan. Zhukov was ordered to replace Feklenko as corps commander.

The 57th Corps was insufficient to cope with what Voroshilov and now Zhukov termed "the Japanese military adventure," especially if the enemy chose to strike "in other areas from other directions." Massive preparations were always a hallmark of Zhukov's battles; in this case, "realizing the great difficulty of the situation," he asked Moscow for air force reinforcements and no less than one tank brigade, three rifle divisions, and heavy artillery units. Within a day the Soviet General Staff advised that it was honoring the requests. During June the following reinforcements were sent to the Tamsag battle zone: the 11th Tank Brigade; the 7th, 8th, and 9th Mechanized Brigades; the 36th Motorized Rifle Division (less one regiment); a heavy artillery detachment; and the MPRA 8th Cavalry Division. More than 100 fighter planes, including the improved I-16 and the I-153 "Chaika" ("Gull"),[4] were also dispatched. So were 21 special pilots, Heroes of the Soviet Union, led by the famous and popular Y. I. Smushkevich.[5]

Japanese sources deny that, with immense amounts of matériel and hundreds of thousands of IJA troops diverted to the China theater, there was either the desire or the capability for large-scale "adventures" in 1939 against the Mongolian People's Republic or the Russian Far East. Still, in many other respects, Japanese accounts resemble the Soviet version of events shortly after the withdrawal of Yamagata from the front. Reports from the Manchukuoan forces that were now guarding the Nomonhan sector and from Japanese scout planes indicated that by 31 May enemy troops had pulled back to the left shore of the Halha and the area was quiet except for some Soviet air reconnaissance activity. From the afternoon of 2 June, however, enemy forces reappeared on the right bank: some 60 trucks and armored cars and eight antiaircraft guns in the Balshagal district. About 400 motor vehicles were also operating on the left side of the river.

According to Japanese intelligence, the Russian authorities held a conference in Chita in early June to consider the advisability of counterattacking on the east Mongolian front and the need for fighter aircraft reinforcements. IJA intelligence also learned, from a usually dependable source, that a special meeting had been convened in Moscow to examine the Far Eastern problem, and that the ailing former ambassador to Japan, Mikhail Slavoutski, had even been called from the Crimea. Closely reflecting Zhukov's record of his recommendation to the defense commissariat was the unconfirmed intelligence received by the Japanese AGS in early June to the effect that the Russians were expecting the resumption of Japanese offensive operations in the Nomonhan region and were enthusiastically preparing a counterattack intended to recapture the line of heights on the right side of the Halha if possible. The air force commander in the MPR eastern military district had reportedly directed that all Russian planes be repainted with Mongolian markings—to mask Soviet participation—a decision that was appealed to Chita for psychological reasons but was upheld because it accurately reflected the intention of the Soviet High Command. Many Japanese intelligence reports alluded to local Russian and Mongolian requests for reinforcements of artillery, munitions, fuel, aircraft, and armor from the Trans-Baikal region.[6]

A number of Japanese army interviewees think that General Komatsubara, still pained by the Azuma debacle, was hoping for revenge. At best, the reconnaissance force's fate rendered the division commander more belligerent in his outlook.[7] The Kwantung Army, however, promised the High Command on 31 May that it would endeavor to avoid disputes requiring protracted confrontation with the enemy. From examination of the other party's situation and of the terrain in the vicinity of Nomonhan, it was not thought that the enemy would commit very large formations to the region. Hence the Kwantung Army did not expect the present incident to escalate into full-scale war. If the foe did reinforce the Nomonhan region and violate the frontier again, the Kwantung Army would inflict severe losses on him intermittently by drawing upon the 23rd Division, available air units, and all other forces under direct command of the field army. Minor affrays could be expected in various areas in view of the general state of tension that existed on both sides.[8]

The rather restrained statements by the Kwantung Army do not reflect the "adventurism" suspected by the Soviet military leadership. Nevertheless, it is possible to interpret as ominous the request made on 31 May that the IJA High Command activate six mobile aviation-repair sections and, in particular, immediately supply river-crossing materials, which were termed the weakest feature of the Kwantung Army's operational resources. Presumably, the contingency of crossing the Halha was already envisaged. It is known that the Kwantung Army possessed only sufficient equipment to construct one 50-meter span across the river, since most such matériel had been diverted from the homeland to the China theater. Kwantung Army apologists observe that the AGS had merely asked for recommendations of reinforcements necessary to cope with enemy threats in the Nomonhan region; within this context the Kwantung Army staff officers were being very modest in their requests. Although assistance was desperately needed in the face of Russian Far Eastern forces, which outnumbered the Japanese by a factor of 3:1 and which were "obstinately provoking an increasing number of border incidents," the Kwantung Army sincerely wanted to avert the diversion of precious materials from the rest of the Japanese army, such as the units engaged in China. From the overall strategic viewpoint the Kwantung Army was therefore determined to limit its demands and its countermeasures, although it did caution all of its subordinate main commanders to buttress defensive preparations.[9]

The Japanese High Command was appreciative of the Kwantung Army's attitude at this stage. On 31 May a joint AGS–war ministry committee drafted an "Outline for the Settlement of the Nomonhan Border Incident" that expressed confidence in the Kwantung Army's policy of endeavoring to localize the affair by chastising Soviet-MPRA land and air invaders of Manchukuo through "elastic military operations." Though the High Command would monitor further actions, it expected the Kwantung Army to end matters by preventing the enemy from entering the right shore of the Halha.[10] As for Komatsubara, he noted on 11 June that he intended to watch and wait, and to attack MPRA invaders when a good opportunity arose. By "invaders" he meant trespassers across the Halha, which was still in all earnestness regarded as Manchukuo's boundary. When his forces sortied, Kwantung Army headquarters would be contacted regularly. If a Manchurian-Mongolian border conference materialized, Komatsubara would expel enemy troops from the disputed sector, for the benefit of his side's negotiators.[11]

During the first half of June, the Kwantung Army played down the border dispute in the expectation that it would run its course, as so many preceding affrays had done. Publicity was restrained, and the Japanese air force, off alert since 10 June, did not challenge enemy overflights but instead concentrated on training and maintenance. Early in the month, map maneuvers and operational conferences at Kwantung Army headquarters, with emphasis on the eastern front, brought a high-ranking team of AGS officers from Tokyo, including Operations Bureau chief Hashimoto Gun, Prince Chichibu, and four Operations officers. The atmosphere was highly congenial and frank opinions were exchanged in many an intimate conversation. The AGS visitors were assured repeatedly by Kwantung Army staff officers, including Tsuji, that the High Command could rest easy, that nothing would be done to enlarge the Nomonhan affair.[12] Although he was an active-duty lieutenant colonel, the imperial prince attracted particular attention from the media. A United Press correspondent told the American consul in Harbin that, after the actions in May, Prince Chichibu had flown to the Manchurian front "to restrain the Japanese from pursuing the enemy into Mongol territory." This surmise was echoed by another American reporter who expressed the private opinion that Chichibu had apparently "counseled moderation" to the Kwantung Army.[13]

During the period of relative quiescence, Soviet-MPRA forces replenished their combat losses and prepared for more serious warfare. Red Army commanders and commissars were reported to be arriving from European Russia to reorganize and improve the combat strength of the Mongolian armed forces. Red ground units became increasingly active on the right bank of the Halha in mid-June, although they did not advance beyond the boundary line claimed on their own maps. Work continued on Soviet-Mongolian field positions along the high ground on the left shore and on both sides of the Holsten. Cavalry patrols were observed scouting fords on 11 and 15 June; more importantly, a third bridge was completed on 18 June at the Halha-Holsten junction. That day, according to AGS intelligence, 200-300 enemy vehicles and 70-80 pieces of artillery were concentrated in the Tamsag area.[14] Between 17 and 19 June, severe ground attacks against Manchukuoan guard units were reported from the west side of Lake Buir and near

Halhamiao, involving enemy tanks, armored cars, mountain artillery, and troops.[15]

The Soviet-MPRA air capability, which had been crippled at the end of May, was rebuilt in eastern Mongolia in June. Zhukov tells how the team of Heroes of the Soviet Union trained new young pilots and taught them battle lessons from Spain. Japanese pilots who reconnoitered Tamsag, inside the MPR, reported on 18 June that 55 small and medium planes parked at the air base. For their part, single Red scout planes appeared over the Arshaan district, southeast of Nomonhan, on 14, 16, and 17 June.

Details of the next events are not entirely clear, but there can be no doubt that the Soviet-Mongolian air force commanders had decided to initiate offensive operations of a limited nature. On the 17th, between 27 and 36 planes attacked an already endangered Manchukuoan outpost southwest of Lake Buir and the hamlet of Kanchuerhmiao southeast of the lake. No particular losses were reported from either place. Next day, 15 Red aircraft struck at Arshaan, killing one Manchurian and wounding three. The attacks were more severe on 19 June. Sixteen enemy planes hit Kanchuerhmiao from an altitude of 300 meters and then dropped dozens of incendiary bombs on targets at Amukulang from only 50-100 meters. Casualties were trifling, but considerable quantities of military fuel and provisions were destroyed, including 400 gasoline drums and 380 bags of grain. In addition to the attacks on Kanchuerhmiao and the supply dumps at Amukulang, a dozen planes hit Halhamiao and Tsagan Obo, where Manchukuoan forces were being encircled on the ground. IJA intelligence estimated that, as of 19 June, the enemy air force in the forward zone numbered one brigade of 40-50 heavy bombers, one reconnaissance battalion of 20-30 light raiders, and two battalions consisting of 50-60 fighters.[16]

The Soviet air raids occurred too far from Hailar to cause any real shock at 23rd Division headquarters, according to senior operations officer Murata; persistent hostile activities in the border region had been anticipated. Air Division commander Giga says he was not really surprised either. He dismissed the assaults as the Russians' method of keeping their air reinforcements' "idle hands busy."[17] At Kwantung Army headquarters, however, the unexpectedness of the Soviet air actions was apparent. It had been thought that the real danger from the Russians lay to the east and particularly to the north, where the Fourth Army had been established at Peian only a year before. The Kwantung Army commander, his deputy chief of staff, and almost all operations officers were absent from Hsinking until 18 June on a series of trips to inspect the defenses and the state of readiness along the distant north Manchurian borders; the deputy did not get back until the 20th.[18]

The messages the Kwantung Army received from Komatsubara on 19

June sounded serious. Not only were Manchukuoan forces in the Lake Buir–Nomonhan region in danger as of the 18th, but formations of 15-30 enemy planes had raided the Arshaan-Kanchuerhmiao area on the 18th and 19th, inflicting considerable damage and causing the terrified natives to flee. The Kwantung Army did not need to be reminded of Komatsubara's local duties under its own border guidelines of April, but it did have to address the general's recommendation of decisive counteraction, for the Nomonhan affair was developing far beyond the purview of any area commander. Why had the Russians chosen to take offensive air action, without any particular Japanese provocation? Perhaps they were testing the Kwantung Army's seriousness of purpose on the MPR frontier, seeking to divert Japanese military attention from the China theater, reassuring Choibalsan and the Outer Mongolians that they would indeed defend MPR territory as earnestly as their own, or retaliating belatedly for some of the Japanese air force's own aggressive activity over the disputed zone and across the left side of the Halha in May. There had been a delay of about two weeks between the sorties of Azuma and of Yamagata; possibly the Soviets foresaw still another Japanese ground excursion, basing their deductions on aerial reconnaissance reports of shipments of fuel and ammunition at Kanchuerhmiao and the always busy rail terminal at Arshaan. From the Japanese standpoint, the ground logistical activities were routine, and mainly for the benefit of the local Manchukuoan army. But of course the Russians would make no differentiation, especially since "Japanese Bargut" forces were still operating on the Halha's right shore, which the Soviet-Mongolian side never ceased to claim. In any case, the Japanese did not doubt that the latest Soviet actions were intended to be a deterrent or challenge or both.[19]

During a half-day of intensive discussions on 19 June among the Kwantung Army staff at Hsinking, Operations Section chief Terada recognized Komatsubara's responsibilities but stressed the larger IJA problem of China, as his Tokyo counterpart Inada had done in May. Only a week before, Japanese forces had imposed a blockade of the foreign concessions at Tientsin, causing a crisis in relations with Great Britain. A confrontation with the Russians at Nomonhan would weaken the Japanese stance against the British at a crucial stage, just as the outbreak of the Changkufeng affair in 1938 had distracted the Japanese High Command from the decisive Hankow campaign. To Terada it seemed better to attend to Nomonhan only after progress was reported from the Craigie-Arita talks on the Tientsin issue.[20]

The Kwantung Army's hawkish officers retorted that Nomonhan was becoming too serious to ignore. Enemy planes were not limiting themselves to tactical actions within a disputed border zone but were striking at supply and transport hubs well inside Manchukuo. If nothing were done, Hailar and Tsitsihar might become the next targets. It was possible that the USSR was seeking to check Japanese pressure on China, but "turning the other cheek" was not the way to deal with the Russians; worse clashes could erupt on other fronts, bringing dangers of all-out war. Nor would the Tientsin parleys be advanced by letting the British conclude that the Japanese army lacked the will or the strength to stand up to Soviet-MPR provocations. During the recent inspection tour of northern Manchuria, several Kwantung Army officers had even considered cheering on the North China Expeditionary Army by sending a telegram of support; but it would be even more encouraging if the Kwantung Army acted out its motto that "actions speak louder than words." [21] The experiences of May did not discourage expectations that the right bank of the Halha could be cleared by meting out one overpowering blow. Indeed, the Nomonhan Incident would be controlled, not expanded, if a forceful policy were adopted. This was the position successfully articulated by Tsuji, who, though only a major, was the dominant figure in the Operations Section. He remained convinced that Terada's mild recommendation—apart from its psychological weakness—would have resulted in the Kwantung Army's counteraction being delayed until autumn and then dragging into the winter of 1939 and beyond. Inada sees close connections between the unforgotten loss of the Azuma unit, the new enemy air raids, and the provoking of the Kwantung Army into abandoning its policy of localizing the Nomonhan affair. [22]

After all of the Kwantung Army's operations officers had come round to Tsuji's aggressive view, other staff sections were consulted and the draft of an "Operational Plan Against Outer Mongolia" was prepared on the 19th. The guiding principle was that Soviet-MPRA forces violating the frontier in the Nomonhan region were to be destroyed, "thus completely frustrating their treacherous designs." The Hulun Buir region must be secured, not only for the sake of Manchukuo's peace of mind and confidence in the Kwantung Army but also for the insurance of high morale among the Japanese forward units themselves. It must be demonstrated that the border guidelines meant what they said. In this respect, the Kwantung Army staff was convinced that there was no danger that the proposed handling of the border problem would escalate into full-scale war.

The key to the Japanese ground offensive, which was scheduled for early July, would be an infantry brigade and other strong components of Lt. Gen. Sonobe Waichirō's elite 7th Division, which would be brought up from Tsitsihar. After concentrating in the Arshaan area, these forces would cross the upper reaches of the Halha, surprise the enemy from his flank and rear, destroy the main artillery concentrations, and then swing toward Nomonhan on the right or eastern bank, capturing as many prisoners and as much matériel as possible and annihilating the foe in the process. Only one infantry regiment from the 23rd Division was to be employed, to cover the Kan-chuerhmiao-Nomonhan sector; most of the division was to be held in reserve at Hailar, with elements detached north to Manchouli to threaten the hostile flank.

Other features of the draft plan included the commitment of two tank regiments and the main strength of the 2nd Air Division. Prior to the ground offensive, the air units were to win aerial supremacy. After enemy ground forces had been cleared from both sides of the Halha, IJA elements would be left to secure key locations on the right bank, while the main force pulled back and kept an eye on the enemy. Meanwhile, Kwantung Army forces would go on alert along all other Manchurian frontiers. For the offensive itself, the Kwantung Army was intending to commit nine infantry battalions, three engineer companies, 92 antitank and 24 antiaircraft pieces, 70 tanks, 400 motor vehicles, and 180 planes. This strength was roughly the equivalent of one division in crack infantrymen and two divisions in gunpower—or, in overall terms, twice the combat effectiveness of the 23rd Division.[23]

Before submitting the draft to Ueda, still on 19 June, Terada and his colleagues took it to the chief of staff, Lieutenant General Isogai, who reacted very cautiously. Though Isogai saw the need to destroy hostile forces invading Manchukuoan territory, he noted that implementation of the offensive plan would require large-scale operations. Consequently, if matters were to proceed smoothly, the Kwantung Army ought to make sure that its thinking precisely matched that of the central authorities. Isogai was of the opinion that the campaign should not be set in motion until approval had been elicited from the High Command. Terada and Hattori countered with various arguments: the situation at Nomonhan had deteriorated; enemy planes dominated the skies at the front; and the security of Manchukuo demanded immediate offensive action, for which prior instructions from Tokyo were not necessary in view of the Kwantung Army's defensive mission. In case the "indecisive" central authorities disagreed with the decision reached in Hsinking, which was probable, another Kanchatzu "mistake" in the chain of command would result, as Tsuji—the sole holdover from the 1937 episode—could attest to personally.

To these heated contentions, Isogai replied that it might be best to wait for his operations assistant, deputy chief Yano Otosaburō, to return from the northern border on the 20th. But Isogai's visitors insisted on the emergency nature of the situation, and the general finally gave his tentative and reluctant approval to their plan. At this important juncture, Isogai showed weakness in judgment and in control over his subordinates, as well as a lack of courage in his own convictions. Long afterward, the hawks admitted that, had they heeded Isogai's unexcited opinion, consulted the High Command, and resorted to negotiations to try to settle matters, it was likely the Nomonhan Incident would not have escalated. At the time, however, emotion prevailed over reason in the minds of the operational staff officers, because of the ineluctable sense of crisis.[24]

The draft of the offensive plan was now ready for submission to General Ueda, to whose office the chief of staff and all the operations officers proceeded in the evening of the 19th. To Tsuji's distress, the commander seemed uncharacteristically impassive as he listened to the detailed explanations. Did he too think that Tokyo must be contacted beforehand? When Ueda finally spoke, his words came slowly and his tone seemed gloomy. Like Isogai, he agreed that chastising the invaders in the Nomonhan area lay within the Kwantung Army's assigned mission. Nevertheless, he wondered about the effect the implied lack of confidence in Komatsubara would have upon the whole 23rd Division, since another division commander was being called on to deal with an affray that had occurred inside the 23rd Division's proper zone of defensive responsibility. If he were Komatsubara, Ueda remarked sadly, he would kill himself. Taken aback but impressed, the staff officers could only reply that the plan was based on simple tactical considerations and map study, that the brand-new 23rd Division had performed unimpressively in independent combat operations in May, and that the 7th was the best division in Manchukuo. Ueda responded that the explanations were sound technically but that principles of command should not be overlooked. He also suggested that consideration be given to an approach route to Nomonhan differing from the one used during the two Japanese forays in May. Terada reassured the commander that the draft would be carefully rethought; but since time was pressing, he requested and obtained permission from Ueda and Isogai to alert air force units on an interim basis.[25]

Working into the night of 19/20 June, the Kwantung Army operations officers revised the offensive plan to reflect Ueda's ideas. Fundamentally, the responsibility for handling the Nomonhan Incident would now be entrusted entirely to Komatsubara, who would concentrate his full 23rd Division in the border zone, mainly in the vicinity of Chiangchunmiao, with a view to offensive operations in the Halha valley. Since the operations staff remained convinced that, under either of their plans, it was imperative to cut off the enemy forces' route of retreat on the left shore, even after they had been beaten on the right side, a new and very powerful task force was created to operate temporarily across the river. In lieu of the entire 7th Division, one of its motorized infantry regiments plus two antitank gun batteries, two regimental gun batteries, and a truck company would be combined with two tank regiments, a field artillery regiment, a reinforced regiment of engineers, an antiaircraft battery, a 120-truck transport regiment, and medical and signal elements. The task force would be named after its chief, Lt. Gen. Yasuoka Masaomi, commander of the 1st Tank Group at Kungchuling. All of these units, as well as field antiaircraft artillery reinforcements, would be attached to Komatsubara's command.

Since much of the rationale for the Kwantung Army's proposed offensive derived from the renewed activity by the enemy air force, considerable thought was devoted to air countermeasures. The air staff, through the operations section, had recommended that Isogai approve simultaneous orders for an aerial offensive against air bases inside Mongolia, but this was rejected out of concern about possible retaliation. Instead, as provided in the original plan, the 2nd Air Division commander was to bring up the 7th (Kungchuling), 9th (Tsitsihar), and 12th (Harbin) air groups. Consisting of eight fighter, six heavy bomber, one light bomber, and two scout squadrons, these forces represented the main strength of Giga's air division. Giga was directed to search out and destroy hostile planes invading Manchurian airspace. Though an air campaign against the MPR was held in abeyance, the Japanese air force could prepare for future offensive operations. Inasmuch as topographical data as well as military intelligence were in very short supply, the Kwantung Army called for prompt photographic reconnaissance of the route from the Arshaan area to the other side of the Halha. Four high-performance observation planes, with crews, were borrowed from the Manchuria Aviation Company at Hsinking.

Thanking his operations officers for their work, Ueda approved the new offensive plan in the morning of 20 June. Major General Yano, the Kwantung Army deputy chief, had been directed to fly back to headquarters from the north but, since weather delayed his return, the Operations staff obtained the approval of Ueda and Isogai for the issuance of a detailed concentration order for the ground forces. Because the 23rd Division was so inexperienced, however, Ueda asked that Kwantung Army staff officers proceed to the front and render Komatsubara every assistance.[26] Tsuji, for one, flew to Hailar on several occasions. On 20 June, he remembers, 23rd Division headquarters was in a state of excitement, for it had been given only ten hours in which to depart for the front. By his own account, Tsuji explained to Komatsubara and Ōuchi the full background of the battle plan, expressed regret for the Operations Section's initial notion of holding the 23rd Division in reserve, and described Ueda's corrective actions and assurance of faith in Komatsubara. Tsuji long remembered the tears of appreciation that welled in Komatsubara's eyes.[27]

Japanese offensive strength to be committed, according to the Kwantung Army's second plan, was the same in terms of tanks (70), trucks (400), antiaircraft guns (24), and planes (180), but provided four more infantry battalions (now 13), two more engineer companies (now five), and 20 more antitank guns (now 112). The increases were necessitated by the weak combat resources of the 23rd Division. As in May, however, the Kwantung Army was more concerned about cutting off the enemy's "route of retreat" than about causing that retreat. The presumably overpowering strength of the reinforced Japanese strike forces, with their tanks, troops, and planes, was often compared to a butcher's axe used to dice a chicken. Or in the picturesque words of another army expression, the mere sleeve of a mail-clad samurai could brush away the foe. Both of the Kwantung Army plans called for the "temporary," "slight" crossing of the Halha into undeniably Outer Mongolian territory for tactical reasons, an action justified by the self-serving provisions of the border guidelines and the fundamental "imperial task" of guarding Manchukuo, as well as by a lack of concern about the danger of war. There was no coordination between the Kwantung Army and the central command, the civil government, or the diplomats.

Since the Japanese border crossing was to be deliberate, not accidental, it really required imperial sanction; but only one IJA interviewee has specifically questioned the legality of the operation, and he served at the Tokyo level—the AGS Soviet Intelligence Subsection chief, Kōtani. He remembers thinking that the envisaged Kwantung Army action—the penetration of MPR (and by extension Soviet) territory—was thoughtless, and going to Inada's office to complain. Kōtani warned that so-called border incidents could escalate into international crisis. At the time of the Changkufeng affair, IGHQ had carefully guided the Korea Army; why was the Kwantung Army not being controlled similarly this time? Inada replied that the Kwantung Army Operations officers were all excellent. "Some are better than we are," said Inada; "even if we don't direct them, they can and will solve matters." Kōtani argued against this. "They may be excellent staff officers," he told Inada, "but there is a big difference between people on the spot and those who see the big picture. You must guide the Kwantung Army." Inada, however, insisted that the Kwantung Army staff officers were all "great men," so "let's not say unnecessary things to them." Perhaps Inada's words were sarcastic, thought Kōtani, but he could not very well defy the stand of the full colonel who headed the AGS Operations Section.[28]

Even within the narrower military context, the 23rd Division's ignorance of the real size and quality of hostile forces behind or at the front can only be termed abysmal. Intelligence was still emphasizing that MPRA forces constituted the main ingredient of the opposition and was typically underestimating them. At the time Komatsubara's forces sortied from Hailar in late June, his intelligence indicated that the enemy possessed only 1,000 men, ten field pieces, ten antiaircraft guns, and something more than ten armored vehicles in the Nomonhan sector. The division was so ill-acquainted with the projected battlefield that it took days to decide upon a suitable site to cross the Halha.[29]

Two particular episodes illustrate the Kwantung Army's overconfidence. At the beginning of July, a pair of AGS officers flew from Tokyo to Hsinking, where they offered to arrange the transfer of the 5th Division from strategic reserve in China. Terada and his associates said it was not needed. In addition, the North China Area Army commander, Gen. Sugiyama Hajime (Gen), told his liaison officer at Kwantung Army headquarters, Lt. Col. Yabe Chūta, to say that four divisions could be spared, if desired. Ueda, delighted with Sugiyama's fraternal offer of assistance, referred Yabe to his Operations Section. There Tsuji declaimed: "Never mind about sending divisions to the Kwantung Army. If you have so many 'spares,' take care of your own campaign against the Chinese bandits." Naturally Yabe censored this barbed statement when he reported to Sugiyama.[30]

Those involved in the day-to-day planning of the Japanese offensive were well aware of the immense difficulties confronting them. They knew that the basis for the Kwantung Army's operational doctrine was swiftness and overkill in springing a trap; logistics, in particular, was a subordinate consideration. Even if one could not be entirely ready with such matters as ammunition stocks and bridging equipment, time must not be "wasted." The Kwantung Army operations officers' approach was the opposite of "slow but sure."[31]

Departing by train from Tsitsihar for Hailar with his 1,500 men of the 7th Division's veteran 26th Infantry Regiment, Col. Sumi Shin'ichirō had his own misgivings. The only Soviet intelligence expert among his division's regimental commanders, Sumi wondered privately whether Komatsubara and Ōuchi were overly optimistic and, on the basis of the misleading experience on the Amur in 1937, were taking the enemy too lightly. Had not Changkufeng revealed new strength on the part of the Russians the year before? It was also known that the Red Army possessed large armored forces. Yet Sumi's regiment had no more than six heavy machine guns, six battalion guns, two mortars, and some unimpressive little satchel charges for antitank defense. Rations sufficed only for two meals per day per soldier, one of rice and one of hardtack. Even the trucks were commandeered, with civilian drivers. Although Sumi hoped that he was not being overly pessimistic, he "feared that we were in for serious trouble, for our equipment was lamentably inadequate."[32]

If this was the real situation inside a regiment of the elite 7th Division, about which the Kwantung Army boasted so often, one can imagine the pathetic conditions in the 23rd Division that caused Colonel Chikazawa, its ordnance bureau chief, to shoot himself on the day the main formations left

Hailar for the front. Although the suicide was hushed up, it was common knowledge on the divisional staff that Chikazawa, a fine officer with a keen sense of responsibility, was appalled by the "awful equipment" that he was powerless to improve. The infantry group commander, a recipient of one of the last testaments penned by the colonel, speculated that Chikazawa had become hopelessly oppressed by such problems as moving out the troops and the ammunition. Komatsubara referred to the probability of excessive "nervous strain."[33]

Gratified by Ueda's trust in him, however, and eager to even the score with the enemy who had destroyed Azuma and his men, Komatsubara threw himself into the task of moving out his division rapidly and well. Capt. Hara Seiroku of the logistics staff felt that the general was growing "emotionally involved" in the operation. Even Tsuji, an inveterate critic, admitted that Komatsubara never grumbled throughout the Nomonhan Incident. The new division sought to prove itself. Although every kind of vehicle was pressed into service—from civilian sources and the South Manchuria Railway as well as the army, including antiaircraft and artillery units' trucks—there was insufficient transportation to move the troops and equipment at once. Scheduled shuttles to Chiangchunmiao, 12 hours each way, were necessary. But the infantry units that were ready in Hailar could not be held for the trucks. Under a fierce red sun—bigger than one ever saw in Japan—with little rest and less water, and hauling 80-pound loads on their backs, the soldiers trudged 250 km. across the treeless steppes to the front. In some units, the field-grade officers were mounted. When the group commander met elements of the foot regiments arriving near Chiangchunmiao on 27 June, they struck him as "rather exhausted" after having been on the march for almost six days. One battalion of the 64th Infantry, numbering 625 men and 41 horses, had covered between 32 and 48 km. during each of the last four days of marching, the rates depending on the distance between food caches and sources of water. According to the records of an infantry company of the excellent 26th Regiment, the unit was on the march between 10 and 15 hours per day for six days.[34]

In retrospect, Kwantung Army and other Japanese officers feel that, apart from Ueda's humane objections to the proposed treatment of Komatsubara, it would have been far better, as originally intended, to use the 7th Division. The latter not only had a splendid reputation dating back to the Russo-Japanese War but also was a four-regiment, "square" division of two brigades. Additionally, it was deployed in reserve in the Manchurian hinterland, whereas the 23rd Division, despite its many weaknesses, was responsible for safeguarding the vast western frontier domain encompassing sectors of far greater importance than bleak Nomonhan. One dangerous feature of the Japanese offensive plan was the inevitable denuding of the vital Manchouli-Hailar defenses. This calculated risk was based on the urgent need to mass forces at the Halha and on the specious premise that escalation need not be feared. Still, the Air Division commander was instructed to take precautionary measures in the Manchouli region at the same time that he was to support the main offensive at Nomonhan. Even if the powerful 7th Division had been employed in toto, the hawks have to admit, it could not have coped with the enormous Russian forces that appeared unexpectedly on the battlefield.[35]

The Kwantung Army's Unauthorized Air Offensive

While Kwantung Army preparations for the ground offensive proceeded, the air war resumed in earnest, 25 days after the major encounters of 28 May. According to the Russian version, 95 Soviet planes shot down 31 of 120 Japanese aircraft over Outer Mongolian territory on 22 June, at a cost of 12 planes. Zhukov adds that many Heroes of the Soviet Union took part in the dogfights and "gave the Japanese a lesson to remember."[1] As would be true throughout the Nomonhan fighting, the Soviet and Japanese accounts are irreconcilable. The Japanese assert that they encountered the largest Soviet aerial formations to date on the 22nd in the Kanchuerhmiao-Amukulang sector, totaling between 140 and 150 I-15 and I-16 fighters. Russian sources may be correct in estimating the Kwantung Army's available aircraft strength at 120, but IJAF records and interviewees indicate that only two Japanese interceptor squadrons, totaling no more than 18 or 19 planes, actually engaged the enemy. The Japanese state that, in two giant battles, 49 Russian aircraft were downed for sure (with another seven probables), at a cost of seven planes, four pilots killed, and two pilots wounded. The Japanese dead included the 24th Group's 2nd Squadron leader, Capt. Morimoto Shigenobu, lost in a melee involving 12 I-15's. One Japanese pilot bailed out and was taken prisoner. Presumably he was among those listed as killed at the time.[2]

Since the dogfighting on 22 June was his first combat experience, the day is recalled with particular vividness by Kira Katsuaki, a 20-year-old staff sergeant aviator at the time. His squadron, the 2nd, which got its 19 confirmed kills in about eight minutes, met 62 enemy planes coming from the Lake Buir area: 12 I-15's and 25 I-16's at 4,000 meters, and 25 more I-16's at 5,500 meters. The Japanese pilots zoomed up from 3,000 meters, with the western sun in their eyes, soared above the Russians (who never saw them), and dived on their tails. Kira used up all of his 7.7-mm. machine gun ammunition in destroying one I-16. There were so many planes in the air that collisions were a serious problem for both sides. Lacking ammunition and without the possibility of reloading, Kira "scared off" an I-15 and two I-16's by acrobatic flying, then joined two similarly disarmed Japanese planes to force two I-15's (abandoned by the speedier I-16's) to crash to earth. After counting the pillars of smoke billowing up from downed enemy planes, the

Japanese pilots ineffectually but aggressively "buzzed" Mongolian troops who were digging positions, and then flew home. The 2nd Squadron had done its fighting on the eastern or right side of the Halha, but the 1st Squadron fought another 100 enemy fighters, plus those fleeing from the 2nd Squadron, in "hot pursuit" over Mongolian territory. For their lopsided successes, the Japanese fighter units received a certificate of appreciation from the Kwantung Army commander.[3]

Already inflamed by the "vulgar" Soviet air raids against targets inside Manchuria, the Kwantung Army air force and headquarters Operations officers were vexed by the impunity with which the enemy sent a mass of 150 aircraft to sweep the skies over the right side of the Halha. Since the Japanese air force had "one hand tied behind its back" and was allowed only to intercept, the enemy might feel free to launch long-range heavy bombers against Hailar and Tsitsihar, perhaps against Hsinking and Seoul, and perhaps, some warned, even against the Japanese homeland itself. Whereas Kwantung Army air strength was finite and relatively small, Soviet aviation resources and reserves seemed unlimited. Although the foe had lost an estimated 118 aircraft from May through 22 June, Giga's 2nd Air Division remained chronically outnumbered, and his pilots were being worn down by the constant flying and fighting. Furthermore the success of the impending ground offensive would be endangered unless the sky was safe.

Hence the air units pressed the Air Division, which pressed the Kwantung Army, to give up the exhausting piecemeal method of flying patrol after patrol to "greet" intruders only inside Manchurian airspace. Instead of waving a fan to shoo off flies, common sense dictated fumigation of the breeding grounds. This would be the most efficient and least costly method of using Japanese air power. To those few who might worry about projecting offensive operations too deeply into the enemy's hinterland, the air officers provided the casuistic reassurance that the Mongolian airfields were battlefield airdromes, not rear bases—i.e. tactical rather than strategic targets. Anyhow, semantic niceties had not prevented the Russians from attacking Arshaan, Kanchuerhmiao, and Amukulang. Advice from Col. Doi Akio, a highly regarded former Kwantung Army staff officer who was now military attaché in Moscow, also encouraged the staff in Hsinking to nip Soviet offensive actions in the bud. The USSR, Doi judged, had no intention of waging a full-scale war in the Far East, given the critical situation in Europe. Giga says he told the Kwantung Army chief of staff and headquarters officers that if the army commander would not authorize a thrust against the air bases across the border, Giga would order it himself.

To document estimates of the hostile aerial buildup inside eastern Outer Mongolia, the Kwantung Army air force released long-range reconnaissance planes to overfly MPRA airdromes. Air staff officer Lt. Col. Miyoshi Yasuyuki, who was naturally very sympathetic to his air force colleagues' pleas for action, took a fast headquarters scout plane from Hsinking in the early hours of 23 June and flew to the eastern salient of the Mongolian People's Republic. At Tamsag, Madat, and Bain Tumen (Sanbeise), he observed a total of about 200 enemy planes on the ground.[4] Miyoshi became more convinced than ever that aerial battles of encounter would not suffice; the Japanese air force must strike at the roots of hostile airpower, for the Soviet attacks against Arshaan and other points must have originated here. As soon as he got back to Hsinking, around 9 A.M. on the morning of the 23rd, Miyoshi presented his findings to Ueda. An hour later, Ueda and his senior deputies had allowed themselves to be convinced by the hawks, and the Kwantung Army finally issued an order unleashing the air force in a positive role. In accordance with Operations Order No. A-1, the Kwantung Army would destroy air units stationed in Mongolia. At an appropriate time, the 2nd Air Division was to attack bases in the vicinity of Tamsag, Madat, and Bain Tumen and wipe out hostile aircraft.[5]

The Kwantung Army's climactic decision was kept unusually secret. Tokyo was not advised beforehand because of private dread that the High Command would cancel the order if it heard about it in time. The unimpressive argument was propounded that no imperial order was necessary for an "internal" matter of the field army. The bad lesson of the bombing raid on Chinchow in 1932 (which embarrassed the Japanese government) was ignored, as was the instructive lesson of Changkufeng in 1938, when the AGS kept the air force on a very tight leash. Tsuji's quaint explanation is that the Kwantung Army had a "playful" notion (*chamekke*) of "making Tokyo happy" by conducting matters silently, achieving great results, and only then reporting the good news. Therefore an Operations officer, Shimanuki Takeharu, who was leaving for Tokyo on 23 June on other business was to report "incidentally" about Operations Order No. A-1, preferably just before or just after the IJAF offensive had been mounted. In Manchuria, only air force officers and selected Kwantung Army staff members were let in on the secret, and the order was not transmitted by telegram but delivered personally by Miyoshi to 2nd Air Division headquarters at Hailar. Operations officers Terada and Hattori had already flown to Hailar to confer with the 23rd Division and the Air Division about synchronization of the air and land offensives. The ground attack had been tentatively scheduled for about 30 June, so it was agreed that, depending on the weather, the air offensive was to begin one to three days beforehand. The Air Division received orders accordingly from the Kwantung Army.[6]

Somehow the AGS did hear rumors about the unilateral air attack plan. Tsuji, Hattori, and other Kwantung Army officers were convinced that Katakura of the civil affairs section "spilled the beans" to Tokyo. Katakura still regards as slanderous Tsuji's allegation that he broke security; working through their mutual colleague Hattori, Katakura forced a retraction in later editions of Tsuji's postwar book on Nomonhan. What happened in June 1939, insists Katakura, is that he was getting ready to fly to Tokyo around the 20th on matters affecting his own section when Terada told him that the Kwantung Army was thinking of conducting an air raid to root out the bases of Soviet aerial attacks against Manchuria. Katakura replied that the Kwantung Army's right of self-defense was probably the best justification. Terada agreed and asked Katakura to "conduct liaison" and convey a "hint" unofficially to the High Command. In Tokyo, Katakura did what Terada had suggested. Katakura stresses that his duties in civil and diplomatic affairs gave him the right to explain operational intentions, but that Tsuji had jumped to conclusions because of hard feelings between them.[7]

Until now, relations between the Kwantung Army and the AGS had been proceeding smoothly. Constantly reassured from Hsinking, the central authorities were convinced that the field army was doing its best to localize matters. There seemed to be sound reasons for the drafting of the ground offensive plan: "operational necessity" apparently justified a temporary sweep across the Halha, although the use of such large forces, in division strength and above, ordinarily should have been reported to higher headquarters beforehand. If the Kwantung Army asked first, the High Command could at least make suggestions and changes easily; but if a post factum report were submitted, it was extremely difficult to modify a decision approved by the very senior full general who always commanded the Kwantung Army. The orders and directives to that army never contained detailed requests but were couched in respectful and often vague or circumlocutory phraseology. After all, Ueda was a fine old general, the Kwantung Army had been cooperative in recent years, and Terada, Hattori, and Tsuji were capable staff officers. Whereas the 19th Division had been a "sitting duck" at Changkufeng hill in 1938, a reinforced Japanese infantry division on the attack ought to be able to dispose of the Nomonhan affair quickly and easily, even though the Russians were not as weak an enemy as the Chinese. There had been dozens of affrays on the Manchurian borders, and none had got out of hand. Of course the High Command was also seriously distracted by more vital considerations than strategically unimportant Nomonhan: the China war, the Tientsin crisis with the British, and the problem of forging the Tripartite Alliance.[8]

For the preceding reasons, the Kwantung Army's ground offensive plan elicited a sympathetic response in Tokyo at an important conference between war ministry and AGS officials about 22 June. Although the war ministry's Military Affairs Section was opposed to the Kwantung Army's aggressive stance, the overall feeling of the conferees was to leave matters to the field army. Even the influential chief of the AGS Operations Section, Inada Masazumi, was basically amenable to the Hsinking staff's handling of the border dispute, though he would later become involved in a career-jarring row with the Kwantung Army. The dissident view left little impression, and War Minister Itagaki, a veteran of the Manchurian Incident, concurred easily with the feelings of consensus. A one-division "demonstration in force" did not displease him.

Thus was lost the best opportunity to restrain the Kwantung Army during the entire Nomonhan affair. Indeed, the High Command went out of its way to help the field army at this stage. On 22 June the AGS Operations Bureau chief sent the Kwantung Army a message expressing concern about the need to provide sufficient strength, especially in artillery, to chastise the Soviet-MPRA forces, given the weakness of the 23rd Division's equipment (as demonstrated in May) and the power of the enemy. Subsequently, it was decided to send reinforcements from the homeland: a 10-cm. artillery and 15-cm. howitzer regiment under a brigade commander, four companies of supply vehicles, balloon and signal elements, and some antiaircraft guns.[9]

In view of the existing rapport between the staffs in Hsinking and Tokyo, the hints of a covert Kwantung Army decision to use the air force flabbergasted the High Command. Maj. Miyashi Minoru, an AGS air staff officer, explains how he was torn between his personal views as an airman and his official views as a staff member. He had not been surprised by the Russians' "battlefield" bombing of Kanchuerhmiao, but the attack on Arshaan, clearly a rear base, was extremely significant and gave evidence of a Soviet intention to enlarge the fighting. In the Japanese air force in those days, the debate about aerial doctrine (between the concept of close support and the Douhet-Mitchell conception of an independent air force) was unresolved. The AGS, which regarded ground battle as decisive, tended to favor the close-support view, but many experienced officers like Miyashi were devotees of Douhet. Not only the Kwantung Army bomber group officers but also Kwantung Army air officer Miyoshi and Giga's senior operations officer Shimanuki Tadamasa were known as strong Douhet men, and the Douhet philosophy was undoubtedly gratifying to vigorous staff officers such as Hattori and Tsuji too. Now, in late June 1939, proponents of the bomber felt that a "wrapping cloth" (*furoshiki*) ought to be draped over the Mongolian air bases. Offensive action was particularly important for the side that lacked numerical superiority, as the Chinese strategist Sun Tzu had taught. Still, bombing the interior of another country might cause unpredictable levels of retaliation, for which the Russians were noted. In the painful struggle between heart and head, the AGS could only regard inland bombing as out of the question. The Nomonhan Incident had to be limited, from the larger view.[10]

Within a day of the secret decision to mount an air offensive, on the evening of 24 June the Kwantung Army received a wire from the AGS deputy chief reiterating that the General Staff was determined to localize the frontier dispute and expressing the belief that this policy accorded with the views of the Kwantung Army. While ground operations were being undertaken to expel invaders in the west, it was imperative that fighting be avoided on other fronts. The bombing of the Outer Mongolian interior was deemed to be inappropriate, for it would cause gradual aerial escalation by both sides against targets across the borders and would delay settlement of the Nomonhan Incident. Lt. Col. Arisue Yadoru was being sent to Kwantung Army headquarters on 25 June for "operational liaison." Miyashi remembers that Arisue, the AGS Operations Subsection chief, volunteered to fly to Manchuria. Since interpretations might vary and telegrams alone could not restrain the "wild horses" at Kwantung Army headquarters, Arisue—a persuasive "debater"—could be expected to do the job.[11]

The AGS message, phrased gently and graciously, represented no order to the Kwantung Army. It embodied open dissent and a covert hope that the field army would stop the air offensive of its own free will. Although addressed to the Kwantung Army chief of staff, the telegram from Tokyo may not have been shown to him or to the army commander; both Ueda and Isogai were responsible general officers who would not have deliberately flouted a communication from the AGS deputy chief of staff. But the Kwantung Army operations officers, who did see the message, were incensed at the dispatch of official cautions about a matter that they had never communicated to Tokyo in the first place. They pondered the source of the leak and, more importantly, the fate of the air thrust, which seemed as important to them as ever. The reports from daily reconnaissance flights were not reassuring. On 24 June, 185 medium and small enemy aircraft were sighted on the airdromes in eastern Mongolia: 135 in the vicinity of Tamsag; 39 southeast of Lake Buir; 11 elsewhere. Four heavy aircraft were also noted at Tamsag. The situation at Madat and Bain Tumen was unclear. Although the weather was poor on 25 June, morning scouts reported 50 planes, including one heavy aircraft, east of Bain Tumen and 44 elsewhere. Soviet air strength in the forward zone was now estimated at four fighter and two scout battalions plus one heavy bomber brigade.[12]

Air battles of encounter were also continuing. On 23 June, one of five enemy fighters sighted over Lake Buir had been downed by two Japanese aircraft, at the cost of a plane and a pilot. Next day, between 12 and 17 out of a total of 60 I-15's and I-16's were claimed to have been shot down south of Amukulang-Kanchuerhmiao by a Japanese fighter squadron. One IJAF interceptor and pilot were lost, and eight planes were damaged. The Japanese encountered three Soviet low-wing fighters this day—I-17's or improved I-16's—that were too fast for them, but a Russian plane that made an emergency landing was retrieved in flightworthy condition.[13] According to Russian records, 25 of 60 Japanese fighters were shot down on the 24th in the course of a "thorough thrashing" by 60 Soviet aircraft, whose losses were only two.[14] IJA intelligence heard that Russian authorities in Chita were being advised by front-line subordinates that, as of 24 June, Soviet fighters were doing better in combat than they had previously.[15]

Since there were very close connections between the timing of the proposed Japanese aerial offensive and the approved ground operations, the Kwantung Army staff officers feared that if they voluntarily suspended the air strikes, the High Command would transmit an imperial order canceling their plan permanently. Arisue's mission could be guessed; perhaps the Kwantung Army operations officers also knew the details, for there were secret telephone connections between them and the General Staff.[16] Apparently some reassurances were transmitted privately to Tokyo. On the afternoon of 24 June, an AGS officer on temporary duty in Hsinking telephoned IJA intelligence in Tokyo to say that the atmosphere at Kwantung Army headquarters was excellent. The High Command could rest easy because certain "countermeasures" were being conducted with "firm faith," and the field army's reporting was fast and trustworthy.[17] Nevertheless, the Kwantung Army felt that it dared not wait for Arisue to arrive in Hsinking. An effort was made to recall Shimanuki Takeharu from his now-unnecessary trip to Tokyo, but the communication did not reach him. To get the jump on Arisue, Tsuji therefore prepared a message on the morning of 25 June, in Terada's name and addressed to the 2nd Air Division chief of staff. For various reasons, said the wire, the time had become ripe to implement the Kwantung Army's instructions for an aerial offensive. It should be launched immediately, preferably next day, 26 June, if possible.[18]

Acting like "children who cannot fathom their parents' thinking" (according to Inada), the Kwantung Army proceeded to "double-cross" the High Command by turning loose the 2nd Air Division. Peeved individuals on the General Staff felt that the Kwantung Army was paying no attention to the domestic or external effects of its actions and lacked composure or vision. Surely Giga or his chief of staff, Col. Kusunoki Nobukazu, to whom the Kwantung Army's message of 25 June was addressed, must have noticed that the instructions originated with the Operations Section chief and did not bear the authentication of the army commander or chief of staff. The recipient should have verified the originator's authority, especially in such a crucial instance. Perhaps there was some "unofficial" coordination, but whether there was or not, 2nd Air Division headquarters was as excited as the hawks at the Kwantung Army and chose to interpret Terada's communication as an order, which it was not.[19]

In Hailar the elated Giga asked no official questions while preparing for the air thrust as soon as possible. Weather cannot have played much of a part in the decision to delay the raid by a day, for there was heavy aerial combat on 26 June. IJAF accounts claim that 16-18 of 50-60 Soviet fighters were downed, without loss.[20] Russian sources assert that on this day 50 Soviet planes intercepted as many as 60 IJAF aircraft over the Mongolryba sector of Lake Buir, shot down 25 at a cost of two or three fighters in a "ruthless dogfight" lasting two hours, and chased the surviving Japanese to Kanchuerhmiao. "Everything showed," Zhukov wrote, "that the Japanese pilots taking part in this battle were more experienced than their predecessors and yet they could not gain victory." Between 22 and 26 June the Japanese had supposedly lost 64 aircraft, although they had brought air force aces from the China theater.[21] One wonders whether the reference to China bespeaks the Russians' covert intention to divert Japanese strength from there (as the Kwantung Army staff had speculated) or at least to convince the hard-pressed Nationalist Chinese government that some relief had already been given.

Last-minute reconnaissance reports available to Giga on 26 June repeated the information that approximately 200 single- and twin-engine enemy aircraft were deployed in the Tamsag complex of eastern Mongolia. That evening the Air Division commander and his chief of staff called in their wing leaders and staff only. In the presence of Kwantung Army officers Yano, Hattori, and Tsuji, who obviously approved of all his actions, Giga announced that the big raid against Tamsag would take place at about 6 A.M. next day, 27 June. It is difficult to ascertain the exact number of planes that took part in the offensive, but the following figures approximate the composition of the strike force:[22]

Parent Unit	Commander	No. and type of planes	Tactical units committed
7th Air Wing	Maj. Gen. Hōzōji Hisao	at least 12 I-100 (Fiat BR-20) heavy bombers	12th Air Group
9th Air Wing	Maj. Gen. Shimono Ikkaku	9-12 Type 97 heavy bombers and 6-10 light bombers	61st Air Group 10th Composite Air Group
12th Air Wing	Maj. Gen. Higashi Eiji	74-81 fighters	11th and 24th air groups reinforced by 1st Air Group

The 24th Group would fly top cover for the bombers; the 1st Group would fly the middle layer; and the 11th Group would conduct follow-up attacks. A dozen fast reconnaissance planes were assigned to assist the three wings.

Eager to participate in the raid, every healthy airman flew. In fact, all three air wing generals and every group leader, except one,[23] took part. Even the high-spirited Giga flew to Tamsag in an unescorted scout plane and arrived over the target in the midst of the strike.[24] The only staff officer who flew that day was the ubiquitous Major Tsuji from Kwantung Army headquarters. He prevailed on Yano and Giga to let him hitch a ride aboard a heavy bomber on the flank of the Hōzōji air wing, and experienced his usual share of hair-raising adventures during the sortie.[25]

Japanese preflight intelligence was very uneven. Fighter Group Leader Matsumura had heard that as many as 500 enemy planes were stationed in the Tamsag region. Although higher headquarters was using the figure of 200, just before the raid Bomber Wing Commander Shimono sent out three separate scout planes which reported sighting little more than 100 aircraft on the ground, mostly fighters. No printed intelligence reached Heavy Bomber Group Leader Mikami. From oral briefings, he heard that there were "many aircraft" in the Tamsag complex; such vagueness was "rough on the pilots." Fiat Bomber Commander Harada felt that the scouting had not been thorough. He saw no aerial photos, and targeting was primitive. As Harada recalls, his mission on 27 June was to "fly to Tamsag air base and bomb whatever you see."[26]

Since the slower Japanese bombers had farther to fly from their bases at Hailar, they left in darkness before the fighters. At his interceptor airdrome at Kanchuerhmiao, Lt. Col. Matsumura had a leisurely breakfast and was astonished to hear the bombers thundering overhead already. The IJAF fighters raced to catch up with the bombers but, when Matsumura was almost across Lake Buir, he could see sunlight glimmering on the wings of enemy fighters taking off, one after another, from the Tamsag area. Matsumura feared that enemy pursuit planes would be waiting for Mikami's heavy bombers, which had arrived over target ten minutes early. Nevertheless, the original surprise must have been complete, for there were no Soviet patrols airborne. Operating at 3,000 meters, Mikami's aircraft had dropped their 50-kg. high-explosive bombs from level flight on the east side of the Tamsag area. Somewhat slower than Mikami's bombers, which were operating under separate orders and with whom he had coordinated by phone only the night before, Harada and his gas-guzzling Fiats could not catch up. Mikami was returning when Harada arrived at Tamsag. He and Matsumura saw clusters of tents in the open field, and some dumps, but no control tower, no hangars, no buildings, and not many aircraft in the open on the ground. Enemy fighters that had been able to take off had already done so.

The smoke from Mikami's bombing had largely cleared. Harada's planes circled once and released their full loads of 600-700 kg. per bomber from about 3,700 meters, just inside the enemy's antiaircraft firing range. The flak was desultory. Harada does not think his bombing was very effective against the scattered targets on the west side; Tsuji adds that half of the bombs missed their targets. Lt. Col. Ōtsuka Torao's light bombers flew in at 4,000 meters at 270 kph. Although the skies were bright, the ground was only partially illumined and the targets were not clear. Only three hostile planes could be observed on the ground. The light bombers dived at an angle of 50 or 60 degrees and released their bombs at 700 meters, concentrating on the airstrip and camouflage nets. No interceptors were encountered, and no Japanese light bombers were hit.[27]

The bombers' first attack had forced the enemy fighters to scramble to avoid destruction on the ground. They came up singly, not in organized units, and were picked off by the dozen by the 1st and 11th fighter groups. It was as easy as "twisting an infant's hand," says Matsumura. Flying "cap" against possible enemy reinforcements, at an original altitude of 5,500 meters, the 24th Group envied its partners, who were "having all the fun." Kira observed black dots rising like ants through the early mist; Tsuji's image was of baby fish jumping out of water. Matsumura saw the shining green wings of the Soviet fighters, the red stars, and the flashing propellers. After the 24th Group was finally allowed to come down, it was almost too late to find hostile aircraft. Kira missed getting two I-16's that escaped into a layer of ground fog.[28]

When Matsumura returned to base between 7 and 8 A.M. on 27 June, the Air Division headquarters was relaxed and very satisfied with the reported results of the raid on Tamsag. Matsumura, however, argued that several hundred enemy planes might still be in the general area. He wanted the force to refuel and strike other important targets before it was too late. Giga authorized another bombing raid after noon, against Bain Tumen, much deeper inside Outer Mongolia, 320 km. west of the Halha. Even the fine Japanese Type 97 fighters needed to attach auxiliary fuel tanks for this long round trip. About the same number of IJAF planes participated in the second raid, less the light bombers. The synchronization of the heavy bomber groups was good this time, but the results were disappointing. Although IJA intelligence had reported a concentration of new Soviet aircraft from the Ural district, Bain Tumen proved to be only a hamlet with an airstrip and barracks. Mikami observed quite a few aircraft on the ground, more inside permanent hangars than outside. There were no enemy air patrols and not more than three planes took off, of which one was downed. Mikami was too busy to note if there was antiaircraft fire, but he remembers none. The bombers dropped their loads on some small buildings, hangars, and storage tanks, yet the raid seemed useless to the participants—especially to the fighter pilots, who saw almost no planes on the ground, had nobody to engage, and had to worry only about their fuel supply as the weather worsened. Matsumura wondered how Bain Tumen could be used as a combat base, so far from Nomonhan; perhaps it was a transient staging and refueling site.[29]

All in all, the great raid on Tamsag had proved to be a magnificent success for the attackers, especially for the fighter planes, during 20-30 minutes of combat. Initial reports indicated that 98 enemy aircraft were shot down for sure in the air, as well as six probables. Moderate damage was inflicted against ten planes on the ground, and slight damage to another ten or 20, quite apart from hits on ground facilities and personnel.[30] The reports were refined in the course of subsequent recording. The 11th Fighter Group's "bag" was given as 50 fighter planes shot down and three unconfirmed; the 1st Group, 45 confirmed and three probables. Flying top cover, the 24th Group claimed only three planes. In addition, the light bombers reported inflicting heavy damage on eight small or medium aircraft, and slight to moderate damage on another 30. The Fiat bombers heavily damaged two small planes and slightly or moderately damaged eight more. Severe damage to three Soviet heavy bombers was observed by the 61st Bomber Group. Even omitting the six planes whose downing was unconfirmed, the air division claimed to have destroyed 98 aircraft, to have heavily damaged 13, and to have moderately or slightly damaged 38, for a grand total of 149.[31]

About 30 percent of the Japanese heavy bombers were hit, mainly by antiaircraft fire, and almost all the fighters from the two main groups incurred some damage. A heavy bomber was downed by an interceptor, two fighters were lost, and one headquarters scout plane disappeared. The heavy bomber aboard which group leader Mikami was flying encountered trouble in one of its two engines while over Mongolia. The pilot nursed it back across the Halha to a temporary airstrip near Chiangchunmiao, where a second bomber picked up Mikami.[32] In all, seven men were killed on the raid and two were wounded. These material and manpower losses were relatively trifling in view of the results claimed.[33]

The atmosphere at Giga's headquarters after the raids of 27 June was one of exultation. It had been the first Japanese air offensive against Russians, and the psychological effects were exhilarating.[34] A Japanese correspondent likened the IJAF victors to "an eagle attacking little sparrows." Although the number of enemy planes claimed to have been destroyed was large, the main consideration was that a Japanese bomber and fighter force had engaged and shattered the foe. Veterans of the raid were much moved by the majestic sight of so many friendly aircraft roaring into action; a formation of over 100 planes was awesome in those days. The airmen also were impressed by the scenes of dogfighting reminiscent of feats they had read about from the First World War in Europe, and by the pillars of smoke rising from enemy aircraft downed in profusion on the plains of Hulun Buir.[35]

Inevitably, there was criticism of the attack forces' large claims. Shimono thinks that the figures may have been excessive by a factor of two or three, and that the number of enemy planes destroyed was closer to 26 confirmed. Matsumura disagrees because of the large number of aircraft caught on the ground or trying to take off—a very vulnerable time for any plane. According to Miyashi, the Kwantung Army did not fabricate its reports; it only conveyed data collected by Giga from his individual pilots. Unintentional duplication was unavoidable. Combat leaders, pressed to report quickly, could not very well doubt, contest, or verify their subordinates' claims. Confirmation was especially difficult when, for example, a hostile plane disappeared exuding smoke behind enemy lines but was not seen to crash.[36]

The Soviet authorities, who commenced press coverage of the Nomonhan Incident only from 26 June, referred to the Japanese thrust of the 27th as "new raids on the territory of Outer Mongolia in the region of Tamsag and Bain Tumen." The IJAF strike force was rather accurately estimated at 80 fighters and 30 bombers, but the claim that 100 of the Japanese aircraft were brought down is ridiculous. Soviet losses were given as 33 planes.[37] IJA intelligence learned that on 27 June the Trans-Baikal military district was advised that, in the raid on Tamsag that morning, 12 headquarters planes were lost and the repair facilities of the Yakovlev mechanized brigade were damaged. Reinforcements of two air brigades had been sent to Bain Tumen.[38] Zhukov slurs over the period between 27 June and 1 July as characterized by almost daily dogfights, "although they were not as fierce as before. In these battles our pilots improved their skill and steeled their will for victory." Although this description is not very helpful, Zhukov is right in surmising that "the increased activity of the enemy Air Force was not accidental. We believed that the activization of the Japanese Air Force aimed to deal a serious blow at our Air Force and gain air superiority to support the forthcoming major Japanese offensive."

Meanwhile, Kwantung Army staff officer Shimanuki Takeharu hand-carried Operations Order No. A-1 to Tokyo, authorizing the 2nd Air Division's attack into Mongolia. He had not received the message asking him to return to Hsinking, and he had used a slow means of transportation rather than take a plane, so that he finally arrived only on the evening of 26 June. Those in the know at Kwantung Army headquarters were personally sorry that he was being put on the spot, and they wondered if he would, on his own initiative, put off reporting until the Tamsag raid had been carried out. It was hoped that he would play a great scene called *haragei*—"belly talk" or psychological dissimulation. There was no need for concern in Hsinking;

Shimanuki Takeharu conducted his task well. He should of course have conveyed Operations Order No. A-1 to the General Staff as soon as he arrived, no matter how late in the day. But he did not report until next morning, when the great dawn raid was over, and he endured whatever criticism he received with stoicism and dignity.[39]

Inada was furious when he learned about the raid and the way it had been handled by the Kwantung Army. He felt particularly betrayed by Shimanuki Takeharu, who had belonged to Inada's own AGS Operations Section and had been assigned to the Kwantung Army recently to enhance relations between the commands, not to "play a prank" when the stakes were as dangerous as at Nomonhan that summer. Inada remembers how Shimanuki sat listening impassively to what he said, giving no excuse and no answer. Some of the Kwantung Army hawks later insisted feebly that the whole episode was the product of sheer coincidence. Shimanuki himself, queried after the war, denies that he was up to anything and insists that "playacting" on his part is an exaggeration.

Relations between the High Command and the Kwantung Army were never the same afterward. When Inada had Terada on the phone from Hsinking and heard the boasts about the Tamsag raid, Inada bawled out his old friend and classmate mercilessly, yelling that combat results were not all that mattered and that the press releases must be "killed" immediately. Terada began mumbling, which struck Inada as strange. Later it was learned that Tsuji and Hattori were by the phone next to Terada. They heard Inada calling their chief a fool, and they saw Terada blanch and his hands shake. Inada admits that he may have acted childishly, but he felt that the Kwantung Army was getting out of hand, and he feared that more air raids were being launched or were being contemplated.[40]

Perhaps Lieutenant Colonel Arisue could have exerted some influence on the Kwantung Army's implementation of the Tamsag raid if there had been time. He was to have reached Hsinking from Tokyo by 26 June, but bad weather delayed his flight and he did not arrive until the 27th. It was by now academic to contest the field army's victorious aerial action. A man of gentle and cheerful personality, Arisue lacked the inclination or the temperament to argue the AGS position with the stubborn self-righteousness of his superior, Inada. Nor could he, a field-grade officer, very well have challenged a decision apparently sanctioned by the full general commanding the Kwantung Army. Why fuss, under the circumstances?[41] Although the similarities are not precise, there are ironic resemblances between envoy Tatekawa's sleeping through the outbreak of the Mukden Incident in September 1931 and envoy Shimanuki's dillydallying en route to Tokyo or envoy Arisue's delayed arrival in Hsinking in June 1939.

The Nomonhan Incident was already troubling the highest authority as

early as 21 June, when the Emperor had discerned possible connections between Outer Mongolian activities and the Tientsin crisis, and had pressed
for an early solution to the latter problem. When the AGS chief requested
authorization on 24 June to send a brigade of artillery reinforcements to the
Kwantung Army, the monarch had approved but at the same time had expressed concern about mutual escalation of the frontier troubles. To his
chief aide and later to the AGS chief, the Emperor remarked that although
the army had spoken of localization in 1931, the Manchurian Incident had
expanded massively. The monarch wondered whether a border settlement
might not be the best approach, although the Kwantung Army apparently
had not wanted such a solution during earlier negotiations. In view of the
worsening military situation on the Mongolian frontier, the Emperor's idea
does not seem to have struck a responsive chord.

Then came news of the Tamsag raid, with its undertones of Kwantung
Army arrogance and violation of the structure of command, since Ueda had
not reported Operations Order No. A-1 beforehand. During a briefing by
his aide, the Emperor intimated that the Kwantung Army commander ought
to be given a warning and some kind of punishment. When the AGS deputy,
Lt. Gen. Nakajima Tetsuzō, advised the Throne about the Tamsag raid, a
rather angry monarch rebuked him and asked who would assume responsibility for the unilateral bombing of the interior of Outer Mongolia. Nakajima replied that military operations were still in progress but that the necessary measures would be taken when this phase had ended.[42]

Inada was distressed that the IGHQ chain of command, which had been
well established since the Changkufeng Incident, was sufficiently impaired
to warrant the imperial reproach of Nakajima. Some "irresponsible" officers
and cronies at the High Command level may have welcomed the Tamsag
raid because the Russians had been acting defiantly of late. Others merely
felt that the IJAF action was unavoidable. But the domestic press was playing up the air war in boastful style, and Inada and a number of his colleagues worried about the next step in the Nomonhan Incident. Though it
was still not generally believed that full-scale hostilities against the USSR
were imminent, there was widespread feeling in the High Command that
border incidents should be settled on the border and that the Kwantung
Army should not play the Russians' game. Had Terada lost his head or been
dragged along by thoughtless, irresponsible juniors? Inada sent him a strong
telegram to the effect that all Kwantung Army staff officers responsible
would be sacked in due course.[43]

On the very night of the Tamsag raid, the Kwantung Army chief of staff
received a radio message from the General Staff, indicating that the bombing of Outer Mongolian territory, which had just been learned of in Tokyo,
was "in fundamental disagreement with the policy which we understood

your army was taking to settle" the Nomonhan Incident. "It is regretted exceedingly," continued the AGS message, "that advance notice of your intent was not received. Needless to say, this matter is attended by such far-reaching consequences that it can by no means be left to your unilateral decision. Hereafter existing policy will be definitely and strictly observed." The communication ended with a request that the Kwantung Army's aerial attack program be canceled immediately.[44]

If the High Command had been astonished by the news of the Tamsag raid, Kwantung Army headquarters was rendered apoplectic by the General Staff's reaction. Just as Inada tended to blame Tsuji for agitating opinion in Hsinking, so the Kwantung Army hawks attacked Inada as the focal point for AGS timidity and rudeness. Inada, griped Tsuji, had not even had any combat experience; the desk warriors in Tokyo did their criticizing on paper, without deigning to send even one staff officer to inspect the real situation at the front. The General Staff was interfering in the details of the Kwantung Army's own business, just as had been done when the field army lost face during the Amur affair in 1937. Admittedly, the Kwantung Army owed Tokyo an apology for the "stunt" of not notifying the High Command about the Tamsag raid in advance. Yet if Inada had had the courtesy to congratulate the field forces for their spectacular success and had then asked for prior notification in future, the Kwantung Army would cheerfully have sent a telegram of apology. The airmen had risked their lives, and some had been lost, in a proper, retaliatory air strike. Now Inada and the doves were impolitely and insensitively hurting the feelings and trampling on the enthusiasm of the front-line troops. Was the AGS "friend or foe"?

In a state of great heat, a reply was drafted in the Operations Section for immediate transmission to the General Staff. The basic policy of the Kwantung Army, said the message, envisaged crushing the enemy's illicit designs at inception and forcing his complete submission, while contributing to the settlement of hostilities in the China theater by strengthening defenses in the north. There appeared to be "certain differences of opinion" between the AGS and the Kwantung Army "in evaluating the battlefield situation and the measures to be adopted," but it was requested that "handling of trivial matters in border areas be entrusted to this army."[45]

It was the High Command's turn to be incensed by what was deemed to be an intemperate, conceited, and insubordinate response by the Kwantung Army. Was the dispatch of over 100 fighters and bombers against the interior of a neighboring country a "trivial matter"? Did the Kwantung Army have the right to impose a war on Japan? Which was the High Command and which was the field army? Although the Kwantung Army's wire was conveyed in the name of the chief of staff, later examination of the message file revealed that Tsuji was the preparing officer and that no higher seals of authority were affixed. Had the Operations Section hawks gone so far as to send a brash message to the AGS deputy chief without going through Ueda, Isogai, or Yano? Inada, fed up, wanted Tsuji ousted from the Kwantung Army, but the chiefs of the personnel and assignments sections of the AGS and war ministry did not agree. Since Inada realized that ultimate responsibility for all officer personnel decisions lay with the war minister, he went directly to see General Itagaki. The latter, however, knew Tsuji personally as an able officer, regarded Inada's complaint as an overreaction, and left matters as is.

A situation had developed in which a mesmeric Kwantung Army staff officer, Tsuji, "defeated" a full colonel on the General Staff. Looking back, Inada thinks that he may have first antagonized the Kwantung Army staff unintentionally during his visit to Manchuria in mid-May. He had had a luncheon engagement with General Ueda on the 15th, but the OSS branch chief in Harbin had delayed him all day. Inada received an angry phone call from a Kwantung Army staff officer regarding his truancy, and a heated quarrel ensued about Inada's unprecedented "ignoring" of an appointment with the commanding general of the Kwantung Army. Inada believes that he was regarded as a "wise guy." Although he apologized subsequently to Ueda for having missed the luncheon, Inada remains convinced that the argument over a relatively small matter did exert a baleful influence on relations between him and the hotheaded Tsuji-Hattori group, at the subjective and emotional level.[46]

As the AGS and the war ministry now viewed matters, a number of crucial steps would have to be taken by imperial decree in order to localize the Nomonhan affair (specifically to prevent further air offensives inviting retaliation), to punish the Kwantung Army miscreants, and to counteract the ill effects of the field army's arbitrary and aggressive border guidelines of April. It would also be necessary to update and revise the very vague basic mission assigned to the Kwantung Army commander in 1932, whereby he was made responsible for the defense of Manchukuo and the Kwantung Leased Territory. Documents were drafted by 29 June, and the AGS chief, Prince Kan'in, obtained approval from the Emperor that afternoon. Learning from Kan'in that the army would give careful attention to the problem of dealing with the responsibility of the Kwantung Army commander, the Emperor remarked that there must be no repetition of recent events. When the monarch spoke with his chief aide in the evening, he indicated relief that the General Staff did not appear to be concealing anything from the Throne and that the AGS seemed to have pronounced views about handling the Kwantung Army's commanding general.[47]

Since "advice" to the Kwantung Army would no longer be sufficient, the High Command took steps to obtain imperial sanction for controlling orders. On 29 June an IGHQ order and an IGHQ directive were issued. Ueda was told that, depending on circumstances, areas where boundaries were in dispute with neighboring countries or where the use of troops was "unfeasible tactically" need not be defended. The Kwantung Army commander should further "endeavor to localize matters in settlement of border incidents."[48] In the IGHQ directive, which as always followed an IGHQ order, the army chief of staff issued specific instructions regarding the handling of the Nomonhan affair: "(1) Ground combat will be limited to the border region between Manchukuo and Outer Mongolia, east of Lake Buir; (2) enemy bases will not be attacked from the air."[49]

Immediately following the IGHQ order and directive came a detailed elaboration from the AGS deputy. The Kwantung Army commanding general was warned that the air raids against Tamsag and Bain Tumen had clearly exceeded mere border operations and therefore had required previous imperial authorization. An IGHQ order had been issued to clarify the fundamental mission of the Kwantung Army as well as the basic policy for dealing with frontier problems; the IGHQ directive indicated the responsibility of the field army to suspend the air offensives. The mission assigned to the Kwantung Army was consonant with the spirit of previous orders and regulations, and the basic concept coincided precisely with policies already pursued by the field army in carrying out its duties. Restraint upon the locale of ground combat was designed to facilitate the Kwantung Army's conduct of the impending offensive by the 23rd Division. Lastly, the AGS deputy addressed the vital question of border-crossing operations by the ground forces. With respect to the April border guidelines, it was regrettable that the Kwantung Army had not seen fit to request imperial sanction to carry out provisional actions beyond the frontier, based on the field army's interpretation of the guidelines as an extension of the defensive mission assigned the Kwantung Army commander. In the event that temporary border operations proved necessary in a "real emergency," the General Staff intended to seek imperial enabling authority, on a case-by-case basis.[50]

Operations Bureau chief Maj. Gen. Hashimoto Gun (certainly not Inada!) was sent to Kwantung Army headquarters to explain the General Staff's thinking in person.[51] Tsuji and his colleagues were not assuaged. Because the High Command lacked confidence in the Kwantung Army and expected that it was going to perpetrate "something terrible," the AGS was "binding the field army's hands and feet" by imposing a nonnegotiable IGHQ order and directive. It was the agony of the Kwantung Army, lamented Tsuji, to have to face "enemies on two sides"—that is, the Soviet-Mongolian forces in the field and the High Command at home. The Nomonhan Incident would have had a "glorious ending" for the Japanese, had it not been for the attitude of the central authorities.[52]

A more detached observer can only side with the Japanese High Command. Tsuji was a brave, able, and forceful officer, egocentric, hot-tempered, and rash; not even his most loyal supporters endorse his behavior in drafting messages emanating from Kwantung Army headquarters in connection with the Tamsag raid. The best explanation is that Tsuji was so trusted by General Ueda that the commander gave him a de facto proxy, with the force of Kwantung Army "orders." Terada would confess later that his Operations Section's hawkish handling of the Nomonhan crisis broke his heart.[53] Inada, of course, is convinced that the Kwantung Army's actions were characterized by amorality and trickery. Even the unemotional military historian Imaoka Yutaka, a former staff colonel, discerns dishonesty and impurity in the field army's actions of June 1939.[54]

18

On to Mongolia:
A Bridge Too Poor

The imperial order of 29 June had been designed to get the Kwantung Army commander "off the hook" at Nomonhan by assuring him that not every border trespass by hostile forces need be extirpated. By the time the order was issued, neither the 23rd Division commander nor the Kwantung Army Operations staff wanted to be excused from the task. Infantry units had begun the long, four- to six-day march of more than 200 km. from Hailar on 20-21 June, under enemy aerial surveillance part of the time.[1] Ammunition and rations were being hauled forward to Chiangchunmiao hamlet in about 350 trucks. Horses carried the machine guns and pulled the artillery, 50 per battery. The need for water sources slowed the horse units in particular.

Maj. Gen. Kobayashi Kōichi, the infantry group commander, had been ordered to the front with a regimental covering force on 22 June. Next day he and his spearhead elements, arriving in 55 trucks, were already in action against a small force of hostile armor, infantry, and cavalry that probed the defenses of the Chiangchunmiao area. All day on the 24th, larger enemy units attacked repeatedly, reaching a strength of 50-60 armored vehicles, 200 troops, and seven guns. Quickly learning from their mistakes, the Japanese began holding their fire until the range was less than 1,000 meters. Results were good on 24 June: 10-16 enemy armored vehicles and trucks were burned or knocked out (of which the foe retrieved four), and seven bodies were abandoned from a total estimated at more than 50 slain. IJA losses were six killed and 20 wounded.

From the initial actions Kobayashi, an experienced infantry commander, derived a number of impressions and lessons, many of which would be repeated during the Nomonhan fighting. Because Japanese cannon were few and ammunition was scant, superior tactics had to be stressed. Hostile tank fire slowed down after 30-minute barrages, perhaps because the gun barrels became overheated. Armor remained in combat from morning until night; when the vehicles withdrew for ammunition and fuel, artillery carried on the fighting. If forced back, enemy tanks could fire from hull-down positions. Since very few infantrymen accompanied armor, its effectiveness was greatly reduced. The secret to successful antitank combat was to draw the armor in close and to open fire during intervals in the bombardment.

Knocking out the lead tanks disconcerted attack formations. Hostile forces sought consistently to retrieve corpses and damaged vehicles left on the battlefield, generally under cover of a protective barrage. Japanese troops showed a regrettable lack of counterattacking spirit, which cost them the chance to capture dozens of vehicles. In addition, on one occasion during heavy rain, IJA soldiers fired excitedly at friendly aircraft.[2]

Whereas the melees in the Halha-Holsten confluence zone occurred in a region of admitted dispute, the enemy was now willing to fight inside an unmistakably Manchurian area at Chiangchunmiao. Additionally, IJA intelligence reported that, in the combat on 23-24 June, the hostile forces were definitely and entirely Russian.[3] Judging that "it would be detrimental to react passively" while enemy preparations were still incomplete, the Kwantung Army issued an attack order to the 23rd Division on 25 June. Komatsubara was to expedite concentration of the divisional main body at Chiangchunmiao and assume control over the Yasuoka mechanized detachment and Manchukuoan cavalry. To accomplish his mission of wiping out MPRA [*sic*] units in the Nomonhan region, the division commander might deploy forces temporarily to the western or left shore of the Halha. The Kwantung Army deputy chief of staff, Yano, hand-carried the offensive order to Komatsubara, who advanced to Chiangchunmiao on 27 June to assume personal command of the forces in the field. Before the 23rd Engineer Regiment commander, Lt. Col. Saitō Isamu, left Hailar for the front, he was told unofficially by the division chief of staff that he might have to build a bridge across the Halha. Most of the troop concentration was completed between 26 and 29 June. Yano remained to assist Komatsubara, joined by Tsuji, Hattori, and Captain Hara of the logistics section.[4]

To reconnoiter the site for a river-crossing operation was no easy matter for the 23rd Division, since the enemy commanded higher ground on the left shore and occupied a large foothold on the right. Komatsubara assigned Lieutenant Colonel Saitō the entire responsibility for selecting the best crossing point. Officer-led infantry and engineer patrols were dispatched to study possible fords and bridging sites and to familiarize themselves with the terrain. Although it had been thought that the Halha was only 50 meters wide, recent rains had swollen the width to 60, 80, or even 100 meters. The precipitation had also increased the river's depth to more than two meters, excessive for men or horses to ford. In some sectors the banks were gentle enough for soldiers to carry machine guns, but in many places there were steep inclines and extensive bogs, 20-30 cm. deep, unmanageable by foot troops. Both Saitō and the division commander strictly ordered the engineer teams "at least to touch" the opposite shore.[5]

An infantry battalion commander, then 36, remembers setting forth with two other officers and three men, all handpicked swimmers. On the first day the patrol tried to operate by daylight, but an enemy sniper, firing from a foxhole and probably using a telescopic sight, picked off and killed one of the Japanese soldiers. Thereafter the team hid in the grass by day, observed the area through binoculars, moved out "like cats" after twilight, and did most of their swimming before dawn, when neither side could see the other too clearly. The river was full of big Lake Buir fish that jumped loudly from the water at night and scared the Japanese into thinking that noisy enemy cavalrymen were crossing. This team did not proceed to the other shore; the best swimmer started across but turned back after testing the water's depth. About 29 June, following three or four days of scouting, the patrol returned to report.[6] On the 28th, an MPRA trooper from the 8th Cavalry Division was captured by Manchukuoan forces. Kobayashi had him sent to division intelligence for interrogation concerning possible crossing points.[7]

As early as 25-26 June, IJA intelligence noted that the enemy had prepared positions along both sides of the Halha; on the right bank three belts were identified. Ground patrols, however, could provide little information about the depth or extent of the Soviet-MPRA defenses, especially across the river, or about the number of enemy bridges. Engineer Saitō says he learned nothing specific about the spans, though he was extremely anxious to know. He suspected the existence of underwater bridges, and indeed Soviet sources reveal that such spans, about one foot below the water's surface, were developed for the first time during the Nomonhan hostilities.[8] To supplement the meager findings of the ground scouting parties, Japanese reconnaissance planes studied the entire Halha valley and reported one enemy pontoon bridge on the Halha at the confluence, another to the north near Hara Heights, and a third below the Holsten. Numerous photographic missions were also flown over the now-quiescent air bases in eastern Outer Mongolia and over the forward zones, with special reference to the region of the scheduled Japanese land offensive. Hostile ground movements were found to be very vigorous; estimates varied from 850 to 1,000 trucks and armored vehicles operating in total each day. One rough aerial count for the period following 20 June showed 655 vehicles on the left bank, 255 on the near side, north of the confluence, and another 60 south of the Holsten.[9]

Japanese air observers carefully photographed the enemy's left anchor at Bain Tsagan Obo on northern Hara Heights, the center positions at the main Komatsu Heights, and the right wing at Sambur Obo on Hamardaba Heights. The Kwantung Army had originally given serious thought to a river crossing somewhere south of the Holsten by Yasuoka's mechanized forces under the army's direct command. But Komatsubara and his staff, who had by now been given operational control of the Yasuoka detachment, judged that the 600 to 1,200 meters of swampland found on each side of the Halha below the Holsten was impassable by tanks and trucks. In addition, the rains had not only caused the river level to rise but had rendered the roads abominable, and the arrival of bridging matériel had been delayed. Consequently the southern plan was discarded. A crossing to the far north, against the region southeast of Lake Buir, was deemed feasible but too remote. Insofar as the engineers were concerned, a number of special desiderata remained to be met. River width could not exceed 80 meters, the maximum bridging capability. The preferred location should have easy transportation access from both sides. From the tactical point of view, the crossing should be away from the enemy concentrations at the confluence but not too far north, where the cliffs increase. For these reasons and on the basis of the information available to him, Saitō recommended and Komatsubara accepted the idea of forcing an infantry passage to the left shore of the Halha from the area of Fui Heights against Hara Heights, while the mechanized detachment struck against the confluence from the right side of the river.[10]

The Kwantung Army had directed the 23rd Division to launch its offensive as soon as preparations were completed. The process was far along when strange intelligence was received on 29 June from aerial reconnaissance and ground patrols: hostile forces seemed to have begun to retreat gradually since the previous night. In particular, many enemy vehicles appeared to be moving back to the left shore of the Halha.[11] Skeptics have wondered whether this unfounded intelligence was not concocted by hawkish Kwantung Army staff officers in order to prod Komatsubara and Yasuoka into faster action while the "therapeutic" effects of the Tamsag air raid could still be felt. Others think that the intelligence reports were authentic but that Japanese observers may have misinterpreted enemy ground movements. There was, of course, the precedent of the MPRA pullback in May when the Azuma detachment first sallied. General Kobayashi, for one, had an "empty feeling" now, lest the Japanese miss the prize by a slight mischance. His infantry group was preparing enthusiastically, with the engineers, for the river crossing. Covering-unit training was being conducted on the 30th when Komatsubara reached his decision: the 23rd Division must commence action quickly from the early hours of 1 July in order not to lose its opportunity. Oppressed by his sense of mission, Komatsubara had now probably become involved emotionally in the Nomonhan campaign.[12]

Drawn up by the 23rd Division at Chiangchunmiao in consultation with the Kwantung Army staff officers, especially Tsuji, the order of 30 June called for pinning and defeating hostile forces on the right shore while the river-crossing units swung around the enemy on the other bank and severed his line of retreat. (See Map 4.) With five infantry battalions from the 71st and 72nd regiments, Kobayashi was to leave Chiangchunmiao on the morning of 1 July; he was to commence his river-crossing action from Fui Heights

MAP 4: COMBAT OPERATIONS, 2-3 JULY 1939

during the night of the 2nd. Moving behind the infantry group, Komatsu-bara would bring up artillery and engineers and proceed across the Halha, too. The motorized reserves—three battalions of the 7th Division's 26th Infantry Regiment transferred from Yasuoka's command—would exploit the anticipated success by crossing the river and operating on Kobayashi's outer wing. On the right shore, Yasuoka's tank corps would follow Kobayashi and Komatsubara to the Fui area and, at dawn on the 3rd, strike toward the Halha-Holsten confluence while the main body of the 23rd Division was attacking across the river.[13] (For a complete list of the units deployed for this operation, see Table 18.1.)

Hara, the Kwantung Army logistics expert, was less than enthusiastic about the prospects for the river-crossing offensive. Although for some reason he had not participated in the operational planning session, he confided to Captain Itō (his successor as 23rd Division logistics officer) that he regarded the crossing operation as impossible. How could it be supported logistically? Itō replied blithely that he foresaw no problem: "We'll just cross the river, deal a blow, and come back." That much might be feasible, said Hara, but nothing more ambitious than a penetration could be supported across the river.[14]

The hurried order for the ground offensive caused immense confusion among the units assembled in the Chiangchunmiao area. Officers and men labored without rest to prepare for a quick departure. By 4 A.M. on 1 July, about 15,000 heavily laden troops had started to march westward some 30-35 km. across an arid plain. Col. Okamoto Tokuzō's 71st Infantry Regiment led the whole Kobayashi infantry group, followed by Col. Sakai Mikio's 72nd Infantry. Only the field-grade officers were mounted. Manchukuoan sentries were the first to sight some enemy armor at very long range, and at midday, with the desert sun beating down, advance elements moving north of Fui Heights came under accurate fire from elevations to the south. Japanese field artillery responded and, in Komatsubara's words, the infantrymen, "whose feet were aching and who were suffering from thirst, perked up." The hostile fire was coming from seven or eight armored vehicles and a half-dozen guns (tractor-pulled field guns and howitzers) emplaced on dunes 2,000 meters away. By evening, after IJA rapid-fire guns had set two or three tanks ablaze and the Japanese troops had advanced another 1,000 meters, the enemy, with about 300 infantry, finally withdrew. Ten bodies were found; the Japanese lost one killed and four wounded. Komatsubara and the division were cheered by this first little victory, and Kobayashi ordered a night attack to clear Fui Heights.[15]

Assembling the troops did not progress properly, however, and it was noon on 2 July before an attack battalion of the 72nd Infantry Regiment could

TABLE 18.1
Japanese Offensive Deployment, 2-4 July 1939

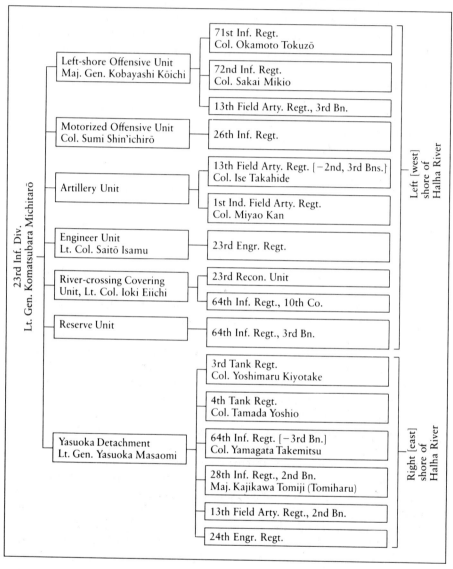

advance against Fui Heights. Even in daylight, there was a mistake in identification. The 1st Battalion occupied the wrong dunes, four to six km. northeast of Fui, an error that was not realized until evening. Col. Sumi Shin'ichirō explains the terrain problem: "When you hear the word 'heights,' you imagine a mountain or at least a hill. But here it meant something like a raised pancake, with a diameter of about three km. The area was like a sandy beach, with weeds as thin as joss sticks overlying the dry surface soil." [16]

Early on the 2nd, Japanese patrols from the 72nd Regiment reported sighting no enemy troops on the right side of the river in the Fui sector. The 3rd Company was sent out to cover engineer reconnaissance elements. Later in the morning, when the company was advancing toward the Halha four or five km. away, it sustained severe crossfire from eight or nine guns and over a dozen machine guns situated on the higher left shore. Soon afterward, 200-300 enemy troops appeared on the right bank, together with some (amphibious?) armor, and attacked the 3rd Company. Colonel Sakai directed the 1st Battalion commander, Maj. Nishikawa Masayuki, to relieve the isolated company. The regiment believed that artillery and air support, which it solicited, finally suppressed the hostile fire and extricated the company, but Major Nishikawa says the enemy merely disappeared after three hours of fighting.

To assume responsibility for the danger into which his 3rd Company had been placed, Nishikawa had sought death in battle. He stood up under fire and pushed back his helmet, in the hope of receiving an "easy" hit through the head; yet he was not shot and, by remaining upright, he could spot three cannon and 15-16 machine guns firing from across the river. Nishikawa refused two orders to pull back but, since the hostile fire was causing numerous casualties among his men who were huddled on the ground, he finally sat down. No enemy bodies were found; to Nishikawa, the action had been an "utter failure." By the time he withdrew after nightfall, his unit had lost 24 killed (including the company commander) and 55 wounded. A distraught and discouraged Nishikawa later reported the casualties to Komatsubara. The general told him not to despair: "Thanks to you, our river crossing succeeded." For, ironically, the mistakes of the Japanese infantry caused the enemy to expect a crossing 15 km. from the real site on the Halha. In this sense, the 72nd Regiment's troubles on 2 July amounted to an unintended but useful feint. [17]

Soviet sources would agree. The Soviet-MPRA military commanders had received no reports of a Japanese river-crossing operation against the left shore of the Halha near Bain Tsagan (Hara Heights), but they had heard of the Japanese tank-infantry offensive movement on the right bank against the Soviet 149th Infantry Regiment and 9th Mechanized Brigade. Already stimulated by aggressive Japanese air force activity in late June, which seemed to presage a large-scale attack, the Russian army command had been planning a powerful counteroffensive while retaining a tenacious foothold on the right side of the Halha. During the night of 1 July, Soviet reinforcements were sent out from Tamsag with orders to conduct a flank attack against Japanese forces on the right shore. The actual effect was to commit the following strength against the Kobayashi task force on the left bank: the 11th Tank Brigade, to deliver a flank attack from the north; the 7th Mechanized Brigade, to pin down the enemy from the front; and the 24th Motorized Infantry Regiment, to strike from the west. The bulk of the MPRA 6th Cavalry Division was to be deployed in the north, on the left side of the Halha 10 km. northwest of Hara Heights, while its 15th Cavalry Regiment moved to the east bank to cover the left flank of the Soviet 9th Mechanized Brigade. The MPRA 8th Cavalry Division would screen the right wing on the western shore.[18]

Actually, the Japanese had still not defined the precise location of their infantry crossing. One of Saitō's reservations about the Fui-Hara crossing route had been the large number of foxholes that could be spotted on the left bank. The Kwantung Army staff officers at 23rd Division headquarters were also very anxious about this potential danger to the crossing force, for they deduced from the aerial mosaic maps that the proposed offensive would encounter the most powerful defenses on the enemy's left flank at Hara, not in the center at Komatsu Heights. Tsuji flew personally in a De-Havilland Moth two-seater to reconnoiter the crossing site, at low altitude through rain clouds. That the slow and unarmed little scout plane could overfly the Halha so easily demonstrated that the air force's Tamsag raid of 27 June had indeed swept the skies clear of hostile aircraft. More importantly, it was found that the enemy's anchor defenses were not as formidable as feared; the holes were unoccupied and seemed to be revetments for tanks. Tsuji and his associates therefore endorsed Komatsubara's plan to cross opposite Hara.

Engineer, infantry, and artillery commanders were instructed to reconnoiter the sector from the air, too. On 2 July, Saitō boarded a small Manchuria Aviation Company Typhoon, a three-seater, in company with the spearhead infantry battalion commander, Maj. Fujita Kanya, and scouted the crossing site. To the officers' relief, they could verify that not one enemy soldier was in the honeycomb of foxholes. Saitō was also pleased to confirm that on the Mongolian side there was a truck road opposite the natural track on the right shore. A bridge built at this bend in the river would link the two routes for the benefit of the crossing force. Reassured by the advice of Saitō and the concurrence of the Kwantung Army consultants, Komatsubara issued the necessary orders to proceed along the Fui-Hara axis.[19]

Once the correct high ground in the Fui Heights vicinity had been occupied and a base of operations had been consolidated,[20] the advance to the river after sunset was ordered by the division at 5 P.M. on 2 July. The spearheads of the crossing force were to be rowed to the left shore, seize the high ground on the northern contour of Hara Heights by dawn on the 3rd, cover the construction of the bridge and, after regrouping, strike south toward the confluence, paying special attention to the security of the right rear of the Kobayashi group. Artillery and the Sumi motorized reserves would traverse the bridge and also strike southward toward Komatsu Heights. It is Sumi's impression that 23rd Division headquarters was still as optimistic as it had been in Hailar, but that all of the regimental commanders were more serious as they discussed details of coordination. In other words, whereas the division regarded the offensive as an easy task, the subordinates comprehended the problems.[21]

Movement forward began at about 8 P.M., but not without new misadventures. Three engineer platoons were to have floated a total of 25-30 pontoons and eight-meter-long plywood boats in the Halha and to have rowed the advance infantry elements silently across at about midnight. In the darkness and difficult ground, one unit mistook a pond (Lake Tagi) for the river, until discovering that no current was moving the boats on the unusually wide waters. Considerable time was lost in resuming movement west to the Halha. A spectacular lightning storm further hampered activities although, according to 72nd Infantry Regiment records, "the gods were giving us a great opportunity to mask our intentions."[22] Maps and terrain were not in accord; for example, the expected route by the river did not materialize. In the 71st Regiment, the infantry point company assigned officers, noncoms, and good soldiers to serve as route guides, 50 meters apart, using compasses, hemp lines, and a sixth sense to maintain direction and convey orders, while the engineer troops rushed to rectify the topographical mistakes.

Sumi recalls one terrain problem that was not the engineers' fault. The division commander had expected engineer equipment to be deployed a certain distance from the center of a heights near the river. But, argues Sumi, the word "heights" was meaningless at Nomonhan; there existed only flat "plates" without clearly defined centers. The division commander, nervous and angry with the engineers, thought that he was standing on the center, but a staff officer disagreed. Examination of a map revealed that the site was really on the edge of the so-called heights. If there had been a mistake in this case, Sumi says, it was attributable to the general.

Komatsubara was conferring with Kwantung Army staff officers Yano and Hattori. It might have been more prudent to delay the crossing by a night, but the element of surprise would have been lost. The 71st Regiment's lead infantry battalion commander, Major Fujita, insisted that it was not too late, and Tsuji (who had volunteered to accompany Fujita) reported optimistically to Kobayashi and later to Yano and Hattori. Crossing operations continued. Engineers and infantrymen ran 500 meters to the Halha, lugging their boats and pontoon sections. The portable boats, not too heavy, came in two parts, borne by four men per section. When carried, the boats looked like boards. Pontoons came in four parts, the first and last fan-shaped, the middle two box-shaped.

At river's edge, the drop was a steep 20-30 meters—"the height of a tall building," gasped one soldier. Fujita ordered his hesitant men to slide down the embankment, at the foot of which a bog awaited them. By 3:15 A.M., when the foot soldiers finally began clambering aboard each engineer platoon's 8-10 boats or pontoons, the van of the 71st Infantry was about three hours behind schedule. Craft shuttled back and forth across the river three or four times, the engineers operating in shifts. One engineer used a pole at the bow and a second engineer sculled at the stern. Using no rope lines, the engineers first rowed against the current and then let it sweep them, with some guidance, to the debarkation point on the opposite shore.

Each portable boat carried the two engineers and about 15 men, one infantry squad. Pontoon boats could haul three engineers and as many as 21 soldiers, but the infantry preferred to load no more than one squad per vessel. Battalion, company, and platoon commanders went with the first increments. The troops and engineers were expecting to have to fight from the river, incurring considerable casualties in the process. Orders for silence were taken seriously, one soldier remembering instructions to keep quiet even if he was being killed. Against the danger of holing of the landing craft, the engineers prepared plugs. Some elements remained on the east bank to provide covering fire if necessary. One of the boats became entangled in bridging cables and capsized; some of the infantrymen were drowned before they ever saw combat.

The regimental gun battery and rapid-fire weapons had been apportioned between the two battalions that made the crossing. Since the bridge was not ready and there were no rafts, the rapid-fire batteries (which had expected to cross by bridge) brought their relatively light weapons across the river on pontoon boats without disassembling the guns. The regimental gun batteries had to dismantle their heavier pieces. One crew was seen to drop a gun shield into the river by accident while boarding.

By 4:30 or 5 A.M., when the boat crossing was completed, the skies were already bright. The 2nd Engineer Company presently transferred pontoons from the rowing operation to help the 1st Company finish the bridge. Although the building of the span was behind schedule, work had proceeded for an hour without the stipulated infantry cover from the left shore, fortunately not needed. It had been intended to lay down the 80-meter-long bridge (Sumi says 60 meters), using the main body of Saitō's engineer regiment, at a point approximately 500 meters upstream from the covering infantry battalion, but both operations ended up askew at roughly the same site. Two platoons of the 2nd Engineer Company handled the rowing, about 200 meters upstream from the bridge. The third platoon, equipped with eight pontoons only, operated downstream. To haul the large old iron pontoons (dating back to the era after the Russo-Japanese War) needed for the bridge, an independent truck regiment of 60-80 vehicles had been assigned to the Kwantung Army. After being loaded near Chiangchunmiao in daylight on the 2nd, the truckers fought mud and fatigue to get to Fui Heights after sunset. Since at that time of year at Nomonhan the sun went down around 9 P.M. and rose about 4 A.M., there would have been insufficient time for sustained movement in the dark. Although the engineers worried about the danger of enemy air attacks in the open during daylight, no hostile planes were observed. But the truck convoy missed the route it was to have followed, and the 23rd Division had to correct its bearings.

The motor regiment commander wanted to unload the pontoons 1,000 meters away from the river and have the engineers carry them the rest of the way. To save time and manpower, Saitō deemed it imperative that the pontoons be trucked as close to the river as possible. The truck commander, however, was apprehensive lest enemy units across the river knock out both the bridging matériel and his vehicles. Saitō insisted that no hostile forces had been detected. While the argument was proceeding, a portion of the truck regiment did offload pontoons 1,000 meters from the riverbank, delaying ultimate commencement of the bridge building even further. A Kwantung Army staff officer, who had been with Saitō at the site from the outset, eventually helped the engineer colonel to win the argument with the truck unit commander.

Moving quietly, without headlights or other illumination, the Japanese trucks carried the pontoons safely along a natural road to the river by about 11 P.M. Engineers hauled pontoon sections the rest of the way. The bridging gear was being deployed when the portable-boat engineers and the spearhead infantry battalion arrived very late on the scene, adding to the disarray near the river. Bridge construction began around 3 A.M., before even one Japanese soldier had been rowed across the river. "In war," Saitō reminisces, "there are always very many unplanned, unexpected developments!"

Saitō was worried, of course, that the bridge could not be completed before daybreak as ordered. The commander of the 26th Infantry, Sumi, was particularly disturbed. He and his motorized regiment had reached the river around 1 A.M. and wanted to get across immediately, but he was told that the bridge would not be available until some time after 6 A.M. This would mean moving 194 trucks, a "snake" six km. long, slowly across a narrow bridge in broad daylight, offering a tempting target to enemy gunners on the high ground on the left shore, especially if the Japanese column bunched up. Fearing loss of control, Sumi shifted his regiment three or four km. behind the river, east of Fui Heights, by about 2:30 A.M.

Komatsubara noted that the bridge was finally completed by 6:40 A.M. Luckily for the Japanese, there was no enemy interference at this stage, and the main body of the division was eventually able to get across unscathed, although not without difficulty. For example, in the 71st Regiment, the three infantry platoons that were supposed to do the hauling of matériel had not been able to catch up. Therefore the regimental headquarters, which had brought its colors across the river, tried to assemble by the riverbank. Confusion reigned.

From Zhukov's account, we learn that before dawn on 3 July, the Outer Mongolians' senior Soviet military adviser, Col. I. M. Afonin, had gone personally to Bain Tsagan Obo to inspect the defenses of the MPRA 6th Cavalry Division. By coincidence, Afonin "stumbled into the Japanese, who at night had secretly crossed the Khalkhin Gol [Halha River]," had attacked the Mongolian cavalrymen, and had driven them northwest of the heights. Shaken by "this new and dangerous situation," Afonin had rushed back to Soviet group headquarters to report to Zhukov.[23]

The last foot soldiers of the 71st Infantry Regiment—the 3rd Battalion—traversed the bridge by about 9 A.M. Field artillery did not cross until 9:10 A.M., followed by division headquarters. Shishkin thinks the crossings were completed between 7 and 8 A.M.[24] Sumi was still waiting helplessly as the morning wore on, with most of his own regiment and the heavy equipment and horses belonging to Kobayashi's units that were already fighting across the river. The Japanese forces had piled up like "flies blackening food." Sumi brought his regiment to the river at about 8:30 A.M., but by noon only one-third had crossed the Halha.[25] Traffic control had proved to be the bottleneck. Saitō remembers seeing no ranking divisional officer handling this responsibility at the bridge site, although Komatsubara's operational order had clearly stipulated priorities of movement. Everybody was eager to get across the river swiftly and first, and many a dispute (*kenka*) ensued. Although Sumi was a full colonel, his regiment was an "outsider," and rank counted for nothing at the bridge. Since struggling was useless, the commanders had to reach compromises involving alternation of their movement across the bridge. Disarray and upset were inevitable.

Major General Hashimoto, from the AGS Operations Bureau, appeared on the scene and asked for the senior officer at the bridge. Sumi replied that it was probably he. "You've got to do something about this mess," Hashimoto said, "before enemy planes come." Sumi responded that he was new, that nobody was acquainted with him, and that there were no 23rd Division regiment commanders in the vicinity. Hashimoto could only smile wryly. The nearest to a traffic controller at the bridge was an engineer warrant officer, who told Sumi that the trucks must be unloaded completely, the soldiers must dismount, and even their knapsacks must be removed from the vehicles. Sumi thought that his heavy gas drums might be allowed aboard, but they were ordered off the trucks too. Worse yet, only one truck was allowed on the bridge at a time: a second could not move forward until the first was gone. Each vehicle had to be guided very carefully, as the bridge was only 2.5 meters wide. All guns had to be dismantled. From time to time the warrant officer would suspend activity entirely in order to conduct repair of the bridge, for 30 or 40 minutes at a stretch. It is small wonder that it took hours to move Sumi's 1st (Adachi) Battalion across the bridge by midday. Komatsubara confided to his diary on 3 July that because the bridge was so very weak, "a tremendous amount of time" had been needed to get trucks and artillery across the river.

When he saw Komatsubara, Sumi told him that, at the present rate of progress, it would be evening before the other two infantry battalions traversed the bridge. The whole regiment should have crossed the night before. Komatsubara decided that Sumi's one lead battalion would have to assume the entire responsibility for carrying out the 26th Regiment's combat mission. The other two battalions must abandon their trucks to the division and become foot soldiers, carrying their own ammunition, weapons, etc. Sumi realized that his remaining infantry would undoubtedly have to fight as part of the Kobayashi group, since it would be impossible to catch up with Maj. Adachi Chikao's one truck-borne battalion. Obviously, Komatsubara's original conception of mobility and maneuver had been wrecked by the problems of the river crossing.

For his part, engineer Saitō certainly comprehended the division's difficulties. If the width of the river had been only 50 meters, the distance between pontoon supports could have been shortened, allowing passage by somewhat heavier loads. But as it was, the engineers had had to expend all of their ancient matériel, which had never been intended to support more than the weight of field artillery in any event, just to complete the span, and there were no additional pontoons to strengthen it further. Not only did the trucks face problems, but it was also patently impossible to contemplate moving armored vehicles across such a bridge. Sumi could see that the Halha was somewhat narrower here, that the current was faster than expected, and that the riverbed was composed of fine gravel and sand, causing anchoring problems for the engineers—and creating a crescent-shaped span. The engineers shared the infantry's unhappiness with the "practically useless" crossing matériel and the second-class (*otsu*) bridge. Of course, the field artillery had no choice but to use the span. But they too were frustrated because they had to disconnect their teams of six horses from each gun and then use artillerymen to tow the pieces across the bridge with ropes.

The only bright spot was the quality of Japanese engineer personnel. Saitō had been troubled by the fact that his engineer regiment had undergone no training in bridge building since leaving Kumamoto in the homeland in 1938, having worked only on the construction of defensive positions at Manchouli before being dispatched to Nomonhan. But the IJA engineer officers and men had proved to be eager, enthusiastic, and hard workers, and they did unexpectedly good work at the Halha. Saitō himself crossed the bridge repeatedly, the first time immediately after it was completed.[26]

19

An Authorized Offensive: The Halha River Crossing

Worse lay in store for the Japanese across the Halha, although that fact was not immediately apparent. Original enemy resistance on the west or left shore was unexpectedly weak, according to the 71st Infantry. At 4:36 A.M., an enemy signal flare went up on the 1st Battalion front, followed by the heavy firing of machine guns, apparently the signal for the foe to retreat. The undefended high ground at Bain Tsagan Obo was seized rapidly by the 1st Battalion as day broke. Only empty tank revetments were found. Komatsubara noted that 100 enemy soldiers, taken by surprise, fled without resistance, that artillery must have been relocated the day before, and that long-range guns had remained entirely silent.

After pressing southward, the 1st Battalion discerned dim illumination several hundred meters away. Tsuji advised Major Fujita to hold up and defend the bridge area, in anticipation of an enemy attack in the morning. The battalion commander directed the digging of a defensive circle of foxholes on the high ground, 15-20 meters above the plain. A half-hour later, before the major's own foxhole was dug or the battalion's deployment was complete, the enemy launched a surprise attack with about a dozen armored vehicles from the west and south. In the words of the regimental record, the Japanese forces "nearly fell into confusion" and Fujita was shot through the head and killed on the spot. Tsuji lamented the fact that this tough combat veteran, his *senpai* (senior), had fallen without a chance to draw his sword. From the right bank, Japanese mortars lent support by firing against enemy machine guns, while on the left slope the senior company commander stood in for the slain Fujita.

The arrival of Japanese rapid-fire weapons (37-mm. antitank guns with armor-piercing shells) was timely, for in conjunction with IJA heavy and light machine guns they stopped the first four enemy armored cars sighted (four- and six-wheel Fords), setting afire two machines that had penetrated between the infantry battalions. One crewman was captured.[1] Having beaten off the counterattack, the elated troops of the 71st Infantry rushed south after the foe, in a scene that resembled a "large-scale stag hunt," directed toward Komatsu Heights seven or eight km. away. Japanese reinforcements caught up during the morning.

By the time the 3rd Battalion came across the river around 9 A.M. and turned south, enemy resistance had stiffened and the fighting became so heavy that no distinction between first and second lines could be discerned. Contrary to the regiment's original plan, the new battalion entered combat immediately. One of the company commanders called the battlefield "black with enemy armor." Under tank fire and heavy artillery barrages, the Japanese offensive lost momentum and gradually degenerated into defensive operations. The soldiers dug foxholes, leaving only their heads protruding. They would wait now to launch a night attack.

Meanwhile, against the masses of enemy armored vehicles, the Japanese infantrymen answered with machine guns and ancient infantry guns that spewed high-angle and direct armor-piercing fire. The enemy's heavy artillery bombardments were of two types: shrapnel canisters, air-burst (*ryūsandan*); and particularly loud ground-burst common shells (*ryūdan*). When the barrages lifted, enemy tanks and armored cars would attack at high speed, sometimes at an estimated 45-50 km. per hour. Since the vehicles were overheated in the sun and were mainly light types and gasoline-fueled, they tended to burn easily when hit at any point.

About 50 enemy tanks and armored cars that launched an enveloping attack were driven back by noon, leaving behind more than 20 machines stopped by rapid-fire weapons and by a platoon of the newly arrived field guns from the 3rd Battalion of the 13th Field Artillery Regiment, which knocked out 14 vehicles in 20 minutes, at ranges as great as 700 meters and as close as 30 meters. Initial firing ranges of 1,000-1,500 meters had proved ineffective, and the gunners learned to wait till the enemy circle contracted.

At 12:40 P.M., with the sun at its peak, the 71st Infantry reported destroying an enemy bridge, presumably the Kita-watashi span southeast of Hara Heights. Indeed, the Japanese were so close to the Halha on the left that they sent a platoon down the gentle slopes to collect drinking water. Twice, at 2 P.M. and at 3:25, some 100 light tanks and armored cars swarmed around the 71st Regiment, but the supply train arrived just in time with stocks of ammunition, and the assaults were smashed: "Dozens of chunks of iron from tanks, etc., lay strewn around the area, and smoke from blazing armored vehicles clouded the sun. It looked like the steelworks of Yawata [on Kyushu]." The field artillery claimed 26 kills since morning at a cost of several enlisted men and many horses killed, but no guns lost. Having gained confidence in their combat capability, the Japanese gunners began to "enjoy" engaging enemy armor, say veterans.

At about 4 P.M., enemy 12-cm. heavy-artillery fire erupted from the area of the confluence, on the Japanese flank. Although the gun flashes were visible to the Japanese, they were beyond the range of friendly weapons. The firing kept up for about five hours, and this added to the particularly severe casualties that the 71st Regiment suffered this day. A company commander remembers that his unit alone lost 12-13 dead and 30-40 wounded.[2]

The 2nd (Kokura or Ogura) Battalion of Sakai's 72nd Infantry Regiment had come across the Halha by 3:50 A.M. and began to advance on the right front at 4:40, uncertain about hostile strength in the area. Approximately 300 enemy horsemen with machine guns counterattacked but were driven off, after 20 minutes of fighting, by the 5th (Harada) Company and machine gunners. This particular action seems to be the one alluded to by Shishkin, who asserts that around 5 A.M. the MPRA 15th Cavalry Regiment had moved up to the river, intending to cross to the right side to support the Soviet 9th Armored Brigade. The Mongolians encountered unexpected enemy elements on the left bank and fought a furious battle, but they were forced to retreat to the northwest "under pressure by superior Japanese forces."[3]

Throughout the late dawn, the 72nd Infantry's 2nd Battalion occupied Hara Heights, covering the regiment's advance and scouting the enemy situation. The main regiment had been rowed across the river by 4:30 A.M., had concentrated on the plain by the shore, and had pushed south toward Komatsu Heights at 5:30 A.M., deployed to the right of the 71st Regiment, which was already in action. Some enemy armored cars and about 100 infantrymen were observed, but they did not put up serious resistance and were defeated without much difficulty.

Maj. Nishikawa Masayuki's 1st Battalion had moved inland from the river without delay and without opposition, heading for Komatsu Heights as easily as on "mobile maneuvers." The unit had advanced south for an hour, traversing three or four km. by about 6 A.M., when it encountered six light tanks, which opened fire at 800 to 900 meters. Lacking the regimental gun battery (presumably held up at the bridge), Nishikawa allowed his eager men to fire the two battalion guns and the heavy machine guns uselessly at a range of 700 meters. Although the projectiles merely bounced noisily off the armor, the tanks withdrew. Nishikawa had not been overly apprehensive, since no foot soldiers accompanied the enemy armored vehicles.

At approximately 7 A.M., 12 or 13 enemy tanks appeared at 600 or 700 meters, opened fire, and closed the range despite nonpenetrating hits by the Japanese machine guns and battalion guns. Japanese "tank-killer teams" launched "human bullet" assaults (*nikuhaku kōgeki*), later made famous as the "special attacks" (*tokkō*) of the Pacific War. Rushing the tanks at close range, the men threw incendiary bottles (*kaenbin*) and explosive charges or leaped aboard the machines and inserted grenades. In one highly publicized episode, a Japanese soldier jabbed his bayonet through the hatch. Within 20 or 30 minutes, ten of the tanks had been burned or immobilized, and at least one prisoner had been taken. "Our men let loose with spontaneous shouts of *Banzai!* and applauded with glee," Nishikawa recalls. Twenty or 30 more enemy tanks attacked next, in groups of five or six, from the right rear of the 1st Battalion at about 9 A.M. Another melee ensued, one tank being knocked out by the battalion gun leader at a range of only five or six meters. One Soviet crewman, a "brave warrior" (*yūshi*), wielded a pistol to resist Japanese soldiers who had clambered aboard his tank with drawn sabers, until he and his machine were incinerated by a grenade.

These were the last enemy tanks encountered directly and destroyed by the 1st Battalion on 3 July. On the 2nd Battalion front, 17 enemy tanks had appeared at 10 A.M. Between them, the two infantry battalions were reported to have smashed 12 of 47 tanks in an hour. Whereas the pyres of blazing Russian armored vehicles reminded some of Yawata, Nishikawa heard a staff officer liken the scene to the factory district of Osaka.

Since the Japanese regimental guns and rapid-fire weapons had been slow to arrive (they did not appear until 9 A.M.), the 72nd Regiment commander had been trying to slow down his zealous front-line units, who were continuing to dash forward. Maj. Hamada Toshio, the regimental aide, says that the men were convinced that the enemy troops would take to their heels as soon as the Japanese got across the river, so the soldiers ran hard into Mongolia in order to cut off the expected retreat. When he and the regimental commander debarked from their boat on the left bank of the Halha, the lead company had already lined up many men to convey messages by voice to regimental headquarters. Before Hamada could utter a word, the runner nearest to him yelled "Advance!" The message was relayed along the front and all of the messengers dashed forward. Hamada shouted "Hold up!" and chased after the messengers to try to get them to stop, but when they saw the major running ahead, they did too. Whereas the soldiers wore comfortable *jikatabi* (split-toed, rubber-soled canvas sneakers), the aide and the colonel wore high boots, which made it difficult to run at all in the scorching heat, let alone keep up with the sprinting foot soldiers.

Hamada finally reached the lead company, which had stopped in front of five strange pillbox-like (*tochka*) positions on the crestline. Suddenly the "pillboxes" started to move; they were tanks, skillfully camouflaged. The Japanese lay on their stomachs and let the machines pass, knowing that there were few friendly troops behind them and that the tanks would eventually return. When the armored vehicles came back, the infantrymen attacked them with improvised firebombs (*kaenbin*) and knocked them all out within an hour.

Thereupon the 72nd Regiment resumed the advance, though it tended to veer left toward the river, which was not its sector, in order to intercept the presumably fleeing enemy. The regiment commander tried to check his forces from heading too close to the Halha, but Hamada says the units continued to dash far southward. According to the regimental records, the 1st Battalion reached the northern edge of Komatsu Heights (actually no closer than 1,000 meters?) by about 9:20 A.M.; the 2nd Battalion arrived soon afterward. Hamada thinks that lead elements of his regiment pushed as much as 20 km. from the crossing point—i.e., about six hours of jogging multiplied by a foot speed of 3-4 km. per hour. According to field artillery Capt. Kusaba Sakae, the Japanese lead elements were eight km. from the crossing site a little after 9 A.M. But apparently no Japanese units ever reached Komatsu Heights itself.[4]

At 9:45 A.M., Major General Kobayashi ordered his infantry group, which had supposedly "achieved its mission completely," to consolidate on the spot and to prepare for pursuit operations against the Tamsag trail. The 72nd Regiment claims that it regrouped by 11 A.M. There is much more to the story than the records indicate. The hour of 11 A.M. sticks in Hamada's memory because that is when his horse finally arrived. But by that time, he could observe an enormous number of enemy tanks and armored cars swarming on the horizon. He had tallied up to 500 when he quit counting; there may have been as many as 1,000 vehicles in total, he guesses. Lacking tanks, artillery, and heavy weapons (or close-support aviation), the Japanese were struggling against massive amounts of hostile armor with puny small arms, hand grenades, light machine guns, and firebombs. Hamada galloped forward, ordering the men to hold up and to dig foxholes immediately. Hamada's recollection of the hour is borne out by Zhukov. At 9:15 A.M. on 3 July, Zhukov had conferred with the 11th Tank Brigade commander, who was with the Soviet lead battalion directing operations. It was "decided to alert our entire air force, speed up the movement of our tanks and artillery, and not later than 10:45 [A.M.] attack the enemy. At 10:45 the main forces of the 11th Tank Brigade deployed for combat and attacked the Japanese troops." The 11th Brigade's 1st Battalion encircled Hara Heights from the northwest, hitting the Japanese from the flank and the rear. Striking from the west, the 3rd Battalion and armored elements from the MPRA 6th Cavalry Division squeezed the Japanese into "a steel semicircle of armor."[5]

Even by noon, however, Japanese digging-in had not begun, for after the pell-mell dashing forward most of the morning, the 72nd Regiment was "completely disorganized" and needed to consolidate and deploy. The actions of the other Japanese regiments were impossible to ascertain. Hamada never did see the 71st Infantry on the flank. Although pretty battle maps may indicate neat sector lines, Hamada reminds us that there were no landmarks and that the terrain was unknown. All that was certain was the general direction of the river to the regiment's left. A field artillery captain remembers maintaining direction by sighting on cloud formations. Imagination had to be invoked even in naming dunes; Colonel Sumi mentions protuberances called bat-shaped (*kōmori*), dharma-doll-shaped (*daruma*), and three-sandhill-shaped (*mittsu sunaoka*). From the Soviet side, Zhukov notes that "for hundreds of kilometers around there was not even a bush in sight." Shishkin calls the left shore of the Halha "a flat and sandy plain, devoid of natural camouflage or hiding places." Direction finding was difficult for ground troops.[6]

Around 1 P.M., the Russians opened fire with heavy artillery from the right shore of the Halha and with four guns from the confluence. A fierce rumbling of tank engines was heard simultaneously from the rear—to the north-northwest of the 72nd Infantry. The troops wanted to fire, but Hamada denied permission for an unrealistic reason: these might be Japanese tanks coming across the bridge behind the infantry. Soon enough, it became apparent that the tanks were hostile and extremely numerous. Several groups of tanks totaling some 100 machines were approaching from the south, too, and a dozen had already started to move against the 72nd Regiment's rear. Except for the five mobile *tochkas*, says Nishikawa, the regiment had not directly encountered enemy armor during the morning push southward.

Against the latest center of gravity of the Soviet armored forces, the Japanese had to reverse their deployment and engage the foe with depleted stocks of firebombs and antitank charges. Some welcome support was rendered by a few old Type 38 field guns, admittedly arriving five hours behind schedule and firing only instant-fuzed common shells, not armor-piercing shells. Had the new swarms of tanks appeared from the Mongolian interior or from the right side of the Halha? Indeed, another reason for restraining the 72nd Infantry's advance had been the suspicion that hostile forces on the right shore had recrossed the river and were massing behind the Kobayashi task force. The presence of the hundreds of armored vehicles sighted by Hamada on the crestline reinforced this estimate.

Soviet battle maps reveal the answers to the questions perplexing the Japanese forces on 3 July. Russian armor was deployed on the left bank as follows: The 2nd Battalion of the 11th Tank Brigade occupied the northern edge of Komatsu Heights. Striking against Hara Heights from the southwest, in two groups, was the 7th Armored Brigade. The 24th Motorized Infantry Regiment was moving west and north of Hara Heights, while the rest of the 11th Tank Brigade attacked Hara from the northwest. The only Russian armor across the Halha east of Hara Heights was the 9th Armored Brigade, which remained engaged fully on the right bank.

Zhukov and Shishkin explain the background to these deployments in detail. As soon as Colonel Afonin came back from the Halha and reported to the command post of the First Army Group (formerly the 57th Special Corps) in the early morning of 3 July, it became obvious that "it was impossible to stop the progress of the Japanese troops in this area and prevent their offensive on the flank and rear of our troops." All of the army reserves were alerted and rushed toward Hara Heights to surround and destroy the Kobayashi force. The bulk of M. P. Yakovlev's 11th Tank Brigade (with as many as 150 tanks) was to conduct a rapid on-the-march attack from the north, while its 2nd Battalion (operating with elements of the MPRA 6th Cavalry Division) was to meet the Japanese frontally and check their movement southward. Supported by an artillery battalion, Lt. Col. I. I. Fedyuninsky's 24th Motorized Regiment was to attack from the northwest, cooperating closely with the 11th Tank Brigade's offensive. Col. A. L. Lesovoi's 7th Armored Brigade (154 armored vehicles) would attack from the south, while an armored battalion of the MPRA 8th Cavalry Division, armed with 45-mm. guns, moved in that direction too.

The Military Council of the Russians' First Army Group rushed to the area of Hara Heights early on the morning of 3 July. The 185th Artillery Regiment's heavy artillery battalion was instructed to send a reconnaissance unit to Hara to engage the Japanese. At the same time, the Soviet artillery operating on the right side of the Halha in support of the 9th Armored Brigade was ordered to redirect its fire against Hara Heights. The entire air force capability was committed to the operation. "It was extremely important for us," wrote Zhukov, "to hold the enemy on the mountain [Hara Heights] in check with aircraft and artillery until the arrival of reserves for the counterblow." The Russians ordered the continuation of shelling and bombing of the Japanese bridge area in order to slow down further crossing by enemy forces as well as their concentration around Hara Heights. As Zhukov noted, "our trump cards were the armored detachments, and we decided to use them immediately in order to destroy the Japanese troops that had just crossed the river, not letting them entrench themselves and organize antitank defense. It was impossible to delay a counterblow [once] the enemy . . . saw the advance of our [unsheltered] tanks."

Around 9 A.M., the first elements of the 11th Tank Brigade's leading 2nd Battalion entered the combat zone and attacked the forwardmost Japanese, who proceeded to dig in around Hara Heights and deploy antitank weapons against the Soviet armored formations. According to Zhukov, the Kobayashi task force concentrated more than 10,000 soldiers at Hara Heights, against only 1,200 Soviet troops. The Japanese possessed about 100 cannon and as many as 60 antitank guns, against approximately 50 Russian pieces, even including the Soviet supporting artillery on the right shore of the Halha. But the 11th and 7th brigades had over 300 armored fighting vehicles between them, whereas the Japanese had none across the river.[7]

Of the antitank warfare on 3 July, the 72nd Regiment historian called the dozens of black pillars of smoke reminiscent of "a picture scroll of the great naval battle of the Japan Sea [Tsushima]" in the Russo-Japanese War. Ten-tank assaults were repulsed several times. But from about 2 P.M., enemy heavy artillery barrages grew "rather severe" from the direction of Balshagal Heights (on the right shore) and Sambur Obo (on Hamardaba Heights to the south), where four guns each were firing. By 2:30 P.M. the wire signal network between regimental headquarters and General Kobayashi's command post was being severed frequently, and communication had become unsatisfactory. Japanese offensive operations were over. By 3:30 P.M. the 72nd Regiment was already pulling back 1,000 meters when the reinforced enemy surrounded the Japanese and attacked with 50 armored vehicles and cavalry.

Describing the same period on 3 July from the Russian standpoint, Soviet military historians admit that the 24th Motorized Infantry Regiment, which was supposed to have struck from the northwest, mistakenly headed northward, then corrected itself by shifting back to the south, and eventually attacked the Japanese from the west at about noon. The main body of the 7th Armored Brigade went into action from the south at 3 P.M. Thus the Kobayashi force was surrounded in the vicinity of Hara Heights from every direction except the east, where the Halha River afforded no escape. Nevertheless, the Japanese fought back tenaciously the rest of the day, relying on their antitank defense and even foiling a coordinated assault from the three sides at dusk, around 7 P.M.[8]

Although the Japanese soldiers did resist doggedly, as the IJA records agree, they "could not achieve the same degree of success" as in the morning. In fact, the Japanese now fired back only occasionally. One field artillery sergeant says the men had actually "reached their limits" by about 1 P.M. According to a Japanese soldier's diary captured by the Russians on 3 July:[9] "Several scores of tanks attacked unexpectedly, causing chaos [among] our troops. Horses stampeded, neighing and dragging gun carriages with them; cars scattered in all directions. Two of our planes were shot down. The morale of our troops fell extremely low. The Japanese soldiers could be heard saying more and more frequently: 'Terrible,' 'sad,' 'ghastly,' etc."

Hamada is of the opinion that his regiment had been engaged frontally by enemy scouting forces only. But by afternoon on 3 July, "a kind of hand-to-hand struggle" had developed—hostile armor against Japanese infantry. IJA artillerymen, for example, never saw enemy foot soldiers. The combustible hostile tanks fought blindly, pushing forward from all directions and firing wildly, which rendered them rather easy to knock out, as attested to by the many "fires on the plain." Still, after the hordes of enemy tanks appeared to the 72nd Regiment's rear and heavy artillery started to hammer the sector, the regiment not only ceased to advance but began to withdraw, especially as hostile strength was built up greatly. For the Japanese, any thought of "pursuit to the Tamsag trail" had become ridiculous.[10]

With only the 1st Battalion (532 men, 78 trucks) of Major Adachi across the river by about 11 A.M. on 3 July, the 26th Regiment commander, Colonel Sumi, pondered whether he ought to stay with the main body or cross the Halha and join the major. The latter, a splendid swordsman, was brave enough, but his mission—using one battalion to conduct a whole regiment's assignment—was extremely difficult, and Sumi wondered if even he could accomplish Adachi's task. Naturally, Sumi would have preferred to team up with Adachi, but the sacred regimental colors were held by the main force. The colonel might be criticized later if he left the colors behind him.[11] Perplexed, Sumi asked his aide, Maj. Maruyama Kōichi, for advice. The aide replied that if Sumi thought Adachi had a chance of succeeding, he should join the 1st Battalion; if not, he should stay with the main body. This very practical counsel, worthy of an "office worker," displeased the colonel, but lacking a better idea of his own he accepted it and decided to go to the other side of the river, about which he knew next to nothing, and at least observe developments from the higher ground there. Sumi says he got into his staff car with his aide and as many more men as could be crammed in and proceeded across the Halha. Adachi and his troops were waiting for the other battalions to catch up on foot. Sumi did not yet pass along Komatsubara's new orders in detail, pending his own visual appraisal of the situation. He merely told Adachi to push forward separately (*dokuritsu*), in accordance with the division commander's on-the-spot instructions. The 1st Battalion then advanced 1,000 meters and ran into enemy armor. Sumi explains the command relationships: "The moment I told the 1st Battalion to advance, it came under direct control of the division, in theory. But from beginning to end I retained the idea of controlling the battalion without particularly waiting for any orders. Thus the period during which the Adachi battalion was supposed to be operating under the division commander's direct control was actually only that phase of their initial advance forward from my location, and the 'control' faded away imperceptibly (*uyamuya*)."

In practice, Adachi and Sumi were fighting on their own initiative, adapting to the realities of the situation. Until the morning of 4 July, in fact, there were no orders from and no contact whatsoever with the division, although Komatsubara had come across the river and set up his command post (near

I P.M., says Sumi) on the 3rd. Similarly, there was no liaison with the Kobayashi force, not more than two or three km. away to the left along the river. The Sumi regiment had no communications facilities, no method of reporting developments or receiving orders, no way of knowing about the situation of the division or the Kobayashi force, which was engaged very heavily too. Even in Sumi's own unit, real regimental orders were impossible. In a battle of encounter, there is no difference between regimental and battalion commanders.

Sumi had gone to the observation post atop the high ground at Bain Tsagan, and from there he saw enemy tanks deploying in the distance, near the horizon or on elevations. It was impossible to count the number of armored vehicles, but they were clustered, hither and yon, in many groups of six to ten machines each, perhaps 40-50 to the left, 70-80 in front, 30-40 on the right. Undoubtedly the tanks were operating in many lines, with only the front lines visible, since the terrain was mainly flat beyond the heights on the left bank. Much hostile fire soon began to be received, some shrapnel at first but mostly percussion shells, although one could not be sure if it emanated from tanks or artillery.

In any case, there was no problem about where Sumi should be situated now, with the enemy visible directly in front, so he ordered the rest of his regiment to march across the bridge immediately and join him in battle. The twelve 75-mm. regimental guns were trundled across the bridge, one whole squad of 16 men easily hauling each piece. There was every incentive to hurry across, since hostile tanks were on the move, and the men had been wasting a lot of time with their packs off. The 2nd Battalion of Maj. Kawai Jiichi was closer to the bridge than Maj. Kikuchi Tetsuo's 3rd, so in the main it got across first, by about noon. The 3rd Battalion was on the left shore by around 12:30 P.M. But the notice to advance was so short, there was little time to sort out the battalions distinctly, and units proceeded in a jumble. Once across the bridge, the battalions deployed in two sectors to the left of the 1st Battalion—i.e., somewhere between the 1st Battalion to their right and the Kobayashi task force to their left.

An important facet of Sumi's preparations now paid off for the 26th Regiment. On his arrival at Hailar on 22 June, he had sent officers to the barracks to visit all the units that had already participated in the first-phase Nomonhan fighting to learn about the battlefield terrain and the lessons from combat. One such lesson was that hand-operated antitank mines (*anpan*), with their small yellow-explosive filling, were not very effective in the ash-like sand. Tanks evaded or merely pushed down the mines, which often did not detonate at all. Firebombs were easier to use and much more effective. The colonel accordingly ordered the collection of empty soft-drink ("cider") bottles and their improvisation as *kaenbin*.

Neither Sumi nor other interviewees was acquainted with the genealogy of the firebombs. Maj. Nishiura Susumu, sent from the war ministry to Spain to observe Nationalist operations in the Civil War, had seen the success of "Molotov cocktails" improvised from wine bottles and had advised Tokyo accordingly in a report dated July 1937. When Nishiura got back to Japan, experiments against Japanese tanks were conducted by the skeptical ordnance bureau, but the tests were a failure because the tank targets were stationary and cold, and their engines were diesel-powered. Lt. Gen. Kawamura Kyōsuke, the 1st Infantry Division commander, heard about the experiments, was impressed by the tactic, and even issued training pamphlets to his units on the employment of *kaenbin*.

As for the use of firebombs at Nomonhan, Murata Masao agrees that somebody must have heard about the Spanish Civil War experience, but regards it as more probable that the technique was devised by some clever Japanese soldier somewhere in combat. Murata appears to be correct. In 1977 it was revealed that a 20-year-old artillery PFC, Okano Katsuma, and two other soldiers assigned temporarily to the 23rd Division as truck drivers had accidentally "invented" antitank firebombs during the first phase of the Nomonhan incident in May. Chased by enemy armor one day, the desperate truckers had shoved spare jerricans of gasoline off the back merely to harrass and impede the pursuit. Surprisingly, the tanks burst into flame when the petrol cans rolled into them. "Thus we learned," Okano says, "that gasoline will ignite a tank."[12]

In addition to fire bottles, Sumi had the idea of installing heavy weapons aboard the regiment's trucks, from which the colonel expected the 26th Infantry to be able to fight. Two of Sumi's platoon leaders remember the optimistic thinking behind the colonel's novel—and "a little too difficult"—idea of using wooden ramps for onloading and offloading the trucks. By the time the powerful Japanese motorized infantry regiment got across the Halha, the foe would have been scared off and in flight. Unless the 26th Regiment raced to the confluence in time to catch up with the fleeing enemy, the Japanese might suffer the "disgrace" of never getting to fire at all, and the offensive would amount to nothing more than a mobile exercise. To gain time, instead of dismantling the guns, they would be emplaced and fired from the trucks. An antitank role was possible, too. In practice, there never was a chance to conduct test-firing of the guns from a truck.[13]

Sumi himself gave his troops a 30-minute lecture at Hailar, including the following injunctions and exhortations: "If necessary, you may ignore everything you learned in the infantry textbooks, regulations, and combat essentials. We must improvise with our original ideas for combat, and prove them with our blood, for they may become the fundamentals for the following generation." Sumi's "junkman" was 2nd Lt. Negami Hiroshi, 26, a quartermaster officer, who was left behind at Hailar to collect the empty bottles and the three-inch-thick planks to be used as ramps and to send them on to the regiment aboard a company of 15-16 supply trucks. The army warehouse contained plenty of bottles, but they were full of soda pop the army had probably imported from the Japanese homeland. Negami must have requisitioned nearly 1,200 bottles, since he was computing the regimental needs at the rate of one per front-line soldier. The quartermaster personnel (typical of all armies) would not issue supplies easily, especially since Negami, for security reasons, could not divulge his real reason for requisitioning so many bottles and planks. By "dealing" hard with the canny quartermaster people, the lieutenant finally wheedled what he needed. Indeed, the Sumi regiment obtained enough bottles to be able to distribute some to the 71st Infantry. That the bottles arrived full, of course, pleased Sumi and all of the thirsty troops. "Negami was one smart lieutenant!" laughs Sumi. He warned the regiment not to throw away the bottles after imbibing the cider; they should fill them with water first and be ready to use them as Molotov cocktails later. Each man, even the colonel, tied one bottle to his waist with string.

At Chiangchunmiao, Sumi had studied the best ways of employing firebombs. The bottle should be filled with about one-third sand for ballast, the rest with gasoline. A cotton piece, the rifle-cleaning patch carried by every soldier, could be used to plug the mouth of the bottle. One then lighted the "wick" with a match and threw the bottle at the target. But on the steppes there was generally a breeze in the open, and striking a match and igniting a wick (or even lighting a cigarette) always posed difficulties. Disturbed by this insoluble problem, Sumi and his men entered battle at Nomonhan.

In combat on the left shore on 3 July, the 26th Infantry at first employed regimental and infantry guns against 80 to 100 enemy armored vehicles at long range. The 75-mm. regimental guns opened up immediately at 1,500 meters, at a rate of a round per minute. Firing no armor-piercing shells, they could merely hope to break a tank's tread. At 800 to 1,000 meters, the infantry guns could register only one effective hit out of every three rounds fired. The tanks had closed to perhaps 100 meters by the time the infantry guns got off more than two or three shots. Throughout the fighting, usually within a range of 500 meters, the regiment's heavy machine guns fired at hostile armor. Since no Soviet infantrymen were accompanying the tanks, Japanese machine gunners aimed at vision slits; the slugs did not set armor afire.

When the tanks approached to 40 or 50 meters, Japanese *nikuhaku* (human bullet) antitank teams sprang into action. The combat was so close and so confused that officers and men—aides, messengers, and even the regiment commander—shouted instructions and pointed out directions of attack to the tank-killer squads. "It was like smashing flies whenever and wherever they appear," explains Sumi. The tanks were not in formation but were scattered, and thus they could be "bagged" one by one. More than ten of the first 20 vehicles encountered were knocked out, by all causes, within the first hour across the river.

The scenes of destruction of enemy armor were entirely new to the Japanese. Originally, it will be recalled, the soldiers had intended to cap the fire bottles with wicks, but the antitank maelstrom erupted very quickly and from many directions. So the men hurled the bottles at the nearest target, by automatic reflex, without igniting them. The results were spectacular and quite unexpected. When a tank is penetrated by gunfire from another tank or from artillery, it usually spews flame and then belches smoke. With *kaen-bin*, the phenomena differed. As soon as a firebomb hit armor, the pop bottle would shatter, the gasoline contents would splatter quickly, and the sheet of fuel would ignite from the heat of the sun and the vehicle. Flames would appear from the bottom of the tank, the way a newspaper burns, giving the impression that the earth was on fire. When the flames licked the top of the tank, the fire would subside with a puff, for the fuel tank had been entered. Now the inside of the tank would catch fire, vomit black smoke, and burn furiously. A truck or a car could be expected to blaze for 30-40 minutes, certainly less than an hour, before going out, but these Russian tanks burned for three or four hours or more. Machines hit in the afternoon of 3 July continued to burn until evening; those knocked out after dusk smoldered through the night. The pyres flamed in various stages, from brand-new kills and from explosions in earlier tank victims. And when flames reached the machine-gun ammunition, loaded in pans or stored around the inside of the turret, the bullets would shoot out crazily in every direction. Cannon rounds, stacked inside the tank, would ignite and explode into the armor or blast up into the sky like fireworks. Japanese troops had to be restrained from approaching too closely, as the direction of the spontaneous firing was impossible to guess. The smoky battlefield resounded with noise as the Soviet armored vehicles went on burning.

When flames burst out inside the tanks, the hatches (customarily closed in combat) would open and the Russian crewmen would appear, jump down, and try to escape to their own positions. The bodies of many were half-burned and they would stagger a few steps in agony. Some tried to help wounded comrades; others sought to hide under blazing tanks. A few Russians even bailed out of undamaged tanks. Individual crewmen reacted in different ways and the sights were diverse. Japanese heavy machine gunners claimed to have cut down most of the escaping Soviet crews. The regimental guns were "too busy shifting fire from tank target to tank target to bother with people." One Japanese infantryman felled a Russian, who tried to resist but was finished off by a pistol. An IJA transport captain remembers watching the scene "as at a festival."

The 26th Regiment claimed to have knocked out 83 enemy machines. Incredulous higher headquarters thought that Sumi was boasting when he reported that unlit pop bottles were incinerating tanks. But, as noted earlier, the sun was fierce (over 100° F.) and the unshielded, gasoline-fueled tanks were very hot after their long and fast rush from Tamsag toward the river, where they were probably seeking to engage a Japanese armored task force on the right bank—an accurate supposition, as we know. Indeed, Sumi was convinced that, just as the Japanese wanted to outflank and knock out the enemy bridge at the Halha-Holsten confluence, so the Russians intended to take the 23rd Division's pontoon bridge, for Soviet armor was attacking the 26th Regiment from all directions.

Though he admits that his regiment's claim of 83 tank kills undoubtedly includes duplications, Sumi thinks the figure is not too far off. After all, these tanks were all knocked out at close range, mainly by *kaenbin* attacks, so verification was not difficult. Sumi suggests an authentic figure of at least 70 tank kills by the 26th Regiment. The regimental guns claimed five on 3 July. Each of the 12 guns must have fired 18-20 rounds that day. Regardless of the claims, Sumi insists, the important thing to note was that the Japanese infantrymen stopped every tank that approached the regiment.

A Japanese platoon leader recounts one problem about firebomb attacks that, understandably, is rarely mentioned in IJA accounts: The Japanese infantry's human-bullet assaults were carried out too early for friendly artillery to fire, lest their own soldiers be hit. Enemy armor irrupted with such suddenness and rapidity that Japanese artillery could not depress their angle of fire to engage them at less than 500 meters. On occasion, Japanese *nikuhaku* men were known to have been cut down by the misdirected fire of their own battalion guns. Fortunately for the Japanese, in general the Russian tanks did not use their machine guns much, concentrating instead on firing their cannon against the heavy weapons. This lightened Japanese infantry casualties and facilitated the fire-bottle attacks.

As for the depth of the 26th Regiment's penetration, a platoon leader notes that the first antitank battle was fought about 500 meters from the bridge. It was another 1,000 meters to the foot of the high ground, up the gentle slope of which the Japanese moved for a distance of some 2,000 meters. This would place the Sumi regiment's farthest movement at 3,500 meters from the bridge by about 3 P.M. on 3 July. Here, the attack bogged down, after little more than two or three hours, with Sumi exerting command over both the 2nd and 3rd battalions from 2:40 P.M., and with Adachi's battalion ahead and alone to the southwest of the main body. Enemy artillery positions were probably a further 2,000 meters up the high ground. AGS intelligence heard that the 26th Regiment had reached a point six km. southwest of the crossing by about noon.

Sumi felt that his men could knock out the front waves of the enemy who reached Japanese lines, but that they could not "repulse" the hostile forces massed ahead. After the fiercest *kaenbin* actions, enemy attacks eased up, and the colonel ordered a resumption of the advance. Concentrated hostile fire, probably emanating mainly from tanks, then hammered the regiment and inflicted many casualties in the 2nd and 3rd battalions. In all, on 3 July, the 26th Infantry and attached units lost 63 killed and 136 wounded. Two of four medical noncoms were killed. From his regimental headquarters, Sumi lost his aides, Major Maruyama and 2nd Lt. Shinoda Kenji, half of his clerks, and his orderly. Maruyama, a veteran officer, was killed by tank fire while returning from delivering instructions to Adachi, there being no direct communications between the regiment and the exposed 1st Battalion. Similarly, Shinoda was slain by an artillery fragment at the moment he got back from contacting the Adachi battalion. Sumi wondered, in fact, if his own new colonel's insignia, sparkling in the sun, were not attracting enemy fire, but he decided against discarding them.

It is very difficult for infantry to move forward under artillery barrages without covering fire of their own. Kobayashi's corps, closer to the Halha, could receive field artillery support; Sumi, getting no such assistance, had to hold up. Although he tried to regain the momentum several times, the task was simply hopeless without artillery. To solicit friendly fire support, Sumi ordered his headquarters clerk, a master sergeant, to use the regimental sedan and head north to contact artillery battalion headquarters. Enemy armor chased the vehicle but did not prevent the sergeant from carrying out his mission and conveying Sumi's request to the artillery. On the way back, though, tank fire riddled the sedan, killing the already injured orderly and another soldier, wounding the driver, and blowing off an arm of the sergeant, who died during evacuation to the rear. The commandeered black staff car was conspicuous against the sandy soil; undoubtedly the enemy believed that a senior officer was aboard. But the sacrifices were in vain; not one round of the promised friendly artillery support was ever fired, Sumi complains.

While waiting fruitlessly for artillery assistance, Sumi pondered his situation. Evening was at hand, the Adachi battalion had been held up, and the regiment was isolated on the left shore. The original mission—to cut behind the enemy and reach the confluence—had become impossible. Ahead, the enemy was deployed in strength; the regiment was out of contact with the rest of the Kobayashi force; and there was no way of predicting how long the operation would last. More enemy tank attacks could be expected, but a canvass of the regiment revealed the unsettling information that only 36 fire bottles were left, insufficient for even one day's combat. By 4 P.M. the 2nd and 3rd battalions had been reduced to one infantry gun and one box of ammunition. Adachi's heavy weapons had run out of ammunition by about the same time.

What did military history teach a regiment commander under such circumstances? Sumi's mind went back to textbook examples from the Western Front in the First World War, when hung-up forces would have occupied a reverse slope. In Sumi's case, this would necessitate a pullback of about 1,000 meters from across the slope. But to retreat any distance without orders was a dangerous problem in the Japanese army. Should he cling to the vulnerable advance positions, or should he protect his unit from enemy fire by falling back and personally assuming responsibility? To retreat was a very difficult task, especially since there were many dead and wounded to evacuate. Still, the regiment could at least protect the bridge across the Halha against an enemy rush; although infantrymen were useless against long-range artillery, they retained their capability in close-quarter combat.

After weighing the pros and cons, Sumi decided to risk a pullback after sunset. Among his many worries was the safety of the regimental colors, which were in danger during such confused combat on the steppes. He accordingly ordered 1st Lt. Kokubu Yoshio's 10th Company to escort the colors back across the Halha.[14] But what of the Adachi battalion, which should be pulled back too? Since contact had become impossible after Sumi's aides and messengers were lost, the regiment commander decided to find the 1st Battalion himself.

Trudging through the darkness, Sumi headed in the direction of Adachi but had still not reached the battalion after traversing about 500 meters. Russian soldiers could be heard yelling as they towed out immobilized armor and sent flares up 20 meters to indicate the locations of those vehicles that were not still burning. Sumi had a new worry. What if he, a full colonel, were captured and thus disgraced? Should he continue forward? Suddenly he espied a form nearby in the gloom—fortunately a Japanese warrant officer. Sumi ordered him to tell Major Adachi to pull back the 1st Battalion and rejoin the regimental main force. Sumi returned to his command post and got ready to "change direction" with the main body. So immensely relieved was he at having been able to convey his order to Adachi, the colonel forgot to ask the name of the faceless warrant officer. If Sumi's recollection is correct, it was his neglect that had fatal consequences for the 1st Battalion.[15]

For Komatsubara, a worrier, there was much to worry about on the night of 2/3 July. The general spent tension-wracked hours in the darkness near the Halha, checking on the frustrating lack of progress of the crossing operation. The bungles in the rowing and the bridging process cost enormous amounts of time, and the coming of daylight on the 3rd—which started cloudy but later cleared and became torrid—brought the danger of catastrophe with the passing of each slow hour. That the Kobayashi task force somehow got across the river without casualties from enemy action Komatsubara attributed to surprise induced by two factors. First, by unintentionally missing the location of Fui Heights on 2 July, the 23rd Division had diverted the enemy from the real crossing site opposite Bain Tsagan Obo. Second, the Japanese tank offensive against the confluence, starting on 2 July, had fixed enemy attention on the right shore. Itching to get across the river personally, Komatsubara had only to hear that the Japanese infantry were achieving "some results" before he ordered his black Buick sedan to take him over the bridge that morning with Major General Yano, his aide, and the *kenpei* (military police) guards. A truckful of soldiers escorted the staff car. Intelligence officer Suzuki came galloping up to the bridge to report to Komatsubara that everything was going well.

Major General Hashimoto, the AGS Operations Bureau chief, would not have shared Suzuki's sanguine appraisal. Hashimoto had come to Kwantung Army headquarters from Tokyo to explain the imperial order of 29 June, which had been designed to limit the field force's activities in general. By coincidence, Hashimoto conferred with Kwantung Army commander Ueda on the very day that the 23rd Division moved to the Halha (2 July) to commence its offensive—an action that certainly did not jibe with the intent of the IGHQ order, although Ueda assured his visitor that he comprehended its import. Hashimoto had had no intention of proceeding to the front, but when Ueda asked if he would like to observe the river-crossing operation, he agreed to take a plane next day for the Halha, via Hailar. He reached the bridge between 10 and 11 A.M. on 3 July, expecting to go by two-passenger light plane or by sedan to the left shore. As noted earlier, however, things were "in a mess," and Hashimoto had to walk across the bridge.

Hashimoto's first impression was that "it was a lousy operation and it is bound to fail." Incredibly, the division commander (whom he never could find on 3 July)[16] was already across the river with lightly equipped infantry only, while the field artillery battalion was still on the right bank and Sumi's regiment was milling around. Even if the enemy were weak (which he proved not to be), it was unsound to disperse an attacking division so badly. Hashimoto knew Komatsubara well from war college days, and he regretted having to think adversely of him, but the operational preparations and the operation itself were undeniably poor. "I felt awful," Hashimoto says. His outlook was not helped when Japanese field artillery arrived on the left bank without a commander. An old artillery officer himself, the major general had to take temporary command of the Japanese guns against enemy tanks that were attacking the vicinity of the bridge.

The severity of the day's action was driven home when Komatsubara himself was almost killed by tanks. In late morning, Capt. Kusaba Sakae's 7th Field Artillery Battery had been assigned to cover division headquarters during the advance. At about 11:30 A.M., the headquarters party pushed ahead of the artillery after sending word, "Excuse us for going first" (*osaki ni*). Suddenly, the troop truck escorting Komatsubara's sedan stopped and the soldiers jumped off. The sedan stopped too, and the officers got out. Tanks could be seen approaching "bravely." Komatsubara's aide thought they might be friendly, and even General Yano was unsure of their identity, for the terrain was undulating and a full view was not possible at this location. Uncertainty ceased when the tanks opened fire at about 300 meters. The Japanese generals and their retinue threw themselves on the ground and lay on their stomachs while enemy gunfire roared overhead. Since Komatsubara's headquarters had no antitank capability, it was decided to try to reach the Kobayashi force, at least 1,000 meters away. Leaving their escort truck behind, the Japanese officers jumped into the Buick and raced off at full speed, while enemy tank shells flew over the fleeing sedan.

Only later did division headquarters learn what had proved their salvation: Kusaba's Type 38 field artillery. The battery, which had just knocked out four tanks, observed 15 more enemy armored vehicles pursuing the general's sedan and only 10 meters from it. At a visual range of 700 meters from the high-speed chase, Kusaba wondered if his guns would kill the general or knock out the lead pursuer. Common shells with instantaneous fuzes were already loaded in the Japanese guns and Kusaba, without time to think, "closed his eyes" and gave the order to fire at will. The first one or two rounds hit, the tank started to blaze, and the Japanese shouted "*Banzai!*" automatically. "What a thrill!" mused Kusaba. After the loss of what was probably their commander's tank, the rest of the Soviet armored unit— "confused or furious"—abandoned the chase and headed straight for the field artillery battery. In a 20-minute action (described elsewhere), which Kusaba called "delightful," the field guns accounted for all 14 remaining enemy tanks at ranges of 30 to 700 meters before noon. Kusaba says that the crew of one slightly damaged tank waved a handkerchief as a token of surrender. But because no tankers emerged and because "there was the possibility of a sudden treacherous attack if we approached to accept the surrender," the Japanese captain ordered his gunners to demolish the Soviet tank, which, after all, mounted a 45-mm. gun and a heavy machine gun.

Komatsubara and Yano had had a hair-raising escape, whose enormity surely affected their operational thinking throughout the rest of 3 July. The unexpected number of Soviet armored vehicles that "came out of nowhere" left its imprint. For his part, Hashimoto was surprised that the 23rd Division's intelligence of the enemy was so poor. Since the Japanese air force controlled the skies, aerial reconnaissance should not have been difficult. The Kwantung Army must have known the details and shared them with the division, and moreover the deputy chief of staff and other Kwantung Army brass were at the front, advising Komatsubara. But the division commander's junior aide, an infantry second lieutenant, remarks upon the unforgettable sight of row after row of enemy tanks pushing forward from the area south of Komatsu Heights around noon. The lieutenant was amazed by the masses of machines; he had never seen so many. Even after very heavy losses, Tsuji observes, the enemy still had more than 200 armored vehicles in action.

Division intelligence officer Suzuki admits that the number of Soviet tanks was not anticipated. Had the Japanese units been able to cut behind the enemy and reach the confluence, then it was expected that Kobayashi might encounter considerable hostile mechanized strength; but in the area of the river crossing only small-scale enemy forces were thought to be deployed. Yet before the infantry had advanced more than one or two kilometers south of the bridge they ran into unexpected Soviet armored strength. Murata agrees that the 23rd Division, which was entirely reliant on the Kwantung Army for its intelligence, knew nothing about enemy forces behind the river line.

The one flimsy bridge, of course, was central to the Japanese west-bank operations. Komatsubara was very concerned about the physical weakness of the span, knowing that its loss would mean the destruction of friendly forces across the river. The general's junior aide remarks that "if the enemy forces had been a little more clever, they could have detoured around the Kobayashi group and concentrated against the bridge. No countermeasures would have been possible." The fear of Hashimoto and other staff officers was that Soviet aircraft would assault the bridge in daylight. Lieutenant Colonel Saitō of the 23rd Engineer Regiment remembers two enemy fighter raids, in three-plane formations, at about 2 P.M. on the 3rd, without prior reconnaissance. Fortunately for the Japanese, the strafings did not hit the bridge below water level. Some of the engineers were wounded slightly by ricochets and fragments. Sumi recalls an enemy three-plane formation flying very low over the bridge, obliging him and his orderly to "hit the deck" but shooting up only a horse and a gasoline drum aboard a truck. Tsuji speaks of 30 enemy bombers attacking the bridge.

Soviet heavy artillery as well as armor brought the area of the bridge under fire. Although no shells hit the span directly, there was some damage on the shore. Standing next to Saitō, a quartermaster officer lost a leg to a shell fragment. Saitō estimates the total of Japanese casualties to enemy bombardment of the bridge district at fewer than ten men wounded, but the appearance of 15-cm. enemy artillery within range of the river crossing disturbed Komatsubara and his colleagues greatly. Including the heavy artillery, observes Tsuji, the Russians disposed of 40 or 50 guns against the Komatsubara force. Suzuki notes that, of the two sedans and two trucks brought across the river by division headquarters on 3 July, only one truck was left by day's end. Soviet artillery fire destroyed the general's famous black sedan and killed the civilian driver in the evening. The combined threat from enemy aircraft and artillery meant that nobody would be able to cross the river, in either direction, in daylight.

The 23rd Division's operational orders had called for the creation of a river-crossing covering unit (*toka engotai*) consisting of the divisional reconnaissance regiment (under its new commander, Lt. Col. Ioki Eiichi) and the 10th (Gotō) Company of the 64th Infantry. These forces were to follow Kobayashi across the Halha and directly cover the Japanese bridge, in conjunction with the 23rd Engineer Regiment, which would provide technical maintenance and protection of the span. One of the more memorable experiences of the covering unit occurred near 11 P.M. on the night of 3 July. Unidentified "strange lights" moving along the ground southwest of the bridge site proved to be three enemy tanks operating flame-throwers at an inexplicably long distance, over 1,000 meters from the crossing. Thereupon the 1st Engineer Company commander, Capt. Kakoi Iwami, ordered close-quarter teams to rush to the left shore. Combat-wise Master Sergeant Asakura took five men, and the bridge commander, 2nd Lt. Jin Torao, dashed across the bridge with a sergeant to do battle with the column of hostile fighting vehicles, now only 300 meters from the span. The infantry company and the reconnaissance unit also sent out tank-killer parties on the left shore.

When Soviet crews detected the approach of Japanese antitank teams, they turned northwest toward the bridge. The boldest of the three tanks, in the lead, came as close as 10-20 meters from the Japanese trenches, where it seemed to stall. By now its incendiary oil must have been nearly expended, for it spit forth a last short burst of flame and then subsided into a hiss, the mouth of the flamethrower merely glowing like a jack-o'-lantern. Only light machine gun and pistol fire emanated from the tank. Covered by one of his riflemen, 10 meters away from the tank, Asakura approached from the rear of his target, set a two-kg. charge on the right-hand tread, and fell back to escape the explosion. When the track blew sky-high, the nearby Japanese soldiers cheered and applauded, reminding Lieutenant Jin of a scene from some Japanese medieval battle. Asakura was running forward to finish off the tank when machine gun bullets tore into his throat. He staggered to his feet but another burst of fire cut him down and shattered his drawn saber. Another soldier was killed at the same time.

Japanese troops surrounded the lead tank and fired their rifles madly at it. Lieutenant Colonel Saitō, now on the scene, calmed his men and called on the enemy crewmen (in Japanese) to surrender. When there was no reply, PFC Kaida defied enemy and friendly crossfire to hurl an explosive charge under the thin belly of the Soviet tank, damaging its front hatch. Sergeant Higaki dragged out a young Russian by the neck, and Kaida bayoneted him. The second Russian tank veered away to the far right and eventually toppled into the Halha River, while the third machine, which never came close, turned tail and got away. To Saitō, the small Soviet tank platoon's whole mode of action was more ridiculous than brave. The blind night firing of the flamethrowers, which fizzled out at the decisive moment, may have been caused by the crewmen's confusion or fear. The only other explanation was the possible use of flame as illumination or as a signal to other enemy forces.[17]

Japanese officers who were on the left shore explain the factors that began to erode their confidence in the feasibility of continuing their operation by the afternoon of 3 July in terms of logistics, terrain, and loss of initiative.

Logistics. Japanese units were fatigued from movement and fighting, and were extremely low on food and ammunition. Komatsubara's junior aide later heard that the infantry had run out of antitank ammunition. As Suzuki puts it, by nightfall on the 3rd the Japanese troops were "naked, unarmed, mere flesh." Fighting in scorching desert heat, the men found no potable water sources on the uplands across the Halha. Most of them had been able to fill their canteens only once, very early in the day, when they had crossed the river. The plight of the horses, originally about 60 per battery, was especially pitiable.

Terrain. Moving up a slope line 2,000 meters long, the Japanese infantry were attacked by tanks before they ever reached the top. This cost the troops the terrain advantage, for they could only glimpse the "tip" from below, whereas the foe could look down on every Japanese movement with the naked eye.

Loss of initiative. Once across the river, the Japanese were bereft of the element of surprise. Indeed, it was Suzuki's impression that the enemy seized the tactical initiative from the outset by striking the Japanese just as soon as they got across the river. Division operations officer Murata feels that the IJA foot soldiers had no targets within their range, especially after hostile armor stopped coming close. Enemy artillery pounded the unshielded Japanese from invisible positions, and only IJA artillery could get at the Soviet guns and armor. By the afternoon of 3 July, says Murata, the Japanese infantrymen were "accomplishing nothing." Their small arms were useless, their momentum had been lost, and the men were merely hanging on across the Halha. The enemy was being reinforced strongly and could be expected to strike again next morning. At the same time, in the confluence area, the Japanese tank offensive on the right shore seemed to have been stalemated too.

What should be done from 4 July? Those Japanese senior staff officers in charge of directing the crossing operation had to reach a quick decision. General Yano and the other two Kwantung Army consultants, Hattori and Tsuji, first conferred among themselves in the mid-afternoon of 3 July. There was little to say on the plus side of the ledger, except that the destruction of at least half of the hostile armor encountered thus far "should be considered satisfactory, in view of the division's combat effectiveness vis-à-vis the numerically superior foe." Still, enemy quantity seemed to be prevailing over IJA quality, and other considerations that were uniformly unfavorable had to be taken into account, such as the exclusive logistical dependence upon the one bridge, which was in imminent danger of destruction next day by air, artillery, and tank attack; the consequent vulnerability of the main force of the 23rd Division on the left bank; and the paucity of ammunition in particular. In elliptical IJA phraseology, enemy retreat "had unfortunately not been cut off entirely." This meant that Komatsubara's original intention of plunging to the confluence and trapping the foe against the river had become an impossibility. In short, little could be expected of operations on the left shore from 4 July on. Therefore the Kwantung Army liaison officers reached unanimous agreement that the Kobayashi task force should be withdrawn, but that the Kwantung Army alone, not Komatsubara, should be held operationally responsible for the matter of advancing or withdrawing.

When asked his opinion, Komatsubara had already indicated to Yano and the others that he would defer entirely to the Kwantung Army's wishes. If the offensive toward the Halha-Holsten confluence were to be continued, the division would attack Komatsu Heights with all of its strength. But if the Kwantung Army preferred to evacuate the left bank and to resume the attack against the enemy in the confluence sector from the right side, the division was prepared to "change course" that very night. Speaking from what he called the overall combat standpoint, Yano now suggested to Komatsubara the advisability of suspending action on the left shore and adopting the "change of course" alternative. Tsuji had the impression that the division commander and his staff were expecting this recommendation. Komatsubara accepted the counsel and issued the necessary order at 4 P.M. on the 3rd.

Lieutenant Colonel Murata, who was present when the final decision was reached, fully shared the opinion that, from the "reasonable" viewpoint, continuation of the left-shore operation would only have meant sacrifice to the point of annihilation. Tsuji says that he was very sorry the division had to return without achieving its objective across the river, but that nothing would have been achieved by hesitating to recross the bridge and leaving the entire Kobayashi group to fend for itself. Since operational prospects had become dim, it was high time to fall back.[18] The rationalization for the Japanese pullback permeated all levels of the chain of command, and was by no means generated by publicists or propagandists. Secret AGS intelligence, for example, heard that, although the right rear of the Kobayashi force had been threatened by enemy armor around midday on 3 July and 50 SB bombers in formation had attacked the Japanese ground forces, especially their rear, "the general situation had developed favorably." The Japanese had stopped some 140 enemy tanks and armored cars, of which no fewer than 100 had been wrecked. At the confluence, the enemy's bridge was gone, probably destroyed by the Japanese. "Having dealt a devastating blow to the enemy mechanized units, and having achieved their objectives," Komatsubara's main forces had been redeployed to the right side of the Halha to clean up the enemy on that shore. Although IJA losses were not yet verified (as of 6 July), they did not seem to have been severe.[19]

Japanese units on the scene, who were in the best position to know, issued orders that inevitably contained morale-building rationalizations of their own. The 72nd Regiment, for example, had had to fight its way out of encirclement by armor and horsemen at 3:30 P.M., and could not reassemble and occupy new holding positions 1,000 meters to the rear until after 4:30. It was admitted that, although the nearest hostile elements had been repulsed, the enemy's main force still occupied the foot of the high ground west of the confluence, in increasing strength. The regimental annals then assert that the left-bank attack force recrossed the river "since we had completely achieved our purpose." The 71st Regiment's history was only one adverb more candid: The Japanese had gone across the Halha and dealt a great blow to the enemy; the purpose of the left-bank offensive had "nearly succeeded." But even this qualification is lost in the preamble to Colonel Okamoto's regimental order issued at 8:20 P.M. on the 3rd; here the 71st Regiment, like the 72nd (and of course the division and the Kobayashi task force), is said to have "achieved its purpose completely." The order added the comforting but misleading information that Lieutenant General Yasuoka's separate offensive had also made good progress and exerted pressure on the foe located on the left shore of the Halha.[20]

Looking back on the period of 3-4 July, the military historian Imaoka endorses the Japanese decision to withdraw from the left side of the river, and points to a danger averted:

It seems proper from the overall standpoint that the 23rd Division's main force was pulled back and transferred, in accordance with the recommendation of the Kwantung Army staff, at the time the combat of the division had not developed as expected. If the 23rd Division had confronted the enemy continuously on the west bank of the Halha—given the thinking of the Japanese army at the time to the effect that retreating was extremely dishonorable—the division would probably have sustained a devastating blow prior to the Soviet army's great offensive in August.[21]

Hattori and Tsuji, however, saw the fundamental problem as the Kwantung Army's backdown in June from the original intention of using the veteran 7th Division, "the best division in Manchuria," instead of the weak 23rd Division to attack Soviet-MPRA forces on both shores of the Halha. Arguing from hindsight that Lieutenant General Sonobe's powerful division could have inflicted far more severe losses than those caused by the Komatsubara-Kobayashi force, the Kwantung Army staff officers nonetheless admitted that the strength to have been committed would still have been insufficient to annihilate hostile forces in the Halha region, since those forces proved to be far larger than had been anticipated at the time.[22]

20

Retreat from the River

Komatsubara's order of 4 P.M.[1] on 4 July called for the swift pullback of the Kobayashi group during the hours of darkness. (See Map 5.) After all casualties were evacuated, the whole task force was to cross the bridge and assemble at Fui Heights by daybreak. The engineer regiment would secure the span and dismantle it after the last soldiers had crossed. If imperative, explosives might be used to demolish the bridge. It was originally intended that Colonel Okamoto's detachment—the 71st Regiment, reinforced with field guns and other heavy weapons—should occupy the elevation around Bain Tsagan Obo by morning and cover the withdrawal by the 26th Regiment, the artillery, and the 72nd Regiment, before itself recrossing. Under the terms of its order of 8:20 P.M.,[2] the 71st Regiment set forth at 12:15 A.M. on the 4th, behind the field artillery, with guard elements 200 meters to each flank, the point battalion 300 meters ahead of the main body, and the rear guard 500 meters behind. Having lost so many horses in action, the field artillery batteries could only draw on about two pairs instead of three pairs per gun.

The Okamoto detachment filed solemnly past the hulks of the many burned enemy armored vehicles strewn on the plain. No large-scale hostile formations had been sighted since evening, other than tank salvage parties. To the northwest, tracer fire could be seen on the Sumi regiment's front. At 5:25 A.M., the Okamoto force reached its destination, the cairn site at Bain Tsagan. Ominously, severe fighting was still raging between the 26th Regiment and powerful enemy units, to the right of the detachment's covering position. Okamoto deployed the field artillery in front and the regimental guns on the flank, against possible tank irruptions. A half-hour later, while the troops were digging in, enemy artillery opened fire from high ground six km. to the west and inflicted some casualties, since defensive construction was by no means finished.

Enemy bombardments continued all day, despite Japanese bomber raids. But the foot soldiers soon learned that the earth was unexpectedly hard at 20 cm. below the surface and, using spades, they were able to dig good shelters, which reduced casualties. "Every last man came to realize," noted the regimental historian, "that construction is vital in every spare moment, not only on the defensive but also on the offensive. Nevertheless, one must beware of ignoring the dictum of always keeping one's eyes open."

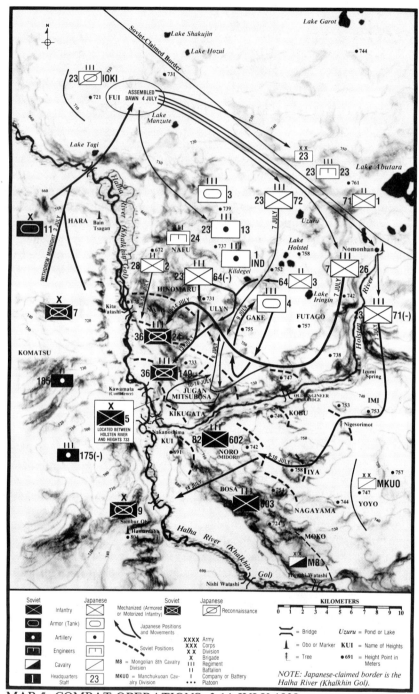

Legend

Soviet	Japanese		Soviet	Japanese
Infantry			Mechanized (Armored or Motorized Infantry)	Reconnaissance
Armor (Tank)			Japanese Positions and Movements	
Artillery			Soviet Positions	
Engineers				
Cavalry			M8 = Mongolian 8th Cavalry Division	
Headquarters Staff	23		MKUO = Manchukuoan Cavalry Division	

XXXX Army
XXX   Corps
X X   Division
X   Brigade
III   Regiment
II   Battalion
I   Company or Battery
•••   Platoon

KILOMETERS

0 1 2 3 4 5 6 7 8 9 10

≋ = Bridge   *Uzuru* = Pond or Lake
⊥ = Obo or Marker   **KUI** = Name of Heights
♣ = Tree   • 691 = Height Point in Meters

NOTE: *Japanese-claimed border is the Halha River (Khalkhin Gol).*

MAP 5: COMBAT OPERATIONS, 3-14 JULY 1939

Having received the Kobayashi group's instructions, Sakai's 72nd Regiment—farthest to have advanced—issued its own pullback order at 7:30 P.M. Starting the withdrawal at midnight, Major Kokura's 2nd Battalion—guarding the left flank—drove back about 50 enemy horsemen at 1 A.M. The regiment proceeded to the river crossing by 4:30 A.M. without further interference. In the distance, enemy tracers and illuminating shells could be seen. Major Hamada, the regimental aide, likened the beautiful sight to the annual fireworks display by the Sumida River at Ryōgoku in Tokyo. The regiment marched back, "enjoying the scene" yet feeling uneasy and saying nothing as they passed knocked-out enemy tanks, barely visible in the darkness but with turret guns still pointed menacingly at them. Major Nishikawa, commanding the 1st Battalion, calls it an easy pullback to the crossing site. Although the enemy must have known the Japanese were leaving, there was no pursuit. The bridge itself was jammed with vehicles, horses, foot soldiers, guns, and headquarters. The 4th of July was bright and hot again, and there was considerable concern about possible hostile air or artillery bombardment of the exposed span. Enemy guns did open a severe all-day barrage from 6 A.M., and about a dozen bombers also struck the area. The regiment got back to the right shore before noon but admitted suffering heavy casualties in the process.[3]

Some IJA records paint a rosy picture of the withdrawal across the bridge, stressing the smoothness of the movement. Capt. Hara Seiroku, who was there both times, says it was worse coming back than going across, though. Everybody wanted to leave first—a natural psychological phenomenon for troops pulling back under fire. But there was a giant traffic pileup, posing the very real danger that the flimsy span would collapse. Again, a traffic controller should have been assigned. Hara, although a Kwantung Army officer, remembers handling traffic for a while until he could turn the task over to some local officer.

The unexpected troubles of the 26th Infantry upset the 23rd Division's pullback schedule and cost the regiment one powerful battalion. Sumi deemed it necessary to pull the regimental main force back 1,000 meters, and he wanted Adachi to rejoin the main body, too, which meant at least double the distance to traverse for the 1st Battalion. After ordering the main force to evacuate the casualties when it fell back, the colonel tried in vain to find Adachi. When Sumi got back to his planned position, the skies were brightening, but the regiment was not deployed yet. The colonel was very pessimistic and unhappy. Entirely on his own, he had converted his mission from an aggressive penetration of the enemy's rear to the merely negative role of protecting the bridge sector. Although he still did not know how Kobayashi was faring, he finally saw some troops from the 71st Regiment, falling back on his left flank. Learning in this way that Colonel Okamoto had not been too successful with the frontal assault either, Sumi was frankly relieved that he was not the only regimental commander who had not done well.

As the day grew brighter, there was no trace of pullback by the remnants of the Adachi battalion, apparently still stuck at the original advanced location. This meant, Sumi remained convinced, that his order had not been transmitted to the 1st Battalion by the warrant officer; there was no way of checking because the colonel did not know the man's name. Peering in the general direction of Adachi's sector, Sumi could see enemy tanks already on the move, presaging new attacks on the regiment, which was very short of its primary remaining antitank weapons—pop bottles for use as *kaenbin*.

At last orders came from the 23rd Division, conveyed by Captain Itō at about 5 A.M., some 13 hours after Komatsubara had issued his instructions. The 26th Regiment was to recross the river immediately and reassemble on the right bank. Sumi replied that he could not do this. Elements of one battalion were still 1,500 meters to the front, encircled by the foe and thus separated from the main body of the regiment. It was too difficult to communicate with the 1st Battalion during daylight hours, so Sumi would have to hold on for another day, wait for darkness, regain control of the battalion, and then carry out the division's order to withdraw. The division may have known that the battalion was in a difficult and separate position, but it clearly had not realized—when the order was originally issued—that the Adachi unit had been trapped and mauled. To last even one more day, however, the regiment desperately needed more cider bottles. Sumi pleaded with Itō to treat this as a matter of ammunition, not of mere bottles. The latter should be flown in, if necessary. Itō promised to help, but Sumi worried privately that he could not depend on him.

When Sumi saw Colonel Okamoto heading back to the bridge, he asked for any cider bottles that the 71st Regiment could spare. Although Okamoto agreed, his front-line units were not generous when Sumi sent a platoon to collect bottles. Only 12 more were obtained, which brought the 26th Regiment's total to a mere 48. Sumi kept eight bottles at his headquarters and distributed 20 each to the 2nd and 3rd battalions. He was convinced that when this insufficient number of fire bottles was expended in battle, he and all of his men would die where they were.

Meanwhile, in the morning hours of 4 July, tragedy befell 23rd Division headquarters, whose command post had been transferred to the right shore. At various times since daylight, Hattori, Tsuji, and Yano had already experienced very close calls from enemy artillery barrages. On high ground north of the bridge, Komatsubara noted, the Japanese were being hammered by long-range guns, in particular by four 15-cm. cannon that laid down "swift, hurricane-like fire." The power of the shellfire resembled aerial bombardment in severity; but whereas bombers could be expected to depart after a strike, the enemy guns went on and on, causing explosions and black smoke in succession, with accurate impact. The cavalry horses were hit at the outset, and over 100 stampeded in all directions. Komatsubara was especially distressed by the sight of one horse, whose leg was shattered, limping away, whinnying pitifully.

Sometime before noon, a formation of perhaps a dozen Soviet aircraft raided the division command post, wounding a visiting staff officer, Lieutenant Colonel Gondō, in the eyes and knocking staff officer Hara unconscious and burying him in debris. Hara regained his senses only when a shovel hit his helmet. From high ground on the left shore, an enemy barrage had been bracketing the area 200 to 300 meters behind Komatsubara, who was directing pullback operations at the cliff's edge. Hara saw the division chief of staff, Colonel Ōuchi, lying 30 meters away, with blood soaking his chest. He knelt by the unconscious colonel, whose pulse was very weak. Ōuchi expired soon afterward without uttering a word. The death of Komatsubara's respected deputy, a brave and steady officer, shook up the division commander as well as Tsuji, Suzuki, and all of their colleagues scattered around the post. Komatsubara seemed concerned lest the division fall into disarray. At a distance from the headquarters, a transport company commander heard that 15-cm. howitzers had pounded the area. He looked in the direction of the bombardment and saw that "the command post had disappeared completely."

The atmosphere of the 23rd Division at this stage is described well by Major General Hashimoto, the AGS Operations Bureau chief, who finally caught up with Komatsubara and Yano on the right bank in the evening on 4 July. Escaping an attack by Soviet planes bound for a raid against the advance Japanese air force base from which his own scout plane had taken off, Hashimoto reached the bridge area before the sun went down. Dirty and muddy, Komatsubara was changing his uniform in a sedan to the rear. Hashimoto waited in the division commander's foxhole, and then chatted with his old war college classmate for about ten minutes. Without knowing the full details, Hashimoto gathered that matters had not gone too smoothly for the division. He felt very sorry for Komatsubara and expressed words of comfort, but the division commander did not strike him as particularly depressed or exhausted.

Although hurried by his pilot, who was anxious to get back to Hailar that night, Hashimoto also had a chance to confer with Yano, who had once been his subordinate in the First Army in North China and whom he knew well. The chat in Yano's foxhole was a disappointment. Now a Kwantung Army senior officer, Yano gave an embellished report. Since the division had achieved its mission, Yano claimed in reply to a question about the progress of the operation, he had recommended that the task force be brought back across the river. Actually Komatsubara had been very aggressive in his outlook throughout and wanted to do more, but it was Yano who had recommended the pullback, and the division commander agreed. Hashimoto listened quietly to Yano's presentation, and then asked for a prognosis. "Repeating this type of combat is feckless," Yano answered. "I'll provide guidance so as to prevent a recurrence." Hashimoto told Yano that he concurred, but inwardly he felt that he had been the recipient of a whitewash.[4]

Sumi's regiment was supposed to have recrossed the river first of the infantry regiments. By now on 4 July, however, it had become dangerous to retain the Okamoto detachment even one more night as a covering force on the left shore. Consequently, the 26th Regiment was going to be the last of the three infantry regiments to return to the east bank.[5] Following a whole day of enemy bombardment, the 71st Infantry came under attack, shortly after 8 P.M., by some two infantry battalions and more than ten tanks, supported by 13 or 14 artillery pieces. Okamoto detachment headquarters reported receiving frequent requests by front-line units for gasoline needed to fill fire bottles.

At midnight on the 4th, the Okamoto force withdrew from the Bain Tsagan cairn site under fire and headed for the bridge. A field artillery master sergeant had been expecting that his battalion would recross the river first. "The chain of command must not have been too good here," he muses, "for some infantry preceded us across. My battery was left behind to cover the crossing. With my one-gun squad, I felt rather scared and alone!" Around 1:15 A.M., the regimental colors were back on the right shore. By the 71st Regiment's own admission, the redeployment was "a bit confused" in all units. For example, most of the 3rd (Hanada) Company could not catch up with the main body of the detachment, and elements of the attached medical unit did not arrive until 8:30 A.M.

On the right bank, the Okamoto force was strafed at 11:55 A.M. by fifteen I-16 fighters flying from the east at very low altitude and firing what were thought to be explosive bullets. Casualties were particularly severe in the field artillery battalion, which was jammed with men and horses. The imaginative regimental chronicler likened the strafing to "raindrops jumping up from the surface of the water during a shower."

Harassed by the 15-cm. howitzers that had already appeared on the left bank near vacated Hara Heights, Okamoto decided at 1 P.M. to move his troops toward Hill 752—well southeast of the IJA bridge over the Halha—

in an effort to get out of range. Despite putting 12 or 13 km. between itself
and the Soviet artillery, the regiment remained within the enemy batteries'
effective range and continued to incur casualties. A platoon leader was
struck and killed, together with horses and other men, while transporting
mortars on horseback. The outgunned Japanese field artillery "returned the
favor" (*oreimairi*), in the words of a company commander, but was ineffective beyond eight km. and accomplished nothing.

First Lt. Nomura Norio's 3rd Transport Company thought that it too had
proceeded beyond the range of enemy bombardment and was catching its
breath when dozens of I-16 fighters swooped in, strafing the trucks at very
low altitude. Soviet SB bombers followed closely and demolished vehicles
that had pulled up. Nomura ordered the trucks to be dispersed 100 meters
apart and the men to dig holes near the vehicles. After the air raid, the exhausted lieutenant stretched out on the meadow. Realizing that he had not
eaten for two days, he munched on some dried noodles and drank a cup of
water that tasted of gasoline. During this lull he pondered his recent experiences, and "the superficial attitude that I had had [toward combat] when we
first set out from [Chiangchunmiao] vanished from my mind." The site
northeast of Hill 752 that was selected for the company's bivouac was unattractive because the terrain was swampy and it had been raining. "It could
not be helped," however, for there was a useful airstrip on the heights. The
night turned cold and wretched, and Nomura's men could not sleep, even
after their earlier exertions.

During the gloomiest period on 4 July, near 3 P.M., claims Tsuji, a liaison
officer with a "tragic countenance" reached division headquarters at Fui
Heights from Sumi's unit. The courier reported on the crisis besetting the
26th Regiment and, "in a trembling voice," asked for *kaenbin* and mines.
Tsuji intimates that Komatsubara was pained by this "sniveling" so soon
after losing Colonel Ōuchi. It must be admitted that Sumi and his regiment
were not exactly popular at headquarters. Since the 26th Infantry was on
loan from another outfit, the 23rd Division knew little about them. Once in
combat, however, Sumi's force conveyed the impression to staff officers that
it had come to "save" the division, whereas it was not that capable in general. In particular, the division staff viewed Sumi as a sort of "tyrant," found
it difficult to employ him, and did not regard him as an efficient combat
commander. The logistics officer considered him to be the most troublesome
of all the infantry regiment commanders to deal with during the Nomonhan
fighting.

For his part, Sumi remains certain that 23rd Division headquarters was
overly optimistic about its grandiose plan of crushing enemy forces on the
left bank and using his regiment for an unrealistic deep exploitation mission

to the confluence. Dramatic proof of the underestimation of the foe was the death of Ōuchi in the strafing, the destruction of the division commander's own staff car, and the fact that Komatsubara had had to walk back across the river and set up his command post on the right bank. Sumi heard that morale at division headquarters had degenerated to the point that "everybody was too depressed to say a word."

As for himself, Sumi says that he was a desk officer, a war college graduate and "instant expert" on the Russians (by dint of previous OSS experience), who was in good if not robust health at the time. He had developed a congenial atmosphere in the regiment and had fostered close relations between officers and men. Majors Adachi, Kawai, and Kikuchi were superb battalion commanders, and their troops from Hokkaido and Kyushu possessed well-known military qualities of seriousness, patience, reserve, and devotion to orders. The 26th Infantry was the best in the 7th Division in terms of marksmanship, swordplay, and marching, says Sumi. He calls it "a superior, nearly ideal regiment."

Staff officers explain their thinking about Sumi's regiment as of 4 July. The 26th Regiment was not being treated differently from the other infantry regiments. Sumi got a better hearing from Komatsubara than did his fellow-colonels. It was, in fact, intended to pull the Sumi unit back across the river before the others, since the regiment was the "guest" of the 23rd Division. But Sumi was still on the left bank, and the engineers could not dispose of the pontoon bridge until the last of his men were brought back safely. The Adachi unit was engaging only tanks, which now operated exclusively by night; so it should have been relatively easy to extricate the battalion in darkness, as stipulated by the division order. Some found it hard to believe that a battalion had been left so far ahead of (or behind) the main force of the regiment.

"Since considerable difficulties were anticipated" in pulling out the 26th Regiment, Tsuji was sent to direct the movement. Tsuji says that, after the death of Ōuchi, there was a shortage of staff officers to send to Sumi, so he volunteered to proceed without any escorts, who would only draw enemy fire. Yano and Komatsubara agreed, the latter gently thanking him for going out of his way so often. En route back across the Halha, Tsuji gulped down two canteens of river water. When he reached Sumi's command post on northern Hara Heights, there ensued a sensational confrontation, which Tsuji has retailed widely in an often-reprinted book whose treatment of the episode is called "disgusting, fallacious, and slanderous" by Sumi. Tsuji asserts:

> I found the regiment commander in the midst of supper, although it was still broad daylight. Strange to say, he was drinking beer. I was amazed that he could

be so inconsiderate . . . while his fighting men were going hungry and thirsty. My displeasure turned to fury. "What happened to the Adachi battalion?" "Adachi? Oh, he dashed forward on his own, and look what he got into. It's too bad. I guess I'll send out a patrol tonight to establish contact with him." While a brave battalion commander of his was in dire danger and heavily surrounded by the enemy, the regiment commander was nonchalantly drinking beer! Is this the brilliant man who graduated from the war college? I eventually forgot my rank and place and I shouted, "Why don't you rescue the Adachi battalion with all of your strength, bearing aloft the regimental colors? As an officer in command, how can you leave [the battalion] in the lurch?" The 2nd and 3rd battalion commanders and the regimental aide, who were nearby, also expressed their dissatisfaction with the regiment commander, in low tones.

Of Tsuji and his denunciations, "expressed in his own peculiar style of writing," Sumi remarks that it was customary for the "hot-blooded" staff officer to show up at front-line positions. "Although there was much to glean from his opinions, some of the regimental commanders found him to be a nuisance." The story of Sumi's drinking beer on the battlefield was a canard. He was sitting alone near his foxhole, his aide and orderly dead, and he was worrying about Adachi. A regimental clerk, a sergeant, felt sorry for the colonel, urged him to eat, and offered him a beer bottle filled with river water. After sipping from it, Sumi left the bottle on the sand. As a matter of fact, he was not much of an imbiber of alcohol of any kind. The only thing he remembers definitely about the conversation with Tsuji was that the latter offered him a drink of sake from a cup that he claimed was the gift of the Emperor. Sumi writes:

> This so-called gift cup, which Tsuji claimed had been presented to him by Prince Kan'in, was always seen dangling from his waist, while his flask was always filled with sake. . . . I was well aware of the fact that his cup was an imitation. . . . [Apart from being weak when it comes to liquor], I just did not feel like drinking sake from an imperial cup forced on me by "imperial aide" Tsuji. Probably my face betrayed my feelings—"Why, you presumptuous little pip-squeak, making a fuss about a gift cup from the Emperor!" Saying "No, thank you, but since you insist, just to be polite," I sipped a little of his sake.

After the war, Sumi once had a new confrontation with Tsuji at Yasukuni Shrine. In addition, one of Sumi's men wrote to Tsuji to acquaint him with the truth about Adachi's relief and the beer versus water controversy, and to demand an apology and retraction. In effect, Tsuji admitted his error with respect to the beer, but insisted that a battalion commander did tell him at the time that Sumi was not enthusiastic about rescuing the Adachi battalion.[6]

To this point, we have mentioned Major Adachi's "lost battalion" from the vantage of Sumi's regimental headquarters, which was characterized by worry and by ignorance of the situation, since communication was nearly nonexistent. Adachi, it will be remembered, had ended up with the only motorized infantry battalion in the 26th Regiment and indeed in the Kobayashi task force. With this one battalion, he had done his best to implement the three-battalion deep-encirclement mission originally assigned to Sumi by Komatsubara. Adachi's 1st Battalion had easily outdistanced the two battalions that followed him on foot (and very late), but he ran into a hornet's nest of enemy armor, Mongolian cavalry, and motorized machine guns and was soon isolated. In fact, the battalion was not even concentrated in one location. Near battalion headquarters were deployed only the 2nd and 3rd infantry companies and three machine gun platoons. To the right, in sight of the Halha but separated from the battalion's main body, were the 1st Company and another machine gun platoon. His remaining rapid-fire and regimental guns, out of ammunition, were similarly isolated from Adachi. The fractionalization of the Adachi unit rendered the regiment's problem of communicating with "the" battalion all the more understandable.

The splinter unit of the 1st Battalion, closer to the regiment, was able to make contact with Sumi's headquarters on the night of 3 July and was ordered to rejoin the regiment. Despite meeting enemy armor, the withdrawing company and machine gun platoon were assisted greatly by a 27th Infantry rapid-fire battery (attached to Sumi), which knocked out two tanks and drove off the rest. En route to the regiment's location, the withdrawing force encountered a messenger from the 1st Battalion. He had been sent by Adachi to contact Sumi, but when he got back to the battalion command post, he found the unit annihilated. The splinter force conveyed this information to Sumi when it reached his headquarters at 2 or 3 A.M. on the 4th.

Hope that the 1st Battalion had not been destroyed was rekindled when, from Adachi's direction, was heard the distinctive sound of Japanese machine guns (a low or heavy sound as opposed to the soprano of Soviet and Czech weapons). Perhaps the messenger met by the splinter force had missed the battalion's command post in the darkness and deduced that the unit had been annihilated from the evidence of corpses he found littering the battlefield. Around 4 A.M. a warrant officer and two messengers arrived at regimental headquarters from the command team of the 3rd Company, a core element of the battalion. Major Adachi and a company commander had been killed and the 1st Battalion was surrounded on three sides, but the unit was still holding out and would try to break through the encirclement and rejoin the regiment.

The circumstances of Adachi's death could be reconstructed only later. His isolated main force had clung to its positions under heavy fire all day on the 3rd, digging foxholes and trying to stay alive. Despite Sumi's conviction throughout that the order to rejoin the parent regiment never reached Adachi, the battalion commander had been preparing to withdraw during darkness on 3/4 July, and it is improbable that such a decision was reached arbitrarily on Adachi's part. At night, medical personnel checked and counted the casualties.

Adachi directed his men to keep low and hold their fire when the withdrawal began. But during the preparations enemy trucks, with headlights on, blundered into the area from behind a dune to the battalion's left. A front-line Japanese soldier, unable to restrain himself, shot down two Russians in the lead truck. Taken by surprise, the enemy fired back in confusion. Instead of proceeding past the battalion site, however, the Russians swung back from the right. Enemy foot soldiers and tanks swept the area with tracer fire. Adachi ordered his 2nd Company to launch a charge (*totsugeki*), and then, as a new wave of enemy pressed near, he sent the 3rd Company forward. The Japanese infantrymen were overrun. When Soviet armor was 200 meters away, Adachi drew his sword and ordered his last soldiers, machine gunners and headquarters men, to follow him in a last charge against the tanks. Lacking rifles, the machine gunners dashed forward with bayonets. From a distance of 50 meters, a Japanese superior private saw a tiny black dot jump aboard a tank, illuminated by an enemy flare. It was Major Adachi, opening a hatch and trying to grapple with the tank crewmen. Tracer fire from another tank shot him off the tank; he fell backward and was run over. The time was about 1 A.M. on 4 July.

Upon the death of Adachi, the commander of the 1st Machine Gun Company, Capt. Kondō Kōjiro, assumed control of the remnants of the 1st Battalion. Although there was some thinking among the surviving company commanders that the unit should try to resume Adachi's effort to pull back, Kondō declined until he was ordered to do so. He sent a warrant officer and a soldier to try to contact regiment headquarters, while the men scooped out holes with their helmets and emplaced their heaviest weapons—machine guns—to the front. The liaison officer managed to make it to Sumi's post after some incredible adventures: becoming lost, getting illuminated by enemy flares, jumping atop a parked tank and throwing a grenade into its open hatch, being knocked off the machine when it spun its turret just before exploding, and squirming with the injured soldier while Soviet armor scoured the area looking for them for an hour.

Hearing the explosion of the tank and thinking that his messengers had been killed, Kondō sent out another warrant officer to report to Sumi. This officer arrived safely, about two hours later. After learning of the crisis afflicting the 1st Battalion, Sumi tried to resupply the unit with some of his own scant ammunition and stores on the morning of the 4th. Enemy armor thwarted this mission. The quartermaster officer, Lieutenant Negami, and a work party had been bringing up supplies from the right shore on 3 July for

Kikuchi's 3rd Battalion: ammunition and food such as rice balls (o-*nigiri*) and tinned beef. Unable to find the Kikuchi unit that night, Negami had entered a small dip two or three km. from the bridge. There, by early morning on the 4th, were concentrated all of the trucks of Nomura's transport company. This had been Adachi's troop-carrier unit but, during the night melee, it had become separated from the 1st Battalion and had had to form close-quarter teams of its own to try to defend the trucks. An infantry platoon leader, a second lieutenant from the 3rd Battalion, arrived at the dip with two squads to carry supplies intended for Adachi. Since it had become dangerous to move by day, Nomura offered the platoon leader two trucks; but the enemy was all around, firing, and nobody volunteered to drive. The officers and men huddled in the dip, and no supplies ever went forward to the desperate 1st Battalion. As soon as they could, that morning, the truckers pulled out of the gully and drove back across the bridge to the right side of the Halha.

Efforts by the regiment to contact the 1st Battalion in daylight failed. After nightfall, Sumi would attempt to relieve his lost battalion. The main body of the 26th Regiment underwent artillery bombardment all day. Movement forward or backward was not possible, but Japanese casualties were light. To Sumi's astonishment, not one enemy tank came closer to the regiment than 400 or 500 meters. The armored vehicles would jam on their brakes, gun their engines, and sink into the sand up to their cannon, which was all they would use. Sumi was impressed by the overnight change in Soviet tactics, by their swift application of lessons learned only the day before. The enemy must have comprehended that tanks versus *kaenbin* were like moths blundering into the flame. Later, the colonel heard that the Russians told their tank units the Japanese possessed some kind of powerful new antitank weapon which could incinerate armored vehicles instantly, so the tankers should not come too close to Japanese positions. In any case, the caution of enemy armored forces on 4 July was heartening, for Sumi's regiment still had only the 48 bottle bombs for antitank combat. Mulling over the envisaged relief operation and commiserating with the plight of his scattered 1st Battalion, the colonel spent what he calls "my own longest day." His regiment and attached units lost 53 killed and 112 wounded on the 4th.

What was left of the 1st Battalion endured an even grimmer 4 July, under enemy attack in searing heat from morning till night. In the words of a superior private, "it was just horrible" that day. A sergeant looked inside his gun cart and found only melted wick stubs left from the long tallow candles he had stored inside. Touching one's steel helmet in the sun would cost a scorched hand. There was nothing for the 1st Battalion to eat but dry hard-tack, without water to wash it down. Stripped to the waist and almost crazed by thirst, soldiers licked blood, while even an officer was heard moaning for water. Some men coated the inside of their mouths with mentholatum ointment. The extent of the soldiers' thirst is suggested by the fact that five or six men launched a bizarre charge against machine guns to get at their water coolant. The couple of soldiers who survived filled all of the canteens with nauseous liquid, which they drank but which proved unpotable because of the 50 percent spindle-oil solution.

The Japanese troops waved their red-ball flag when IJA aircraft circled over them, bombing nearby enemy lines but caving in friendly trenches in the process. Later, Japanese planes returned to drop ammunition for rapid-fire and regimental guns, of which the 1st Battalion had not one left. Messengers sent to regimental headquarters never came back. Dusk arrived, with no sign of a rescue unit. The battalion concluded that it was being abandoned on the supposition that it had been annihilated. Captain Kondō and his men decided to make one last, improbable charge at midnight. It would be directed not toward the regimental command post or the bridge across the Halha, but toward Lake Buir, perhaps 15 km. ahead of them, deep in enemy territory—shimmering Lake Buir, where everybody could die a glorious death while gorging themselves on water. Kondō checked the number of survivors and was pleased to find that there were still quite a few men left. Waiting for midnight to come, hungry and thirsty, bitten by swarms of relentless mosquitoes, soldiers collected mementoes from slain comrades or gathered dead men's puttees, which would be useful later.[7]

Despite Tsuji's insulting remarks, it is unthinkable that Sumi had written off the remnants of the 1st Battalion. On the morning of the 4th, he had told 23rd Division staff officer Itō what he had in mind, and he worried about the battalion all day. The new division order for the 26th Infantry, now the last part of the Kobayashi force on the left shore, to recross the Halha that night was issued at 3 P.M. and reached Sumi at 5:30 P.M. The colonel was still pondering the best way of extricating the 1st Battalion yet getting the whole regiment back across the river before daylight on the 5th. Entering into his thinking was the fact that though the sun would be down at 9:30 P.M., the area would remain bright for another half-hour, during which time unobserved movement would still be impossible.

At 10:10 P.M. Sumi issued a regimental order directing all units to clean up the battlefield (*senjō seiri*), recover the dead and wounded by 1:30 A.M., disengage from combat, and proceed to the river crossing. Maj. Kikuchi Tetsuo would take the 2nd Battalion and conduct a night attack designed to rescue Adachi's men. Ordinarily, Sumi should have remained at regiment headquarters with Maj. Kawai Jiichi's 3rd Battalion, but the colonel was determined to fulfill his sense of responsibility for the Adachi battalion's isolation and to die with his men in battle if the rescue operation failed. So Sumi ordered the colors to be sent back across the river and the guns to be left at the regimental command post, which Kawai was to defend.

The two warrant officers who had made it to regiment headquarters from the Adachi unit the night before were ordered to guide the relief force, since they presumably knew the location of the lost battalion. But although they studied the terrain all day, they could discern no landmarks to suggest even the general direction of the objective. After preparations were completed at 11:40 P.M., Major Kikuchi led forth 285 men of his battalion plus the splinter company and machine gun platoon from the Adachi unit and volunteers from attached units. The troops traveled light and were organized into a charging unit followed by a casualty-retrieval force. Sumi claims that the movement proceeded precisely and easily, but one of the warrant officers says that only the distant sound of machine gun fire enabled the relief force to gain a bearing. The guides scurried around frantically, sighting on compasses and the Big Dipper, while the column of troops moved along silently, sometimes extended and sometimes compressed, giving the impression of a "wriggling worm."

Two or three hours passed. The Adachi battalion must be nearby, but still it could not be detected. Sumi conferred with the guides. When the charging unit had approached the objective, it should break the enemy encirclement and secure positions, while the retrieval force did its task and got out quickly. Word should first be conveyed to the 1st Battalion and then a pistol signal discharged to alert the relief elements.

Unexpected firing erupted ahead. Apparently the lost battalion was trying to break out, but after about ten minutes the shooting stopped. Had this been Kondō's last charge to reach the waters of Lake Buir? An officer guide dashed forward, heard some moaning, then saw enemy flares illumine the area. To evade hostile bombardment, the officer jumped into a trench. It was Kondō's battalion headquarters. After learning that Colonel Sumi had brought relief forces, Kondō passed the word along the trenches. The battalion "perked up," and the guide fired his pistol signal. It had, in the literal sense, been the survivors' "last hour."

Retrieval work did not progress as well as desired because of the darkness, the hurriedness, the confusion, and the firing by enemy infantry. A special effort was made to extricate the bodies of Major Adachi, the battalion aide, other officers, and noncoms. Puttee strips were tied to corpses and pulled along. Adachi's body was alternately dragged and slung on soldiers' backs. The first troops got out in fairly good order, but later, delayed and dispersed elements had to dash away and try to outrun the pursuing enemy. A warrant officer fears that many severely wounded men as well as corpses were left behind. Certainly those dead who had already been buried in shallow graves could not be dug out and removed.

Inside the defenders' perimeter, a wounded superior private saw welcome canteens of water being thrown to the survivors. But the retrieval unit was rushing to evacuate whatever dead and wounded it could find, and the machine gunner had to get out in only ten minutes. What to do with the body of his brother-in-law, his slain subordinate? Because of his own wounds and the shortness of time, he could only cut off a hand of the corpse and bear it back with him.

Actually, there were more wounded than dead. Their evacuation was difficult enough, says Sumi, but it was even harder to remove the corpses. Manpower requirements were great. Four unloaded soldiers, for instance, were generally needed to haul each dead man. This unexpected task, although obviously important in such an operation, received no attention in peacetime troop training. Additional manpower was needed to carry captured or lost matériel. Some equipment that could not be removed had to be buried. For example, a machine gunner, wounded in the hand and the foot, could not carry out his precious Type 92 heavy machine gun, the newest IJA model, which weighed a hefty 35 kg. Pressed for time, he had to leave the gun barrel and tripod as is, and only take apart the firing mechanism and hide it in the sand.

The charging unit had pressed forward in the van with Kikuchi's machine gun company firing their eight weapons on both flanks. A confused melee developed in the dark. Soviet tanks usually pulled back at night, and Soviet infantry did not relish bayonet fighting. Therefore most of the enemy attacks involved grenades. Kikuchi launched three charges designed to give time for the wounded, the able-bodied, and the retrieval men to get out. During the third charge, a hand grenade exploded against the front of the major's helmet and he fell unconscious. Four soldiers carried the mortally wounded Kikuchi back to the river. Fragments of the same grenade hit a medical lieutenant in 16 places, but he survived. Machine gun bullets struck another lieutenant in the neck, wounding him fatally.

Somewhere between 3 and 4 A.M. on the 5th, Sumi, the mauled relief force, and the remnants of the Adachi battalion straggled back to the Halha. Kawai brought out the 3rd Battalion and the regimental headquarters, too, hauling the wounded and the dead. Sumi called to Kikuchi, whom the soldiers were carrying on a litter across the bridge, but the major was still in a coma and died soon afterward.

According to the Russians, Soviet and Mongolian forces launched a coordinated offensive during the evening of 4 July along the entire front. In the fierce fighting, which raged throughout the night, the Japanese struggled desperately to hold the Bain Tsagan sector at all costs. By 3 A.M. on the 5th, under Soviet-MPRA pressure, especially by armor, Japanese resistance was overcome in hand-to-hand fighting. The eastern slopes were littered with enormous numbers of dead and masses of matériel—supposedly thousands of corpses as well as the "carcasses of horses, a multitude of crashed and broken guns, mortars, machine guns, and cars."

The Japanese engineer regiment commander, Saitō, had been waiting at the bridge since midnight. By 2 A.M., with early dawn not far off, Kobayashi's main force had come back across the river, with their wounded and their dead, but the 26th Regiment was still on the left bank. A division staff officer asked Saitō what he was going to do about the bridge. Could it possibly be dismantled and piled up on the right shore? Saitō insisted that he could not do a thing until the entire 26th Regiment had returned. Couldn't the forces be rowed back? Portable boats were a possibility, but the disappearance of the bridge would unsettle all of the troops still on the left side of the river. Saitō felt that, if only he could get started by about 3 A.M., he could somehow manage to take apart the span, and preparations were made accordingly. Around that hour, however, heavy fire was heard in Sumi's direction and the 26th Regiment was just beginning to recross the bridge in small groups—a "sad scene," with the walking wounded supporting more severely injured comrades or dragging dead friends along with ropes.

The retreating Japanese troops appeared at first in unit size. To Negami, the troops' morale seemed "lost," and the soldiers were rather disorganized as they retreated under fire. Many an eerie sight was visible. One PFC, carrying a corpse wrapped in a tent, passed a soldier resting at mid-bridge with a wounded man whose nose had been destroyed by a shell fragment, leaving maggots swarming over the hideous gash. Lugging his own burden, the PFC was also horrified to see, bobbing crazily on the backs of soldiers trudging across the bridge ahead of him, the gory frozen faces of other corpses protruding from body-bag tents.

Saitō stood on the left bank. By now it was a little past 4 A.M., and it had become almost hopeless to think of dismantling the bridge. Tsuji came up and asked the engineer commander what he was going to do. Saitō responded that he had no choice but to demolish the span, which he would do only after the 26th Regiment was all safe. Tsuji agreed and recrossed the bridge. Reluctantly, two squads of demolition engineers set two 1-kg. yellow explosive charges on individual pontoons, with electric fuzes linked by cables extending 1,000 meters from the shoreline to avoid casualties from enemy fire. Saitō felt terrible. Destruction of the Kwantung Army's only existing bridging equipment, poor as it was, meant that a second offensive into Mongolia would have to be forgotten in the foreseeable future. IJA engineers, of course, had had experience demolishing bridges, but never in their long history had they blown up one of their own. Tormented by a sense of responsibility, the engineer commander even thought of committing suicide.

Meanwhile, Saitō tried to reassure his haggard old friend and classmate

Sumi, whom he had known since the age of 14, that the bridge would not be demolished before the entire hard-fighting 26th Infantry had returned safely. As the returning forces dwindled to a mere trickle, Sumi would stand on the left shore and anxiously ask solitary stragglers if they were the last on that side. The men would say they thought so, and the colonel would walk with them to the right bank. But worry still gnawed at him. There might be walking wounded slowly trying to reach the bridge. So Sumi would go back to the other side—a process he repeated three times. He kept asking Saitō to delay demolition. Even when no more soldiers appeared, Sumi was apprehensive and hesitated to leave. Finally, a lieutenant came to Sumi from regimental headquarters and told the colonel he would have to stop at some point. Sumi thanked Saitō for his forbearance, called the operation completed, and went back to his command post on the right shore, just behind a machine gun company.

A little after 5 A.M., dragging his sword and trying to help some wounded, an infantry battalion officer made it to the bridge and assured the engineers that he was the last man out. Sumi had recrossed a little earlier, and Saitō deemed it safe to destroy the bridge now. Moving up the high ground on the right shore, the engineer commander peered intently across the river. No more Japanese soldiers were in view, but up to 80 enemy tanks could be sighted "napping" on the heights to the west—watching and waiting in broad daylight. Sometime around 6 A.M., Saitō ordered the bridge blown up. A noncom waved a flag from the high ground. Thereupon the lieutenant in charge of the demolition unit detonated the charges and blew the span sky-high. The enemy tanks "awoke" and began firing, but the Japanese sapper squads made it back to their headquarters safely. Saitō left only after he was certain that the span had been wrecked. Tsuji recounts a cock-and-bull story that the bridge was blown up while enemy armor was dashing across in pursuit, and that tanks were plunging into the Halha when the span collapsed.

Other Soviet tanks apparently came across the river on an invisible underwater bridge two km. upstream and chased some engineer trucks on the right shore, causing the men to jump off the vehicles and run for cover. Meanwhile, with suicidal feelings, Saitō reported to Komatsubara that the Japanese bridge had had to be demolished. The division commander did not reproach him but was concerned mainly whether every last 26th Regiment soldier had escaped. Reassured that they had, Komatsubara seemed relieved and pleased, as was Saitō for the additional reason that he did not have to kill himself now!

As for the bridge itself, Lieutenant Negami remembers only the center of the span having been destroyed, leaving enough to reveal the configuration of the bridge. Going to the river soon afterward to recover supplies, he could see Russian troops repairing the center portion. In the shallows, pilings were still visible. Saitō responds that, although only portions of the pontoons may have been shattered, all were rendered unusable, at the least. The surfaces may have been floating but the hulls themselves sank. On the right shore, the four pilings had been removed. Not a man could have walked across the bridge after the demolition, and certainly not a vehicle could have passed. Perhaps the Russians were able to put in new pontoons and other gear, but to this day Saitō doubts that the bridge could have been made usable.

Most recently, the writer Onda Shigetaka has taken up the question of whether the Japanese bridge was destroyed. He notes that the combat diary of the 1st Battalion of the 71st Infantry refers to the decision to blow up the span but does not say anything about actual destruction. Onda has also seen a Russian photograph showing the Japanese bridge in almost intact condition. Lastly, he cites evidence conveyed at the time by a 3rd Battalion aide of the 71st Regiment to the effect that there was a growing probability the enemy was using the Japanese bridge. In fact, on the night of 10 July, the front-line infantry formed a do-or-die unit (*kesshitai*) to blow up the span. The raid failed.[8]

With respect to the portable boats, all remained operational but, in the absence of truck transportation, they had to be hauled away from the river on the shoulders of an engineer platoon. Making slow progress because of the weight of the craft, the unit became separated in the dark, felt insecure, and hid the boats in the grass. The men then proceeded to Saitō's headquarters in the Lake Iringin area. Explanations availed them naught when the irate engineer commander learned of their action. He ordered them back to retrieve the boats, at the risk of their lives.

A similar problem befell the 26th Infantry. When the 2nd and 3rd battalions had originally crossed the river on foot, they had left their sacks on the right shore. Now, when they returned, some picked up their belongings; others did not. Coming under fire, the men began to run away up the hill, and some dropped their sacks. Even the trucks fled on the Japanese side of the river. Dumped by the shore were canned goods, hardtack, rice, personal effects, and even ammunition. Next day, a company had to be sent to the area to try to recover the sacks, whose contents were needed for the next operations.

Kwantung Army staff officer Hara underwent a disconcerting experience of his own on the morning of the 5th. At the division command post, Komatsubara told him that Tsuji was missing and that he, the division commander, would have to commit suicide if Tsuji were lost. Intending to cross to the left bank to seek Tsuji, Hara took a truck and a dozen soldiers to the bridge area but encountered a young engineer officer who said that he had just blown up the bridge and that crossing was impossible. Returning to division headquarters, Hara and the truckload of soldiers were attacked by 20 or 30 low-flying Soviet planes. Everybody leaped off and ran from the truck, which was strafed. When Hara and his party finally got back to division headquarters, Tsuji was there, safe and sound. Hara was unnerved. "Tsuji owes me something to this day!," he told the author.

Undoubtedly a number of Japanese soldiers, unhurt or wounded, never made it back across the Halha. Major Nishikawa confirms the case of a master sergeant from the 72nd Regiment, who was badly wounded in the leg and unable to walk. Lying to one side in the dark, he was easily missed by his retreating unit. That he was captured by the Russians became known only by the fact of his repatriation after the Nomonhan Incident. Even IJA records, which are always reticent about missing men, admit to 11 missing and presumed dead. It is said that some who had been hiding from tanks in tall grass along the left bank got to the river, as did wounded seen staggering into the water. A number tried to link hands and swim across, only to be swept away by the swift current before the helpless gaze of engineers stationed on the right shore. A platoon leader in the 26th Regiment knows of one infantry-gun soldier who lost his way on the left side but followed footprints and reached the riverbank after the bridge was destroyed, perhaps the next night. Although not under fire at the time, the man had to struggle against the current and the cold water, but he alone made it safely across—truly the last man to return. Negami, an Olympic swimmer (Amsterdam, 1928), remarks that no "normal" swimmer could have made it across the Halha, but that the 26th Regiment included many strong fishermen from Hokkaido.

The Soviet version of the IJA pullback is understandably unflattering to the Japanese. After being crushed on Bain Tsagan by 3 A.M., the Japanese troops began to retreat in disorder to the river crossing. Frightened by the breakthrough by Soviet armor, Japanese engineers prematurely blew up the only Japanese pontoon bridge. Panic-stricken Japanese soldiers and officers in full uniform leaped into the Halha and drowned in front of the Russian tank crews. Only the swampy riverbanks and the depth of the river prevented Soviet-MPRA mechanized units from pursuing the defeated enemy to the right bank.[9]

When Sumi got back across the river to the new site of his headquarters, he was so relieved to have brought out his regiment that he had hardly enough energy to speak. Having gone without sleep for three nights and three days, he felt that he had reached his limits. During the night fighting on the way back from rescuing the remnants of the Adachi battalion, Sumi saw the legs of his troops looming black amidst red flashes and tracer fire;

he visualized the trunks of pine trees seen from the window of a train passing through the woods, or the legs of horses galloping at high speed. His own limbs seemed especially fat to Sumi. Whenever he heard the sound of bodies falling to earth, he imagined that his men were being shot in the legs and that, if he were hit, it would be in the legs too. The colonel's vision was so disturbed that, on the way to the bridge, when he passed knocked-out and stationary tanks in the field, he thought he saw them moving.

Psychologically, of course, Sumi was distressed that he and his regiment had had to retire from the battlefield "drenched with the blood of our comrades." In three days of fighting, the colonel found after checking his casualties, the 26th Infantry and attached elements had lost 143 officers and men killed and 278 wounded, or a total of 421 out of about 1,500 in the regiment. Although the numbers amounted to somewhat less than one-third of the Sumi force, the dead included most of the key personnel—three of four majors (including two battalion commanders), over half of the company commanders, and a large part of the regimental headquarters staff. Sumi felt very depressed and lonely. How painful it would be to have to report to the 7th Division commander, Lieutenant General Sonobe, that Major Adachi—the expert *kendō* fencer and fine singer—was dead along with Major Kikuchi—the sharp and quick hero of the Manchurian Incident. Indeed, Sumi heard that rumors were rife in Tsitsihar that the regiment commander had been killed or severely wounded, or that he had survived but was weeping over the death of his men. General Sonobe in fact sent Sumi a gracious letter. But privately Sumi was wondering if his force could carry on as a "regiment" with its remaining strength. For the next ten days, he worked to rebuild his own and his men's health and to reconstruct the regiment, largely by shuffling personnel.[10]

A CRITIQUE OF THE OPERATION

Kobayashi's task force of seven and a half infantry battalions had spent little more than 50 hours across the Halha. Though Soviet sources round off estimates of Japanese strength on the left shore at 10,000 men, the figure was probably closer to 8,000. Of these, the Japanese lost nearly 10 percent killed and wounded, half in the 26th Regiment, most particularly in Adachi's 1st Battalion.[11] According to Tsuji, IJA intelligence learned that Soviet frontline forces had reported to their central authorities that they had incurred severe casualties, and the hospitals east of Baikal were full of wounded men.[12]

Japanese tallies of enemy tanks and armored cars burned or knocked out on 3-5 July are high: the 71st Regiment claimed 164 ("a whole tank brigade," says Nishikawa); the 72nd Regiment claimed 97; and the 26th Regiment claimed 83. In addition to these 344, claims by the Japanese field artillery units would bring the total to about 400. One infantry major thinks the data are inflated by a factor of three. Sumi admits that duplications may have inflated his regiment's figures by 20 percent; others suggest an overall factor closer to 30 percent. The range of Soviet-MPRA mechanized losses would thus be 280-320 vehicles, still an impressive kill rate.[13] The upper limits can be further reduced by the known fact that the Russians sent salvage teams to tow back immobilized machines. Regardless of the exact number of armored vehicles incapacitated, there can be no doubt that the Soviet-MPRA side paid a high price for checking the Japanese left-bank offensive. The Russians, indeed, may have exaggerated the number of Japanese artillery pieces and antitank weapons[14] because they could not credit the *nikuhaku* teams and fire bottles with such murderous efficacy.

General Kobayashi, the able task force commander, was one Japanese officer who regarded the pullback order with displeasure. He had considered the advances by the 71st and 72nd regiments on 3 July as "utterly ideal," comparable to grand maneuvers. To have withdrawn before attaining the objective, well within sight, struck Kobayashi as inconsistent and irrational. The fighting would have progressed favorably if the offensive had been conducted thoroughly and without letup. Operational guidance was not effective because the division commander had advanced to the front too soon and had overreacted to tactical developments. If Komatsubara had stayed near the river crossing and had evaluated the situation and directed actions coolly from the rear, the outcome would have been different. Kobayashi felt that it was a regrettable and incoherent misuse of forces to fall back without having fully employed the 26th Regiment or the artillery.[15]

That the Japanese ground forces ever got across the river in the first place, and that the bridge survived the entire operation under fire, was admittedly "miraculous." Usually, in the case of enemy air attacks or ground bombardment, the engineers would dismantle a pontoon bridge, hide the matériel, and then try to reassemble the span. But in the Halha operation, the bridge was defended and remained remarkably intact until the time came to destroy it. Some of the IJA veterans feel that too much attention was paid to the preservation of the bridge and to the rear. If the enemy had been routed from Komatsu Heights and the left shore opposite the confluence, retention of the bridge would have become irrelevant.[16]

Among the more aggressive IJA officers there was an opinion that, if only the Japanese infantrymen could have worked their way up to the hostile artillery positions and have held on till sunset on 3 July, it would have been possible to conduct a night attack and to seize the weakly defended positions. After all, Soviet infantry units were still outnumbered by the Japanese. According to this tough-minded contention, it is the true function of commanders to be heartless "devils" on the battlefield and to drive listless or exhausted troops to accomplish seemingly impossible tasks. German handling of the battles of Tannenberg and Lodz in the First World War is cited as a splendid example of the triumph of "mind over matter" that should have been emulated by the 23rd Division on the left bank of the Halha on 3 and 4 July. Japanese critics respond that the exaggerated IJA devotion to the night attack concept was already being rendered obsolete by modern firepower and powerful fortifications. In this view, Kobayashi's battered force might well have suffered the tragic fate of Col. Ichiki Kiyonao's detachment on Guadalcanal only three years later.[17]

Certainly there was no feeling of defeat at the level of the Kwantung Army and the 23rd Division, or among most of the front-line commanders. Checked on the left shore, the Japanese ground forces were soon undertaking fierce offensive action on the right bank, surely evidence of unimpaired morale. Although IJA casualties had been considerable, the enemy seemed to have sustained even greater losses. Division staff officer Suzuki calls the operation a success, not a failure. The Japanese troops were on foot, in the face of enemy armor, so no linked lines could be established; Soviet fighting vehicles could penetrate and attack from every direction. But to have knocked out 200-300 machines, which burned for half a day and elicited constant Japanese cheers of "Well done!"—this scene lingers vividly in Suzuki's mind to this day. The fact of a "tactical withdrawal" meant, at worst, a "draw."[18]

Even Colonel Sumi, who did not consider the left-shore operation a victory, felt that his regiment had succeeded in securing the bridge by holding the Bain Tsagan elevation and thus enabling all the other ground units to recross the Halha. It was no mean feat to have remained alone across the river for an extra day. But Sumi disliked the higgling language used to mask the "failure" of the first Japanese offensive: "Those in charge of operations deceived people by claiming that it was not a retreat (*taikyaku*) we had experienced but a change of direction (*tenshin*). By saying this, they were comforting themselves and planning new operations. How could one be sure of success, though, after the division had been wounded once?"[19]

Some of the Japanese troops thought they were recrossing the river to detour the enemy's main force and come back to the left shore at a different point. Inevitably, differences in outlook depended on the casualties incurred by individual units in the fighting of 3-5 July. Major Hamada of the 72nd Infantry, for example, is of the opinion that his regiment's losses were relatively light and that the objective had been accomplished. Therefore he and the soldiers felt that they had won their battle. Only later did Hamada learn that the other regiments and division headquarters had suffered heavy casualties. Similarly, Major Nishikawa of the same regiment still wonders why the Japanese did not push on to the confluence and destroy the enemy bridge, since lead elements were already so near Komatsu Heights. Perhaps the Soviet heavy artillery bombardment "shook up" the division staff? Nishikawa only pulled back because of orders from higher headquarters, which told him not to leave behind even a single piece of paper. But Kwantung Army staff officer Hara admits that the Japanese infantry had no idea why they had gone across the river or why they had pulled back.[20]

From contemporary documentation and from reminiscences, we know the main Japanese military criticisms of the conduct of the left-shore operation.

Underestimation of the Enemy, Overconfidence in Self

In the words of an AGS Operations Section staff officer, Maj. Imoto Kumao, the IJA attitude toward the handling of border incidents was imprudent. The transport company commander, Lieutenant Nomura, originally thought that the Russians could be "polished off" in ten days and that he could go home in triumph. On leaving for the front, the division staff, he heard, packed their bags with necessities for little more than a week. At first, Nomura admits, the mood of the troops across the Halha was "more festive than fighting." Little attention was paid to positions, construction, or deployment. Though certainly brave in antitank warfare, the Japanese troops were also rash and reckless, typical of soldiers first entering combat. The Japanese attitude toward battle was conceited and extremely superficial, says Nomura. Interviewees agree that the enemy was supposed to flee at the first appearance of Japanese regulars, whose exclusive emphasis was on the offensive.

In a private letter to Sumi dated 10 July 1939, the 7th Division commander, Lieutenant General Sonobe, wrote that judging from reports on the recent operations, the "superiors" (the Kwantung Army) appeared to be taking the foe very lightly. There seemed to be little comprehension of enemy strength or of friendly limitations. To Sonobe, this was impermissible. "Never make light of an enemy," he warned Sumi, "even a weak one."

There should have been no need for fire bottles in the first place, but apart from material deficiencies on the Japanese part, intelligence did not prepare Komatsubara and Kobayashi for the hundreds upon hundreds of Soviet-MPRA armored vehicles that swarmed toward the Halha by 3 July. Yet Maj. Shimanuki Takeharu, a Kwantung Army staff officer, went out to the Tamsag area on aerial reconnaissance as early as 20 June and observed many tank units on the heights across the Halha, clustered "like villages" and leaving tread marks everywhere. Shimanuki's report caused no stir and was played down by Kwantung Army headquarters. Intelligence of enemy rearward strength was particularly weak.

Poor Strategic Direction by Higher Headquarters

General Kobayashi, commanding the task force, expressed dissatisfaction with the 23rd Division's handling of the transriverine operation, as we have seen. But the Kwantung Army drew covert and well-deserved criticism too. General Sonobe, for one, believed that higher headquarters was conducting operations without proper planning. Because of the locale of the Halha battle, which Sonobe insisted was favorable to the Soviet-MPRA side (a notion the Soviets deny), the enemy could bring immense power to bear locally. The Kwantung Army did not realize the "true situation."

After observing the Halha operation, General Hashimoto had stopped off at Hailar and learned, "pretty much," what had happened on both sides of the river. When Hashimoto went on to see General Ueda, the Kwantung Army commander seemed to think that the operation had been a success, on the basis of reports from his chief of staff, Yano, and the other observers. Although Hashimoto's own critique was based on impressions and not details, he gently asked Ueda to be more cautious thereafter. Tsuji, however, was furious with Hashimoto and the Army General Staff for "misreading" the battle situation. In particular, the Operations Bureau chief, he charged, drew erroneous conclusions on the basis of a flying visit to the front and perfunctory observation of enemy bombing of the bridge area. This, Tsuji claimed, contributed to future mistakes by the High Command in Tokyo.

Weakness of the 23rd Division

The mission assigned to the new, three-regiment 23rd Division far exceeded its capability in terms of manpower, training, experience, and equipment. Attachment of one 1,500-man infantry regiment from the 7th Division was insufficient reinforcement. In an entry dated 8 July, AGS Major Imoto referred to a lack of spirit (*mukōiki*), and the pressing need for "full-scale, down-to-earth" training.

Inferiority of IJA Artillery

The Japanese lacked 10-cm. and 15-cm. firepower to support ground operations on the left shore. Field artillery batteries were outnumbered and consistently outranged by excellent Soviet guns emplaced on higher ground. Again reflecting the low opinion of enemy strength, the Japanese unwisely divided the relatively few batteries of Colonel Ise's 13th Field Artillery Regiment. Only Maj. Seki Takeshi's 3rd Battalion went across the river with the Kobayashi force, bringing eight field guns and four 12-cm. howitzers of the 36 pieces of the regiment.

Logistical Weaknesses

To form even one motorized infantry regiment, it had been necessary to commandeer about 200 civilian vehicles in Tsitsihar. But, in the confusion and delay involved in spanning the Halha, only one infantry battalion ever had the use of trucks on the left shore. All of the 23rd Division's infantry units marched from Hailar to Chiangchunmiao and on to the front. A military rail line was needed between Arshaan, Handagai, and Chiangchunmiao. General Sonobe stressed that Soviet propinquity to bases gave the enemy a pronounced edge and facilitated his "thorough operations."

Against the hundreds of enemy armored fighting vehicles encountered on the left shore, the Japanese expended almost all of the antitank ammunition for their heavy weapons. Resupply efforts were negligible; rations were not plentiful, as a lightning campaign had been anticipated; and potable water was not found on the high ground across the river.

Feebleness of Bridging Capacity

The attack across the Halha is the only historical instance of Japanese army river-crossing operations in battle against the Soviet army. The Kwantung Army had been importuning the Army General Staff for first-class bridging gear since long before the Nomonhan Incident, but older materials suitable for tanks had been committed to the China theater, and new equipment was scheduled for later issue. Meanwhile, separate bridging gear was required to support passage by armored vehicles and heavy artillery. As for the engineers, the 23rd Engineer Regiment did not even possess the usual organic bridge construction company. Pontoons had originally been brought from Kumamoto only for training purposes in the Hailar area. As mentioned earlier, the survival of the bridge for two days after its discovery by the Russians was regarded by the Japanese as a "miracle."

Primitive Antitank Capability

Japanese antitank weapons, says Colonel Sumi, were "cute little toys." His infantrymen called enemy projectiles "the real thing." In Sumi's words, battling the Soviet armor was like taking part in a fixed fight. Fire bottles were used with great effect against light armor at the outset but the human-bullet leaps aboard tanks resembled "wielding an axe against a stone lantern." Revolving a tank turret at high speed sufficed to fling away any close-quarter soldier. In Adachi's case, one recalls, a tank machine-gunned the major from the hull of another vehicle. Against closed hatches, hand grenades were ineffective, as were puny land mines. General Sonobe termed enemy equipment excellent overall, whereas the Japanese were entirely "naked."

Insufficient Communications

Coordination was poor between the division command post and the infantry regiments, and between regimental headquarters and the infantry battalions. The problem was especially acute with respect to the 26th Regiment, whose original mission called for motorized operations to encircle the foe at high speed, but which lacked radio or wire connections once the trucks were diverted on 2-3 July. Radio equipment finally caught up with the regiment on the night of 3 July, but communication was not established until the operation was over. In view of the absence of wire or radio contact, messengers (*denrei*) had to be used mainly. Their movement was difficult if not impossible by daylight, however, under enemy observation and bombardment. Sumi's isolated 1st Battalion paid an especially severe price for the inability to communicate.

Related to communications problems was the matter of ground forces' mistakes in identification of friendly aircraft. On 3 July, for example, machine guns of the 64th Infantry on the right shore shot down a Japanese scout plane that had come to drop a communications tube warning of the approach of enemy armor on the left bank.[21]

From the battles on the left shore of the Halha, the Russians learned that "tank and motorized troops skillfully cooperating with air force and mobile artillery are a decisive means for carrying out swift military operations." As Shishkin puts it, "Soviet-Mongolian military actions around Bain Tsagan represent [a classic example] of active defense, resulting in a decisive defeat for the hostile striking force. Tanks and armored cars played the primary role in destroying the enemy. Experience in combat indicated that mobile armor (which combines the ability to maneuver and to strike) can be effectively employed not only during the attack but also during the defense." It was essential to synchronize the organization of combat missions with the capabilities of armored fighting vehicles; to exercise able direction of armored forces at the level of overall command and of tactical control of armored units; and to coordinate armored action with other types of weaponry.

Special praise was earned by the Russians' 11th Tank Brigade and 7th Armored Brigade, the 8th MPRA Armored Battalion, and the artillery and air force units that rendered support. As the Russians exulted, the Japanese, who had "sought to surround and wipe out the Soviet-Mongolian forces, were themselves encircled, with the consequent annihilation of their main body." They never again tried to cross the Halha.[22]

21

Trying It with Tanks

The Kwantung Army had no original intention of using armored forces at Nomonhan. Several weeks before the Halha river-crossing operation just described, between 4 and 7 June 1939, regularly scheduled map exercises were conducted in Hsinking. In attendance were all the senior men, from General Ueda down to division chiefs of staff and divisional staff officers from East Manchuria, as well as an AGS team of seven officers from Tokyo. War-gamed according to current operational plans, the maneuvers mainly concerned the eastern front. Other than air force matters, which affected all of Manchuria, the remaining sectors were merely alluded to. The Nomonhan front was not gamed. Indeed, Tsuji assured the AGS team that the Nomonhan affair was over, and that the Kwantung Army had nothing further in mind. Relieved by this affirmation, the AGS officers set off on various inspection tours after the map exercises were over. On 9 June, Maj. Gen. Hashimoto Gun and Maj. Imaoka Yutaka visited Kungchuling in South Manchuria, headquarters of the mechanized brigade commanded by Lt. Gen. Yasuoka Masaomi.

Small though they were, Yasuoka's two tank regiments—Col. Yoshimaru Kiyotake's 3rd Tank Regiment (Medium) and Col. Tamada Yoshio's 4th Tank Regiment (Light)—comprised almost all of the Kwantung Army's armor.[1] Plans called for doubling the tank force by organizing two new regiments (the 9th and 10th) at Kungchuling by August with Type 97 medium armor from the homeland at the core.[2] But as of early June, nobody suspected that Yasuoka's existing brigade, still in normal peacetime status (*heiji hensei*), was destined to fight at Nomonhan. Indeed, Yasuoka told his AGS visitors that his mission, in conjunction with spearhead infantry, was to exploit the penetration of the powerful enemy fortified positions on the eastern Manchurian borders in case of war with Russia. This was the type of operation stressed in training, not action on broad steppes—although theoretically this one mechanized brigade of the Kwantung Army must be available to fight on any front.

Yoshimaru's 3rd Tank Regiment, numbering 376 officers and men, included the following combat tank strength: 26 Type 89 (*Otsu*) medium tanks, organized into two line companies; 4 Type 97 (*Chi-ha*) medium tanks; 7 Type 94 (*TK*) tankettes; and 4 Type 97 (*Ke-te*) tankettes. Tamada's 4th Tank Regiment, numbering 565 officers and men (128 of whom were in the regimental Supply and Maintenance (*danretsu*) Company), included the following elements: 35 Type 95 (*Ha-go*) light tanks, organized into three line companies and one reserve company; 8 Type 89 (*Kō*) medium tanks in one line company; and 3 Type 94 (*TK*) tankettes.[3]

The medium tanks assigned to the brigade represented both the best and the worst of Japanese tank design. The low-silhouette Type 97 (*Chi-ha*) medium tanks were the newest and probably the best-designed of their class, and came to be the most representative Japanese tank. At the time of Nomonhan, the Type 97's were still experimental and had mainly been committed to the China theater. By contrast, the two variants of the Type 89 medium tanks (*Otsu* and *Kō*) were the worst of the current IJA armor, and the oldest. These were the first Japanese-built main battle tanks, and they had operated well during the Manchurian Incident. The *Otsu* incorporated a six-cylinder diesel engine developed for tank use after 1934, which enabled it to be slightly heavier and have a 20 percent greater range than the gasoline-powered, water-cooled *Kō*. All three medium tanks had crews of four men and carried the same main armament—one unimpressive 57-mm. gun—but the Type 97 tank had two 7.7-mm. heavy machine guns instead of the two 6.5-mm. light machine guns mounted on the Type 89. The powerful V-12 diesel engine and excellent suspension system of the Type 97 enabled it to carry heavier armor and move farther and faster than the older Type 89's (armor 20-25 mm. versus 15-17 mm.; range 210 km. versus 170 or 140 km.; speed 38 kph versus 25 kph).

The Type 95 light tank (*Ha-go*) had the same 120 HP, 6-cylinder, air-cooled diesel engine as the improved *Otsu* medium tank, but at just over half the weight of the Type 89 (6.7-7.4 tons versus 12.1-13 tons), and with lighter armor and armament (armor 8-12 mm.; one poor 37-mm. gun and one 7.7-mm. heavy machine gun), the *Ha-go* could attain a maximum speed of 40-45 kph and had a range of action of 250 km. This was the newest IJA light tank in production, its speed and mobility designed to enable it to keep up with wheeled vehicles. It took a crew of three men.

The two models of tankettes assigned to the brigade were the Type 94 (*TK*) and the newer Type 97 (*Ke-te*). Both were designed for towing vehicles and supplying ammunition to the front, and were excellent for reconnaissance, guarding, and liaison. They were not intended for offensive actions, the normal armament of both being a single 7.7-mm. machine gun (the Type 97 could substitute a 37-mm. gun for the machine gun). Both carried crews of two men and could attain top speeds of 40 kph. The older, gasoline-powered Type 94 weighed 3.2-3.5 tons, carried 8-12 mm. of armor, and had a maximum range of 200 km. The diesel-powered Type 97 weighed 4.25 tons, carried 8-16 mm. of armor, and had a maximum range of 250 km.[4]

All of the unit commanders at Kungchuling stressed the need for beefed-up ordnance sections and more and better equipment—a view with which Imaoka agreed. Of the nine units he and Hashimoto inspected, all were at about the same stage of readiness: under construction, not complete. The tank regiments lacked replacement capabilities in tanks and personnel. Imaoka, a logistics expert, came away with the conviction that operations staff officers, in devising plans against an enemy, needed to comprehend the difference between actual strength and planned (hypothetical) strength of units. Yasuoka's tank regiments were showy facades without depth. Tamada calls his own unit a very weak regiment in terms of military power.[5]

The top commanders and staff of the Kungchuling tank brigade, however, were excellent officers, with an infantry background.[6] Yasuoka, from Kagoshima, a lieutenant general since 1938, was a graduate of the 18th military academy class of 1906, and of the army war college. At the time of Nomonhan he was 53. He became Tank School commandant in 1936, and in 1938 commanded the 1st Independent Mixed Brigade at Kungchuling and then the 1st Tank Brigade upon the former unit's deactivation. To Maj. Noguchi Kamenosuke, who worked with him constantly, on the outside Yasuoka seemed like a feudal lord (*tonosama*), conveying an aura of haughtiness (*ibaru*). Maj. Masuda Umeki, Yasuoka's senior aide, calls him rather gentle but strong on the inside, a real combat type who took good care of his troops. The general was tall and husky, with thinning gray hair and a bald spot. He wore glasses for reading, smoked, and drank "pretty much." Noguchi was particularly impressed by the fact that Yasuoka was always prepared beforehand for combat formations and operations. For example, he "did his homework" while still in Kungchuling and thus never had occasion to become perturbed while at the front. The general drafted orders alone aboard his command truck, and was able to dictate without notes. Masuda found the general easy to work with, quite different from Yasuoka's brilliant but cantankerous predecessor Lt. Gen. Sakai Kōji, who had made his own aide sick until "thick-skinned" Masuda was assigned.

Yoshimaru, nearly 47 years old in 1939, was a graduate of the 26th military academy class of 1914. In 1936, as a lieutenant colonel, he was assigned to the 2nd Tank Regiment; the following year he served in China. At the end of January 1939, he became commander of the 3rd Tank Regiment at Kungchuling; he was promoted to full colonel in March. Masuda remembers mustachioed Yoshimaru as a fine commander who loved his men, quiet and gentle, with a good sense of humor. Noguchi and 1st Lt. Irie Tachio, one of his platoon leaders, call Yoshimaru a "pure samurai" (*hagakure bushi*) from Saga on Kyushu. Another of his platoon leaders, 1st Lt. Takeshita Iwao, says that the colonel was excellent, universally respected, always stressing the spirit of attack. Although strict and severe in training, Yoshimaru was personally considerate and nice. Inspired by the colonel, the regiment was high-spirited, splendidly united, and good at teamwork.

At the time of Nomonhan, Colonel Tamada was a year older than Yoshimaru. He had been a class ahead of him at the military academy, and had also attended the army war college. In December 1933, as a major, he was sent to a tank regiment for training, and in April 1934 he joined the 4th Tank Regiment of the Independent Mixed Brigade. At the end of 1936, a lieutenant colonel, he became an instructor at the Tank School. Promoted to full colonel in July 1938, he took command of the 4th Tank Regiment. Short and stocky, he did not drink or smoke. He says of himself: "I'm from the *Tōhoku* [northeast Japan] and am personally rather slow in reaction and unexcitable (*donjū, donchō*). So I wasn't really cut out for the tank branch. And, since I was a newcomer in tank circles, my opinions on armor were not highly esteemed." But to his subordinates, Tamada seemed very happy with tanks. He struck them as deliberate, rather stubborn, extremely serious, precise, intellectual, detailed in his thinking and his orders, and considerate of and gentle to his men. Tamada's very rigorous training would pay off in battle.

Ogata Kyūichirō, the offspring of a Kagoshima family, figures in the Nomonhan campaign as Tamada's regimental aide, in the rank of major. A graduate of the 32nd military academy class, Ogata was nearly 40 years old in 1939. He was well acquainted with Tamada, having served four times with him, including their initial 90-day training stint with the Narashino tank regiment from December 1933 to March 1934, and their first posting to the Kwantung Army in the spring of 1934. After serving as the most senior captain in the 3rd Company of the 4th Tank Regiment, Ogata took charge of training under Col. Murai Toshio. Assigned as regimental aide after Tamada took over, Ogata often had occasion to converse and argue with the colonel, mainly about training matters. Since both officers were "nonspecialists," Ogata would collate the junior officers' recommendations and complaints and bring them to Tamada for consideration. Ogata calls himself quick and bold, quite opposite in personality to the colonel. Nevertheless, they "clicked" and worked well as a team, blending as in a good marriage, in the words of Ogata. The latter continuously prodded the colonel, and undoubtedly exerted great influence upon him. Ogata had had combat experience, between July and December 1937, when the Sakai detachment (named after Maj. Gen. Sakai Kōji) went to North China. As aide to an infantry colonel without armor experience assigned to the tank unit and to the China battlefront, Ogata actually ran the tank regiment, whose achievements he considered insufficient—an experience that would color his outlook at Nomonhan.

With the heating-up of the border incident by mid-June, and after General Ueda's decision to entrust the Halha offensive to the 23rd instead of the 7th Division, the Kwantung Army operations staff, especially Tsuji, came up with an idea involving the use of armor. As early as 16 or 17 June,[7] Tsuji tried out his first amorphous notion on Maj. Noguchi Kamenosuke, a tank specialist in the 1st Section (Operations). How about attaching the two tank regiments at Kungchuling to an infantry division (presumably still the 7th Division, at this early stage), crossing the upper Halha west of Handagai, plunging north toward the junction of the Holsten, and catching hostile forces from the rear in a pincers operation coordinated with more infantry striking at the confluence from the east?

Noguchi questioned the feasibility of tying armor to infantry, and a genial argument ensued. Infantry was to be attached, Noguchi reminded Tsuji, because one tank brigade was not strong enough to accomplish the mission alone; but an ordinary infantry division without trucks was not fast enough to keep up with tanks. Speed would be lost as a result, for the armor could not afford to outstrip the infantrymen and would have to slow down to their pace. Tsuji thereupon revamped his proposal to create a detachment that, in addition to the medium and light tanks, would draw entirely on motorized infantry, engineer, and field and antiaircraft artillery units stationed largely around Kungchuling. The Yasuoka detachment, in Noguchi's words, was "born in one night." Kwantung Army headquarters, with Tsuji as "project drafter," issued the appropriate ten-hour combat-alert (*ōkyū-hahei*) and concentration (*shūchū*) orders in the evening of 19 June and early afternoon of 20 June. By this time it had been decided that the Yasuoka detachment would replace the main body of the 7th Division in the attack against the left bank of the Halha. A Kwantung Army staff officer flew to Hailar to deliver the new combat-alert order to Komatsubara, and another staff officer followed with the concentration order.

Major Noguchi learned on the 19th that he was being assigned to Yasuoka for staff liaison. He proceeded by air from Hsinking to Kungchuling, which he reached before nightfall on the 19th. At Yasuoka's official residence, he instructed the general on the Kwantung Army's conception of assembling the tank brigade's organic and attached units between Arshaan and Handagai, and of preparing for operations in the Nomonhan sector in conjunction with the 23rd Division—i.e., to cut off the enemy's "escape route" to the left shore. From the look on his face, Yasuoka seems to have had not the slightest inkling of the Kwantung Army's notion of forming the detachment. None of the general's staff was present, and it took time to get organized.

Specially attached to the Yasuoka detachment, whose core remained the two tank regiments, were Col. Miyao Kan's 1st Independent Field Artillery Regiment, a battery of antiaircraft guns, and a tractor company from a heavy artillery regiment (all from Kwantung Army artillery formations); and Col. Kawamura Shichirō's 24th Engineer Regiment, a company from an independent engineer regiment, a radio platoon from a signal regiment, and the 3rd Motor Transport Regiment consisting of about 120 trucks in three companies. From the 7th Division at Tsitsihar were to be sent a medical unit as well as a reinforced battalion of the 28th Infantry Regiment to cover the concentration of the main body of the Yasuoka detachment and to come under its command when it reached Arshaan.[8]

The "motorized reserve" of the 23rd Division was to be a seasoned regiment loaned by the 7th Division—Sumi's 26th Infantry, loaded aboard the trucks of a motor transport company and reinforced with two antitank gun batteries and two regimental gun batteries. After his regiment reached Hailar by train about 23 June, Sumi was told by a confident General Komatsubara (with whom he was acquainted since a tour in the Soviet Intelligence Subsection of the AGS) that he was to join the Yasuoka detachment near Lake Dorot (about 45 km. southeast of Chiangchunmiao), board trucks, and be ready to cross the Halha under Yasuoka's cover. As Sumi understood it, the battalion from a sister regiment of the 7th Division—Maj. Kajikawa Tomiji's 2nd Battalion of the 28th Infantry—was to come under his command. There were no details yet, only the outlines of a draft. Sumi heard much the same thing from Komatsubara's peppy chief of staff, Colonel Ōuchi, another Russian-speaking officer whom he knew very well from prep school, war college, and Harbin OSS days. Like Komatsubara, Ōuchi indicated that the offensive was still in the planning stage, subject to change on the spot. Sumi should "play it by ear," abandon all of his useless regimental horses, and draw a staff car for himself. "In any case," Ōuchi grinned, "I'll arrange for you to win the Order of the Golden Kite!"

Meanwhile, farther south, General Yasuoka had been transporting his detachment by train to the front along the single-track Paichengtzu railway. One tank platoon leader, 1st Lieutenant Takeshita, calls the rail line very poor; he remembers how his whole train, loaded with armor, would slip when struggling to traverse a rise. Still, Noguchi was impressed by the speed with which the many trains and well-organized units were loaded aboard flatcars and moved out from Kungchuling, starting at 9 A.M. on 20 June, after having received their orders only the preceding evening.[9] In fact, Noguchi smiles sadly, everything proceeded smoothly until the time of battle!

From the platoon leader's level, however, 1st Lieutenant Irie of the 3rd Tank Regiment recorded myriad problems, large and small: "Mobilization was a failure. We did not attend to details or check [our equipment]. There was a shortage of helmets and gas masks. We did not have time to attend to personal affairs. During our movement forward, dysentery occurred. It was imperative that we have more time to study and to train regarding battlefield conditions and both sides' tactics. We could not exert sufficient 'hold' over the men.''

It took two days to move the whole detachment to Arshaan; Yasuoka began unloading his two tank regiments by 22 June. The units checked their vehicles for mechanical defects and damage; none had to be left behind. Special attention was paid to the status of ordnance and ammunition, and gunnery exercises were conducted immediately, with good results. In the absence of dummy training shells, however, precious live ammunition had to be used. As for pistol-firing practice, Irie noted that the skill level was unsatisfactory.

From 24 June, the Yasuoka detachment moved out of Arshaan and concentrated near Handagai, about 65 km. away, in preparation for the advance to the Halha. Tank radios were found to be broken, says Irie, and tables of organization and equipment had to be changed. With respect to intelligence, ever since the Tauran affair in the spring of 1936 the Kwantung Army had accumulated information concerning the terrain and general features of the sector between Chiangchunmiao and Handagai, which proved useful for operational and logistical purposes. Now Yasuoka's staff and commanders devised deployments of advance, sent ahead route repair parties, erected markers, and designated traffic-control teams. But at Handagai, Noguchi soon noticed and was disturbed by the fact that the Japanese armored columns were arriving without trucks. Recent rains, especially on and after 23 June, had turned the tracks to a quagmire, for there were neither paved nor improved roads across the steppes. Roads in name only, the "caravan routes" became wetter, more swampy, and lower in the Halha valley.

Using planks and boards, the tankers and soldiers somehow got their caterpillar machines through, but the primitive pathways deteriorated as the tanks churned their way forward, and no wheeled vehicles could move. One stretch of several kilometers resembled a river. Some truck units advanced as little as one kilometer a day on occasion. OSS Maj. Nyūmura Matsuichi speaks of mud to men's ankles and to trucks' axles. Tanks had to be used to tow the wheeled vehicles. Bog-downs and mechanical failures were frequent. It became even more difficult for the trucks when the route ascended into hill country.

One PFC from the 3rd Regiment's supply company was driving a brand-new, six-wheel diesel truck loaded with tank shells, mines, and machine guns. He left Arshaan around midnight on 23 June and ran into the morass after dawn. Several dozen trucks became mired, deeper and deeper, fighting to pull out. Dozens of soldiers attached ropes and cables as they pushed and pulled to extricate the vehicles. Of the PFC's 17-truck company, only his and eight others made it to Handagai by 25 June. The Kajikawa infantry's records are in agreement that it took two days, from 1:40 P.M. on the 23rd until the 25th, for the entire battalion to reach Handagai.[10]

Yasuoka reminded Noguchi that tanks without fuel were helpless—like "dead fortresses." The major apologized and said that the engineers were chopping wood for roadway planks. Still, there was no way of predicting when the trucks would get through. At present, a farm tractor was being used to haul trucks out of the mire, one by one. Yasuoka remarked that it was good to have the engineers but that they should have been mechanized in the first place.

At first, the Yasuoka detachment was not overly worried by the fact that the infantry might have to move forward while the tanks were still waiting for fuel. After all, the armored formations could proceed very rapidly once they were fueled up. But Tsuji's original conception had called for striking against the enemy's rear, across the river; now the detachment had barely enough fuel to move, and lacked matériel to bridge the river. Japanese tanks, as we have seen, could not have crossed the frail IJA pontoon bridge eventually thrown across the Halha. How did the Yasuoka detachment, which lacked a bridging capability of its own, hope to get to the left shore? Theoretically, the tanks could ford to a depth of one meter,[11] but of course this required an intimate knowledge of the river and would depend in particular on the solidity of the stream's bottom. At the site of the envisaged Halha crossing, the river proved too wide and too deep. Discouraging reconnaissance reports only reinforced the overall estimate that fording two tank regiments was not feasible. Some alternative was necessary. If worse came to worst, Noguchi thought privately, the Japanese might even have to use a portion of their own tanks as piers to support an improvised bridge. There was also a bizarre Japanese idea of using enemy bridges. The Soviet-MPRA forces had moved armor to the right bank, so why not use their bridges, of which there may have been as few as two and as many as five at the time, to send Japanese tanks to the other shore? If the enemy blew up their spans, Yasuoka's attached engineers would repair them.[12]

The lack of a realistic way to cross the river or to traverse swampland was only aggravated by the tank units' shortage of fuel to support sustained combat—a situation that posed hardships never before experienced by staff officer Noguchi. Medium tanks, in particular, gobbled up precious fuel.[13] IJA transport units, however, tended to emphasize troop movement at the expense of fuel, rations, and ammunition, pursuing the maxims "logistics follow operations" and "the front lines come first." Noguchi felt that the tanks' fuel needs, in this case, should take precedence over the hauling of troops or pontoons. Trucks could not make it to the river, given the fuel shortage, but the armor must be enabled to reach and presumably to cross the Halha. Noguchi's greatest fear was that, with only one or two days' supply of fuel, the tanks would grind to a halt across the river. He therefore focused his prime attention on moving fuel to Handagai from the dumps at Arshaan, to which the trains could operate without delay. At Arshaan, in fact, Noguchi had aired his complaints for several days to Capt. Katō Shōhei, a Kwantung Army staff officer and an old roommate. Although a Kwantung Army officer himself, Noguchi could not very well voice recriminations while attached to the Yasuoka detachment; but Katō probably could, and so could army liaison officers advising the 23rd Division, such as strong-willed Tsuji. The Kwantung Army logistics staff requested the Manchukuo government's transport bureau to repair the worst stretch of roadway. Several hundred laborers were put to work by the civil engineering section, but results were unimpressive.[14]

Colonel Tamada, pressing Noguchi about the fuel problem, told him that 1st Lt. Shinoda Hangorō had already died on 26 June because of it. The 4th Tank Regiment had been scouting sites to cross the Halha to link up with the 23rd Division in the Komatsu Heights area, but because of the desperate fuel shortage patrols were borrowing Mongolian ponies from the Manchukuoan army's Hsingan cavalry.[15] Lieutenant Shinoda and some enlisted men, galloping off to reconnoiter three or four kilometers ahead, had been chased and overrun by enemy armor or truck-borne infantry. His escort of two or three Manchurian cavalrymen, scared off by the foe, had fled back and reported the skirmish, including the fact that Shinoda had been wounded and had fallen unconscious. Capt. Tamaki Sōichi's 3rd Tank Company was sent to investigate. Despite an intensive search, Tamaki unearthed no trace of the lieutenant or his men. There were tread marks in the vicinity, however, and several scattered enemy soldiers, probably Outer Mongolian horsemen, were watching the scene.

It was thought that, if conscious, Shinoda may have committed suicide to avoid the disgrace of capture. That the enemy had seized the Japanese scouts, dead or alive, was confirmed by Colonel Tamada when a missing Japanese noncom was exchanged after the Nomonhan campaign.[16] A platoon leader, two years junior to Shinoda, suggests that the lieutenant (whom he calls a fine young officer) may have been picked up while still unconscious. Later, realizing that only suicide or execution after court-martial awaited a repatriated Japanese officer, Shinoda may well have opted to remain permanently in the Soviet Union, as an appreciable number of IJA prisoners are known to have done. Tamada, feeling helpless, regarded the Shinoda episode as meaningless and ridiculous: "Imagine, a tank officer killed on horseback!" Noguchi shared the colonel's dismay. He sought to appease the line unit commanders while coordinating with the truck forces, which were struggling "superhumanly," day and night, to get stores through.

While the Yasuoka force was held up in the Arshaan area, rumors reached the detachment staff that the general was being criticized by the Kwantung Army for "dallying at the [Arshaan] hot springs." Noguchi denounced the canard (*dema*), but some of the older officers, such as Major Masuda (Yasuoka's training officer) and Lt. Col. Takazawa Hideteru (the senior staff officer), vented their frustration by proposing a mad plan designed to resume the momentum: the tanks should move forward as far as their fuel held out "for the sake of the detachment's honor." Then the crews should dismount, remove the machine guns, and manhandle them on foot against the enemy. Thus would every effort be made to achieve the mission of the detachment. Noguchi retorted that the idea of a tank brigade fighting on foot was irresponsible and useless.

This was the period just before the Japanese air force's great raid of 27 June against the enemy air base at Tamsag inside Outer Mongolia. The Kwantung Army was highly desirous of mounting the ground offensive immediately after the air force had won control of the skies. Reports from Komatsubara indicated that hostile ground forces in the Nomonhan district had been reinforced steadily and that, on the 24th, the Kobayashi task force had been heavily engaged near Chiangchunmiao. Since counteraction seemed imperative, the Kwantung Army issued a new operations order on 25 June. In addition to authorizing Komatsubara's left-shore offensive, Hsinking released the Yasuoka detachment and the Manchukuoan army's Hsingan (Kōan) division from its direct control and attached them to the 23rd Division. Komatsubara was to annihilate Outer Mongolian forces in the Nomonhan sector after completing the concentration of the 23rd Division's main body.[17]

Colonel Sumi's 26th Infantry (Komatsubara's motorized reserve), which had already proceeded to Lake Dorot as ordered, still expected to rendezvous with Yasuoka and to draw trucks for the combined thrust across the Halha. But when Sumi reached Dorot, he found no further orders and no trucks, so he and his men supplemented their diet by digging up edible roots and herbs or fishing in the lake. On the evening of 27 June, Komatsubara and Ōuchi caught up with Sumi by car. As Sumi recalls their conversation, he was told that the river-crossing plan was being changed. Since Japanese tanks could not traverse the Halha at the point that had finally been selected, Yasuoka's mechanized force would be used on the right shore, under Komatsubara's command. The three battalions of the reinforced 26th Regiment would still provide the motorized punch for the 23rd Division on the left bank. They should leave next morning for Chiangchunmiao, where trucks would be made available.[18]

Though Sumi's recollection is consistent on the basis of internal evidence, the Yasuoka detachment did not yet know that its mission was being changed from penetration on the left shore to frontal assault on the right.

Directed by the 23rd Division to "get going," on the evening of 29 June Yasuoka instructed his forces to proceed next morning toward the Halha sector, Tamada from about 9 A.M., Yoshimaru at 11 A.M. To provide mobility for Major Kajikawa's 2nd Battalion of the 28th Infantry—attached to the 4th Tank Regiment, reinforced by the 1st Tank Company, and given the assignment of conducting reconnaissance immediately—Tamada directed his supply and maintenance company to release 12 trucks to Kajikawa; Yoshimaru's regiment provided eight more. Kajikawa was to depart at 6 A.M. The engineers, too, would need trucks for their road repair work, so Yasuoka had ten loaned to them by the independent artillery regiment, and two by the antiaircraft battery. Manchukuoan army cavalry elements from the Hsingan division would screen the right flank. Tamada reminded his units to carry lunch and supper rations. A captain with a truck was assigned to handle traffic control and construction duties.[19]

Noguchi was still uncertain about the precise locations of the detachment's battle targets—a recurring complaint of the tank officers throughout the period. Though trucks had begun to get through to Handagai, only half of the necessary fuel had been collected, and bridging materials had not arrived. But at 11 P.M. on 29 June, an even more pressing order was issued by detachment headquarters, on the basis of intelligence from the 23rd Division that there were signs of enemy retreat. The engineers must immediately set to work repairing the roadway, for the move-out time of the Tamada regiment was now advanced to 1:30 A.M. on 30 June, and the Yoshimaru regiment to 3:30 A.M. Taking a shortcut, Kajikawa's infantry battalion was to depart at 4:30 A.M. (it actually left at 6:30 A.M.). An officer-led patrol should set forth promptly to conduct reconnaissance, with particular reference to the enemy's presumed route of retreat and the river-crossing site on the Halha. Capt. Kitamura Ryōichi's 2nd Tank Company would spearhead the Tamada regiment's movement, two kilometers ahead of the main body, and mark the route of advance. With the exception of one radio apparatus located at regimental headquarters, signal silence must be maintained.

The shortage of fuel prevented the sortie by the entire Yasuoka task force. From Tamada's regiment, Capt. In Sanji's 4th Company, made up of gas-guzzling medium tanks, had to be held at Handagai. So did Capt. Kamiyama Tamotsu's supply company, with its large amount of matériel including supplementary tank gun ammunition, because of the subtraction of the dozen trucks assigned to Kajikawa's infantry. Only when the Kajikawa battalion returned the trucks would Kamiyama be able to catch up with the 4th Regiment.[20]

Earlier, mention was made of the erroneous IJA intelligence that the enemy had been retreating gradually from the right shore since the night of 28 June. It was suggested that the Kwantung Army and the 23rd Division may have used this device to prod forward the Yasuoka detachment and other advance forces, or that the local military authorities merely misinterpreted hostile local movements.[21] Tamada remembers many reports, then and earlier, of an enemy pullback and of supply difficulties. He agrees that the Yasuoka detachment was in a great hurry. Indeed, it is his impression that the Japanese units were being used in something resembling a pursuit operation. By all accounts, the Kwantung Army operations staff nurtured from the outset the unrealistic notion that enemy forces would disengage before they could be forced to stand and fight.

Maj. Nyūmura Matsuichi, commander of the special combat intelligence unit attached to the Yasuoka detachment, has the best explanation for the sequence of events that caused the Japanese armored task force to be rushed toward the confluence. The Soviet consul in Harbin had apparently planted a double agent in the Japanese OSS branch in that city. Through this channel, the OSS picked up a telegram ostensibly addressed by Major General Yakovlev, the 11th Tank Brigade commander, to the 57th Corps commander, Zhukov. The gist of the message was that "because of the daily rains, the roads have become muddy and many of our tanks are bogging down, one after another; it has therefore become imperative to pull back one time to perform the necessary repairs."

The OSS experts in Harbin later insisted to Nyūmura that they knew the telegram was merely one piece of unconfirmed, raw intelligence, and that they had transmitted it to the 23rd Division "for reference" only. The division, however, took things literally and concluded that the enemy would pull back immediately. Undoubtedly, division intelligence officer Suzuki was at fault on this occasion, but even Nyūmura was taken in by the explicit report of signs of enemy retreat. After all, it had been raining and had become very muddy in the Arshaan-Handagai sector where Nyūmura and the Yasuoka detachment were deployed. Later the Japanese learned that the sandy Halha area was not muddy at all; when rains fall on dunes, the sand becomes hard as concrete, like the part of a beach pounded by tides. Yakovlev was actually dashing toward the Halha, but the Japanese were deceived into thinking that the reverse was true. As Nyūmura puts it, the histories may say that the tank offensive was planned, but he was on the scene, and he felt that the Japanese were in unseemly haste to catch the foe. He remains conscious of some responsibility for this important mistake; as an intelligence specialist, he should have recommended caution, but he believed the information at the time. To Nyūmura, the Yakovlev message is a perfect case of the Russians' excellent "inspirational information." He had found that Soviet intelligence does not simply plant false information but feeds correct data until the decisive moment, when "inspired" information is released, resembling fact and thus highly credible when intercepted. The Soviet use of double agents was especially troublesome, in particular those orchestrated from Harbin.[22]

As Yasuoka's units moved out, more or less on schedule, the line officers and the men were in high spirits, says Noguchi, since they knew nothing about the real state of affairs. But the detachment commander and his staff were suffering, for "the Komatsubara corps was playing the part of sacrificial lamb for the whole Japanese expedition, and the Yasuoka force for the Komatsubara corps." The 4th Regiment's light tanks led the advance toward the point on the river (opposite Komatsu Heights) that reconnaissance elements had scouted. Noguchi saw an enemy plane flying parallel with the detachment for a while, undoubtedly reconnoitering.

The advance of the Japanese task force was characterized by ignorance of the terrain and of directions, and was complicated by dense fog and the darkness of a moonless night. Afflicted by wet patches and bogs, the roadway did not hold up, despite repairs by the engineers, and the situation only became worse with the constant movement of the tanks. The men of the armored units labored with the engineers to render the route passable, detouring where feasible. Away from the soft stretches and low ground, the soil was generally sandy; the tanks had to stop occasionally to cool their engines, overheated from sustained operation. Trucks, in particular, found the going extremely difficult.

By about 9 A.M. on the 30th, Tamada's spearhead unit—the Kitamura company—had reached a point seven kilometers northwest of Handagai pass, opening a gap between it and the main force. Tamada tried to redeploy his units and to contract the columns, which had become very elongated as a result of the execrable roadway, as well as to reconnoiter the area ahead. At this time, Noguchi roared up in his sidecar to advise Tamada that his force, renamed the Advance Unit, was to assume command of the reinforced Kajikawa infantry battalion.

Tamada was in the process of assembling his scattered units and letting the engines cool off after the strenuous off-the-road movement when a liaison second lieutenant arrived from the spearhead company at 10:35 A.M. Captain Kitamura had discovered eight or nine enemy BT tanks,[23] three armored cars, and two rapid-fire guns at 8:50 A.M., and a half-hour later had begun to engage them with the light tanks of his 2nd Company. Although Tamada had only two light tank platoons, a repair platoon, and a field artillery battery at regiment headquarters at the moment, he decided to rush forward in support of Kitamura, lest the 2nd Company become isolated and the splendid high ground south of Lake Dorot be lost. En route, Tamada passed the Kajikawa battalion, from whom he "borrowed" an antitank battery. At 12:30 P.M., with engines overheated again from traversing the slopes, the colonel reached the Kitamura unit and learned that it had quickly driven off a force of eight or nine enemy tanks supported by anti-tank guns, three armored cars, and horsemen, had secured the high ground (Heights 893 in IJA terminology), and was scouting the area within sight of the Halha River.

With reinforcements from the 1st Tank Company and from a Man-chukuoan cavalry squadron, Kitamura subsequently discovered, at 1:20 P.M., what appeared to be an enemy armored car moving east to reconnoiter at a distance of three km. Tamada, who was also observing the enemy, approved the captain's request to try to capture the fighting vehicle. Kitamura got behind the foe and began to close in toward the northeast. It turned out that the enemy consisted of a truck carrying ten soldiers and towing a rapid-fire gun. This element did not try to flee when the Japanese cut off retreat, but swung around and took cover in a shallow dip on a dune at 1:50. The enemy troops dismounted, while their lieutenant readied the antitank gun to fire at point-blank range—about 30 meters.

Kitamura led the charge up the rise, into the ambush. The enemy rapid-fire gun smashed and burned his Type 95 light tank, perhaps with one shot, killing the captain and fatally wounding a crewman. Noguchi remembers that Kitamura had been very fond of the excellent engine in his tank and always used to outdistance the rest of his unit. This time, unluckily, he had penetrated too fast and too far alone, and was cut off and destroyed.[24] The rest of the Japanese tank company surrounded the hostile force and killed the gun crew, dispersing the others and finally annihilating them by 2:40 P.M. The antitank gun and 200 shells aboard the truck were captured, as was one live enemy soldier, a badly wounded Russian sergeant, the only survivor. Soldiers came to the Yasuoka detachment from the 4th Tank Regiment to apologize for having lost the company commander. As a measure of revenge, they brought ten caps and knapsacks taken from the slain enemy.[25]

Tamada remembers the antitank gun as excellent, and the armor-piercing shells as much more effective than Japanese ammunition. As one IJA officer put it, the Japanese tanks had a muzzle velocity of only 400 meters per second, and the flight of the shell could be observed; but, with respect to Soviet antitank guns, "hardly had we seen a flash than there was a hole in our tank; their accuracy was wonderful too." Noguchi later used the captured gun to defend the headquarters. It was significant, Tamada notes, that the enemy attached antitank guns to BT tank units. From this daylight action, the colonel learned that Soviet equipment was good, enemy reactions were rapid, and the foe was both tenacious and possessed of high fighting spirit. As the regimental diary concluded, it was necessary to be more cautious regarding tactics and approach. In other words, the quality of the enemy was much better than had been expected.

Nyūmura personally interrogated the Soviet prisoner, "a fine noncom, as good as a Japanese." The Russian's mouth had been partly shot away and he resisted answering at first. Finally he began to talk, although it was hard to understand him. At Ulan Bator the Russians had stationed a special corps. The particular unit engaged by Tamada was the Bykov armored car battalion, to whose artillery the sergeant's platoon belonged. But Bykov himself (who had come to the front from Borzya) had been relieved for alleged failure in the first phase of the Nomonhan affair.[26] At Undurhan there was a mechanized brigade, the 11th, with 80 amphibious tanks and two field artillery batteries totaling eight 76-mm. pieces. Antitank guns of 45-mm. caliber fired three kinds of projectile: armor-piercing, instantaneous fuzed, and short-delay common shells. Of Soviet grenades, shaped like tortoiseshells, there were both defensive and offensive models, the latter being employed for the first time at Nomonhan. The enemy had been taught that since Japanese tanks were slow and lacked firepower, there was nothing to fear from them. But the facts went contrary to this notion, and the men did dread Japanese armor.

Nyūmura and his combat intelligence men searched the Soviet bodies and collected papers, including the identification found on each individual. The Russian officer, a first lieutenant of artillery, was very handsome, says Nyūmura, who was sorry to see such a young officer slain. In the lieutenant's bag were found a field diary and map. It was now apparent that the Bykov unit, originally from the Trans-Baikal region, had arrived at the front two or three weeks earlier and had been practicing firing and scouting actions every day. It seemed ominous to the Japanese that the Russians had been setting up markers for prearranged artillery fire against anticipated Japanese routes of advance.

This was the first hard intelligence on the 11th Tank Brigade. Nyūmura now realized that the right bank was held by Soviet forces, not Outer Mongolians. Until then, based on the experience of May, it had been thought that the main hostile force was MPRA, with some Russians in support. Obviously, the order of battle must be reversed; this scale of Russian participation had not been expected. Nyūmura reported his findings by wireless to the 23rd Division, the Harbin OSS, and Kwantung Army headquarters. But the information was obtained too late to affect the offensive by Yasuoka, whose detachment kept rushing forward.[27]

At 2:50 P.M., from the high ground east of the Halha, Tamada's regiment observed eight hostile vehicles (perhaps tanks), accompanied by guns, moving toward them on the left side of the river. Both Tamada's 3rd Tank Company and Kajikawa's infantry battalion scouted the right shore and encountered no enemy. The hostile unit on the left side did not take aggressive action, and since it was beyond range anyhow, Tamada's forces did not fire.

Noguchi had caught up with the Tamada regiment and was chatting with the colonel in the afternoon, after 3 P.M., when a Japanese plane with Kwantung Army staff officer Katō aboard flew in from the north. It circled low overhead and dropped a communication tube containing the gist of new instructions for the Yasuoka detachment from the 23rd Division. According to this preparatory-alert message, to be followed by more complete orders, Yasuoka was to veer away from the Halha and head north for Chiangchunmiao in order to render support to the 23rd Division's own forthcoming crossing of the river. A map enclosure showed where fuel had been cached en route, southwest of Lake Dorot; the columns were to refuel there and proceed to their destination.

Tamada and Noguchi were very relieved that the tank force would no longer have to negotiate the river with skimpy fuel supplies or lug machine guns on foot. The fuel stocks had been brought in by air, and Noguchi suspected that his friend Captain Katō had prevailed upon the other Kwantung Army staff officers at 23rd Division headquarters to arrange the aerial resupply. As for the reasoning behind the sudden change in offensive plan and the shift to Chiangchunmiao, Noguchi is of the opinion higher headquarters had decided (1) that it was too far to send the armored detachment across the Halha from Handagai, at least in the absence of heavy bridging gear to span a river higher than usual, and (2) that hostile ground forces posed a threat to the rear of Kobayashi's main river-crossing group that the tanks could deal with on the right side of the confluence. At the time, Noguchi thought that the detachment, after clearing the right bank, might still be able to pursue the foe to the other shore.

The formal order of the 23rd Division had been issued at 3 P.M. on 30 June, outlining the missions of the Kobayashi force on the left shore, of Sumi's motorized reserve regiment at Chiangchunmiao, and of the armored detachment. Yasuoka was to follow Kobayashi and Komatsubara to the Fui Heights area and strike southward toward the confluence. Manchukuoan cavalry units would attack Noro Heights (south of the Holsten) and Balshagal Heights (north of the Holsten) to cut the enemy's route of retreat in that direction.

Although the Yasuoka detachment had only concentrated the bulk of its tracked vehicle units, it had become imperative to press forward promptly, so as not to be late for the river crossing and the offensive by the main force of the 23rd Division starting on 2-3 July. Yasuoka's thinking, which certainly reflected the Kwantung Army's and Komatsubara's, has been recorded as follows: "The opportunity to smash the foe has arrived, since the facing enemy has already lost his fighting will. Our detachment intends to smash the enemy north of the Holsten River, in concert with the division main force's attack on the west bank of the Halha, slated to begin on 3 July.

The scheduled time for opening the offensive is morning on that date, but if there are signs of enemy retreat, we will start our offensive before the stipulated time."[28]

Probably because the Kajikawa battalion had been delayed, however, Komatsubara attached the 1st and 2nd battalions of Yamagata's 64th Infantry to Yasuoka, retaining the 3rd Battalion as division reserve. Yamagata's regiment had already reached Chiangchunmiao late on 28 June. Komatsubara may have intended to beef up the Yasuoka-Kajikawa task force, but in practice Yamagata's two battalions fought as substitutes for Kajikawa's battalion.

At 5 P.M. on 30 June Tamada's Advance Unit designation was rescinded, and all elements were ordered by Yasuoka to head for the assembly area southwest of Lake Dorot, bound for Chiangchunmiao. Tamada, however, decided to defer movement except by the artillery until after sunset, partly because of the need to conceal Japanese intentions but also because contact had been lost with the attached Kajikawa battalion. Much of Kajikawa's problem stemmed from the repeated changes in status of his infantry unit. At Arshaan, which it reached on 21 June, the battalion had been given trucks in order to operate with Yasuoka's armor. When the trucks broke down in the morass past Arshaan, most of Kajikawa's men ended up slogging over 60 km. to Handagai. There, Yasuoka ordered his own detachment to loan some of their precious trucks to the infantry. But since the battalion was under the direct control of Yasuoka from 27 June, even after being attached to Tamada's Advance Unit, it apparently had not been notified early enough of the tank regiment's advance. Now, with the relocation to Chiangchunmiao, the mechanized units wanted their trucks back immediately, and most of Kajikawa's men were obliged to march again. As the 4th Tank Regiment's diary says, because the Kajikawa battalion did not move to its rendezvous as rapidly as ordered, the transfer to Lake Dorot became badly delayed. This is but another of many cases of poor synchronization between Japanese tank and infantry cross-country mobility.[29]

Sunset came at 8:10 P.M. on 30 June. Shortly afterward, Tamada commenced the assembly of his leading regiment, and by about 9 P.M. his forces set out for Lake Dorot, impeded again by rain, darkness, mud, and difficult direction finding. To traverse only 23 km. took the detachment over six hours, instead of the one that that distance would require in good terrain. At about 3:30 A.M. the Japanese units finally completed their concentration at the lake. Tamada complained that the movement should have been controlled more quickly by the Yasuoka detachment, which should have sent guides to conduct reconnaissance of the route of advance and to mark the road.

At the Lake Dorot assembly area, on the morning of 1 July, Captain In's

4th Company (the only one consisting of medium tanks) and the main body of Captain Kamiyama's regimental supply company finally arrived from Handagai. Yoshimaru's 3rd Regiment of medium tanks also pulled in, following Tamada's force. Having begun its march to Lake Dorot at 9 P.M. on the night before, the Kajikawa infantry battalion finally arrived fourteen hours later, at 11 A.M. Between 10 and 11 A.M. Yasuoka issued orders to his detachment to leave at 1 P.M. for Chiangchunmiao, with the ultimate objective of smashing the enemy on the right shore of the Halha. Tamada was to provide the point company, assign one platoon for labor duties, and lead the detachment's main force with the rest of his regiment. Yasuoka then flew to Chiangchunmiao to coordinate operations with Komatsubara.

At 11:30 A.M. on 1 July, Tamada ordered his forces to prepare to depart again.[30] Guided by Noguchi, the detachment left on schedule at 1 P.M., shadowed occasionally by enemy scout planes. By 5:10 P.M. on 1 July, the force reached the bivouac point at a lake eight km. east of Chiangchunmiao, where it linked up with the 23rd Division. Yasuoka, who had returned from division headquarters, issued a new operations order at 12:30 A.M. on 2 July. The 23rd Division and 64th Infantry Regiment having moved toward the front already, the armored detachment should send out an advance guard at 4 A.M., this time led by Yoshimaru's 3rd Tank Regiment and a battery from Colonel Miyao's 1st Independent Field Artillery Regiment. About a kilometer behind should come the main force of the 1st Echelon: detachment headquarters, the 4th Tank Regiment, the rest of the artillery regiment, medical and signal troops, and the water supply section, which was to reconnoiter every pond along the route. All regimental supply and maintenance companies were to follow the main unit. A 2nd Echelon, under Major Kajikawa and including his infantry battalion, a light tank platoon, an antiaircraft battery, a tow-truck company, an independent engineer company, and a medical element, should also move forward on the 2nd after taking a long rest upon arrival at Chiangchunmiao. Probably influenced by the Kitamura episode, Tamada's order added the injunction that each of the tank companies should designate a platoon beforehand assigned exclusively to neutralize enemy antitank guns.[31]

After having marched 14 hours and rested about eight, the Kajikawa infantry battalion left Lake Dorot at 7:10 P.M. on 1 July. Those aboard the 20 trucks reached Chiangchunmiao at 2 A.M. on the 2nd; those who marched got to their destination at 7:30 A.M. Assigned to Yasuoka's 2nd Echelon, Kajikawa was ordered to catch up with the armored detachment as soon as possible. The battalion set out again from Chiangchunmiao at 1 P.M. on the 2nd, some on foot, others on trucks. Yamagata's 64th Regiment, necessarily filling in for the truant but tired Kajikawa unit, had begun its foot march to the front from Chiangchunmiao the day before, at 4:30 A.M. on 1 July.[32]

At 4 A.M. on 2 July, the Yasuoka detachment left the Chiangchunmiao area. By 7 A.M. Tamada's lead elements, some 20 km. to the west of Chiangchunmiao, heard the sound of artillery fire in the far distance to the southwest. The units pressed ahead, ready to fight. A wet area did not impede the tanks greatly but slowed down the trucks as usual. At the bivouac east of Lake Hozui, at 2 P.M., Yasuoka's order noted that Yamagata's 64th Infantry had been in combat since noon and that the detachment was to catch up quickly. The signal for the advance would be the waving of a Japanese flag. Tamada's regiment headed south in diamond formation at 2:20 P.M., paying particular heed to the areas ahead and to the right. Time was lost because of difficulty locating the rendezvous and because of obstacles posed by the roadway. By 3:15 P.M. the lead elements had reached the east side of Lake Manzute and were preparing rapidly to go on the offensive, sending out patrols and security forces. Suddenly enemy artillery shells flew in from the direction of the high ground on the left bank of the Halha and struck in front of the bivouac area.[33]

Japanese scout planes landed occasionally near Yasuoka's command post and conveyed information from the 23rd Division. At 4 P.M. the division ordered Yasuoka to attack the confluence from dawn on 3 July. The general was in the process of working up his offensive order when a plane brought intelligence—again—that there was evidence of an enemy retreat in groups of two and three vehicles. Around 5 P.M. Yasuoka called Colonels Yoshimaru, Tamada, and Yamagata to his command post and revealed his new tactics for attacking the enemy. Before the division's main force crossed the river during the coming night, mopped up left-shore resistance next morning, and advanced toward the confluence, the Yasuoka task force (with Yamagata's infantry regiment and a field artillery battalion newly attached) would press forward quickly to pin down and smash the foe on the right bank above the Holsten. Yamagata was to attack along the dunes and press the enemy to the bridge at the junction, with Yoshimaru's medium tank regiment in support. Operating as the left wing in the second echelon, Tamada's 4th Regiment (without infantry) was to assist the 3rd Regiment from the left rear and strike for the bridge too, from the outer flank. The field artillery should neutralize enemy guns on both shores and support the tank and infantry actions, those of Yamagata in particular. The jump-off time would be 6 P.M. In other words, Yasuoka, in great haste and on his own initiative, wanted to launch his offensive in the evening of 2 July, not the morning of the 3rd, to catch the enemy off balance and facilitate the main river-crossing operation by the 23rd Division.[34]

Noguchi remembers how tired Colonel Yamagata was from his regiment's long march to the front and how he was using his sword as a cane. Yasuoka kept the colonel at the command post as long as possible, so that he could be given a sedan to catch up with his unit. Meanwhile, Yamagata passed along what little information his infantry had acquired concerning the enemy, whose tanks were conducting a "roving defense" in certain areas on the right shore. The terrain, swampy or sandy in places, would make it rather difficult for the Japanese tanks, but essentially it was a vast plain characterized by gentle slopes. One of Tamada's own patrols reported generally feasible cross-country mobility. Yamagata, Yoshimaru, and Tamada coordinated their envisaged deployments and routes of advance. They drank some cider and wished each other well. Irie, in from patrol aboard a tankette, wondered if the colonels were toasting farewell or victory, but his less profound thoughts centered on his own thirst and his envy of the soft drinks. Tamada returned to his unit and exhorted the 4th Regiment, noting that they were to seize a good opportunity to enter combat. He says he was aware of his operational objectives in general terms only.[35]

It was significant that the latest 23rd Division instructions on the afternoon of 2 July had called for the attachment to the Yasuoka detachment not only of Yamagata's 64th Infantry Regiment but also of different field artillery, Maj. Morikawa Shin's 2nd Field Artillery Battalion, part of Col. Ise Takahide's 13th Field Artillery Regiment organic to the 23rd Division, and consisting of two batteries totaling eight 75-mm. field guns and one of four 12-cm. howitzers. Ise's regiment had originally been assigned to support the division main force's left-bank offensive, whereas Yasuoka was to have been covered by the 1st Independent Field Artillery Regiment of Miyao—two tractor-drawn batteries numbering eight Type 90 75-mm. field pieces. Though Yasuoka now found himself with more guns, they were old ordnance dating back to the era of the Russo-Japanese War. Morikawa's 75-mm. guns were not even of the "improved" model and had an effective range of only 6,800 meters, and his equally old howitzers could not fire much beyond 5,000 meters. By contrast, Miyao's long-barrel 75-mm. guns, equipped with distinctive muzzle brakes, were of the newest type (1930) and possessed a long-range capability of perhaps 14,000 meters.

Convinced that the enemy was in retreat, and anxious to hasten the river-crossing operation while neutralizing enemy guns on the higher left shore, Komatsubara and his Kwantung Army staff advisers made the clumsy, last-minute decision to swap Miyao's fine unit for Ise's ancient horse-drawn batteries. Noguchi remembers that the "deal" was designed to replace Miyao's eight guns with a full regiment of field artillery. In practice only one battalion of Ise's regiment was able to enter action on 2 July, and was no substitute for the tractor guns. To bring up Miyao's force (with its 95 tracked and wheeled vehicles), says Noguchi, had been extremely difficult, but now all of the Type 90 mobile guns were taken away to Fui Heights to help the division's left-shore offensive. At the very time the Yasuoka detachment was going to plunge against the foe on the right bank, the task force was weakened by being deprived of its tractor-hauled artillery as well as its motorized infantry.[36]

As usual, only limited intelligence was available to the Japanese commanders regarding Soviet-MPRA strength. Tamada remembers merely rough markings of hostile positions on 1:100,000 aerial maps. According to Noguchi, the maps were copied from reconnaissance photos and, instead of being up to the minute, were probably two or three days old. Nyūmura agrees that the cartography was understandably better after the combat. According to intelligence, no fewer than two enemy divisions had been deployed southeast of Nomonhan and on both shores of the Halha since 20 June. Air reconnaissance had reported many enemy vehicles, but it was not clear if they were tanks or trucks, and it was difficult to analyze concentrated, stopped formations. In short, Nyūmura admits, the Japanese had almost no idea of the size or strength of enemy units lying ahead. On the right bank, the foe was known to have constructed a triple belt of strong positions with wire entanglements. But firsthand information, beyond scouting reports, would have been useful, especially since dunes blocked the view. Therefore, serious efforts were made to take prisoners—even one, says Nyūmura. The results were fruitless. For example, Kajikawa's infantry battalion had been ordered to conduct a night assault on 28 June against 100 Outer Mongolian soldiers, in the direction of the Halha west of Handagai, with a view to seizing captives and matériel. The reinforced Japanese infantry company conducting the attack marched for seven hours but found no enemy troops. Again on the morning of 30 June, Kajikawa sent an infantry platoon, supported by heavy machine guns and light tanks, to take prisoners—without success.[37] Now, on 2 July, Kajikawa's unit was expected to assemble in the Lake Manzute area by evening, but contact had been lost with him.

Noguchi did not really believe that the foe was pulling back; in fact, he was of the impression that enemy positions on the right shore were being reinforced. Nevertheless, it was clear that higher headquarters wanted Yasuoka's tank force to hurry. Japanese orders, says Irie, often did not fit the actual situation; they consistently read "Attack, attack, attack . . . charge . . . to the Halha, across the Halha . . . to Tamsag, etc." Irie felt as though his seniors were always "kicking him in the ass," from corps to regiment to company to platoon, down the line. He was terribly irritated, for he knew that the detachment simply was not ready to go into action yet. Still, orders were orders, although all ranks believed they were both grandiose and nebulous in this case. Pushing forward pell-mell posed special problems. The Japanese units were well trained individually, but Yasuoka's elements were new to each other and had never operated or practiced together until the detachment was activated about 10 days earlier. In an effort to foster unity and coordination as soon as possible, Yasuoka ordered the tanks to advance in an unusual line of combat columns, although the enemy was still far off.

Each Japanese tank bore a distinctive name, as warships did. In the 1st Company of the 3rd Tank Regiment, Takeshita's platoon took the names of mountains; the lieutenant's own tank was called *Aso*. The tank of another platoon leader, 2nd Lt. Koga Yasuo, was named *Hayabusa* (Falcon); his second machine was *Hiryū* (Flying Dragon); his third, *Fubuki* (Snowstorm)— all "things that fly through the sky." Other platoons named tanks after rivers, flowers, etc. The names were spelled in *hiragana* phonetics, in white enamel. A red-ball flag, the full-color *hinomaru*, adorned both sides of the turret, clearly visible with binoculars but too small to be dangerous as a target. In addition, each company numbered its tanks in two-digit arabic numerals, like a license plate.[38]

Despite the many problems facing the Yasuoka detachment as it prepared to attack, unit morale was high. Major Ogata was joshing the tanker noncoms and men of the 4th Regiment. "A soldier's corpse," he grinned, "is usually placed in a very cheap, white wooden box. But if we tank men die here, our wonderful caskets will be worth ¥100,000 each. Ours is certainly a better fate than that of mere soldiers!" The troops clapped their hands and guffawed in response to Ogata's black humor.

In the 4th Regiment, 2nd Lt. Sunouchi Seiichi assembled his platoon of the 4th Company and shared what might be called a "last supper," featuring canned tangerines and beer. Everybody looked hale and hearty, but as he gazed at each tanker's face, Lieutenant Sunouchi was determined not to lose a man. Meanwhile, a tank corporal in the company gathered the new first-year soldiers and joked with them: "This may be the last chance for you guys to enjoy my bearded puss, so take a good look!"[39]

In the same way that Yasuoka had pushed the timing of the tank offensive ahead of the division's river crossing, Tamada could not wait to get going too. Negative facts became inverted justifications for speed. In the words of the 4th Tank Regiment's chronicle for 2 July: "From here to the confluence was still about 20 km. as the crow flies. In addition, the enemy situation and the terrain were unknown, and evening was approaching gradually. So we were afraid of losing our chance by dragging things out needlessly." At 6:10 P.M. on 2 July, Tamada got his unit under way, ahead of the Yoshimaru regiment, he claims, and on his own initiative.[40] Light armor, more mobile than Tamada's medium tank company, led the line of columns in diamond formation. The first and last Japanese tank participation in the Nomonhan fighting was finally at hand.

Tanks Dare the Night

Even before the Yasuoka task force launched its offensive in the evening of 2 July, Colonel Yamagata's 64th Infantry Regiment and the Morikawa field artillery battalion were mauled by the enemy. At 10 A.M. the Yamagata regiment's 2nd Battalion, commanded by Lt. Col. Tokumaru Mitsuru, had begun action against Heights 739, four kilometers south of Lake Manzute. For once, matters went well for the Japanese at first, and the enemy was driven back. "It was like a pursuit," a sergeant reminisces. "Although only two or three hours were involved, never again did I feel so good throughout the entire Nomonhan Incident." But as soon as the foot troops gained the high ground, Soviet artillery emplaced around Hara Heights on the left bank of the Halha pounded the Japanese. The number of enemy 15-cm. howitzers in action did not seem to exceed a battery of four, but the gun flashes could be seen at a distance of five or six kilometers, and the impact of the hurtling shells resembled lightning bolts or buzz saws, kicking up blinding pillars of sand and dense smoke. Casualties were reduced by the cushioning effect of the sandy soil, although direct hits could be murderous. The Japanese infantrymen were awestruck by the "indescribable" enemy barrage, which lasted for about two hours. Shaken IJA officers and men who had seen combat in the Nanking campaign said the effectiveness of the Russian artillery fire was beyond anything they had experienced in China.

During the movement forward, the riflemen had scattered to evade the bombardment and had tried to thread their way through the barrage as best they could. Now exhaustion began to take its toll. The foot soldiers had been on the march for days, with little rest, although they do not seem to have been speedsters at any time. During the long and arduous hike from Hailar, the better-conditioned 26th Regiment, according to Sumi, had even requested and received Yamagata's permission to leapfrog his 64th Regiment. By 2 July the marching ability of the Yamagata unit must have been reduced to four kilometers per hour, not the six ordinarily expected of infantrymen. A corporal explains: "We were simply exhausted, having expended our strength during the forced march . . . to Chiangchunmiao and the front. Things got so bad, we had to make desperate efforts just to keep up, let alone avoid enemy artillery shells or aircraft. Along the wave-shaped crestlines, we ought to have been able to enter dead angles if only we could have pushed forward a bit more. But when you have no energy, your body does not respond the way it should."[1]

The 2nd Machine Gun Company of Capt. Uchida Tadaaki had been using its 33 horses to haul its heavy weapons and ammunition to the front. When the march was to be followed by combat, the men unloaded the horses and tethered them two kilometers to the rear to avoid artillery fire. With the horses, the troops left their knapsacks, rations, and tents. But the long reach of the Soviet artillery came down on the horses and wiped them out, together with all of the soldiers' gear.

The absence of infantry support posed a serious problem for Colonel Yoshimaru's 3rd Tank Regiment. Yamagata and Yoshimaru were supposed to attack in concert, and Lieutenant General Yasuoka had tried to link up the armor and the riflemen from the start. Nevertheless, when the Japanese tank offensive got under way on the evening of 2 July, there was still no sign of movement by the 64th Infantry. Rightly fearful that Yoshimaru's fighting vehicles, ahead of the foot troops, would become isolated, Yasuoka pressed Yamagata to advance promptly. Yoshimaru had also contacted Yamagata about their regiments' envisaged coordination. At 7:40 P.M., in driving rain, a Japanese plane dropped a message tube at detachment headquarters repeating the intelligence that enemy forces were allegedly retreating westward constantly through the river crossing, and reminding Yasuoka that it was imperative to launch an immediate pursuit. Again Yamagata was prodded to begin moving, and his weary soldiers finally advanced, shortly before 8 P.M.

Tank staff officer Noguchi was well aware that the 64th Infantry was worn out and suffering from thirst. Dispatched by Yasuoka to maintain liaison with Yamagata on the night of 2 July, Noguchi and his colleagues had at first been moving on foot, keeping tank speed down to that of the very slow riflemen. Noguchi remembers instructing the foot soldiers to maintain proper intervals and take cover. The atmosphere of the 64th Regiment seemed to him rather gloomy. Yamagata well knew the problems of the local battlefield, having operated in that terrain in late May; indeed, the infantry colonel could not have forgotten his very unsuccessful experience little more than a month earlier when Azuma was annihilated. Undoubtedly to avoid any reference to that episode that might be taken as pessimistic about the present operation, Yamagata said nothing at all in Noguchi's hearing.

The colonel, like his seniors, was caught up by the idea that the foe showed signs of retreating, as we know from a regimental order Yamagata issued as early as 2:30 P.M. on 1 July. As he conceived of his mission (approved by Yasuoka), the 64th Regiment would mount another night attack on 2/3 July against the estimated battalion of enemy infantry defending the Heights 731 sector about six kilometers northeast of the confluence. Then Yamagata expected to break through to the Halha and somehow cross the river on the enemy's bridge at the junction.[2]

Yamagata's concept, although never realistic, has a connection with the mission given by Yasuoka on 2 July to Capt. Yabuuchi Retsuo, 1st Company commander in Kawamura's 24th Engineer Regiment: to capture the Russians' bridge. If this proved impossible, Yabuuchi was to blow up the span in order to cut off the retreat route of the enemy on the right shore. Demolition engineers hoisted a total of half a dozen 10-kg. packages of explosives on their shoulders and joined the rest of the 200-strong company in a dash for the crossing. This force was the first of Yasuoka's detachment to commence the so-called pursuit action on the evening of 2 July, operating like a "special attack unit" (*teishintai*).

After charging southwest in the gathering darkness and then in a thunderstorm, Yabuuchi's company encountered a deep belt of barbed wire on a front of four to ten meters. Judging that such defenses presaged the enemy's main positions, Yabuuchi stopped his unit. Presently, Soviet machine guns, whose presence was anticipated but whose numbers were not, opened fire. Including one tracer in ten rounds, the "beautiful pyrotechnics" flew low above the heads of the Japanese. Although Yabuuchi's men suffered no casualties, they could hear the ominous rumble of armor, followed by tank gunfire. Isolated from the rest of the Yasuoka detachment, Yabuuchi deemed his prospects to be hopeless, so he pulled back the engineer company gradually and had the men dig in and wait for daybreak. It was frustrating for the Japanese engineers, who could already discern the confluence clearly ahead, not to be able to break through to the bridge. Yabuuchi sent several messengers to contact the main force; they did not make it back until around noon on 3 July. Naturally, the engineer regiment commander, Kawamura, was worried about the fate of the 1st Company, with whom he was still out of contact as of 9 A.M. on the 3rd. The colonel therefore asked the 3rd Tank Regiment to look for his missing unit.[3]

When most of the Yamagata regiment, outdistanced by the tanks, holed up for the night somewhere around Heights 731 past 10 P.M., over 12 hours after beginning action on the 2nd, the men of the 2nd Machine Gun Company had only some biscuits in their bags, and no shelter against the thunderstorms dousing them. The troops pulled up grass, draped it on the bottom of their foxholes, and slept wretchedly with their helmets tilted over their faces.[4]

As for the Japanese field artillery, Yasuoka was of the impression that Major Morikawa had unlimbered counterbattery fire from about 7:20 P.M. In fact, the horse-drawn 2nd Artillery Battalion had been pinned down from the outset. Reassigned from the Fui Heights area, Morikawa's column came under severe enemy long-range 15-cm. fire from the left shore after finally reaching Heights 739 around 2 P.M. The Japanese gunners lay prone in a dip, unable to move. Like their infantry counterparts, the veteran artillery officers and men muttered about the difference from their experience in China. One observation lieutenant called the Soviet barrage "tremendous." By 8 p.m. the battalion commander, growing concerned that his guns would be destroyed by enemy fire, decided to relocate his unit, presumably rearward. Soviet howitzer barrages were so severe, however, that Morikawa felt compelled to defer any movement until it was pitch-dark. The Japanese guns and draft horses, which had had to be separated, were hidden in a dip while the battalion observation teams and the batteries dug in on the dunes. An effort by Capt. Sonoshita Zenzō's 1st Company of Yamagata's 64th Infantry to rescue the Morikawa artillery battalion during the middle of the night failed when the foot troops got lost. The artillerymen lay flat most of the night, without pitching tents, even in the driving rain.[5]

Yasuoka's troubles with Morikawa's horse-drawn artillery, Yoshimaru's armor, Kajikawa's and Yamagata's infantry, and Yabuuchi's engineers illustrate fundamental dysfunctions in doctrine, training, and practice. The spirit and the ideas of the various arms differed markedly. So far as the tankers were concerned, they always regarded themselves as the spearhead for the infantry, adopting the "corps method" (*heidan yōhō*), launching surprise attacks, and charging ahead into enemy positions. This was the armored forces' notion of direct support (*chokkyō*), which bred a "tank-as-the-main-element philosophy" (*sensha shuryoku shugi*). Such an approach served the Japanese army well in the China theater, where the enemy had no armor and the IJA tankers were almighty "battle heroes," convinced that they were the stars who won the engagements, that no enemy could withstand them, and that the infantry—the traditional "queen of combat"—must envy them. For operations in North China, a mechanized corps (the Sakai detachment) had been formed, including truck-borne infantry. Since the experiment was not regarded as successful, it had been deactivated and the infantry were put back on their feet by the time of Nomonhan. On the flatlands of Hulun Buir, however, the tanks could have achieved far better results if only they had been accompanied by motorized infantry. Noguchi, for one, missed the Sakai detachment or its equivalent at Nomonhan.

In the fighting of 1939, it soon became apparent that the Russians stressed tank-infantry-artillery mutual-support tactics (often assigning ten foot soldiers per machine), and that they regarded tanks as mobile, armored artillery. But the Japanese tank command, emphasizing mechanized mobility, had conducted almost no training for cooperation with other arms, especially in open terrain. The inclination for tanks to operate separately from infantry customarily drew criticism at armored schools and at joint maneuvers—"a lousy tendency," which reached extremes at Nomonhan, says the 3rd Tank Regiment's Lieutenant Takeshita.

Many Japanese infantrymen and artillerists never saw a friendly tank in action on their sectors at Nomonhan. A lieutenant in the 13th Field Artillery remembers a tank noncom driving up to his battery and pleading desperately for the loan of a gunner to replace his slain tank gunner. The battery commander felt obliged to reject the request, whereupon the tanker drove away sadly, leaving the artillerymen regretful too. It was the one time they ever met a Japanese tank. In the 64th Regiment, a soldier recalls his pleasure at observing friendly tanks, flying the red-ball flag, before the offensive of 2 July began; but he never saw another during the subsequent confused combat. Naturally, foot troops could not keep up with the tanks, yet the tankers were complaining that the infantry did not support them. "To tell the truth, however," a foot soldier responds, "I remember feeling disappointed that it was the tanks which could not be depended upon by us." The infantry made no claims that coordination with the armor was satisfactory. Nevertheless, the soldiers were truly grieved to see friendly tanks burning. "Every time we passed one," says a machine gun company commander in the Yamagata regiment, "we would silently thank them for their sacrifice and mourn the dead, with our hands clasped together in reverence."[6]

The Japanese tankers, for their part, argued that infantry were useless in a mobile offensive, especially in the case of high-speed pursuit. Foot troops could never have proceeded as far in the direction of the confluence as the armor did, "even in a month or two." At Handagai, Yasuoka had called in Yoshimaru and Tamada and asked their opinions regarding the employment of infantry with tanks in the river-crossing operation. Yoshimaru opposed their use in this case because of the slowness of riflemen. But Tamada, the newer tank officer, felt that armor possessed offensive and defensive limitations that must be taken into consideration. Mass, for instance, had as great significance to tanks as velocity. In addition, once stopped on the steppes devoid of natural cover, tanks became vulnerable to artillery emplaced on high ground. The best time to pause was during darkness, but then in particular infantrymen were needed to guard and support the armor.

The 3rd Regiment's Irie agrees that the tank forces' elitist spirit went too far, warped by the experience in China. Though it was very difficult for armor to work closely with infantry, he admits candidly that the tankers had no real intention of collaborating in the first place: "That the tanks could not cooperate with foot soldiers is only half the story. That they *would not* is the other half." Takeshita adds that Japanese armor, in his experience, received no close support from the infantry, but he has to confess that the tanks were to blame, for they operated rather independently too.[7] These insights help to explain the fact that, from beginning to end of their combat participation at Nomonhan in July, the Japanese tanks operated essentially alone and "naked."

Moving forward under dark clouds in the rain on the evening of 2 July, Japanese armored forces, like the infantry and artillery earlier, came under artillery fire from the left shore of the Halha. Near 8 P.M., far off to the northwest in the direction presumed to be that of Yoshimaru's 3rd Tank Regiment, Tamada discerned heavy smoke and firing, but no courier could get through. Although Yasuoka's detachment headquarters also observed burning vehicles, it could not ascertain whether friendly or hostile machines were aflame. Actually, Yoshimaru had advanced on schedule, moving through dips and gentle slopes on the plain at a speed of about 15 kilometers per hour until his unit encountered the fire of heavy artillery, 10-cm. cannon and 15-cm. howitzers emplaced on the left bank of the Halha. Smoke blanketed the area, giving the impression that some tanks had been wrecked, but in fact none of the vehicles had been hit yet. Irie conducted what he called test-firing, but this was regarded as premature, and he was scolded by the company commander.

Once past the zone of barrages, the Japanese tanks charged into enemy outposts, probably manned by motorized infantry, who were overrun. As one Japanese gunner put it, "We passed through pleasantly." About 700-800 meters beyond, Soviet gunline positions were encountered, consisting of armored vehicles and antitank weapons, whose intense fire posed an even greater threat to the advancing Japanese armor than the high-explosive shells of the long-range heavy artillery.[8] When their defenses were penetrated, the Russians abandoned a number of tanks and armored cars, leaving them scattered on the plain. Certain elements escaped aboard trucks; others, left behind, waited for night to get away. Some enemy rapid-fire guns and foot soldiers were observed taking cover on the wings.

By about 8 P.M. the 3rd Tank Regiment had reached the high ground that sloped down toward the confluence, a sector of complicated terrain where the Russians apparently concentrated their antitank defenses. One Japanese soldier likened the area on the right shore to a small-scale replica of volcanic craters. Though the IJA armored units had generally managed to maintain their formation, a tank from the 1st Company had stopped to fire and became lost. Trying to catch up, this tank was hit in the turret by several slugs fired by a Soviet heavy machine gun operating from the flank. The crew compartment heated up as if the tank were on fire, but the armor had not been penetrated, and no casualties were incurred.

As Yoshimaru's regiment tried to push to the confluence, the Russians concentrated guns, infantry, and armor in the narrow zone by the river and launched counterattacks from three directions. The Japanese made some progress, but their tank radios were overpowered by enemy transmissions, and Soviet artillery fire grew more intense. Russian mechanized reinforcements moved steadily across the Halha from the left shore. Several enemy armored cars could be seen burning, but the Japanese began to sustain losses of their own. Some of Yoshimaru's tanks had to engage in combat while towing inoperable friendly machines.

Shortly after 9 P.M., "realizing the disadvantage of lingering at the present location for long" without infantry or artillery support, Yoshimaru had decided to pull back and reassemble the regiment to the rear for the time being. Night's darkness was at hand. Signaling "Follow the commander," Yoshimaru's headquarters and reserve platoon headed for a dip near Heights 731, sent out teams to conduct liaison, and waited for the scattered companies to concentrate—a far from easy task. All units struggled to assemble throughout the rest of the night, leaving Yoshimaru unable to exert effective control.

Capt. Miyatake Masajiro, the 1st Company commander, was in high spirits when he finally pulled in, towing a captured armored car and one of the three or four truck-pulled 57-mm. guns that had also been seized. But three of Miyatake's platoon officers had already died in action.[9] Part of the losses had been incurred when, around 8 P.M., the company commander lost contact with 2nd Lt. Shimizu Saburo's 2nd Platoon and dispatched Koga's tankette platoon to the rescue. The Japanese vehicles' radios were still drowned out by Russian voice transmissions, and the terrain was typically undefinable. Soviet soldiers could be sighted moving in their positions, and Captain Miyatake, clowning around, yelled "Hallo! Hallo!" to them. More seriously, artillery fire could be heard in the probable direction of Shimizu's unit, which was why Miyatake sent Koga to knock out the remaining enemy antitank guns.

Near the Soviet artillery emplacements, Koga's platoon detected strange-looking wire resembling green grass—the infamous piano wire entanglements that will be discussed in greater detail in chronicling the disastrous events of 3 July. Koga's own tankette managed to traverse the wire and proceed forward, but it disappeared into a gloom punctuated only by enemy gun flashes. A subordinate tankette commander, Wakabayashi Itsuo, ordered his driver to ignore the piano wire, but the driver sensibly evaded the entanglements and detoured safely to the right. Wakabayashi was not particularly worried about hostile artillery fire—which supposedly could not penetrate Japanese armor—but enemy tanks were another matter. At a range of 300 meters, four unidentified hulks attacked suddenly from the left flank. Wakabayashi broke out a red-ball flag and tried to wave off what might be elements of Tamada's 4th Regiment. All doubts about the identity of the attacking tanks were eliminated when they redoubled their fire.

Wakabayashi was heading for cover in a dip when his tankette was hit on the right rear. Fortunately for the crew, the shell was a dud; only the fuze detonated, while the projectile itself landed behind the ammunition box. Wakabayashi's tankette continued moving, but fire broke out among the three smoke candles stored inside, and the machine gun ammunition began exploding. Although the tankette's battery was damaged, the fuel tank remained intact. Actually, the Japanese vehicle was saved by the fact that the burning candles emitted billows of smoke, causing the enemy to think that they had destroyed their target, which they stopped engaging. Using a fire extinguisher, Wakabayashi tried to douse and eject the candles. The smoke was choking the driver, who opened the front exit and the hatch, kept his foot on the gas pedal, and continued driving the tankette, occasionally sticking out his head for air. Eventually the crew managed to throw out the smoke candles.

To the right, Wakabayashi discerned two Japanese medium tanks, silent and inanimate, although three Russian corpses lay nearby. It was later established that these were the shattered tanks belonging to Lieutenant Shimizu's ill-fated platoon. Although Wakabayashi had lost his bearings, he kept going until his tankette fell into a trench and its engine stalled. Luckily for him and his men, the trench belonged to a unit of the 64th Infantry Regiment. Dazed and hallucinating, Wakabayashi was treated for burns on both hands and for leg wounds caused by a spontaneously fired machine gun bullet. The time was about 10 P.M.

A tankette could be seen burning off to the left—platoon leader Koga's destroyed vehicle. The lieutenant's tankette, after negotiating the first entanglements and overrunning enemy gun positions, had become enmeshed in a third belt of piano wire, which caught the drive wheels and set up the immobilized machine for destruction by enemy gunfire. When Wakabayashi went out to recover his platoon leader's corpse, he found that the lieutenant had been incinerated, his goggles burned, his saber deformed. Some say that Koga, loyal to the Japanese tank officers' tradition, had committed suicide. The driver's upper body was charred to a crisp. Wakabayashi tried to manipulate the tankette's controls, but they were wrecked and inoperable.[10]

A disoriented tank crew from the 1st Company had been moving through the storm with hatches open, pelted by the rain and feeling rather uneasy about being lost and isolated in the night, when they saw platoon leader Irie and some soldiers running along on foot. This struck them as very curious, but their attention was soon diverted when they sighted three or four tanks from the 2nd Company. Efforts were made to establish the location of the regiment's original jump-off site, but, perhaps because of the lightning, the compasses proved unhelpful. Since one could not rely exclusively on the sense of direction of the tank drivers, several of the crewmen dismounted, draped patches of white cloth on their backs, drew their pistols and sabers, and tried to guide the tanks on foot. Finally, it was found that the force was merely describing one large circle in the storm and the darkness. The tank commanders decided to remain where they were, posted sentries, and waited for daybreak.[11]

In the 2nd Company, the commander and two of his platoon officers were slain this night.[12] Maj. Kinomoto Morinosuke's tank had pressed deeply into the confluence sector and was facing across the crestline when the company commander was killed by an artillery shell. The rest of the 2nd Company's tanks had not been able to keep up with the plunge forward by Kinomoto. Operating behind him, platoon leader Irie thought that the unit had almost reached the Holsten, a few more dunes away, when at about 9:30 P.M. he saw his own driver slump over at approximately the same time that Kinomoto was killed. A ricocheting tank shell, fired from the flank on the right shore, had penetrated the thin belly armor of Irie's medium tank and come up and mangled the driver's thigh. The drive shaft of the tank had been broken; the engine was rotating but the vehicle could not move. With the idea of resuming command of his platoon from another of his armored vehicles, as required, Irie dismounted and waited for his other two tanks to come up, little knowing that both had bogged down in sand and had never entered combat.

IJA regulations forbade the abandonment of a tank under fire, even if the machine were knocked out. As platoon leader Koga of the 3rd Regiment always insisted, crewmen must share the fate of their tank, saving their last bullet to commit suicide. Looking back, Irie calls the practice wasteful, as indeed it was in his case: his immobilized tank, now a sitting duck, was hit a dozen times and burned by enemy gunfire. The crew were not allowed to bail out. Consequently, Irie's noncom gunner was killed and the wounded driver was captured (later to be repatriated), although the details were unknown at the time. Irie would suffer grievously over the casualties caused by the unnecessarily rigid military code.

Hitching a ride on a tankette, Irie went looking for the rest of his platoon. After full darkness fell, he changed to a reserve tank which had come to deliver the orders to reassemble. Eventually the tank encountered a noncom and two men marching along—the crew of another of Irie's vehicles, this one merely stranded. The soldiers were lugging the machine gun removed from their tank and fighting as infantry, something demanded by army regulations when a fighting vehicle had bogged down but was not under fire. Joining the crewmen on foot, Irie trudged northward all night, through the enemy positions, where Russians could even be heard talking. The Japanese tried to follow tread marks but only got lost. During their aimless wanderings, they were soaked by the torrential thunderstorm. Having gone almost without water for a day, the men were grateful for the rain. They lay on the ground and lapped up muddy water, and they collected rainwater in their helmets, soaked handkerchiefs in them and sucked the cloth. Near dawn on 3 July, the party stumbled into the 64th Regiment, which was not moving. Irie went to Yamagata's command post, asked questions about the confused situation, and set out once more to find his tank regiment. Later it was learned that, on the death of Major Kinomoto, the 1st Platoon leader (1st Lt. Sakamoto Moriaki) had tried to reassemble the company as directed by Yoshimaru. Sakamoto encountered many difficulties because of the number of tanks that had been incapacitated or destroyed, the dispersion of the platoon, and the severe artillery fire emanating from the flank.[13]

During the Japanese tank forces' night actions of 2 July, none of the senior commanders was in touch with anybody else. Tamada later recorded his painful reactions in the unit diary:

> Among the things from which I suffered most as commander were insufficient communication and uncertainty about location. Because there were absolutely no communication facilities between us and higher headquarters or neighboring units, contact had to depend on messengers. Despite wide-open terrain, there were no particular landmarks in the area; so it was extremely difficult to perceive locations or to find units. Not only were messengers' actions delayed as a consequence, but it is also clear that many errors and discrepancies in orders, bulletins, and reports were caused by the fact that recognition of locations mentioned in orders issued during the process of combat differed [from reality] on occasion.

For his part, Yasuoka had dispatched a pair of tank patrols, consisting of two expert officer drivers each, to try to coordinate with Yoshimaru and Tamada. The patrol sent to find the 3rd Regiment returned without success next morning; the other, looking for Tamada, got lost, overslept, and disappeared for a while.[14] Caught in crossfire, it was not extricated by the infantry until 4 July.

Major Noguchi maintained detachment liaison with the 64th Infantry until about midnight, when Yasuoka sent a sidecar for him. Noguchi had the motorcycle lead the way back to detachment headquarters, and he walked alongside it with a dozen infantrymen. This allowed the major to retain his bearings, for he feared that a swing too far to either flank might lead to a collision with the enemy, although the Yamagata regiment was located little more than 1,000 meters from Yasuoka's command post. Major Ogata of the 4th Tank Regiment took a light tank, around 8 P.M., in an effort to contact Yasuoka's headquarters, and he got perhaps halfway there. In the murk, however, ignorant of the terrain and of the exact location of the detachment post, Ogata decided it would be better to stay with his regiment, about which he was worried, so he returned to Tamada. Although the sounds and sights of distant battle could be discerned on Yoshimaru's front, the 4th Regiment was obliged to operate that night, as we have seen, without the support of rifle units or artillery.[15]

Moving to the left rear of Yoshimaru in the drive toward the confluence during the early evening, Tamada's 4th Tank Regiment had great difficulty maintaining direction through a zone of connected dunes. The maps were too small in scale, and the magnetic compasses were affected adversely by the steel plate of the tanks' armor. Lacking landmarks as always on the trackless plain, the units selected low spots for the advance in order to avoid Soviet barrages from the right wing. Lieutenant Sunouchi remembers his baptism of fire and how he trembled with excitement, although the enemy howitzer shells were falling between his reserve 4th Company and the supply company to the rear. The nearest round landed two meters behind his tank, but Sunouchi occasionally lost sight of the other two tanks in the platoon, which were obscured by bursts of smoke. Inspired by his company commander's style of observation, Sunouchi began to stick his head in and out of the turret. "I did not feel scared," he says. "It did not seem at all different from maneuvers."

Under enemy bombardment from the right flank, the 4th Regiment tended unintentionally to veer southeast instead of proceeding due south as envisaged in the original detachment order calling for Tamada to assist Yoshimaru and to strike for the river junction from the left wing. Second Lt. Tomioka Zenzō, one of the platoon leaders, insists that the tankers, instead of trying to avoid the artillery fire, were searching for enemy positions. There were no orders to shift course; individual platoon leaders merely sought to follow the regiment commander's and the company commander's lead. Certainly the light tanks that predominated in the 4th Regiment moved much faster cross-country than the medium armor of the Yoshimaru unit. Adverse terrain and confusion in placement also played a big part in the strategic dislocation, for Tamada's regiment missed Heights 752 entirely and by 7:30 P.M. ended up southwest of Uzuru pond, although they did not know it at the time. The skies were still lowering but the rain had let up, and enemy artillery fire from Hara Heights on the left shore had stopped for the moment too. At this point, Captain Matsumoto's leading 1st Company reported hostile antitank fire, sentry positions, and heavy weapon sites along the dunes to the southwest. While the regiment's main body concentrated in a circle around the headquarters tanks, Matsumoto's armor drove off the immediate foe.

After reconnoitering the area, Tamada decided to detour the dunes and advance through the plain to the southeast instead. At 8 P.M. the regiment started out again, burning every cluster of sedge that might conceal antitank weapons along the way. During the first phase, the Japanese tanks engaged antitank guns roving along the crestline to the south and armored cars operating in the Holsten valley to the east. Sunouchi found it "really enjoyable" to fire against the Russians, although one enemy round that fell three meters behind his tank, showering soil on him, came too close for comfort. Immediately after he had moved the tank forward one length, a Soviet shell hit the spot he had just vacated. By 9 P.M. Tamada's force had advanced two or three kilometers southeast of Lake Iringin, fighting an enemy estimated to possess five or six antitank guns. Although the Japanese thought they had suppressed the hostile fire, the Russians took skillful advantage of the terrain to regroup and to resume bombarding the Tamada regiment with over ten pieces of field and heavy artillery from north of the Holsten. Tamada believes that 100 rounds, probably fired blindly by 12-cm. howitzers, rained down on his unit. It was a miracle, he adds, that none of the tanks was hit, although some casualties were incurred in the advance supply elements situated to the rear. Constant shifts in tank location were imperative.

First Lt. Itō Yoshihisa, the acting 2nd Company commander since the death of Captain Kitamura on 30 June, pressed Tamada to resume action. Inasmuch as the Japanese tanks were parked in a dip, however, the colonel expected that they would be sighted by the enemy whether they moved or not, so he preferred to hold up. Counseling caution, he continued to peer through his binoculars atop his turret in the dusk. Piecing together the information available to him, Tamada judged that two or even three Soviet batteries were emplaced on high ground at a distance of three kilometers to the southwest; forward observation posts were located on their right front. Two kilometers to the south, hostile positions could be confirmed on the crestline, with undetermined strength on the reverse slope. To Tamada's left, on his side of the Holsten, enemy armored cars, infantry, trucks, and antitank guns were operating. No movement was detected across the Holsten.[16]

Tamada now engaged in some serious tactical thinking, the details of which he explains as follows. Ever since the regiment had embarked for the front at Kungchuling, he had been pondering how his 40 or so light tanks could best engage an enemy endowed lavishly with armor and guns. "My dull mind," he says, "could come up with nothing." About all that he could think of was to endeavor to attack from a flank. During the evening movement of 2 July, the colonel was intending to swing right, in Yoshimaru's direction, toward the confluence; but now Tamada felt that he would run into a crossfire trap if he tried. Shortly after 9 P.M., when he observed Russian infantry and trucks moving slowly away, he thought that they were pulling out as expected. Consequently, he wanted to pursue them and, if possible, get to the confluence. Since hostile artillery lay between the Japanese and the junction, Tamada's first intention was to smash the gun positions. After all, the orders from the detachment were vague and spoke of "seeking a good opportunity," so he felt that he had leeway to employ limited initiative in the tactical sense. Tamada's solution was to unleash an unheard-of night attack by all of the tanks in the regiment.

The 4th Regiment's records are silent about the lack of consensus among the tank officers. From Tamada himself, however, and from Major Ogata, we know that the colonel consulted his company commanders and that they all were opposed to the idea of a night attack. It was "only natural for them to disagree," Tamada admits, "because our tank manuals [*sensha sōten*] made no provision for a tank regiment to conduct an independent night assault." Armored actions at night were permissible only in cooperation with infantry, and were never to involve more than a tank platoon or so. As the colonel says, he had not intended to conduct any night attack until tactical circumstances imposed it on him. The company commanders, however, had good reason to oppose the scheme. Ogata notes that no details of the enemy situation were known—merely that hostile forces were "roughly in that direction" and that artillery was "over there," for the simple reason that shells were emanating from "over there." Platoon leader Tomioka adds that the regiment had never undergone night training with tanks alone, and Masuda points out that night operations by armor are ordinarily very hazardous, entailing the danger of bogging down in holes and of overturning. At night, tanks were supposed to pull behind their daytime conquests and be guarded by backup infantry.

The only officer who supported Tamada was Ogata, who had recently returned from his feckless effort to reach detachment headquarters, and whom the colonel had consulted even before the conference with the company commanders. Ogata argued that the regiment had its objective laid down by Yasuoka. Failure to attack toward the confluence would violate direct orders. What was the regiment going to do to carry them out? As for tactical considerations, Ogata did not think that direction finding and movement would be too difficult, for the regiment had been conducting as much reconnaissance as possible on the flat and vast terrain. The aide had a last, personal reason for advocating the night mission: as the regiment's senior staff officer, Ogata realized better than anyone how poorly the unit had performed in combat at Tauran and in North China. Inaction on the night of 2 July would undoubtedly leave an indelible blemish on the regiment's precious military tradition, as veterans in the detachment would certainly agree. All in all, Ogata deemed a night attack feasible, although some losses would be inevitable. If the operation did not go well, however, the aide would be in the position of having to commit suicide; probably the regiment commander had similar thoughts.

The 4th Regiment's combat diary would have us believe that Tamada issued his order for the night attack at 9 P.M. sharp. Such chronology leaves little leeway for prior combat and for the advance toward Heights 757 (where the order was finally issued), or for meaningful consultation with the company commanders. Ogata, in fact, recalls that the discussion with the subordinate officers lasted about an hour, after which Tamada reflected for another considerable period, during which time the aide was called in again for his views. He thinks that his opinion may have proved decisive, but Ogata cannot be sure whether or not Tamada would have delayed the attack until dawn if he had not spoken out. Although the colonel and his aide were very well attuned, Tamada did not explain his reasons in great detail, instead stressing the importance of unit mission, which was why he would require "fullest solidarity, unity, and desperate resolve" on the part of all the company commanders. It is probable that he also felt a covert sense of urgent responsibility caused by the fact that the 4th Regiment had been drifting to the east while Yoshimaru was engaged in fierce combat and heading straight for the confluence.

Probably close to 10 P.M., Tamada addressed some very special and emotional instructions (*kunji*) to all of his officers of company commander rank and above:[17]

> It is regrettable that the regiment did not break through the enemy facing us during the daylight hours, but the mission does not admit of delay. If we let things ride, a blot would remain in history for a long time. Yet, if we carry out this advance at night with determination, there is hope of breaking through. Consequently, from now the regiment will seek and destroy the foe, wherever encountered, while advancing toward the confluence. It seems foolhardy to commit a large tank unit to battle at night without knowing the enemy situation and the terrain; but the mission demands it, and I therefore earnestly desire that all officers and men blend into one, centering on the unit commander and, for the honor of the regiment, push forward at the risk of annihilation.

Ogata was pleased with Tamada's instructions. "They contained," he says, "precisely what I had been recommending."

Moments after issuing the *kunji*, Tamada spelled out details in an operations order.[18] Beyond what could be observed immediately in front, neither the situation of the enemy nor that of friendly forces was known. The offensive would be launched after darkness, the exact time to be signaled later. Captain In's 4th Company of medium tanks, leading the regiment and deployed abreast, would constitute the cutting edge of the attack. Regimental headquarters would proceed immediately behind In, with Matsumoto's 1st Company to the left rear and Tamaki's 3rd Company to the right rear, all moving in column of echelons. Bringing up the center rear and advancing in lateral formation would come Itō's 2nd Company, now to be the regimental reserve. The space between units should be 30 meters; between tanks, 6 meters. Whether to smash the enemy positions by overrunning them or by turning on headlights and firing at them, Tamada left to the decision of the individual company commanders.

Once the colonel had reached his decision and issued the operational order, there were no complaints and no grumbling. The atmosphere was one of "grim resolve" (*hisō*). If there was any tinge of "tragedy," it was in the sense of dying gloriously, carrying out the tank corps' credo, "Attack, attack, attack!" Though all possible preparations had been made, they were not satisfactory. Consequently, there was not pessimism but uncertainty about the outcome, a lack of the usual confidence of sure victory. Inwardly, the men felt that "now we can depend only on heaven's fortune." [19]

By 10:30 P.M. the region of the 4th Regiment was pitch-dark, and storm clouds covered the sky. In the 4th Company, In assembled his platoon leaders, offered them cigarettes, and issued instructions in detail: each tank was to fly the Japanese flag, each unit was to attack in disciplined array centering on the company commander. Platoon leader Sunouchi remembers lining up his second and third tanks at the jump-off site and directing the tank commanders to maintain careful linkage. The lieutenant was excited that the night attack was finally at hand—"something never seen before in the military history of the world." A little before 11 P.M., the regiment commander ordered the units to advance. At first, In's Type 89 medium tanks moved forward in second gear at minimum speed, about five kilometers per hour. The captain had ordered the crews not to fire until fired upon. As the tanks advanced, only the clanking of their treads could be heard.

From the standpoint of stealth, the weather was ideal for a night attack: low clouds, no moon, visibility of 10-20 meters. The temperature of 65° F. was comfortable, and the terrain consisted of gentle undulations. Everyone had been concerned about maintaining direction, and there was talk about assumption of responsibility. Ogata, who prided himself on his "sixth sense" and who had already learned a lot about the terrain from his liaison trips, volunteered to guide the regiment and clambered atop the turret on In's tank. The regiment tended to straggle and head to the left or southeast, and Ogata stopped occasionally to adjust direction, with all of the following tanks aligning themselves in terms of In's point vehicle. Platoon leader Tomioka can recall getting out of his tank and going up on a rise with his six-power field glasses. In Ogata's words, contact between units was "difficult, though not impossible." At one point, Sunouchi waved a national flag in an effort to speed up the advance of his dawdling third tank. When this seemed to have no effect, the lieutenant leaped down and yelled to the truant tank driver to hurry up.

Since the tanks were jammed so close together for night action, use of radio would only cause confusion; hence visual sighting and verbal commands were much preferred. Momentary flashes of lightning greatly facilitated orientation, observation of the terrain, and location of enemy positions. Around midnight, Ogata discerned a track on the plain that, according to compass readings, led southwestward to the confluence. This discovery (later verified) served to bolster Ogata's confidence in the general accuracy of his bearings, and the regiment now followed the path to the southwest.

The first elements of the enemy to be encountered were pickets in holes. Tamada ordered them to be destroyed, a task that was accomplished easily. Realizing that the main hostile defenses must be very near, the colonel instructed the 4th Company, which had asked if it should storm enemy forces, to follow his orders and fight without hesitation. When a driver in Sunouchi's platoon sighted several figures crawling on the right and requested permission to crush them, the lieutenant instinctively ordered him to do so, while he fired his own pistol at what could only be enemy soldiers.[20]

After the regiment resumed its advance past midnight, a spectacular thunder and lightning storm erupted, providentially illuminating the Russian positions. Most of the Japanese tank commanders operated with turret lids open since the vision slits were too limited to afford meaningful observation, especially at night. But when torrential rains pelted the tanks, the commanders found it difficult to breathe or to keep their eyes open. Sunouchi put on his goggles, which helped his vision, not his breathing. The platoon leader then hit upon the clever idea of donning his gas mask, which worked well in the violent downpour. None of the tanks was hit by lightning, but the bolts seemed close, and Tomioka thought they struck something.

Tamada asserts that it resembled a "miracle" to have been able to detect the Soviet defenses before closing with them, thanks to the electrical storm. Though Ogata thinks that "miracle" is too strong a word, he understands why the regiment commander felt that way. Many Japanese sources compare the night action to Oda Nobunaga's famous sixteenth-century surprise attack at Okehazama, fought and won in a great storm.[21]

Apparently lulled by the night and the gale, the Soviet defenses did not come to life until the lightning flashes suddenly disclosed the Japanese tank force drawing near. Thereupon the Russians opened fire, especially from the center and right, with heavy machine guns, antitank weapons, and artillery. At such close range, the artillery was particularly useless. Although the guns were depressed to minimum elevation, the shells flew crazily high over the Japanese tanks.

At about 12:20 A.M. Tamada ordered his regiment to charge. The timing could not have been better, from the Japanese point of view, for the storm was at its peak and the lightning constantly spotlighted the enemy positions. To Lieutenant Sunouchi the advancing tanks, which had picked up speed, looked like "wild bulls enraged." Automatically removing his gas mask, breathing deeply, and yelling again, the platoon leader kept one eye on the enemy, the other on the company commander. He ordered his cannoneers and machine gunners to fire at point-blank range, while he clutched his pistol and prayed for victory. Tamada and most of Captain In's company of medium tanks plunged 1,000 meters through the enemy's infantry positions. In his three-man light tank, the colonel himself fired the cannon while the regimental signal officer, 1st Lt. Nakajima Hideo, directed the driver, estimated range, and operated the machine gun. The crew was too busy at the time to investigate the identity or the fate of a friendly tank seen in flames in the distance.

While In and the regimental headquarters pushed straight ahead, Tamaki's 3rd Company advanced on the right flank against the artillery emplacements. One of In's platoons, under 1st Lt. Shiragata Takurō, became lost and veered into combat to the left of Tamaki. Despite coming under heavy fire, the Japanese tanks did not slow down. Tomioka's platoon did not open up with its cannon and machine guns until enemy guns, soldiers, and ammunition were clearly visible at 100 meters, up a slight rise. Again the lightning played a vital role, because the Tomioka unit, although the anchor platoon covering Captain Tamaki, was out of touch with the rest of the company, could not catch sight of the commander, and had to operate independently in combat.

In the lead, Tomioka's tanks employed "corkscrew" tactics. They shot up each enemy position, crashed into the guns, cut the clutch, overran and toppled the artillery, and riddled the ammunition, causing fires and explosions. Although drenched by the rain, Tomioka kept the tank "unbuttoned," and his driver opened his hatch too, the better to spot targets. The lieutenant barked orders to the platoon to fire first the cannon, then the machine guns. Enemy batteries were sandbagged in the open and manned by about three soldiers per site. Communication trenches were shallow—perhaps half a meter deep—and only useful for crawling. There were about two square infantry holes per gun emplacement, each capable of holding four or five men handling observation and ammunition supply duties. In all, there must originally have been 50 or 60 soldiers in this sector, deployed on a front of some 700 meters and to a depth of 500 meters. All twelve of the Russians' artillery pieces were knocked out by 2 A.M.

Two features of the Soviet defense attracted Tomioka's attention. First, the enemy made no effort whatsoever to launch close-quarter attacks against the tanks. Under similar circumstances, the Japanese would un-hesitatingly have employed antitank suicide teams. Second, the layout of the Soviet artillery emplacements was unusual. In front of the guns, the Rus-sians had dug holes all over, from which spotters with binoculars could re-port targets by radio. Deep enough to reach the face of a standing Japanese soldier, the holes had been scooped out with such vertical edges that boxes could have been inserted in them. Japanese soldiers typically dug holes whose sides slanted outward, and they piled up the earth in front, in place of sandbags; these earthen parapets naturally drew hostile attention and gun-fire. But Tomioka noticed that the Russians got rid of all the soil they dug out, undoubtedly using considerable amounts of machinery. Consequently, dan-gerous Soviet holes "popped up" unexpectedly throughout the flatlands.[22]

On the 4th Regiment's left flank, the light tanks of Matsumoto's 1st Com-pany were observed passing In's medium tank company, apparently in a swift pursuit operation. The regimental diary adverts very briefly to Matsumoto's overrunning enemy infantry and deeply penetrating hostile positions to the southwest. Maps present a neat and orderly offensive progression, but Ta-mada admits that Matsumoto moved too far to the left, against light resis-tance and few infantry. Platoon leader Kuwabara Katsushige lost his bear-ings and joined combat to the left of Tamaki's 3rd Company.

As for Lieutenant Itō's 2nd Company, the regimental reserve had entered battle on the difficult right wing, between In and Tamaki, where its support was most needed. An antitank or artillery shell penetrated Itō's ammunition compartment behind the driver, exploded, and set the fighting compartment ablaze with yellow flame. Itō was severely burned in the face and limbs. The enlisted gunner's face and hands were also burned, and he was wounded by shell fragments. Flames seared the back of the corporal driver, who was cut by fragments too. The tank's engine stopped and could not be restarted. After fruitless efforts to put out the fire, Itō decided to evacuate the tank. He struggled out of the turret, fainted from pain, and toppled to the ground. The driver managed to drag himself out of his seat, and the gunner painfully revived Itō when he accidentally fell on him. Visible to friend and foe be-cause of the flames, Itō's tank drew continued gunfire.

Oppressed by the need to resume command of his company, the lieutenant limped off with his men, the three of them leaning on one another, in search of friendly armor. After staggering 150 meters, Itō and his driver were picked up by the 2nd Platoon leader, 2nd Lt. Niikura (Shinkura) Masakichi, while the gunner, who could not get inside Niikura's vehicle, was rescued by another tank.[23] Niikura remained in combat, engaging armored cars and overrunning enemy defenses. Having become separated from his own company by now, he managed to catch up with Captain In's main force at the corner of the attack. Itō, blinded, lay inside Niikura's tank, unable to command his company. Throughout this period, as noted, regimental headquarters remained ignorant of the identity and fate of the wrecked Japanese tank.

The great storm subsided after the 4th Regiment had penetrated far into the Soviet defenses. When things calmed down suddenly, Colonel Tamada—who had been very busy until now, serving as a tank commander—realized that he and his combat headquarters staff were entirely alone. Without the lightning to illuminate the battlefield now, he had no idea of the whereabouts of his companies. The crews of the headquarters dismounted from their vehicles and conferred. It was obvious that measures must be taken immediately to concentrate the regiment, which must have become scattered around a 1,000-meter circumference in the darkness. Captain In, the 4th Company commander, who had joined Tamada and Ogata behind their tanks, signaled by flag to platoon leader Sunouchi. The latter jumped down from the turret of his medium tank, saber in hand, and ran to the colonel's party. Tamada's loud call for assembly was followed by Ogata's calm order to regroup around the regiment commander's tank. Sunouchi dashed back to inform the rest of his platoon, only to learn that one of his sergeants had just been killed, presumably by an antitank round.

At this first stage of reassembly, Tamada controlled only four tanks: his own and those of Ogata and In, plus one of Sunouchi's. Concentration might prove impossible this deep in enemy territory. The colonel was depressed. "Since the night attack was entirely my own idea and I had apparently lost the whole regiment," he states, "I felt that I must take responsibility." Ogata remembers Tamada saying, in an unexcited tone, "Ogata, how about around here now?" The aide knew instantly what his commander meant. In the civil war of 1877, the great rebel leader Saigō Takamori, wounded mortally in the belly, had asked a friend to lop off his head and had uttered the same famous words. Obviously, Tamada was influenced greatly by Saigō. So was Ogata, a native of Kagoshima too; but the battle-hardened aide knew that there were mitigating circumstances this night. In particular, this had been Tamada's first taste of combat. The colonel seems to have regarded the situation as the worst possible, an appraisal that Ogata did not share, for elements of the 4th Company were not far away, and platoon leader Niikura (from the 2nd Company) was already there.

The aide decided to assuage Tamada's fears. Recounts the colonel: "When I told Ogata that I must assume responsibility, he replied, 'Please wait a while longer. I'll try to locate and assemble the unit.'" First, Ogata sent 2nd Lieutenant Niikura out with his tank to make contact with the others. Headquarters clerks followed. Later Sunouchi dashed off, on foot, to see if the 1st Company was in the direction from which tank sounds could be heard. Then, privately fearful that if he remained with Tamada he would have to help with the suicide, the aide said he would like to go to the front for a moment. Ogata proceeded on foot with two noncom clerks, carrying a huge Japanese flag mounted on a bamboo pole. Although the *hinomaru*, of course, has a large white field, the aide realized that he was enhancing his visibility by little more than 30 meters. But his main intention was not really to assemble the dispersed tanks: "I only took this action because of the commander's crisis and because I wanted to do something to reassure him, though I knew that flag-waving was not very effective." As the clerks advanced with Ogata, they hollered "*Oi! Oi!*" into the gloom. No flares were fired, lest the enemy be afforded a target.

Twenty or 30 minutes later, Niikura's tank came circling back, the lieutenant peering tensely from the open turret. Probably before Ogata's party could wave its flag, Niikura opened fire with his machine gun. Screaming at the lieutenant to stop, the aide and his men managed to escape the fusillade and get Niikura to desist. From the lieutenant, Ogata learned what he already knew—"that the situation was really confused and that our tanks were scattered all over the landscape!" Thereupon, the aide returned to headquarters with his clerks and Niikura, determined to mollify the colonel with some creative intelligence: "Although details are not known, our forces are operating well. Let's pull together the 4th Company and other known elements where we are." Matters improved afterward, as Ogata had expected all along. The question of suicide did not recur.

With In's 4th Company well in hand and shellfire emanating only from enemy positions far to the Russian rear, Ogata recommended that Tamada's nucleus force move carefully leftward and try to concentrate in the area where Matsumoto's 1st Company was supposed to have been operating. At the moment, the projectiles were flying in as high as 50 meters over the tanks, which elicited a gratifying "*daijōbu*" ("not to worry") from the Japanese. But if the foe corrected his range, the laager might become untenable. The colonel agreed, and soon afterward noises were heard from the area where the 1st Company was expected to be found. After some anxious moments, Sunouchi confirmed the identification of Matsumoto's unit, which was trying to pull itself together after its wide sweep to the south. Tamada was thus able to reintegrate the 1st Company into the regiment.

From the north, unidentified tanks appeared with their headlights on. Fearing an enemy counterattack, Tamada and his staff prepared to fight. Fortunately for the Japanese, the tanks proved to be the main body of Tamaki's 3rd Company, sprinkled with stragglers from the 1st Company and elements of the 2nd Company, which had moved up to the right during the battle and had circled all the way around. Details of the deployment were all new to the confused headquarters, which had lost control of the units from the outset of the fighting. When Ogata learned that Tamaki had returned, he was "more than glad"; it was apparent that more than half of the regiment had been reassembled by now. As for Tamaki, he reported that his company had destroyed the Soviet field artillery, and he asked Tamada if he should occupy the gun sites. Since the colonel was still concerned about a possible enemy counterassault, and since he needed every crewman to operate the tanks, he lacked strength to hold the positions or to remove the artillery that had been overrun. Therefore Tamaki's suggestion was turned down.

The Japanese tank force was still isolated inside the enemy defenses, and artillery fire was still hurtling in. Although the volume of fire, Ogata remarks, was not as great as the records estimate, it was too hazardous to remain so far forward. Consequently, the aide recommended a further pullback. Between 1:30 and 2 A.M., guided by Ogata, the units proceeded another 1,000 meters east by northeast. By this time, about two-thirds of the regiment had been concentrated. It was here, according to Ogata, that the regiment learned that the knocked-out Japanese tank it had seen burning was from Itō's company.

So soon after having contemplated suicide, Tamada regained his confidence and began to speak of re-forming the regiment and launching a new offensive against the remaining enemy. Ogata responded that this would be very difficult under the circumstances. Other than having collected more of its tanks, the regiment was beset by the same negative considerations that had dictated withdrawal to the second assembly site. Even worse, a ragged deployment still prevailed, and it would be impossible to control yet another night assault. Daylight, which would arrive in a couple of hours, would surely expose the surviving strength to enemy barrages from the west. Instead of advancing, the Japanese force should withdraw even farther and regroup at the original jump-off site. Tamada was convinced, and the movement began, in line of columns.

Platoon leader Sunouchi felt utterly lost, but Captain In exuded great confidence in guiding the 4th Company back. Far to the west, flashes from Soviet artillery could be discerned atop considerably higher ground. Deployed at the extreme left of the leading In company, Sunouchi became "terribly uneasy." He ordered his platoon to train its guns to the left and he prayed for the salvation of the Japanese columns. Enemy shells were still flying very high overhead but, after 20 or 30 minutes, even that fire subsided.

By about 3 A.M., as the skies brightened, the regiment had managed to traverse three kilometers to the northeast. But the location of this third laager was still four or four and a half kilometers from the jump-off site. Lieutenant Sunouchi correctly noticed the discrepancy, for the assembly area seemed closer to the Holsten than to Uzuru pond, on the basis of elapsed times of movement. Ogata, nevertheless, was pleased with the site, for the terrain shielded the tanks at last, and the foe was nowhere to be seen. With the integration of the strayed 2nd Company, whose arrival had not been noticed, the massing of the 4th Regiment was essentially complete.[24]

The regiment commander, however, was distressed that two of his officers were missing: Maj. Miyazaki Kiyo'omi, in charge of training, who had gone out in a sidecar; and Lieutenant Itō. Later, it was determined that Miyazaki's sidecar had broken down, that the major and his motorcycle driver had made repairs, and that they had tried to catch up but got lost before finally rejoining the regiment. Itō's fate was established before dawn when a dim light was espied and the distant clanking of treads was heard by the 4th Company. In's crews reboarded their medium tanks and got ready to engage a possible enemy force. A sergeant who took off to reconnoiter the situation encountered Lieutenant Niikura's light tank carrying the badly burned Itō. The latter, lifted from the vehicle, apologized to the colonel for the charring of his tank and reported on the wounding of the driver. Tamada responded graciously, lauding Itō and his crew for their fine performance.

Ramifications of the action involving the unfortunate Itō remained to haunt Tamada, the 4th Regiment, and presumably the lieutenant. It was not reported immediately to the colonel that Itō's tank had been abandoned on the battlefield. Intensive searches had to be conducted. For example, one reason the 2nd Company was so slow in catching up with the regiment during the night was the effort mounted to find Itō and his tank after it was learned they were missing when unit strength was tallied at the second assembly point. The senior platoon leader, 1st Lt. Kajiya Tsuneichi, was thinking of turning around and attacking south again with all of the company's tanks then available. The risks seemed exorbitant, however, so Kajiya set out with only one other tank, drove west on the route to the confluence, and infiltrated hostile territory, avoiding scattered enemy forces and escaping the fire of outposts. No trace of Itō's tank was discovered. The thunderstorm had undoubtedly put out the flames and the search officers could not be sure that they were scouring the exact area where Itō's tank had been hit. At 4 A.M. Lieutenant Niikura drove out to tell Kajiya that he had just brought Itō to regimental headquarters. Kajiya and his companion tank rejoined the regiment at the third laager.

Only after the fighting on 6 July did Tamada learn the circumstances attending the loss of Itō's tank. It had vanished by then, only to reappear later in a Soviet photograph showing six exultant Russian soldiers clambering over the vehicle. The problem for the Japanese, as explained earlier, was the practice in the IJA tank corps for crews to meet the same fate as their vehicles. As Tamada tells it, "Somebody came from Japan [the war ministry?] and apparently went to see General Yasuoka. It was said that I, as the regiment commander, had to assume responsibility for this regrettable episode.

The general, however, defended me and reached a generous decision: that cases such as this one could very well occur during close, confused combat." Consequently, Tamada was not obliged to commit suicide or be otherwise disgraced, although the matter troubled him deeply. The colonel insists, nevertheless, that final responsibility did not belong to Itō, the acting company commander—a statement that does not jibe with the attitude of even a platoon leader such as Koga. Tamada also claims that Itō, evacuated to a hospital, was not punished. But a platoon leader from the 3rd Company retorts that the behavior of Itō was reprehensible for a military academy graduate, and that the lieutenant was punished for it. The fact that Russian propagandists could gloat about their capture of the Japanese light tank was particularly rankling to fellow officers in both the Tamada and Yoshimaru regiments.[25]

By dawn on 3 July, the time seemed ripe to Tamada and his staff to hasten all the way back to the jump-off site. There was no longer any need to search for lost personnel. Itō's missing tank could undoubtedly be located and retrieved in the morning. Even if found during the night, it would be difficult to tow out. Fuel, ammunition, and rations were short, and casualties needed to be evacuated. To resume the offensive on the 3rd, it would also be best to utilize the services of the forward supply and maintenance unit, for there had been no contact with the main body of the regimental *danretsu* company since it had arrived at Lake Manzute only the day before.

Between 4:30 and 5 A.M. the 4th Tank Regiment was finally in bivouac southwest of Uzuru pond, which was mistaken for Lake Iringin. In other words, the unit had proceeded north of the third assembly point instead of west—typical of the botched direction finding that consistently plagued the regiment. Exhausted from at least a day without sleep, many of the crewmen dozed in their tanks. In this area around Uzuru, the 4th Regiment encountered a company from the 64th Infantry and a new scouting unit sent up by the Manchukuoan army's Northern Garrison Force.

While his tank companies were regrouping with the help of the supply unit, Tamada sent Major Ogata to find Yasuoka's command post, learn what had happened elsewhere the preceding night and what the detachment intended to do next, and report on the 4th Regiment's night attack and its current plans, which were to strike again for the confluence, by daylight, as soon as preparations were complete. In the meantime, it was learned that Tamada's rear echelon, the regiment's main headquarters section, had been waiting since 10 P.M. west of Uzuru pond, and that at dawn a straying truckload of perhaps 12 Soviet soldiers had blundered into the Japanese. Men under 2nd Lt. Tashiro Sōtaro, the regimental liaison officer, knocked out the truck, captured one prisoner, and drove off the rest of the enemy soldiers. From the nature of the seized matériel, which included ten rolls of phone wire and five telephones, it appeared that the wandering Russians were a signal party.

Tamada tallied his regiment's losses and found them to be remarkably light: one soldier killed and one officer and eight men wounded,[26] from a participating strength of 13 officers and 302 men in the four line companies. Neither Matsumoto's 1st Company nor regimental headquarters had incurred any casualties. Apart from a minor amount of small arms (mainly pistol) ammunition, the regiment had expended over 16,000 machine gun cartridges, 1,100 light tank 37-mm. cannon rounds, and 129 medium tank 57-mm. projectiles. In's 4th Company and the regimental supply company each had consumed approximately 3,000 liters of fuel; the regiment headquarters, 1,200 liters; the three light tank companies, a total of 7,000 liters. The regiment's total fuel consumption amounted to 14,600 liters by the time the last laager was reached after 4:30 A.M. on 3 July.[27]

Putting together what had been destroyed during the night action with what was ascertained afterward by Lieutenant Tashiro and other scouts, the 4th Regiment estimated that it had encountered a four-piece battery each of 12-cm. howitzers, 10-cm. cannon, and 75-mm. field guns, plus ten armored cars and two BT tanks, seven towed antitank guns, 150 infantry, five infantry mortars, a dozen vehicle-mounted machine guns, and 20 trucks. The Japanese correctly believed that a Soviet mechanized brigade was present, and identified the Bykov motorized regiment. Enemy positions southeast of Heights 755, into which the 4th Regiment had charged, must have constituted the wing defenses of hostile forces on the north bank of the Holsten.

Ogata was in his tank, en route to detachment headquarters with bits and pieces of information and many questions, when he sighted and picked up his old friend from Kagoshima, Lieutenant Irie, the platoon leader from the 3rd Regiment who was still wandering around on the plain with a soldier or two after having had his tank shot out from under him hours earlier. Irie brought Ogata the first tidings of Yoshimaru's battle, including the sad news of the death of Major Kinomoto, Ogata's military academy classmate and driving instructor from days in Chiba. Ogata, in turn, told Irie about the bizarre experiences of the 4th Regiment.

Tracing the tread marks of Japanese tanks, Ogata was able to locate detachment headquarters. Irie dismounted from the tank, wolfed down four hardtack biscuits and some water—his first "meal" since leaving Handagai—and "came to life again." Ogata went on to report to Yasuoka, who had not breakfasted yet and was completely in the dark and extremely worried about the activities of the 4th Regiment. Amazed at the information that Tamada had launched a night offensive, the detachment commander seemed satisfied to learn that, although one light tank had been burned, the battle had gone well. "*Yokatta!*" ["That's a relief!"], remarked Yasuoka.

The general then approved Tamada's intention of resuming the attack toward the confluence. Ogata saw nothing of the 3rd Regiment, but detachment headquarters knew then or soon afterward that Yoshimaru had lost five officers and 16 men killed, and two soldiers wounded. (The killed-to-wounded ratio is generally much higher in tank than in infantry units, given the "all or nothing" nature of an armored fighting vehicle.) Though reports were still fragmentary, Yasuoka drew the conclusion from recent events that "the furious attacks by our tank units seem to have caused the enemy great fear and apprehension."[28]

About the events of 2/3 July, Soviet sources—despite being laconic, as we saw in connection with the Japanese left-bank offensive—make three points. The Russians heard about Yasuoka's attack well before they knew that an enemy force was crossing the Halha. Although subsequent Soviet concentrations of reserves were designed to strike the Yasuoka detachment from the flank, they had the practical effect of hitting the Kobayashi corps on the left bank. Defending the Russian foothold on the right shore were the 9th Armored Brigade and 149th Infantry Regiment. The 15th (MPRA) Cavalry Regiment, which was ordered to cross the Halha to cover the left wing of the 9th Brigade, was prevented from getting across the river by the outnumbering Japanese forces, specifically engineers, in the early morning of 3 July. As for Yasuoka's offensive, Russian sources confess that the defenses of the 9th Brigade and the 149th Regiment were pierced on the 2nd and that, during the night battles, the Japanese drove the Soviet-Mongolian left flank back in the southwest and cut into the positions. In particular, IJA tanks admittedly reached Russian artillery sites.[29]

23

Foiled by Piano Wire

After the turbulence of the night of 2 July, dawn brought a beautiful-looking day. Mauled units tended to their wounds, lost units tried to regain their bearings, and pinned-down units sought to resume their momentum. For example, elements of Major Morikawa's 2nd Field Artillery Battalion were finally able to emerge from cover, thanks to the sacrifices of Yoshimaru's 3rd Tank Regiment. By 5:30 A.M. the field guns had advanced to a site a couple of kilometers north of Heights 731, not far from Colonel Yoshimaru's jump-off site the night before. The infantry of Colonel Yamagata's 64th Regiment were deployed ahead, intending to seize Heights 731. Morikawa set up an observation post 500 meters beyond the guns, linked to them by telephone.

At 5:50 A.M. the Japanese field artillery commenced firing against specific enemy targets in the Heights 731 sector—an observation post, several armored vehicles, and a grouping estimated at 100 infantrymen. Gunners reported excellent results, including the destruction of a Soviet tank at about 8:30 A.M., a feat that reportedly encouraged the 64th Infantry to try to capture Heights 731. Not everyone was as laudatory in the artillery's sister units. Tank Lieutenant Irie calls the field artillery's firing unskillful and inexperienced (*mijuku*). His 3rd Tank Regiment chronicler remarked that IJA artillery was ineffective because of dead angles and counterfire. Artillery veterans mostly remember firing against Maxim heavy machine guns, in support of the Japanese infantry. One memorable incident occurred around 11 A.M. when more than a dozen I-16 fighters flew in at low altitude and strafed the Japanese observation post, gun emplacements, and front-line troops before disappearing to the west. No casualties were reported in the artillery.

Yasuoka detachment staff officer Noguchi asserts that Morikawa's parent unit, Colonel Ise's 13th Field Artillery Regiment, found it difficult to keep up, largely because the guns were horse-drawn and the unprotected animals, fatigued and thirsty, made good targets. General Yasuoka wanted to push the artillery forward but was thwarted by lack of communications. Ignorant of the guns' location, the general decided to take his own command post ahead of the Japanese tank lines as an "incentive" to friendly artillery. Major Noguchi did not appreciate this dangerous action but was obliged to accompany the detachment commander. Yasuoka's idea worked, for Ise now caught sight of headquarters and felt such pressure to respond to the general's example that he egged on Morikawa's battalion to advance. This unit, in fact, got ahead of the armor and dared to fire in an antitank role, which caused the Japanese tanks, in turn, to move forward to protect the guns.[1]

From the western flank of the Yasuoka detachment, the southward progress of the Kobayashi infantry corps on the other shore of the Halha could be discerned—or at least could be gauged by the pillars of black smoke rising skyward from burning tanks and armored cars. Since the Japanese did not possess even one tank across the river, it was obvious that enemy armor was aflame. The sight was not only gratifying to Yasuoka's unit but served as an encouragement to keep pushing for the confluence from the right bank, too. Noguchi admits, however, that he "felt like clasping [his] hands in prayer as [he] thought of a plain infantry division plunging into hordes of enemy tanks."[2]

In the 64th Regiment, Yamagata certainly wanted to regain the initiative, although the fatigue and thirst of his infantrymen were apparent. There was also a scare in the 1st Battalion at about 6 A.M., when a strange and powerful odor was detected at the assembly area two kilometers northeast of Heights 731. Although poison gas was suspected, nothing came of it. At 7:10 A.M. the foot soldiers tried to advance, but they were soon attacked by enemy armor and strafed by 17 I-16 fighters firing incendiary bullets. Yamagata kept calling for his units to drive to the junction, yet as Noguchi puts it, their progress was "not fast." By 11:30 A.M. the infantry knew that the tenacious enemy was constructing positions south of Heights 731 and, significantly, that antitank barbed wire entanglements had been set up in several lines. Engineer Captain Yabuuchi remembers joining the infantry in a charge into the wire and getting pinned down, armed only with a rifle.[3]

Yasuoka felt that it was imperative to pin the foe on the right shore at the confluence "at any cost" while the main force of the 23rd Division was pressing the left-shore offensive. In other words, the detachment commander was still indulging in wordplay—thinking of pursuing an enemy who was not retreating. There was no time for detailed reconnaissance and thorough preparations. The Japanese historian Gomikawa Junpei finds Yasuoka's thinking incomprehensible. What had occurred the preceding night exerted little practical effect on the detachment, other than spurring efforts to improve tank-infantry coordination. Yet both tank regiment commanders had pulled far back to laagers by dawn to avoid enemy gunfire, which was expected only to intensify after first light. What remaining chance of success did Yasuoka discern? Was a frontal assault in broad daylight the best tactic that this general officer could devise? Would a charge by "unstoppable" tanks solve problems that were insoluble? Gomikawa castigates "feudalistic" IJA thinking based upon a destructive type of decisiveness, self-righteousness in underestimating the foe, and illogical optimism—an example being the notion that "no one could tell what would happen unless one tried; and if one tried hard enough, a way could be found."[4]

The 3rd Tank Regiment's Yoshimaru had tried several times to insure cooperative arrangements with both Yamagata and the artillery, as well as to contact his own battered 2nd Tank Company and to scout the area between Heights 733 and the Halha.[5] Although it was learned that enemy armor and rapid-fire guns were using hull-down firing tactics (*hōtō shageki*), the anti-tank barbed wire traps had still not been discovered. On the basis of his careful reconnaissance measures, Yoshimaru decided that offensive emphasis should be shifted to his right flank, closer to the river. The colonel went personally with a captain to see Yamagata, atop a dune 1,000 meters to the right or southwest front of the 3rd Regiment. They reviewed matters of reconnaissance and of tank-infantry linkage.

Around 11 A.M., Yoshimaru's aide, Capt. Koga Ototo, brought a detachment order reconfirming the tank regiment's mission. Upon returning to his unit south of Heights 731, Yoshimaru issued a regimental operations order that incorporated Yasuoka's injunctions to work with the infantry, pursue the foe toward the confluence, cut off the route of retreat, and annihilate forces on the right bank of the Halha. The colonel gave especially detailed instructions to Captain Miyatake, whose 1st Company would conduct the main "pursuit" thrust on the right while the 2nd Company charged on the left. Even the tank platoon of Yoshimaru's supply and maintenance company, which was to repair incapacitated armor, must be ready to enter combat and participate in the pursuit to the junction, behind Miyatake. The colonel would advance with the 1st Company.

Anticipating tough fighting, Yoshimaru ordered Maj. Harada Kazuo to assume command if he was killed, and Captain Koga to step in if something happened to Harada. After making some hortatory remarks, the colonel gave his unit commanders specific advice: to abstain from fighting in individual and dispersed fashion, to avoid attacking along routes that could be anticipated by the foe, to take best advantage of terrain features, and to conduct hull-down firing, especially on crestlines. In particular, the tanks were to cooperate with artillery and infantry, helping the latter as much as possible. Supply platoon leader Sakano Nobuo, a captain, had brought a bottle of *Gekkeikan* ["laurel crown"] sake and one of cider, which Yoshimaru shared with his officers in a farewell toast. Twenty-nine Japanese fighting vehicles were readied for the daylight attack—one Type 97 and 21 Type 89 (*Otsu*) medium tanks, and seven tankettes.

Miyatake's company was supposed to proceed to the right rear of Yamagata's regiment, but there was no sign of movement by the infantry. Harada was therefore sent to press Yamagata again to begin advancing promptly and to remind him that the foot soldiers and the armor must not become separated. There were good reasons why Yamagata could not get going at the tempo required by the tankers, but the tragic result was the collapse of tank-infantry collaboration even before Yoshimaru began his charge. The foot soldiers wriggled along the ground like worms, scraping out trenches with their shovels.[6]

At 12:15 P.M. Yoshimaru led the assault by his tanks through an area of dips and folds, with many slopes to climb. The enemy resisted ably, conducting hull-down fire and maneuvering in all directions. At given base points there might be as few as three or four hostile tanks, or as many as ten. Between the topography and the gunfire, the attacking Japanese armor began to lose cohesiveness of formation and coordination of firepower. The Russians supplemented their tanks with powerful antitank weapons and with some infantry.

The 3rd Tank Regiment did its best, overrunning outlying defenses and drawing concentrated enemy fire away from friendly foot troops, but essentially it accomplished little. "It was rather difficult," Major Noguchi observes, "and things were not going well." Yoshimaru wanted very much to hack a path forward for the stalled infantry, but worse was yet in store for his regiment, in the form of almost invisible fine strands of steel known as piano wire. The configurations varied, but no man who survived the ordeal can forget what he encountered. To the Japanese, piano wire was something utterly unexpected, for which the tank corps had never been trained.[7] "Something strange" was the reaction of those who first sighted it; perhaps it was a recently developed innovation of the Russians.

A Japanese machine gunner saw two-meter rolls of troublesome piano wire that was thin, flat, and strong, like the mainspring of a wristwatch. At various points it was tightened sideways in a shape resembling electric coils. The elastic, indestructible wire was strung in more than one line, conveying the impression of "cotton carpeting the earth." Foot soldiers felt that they could have cut it if it was ordinary barbed wire, but even artillery shells could not break piano wire. One infantryman encountered piano wire that was not coiled but instead posted "up, down, and sideways," forming cross-shaped netting amid grass 30-40 cm. high. Two or three meters wide, and as long as an *obi* sash, the wire was stretched along the anticipated routes of advance of the Japanese. In certain cases, foot soldiers succeeded in getting across the entanglements, under fire, although hobnails tended to catch. Elements of the 64th Infantry's 1st Battalion, for example, broke through by draping tent covers over the coils and then walking over the flabby wire.

Lieutenant Irie describes the entanglements as low barbed wire intended primarily against foot soldiers. Nearly invisible when concealed in grass, collapsible and easily portable, the piano wire was a "very handy" defensive weapon. In many instances it separated tanks from infantry support, as intended by the enemy. A machine gunner from the 2nd Battalion of the Yamagata regiment remembers a rare instance of tank-infantry cooperation near Heights 731, when three machines tried to move up in support of the foot troops and ran into piano wire entanglements. The wire coiled up deeper and deeper in the treads. "Like butterflies caught in a spider web," the tanks could move neither forward nor back, and enemy gunfire pounded them mercilessly. Smoke billowed from the stricken vehicles, which won the admiration of the infantry by continuing to fire their machine guns despite their helplessness. Within 30 minutes the tanks had been scorched to destruction.

Some tanks could manage the wire. Irie says the key was not to turn in it; otherwise the strands would "eat" into the gears of the treads. Most of the Japanese armor could not traverse the entanglements cleanly.[8]

Unable to break through or to extricate themselves from the piano wire spirals, Yoshimaru's tanks tended to line up abreast and to fire. There was little movement, and no close tank-to-tank combat ensued. Japanese tank guns were outranged decisively by those of the Russian tanks, which had an effective range of 2,000 meters. Against the stalled IJA vehicles, the enemy also employed excellent long-barrel 45-mm. or 47-mm. antitank weapons, firing from behind hillocks at perhaps 700-800 meters. Judging from the muzzle flashes, many tanks and antitank guns were dug in, and they were supplemented by quite a few small caliber weapons. Their engines overheated and their fuel at high temperature, even the diesel-powered Japanese tanks began to catch fire when hit by armor-piercing projectiles. Whereas Japanese cannon shells sometimes bounced off enemy armor, Soviet shells—even ricochets—could penetrate the belly of IJA tanks at even a "flat" angle of only 15 degrees. The Russians' antitank rounds were especially effective, with capped cones of soft metal that clung to targets and facilitated penetration by the hard-base shells, which spun and scooped their way through armor plate as thick as 20 mm. By comparison, Japanese shells resembled lazy fly balls.

Yoshimaru encouraged his subordinates by personally firing at targets, and particularly delighted his crews by clapping his hands and stamping his feet whenever he scored a hit. Meanwhile, attempting to overrun the piano wire, 1st Lieutenant Takeshita became separated from the rest of the armor in his platoon of the 1st Company. On the "sea-cucumber-shaped" crestline ahead, two or three other Japanese tanks could be seen, including the colonel's somewhat in the lead. It looked as if Yoshimaru were backing up slowly. Takeshita wanted to follow, but it soon became apparent that the rear bogies of the regiment commander's tank had become trapped in the wire and that he was really trying to escape, dragging the mesh. The enemy, as usual when a Japanese tank was ensnarled, concentrated gunfire on it. Just as IJA tanks aimed at the enemy's lead vehicle, which carried the commander, so the Russians focused on the Japanese leading tank. A dozen Soviet tanks and armored cars plus antitank guns struck from the left. Apparently the first shell hit the turret of Yoshimaru's machine, resulting in fatal head wounds to the colonel and serious injuries to Capt. Higuchi Yoichi. Despite his wounds, Higuchi and the machine gun sergeant jumped down and tried to guide the tank driver into the shelter of a dip below the crestline. But the piano wire had entangled the guide rails and drive wheels, and the reversal of direction only served to ruin the drive train of the machine. After the tank had struggled only 40 meters to the rear, it broke down completely.

Another Japanese tanker, Master Sergeant Honda, 300 meters away in the 1st Company, saw Yoshimaru's tank move back very slowly and then stop, dangerously exposed. Enemy shells hit the drive wheels and the hull. Three or four rounds struck the engine vent, causing dense smoke to pour from the compartment. Then the whole tank burst into flames and the ammunition started to explode. Captain Higuchi was killed by machine gun fire and his machine gunner was critically wounded. Honda emerged from his neighboring tank and crawled as close as he could. The colonel's body, wedged behind the engine, could not be retrieved from the pyre of his tank. Only Yoshimaru's gunnery sergeant escaped unscathed. Some of Yamagata's infantrymen came up and covered Honda's withdrawal. It was about 2 P.M. when Yoshimaru died.[9]

Moving to the left of Yoshimaru, Captain Koga's tank had been firing against the enemy's rear. After the colonel was killed, Koga dismounted and paid his respects to the slain commander, then returned to his tank and continued to engage the Russians on the left. It is said that the captain knocked out four or five tanks and armored cars before his own machine was smashed and burned by gunfire, killing him and his entire crew.

Major Harada, having returned from coordinating with the 1st Company, was fighting to the right of Yoshimaru when he saw the colonel's tank afire. Assuming command of the regiment, Harada moved over to the left and fought on with the 2nd Company. Temporarily commanded by 1st Lieutenant Sakamoto, the 2nd Company claimed to have achieved revenge for the death of Yoshimaru. Casualties were relatively lighter on this front, although Harada was wounded.

Capt. Yoshitake Kanji, the regimental supply company commander, brought up four medium tanks from reserve and joined the right flank of the 2nd Company in battle. Plunging deeply into the enemy defenses, Yoshitake effectively engaged armor and antitank guns until he and his crew were killed by concentrated gunfire. His tank, alone, could be seen knocked out on the downslope leading to the Halha, utterly exposed to fire from the left shore. Eleven abortive attempts were made to recover Yoshitake's corpse and to salvage his tank. Not until about 6 July did a night patrol manage to traverse the piano wire, recover the mangled and stinking bodies and some of the charred personal weapons, evade enemy armor, and trace the way back by stumbling onto a friendly communications line. Later, Irie's platoon was able to extricate Yoshitake's smashed tank.[10]

A resupply truck, carrying shells with fuzes installed, had been trying to locate the 2nd Tank Company, which was reportedly low on ammunition. Enemy gunfire, especially from fast armored cars, always grew fierce when a truck ascended a crestline. The spectrum and quantity of Soviet firepower awed the truckers, who were, by the same token, saddened to see Japanese tanks ablaze. Scenes that long remained in their memory included the sight of a Japanese tanker with a leg blown off, the sun glistening on the hobnails of a dead man's shoes, a soldier wandering dazed on the battlefield without a weapon, and two truckers buried alive when a shell hit a foxhole near the 2nd Company.[11]

In the 1st Tank Company's sector, to the right, the terrain proved to be constricted and difficult to traverse. The enemy's roving attacks were also rendering the company's position untenable. Since the 2nd Company seemed to be having more success and a path for the infantry was still needed, the 1st Company was transferred to the left, with instructions to provide flanking fire. Lieutenant Takeshita's tank was hit in the fender and in some unimportant parts, but incurred no fatal damage. The other officers were less fortunate: the company commander, Captain Miyatake, and all three remaining platoon leaders were soon dead. Indeed, Takeshita—the acting company commander, of necessity—thinks that almost every tank in the company sustained some hits. Not only was the power of Soviet shells impressive, but Japanese crewmen were also surprised to learn that the design of the IJA turrets was incapable of deflecting high-velocity enemy armor-piercing rounds.

The surviving Japanese crews fought on as best they could. The 1st Company claims it shot up about 20 armored cars and smashed eight antitank guns and four artillery pieces. First Lt. Sakamoto Moriaki, now commanding the 2nd Company, took on 40 or 50 high-speed BT tanks firing from the southwest, fought for about two hours, and knocked out or drove away about a dozen vehicles, enabling his company to advance to the south of Heights 733 by 3 P.M. Regimental headquarters tanks may have smashed five or six armored cars on high ground ahead. By 4 P.M. the Japanese tanks were running out of ammunition, for on this day they expended 1,394 common and 896 armor-piercing shells. Efforts were made to reload behind the crestline and to resume firing. The regimental supply company performed field repairs, provided ammunition, and sought to locate and extricate inoperable tanks. But without infantry cover, there were cases of tankers being felled while working in the open to repair their machines.

According to the 3rd Regiment's boastful combat diary, the unit repulsed a series of counterattacks by tanks, armored cars, and 200-300 infantry along the entire regimental battlefront (especially the right flank at night), and "chilled the innards" of the enemy. Nevertheless, at about 7 P.M., detachment headquarters ordered the regiment to reassemble and recuperate with a view to resuming the offensive at dawn on 4 July, after the 64th Infantry had pulled itself together too. The remnants of the 3rd Regiment fell back to the original take-off site south of Lake Manzute. "Fortunately," notes the detachment journal, "enemy forces had not tried to break through our front, although our advance locations were too broad for our strength."

As the detachment understood the 3rd Regiment's casualties on 3 July, it had lost six officers (including Yoshimaru) and nine men killed, and one officer and ten men wounded. This brought the toll since the 2nd to eleven officers and 31 men killed, plus 13 personnel wounded; i.e., approximately 16 percent of the regiment's manpower had fallen in battle, including more than half of the 20 officers. Over 50 percent of the 29 Japanese armored vehicles that had joined in the attack were knocked out: ten of 21 Type 89 tanks, the one Type 97, and most of the seven tankettes. Five of the medium tanks and one or two of the tankettes were a dead loss, trapped and riddled in the piano wire.[12]

According to Soviet sources, gunfire accounted for about 30 Japanese tanks, and 11 IJA crewmen were taken prisoner.[13] This figure may include attached Japanese infantry, for Yasuoka detachment records as late as 10 July list only one noncom and one enlisted man missing from the 3rd Tank Regiment, plus one officer and two soldiers from the 4th Regiment.

The 3rd Tank Regiment claimed to have knocked out 32 tanks and 35 armored cars. Captured equipment included ten of the tanks and ten of the armored cars, in addition to one field piece, 17 trucks, five heavy machine guns, and 20 light machine guns.[14] Gomikawa rightly points out that even if the very large claims of the 3rd Regiment can be accepted, they would still represent "a drop in the bucket" for the Russians in terms of replenishment, whereas Yoshimaru's losses were nearly fatal to the Japanese armored force.[15]

On Yasuoka's left flank, after dawn, Tamada was still unaware of the situation of the detachment or of enemy deployments in the direction of the confluence. Nevertheless, the colonel hurried resupply and repair and, at 7:30 A.M., again ordered the 4th Tank Regiment to advance quickly toward the junction even before Major Ogata could get back from reporting to

Yasuoka—"in view of the mission." Captain In's medium tanks were to lead the attack, as before, in line of columns and in diamond formation. Each company should designate one platoon for an antitank role.

At 7:50 A.M. Ogata returned from detachment headquarters with word that Yasuoka approved resumption of the offensive. When the regiment, after mopping up remaining enemy positions, reached the dunes northwest of Heights 755 around 9:30 A.M., artillery fire was received from the sector of the confluence. The companies took advantage of waves in the terrain and of intervals in the enemy barrages to advance 1,000 meters southwest of Heights 755. Without infantry, reconnaissance was difficult, but Tamada learned that strong enemy positions dotted the crestline another 1,000 meters to the southwest: 400-500 infantry, with several antitank guns and field pieces. At 10:10 A.M. Tamada ordered bombardment by the 4th Company on the right and the 1st Company on the left.[16] When the two tank companies went into action, they were answered by eight rapid-fire guns and eight field artillery pieces, all well sited. Other artillery fire emanated from the direction of Noro Heights, south of the Holsten. The enemy forces exploited the terrain, shifted position rapidly, and "responded cleverly."

Some 700 meters northwest of the 4th Tank Regiment, it was learned, friendly forces were trying to rescue a platoon of the 64th Infantry Regiment that had become isolated after advancing too far the night before. The relief unit—Capt. Sonoshita Zenzō's 1st Infantry Company from the 64th Regiment and 40 Manchukuoan horsemen—was being mauled, in turn, by Soviet weapons and armored cars. Tamada rushed the 3rd Tank Company and then the 2nd Company to help.

At approximately 10:30 A.M., one of Tamada's lieutenants, who had been sent to detachment headquarters the night before and had been looking for the 4th Regiment all morning, caught up aboard a supply company tank, with an order from Yasuoka to support Yamagata's combat operations. The officer also reported that, since 9 A.M., Yamagata and Yoshimaru had been advancing southwest in the area about 3,000 meters to the northwest of Tamada. Despite the change in mission, Tamada obtained no precise information on the Yamagata regiment's location. Across the Halha, smoke and fire could be seen around Hara Heights; the 23rd Division's main offensive seemed to be progressing, although again no details were known.

Near noon, seven or eight Soviet BT tanks and armored cars pushed north, supported by 50-60 infantry and covered by artillery, forcing back a Manchukuoan cavalry platoon deployed 500 meters to the left of the 4th Regiment. Then the enemy forces launched an outflanking assault against Tamada's left. Elements of the 4th and 1st companies, aided by a tank from the supply company, let the enemy get within 700 meters and then opened fire, burning three armored vehicles in short order and driving back the rest.

The 4th Company also neutralized three antitank guns and some infantrymen. Tamada, however, says he was receiving disquieting reports that Japanese cannon projectiles were bouncing off enemy armor. At about 3 P.M. the main regimental supply company sustained an air raid at Lake Manzute, but it continued on toward Uzuru pond.

Operating much more cautiously than he had the night before, when terrain and weather seemed favorable, Tamada decided to suspend offensive operations for the time being. Attacking across a dip alone would be too dangerous, the colonel says, and the nature of the enemy's resistance betokened main defenses, complemented by many rapid-fire weapons. The enemy was building up for an attack of its own against the Japanese left wing. Although the actions of the rest of the detachment were still unknown, the units were obviously dispersed; and from the sounds of small arms and artillery fire, it was hard to believe that there had been much progress. If the 4th Regiment launched a charge, on its own and without support, there was insufficient strength to secure objectives, and only a "dent" would be achieved at best. It would be wiser to reconnoiter, complete preparations, and attack only in cooperation with friendly infantry and artillery—none of which had been done the previous night.

Tamada left some elements on the crestline for scouting purposes; then, to protect the tanks and conserve ammunition, he had the rest of the regiment take cover behind the rise on his side of a dip. Major Ogata was sent off by sidecar to locate friendly forces. Enemy barrages continued, as did sallies by armored cars against the Japanese left flank. Scouts reported that the Sonoshita infantry company had indeed been chewed up badly, although Tamada suspected an enemy intention to entice his whole regiment into a trap. Near 5 P.M. a master sergeant returned from detachment headquarters with news of the death of Yoshimaru and with an optimistic order issued at 3 P.M. According to Yasuoka, the 23rd Division had crossed the Halha smoothly and lead elements of the "pursuing" regiments were apparently advancing southward across Hara Heights already. Still obsessed with the notion of pursuit (although, as we have seen, the 3rd Tank Regiment had already been lacerated), Yasuoka directed his detachment to annihilate the immediate enemy and push at once to the left shore of the Halha in pursuit of the foe. The 64th Regiment and attached engineers were to follow the enemy retreat and quickly occupy the bridge across the Halha to enable the detachment to cross. Both tank regiments should cooperate with Yamagata's assault upon the bridge positions, pin the enemy on the right shore, and destroy him. Under Colonel Miyao, reassigned to the detachment, the artillery was to press close to the Halha and support Yasuoka's envisaged river-crossing operation.[17]

Even after receiving Yasuoka's unrealistic order, Tamada showed no haste to resume the offensive. It was obvious to the colonel that the foe was not on the run. At 6 P.M. Ogata reported that the Yamagata regiment, with the 3rd Tank's support, had captured a portion of the enemy defenses on its sector, but that there had been no further progress. Locations, details, and intentions were unknown. Since it was impossible to coordinate with Yamagata as Yasuoka had directed, Tamada ordered his regiment to secure its laager for the night. Patrols should operate until nightfall, and one-third of the personnel should prepare a defensive perimeter, with machine guns and small arms. The units should attend to resupply of ammunition, fuel, food, and water, be careful with flame, and beware of artillery fire.[18] Enemy harassing fire continued during the evening. Once arrangements for the night had been completed, Tamada left the senior officer in charge and set off on foot at 7:30 P.M. to find and confer with Yamagata and the infantry, taking with him Major Ogata, all four company commanders, and two runners.

The performance of the Japanese infantry on the right bank during the travails of the armor was uneven but difficult on 3 July. Kajikawa's excellent 2nd Battalion of the 28th Regiment, for example, was still hopelessly lost (as it had been since the 2nd), a condition which did not stop the major from fighting hard wherever he could encounter enemy forces. Early on the 3rd, the sounds of firing could be heard in the presumable direction of the Yasuoka detachment. On his own initiative, Kajikawa left Lake Manzute at 6 A.M., heading for the combat area on the right shore. En route, four km. west of Heights 739, the battalion encountered a battle in progress; again without orders, Kajikawa joined in support of friendly forces. Apparently the very heavy fighting across the river, visible to the 2nd Battalion, accounted for the "comparatively easy" combat on the right side, where only sporadic firing was encountered from artillery, riflemen, and machine guns. Kajikawa's front-line companies deployed snipers mainly, while the 37-mm. battalion weapons and heavy machine guns targeted enemy infantry and machine guns. Shortly after going into action, the 2nd Battalion was attacked by more than 20 planes, one of which was shot down. At 7 P.M. Kajikawa assembled his forces, deployed them defensively for the night, and stayed on the alert. Runners failed to find the Yasuoka detachment.[19]

As for Yamagata's regiment, which was in contact with Yoshimaru's tanks, the two infantry battalions bestirred themselves after noon when the Japanese armor pushed into the piano wire entanglements. On the left flank, the 1st Battalion's 4th Infantry Company under 1st Lt. Someya Hatsuo attacked enemy positions, supported by the four platoons of the machine gun company pressing through wire on the right. The rapid-fire guns laid down fire against enemy armor, helping to clear the approaches to Heights 731. During close-in fighting, the Japanese infantry found grenades effective in driving out the foe. Some 200 meters from the Russian positions, 1st Battalion commander Maj. Tazaka Yutaka raised himself to reconnoiter atop a rise just vacated by advancing platoons of the machine gun company. Zeroed-in on this target, an enemy tank got off a shell that struck Tazaka in the head and killed him on the spot. All that was found of him was the red tassel of his saber.

By 4 P.M. the 1st Battalion on the left and 2nd Battalion on the right claimed to have cleared Heights 731. Several hours later, while digging in, the battalions received an order from Yamagata essentially instructing them to take a breather and recoup their strength. Enemy forces were still occupying defenses east of the confluence, basing artillery on Noro Heights south of the Holsten, and operating in strength across the Halha from the Komatsu Heights sector southward, although the division had pushed to the southern edge of Hara Heights and was continuing the offensive. The 64th Regiment should readjust its lines, replenish its ammunition and its supplies, place one-third of the men on standby alert, send out probing patrols until dawn, clean up the battlefield, and recover casualties promptly.[20]

It is clear that Yamagata's order was affected by such considerations as the failure of Yoshimaru's tanks to reach the confluence and their subsequent pullback; the unexpectedly tenacious resistance and great firepower of the enemy; the consequent heavy consumption of Japanese lives, ammunition, and ordnance; and the psychological and physical exhaustion of the 64th Infantry. This was the atmosphere in Yamagata's command post when Tamada, having been ordered to take over coordination after the failure of Yoshimaru's fierce daytime battle, set out at 7:30 P.M. from the 4th Tank Regiment to find the infantry's headquarters.

Moving northwest through areas swept by enemy artillery fire, Tamada's party slowly traversed the five kilometers to Yamagata's sector. After dropping off his company commanders for purposes of liaison when he contacted infantry battalion outposts, at about 9 P.M. Tamada proceeded with Ogata and the two runners to Yamagata's post behind a dune southwest of Heights 731, some 200-300 meters from the infantry lines. The tank colonel conferred with Yamagata and the 24th Engineer's Col. Kawamura Shichirō, both of whom he had not seen since the good-luck toast at Lake Manzute on the 2nd. When Tamada described his intention of launching an infantry-supported offensive next day, Yamagata responded that careful study and preparation were required and that his regiment was not ready to attack in the daytime on the 4th. In view of this day's actions by Yoshimaru, the difficulty of advancing with tanks alone was evident. To attack main defenses, a night assault would be best. Tamada agreed, adding that a joint infantry-tank-artillery offensive was next best. Tactical emphasis might be preferable in the Tamada area, where the terrain was less corrugated and thus favorable for tank movement. In any case, since the tanks had been ordered to cooperate with the infantry, Tamada hoped Yamagata would provide notice when the 64th Regiment could resume offensive operations, so that further coordination could be conducted. Thus both line colonels agreed that the attack should recommence, in prearranged instead of extemporized fashion; but no concrete plan was devised, and no date could be set. Tamada had the impression that the infantry might not be ready for a day or two. "Anyway," he remarks, "as long as the Yamagata unit did not start the offensive, there was nothing my regiment could do."

After the conference, a small-caliber enemy artillery shell landed in the sand near the feet of the three officers but did not explode. Tamada headed back for his regiment in the darkness. On the way, very close to the enemy, he saw several knocked-out Japanese tankettes, and a Type 97 medium tank entangled in thin piano wire and riddled like a beehive—Yoshimaru's doomed vehicle. Tamada paid his last respects and proceeded in the moonlight. At midnight he got back to the 4th Regiment; two hours later the company commanders returned after conferring with the infantry. Japanese units spent the night of 3/4 July on the *qui vive*. Enemy flares were observed, and there were signs of a Soviet night attack, but none materialized. Unknown to Tamada, Yasuoka had issued an order at 9 P.M. on 3 July, directing the 64th Infantry, the 4th Tank, and the artillery to launch a dawn attack on the 4th. Yamagata was even supposed to conduct a secondary surprise assault against armored cars south of the Holsten. Tamada did not hear about this until 7:30 A.M. on 4 July, since the messenger from detachment headquarters could not locate the 4th Regiment.

As for Yamagata, his regiment sustained a tank-infantry counterassault at midnight and beat it off after 30 minutes of heavy fighting. Detachment headquarters also repelled an attack by 200-300 infantry and several armored vehicles, north of Heights 731. Although, as he had told Tamada, Yamagata did not want to attack yet, he received Yasuoka's order after the tank colonel had departed, and felt obliged to prepare the infantry for a dawn assault, which obviously would have lacked armored support. From Yasuoka's point of view, Yamagata's offensive had only been postponed from the 3rd to the 4th because of the infantry's fatigue and shortage of water. The general directed his water supply staff to accelerate issue to the 64th Regiment.

At 3 A.M. on 4 July, the Yamagata regiment was able to call off the plan for a dawn assault for the time being and to concentrate on repairing its defenses in anticipation of Soviet artillery barrages after daybreak. The infantry gave as its reason insufficient reconnaissance of the enemy's situation and of the terrain. According to the Yasuoka detachment, the dawn offensive had to be postponed because the front-line forces were worn out and because, in particular, severe artillery fire had prevented the arrival of water supplies.[21] Thus, as dawn broke on 4 July the Japanese on the right bank of the Halha were not much closer to the confluence—their constant objective—than they had been on the morning of 3 July, despite enormous effort and heavy losses.

With the slain Yoshimaru's 3rd Tank Regiment effectively out of action on 4 July, the main burden of Japanese armored combat fell to Tamada's 4th Regiment, southwest of Heights 755. Soviet artillery opened accurate fire after 6 A.M., suppressed Tamada's counterfire, scored some hits on In's medium tanks, and forced the Japanese armor to seek cover. At 7:30 A.M. Capt. Hirose Kōkichi arrived from headquarters with Yasuoka's sanguine order issued the night before.[22] The general was of the impression that his tanks and infantry had pressed the enemy to a line 2,000 meters from the confluence, and that on the left shore the divisional main force's offensive had proceeded well and had reached a point about six kilometers north of the junction. In particular, Tamada's regiment and Maj. Morikawa Shin's 2nd Field Artillery Battalion were to cooperate with Yamagata's infantry actions from dawn on the 4th, while Miyao's independent artillery regiment undertook to neutralize enemy guns on the high ground across the Halha and the Holsten.

Tamada told Hirose that it was too late to carry out detachment instructions devised over ten hours earlier. Reflecting the substance of his own unproductive discussion with Yamagata on the 3rd, the tank colonel asked that Yasuoka be advised of his thinking: since a new offensive by the 4th Regiment alone would be costly and ineffective, Tamada would conduct preparations for an attack until Yamagata sent word that his infantry regiment was ready to proceed. No such word was forthcoming on the 4th; nor did artillery cooperation become available, although a spotter arrived from the field artillery battalion. Hostile infantry and armored cars were operating vigorously on the left flank from the direction of the Holsten valley. By midday enemy barrages had grown more severe and gradually more encircling. Manchukuoan cavalry, deployed north of the Holsten six kilometers southeast of Heights 755, were driven eastward, away from the 4th Regiment.

Tamada relocated his companies on high ground to the rear, for the enemy had zeroed-in on the previous site, and the Japanese tanks were hampered by their short-range guns. The Russians drew closer under artillery cover. On the 4th Company's front on the right, 200–300 enemy infantry could be observed, with heavy machine guns, 7-8 rapid-fire guns, and 5-6 BT tanks and armored cars. A force of 200 infantrymen with machine guns, plus 5-6 BT tanks and armored cars, engaged the 1st Tank Company on the left, never closer than 700-800 meters. In addition, 30-40 enemy foot troops with machine guns and one or two rapid-fire guns, and 4-5 BT tanks and armored cars appeared in the neighboring sector of the Sonoshita infantry company, to the right, and fired on the 4th Tank Regiment at a range of 500 to 1,000 meters.

In's 4th Company pressed forward 400 meters and drove back the foe, with the help of elements of Matsumoto's 1st Company on the left. The battle raged for two or three hours until 3 P.M., with the tank units reporting good progress against what Tamada thinks may have been a reconnaissance in force. Sonoshita's infantry company, however, had incurred grievous casualties and began pulling back around 4 P.M., causing Tamada to rush Tomioka's tank platoon from the reserve 3rd Company to help the foot soldiers. Tomioka knocked out Soviet armor, then drove off enemy infantry and cleared a path for Sonoshita to return by advancing 1,000 meters. This enabled the Japanese infantry to regain their original positions by 6 P.M.

During the daylight fighting on 4 July, Tamada's units reported inflicting considerable but unspecified losses among the enemy infantry. In addition, the 1st Company claimed to have knocked out two armored cars and three rapid-fire guns; the Tomioka platoon claimed two BT tanks, two rapid-fire pieces, and two machine guns.

Since nothing further had been heard from Yamagata, Tamada ordered his regiment to prepare a perimeter defense for the night.[23] All of the supply units were to organize close-quarter antitank teams, and every crewman was to stay in his vehicle. But the Russians gave the Japanese no rest. At about 7 P.M. a counterattack began on the 1st Company sector, involving 50-60 foot soldiers, four rapid-fire guns, 5-6 BT tanks, and 4-5 armored cars, with artillery support. In the ensuing fighting, Matsumoto's command tank and one or two others were knocked out.[24] One of the wrecked tanks belonged to First Lieutenant Kuwabara, whose platoon had been sent to reconnoiter the grassy field north of the Holsten. Tamada saw the Japanese platoon returning with one light tank in tow. The platoon leader and his crew were dead.

After learning of the 1st Company's straits, at 8:20 P.M. Tamada dispatched Tamaki's 3rd Company to assist. Meanwhile, the Manchukuoan cavalry on the left wing was also under renewed attack by 200 infantrymen, six BT tanks, and several armored cars, and its retreat uncovered the Holsten flank to the southeast. Near dark, a company of 7 or 8 enemy tanks was reported to be moving up to take advantage of this opening. Tamada decided to commit every operational machine against the foe, leaving behind only his supply unit and the damaged tanks. The Japanese force sallied after 9 P.M. About 1,500 meters away, four or five enemy armored cars could be seen fleeing toward the Holsten, with some 1st Company tanks in pursuit. Soviet guns fired from the southwest and east, but the 4th Regiment raced ahead until several enemy tanks were discovered in ambush, 600 meters from the Holsten, at 9:30 P.M. Tamada pulled together the 1st Company and deployed on the crestline, knocked out three or four of the armored vehicles, and drove off the remainder to the southwest.

Hampered by low clouds, darkness, and problems of direction, Tamada had to abandon any thought of pursuit. He had wanted to outflank the enemy, but the Soviet tanks were faster than his and the range was great; the foe got away. In the distance he could see one or two enemy tanks burning. Tamada withdrew 1,000 meters and assembled his forces. The 1st Company was ordered to retrieve its knocked-out vehicles. By 11 P.M. the regiment had returned to its original bivouac site—albeit with difficulty. During the evening's actions the regiment claimed officially to have achieved the following results: headquarters, to have burned two BT tanks and possibly damaged a third; 1st Company, to have knocked out two armored cars and two rapid-fire guns; 2nd Company, to have driven off two BT's and infantry.[25] In all, the 1st Company lost four killed on the 4th, including Lieutenant Kuwabara; another lieutenant and two men were wounded. One man was also injured in the 2nd Company, and another in the 3rd.

At the bivouac site Tamada learned from detachment headquarters that, as of 9 P.M., an enemy counterattack was expected from the south by 200-300 troops and 5-6 tanks. One of Yamagata's infantry companies was to assist Tamada in driving the foe back toward the Holsten. Two tank officers sent to guide the infantry were unable to make contact, but they brought the unexpected word before dawn that the 23rd Division's main body was returning from the left shore of the Halha and was bound for the Tamada sector in the near future.[26] To cover the division's movement, Tamada felt that he must retain his present location, although he did order some tactical adjustments for the purpose of mobile defense.

Although the night rains had let up, the skies were overcast—weather particularly conducive, in Tamada's view, to enemy use of gas; at 8 A.M. on 5 July, the colonel ordered a "gas alert."[27] Except for sporadic and weak hostile artillery fire, and a few unaggressive enemy scouts and snipers, Tamada's area remained generally quiet; the colonel dispatched patrols to scout the Holsten sector. In the afternoon the Manchukuoan forces reported an outflanking movement in the Holsten valley by enemy armor and rapid-fire guns. At 3:30 P.M., Tamaki's 3rd Company, reinforced by a platoon from the 2nd Company, was sent out to reconnoiter the endangered region and assist the "bothered" Manchukuoan cavalry. Tamaki detected 5-6 BT tanks, three armored cars, and three rapid-fire guns. Despite artillery fire from somewhere south of the Holsten, the Japanese tanks drove the enemy mechanized unit off to the southwest and returned safely to regimental headquarters by 6:30 P.M.[28] The colonel heard from Tamaki that the Manchurian horsemen were so pleased, they gave the Japanese tankers gifts of sheep and meat.

While the Tamaki unit was away, at 4 P.M. Tamada received typically optimistic and aggressive word from Yasuoka.[29] Issued at noon, the general's operations order stated that "the enemy, who had been trying to conduct final resistance in the triangular area between the Halha and the Holsten, seems to have started to retreat since morning." The detachment would launch a new offensive on 6 July (the timing was later stipulated as twilight), using the newly attached Kobayashi force of three infantry battalions and one artillery battalion. The old language about "cutting the enemy's route of retreat" appeared once more. As for the Japanese tank units, Tamada's regiment was to cooperate with Kobayashi, and the 3rd Regiment was to remain in reserve.

Tamada's tanks were running short of ammunition, especially after the heavy expenditures of 3 July. On the 4th, the 1st Company alone fired 336 37-mm. rounds; the 4th Company fired 125 57-mm. shells. Next day, the 3rd Company fired 147 rounds and the 4th Company 152. Therefore, on 5 July, Tamada drew upon the ammunition stocks of the inactive 3rd Regiment and distributed shells in the evening.

At twilight on the 5th, supply troops on guard reported to Tamada that enemy infantry were deploying forward. Covered by artillery and supported by rapid-fire guns, 150 Soviet foot soldiers attacked the right front of the regiment—In's 4th Tank Company—which knocked out one gun and drove off the infantrymen. After nightfall the enemy launched a new encircling assault, with 200-300 troops and heavy weapons, coming as close as 200-300 meters from the 4th Company by 9 P.M. Nevertheless, on the 5th, Japanese tanker casualties numbered only one man wounded in In's company.

According to Yasuoka's order of 9 P.M. on 5 July, received by Tamada around midnight, the 4th Regiment was to support the newly formed Left Wing Unit of infantry and engineers under Major General Kobayashi. (The Right Wing Unit was made up only of Major Kajikawa's heavily engaged, reinforced infantry battalion, with whom contact had finally been made.) Like the other unit commanders, Tamada was to conduct vigorous reconnaissance and enforce strict defense against surprise attacks by armor and against air raids. The latter were especially mentioned because, on the 5th, Yasuoka recorded seven aerial attacks, involving 35 I-16 fighters and 88 TB bombers. Tamada's regiment, by contrast, noted no air assaults.[30]

During the night of 5/6 July, the Russians continued to build their strength on Tamada's front, not only near the 4th Company but also 200-300 meters from the 1st Company. The enemy was digging in and gradually surrounding the Japanese positions. Tamada ordered all crews to board their tanks and prepare for combat, and he sent liaison officers to Yasuoka to report and to ask for infantry support. After 3 A.M. Maj. Fukumura Yasuhide, commanding the 3rd Battalion of Yamagata's 64th Infantry, reported to Tamada's post with word that he had been directed to cooperate with the tanks. Since the situation was quiet at the time, Tamada released Fukumura. A little before sunrise on 6 July, however, the enemy sent up flares and launched an attack. Tamada could see the troops crawling forward—400-600 infantrymen with heavy machine guns, light artillery, and rapid-fire weapons visible in the front waves. Three Soviet antitank guns, operating in a salient southwest of the 1st Company, were particularly effective, hitting the left flank of In's 4th Company and knocking out four medium tanks and a tankette in quick succession. Casualties were heavy, including 1st Lt. Shiragata Takurō killed. Russian observation posts moved forward and directed artillery barrages.

As the situation deteriorated after sunrise, Tamada wished he had Fukumura's foot soldiers after all. Before 6 A.M. the colonel rushed officers to ask Yasuoka to bring up infantry to help the beleaguered tanks, but reinforcements were slow to arrive. In order to neutralize the murderous enemy antitank guns in the salient, Tamada dispatched the Tomioka platoon from the reserve 3rd Company to high ground between the 1st and 4th companies. Between 6 and 7 A.M. the 4th Company came under especially severe fire from the right flank. Sent up to assist, the rest of the reinforced 3rd Company—"a very brave company," says Tamada—took positions on high ground 800 meters northwest of the 4th Company and, at point-blank range, engaged a force of 100 infantrymen, 5-6 heavy machine guns, five rapid-fire guns, five field pieces, three BT tanks, and three armored cars. Gradually joining in the fight were Tomioka's platoon, the tank company's support soldiers, and the rapid-fire gun platoon of Fukumura's infantry battalion. The Japanese tanks overran the foe several times and drove them back after an hour and a half of hard fighting.

Since the 4th Company had been hurt badly and was having difficulty hanging on, Tamada decided at 8 A.M. to transfer it to the right, to link up with the 3rd Company. Redeployment was accomplished by 9 A.M., at which time the 4th Company had moved 500 meters to the northwest. Fighting intensified after 10 A.M. when the Russians on the old sector, with heavy weapons and armor, teamed up with reinforcements of 300-400 truck-borne infantry, rapid-fire guns, and tanks, trying to encircle the 3rd Company. Assailed by severe flanking fire, the 3rd Company fell back toward the 4th Company. The two Japanese tank units clung to their positions until noon, but losses were mounting. Consequently, the tanks pulled back again to a point about 500 meters on the right wing of the regiment, where they covered the flank and rear and withstood air attacks till 1 P.M.

In the fighting, the 3rd Company lost five light tanks to rapid-fire guns.

None of the Japanese vehicles sustained a direct tank gun hit, but 2nd Platoon leader Tomioka's own tank was dented by 130 machine gun slugs. Several men, including a master sergeant, were killed. The wounded, all felled by machine gun fire, included the company commander, Captain Tamaki, and Lieutenant Tomioka. Tamaki, who had alighted from his tank to observe, was hit in the hand. A Japanese noncom machine gunner opened his hatch to see better and was shot in the head. Tomioka kept his hatch closed and was peering through the 10-cm. vision slit, with his padded cap on his head, when a burst of fire struck the slit. A cartridge ripped into the lieutenant's forehead and fragments scarred his eyes. Feeling as if he had been hammered on the skull, and blinded by blood, Tomioka ordered his driver to pull back a little. He managed to dismount and told Tamaki he was all right, but since he was blind in both eyes (and remained so for two months), his machine gunner took command of the tank. Tomioka was sent by truck 1,000 meters to the rear to a first-aid station. From there he was trucked to the field hospital in Chiangchunmiao, where he was treated for a week before being evacuated by train, with many other wounded (especially from Fui Heights), to Harbin army hospital. The cartridge could never be removed from his skull; only the bullet fragments were extracted.[31]

During the first phase of combat on 6 July, the 3rd Tank Company claimed to have knocked out three BT tanks and an armored car, and to have literally overrun one antitank weapon and eight heavy and five light machine guns. In addition, considerable losses were inflicted on the 200-300 enemy infantry, and 5-6 field pieces and an antitank gun were neutralized. The 3rd Company captured one soldier and a heavy machine gun. According to the 4th Tank Company, it helped to defeat the Soviet infantry, stopped two armored cars, and damaged a machine cannon, an antitank gun, a field piece, and four heavy machine guns.

On Captain Matsumoto's sector, the 1st Tank Company began action at daybreak, at a range of 200-300 meters, against an attacking force of 200-300 Soviet infantrymen with many machine guns and rapid-fire weapons plus several artillery pieces. Supported by field and heavy guns that moved forward gradually, the enemy coordinated the assault with other forces on the 4th Company front and drew as close as 50 meters at some points by 8 A.M. Operating on Matsumoto's left rear, reserve elements of the 2nd Company helped to check the foe. Matsumoto's casualties were not severe, says Tamada, because the 1st Company had dug in ably.

Meanwhile, at detachment headquarters, Tamada's two liaison officers had arranged the assignment of Fukumura's 3rd Infantry Battalion and some rapid-fire guns. The latter and one infantry company were rushed to the 4th Tank Regiment under fire by 8 A.M., aboard tanks as well as trucks of the regimental supply unit. Tamada sent the reinforcements to assist Matsumoto's tank company. By about 9:30 A.M. the bulk of Fukumura's battalion had arrived, and Tamada deployed them on his exposed left wing. Additionally, the colonel sent an officer to make contact first with the 2nd Battalion of Ise's field artillery regiment, now located two kilometers northeast of Tamada's unit, and then with Sakai's 72nd Infantry Regiment, which had been relocated near Heights 755. Around 11 A.M. the Japanese artillery opened fire against enemy forces on the Matsumoto sector and the old 4th Company front. Hostile artillery continued to pound the areas of the 1st and 2nd companies and regimental headquarters, causing some casualties.

In the course of the fighting, the 1st Tank Company says it knocked out two antitank weapons and four heavy machine guns, neutralized several artillery pieces, and smashed 70 or 80 infantrymen and beat off the rest. The company's casualties included a master sergeant. Considerable damage was sustained by the Type 95 light tanks.

Tamada had remained at his command post, waiting to move forward once the infantry was in place, when at 1 P.M. he heard from the 1st Tank Company that new enemy forces—200-300 troops with 7-8 tanks and 4-5 antitank guns—were approaching the regiment's left flank under artillery cover. Fearing envelopment unless prompt action were taken, Tamada prepared a counterattack based on a dip east of the 2nd Company. With field artillery support from the rear, Tamada sortied with the main force of his regiment—the headquarters and the 3rd and 4th companies—at 1:20 P.M. and drove the foe to the south after about 50 minutes of fighting. At 2:30 P.M. the Japanese tanks reassembled at the regimental command post. Four or five enemy armored cars, attempting to attack the regiment from the direction of the 4th Company's old front on the right, were repulsed by the 1st Company at 3 P.M. As a side note, around 1 P.M. the regimental supply company, deployed three kilometers north of the main force, had detected two enemy tanks advancing against friendly artillery positions, had attacked immediately, and had captured one tank.

During the Japanese assault, hostile antitank fire damaged the 37-mm. cannon of Major Ogata's Type 95 tank. In the 3rd Company, two light tanks were knocked out by rapid-fire shells, and several men, including a master sergeant, were killed. The 4th Company lost two of its medium tanks to rapid-fire guns, and sustained a number of casualties, including a warrant officer killed.

On the attack, the 3rd Company reported merely stopping a BT tank and driving off armor and infantry. In place to the right of the assault, the 1st Company knocked out an antitank weapon and two heavy machine guns, burned two armored cars and hit three others, and inflicted heavy losses on infantry. The main body of the 2nd Company knocked out one antitank gun, hit two BT tanks and two armored cars, and gunned down 20 or 30 foot soldiers; the detached Niikura platoon (the 2nd Company's 2nd Platoon) knocked out one rapid-fire gun and one truck, and shot up about 20 infantrymen.

Despite the 4th Tank Regiment's claim to have driven off most of the facing enemy, hostile elements remained near the crestline ahead. At 3:30 P.M. Tamada directed defensive deployment, security arrangements, and reconnaissance patrolling. Soon afterward, before 4 P.M., Tamada received the text of a decisive order from General Yasuoka, issued at noon on the 6th.[32] Specifically, the Japanese tank forces were to be replaced by Kobayashi's infantry—the Left Wing Unit—and were then to withdraw to the location of their regimental supply companies, where they were to "recover their combat strength and prepare for further operations." As the detachment records explain, first the Fukumura battalion and then elements of the 26th Infantry would take over the sector of the Tamada regiment, which would concentrate south of Lake Iringin "because of the need to conduct maintenance on its vehicles as the result of the daily combat." Tamada knew what the detachment order meant: "My mission was over, and I must pull back."[33]

Tamada immediately issued his own instructions at 4 P.M.[34] Particular attention must be devoted to the retrieval of casualties and the salvage of immobilized vehicles, especially after sunset, on the part of the line units, the supply company, and the small medical staff (one first lieutenant, two second lieutenants, and six medical corpsmen). Ready to engage the enemy if necessary, the 1st and 2nd companies and the maintenance elements were to assist the main work undertaken by the 4th Company's medium tanks. In the absence of organic ambulances, the 3rd Company should assign two 6-wheel supply trucks to transport the casualties (including those of Fukumura's infantry) quickly to Chiangchunmiao (this was how the blinded Lieutenant Tomioka had been evacuated, as mentioned earlier). For the moment, one light tank platoon from the 1st Company would be left behind to cooperate with Fukumura's infantry battalion. Eighteen Soviet bombers raided the supply company site around 5 P.M., but they were driven off and caused no casualties. At 9 P.M. Yasuoka ordered Fukumura's unit transferred from the control of Tamada to that of Kobayashi, with the intention of covering friendly field artillery to the east.[35]

With the approach of sunset at 8:50 P.M., the battlefield grew quiet. Observing the movement of small enemy infantry patrols, Tamada decided to conduct the transfer of his regiment only after all the units had been concentrated and the Fukumura force had occupied its positions. Meanwhile, the salvage of Japanese armor proceeded, but a distressing number of vehicles could not be hauled out and had to be left behind for the time being (one light and three medium tanks). All of Tamada's companies finally pulled back at 1 A.M.; they reached the supply company bivouac site, about four kilometers away, an hour later.

On 6 July the Tamada regiment expended 1,063 37-mm. and 279 57-mm. shells, and consumed 1,454 liters of fuel. Yasuoka's detachment was able to receive and distribute welcome stocks of tank gun shells and gasoline that day, as well as armor-piercing rounds for the field artillery. But it is ironic that Tamada's tank unit incurred its worst—and final—losses on a day when the regiment was in a relatively static situation, not during the wild actions of 2 and 3 July. Indeed, on the 6th, the Tamada regiment suffered 18 killed and 24 wounded, mainly in the 3rd and 4th companies.[36] The 4th Company lost six medium tanks and a tankette; the 3rd Company, five light tanks. Nevertheless, as Tamada puts it, "My unit was almost surrounded by attacks this day, yet we repulsed them all."

Japanese tanks' participation at Nomonhan wound down after 6 July. Starting on the 7th, Yasuoka directed Tamada to be ready to support Sakai's 72nd Infantry, while the 3rd Tank Regiment was to help Yamagata's unit. The tankers worked on maintenance, repair, and consolidation. On 8 July, elements of both armored regiments moved up to the right rear of each infantry regiment belonging to Kobayashi's Left Wing Unit. This deployment stemmed from the fact that Yasuoka was again receiving information from aerial surveillance suggesting that hostile forces were retreating to the left shore that morning. So Yasuoka, once more, called for "pursuit attacks" toward the confluence. The Japanese started to advance, but of course the intelligence was in error and enemy barrages checked them in their tracks. Komatsubara tried to get the offensive under way all day, without success.

On the afternoon of 8 July, Tamada dispatched elements of his 1st Company to assist an engineer-infantry assault by 60 men against the enemy bridge on the Halha just above the confluence. According to the infantry platoon leader from the 72nd Regiment in charge of the operation, two light tanks assigned to support the raiders were knocked out at the outset, in broad daylight. Without armored assistance, the demolition mission had to be suspended until nightfall.[37]

On 8 July, three of Tamada's tank officers returned from detached duty at the tank school in Kungchuling. At the same time, Maj. Kurusu Einosuke flew to the front from Kungchuling with replacement personnel for the crippled 3rd Tank Regiment: three officers, four noncoms, and 20 soldiers. Within 24 hours, the eager Major Kurusu was in combat. Around 3 P.M. on the 9th, two or three Soviet infantry companies, with tanks, attacked the right-flank battalion of the 64th Infantry. On the 3rd Tank Regiment's sector, northwest of Heights 738, seven or eight BT tanks appeared with some antitank and heavy guns. Staff officer Noguchi, who had strayed through friendly lines and was in the process of getting lost aboard his motorcycle sidecar, observed Japanese medium tanks advancing unexpectedly to engage the hostile armor. Although Noguchi did not know it at the time, apparently Kurusu and the regimental mechanics had "bound the wounds" of the depleted 3rd Regiment by placing surviving or replacement personnel in six or seven repaired or reserve tanks and were seeking a modicum of revenge by conducting a spontaneous sortie. Noguchi was much moved: "Detachment headquarters had not given any offensive order to the Yoshimaru regiment because they were in such a tragic condition. Since they had lost their combat companies, no fighting potential was any longer expected of them. The half-dozen tanks of the supply and maintenance company represented what was left of the whole regiment operationally."

Fortunately for the Japanese, the enemy armor was maneuvering "stupidly" in line, exposing its flanks, at an initial range of 1,000-1,500 meters. Perhaps the Russians were heading toward Tamada's front and were taken by surprise by the 3rd Regiment's "resurrected" tanks. Without loss to the Japanese, four BT tanks were burned in six or seven minutes, another was stopped, and the rest fled, one spewing black smoke. The foe had resisted "rather tenaciously," Kurusu wrote later. All of the enemy soldiers were Russian, 18 to 20 years old. Naturally, Yasuoka was delighted when he received the battle report.[38] It was the Japanese tankers' last occasion to exult during the Nomonhan Incident.

24

The End of the
Yasuoka Detachment

On the afternoon of 9 July, "out of the blue" so far as Lt. Gen. Yasuoka
was concerned, Kwantung Army headquarters dispatched the gist of an order to the 23rd Division directing deactivation of the tank detachment next
morning. Units other than armor would be placed under the 23rd Division's
command; the tank forces were to return to Kungchuling via Hailar. But
there was much more to the order than met the eye. Colonel Terada, head of
the Kwantung Army's Operations Section, had arrived at Komatsubara's
command post on 6 July, the same day that Deputy Chief of Staff Yano and
staff officers Hattori and Tsuji felt free to return to Hsinking. On the 7th,
Yano's chief, Lt. Gen. Isogai, joined Terada. Tsuji and Hattori, in particular,
brought back the opinion to the Kwantung Army that, although the Yasuoka
detachment had fought well and achieved great results, its services were no
longer necessary or desirable, now that the main body of the 23rd Division
was about to clean out enemy forces on the right shore of the Halha.
Yasuoka's two armored regiments had been severely weakened by the loss of
about half their tanks. Further combat would only cripple the Kwantung
Army's treasured armored assets, its "tiger cubs" (*tora no ko*), which were
in the midst of major reorganization and buildup in mid-1939. Anyhow,
adds Tamada, the knockout blow to the enemy was supposed to be administered by Japanese heavy artillery, which was already being advanced to
the front.

To Tsuji and Hattori, moreover, the chain of command at the front was
skewed. Komatsubara was Yasuoka's nominal superior, although they were
academy classmates and both lieutenant generals. But to the Kwantung
Army staff officers it was as if "a roof had been constructed on top of another roof," for Yasuoka was in de facto control of most of the ground forces
on the right bank, thereby conveying the impression that Komatsubara was
not in actual command of his own division's main body.

The Kwantung Army commander, General Ueda, gave his approval to the
draft order submitted to him through Yano, presumably on the morning of
9 July. Hattori was specifically reminded by Yano, however, that the timing
of the deactivation required careful attention and should be synchronized
with actual conditions at the front, to lessen the impact of the decision. In

other words, one should wait until the success of the 23rd Division's offensive had been verified. In the early afternoon, Tsuji came up with an effective date of 6 A.M. on the 10th, which Hattori accepted casually. Their thinking was that Yano's injunction meant a very short lead time to deactivate the Yasuoka force. A half-day seemed more than sufficient to allow the division's offensive to succeed, since Tsuji and Hattori were convinced—for some reason by their experience with the left-bank operation a week before—that the new Japanese infantry attacks of 9-10 July "or so" would conquer the enemy on the right shore of the Halha. Thus, prompt issuance of the order to dissolve the Yasuoka detachment could be expected to expedite the 23rd Division's own offensive. At 2:10 P.M. on 9 July, the draft of the order was transmitted by Tsuji from Hsinking.[1]

Although the soundness of the sanguine tactical appraisal by Hattori and Tsuji is questionable, there can be no doubt that Yano's concern about the effective date of the order to Yasuoka was well-founded, and that the method of transmission was botched. The telegram was addressed to the 23rd Division's new chief of staff, Col. Okamoto Tokuzō (commander of the 71st Infantry Regiment before the death of Colonel Ōuchi), who naturally showed it to Komatsubara immediately. The division commander shared the unsettling news with Yasuoka, and then with Isogai and Terada. Although Komatsubara asked the Kwantung Army officers to consider postponing the deactivation of the detachment for a while, since the tank corps was in the midst of combat, the psychological damage had already been inflicted on Yasuoka and his corps. The problem could have been avoided or mitigated if the telegram had been sent directly to Isogai, or if Komatsubara had evinced greater sensitivity and had consulted the Kwantung Army chief of staff before showing the message to Yasuoka.

As a Kwantung Army diarist admitted, the issuance of the order to Yasuoka at this particular time was "unnatural" in terms of the combat situation on the spot, and Noguchi has confirmed that the tank general was disgusted at first.[2] Masuda affirms that Yasuoka was very upset. Quite apart from the fact that Japanese commanders did not, in general, like to be recalled, in this case Komatsubara was still in action and only Yasuoka was being pulled out, although he had been in the midst of directing forward operations on the right bank. Were his warrior's spirit and his ability being impugned? To Masuda, the matter of rank and of "subordination" did not seem to pose much of a problem at the front. Everybody knew that there was nothing personal involved in the command relationship, and it was a basic rule that there must be only one chief in combat.

Colonel Tamada reveals other dimensions of the Japanese forces' shock and discomfiture. To the tankers, the Kwantung Army's order was hard to understand; the reasons for it were unknown. The men were incredulous as they prepared to pull back, "wondering why." It went against the principles of command to relieve a chief and withdraw his detachment while the outcome of combat was undecided. Of equal importance was the potential effect on troop morale. Unfair rumors spread that Japanese armor was useless, which was why the tanks were being "dismissed." Major Ogata remarks, "I felt funny. Aren't tanks needed in this battle?" But so far as the tankers were concerned, they had sacrificed themselves to the maximum and had paid exorbitantly for their efforts, always fighting alone and unsupported. It was small wonder, says Tamada, that Yasuoka "blew his stack" when the Kwantung Army acted so selfishly and carelessly, drawing up a paper plan based on a rosy estimate of the situation and delivering it to an infantry division commander who was entirely unacquainted with Japanese tank-branch planning on the larger scene.

Yasuoka vented his humiliation and frustration by firing off a message on 10 July directly to General Ueda, expressing disappointment that his detachment was being sent back in the middle of combat. This evidence of vexation elicited a prompt response from Hsinking at 2:20 P.M. on the 10th, commending the detachment for its brave fighting, asking for Yasuoka's understanding, and indicating that the timing of return would be the subject of further orders—i.e., that the force would not be deactivated overnight.[3]

Isogai and Terada had already reached the opinion that the timing of the Kwantung Army's order was not appropriate. In response to Komatsubara's plea for a delay, they instructed the division commander to disregard the effective date for dissolution of the Yasuoka detachment. After having patched up the problem in this unusual way for the time being, Isogai rushed back to Hsinking on 10 July to straighten things out. At Kwantung Army headquarters, Isogai and Yano pointed out to Hattori that the timing of the order was faulty, and they reminded him that the wire should have been addressed to Isogai in the first place. Hattori then had Tsuji dispatch a new order, addressed to the 23rd Division chief of staff for delivery to Terada, indicating that the deactivation of the Yasuoka detachment still stood, but that the timing would be stipulated later.[4]

But a second and even more basic disagreement concerning the future of the 23rd Division had to be resolved too. When they formed their opinion about deactivating the Yasuoka force, Tsuji and Hattori had also concluded that despite inflicting losses double its own during ten days of hard fighting against a numerically superior foe, the 23rd Division had failed to accomplish its main objective of ending the Nomonhan affair by offensive action. On the left shore of the Halha the Russians retained commanding heights, with vastly superior artillery capability. Continued deployment of the 23rd Division in the confluence area, in an effort to climinate the hostile bridgehead on the right side, would lead to protracted combat and increasing casualties. New guidance of the division's operations was necessary, entailing re-deployment to cope with the enemy's further attacks.

The Kwantung Army order to the 23rd Division on 9 July dissolving the Yasuoka detachment also conveyed word that staff officer Lt. Col. Miyoshi Yasuyuki would arrive next day with the full text of the plan affecting the operational prospects of the division. Soon enough, Komatsubara and his staff learned what higher headquarters had in mind. The Kwantung Army order began by claiming, in typical boastful fashion, that most of the invad-ing enemy's bridgehead on the right side of the Halha had been eliminated and that remnants had pulled back to the left bank. While securing key points in the frontier zone, the Kwantung Army would "choke off" Soviet-MPRA activities. To accomplish this, the 23rd Division was to redeploy its main body in the Nomonhan-Chiangchunmiao sector. Forward elements of the division would secure the following specific points: Kanchuerhmiao (45 km. to the northwest), Amukulang (40 km. to the northwest), Fui Heights (on the division's right wing), important locations on both sides of the Holsten (Balshagal on the north and Noro Heights on the south), and Handagai (30 km. to the southeast).[5]

Terada had been well aware of his operations section's thinking when he arrived at the 23rd Division's command post on 6 July. But after conferring with Komatsubara and observing the battle situation on the spot, Terada—reinforced by Isogai's presence—undoubtedly realized that the progress of the Japanese forces in the confluence area did not support the recommenda-tion by Tsuji and Hattori that the main body of the 23rd Division be pulled to the rear immediately. In other words, the enemy bridgehead on the right shore was hardly on the verge of eradication. Just as Terada and Isogai had agreed that the Yasuoka detachment ought not to be dissolved at 6 A.M. on 10 July, so the two senior officers concluded that the 23rd Division should not be redeployed at that time either. That feature of the original Kwantung Army order was accordingly suspended too.[6]

Meanwhile, appeased by Isogai personally, Yasuoka cooled off. Isogai ap-parently devised a rationale that the order to deactivate had really referred to the structure of Yasuoka's original detachment, not to the present beefed-up force. Yasuoka said he understood the situation, especially the matter of his command relationship with the division commander. Indeed, he admit-ted the propriety of early deactivation of the detachment. At 6 P.M. on 10 July, the general ordered his corps to concentrate around Lakes Iringin and Holstei, appending the ritualistic and face-saving stipulation that the units should "recover their strength and prepare to take part in combat on occa-sion as necessary." Both armored regiments were to strive to retrieve all im-mobilized tanks before moving to the rear.[7]

Yasuoka bravely went out in a sedan with Noguchi and visited all of the forces remaining in the Left Wing Unit, bidding them farewell and thanking them for their assistance. He also conveyed his appreciation to the elements of the Right Wing Unit. In turn, Kwantung Army commander Ueda sent his thanks to Yasuoka and boxes of sweets to the detachment's unit commanders. Tamada thinks that disengagement from the front was effected on 12 July, although this did not mean that the tank regiments left the general area of the forward zone. Indeed, the colonel heard Yasuoka say that he "could not tamely go back yet"; he would only do so after the Japanese artillery's forthcoming general offensive, scheduled around 19 July.

Noguchi came to say goodbye to Tamada, bringing considerable intelligence—for instance, that the enemy's logistics were in disarray, and that his casualties were severe, as betokened by full field hospitals and crammed westbound military trains. Consequently, the Russians were said to be pondering a delay in their own offensive. It was the Kwantung Army's opinion that the enemy might commit two more divisions to the Nomonhan sector.

Tamada remembers telling Yasuoka that he wanted to see again the area of the 4th Regiment's night attack of 2 July. Yasuoka not only agreed but also accompanied the colonel. Furthermore, Tamada recalls being troubled by the matter of Lieutenant Itō's abandoned tank—although, as we have seen, Yasuoka defended the colonel from censure by higher headquarters.

The salvage of smashed tanks proceeded slowly and with difficulty. Irie remembers many feckless searches for lost armor. Although it took about 20 days to do things properly, he boasts that the 3rd Regiment managed to collect and evacuate every one of its tanks. Machines that had simply bogged down were hauled out, but gutted tanks had to be cut into manageable pieces with acetylene torches before removal.

There was only one flurry of combat activity for the Japanese tanks during this last period of their deployment near Nomonhan. Lt. Col. Ioki Eiichi's new 23rd Reconnaissance Regiment (the replacement for Azuma's unit destroyed in May) had been sent to occupy Fui Heights on 10 July, guarding the 23rd Division's right flank. When Ioki and Manchukuoan forces to the northeast came under severe enemy pressure, on 15 July, Komatsubara ordered Yasuoka to reconstitute his armored detachment for the moment and dispatch a company from each of the tank regiments in support. Tamada remembers no such action; at most, he suggests, the tank units voluntarily supported Japanese infantry from the rear.

From the 3rd Regiment, however, Lieutenant Takeshita recalls receiving orders to sally with his medium-tank platoon to cover the endangered right flank of Ioki on Fui Heights. Takeshita's three tanks, camouflaged with nets and grass, entered hull-down firing positions in huge pits dug in a dip to the north, as directed by Ioki. In the evening of the 15th, the foe attacked Fui from both flanks, firing at short range. Well emplaced, Takeshita's unit suffered no hits. "Somehow or other" the enemy was compelled to pull back. The Japanese tank platoon remained another two or three days, but there was no further attack on Takeshita's sector. It is said that the presence of Japanese tanks encouraged the Ioki unit but that it also had the effect of drawing hostile strength to the Fui area.[8]

Conducting solitary "self-reflection" in his tent near Lake Holstei, Tamada concluded that he owed Yasuoka a profound apology for "insufficient efforts." Around 17 July, determined to die like a warrior, Tamada went to see the general. He could no longer helplessly watch the 23rd Division in combat. Soldiers must help each other (*bushi wa aimitagai*), and he wanted to fight, Tamada beseeched Yasuoka. The impending major offensive would provide a splendid opportunity for combined tank-infantry-artillery operations. "So you feel that way *too?*" the pleased general responded. When Yasuoka conferred with Komatsubara presently, the division commander was very appreciative but stressed the need for restraint, since tanks were too precious to the Japanese army as a whole to justify their wastage. Komatsubara assured Yasuoka that the division could cope with the fighting by itself, so the armored units should just stand by (*taiki*). The division commander, Tamada speculates, reached this decision because he now knew that the Kwantung Army's armored formations were being expanded and reorganized, and that Yasuoka's tanks, scheduled for return to south Manchuria, were to be saved for incorporation into a new corps.[9]

Around 20 July, the Japanese tank units moved six kilometers back from Lake Holstei and camped west of Lake Manzute, where enemy scout planes sighted them during the offensive of 23-25 July. On the afternoon of the 25th, a Kwantung Army staff officer arrived at Komatsubara's command post with orders to implement the deactivation and return to Kungchuling of the Yasuoka detachment—at last. Komatsubara released the tank corps, effective 9 P.M. on 26 July.[10] Uselessly camouflaged, the Japanese tanks left for the rear during the night. Tamada dozed in his sedan, distressed because his regiment was carrying the funeral urns of about 30 of his men. Two nights later the units reached Hailar, but they bivouacked northwest of the town for security reasons; personnel were kept out of sight, so far as possible. Tamada did get to visit his officers and men who were in the army hospital. The colonel also saw the Hailar garrison commander, who had heard that Tamada was dead.

On 1 August, aboard flatcars, Yasuoka's forces got back unhurriedly to Kungchuling. There the general learned that he was being transferred routinely to command the 3rd Depot Division at its headquarters in Nagoya.[11] He stayed in Manchuria until the joint memorial services for the Nomonhan dead were conducted. Lieutenant Irie was disgusted with the situation in Kungchuling. Like many a combat man returning from a war, he was surprised and infuriated by the difference in atmosphere between the battlefront and the rear. Irie was also unhinged for several days by the sight of his own mortuary plaque (*ihai*), which an irresistible combination of vanity and curiosity had induced him to view.[12]

Though the reports of the deaths of Tamada and Irie were, as Mark Twain said of an experience of his own, "greatly exaggerated," the demise of the Yasuoka detachment was very real. As of 10 July, the 3rd Tank Regiment had lost 42 killed (including 12 of 25 officers), 20 wounded, and two missing, from a total strength of 376. The figures for the larger 4th Regiment were 28 killed (including three officers), at least 44 wounded, and three missing, from a strength of 565. Without including four killed or wounded in detachment headquarters, Yasuoka's manpower casualties in the tank units totaled 139, or some 14 percent of the personnel strength. Of particular importance were the losses among the detachment's tank commanders, who always led their formations: 15 officers killed and eight wounded, from a total of 170. As Major Masuda points out, it proved to be customary for all key Japanese officers to be annihilated in combat on the relatively small atolls in the Pacific in the Second World War; but such an incidence of line-officer casualties had not been expected in the open plains of Nomonhan.[13]

According to the best data on the number of Japanese tanks disabled in both regiments during the July fighting, 13 were wrecked irreparably by gunfire, 11 to 14 others were repaired after the return to home stations, and 17 more were restored to action before the return. In other words, from a total of 73 light and medium tanks committed, 41 to 44 machines (about 60 percent) were immobilized in varying degrees. Major repairs could apparently be performed eventually on three Type 89 (*Otsu*) medium tanks belonging to the 3rd Regiment, on seven of Tamada's light tanks, and on four of his *Kō* mediums. Utter losses included Yoshimaru's own Type 97 and five of his *Otsu* medium tanks, in addition to four light and three medium machines from the 4th Regiment.[14]

The itemization of Japanese personnel and tank losses suggests the extent of the armored detachment's laceration within what was essentially only a week of combat. To that degree, the Kwantung Army's concern about conserving the remaining armor is understandable. Tank veterans, however, stress that positive considerations must be borne in mind.

First, the Yasuoka detachment pinned enemy forces in the confluence area on the right shore of the Halha. Analysis of data obtained by Major Nyūmura and his team led Japanese combat intelligence to report the presence in the confluence sector of the Soviet 36th Rifle Division and, from the 57th Corps, of an armored brigade that had arrived at the front on 4 July. In the

Russian counterattack of 6 July (to be described in the next chapter), the enemy committed 75 tanks, 800 motorized troops, and a rifle regiment. Tamada's regiment estimated hostile strength, in its area alone, as shown in Table 24.1.

Second, Yasuoka's tank forces not only facilitated the 23rd Division's river-crossing offensive but also played a big part in the subsequent fighting on the right bank. Among veterans of the tank combat, there was the feeling, then and later, that the Japanese lost their chance to prevail when their armor was withdrawn. As long as IJA tanks were deployed at the front, enemy armored units did not ordinarily come very close. After all, the excellent Soviet tank cannon, firing armor-piercing rounds, could strike at 2,000 meters, with an effective range of 1,500 meters. Noguchi explains the confrontation: "The front lines of both sides were spread out, quite inappropriately, across an expanse as broad as an ocean. Neither side penetrated the other's center. Even if attempted, such an effort would probably have failed, because tanks—which possess mobile power—were deployed there on both sides, watching each other." News of the withdrawal of the Japanese tanks, many interviewees remain convinced, only encouraged the Russians to unleash their offensive in August. Conversely, the continued presence of Yasuoka's two small tank regiments might have restrained the foe. The credibility of this argument is enhanced by the fact, mentioned by Noguchi, that after the deactivation of the detachment, the Kwantung Army received pleas for the commitment of "even one Japanese tank." [15]

Third, despite their own heavy casualties, the Japanese forces inflicted relatively enormous losses upon the foe. According to "minimum" figures compiled by Yasuoka's staff, by 10 July the detachment as a whole had knocked out 66 tanks (including seven heavy machines), 20 armored cars, 20 trucks, four 12-cm. howitzers, seven field guns, six antitank weapons, and three heavy machine guns. In addition, 400 troops were eliminated,

TABLE 24.1

Numbers and Armaments of Enemy Forces Encountered on the Tamada Regiment Front, 3-6 July 1939

Element	3 July	4 July	5 July	6 July
Infantry	400-500	700-800	none	1,200-1,300
BT tanks	4-5	12-13	5-6	12-13
Armored cars	4-5	14-15	3	5-6
Artillery pieces	at least 7-8	7-8	5-6	none
Antitank guns	at least 7-8	12-13	3	15-16

SOURCE: 4th Tank Regiment [134].
NOTE: Some machine-cannon and light-machine-gun fire was also reported.

three bombers and nine fighter planes shot down, and another 14 fighters forced to crash-land. Apart from taking 32 prisoners, the Japanese reportedly captured four tanks, seven armored cars, seven trucks, two 15-cm. howitzers, five field-artillery pieces, two antitank guns with 480 rounds, and several heavy machine guns. However, to Tamada's regimental aide, Major Ogata, the Japanese tank forces' achievements were good but quite limited, and in this sense the Yasuoka detachment was a failure.[16]

The nagging question remains: Should the Yasuoka detachment have been deactivated? Some IJA officers discern reasons beyond those expressed earlier. By mid-July, there seemed to be a relative lull in the action. The river-crossing force had entirely returned. The terrain and the region were useless, the frontier meaningless. There was no need to get overly "excited" or to become overcommitted. Rapid creation of the first Japanese armored division and eventually of a whole mechanized army made more sense than leaving the two core tank regiments hanging around Nomonhan and, if matters went badly, expending them. Tamada's comments sum up the view of most of his tanker colleagues: "From the standpoint of organization, deactivation was not a mistake. But strategically, no doubt it was." Even Tsuji and Hattori, who had pressed for dissolution in the first place, later called the decision an error.

Noguchi feels that even though the Yasuoka detachment was deactivated, the armored brigade should have been left at the front. Tank losses could have been replaced, for there were enough reserves in the rear to double Yasuoka's surviving strength. It did matter very much to the Japanese infantry if friendly tanks were no longer in the area. Admittedly, the IJA machines were not very good in the tank-versus-tank role, but the training and unity of the Kungchuling detachment were excellent, and the tankers would have made up for any deficiencies by adapting nicely to the Nomonhan terrain. Ogata wished that the Kwantung Army had had the strength to commit a tank detachment on a much larger scale, capable of achieving decisive results.[17]

As for the task assigned to the Yasuoka detachment—to clear the area of the confluence—Tamada still thinks the mission was appropriate. Ogata agrees. The Halha posed a great obstacle and, from the standpoint of the terrain and of the enemy situation, the only way to have used the Yasuoka detachment was the way that was chosen. With respect to the tactics, Tamada asserts: "My method of striking from the flank, where the enemy was weaker, was a good idea, in the face of hostile positions dotted with antitank weapons deployed to the rear and very difficult to find." Of course, Tamada adds, "if I had been ordered to attack frontally, like Yoshimaru, I would have had to do so." But the fact that his instructions allowed some margin enabled him to adopt a more flexible approach.

Considerable criticism has been leveled against the composition of the Yasuoka detachment and the haste with which the task force was organized by the Kwantung Army. It would have been preferable, Tamada remarks mildly, if the detachment had conducted better preparations. Censure by other IJA tank officers is more pungent. First, Yasuoka's detachment was thrown together overnight like an unready samurai who in an emergency dashes into the fray with only his sword (*ottorigatana*). Second, since the Japanese army lacked mechanized-brigade organization at the time, units were unfamiliar with each other and lacked joint training and teamwork. Third, it was amateurish to try to meld foot soldiers, horse-drawn artillery, motorized or tractor units, and a variety of armor. Fourth, the task force was rushed to the front and hurled into combat as soon as it reached the battlefield, without much awareness of hostile strength or tactics. And fifth, not only was there inadequate comprehension of the enemy, but the tank forces lacked familiarity with local terrain, topography, obstacles, and weather.[18] The Yasuoka force ended up in a remote and difficult region abutting Mongolia, about which it knew next to nothing. Indeed, it will be recalled that the Kwantung Army was thinking originally of sending the tanks across a river when there was no Japanese bridge on the scene that could support the passage of armor.

In the case of the Yasuoka detachment, Noguchi observes, everything had to be improvised from scratch: "The earlier the departure, the greater the sense of anxiety among those who understood the situation. But nobody said a word, since a unit exists for operational purposes only." The price was severe in human terms. Sent to Yasuoka from Kwantung Army headquarters, for example, Noguchi drove himself so hard to get the detachment ready for combat that by 3 July he had expended all of his energies and fell ill. He was feeling relieved psychologically but was lethargic and worn out physically. It was not widely known at the time, but Maj. Nakamura Mitsugu, a brilliant and combat-experienced officer sent by the Inspectorate General to study tank warfare at Nomonhan, had to take over Noguchi's operational staff work for two or three days. We also know that in the 3rd Tank Regiment, the major commanding the 2nd Company was exhausted physically and mentally by the time he reached Handagai.[19]

Tactically speaking, there had been much dissatisfaction with the leadership of the Japanese armored detachment. In the words of one postwar Japanese military critic: "Improperly used, the detachment suffered heavy losses and was driven from the battlefield after one struggle."[20] Numerous earnest efforts to coordinate the tanks with infantry and artillery generally came to naught. Worse yet, the armored regiments operated separately (*heiryoku bunri*), probably 3,000 meters apart or more, regardless of tidying-up attempted in the after-action maps. There was neither liaison nor cooperation nor connection between the regiments, let alone with support units or with the detachment command post. Whereas on the east Manchurian front facing the Soviet Union, no Japanese tank commander would have dreamed of trying to break through enemy defenses with armor alone, the Yasuoka detachment seemed to operate as if "infantry is infantry, and tanks are tanks." One reason may have been the wide-open (although complicated) terrain. A second may have been contempt for the Mongolian theater of operations.

Still another major contribution to the problem of poor IJA higher-echelon leadership was Yasuoka's woeful misunderstanding of actual conditions and his constant conviction, fed by headquarters above him, that the enemy was on the run and would collapse when the "invincible iron monsters" attacked. It was the old story of supposedly "knocking over sparrows with an elephant gun"—an obsession with springing traps and conducting pursuit-annihilation operations (*hosoku gekimetsu*) that bordered on psychosis. Recollection of the Azuma debacle in May ought to have dictated greater caution. But prior reconnaissance was incomplete (partly to avoid tipping the Japanese hand), and subsequent consolidation of information was nonexistent. In addition, Yasuoka chronically underestimated the distance to the confluence or, more precisely, overestimated the extent of progress achieved by his units.

Commanders' tactical styles played a major part in the orchestration of the tank battles, but one delicate problem is almost never mentioned: the covert existence of poor relations between the two tank regiments. Interviewees from the 3rd Regiment have voiced indirect criticism of the slowness and ineffectiveness, if not the timidity, of the 4th Regiment, which was far off "chasing ghosts" at little cost on 2 and 3 July while Yoshimaru and most of his officers were giving their lives in a direct push for the Halha bridge. The abandonment of a light tank to the Russians attracts particular bitterness or indignation from 3rd Regiment survivors. Understandably, however, the veterans prefer to ascribe possible disharmony and lack of coordination to unit rivalry, not hostility. In this sense, the 3rd Regiment was the "older brother" and was equipped exclusively with more powerful medium tanks suitable for frontal assaults.

The men of the 4th Regiment remain proud and awed by the success of their unusual, large-scale night offensive. As Tamada insists, his unit veered away from the Yoshimaru regiment without knowing it, only because of the terrain and direction-finding problems. Upon his return from the front, the colonel recommended that a surveying section accompany front-line units to help orient them quickly and to establish effective communications whenever operating in wide-open, rippled terrain like that at Nomonhan. To rectify the tendency to underestimate distances visually, the Japanese needed field glasses with improved magnification. More accurate compasses and small-scale maps on a scale of 1:50,000 were essential, and tank units must master operations in flatlands using larger-scale, 1:100,000 cartography.[21]

Tamada also deplored the Japanese tank communication system, whereby radio contact during combat was supposed to be handled from the regiment commander's own tank. "This is feasible in theory," he wrote, "but in the midst of actual combat it is nearly impossible for the commander to evaluate the enemy situation by himself, to transcribe his observations, to conduct firing, and to attend to communication at the same time." During battle, rather simple electrical apparatus would suffice, but for more complicated tasks it would be advisable to have a regimental signal section and to assign special tanks to handle signal functions exclusively. The tank radios then in use were worthless in battle; most could not be operated at Nomonhan. Swift improvement of radio equipment was imperative. Irie adds that air-to-tank relay of messages by dropping tubes was not very effective.[22]

After the Nomonhan fighting, teaching as an instructor at the Kungchuling tank school, Ogata used the 4th Regiment's night attack as a good combat example. The Japanese army also issued a training document citing this instance of "achieving great results by attacking enemy artillery positions at night with tanks alone." Though admitting they lacked details, the authors of the manual wondered why it took the 4th Tank Regiment so long—four hours—to reassemble after the assault. The delay must have accounted for the regiment commander's decision to reverse course instead of plunging all the way to the confluence as intended. Shouldn't the colonel have bypassed the enemy artillery sites in the first place?[23]

The questions raised in the IJA training document are mild compared to others' censure. Some have charged that portions of the 4th Regiment's after-action chronicle were embellished and that Tamada only launched the night attack because his regiment got lost and had accomplished nothing after many hours of stop-and-go "mucking around." In this view, it was illogical if not "crazy" to launch a night assault alone and without scouting or preparation. The tanks were "deaf and blind" in the face of a dug-in enemy and were in violation of accepted armor doctrine of the time.[24]

The preceding strictures are not fair to Tamada. When he overcame the objections of all his company commanders, with Major Ogata's help, and finally decided to unleash the night offensive, he included in his instructions the comment that the urgency of the mission overrode customary prudence. In his after-action summary, Tamada detailed his rationale at length:

> Generally speaking, I think that the night attack is a very advantageous tactic against Soviet forces, and especially against mechanized corps. . . . Though a night assault by tanks is not advisable in general, signal success may be achieved sometimes if you reach a firm resolve and advance when conditions of weather

and terrain and the like are appropriate, as they were this time. In particular, it is feasible to conduct this type of battle against enemy tank units during maneuver combat; so it cannot be said that there is absolutely no chance of victory [for armor attacking at night].[25]

One of the obvious advantages of night operations, Tamada pointed out, was the element of possible surprise. After dark, the Russians tended to concentrate their armored strength, even when preparing or in the middle of an attack operation. Some tanks would be assigned to guard duty, but nighttime security was not tight, and Soviet activities were noisy. When Tamada's regiment attacked in the storm on 2/3 July, the Russians were in great confusion and their fighting spirit was poor. Nonetheless, the colonel admitted that it was difficult to orchestrate a night assault by large-scale units, such as a full tank regiment. Ideally, only one tank company should be used as the strike force, with infantry attached if possible, and with the rest of the tank regiment in support. Having launched his night attack without sufficient preparations, Tamada was aware that fighting and maneuver would have been facilitated greatly if there had been careful planning and prearranged communications, reconnaissance, and logistics. A shortage of fuel, in fact, prevented pursuit after the night assault. Avoidance of employing tanks without support, especially by infantry and artillery, is Tamada's constant refrain, especially since the Russians always systematically combined armor with antitank guns and artillery. During night attacks, even successful ones, it would be impossible to secure the results using only tanks. Tamada concluded that it was imperative to "conduct training for and greatly emphasize night attacks as the unique tactic of the imperial army."[26]

The previously mentioned IJA training manual, accepting Tamada's view, admitted that an armored unit could fight at night, depending upon the situation, the terrain, and leadership. Surprise could be facilitated by making best use of weather—in Tamada's case, a fortuitous lightning storm. Japanese postwar official historians admit the dangers and term the night attack "only an emergency expedient." But Noguchi presents a glowing defense of Tamada's action: "Even infantry—the vaunted night-assault experts—would have had trouble attacking on the same night that they arrived at the front." The feat accomplished by the puny tanks of the 4th Regiment was splendid, thanks to Tamada's fearlessness and sense of responsibility, and the unit's fine training, unity, and teamwork. It was the warrior's *bushidō* spirit of the 4th Regiment, argues Noguchi, that "prohibited them from abandoning their comrades of the Yoshimaru unit and impelled them to dare the night attack—a spirit of self-sacrifice." The results "transcended all logic," and the regiment achieved what "even today's weaponry can hardly do."[27]

Even Yoshimaru has been criticized for a suicidal rashness that set a bad example and led to his own death and the mangling of the 3rd Regiment in broad daylight on 3 July.[28] Noguchi supplies the most effective rebuttal, stressing that Yoshimaru, an intelligent and ordinarily cautious tank officer, believed in cooperation with infantry, as proved by his repeated visits to Yamagata, who could not get the foot soldiers under way. It was Yoshimaru's selfless concept of quickly helping the 23rd Division's offensive on the left bank of the Halha that underlay the decision to charge alone on the right shore. To quote Noguchi:

> Although the colonel was a brave man, he was in no sense a wild boar. As a result of careful consideration of the responsibilities of the Yasuoka detachment vis-à-vis the corps fighting desperately across the river, Yoshimaru advanced and attacked the foe, because it was the only thing he could do. Later, some of the people who came from Tokyo looking for lessons voiced criticisms based solely on the outcome. This was an example, they charged, of enlarging losses, of separate fighting by infantry, artillery, and tanks. But those people don't at all comprehend the heart of the samurai [*samurai no kokoro*] on the spot. Who would plunge into a deadly area on a lark or with an irresponsible attitude?[29]

Though they may disagree about leadership ability and tactical prowess, IJA tank corps interviewees consistently identify common technical problems affecting their machines, equipment, and ordnance. The most frequent complaint centered on the short-barrel, low-velocity 37-mm. and 57-mm. cannon of the light and medium tanks. These weapons were excellent in the infantry-support role, firing high-explosive rounds against "soft" targets, as in China and in the "promenade" through Southeast Asia during 1941-42. In range, destructiveness, and ability to penetrate armor, the Japanese guns were outclassed in tank-versus-tank combat at Nomonhan by the Russians' BT and T-26 machines. The inferiority of IJA tank armament is colorfully described by a machine-gun company commander of the 71st Infantry who on 3 July was peering through binoculars from the higher left shore of the Halha at the opposing sets of "matchbox" tanks slugging it out on the right bank with a crestline between them. "It's embarrassing to say," this infantry captain remarks, "but the Japanese tank-gun barrels looked like a little boy's penis, just protruding, whereas the Russian barrels were really long. 'No contest!' I thought. . . ."[30]

Platoon leader Takeshita of the 3rd Regiment proffers interesting comments on the Soviet philosophy of tank design: Armament was regarded by the Russians as the key, and both tank cannon and machine guns were excellent; everything else, being of less importance, was poorer. "Observing Russian forces in action, one derived the impression that individual equipment was inferior: cloth briefcases, boots with leather soles but fabric tops, coats of thick cloth. Tank chassis looked rough—unpainted and rusty. Even the welding points were obvious. But the guns were another matter, although there was nothing special about their accuracy."[31] Soviet armor impressed the Japanese as well-suited for mass production.

Tamada wanted a tank cannon that was effective beyond medium range—that is, out to 2,000 meters. (Tomioka says the Japanese light tanks had an effective firing range of less than 700 meters.) Tamada also felt that tank cannon and machine guns must be capable of shooting at night. On 2/3 July, the Japanese operated at point-blank range, observing from open hatches, estimating targets crudely, and firing "from the hip" (*koshidame*). Illuminating shells, flares, and smoke were needed. In addition, Tamada desired a "special kind of gun" designed mainly to neutralize antitank weapons that had low silhouettes, used terrain and camouflage well, and were hard to detect and knock out. As the Russians used them, such antitank guns had a high rate of fire, changed positions often, and were more dangerous to Japanese tanks than were artillery and armor. Tamada also noted how hard it was to achieve hits on the battlefield while on the move, because of problems with target detection (especially against antitank guns and armor), bumpiness caused by rough terrain, and overreliance on a sixth sense. Vision slits were tiny and few, and no periscopes had been developed yet. Of course, stopping to shoot was a two-edged sword: gunnery was more reliable when stationary than when on the move (except at point-blank range), but a standing target invited enemy fire. In stopping to shoot, it was imperative to implement the "one shot, one hit" technique immediately. Soviet armor fired well when stationary.

Because of their primary mission of cooperating with infantry, IJA tanks were designed with less emphasis on speed and armor plating. It was said that Soviet tanks could operate on treads cross-country at 40-55 kph, or on wheels on roads at a reputed top speed of 78 kph—"like trucks." Using caterpillar treads solely, Japanese medium tanks could move at only 25 kph; light tanks could attain perhaps 40-45 kph on roads. IJA tankers were pleased with their diesel engines, but the records report many instances of starting trouble among Type 89 tanks. Tomioka speaks of lack of ventilation in the tanks when the hatch was closed. Fumes, engine heat, and gun smoke were troublesome, though the busy crews could not allow them to interfere.

With respect to steel plating, Tamada notes that his tanks' armor could even be pierced at perpendicular angles of merely 5-6 degrees. The rounded shape of IJA plate proved surprisingly ineffective; ballistic design of Soviet armor shielding was superior. Firing splendid high-velocity armor-piercing ammunition, Russian 47-mm. tank and rapid-fire guns could easily penetrate the mere 15-17 mm. of main plate on Japanese Type 89 medium tanks and, of course, the 8-12 mm. armor of the light tanks. Ricochets through the even thinner belly plates could be fatal.[32]

The Russians possessed flame-throwing tanks, amphibious vehicles, and, toward the end of the Nomonhan fighting, heavy armor. In none of these categories did the Japanese have comparable tanks. Among Tamada's suggestions was the need to equip the maintenance units with ambulances, instead of resorting to tanks for immediate removal of casualties and to trucks for evacuation to the field hospital.

Japanese tank treads were somewhat noisier than the Russians', although engine sound was about the same. IJA armor operated well on bad roads and over obstacles, but Irie says the treads often fell apart. Swampy areas created particular hazards. Dips in dunes, across which tracked vehicles could generally move at 20 or 30 kph in fine weather, frequently posed special difficulties after rain. Soviet armor—the BT tanks in particular—possessed superior cross-country mobility, especially because of their versatile track/wheel capability mentioned above.

Logistics, affected by optimistic estimates too, caused constant problems that were particularly acute in the case of armored units. When a company lost even one tank, the effect was far more deleterious than in other combat arms. Crew casualties were proportionately higher, especially in the officer category; and though enlisted men were often thrown in as replacements, Tamada says "there was a feeling that this was not satisfactory to maintain combat power." Thus an overstrength allotment of officer personnel to tank units was required. Spare parts were in short supply, and damaged or immobilized tanks had to be cannibalized to maintain companies at minimum levels of strength. Captain In's 4th Company of the 4th Regiment posed a special problem, for the old Type 89 *Kō* medium tanks had traveled more than 10,000 kilometers even before Nomonhan, and they were wearing out.[33]

There were severe ammunition shortages, and resupply efforts were slow and inadequate. Yoshimaru's 3rd Regiment ran out of shells by the afternoon of 3 July. Later, in the 4th Regiment, the tanks were down to five rounds each, and Tamada had to scrounge ammunition from the mauled sister regiment. Lieutenant Takeshita remembers being admonished daily not to waste shells, and to fire only at targets within range. The problem would have become acute if the IJA tank units had remained in combat much longer.

Fuel was a vexatious question, particularly since wheeled support vehicles had to be used in difficult soil and available tanker trucks were insufficient for sustained operations. When the weather was adverse, as in late June in the Arshaan-Handagai sector, the tank units' radius of action was diminished by a fuel shortage, and thus the combat mission was endangered from the beginning. One might somehow economize on ammunition, but there could be no economizing on fuel.

In semiarid regions such as Nomonhan, the acquisition of drinking water posed constant difficulties, especially on the higher ground. At the outset, the tankers drank salty water provided by the regimental supply and maintenance company. Later, potable water became available from the water-supply section. Nevertheless, although the situation was better in mechanized than in foot or horse units, and although he was attached to detachment headquarters, Noguchi could not wash his face for 20 days and of course could not shave. Apart from trying to drink from saline ponds, the men dug "wells" two meters deep, drawing a trickle of water into a can.

Noguchi says the detachment possessed adequate rations of dried vegetables, canned goods, rice, and the ever-present *kanpan* hardtack. But the food situation varied from unit to unit. Lieutenant Tomioka says food (mainly *kanpan* and *miso*) was not a special problem—there was just not enough. Lieutenant Irie recalls bouts with hunger, and says his weight had dropped to 115 pounds from 140 by the time his 3rd Regiment left the Nomonhan battlefront. Major Harada had two suggestions based on experience in the same regiment: first, supplement the rations locally (as with Russian bread acquired at Arshaan and with edible wild vegetation picked by troops in the field); second, stock extra food aboard trucks, for possible emergency issue.[34]

The most telling Japanese complaint dealt with the disparity in the number of tanks and other vehicles on both sides. According to Japanese combat intelligence, Soviet mechanized brigades possessed battalions with 25 BT tanks and 37 armored cars each; a motorized infantry battalion had 100 trucks and 900 infantry; a reconnaissance battalion, five armored cars and 18 amphibious vehicles. And all of these elements had artillery and antitank guns in support.[35] By comparison, the fighting at Nomonhan demonstrated that the Japanese tanks were far too few to exploit combat achievements or to keep up with attrition. Thus whenever Tamada dispatched a company on an independent mission, or whenever a company suffered losses in battle, he was obliged to add to it elements of a second company. In future, the colonel felt, tank companies should always be made up of four platoons. Indeed, he had been pressing for an increase from three to four platoons since before the outbreak of the Nomonhan Incident.[36]

To compensate for numerical and technical deficiencies, the 4th Regiment emphasized the negation of the enemy's range superiority by exploiting terrain cover, firing from hull-down positions, and operating at twilight. But the Japanese tank units lacked a self-defense capability, especially in the absence of friendly infantry to cope with the possibility of enemy infiltration threatened by the open terrain. *Danretsu* (supply and maintenance) and line soldiers were insufficient to provide all-around protection. Tamada's whole regimental supply company, for example, started out with a mere six officers and warrant officers, 95 noncoms and soldiers, and 27 mechanics. When the *danretsu* unit was obliged to release every one of its reserve machines (five light tanks and one tankette) to the wounded line companies, it ended up with almost no antitank capacity. A tank regiment, Tamada suggested, needed to be armed with more machine guns, antitank weapons, land mines, and grenades.

Russian tactics were marked by mass and by the combination of tanks, infantry, and artillery. Tamada was unusually honest in evaluating Soviet combat ability:

> We have had the preconception that Russian forces fight pigheadedly and crudely; but, on the basis of seeing them in action . . . that is not necessarily so. For example, they used armored cars as decoys to lure out our tanks into antitank or armored ambush; and they shifted their rapid-fire guns quickly and expertly. . . .
>
> The enemy's fighting spirit should not necessarily be despised. Apparently because their organization, matériel, and strength were superior to ours, their counterattacks between 3-6 July were repeated tenaciously. On occasion, when we fought at close quarters in certain sectors, they refused to retreat, and some of them even blew themselves up with grenades.

During the Japanese night attack, it was true, Soviet tanks and artillery had abandoned their positions. Many of the remaining infantry were panicked, and the number of those willing to fight at close quarters was scanty. Nevertheless, gasoline bottles and antitank mines were found strewn around, "so it is not proper to judge that the enemy has no fighting will at all." Contrary to Tamada's fair appraisal, however, most Japanese tankers were not overly impressed by the Russians' fighting skill or spirit.

In overall terms, observed Tamada, the Russians' offensive tactics may have been dispersed and uncoordinated. Still, in local actions, they linked their tanks and rapid-fire guns effectively and fought well. There was a feeling that the enemy had very carefully studied and prepared for operations on the plains. The Soviet method of attack was to soften up the Japanese with artillery first while advancing tanks and infantry—though the latter did not move very close to the barrages. Firepower was the key to Russian combat. Antitank defense was conducted mainly by towed rapid-fire weapons and armor firing effectively at a range of 1,500 meters or more. The infantry hurled grenades but did not launch charges too close for hand-to-hand fighting, and tanks did not overrun positions. Enemy snipers were excellent, even at 700-800 meters; Japanese snipers, by contrast, equipped with scopes one-third as strong, generally fired at only 300 meters.

Profiting from the long-range firing ability of their main armament, Soviet tanks and armored cars could also disengage from action by exploiting their superior speed as necessary. There was no evidence of employment en masse.

Armor used stop-and-fire tactics and hull-down emplacement. On the defensive, the enemy preferred reverse-slope positions, sallying from the flank under artillery or rapid-fire support, and roving tactics.

Russian artillery fire was not concentrated in terms of time or space, but the expenditure of shells was abundant and duds were few. Since the IJA tank units lacked foot soldiers and artillery that might have interfered, most of the Soviet observation posts could be advanced into their own infantry lines, and the Russian spotters were able to direct the opening of fire and the shifting of targets rapidly by telephone. In general, however, Soviet guns fired blindly and routinely—morning, noon, and night, at about the same time each day.

To sum up the preceding critique by Japanese tankers: although no dread of the Red Army was instilled in them, there was no underestimation of the level of the enemy's mechanization and his quantitative superiority in matériel. "Our situation was one of 'always less, always worse.'" If the Japanese had had comparable equipment and ordnance, it was often said, there would have been not a thing to fear from the Russians.[37]

Quite appropriately, Soviet sources have exalted the success of their forces on the left bank of the Halha in the face of the Japanese river-crossing offensive of 2-5 July. It had, after all, been a threat from which the Russians "had only escaped by the skin of their teeth," and which owed as much to "good luck as good management."[38] The demands of Soviet propaganda were also served by the fact that the invaders had been evicted from territory that indubitably belonged to the USSR's client state, the Mongolian People's Republic.

It was the right shore of the Halha that was in dispute, however—at least as interpreted by the Japanese and their own satellite, Manchukuo. Thus Soviet retention of the bridgehead on the eastern bank, compressed to five or six kilometers from the river, was essential to Zhukov's plan. That mission was handled tenaciously and effectively by the 9th Armored Brigade on the left wing (facing Yoshimaru) and by Major Remizov's 149th Infantry Regiment (less one battalion) from the 36th Division on the right flank (facing Tamada). These Russian forces were certainly not in retreat to the left bank, as Yasuoka was told so constantly.

The Russians are essentially correct in their judgment that, after some limited success, the Japanese armored units were soon checked by artillery fire, incurred severe losses, and accomplished little. Though Zhukov admitted to Stalin in May 1940 that the Russian BT-5 and BT-7 tanks were "too fire-hazardous" (an undoubted allusion to the IJA success with fire bottles), he called the Japanese tanks of the type of the Soviet MS-1 "definitely obsolete . . . slow, poorly armed," and very limited in radius of action. Still,

Soviet historians do not improve the luster of their army's achievements by inflating the size of Yasuoka's force to 130 tanks and six armored cars [tankettes]—nearly double the actual number of Japanese machines in action.[39]

When, as Shishkin says, the Japanese found that their armor was incapable of maneuver, they assigned the tanks to the task force that had the mission of pinning down Soviet elements on the right shore. Consequently, the Japanese were deprived of "swift punching power." The success of the Russians on both sides of the Halha, writes Zhukov, "proved an important stimulus for boosting the morale of our troops as well as that of their Mongolian counterparts."[40] While preparing methodically for a giant counteroffensive in August, the Soviet command would soon have to address a new series of Japanese ground assaults on the right shore, directed against the confluence sector.

25

Trying It with Cold Steel

And we are here as on a darkling plain
Swept with confused alarms of struggle and flight,
Where ignorant armies clash by night.

—Matthew Arnold, "Dover Beach"

When Komatsubara got back from the blunted left-shore offensive on 4
July, the notion of striking to the confluence still beckoned, this time from
the right bank. As higher headquarters understood it, by 2 P.M. on the 4th
the Yasuoka detachment had advanced as close as four kilometers from the
Halha-Holsten junction, and by evening may have come within one kilometer of it.[1] In a sanguine order issued at 3 P.M., Komatsubara stated that
the main body of the 23rd Division had been transferred to Yasuoka "as
planned" and would now annihilate enemy forces on the right side of the
Halha.[2] The division commander's thinking, however, was far ahead of realities: neither the 71st Infantry and its supporting field artillery battalion nor
Sumi's 26th Infantry had come back across the river yet. Kobayashi's infantry corps—Sakai's 72nd Regiment, a battalion of Yamagata's 64th Infantry,
and the rest of the 13th Field Artillery Regiment—were still in the process
of entering Yasuoka's command.

Sakai had had to traverse 28 kilometers from Hara Heights to a site
northeast of Heights 755. The 71st Regiment would have to move 40 kilometers from Hara to Heights 753 on the south side of the Holsten. From
Bain Tsagan to the vicinity of Lake Manzute, Sumi's assignment, was 13
kilometers. Although these distances were by no means enormous, and
although the Japanese decision to withdraw from the left bank was more
or less voluntary, Russian heavy artillery and aircraft were interfering with
the redeployment. The movement of the tired troops and the assignment
to them of a new mission were devouring precious time and causing
confusion.[3]

The only forces theoretically available for Komatsubara to order into action on the right shore at this time were Yasuoka's two tank regiments, the
bulk of Yamagata's 64th Infantry, Miyao's 1st Independent Field Artillery,
and Kajikawa's infantry battalion from the 28th Regiment. But even this
strength was not fully functional: the front-line foot soldiers were unready,
Kajikawa's whereabouts was unclear, the 3rd Tank Regiment had been

pulled to the rear to lick its wounds, and the 4th Tank Regiment itself was being attacked on the night of the 4th.

Kobayashi finally caught up with Yasuoka and came under the detachment's command early on 5 July. Setting up his command post south of Uzuru pond, Kobayashi tried to consolidate his scattered units and prepare for the offensive so ardently desired by Yasuoka and Komatsubara. The task was complicated tremendously by problems of location. "All of us thought that we were much closer to the confluence than was the case," says Tamada. Whereas Yasuoka, as we have seen, estimated that he was two kilometers from the junction, aerial surveillance suggested a figure closer to four. The difficulty of maintaining direction on a trackless plain and of establishing liaison was "unimaginable," Kobayashi wrote. Although Sakai arrived by noon, there was no communication between units. Telephone lines had not been set up, and runners were not getting through. "I spent the whole day 'in a fog,'" Kobayashi lamented.[4]

Ground action on 5 July was not pronounced in Yasuoka's sector, but enemy fighter and bomber activity was vigorous. Japanese losses were not severe, however: five engineers and two antiaircraft gunners wounded, and a truck burned.[5] After his plans of 4 July did not materialize, Yasuoka organized a Right Wing Unit (now that Kajikawa's battalion had been located) and a Left Wing Unit. Continuing his repeated calls for offensive action north of the Holsten, and making use of the new strength brought by Kobayashi—one artillery and three infantry battalions, plus engineers—the general issued another operations order at 9 P.M. on 5 July, prescribing a dusk assault next day.[6]

From his latest decisions, there is evidence of a certain modification of Yasuoka's tactical thinking—namely, stress upon coordinated operation. With Ise's as well as Miyao's artillery becoming available, Yasuoka would use guns to soften up the foe with a short barrage. Then, before hostile fire became too powerful, the infantry should charge at dusk. Tanks were to be employed only as needed in the main sector, with the 3rd Regiment held in reserve. In other words, the tank general was emphasizing direct infantry action, not surprise and pursuit strikes—of which he was so fond—by his armored formations.[7]

Meanwhile Major Kajikawa, as we saw in Chapter 23, had been displaying initiative and fighting a successful "private war" of his own. In the early morning of 4 July, the 880 men of his battalion moved forward 1,000 meters to the southwest from their campsite west of Heights 739, since the foe had pulled back during the night. Two air attacks caused no losses. Kajikawa's battalion advanced rapidly against trifling resistance, for apparently the enemy's main attention was focused on the left bank or on the Yasuoka front.[8]

Deciding to sever hostile lines of communication, Kajikawa sent out a patrol to try to blow up the bridge across the Halha at the confluence.

While the demolition party was away, Kajikawa learned from scouts that enemy defenses in the Halha-Holsten apex area were not strong, although barbed-wire nets and piano wire, something new to the battalion, had been laid in front of the Soviet positions, obviously with the intention of separating tanks from infantry. Kajikawa decided to launch a dawn assault toward the confluence on 5 July. When friendly troops were encountered to the left—the 8th Company of the Yamagata regiment—it was decided to team up for the dawn attack. To 2nd Lt. Takashima Masao, one of Kajikawa's platoon leaders, the Yamagata men looked like real combat veterans, indifferent to fire, with hollow cheeks and glassy eyes. In their *hangō* mess kits they had rice, whereas Kajikawa's soldiers lacked even dry biscuits.

At daybreak on the 5th, Kajikawa's troops could hear the sounds of explosions and then the "hated Czech machine guns" from the direction of the bridge. From a patrol, Kajikawa learned that the span was well-guarded by tanks and armored cars. The bridge itself was underwater, since the Halha had been rising, but was functioning nicely.

By 6 A.M. the Kajikawa battalion had jumped off, in light rain, under enemy artillery fire that grew particularly heavy after the unit advanced 1,500 meters. The gunfire cut swathes in the grass and shot off the dew. Coordination with Yasuoka was still impossible, and to some the "blind" advance seemed reckless. Around 11:30 A.M., dashing from dip to dip, the battalion reached a point estimated by Kajikawa to be 1,800 meters northeast of the bridge at the confluence. Resistance grew more severe, and 14 or 15 enemy tanks were seen approaching, beyond effective range of the Japanese rapid-fire battery. Thereupon the battalion-gun platoon engaged the enemy and burned one tank. Since smoke obscured observation and ammunition was running low, the Japanese infantry prepared human-bullet antitank teams to bound forward. But the enemy armor held up at a distance of 1,400-1,500 meters and bombarded the Japanese lines, while the foe brought up more troops and intensified the artillery fire. Gradually the enemy encircled the Japanese from both flanks and the front, and casualties mounted. Ordering his battalion to dig in, Kajikawa repeated his efforts to contact Yasuoka.

Eventually, at midday, a master sergeant made it back from detachment headquarters with orders to prepare for offensive action. In view of his difficult tactical position, Kajikawa decided to wait till darkness to pull back and consolidate. Enemy actions became larger, nearer, and more aggressive until, by 2 P.M., hand-to-hand combat was in progress. At such close quarters, the Japanese rapid-fire guns were more effective, smashing two tanks and stopping another. The armor veered to the left flank of the infantry, which sent out tank-killer teams in twos and threes that accomplished little and lost a second lieutenant in the process. A minor but cheering development was the appearance of one Japanese plane, which bombed the enemy. Soviet pressure did not let up all day. From the area along the Halha, 100 soldiers and two tanks closed in on Kajikawa's right flank, and enemy artillery became more accurate. Finally, the rain and the clouds of nightfall brought merciful darkness. Wet and covered with sand, says Takashima, "we looked like sewer rats." Bodies felt heavy; thoughts raced although the mind seemed paralyzed; only the eyes moved.

Kajikawa ordered his front-line companies to pull back to the battalion command post, bringing as many of their dead and wounded as possible. Using tents, the troops improvised four-man litters. Generally unimpeded by the enemy, the units assembled at 7:40 P.M. They were back at the original jump-off location by 9:30. As a morale-builder, Kajikawa told his men that it had not been a withdrawal. "In order to achieve the more important missions ordered by the Yasuoka detachment," he said, "we have merely disengaged from the enemy for the time being." By 11:30 P.M. the Russians must have lost contact with the relocated Japanese, for they sent up illuminating shells in the murk. Takashima's ears were ringing, he felt dizzy and had a headache, he was sleepy but could not sleep, and mosquitoes swarmed around.

Kajikawa estimated that enemy casualties exceeded 300 on 5 July. Four tanks had been knocked out, and two water-cooled heavy and three light machine guns captured. But Japanese losses had been heavy, especially in the 5th Company, whose commander, Capt. Aoyagi Kin'ichirō, was slain, charging a tank with saber in hand. In all, two officers and 16 men had been killed; three officers (including a medical lieutenant) and 30 men had been wounded.

Looking back on the events of 5 July, Kajikawa recorded the following criticisms: (1) no support by artillery; (2) insufficient cooperation and liaison with neighboring units; (3) no way of communicating with Yasuoka detachment headquarters; (4) insufficient ammunition; and (5) disadvantageous terrain (the Japanese were good targets for tanks and artillery on the slopes of the high ground). Most importantly, the main body of the 23rd Division had stopped its offensive against the left shore from Fui Heights and had moved to the right bank, thereby freeing enemy strength for commitment to the Kajikawa sector.

At dawn on 6 July, the three-man bridge-demolition team that had gone out on the 4th returned. They had somehow made it near the span, which was being used constantly by tanks and trucks and was defended by 23 soldiers armed with heavy machine guns. Unable to reach the bridge itself, the Japanese had passed themselves off as Russian soldiers, had set charges on the approaches 50 meters from the bridge, near daybreak, and had then taken cover. The lead tanks of two columns were stopped, and a chain of collisions had occurred, causing great confusion. Although the Russian machine guns had opened fire promptly, the three Japanese soldiers got away. One private, though shot in the arm, played dead and then "wriggled away like a worm." The men hid all day in bushes on the shore, digging shallow holes with their helmets. Russian soldiers could be heard humming a few steps away, as they came to get water from the river. At first the Japanese soldiers were tense, but eventually, they claimed, they were able to doze and even snore. On the way back at night the team decided to "raise some hell," since they were still in enemy territory. They added to their exploits by cutting enemy telephone lines in five or six places. Kajikawa and the battalion were, of course, delighted that the bold patrol had not only returned safely but had committed so much mayhem.

Now, on the morning of 6 July, Kajikawa received Yasuoka's order, issued the night before, decreeing creation of a Right Wing Unit based on the battalion and calling for a new offensive at dusk. While making preparations, Kajikawa's unit was spotted by the enemy, who unleashed air assaults and accurate artillery fire. The battalion dug in and awaited further orders. When new Soviet positions were detected under construction, 2,000 meters away, Kajikawa on his own initiative directed his battalion guns, rapid-fire battery, and heavy machine guns to harass and destroy the emplacements. But in the absence of the go-ahead from Yasuoka, Kajikawa launched no offensive on 6 July.

Near midday on the 7th, a signal liaison team arrived from detachment headquarters with details of the on-again twilight offensive. Soon afterward, while continuing offensive preparations, the Kajikawa battalion detected 150 enemy troops, with two heavy machine guns and two towed field pieces, which had traversed the Kita-watashi crossing. Now only 200 meters from the Japanese, these forces were blundering against the right rear of the battalion, obviously ignorant of its presence, since it was very well dug in. Lieutenant Takashima remembered seeing tall strange men in unfamiliar greatcoats approaching nonchalantly, "innocent and chattering." The Japanese waited until the enemy had come as close as 40 meters, whereupon the 7th Company ringed the Soviets with surprise fire, mowed them down, then charged. Takashima tells of the massacre of 60 Russians on his sector—the chance to blood his own saber, the "happy" slashes of bayonets and swords, the hurling of grenades, the desperate sprinting-away by hunched-up enemy soldiers.

By 4 P.M. the battle was over. The Russian field guns had been demolished and the machine guns had been captured; 102 bodies were found strewn on the field, "all on their backs, large figures sprawling in black blood." But the

Japanese paid for their zeal to charge. One platoon, having bounded across the crestline, found itself exposed on flat terrain. Two Japanese platoon leaders died in the fighting, and a third officer was wounded. Enemy heavy weapons unexpectedly tore into the Japanese pursuers and cut down a number of soldiers, until suppressed by the expert fire of a heavy machine gun squad and the battalion-gun platoon. "The enemy's confusion boosted our morale," noted the battalion records. Kajikawa commended 1st Lt. Saitō Seikichi's 7th Company, particularly for the action of the 1st Platoon. Lieutenant Takashima was amazed and shaken to have emerged unscathed. Back in the Japanese trenches, rewards of sake and sweet bean-jelly waited, but some men wept, in the silence after combat, for slain comrades who lived on in the souls of the survivors.[9]

Elsewhere on the Yasuoka detachment front, Soviet tank and infantry forces with heavy weapons had launched attacks from dawn on 6 July. Hardest hit was Tamada's tank regiment, located on the far left near Heights 755. Russian troops and 25 to 50 armored vehicles also assaulted the 64th Infantry sector, to the right of Tamada, where a battery of Miyao's field artillery claimed to have knocked out five machines. Another IJA artillery battery fired at armor approaching the Halha crossing from the left bank. The 72nd Regiment, on the right wing, was attacked by infantrymen supported by machine guns and artillery.[10]

Problems of communication continued to plague the Japanese command to the extent that, when Komatsubara came to inspect the front on 6 July, he directed Kobayashi to take all of his unit commanders aboard aircraft and scout the situation at firsthand. Even this measure did not eliminate the confusion, for Yamagata—whose regimental site was supposed to have been the pivot of the Left Wing Unit's dusk offensive on the 6th—still insisted that he had plotted *his* location accurately. Since proper alignment of the forces was impossible until the cartographic disagreement was worked out (in Yamagata's eventual favor, incidentally), Yasuoka had already by noon postponed the twilight offensive till the 7th. The reason he gave officially was the necessity for full combat preparations, particularly supplies of ammunition and fuel.[11]

Another problem troubling Komatsubara was the situation on the south side of the Holsten, where the Manchukuoan cavalry division's combat performance, in his words, "had not been too good, since they had a tendency to be overwhelmed by the enemy." Tamada, on the north shore of the Holsten, had been complaining about the Manchurian screening units too: "Insofar as possible, it would be best to avoid using friendly forces that do not possess sufficient operational strength to close gaps between units, or to cover the flanks. Our unit [4th Tank Regiment] was always worried about the left wing because of pullbacks by friendly forces [deployed there]."

On 6 July, Komatsubara therefore organized a detachment made up of the 71st Infantry Regiment (less one battalion) and the 1st Field Artillery Battalion, to be headed for the time being by Col. Okamoto Tokuzō, the 71st's commander, who would shortly become division chief of staff, now that Colonel Ōuchi had been killed. This new unit would cross to the south shore of the Holsten, seize Noro Heights, and strike the enemy in the confluence area from the right rear. The Manchukuoan Hsingan (Kōan) division was transferred simultaneously from Yasuoka's operational command to that of Okamoto. Saitō's 23rd Engineer Regiment would construct a bridge over the Holsten.[12]

North of the Holsten, Komatsubara ordered Yasuoka, now reinforced by Sakai's 72nd Infantry and the field artillery regiment, to mount a combined offensive against the confluence. Sumi's 26th Infantry Regiment was to detach a portion as a feint in the Fui Heights sector, where Mongolian cavalry had been operating. The main body of the 26th Regiment would stand by near Lake Manzute. (For a schematic rendering of the Japanese deployment, see Table 25.1.)

Soviet defenses in the confluence area were well constructed, camouflaged cleverly, protected by entanglements, and deployed to a depth of several lines. The advance positions were anchored at Heights 733, on the West Balshagal (Barunishi) elevation, with particular emphasis on well-fortified "Loophole" and "Three-Bush" heights (Jūgan and Mitsubosa).

Strategically, Komatsubara and Yasuoka were now thinking of a pincer operation from both sides of the Holsten instead of both sides of the Halha. But the Japanese ground forces would have to breech the tough defensive belt north of the Holsten if they were to make it to the river junction. The task was complicated by the average 50 meters' disadvantage in height vis-à-vis the left shore of the Halha. In addition, IJA firepower was notably inferior to Soviet in numbers and quality, and friendly tanks were virtually out of action.

Thus, tactically, Komatsubara's choices were highly limited. Daylight attacks were out of the question. Dawn assaults required artillery and tank support. Komatsubara therefore adopted the technique of the dusk attack (*hakubo kōgeki*). Sunset occurred at about 9 P.M. and was followed by an hour of twilight when diminishing visibility would suffice for the Japanese attackers but would be insufficient for enemy artillery, especially batteries firing beyond medium distance. Once darkness came, the spirited IJA infantrymen would be "in their element," for their unique historical forte was close combat, cold steel, and *yashū*, or attack by night, when goblins haunt

TABLE 25.1

Japanese Offensive Deployment, 6–13 July 1939

23rd Inf. Div.
Lt. Gen. Komatsubara Michitaro

- Yasuoka Detachment
  Lt. Gen. Yasuoka Masaomi
  - Right Wing Unit
    28th Inf. Regt., 2nd Bn.
    Maj. Kajikawa Tomiji
  - Left Wing Unit
    23rd Inf. Corps
    Maj. Gen. Kobayashi Kōichi
  - Tank Unit
    3rd, 4th Tank Regts.
    Col. Tamada Yoshio
  - Artillery Unit
    1st Ind. Field Arty. Regt.
    13th Field Arty. Regt.
    Col. Ise Takahide
    - Right-sector Unit
      64th Inf. Regt., Col.
      Yamagata Takemitsu
    - Left-sector Unit
      72nd Inf. Regt.,
      Col. Sakai Mikio
    - 24th Engr. Regt., Col.
      Kawamura Shichirō

- Sumi Unit
  Col. Sumi Shin'ichirō
  - 26th Inf. Regt.
    - To left side of 72nd
      Inf. Regt., 8–9 July
      To right side of
      Kajikawa Bn., 10 July

- Engineer Unit
  Lt. Col. Saitō Isamu
  - 23rd Engr. Regt.

- Reserve Unit
  Lt. Col. Ioki Eiichi
  - 23rd Recon. Unit
    71st Inf. Regt., 1st Bn.

- Okamoto Detachment
  Col. Okamoto Tokuzō
  - 71st Inf. Regt. [− 1st Bn.]

Right [north] shore of Holsten River

Left [south] shore of Holsten River

the mind. The Russians were supposedly unenthusiastic about the use of swords and bayonets. One IJA officer claimed that Soviet troops "fled weeping" from saber-wielding Japanese infantry. In addition, the Russians were said to be inadequately trained for night fighting, whereas IJA soldiery were known for the "boldness, quickness, and diligence that are part of the traditional Japanese character"—a perfect complement to the restrictive, beneficial effects of darkness.[13]

The combined dusk assault envisaged by Komatsubara when he had come back across the Halha was supposed to have been unleashed soon enough to catch the enemy off balance. Instead, it took about two and a half days to get ready to jump off for the first time on 7 July. At least the weather favored the attackers—cloudy, windy, cool, with occasional showers. To facilitate the charge, artillery was to soften up the enemy with a short barrage of about 30 minutes' duration, paying particular attention to neutralizing hostile artillery batteries on the left shore of the Halha. Once the front-echelon infantry had seized their objectives, elements of the friendly artillery should proceed immediately to the forwardmost lines and prepare for the resumption of action at dawn.

Yasuoka's intention was to preempt an anticipated assault involving 70-80 tanks, a rifle regiment, and 800 motorized troops. There was already considerable evidence of intensifying enemy action on 7 July. Around 10 A.M., an infantry company with a rapid-fire gun had pushed into the zone between the wing units until driven off by Miyao's artillery. Before noon, scout planes detected 50 or 60 Soviet tanks operating southeast of Heights 755 and six guns being emplaced three to four kilometers southwest of that elevation. Kajikawa reported reinforcement of enemy positions on his front, especially with piano wire; frequent movements of hostile armor and trucks toward the sector of the Left Wing Unit; and heavy artillery fire from the left side of the Halha. The barrages, says Lieutenant Takashima, caved in his platoon's foxholes and enlarged them into one long "group trench."

Originally, in the afternoon of 7 July, Kajikawa was directed to strike southeastward and seize enemy positions three kilometers from Heights 733. But at 8 P.M. Yasuoka decided to suspend the offensive by the battalion, which was ordered to maintain its present positions and cover the right flank of the detachment. Kajikawa's men dug deep kneeling-trenches and conducted reconnaissance. It was learned that the level of the Halha had risen further, inundating and undermining the river banks. Crossing by enemy foot soldiers became impossible, and armor found it difficult to operate. Consequently, Kajikawa reported, defense of his area had become relatively easy.

To cope with enemy activities in the Holsten valley near Heights 747, on the morning of 7 July Komatsubara ordered the 26th Regiment to attack the foe there, on the far left flank of the forthcoming twilight assault by the

Yasuoka detachment.[14] Sumi therefore took what few forces were then available to him (about 435 men), left the Lake Manzute reserve area, and reached the division concentration zone at Lake Iringin to the south by evening. Proceeding to an elevation near Heights 755, he began his southwestern advance, north of the Holsten.

Throughout the day on 7 July, since 9 A.M., Miyao's field artillery regiment had been engaging Soviet heavy guns on Komatsu Heights across the river, expending 258 shells in the process. At 9 P.M., all available Japanese artillery—32 field pieces and howitzers—opened counterbattery fire for 30 minutes. Kobayashi called the friendly barrage ineffective because of the rain. Air support had also been requested, but the bad weather prevented it.[15] Thus, in practice, the "combined" offensive consisted preponderantly of infantry.

Kobayashi's Left Wing Unit conducted the actual twilight assault, with the three battalions of the 64th Infantry on the right flank and two battalions of the 72nd Infantry on the left. The emphasis of the offensive was to be the belt of dunes 3-4 kilometers southeast of Heights 733. Code words would be *Hisshō* ("certain victory") and *Shinnen* ("conviction").

After the Japanese artillery had supposedly "dominated the enemy" for a half-hour, at 9:30 P.M. the infantry moved out. According to the simplistic record of the Yasuoka detachment, the assault proceeded smoothly because it was raining heavily at the time, and the objectives were reached by 3 A.M. Of course, the actions were far more complicated on the scene. In the 64th Regiment, for instance, Major Tazaka's 1st Battalion, on the far right, had been under attack and bombardment since noon on the 7th. Not only was this battalion not able to charge by 9:30 P.M., but it also had to struggle to extricate itself from its own battle by midnight. Not until 1 A.M. on the 8th did it begin its attack—hardly a twilight operation. Hard fighting ensued against enemy pickets and about 60 armored vehicles. The Soviet positions were penetrated and the armor repelled, but dawn was approaching and the terrain ahead was unfavorable, sloping downward to the enemy. Therefore it was decided to withdraw the 1st Battalion to the jump-off site.

To the left of the 1st Battalion, adjoining the sector of the Sakai regiment, Yamagata's 2nd and 3rd battalions were able to commence action on schedule, although they had been receiving enemy barrages before jump-off time. By 2:30 A.M., Lt. Col. Tokumaru's 2nd Battalion had reached the enemy defenses on Heights 733. Scouts reported that it was an artillery site without many foot troops. Supported by heavy machine guns, the battalion stormed and occupied the position by 4 A.M.[16]

Sakai's 72nd Regiment had seen considerable action since 6 July, when its advance against the Heights 755 area encountered severe artillery barrages as well as tank and infantry counterassaults. During preparations for its own offensive on the 7th, a little before evening, the regiment was struck by a very powerful heavy-artillery bombardment. Playing down the effects, the regimental chronicler merely noted that, although numerous casualties were incurred, the Japanese operation commenced at about 9 P.M. Sakai and his headquarters moved forward behind the front-line battalions, whose frontage was intended to be less than one kilometer.

Survivors are more explicit. The regiment was on the verge of starting when a barrage of enemy artillery rounds hurtled in, one shell alone killing or wounding eight men and four horses. In the resulting chaos, the unit flinched until Colonel Sakai personally pulled the troops together by shouting words of command and encouragement. Despite continued bombardment as long as there was light, the regiment jumped off, taking advantage of crestlines and supposedly supported by the 3rd Field Artillery Battalion. It had been drizzling constantly, and the region became black when night came. Enemy defenses could not be discerned clearly, and lateral contact was lost by the battalions—Major Nishikawa's 1st, Major Kokura Keiji's 2nd.

Assisted by an engineer platoon per battalion, the 72nd Regiment pressed forward into the enemy's defensive lines in the Heights 733 sector. The left-flank 1st Battalion overran sentry posts and moved against the main positions. Intense Soviet machine-gun fire caused grievous casualties, including the 2nd Company commander, 1st Lt. Katsuki (Kazuki) Norihisa, slain. The right-flank 2nd Battalion veered left gradually and lent assistance, both units ending up at almost the same location. Casualties increased while the troops consolidated their deployment and dug in during the rest of the night.

Unaware that the 2nd Battalion originally ahead of it had moved to the left, the regimental headquarters with the unit colors advanced straight forward, escorted by the color-guard 4th Company. When empty enemy emplacements were encountered, the Japanese subordinate commanders wanted to hold up, since they were entirely out of touch with the forward battalions and they did not know where the main hostile forces were located. But Colonel Sakai got the men moving again, reminding them that the confluence remained the objective, the battalions could be contacted in the morning, and the less enemy met, the better. Thereupon they stopped milling around and proceeded through the piano wire at the deep but deserted second defense line and the barbed wire at the third, until a separate heights behind the enemy defenses was reached before daybreak. Apparently the regiment commander was now over 1,000 meters ahead of the forwardmost Japanese infantry battalions.

Sakai was deploying his headquarters force and trying to locate the two battalions when a hostile motorized unit appeared with between 150 and 300 troops, trucks, and some armor. The enemy may originally have been retreating, but when they realized that the elevation was in Japanese hands and weakly held, they encircled and attacked the position. In this emergency, "as calm and cool as Mount Fuji," Sakai encouraged his men. Realizing the dual threat to the regiment commander and the colors, the reserve troops fought very well, none harder than 2nd Lt. Ryūzu (Ryūtō) Noboru, acting commander of the 4th Company.

At approximately 5 A.M., a runner from the 4th Company staggered through to the 1st Battalion, bringing word of Sakai's plight. Nishikawa was horrified when he realized that the colonel and the colors had advanced 1,000-1,500 meters beyond the main infantry. The major rushed forward with his battalion, meeting a regimental staff officer, sent by the colonel, on the way. Within 20 minutes the battalion had driven off the enemy forces and reached the right rear of the 4th Company. When the relief unit arrived, Sakai shook hands with Nishikawa and thanked him warmly instead of bawling him out. The major was both touched and relieved.

The 72nd Regiment estimated that the foe had been hit hard during the night. In addition to the 250 corpses abandoned on the battlefield, 20 trucks and armored vehicles were reported to have been captured by Lieutenant Ryūzu's reserve company. These represented only the enemy's visible losses. But Japanese casualties had been very severe too: six officers and 95 men killed, another six officers and 185 men wounded. Most of the casualties were incurred during the artillery barrages that preceded the offensive advance.[17]

Still digging in at Heights 733, Kokura's 2nd Battalion repulsed a counterattack at 8 A.M., after which the fighting abated. At detachment headquarters, Yasuoka was pleased with the first reports he received at dawn. Maj. Seki Takeshi's 3rd Battalion of the 13th Field Artillery Regiment was reported to have displaced to the area south of Heights 733. On the basis of information from the two infantry regiments, Yasuoka and Komatsubara were convinced that all of their objectives had been seized.[18] In the case of Sakai, for example, it was thought that the entire Heights 733 defense complex had been secured. After-action maps, however, reveal that the infantry had merely occupied the front edge of the positions on the south side of Heights 733 near the Holsten. This meant, in short, that the Japanese had not really progressed appreciably from their take-off location, despite the fierce combat.

According to Soviet sources, after being defeated on the left shore of the Halha River the Japanese regrouped and resupplied their forces. New Japanese attacks, however, would eschew deep encircling maneuvers and would have to settle for a limited objective—namely, depriving the Soviet-MPRA forces of the bridgehead on the right side of the Halha by means of frontal attacks. The 149th Infantry bore the brunt of the first Japanese night assault, which admittedly took the Russians and Mongolians by surprise. Forced to retreat toward the Halha, elements of the 149th Regiment dug in around high ground three or four kilometers from the river. During the ensuing combat the regiment commander, Maj. E. M. Remizov, was killed on 8 July. In recognition of his gallantry, the major was posthumously proclaimed a Hero of the Soviet Union and the site of his command post was renamed Remizov Heights.[19]

Just as combined actions and a twilight advance failed to characterize the Japanese attack of 7/8 July in practice, so too did the Holsten jaw of the envisaged pincers fail to materialize. Although Komatsubara did not know it at the time, the Okamoto detachment went astray and could not team up with the twilight offensive.

In accordance with a division order, at mid-morning on 6 July Colonel Okamoto had set out to cross the Holsten and attack Noro Heights from the east. Soon after traversing the river at 12:15 P.M., the detachment was detected by the enemy and came under interdiction fire. Long-range, preset gunnery was suspected, from the direction of Heights 738 on the north side of the Holsten. Around 5 P.M., while the detachment was taking a break on high ground, a scout plane dropped a sketch and a divisional message advising the unit that it was really near Imu (756) Heights—i.e., it was too far south of the Holsten. Komatsubara wanted Okamoto to advance along the valley and said he expected a good fight by the detachment.

Japanese army commanders were supposed to follow orders to the letter, but in this case Okamoto ignored his instructions, for he deemed the Holsten valley to be an enemy "re-entrant" salient. Consequently, Okamoto stayed near Imu, with the intention of checking with the Manchukuoan (Hsingan) Kōan cavalry division operating south of the river, and of reconnoitering the enemy situation and the terrain through the night. At 9 A.M. on 7 July, the Hsingan division was contacted and asked to assist the Japanese by striking from south to west. Okamoto had concluded by now that it was inappropriate to move along the valley because powerful enemy forces, which lay athwart the route, could inflict severe casualties by aimed fire. This estimate is hardly supported by IJA intelligence, which put enemy strength in the Noro Heights area on 7 July at only 200-300 infantry and a dozen armored vehicles.[20] But Okamoto was undoubtedly concerned about the threat from hostile forces, especially artillery, deployed just north of the Holsten too.

Breaking camp in the morning, the 71st Regiment headed west. At 1 P.M. a scout-plane pilot dropped a message that he could see enemy forces south of the Holsten, eight kilometers ahead. At 2:30 P.M., hostile artillery fire was received. Since the Japanese columns were stringing out, the units redeployed. When it was learned that the enemy was not advancing but occupying rather strong positions, Okamoto ordered the reinforcement of his spearhead elements by assigning the right-flank guard to the advance force, with rapid-fire and heavy machine guns. Support was to be rendered by the 1st Field Artillery Battalion, which commenced counterbattery fire at 3:30.

Before 4 P.M., three enemy armored vehicles opened fire from behind the Japanese. Okamoto was displeased with the fact that the infantry depended only on the rapid-fire guns and evinced no enthusiasm for forming close-quarter antitank teams. Lt. Col. Higashi Muneharu was sent up to control the situation and encourage the lagging troops. Maj. Murata Mosuke's 3rd Battalion, in particular, was always slower than Maj. Baba Susumu's 2nd Battalion in advancing or in occupying designated objectives, especially before sunset. It was true that there had been poor transmission of orders, occasioned largely by the inaccessibility of regimental headquarters, but the 3rd Battalion had been continuing to operate "somewhat negatively." Higashi pressed the unit to act more aggressively and finally rectified matters by evening. Capt. Onozuka Kichihei, 9th Company commander on the flank, retorts that his 3rd Battalion had a greater distance to traverse and was under fire all the way.

Resuming the advance at 7:30 P.M., the detachment occupied what it thought was Heights 758 two hours later. At least that was the location the Japanese say they were given by the Manchukuoan cavalry, already on the spot. If accurately identified, the hill was only three kilometers from Noro. Okamoto had his doubts, however; so instead of launching any twilight or night attack, he bivouacked for the night.[21]

Not for days did the Japanese comprehend that all of the presumed locations south of the Holsten were incorrectly labeled. For example, Okamoto's men had not reached Heights 758 on the night of 7 July, but were at a point just west of Nigesorimot, which meant they were nine kilometers from Noro Heights, not three. Imi Heights, which the detachment thought that it had occupied at 3 P.M., proved to be the vicinity of Heights 749.[22] In short, Noro was not close to seizure and the Japanese forces south of the Holsten were no nearer to evicting the enemy bridgehead than were their comrades north of the river. Komatsubara's idea of a concerted offensive remained a paper plan.

The Japanese command was typically upbeat on 8 July. Kwantung Army commander Ueda sent Komatsubara a telegram congratulating him on the success of the night attack and the subsequent pursuit, and exhorting decisive combat results. Komatsubara relayed the commendation to his subordinate commanders. Wishful thinking was resuscitated. At 8:30 A.M., Kobayashi heard a familiar refrain from the air force—that the immediate enemy seemed to be in retreat. An hour later, Yasuoka was ordering both wing units to send powerful elements to chase the foe to the Halha and exploit the effects of the action the preceding night, while artillery blocked routes of retreat. Kobayashi's order called for Sakai and Yamagata to conduct the pursuit and destroy the Soviet bridges. There was no emphasis on twilight or night operations now—only a haste to push forward as soon as possible to "finish off" the enemy. A scout plane was sent to the 71st Infantry at 10 A.M. with divisional orders to resume the attack against Noro Heights and thus facilitate the Yasuoka detachment's combat north of the Holsten.[23]

Japanese actions did not proceed as smoothly and rapidly as Komatsubara had hoped and expected. Kobayashi was suffering from the usual frustrating and worrisome problem of trying to communicate with the Yamagata and Sakai regiments, with whom he had been out of touch throughout the night and well into the day of the 8th. The general displaced his command post as far forward as possible, eventually to a point two kilometers east of Heights 733, but telephone lines still had not been laid down. At 3 P.M., Komatsubara pressed again for resumption of the offensive. Yasuoka conveyed the injunctions to his detachment and at 6:50 P.M. took steps to reinforce Kobayashi's group with a portion of Sumi's regiment and with an engineer platoon.[24] But night was approaching by now.

One exception to the low level of Japanese daytime action on 8 July occurred on Yasuoka's right wing, where enemy shelling of Kajikawa and his battalion had let up. Around 10 A.M., the major received word that the enemy was falling back to the left side of the Halha and that the battalion was to pursue the foe and cut off his retreat route. 1st Lt. Sawada Tetsurō was immediately ordered to set out with his reinforced 6th Infantry Company supported by heavy machine guns, rapid-fire guns, and battalion guns. Moving forward at 11 A.M., Sawada and his men advanced 2,000 meters, overcame small enemy elements, and seized the north edge of an *obi*-sash-shaped hill—"Rising-Sun Flag" or Hinomaru Heights. A tattered pennon always flew on the heights, perhaps dating back to the period of the Azuma debacle in May. There the Japanese were checked by a powerful counterattack. It was apparent to Sawada and Kajikawa from observation and patrol reports that the foe had no intention of retreating and was instead reinforcing the units in the area in order to attack and recapture Hinomaru Heights. Kajikawa reported these findings to Yasuoka, brought up the main battalion to reinforce Sawada, and canceled plans in progress for a night attack.

At 10:30 P.M., after frequent flares appeared, two enemy infantry companies counterattacked Hinomaru Heights, yelling "Hurrah!" and firing heavy and light machine guns with a profusion of tracers. Since Sawada had been getting ready for his own assault, he was fairly well prepared for the onslaught. The Japanese machine guns held their fire until the foe drew close, and then opened up till their barrels grew searing hot, stopping the enemy's forward movement. Thereupon Sawada charged deeply into the left rear of the foe.

Kajikawa lost contact with the 6th Company. Although the major had a rough idea where Sawada was, because he could be heard shouting inside the hostile positions, enemy artillery fire was still coming down on the battalion, and Kajikawa accordingly held up the movement of the main unit and shifted forces to the right flank of the enemy. Three noncoms were sent to locate Sawada but they failed to get through, for the enemy was strengthening the positions and reinforcing the sentry network.

Past 3 A.M. on the 9th, when the firing had abated, Sawada returned to the battalion with one-third of the men with whom he had started action. The lieutenant had been shot in the chest, as had Master Sergeant Iwakoshi. Collating the men's reports, Kajikawa estimated that Sawada's unit had killed 150 of the enemy, including eight (some say 12 or 13) cut down by Iwakoshi, a master swordsman. At sunrise, the battalion main force returned to its original lines and concentrated there. The wind swirled sandy dust over the trenches. Some of the men boasted to each other about their combat exploits; others dozed and dreamed of home in Hokkaido. Supported by one platoon each of infantry, heavy machine guns, and rapid-fire guns, 2nd Lt. Kijiya (Kijitani) Tomizō and his platoon of battalion guns were left to defend Hinomaru Heights against the enemy counterattacks.

All of Kajikawa's after-action reports are characterized by candid critiques. Of the operation of 8/9 July, especially Sawada's thrust, the major noted that there had been poor communication between the battalion and the attack force. The night assault itself had been insufficiently prepared, because of lack of training. That is to say, most of the newest recruits, who had completed only the first 90 days of basic training, lacked night-attack practice. The enemy positions contained trenches and passages that rendered movement difficult. Some of the Japanese soldiers stopped advancing when the enemy threw hand grenades; others held up because they lost their bearings. Indeed, most of the trouble stemmed from the fact that nothing was done to maintain direction. Lastly, objectives were not clear and the Sawada unit penetrated too deeply into the hostile positions, although this action did prove effective by causing confusion among the enemy.[25]

In the Left Wing Unit, Sakai's 72nd Infantry—the left-flank regiment—responded fairly promptly to Yasuoka's and Kobayashi's attack order received at 10:30 A.M. on 8 July. First Lt. Ōtake Sakae's 8th Company and a machine-gun platoon were sent out "in pursuit" around 2 P.M., with the concurrent mission of cooperating with a couple of light tanks from Tamada's regiment in covering a demolition team's raid against a bridge over the Halha. The Japanese emphasis on destroying the bridges stemmed, of course, from the fact that the spans handled the enemy forces' main supply lines and were thus the keys to their retreat or advance. In all, it was now thought there were a total of 7-9 bridges across the Halha and the Holsten. Ground and air scouts were having difficulty locating the spans, which were often underwater. Engineer regiment commander Saitō says the engineer and infantry patrols could hear the water making noise when enemy tanks and trucks crossed bridges, but they could not make out the spans, though they tried their hardest. While IJA bombers and ground parties did their best to wreck the bridges, enemy tanks, trucks, guns, and infantry continued to operate across the river with impunity. The survival of the spans was a source of unending "humiliation" to the Japanese.

Typical of the IJA demolition raids was the action of the Sakai regiment's 8th Company, which sent out 2nd Lt. Takayama Shōsuke with an engineer platoon and his own supporting infantry platoon on the afternoon of 8 July to attack a bridge across the Halha. After losing the two light tanks that had been sent to help, the Japanese—pinned down by enemy fire—could advance no more than two kilometers in the daylight. Takayama decided to wait for nightfall. Since direction-finding was difficult, the lieutenant took his 60 men to the north side of the Holsten Valley under the stars and then groped his way westward. The unit fought through a series of pickets, lost one man, and got to the broader and deeper Halha by about 2 A.M. on the 9th. Takayama let his soldiers gulp the water while he tried to figure out where the bridge was. In the distance, he could discern flashlights signaling to each other, back and forth across the stream. Obviously the enemy was having trouble, too, locating the bridge in the darkness. Takayama led his party toward the blinking lights.

Enemy troops were camped on sandbars in the wide river. Figures could be distinguished, but not identities, in the 20 meters of visibility. From a sandbar came a challenge in Russian. Takayama answered in pidgin Russian that it was a patrol returning from reconnaissance. The enemy's suspicions were not allayed. Slinking along the shore, the Japanese were followed by sentries for 30 to 40 meters. Takayama restrained his nervous men from firing and kept them moving toward the span. Apparently the Russians lost interest, for it must have seemed unbelievable to encounter Japanese inside the three or four defense lines of the Soviet bridgehead.

When he was 30 meters from the bridge, Takayama could make out two guards. The lieutenant hurled a grenade but, in his haste, he had forgotten to pull the pin, and the thud of the grenade brought the sentries running. Takayama's second grenade went off, killing both guards. Leaving seven men behind to cover him with light machine guns, the lieutenant and his raiders dashed onto the big bridge. It was close to 200 meters long and six meters wide, built of boards 7-8 cm. thick. The Japanese ran past the middle of the span and then came back, pouring gasoline from five-gallon jerricans and planting 10-cm. and 15-cm. squares of explosive every 10 or 15 meters. Back on shore, the attackers lit the trail of fuel with matches and blew the bridge sky-high at about 3 A.M. Despite drawing a flurry of machine-gun and small-arms fire from troops and trucks on the sandbanks, Takayama and his audacious team escaped unscathed. When the lieutenant recounted his party's exploits at 23rd Division headquarters, the division commander was delighted and the chief of staff shared sweet bean-jelly with him.

Takayama learned that his was only one of four engineer-infantry bridge-demolition teams dispatched from the two regiments that night. From the Sakai regiment's 6th Company, a platoon of 50 infantrymen had teamed up with 20 handpicked engineers led by 1st Lt. Amiya Kiichi—albeit without hoped-for tank support—to destroy a bridge over the Holsten. Commencing action well before the midnight attack to be launched by the main 72nd Regiment, Amiya's unit (like Takayama's) moved along the Holsten, used only sabers to eliminate two or three sentry outposts, and reached the bridge without loss by 1 A.M., just before the half-moon rose. This span was designed to be used by tanks. Log pilings had been driven into the riverbed, but boards were laid only on the edges of the bridge, twice the width of a tank's treads. The space between the edges of the bridge had been left open; the Russians "must have been conserving lumber," guessed engineer Amiya. Although the Holsten was narrow at this point, the bridge was about 100 meters long, for both shores were swampy.

Amiya's men planted 60 kilograms of yellow explosive at the center of the bridge, and detonated the charges electrically. A pillar of flame shot up, well over 100 meters high, and enemy tanks parked near the shore scattered in all directions. Amiya's team did not have to use the 40 kilograms of explosive that had been saved for antitank combat; "we were probably lucky, too," he admits. Escaping without loss, the raiders encountered the Sakai regiment sallying for the night attack along the same route taken by Amiya. Code words were exchanged, and no clash ensued in the dark. The demolition team wished the infantry well and headed back without incident.[26]

Komatsubara's original intention of dashing to the confluence was more than half a day behind schedule. Responding to Kobayashi's order received before 9 P.M., Sakai assembled his line commanders and, at 10:40, directed them to mop up the enemy on the right side of the Holsten in the confluence triangle and have the engineers blow up the bridges this night. The jump-off time, set for midnight, was met on schedule. Heading for Heights 733, Nishikawa's 1st Battalion advanced on the right, Kokura's 2nd Battalion advanced on the left, and the 4th Company guarded the rear. Unlike the preceding night, the moon was out, and the regiment was astounded to meet merely trifling hostile elements en route to the Holsten valley. In fact, according to the 1st Battalion aide, 1st Lt. Nomura Haruyoshi, the only difficulty encountered was in maintaining direction. For once, the Japanese aerial reconnaissance reports may have been correct in reporting that hostile forces in this area had been pulling back. But this was not the same as saying the Russians were abandoning their foothold on the right shore. Undoubtedly they were consolidating and adjusting their defensive deployments after the night combat of 7/8 July. At 7 P.M. on the 8th, Sakai had recorded intelligence that 300-400 enemy troops with armor were in the Holsten triangle, probably intending to launch a counterattack on the regimental sector.

By 2:30 A.M. on the 9th, Sakai's regiment reached the valley of the Holsten and got almost as far as the Halha. Gunfire and tank engines could be heard and tracers could be seen in the direction of the confluence, in Yamagata's adjoining sector. Instead of proceeding farther or keeping the whole regiment in possession of the objective, Sakai ordered a green starshell to be fired at 4:30 A.M., signaling "return to the jump-off site." Behind him, however, the colonel left 1st Lt. Moriyama Yasoichi's 7th Company, reinforced by a platoon each of infantry guns and heavy machine guns from the 1st Battalion, to conduct reconnaissance and provide a secure base for future offensive action.[27] The colonel said the regiment had "masterfully achieved its assigned mission" and had "finished cleaning up the enemy." But presumably he was deterred from staying too close to the river in force by the usual constraints: first, the tremendous Soviet artillery capacity by day; second, the inferior Japanese firepower; and third, the lower and hence disadvantageous terrain on the right bank. Thus, as we shall see, a steady but grueling pattern of IJA infantry action now emerged: first, penetration of enemy defenses during hours of darkness; then, withdrawal before daylight, leaving elements behind, ever closer to the river junction.

To the right of Sakai, on the night of 8 July, Yamagata's 64th Infantry commenced its attack even later, in general, than the 72nd Regiment. The exception was the 1st Battalion, off to the far right flank by itself, southwest of Heights 731. This battalion jumped off at 11 P.M.; by 1 A.M. it had reached its objective, the high ground north of 733, without encountering enemy forces. An officer patrol was sent forward to reconnoiter and, after dawn, a team was dispatched to regimental headquarters, east of Heights 733, to report on the completion of the mission.[28]

In general, then, almost no resistance was met on 8/9 July by Yamagata's flank battalion on the right or by both of Sakai's battalions on the left. Things were different in the center of the Left Wing Unit, where Yamagata's 2nd and 3rd battalions had to fight for any ground gained. Deployed at the front edge of Heights 733, the 2nd Battalion jumped off in the middle of the night, at 1:30 A.M. The first position to be encountered was a howitzer-battery site, which was overrun. Proceeding toward Mitsubosa (Three-Bush) Heights, by 3 or 3:30 A.M. the battalion seized the elevation, which Komatsubara placed as one kilometer east of the Halha. At 4 A.M., orders were received from the regiment to withdraw to the take-off location. The battalion got back at 5 A.M., having lost an officer and four men killed, and seven soldiers wounded in the night's combat. Enemy losses were given as 30 men cut down and two taken prisoner, plus the four 15-cm. howitzers, one tractor, and five trucks knocked out.

To the left, past 1 A.M. on 9 July the 3rd Battalion had gone over the top. Fierce resistance was encountered, replete with attacks and counterattacks, in the course of which the battalion commander, Major Fukumura, was wounded. The 3rd Battalion, too, had been given a bridge-demolition assignment. But whereas the Sakai regiment's raids succeeded, Yamagata's failed, for enemy defense of the confluence area seemed to be concentrated in this sector. Since the 10th Company could not make it to the bridge, it joined in the fighting waged by the parent battalion.[29]

Apart from the Sakai and Yamagata regiments and the Kajikawa battalion, two other infantry regiments were supposed to collaborate in the division's actions of 8/9 July: Sumi's 26th, north of the Holsten; and Okamoto's 71st, to the south. The Sumi regiment was still located four kilometers west of Heights 755 on the morning of the 8th. Maj. Kawai Jiichi's 2nd Battalion of the 26th Regiment arrived from Lake Manzute and rejoined the main body at 2 P.M. In accordance with Yasuoka's order of 6:50 P.M., Major Kawai's 2nd Battalion and the 3rd Battalion (temporarily commanded by 1st Lt. Kokubu Yoshio) got ready for a night attack under Kawai, supposedly in cooperation with the Sakai regiment. The rest of the 26th Infantry was to enter detachment reserve.

Operating behind Sakai, Major Kawai's force advanced easily during the night. As Lieutenant Negami says, "It was fun chasing after the enemy; we weren't thinking of the potential danger." The timing of the two regiments' movements was not synchronized. That Sakai was already returning, adds Negami, did not bother the Sumi unit, which plowed forward and lost its bearings several times. Sumi says he went up to reconnoiter with a couple of officers, got 1,500 meters ahead of the main body, and at one time found himself alone with the mosquitoes. Fortunately for him, the enemy had been pulling back all day north of the Holsten, well beyond Japanese close-quarter attack range. Sumi's troops took a number of Soviet positions and captured weapons, ammunition, and supplies. On the left flank, the only Russian was found, a wounded first lieutenant. The Japanese tried to seize him but he killed himself with a pistol. On his body were found a map, a manual, and other materials useful to IJA intelligence. When daybreak came, the only visible enemy positions were on the chrysanthemum-shaped dune (Kikugata) two kilometers south of Heights 733.[30]

South of the Holsten, on 8/9 July the 71st Infantry was supposed to strike the right rear of enemy forces confronting the Yasuoka detachment in the confluence sector. In mid-course, however, there had been a change of command. At 5 P.M. on the 7th, a plane had brought Col. Nagano Eiji (from the 8th Border Garrison Unit) to the front to take over the regiment, since Colonel Okamoto was scheduled to replace the slain Ōuchi as 23rd Division chief of staff. At 2 A.M. on 8 July, Nagano arrived at Okamoto's command post, where the two officers conferred. At 8:30 A.M., both colonels addressed the regiment.

A Japanese scout plane dropped a message tube at 10 A.M., directing the unit, now called the Nagano detachment, to capture Noro Heights and cooperate with the actions of the Yasuoka force, which had launched a night offensive on 7/8 July. At 1:25 P.M., Okamoto issued the last order in his capacity as regiment commander. Enemy forces on this front, he said, were very weak. Yasuoka's offensive was progressing nicely, and apparently his whole command was pressing the foe to the river junction. Baba's main 2nd Battalion, on the right flank, should attack north of Noro and seize the heights, while other elements occupied the dunes three kilometers to the northwest, in order to interdict the enemy's path of retreat. On the left, Murata's 3rd Battalion should take Noro from the south. After seizing their objectives, the infantry battalions should try to hold down losses inflicted by hostile artillery operating on the left bank of the Halha. Simultaneously with the foot soldiers' advance, the 1st Field Artillery Battalion should open supporting fire against Noro. Once the heights had been taken, the IJA batteries should deploy forward quickly and suppress enemy guns on the left shore of the Halha, especially pieces on the Yasuoka front. Manchukuoan forces were to assist the actions of the Japanese left flank. No specific times for the attack were announced yet.[31]

As usual, the 71st Regiment thought it was occupying positions farther west than was the case. Judging that it was located at Heights 758, the field artillery battalion opened fire at 4 P.M. against what was supposed to be Noro Heights. There was no response. Urged by the division to press its advance, the detachment started forward at 5:25 P.M. Immediately, the right flank was hit by severe artillery fire from across the Holsten. "The Yasuoka detachment," lamented the regimental chronicler, "does not seem to have made as much progress as we had been told." Enemy barrages cut communications at many points. After sundown, there was great confusion in conducting telephone liaison and bringing up supply trucks from the rear, especially because the locations of detachment headquarters and of subordinate units were not clear. Nevertheless, Colonel Nagano pressed forward. At 9:15 P.M. the 7th and 12th companies led the battalions in seizing high ground. It was still not Noro but Funagatayama, the "Boat-Shaped Hill." [32]

On 9 July, Komatsubara inspected the battlefield and visited Yasuoka and Kobayashi. The division commander was in an impressionable mood as he rode in his sedan to the Left Wing Unit's command post across a wide-open plain. By the pathway, he saw corpses of two Japanese soldiers sprawled in the sun, and eight dead, saddled horses, their legs in the air as if they were jumping. A 15-cm. cannon shell crashed nearby, kicking up dense smoke— undoubtedly the ordnance that had killed the soldiers and the horses. The scene reminded Komatsubara of an oil painting that hung in an art gallery in Moscow, depicting an old battlefield: a pale young warrior dead in the grass, with an arrow through the armor over his chest, while wild birds gorged on his dead horse. To the general, today's scene recalled the feelings engendered by the old one: "It tells of the misery of battle." [33]

As for the disconnected actions of 8/9 July, Komatsubara had mixed emotions. That demolition teams from the Sakai regiment had hit two enemy bridges was a source of gratification, but Nagano was even now not at Noro Heights and the night offensive north of the Holsten had not succeeded in general. The reasons, as Komatsubara saw them, were the lack of coordination between the 64th and 72nd regiments, and the fact that withdrawal instructions were issued at the same time as night-attack orders. In addition, the division's basic operations order had been issued at 3 P.M. but, since the jump-off time was not stipulated specifically, the offensive became disorganized and Yamagata, for example, did not commence action until 1 A.M. on the 9th. Although it was between four and six kilometers to the river, the Japanese did not reach the enemy defenses until 3 A.M. or so. Yet the troops had to get back to the jump-off site by sunrise, around 4 A.M. Given the tight time frame, they could not make it to the river. [34]

As Yasuoka put it, the hard-fighting units had pressed the foe to the shore, but small portions of the enemy remained active on the right side of the Halha because the Japanese had to return to their original locations. Within three days, the Soviet forces seemed to have regained their strength, after recovering from the shock of the first Japanese night attack and the loss of bridges during the second assault. In the face of increasingly vigorous Russian actions, the Japanese command decided upon a third night attack against the Heights 733 defenses north of the Holsten. At 1:40 P.M. on 9 July, Yasuoka ordered his detachment to resume the offensive and mete out a smashing blow. That night, elements of both wing units should seize key points on the Halha while teams reconnoitered and blew up the bridges remaining on the river. The Kajikawa force would come under Sumi's 26th Regiment, two of whose battalions were being transferred from the left to the right wing. Sumi, in turn, would be reinforced with a platoon of engineers from the 24th Regiment. Friendly artillery should neutralize hostile batteries below the Holsten.[35]

While steps were being taken to prepare the third night offensive by the infantry, there were important developments in the Japanese forward command structure on 9 July. Having decided to commit new heavy artillery and to dispense with the battered tank units, the Kwantung Army sent its chief of staff, Isogai, to coordinate plans and operations with Komatsubara. Notice of the deactivation of the Yasuoka detachment was transmitted to the 23rd Division, as we saw in Chapter 24, and Maj. Gen. Uchiyama Eitarō, the Kwantung Army's artillery commander, arrived at the divisional command post to come under Komatsubara's control in connection with the impending Japanese big-gun offensive.[36]

Upon receiving orders from the Yasuoka detachment on 9 July, Sumi transferred his available forces, essentially the 1st Battalion at this time, from the far left flank above the Holsten to Kajikawa's sector on the far right flank. Regiment headquarters and the 1st Battalion, under the temporary command of Capt. Kondō Kōjirō since the death of Major Adachi, reached the detachment command post at 5:40 P.M., where Sumi conferred with Yasuoka. He also met the Kajikawa battalion aide, 2nd Lt. Muranaka Shōichi, whom the major had sent to make arrangements after learning at midday that he was to come under Sumi's command. Muranaka guided the regiment in extended order to its destination, about 1,000 meters from the enemy. The terrain was made up of continuous irregular dunes 10 or 20 meters above the plain, pitted with conical dips, in a zone roughly one and a half kilometers wide by two kilometers deep. Sumi's troops began to dig, automatically, while the colonel peered through a scope in the direction of enemy machine-gun fire. An aide came to tell Sumi that his thigh-deep foxhole was ready, but the colonel was in more urgent need of a toilet pit at the moment.

It was clear to Kajikawa that his battalion was to constitute the far right wing but, from Muranaka's report, there was confusion about the exact line of deployment. Since Sumi thought the battalion was 1,500 meters behind the location he wanted to secure, Kajikawa had to go to the 26th Regiment command post to straighten out the discrepancy in map plots. Perhaps Sumi had not realized that Lieutenant Kijiya was at Hinomaru Heights, which the colonel could see was the anchor point on the right.

On Hinomaru, Kijiya's forward unit had undergone a pounding by artillery and had had to beat off attacks in the afternoon by two or three infantry companies (perhaps 300 men), five tanks, and a dozen guns. The lieutenant estimated that his men and the heavy weapons caused 100 casualties and knocked out two tanks. The Soviet assaults continued, however.[37]

At 8 P.M., Sumi decided to launch a twilight attack to occupy dunes 1,800 meters west of Heights 731. Enemy artillery, which intensified its action after sunset, seemed to have preregistered key targets, but it was not saturation fire, and the IJA infantry found it relatively easy to evade the clusters of rounds. The objective was taken by 9 P.M. Anxious to retain the initiative and control the high ground, Sumi wanted to move his lines 1,000 meters farther. The 1st Battalion was ordered to scout the area prior to a night attack scheduled for midnight. At the appointed time, Captain Kondō took the main force and headed for a dip on the south side of Hinomaru Heights. First Lt. Kimura Yoshio's 7th Company (from the 2nd Battalion) charged against fierce resistance and seized its objective at about 4 A.M. on the 10th but was unable to make contact with the Kajikawa battalion to its right. Sumi was certain that Kondō had succeeded by dawn; but the colonel says he was out of touch with the unit because of the complicated terrain and the heavy enemy fire.

In a correlated operation, Sumi had thrown the 2nd Company, temporarily commanded by Warrant Officer Fujii, directly against Hinomaru Heights. Seriously understrength after the combat on the left side of the Halha, the 33-man spearhead company had the toughest nut to crack. After conducting reconnaissance, the troops advanced 200 meters, hunching low and then crawling "like mink." About 30 enemy infantrymen and three armored cars were deployed in front, laying down accurate cannon and machine-gun fire. Although later reinforced by 2nd Lt. Hachida Takashi's little platoon of two heavy machine guns and ammunition men, the 2nd Company was pinned down in the moonlight. The Japanese sought shelter in tank trenches and waited for day to resume the attack under cover of the milky morning mist.

Some 50 to 100 enemy soldiers with three heavy and six light machine guns plus more than a dozen automatic rifles were concentrated on an elevation 700 meters to the southwest by dawn. At first light, the 2nd Company jumped off and dashed by bounds to the creased crestline. Zigzag trenches, two meters deep, cut the heights, approached by six or seven steps that terraced the slopes. Fighting his way into and back from the hornet's nest of Soviet defenses, Fujii lost 18 of his men, including the platoon sergeant. The Hachida machine-gun platoon, desperately trying to cover the pullback by the infantry remnants, was deployed disadvantageously on a bottom rung and was cut to pieces. Later it was estimated that no fewer than 300 enemy riflemen had been fed into this sector from a dip to the rear, from about 5:30 A.M. on the 10th.

Major Kawai's 2nd Battalion and First Lieutenant Kokubu's 3rd Battalion played no part in the Hinomaru-district action yet. Deployed near Kikugata Heights in the Sakai sector, these forces under Kawai's combined command came under attack in the evening of 9 July and had to fight their way back through the night. Further slowing their effort to rejoin the parent 26th Regiment was the fact that the battalions lost their way en route.[38]

Yamagata's 64th Regiment, to the left of Sumi, scheduled its own night offensive for 10 P.M. on 9 July. The task assigned to all battalions was the usual: eradicate enemy forces on the right shore of the Halha. The 2nd Battalion, ready by 10 P.M., jumped off an hour later. At midnight, the battalion was storming enemy lines. On the right front, the 5th Company took Mitsubosa Heights.

The 1st Battalion, which had been given the additional mission of helping the engineers to blow up a Soviet span over the Halha, set out at 10 P.M. as ordered. Breaking through sentry lines and gaps in the enemy defenses, the battalion headed for the confluence. At 1:40 A.M. on the 10th, near the river, 1st Lt. Someya Hatsuo's 4th Company was detached to cooperate with an engineer platoon in wrecking the bridge, covered by the main battalion. Proceeding through enemy lines and armor, the raiding party reached the crestline. Lights could be discerned 700 meters down the slope. Hostile infantry and about 20 armored vehicles were guarding the bridge. With day breaking, Someya aborted the mission.

Leaving the 2nd Company on the dunes northeast of the bridge as a "key-point occupation unit," the 1st Battalion withdrew to its original location a kilometer north of Heights 733 at 4:40 A.M. Soon afterward, it was learned that the 2nd Company was under attack. At 6 A.M., two enemy infantry companies and more than a dozen tanks, with artillery support, were engaging the 2nd Company. The 1st Battalion thereupon sent out a relief force— the 1st Company and a machine-gun platoon—and asked regimental headquarters for artillery help. By about 10 A.M. on 10 July, the enemy was reported to be in retreat.[39]

Whereas the Japanese right-wing forces—Sumi's regiment and Yamagata's 2nd and 3rd battalions in particular—met strong enemy resistance on 9/10 July, Sakai encountered negligible opposition on the left flank near Heights 733. Pursuant to the operational order received from Kobayashi at 6:30 P.M. on the 9th, the 72nd Regiment decided to employ Maj. Kokura Keiji's 2nd Battalion, supported by engineers for bridge-raiding, to conduct a night attack aimed at eliminating hostile forces clinging to the right shore of the confluence zone. To prevent enemy observation and incursion, the reinforced 8th Company should hold Kikugata Heights toward the junction, while infantry and machine guns from the 6th Company should occupy high ground two kilometers to the east, above the Holsten. The starting time was to be 11 P.M.

Enemy infantry and armor had been very active on the regimental front since morning, causing pronounced exhaustion among the Japanese troops. But, to the pleasant surprise of Kokura, his men met almost no hostile forces when they jumped off. The 8th Company and 2nd Lt. Hayama Tatsuo's platoon from the 6th Company were detached without difficulty to secure their designated objectives. Kokura's main battalion headed back, as was now the practice, at 4:15 A.M. on the 10th. Around dawn, however, enemy units began to counterattack, the Japanese explanation being that they must have come back again from the left bank. Of particular importance, Soviet artillery strength was built up steadily on the right shore and "came to interfere greatly with our combat."[40]

Not only had the Japanese been anxious to eliminate the Soviet bridges, but as early as 6 July the 23rd Division had also called for the engineers to throw a span of their own across the upstream Holsten River. An effort to do the job on 8 July was thwarted by the enemy, but on the 9th, men from the 23rd Engineers, using two pontoons, succeeded in building a 20-meter span that became known as Kōheibashi or Engineer Bridge.[41]

There are obvious connections between the 23rd Division's desire for its own bridge over the Holsten and the increasing attention paid to Japanese actions south of that river. As of 9 July, Colonel Nagano was still unaware of the situation on the Yasuoka detachment's front. To the left of his own regiment, Nagano heard from the Manchukuoan cavalry division that there were now 30-40 hostile armored vehicles in addition to the 200-300 infantry reported earlier. At 8 A.M., an artillery exchange began. Tractor-towed enemy field artillery had appeared, and 15-cm. howitzers were emplaced across the Holsten.

Needed rations arrived for the 71st Infantry. But though the days were very hot, the water-supply unit was not providing sufficient drinking water, so the troops drew as much water as they could for themselves and the horses directly from the Holsten seven kilometers to the north. Indeed, one party headed an equal distance to the west, reached the Halha triangle, frolicked in that river, came under fire, lost their horses, and straggled back.

At 1 P.M. on the 9th, the divisional logistics staff officer, Captain Itō, visited Nagano's command post to convey Komatsubara's intentions plus news of the impending IJA artillery offensive, and to present a sanguine interpretation of the current battle situation. This optimism is reflected in the order that Nagano issued at 2 P.M.: matters had been developing favorably on Yasuoka's front, to the extent that elements of the detachment had already pushed to the confluence. The enemy facing the Nagano force was very weak and had been losing fighting spirit since morning. Nagano's main body, centering on Baba's 2nd Battalion and supported by the field artillery, would attack the foe on the dunes three kilometers northwest of Noro Heights. Murata's 3rd Battalion was to occupy Noro itself and the area to the southwest, screening the left flank of Nagano's offensive. Once the objectives were taken, the regiment should pursue without letup, sending a reinforced infantry company westward to Kui (691) Heights immediately.

At 3:40 P.M., however, a friendly scout plane dropped word from the division chief of staff that the Nagano unit was still mistaken about its location—that it was in the Heights 758 area, not one kilometer east of Noro. Since this correction agreed with a recommendation made by the 5th Company commander (Capt. Nishimura Taizō), Nagano adjusted his attack plan to reflect the greater distances involved. Meanwhile, enemy activity increased markedly, and several tanks approached the Japanese positions at 5:50 P.M. *Nikuhaku* ("human bullet") teams knocked out two machines.

Even after the Nagano unit launched its night attack on 9/10 July, the troubles with location were by no means ended. Driving off enemy elements, the battalions advanced. At 1:55 A.M., the 3rd Battalion stormed high ground deemed to be Noro Heights at last. Alas, it was still only Heights 758, three kilometers away. The 2nd Battalion seized a similarly misperceived objective, and Nagano's headquarters merely arrived atop Funagatayama, which had been taken by forward infantry the preceding night.

Nagano did not abandon the idea of the thrust to Kui Heights, another four kilometers to the west. Captain Nishimura objected strenuously. The coming of daylight would expose his isolated 5th Company to enemy artillery's domination and to possible annihilation, evoking painful memories of the fatal mission assigned to Azuma's unit in May. Nagano was not unmoved. Still, the message sent by the 23rd Division on the afternoon of the 9th not only had tried to correct the Nagano regiment's location but also had said, "The Yasuoka detachment is continuing the offensive. Your unit should force the attack too." Nagano interpreted this to mean that he had no leeway—that Kui Heights must be seized, using the full strength of the regiment if necessary, and even at the risk of losing the whole Nishimura company. Therefore, wrote the regimental chronicler, Colonel Nagano "gave a stern and cold order to company commander Nishimura and his men to die for Kui Heights, and he sent them on their way." Reinforced by a platoon each of heavy machine guns and rapid-fire weapons, Nishimura advanced in the moonlight toward Kui, supposedly "in high spirits," reaching his objective by dawn. There had been no resistance yet, but on the morning of 10 July the regiment received a radio message from Nishimura to the effect that there were 20 enemy tanks, 100 infantrymen, and 10 trucks at Kui Heights.[42]

Regarding the progress of the night attacks of 9/10 July, Yasuoka knew only that the various units had begun action from about 9 P.M. Afterward, communication lines were cut, and 10 July came with the detachment commander in ignorance of the front-line situation. During the morning, Yasuoka heard that his Left Wing Unit had reached the confluence, had posted elements to guard key points, and had pulled back the main forces and concentrated them in the rear. Maj. Gen. Kobayashi seems to have been less than pleased with the results of the latest night operation in his subordinate corps command.[43]

Komatsubara, however, apparently thought the Russians on the right bank of the Halha had been weakened very seriously by the Japanese infantry's nightly attacks. Consequently, at 7 P.M. on 10 July, the division commander issued an operational order calling for the "mop-up" of enemy forces in all sectors.[44] This outlook helps to explain the overoptimistic estimates underlying the Kwantung Army's decision to deactivate the Yasuoka detachment and even to thin out the 23rd Division at the front. Despite the mishandling of the matter by Tsuji and Hattori, the Japanese tank units were pulled out, and Komatsubara set about restructuring his forces to incorporate those elements that Yasuoka would not be taking back to Kungchuling.

On the far right flank, Kajikawa's battalion was in close contact with the enemy on 10 July. At Hinomaru Heights, in particular, Lieutenant Kijiya's men repulsed infantry and tank attacks while withstanding constant artillery barrages that deformed the high ground. Later, Kajikawa personally commended his "Hinomaru unit." Overhead, around 1 P.M., dozens of Soviet and Japanese fighter planes engaged in dogfights, regarded in silence and awe by the ground troops on both sides. White parachutes could be seen floating "like jellyfish" in the sky. At 4 P.M., Kajikawa learned that another night attack was scheduled. Smoke was laid down at twilight to screen the offensive advance by Kondō's battalion on the adjoining Sumi front. Kajikawa also used smoke when his own battalion charged forward at 11 P.M. The objective was reached by 12:30 A.M., against almost no resistance.[45]

On the morning of the 10th, Sumi was pleased to receive messages congratulating the 26th Infantry for its successful action the preceding night from Yasuoka (who was relinquishing command of the two wing units) and from the 23rd Division chief of staff. All day, though the enemy infantry was relatively quiet, Sumi's positions were bombarded by artillery emplaced across the Halha. The colonel ordered his regiment to resume the attack that night at 11 P.M.[46]

To the left of Sumi, Yamagata's regiment was anxious to blow up the Halha bridge at the confluence, having failed to do so till now. At 9 P.M., the 1st Battalion was again given the task on 10 July, with infantry and machine guns assigned to support an engineer demolition platoon and an infantry team assigned to raid an enemy tank laager. The whole operation bogged down in the face of tenacious resistance. Engineer scouts reported that the enemy bridge was much too strong to be blown up by the meager explosives—portable mines—which the Japanese sappers were carrying. The senior officer, machine-gun unit Capt. Funakura Eishirō, called off the mission. Once again, the 64th Regiment could not wreck a bridge.[47]

The 72nd Regiment, which had had success against the river spans, tried again on the night of 10 July. Orders were issued for infantry and machine-gun support of an engineer raiding platoon, but the sappers failed to find their target and came back empty-handed before daylight.[48]

On the Nagano front, enemy aerial activity was pronounced on the 10th—a day of broiling heat south of the Holsten. But, according to the chronicler, the 71st Regiment felt that it was "getting good" at distinguishing between hostile and friendly aircraft (from their whirring sound) and automatic weapons (from their rapidity and noise of fire). At 8:20 in the morning, word came from the division that, although the enemy on the right side of the Halha had been almost destroyed by the severe Japanese assaults, artillery on the left shore was still vigorous. The division planned to knock out those batteries upon the arrival of its own artillery reinforcements. All units should cooperate with the firing preparations of the artillery corps, while getting ready for further advances and the cleaning up of the remaining enemy forces.

In drafting his regimental order at 9 A.M., Nagano added that his own unit had nearly wiped out hostile elements below the Holsten. The infantry battalions should continue their offensive, especially now that the remaining foe was observed to be in retreat. In addition to cooperating with the "clearing" operations, the field artillery battalion should suppress enemy forces facing the Yasuoka detachment, especially those near the confluence bridge. As for the Nishimura company at Kui Heights, it should come under Nagano's direct control, interdict the enemy's retreat route near the Halha bridge and near Kui, and try to "trap the defeated foe." The Manchukuoan forces were to move up to Kui and "cooperate positively," as they were instructed to do when a liaison officer arrived at 9:45 A.M. from the Hsingan division.

From 11 A.M. on 10 July, small-arms fire emanated from Nagano's left flank. There was no enemy artillery bombardment, however, and only skirmishes occurred throughout the day. At 2:30 P.M., the 9th Company commander, on the left flank, reported signs of an enemy attack by two infantry companies, six motorized artillery pieces, and two heavy machine guns. Nagano sent word to the field artillery battalion and ordered his line companies to be on strictest guard. The enemy assaults, along the whole Nagano front, came at midnight. Soviet shouts of "Hurrah!" could be heard at 800 meters' distance, but the enemy hugged the ground and approached no closer than 300 meters in general. Strong forces, however, did penetrate as far as the right front of Nagano's headquarters location at 3 A.M. on the 11th, until beaten off by the regimental guns. Fighting continued all morning.[49]

On 11 July, the men of the Kajikawa battalion on the extreme right of the front, like the Japanese soldiers on the other sectors, were delighted to hear that IJA heavy artillery was arriving soon and would squelch the baneful Soviet batteries across the Halha. "We yearned for our artillery's fire against the barking enemy," said Lieutenant Takashima. The day before, he was "saved by a hair" when a Russian shell had exploded and buried him under a mound of sand and soil. Worse took place near Kobayashi's command post to the south on the 11th: an enemy 15-cm. cannon projectile hit a Japanese 12-cm. ammunition truck and blew apart the vehicle and 13 gunners.

At Hinomaru Heights, 11 July opened and closed with enemy bombardments. Pinned in the trenches, Takashima could guess what Verdun must have been like. In frustration, he wished the troops could launch a charge and "get it over with," winning or losing the battle right away. Meanwhile, somebody in his unit had located a puddle of water, and a party went out to get some. Sniped at by 15-cm. howitzers on the way back, the team juggled the biscuit cans it was using and got back with the water. Soviet troops, who in the meantime had drawn as close to Hinomaru as 400 meters, could be detected laboring on defenses. Japanese heavy machine guns and battalion guns smashed the enemy machine guns and shot at the work parties. The IJA firing, however, exposed friendly positions and drew severe artillery counterfire. One Japanese three-man patrol, sent out for liaison, lost its bearings, blundered into a Russian machine-gun emplacement, and barely got away.[50]

Throughout the day, portions of Sumi's 26th Infantry continued to straggle back from their old locations in the Sakai zone. Other elements were still lost en route to the regimental command post at Heights 731. Sumi's main body repulsed attacks by an estimated two enemy infantry companies. When Kokubu's 3rd Battalion headquarters arrived with one and a half of its companies by 8 P.M., Sumi ordered the battalion to attack Kōmoriyama ("Bat-Shaped Hill") that very night. Jumping off at 9 P.M., the unit took the elevation an hour later.[51]

To Kobayashi, however, the elimination of enemy bridges was still essential to clear the right shore, especially in the Yamagata regiment sector, where demolition efforts had failed two nights in a row. At 11:30 A.M. on 11 July, having convinced Komatsubara, General Kobayashi ordered the 64th Regiment to hurl its entire strength into a night attack against the Heights 733 sector, assisted by elements of the Sakai regiment. Yamagata issued his operational order at 3 P.M., calling for the infantry to wipe out the bridgehead downstream from the junction and for the attached engineer company to handle the actual bridge-demolition assignment. On the right flank, the 1st Battalion, commanded temporarily by Capt. Sonoshita Zenzō, had donned its white crossbands for ease of identification in the dark and was ready by 10 P.M. It had to wait for the main regiment to catch up by jump-off time, already pushed back to 10:30 P.M. Unfortunately for the unit, the main body got lost and could not make it until midnight, setting back the offensive until 2 A.M. on the 12th.

Taking advantage of terrain cover and breaking through gaps in the Russian positions, the 1st Battalion passed such eerie remains of Azuma's defeat in May as saddles and mess tins. In the mist before daylight, birds began to screech in unison, and lights could be seen dimly at the enemy bridge. There were food and ammunition dumps in many places, and the tread marks of tanks and trucks were visible throughout the area. Soviet armor detected the Japanese sappers, the 1st Battalion charged against the bridgehead, and all hell broke loose. Two of the tanks were knocked out by suicide teams. Taken by surprise, the enemy troops and armor fell back to the span in confusion. At this auspicious stage for the Japanese, regimental headquarters was at last on the edge of the high ground on the right shore of the Halha, and the 1st Battalion was by itself, 1,500 meters on the downslope from the confluence, as the skies brightened.

Exploiting crests and dips, elements of the 1st Battalion got as close as 500 meters from the river, but 30 Soviet armored vehicles guarding the bridge pinned down the Japanese at 4:30 A.M. A half-hour later, two enemy infantry companies with 15 tanks and armored cars launched a counterattack from high ground on the left. While the 2nd Company and the rapid-fire guns engaged the foe, four enemy artillery pieces hit the 4th Company from the flank and rear, causing heavy casualties. Trying to cover the engineer raiders, the 1st Battalion dug in and returned the fire. On the right, the 1st Company was counterattacked by infantry and armor concentrated on the north side of the bridgehead. The Japanese rapid-fire guns struck back at the swarming tanks and armored cars but were hammered, in turn, by hostile artillery emplaced across the Halha. Two IJA guns were smashed, and their crews annihilated. When one enemy tank was stopped by gunfire and set ablaze by fire bottles, the Japanese "felt fine" and yelled "*Banzai!*" Another cheer ensued when two Soviet crewmen were cut down by saber and bayonet.

The engineers were approaching the span from downstream when they encountered two groups of 50 armored vehicles each, defending the bridgehead. Gunfire struck and blew up most of the explosives carried by the engineers.[52] The survivors had no choice but to fall back and rejoin the infantry at 6 A.M. The 1st Battalion sought to veer to the left, where the 2nd Battalion had been advancing. Radioing its situation to Yamagata, the 1st Battalion requested a full-scale supporting attack by the whole regiment; "but matters did not proceed as we wished."

Enemy riflemen, covered by tanks and armored cars, had by now encircled the 1st Battalion. Soviet reinforcements arrived steadily, and artillery barrages continued from the high ground, especially after daybreak. Rashly disclosing its emplacements by responding, 2nd Lt. Oki Tadashi's rapid-fire battery and its two remaining guns were demolished by counterbombardment. One Japanese gun barrel could be seen shattered; the other wrecked piece had toppled over, its wheels in the air. Grenade battles raged at distances of 30 to 50 meters, close enough to hear Russian voices, as the survivors gathered in dips. At one point, the Japanese saw yellow smoke, mistakenly thought they were under gas attack, and donned gas masks. Even three Soviet flame-throwing tanks entered action. The din of battle was literally deafening. Dying or wounded soldiers lay pleading for water or groaning. Little movement was possible throughout 12 July.[53]

Kobayashi's battle plan for 11-12 July had placed the main emphasis on the 64th Regiment's front, with Sakai advancing his positions to assist Yamagata on his right and link up with Nagano across the Holsten on his left. The latter sector was particularly troublesome to the 72nd Regiment because the Nagano detachment's advance to the shore of the Holsten was behind schedule, thus leaving Sakai's unit exposed to flank fire by enemy tanks and machine guns from across that stream. Sakai issued an order at 2 P.M. on the 12th detaching the 7th Company, a squad of heavy machine guns, and an engineer demolition platoon to support the 64th Regiment's night actions from 10 P.M. by helping to knock out the strong enemy bridge near the river junction. Meanwhile, the Russians had attacked the 8th Company, the "river-bank security unit" on Kikugata Heights, at 1 P.M. and again at 7 P.M. The company fought off the assaults, using regimental and rapid-fire guns to repulse the second attack by 100 soldiers and 10 armored vehicles.

Emplaced to the east of Kikugata, Lieutenant Hayama's isolated little platoon of 38 men was hit particularly hard from the morning of the 11th. Around 5:30 P.M., the enemy made one final offensive effort, employing several dozen infantrymen and three tanks. The situation "grew critical," and Hayama sent his classified battle map back to the company commander to prevent its falling into hostile hands. Fighting desperately, Hayama and his men beat off the last assault by 6:20 P.M.

But even after the strenuous combat of the day, Hayama was not through. Donning the uniform of an enlisted man and carrying a rifle, that night he took two noncoms and went out on a deep and daring reconnaissance patrol. First he swung left, around the flank of the Soviet forces facing his platoon; then he penetrated the defense lines at the bridgehead and made it all the way to the Halha. At the confluence, he observed no fewer than three enemy crossing points. Taking the difficult way back, the lieutenant sneaked through the rear of the Russian positions facing the Japanese troops at Kikugata Heights and other enemy emplacements facing his own platoon toward the east. At 5 A.M. on the 12th, Hayama's patrol got back safely and transmitted its findings to battalion headquarters to the rear. Just north of the crossings at the confluence there were 20 enemy tanks, 70-80 soldiers, and 35 trucks. Immediately opposite the Hayama platoon, the Russians had deployed two tanks, 20 infantrymen, and two heavy machine guns. In the Kikugata area, a company from the 71st Regiment (Nishimura's company, although Colonel Nagano did not know about it yet) had reinforced elements of 1st Lt. Ōtake Sakae's 8th Company of the 72nd Regiment.

Meanwhile, "catching the enemy unawares," the Sakai regiment's 1st Battalion had displaced forward on the right at twilight, followed by the 2nd Battalion and regimental headquarters on the left at 10 P.M. Some 400 meters beyond the old lines, the units proceeded to dig in.[54]

On Nagano's front south of the Holsten, regimental guns and grenade launchers were instrumental in finally forcing the immediate enemy to withdraw by 11:30 A.M. on 11 July, after hard fighting. Toward 4:30 P.M., there were signs that the foe holding a line 1,000 meters away was starting to pull back. Nagano ordered his regimental guns and the field artillery to fire. The latter used mainly shrapnel shells because the "common rounds" were mislabeled.

Of particular concern to Nagano was the fate of his Nishimura company, which he had "forced" to advance to Kui Heights on 9/10 July. During the interim, much of the regiment's wireless network had become inoperable—destroyed by gunfire, thwarted by terrain or breakdowns. In any case, nothing had been heard from Nishimura since evening on the 10th. Next day, Nagano ordered out a patrol of five infantry noncoms under a machine-gun company commander, 1st Lt. Takada Kiyomi, to seek the whereabouts of Nishimura. That night, Takada's party infiltrated the confusing no-man's-land around Kui. No trace of Nishimura and his men was found. Takada returned and reported that the 5th Company was "missing in action."

Nagano assembled his commanders late on the 11th and gave them their missions for next day. Although the overall situation was "developing favorably," hostile forces facing the regiment were increasing again and artillery across the river was domineering. The Nagano unit would press the enemy toward the confluence, destroy the bridge north of the sandbar (*nakanoshima* in Japanese) in the Halha as requested by the division, and try to rescue the Nishimura company. Specifically, the 2nd Battalion should attack Kui on the right flank, mop up the enemy, beware of hostile artillery, and look for Nishimura. Advancing in parallel, the 3rd Battalion should do much the same on the left and assume the additional task of sending suicide teams by night to destroy the bridge with gasoline and grenades. The starting time for the offensive was set for 6 P.M., and the reserve elements should be especially careful to guard the regimental colors. In addition to advancing the observation posts of the field artillery and the regimental guns as far to the front as possible, Nagano was asking the division to try to suppress enemy batteries across the river, and to deploy the Manchukuoan screening forces to the left.

Unknown to Nagano, Captain Nishimura had taken his company across the Holsten, probably because there was a much greater danger to Ōtake's 8th Company (from the 72nd Regiment) in the vicinity of Kikugata Heights than there was at Kui south of the river. Since the search party sent by Nagano had found no evidence of Nishimura at Kui on the night of 11/12 July, the captain's company must have forded the Holsten during the preceding night—no difficult task, of itself, since the stream was shallow and only about 10 meters wide. Ōtake's unit had been pounded hard since the 11th. Trying to defend its positions, the company incurred very heavy casualties and became "utterly helpless." To help Ōtake as well as to get behind the enemy forces undoubtedly accounts for Nishimura's decision.

From early morning, presumably on the 11th, the Nishimura company came under serious attack. At midday the unit found itself completely isolated, without communications, and short of ammunition, food, and water. By 4 P.M., facing annihilation of his company, Nishimura ordered the destruction of confidential documents and of the top-secret IJA gas masks,[55] and waited for the end to come. Nevertheless, his unit eventually managed to fend off its crisis by launching close-quarter assaults against the enemy's armored vehicles.[56]

26

Stealth Suspended

Japanese division headquarters had lost its communications on the night of the 11th. Regarding the operations of 11/12 July, Komatsubara understood only that the night attacks had progressed smoothly in general, although the Yamagata regiment had run into about two enemy infantry battalions and 150-60 armored vehicles, and thus had not been able to reach the confluence bridge by daylight. Kobayashi learned, however, that Yamagata's main force had got lost on its way to join the 1st Battalion, and had held up the offensive by more than three hours. From Yamagata's sector, Kobayashi could hear increasing gunfire after 3 A.M. on the 12th. With the coming of daybreak, the bridge-demolition mission had not been accomplished, and night action had been succeeded by daylight combat. That morning, after being visited by Komatsubara, Kobayashi observed the status of the ground fighting at firsthand when he went to help Yamagata. Painful messages reached the regimental command post all day from the 1st Battalion, to the effect that the unit was undergoing counterattacks and was taking considerable casualties.[1]

Indeed, Yamagata's 64th Infantry sustained no fewer than five counterattacks on the 12th and incurred severe casualties. Enemy artillery pounded the Japanese entrenchments clawed from the slopes near the Halha. Foxholes collapsed under the bombardment. Machine gunners and infantrymen who raised their heads were picked off by snipers. The existence of a unit could only be confirmed by the men's yelling to each other. Near sundown, with enemy tanks and infantry closing to 200 meters on the 3rd Company's sector, and with soldiers falling on all sides after being hit in the head by gunfire, 2nd Lt. Miura Akira decided to preempt the foe by charging from the trenches. "Anybody who survives this," he said to the vestige of Japanese infantrymen, "try to cut off at least one of my fingers and take it back with you." The troops responded, "*Tennō heika banzai!*" Miura shouted back an even louder cheer, jumped over the top, and charged to his death.[2]

The Ise field artillery regiment's 3rd Battalion, commanded by Maj. Seki Takeshi, had not been able to assist the infantry (or, as the artillery put it, they had not been asked to fire) during the night of 11/12 July. When artillery signalmen finally laid 4,000 or 5,000 meters of telephone wire to the 64th Regiment in the morning, Yamagata was so pleased that he gave the lieutenant in charge a precious bottle of cider. Another 1,000 or 2,000 meters of wire had to be strung to 1st Battalion headquarters. The Japanese rapid-fire guns had been wrecked by now, and artillery support was badly needed. At 1:40 P.M., Capt. Kusaba Sakae's 7th and Capt. Imoto Kazuichi's 8th batteries finally brought the enemy's underwater bridge under fire. Fragments could be seen flying up from the river, and armored vehicles no longer came across.

Capt. Kai Mansuke's 9th Battery, equipped with 12-cm. howitzers whose maximum range was only 5,500 meters, could not reach targets at the confluence when it conducted test-firing. At 3:40 P.M., the 7th and 8th batteries opened up for two minutes of concentrated bombardment against Soviet 15-cm. howitzers south of the bridge, and claimed to have silenced them. When the hostile guns resumed firing at 4:40, the 7th Battery responded, causing the enemy artillerymen to abandon their pieces, the gunners boarding trucks and departing. One Japanese shell was seen to hit a fleeing truck. At 6:30 P.M., the three IJA batteries smashed an attack by 200 infantrymen against Yamagata's front. Another assault by tanks and 300 soldiers attacking in the Mitsubosa area on the adjoining Sakai regiment sector was checked by two batteries at 7 P.M.[3]

As a Japanese soldier remembers it, with the coming of darkness on 12 July almost all of his platoon had been killed or seriously wounded. The enemy tanks and infantry were "going as strong as ever." "Those of us who were still breathing, or who could walk, called to each other and waited for the opportunity to launch a last charge." But "for some reason" the enemy withdrew, their tank treads clanking noisily as they went. One explanation may have been the mid-range effectiveness of Ise's artillery batteries.[4]

Earlier on the 12th, Komatsubara had received a congratulatory message from Kwantung Army commander Ueda: "I am delighted that you have chastised the Outer Mongolian and Soviet forces by your swift and appropriate operations, secured the frontier, and achieved brilliant combat results; and I thank you for your efforts. May I also take this occasion to express my deepest reverence to the spirits of the officers and men who were killed in action." Against the backdrop of Ueda's commendation, Komatsubara reached a reluctant but important decision that day: to abandon the use of infantry to get to the river, and to wait for the arrival and deployment of the Japanese heavy artillery. A mighty general offensive would then eliminate the Soviet bridgehead and neutralize the batteries across the Halha.

This strategic thinking undoubtedly dominated the conversation that Komatsubara had with Kobayashi when he visited the infantry group headquarters on the morning of the 12th. There were a number of contributing considerations. By the evening of the 11th, Komatsubara learned, Japanese casualties had reached 1,470—an increase of 300 since the 9th. Some 250 horses had been killed, 261 were injured, and 69 were missing. Despite the constant talk of enemy retreat, the Yamagata regiment alone had just encountered as many as 200 armored vehicles and a couple of infantry battalions. The river bridges had not been blown up, and hostile artillery was firing unimpeded from the left shore. On 12 July, one shell had already exploded in a dip at Kobayashi's command post, killing six signalmen and wounding two, as well as slaying 12 horses. Enemy spotters were known to have stayed far behind, in the area of the Japanese headquarters, to guide Soviet artillery fire by telephone and by the use of signal pistols. Some of these men were living in holes.[5]

Kobayashi cannot have been surprised when division staff officer Murata arrived in the afternoon with Komatsubara's instructions to pull back every unit to the location of the main regiments, leaving no advance elements near the river. The appropriate operations order was issued promptly by infantry group headquarters at 5 P.M. But Yamagata, in Kobayashi's words, "did not go along with it easily." In fact, the colonel made a recommendation (*iken gushin*) against pulling back to the jump-off site immediately. His troops were "a stone's throw" from the confluence already, only one or one and a half kilometers north of it. With one more night attack, they would certainly make it to the Halha and destroy the bridge.[6] In view of the regiment's repeated efforts and heavy expenditure in casualties, Yamagata's resistance is understandable, but he could not prevail upon his superiors to yield.

By 10 P.M., Yamagata had bowed to the pressure exerted on him and reluctantly issued his operations order. Hostile forces on the right shore of the Halha, he began, had been overwhelmed by the regiment's very powerful offensive. But the 23rd Division was planning to annihilate the enemy still on the right bank plus the batteries across the river "in one fell swoop," which necessitated waiting for the commitment of all of the Japanese artillery reinforcements. Front-line units were thus to secure those points they had held before the night attacks toward the confluence, and were to prepare for future offensive action. Now, as of the night of 12/13 July, all forward units and river-security elements were to cease their attacks and, under cover of darkness, to return to the location of the parent body.[7]

At 11 P.M. the forwardmost 1st Battalion received the order to pull its units together, retrieve its casualties, and prepare to withdraw from the river area. Except for sentry troops, all of the surviving able-bodied officers and men picked up as many dead and wounded as they could—about 160 in total—and carried them to the rear of the positions by 2:30 A.M. Those corpses that could not be moved were buried for the time being. But when the 1st Battalion got back to the site of the regimental command post, the headquarters had left already. Joining the 2nd Battalion, the Japanese troops headed sadly back at 4:30 A.M. There was some enemy artillery fire, but no further losses were incurred. When a small hostile force pursued, the Japanese dug in and checked the foe, while administering first aid to the wounded. As Komatsubara noted in his diary, since Yamagata's men had reached point-blank distance from the enemy, the need to disengage delayed the pullback, and they did not return until 6 A.M. on the 13th.[8]

Yamagata's total casualties on 11-13 July, evacuated or not, were reported to be 79 killed, 167 wounded, and 10 or 20 missing. In the 1st Battalion alone, there had been 212 casualties since 7 July—about half the unit's strength. Someya's 4th Company of approximately 100 men was down to 15 able-bodied soldiers by 14 July; 38 had been killed. In the 3rd Battalion, the 10th Company suffered 30 casualties; the 12th Company, 40. In all, the Yamagata regiment had lost about one-third of its strength in the fighting between 7 and 12 July. Four Japanese machine guns and four rapid-fire guns had been knocked out during the night attack of 11/12 July. But enemy losses were said to have been severe on that night—300 abandoned corpses, and 45 armored vehicles and three antitank guns knocked out. Eight Soviet artillery pieces and 10 machine guns were captured.[9]

To the left of Yamagata, the main body of the Sakai regiment occupied its new lines and reinforced its works on 12 July. Enemy bombardments cut communications at many points. Lieutenant Hayama continued to cling to his advanced positions. At 3 P.M., when word was received that the Yamagata regiment was in trouble, Sakai took steps to send assistance. Soon afterward, however, at 5:20 P.M., the new order arrived from Kobayashi. But whereas Yamagata had been told to return to his original location, Sakai was directed to secure the present line in general. The 72nd Regiment therefore called off plans to destroy the Halha bridge north of the Nakanoshima sandbar, below the confluence. Ōtake's 8th Company, the riverbank occupation unit, was to pull back to its parent battalion's area during the night. Each battalion should secure key points in front of its positions. In keeping with this injunction, at 10:30 P.M. the 2nd Battalion sent an infantry company to occupy high ground behind Hayama's defenses, to backstop the lieutenant's indomitable platoon.

Although higher headquarters had suspended further offensive operations for the time being, Sakai apparently regarded tactical adjustments as acceptable. At 7 P.M., the 2nd Battalion was directed to launch a night attack against Mitsubosa Heights, on the 1st Battalion front, after preparatory artillery fire. The 5th Company drew the assignment, jumped off at 9 P.M., and encountered unexpectedly strong resistance, especially grenades. Responding with captured Maxim machine guns, the Japanese inflicted heavy casualties before returning at 5 A.M. on the 13th. Meanwhile, Lieutenant Hayama conducted two more deep reconnaissance patrols, returned safely, and submitted very helpful reports.

Whereas the Yamagata regiment had lost about one-third of its effectives by the time the night attacks were suspended, Sakai's 72nd Infantry had been reduced by about one-fifth after the battles of 5-10 July. That is to say, from participants numbering 1,600, the regiment lost seven officers and 100 men killed, and 10 officers and 211 men wounded, for a total of 328 casualties.[10]

Sumi, to the right of Yamagata, dispatched a rapid-fire gun battery at 8 A.M. on the 12th to reinforce the 3rd Battalion on newly captured Kōmori (Bat) Heights. Although the guns knocked out an armored car, enemy tanks followed by 200 riflemen counterattacked the battalion. In the afternoon, one of Sumi's machine-gun and two of his infantry companies finally reached the regiment from their previous locations on the left wing. One of the straggling companies, the 9th, now in the line, was hit that very night by Soviet tanks, machine guns, and foot troops. Learning from the recent tragedy of a platoon that had charged into an ambush and been wiped out, the 9th Company repressed its impulse to counterattack, waited for the enemy to come within hand-grenade range, and withstood the assaults.[11]

The Kajikawa battalion, beyond Sumi on the right wing, was pounded by artillery for an hour after 9 A.M. on 12 July. Kajikawa's heavy machine guns and battalion guns responded. During the day, the latter claimed to have knocked out one enemy artillery piece and two machine guns. A liaison lieutenant arrived from Sumi's headquarters, conveying instructions for Kajikawa to send a squad to the Heights 673 area, six kilometers below the confluence, to ascertain whether a crossing existed there. If so, the squad should secure the shore. Having sent a series of patrols to the region from the outset, Kajikawa already knew the answer, but he dispatched yet another patrol and later reported in detail to Sumi that there was no place to cross near Heights 673 and no trace of enemy movement in the area. Because of the recent rise in the water level, the river banks were soggy and difficult to traverse by armor. As of the 12th, the Halha's depth was 1.3 meters—impossible to ford on foot.[12]

To the south of the Holsten, Colonel Nagano finally learned at 10:45 A.M. on 12 July what had happened to the vanished Nishimura company. A warrant officer sent by Nishimura broke through to report that the company had crossed to the north side of the Holsten and was fighting hard at the rear of the enemy forces facing the main body of the division. "I was relieved at last," said Nagano, "but it was unfortunate that actions exceeding the assigned mission had been undertaken." For a while, wireless messages began to be received from Nishimura. According to one, a prisoner had revealed that enemy tank groups and some 6,000 troops were going to launch a general offensive shortly. Communications were lost again soon afterward.

At 12:45 P.M., Nagano modified the operations order he had devised the night before. The Nishimura unit, he commenced, "has penetrated deeply into the enemy area and is isolated, but it has been persistently and aggressively pursuing its mission and is fighting strenuously." For the impending twilight attack by the 71st Regiment, the 2nd Battalion should concentrate gradually, strike its target, and quickly relieve the Nishimura company, which would revert to regimental reserve. The 3rd Battalion, after reaching its objective, should leave the 12th Company to defend Kui Heights.

The twilight operations became a night attack. Well after 9 P.M., in drizzle, Nagano's units set forth, hours behind schedule. Enemy resistance was trifling. The Japanese eliminated two sentries but incurred a couple of casualties in the process. Thereupon the forward elements "lost heart, and the advance ceased." Nagano called off the main attack. According to the records, the immediate enemy amounted only to an outpost unit and a few tanks; but the regiment concentrated on destroying the bridge and sent the rest of the units back to their original positions by 4 A.M.

Though the poor performance of Nagano's main attack force is astonishing, it is true that the regiment had been prodded repeatedly by the division to retain the mission of knocking out the bridge north of the Nakanoshima sandbar in the Halha. The 12th Company, commanded by 1st Lt. Kimura Takeshi and reinforced by heavy machine guns and rapid-fire weapons, was ordered at midnight to support the engineer platoon in the raid on the bridge. Kimura proceeded to Kui Heights, whence he was about to head for the river when he received an order to pull back to regimental headquarters by dawn. Thus, even the demolition assignment came to naught.

Nishimura, who was supposed to be saved by the regiment on 12/13 July, had redeployed his company north of the Holsten on the basis of his most recent combat experience. The expected new enemy assaults did not materialize by twilight. Having received the order to rejoin the regiment, Nishimura recrossed the Holsten and proceeded to the dune where he expected to rendezvous with the main body by dawn. There was no sign that the regiment had ever sallied this far, although the original orders had spoken of an afternoon jump-off time and an advance to the confluence area during the night. Nishimura kept moving, again on his own, and made it to the location of Nagano's command post by 11 A.M. on the 13th. In a sense, he had rescued himself, given the rather inept operations of the regiment.[13]

By 13 July, Sumi had learned about the forthcoming Japanese general offensive employing heavy artillery. During the day, the 26th Regiment came under bombardment, including mortar fire for the first time. After nightfall, however, the sector became unusually quiet. If enemy forces had really pulled back or were consolidating, the colonel thought, it would pose a splendid opportunity to clear the area and perhaps even destroy the bridge at the confluence. After pondering through the night, Sumi ordered an attack at dawn on the 14th. Moving in 100-meter bounds, the spearhead 5th Company reached the first objective at 6 A.M.; all the other companies followed within the hour. By 10 A.M., advance elements were only 500 meters from the confluence, and the famous bridge could be seen by some. The closer the troops came to the river, the heavier the shelling became from the left side. As the Japanese ran forward, they seemed to be followed by enemy artillery. After about 1,000 meters, Sumi was only able to walk fast, not run. No site seemed safe for the headquarters, and the regimental guns were useless at this range. One officer counted 300 Soviet shells per minute. Maj. Ikuta Junzō, formerly a 7th Division aide, arrived at midday, through a hail of fire, and was immediately given command of the slain Adachi's 1st Battalion. During his stop at 23rd Division headquarters, said Ikuta, he had been told that the 26th Regiment was pursuing the foe toward the confluence on its own initiative, so he should go forward quickly.

The good news of Ikuta's arrival was followed at 4 P.M. by a vexing phone call from division staff officer Murata. Sumi's regiment, Murata complained, had advanced too far and should pull back to its former positions (as the new order of 12 July had required). Sumi was disgusted. Racing to the confluence was certainly his idea and had been begun on his own initiative; but it had been reported early to the division commander and had been approved by him, Sumi insisted. The thrust had been a triumph, the enemy had been taken by surprise, Japanese losses were light, and the 26th Regiment had reached the confluence for the first time. Nevertheless, according to Sumi, his very success contributed to his eventual punishment by higher headquarters when the Nomonhan Incident was over.

It seems that Komatsubara had asked Kobayashi if the enemy forces were really pulling out and had been told that they were not. The division commander was thinking of covering Sumi's advance with an artillery battery, but wanted to use a portion of the Yamagata unit to cover advance observation posts. Despite his urgings, Komatsubara was told that elements of the 64th Infantry would not suffice—that the whole regiment would have to be committed. Since such employment did not fit the scheme of the all-out offensive, the general decided to conserve the Yamagata regiment, gave up the support idea, and ordered Sumi to pull back too. The colonel reluctantly "consolidated his lines" and waited for the general offensive. Morale had been boosted by the race to the bridge, however, and the soldiers boasted of having "terrorized" the enemy, an attitude that Sumi encouraged gladly.[14]

On the far right flank, on 13 July, Kajikawa estimated his battalion's sinuous frontage at 400 to 1,000 meters. Lieutenant Takashima dozed in his trench, soaked to the skin by the rain, while the sounds of enemy machine guns and artillery could be heard. Sumi called Kajikawa to the 26th Infantry's command post and, at 2 P.M., ordered him to move his unit closer to the regiment's right-wing Kondō battalion in order to tighten the linkage. Kajikawa asked for and was allowed two nights in which to accomplish the relocation.

In the early evening, while the battalion was preparing to move, the enemy attacked "more heavily than ever," with infantry and artillery. To mask his intention of relocating, Kajikawa ordered counterassaults all along the sector. After checking the foe, the battalion disengaged and at 10:30 P.M. headed for an elevation 1,000 meters west of Heights 731. By now, the soldiers knew the terrain extremely well. Near 1 A.M. on the 14th, they had reached their first objective without losing their way in the murk. The men dug trenches and "settled in." Takashima was pleased that the new location would avoid enemy flanking fire from the heights across the river, but it proved to be the site of an earlier battle, whose stench of blood was wafted on the wind when the weather cleared next day. There had been no opportunity to attend to the Japanese dead, but now they were buried for the time being, with the smoke of cigarettes substituting for incense.

Since it would still be very difficult to move by day, Kajikawa intended to resume the relocation on the second night and to make contact with the Kondō battalion. The regiment, however, now sent word that Kajikawa's unit should move to the rear of the 26th Infantry and become Sumi's reserve. This, too, Kajikawa expected to undertake after darkness. Takashima volunteered to lead a four-man patrol to the left. Toward the high ground near the confluence, he says, smoke could be seen and the shouts of Sumi's charging infantrymen could be heard between shell bursts. Despite the enemy bombardments, the Japanese looked as though they ought to be able to make it to the river with "just one more push," Takashima reported to Kajikawa. The lieutenant provides a rare picture of his chief: "The winner of a fifth-class Order of the Golden Kite (*Kō-gokyū*) and master of the sixth *dan* in *kendō* fencing, our tall and slim battalion commander stood on a crest, observing [through binoculars]. His cheeks were hollow, his eyes were sunken, and his scraggly beard was streaked with gray. The commander had suffered most of all, leading his independent unit throughout the entire combat to date."

Starting out at dusk on the 14th, Kajikawa brought his battalion to the area of the regimental headquarters by midnight. Sumi and his units were off on their offensive toward the confluence, but orders were waiting for Kajikawa to disregard the earlier instructions and instead to seize Hinomaru Heights. The major was confronted by a dilemma. He did not know the way to Hinomaru, and before he could reach it the sun would rise, so that his unit would incur severe casualties. Yet if the battalion simply waited where it was, the opportunity to advance would be lost. Having concentrated his forces behind the regimental headquarters and sent out scouts, Kajikawa decided to move to Hinomaru after all.

In about an hour, the battalion encountered the 26th Regiment falling back. According to Kajikawa's account, Sumi had apparently decided to return to his location as of 13 July, out of concern for the threat from enemy artillery. Conferring with the colonel, Kajikawa said that if his battalion went on to Hinomaru, it would be isolated. Sumi then changed his orders once more and returned the battalion to its reserve assignment behind the regimental command post.

At 2 P.M. on 15 July, Kajikawa was moved to the dunes northeast of Hinomaru Heights, again becoming the far-right element of the whole Japanese front. On the next day, however, Komatsubara sent an order transferring the battalion to his direct control, in divisional reserve near Heights 731. Kajikawa's attack phase was over for the moment, and his men dug in under the hot sun on 18 and 19 July, during the lull before the next storm.[15]

On Sakai's front, about 200 enemy troops, occupying positions 700 meters from the 72nd Infantry, engaged the Japanese, but in general the situation was unusually quiet. Ahead of the regiment, Lieutenant Hayama's platoon was still dug in. Starting near 1:30 P.M., he was attacked and surrounded on three sides by 200 soldiers equipped with machine guns and supported by artillery and tank fire. Aided by another platoon, Hayama's men waged an eight-hour battle, punctuated by close grenade exchanges.

Around 8 A.M. on 14 July, Kobayashi's headquarters phoned Sakai to report that the Sumi regiment, having concluded that there had been a pullback by the enemy, had advanced to a point only 300 meters from the Holsten. As a result, Sakai prepared to launch a pursuit operation of his own. At Kobayashi's urging, Sakai also intensified the regiment's observation efforts and reconnaissance activity. Patrols conducted by Lieutenants Hayama and Takayama were especially vigorous on the 14th and 15th, but there was dissatisfaction with the progress of the neighboring Yamagata regiment. Despite promises to resume the advance, its night-attack force had only reached a dune 300-400 meters to the right of Sakai's 1st Battalion. From Sakai's standpoint, the situation improved neither on 15/16 July nor on 16/17 July.

Meanwhile, at dawn on 14 July, the 72nd Regiment had celebrated the first anniversary of the bestowal of its colors. At his command post, Sakai drew up his headquarters and his reserve company and delivered an address. The line battalions saluted the colors from where they were deployed.[16] It would be the regiment's last review at Nomonhan.

South of the Holsten, on 13 July, Komatsubara and staff officer Murata Masao came to confer with Nagano at his command post at 1:40 P.M. They explained the division's idea of waiting for the deployment of the friendly heavy artillery corps before mounting a general offensive. Meanwhile, the 71st Regiment was immediately to reconnoiter and blow up the two important enemy bridges connecting the Noro Heights area with the west side of the Halha, south of the confluence near Sambur Obo. This meant that Noro itself would have to be cleared at last—something that Komatsubara had first ordered on 7 July but that had continued to be delayed by problems of terrain identification.

Around 9 P.M. on the 13th, Nagano's detachment began its advance—after an attack by 150 enemy troops was beaten off by the 7th Company on the extreme right, delaying the 2nd Battalion's departure a bit. The spearhead 6th Company, from Baba's 2nd Battalion on the right, charged onto the edge of Sankaku (Triangle) Hill on the Noro elevation by 2:40 A.M. Stubborn opposition was met, and casualties were heavy, including the acting company commander wounded. At 5 A.M., the main body of the 6th Company was reported to have taken Sankaku Hill itself. Maj. Murata Mosuke's 3rd Battalion, in seesaw fighting, broke the resistance of an estimated two infantry battalions and three artillery batteries. At 5:45 A.M., Colonel Nagano arrived at the front line to direct operations, based on Komatsubara's orders. It was an auspicious beginning for the first anniversary of the receipt of the regimental colors: "The sky was wonderfully clear, the sun glared down on the fleeing enemy, and our morale soared along the whole front."

Division staff officer Suzuki phoned the 71st Regiment command post after 7 A.M. and conveyed the following information: on the Japanese right wing, the enemy was in retreat and friendly forces had begun the chase toward the confluence; on the left wing, the foe was faltering, and the Japanese were preparing to pursue. Nagano should press the enemy to the bridge in the vicinity of Sambur Obo and try to follow quickly, using trucks. A runner was sent with the order to Nagano but, when he caught up, it was 7:30 A.M.—"a hair too late." Although the detachment headquarters had started forward with the colors, "the chance of pursuit seems to have been lost." Since the location of both battalions' headquarters was unknown, runners could not be sent; and telephone links were snarled.

The 3rd Battalion, on the left side, sent the 9th and 11th companies, each reinforced with a heavy-machine-gun platoon, toward the Sambur Obo bridges. Both companies got to the river under fire, after some strenuous running—the 11th Company to the northern bridge at 10 A.M., the 9th Company to the southern bridge ten minutes later. En route, a body of Russian troops, appearing from the crestline on the right—probably having been evicted from the Kui zone—blundered into the advancing Japanese and were cut down. Within an hour, by 11 A.M., both main battalions came up to the river line. While they were taking a break, the division's instructions finally caught up with them, about three and a half hours late.

A PFC from Capt. Miki Toranosuke's 11th Company, deployed on the right, remembers dashing down the slopes, under bombardment, and reaching a terrace 50-60 meters above the river, perhaps 500 meters away. After charging forward another 300 meters through short reeds, the Japanese encountered a gentler slope, although Maxim machine guns firing from across the river were felling soldiers in succession. Propelled by their own momentum, several of the men kept going, onto the upstream wooden bridge in their sector; but they were eventually driven back, leaving one PFC lying at the edge of the span.

The 11th Company jumped into the recently vacated Soviet trenches, built in a half-moon around the bridge. Forty or 50 meters in radius, and designed to defend against attack from the Nomonhan direction, the emplacements were not too effective against gunfire emanating from the left shore. To the Japanese, the Mongolian cliffs appeared to be "seven stories high," with Maxims shooting from the "windows." Along the ridges, little tanks could be seen moving up and down a zigzag road connected to the bridge at the level bottom.

The Soviet span itself, not made of pontoons, was similar to sturdy bridges found throughout rural Japan. It seemed wide enough for five soldiers to cross abreast, and stable enough to support trucks, although the current was fast. The Japanese speculated that the Russians had used cement to harden the underwater pilings. One of the men who had gone onto the bridge said it was like tramping along an ordinary road, not wooden boards. Wires were strung as guiderails, too strong to be cut when a soldier slashed at them with his bayonet.

Armed with nothing more powerful than grenades, the Japanese infantrymen clung to the trenches. At 11:30 A.M., Soviet troops came back down from the high ground and counterattacked from across the bridge, with one infantry company and three heavy machine guns. The enemy foot troops fired their rifles from the hip. Incurring increasingly heavy casualties (especially from the Maxims) and running low on ammunition by 3 P.M., the 11th Company began to give ground. The company commander was wounded, and the battle situation grew "uneasy." A sergeant took four men and went back for ammunition at the terrace above the river, where the 10th Company was standing by. The party borrowed as many cartridges and grenades as it could stuff into bags or haul on its shoulders, ran back, but went astray. Maxims could be heard chattering and Soviet troops yelling "Hurrah!" Since the 11th Company must be out of ammunition by now, the sergeant ordered a do-or-die rush. Only one soldier made it unscathed. There were still many hours until nightfall, but the firing finally diminished.

At night, some engineers arrived to demolish the span. Guided by the indestructible PFC, the sappers made it to the target and produced an explosion that sent a pillar of water into the sky. Afterward, the 11th Company pulled back, carrying its casualties. Of the 120 men, half were dead or wounded, including Captain Miki injured.

On the left flank, Captain Onozuka had taken his 9th Company, supported by a machine-gun platoon, toward the southern bridge. The enemy had abandoned the positions on the way, and had left even artillery behind. Although the guns were well camouflaged, the company found them, marked the ammunition boxes "captured by the Onozuka unit," and pressed ahead without taking the time to destroy the pieces. Two hundred meters from the enemy, in the swamp by the river, Onozuka and his men hid in the reeds, with water as high as their chests and with their ammunition slung around their necks. Onozuka sent his attached engineers to blow up the bridge. They reported having accomplished their mission, although the captain— engaged in heavy combat at the time—heard no explosion and saw no spout of water. Like Miki's unit, the 9th Company was running out of ammunition until resupplied by brave 1st Lt. Hatanaka Sanjirō, who broke through from regimental headquarters with a vital truckload of machine-gun cartridges. Hatanaka was shot in the chest. Finding it increasingly difficult to hold on, Onozuka withdrew his company that night.

Onozuka estimates the time of the first engineer raid against the bridge in his sector as 5 P.M. But this effort may not have succeeded, for engineer 1st Lt. Nagatoshi Toshio's party of 14, reinforced by a machine-gun platoon, did not make it onto the pontoon bridge until night. The team had proceeded by truck to the river at 2 P.M.; Nagatoshi was wounded near the river, and the party was divided into two. The first team went to the site of the wooden southern bridge but reported that it was already inoperable. The second team headed for a 15-meter pontoon span. Since Soviet machine-gun fire was severe in the area, the unit waited until dark and, it reported, blew up the bridge at 10:40 P.M.

Nagano, who would have wanted to retain his advanced lines, at 6 P.M. on 14 July issued an optimistic and aggressive order. By hard fighting, he said, the regiment had defeated enemy forces estimated at two infantry battalions who had been counterattacking since the preceding evening. On this day, the 14th—"the anniversary of receiving our colors"—the enemy had been pressed entirely to the Halha. Fighting on the north side of the Holsten was also developing favorably. The Nagano force would spend the night at its present location, deploying a tight guard net; watch the Halha crossing points with strong elements; and scout the situation on both sides of the river for the purpose of further offensive operations.

At 7 P.M., however, the 23rd Division phoned orders to Nagano to pull back that night. Starting around midnight, the entire detachment withdrew, reaching Noro Heights by dawn on 15 July. Nishimura's long-lost company escorted the colors. That the Russians had not been cleared entirely from the district south of the Holsten became apparent at 6 A.M., when an enemy infantry company and five tanks moved against the right rear of the 7th Company, prompting Nagano to ask for supporting fire by friendly artillery.[17] But it can be said that the 71st Regiment on 13/14 July redeemed its sluggish performance of the night before by sweeping past Noro Heights to the Halha at last and by knocking out two enemy bridges.

The series of dusk-to-dawn attacks by Japanese infantry petered out at a time when, at first glance, it seemed that Komatsubara's forces were finally winning at Nomonhan. A total of five Soviet bridges had been knocked out, and Japanese elements were deep in enemy territory or near the confluence. Each of the four IJA regiments (plus the Kajikawa battalion) had something to crow about. Komatsubara had tabulated an impressive listing of enemy losses as of 12 July: abandoned corpses, at least 1,700; prisoners, 40; tanks and armored cars knocked out, 400; armored vehicles captured, 15; guns captured, 4 heavy, 7 light, and 30 machine guns; and trucks seized, 40.[18]

But on 13 July Komatsubara cooled down the infantry in the center—as he had the units on the far right and south of the Holsten the day before. We know from the division commander's diary that as early as the 13th he had grave regrets, especially with respect to the 64th Regiment, which had broken through to the river. Ordered to pull back on the verge of achieving his mission, Yamagata must have been dejected, wrote Komatsubara. The colonel's petition to Kobayashi for authorization to attack and advance one more time was certainly understandable.[19]

> As division commander [Komatsubara continued], I grieve for those who were killed in battle, and I feel remorse. If only I had known of the actual existence of such a high offensive spirit, I would have wanted to let [the unit] accomplish the objective. But the telephones had been out of action since the night before, and I had no way of knowing the situation. Therefore I issued the orders yesterday from the broad standpoint. I had my reasons, but even so, I cannot evade responsibility for breaking the attack spirit of subordinates.

The period of the Japanese night assaults may appear "drab" at first glance, and the actions themselves unimportant and minor. But great significance can be detected in the tactical sense—the small-scale thrusts designed to smash the enemy within the "inner radius" of 100 meters to four kilometers. Sakai's regimental aide, Major Hamada, says it was warfare by platoons, often by squads, very rarely even by companies. Gaps were many, and infiltration was easy, as best shown on maps of 1:25,000 or 1:50,000 scale. Yet though it was true that the Russians generally reoccupied by day what had been lost at night, they were always a step behind what they had had the day before. In this sense, the Japanese forces were gaining ground, slowly but surely.

With the benefit of hindsight, we can also see that the Japanese never enjoyed more than two real opportunities, during the Nomonhan fighting, to eliminate Soviet-MPRA forces in the confluence zone, the first being the transriverine offensive that was supposed to have reached the enemy artillery batteries on the left shore. The night attacks on the right bank were conducted by the peerless "queen of battle," the infantry, after the IJA armored units were neutralized and before the heavy artillery corps commenced action. The period of night attacks was also the most difficult stage for the Russians, since attrition was relatively costly before early August, when they were at last able to augment their positions and reinforce their troops (especially infantry) to overwhelming strength. Some IJA analysts suggest that the Japanese "piston" assaults were so powerful and so effective, they could have annihilated the enemy forces within only another two or three days, and certainly in four or five.[20]

The crux of the Japanese infantry's problem was, of course, the superiority of the enemy artillery and the absence of countervailing friendly heavy batteries. Major Hamada observes that to stay at advanced positions, low and easily spotted by guns and tanks, meant death in the daytime. One had to pull back behind elevations, away from the river, and try to hide till dark. A favorite motto of the infantry was "Hell in daylight, paradise at night." Meanwhile, the enemy was free to cross or recross the river, covered by artillery and armor. "Battle under such conditions was folly," asserts Hamada. "Of what use were infantry rifles? All we could depend upon was the shovel, to dig in." Certainly the front-line troops did not want to fight this kind of war. Responsibility for it lay "above the division commander, at the highest level." What did Sakai think about it? "He kept silent," replies Hamada, "as did I in those days."

Could the Japanese infantry have made it to the river en masse in a few days more? "To say quite that much is rather difficult (*chotto muzukashii*)," Hamada responds. Battalion commander Nishikawa, from the same (Sakai) regiment, concurs: "It wasn't really that easy at the time." Nishikawa adds that his men accomplished every order given to them—to launch night assaults, seize heights, etc. "It was the other [regiments] that couldn't keep up. 'You've advanced too far,' they would tell us." When Nishikawa's battalion pushed forward and occupied objectives, for example, the Yamagata unit on the right did not budge, and Nishikawa was exposed from the rear. [21]

A machine gunner from the 64th Infantry tells what a typical night attack was like. Rice would be cooked in the evening and eaten from individual mess tins (*hangō*); since many hours of effort lay ahead, the men would "stuff" themselves. After night fell, the unit would depart at around 10 or 11 P.M. Maintaining silence, the troops would creep forward until enemy lines were reached. The company commander was always in the lead. To maintain direction and keep up, the soldiers behind him on right and left would wriggle forward, touching one of his legs, and the men following them would touch one of their legs in turn. The troops were told never to fall asleep during the advance, but since they were so exhausted, some of the newer soldiers dozed off and got lost. In front of the enemy, the column would open up laterally and commence traversing fire (*chisha*). When the Russians fled, they would leave ammunition and rations behind. Sometimes there was hand-to-hand fighting, with the Japanese running forward and slashing the enemy with sabers and bayonets. But when the Russians counterattacked, the Japanese troops would engage them and then get away quickly. The enemy used flares and illumination shells and brought down supporting fire.

Typically, Soviet troops and armor emerged in the morning or evening. A plane would fly in to reconnoiter, artillery would lay down concentrated fire, tanks and armored cars would approach, and finally the infantry would advance. In the face of stiff resistance, the Russians would pull back the foot troops and then the armor, after which they would fire, generally from beyond range of the Japanese. If the latter pursued carelessly, they would often run into an ambush. Using sniper scopes, Soviet riflemen were excellent.[22]

Under these circumstances, the green 23rd Division was learning to fight through "on-the-job" training. But the price was high and escalating. Hamada, for example, remembers losing about a dozen men killed per day in the 72nd Regiment. As of 12 July, Komatsubara learned, the Japanese had lost 80 officers (41 killed, 37 wounded, two missing) and 2,042 men (538 killed, 1,500 wounded, four missing). The total of 2,122 casualties represented more than 25 percent of the approximately 8,000 ground troops in combat at the time.

Komatsubara's figures for knocked-out Japanese weapons and equipment, also as of 12 July, included two Type 90 and two Type 38 field pieces, three mountain guns, eight rapid-fire and three battalion guns, and 39 heavy or light machine guns. In addition to tank and tankette losses (mentioned elsewhere), 16 Japanese trucks and four sedans were wrecked.[23]

Just as hard-nosed Japanese military critics have insisted that the offensive across the Halha could and should have been pushed beyond the limits of human endurance in order to succeed, so has it been argued by a few that the danger to the Japanese infantry was exaggerated. In modern war, it is contended, foot soldiers are dispersed and dug in. Like aircraft, cannon and howitzers cannot usually engage individual targets, especially along a front that is 14 kilometers wide as at Nomonhan, necessitating a multiplicity of observation posts and ranging facilities. After the Japanese attacked, they never returned to their precise jumping-off locations; a discrepancy of merely five meters would suffice to nullify enemy accuracy and eliminate fear on the part of the defenders. Though Soviet artillery was very good at pre-planned firing, it was not very effective against targets of opportunity. Much more dangerous to the Japanese infantry would have been a systematic enemy firing network, closely and simultaneously melding batteries with riflemen and armor and aircraft. As long as only artillery was employed, conducting area bombardment, the threat was far less fearsome. It must be stressed, however, that the preceding views are held by IJA officers who, regardless of their knowledgeability about combat, did not fight in the zone of the Halha-Holsten confluence.[24]

A more prevalent IJA criticism of the decision to suspend the infantry's night attacks centers on the fact that the Soviet-MPRA side was given the time to repair damage to the Halha and Holsten bridges that had taken so many lives and so much effort to wreck. This was all the more frustrating because Soviet bridging equipment was better than the Japanese, and because enemy engineers were apparently more advanced in techniques. Unlike the Japanese, the Soviet army gave no evidence of having bridging difficulties. Their spans were numerous, took heavier loads, were hard to spot, and were quickly constructed, disassembled, or relocated. In addition, the Russians could rely on the Outer Mongolian cavalry for intelligence on fording sites.[25] During a breathing spell of about ten days, in the two river valleys now essentially free of hostile troops, the Russian command could prepare unhurriedly to cope with the expected Japanese general offensive.

With respect to the early part of July, after the Japanese had pulled back from the left bank of the Halha, Russian sources highlight two particularly fierce actions: the first on 8 July, when Major Remizov was killed; the second on 11 July, another time of danger for the Soviet bridgehead on the right shore. Until the 11th, say the Russians, the Japanese launched repeated night assaults in various sectors, with no substantial success.

Then, on 11 July, the Japanese attacked "with all of their strength," focusing the main effort at Remizov Hill (Heights 733 to the Japanese), north of the Holsten. Enjoying "considerable numerical superiority," the attackers were able to occupy the hill, but further progress was checked by the heroic Soviet-MPRA forces. The Japanese were aiming to break through to the Halha crossing, but only one company (undoubtedly from the 1st Battalion of the Yamagata regiment, as we have seen) managed to penetrate the defenses. Thereupon the Japanese tried to dig in on the dunes, until supposedly annihilated by the combined action of infantry and armor from the Soviet 11th Tank Brigade. M. P. Yakovlev, the brigade commander, who personally led the counterattacks, died "a glorious death" and, like Remizov, was made a Hero of the Soviet Union. Soon afterward, on 12 July, the Russians sped reinforcements to their units on the right side of the Halha.[26]

There is evidence from the Soviet side that the defenders of the bridgehead were exhausted by the almost ceaseless nightly combat. Of much greater importance, however, are the Soviet revelations in 1979, from documents in the archives of the Ministry of Defense, concerning the Russian command and control structure at Nomonhan in July 1939. On the 5th of that month, with the Japanese offensive across the river coming to a hasty end, Voroshilov announced that all Soviet forces in Siberia and the Far East were to be placed under a Front Group, nomenclature used rarely before or afterward, commanded by G. M. Shtern and based in Chita. This huge force consisted of the 57th Rifle Corps based in Outer Mongolia, the First and Second Red Banner armies, the Trans-Baikal Military District, and the Pacific Fleet. Red Army Chief of Staff B. M. Shaposhnikov was directed to supervise the Front Group's staff, and "super commissars" E. A. Shchadenko and L. Z. Mekhlis of the Red Army's Political Administration were designated the "watchdogs." Parrish suggests that the directive of 5 July may have meant that the Russians were expecting a major campaign against the Japanese or were trying to impress them. A second document, dated 9 July and signed by Shaposhnikov, explained the duties of the Front Group.

During the week after the Japanese suspended their nightly offensives, Voroshilov signed a third directive, dated 19 July, decreeing the redesignation of the 57th Rifle Corps as the First Army Group, another item of unusual language, to be commanded by G. K. Zhukov. Since this document does not mention the Front Group, Parrish takes it to mean that Gen. A. T. Stuchenko was correct when he claimed that Zhukov (the former head of cavalry forces in the Belorussian District, and "a man with no experience in the Far East") "ignored his nominal superior, Shtern, and reported directly to Moscow."[27]

Thus before the appearance of the IJA heavy artillery, the Russian forces at Nomonhan acquired an unusual new Far East command organization and at least two posthumous Heroes of the Soviet Union.

27

Trying It with Big Guns

An observer unfriendly to the Japanese cause might conclude, on the basis of events at Nomonhan from late June through mid-July 1939, that the Kwantung Army had only briefly neutralized Soviet air power, had been evicted quickly from Outer Mongolian soil across the Halha, and had penetrated but not eliminated the Russian-MPRA foothold on the right bank of the river. The staff at Hsinking, however, subscribing to the view that "the inner half of every cloud is bright and shining," generally wore their clouds "inside out to show the lining."[1] By early July, the Kwantung Army was convinced that Giga's air division had rendered the Soviet air force impotent, that the combined efforts of the 23rd Division on the left bank and of the Yasuoka detachment on the right had chewed up the core of Russian armor, and that the night attacks had brought the Japanese infantry regiments figuratively within the famous "last five minutes that precede victory." By 7 July, the Kwantung Army, so confident of the infantry's attack prospects, reported to Tokyo that "it is only a matter of time before we destroy the enemy on the right shore." This, "despite the heat, disadvantages of terrain, interference by enemy artillery from across the river," and the fact that the Japanese troops were still about eight kilometers from the confluence as of the preceding evening.[2]

According to the cheerful estimates by the Kwantung Army, the main surviving element of Soviet strength was the heavy artillery emplaced on the higher left shore. As early as 6 July, it had been decided to focus tactics on artillery combat in case the infantry assaults somehow came to a standstill. Reinforcement of the very limited IJA artillery forces at the front with powerful new batteries could be expected to finish off the hostile guns. Elimination of their nemesis would then enable the infantrymen, who had reached the enemy's fourth-line defenses around the Halha-Holsten confluence by 12 July, to "waltz" to the Halha and thus bring about a triumphant ending to this stage of the Nomonhan fighting. It will be noticed that the Kwantung Army's offensive plan contained no elements of surprise or suddenness.[3]

Kwantung Army commander Ueda was an ardent proponent of the new scenario. The AGS Operations Bureau chief, Major General Hashimoto, who visited the battlefront at the time of the river crossing, also felt that it was only natural and proper to introduce heavy artillery. From this standpoint, the 23rd Division had been conducting operations by "blind push-ing—like a wild bull." Division staff officer Murata adds that, although the commitment of heavy artillery was a Kwantung Army notion in general, the 23rd Division was "pleased indeed."[4]

Since Soviet units had to come from Borzya, the nearest point on the Trans-Siberian Railway, some 700 kilometers away, the Kwantung Army did not expect the enemy to commit more than one and a half or at most two rifle divisions in the Nomonhan region. The artillery routinely assigned to support these divisions could be smashed, it was thought, by the 35 guns that the Kwantung Army could draw from stocks in Manchuria or from the homeland. This was not a case of "sending a boy to do a man's work"; as one AGS officer puts it, if the true strength of the Russians at Nomonhan had been comprehended before the offensive, "even the stubborn Kwantung Army would never have dared to mount such an operation." But, as we have seen repeatedly, faulty Japanese preconceptions worsened actual mistakes of estimation. The Kwantung Army seemed still to be regarding the war at Nomonhan as "only a wee bit more intense than the China Incident."[5]

The ease with which the Kwantung Army obtained heavy artillery from Japan, Colonel Inada reminds us, did not originate from the needs of the fighting at Nomonhan. Ever since Inada took over the AGS Operations Section in March 1938, he had been convinced that the Kwantung Army lacked the firepower to implement the wartime contingency plan against the USSR (Plan No. 8, or *Hachigō sakusen*). Since heavy artillery was not suitable for use in homeland operations anyhow, it was on standing offer to the Kwan-tung Army. Nomonhan merely hastened the transfer process to Manchuria in mid-1939, where it could be employed in the second phase of the fighting. If it helped to win the battle, Inada would be all the more pleased, since this would accord with the intention of his AGS section: to localize the conflict and bring about an early settlement, while achieving the operational objec-tive of meting out a devastating blow to the Soviet-MPRA forces.[6]

On 24 June, Maj. Gen. Hata Yūzaburō's 3rd Heavy Field Artillery Bri-gade received mobilization orders (*ōkyū dōin*) at its base at Ichikawa in Chiba prefecture. The brigade headquarters began with draft horses, but in order to keep up with the motorized regiments, it asked the Kwantung Army to provide it with trucks. Hsinking agreed to make the change at Hailar.

Hata's brigade consisted of two regiments. The 1st Heavy Field Artillery Regiment, commanded since March 1939 by Col. Mishima Giichirō, 44 years old and a graduate of the 28th military academy class, consisted of about 1,600 men in two battalions of two batteries each. There were four 15-cm. Type 96 howitzers per battery, as well as 15 tractors, seven trucks, two sedans, and one observation vehicle. Including the regimental train, Mishima had a total of about 100 tractors, 104 trucks, 21 sedans, six side-car motorcycles, ten observation vehicles, and three repair trucks.

Mishima's unit was the only completely motorized artillery regiment with the 15-cm. Type 96 howitzer of 1936 in the whole Japanese army. Together with its sister 7th Regiment, Mishima's force was regarded as the "most pre-cious" artillery in the army and was not sent to the China theater, although about 50 percent of its veteran personnel had had to be transferred there because of the desperate fighting. Nevertheless, two-thirds of the men were regulars, and even the conscripts were experienced. Battery commanders and above were excellent active-duty officers; indeed, one battery com-mander was an imperial prince, Higashikuni Moriatsu. There seems to be a connection between the presence of Higashikuni and the hasty transfer from the China battlefront of Tsuchiya Masaichi, a 27-year-old artillery captain with two years of combat duty. Two days after he got back to Japan, Tsuchiya reported to his unit, hoping privately that he would be granted some leave. But the regiment was already mobilizing, and Tsuchiya—at-tached to the unit without a specific assignment—was rushed to Manchuria before any of his personal effects had arrived from China. Did higher head-quarters handpick him, he wonders, because the unit contained a prince, and therefore at least one battle-experienced officer was needed to serve in the regiment? (Mishima, however, had fought in the Wuhan operation in China during 1938.)

In any case, the high quality of the 1st Regiment's manpower is suggested by the fact that at least one officer per battery in addition to the battery commander was a military academy graduate. Battalion commanders and observation team chiefs were instructors from the artillery school. Past regi-mental commanders were to prove themselves outstanding in the Second World War—notably Wada Kōsuke, who was artillery commander on Oki-nawa in 1945, and Shimomura Sadamu, who became war minister in 1945. Motorized for about a year before Mishima took command, the formation enjoyed the best conditions available to an artillery regiment and could be termed an elite or model unit.[7]

The Hata brigade's second unit was the 7th Heavy Field Artillery Regi-ment, commanded by Col. Takatsukasa Nobuteru (Nobuhiro), a baron. The organization of this motorized regiment was about the same as that of Mi-shima's, but the ordnance consisted of sixteen 10-cm. cannon, Type 92, which went into service in 1932.

Apparently the Kwantung Army expected the heavy artillery reinforce-ments to reach the front after 10 July, and to participate in the offensive on or about the 19th.[8] In practice, mobilization took about ten days, and the units began to leave Chiba for Osaka between 4 and 7 July. From Osaka, the artillery forces went by ship to Pusan, Korea, and thence by train on the main line to Hailar, which they reached by 19 July. It was, of course, another 200 kilometers cross-country to the battlefront.

On 6 July, the Kwantung Army ordered the reinforcement of the 23rd Division by an artillery corps headed by Maj. Gen. Uchiyama Eitarō, its senior artillery officer. Uchiyama was to command three components: the reinforcements arriving from Japan under Hata; the units already at Nomonhan (Ise's 13th Field Artillery Regiment and Miyao's 1st Independent Field Artillery Regiment); and two regiments drawn from the Kwantung Army's own inventory. The new units from Manchuria were the following: the Muleng motorized heavy artillery regiment of 525-600 men under Lt. Col. Someya Yoshio, with four 15-cm. Type 89 cannon (two batteries), plus two more cannon (one battery) from the Port Arthur fortress (under direct command of the Kwantung Army); and the motorized 1st Artillery Intelligence Regiment from Acheng, under Lt. Col. Fukuda Kazuya, with approximately 550 men organized into survey, flash-plotting, and sound-locator companies, photographic and meteorological teams, and the regimental train. It took the reinforcements from Muleng three days and two nights to get to Hailar, whence they proceeded cross-country to the east side of Heights 755.[9]

Under General Uchiyama's corps command, two artillery groups were organized: the 2nd Group, under Colonel Ise, commanding those field artillery forces that were in action already; and the 1st Group, under Maj. Gen. Hata, incorporating the new heavy formations from Japan and Manchuria. Mishima, among others, feels that the command structure was much too cumbrous—"like five wheels on a coach."[10]

Before the artillery reinforcements were in place, commanders and staff officers conducted preliminary liaison and observation. The Hata brigade's observation team leader, Capt. Ida (Iwata) Masataka, proceeded quickly to Kwantung Army headquarters about 6 July and spent a day or two conferring mainly with the Operations Section. Ida reported on the status of the brigade and was briefed about the combat situation at Nomonhan, the envisaged role of the heavy guns, and the structure of the corps command under Uchiyama. (For the IJA deployment for this stage of operations, see Table 27.1.) From Hsinking, Ida went to Uchiyama's command post at the front, via Hailar. The headquarters was in tents near Holstei, west of the Abutara depression, a district that struck Ida, fresh from Japan, as singularly devoid of houses, trees, and women. Uchiyama mentioned the fact that the Japanese infantry were looking forward to the arrival of the friendly heavy batteries to commence the general offensive. Returning to Hailar, Ida waited for Hata to come in a few days.

TABLE 27.1

Japanese Offensive Deployment, 23–25 July 1939

23rd Inf. Div.
Lt. Gen. Komatsubara Michitarō

- **Artillery Corps** — Maj. Gen. Uchiyama Eitarō
  - **1st Arty. Gp.** — Maj. Gen. Hata Yūzaburō
    - 1st Heavy Field Arty. Regt. — Col. Mishima Giichirō
    - 7th Heavy Field Arty. Regt. [−2nd Bn.] — Col. Takatsukasa Nobuhiro (Nobuteru)
  - **2nd Arty. Gp.** — Col. Ise Takahide
    - 13th Field Arty. Regt. [−1st Bn.]
    - 1st Ind. Field Arty. Regt. — Col. Miyao Kan

- **Right Wing Unit** — Col. Sumi Shin'ichirō
  - 26th Inf. Regt.

- **Left Wing Unit** — Maj. Gen. Kobayashi Kōichi
  - 64th Inf. Regt. — Col. Yamagata Takemitsu
  - 72nd Inf. Regt. — Col. Sakai Mikio
  - 24th Engr. Regt. — Col. Kawamura Shichirō

- **Yasuoka Detachment** — Lt. Gen. Yasuoka Masaomi
  - 3rd, 4th Tank Regts. — Col. Tamada Yoshio
  - 23rd Recon. Unit — Lt. Col. Ioki Eiichi

- **Engineer Unit** — Lt. Col. Saitō Isamu
  - 23rd Engr. Regt.

- **Reserve Unit** — Maj. Kajikawa Tomiji (Tomiharu)
  - 28th Inf. Regt., 2nd Bn.

- **Nagano Detachment** — Col. Nagano Eiji
  - 71st Inf. Regt.
  - 7th Heavy Field Arty. Regt., 2nd Bn.
  - 13th Field Arty. Regt., 1st Bn.

Right [north] shore of Holsten River

Left [south] shore of Holsten River

When Captain Tsuchiya stopped at Kwantung Army headquarters in early July, he was told that there was no longer any need for the heavy artillery regiments to bother to go to the Nomonhan front. "Our troops are crossing the Halha today," one staff officer said, "and we shall dump the enemy into the river. Why don't you go to Tsitsihar or someplace and find accommodations for your unit there?," they joked with Tsuchiya. But when the latter reported again next day, in a relaxed mood, the attitude of the Kwantung Army was completely reversed. Tsuchiya was pressed to hurry his regiment forward. "We need even one howitzer as soon as possible," he was now told. Taking the request literally, Tsuchiya wired his regiment to send ahead one piece immediately. It would take time for the whole regiment to arrive, but one howitzer could be easily detached.

Hata's diary corroborates the gist of Tsuchiya's recollection. The general knew that enemy artillery was deployed on the heights near the Halha and was firing down on friendly infantry. Although the bombardment was unsystematic, the infantrymen were helpless, and IJA field-artillery fire could only reach the river. Hata saw the advantage of responding promptly, even with one of the 15-cm. howitzers. But the idea was abandoned because of the disadvantages of exposing the Japanese heavy artillery's own strength and intentions before the offensive.

The regiment commanders visited the Kwantung Army too. Mishima, for example, went by train with an aide from Pusan to Hsinking. There he reported his arrival to General Ueda, who told him to do his best. The headquarters staff briefed him on operations, intelligence, and logistics matters. To Mishima, the attitude of the Kwantung Army officers seemed quite optimistic. They said they had been waiting for the arrival of the elite artillery units, and like Ueda they exhorted him to do his best. In fact, Mishima was "worried" that, if he did not hurry, the fighting would be over.

At dawn on 9 July, Hata reached the port of Pusan, where he received his first orders and transport plan from the Kwantung Army. Proceeding to Hsinking via Seoul on the same day, Hata visited Ueda and conferred with the staff. Among other matters, he learned about the Kwantung Army's policy for handling the Nomonhan affair, about the battle situation of the 23rd Division, about the terrain at the front, and about the enemy, especially the Soviet artillery. Hata was also told of the probability that the fighting would drag on. Since available Japanese stocks of shells were not plentiful, it was suggested even at this early stage that ammunition be conserved to the extent possible.

On the morning of the 11th, Hata and his first-echelon officers went to Hailar. That afternoon, the general flew to Uchiyama's command post with a party including Ida and Tsuchiya. Starting early on 12 July, Hata went out to reconnoiter personally. Colonel Takatsukasa and three officers of the 7th

Regiment had already arrived. After assigning missions and sectors, Hata ordered them to scout the firing positions that were to be occupied. The brigade commander took control of Someya's newly committed unit, "adjusted overall deployments, and carried out combat preparations and emergency training for improvement of firing accuracy." Hata also contacted Fukuda's intelligence regiment about the collection of needed data. All in all, the preparations were progressing nicely, in Hata's opinion.[11]

Tsuchiya says that Hata directed him to study firing sites for all the heavy-artillery units. The captain was sorry that he had brought no men with him to help, for there was nobody at the command post who knew the district or where to go. Lack of landmarks posed the usual problem and Tsuchiya could never relax. If, for instance, he could not find a pond he was looking for, he would tell his driver to turn around, go back, and start over again. Although Japanese infantry elements were deployed at the front, there were vast gaps between them, and one never knew where friendly territory ended and enemy lines began. Tsuchiya would alight from his vehicle and stroll around likely locations. Eventually, he found three places suitable for Someya and the regiments, marked circles on his map, and showed his findings to Hata, who accepted them. When the artillery arrived at Hailar station, Tsuchiya had to guide the units separately to their sites, shuttling back and forth from the front, for he was the only officer who knew the area well. He did not sleep for days, and his bloodshot eyes showed it.

As for Colonel Mishima, he had taken the train from Hsinking to Hailar, which he reached on the morning of the 12th. He flew to the front next day. More details were available at 23rd Division headquarters and at Uchiyama's command post, about seven kilometers from the confluence. From the dunes, the corps commander pointed out the general area of the 1st Regiment's scheduled deployment and described the operational mission and the terrain. Uchiyama, like the Kwantung Army staff, struck Mishima as optimistic (*nonki*) and open (*gōhō*). The colonel borrowed a truck and set forth on position reconnaissance with his second lieutenant. But something was troubling him: Uchiyama was a fine commander, and there were many officers at the command post, yet the intended location of the 1st Regiment was designated only by (Tsuchiya's?) rough circles in pencil on a poor, large-scale map. Mishima says that had he been in the corps commander's position, he would have attached at least one staff officer to a newly arrived regimental commander and his junior aide, neither of whom knew the area.

Moving toward the front, under occasional fire, Mishima could see Japanese infantry dug in behind the dunes, and supplies and ammunition being brought up from the rear. Remainders of burned-out tanks were visible, as were many piano-wire barricades and corpses of Soviet soldiers, who

seemed to be rather older than regulars. Were the elite forces being conserved for later use? From Mishima's truck, the gently undulating plains
seemed like an ocean, difficult to delimit and leaving the colonel "really at a
loss." The 15-cm. howitzers' relatively short range meant they had to be displaced far ahead, but this was precisely where the Japanese would be utterly
exposed to forces on the left shore. Cover was imperative but lacking. Usually a regiment commander had only to scout and designate general deployment zones of several hundred meters for his battalions. Mishima, however,
had such an unpleasant experience on the 13th that he decided to help the
battalion commanders, when he brought them up, by personally indicating
the sites for every battery and every gun. Since complete shelter was impossible, the colonel settled for "half-covered" sites; i.e., the enemy might be
able to see gun flashes but not entire pieces. The 1st Battalion would be deployed on the right, the 2nd Battalion on the left, in the Heights 733 area;
the regimental matériel unit would be based in the Nomonhan sector.

At sunset on the 13th, Mishima returned to Uchiyama's tent, where the
two officers chatted. The general did not go into specifics, but Mishima
mentioned the problems of terrain and shelter. Next morning, anxious
about the progress of his regiment, the colonel returned by air to Hailar,
where he conferred with brigade commander Hata. After a few days of
waiting for the regiment to arrive, Mishima flew back to the front with his
two battalion commanders and, as he had intended, pointed out the deployment of the guns to them on the spot. One problem still troubled Mishima
greatly: could his senior aide, a recalled reserve officer, handle the movement
of the regiment all the way from Hailar to the front across an uncharted
area devoid of trees and real roads? Without alluding to Tsuchiya's presumable role, Mishima asserts that the unit made it safely, using compass
and stars.[12]

The gist of the Kwantung Army's order of 6 July, organizing the support
corps of artillery, was transmitted to Komatsubara by operations chief
Terada on 8 July. Naturally, the division commander had no objection to
being sent heavy-artillery reinforcements. On the 10th, he ordered his
forces to provide cover for the arrival and deployment of the big guns and to
assist with their firing preparations. As for the timing of the general offensive, shortly after Hata got to the front on 11 July, he recommended that the
23rd Division schedule the attack for 21 July, a recommendation accepted
promptly by Uchiyama.[13]

On 11 July, Komatsubara convened an important meeting in his command tent attended by Uchiyama, by Kwantung Army Operations Section
chief Terada, and by his own operations officer, Lt. Col. Murata Masao. The

main topic was the general offensive,[14] and Uchiyama described what his attached artillery corps proposed to do with an optimism that mirrored the Kwantung Army's own, despite the shortage of ammunition and the heavy artillery's lack of experience with counterbattery fire. Deployment of the artillery was scheduled to be completed by 19 July at the latest. The corps then intended to smash the foe with all of its strength; but in case the enemy began to attack or retreat beforehand, the IJA batteries would commence action without waiting to deploy entirely.

At this point, Uchiyama made a startling request: that the division suspend its own attacks immediately. His central argument was that the artillery corps dreaded a withdrawal of enemy guns beyond range of friendly batteries but still within range of the front-line IJA infantry. It was most desirable to draw enemy artillery forces to the front edge of the left shore, thus exposing them to IJA heavy guns. After most of the hostile firepower had been eliminated, the corps would appreciate it if the infantry launched a night assault to "finish the job." Despite the gracious and roundabout language employed by Uchiyama, it was apparent that he wanted the Japanese infantry pulled back, giving the friendly guns a free field of fire on the right bank and keeping the enemy batteries near the river's edge on the other side of the Halha.

Komatsubara and Murata responded that the infantry's nightly attacks had been gaining ground steadily and that infiltration was progressing. They argued that it would be advisable to continue the assaults and commit the heavy artillery to battle piecemeal as it came up. Uchiyama was told that infantry group commander Kobayashi fully shared Komatsubara's views and in fact had been strongly recommending continuation of the night assaults. This very night, 11 July, at Kobayashi's urging, Yamagata's entire 64th Regiment was being hurled against the enemy bridgehead on the right bank. Infantry morale and confidence remained high, even after word was received that the heavy artillery was coming. Indeed, although Komatsubara may not have been able to say so directly, it was apparent that the Japanese infantry wanted to overwhelm the Soviet-MPRA forces before the friendly artillery corps arrived.

Within two weeks Komatsubara would have occasion keenly to regret his decision, but on 11 July he yielded to Uchiyama. It was difficult to resist, for the idea of an artillery offensive was the Kwantung Army commander's brainchild, and Uchiyama was Ueda's deputy for artillery. In addition, Colonel Terada was supporting Uchiyama vigorously, arguing that once hostile batteries across the Halha had been eliminated, the enemy toehold on the right shore could be destroyed with ease.[15]

During the American war in Vietnam, it was sometimes suggested—not entirely in jest—that victory should be announced unilaterally, and then a withdrawal effected. In the case of the Kwantung Army, one wonders whether a similar notion underlay the issuance of a press release in Hsinking at 5:30 P.M. on 11 July, the day of Komatsubara's meeting with Uchiyama. As the result of offensive action between 2 and 11 July, it was announced, the Kwantung Army had smashed Soviet-MPRA forces operating on the right bank of the Halha and had driven them back across the frontier from the Noro and Balshagal Heights areas. Only enemy remnants remained to be mopped up.[16] Might this communiqué have been intended to justify publicly, or to signal to the Russians, the impending suspension of Japanese ground action in the area of the confluence—at least until the IJA heavy-artillery offensive was revealed?

Regardless of the Kwantung Army's motives in releasing the "victory" communiqué of 11 July, Komatsubara implemented the secret decision reached at his command post that day with an operations order on the afternoon of the 12th.[17] Deployment of the entire strength of the heavy artillery was being awaited, after which the offensive would be launched on X-day (21 July was not stipulated officially) with the objective of destroying Soviet-MPRA forces in the confluence area and enemy artillery on the left-bank high ground "in one fell swoop." As noted earlier, the infantry units were directed (1) to secure key points near the front-line main body in general, as of the period before the night attacks, (2) to withdraw for the time being those elements that were occupying areas near the riverbank, and (3) to prepare for further offensive action. Artillery corps commander Uchiyama should assume control of the division's field artillery, allot elements to support both wing units, and get ready for the offensive, making special efforts to conceal his intentions. All available engineer units should assist the deployment of the artillery corps while readying for the offensive.

Doubts must still have been gnawing at the division commander about the wisdom of stopping his rifle regiments' night attacks, especially when he learned at last that Yamagata's infantrymen had ripped their way to the river on 11/12 July. Komatsubara gave his reasons for issuing the operations order of 12 July in his private diary entry of that day.[18] First, the division was confident of being able to destroy the foe by infantry forced attacks, but when the artillery battle ensued, enemy guns would be pulled back, deep to the rear of the left shore, and IJA artillery would be unable to fire effectively (i.e., would be outranged). It would be advantageous to force the enemy to fight the kind of battle—the combined infantry-artillery operation—that the Japanese had in mind, and thus it was important to prevent hostile artillery from withdrawing too far from the left bank of the Halha. Second, considerable further casualties were to be expected if the Japanese infantry continued to secure the river shore—"needless losses that would mount daily" if the troops stayed too close to the enemy at this stage. Third, it was true that the pullback of the shore-watch units for the time being would cheer the enemy, incite feelings of contempt toward the Japanese, and allow the foe to reinforce his positions. But, wrote Komatsubara, IJA forces would thus be able to achieve even better combat results in the great and decisive artillery battle that was forthcoming.

It would seem that Komatsubara was trying to convince himself by rationalizing his difficult decision to go along with Uchiyama's request. Meanwhile, the reinforcements of heavy artillery continued to move up on schedule. Takatsukasa's 7th Regiment arrived from Hailar on 17 July. Maj. Sakuma Yoshio's 1st Battalion was to be deployed on the south side of the Holsten, with the special mission of supporting the Nagano detachment located ahead of it by neutralizing Soviet artillery that had been firing from the left shore of the Halha near Sambur Obo. Takatsukasa's regimental command post would be set up 200-300 meters behind Sakuma's battalion. Across the Holsten, on the north bank, Maj. Kondō Toranosuke was to emplace his 2nd Battalion. Takatsukasa's units entered their positions between 19 and 20 July.[19]

On 18 July, Mishima's 1st Regiment assembled near Uzuru pond, and during the night of the 19th it moved into sites west of Heights 755. Based upon previous reconnaissance, Maj. Hayashi Tadaaki's 2nd Battalion was placed on the left wing, and Maj. Umeda Kyōzō's 1st Battalion on the right. Prince Higashikuni's 1st Battery was held in reserve near Mishima's regimental observation post.[20] Someya's 15-cm. guns arrived on 18 July, were deployed two kilometers behind Mishima's howitzers with about 100 meters between pieces, and underwent low-level strafing while entering their positions.[21]

As important to the artillery as the selection of battery sites was the pinpointing of "invisible" targets on higher ground and at long range. While the Japanese artillery troops labored day and night on the positions, observation teams worked on target-spotting and fire-control data for five or six days, the battalion being the basic tactical unit and the battery the basic firing unit in battle. There were enough trained observers, says Ida, and they were comparatively good. On the basis of Fukuda's excellent intelligence regiment's basic surveying and location of enemy gun sites, the combat units were able to delineate firing sectors. The artillery group's observation post section dealt with "general effectiveness."

The problems faced by the artillery observers were numerous. Enemy "bugs" could be seen at the front of the Halha ridges, but nothing was visible on the reverse slopes. The closer one pushed observation sites to the river, the more difficult it became to make out targets. At artillery firing ranges in Japan, there were always landmarks to be used as reference points for observation, orientation, and orders. "What a terrible place!," Ida said of

Nomonhan. The road down to the Halha, across the river, was a good reference feature, as was Sambur Obo in particular. It was still necessary to sight upward on enemy gun flashes and try to correlate them with aerial reconnaissance photos, but the latter did not show Sambur Obo. The enemy also moved the artillery and built dummy positions. As a result of confusion of target locations, one gun site might turn up on the maps as two or three targets. Conversely, several distinct targets might be confused as one.

Although the Japanese possessed good optical instruments, there was a chronic problem of underestimation of range because of reliance on visual judging, considered most important by the artillery. On the Mongolian plains, vast like the sea, the skies were usually brilliant, the air was pure, and there were no obstacles to vision. At 10,000 meters, with the naked eye, one could see a man's head. Range finders could operate clearly to 24,000 or 25,000 meters, but whereas a finder would disclose a distance of, say, 10,000 meters, the corresponding visual estimate might be only 6,000 meters. Units had 16-power military range finders, which the battery commanders used for close spotting. But battalion commanders need a wider field, so Hayashi relied on his eight-power personal binoculars. Since the twin periscopes of the range finders offered good targets to the enemy, Mishima tried to emplace them as low as possible. Heat shimmer often interfered, however, and it became necessary to raise the periscopes (less than one meter if possible).

Light played an important part in artillery observation and firing. In the morning—which came early—the Japanese, located to the east, had the advantage of the sun, which was in the enemy's eyes for one to one and a half hours in those latitudes. The situation was reversed when the sun set. Soviet artillery fired throughout the night, but if traffic interdiction was intended, it was not very accurate, and if psychological harassment was intended, it was not very effective. The Japanese artillery preferred to fire by day.

Mishima's men put up observation towers, which drew enemy fire but were hard to hit. The observers would stay up until driven off, then come down, take cover in a hole under the tower, and compute their calculations. Sometimes, to attract fire, smoke shells were detonated and dummy positions (not dummy guns) were constructed, since digging was so easy. Observation had to be conducted repeatedly, data exchanged, cartography verified, and targets corrected. During the period before the offensive, an intelligence meeting was held every evening at artillery corps headquarters, drawing upon all the observation team leaders from battalions upward. Scout planes from Col. Abe Katsumi's 15th Air Group were to handle aerial reconnaissance and photography, and to perform fire-control missions. Although Ida remembers seeing the air photos two or three times, he does not rate them highly because, in the absence of landmarks, even mosaics could not be meshed accurately and targets did not jibe with ground surveys. There was some thought of having the regimental and battalion commanders fly over the battlefield, but the missions were canceled.

Major Hayashi, for one, was satisfied with the preliminary work done by the artillery observers. Their materials were "good, precise, and prepared in detail." By the time of the offensive, almost all the enemy gun sites on Hayashi's sector were known and plotted. But, in general, IJA analysts have concluded that the Japanese heavy artillery proved unable to conduct sufficient prebattle search for objectives, observation of targets, and determination of range, largely because of adverse terrain and limited aerial surveillance.[22]

From mid-July, the Japanese artillery's combat preparations were intensified. Construction materials—sandbags, boards and beams, nails, etc.—were amassed and issued. Individual guns, about 20 meters apart, were draped with brown shelter nets (*shahei-mō*) and decked with branches and grass for camouflage. Mishima paid special attention to the digging of connecting trenches. Thus men, unless they took direct hits, could be moved safely, as could ammunition, which in the case of the 15-cm. howitzers weighed 40 kilograms per shell. Taking advantage of the fact that his regiment had so many trucks, Mishima had the excess soil hauled and dumped far away, around Lake Abutara. In the absence of color changes in the earth around the emplacements, the enemy would be less able to detect the Japanese batteries, even using aerial photography. Movement between positions was very dangerous at night, however, and the men had to learn to use their sense of smell. By day, they would note and remember the location of putrefying horses and enemy corpses, so that by night they could plot their course by the stench.

Of enormous importance to the heavy artillery, naturally, was the amount of ammunition that could be stockpiled for the offensive. Individual firing loads (*kisū*) varied with the type of ordnance: 40 rounds for the 15-cm. howitzer, 30 or 40 for the 15-cm. cannon, 50 or 60 for the 10-cm. gun, 100 for the field or mountain pieces.[23] For their units, Generals Hata and Uchiyama were thinking in terms of five *kisū*, which amounted to the following totals by main category: 10-cm. cannon (Takatsukasa), 4,800 shells; 15-cm. cannon (Someya), 900 shells; 15-cm. howitzer (Mishima), 4,000 shells.[24]

The ammunition was preponderantly of the high-explosive type—common rounds and shrapnel. There were some smoke but no armor-piercing projectiles. The 3rd Brigade's truck unit made a daily round trip shuttling ammunition between Hailar and the front. Each morning, every available truck in Hailar would be loaded with 36 heavy wooden ammunition crates, one shell per crate. The convoys would depart at 9 A.M.; traverse the 200-plus kilometers by 4 P.M.; unload, stack, and camouflage the ammunition at the heavy artillery regiments' rear dumps; and then head back for Hailar to repeat the process.[25]

While the battle preparations were proceeding, Komatsubara was pondering the optimum format of the general offensive, in concert with Uchiyama. A divisional attack plan was drafted on 17 July, and the operations order was issued officially two days later. Given the chain of command, Uchiyama's and Hata's battle plans and orders closely paralleled those of Komatsubara.[26] So far as the artillery forces were concerned, all combat units were to move to the assembly sites under cover and approach their positions during the two nights preceding X-day, enter the gun sites the night before, and be ready to open fire by 5 A.M. on the day of the offensive. Preparatory firing should begin at 7:30 A.M., designed to draw enemy batteries' counterfire and thus confirm their locations and allow adjustment of sighting and lines of fire. This preliminary stage was to last approximately 30 minutes.

At 8 A.M. on X-day, stipulated the commanders, all of the Japanese guns should launch "sudden and overwhelming" fire. During this "Period 1/Phase 1," lasting two hours, the identified enemy artillery and bridges at the Halha-Holsten confluence were to be destroyed. During the second half of the phase, friendly bombers would join in attacking the enemy heavy artillery. Specifically, Hata's 1st Group (the two heavy field artillery regiments) should allocate most of its firepower to smash hostile guns between Bain Tsagan and Sambur Obo, with the remainder destroying bridges, interdicting traffic, and directly supporting the Nagano detachment. Ise's 2nd Group (the 13th and 1st Independent Field Artillery regiments) was to cooperate mainly with both of the infantry wings north of the Holsten.

"Period 1/Phase 2" was defined as the time between the front-line infantry units' jump-off (at the end of the first phase) and their reaching of the Halha, in about two hours. During this second phase, the 1st Artillery Group was to destroy any hostile guns that made an appearance while Ise's group assigned its full strength to support the infantry. Ammunition expenditure during Period 1 was set at about 70 percent of the available total of 14,000 shells. In "Period 2," scheduled after noon on X-day, IJA artillery was to demolish the enemy's remaining guns and break his fighting spirit. After X-day, the actions of hostile artillery were to be "blockaded completely" (*kanzen ni fūsa*), and any recrudescence of the enemy's fighting will was to be shattered.

From the preceding plans, it can be seen that the Japanese artillery command was indulging in wishful thinking (*amai kangae*), as Tsuchiya terms it. That is, on the very first day of battle, it was intended and undoubtedly believed that the IJA heavy batteries would silence every enemy gun site whose location had been computed and thus enable the infantry to dash to the Halha, and that on the second day the "omitted" targets would be finished off.[27]

On the night of 19 July, Hata moved all of his artillery group's units halfway forward to the selected firing positions. (See Map 6.) Next day, he invited Colonel Abe and his 15th Air Group staff to his command post to make mutual arrangements for aerial spotting. The commanders were still thinking of 21 July as X-day, but it had started to rain on the afternoon of the 19th, had grown worse during the night, and had continued occasionally next day. In the afternoon of 20 July, a staff officer came from Uchiyama's headquarters with the corps commander's suggestion that since the weather was not good, the 23rd Division should be advised to postpone the offensive by one day. Generally, artillery ought to be allowed 24 hours of fine weather before a major operation, in order to complete final preparations to fire. Since visibility was extremely poor on the 20th, Hata willingly concurred with Uchiyama's proposal. Artillery corps headquarters issued the delaying order in the evening. Hata, however, did not mention the postponement to his formations, which went about entering their firing positions as scheduled and trying to provide sufficient shelter. The group commander was obliged to admit privately that the process was "very confused and very noisy," and that "the units exposed their inexperience with this kind of training."[28]

On 21 July, a fine day with only occasional clouds, Hata received a report at 5 A.M. that the various units had finally taken up their positions. The general asked that the artillery group improve its firing accuracy, now that the offensive had been put off one day. At about 6:30 A.M., two enemy scout planes flew in at very low altitude and strafed the Japanese ineffectually. Hata and Uchiyama went out at 8:30 to inspect the preparations of the battalions and some of the batteries. Mishima's regiment had completed its work properly. Praise was especially lavished on Prince Higashikuni, whose battery was "in perfect shape," a "model" for the artillery group. But Uchiyama and Hata, in addition to providing operational guidance and trying to boost the morale of all the units, generally had to call for improvement. Takatsukasa's regiment, in particular, evinced a "lack of care, to some extent," perhaps because it had incurred casualties during a bombardment the preceding evening.[29]

On 22 July, the day when the general offensive was now scheduled to commence, the Japanese artillery units reported by 5 A.M. that they had completed firing preparations. Hata did some last-minute checking and, a

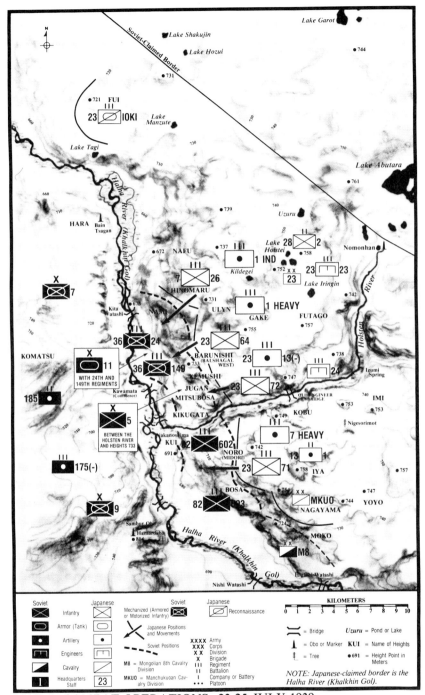

MAP 6: COMBAT OPERATIONS, 23–25 JULY 1939

506   *Trying It with Big Guns*

little before 6 A.M., was ready to recommend that the bombardment begin, since visibility was satisfactory and the weather was fine. At that moment, he received an order from Uchiyama (based upon instructions from the division) that the offensive was to be delayed one more day. According to the latest weather report, rain was forecast on the afternoon of the 22nd, and higher headquarters did not want to have to suspend the climactic battle in mid-course for reasons of weather. There was considerable dissatisfaction among the infantry and the gun batteries, although some of the artillerymen admit that "every bit of extra time was welcome" in getting ready for the sustained barrages. When the senior staff officer of the artillery corps came to offer the services of the intelligence regiment in connection with ranging, Hata was delighted. He asked that officers be sent to help Takatsukasa's regiment, which needed to better its firing accuracy. The 1st Regiment was in very good shape, but other units had had difficulty stockpiling ammunition. Some participants, in fact, think the delay stemmed less from the weather than from the incompleteness of firing preparations, which were all the more critical by virtue of the known shortage of ammunition. Indeed, one infantry company learned officially at 6:30 A.M. on the 22nd about the deferment of the general offensive "for reasons of artillery ammunition." [30]

The 23rd of July dawned clear and hot. Visibility was unlimited. This time, the Japanese artillery was directed by the 23rd Division at 5 A.M. to commence action on schedule. But Uchiyama had modified his plan a bit and ordered the field guns to start shooting first, at 6:30 A.M., in order to draw counterbattery fire. When the enemy obliged vigorously, Japanese spotters hastened to confirm targets revealed by the gun flashes, whereupon the full IJA artillery offensive got under way at 7:30 A.M. as planned. After a half-hour of preparatory bombardment, which "nearly achieved its purpose" (as Hata said), at 8 A.M. every IJA battery began to fire for effect. Hearing the thunder of the guns and seeing smoke bursts kick up in profusion across the Halha, the long-suffering Japanese infantrymen let loose with cheers and applause. For the stipulated two hours the IJA barrages continued. But the smashing of the enemy positions proved incomplete, and it was decided to continue concentrated firing for one more hour.

On the 1st Regiment's sector, west of Heights 755, Mishima's 15-cm. howitzer batteries engaged Soviet heavy guns emplaced around Komatsu Heights, seeking to deliver maximum fire in minimum time. The colonel calls the effort "overwhelmingly successful" on this first day. On a front of some eight kilometers, firing in brackets of three rounds, the howitzers were thought to have almost entirely neutralized approximately eight designated objectives. They had fired at targets of opportunity as well. When the 64th Infantry began its delayed attack at 11 A.M. (Period 1/Phase 2), Mishima's regiment shifted fire against enemy positions ahead of the foot troops. Dur-

ing Period 2 (which probably did not commence until 1 P.M.), Mishima remembers wearing down the stubborn resistance of the enemy artillery batteries and largely suppressing them by about 3 P.M.

Whenever the Japanese howitzers scored a direct hit, enemy bodies and
fragments of guns and wheels could be seen flying into the air. Through six-
power binoculars, it was not difficult to discern Soviet soldiers fleeing in
trucks, dispersing batteries beyond IJA range, and seeking cover in shelters.
Along the crestline, enemy tractors towing away operational pieces drew
concentrated fire. It was noticeable that, on the road to the Halha across the
river, Soviet trucks ignored IJA field-artillery fire and kept moving. But
when Japanese howitzer shells exploded even nearby, the enemy trucks
would turn around and go back, or the soldiers would dismount and take
cover—evidence, says Mishima, of the psychological as well as the tangible
effectiveness of howitzer fire.

Umeda's 1st Battalion, located on Mishima's right flank, fired at an initial
range of 7,000 to 8,000 meters. Tsuchiya recalls engaging five or six enemy
gun sites and firing one mission in close support of friendly infantry. The 1st
Battalion fired all day, for 14 hours, expending a total of 465 rounds, or 58
per piece. But contrary to the situation on the 2nd Battalion front, enemy
shells began landing all around Umeda's battalion within a half-hour of the
commencement of firing for effect at 7:30 A.M. The effectiveness of hostile
fire was greater than anticipated by the 1st Battalion. Around 8:40 A.M., a
15-cm. cannon round exploded at the 2nd Battery and blew off the head of a
platoon leader, a second lieutenant.

On Mishima's left wing, Hayashi's 2nd Battalion fired at a particularly
effective opening range of 6,500 meters. Later, the distances opened to
8,000-10,000 meters, but there was still shorter-range fire against enemy
guns that had sought cover and then reappeared. Stripped to the waist, the
crews sweated profusely at their work. The battalion's expenditure of ammunition was lavish by Japanese standards. It was the first time the artillerymen had ever fired so many rounds at once. The barrels grew extremely
hot—not too hot to fire, but too hot to touch. Hayashi's forward observers
were effective, sighting on gun flashes and smoke, and calculating standard
deviation down to the meter on the grids. Sometimes several ranging rounds
would be aimed against a target, but when the plotting became more precise,
only long or short rounds needed to be fired. On the regimental sector, there
were about 20 hostile cannon; Hayashi's unit engaged ten and knocked out
"at least 70 percent." He had thought that every enemy piece had been silenced, for at one time in the morning there had been no reply at all. Physical evidence of hits on the enemy guns and disturbance of their positions
could be discerned, "so, to some extent, we did get them."[31]

North of the Holsten, Takatsukasa's 7th Regiment had deployed Major

Kondō's 2nd Battalion. In action all day, from 7:30 A.M. until about 8:30 P.M., Kondō's 10-cm. cannon fired 937 rounds, or 117 per gun, at ranges between 7,800 and 14,800 meters. During peak periods of bombardment, the gunners were ordered to pump off one shell per minute for three minutes. Enemy counterfire often exploded near the observation posts and gun positions. One observation-post soldier was killed and another wounded at 10:40 A.M.

Most of the Kondō battalion's firing was done by 1st Lt. Ozaki Masamichi's 3rd Battery, which expended 693 rounds on the 23rd. Illustrating the possible deceptiveness of figures, however, is the fact that most of the firing was conducted by one squad's base-gun, the key piece that aims for range and elevation. (The supports for one of the battery's four guns had broken down soon after the bombardment began, and those for a second piece collapsed after about 100 rounds had been fired.) Emplaced in a depression near the Holsten and thus concealed from enemy observation (he hoped), Ozaki could not see his targets but fired on order from the battalion. Nobody came to the battery during the day. Spotting reports were relayed by phone from the forward observers to the battalion, on to the battery, and down to the platoon leaders. The latter, in turn, told their crews, who cheered when the news was good.

Although the roar of their own cannon was deafening, the officers and crews at gun sites rarely used cotton earplugs. In the 3rd Battery, one platoon leader had been wounded on the 23rd, but the other officer was still preparing to fire in the evening when the order came to cease action for the day. Since the base-gun had already been loaded, the second lieutenant in charge of the platoon asked the battery commander's permission to get off a last round. During the process of verification, tragedy befell the crew. The shell, inserted too long in the overheated barrel, went off spontaneously, recoil shattered the undercarriage, and four men were killed on the spot. Ironically, enemy fire had scored no hits on the battery that day.

Only 244 shells were fired by 1st Lt. Watanabe Hatsuya's 4th Battery on the 23rd. Enemy counterfire on this sector was severe; bursts of sand and smoke obscured friendly gun sites, and "the earth and the sky shook." But hostile batteries were also revealing their positions, and the powerful new IJA 25-power range finders available here were able to help the Japanese guns strike at the exposed targets. Even with the naked eye, the master sergeant at the battery observation post could see "poppy seeds sprinkling the air" over the Soviet positions—perhaps pieces blown up from the shelters. To a noncom, it was "like watching a movie through a matchbox," and the effectiveness of the Japanese heavy cannon made him very proud indeed.

Major Sakuma's 1st Battalion was the only heavy artillery unit located south of the Holsten, on the Nagano detachment's front. Sakuma's batteries engaged targets across the Halha, from the right side of Sambur Obo to the confluence, at ranges of 10,000-12,000 meters. Preliminary bombardment at 7:30 A.M. elicited a hurricane of enemy counterfire and some air attacks, but the battalion incurred no casualties. Hostile batteries' response abated for a while after the Japanese began to fire for effect. Sakuma estimates his battalion's ammunition expenditure at one and a half or two *kisū*, which would amount to some 700-950 rounds—probably nearer the lower figure, for we know that, at least in the 1st Battery, firing was suspended around 2 P.M. The battery's base-gun had fired some 40 rounds when one of the crew was allowed to go to the rear because of deafness. Gun barrels overheated, the brass shell cases became stuck, and raising the barrel no longer ejected the cartridges. Firing had to be stopped and ramming done—a dangerous and slow process known to the field artillery too. Despite the abbreviated operation, Sakuma reported that on his front the firing had been "effective to a certain degree." [32]

To the rear of Mishima's regiment were emplaced the three 15-cm. cannon batteries of the Someya unit, firing at a range of 12,000 meters. After the preliminary bombardment, "fire at will" was signaled, the maximum rate being two rounds in three minutes. Probably 100 shells were expended on 23 July by the 1st Battery. The Japanese barrages continued until gun barrels turned red-hot. Wrapping the overheated tubes with wet cloth, the crews poured water over them, until the black cannon took on a whitish hue. On Someya's sector, the firing was deemed effective. [33]

Colonel Ise's 2nd Artillery Group, consisting of the field artillery that had been involved in the fighting since the outset, had a largely infantry-support role and was not very well regarded by the heavy-gun units, owing to the dubious effectiveness of its guns and their limited firing range. Although Miyao's Type 90 motorized 75-mm. guns had a respectable effective range of 8,000 meters, the light but old Type 38 field pieces had an effective range of only 3,000 meters and a maximum of less than 5,000. A 75-mm. squad sergeant says the field gun was easy to handle against tanks but was "wretched" against long-range artillery. He could see the field artillery's rounds falling very short. IJA batteries generally aimed at observation posts, but the enemy had reserve sites, moved the locations, and resumed firing. Of course, field artillery was designed for the close support of riflemen, but at Nomonhan in July there was more enemy artillery than infantry. As for the bigger 12-cm. howitzers, whose maximum range was only 5,600 meters, "they stayed in their holes to the rear," says a 1st Regiment officer, "and accomplished 'zilch.'" [34]

Despite the technical limitations of this ordnance, Ise certainly did his best. He issued detailed operational orders and directed his units to construct various dummy projects such as gun positions, range finder facilities, and figureheads, and to conduct fake artillery fire. For the larger purposes of the general offensive, he handled the decoying of enemy counterbattery fire on the Yamagata and Nagano sectors prior to the commencement of the Japanese preparatory barrages. During the latter, the field guns were to determine ranging points without engaging enemy observation posts or artillery trains. To signal the beginning of the Period 1/Phase 2 infantry operation, Ise's forces were to conduct shrapnel timed-fire against the forward slopes across the confluence. The following basic ammunition loads per gun were stipulated for Periods 1 and 2, respectively: field artillery, 70 and 33; Type 90 guns, 230 and 95; 12-cm. howitzers, 60 and 23.[35]

From surviving unit records, we know how the main battle unfolded for the three batteries of Major Seki's 3rd Battalion of the 13th Field Artillery Regiment, on the Sakai regiment sector.[36] From the morning of 22 July, and with increasing severity in the afternoon, enemy guns from the right shore of the Halha had the battalion under attack. The 8th Battery train was hit by 15-cm. howitzer fire, which caused seven casualties and some gun damage. Until after 3 P.M. the battery held its fire in order to conceal Japanese intentions, since X-day was scheduled for next day. When enemy artillery, with two guns exposed, appeared at 5:25 P.M. across the Holsten and pounded the left front, the 8th Battery engaged it in particular. At 8:15 P.M., orders were received that the ammunition load for 23 July was being increased to three and a half *kisū*.

Confirmation of the offensive was phoned to the 3rd Battalion by Colonel Ise himself at 6 A.M. on the 23rd. Decoy firing was begun at 6:50 against enemy artillery positions near the confluence. The Russians responded from many sites. When fire for effect commenced, the following ranges were employed, reflecting the primary support function of the 3rd Battalion: Capt. Kusaba Sakae's 7th Battery, 1,450 meters; Capt. Imoto Kazuichi's 8th Battery, 1,550-1,625 meters; Capt. Kai Mansuke's 9th Battery, 1,300-1,600 meters. Enemy counterfire hit the battalion train and observation posts and cut communications. There was no respite for the battalion even on the night of the 23rd. New missions were ordered in support of the infantry, who would jump off at 10:20 P.M. after five minutes of preparatory fire by the field guns at the rate of two shells per minute. A short checking barrage would follow, aimed toward the confluence bridge. The 7th Battery was still in action at 10 P.M. During the long day of firing on 23 July, the 3rd Battalion expended 2,627 rounds, or 219 per gun. Captain Kusaba estimated his battery's consumption of 75-mm. shells at 1,000 in 15 hours of firing beginning at 6:50 A.M. One of his gunners says each piece in the battery fired at least 100 rounds on X-day, and that the sights on two of his replacement guns were the oldest he had ever seen. The firing rate was so fast and furious that shells were not left aboard the ammunition carts but were loaded right from their boxes, which were placed next to the pieces. Ejection of cartridges proved more of a problem than overheated barrels. On one occasion, a shell and fuze remained lodged in the gun tube. Since his squad had lost its ramrod, the sergeant pushed a stick into the mouth of the barrel and finally pried out the very live shell.[37]

According to General Uchiyama's standard, about 70 percent of the corps' 14,000 rounds were to be fired in Period 1. At an average of two *kisū* per piece, the following theoretical numbers of shells would have been fired on X-day: Mishima regiment, 1,280; Takatsukasa regiment, 1,920; Someya unit, 360; Miyao regiment, 1,600; Ise regiment, 4,800 (75-mm. guns) and 1,440 (12-cm. howitzers). The grand total comes to 11,400 rounds.[38]

The Japanese artillery offensive of 23 July, according to the expectations of the Kwantung Army and the local command, would administer "a last iron blow" to the remaining elements of the huge enemy artillery group across the Halha and cause the right-bank bridgehead to collapse, almost of its own weight. After the expenditure of about two *kisū* of ammunition by the IJA batteries, how closely did the results in practice approximate the hopes?

Japanese firing for effect, it will be recalled, had had to be extended an hour beyond 10 A.M. owing to "insufficiency of results." When enemy counterbattery fire slackened or ceased, Kwantung Army staff officer Shimanuki Takeharu, at the 23rd Division command post, drew the optimistic conclusion, as did most other observers, that the Soviet artillery had been neutralized. Period 1/Phase 2 firing began with the assignment of only a portion of the IJA heavy guns to overwhelm hostile artillery, "barely alive now," as Hata saw it. But as soon as the Japanese infantrymen, enthusiastic until now, launched their attack at about 11 A.M., they ran into a storm of fire from both sides of the river by the "revivified" enemy batteries. Shimanuki guessed that the latter had been merely relocating their gun sites. Despite desperate efforts, the IJA infantry could accomplish little the rest of the day. To put it mildly, Shimanuki (and the Kwantung Army, by extension) had expected greater results from the Japanese heavy artillery.[39]

Though General Hata could discern his heavy artillery group's deficiencies in achievement, he understood from his regiments that two or three enemy batteries had been smashed and another five or six put out of action. In this sense, Soviet firepower could be termed "weakened considerably." Under concentrated Japanese bombardment, the enemy gun crews were scattered and were compelled to suspend their fire. But as time progressed, the Russians recovered, and "not a few resumed firing from other positions." It was noticed that the Soviet 15-cm. pieces, excellently sheltered, were able to continue firing without changing sites. Mishima asserts that, on his sector, the main force of enemy artillery withdrew beyond Japanese firing range on the night of the 23rd.

Two other observations may be made about the operations of 23 July. First, the Japanese dummy observation posts and firing positions proved useful, drawing considerable hostile fire. Second, the air spotting effort was ineffective. In part, this was a result of the fact that, as Komatsubara admitted, the Japanese air force had lost control of the skies over the battlefield. Soviet SB bombers were operating freely, and three Japanese scout planes were knocked out by them on the 23rd. Hata identified an additional problem with air spotting: insufficient basic training and joint air-ground experience. For that matter, Japanese air force spotters from the 15th Air Group were displeased with the heavy batteries' performance. Admittedly, the terrain posed problems, but IJA artillery skill levels seemed poor. One artillery officer spotting from the air was so disgusted by the ragged and unsystematic barrages that he was heard yelling by radio to a heavy battery commander, "Knock off that lousy firing!" [40]

Nevertheless, before the day of 23 July was out, Komatsubara decided to try to recapture the initiative on the right bank, once his infantry offensive bogged down despite the cacophony of IJA heavy artillery. The division commander's operations order of 4:20 P.M. began with the usual positive assertion, in this case the claim that most of the enemy's artillery had been smashed or neutralized through the close combat coordination of the Japanese infantry, artillery, and air force. Explaining what was to follow, however, the order admitted that a "portion" of the hostile artillery was continuing action. There was no change in the Fui Heights area. All units of the 23rd Division were to continue the offensive, smash the foe, press to the right shore of the Halha after dusk, and destroy a bridge that had appeared at the bend in the Halha two kilometers northwest of the confluence. By day on 24 July, the main body of the division was to secure the river line in general.

Despite the sanguine tone of Komatsubara's order, of course the general knew that most of the enemy batteries were still "alive and well," and that friendly ordnance was ordinarily outranged. Therefore he requested the artillery corps to push forward its positions, insofar as possible, under cover of darkness, to facilitate the infantry's advance after dawn on the 24th. Since Uchiyama's own views had been accepted earlier by the division commander, the artillery chief was amenable this time to Komatsubara's intention, for he too was troubled by the limited reach of the Japanese heavy guns.

In the evening of 23 July, Uchiyama issued his operations order calling for the 1st Group to advance portions of its main units with a view to assisting the division's battle as well as annihilating the hostile artillery. Someya would move up to the area two kilometers southeast of Heights 733; Takatsukasa, as close as possible to the Halha south of the Holsten; and Mishima, east of Heights 733. Ise's group, too, was to displace forward after the infantry set forth at twilight. Firing preparations must be completed by 6 A.M. on the 24th. Ammunition resupplies could be drawn from the dump at Uzuru pond after 8 P.M., and the next day's allocation was set at about two *kisū* per piece.[41]

When Uchiyama consulted Hata, however, the latter did not go along with the idea of moving up all kinds of heavy artillery. Through his senior aide, Hata promptly voiced a number of objections to the corps commander. For example, Hata stressed the vulnerability that would be caused by the terrain ahead, particularly the downslope to the Halha in full view of the enemy's heavy batteries atop the ridges on the left bank. At best, elements of Mishima's regiment might be displaced, using the high-angle howitzers and not the longer-range cannon, to assist friendly infantry. But even here, Hata wanted no more than a battalion moved. Additionally, the group commander felt that redeployment would result in insufficient firing preparations, which were always arduous and time-consuming. In this connection, the topographical problem would again exert negative effects, for the establishment of good observation posts would be very difficult, the distances would be increased between the guns and the posts, and there would be greater dependency on scarce and inefficient air spotting.

Since Uchiyama did not see eye to eye with Hata in this matter, he invited the group commander to his command post before daylight on the 24th. Komatsubara, explained Uchiyama, wanted closer support of the infantry by the heavy artillery in order to suppress the firepower that was thwarting the progress of the brave foot soldiers. Uchiyama was convinced that the main reason for the less-than-satisfactory results on X-day stemmed from the excessive range requirements. It made sense to him to move up the heavy artillery so as to get within realistic distance of the enemy batteries. Certainly an advance of two or three kilometers was feasible, and the condition of impaired firing preparations would prove transitory. Lastly, Uchiyama intimated that there was a danger that the fighting spirit and morale of the heavy artillery would be called into question if there was hesitancy in pushing the gun sites forward.

To Hata, Uchiyama's plan looked fine on paper only. There was much more to be lost than gained if the heavy artillery were relocated—a poor choice in both theory and practice. The relatively good present positions, for instance, had been laboriously selected by Hata and his officers after studying the terrain on the spot during a period extending from a few days to two weeks. It would be another matter if the Japanese infantry could seize a foothold across the Halha, whereupon friendly artillery could push ahead the observation-post system and then dominate enemy guns on the left bank. But the Japanese infantry had hardly advanced far enough to create preconditions for displacement of the artillery corps, whose main mission was to engage in counterbattery action anyhow. In any case, Hata insisted, the 15-cm. guns were technically ill-suited to perform the mission Komatsubara and Uchiyama were propounding.

The discussion between the artillery generals went on for two hours, until the approach of the original time for opening fire at 6 A.M. on the 24th. A compromise was eventually reached whereby none of the 15-cm. cannon would be moved forward, and only one battalion each of the 10-cm. guns and 15-cm. howitzers would be. Takatsukasa would advance his 1st Battalion on the Nagano front; Mishima, his 2nd Battalion on the Left Wing Unit sector. By now, however, no hours of darkness were left for conducting the relocation, which had to be rescheduled officially for the night of 24/25 July.

The controversy was by no means settled, and the depth of Hata's displeasure is reflected in his private thoughts, recorded later. Changing positions on 23 July, he wrote, proved to be an utter failure. Regrettably, it was caused by ignorance and "unwholesomeness," involving an attempt to sell oneself after receiving a request from infantry who were ignorant about artillery. It was sheer vanity to believe simplistically that displacement forward involved merely bravery and nimbleness, without comprehension and careful consideration of the special features of the enemy, the terrain, and the singularity of the mission. True infantry-artillery coordination demanded an effort to inculcate in the foot soldiers an understanding of the capabilities and limits of artillery, instead of harping on the pushing forward of heavy guns. "It is both unwise and sinful," wrote Hata bitterly, "to sacrifice precious subordinates because of acts of self-advancement by commanders or staff officers."[42]

Weather conditions were fine again on 24 July. The second day of the Japanese general offensive resembled the first, except that there was less artillery ammunition available, the batteries' performance was generally better, and action was delayed until 8 A.M. because of the controversy about advancing the heavy guns. From the artillery command's standpoint, operations on 24 July profited from the combat experience acquired the day before and from more effective air spotting. The lighter enemy guns had been mainly relocated, but the heavy pieces were at their old sites. With undisguised pleasure, General Hata remarked that Takatsukasa's two battalions of the 7th Regiment achieved outstanding results by comparison with their performance on the 23rd, and he found occasion to praise them. The group commander also noted that Hayashi's 2nd Battalion of the Mishima regiment had moved its positions forward and had directly supported the new attack by the infantry. Hayashi says his greatest attempt at assistance was to bombard enemy bunkers on the right shore, observation posts about 200 meters from friendly posts, and the confluence crossing, to prevent enemy armor from moving to the right bank. With respect to the bridge, 5,000 meters away, Hayashi could observe only a portion. It may have been an underwater span, for when the target was hit, water plumes and not fragments flew skyward.

But Hayashi's battalion paid a price for advancing, as Hata had warned Uchiyama. Regardless of the official predawn decision by the artillery generals to defer the movement forward, according to Hayashi's recollection the order was merely suspended once after issuance on the evening of the 23rd. By 3 A.M., the major had managed to push his two batteries ahead 2,000 meters to a point behind the foot troops. Regardless of the timing, Hayashi insists that he had had to give up an area which, although not ideal, was still the best that could be found. The new site was not entirely exposed, but there was frightfully little time to move and to prepare positions. Obviously the enemy could observe the Japanese gun flashes, for Hayashi's right flank was pounded soon after his guns were emplaced and in action. Within an hour and a half of the commencement of actual ranging fire by each of the two Japanese batteries' base-guns, about four Soviet batteries unleashed concentrated barrages from front and flanks at a range of some 10,000 meters. Enemy guns, probably 10-cm. cannon, scored direct hits on both of the Number 1 guns. The 4th Battery of 1st Lt. Magari Toshirō, on the right, lost seven men killed, including the squad leader. On the left, the 1st Squad of 1st Lt. Yatabe Daijirō's 3rd Battery was decimated when a shell detonated the ammunition cache, killing seven and wounding five of 14 crewmen and ammunition carriers. Still another shell exploded five meters in front of Yatabe's trench at the battery observation post, nearly burying the lieutenant in debris.

Actually, the Japanese ranging fire had been called off, but the order did not reach the battalion commander in time because signal communications had been broken. Consequently, only the two base-guns had fired, and it was they that drew the torrents of enemy bombardment. Firing by the remaining Japanese howitzers was suspended. When Generals Komatsubara, Uchiyama, and Hata visited the scene, they expressed their condolences and cheered the battalion with promises of revenge. The surviving squad leader remembers the tears in the division commander's eyes.

Hata understood that one of the 15-cm. howitzers had been demolished, but Mishima says his regiment lost three of the pieces on 24 July—two were lost "semipermanently" and one was repairable. Thereafter, the two wounded batteries had to operate with only three howitzers each, since the Kwantung Army possessed no organic ordnance of this type, and replacements from Osaka could not reach Nomonhan before the end of the fighting.

Umeda's 1st Battalion, which had retained its former positions on 24 July, sustained enemy counterbattery barrages that were not only accurate but also extremely plentiful, outmatching Japanese fire to a very considerable degree. Having lost its platoon leader on the 23rd, the 2nd Squad lost a gunner on the 24th. At 12:15 P.M., an enemy shell struck the ammunition dump behind the battalion, killing two and wounding two men. Dogfights raged above the unit, and Soviet fighters strafed the gun line. In all, casualties in the 1st Battalion reached 40 on 24 July.[43]

Though Hata had grudgingly consented to move up a battalion of Mishima's howitzers, he had never agreed to displace any of Someya's 15-cm. cannon. Nevertheless, the 2nd Battery advanced about four kilometers during the night of 23/24 July, reaching an area only 500 or 600 meters behind Yamagata's 64th Infantry. When the battery commenced firing in the morning, it was hammered by enemy artillery. None of the Japanese guns was knocked out, but one Soviet round blew up a squad's powder cache and tore four soldiers to pieces. As soon as Hata learned that Uchiyama had directly committed the 15-cm. battery to an infantry-support role without going through the artillery group, he took immediate steps to get the unit pulled back, especially in view of the battering Mishima's 15-cm. howitzers were taking on the 24th. Ordered to withdraw, the 2nd Battery waited for nightfall before returning to its old positions.[44]

The bright spot on the 24th, from the standpoint of Hata, was the vastly improved performance of Takatsukasa's regiment, as noted previously. Yet whereas Mishima and even Someya had ended up advancing some of their elements, matters were different in the 7th Regiment. Major Sakuma was supposed to move 1st Lt. Yamada Kanji's 1st Battery close to the Halha on the south side of the Holsten by 5 A.M. on 24 July, in order to assist the Nagano detachment. Yamada, however, convinced the battalion commander that the battery itself did not need to be moved into the front lines. It would suffice, he said, to shift the battery's observation post to Nagano's headquarters, from which requests for support could be transmitted to the guns. In the event, only the observation posts of the 1st and the 2nd batteries were sent ahead.

The Sakuma battalion's targets on 24 July, as on the preceding day, were the Soviet batteries across the Halha to the right of Sambur Obo, as well as artillery emplaced on the sandbar in the Halha south of the confluence, from which fire had been directed against the Nagano detachment advancing toward Kui Heights. Action began at 7 A.M. with a giant air battle overhead. Antiaircraft batteries drove off raiders, and one enemy pilot who parachuted to safety was captured by the supply soldiers of the 1st Battery. Enemy shells "fell like rain," and their accuracy improved. The undercarriage of a 10-cm. cannon collapsed and the piece became inoperable. In the evening, when Nagano was directed to launch a night attack, Sakuma received orders to assist by advancing observation posts to the high ground 400 meters west of Heights 742.

On Major Kondō's 2nd Battalion front north of the Holsten, enemy artillery came to life on 24 July. Soviet barrages grew intense, the telephone lines between the Japanese gun positions and the 3rd Battery commander were severed constantly, and repairs could not keep up with the damage. Gunfire duels went on throughout the day. Kondō's two batteries fired 412 rounds between 9 A.M. and 9 P.M.[45]

Overall ammunition expenditure by the Japanese artillery on 24 July was down to about one and a half *kisū*. Tsuchiya provides the following ammunition data for the 1st Battalion of the 1st Regiment: 1st Battery, 254 common rounds and 32 shrapnel (down 261 and three, respectively, from 23 July); 2nd Battery, 335 common rounds and 37 shrapnel (down 385 and 43, respectively).[46]

It was estimated by the Japanese local command that three or four enemy batteries had been demolished, another four "considerably damaged," and three neutralized. Against these claims, IJA ordnance losses were not light, as Komatsubara was told on the 24th. In addition to the reported incapacitation of one of Mishima's big howitzers, no fewer than eight of Takatsukasa's sixteen 10-cm. guns were out of action, as was one of Miyao's Type 90 field pieces. Komatsubara also learned of the following losses: field guns, 3; mountain guns, 4; rapid-fire guns, 19; infantry guns, 5; antiaircraft guns, 2; heavy machine guns, 18; and light machine guns, 44.[47]

Most importantly, however, the Japanese infantry again achieved almost no progress on 24 July, in the face of undiminished fire by enemy field and heavy artillery. Hence Komatsubara decided to continue the infantry offensive, starting with night operations on 24/25 July. From the viewpoint of the IJA heavy artillery, part of the problem stemmed from the continuing lack of precise reference features. The condition worsened on 24 July. Whereas the day before, Sambur Obo had proved useful for plotting purposes, Mishima says that the foe dealt the Japanese a blow on the 24th by deliberately knocking out the *obo*. Conversely, field artillery Sergeant Tanaka remembers, the enemy had apparently constructed prior to the operation triangular mud hills to serve as man-made reference points on the right shore of the Halha, and they heightened the effectiveness of Soviet fire when Japanese forces approached. According to Captain Kusaba, the Russians' shelling was also comparatively accurate against positions taken from them by the Japanese, since the enemy relied upon mounds built before abandoning the sites for ranging purposes.[48]

The outlook of the IJA artillery commanders, as 24 July came to a close, is summed up in Colonel Ise's cheerful order issued at 8 P.M. Only defeated enemy remnants survived on the right shore of the Halha. Hostile artillery had been reduced in numbers, and their fire had become unaggressive. The 23rd Division was going to continue the offensive, advance to the Halha River on 24/25 July, bombard the bridge, and secure key points on the right bank. Uchiyama's artillery corps, in addition to cooperating with the division's attack, would seek and destroy enemy artillery. There is nothing new about these missions, but the ammunition allowance for 25 July was still set at approximately two *kisū* only.[49]

The 25th of July was fine until midnight, when rain commenced. Artillery dueling began at 7 A.M., and grew especially severe by afternoon. On Mishima's sector, the coordination of spotting between the 1st Artillery Regiment and the air force was working better, and the 1st Battery reported success in neutralizing hostile guns in the morning. But Soviet firing was plotted well, and the gun line of the 1st Battery was hit squarely, killing a squad leader. Under concentrated enemy barrages, the Japanese battery was ordered to suspend firing.

The 2nd Battery also did well in the morning, smashing a battery on the road down to the Halha, across the river. Action was intense around 4 P.M., when the three remaining Japanese howitzers fired one after another, but the hostile guns, far from suppressed, unleashed a counterbattery bombardment. At 5:20, an enemy shell struck a shelter, killing a squad leader and another soldier and wounding four men seriously.

Tsuchiya's figures for ammunition usages on 25 July show that the 1st Battalion fired at about the same rate as on the preceding day, although expenditure of shrapnel went up a bit: 1st Battery, 223 common rounds (down 31) and 64 shrapnel (up 32); 2nd Battery, 304 common (also down 31) and 81 shrapnel (up 44).

Hayashi's 2nd Battalion, which had been moved forward to assist the infantry, worked until midday on the 25th to reinforce its rather exposed positions. For a while, hostile 15-cm. guns, which had been very active on the 24th, were suppressed by Japanese air bombing and by Takatsukasa's 10-cm. cannon, but the enemy guns resumed bombardment later. Soviet tanks also fired heavily at 4 P.M. Finally, around 6:30, Hayashi's battalion of howitzers took a 15-cm. unit's observation post under fire and hit it, but this drew a fierce new barrage an hour later.[50]

Among other noteworthy actions by IJA artillery units on 25 July was the combat of Ise's field guns. In particular, Seki's 3rd Battalion detected enemy efforts to repair the confluence bridge under cover of bombardments that began at daybreak and were directed against IJA gun sites and infantry lines. The 9th Battery took under fire Soviet troops seen working on the span and matériel piled up around it. In addition, the 7th Battery engaged in antiartillery bombardment all day, trying to neutralize emplacements on the high ground across the Halha, and to "check and confuse" hostile guns and columns of trucks that could be observed moving on the left bank.[51]

The Japanese army had used observation balloons effectively in the China theater, where friendly aircraft possessed almost uncontested air supremacy. To supplement the weak IJA infantry-artillery spotting capability at Nomonhan, a 200-man unit with two balloons from Lt. Col. Kōketsu Tetsuzō's regiment based at Chiba had been ordered to Manchuria at the same time the heavy artillery was transferred from the homeland. About 17 or 18 meters in height and 7 or 8 meters in diameter, the main blue-silk balloon carried a crew of two observers in a suspended gondola. Artillery Captain Tsuchiya, back from the China front, was among those who recommended strongly that balloons be used for spotting at Nomonhan.

The independent company, with its one balloon (called No. 101), arrived behind the lines on the afternoon of 24 July and was immediately attached to Maj. Gen. Hata's artillery group. A smaller reserve balloon stayed with the platoon left in Hailar. Hata directed the balloon company to cooperate with his cannon batteries. Antiaircraft guns were deployed at the balloon launching site, and fighter planes were ordered to provide cover.

No. 101 went up three times on the morning of 25 July, starting about 7 A.M. The first two times, the unit commander and a spotting officer were aboard as the balloon soared to 900 meters and remained aloft for about 10 minutes. Danger from hostile planes forced the balloon to be hauled down after the second mission. When it was decided to send the balloon up once again to 1,000 meters, around 11 A.M., air cover was absent but the observation crew was anxious to help improve the accuracy of the artillery's firing for effect. Suddenly, from a concealed airstrip across the Halha, three Soviet I-16 fighters darted out. Gunfire barely repelled them once, but on a second pass five minutes later they cut their engines, dived very low, then zoomed up over the crestline near the Japanese positions and easily raked the balloon with machine-gun fire. In a twinkling, it burst into scarlet flame. The gondola failed to separate and both officers—Captain Kobayashi and 2nd Lieutenant Miura—died in the crash.

Almost all the IJA front-line troops could see the death of the blue balloon. When it first rose, the men had been cheered greatly, not only because of its spotting value but also because it showed the supremacy of the Japanese in the skies. There was a hushed feeling of helplessness when the balloon was attacked. The I-16 fighters' balloon-busting was, in Komatsubara's words, "like a hawk pouncing upon a sparrow." The well-trained Soviet air force's low-level ground-strafing ability in general, wrote the division commander, was superior to the Japanese. Balloon observation in combat against the Russians therefore demanded "special attention and study."

Nevertheless, the Japanese continued to use observation balloons even after the fiery loss of No. 101. The reserve balloon, "Fusan," was brought up from Hailar around 9 August, and its one-man crew got away with spotting almost every day. While airborne on 23 August, "Fusan" was destroyed, but the lieutenant aboard parachuted to safety. Meanwhile, a replacement for No. 101 had arrived in early August and was sent aloft repeatedly. In mid-August, at anchor on the ground, it was incinerated by a 15-cm. cannon shell.[52] Like the IJA "knights of the sky" who engaged in dogfights throughout the hostilities, the anachronistic Japanese balloonists in their open gondolas on the exposed plains at Nomonhan bring to mind the First World War in Europe as well as the China conflict from 1937 on.

Hata was essentially pleased with operations on 25 July, the third day of the general offensive. Little more than one *kisū* of ammunition had been expended as a whole, with "splendid results." Approximately two enemy batteries had been smashed and three damaged considerably. Japanese losses were light. Apparently, the artillery offensive was paying off for the infantry, as had been hoped. Though by no means decisive, the rifle units' attacks were finally making progress in penetrating Soviet defenses.

In the three days of artillery combat, ammunition expenditure had approximated four and a half *kisū*.[53] Using no more than 34 or 35 heavy guns

TABLE 27.2

Results of the Japanese Artillery Offensive, 23-25 July 1939, by Type of Soviet Artillery

Type of Soviet artillery	Number at outset (confirmed)	Number destroyed	Number neutralized	Number remaining
15-cm. gun	12	4	2	6
15-cm. howitzer	12	3	2	7
10-cm. gun	24	3	4	17
12-cm. howitzer	16	5	1	10
Field piece	12	9	1	2
Total	76	24	10	42
Percent	100%	32%	13%	55%

SOURCES: Y. Hata, "Nikki" [5], 25 July 1939; Komatsubara [25], 24 July 1939.

in the strictly antiartillery role, the Japanese batteries had engaged something like 100 Soviet pieces: an original, confirmed number of 64 cannon and howitzers, plus 12 field pieces, on the left shore; and 20 or 30 field guns on the right. These figures excluded still other firepower emplaced outside the 1st Artillery Group's immediate sector. Yet although hostile artillery was still resisting stubbornly, Soviet losses were judged to have been severe. By the evening of the 25th, Hata says he was able to confirm the fact that the foe's firepower had been reduced gradually by about one half since the commencement of the Japanese offensive (see Table 27.2).[54]

For differing reasons, the local Japanese artillery and infantry commands were more than ready to resume the attack on 26 July. Higher authority, however, had decided otherwise. On the afternoon of the 25th, Kwantung Army staff officer Shimanuki Takeharu conveyed word from Hsinking that the 23rd Division was to suspend the offensive immediately and to fortify its advance positions without waiting to eliminate the enemy bridgehead on the right side of the Halha. This represents an admission by the Kwantung Army that the much-heralded general offensive had not really succeeded. On the evening of 25 July, Uchiyama told Hata that the decision had been reached at Hsinking from the "larger standpoint," including the problem of artillery ammunition. Hata's group must be ready to go on for another two months.[55] To understand these developments and how they affected both the 23rd Division and the artillery corps, we must now consider the Japanese infantry's part in the operations of 23-25 July.

28

Komatsubara's Last Push Toward the River

There is nothing that cannot be accomplished. If you have the will, you can penetrate heaven and earth.

Hagakure, 144 [1]

At the meeting with Komatsubara on 11 July, Uchiyama had prevailed upon the reluctant division commander to suspend his infantry's night attacks, to pull back all advance elements from the Halha River zone, and to stake everything on a general offensive. But the momentum of the night assaults could not be checked immediately. South of the Holsten, the Nagano detachment fought its way atop the Noro complex on 13/14 July and headed for the Halha opposite Sambur Obo. On the right wing, Sumi took advantage of the Soviet disarray and advanced toward the river on the 14th. Such aggressive actions violated the intention of the Kwantung Army, which wanted the 23rd Division to focus all its efforts on the general offensive. Staff Maj. Kurasawa Kinzaburō was dispatched from Hsinking to convey strong word directly to Komatsubara to "consolidate the lines" (*sensen seiri*). Consequently, Sumi was "chewed out" by the division and forced to withdraw on the 14th, and Nagano—who had had to be pushed forward originally—was now directed to fall back on the same day. [2]

Komatsubara's decision to pull out was a godsend for the Soviet-MPRA side, which was particularly outnumbered in infantry during July and had had to leave weakly defended gaps of one or two kilometers between groupings. The Japanese had been striking into these interstices during the constant night attacks, say the Russians, necessitating the quick transfer of entire units from one sector to another—sometimes across great distances—and their commitment to battle from the march. Fortunately for the Soviet command, it was able to detect Japanese offensive preparations ahead of time. Into the unexpected vacuum created by the unilateral IJA withdrawal from the right bank poured Soviet and Mongolian reinforcements, starting on the very day Komatsubara issued his pullback order, 12 July. Among the reserves rushed up were Lt. Col. I. I. Fedyuninsky's 24th Motorized Infantry Regiment and the 5th Infantry Machine Gun Brigade. [3]

During the 10-day period preceding the Japanese general offensive, there was considerable combat along the entire front. But it was the Russians who maintained the pressure now, launching very aggressive infantry and armor probes, supported by aircraft and the unrelenting artillery. The 71st Regiment, for example, reported incurring one barrage of 120 artillery rounds in a period of 30 minutes on 18 July. All IJA infantry unit records refer to the enemy's constant construction and improvement of defenses and steady buildup of forces, a buildup so pronounced that a soldier from the Nagano detachment said the region south of the Holsten was swarming with Soviet forces. It seemed to him as though hostile troops were "hiding behind every little dune." According to the Sakai regiment, even when IJA heavy artillery moved into position on 20/21 July, the enemy outposts did not pull back. In fact, Soviet guard measures were so tight, it became difficult for IJA patrols to infiltrate the Russian lines.

The Japanese infantry units, traditionally uncomfortable in the under-emphasized defensive role, found themselves fettered further by the priorities assigned to the artillery corps, from whom so much was expected. In the words of the 71st Regiment chronicler: "Our detachment had merely been staying in the positions and had left the initiative to the enemy, while waiting until the artillery's preparations were complete. [Despite severe enemy assaults and penetrations] we avoided replying. Our stance was very negative and conservative, compared to the foe's positive, active attitude."

Later, there was a feeling in Japanese military circles that the Soviet side made far better use of the lull, which was, after all, equally long for both parties. While the Russians built "amazingly strong" positions, the Japanese infantry "took it relatively easy." This interpretation is buttressed by the notes of an officer in the Nagano regiment: "During the period of 15-22 July, while waiting for the buildup of the heavy artillery, we did not conduct defense because we were thinking [exclusively] of offense."[4] The difference in preparation would prove extremely important once the Japanese offensive got under way. In this regard, the experience of a field-grade officer in the 64th Infantry Regiment is illuminating.

The 3rd Battalion had acquired a brand-new commander, Kanaizuka Yūkichi, a 45-year-old major, transferred from the border garrison unit at Sunwu to replace the wounded Major Fukumura. Rushed to the front on 20 July by train, light plane, truck, and foot, Kanaizuka had no time to be briefed. Kobayashi, for example, told him to hurry to his regiment; the general offensive was scheduled to begin the very next morning, and he should learn about the situation and study the terrain while there was still light. Enemy artillery fire had begun, so Kanaizuka and the battalion aide walked 500 or 600 meters from Kobayashi's headquarters to the 64th Regiment's command post (consisting of tents in a dip), where he met Yamagata for the first time and officially reported his arrival. The colonel was energetic (*genki*), and everybody was in high spirits (*teki o nomu*). The regimental flag was uncased for him, the colonel placed imperial sake before it, and Kanaizuka saluted, bowed, and venerated the colors.

In a lull between bombardments, Kanaizuka and the aide ran about 1,000 meters to his battalion command post, situated in an uncovered trench. The acting commander, Capt. Gotō Chikashi, showed him the rough regimental orders and told him about the offensive slated for the next day. Kanaizuka had not heard any details before, but he "was expecting this anyhow." When all the company commanders assembled, they told him to his face (but respectfully) that he had seen no combat and would only order them to charge. The battalion had incurred very heavy casualties; only about 900 men were available from an assigned strength of nearly 1,500. It was obvious that the officers were worried and fearful of irresponsible charging. Kanaizuka retorted that he had had lots of battle experience. As a company commander in the 63rd Infantry, he had fought more than 30 times— throughout Manchuria (including engagements against Chang Tso-lin's regulars), and in North China at Shanhaikuan and elsewhere. "I know how to fight," he told his officers, "and you must follow me." They seemed relieved to learn the new battalion commander's attitude.

After his first night in the trenches—a quiet night—Kanaizuka awoke to learn that the offensive plan had faded out for the day. It was not possible to conduct terrain inspection by daylight because of the enemy's sector barrages (*chiku shageki*)—lines of fire at varying angles. Kanaizuka could already see how difficult the conveyance of orders would be in such flat and misleading terrain, where measurement of distances might have to be done by aiming one's hands and gauging from a knoll or tree. In the afternoon, Yamagata called in all his unit commanders and issued revised orders. In particular, he assigned new and systematic sectors based on the terrain, whereas previously the battalions had been merely "lined up" on the plains. About ten men, mainly runners, were being killed every day when exposed on the slopes by snipers firing from high ground 1,500 meters away. The colonel insisted that a communications trench (*kōtsūgō*) be dug around the rise to protect the runners. This time, he said, he would not budge until the trench was actually dug, and he waited two hours until a large number of soldiers had finished the job. Kanaizuka surmised that since the Japanese infantry was planning an offensive, the platoon leaders must have wanted to rest their men and not expend labor on the trench project. The sloppiness and laxness that Yamagata was resisting and that Kanaizuka was observing so soon after his arrival at the front were complemented by a collateral matter of nerve, as revealed in the following episode. Anxious to study the terrain and the layout of his companies, Kanaizuka peered through the periscope at his command post, under fire. While he was curiously and unconcernedly observing, "the other officers were cringing, covering their faces as if they were dead."[5] Yet this was one of the line infantry battalions that was to jump off on the morning of the general offensive, hardly 48 hours after Major Kanaizuka met it for the first time.

Part of Komatsubara's rationale for suspending the night attacks had been the need to conserve and to rehabilitate his depleted manpower, while acquiring replacements for the thousands of casualties. On 14 July, the 23rd Division and attached infantry units received an increment distributed as follows: Yamagata regiment, 275; Nagano regiment, 290 (including a new commander for the 1st Battalion, Maj. Sugitachi Kamenojō); Sakai regiment, 325; Sumi regiment, 230; Kajikawa battalion, 40.[6] These 1,160 reinforcements were a modest augmentation but were certainly welcome, especially since the availability of manpower had been further reduced by serious outbreaks of amoebic dysentery, caused largely by problems with drinking water. The epidemic debilitated entire units. Sergeant Tanaka, a field-artillery squad leader, remembers a fever of 102° F., loss of appetite, and 17 or 18 trips to the latrine in the five hours of darkness. From the second day, lacking the strength to climb out of his trench, he had to dig a toilet pit in the ditch itself. About the best that Tanaka can say about this miserable period is that he was "lucky" to get sick during the two-week "slightly slack" phase prior to the general offensive. Many other officers and men had to be evacuated from the lines and sent to the hospital.[7]

The Kwantung Army and the 23rd Division, however, were expecting the Japanese infantry not only to retake the ground that had been abandoned after the suspension of the night attacks but also to push all the way to the Halha with relative ease. Komatsubara was still relying on three main infantry forces: a rather weak right wing consisting of Sumi's 26th Regiment; a strong center, with Kobayashi controlling two regiments, Yamagata's 64th and Sakai's 72nd; and another weak wing across the Holsten on the left consisting of Nagano's 71st Regiment plus Manchukuoan cavalry. Kajikawa's battalion was in divisional reserve. Colonel Ise's 13th Field Artillery continued to provide the closest firepower support—one battery backing Sumi, two batteries with Kobayashi's group, another two batteries assisting Nagano. In short, with Yasuoka's tanks out of action, the Japanese ground forces to be committed to the general offensive were the same as had been used since the 2 July operation, except for the introduction of the approximately 35 heavy guns under Uchiyama and Hata.

The plan that the Japanese command devised in mid-July for the general offensive called for the infantry to jump off for the Halha in Period 1/Phase 2 at 10 A.M., after two hours of softening-up fire by the artillery corps. In addition to receiving the cooperation of the entire field artillery, the rifle units would be assisted by the 15-cm. howitzers and the Type 90 field guns in particular. The air force would provide cover, bombardment support, and reconnaissance. Once the infantry had reached the riverbank, supposedly by midday, Period 2 would begin. Rifle elements would guard the line of the Halha, while the main body would assemble in key areas to the rear. If the situation permitted, positions should be constructed. During Period 2, presumably only a portion of the artillery would be needed to assist the infantry. After all, the bridgehead on the right shore would have been "choked off and annihilated" by now, freeing the heavy guns to engage what remained of enemy artillery across the Halha. Engineers, moving behind the Kobayashi group, would take care of "cleanup" operations near the confluence bridge.[8] The whole scenario reeked of the paper plan, very hopeful but very unreal.

On the Sakai regiment's sector, Major Nishikawa had been anxious to hurl his 1st Battalion against Jūgan and Mitsubosa heights ahead of the main infantry offensive, because those hills dominated the confluence sector. Although Sakai accepted Nishikawa's recommendation at first, on 22 July he reversed himself after receiving divisional orders. Since there would be danger of drawing concentrated enemy fire otherwise, the Nishikawa battalion was to jump off at the same time as all the other units—10 A.M.

X-day, 23 July, began on this front with all three batteries of Seki's 3rd Battalion of the 13th Field Artillery Regiment moving up their forward observers and hammering the Jūgan and Mitsubosa targets at ranges of 1,300 to 1,625 meters between 7:30 and 8 A.M. Enemy bunkers on Jūgan proved to be particularly sturdy, but by approximately 9 A.M. the batteries, aided by infantry heavy weapons, reported success in knocking out embrasures, observation posts, and heavy weapons, as well as guns on the reverse slope. Nevertheless, enemy counterbattery fire continued to hit the Japanese observation posts and battalion train, and to tear up communications. It became apparent to the Japanese artillery command that the stipulated two hours of firing for effect were not achieving the desired overall results. Sakai was told at 9:30 that the starting time for his infantry to attack had been set back to 11 A.M.

At Kemushi (Caterpillar) Heights, Nishikawa had been ready to attack since 7 A.M. He and his men watched the great barrages by friendly batteries with pleasure and hope, but no word reached them (or the attached field artillery battalion, for that matter) of the extension of the bombardment by one hour. Nishikawa sent up a star shell and began his advance a little before 10 A.M. About 200 or 300 meters from Jūgan Heights, the battalion prepared to charge. But when Nishikawa got through by phone to Sakai, the latter barked, "Who told you to go?" Nishikawa has a quaint explanation for his companies' failure to hold up. First he yelled "*Tomare!*" ("Stop!") to his men, and when that did not work, "*Teishi!*" ("Halt!"). Later, when the major asked the troops about it, they said they heard "*Mae!*" ("Forward!") for "*Tomare!,*" and "*Zenshin!*" ("Advance!") for "*Teishi!*" So they kept on going.

Major Seki, observing the Nishikawa battalion storming up Jūgan Heights at 10:20, immediately ordered his 9th Battery to strike the dip behind the hill, and his 7th Battery to neutralize the flanking fire from Mitsubosa Heights. Lines were unavailable to the 8th Battery, but on his own initiative its commander lifted the range to hit behind Jūgan.

First Lt. Nakao Sukeo's 1st Infantry Company made it up Mitsubosa, and 1st Lt. Morimoto Takeshi's 2nd Company up Jūgan, by 10:30 A.M. The field artillery units were pleased when Morimoto thanked them for their help; he said he had expected severe casualties, but the supporting fire had enabled his company to take Jūgan with light losses. After the 9th Battery pounded Midori (Green) Heights on the flank, 2nd Lt. Hamada Gajō's reserve 3rd Company seized that objective too.

Seki ordered all his artillery observation posts to keep up with the infantry, but when he was about to move his command post atop Mitsubosa Heights, hostile remnants were discovered on the hill. The artillery battalion's observation-post chief joined an infantry platoon in evicting the enemy and setting up an observation post by 10:40 A.M. Numerous shells from friendly artillery continued to hit the hill.

On Nishikawa's sector, the Russians abandoned about 130 corpses in all, plus quantities of machine guns and small arms; but by advancing prematurely, the 1st Battalion exposed its right flank and rear to fire from the higher ground on the Yamagata front—i.e., Heights 733. Peering from Jūgan and Mitsubosa Heights, Nishikawa could see many more dunes extending toward the confluence, "so apparently we had not accomplished as much as I had expected." Although both heights were reported secure by noon, Sakai feared that the 1st Battalion would become isolated if it proceeded farther, so he ordered Nishikawa to hold up. But of course the enemy had preregistered the locations of the hills they had lost, and could bring down accurate barrages upon them.

To the left of Nishikawa, Major Kokura's 2nd Battalion had deployed on the crestline and begun its advance at 11 A.M. The 6th Company, which had been under attack since the 22nd, encountered strong resistance at positions on the high ground to the south, where the barbed-wire entanglements were dense. From midday, the battalion came under flanking fire from the Nagano sector across the Holsten, but after some hard fighting it reached a line almost abreast of Nishikawa's progress by 3 P.M. The failure of Yamagata's operation in the Heights 733 zone, however, exerted an adverse ripple effect on both Nishikawa and Kokura.

Sakai had moved his regimental command post to the location of the Kokura battalion's 7th Company by 1 P.M. and to Mitsubosa Heights by 3 P.M. There were problems, however, with friendly heavy artillery, one of whose shells exploded too close to the infantry's front lines at 5 P.M. The troops frantically waved the red-ball flag, but nothing helped, and a second round slammed into the 2nd Battalion's positions, fortunately causing no losses. Sakai kept trying to get the heavy artillery to stop firing. But there was only praise for Seki's 3rd Field Artillery Battalion, which cooperated very closely all day and engaged such targets as tanks, observation posts, heavy weapons, and artillery, and also attacked the bridges at the confluence. The commander of the 9th Battery, Capt. Kai Mansuke, was killed by tank fire in the afternoon while observing from Jūgan Heights.

Directed by Komatsubara, through Kobayashi, to resume the infantry's offensive toward the Halha during the hours of darkness, Sakai issued detailed attack orders between 8 and 8:30 P.M. Among the targets to be eliminated in the bridgehead on the right shore were the Halha spans, four of which had now been located in the general area of the confluence. En route to the river line, which was to be secured by daylight on the 24th, the regiment would rendezvous at a particular sand dune. Jump-off time was set for 10:30 P.M.

Preparations were not completed until 11 P.M., at which time the units began the advance, with Nishikawa's 1st Battalion in the lead. The first objective, 700 meters ahead, was seized by midnight. Armored vehicles and 80-90 enemy infantrymen, who had sent up flares and fired machine guns, were driven off by the 2nd Company's "shouting charge" with the bayonet. To the left, Kokura's 2nd Battalion softened up the first lines at 1 A.M. and then penetrated the positions with almost no loss. Discerning signs of enemy retreat, the battalion pressed ahead, took the second lines by 4 A.M., dug in, and linked up with Nishikawa's unit. Sakai dispatched reserves to mop up 20-30 Soviet soldiers, with machine guns, who were found holding out behind the farthest point of the Japanese advance.[9]

To the right of Sakai's regiment, Yamagata's 64th Infantry awaited jump-off time to strike against the Heights 733 district. Southeast of the objective and east of Mitsubosa Heights, the 3rd Battalion was deployed, holding the left front of the regiment. Although the new commander, Major Kanaizuka, had discerned certain qualitative weaknesses in his battalion, as we have seen, the men's morale was high as they looked forward to the appearance of the air force and the heavy artillery (including Prince Higashikuni's battery) to pave the way for their seizure of objectives. Enemy fire, however, had prevented Kanaizuka from inspecting his individual companies or from using more than periscope and binoculars to appraise the terrain, although he did send out several patrols between 20 and 22 July.

Japanese planes appeared at dawn and air fighting ensued, but the IJA aircraft flew away without bombing the enemy. This was disappointing to the infantry, but at least the supporting 15-cm. howitzers, 500 meters to the rear, opened fire on schedule at 7:30 A.M. New frustrations were in store, however. The Soviet artillery units replied immediately, and their fire, instead of abating, grew more severe. Their range was so much better that they could fire without hindrance. Indeed, enemy soldiers could be seen in the open near their guns on the heights. The Japanese artillery batteries started to shoot without apparent knowledge of the range; once they learned that they could not reach the hostile guns, they soon stopped their useless firing. But the enemy continued to bombard IJA positions all day, probably returning three or four shells for every one fired by the Japanese.

The exact timing for the infantry jump-off was supposed to be the subject of separate regimental orders, but Kanaizuka heard nothing by radio or phone, perhaps because communications had been knocked out. Meanwhile, the enemy artillery, which had been firing at the infantry positions, lifted to engage the batteries to the rear. Immediately, without specific instructions from the regiment, Kanaizuka ordered the advance elements of his battalion to move forward against a hillock lying 500-800 meters ahead. The 12th Company attacked on the left and the 9th Company on the right, supported by some heavy machine guns and the two battalion guns, which tried to provide cover by firing against the enemy positions and heavy weapons. In the face of withering machine-gun fire from the hillock, which hit them when they had advanced only 40 or 50 meters, the Japanese riflemen crawled ahead and, by 11:20 A.M., managed to storm through the barbed wire and into the trenches. There had been only about 30 Russians on the hillock, and they fled, leaving no casualties or prisoners behind. Kanaizuka ran ahead to join his companies.

Examining the scene, the major realized that the hillock was an isolated position below the main hostile defenses on the heights another 500 or 600 meters to the front. All kinds of enemy fire rained down on the battalion, pinning down the headquarters, the battalion guns, the machine guns, and the two reserve companies that were supposed to follow the attack units. On the hillock was the 12th Company, with the 9th Company on the right and nothing on the left. The two front-line companies were separated not only from the rest of the battalion but also from each other. Kanaizuka could see enemy artillery burning the ground in front and all around, apparently scorching his crawling men. Flamethrowers were suspected, but the fires proved to have been accidentally caused. In any case, no further advance was possible.

At 11:40 A.M., the Russians launched a counterassault down the slope from the heights ahead, sending forward five medium tanks firing machine guns and 37-mm. cannon, followed by 250 infantrymen crawling through the grass, which was still burning in patches. The armored vehicles must have possessed 1,000 cannon rounds each, for they sprayed shells like machine-gun bullets. Kanaizuka had his battalion heavy weapons engage the tanks, which turned back without being hit.

Kanaizuka's men had to stay where they were all day. Although the major sent runners to advise Yamagata of the seizure of the hillock, there was no direct communication with the 64th Regiment or with Sakai's infantry 1,000 meters to the left. Fifteen or 16 of Kanaizuka's men had been killed, mainly in the attack on the hillock, and especially in the 12th Company. There were more dead than wounded, although the 9th Company commander, 1st Lieutenant Nishimura, was injured by machine-gun fire and had to be evacuated next day.

With the other Japanese battalions bogged down and his own unit jutting forward alone, Kanaizuka waited until twilight, around 8 P.M., to resume the advance, again on his own initiative, against the main enemy defenses on the high ground. Once more, the 9th and 12th companies were in the lead, supported by heavy machine guns. The Russians laid down machine-gun fire of their own, characterized by one tracer in ten. Before the Japanese penetrated the first lines, the enemy fell back to second positions on the downslope 50-100 meters below. A runner who was sent to report to Yamagata brought back word that the colonel was very pleased with the Kanaizuka battalion's actions and would send up the 1st Battalion to provide support from the right.

The Kanaizuka unit received fire from the second line and at 11 P.M. was counterattacked by Soviet infantrymen, who were pushed back in 50 minutes without hand-to-hand fighting. By 12:30 A.M. the battalion had occupied the entire first line and was starting to dig in. At 1:30, Kanaizuka ordered a new attack, against the second positions; but the Soviet machine guns fired upward against the Japanese over the crestline, and even their blind shooting was deadly. Kanaizuka's men never made it to the second line, and they fell back to the first positions. The major found it difficult to consolidate the troops in the confusion after the foiled attack. Later, he heard that Yamagata had asked the 1st Battalion why it did not help. The reply was that casualties had been heavy, morale had been damaged, and movement had proved impossible.

Kanaizuka had his men build up the breastworks at the former first line of the enemy, but facing the other way now. It was a wise move, for at 4:30 A.M., three Soviet tanks led 100-200 infantry in an attack up the slope on the 12th Company front. A nearly full moon made the field as bright as day, and visibility extended to 1,000 meters. This time, the enemy faced the same kind of problems encountered by the 3rd Battalion in the attempt to seize the Russians' second line. Japanese regimental and rapid-fire guns were instrumental in beating back the assault, without casualties to the IJA infantry. Finally, at dawn, the 1st Battalion showed up on the right, to the rear of the 9th Company. Runners reached Kanaizuka from the regiment with orders to maintain the occupied positions using the 1st Battalion reinforcements; the 2nd Battalion remained in reserve.

To the right of Kanaizuka's unit the 1st Battalion, about which so much has been said, was also the victim of diminishing expectations on 23 July. It, too, had a new commander, Maj. Akai Toyosaburō, who had taken over on the 21st. In the trenches the day began with high hopes. A couple of company commanders, in a recent toast by an exuberant staff officer, had been assured that, once the Japanese heavy artillery opened up, the enemy would flee across the Halha and the infantry would be able to get to Komatsu Heights "with their eyes closed." The keyed-up soldiers were thrilled by the fact that an imperial prince commanded a battery behind them, and during breakfast joked about climbing the banks on the left side of the river by evening. Four enemy armored vehicles appeared at 5 A.M. but withdrew before they could be engaged.

Friendly artillery commenced the bombardment on schedule, but enemy counterfire did not let up, and shells flew over with the raging sound of a typhoon. At about 11 A.M., the Sumi regiment could be seen moving forward on the right. Akai deployed his 1st and 2nd companies forward around 11:30, with the heavy machine guns in support and 1st Lt. Someya Hatsuo's 4th Company in reserve. Through his binoculars, Someya could observe that the advancing companies were having a hard time and that men were falling all around. For example, on the 2nd Company front, a figure in a white shirt could be seen waving a saber until he toppled to the ground. He proved to be a rifle platoon leader, a second lieutenant who had just returned from the infantry school. He and a machine-gun platoon leader were both slain at noon by flanking fire laid down by some ten tanks that irrupted from the right because Sumi's unit was not making any progress there. Akai's battalion had hardly advanced 500 meters when its casualties mounted to 80. The supporting 6th Field Artillery Battery sought to suppress enemy heavy machine guns on this sector at 12:30 and again at 2:30 P.M.

When Akai ordered the 4th Company into action, Someya led his unit forward under fire, through the dead and wounded of the 1st Company. A platoon leader, a second lieutenant, lay sprawled on the ground, hit in the thigh. Someya told him to drag himself into the relative safety of a crater, wished him well, and crawled on. The barbed wire and trenches of enemy positions could be sighted, 300 meters ahead. Someya jumped up, dashed forward, and was shot through the chest. He wanted to struggle ahead, since the enemy was on the run, but his throat seemed to be on fire and breathing became difficult. Someya raised his saber and tried to tell his men where their company commander was. Evacuated to the rear, the lieutenant said his greatest regret was to have lost the chance to climb Komatsu Heights into Outer Mongolia.

Supported by the battalion's heavy weapons and by the 6th Battery, with Someya's company on the right, the 1st and 2nd companies managed to seize the crestline by seesaw fighting around 4 P.M. But the 1st Battalion's casualties had been heavy, amounting to 122 on 23 July. Losses of commanders were particularly severe. In the 1st and 2nd companies, both machine-gun platoon leaders and three other officers (including an infantry platoon leader) were killed. The wounded included an infantry platoon leader in the 1st Company; the 2nd Company's commander, Capt. Kawai Sadamu, and another officer; and the 4th Company commander, Lieutenant Someya.

This was the situation when, as Kanaizuka phrases it, Yamagata "prodded" the 1st Battalion to catch up. At 5:30 P.M., in keeping with Komatsubara's desire to regain the initiative, the regiment commander ordered that Mitsubosa Heights be taken. Akai's battalion spent a lot of time pulling the units together and retrieving the many casualties. Completing its assembly at 2 A.M. on 24 July, the battalion began the night offensive an hour later, headed for the saddle on the left of Mitsubosa, cleared the objective at 4 A.M., and finally linked up with the 3rd Battalion. Although Kanaizuka knows of Akai's heavy casualties, he says that the 1st Battalion did not have to fight to take the open sector to his right. Waiting until dawn for the 1st Battalion to arrive was obviously troublesome for Kanaizuka. To this, the Akai battalion's chronicler responds obliquely that the left-front 3rd Battalion seemed gradually to have been "propelled ahead" (*suishin*) as the result of "scant consideration of the flank and the advantages of terrain." [10]

Sumi's 26th Regiment, deployed to the right of Yamagata, was delighted when friendly heavy artillery opened fire on the morning of 23 July. It was the first time at Nomonhan, says Sumi, that the infantry heard Japanese ordnance heavier than a regimental gun. But the scale of the enemy's response was staggering. An IJA artillery officer later told the colonel that the Soviet guns fired 30,000 to the Japanese guns' 10,000 rounds. One platoon leader remarks that the roar of the enemy artillery was much more thunderous—something like "carpet bombing." [11] As Sumi says, the enemy was clearly forewarned, but the colonel had to send his men into the teeth of the storm, as ordered.

The 3rd Battalion, temporarily commanded by 1st Lieutenant Kokubu, on the left front of the 26th Infantry and thus nearest to the Akai battalion of Yamagata's regiment, pressed its attack before noon. Under fierce fire, it began to lag behind and ended up on the right rear of the 2nd Battalion. This explains the complaint of the 64th Infantry that the adjoining regiment's offensive did not progress well.

Leading the assault on Sumi's right front was Major Kawai's 2nd Battalion. His main force was to attack three dune positions dubbed "I," "Ro," and "Ha," after which elements were to be sent toward the bend in the Halha. Kawai's spearhead unit would be the 76 men of 1st Lt. Kimura Yoshio's 7th Company, supported by heavy machine guns. Reconnaissance had already been conducted on 22 and 23 July by 2nd Lt. Hikime Eizō. The lieutenant's patrol found no enemy defending the high ground 1,000 meters away but, after giving up crawling, had run into machine-gun fire at the main positions 300-400 meters farther. Many large and very deep holes had been dug in front of the defenses, and to the rear, considerable movement of armor was visible. Although none of Hikime's patrol was hit, he beat a hasty retreat, for the sun was rising, the squad was becoming exposed, and he was "extremely worried about getting killed before the main operation got under way."[12]

At 11:50 A.M., the 7th Company jumped off. Smoke from enemy shell bursts greatly reduced the infantrymen's vision, but by 12:40 they had reached the designated initial line, some 1,000 meters from the start. Scouting efforts were not fruitful. Kawai came up and ordered the company to take advantage of intervals in the bombardment to rush against the objective—"black-and-white-stained trenches"—on the heights lying straight ahead. Kimura issued his own orders. One platoon was to lead, with two platoons following. The heavy machine guns should engage enemy heavy weapons expected to appear on the "comb-like cliff" to the left. Once the company reached its objective, the men must immediately dig in against enemy artillery fire.

Despite barrages, Kimura's company advanced. There were no intervening positions and no targets for rifles to engage. The infantry, says Hikime, would run and drop, run and drop. By 1:30 P.M., two of the three objectives, "I" and "Ha," had been penetrated with few casualties. The dunes afforded an excellent vantage point from which to observe enemy positions toward the Halha, but the Russians knew this and had preregistered the zone. Squad and platoon leaders tried to find dead angles in which to conceal their men.

Hikime, commanding the 2nd Platoon, borrowed a range finder and discerned enemy tanks in a dip. But the river was not visible, although the men had been expected to reach the Kita-watashi crossing "in one stride." The company had pushed too far ahead, was the first to be hit, and lost touch with the battalion. Fire of all kinds was pouring in—machine cannon, mortars, machine guns, grenade launchers, tank guns. Rounds from hostile long-range weapons, emplaced across the Halha, began to dance in from both sides.

Caught in the middle, Hikime knew that the shells would reach his platoon soon, but he was stuck and "could not budge an inch." To stick out one's head was to get it blown off. It was a helpless feeling, especially for the platoon leaders. Officers led with their sabers, keeping pistols holstered; so, when pinned down, they had no means of self-defense. Since they also lacked entrenching tools, Hikime had picked up an abandoned Russian shovel on the way back from his patrol and started to dig in. His squad leader offered the lieutenant a deeper hole and was scooping out the old one for himself when an artillery round exploded nearby. Instinctively, Hikime tried to pull the soldier into his hole. But this required lifting his head and, at that instant, a shell fragment tore into Hikime's jaw, nearly severed his tongue, knocked out two teeth, and lodged behind his ear. The squad leader emerged unscathed by lying flat. It was a little after 2 P.M.

Hikime lay mute in the hole until the battalion aide came up when the bombardment eased a half-hour later. The battalion had had a difficult time locating the Kimura company, said the aide. A tourniquet was applied to Hikime; he shook off the suggestion of a lift on the aide's shoulders, and staggered back to the battalion command post. There, Major Kawai thanked him for his fine performance and assured him that he would recover soon. "Now I knew that I was dying," Hikime remembers, "but I was opposed to that, so I tried desperately to make myself understood." A litter eventually came to evacuate him, but the rest of his story borders on the miraculous, the high point being a makeshift operation in a truck at the field hospital during an air raid. A young intern cut a hole in Hikime's throat and inserted a banana-size rubber pipe in it, enabling him to breathe and saving his life. Later, his tongue was sewed together.[13] Colonel Sumi, pleased by Hikime's survival, was amazed because, as he remarks, a common method of Japanese suicide is to bite off one's own tongue deliberately.[14]

With four more men wounded at 4 P.M. and a master sergeant temporarily in charge of Hikime's platoon, company commander Kimura recommended that the third Soviet position at "Ro," about three kilometers north of the confluence, be captured by a night attack. The battalion issued the enabling order at 6:30 P.M., calling for the 7th Company and a machine-gun platoon to strike at 10:30 P.M., for the other units to continue to defend point "I," and for a patrol to advance to the Halha to reconnoiter the new bridge after "Ro" had been taken. Kimura's follow-up order stipulated that the company would seize the western corner of "Ro," cut off the enemy's retreat route, blow up the confluence bridge, and provide the springboard for the main regiment's offensive. The code words were *Hisshō* ("certain victory") and *Shinnen* ("conviction").

The 7th Company jumped off on schedule, using the compass on a moonless night. Five hundred meters ahead, an enemy outpost was encountered, covered by tanks and machine guns. Kimura veered right while his own machine guns drew fire. Despite difficulty in locating it, "Ro" was discerned by starlight and penetrated at about 1:30 A.M. Tracer fire could be seen on the left, where elements of Kokubu's battalion were advancing too, but it was not possible to identify the location of the main emplacements of the Russian heavy machine guns, whose tracers were flying very high. Around 2 A.M., a scout hollered that the gun nests were on the high ground on the right; he was cut down by enemy fire immediately. A master sergeant charged alone against one machine gun, knocked it out, and was killed in the process. Soon after 2 A.M., the company was able to storm onto the edge of the "Ro" position from the rear. During this phase, three had been killed and four wounded.

The Russians fell back a bit, leaving some corpses and many machine guns behind. Then they reassembled and concentrated small-caliber weapons against the Japanese; the sound of armor could also be heard. Enemy machine-gun emplacements on a dune to the left were particularly dangerous, and Kimura "accepted volunteers" for a last charge to seize the nest before dawn. Since everybody offered to participate, lots were drawn for 18 men to attack. Taking advantage of dead angles, 2nd Lt. Horibata Yūji, the 1st Platoon leader, led the main unit in from the front while Sergeant Murakami rushed with a squad from the rear. The enemy resisted with machine guns, grenades, and tank cannon, but the Japanese launched charge after charge, fought hand-to-hand battles, and killed more than 20 of the 30 Russians who were manning a total of seven covered machine guns. When Horibata was slain, riddled a dozen times, Murakami took over. The sergeant slashed his way forward and, in the course of one grappling match with a Russian officer, it is said, lost a thumb to the enemy's teeth. By 3:30 A.M., the last of the seven Soviet emplacements had been overrun, and "Ro" was secured. A runner was sent by Murakami to report the unit's success to battalion and regimental headquarters. In addition to Lieutenant Horibata, four soldiers were killed and three were wounded. The commander of the supporting heavy machine gun company, a first lieutenant who had rushed back from the infantry school in Japan, was slain on his first day of combat while directing fire 100 meters from "Ro."

Regimental commander Sumi, of course, was pleased that the night operations resulted in the complete clearing of the three dunes—by Kokubu's battalion at "Ha," reportedly around 1 A.M., and by Kimura's company at

"Ro" by 4 A.M. In particular, Lieutenant Horibata's action was known to the colonel as "seven charges, seven machine guns." Nevertheless, the attached engineers did not show up, and there was no chance to blow up the confluence bridge, only 500 meters away. Total casualties of the 26th Regiment on 23/24 July were 135, with particularly severe losses of officers: 11 officers and 24 men killed, five officers and 95 men wounded.[15]

South of the Holsten, Soviet-MPRA offensive action had increased markedly since 16 July. From the left side of the Halha, the enemy fired 15-cm. howitzers, supplemented by the barrages of tractor-towed field artillery and tanks that came across the confluence. On the 17th, before noon, 180 howitzer and 20 field artillery rounds hit the area around Colonel Nagano's headquarters in an "equally dispersed" pattern. Next day, at about the same time, 120 shells struck again in a 30-minute period, burying several officers and men in piles of sand, without harm. On 18/19 July, Russian tanks did not even bother to go back across the Halha, as was their practice each night, probably because the Japanese made no effort to attack them this time.

Enemy ground and air attacks continued on the Nagano front. On 20 July, about 40 Soviet fighters employed the rather unusual technique of dive-bombing the 71st Regiment's command post and the artillery. Although Japanese stockpiling of ammunition and rations, and reinforcement of rapid-fire guns, was essentially completed by the afternoon of 21 July, enemy artillery bombardment went on between midnight and dawn on 21/22 July and again on 22/23 July, just before the Japanese offensive. Apparently, the Russians were trying to cut off IJA road movement.

For the general offensive, Nagano deployed Baba's 2nd Battalion on his right, with the main spearhead mission of driving toward the river via the Kui area, paying particular heed to the danger of enemy armor irrupting from the direction of the sandbar in the Halha south of the Holsten. In the center, the new commander of the 1st Battalion, Major Sugitachi, was to attack south of Kui. The objective of Major Murata's 3rd Battalion on the left was the river crossing opposite Sambur Obo. There was need for care in reconnoitering the bridges, which were sometimes underwater. The engineers were to verify the existence of the spans and take charge of blowing them up after Kui had been seized.

At 7:40 A.M. on 23 July, Japanese batteries opened bombardment on the 71st Regiment front. It seemed to the infantry that the supporting 10-cm. battalion was neutralizing artillery across the Halha. Onozuka remembers that enemy guns were silent when the IJA batteries fired, but that when the Japanese let up the Russians replied with 300 to 500 rounds for every 100 they received. Most importantly, there was no doubt in Nagano's mind that enemy firepower directly ahead of the detachment had not been suppressed as intended during Period 1/Phase 1. Division headquarters notified the colonel by phone that jump-off time for his unit had been delayed until 11 A.M. The timing was confirmed in a message dropped by air.

Nagano moved the regimental colors to the front line of the 1st Battalion in the center, but the infantry's advance did not go well. Resistance was unexpectedly strong, and losses mounted. It was becoming apparent that the Russians had used the preceding week to prepare a firing net in minute detail, exploiting their ability to construct fortifications rapidly. Although the obstructions consisted only of low barbed wire, the enemy had cleverly established firing sites on the reverse slopes. In addition to tank guns and other heavy weapons operating from positions ahead, Soviet field artillery pounded Nagano's flank from the direction of the confluence.

By about 2 P.M., says the 71st Regiment's chronicler, "our offensive had already bogged down for the time being." The 1st and 2nd battalions had progressed no more than two or three kilometers in the push toward Kui Heights. Casualties had been grievous, especially among the officers. In the Sugitachi battalion, the 1st Company commander had been wounded critically and one of his platoon leaders had been killed. The regimental aide and the regimental-gun battery commander had also been slain.

Only on the Murata battalion's sector, defended somewhat less strongly at the moment and farthest to the left from the Holsten, was there any degree of Japanese success. The unit managed to launch an assault in the direction of a little key point two kilometers east of the Sambur crossing, Ichimonji (Beeline) dune, which was 50 meters long and a mere 3-4 meters above the flat plain.

In addition to the fire support attempted by the 10-cm. cannon batteries, Ise's field artillery assigned the 1st Battalion to cooperate with Nagano's offensive. The four field pieces of the 2nd Battery engaged 26 targets at ranges of 2,200 to 6,000 meters, and fired 772 rounds between 6:30 A.M. and 10:30 P.M.

Since the Nagano detachment's daytime operations, like those of many other Japanese infantry units on 23 July, had proved inconclusive, in the afternoon Komatsubara called for a night attack to reach the river and destroy the bridges. The 2nd Battalion tried to advance on the right at twilight— 8 P.M.—but was held up before the deep enemy positions and had made negligible progress when daybreak came. In his sector, 1st Battalion commander Sugitachi led the charge and gnawed at the defenses straight ahead, destroying a pair of armored cars in the process. Here, too, the offensive bogged down.

On the left flank, out of touch with the regiment, Murata had led the attack by two companies against Ichimonji dune on his own initiative. Company commander Onozuka Kichihei, an ever-confident *kendō* expert, engaged in another series of charges with his famous sword. Too keyed-up to think normally or to be afraid, the captain concentrated almost automatically on protecting himself and cutting down or running through any enemy soldier he found in a trench. Casualties were heavy but the elevation was largely cleared. Unfortunately for the Japanese, however, contact could not be made with Nagano's command post. Not only was the regimental commander unaware of the seizure of the Ichimonji hillock, but he was also apprehensive about the fate of the 3rd Battalion.[16]

The local Japanese artillery and infantry commands inevitably differed in their views of the results of the first day of the general offensive. Though Uchiyama and Hata might call Soviet firepower "weakened considerably," it was clear that the rifle units had not been enabled to eliminate the bridgehead on the right bank, especially by day. In this sense, what had been accomplished by suspending the infantry night attacks that had pierced the Soviet-MPRA shore defenses, by abandoning the territory taken at such cost, and by starting afresh against a rejuvenated enemy?

Komatsubara understood that, on 23 July, Sumi's regiment had reached the three dunes "I," "Ro," and "Ha," that Yamagata and Sakai had attained a line three kilometers east of the Halha, and that Nagano had advanced two kilometers beyond Kui Heights. Further progress had become difficult, said the division commander, because of "subjugation by enemy artillery." Enemy planes held sway above the battlefield. Infantry group commander Kobayashi shared the evaluation insofar as it applied to his sector in the center. Friendly heavy artillery simply had not succeeded on Sakai's front. Consequently, wrote Kobayashi, the main offensive by the infantry at 11 A.M. had had to be launched without first obtaining neutralization of hostile firepower. This explained the difficulties encountered by the Nishikawa and Kokura battalions of the 72nd Regiment. In Yamagata's sector, the problem was compounded by misjudgment of direction and location, so difficult to correct.[17] To break the impasse, Komatsubara decided to revert to night attacks by the infantry immediately, and to ask the artillery corps to move the heavy batteries close to the rifle units.

Kobayashi judged that the Japanese night actions of 23/24 July on his front were not particularly successful and that considerable time had been spent on "consolidation." Though it was true that Sakai's 72nd Infantry had entered the zone south of Kikugata (Chrysanthemum) Heights, Yamagata's 64th Infantry had not been able to clear Mitsubosa entirely.[18] From the Japanese infantry's point of view, the second day of the general offensive brought essentially no improvement—certainly not during the daylight hours. At daybreak, Soviet artillery resumed the bombardments from across the Halha and from the bridgehead. In Sumi's sector on the right wing,

Kimura's advanced 7th Company, in the "Ro" positions, was bombed by six aircraft at 8 A.M. on the 24th, and was attacked three times by infantrymen, who left more than a dozen corpses behind them on the field. Liaison with the Yamagata regiment was impossible because enemy fire prevented passage of the crestline. In the great heat, supplies of water ran out, and the Japanese had to resort to emergency drinking from captured sources—Soviet canteens and Maxim machine-gun coolant.

At 9:30 P.M., Kimura was ordered to break out of the encirclement and return to the battalion's location. His company picked up its dead and its weapons, as well as captured matériel, and adopted a night-attack formation to deceive the enemy. The latter did become "noisy," but Kimura's men pulled out in formation after the moon went down at 11 P.M., got past enemy sentries, penetrated a dip between Soviet firing points, and reached the destination safely by 4:30 A.M.[19]

To the left of Sumi's regiment, on the morning of 24 July the 64th Infantry's Kanaizuka battalion was ordered to "enlarge its battle accomplishments"—a very difficult task in daylight. Nevertheless, the fresh 10th Company had arrived from reserve during the night, and at 11:20 A.M. Kanaizuka ordered it to advance with the support of the battalion's heavy weapons and seize the portion of Mitsubosa Heights ahead of it, the same objective stipulated in the preceding night attack. From behind the IJA infantry, Kanaizuka's battalion guns, firing first, apparently drove off most of the Soviet troops. The 10th Company advanced at noon, found some defenders, charged with cold steel, and drove them off by 1 P.M. without loss. Only one Soviet body was found—that of an officer—but two or three soldiers were captured. Kanaizuka was surprised that the Russians were "very small—even smaller than the Japanese." The Soviet uniforms struck the major as of poor quality. Among the ordnance taken by the Japanese were four Maxim and five light machine guns; also captured was a Russian battle map.

Barbed wire was encountered by Kanaizuka's men only in front of the position; the entanglements were half-completed and consisted merely of stakes and strands. The Soviet firing sites were unconnected, about 20 meters apart, and each was capable of holding one squad. Some enemy forces were dug in among trenches just behind the heights, but the tanks must have pulled back toward the Halha. In this particular situation, enemy artillery located across the river could not be employed directly, for the Japanese were only 100 meters from the nearest Russian positions.

Kanaizuka sent the prisoners and the map back to regimental headquarters and reported that his 3rd Battalion had taken its objective. Yamagata sent orders to the front-line units to push ahead to the Halha. But the confluence sector was a zone of death by day, and it was not possible to advance from the heights. Nobody on the central sector moved at all. Some battalion commanders, says Kanaizuka, felt that the river was a futile objective anyhow, since it lay just below enemy positions on the western heights. In addition, he remarks, the adjoining units, including the Sakai regiment, were too far behind the salient created by the 3rd Battalion's advance. So Kanaizuka spent the day consolidating his positions and waiting for nightfall, when he could redeploy his troops and his firepower.[20]

On Sakai's 72nd Regiment front, to the left of Yamagata's infantry, enemy shells "fell like rain" on 24 July, regardless of friendly artillery's efforts to silence the Soviet batteries across the Halha. Just as Kanaizuka of the 64th Regiment said that his unit had carved out a forward salient, so the 72nd Infantry chronicler claimed that that regiment "had advanced greatly, by comparison with the other regiments, and therefore we were receiving not only concentrated artillery barrages but also flanking fire against both wings" by heavy weapons and by tanks at Heights 733 and on the left side of the Holsten. But the regimental gun battery took the confluence bridges under fire and reported smashing one of them. At 3 P.M., enemy planes conducted some ineffectual bombing and strafing runs. The biggest scare, however, took place after midday when three Russian tanks penetrated the gap between the front-line units and headed for Nishikawa's 1st Battalion, probably mistaking it for nearby Soviet positions. One of the tanks came as close as 50 meters behind Nishikawa's command post, realized its blunder, and began to use its flamethrower and machine guns. A Japanese "human-bullet" soldier saved the day for the battalion headquarters by detonating a mine against the armored vehicle, blowing up the tank and himself.[21]

For Nagano's 71st Infantry, below the Holsten, 24 July proved to be a very difficult and painful day. Enemy fire was severe from the outset, and as early as 7 A.M. more than 30 fighter planes from both sides could be seen fighting overhead. But Nagano still had no idea of the whereabouts of Murata's 3rd Battalion, and the other two battalions were making no progress against unexpectedly powerful enemy positions and resistance. At 10 A.M., Komatsubara took the unusual step of telephoning Nagano directly to complain and to exhort. On the division's main front, the general claimed, the offensive had developed well. All the other units had advanced close to the Halha, and Komatsubara's own command post was moving to Kikugata Heights. Therefore Nagano should kindly force the attack and quickly advance to the designated line of Kui Heights.

Taking the general's "request" very much to heart, Nagano initiated some desperate steps. After he had ordered his units to redouble their attack efforts, the colonel brought forward his own headquarters, the regimental colors, and his reserve elements into the center of the front lines on Sugitachi's 1st Battalion sector. With the colors right behind him, Nagano personally led the charge, across the crestline and against the enemy positions lying ahead. Soviet heavy machine guns cut down Japanese soldiers on all sides. Since neither the 1st nor the 2nd Battalion could allow the regimental commander and the colors to precede them in combat, Sugitachi and Baba drove their troops ahead as best they could.

With a dozen men, Nagano stormed onto the dune in front of the 1st Battalion and seized the position by 11:20 A.M. Intending to resume the advance, the colonel stood up to observe 10 minutes later; but the enemy had concentrated fire on the dune, and an artillery shell fragment shattered his left leg. Unable to move, and with dead and wounded lying all around him, Nagano was concerned about the negative psychological effects on the regiment and on its ability to comply with the division commander's intention. Lt. Col. Higashi Muneharu was ordered to assume command of the detachment. First, however, Nagano drew up an order, on his own responsibility, intended to prevent an increase in needless casualties as well as to get Higashi "off the hook." The daytime assault should be suspended, the battered units reorganized and pulled together, and a night attack prepared. Lamented the regimental chronicler: "Our offensive did not turn out as we had wished."

There was one favorable development at midday. Peering in the direction of the lost 3rd Battalion, regimental headquarters was delighted to discern a Japanese flag fluttering atop Ichimonji dune, toward the Halha. Obviously, it was Murata's unit that had made it to the hillock. But, to the regiment's regret, the position was nearly surrounded by the foe, smoke kicked up by enemy heavy-artillery bursts blanketed the area, and liaison was still not possible. Worse news lay in store: Major Murata had already been killed.

Despite the nature of Nagano's special instructions to his successor, Higashi, the division took no action to countermand them. While the regiment was getting ready for the night offensive, at 8 P.M. staff officer Itō telephoned higher headquarters' approval. Higashi's resulting order of 9 P.M., issued 1.2 kilometers west of Noro Heights, asserted that the facing enemy had fallen back to the Kui area (with elements occupying two strong positions ahead of Kui), as well as to the Sambur crossing. The detachment would stop attacking Kui and would secure its current locations, while preparing for further offensive action. But Sugitachi's battalion was ordered to proceed with its night assault to clear the enemy at the front edge of the dunes. Attacking at midnight, Sugitachi reported that his unit succeeded in its mission. A strange and eerie silence ensued along the entire front south of the Holsten.

On 24 July, the 71st Regiment had taken heavy casualties—97 killed and 25 wounded. The dead included two majors (one of whom was battalion commander Murata), one captain, and four lieutenants (among them the regimental intelligence officer). In addition to Colonel Nagano, the senior regimental aide, a major, was hurt. Komatsubara expressed private sorrow at the serious wounding of the regiment commander. He realized, the general told his diary, that his urging must have influenced Nagano greatly and forced the advance. It was his fault, Komatsubara admitted, and he felt remorse and regret.[22]

The actions of 24 July were supposed to have been part of the artillery offensive's second day. But, as we have seen, Japanese riflemen and the infantry records have very little to say about the participation of friendly artillery and much to say about Soviet artillery. After two days and two nights of great effort, the IJA rifle regiments were behind schedule and had still not reached the river or the positions they had once occupied during the night-assault phase earlier in the month. Komatsubara heard that the foe had built clay bunkers and positions guarded by barbed wire 1,000 meters in front of the confluence crossing. A route safe for enemy traffic, leading south of the Holsten, existed behind the Soviet defenses. Komatsubara was under the erroneous impression that Sumi's regiment had blown up the bridge at the bend in the Halha during its night action of 24/25 July.

As for the Japanese infantry units in general, Komatsubara observed that the front lines had been bombarded by field and heavy artillery on 24 July, so that the offensive did not develop in any area as intended. Only the Sakai regiment had approached the vicinity of the bridgehead positions, although still three kilometers from the Halha. Komatsubara understood that a corner of Heights 733, Yamagata's avowed objective, continued to be held by the enemy, and that the 64th Regiment had not been able to advance to the ordered locations. The Nagano detachment had finally completed its concentration and had reached the edge of the dunes northwest of Noro Heights. Hence another night offensive had become necessary.

Both Komatsubara and Kobayashi were troubled by several serious problems that centered on the infantry regiments themselves. For one thing, there was the question of why Yamagata had apparently held up his forces on the 24th instead of advancing them as ordered. For another, "all of the units lacked a clear perception of their location," as Komatsubara put it. Surveying by range finder, for example, revealed to the division commander that they were three or four kilometers from the confluence. As for designated objectives, the 64th Regiment set out to attack Mitsubosa Heights, which the 1st Battalion of the 72nd Regiment said it had already seized. Unless there were two heights with the same name, one of the regiments had stipulated the wrong target. Not until 25 July was the confusion resolved, when two Kwantung Army staff officers in the rank of lieutenant colonel arrived and studied the lines. They found that Yamagata's objective was really Heights 733, northwest of Mitsubosa Heights. As for Sakai's point of occupation, it proved to be not Kikugata Heights but a contour line 700 meters away.[23]

Still another problem for the infantry derived from the casualty situation. It seemed to Komatsubara that, as the result of losing many capable officers, the offensive capability of all the units had diminished considerably from what it was in early July, and their "thrusting power" had become weak. This estimate was supported by information available to Kobayashi as of 24 July, to the effect that elements of the 72nd Regiment had suffered drastic losses. The 5th Company was down to 30 men and the 6th Company to 40; the other companies averaged 60. The 2nd Battalion, with 500 men when the general offensive began, now had only 200. As a result, noted Kobayashi, the offensive frontages had to be narrowed, and serious gaps were appearing between regiments—for instance, an opening of 1,200-1,300 meters between the 72nd and 64th regiments.[24]

With respect to operations on the third day of the general offensive, 25 July, the Japanese artillery corps spoke of "splendid results" and thought that the infantry attacks toward the confluence were beginning to succeed. Komatsubara knew better, for his command post was still on a dune no closer than five kilometers northeast of the confluence. At the same time, Soviet bombardments on the 25th seemed as furious as ever, from the outlook of the Japanese infantry all along the front. For instance, Kobayashi's headquarters was hammered by 15-cm.-shell fire in the afternoon, and 24 Japanese trenches were caved in. On the right wing, Russian mortar shells struck the forward lines of Kimura's 7th Company in the evening, wounding the lieutenant and five men.[25]

On the Yamagata front, Kanaizuka's 3rd Battalion was attacked by enemy troops all day on the 25th. At dawn, the 10th Company fought for an hour to beat off the first assault, which cost the Russians 120 dead and four heavy machine guns. There were another half-dozen attacks by evening. Since the regiment had not been able to evict the enemy from Mitsubosa Heights (actually Heights 733), General Kobayashi went to Yamagata's command post in the afternoon to inspect the situation and to encourage offensive movement. At 4 P.M. a night attack was ordered; three hours later, the 3rd Battalion received the mission of mopping up enemy forces on the edge of Mitsubosa Heights. Kanaizuka threw his 10th and 12th companies against the objective at 11 P.M. and reported taking it. Next morning, at 6:40, 70 or 80 enemy troops counterattacked on the 10th Company's sector, and a smaller body on the 12th Company's.[26]

From dawn until 9 P.M. on 25 July, the Sakai regiment came under severe fire too, from heavy artillery and tanks across the Halha. To defend their bridges over the Halha, the Russians put up a network of barbed-wire entanglements in front of their positions, 500 or 600 meters from the river.

Exploiting folds in the terrain, Soviet infantrymen, tanks, and armored cars also pressed against Sakai's lines, but were repulsed. By now, Lieutenant Hayama's famous platoon from the 6th Company had been wiped out.[27]

At 9:30 A.M. on the 25th, while enemy bombardment raged, the 71st Regiment was finally able to make telephone contact with the slain Major Murata's 3rd Battalion, isolated below the Holsten and still surrounded. Lieutenant Colonel Higashi recommended to the division at 11 A.M. that he be authorized to attack Kui Heights, in the direction of the Sambur Obo crossing. Staff officer Suzuki phoned back at noon to say that the span at Sambur had been blown up and that no sizable enemy forces were expected to irrupt from that area, so the regiment should merely concentrate its strength where it was. Higashi immediately issued the necessary order. After sunset, the 3rd Battalion was to pull back gradually to the main detachment's site, by moving along the telephone wires. A truck platoon would be sent to assist. Manchukuoan cavalry should keep an eye on the left flank. Higashi withdrew to the original jump-off location at 10 P.M. that night. By dawn of the 26th, the 3rd Battalion had extricated itself from its advanced positions.[28] For all intents and purposes, the combined Japanese artillery-infantry offensive was over.

Assessing the outcome of the general offensive, the local Japanese commands collated sets of claims to inscribe on the credit side of the battle ledger. According to 23rd Division estimates as of 28 July, the following results had been achieved: Soviet-MPRA dead, 3,000 abandoned corpses; prisoners taken, 54; artillery batteries neutralized, 19 (including 7 smashed); tanks and armored cars knocked out or burned, 500 (not counting 28 captured); aircraft downed, 45; machine guns (heavy and light) captured, 90; and rifles captured, 205. It was judged that Soviet combat strength on the right shore had been reduced to one-third or one-fourth starting strength.[29]

In the simplest sense, however, the accomplishments of the general offensive could be gauged by the visible progress of the infantry units. Their failure to smash the enemy's bridgehead must therefore be largely attributable to the performance of the friendly artillery, from whom so much had been hoped. The heavy artillery corps commander, Hata, confessed that the general offensive had not lived up to the expectations of the Kwantung Army. The latter, in turn, admitted privately that the artillery bombardments starting 23 July had been a failure.[30]

We have seen how shortages of ammunition hampered the effectiveness of the IJA heavy artillery at Nomonhan. The difficulty with ammunition plagued the entire Japanese army but was particularly troublesome for heavy ordnance. Yet in only two days of action, the batteries had expended about two-thirds of their whole allocation. It has been estimated, in fact, that 70 percent of the Kwantung Army's entire artillery stocks were allotted to the general offensive. At Nomonhan, every ammunition load could have been expended in one day. When the objectives of the attack were not achieved by the second or even third day, there were scant reserves from which to draw, for the Kwantung Army had much more of Manchuria to worry about defending than the Mongolian front. Even if all the shells in Japan could have been amassed for the Nomonhan operation, there would still not have been enough. The artillery command underestimated its requirements (whether or not they could be met), largely because of lack of experience with artillery-versus-artillery combat. It was thought simplistically that enemy batteries could be neutralized with "so many guns and so many shells." Insufficient targeting preparations often caused further waste of shells for ranging purposes, complicated by the "jumbling" of shells and by the smoke kicked up on the broad frontage of five or six kilometers on the left shore.[31]

Coupled with the basic fact of ammunition shortage was the related problem of transport insufficiency. The 700 trucks that the Kwantung Army could assign to the Nomonhan theater were simply too few to handle such tasks as the movement of ammunition, fortification materials, wintering supplies, and troop reinforcements. Four or five times as many trucks could have been used, for the available horses were proving nearly useless, and airlift capability was trifling.[32]

A recurring theme in the artillery phase of the general offensive was the inadequate range of the Japanese heavy batteries. For example, although the 15-cm. howitzers were new and well regarded at the time, they often had to fire at maximum or ineffective range. In practice, they operated at their highest elevation, using their most powerful powder charges with four separate propellants at the longest range. Japanese gunners were simply not trained to fire beyond 5,000-6,000 meters (for cannon) and 4,000-5,000 meters (for howitzers). They were certainly not prepared to shoot at the outer limits, with such heavy propellants and in such profusion, against high targets beyond the Halha, where Soviet batteries were emplaced in several lines, originally 8,000-10,000 meters away. Beyond this distance, there were other enemy guns, especially 15-cm. cannon, that the IJA pieces could not even try to engage but that could strike the Japanese gun lines at 14,000-15,000 meters. Mishima says his regiment was once attacked by 15-cm. guns at an effective range of 18,000 meters. Indeed, the Soviet 122-mm. cannon (1931) could fire at 20,800 meters, and the 152-mm. howitzer (1937) at 16,000-17,000.[33]

Unexpectedly severe technical difficulties arose in combat, such as the breaking of undercarriages from excessive recoil and the overheating of barrels, which caused jammed rounds. But it was the rudimentary firing doctrine and incomplete training that hurt the IJA batteries even more. The Japanese army had been studying antiartillery battle in theory; there had been no such combat experience in the First World War or since. Counterbattery operations demanded huge amounts of artillery pieces and ammunition, but these had not been available in maneuvers, and firing drills using live ammunition had not been conducted.[34] There was also insufficient aerial spotting, typified by the resort to balloonists at a time when the Japanese air force was no longer in command of the skies.

The background of the highest IJA artillery commanders and the kinds of ordnance they had at Nomonhan exerted a serious influence on the way the offensive was conducted. The improvised command possessed a mix of old and new field guns, 15-cm. siege batteries, and heavy field pieces. Thus, whereas field artillery normally cooperated with infantry in front-line combat, 15-cm. cannon belonged to the category of siege guns employed against fortified positions (*kōjōjūhō*). Yet the primary mission of the Japanese artillery corps was to dominate the main body of enemy heavy artillery across the Halha. Despite the difficult task and the variegated weaponry, no real expert as such was in charge. Although Hata came from the heavy artillery, the top man—Uchiyama—came from the field artillery.

We have seen some of the differences between the Japanese artillery generals concerning the use of heavy batteries in close-support functions. And, as Komatsubara gathered later after talking with Col. Kanaoka Takashi (Kyō), senior artillery staff officer, the tactical doctrine employed on 23 July had been technically defective. In this view, after conducting preparatory fire for two hours, it would have been better to seek mass impact by laying down concentrated battalion bombardment, followed by individual destructive fire. Such an approach would have had important psychological as well as practical effects.[35]

Still, no degree of improvement in IJA artillery command and tactics alone could have prevailed on 23-25 July. The Japanese might boast of their firing skill and their training, but there can be no doubt that the Russians had many more and far better heavy artillery pieces, "luxurious" supplies of ammunition, and the capacity to move effectively and fast. Tactically speaking, the Soviet artillery forces dispersed their sites well, built dummy positions, used camouflage cleverly, and redeployed to previously prepared emplacements. Nevertheless, the Japanese artillery command (like its sister branches) consistently underestimated the Soviet side's material strength and tended to think in terms of 1904-5 instead of 1939. As one IJA officer admitted afterward, "Underdog tactics may be fine for infantrymen, but not for artillery."[36]

Of course, there were Soviet shortcomings, such as the employment of training shells and old explosives (the Japanese had used theirs up in China), blind and repetitive fire by the new, highly efficient 122-mm. battalion-level howitzers, and some weird scouting tactics—e.g., instances where the same two "red horses" always appeared when 122-mm. howitzers were about to fire, and the infiltration of a large flock of sheep by Russian observation men dressed in sheepskin coats. But at Nomonhan the Soviet artillery commanders, who had been operating in the area since May, knew the right shore of the Halha and the flat left bank of the Holsten like the back of their hand. They not only used good spotting techniques but also had preregistered targets, often using mounds and flags as reference points at key locations. To some Japanese officers, the region seemed like nothing less than one vast Russian firing range.[37]

Of the performance of the Japanese infantry on 23-25 July, there is much less to say. Originally, tanks had been sent to help them; then, heavy artillery. But essentially the same infantry units had been fighting in the area ever since they arrived at the front toward the end of June. The riflemen had tried to smash to the right-bank confluence, first with Yasuoka, then by themselves during the night-attack phase, and finally with the artillery's assistance in the period of the general offensive. Yet they were farther away from the confluence by 25 July, in general, than they had been on 14 July, despite their efforts and their losses. Heavy weapons were weak, armor was lacking, air support was ineffective, and artillery power was insufficient. The survivors were more battle-skilled by now, but they were certainly more exhausted and often sick or debilitated by the dysentery epidemic. There is scant reason to wonder that, under severe fire, some Japanese units hesitated to emerge from their shelters and thus caused delays in jumping off. Under particularly murderous barrages, infantrymen and engineers often dug in and hid where they were, advancing only during intervals in bombardment. In a number of cases, overconfidence stemming from the predicted "ease" of victory caused lax preparations, sluggish scouting, and thus very heavy casualties in the actual battle, particularly among officers and noncoms.[38]

There would be much more fighting and dying at Nomonhan, but the Kwantung Army's dreams of the confluence faded, in practice, during the indecisive general offensive—the last push toward the elusive river.

In the Soviet literature, the brilliance of the Russian defense of the Halha bridgehead continues to be overshadowed by Zhukov's offensive of August. Of the preceding IJA general attack, the Russians say relatively little. At 6:50 A.M. on 23 July, the Japanese opened bombardment against the forward edges of the Soviet-MPRA defenses and against artillery sites. The Russians held their fire to prevent revealing their positions. At 9 A.M. the

Japanese attacked along the front below the Holsten and continued the bombardment north of the river. At 10 the barrages were followed in the north by a ground offensive. The Russians have every right to conclude that the failure of the Japanese to concert their offensive along the whole front enabled the Russian artillery to throw back the assaults, first in the south and then in the north. Several efforts to storm the Soviet-MPRA defenses along both sectors on 23-24 July were defeated with heavy losses to the attackers. As a result, say the Russians, the Japanese suspended their feckless series of attacks on 25 July and went over to the defensive. By preserving the bridgehead and preventing the foe from reaching the river line, the Soviet forces had successfully guarded the frontier that they claimed, and insured an "advantageous base" for the decisive Soviet-Mongolian offensive of August in the process.[39]

29

Digging In

Since the actions of the Japanese infantry regiments on 25 July did not bespeak notable success, Komatsubara and Kobayashi were still grappling with ways to break the impasse. Once the two staff officers sent by the Kwantung Army had uncovered the surprising errors of cartographic location, Kobayashi sent aides to Yamagata and to Sakai to notify them. The division chief of staff, Okamoto, came to see Kobayashi and to observe the front. After visiting Yamagata and urging him to resume the attack, Kobayashi in turn was called to the division command post, where he conferred with Komatsubara and Okamoto at 2 P.M. about the whole problem of the offensive. One of the matters that came up for discussion was the need to find out why the Yamagata regiment was evidently not carrying out its orders. On the larger level, Kobayashi recommended that offensive emphasis be focused on the confluence zone and that Sumi's Right Wing Unit—now under direct control of the division—therefore be incorporated into his own infantry group command en bloc.

Komatsubara agreed readily with Kobayashi's aggressive proposal. As the division commander confided to his diary, it had proved impossible to smash the Soviet batteries on the left side of the Halha in the one or two days (let alone the two or three hours) originally predicted to him by the Kwantung Army and Uchiyama's corps. The Japanese artillery's actual accomplishments, wrote Komatsubara, "ran counter to my expectations." Although most of the enemy guns had been withdrawn beyond sight across the river, they were still able to operate vigorously. In short, Soviet artillery strength had not been weakened in the slightest. Komatsubara derived the reluctant impression that the enemy's artillery, with its plentiful ammunition, was superior to the friendly batteries. Advance by the Japanese infantry units, concluded the general, would remain extremely difficult if they waited for the overblown IJA artillery to pave the way forward.

The delay of ten days before the Japanese general offensive, Komatsubara felt, gave the Russians leeway to bring up two or three more rifle regiments and to construct bunkers and entanglements at the shoreline. Enemy night attacks had become even stronger than they had been at the time of Yasuoka's tank offensive earlier in the month. Komatsubara therefore recommended to the Kwantung Army that artillery and aviation be combined with the full strength of the infantry regiments (as his trusted associate, Kobayashi, had suggested) in one last offensive to destroy the Soviet-MPRA bridgehead on the right bank, sector by sector, position by position. To accomplish this objective, Komatsubara insisted, he would need a copious allocation of ammunition—no less than one full battle load (*kaisenbun*). This emphasis upon ammunition had been impressed upon the general by the Soviet expenditure of as many as 1,000-2,000 rounds per day throughout the second stage of the Nomonhan fighting. On 23-24 July, in particular, the enemy's use of ammunition was enormous. Even if the Russians were deprived of their toehold on the right shore, they would undoubtedly continue their artillery operations from the left side for a long time. Consequently, Komatsubara felt strongly that "the key to victory or defeat in artillery combat will depend upon ammunition supply from now on."[1]

The Kwantung Army, however, had other notions. As early as 9 July, it will be recalled, Tsuji and Hattori convinced themselves that the Japanese infantry's attacks against the confluence were on the verge of succeeding.[2] Therefore it would be necessary for the 23rd Division to leave only forward elements in the Halha zone, along a line from Kanchuerhmiao to Amukulang, Fui Heights, Balshagal, Noro, and Handagai. With the Yasuoka detachment still in action, however, the scheme came to be regarded as ill-timed and had to be suspended. But now that the IJA heavy artillery corps had been committed, it was expected that the general offensive would annihilate the Soviet-MPRA foothold on the right bank in a matter of days or even hours.

To the Kwantung Army, it had become necessary to plan for the consequences of Japanese victory at the confluence. By the time of the staff meeting in Hsinking on 24 July, the second day of the vaunted general offensive, it was decided, in effect, to resurrect the Tsuji-Hattori idea of the 9th. Among the considerations weighing on the staff officers' minds was the danger of an enveloping attack by the enemy from the right flank at Fui Heights or from the left across the Holsten. In addition, there was concern about the front lines' readiness to meet the approaching winter season at bleak Nomonhan. These problems would be explored in depth during the coming weeks, but first the 23rd Division had to be given the basic order issued by the Kwantung Army at 2 P.M. on 24 July. Staff officer Shimanuki Takeharu conveyed it to Komatsubara on the afternoon of the 25th.

The division commander already realized that his recommendation of a new and powerful offensive had become academic. Problems of ammunition alone, he was told separately by the Kwantung Army, militated against it anyhow. According to the latest order from Hsinking, the 23rd Division was immediately to carry out fortification of the area on the right bank, without waiting to complete the destruction of enemy forces in the bridgehead. All units must secure positions near the front of the fortified zone. Artillery batteries should engage enemy guns when opportunity arose. To guard the northern flank, the divisional reconnaissance regiment in the vicinity of Fui

Heights should be reinforced and assigned the task of defending the up-stream Halha area.

Komatsubara thanked Shimanuki for delivering the order, read it quietly, and merely remarked calmly, "I see, I understand." To Shimanuki, it seemed that the general must have known the Kwantung Army's thinking already and was therefore not at all taken by surprise.[3] Nevertheless, whether or not the army order said so explicitly, it meant the abandonment of the offensive by the division and transition to a period of protracted defense. In other words, after having surrendered any advantages his infantry had achieved during the expensive night-attack phase and having squelched the forward momentum for the "greater good" of the lumbering artillery offensive, Komatsubara was being told to desist again for keeps, on the third day of the inconclusive joint operation. In his diary, the general revealed his private discouragement, now that the Japanese artillery had not lived up to its promise and his own proposed offensive of last resort had been turned down too.[4]

> Under these circumstances, when could I ever destroy the enemy and accomplish my mission? Confrontation positions must be built up and equal battle continued for a protracted period. I have no words adequate to console the spirits of the many fallen heroes who sacrificed themselves in hard-fought night attacks advancing to the riverbank for the purpose of destroying the remaining foe. I regret that I did not continue the [original] offensive without expecting any assistance from the artillery. I erred.

Kobayashi had hardly returned to his command post when he was called back to division headquarters at about 3 P.M. to be briefed about the newly received Kwantung Army order. Publicly, of course, Komatsubara voiced no objections. At 5:30 P.M., the division commander issued the required operations order.[5] According to the customary prefatory justifications, "as the result of our powerful daily attacks, coordinating air and ground forces, we inflicted severe losses on the enemy and achieved our purpose of chastisement." By order of the Kwantung Army, mentioned specifically, the division was going to prepare fortifications right away without waiting for the completion of the mop-up of hostile forces remaining on the right bank of the Halha. All the combat units were directed to secure designated lines and key points, keep an eye on the enemy, and smash any attacks in the general area of their positions. The Yamagata regiment would have to advance a bit to attain its mission, and field artillery would assist. Yasuoka's detachment was finally being deactivated and returned to duty stations, except for the reconnaissance regiment, which was to be left at Fui Heights, helped by Manchukuoan forces and reinforced by one field artillery battery and by an infantry company and rapid-fire battery from the Sumi regiment. The artillery corps was to allocate its main strength in support of Kobayashi's infantry group, assist the wing units with a portion, and neutralize enemy artillery when convenient. Engineer units should prepare to fortify the positions. Details of the program would be conveyed separately.

The unexpected divisional order affected the line units differently on 25/26 July. On the 26th Regiment's front, the 2nd Battalion's Kimura company, now commanded only by sergeants at the company and platoon levels, was preparing for a night attack that at 10:30 P.M. was called off. At 2:30 A.M., the 2nd Battalion issued an order for all units to return to and guard the locations occupied before the general offensive had begun. Movement commenced at 3:30 A.M. and was completed by 4:20 A.M.[6]

After issuing his order to the 72nd Regiment at 8 P.M., Sakai waited for darkness and pulled back his advanced positions a little, "owing to the consolidation of the battle line." Special attention was devoted to tight linkage between battalions and with the adjoining Yamagata regiment. Concentration was completed by 5 A.M., and was followed by construction of positions at the western edge of Kikugata Heights.[7]

Kanaizuka's 3rd Battalion of the 64th Regiment proceeded with its night attack at 11 P.M. to clear the edge of Mitsubosa Heights. Higashi's 71st Regiment received the gist of Komatsubara's order by phone on the 25th. The isolated 3rd Battalion made it back to detachment headquarters by dawn, and the 2nd Battalion "also consolidated at the site preceding the date of the general offensive." But there would be some terribly costly tactical problems for the 71st Regiment, which had been ordered to secure a line that the division did not seem to know had never been reached. Higashi was determined to honor his order literally, which would entail dogged offensive action on this "hottest" of sectors.[8]

In the evening of 25 July, General Hata was called to Uchiyama's artillery corps headquarters and advised of Komatsubara's order. The 23rd Division was being shifted to strategic defense, having been directed to protect the frontier by establishing "key point" positions (*kyoten*). Hata heard that the Kwantung Army had reached this decision "from the broad standpoint," which included the problem of insufficient ammunition. In view of the circumstances, Hata's artillery group might have to last for two more months. Every effort was still to be made to dominate hostile artillery.

Since relocation was supposed to begin immediately, later that night Uchiyama asked Hata's opinion about pulling back the heavy batteries. Hata pointed out that the division wanted artillery support for a further assault by part of the infantry on the 26th, and that it would be difficult to complete a withdrawal by dawn anyhow. Therefore he recommended that the movement not be undertaken until the next night. Uchiyama agreed.

Meanwhile, Hata pondered the division's latest policy and combat instructions, in terms of the ammunition shortage and the status of the surviving enemy batteries. For the purpose of resuming antiartillery operations, he made up his mind to carry out "more strict and precise" preparations and to conduct firing with limited amounts of ammunition. In this regard, we know from Ise's instructions on the night of 25 July that his ammunition allowance for the next day was generally only half a *kisū*.

It rained hard on 26 July and visibility was very poor. Hata decided to suspend counterbattery operations and to concentrate on assisting Kobayashi's group with two battalions of heavy artillery. But when the infantry attack was called off, Hata stopped action by his units too. There was, accordingly, only some field-artillery fire by the Japanese on the 26th, although enemy guns continued "blind firing" against the front lines. On the night of 26/27 July, those IJA heavy artillery units that had been sent forward around the 24th to provide direct support to the infantry were pulled back to their original sites. Ise further reduced the ammunition quota for 27 July to one-fifth *kisū*.[9]

While the IJA artillery corps was still in existence, the only severe Japanese offensive action took place south of the Holsten, where Higashi ordered a dawn attack to clear the powerful positions (dubbed "Shi," "Mi," and "Ki") lying 1,000-1,500 meters ahead of his detachment on 27 July. Friendly artillery was to play a key role, conducting softening-up operations between 5:30 and 6 A.M. while the rifle units advanced. If further bombardment was needed, the front-line infantry battalion would set off a smoke pot, which would signal the supporting guns to fire at increased range for another five minutes. Higashi conferred personally with Maj. Matsutomo Hideo, the commander of the supporting 1st Field Artillery Battalion, and with a liaison officer sent from one of the 10-cm. cannon battalions belonging to the Takatsukasa regiment. These supporting units were deployed to fire at a range of 1,700 to 2,000 meters.

Though the artillery made every effort to cooperate with the ground assault on cloudy 27 July, the brunt of the fighting, as usual, was borne by the infantry. During the first hour of the grueling battle, the riflemen made fairly good progress, under cover of fog. But the rest of the day proved nearly disastrous, in the face of tenacious resistance at the broad and deep Soviet positions. Mortar and 12-cm. howitzer fire rained down on Baba's right-flank 2nd Battalion. The Japanese suffered mounting casualties and ran out of battalion-gun shells and grenade-launcher ammunition. Higashi radioed the division for increased artillery support and more ammunition. Flanking fire from the very dangerous Ki position grew worse. Baba and an aide were wounded, and the front-line 5th and 8th companies were being chopped up.

By 10 A.M. the 2nd Battalion was cut off, and the only things the regiment could make out were two Japanese flags stuck on rifle bayonets. Not until 1:20 P.M. did some ammunition trucks reach the regiment, but soon afterward, shouting "Hurrah!," about 400 Russians charged against the 2nd Battalion. A battle ensued that the 71st Infantry chronicler called "heart-rending and ghastly." The 2nd Battalion tried to get the field artillery to neutralize the Ki position but, according to the regiment, Matsutomo's batteries found it difficult to find the range of the front lines and were "perplexed" in firing against Ki.

From north of the Holsten, Mishima's 15-cm. howitzers and Sakai's regimental guns laid down effective flanking fire. Nevertheless, around 11 A.M. Higashi also lost contact with his 3rd Battalion on the left. Every runner sent to break through to the unit was killed. As for the battalion, it could no longer reach its own 9th and 12th companies, which had been separated and mauled severely.

Higashi reassessed the situation in the late afternoon, concluded that Komatsubara may not have wanted him to storm Ki after all, and decided to concentrate his infantry's efforts against Mi on the right front. But this became only a matter of degree after Takatsukasa contacted him at 5:40 P.M., offering the full support of his 10-cm. batteries and suggesting a new offensive after twilight. It was decided that the artillery would fire at 9 P.M. for four minutes against Mi and for six minutes against Ki. The 2nd Battalion was to seize Mi, and the 3rd Battalion was supposed to assault Ki after all, once the artillery's supporting fire had ceased. Upon taking its objective, the 3rd Battalion should assist the other battalion and pull back the following night.

Somehow, a platoon leader and two men of the 8th Company had been clinging to the left edge of the 2nd Battalion's lines since morning—the place where the two red-ball flags had been hoisted. Finally, after 9 P.M., the battalion pushed forward against a torrent of Soviet grenades, engaged in close combat, and cleared the Mi position. But fire continued to pour from Ki, lighting up the night "like a seething blast furnace." The 3rd Battalion was having a terrible time in the Ki area, and communication with it was impossible. It was later learned that the enemy positions were very strong, girded with low barbed-wire entanglements, and covered by flanking fire. When dawn came, elements of the 3rd Battalion found themselves only two or three meters from the enemy, a range which invited continuous duels with grenades.

Casualties had been worse than feared. The 2nd Battalion, for example, had only 82 men in fighting condition by daybreak, under Captain Nishimura and a second lieutenant. Higashi's headquarters was in an exposed location, and the regimental colors seemed in such danger that at 1 A.M. on the 28th, Higashi secretly ordered his color-bearer, 1st Lt. Kawazoe Take-hiko, to transfer the pennon to division headquarters, report the situation on the Holsten front, and hurry back. Fixing his direction with the help of illuminating shells dropped blindly by the enemy, Kawazoe's party set forth, hitched a ride aboard some trucks, and by dawn made it across the Holsten to the division command post, where the colors were stored safely in the chief of staff's tent. To his surprise, Kawazoe learned that the division's attitude was very cautious (i.e., unaggressive) and that an attack against Ki really went beyond Komatsubara's intention. To reinforce Higashi, however, the division was sending the Kajikawa infantry battalion from reserve, as well as a 12-cm. and a 15-cm. howitzer battery.

On 28 July, Higashi stopped the wild charges and complied with the true defensive sense of Komatsubara's order, pulling back to the original lines during the night. On paper, Higashi realigned his depleted forces. The 3rd Battalion, whose senior officer was now Captain Onozuka, would be pulled into reserve at first. But the regiment had not been able to make contact since the afternoon of the 28th, and no patrols could get through. Finally orders reached Onozuka, and after the moon set he started to disengage, covered by his machine gun company. He returned with only two officers and little more than 100 soldiers.

The arrival of Kajikawa's crack battalion at 9 A.M. on the 28th cheered Higashi's survivors. But there was a new frustration in the morning when the regimental radio set first lost its battery power and ceased receiving, and then was finished off for good by artillery fragments. Finally, when the situation had "stabilized a little" on the 29th, Kawazoe was sent back to division headquarters to retrieve the regimental colors.[10]

In supporting the last-gasp Japanese infantry offensive below the Holsten, Uchiyama's artillery corps was experiencing its own final days as an entity at the front. The persistent and insoluble shortage of ammunition is betokened in firing allocations and consumption. While trying to assist Higashi's forces from the north on the difficult day of 27 July, for example, the Umeda battalion's two batteries of 15-cm. howitzers fired only 44 common shells and 118 shrapnel rounds. Ise allowed his units a trifling amount of ammunition on 28 July: Type 38 field artillery and 12-cm. howitzers, 0.15 *kisū*; Type 90 field guns, only 0.05 *kisū*. On the 29th, Kobayashi noted, the ammunition limits amounted in practice to 15 rounds per field gun, 5 per Type 90 field piece, and about 15 for the heavy artillery.[11]

General Hata continued to wrestle with optimum ways of stretching his restricted means. For example, he advised Uchiyama on 28 July that he was still opposed to sending some of the 15-cm. howitzers below the Holsten. They could render support from the northern side instead, whereas direct cooperation could be afforded by 12-cm. howitzers. Counterbattery fire was still the main mission for the 10-cm. and 15-cm. cannon and 15-cm. howitzers—although it should be avoided in ordinary circumstances. When it had to be done, a stocked one-*kisū* load ought to be spent in concentrated fashion in order to demolish enemy gun sites. In general, however, average expenditure of ammunition would be limited to one-tenth *kisū*. Additionally, Hata recommended, firing accuracy and observation should be improved in order to maximize ammunition consumption, and better use should be made of the artillery intelligence unit. Construction of reserve positions and of dummy sites was to be encouraged.[12]

Kwantung Army commander Ueda came to the battlefront on the afternoon of 29 July for his first and last inspection. By the time he finished his morale-building trip next day, he had visited the division command post, the reconnaissance regiment, the field hospital, and the artillery corps headquarters. Kobayashi and his regiment commanders Sakai and Yamagata had occasion to brief him during a 30-minute conference; the artillery chiefs had a separate chance too. Hata was pleased by Ueda's words of praise for the artillery.

The most important command decision on the day of Ueda's arrival was the announcement that Uchiyama was being released immediately from his artillery corps command under Komatsubara and that he and his headquarters were to be returned to the Kwantung Army. Hata, the 3rd Brigade commander, was made the division artillery corps commander, in charge of the same units that had been assigned to Uchiyama. In his diary entry this day, Hata recorded his elation: "Thus the setup of a 'roof over a roof' has been rectified," he wrote. "The time has arrived for me to display my skills." The corps would now "reveal its true capacity, even more, with wholehearted cooperation between the infantry and the artillery."

On the 30th, after Uchiyama officially turned over the artillery corps command to Hata, Komatsubara discussed his tactical ideas in some detail with the latter. Motorized deployment of artillery as "fire fighters" should be planned against the threat of enemy envelopment attacks against both wings. The use of artillery was imperative to relieve the heavy pressure exerted on the Higashi detachment front below the Holsten.

Hata directed concentrated firing by the 12-cm. howitzer battalion south of the river and the 15-cm. howitzer battalion from the north, aimed against the Mi and Ki bastions facing the 71st Regiment. The enemy pressure was relieved considerably as a result, according to Hata, and the infantry units "came constantly to thank us." When Hata visited all of his artillery formations and each rifle-unit commander on 31 July, in his new capacity as corps commander, he was touched by the fact that he was accorded "unexpectedly great confidence." The heavy artillery was the object of special praise, to the extent that Hata became concerned lest the infantry's extreme reliance upon heavy ordnance weaken its own offensive capability.[13]

The presumably routine transfer of a Japanese artillery first lieutenant would not ordinarily warrant our attention, but the officer happened to be Prince Higashikuni, and his case possessed national, servicewide, and dynastic ramifications. Higashikuni had commanded his 15-cm. howitzer battery well during the general offensive and was credited with knocking out a confluence bridge. Certainly his presence, his seriousness of purpose, and his professionalism cheered the troops at the front. But although he never put on airs, he could not be treated as just another junior officer, for in addition to his own royal status, he had been affianced since 1937 to the eldest daughter of the Emperor of Japan. Thus as soon as he arrived in Manchuria, he was visited at Ssupingchieh by no less a personage than the Kwantung Army chief of staff, who paid his respects and explained the battle situation to him.

Unfortunately, on the morning of 24 July the prince's petty equerry, a member of the imperial household staff, was fatally wounded in an air raid. Greatly alarmed, the Army General Staff queried the Kwantung Army, and Tsuji drafted the reply next day. Meanwhile, from Hailar, the artillery brigade rushed 200 railway ties by truck for use in shoring up the prince's trench. The regiment commander, of course, from the outset had been very worried about the safety of his imperial battery commander, whose fate would be his fate. Now, with the death of the equerry, Mishima hoped very much that Higashikuni would be transferred before harm befell him. In this instance, the wheels of personnel management moved very smoothly, and the prince received informal advance notice that he was to take command of a battery at Acheng, as part of the routine transfers that always took place in August.

But on 27 July the Kwantung Army chief of staff received a wire from the 23rd Division stating that the prince had flown from the front to Hailar that morning "on business," was staying at the division commander's official residence, and would remain for an undetermined period. That Higashikuni had "left his post" before issuance of his official orders conveyed a "strange impression" at Kwantung Army headquarters. Complicating matters was the fact that the prince flew back to the front on the same day (29 July) that General Ueda went there. As Komatsubara described Higashikuni's visit, the prince had come to division headquarters for "observation and study."

Although Higashikuni returned to Hailar the same day, Kwantung Army Operations Section chief Terada (who had accompanied Ueda to the front) told division chief of staff Okamoto in no uncertain terms that the prince's departure on the 27th had not been at all proper. What had really happened, however, was that after the wounding and death of the imperial household man and the notification of the prince's transfer, Higashikuni's officer in attendance, a lieutenant colonel, had pressed the regiment commander very hard to get the prince away from the battlefield as soon as possible. Mishima, who agreed entirely, suggested to Higashikuni that he leave for Hailar promptly to prepare for his new assignment. Naturally, the colonel's proposal was cleared with the artillery group commander beforehand, as General Hata's notes confirm.

As for the prince's return to the front on 29 July, Mishima explains that Higashikuni had heard that seven or eight of his old subordinates had fallen just after he had left the battery, and that he wanted to revisit the unit and console his men. The colonel says he "scolded" the prince, who apologized and flew right back to Hailar. In any case, despite the brouhaha at Kwantung Army headquarters, nobody who knew Higashikuni the artillery officer casts the slightest aspersion on his bravery or upon the rapport he had established with his subordinates and colleagues. Perhaps the best of accolades is the fact that even Tsuji spoke very favorably of the prince.[14]

During the first week after the announcement of the 23rd Division's fortification program, the line units worked on preliminary projects. On the afternoon of 26 July, for instance, the 7th Company of the 26th Infantry received the Right Wing Unit's construction plan for Phase 1, calling for the completion of the following tasks by 1 August: the erection of barricades and barbed wire 40-50 meters ahead of positions, the repair of trenches and other works, and the preparation of auxiliary facilities such as latrines. In the course of Phase 2, commencing on 2 August, permanent construction would be undertaken in accordance with instructions forthcoming from the division and the engineers.[15]

Given the scarcity of building materials in the Nomonhan region, the units started by calling for the collection of almost anything usable: empty ammunition boxes, ration crates, cans, and captured matériel. Major Kanaizuka had parties go out by night on 27 July to retrieve and distribute 120 stakes from enemy barbed-wire entanglements. Lieutenant Takashima says that on the 28th his battalion (Kajikawa's of the 28th Regiment), although of serious mien, looked as if it was conducting a "masquerade procession." The soldiers were lugging all kinds of "necessary" items: buckets, mats, barrels, fuel drums, poles, boxes, cans, and litters of junk. One of Ise's field artillery battalions directed that grass be collected for fodder and that empty containers be conserved.[16]

Engineer Lieutenant Colonel Saitō had not been pleased with the strength of the shelters his men had been building for the heavy artillery and the infantry, using only the boards and soil available. A thickness of one meter was entirely insufficient against anything bigger than field pieces of the howitzer class. To withstand hits by 15-cm. shells, the covers needed to be at least four or five meters thick in such sandy soil. Now Saitō sent half of his 23rd Engineer Regiment to the Holsten to produce concrete blocks, although the river was very low and the engineers had to dig to the bottom for sand. From his location near the division command post, Saitō farmed out engineers to help the infantry with construction. But the three weeks Saitō had before the Soviet offensive erupted in August were not adequate to produce and to use enough of the blocks, which later ended up, ironically, as tombstones for the war dead.[17]

Situated 500-600 meters from Saitō was the understrength 24th Engineer Regiment under Lt. Col. Numazaki Kyōhei, who had replaced Kawamura, slain earlier in July. In addition to working on the defenses with new materials sent up by the Kwantung Army, Numazaki's men constructed a long wooden trestle bridge over the Holsten and its swampy banks, farther forward than the rickety old span and strong enough to have supported even tanks.

Numazaki, however, was unhappy with the concept and location of the fortification program as it was evolving. Around 28 July, Col. Kawada Suesaburō, the chief of the Kwantung Army's fortification staff, came to confer with the division commander, chief of staff, and unit commanders. Numazaki recommended that, to take advantage of the terrain, points be constructed a little to the rear of the lines now occupied. After all, the current locations had not been selected beforehand but merely represented a disconnected line imposed by the random progress of combat, generally during hours of darkness. In the event of an enemy offensive, argued Numazaki, the existing sites would prove unsatisfactory to defend. But Komatsubara and Okamoto seemed still to be thinking in terms of the offensive, and they did not want to yield even an inch of the soil they had fought so hard to attain. Therefore they insisted that the key points be built along the existing lines, and Kawada agreed. Numazaki respected the infantry's high-spirited view, and he did not want to press his cautious, conservative approach. He thinks that some of the other conferees may have shared his viewpoint, but undoubtedly they too were hesitant to oppose the aggressive philosophy.

The resulting positions proved as weak as Numazaki had feared. The Japanese engineers suffered from a chronic lack of machinery and heavy construction equipment, although they were clever carpenters and artisans, working with little more than hammers, saws, and shovels. Nevertheless, problems of location and direction troubled them as much as their comrades. Numazaki recommended that the Kwantung Army send surveyors and cartographers, and perhaps a dozen did arrive. They performed good work, but of course they could only clarify locations within the Japanese lines.[18]

Lieutenant Colonel Numazaki was not the only Japanese officer who entertained misgivings about the system of so-called strong points and about the defenders' ability to withstand both an enemy offensive and the cruel Mongolian early winter. Artillery Colonel Mishima, who had once served on a North Manchurian weather-research team, knew that June and July were the only months in these latitudes when the temperature did not drop below freezing. Although the days were still very hot (106° F. on 29 July), Mishima awoke around 1 August to find that a frost had already withered the grass to charcoal brown. Yet the Japanese troops were still clad in summer uniforms, he hastened to point out to division chief of staff Okamoto and the new artillery corps commander, Hata. As Mishima says, although ammunition shortages were certainly a problem, his greatest anxiety was the matter of wintering.[19]

Infantry Colonel Sumi, another worrier, felt that it was imperative to prepare for winter, which would afflict the region by September, when snow would arrive. "Even a mere regimental commander such as I," says Sumi, "was of the opinion that we ought to pull back to the area of Chiangchunmiao, where the ground was higher and undulating. But nobody came to ask my opinion." When he learned that the division was going to set up positions in the wilderness, relying only on "poles and holes," Sumi thought to himself, "What foolish staff officers!" Sumi's quartermaster officer, Negami, adds that about the only "wintering" preparation that he handled was hauling the regiment's blankets to the front from Chiangchunmiao. According to the diary of Komatsubara, however, on 27 July the general did tell his intendance section that protracted combat required plans for clothing—winter garb in particular—and the requisition of tents. The circumstances of the front-line units and their wishes should also be examined closely.[20]

During this period, Komatsubara, Kobayashi, and the 23rd Division staff were concerned with a number of serious problems. First, there was a pressing need for troop replacements, since by 25 July casualties amounted to some 4,400 men (over 200 of them officers), and another 800 were ill.[21] Consequently, on the 27th, Komatsubara requested that the Independent Garrison Units in Manchuria provide some 1,600 replacements for his division and another 600 for the elements of the 7th Division. Second, Komatsubara and Kobayashi criticized imprudent deployments and sloppy entrenchment. When the division commander visited Kobayashi's command post on the 29th, the generals discussed the fact that many of the front-line battalions were bunched up in dips or on dunes. This rendered them especially vulnerable to high-trajectory fire by 15-cm. howitzers and infantry mortars. In addition, when Komatsubara inspected the foxholes and trenches of the troops, he found them to be less deep than those of the Russians. "We have not been serious enough about construction," commented the division commander.[22]

Still other problems attracted the attention of the Japanese infantry commanders and led to the issuing of directives daily. To reduce casualties, communication trenches and individual shelters should be constructed. Much better camouflage and covering were imperative, even for motor vehicles and guns, not only to protect them but also to reduce the chances of detection. Particularly dangerous were the wide gaps between adjacent units. For instance, Sakai noted on 27 July that although the neighboring Yamagata unit had adjusted its front line, there was still a hole of 800 meters between the regiments. Dips in the undulating interval facilitated infiltration by enemy patrols. Infantrymen and rapid-fire guns were sent to occupy key points and plug the gap, although technically they lay beyond the 72nd Regiment's combat sector.[23]

But the greatest fear of the Japanese local command was that the frontline units would adopt a purely negative outlook. A few units had abandoned objectives taken during the general offensive and had pulled back all the way to positions held earlier. Other units "lacked the spirit" to hold key points needed for strategic defense. After reading a book about Gen. Nogi Maresuke, a famous commander in the Russo-Japanese War, Komatsubara noted privately that "it used to be said, wars cannot be fought if one builds forts." The saying meant, the general explained, not that one should scorn constructing fortifications, but that one should not cling to them—or become too comfortable in them. Reflecting Komatsubara's public injunctions, the 13th Field Artillery Regiment's 3rd Battalion issued some sage counsel for unit commanders on 27 July: "Be particularly careful not to render the combative spirit negative in general, as the result of securing the present [defensive] positions."[24]

It goes without saying that Japanese insistence on the Halha as the boundary of Manchukuo underlay the Kwantung Army's obsession with the elimination of the enemy bridgehead and the notion of garrisoning the river zone. This had become apparent on 20 July when Kwantung Army Chief of Staff Isogai conferred in Tokyo with the central authorities, at their urgent request. One of Isogai's main points was that it was absolutely necessary to secure the area on the right shore of the Halha "to the last." The General Staff responded with the draft of a policy for solving the Nomonhan dispute that included a provision for pulling Japanese forces away from the frontier claimed by the Soviet-MPR side. Heated discussion ensued.

As far as the Kwantung Army was concerned, retorted Isogai, the AGS idea might have been relatively acceptable if the district in question had not been the scene of hostilities. By now, however, the Kwantung Army could not abandon the area after several thousand men had fallen in action. Indeed, Isogai wondered, if the High Command continued to insist on withdrawal from the Halha, did this mean that the central authorities were softening their claim to the Halha as the frontier? Operations Bureau chief Hashimoto answered that this was indeed a possibility. Isogai bristled, for he had only expected to confer with the war minister and the AGS deputy chief; the Kwantung Army commander, he asserted, was not about to take such a new and far-reaching decision immediately in response to the opinion of a mere bureau chief, especially since questions of responsibility were involved.

Hashimoto remembers asking Isogai about the Kwantung Army's intentions for Nomonhan. Isogai had answered that the field army planned to have the advance units winter in the area, with *tochka* bunkers constructed on the spots now held; there was no intention of pulling back. Although the High Command did not really like the notion, for reasons of logistics among others, Hashimoto told Isogai that *tochkas* were a good idea, "but why not build them along the Russian-claimed line?" Isogai disagreed, of course.

AGS deputy chief Nakajima Tetsuzō checked Hashimoto by assuring Isogai that changes in the border could not be decided at this conference. The vice minister of war, Lt. Gen. Yamawaki Masataka, added that frontiers were a matter of national policy lying beyond the purview of the General Staff's own authority. Although the argument blew over, Isogai returned to Manchuria on the 22nd with a bad taste in his mouth and with an AGS draft, part of which he and his colleagues regarded as little better than scrap paper.[25]

Soon after Isogai came back to Hsinking, on 24 July, the Kwantung Army went ahead with its strategic-defensive instructions to the 23rd Division. What the Kwantung Army had in mind was the construction of fieldworks strong enough to be held independently against attack for about a month. In addition, it was intended to build housing facilities to the rear of the defenses, and to prepare wells for a water-supply system. These hopes proved unrealistic, for it was soon found that the front-line units lacked strength to do more than work on minimal position construction, which progressed very slowly.[26]

General Ueda's brief visit to Nomonhan on 29 July served to intensify his concern about the vulnerability of the front to a possible enemy enveloping offensive in August. Applying the experience acquired during their river-crossing operation and fighting from existing divisional key points, the Japanese ought to be able to repulse assaults against the wings. But if the enemy attacked the front-line sectors by erosion, one by one, would the present strength be sufficient? Shouldn't the 7th Division be committed, Ueda wondered, or at least moved up to Hailar? In full agreement with the commander's estimate, Deputy Chief of Staff Yano saw the advisability of adding the 7th Division to cope with the possibility of enemy outflanking action as far as Amukulang, north of Nomonhan.[27]

The Kwantung Army's operations staff conducted extensive studies of the best use of the 7th Division. There was considerable reluctance to redeploy this excellent division to the defense of the Nomonhan area, in view of the role assigned to it on the eastern front in the wartime contingency planning for the security of Manchuria as a whole, for which there were few divisions as it was. Directly related were the problems of logistics and transport, in particular the shortage of trucks. A check of inventories revealed 400 trucks supporting the front-line units and another 600 operating on the lines of communication. But these were maximum figures, reduced further by an out-of-service factor approximating 25 percent. The logistics and ordnance officers had pleaded with Tokyo for more trucks and had badgered visitors constantly, but the prospects seemed close to nil.

The conclusion that emerged from the Kwantung Army's studies and discussions was that the front could not be reinforced, unless one abandoned the whole idea of wintering, thereby releasing a vast number of trucks. In the words of the Operations Section's secret diary: "We had decided to have a portion of the front-line strength hold out at the battlefield through the winter. This was because, even during winter, the enemy would invade again if we did not secure the present lines, where so much blood had been expended. A third-phase incident must not recur foolishly next spring, as had been the case in the first phase [May] and the second [since June]." Another consideration was the urgent need for trucks to move emergency troop reinforcements in case of an enemy offensive.[28]

Having decided that defense of a winter line near the Halha overrode the idea of "wasting" the whole 7th Division on the western front, the Kwantung Army staff could recommend nothing better than that one further regiment be committed and that the 23rd Division's casualties be replaced as soon as possible. A draft prepared on 31 July under the title "Essentials for Expediting Operational Preparations in Connection with the Nomonhan Incident"[29] indicated that an enemy offensive was expected in mid-August and that it was to be smashed in front of the Japanese positions in the Nomonhan area and on the wings at Fui and Noro heights. The target date for expediting preparations would be 10 August. Three sets of replacements totaling 4,300 men were to be brought from Japan, and concentrated and trained at Hailar. Platoon leaders would be replaced from within the Kwantung Army, but company commanders and above would be requested of the

High Command. Ammunition for artillery would be stockpiled in the battle zone in the amount of 10 *kisū* per piece.

The Kwantung Army plan called for fortifications to be constructed rapidly, and later strengthened gradually, at Kanchuerhmiao, Amukulang, and the anchor locations from Fui to Noro. The 23rd Division should concentrate one of its infantry regiments in the vicinity of Nomonhan, and should prepare to deploy the following troubleshooter units on the outer flanks: two more of the infantry regiments, with at least eight antitank batteries; and three artillery battalions equipped with Type 90, 10-cm., and 15-cm. pieces. As for the modest troop reinforcements promised, the Kwantung Army would authorize movement to Hailar of the 7th Division's 14th Infantry Brigade headquarters, the rest of the 28th Infantry Regiment (Kajikawa's 2nd Battalion having been committed from the beginning), and an artillery battalion. These forces would be retained under direct control of the Kwantung Army, but one small unit would be assigned to the 23rd Division: the 6th Battalion from the 1st Independent Garrison Unit at Mukden. Air defense of the Arshaan area would be strengthened, and Manchukuoan forces were "roughly to complete" defenses near Handagai. Railway construction between Arshaan and Handagai was to be expedited, as was the preparation of winter quarters near the battle zone.

Having given the cold shoulder to the High Command's cautionary injunctions and having decided to dare the Manchurian winter near the Halha, the Kwantung Army promptly went off on a tangent. However briefly espoused, the new idea reflected a lingering disdain for the defensive and a mesmeric attraction to the offensive, regardless of the realities of the situation. The flight of fancy arose from a "workshop" conducted by the Kwantung Army's Intelligence Section in early August on the subject of battlefield water supply, and attended by Lieutenant Colonel Hattori from the Operations Section. Among the matters that had been intriguing the intelligence experts and military geographers was the question of why the Soviet-MPR side had been so stubbornly clinging to the small sector on the right shore of the Halha. One way of looking at the problem might be to regard the struggle at Nomonhan as a battle for water. In the absence of water on the high ground on the left bank, the Russians must have desperately needed to retain the source of water represented by the river in the confluence area.

The preceding "revelation" exerted a great influence on Hattori. He came up with the notion of administering a "heavy hammer blow" to the enemy before entering winter. By seizing key points in the Sambur Obo sector, the Japanese would compel the foe to withdraw because of the loss of easy access to the water supply from the river. Although one wonders about the alleged novelty of this latest intention of eliminating the hostile bridgehead, at least insofar as the objective was concerned, Hattori enthusiastically brought his idea back to the Operations Section—to the chief, Colonel Terada, and his fellow officers Murasawa Kazuo and Shimanuki Takeharu. (Major Tsuji was off inspecting the eastern frontier at the time.) Everybody liked Hattori's reasoning. Terada saw an advantage to capturing the right shore just before real winter began in mid-October, for then the enemy would lack time to establish wintering facilities of his own. Even if friendly forces withdrew during the winter, it would be difficult for the foe to advance to the shoreline. Thus the Japanese would be able to sacrifice their winter-camping program to a certain degree, in turn enhancing their capability of reinforcing offensive strength with the same number of trucks.

Foreseeing difficulty in securing the shoreline with existing strength, Shimanuki pulled together the various suggestions and devised an alternative plan involving operations across the river. Although, as we have seen, all kinds of reasons had been adduced to prevent the commitment of the 7th Division for the defensive program, Shimanuki now recommended that the division be brought up by the end of August and that another river-crossing offensive be launched in early September, to capture bastions along the opposite shore. Two infantry battalions would be deployed in the Sambur Obo region, and two companies at key points to the north. These forces would be expected to hold on through the winter. Based on previous plans, winter camps would be established on the near bank too. Given the importance of the Handagai district, two more infantry battalions should be assigned to winter there.

Inasmuch as the offensive plan represented a radical departure in the approach to settling the Nomonhan affair, the operations staff eagerly awaited the return of Tsuji, the old Manchuria hand. When Tsuji got back on 10 August and was shown the draft, he said that the concept of seeking a solution by means of an offensive was laudable but that the problem of weather at Nomonhan had been underestimated. The Japanese army, he observed, had never spent the snows of winter in the field at temperatures that could sink to $-60°$ F. It was a fundamental mistake to think it feasible to survive on the basis of the simple construction program now under way. To cope simultaneously with the requirements of winter camping and of a new offensive was impossible without a great reinforcement of trucks. Wintering must take precedence, Tsuji concluded; the offensive plan could not be implemented.

Since everybody in the Operations Section except Tsuji was relatively new to the post, there was no pretense of matching his knowledge of winter in Manchuria. It must have been particularly noteworthy, too, that such a hawkish officer was recommending caution. Terada therefore advised Generals Ueda, Isogai, and Yano that the plan for the autumn offensive was being dropped.[30] One can only wonder how the Kwantung Army's operations staff, including the ordinarily prudent Terada, could have given serious thought to an offensive in September, even reinforced by the rest of the 7th Division, when a series of expensive assaults throughout July, abetted by tanks and heavy artillery, had not succeeded. In view of the near-fiasco with the one bridge in early July, how were attack forces to get across the Halha once more? Moreover, considering the High Command's desire to end the fighting and its willingness to abandon the river as the frontier, how could troops be hurled arbitrarily into Outer Mongolia again? It is apparent that the Kwantung Army was not taking the threat of a Soviet counteroffensive in mid-August very seriously.

The definitive policy for this period was drafted by Shimanuki and issued by the Kwantung Army on 12 August.[31] There were the usual timeworn strictures about compelling the enemy to abandon his ambitions by smashing the effectiveness of the Soviet-MPRA forces and doggedly overwhelming protracted resistance. Hostile offensive action would be defeated, and the foe destroyed on the right bank of the Halha. Once these vague, hortatory declamations were recorded, however, the Kwantung Army laid down details that reflected the most recent staff discussions. Efforts would be made to terminate the operational activities of the Japanese main force by winter 1939. The prearranged program of constructing fortifications and facilities for winter quarters must be expedited, in order to secure the gains already acquired, even in the depth of winter. Although major operations were not to be conducted on the left shore, the army planned to dominate the Halha "if necessary," paying particular attention to the exploitation of the ice-drift period on the blocked river. The shore sector would be secured with powerful elements, in position before the severe cold set in. In the Handagai area, winter facilities would be built to accommodate one artillery and two infantry battalions, two transport companies, and two antiaircraft artillery units. To assist with the construction tasks, the Kwantung Army was assigning trucks, infantry, and engineers: its own motor transport command; the 7th Division's 14th Infantry Brigade and engineer regiment, plus one of its truck companies; the 2nd Motor Transport Regiment; and the 6th Battalion of the Independent Garrison Unit, now at Hailar.

According to the Kwantung Army's guidelines, efforts would be made to limit the zone in dispute to the Holsten shores, and to avoid outbreaks west of Lake Buir. Fortifications should be constructed in the Kanchuerhmiao-Amukulang and Handagai-Arshaan areas, defended by the Manchukuoan army if the situation permitted. The necessary air units should remain at the front through the winter, cooperating with ground forces. Staging bases should be equipped with wintering facilities.

In the larger sense, ominous connotations are to be found in the Kwantung Army's stipulation of the need to expedite preparations for operations in case (1) large-scale fighting resumed at Nomonhan in the spring of 1940, and (2) the Nomonhan affair expanded into all-out war between Japan and the Soviet Union. Contingency planning demanded speedy construction of the railway between Arshaan, Handagai, and Chiangchunmiao in particular.

Commanding the new and old units at the front, and directing their operational activities, was the recently activated Sixth Army, with headquarters in Hailar. It was not organized specifically to deal with the Nomonhan fighting. IGHQ's annually revised "Army Expansion Guide" called for the systematic buildup of the forces in Manchuria, one example being the transfer of heavy artillery units from Japan, as noted earlier. There was a logical structural need for a numbered army on the west Manchurian front, paralleling the Fourth Army in the north at Peian and the two armies in the crucial east—the Third at Mutanchiang and the Fifth at Tungan. (The establishment of the Fifth Army had only been ordered in May 1939.) Originally conceived in the AGS Operations Section around 1936 or 1937, the Sixth Army was to have been formed at last in the autumn of 1939. Nomonhan merely "overlapped," accelerating the organizational process a bit, and IGHQ officially decreed the activation on 4 August.[32]

The commander of the Sixth Army was Lt. Gen. Ogisu Ryūhei, age 55, a graduate of the 17th military academy class of 1905 and thus one class senior to Komatsubara. Ogisu had been Taiwan Army chief of staff (1935-37) and then commander of the excellent 13th Division during the "brilliant" Hsuchow operation in central China. Energetic and aggressive, he struck some as a glory-seeker. Ogisu's chief of staff, Maj. Gen. Fujimoto Tetsukuma, came to the Sixth Army from an air force command at Pyongyang in North Korea. Calm, capable, and experienced in combat, he handled the headquarters very smoothly. Colleagues call him a man of integrity who disliked outside interference.

The senior staff officer was Col. Hamada Sueo, who had been a member of the Kwantung Army's Research Section since the summer of 1937. He had been earmarked for the staff of the new Fifth Army until Lieutenant Colonel Gondō, who had been intended for the Sixth Army slot, was wounded badly in early July. A former artillery school instructor, Hamada had most recently been studying such relevant matters as river- and swamp-crossing actions, water supply, and winter operations. He was the only Sixth Army staff officer who knew Manchuria well. At the time of the offensive on 23 July, he had visited the Nomonhan front north of the Holsten and had talked with the reconnaissance regiment commander, Lieutenant Colonel Ioki, at Fui Heights, as well as with Generals Komatsubara and Kobayashi and Colonels Sumi and Yamagata. Rounding out Ogisu's staff were Capt. Hirai Bun (Hitoshi) (Operations), Lt. Col. Tanaka Tetsujirō (Intelligence), and Capt. Iwakoshi Shinroku (Logistics). Later, Lieutenant Colonel Shiraki was attached from the Harbin OSS branch, and Major Hongō from the Kwantung Army.

The Sixth Army staff started to assemble in Hsinking at the beginning of August. Hamada reported that the core had been formed on the 6th. Fujimoto flew to Hailar, conducted liaison, and inspected the front. Sections proceeded gradually to Hailar, which was new to everybody, and prepared to open the headquarters. Ogisu arrived on 12 August and visited the battlefield next day. There was some thought of advancing the combat head-quarters to Chiangchunmiao immediately and of attaching a staff officer to the 23rd Division. It was decided not to impose additional burdens on the division, since the Sixth Army lacked security troops and signalmen of its own. Another consideration was that Ogisu's army, charged with the de-fense of all of Hsingan Province, was not in a position to concentrate exclu-sively on the Nomonhan affair. Consequently, the Sixth Army command was still located well behind the front when the storm broke, only a week after its arrival in Hailar.

The Kwantung Army, however, was very pleased with the creation of the subordinate Sixth Army. No longer would large forces such as the 23rd Di-vision and the 8th Border Garrison Unit have to be controlled directly from Hsinking. There had been earlier problems with multilayered horizontal and vertical chains of command involving the 23rd Division, the Yasuoka detachment, Uchiyama's artillery corps, and the artillery groups of Hata and Ise. Terada advised his Kwantung Army operations staff that they should try to leave detailed guidance to the Sixth Army now, and not interfere.[33]

With respect to the outlook of the Sixth Army command itself at the time of formation, the best insight is provided by Colonel Hamada. When he in-spected the Nomonhan battlefield during the Japanese artillery offensive, he reacted as follows to what he saw and to what he was "in for":

> I regretted my assignment, and I suffered about it. My heart sank when I studied the terrain on the spot and I realized the feebleness of our resources. After observ-ing the fighting strength of the two sides, my intuition made me doubtful about the success of our [general] offensive under such conditions. In particular, I was shocked by the piddling allocation of ammunition, after all those speeches by the Kwantung Army staff about "using overwhelming firepower this time." I felt that the episode of our balloonists typified the real situation of our forces: knowing for sure that they would be shot down, but having to raise the balloon anyhow.
>
> To be frank, I felt that the geography and the ammunition problem were hope-less for us. "How unlucky to have been sent here," I thought to myself. "What a place! And what a mess I'm getting into!" Although I was at quite a loss about the situation and I fully realized the difficulties facing [the Sixth Army], I was deter-

mined to do my best. But I did think the fighting ought to be settled politically as soon as possible. If the Japanese army was serious about winning, the size of our forces would have to be increased greatly.[34]

Apart from the difficult circumstances in which the brand-new Sixth Army found itself, the front-line Japanese forces were facing the coming of the early Mongolian winter with rudimentary shelter and fieldworks. From the beginning, there had been serious disagreement between the Kwantung Army's Intelligence and Operations sections concerning priorities. The Intelligence Section warned that in the event of a large-scale enemy offensive, everybody would die in battle unless countermeasures were prepared. The operations staff retorted that a Soviet general offensive might or might not materialize, but that winter would come for sure. Then the troops would die from the cold and not from combat. "Which of the alternatives makes better sense to you?," asked the operations officers.[35]

IJA intelligence experts on Manchuria could only agree about the threat of winter. Soviet soldiers were known to be able to work with bare hands aboard trucks at $-10°$ F., and to handle rifles at $15°$ F. Even Japanese troops from Hokkaido (such as the 7th Division) could not cope with such conditions. IJA light machine guns did not operate below $-20°$ F. without heating, and the recoil liquid of Japanese artillery froze at $-10°$ F. Soviet ordnance and equipment worked at such temperatures. As intelligence Major Nyūmura says, whenever he went out on reconnaissance in North Manchuria in the depth of winter, he always took White Russians with him, not Japanese.[36] Thus Tsuji's warning of temperatures as low as $-60°$ F. at Nomonhan sobered his auditors, and wintering preparations were supposed to receive precedence.

On 1 August, the Kwantung Army received an information copy of a message prepared weeks before by the military attaché in Moscow, Col. Doi Akio. Though abandoning the Nomonhan area in general was highly inadvisable, said Doi, the Japanese must not fight large-scale battles of attrition. Impregnable fortifications should be built quickly "at appropriate locations away from the Halha River." Border lookout posts needed to be fortified for permanent retention, thereby thwarting hostile intentions of regaining the border zone. By constructing powerful defenses in a region where friendly forces could manifest their firm determination to secure the frontier and by retaining the area for a long period, the Japanese would cause the foe eventually to abandon hostilities. Meanwhile, one must be prepared to smash an enemy offensive.[37]

The Kwantung Army savored the aggressive tone of the attaché's message and ignored the remarks about building the fortified line back from the Halha. Doi's recommendations, said Hattori, agreed essentially with the guidelines prepared in Hsinking. Yet when Nyūmura saw his friend Doi in person at Harbin station in early August, the attaché stated clearly that the Japanese ought to pull back a little and establish their positions along a more defensible line. Doi's arguments against major Japanese offensive operations in the autumn undoubtedly influenced Kwantung Army thinking about tactics, but not about fieldworks, although his views were shared widely at the High Command level.[38]

On the spot, construction proceeded disappointingly. After only two or three weeks of hard labor, the 23rd Division was supposed to have built powerful defenses, something perhaps feasible in a training exercise in a built-up area. But, as Hamada points out, school studies call for construction at topographically suitable locations, whereas at Nomonhan the haphazard choice of positions represented the poorest possible layout. There was no capability of defense against armor, for the outer wings were wide open, antitank weapons were scarce, barriers were almost nonexistent, and materials were in short supply. The entire zone remained under observation and fire from across the Halha.

It was comparatively easy to dig in the sandy soil near the river, but it was even easier to be caved in by artillery bombardment and air bombing. The strongest of the covered sections at the Sixth Army's advance signal and command site did not meet the protective standards of a "medium bunker." Many of the front-line soldiers still had to rely on tent covers to ward off the dew, although Kusaba says that carpenters, plasterers, and artisans in his battery built "Nomonhan apartments"—dugouts capable of accommodating four or five men, replete with curtains, desks, beds, and memorial tablets. But the walls and roofs of these facilities were made of nothing stronger than ammunition boxes and boards.[39]

The 23rd Division had tried to convert rapidly from an offensive to a defensive stance in the worst of locations, particularly vulnerable to encirclement. Certainly the Russians were not taken in, for they could cross and recross the Halha with ease now. Zhukov knew that the Japanese were "actively building defense lines all along the front: timber was brought in, dugouts [were] built, engineers strengthened the defenses."[40] Imaoka notes the difference between wintering and operational preparations, adding that there were great contradictions and confusions in the planning—notably constructing positions designed mainly against cold weather despite the danger of an enemy offensive in August. The defensive frontage was overextended, but the 23rd Division may have been reassured by Kwantung Army talk of merely holding on for a month or two and then returning the main body to Hailar before the worst of winter set in. Here, too, Imaoka discerns a contradiction. Why construct wintering facilities in the Nomonhan zone if the division was to head for Hailar by, say, 1 October? Meanwhile the so-called key points were to be defended "as is," which was all right if the Japanese were going to attack, but not if defensive combat proved necessary.

Was it complacency and optimism, one wonders, that caused the Kwantung Army's highest leadership and staff to allow the 23rd Division to proceed so dangerously? As one critic put it, the construction of positions so near the Halha, well within reach of the Soviet fire network, amounted to a "sentence of death" for the front-line Japanese units. It is small wonder that, when Nyūmura had the chance to go to Harbin for a couple of days in early August, he seized the opportunity to see his family.[41] Zhukov and his associates, of course, were bending every effort to make it a last goodbye, not only for Nyūmura but also for the entire Sixth Army.

30

Forging a Second Cannae: Zhukov's Masterpiece, August 1939

In many ways, this operation resembles Hannibal's campaign at Cannae. I think it will become the second perfect battle of encirclement in all history.

—Col.-Gen. G. M. Shtern[1]

The Kwantung Army detected, or thought it detected, dangerous signs of Russian escalation of the Nomonhan hostilities even before the Japanese artillery offensive was attempted. Whereas it had been presumed earlier that the Soviet Union was disinclined to wage all-out war against Japan, by mid-July reconnaissance reports from Manchurian border sectors other than at Nomonhan indicated that the Russians had massed forces in every forward zone along the eastern borders. By the middle of July, Kwantung Army intelligence judged that Soviet forces in the Far East had already been mobilized. Then, in the early hours of 16 July, a Soviet plane penetrated deeply into Manchuria and attacked the railway bridge at Fulaerhchi, west of Tsitsihar on the route to Hailar. The raid caused trifling damage but it had important psychological effects.

Having itself demonstrated the effectiveness of serious diversionary actions at the time of the Changkufeng affair in 1938,[2] the Kwantung Army saw the importance of going on combat alert now on almost all fronts and of issuing wartime air-defense orders. Tokyo was asked for permission to raid air bases in Outer Mongolia again. But the High Command was not interested in war against the USSR as a means of settling the Nomonhan dispute. Dislodging the Russians from the right bank of the Halha would suffice. Since prompt permission for retaliation was not forthcoming, the "emotional antagonism" between the staffs in Hsinking and in Tokyo grew worse.[3]

As for the Nomonhan front in particular, the OSS branch in Hailar had picked up various pieces of information in July, ostensibly based upon communications from Soviet military headquarters in Khabarovsk and addressed to the Army Politburo in Moscow. Logistical problems were supposedly proving very severe, and supply personnel were meeting at Chita to try to work things out. But despite requests by the Soviet local command for postponement of the offensive because of insufficient preparations, the plans were proceeding, and X-day was scheduled between August 5 and 10. The latest estimates by Kwantung Army intelligence suggested that the enemy offensive could be expected around the 14th.[4]

Of course, one cannot be sure of the authenticity of the raw intelligence that formed the basis for the Kwantung Army's appraisal. Zhukov speaks of Soviet secret efforts to misinform the Japanese—to convey the impression that no preparations were being made for an offensive and that the Russians were merely building up their defenses, "nothing else." Since it was known that the Japanese were tapping telephone lines and intercepting radio traffic, the Soviets devised a welter of deceptive radio and phone messages mentioning only the construction of defenses and preparations for autumn and winter. In all radio communications, a code was employed that could be broken easily.[5]

Japanese radio-intercept activity from mid-July does seem to reek of Soviet "inspirational intelligence."[6] Nyūmura's combat intelligence unit, beefed up to battalion strength of over 200 specialists, broke some of the simpler Soviet radio codes—the three-letter blocks only. In addition, through double-spy activity in Harbin, the Japanese OSS heard that the Russian combat commander in Tamsag had advised Moscow by telegram to make up for "aerial inferiority" by compensating with artillery reinforcements. This intelligence seems suspect because Soviet air strength was already on the rise by late July. But although the information in the telegram may have been a plant, Nyūmura is still not sure. Since the purported inferiority could have referred to qualitative problems, the message was "not necessarily untrue." Firmer information emanated from attaché Doi, who had traveled from Moscow across the Trans-Siberian Railway and reached Harbin around the beginning of August. Doi told Nyūmura that the rail line east of Chita was clogged with military trains heading east, betokening the great importance that the Soviet Union ascribed to the Nomonhan crisis. Specifically, Doi reported to the Kwantung Army that he had observed at least two Russian rifle divisions and 80 heavy guns moving eastward.[7]

Nevertheless, whereas the Russians say they were striving to divert Japanese attention from the forthcoming offensive, front-line IJA commanders were conscious of aggressive Soviet probing and truck movements from around 28 July, especially south of the Holsten. Komatsubara's private explanation in general was as follows.[8] Since the Japanese prime minister, Hiranuma, had been stating that the Nomonhan affair would not escalate into all-out war, and since articles in this vein were appearing in the Japanese press, the Soviet command was enormously relieved and was able to tailor the massive commitment of troops, ordnance, and equipment to the needs of a localized struggle, drawing from the entire Russian armed forces as required.

Moreover, although details were never revealed by the Japanese, Komatsubara and others were convinced that the most secret operations orders detailing the composition and structure of the Kwantung Army, the 23rd Division, and the 2nd Air Division had fallen into enemy hands during the left-shore offensive on 3 July. Long after the Second World War, Soviet sources disclosed that important IJA documents did fall into Russian hands, including a Kwantung Army order dated 20 June and a 23rd Division order dated 30 June. As for classified Japanese air force materials, the Russians have revealed that a briefcase was captured containing orders and other documents issued by Lieutenant General Giga. MPRA sources add that a high-ranking Japanese air force officer carrying plans and documents was seized when Mongolian ground fire brought down an IJAF plane on 2/3 July.[9] Might this officer have been Lt. Col. Shimanuki Tadamasa, Giga's senior operations expert, who disappeared with his scout plane across the Halha on 2 July? A Russian-speaker and the first IJA airman to have been sent on officer exchange to the Soviet Union, Shimanuki had an unexcelled knowledge of IJA matters as well as access to top secret materials.[10]

Evidence that the Russians were "leaking" planted information to the Japanese can be found in the visible incidence of radio usage. It was a fact that, since 1938, the Soviets' reliance on radio signals had decreased and their use of more secure wire communications had increased markedly, accompanied by modification of codes to complex five-letter blocks, often changed. Nyūmura had been suffering from the diminished Soviet use of wireless, since the latter could allow his unit to home in on enemy radio sites and movements at the division and brigade levels. Ordinarily, shorter code blocks or uncoded transmissions were employed only when time was short and operations were difficult—certainly not true of late July and the next weeks, so far as the Russians were concerned. Significantly, after the deliberate windfalls of early August, Soviet use of radio dwindled. Even when they did not know the meaning of messages, the Japanese had been able to gauge their importance by the frequency of transmission as well as the layout of the network. By about 15 August, however, the 10 or 15 Soviet receivers were handling only about 20 transmissions a day, whereas the 6 or 7 IJA receivers were dealing with 230-50 messages daily. Russian radio traffic was near zero by the 17th or 18th of August—an ominous blackout typical of tight communications security measures.[11]

Amid this atmosphere of confusing indicators, the Japanese continued to operate as if time were working on their side—which it was not. Colonel Hamada wondered privately how reinforcement by a mere battalion of field artillery and one infantry regiment could suffice to stave off the anticipated

Soviet offensive. Ogisu was worried about the weakness of the 23rd Division, too, but though the general did not exactly underestimate the Russians, he did not seem to esteem them highly. Gaps in thinking existed at every level. The Kwantung Army operations staff, for instance, often boasted that the Soviet-MPRA side could be dealt with by Japanese forces at a 1:3 ratio. To the concern expressed by intelligence and other experts that the IJA right and left flanks were exposed, operations officers retorted that the openings were deliberate—designed to suck in and destroy the enemy. Hamada feels that although the Kwantung Army operations staff were talking optimistically and aggressively, they must have been deeply worried. The Sixth Army officers were too new and too unfamiliar with conditions in Manchuria to know better, and seemed even more sanguine. Indeed, Ogisu's initial reports struck even the Kwantung Army as deliberately reassuring. As for Komatsubara, Hamada heard nothing from him that betrayed weakness. The division commander sounded optimistic and conveyed the impression that the Japanese were "winning," but in his diary entry for 15 August he noted that the Sixth Army and the 23rd Division needed to improve their "operational will."[12]

Complicating Japanese prognostications was the fact that the Russians did launch some very brisk attacks in early August involving armor, artillery, and infantry striking along both sides of the Holsten. At about 3 A.M. on 3 August, after an hour's artillery preparation, 1,000 enemy troops with a dozen tanks attacked on the Kobayashi front, mainly against the gap between the Yamagata and Sakai regiments. At a cost of 10 killed and 15 wounded, the Japanese eliminated 430 enemy soldiers.[13]

Shishkin, however, refers only to a Soviet-MPRA operation on 7-8 August designed to improve the tactical situation of the foothold 3-5 kilometers east of the Halha.[14] On the evening of the 7th, the 71st Regiment's records agree, 300-500 enemy infantry and cavalry penetrated deeply into the gap at vital Sankaku (Triangle) Hill east of the Noro Heights area. Russian bombardments were severe on the 8th, and enemy observation posts were moved up all around the high ground. Col. Morita Tōru, the new regimental commander, arrived after noon and gave an impassioned speech to the troops. The brunt of the fighting on 8 August, however, was borne by Col. Hasebe Riei's detachment from the 8th Border Garrison Unit, which had been taking over from the crippled 71st Regiment and the ruined Manchukuo cavalry[15] since 6 August. Kajikawa's veteran battalion, now attached to Hasebe, reported that the enemy lost about 360 men on 7/8 August and over 50 on the 8th. The latter toll included 20 telephone-equipped Russians, probably an artillery observer group, who lost their way while cooperating with infantry and blundered into the Japanese positions. No prisoners were taken, noted Kajikawa, as the enemy fought to the last man. In general, Soviet grenadiers, although laden with grenades, lacked rifles and were helpless in hand-to-hand fighting. Japanese grenade launchers seemed to be particularly awe-inspiring. A lucrative target was to shoot down enemy soldiers who were collecting arms and casualties after dark, or who were moving around carrying tea or water at any time. Kajikawa also stressed the great defensive importance of ordinary, covered IJA fieldworks.[16]

The 72nd Regiment had come under increasing bombardment and fighter attack since afternoon on 7 August too. Barrages from the left bank of the Halha and from across the Holsten were particularly severe, cutting communications and reducing visibility to a foot. Supported by the artillery and by tanks, 200 Soviet infantrymen attacked on Sakai's right and 400 on his left. Another 400-500 troops struck on Yamagata's sector. In the course of hard fighting into the night, Sakai's regiment claimed to have inflicted 230 casualties and to have knocked out two to four tanks, at a cost of 12 killed and 21 wounded. More fighting ensued on the 8th, marked by particularly close combat at 50 meters on the left flank, where the enemy "did not quite retreat" until hand-to-hand assaults "scared the foe off" to a barbed-wire dip.[17]

The preceding actions attracted the close attention of the Kwantung Army, which had been expecting a serious Soviet drive a bit earlier, on 6 August, the anniversary of the big Russian push at Changkufeng the year before.[18] As Kwantung Army headquarters understood matters, powerful enemy assaults on 7-8 August[19] north of the Holsten were repulsed at the Japanese defenses, costing the attackers 300 dead and the defenders about 40. Below the Holsten, the enemy left 200 corpses, against Japanese losses of only 20. Had this been the full-scale August offensive of the Russians? Some thought (or hoped) so, but the consensus was that the scale had been too small, and that the recent assaults were merely preliminary feelers. Nevertheless, the Kwantung Army was delighted with the defensive performance of the much-maligned 23rd Division. There was new confidence that the division had finally become attuned to combat.[20]

The Japanese undertook one small "tactical adjustment" of their own on 12/13 August: a dawn attack by the 71st Regiment with artillery support against the hilly sector south-southwest of Nigesorimot. According to prisoners, the immediate enemy belonged to the 22nd and 23rd regiments of the MPRA 8th Cavalry Division. The front-line IJA units reported that the foe fled in "laughable confusion"—two men escaping on one horse, for example, and others running away naked. A more pitiable scene occurred when ten enemy fighters repeatedly strafed the fleeing Mongolian horsemen; "even though they were enemy, the sight made you want to cover your eyes." From hostile forces numbering 500 men, several guns, and eight tanks, it was estimated that at least 100 soldiers had been killed. Two guns, 100 horses, and two prisoners were taken.[21] Although Soviet sources naturally omit unpleasant details, Zhukov does speak of an attack against the MPRA 22nd Cavalry Regiment on 12 August by almost one regiment of Japanese infantry supported by artillery, armored vehicles, tanks [*sic*], and 22 bombers. The Japanese succeeded in occupying the hills.[22]

At 23rd Division headquarters, in mid-August, Komatsubara remarked that matters were fairly quiet locally. He was pondering how to hasten the construction of fieldworks, collect fuel, deploy his forces in depth, thin out the front lines, and retain large reserves. It would be desirable to pull back gradually, once the threat of an enemy advance had passed; yet the foe must not be provoked into taking countermeasures "for the sake of honor," thus hindering any withdrawal. Meanwhile, the Japanese line companies were in particularly bad shape owing to casualties. After a hair-raising visit to the 71st Regiment on 7 August, Komatsubara noted that 27 officers were dead and about 60 wounded; seven companies lacked commanders. The overall casualties of the division as of the 5th included 4,353 wounded and 1,155 sick. Every day, about 40 men were being wounded. Since replacements were green, "on-the-job" training was vital. It was necessary to enhance morale, offensive spirit, and discipline, and to explain the true purpose of the current low-key operations.[23]

Matters were not progressing smoothly at Sixth Army headquarters. Ogisu not only was responsible for combat operations but also had provincial functions, and he needed more staff officers to handle both. The Kwantung Army's hands-off policy toward the Sixth Army was proving to be no boon, and the battle came to be viewed through different eyes—the difference between theory and practice. Just as the Kwantung Army was blaming the AGS for ignorance of local conditions, so the Sixth Army felt that higher headquarters officers failed to help by directing or involving themselves in the combat. But, as Tsuji put it, the Kwantung Army was extremely sorry to have had to turn over to the Sixth Army "a half-broken hut with a leaking roof."

Most importantly, the Sixth Army was simply not anticipating or ready for the enemy's August offensive. Personnel were misplaced, the organization was defective. As Imaoka puts it, "If the Sixth Army had arrived on the scene with loads of ammunition and supplies, it would have helped. But the army was just a headquarters without backup." Hamada ascribes the main responsibility to the Tokyo and Hsinking command levels. That IJA logistics were in comparatively good shape, he says, was only because the enemy did not interfere between Hailar and the front. Division operations officer Murata adds that "nothing much changed" as far as the 23rd Division was concerned when the Sixth Army was organized, except that "the pressure of responsibility was somewhat lightened for us."[24]

The situation as of mid-August, then, was that the Japanese were rather pleased with themselves and not overly nervous about the enemy. Soviet reconnaissance and combat patrols continued to be encountered, however, and "rather many" trucks and tank units were sighted. On 18 August, for example, the 71st Regiment reported that, starting at 5 P.M. and continuing through the night, the sounds of tanks and vehicles could be heard in the Higashi-watashi crossing area on the Holsten south of Heights 744. "Undoubtedly the enemy intends to encircle our left wing by gradually moving farther east."[25]

On the larger scale, 23rd Division intelligence knew that about two Russian rifle divisions, Outer Mongolian regiments, and at least 500-600 tanks and armored cars were at the front.[26] A specialist on Soviet affairs, Hata Hikosaburō, the able head of the Harbin OSS branch and a major general since March, tried to convince the Kwantung Army operations staff that the Russians were massing three to four rifle divisions and 800-1,000 tanks for the August offensive. Although General Ueda was impressed and wanted to reexamine the Kwantung Army guidelines, his operational subordinates seem to have been unenthusiastic. Lt. Col. Suzuki Yasushi, an officer on the Kwantung Army intelligence staff, adduces a number of explanations: "Even if the calculations were accurate, Japan was tied up in China and the weak Kwantung Army could not be reinforced by Tokyo anyhow. Since the estimates were too large to cope with, try to overlook the cold facts, don't talk about them, and maybe they will go away. What's the use of 'fiddling around' with intelligence, since nothing can be done about it in any case?"[27]

As a result, the Kwantung Army was not prepared for the Russians' enormous August offensive. In the words of the Kwantung Army's secret but misleading apologia: "We had no prior clue from intelligence at any level, from the front to army headquarters, to lead us to expect there would be an offensive on such a scale at this time."[28] The High Command, overestimating Soviet difficulties with logistics and transport, and suspicious of intelligence from double agents, was no more prescient, although an excellent overall estimate of Soviet strength was on the books as of 13 August: 30 rifle battalions, five tank and armored car brigades, 130 field and 50 heavy guns, plus two MPRA cavalry divisions.[29] As always, a wide gap existed between the generators of intelligence and the users.

In the close confines of Zhukov's First Army Group headquarters, meanwhile, plans were being devised for a general offensive to be launched no later than 20 August and designed to clear the Japanese from the soil claimed by the MPR. The target date of the 20th was selected for two main reasons. Strategically or geopolitically—although this is not detailed in Soviet sources—there was consideration of the crisis in Europe: Franco-British parleys with the USSR were collapsing, Nazi German negotiations were about to produce the vital nonaggression pact with the Russians (dated 23 August), and Poland was on the verge of being invaded by the Reich (a week later). Tactically, Zhukov's army group preferred 20 August because it was a Sunday and the lax Japanese command had allowed generals and other senior officers to take leave. Many were far from their front-line troops, in Kanchuerhmiao or as far as Hailar. To Zhukov, this was an important factor to take into consideration. An ancillary argument widely advanced by the Russians was that the Japanese planned an offensive of their own on 24 August. This makes no sense, is unsupported by documentation, and is unnecessary for the Soviet rationale.

For purposes of security, only a few key officers worked on the basic project: Zhukov himself, a member of the Group's Military Council, the head of the Political Department (Division Commissar P. I. Gorokhov), the chief of staff, and the head of the operational branch. Zhukov's deputy, Kom-Brig (Brigade Commander) M. I. Potapov, handled contact between line units and supporting services; the chiefs of logistics and of arms and services were limited to their separate and restricted functions in the master scheme. Indeed, only one typist was allowed to work on the operational plan, combat orders, and related documents. To facilitate coordination and administration, a liaison section was set up at group headquarters with 12 officers and organic transport, supported by a double-wire network connected to the units.

Whereas the Japanese thought in terms of committing a battalion here and a regiment there, the Russians were "thinking big." That is, Zhukov was authorized to draw whatever forces he deemed necessary to wipe out Japanese units east of the Halha. From the Soviet interior he was sent such reinforcements as the 82nd and 57th rifle divisions; a regiment of the 152nd Rifle Division; the 6th Tank Brigade; the 212th Airborne Brigade; the 126th Artillery Regiment; the 85th Antiaircraft Regiment; independent tank companies; antitank, machine gun, and signal units; and aircraft. Eventually, according to the Russians' data, they had massed forces generally intended to surpass the Japanese in the following strength: infantry battalions, 35 to the IJA 25; cavalry squadrons, 20 to 17; machine guns (light and heavy), 2,255 to 1,283; 75-mm. and larger guns, 216-66 to 135; antitank and battalion guns, 286 to 142; mortars, 40 to 60; armored cars, 346 to ?; and tanks, 498 to 120 [*sic*].[30]

To assemble such large forces in an inhospitable area required a logistical effort of enormous proportions—something the Japanese side did not think could be done. As Zhukov later told Stalin, his greatest difficulties involved material and technical supplies for the forces. Everything needed had to be transported overland from the nearest supply bases and railheads in G. M. Shtern's Trans-Baikal Military District headquartered in Chita. "Even the firewood for cooking food," said Zhukov, "had to be brought 600 kilometers."

Zhukov's planning group estimated the following supplies had to be amassed for the general offensive: artillery ammunition, 18,000 tons; bombs, etc., 6,500 tons; liquid fuel and lubricants, 15,000 tons; solid fuel, 7,500 tons; and foodstuffs, 4,000 tons. Another 4,000 tons of miscellaneous items brought the total to 55,000 tons, supplies on an order of magnitude requiring 3,500 trucks and 1,400 tankers. Inventories did not suffice—even after the arrival of substantial reinforcements of over 1,200 trucks and 375 tankers from other parts of the USSR in the week before the offensive—but somehow the overworked Soviet drivers, braving extreme temperatures and "horrible winds," brought up the required tonnage. The consumption of fuel on these 1,400-kilometer round trips of five grueling days apiece was "unheard of," but, as Zhukov admits, "we had no other way out." The Russians were somehow able to accumulate all categories of ammunition at a combat factor of 6; tank ammunition, 9; and fuel, as much as 5.[31]

Soviet truck usage dwarfed IJA capabilities and thinking at the time; the Japanese regarded 100 kilometers as "far" and 200 trucks as "many." To sustain one day of Japanese operations at Nomonhan necessitated the logistical equivalent of 320 truckloads operating across the less than 200 kilometers from Hailar. From the Trans-Baikal District, the Russians would need at least 1,300 daily truckloads. Since the Soviet command achieved its full and sustained buildup, however, IJA military observers have become convinced with the benefit of hindsight that the Russians may actually be underestimating the case when they say they used "only" about 4,000 trucks. Some Japanese think that Zhukov actually drew upon 10,000 or even as many as 20,000 motor vehicles, if the combat units' own trucks are included. Although the Soviets have stated that 720 of the First Army Group's vehicles were engaged in transporting 18,000 reinforcements,[32] a number of Japanese sources go so far as to claim that many or most of the new Russian troops marched all the way from the Borzya railhead to the front and that the trucks were used to haul only the fuel, ammunition, and foodstuffs. In any event, IJA intelligence experts remain awed to this day by the amount of men and matériel moved so ruthlessly.[33]

The Soviet command devoted special attention to concealing the concentration and regrouping of reinforcements and existing troops and matériel on both sides of the Halha. Before 17 or 18 August, it was expressly forbidden to advance forces into the attack areas from which the encircling operations were to be staged. All deployments were limited to nighttime, when enemy observation was minimal. Only as the date for the offensive drew very near were local commanders acquainted with Zhukov's operational intentions—from four days to one day before the actual assault. The noncoms and troops learned of the offensive on the preceding night, and received their exact battle orders only three hours beforehand.

Reconnaissance was of the greatest importance to the Russians. Reflecting the impatience of operations officers with intelligence personnel, who often "misled the Command by tentative assumptions based on pure speculations," Zhukov castigated "doubtful intelligence" and wasted efforts. What was most necessary, he insisted, was information on the precise location and numerical strength of the Japanese. This was hard to get because there were no local inhabitants and no Japanese deserters, and because Manchukuoan defectors were ignorant. Combat reconnaissance produced the best intelligence, but this concerned only the main line of resistance and the nearest artillery and mortar sites. Infiltration of enemy lines by patrols was prevented by tight Japanese perimeter security. There had been considerable inexperience, at the outset, on the part of commanders, staff, and intelligence men. Commanders involved in on-the-spot scouting now donned enlisted men's uniforms and resorted to trucks. Thanks to some resourceful "reconnaissance stunts," useful information was acquired by scouts.[34]

Soviet reconnaissance planes provided photographic intelligence in greater depth. A special scout squadron was set up consisting of fighter aircraft under direct control of the Liaison Section chief and stationed near his command post. Nevertheless, great care and cross-checking had to be applied to the interpretation of aerial mosaics because of enemy camouflage and dummy installations.

Just as Ueda and his more astute colleagues had surmised, Zhukov focused attention on encircling the exposed Japanese flanks while pinning the enemy frontally. The wings seemed particularly vulnerable to attack by shock troops since they were screened by the least reliable elements—Manchukuoan cavalry. Although the Russians claimed an insignificant edge in troop strength along the entire battlefront of 74 kilometers, they sought to achieve decisive preponderance in the sectors of their main assault. The central effort was directed against the area south of the Holsten; the defenses were less substantial, for this was where the Japanese least expected the offensive. From the Russians' standpoint, the southern sector was excellent because they occupied advantageous positions from which a decisive strike could be launched northeastward, against the Japanese rear, by the shortest route.

On the basis of careful study, the Soviet command concluded that a weakness of the IJA defense system in addition to the flanks was the lack of mobile reserves. It was judged, in particular, that the Japanese would be unable to shift units rapidly from the rear or from secondary sectors, since they lacked good armored formations or well-trained motorized units. The terrain, however, was very difficult for offensive forces, and the Japanese were reportedly digging in well. IJA military sources are far less flattering to the status of the works; Hayashi estimates the program at only one-third completed. But the Russians say that the entire network constituted a solid defensive belt, well adapted to the terrain and constructed in accordance with a carefully devised fire plan. The lines were made up of supporting and resistance knots dug into the dunes and linked by passages. Shelters had been prepared for motor vehicles and horses. Trenches were deep, and the camouflaged bunkers could supposedly withstand the impact of 152-mm. shells. Anchor heights had been particularly fortified—for example, around Noro on the south and Fui on the north.

The key to Soviet victory was operational surprise—a major task in view of the size of the offensive and the considerable lead time. Apart from the measures of concealment and misinformation mentioned earlier, the Russians invoked a broad spectrum of "white magic." Thousands of leaflets titled "Reminders for the Soviet Soldier on the Defense" were printed, distributed, and "passed on" to the Japanese. To substantiate the impression that the central sector was being fortified, a radio station was operated only on that front. Broadcasts conveyed false information about defensive construction and requests for engineering equipment. Sound and noise were also employed in various ways to deceive the Japanese. Powerful transmitters were brought up to emit sound effects mimicking tanks, aircraft engines, and the hammering-in of beams. The Japanese, apparently fooled at the outset, would open fire in the direction of the noises. Later they became accustomed to the sounds or realized what they were and ignored them. This "was exactly what we wanted," Zhukov remarks, "because it was extremely important for us during the real regrouping and concentration of forces." The special sound equipment went into use 12-15 days prior to the planned movement of the strike units.

Additionally, the Russians used real noise generated by bombers, and by machine guns, artillery, mortars, and rifles firing on schedule, to drown out night movements and the rumble of armored concentrations. A particular effort was made to accustom the Japanese to the sound of armor. Ten or 12 days before the offensive, trucks were driven along the whole front with engines racing and mufflers off. Soviet planes went out on routinely scheduled flights, day and night, so that the Japanese would become used to systematic sorties and not associate them with specific offensive operations.

As late as 18 August, the Soviet command had deployed merely four infantry regiments and a machine-gun brigade in the bridgehead to the east of the Halha, with the two MPRA cavalry divisions on the flanks.[35] The rest of the attack force was held on the left shore and only began to cross on the night of 18/19 August, a day before jump-off. Final concentration took place in the early hours of the 20th. Men, vehicles, and matériel had to be concealed by dawn in specially prepared blinds along the shore, among the shrubbery and under improvised camouflage nets. The measures were so successful that the Japanese did not notice or interfere with the crossing of the river or the subsequent actions on the right bank. In fact, only the 6th Tank Brigade was delayed in traversing the Halha because rains and high water necessitated its diversion to the less suitable ford allocated to the 57th Rifle Division. The brigade's crossing and concentration were completed by the end of the first day of the offensive.

Of the many Japanese who were the targets of the elaborate Soviet deception measures in August, Nyūmura, commander of the IJA combat intelligence detachment, has particularly instructive recollections.[36] For a week until about 17 August, a single SB bomber would come in very low, night after night, regardless of weather. It would circle endlessly, make noise, and interfere with everybody's sleep, since the hours of darkness were short to begin with. Nyūmura suffered from acute insomnia. At the same time the bomber flew over, the IJA front-line units could hear the enemy hammering posts, all through the night, every night. The Japanese surmised that the Russians were building defensive positions and wintering facilities designed for protracted hostilities. This seemed all the more convincing when the limited Soviet attacks of 7-8 August were not followed by larger assaults, when the "danger period" of 14-15 August passed without incident, and when the nightly hammering sounds continued.

Komatsubara confirms the psychological effects caused by Soviet night "snoopers." At 2 A.M. on 19 August, three enemy bombers flew over, three times each, dropped illumination flares, and released bombs. Although no losses were incurred, an air raid in the middle of the night was disconcerting; and, Komatsubara added, the situation would only deteriorate once the Russians improved their equipment and "practiced more." The Soviet air force was certainly more imaginative than the Japanese, remarked the general. In addition to night bombings and ground support missions, the Russians sent three fighter planes over on 15 August to reconnoiter the entire Japanese front at high speed. Such speed militated against detailed reconnaissance but also defeated all efforts by ground troops to shoot down the aircraft. Certainly the Soviet planes were able to discern the layout of the Japanese positions, movements of reserves, and general deployment.[37]

Nyūmura heard no tank sounds before the offensive. To prevent such noise, the Russians removed the metal treads from the armored vehicles and ran them on their wheels. Moving only at night, the tanks were also "jammed" by the distracting special effects, as stated by Zhukov. The latter noted that tank units were moved to the jump-off locations in small groups from different angles, exploiting their speed, just before artillery preparation and air support began. As for the deceptive pamphlets distributed by the Russian command, Nyūmura did not see any of the "Reminders for the Soviet Soldier on the Defense," but he did peruse notebooks with misleading information planted on Russian soldiers who were subsequently killed or captured by the Japanese. Nyūmura notes that the Soviets did bring up poles and lumber for the construction of some defense works. He suggests that the Russians may have sought to fool their own men, too, about their alleged defensive intentions, the better to fool the enemy.

Immediately prior to the August offensive, says Nyūmura, Zhukov's First Army Group stopped wireless communication, except in unimportant cases, as mentioned earlier. This countermeasure effectively masked divisional movements. In the absence of prior aerial reconnaissance, deserters, or other warnings, Nyūmura's combat intelligence unit was "taken in completely" and had no idea that Soviet divisions were moving toward the Japanese flanks. Once the offensive had been launched and signal security did not matter to the Russians, Nyūmura's radio monitors picked up messages transmitted *en clair*, mainly at regimental or battalion level, or between infantry and artillery. The Japanese could even hear the Russians openly ordering attacks in various directions. But such intercepts had no tactical value to the Japanese in a fluid, fast-moving, and deteriorating combat situation, as the Russians well knew.

The various sectors of the Nomonhan battleground were by no means quiet on the verge of the Soviet offensive. As Shishkin says, the Russians sought to baffle the Japanese and win strategic and tactical surprise by launching a number of local assaults prior to the general attack.[38] On 16/17 August, for example, the Sakai regiment detected enemy patrols pressing near the IJA positions during the night, and Russian mortar fire rained down after dawn. The Japanese responded with field artillery, infantry mortars, and battalion guns. Such activities by the Russians caused the regimental chronicler to ask: "Are they intending to resume the offensive? Do they plan an attack against the other sectors—the 64th Regiment on the right or the Nagano detachment on the left? It seems that they are changing their entire policy, [although] their recent actions have been rather in response to our own and are not particularly aggressive."[39]

Artillery duels continued throughout the period of prelude, despite the chronic Japanese shortage of ammunition for the heavy guns and howitzers. Colonel Mishima, commanding the 1st Artillery Regiment, was wounded on 9 August and evacuated. The Russians had constructed sheltered gun sites for their 15-cm. howitzers, not on the heights but deep in the valley of the Halha opposite Colonel Hasebe's detachment south of the confluence.

IJA field guns and 10-cm. cannon lacked the angle to be effective, and the 12-cm. howitzers lacked the range, as usual. But General Hata ordered two major bombardments—on the 12th and 18th—especially in view of intelligence reaching him that the Russians were relatively quiescent for the moment only because they were engaged in replacing their heavy losses, building up their strength, and laying in ammunition stocks. On the 18th, the 1st Regiment's 1st Battalion expended the most shells since 27 July—94 by the 1st Battery and 148 by the 2nd Battery. But the results did not entirely please the corps commander, who ordered a hurried new effort. The weather was poor on the 19th, however, and from the 20th the "sudden change in the combat situation" rendered any further Japanese artillery offensive action academic.[40]

Interestingly, on the basis of increased hostile scouting activity and movements of armor and trucks, the 72nd Infantry speculated that the Russians were on the watch for an IJA general offensive following the Japanese heavy-artillery bombardment on the 18th. From this, noted the 72nd Regiment, "we concluded that enemy forces were stepping up preparations to go over to the offensive [themselves]." But although Hata said the weather prevented significant artillery action on 19 August, the 72nd Infantry notes that on that day Japanese 15-cm. howitzers fired on and smashed one of the confluence bridges. The span was under repair, probably because the water level of the Halha had risen as the result of the daily rains—a phenomenon alluded to by the Russians in explaining the difficulties encountered by the 6th Tank Brigade in traversing the Halha on the 20th.[41]

Graphic contemporary evidence that Japanese front-line troops sensed more about the imminent Soviet offensive than did higher headquarters emanates from a company commander in Lieutenant Colonel Ioki's reconnaissance regiment at the terribly exposed Fui Heights. According to Capt. Ishikawa Yasoji's notes, the enemy began crossing the Halha from around 17 August, battalion after battalion, with tanks and artillery. If only friendly planes would bomb them, mused Ishikawa, immense losses could be caused. By the 18th, the captain learned that the enemy on the Fui front numbered a rifle division, one tank brigade, two cavalry regiments, and a heavy artillery brigade. (These estimates are not far off from the actual Northern Force strength, it should be noted.) The 23rd Division was constantly apprised of the disparity in strength of the opposing forces on this sector. Meanwhile, the Ioki unit issued three days' supply of food and ammunition, and stood guard day and night.

At dawn on 19 August, Ishikawa observed Soviet troops in black greatcoats in extended formation across the front of the Japanese positions at Fui Heights. The infantry were followed by tanks and then mechanized artillery, kicking up dust. It was like a parade, thought Ishikawa, repeated in serried sequence. Obviously—despite all that has been mentioned previously about the Soviet obsession with secrecy and concealment until the eleventh hour—the Russians were not at all worried about what the garrison at Fui Heights saw on the 19th. The Soviet local offensive was being launched against the Manchukuoan cavalry screening force stationed at Honjinganga, about eight kilometers to the north. Fighting could be heard in that area from 5 P.M.; at night, the sounds of gunfire stopped. The Manchurian elements had been driven not only from Honjinganga but also from the gap between Ioki and the Yamagata regiment to his left, leaving the site at Fui Heights more isolated than ever—even before the start of the main Soviet offensive on the 20th.[42]

Of at least equal importance is the fact that Capt. Ōizumi Seishō (Norimasa), an air squadron commander from the 15th Air Group, actually uncovered the advanced Russian deployments on the afternoon of 19 August. One or two Japanese scout planes had been going out almost every day but had sighted nothing unusual. Then a sustained period of heavy rain (unmentioned as a boon in Soviet sources) had deluged the front from the night of 17 August until midday on the 19th. It was very dangerous for aircraft to take off or land on the unpaved airstrips on the plain under such conditions, and visibility aloft was poor in any case. Thus there was no Japanese aerial reconnaissance during one and a half vital days. When the skies cleared on 19 August, Ōizumi was anxious to observe the area himself.

Ōizumi flew west above the Holsten to the confluence and then turned southward along the Halha. In the sector around the distant Minami-watashi crossing, where there had not previously been anything worth scouting, the captain detected movement among dense river willows. Descending to 1,000 meters, he could make out moving vehicles. There were also tanks under the willows. No bridge had been thrown across the river, but pontoons were stored in the copse, parallel to the shoreline. Suspecting some deployment from the left bank, Ōizumi scrutinized the situation on the right. Enemy tanks and troops were indeed advancing a short distance from the river, not in column of march but already in dispersed combat formation, with one tank per rifle squad. This must be the spearhead of a serious offensive, the captain realized, and he sped back to base to convey his disconcerting findings. En route, he dropped a message tube to the front-line Japanese ground forces. After landing, Ōizumi hastened to division headquarters. The 15th Air Group commander immediately sent a squadron to reconnoiter the northern flank at Fui Heights. Soon afterward came the report that, as expected, Fui was being encircled too.[43]

Thus it was known by 19 August, at a number of levels of the Japanese front-line forces, that the Russians had pressed forward on both wings. The visual observations by the men at Fui Heights and by the reconnaissance pilots, in particular, suggest that the vaunted Soviet security measures were already compromised on the eve of the great offensive. Nevertheless, there is no evidence that the last-minute hard intelligence exerted any effect on the Japanese command's alertness or readiness.

While the Russians were keeping the Japanese off balance by a combination of lulling them, distracting them, and even defying them, the Kwantung Army and the 23rd Division remained ostensibly calm and the Sixth Army scurried around its new quarters well behind the front. At Sixth Army headquarters, a Kwantung Army intelligence officer was considering what the Russians would try next. Having done rather poorly with planes and flammable armor, would they now introduce gas? This officer remembers asking, at midday on 19 August, if the Sixth Army could cope with gas warfare. If not, specialists and equipment must be provided quickly.[44]

On the same day, line units issued warnings and instructions concerning possible enemy gas attack. The Russians were thought to possess gas shells containing phosgene, picrin (transient gas), and yperite (lingering mustard gas). Targets would be artillery sites and rear positions, struck suddenly. Units should train the men about detection, symptoms, and countermeasures, and should inspect the gas masks. Sand was a defense against lingering gas.[45] Undoubtedly, recent intelligence affected IJA thinking—namely, espionage information that more than 500 men belonging to the Russians' Far Eastern Chemical Warfare Battalion had debarked from a train at Borzya on 1 August and proceeded forward. The train had reportedly included four freight cars laden with asphyxiating gas, which had also been unloaded and sent ahead.[46]

Of course, careful preparation against likely contingencies is commendable, but in this case one wonders whether wishful thinking was not the main reason for Japanese higher headquarters' ignoring of statistically significant and very real indicators of danger close at hand. Some IJA veterans deplore the fact that phony signal intelligence commanded more attention than tactical encounters and deductions.[47]

By daybreak on 20 August, Zhukov had moved all of his main forces (except for the 6th Tank Brigade) across the river, deployed in three groupings.[48] (See Map 7.)

First, the very strong Southern Force under Zhukov's deputy, Colonel Potapov, consisted of about three mechanized brigades (the 8th Armored; the 6th Tank, less one battalion; the 11th Tank, less two battalions; and a company of OT-130 flamethrower tanks) plus the three regiments of one infantry division, the 57th Rifle. The 8th MPRA Cavalry Division screened the claimed border on the far right. In accordance with Zhukov's order dated 17 August, the Southern Force was to strike toward Nomonhan after

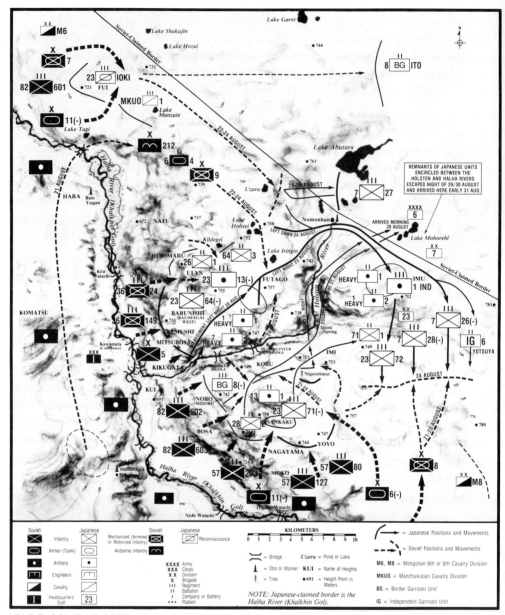

MAP 7: COMBAT OPERATIONS, 20-31 AUGUST 1939

destroying Japanese units north of the Holsten. Constituting the right wing of the First Army Group, Potapov's force faced north.

Second, the less powerful Northern Force, originally commanded by Colonel I. V. Shevnikov, was made up of the 7th Armored Brigade and two battalions of the 11th Tank Brigade, working with only one infantry regiment (the 601st) of the 82nd Rifle Division. Coverage on the outermost northern sector was to be provided by the 6th MPRA Cavalry Division. Shevnikov was supposed to roll up the Japanese north flank at Fui Heights, head southwest for the hills above Nomonhan, and join with the other forces to surround and destroy enemy units north of the Holsten. Operating on the Soviet left wing, the Northern Force began by facing east.

Third, on the broad center of the front, where Zhukov was located, KomBrig D. E. Petrov directly commanded the Central Force. Whereas the other strike forces encircled both flanks of the Japanese, this grouping was to engage the enemy's main strength by frontal attacks. Needing no organic armor, Petrov deployed about two infantry divisions (the 602nd and 603rd regiments of the 82nd Rifle, and the 149th and 24th regiments of the 36th Motorized Rifle), plus the 5th (Mixed) Machine Gun Brigade. The 82nd Division, facing northeast, would operate below the Holsten, its left flank anchored on the river, its right on the adjacent 57th Division of the Southern Force, with whom it was to cooperate in destroying the Japanese units in the south. To the north of the Holsten and facing east, the 36th Motorized Division and the 5th Machine Gun Brigade were deployed in the Remizov (Heights 733) sector of Balshagal two to three kilometers from the right shore of the Halha. This left portion of the Central Force had the mission of encircling and annihilating Japanese elements above the Holsten, in collaboration with the Northern Force and the 82nd Division to the right.

Southwest of his command post in the Hamardaba range, Zhukov controlled strong mobile reserves ready to move out to exploit successes achieved to south or north: the 9th Armored Brigade, the 4th Battalion of the 6th Tank Brigade, and the 212th Airborne Brigade, which operated as infantry.[49] That Zhukov's headquarters was located on the left side of the Halha, below the Holsten confluence and behind the 82nd Division, suggests the Soviet emphasis on the southern axis of attack.

The Russians devoted great care to the artillery aspect of the general offensive, in part to offset mistakes made the year before at Changkufeng. In addition to nearly 300 antitank and battalion guns, more than 200 field and heavy pieces were available to Zhukov.[50] An artillery group provided close support for each rifle division on the right shore of the Halha, above and below the Holsten. Thus, the Southern Force's 57th Division was assisted by its organic field artillery regiment and howitzer regiment and by an antitank battalion. In the Central Force, the two infantry regiments of the 82nd Division received close support from the divisional field artillery regiment and from a field artillery regiment of the 5th Machine Gun Brigade; and the 36th Division was assisted by two battalions from the 175th Artillery Regiment. The howitzer regiment of the 82nd Rifle Division and one antitank battalion were assigned to the Northern Force. Each infantry-support artillery headquarters was directed to designate those batteries that were to advance right behind the rifle units.

Deployed on the left shore of the Halha, a number of heavy artillery formations furnished long-range fire support. Missions given to these powerful 122-mm. and 152-mm. units included neutralization of Japanese artillery on both sides of the Holsten, pinning-down of reserves around Nomonhan and southeast of the Holsten, and interdiction of movement by reinforcements. To the Central Force were assigned two battalions from the 185th Artillery Regiment, one battalion from the 126th, and a battery from the 297th. The third battalion of the 185th Artillery provided long-range support for the Southern Force.

The artillery barrages opening the Soviet offensive were to last two hours and 45 minutes. During the final quarter-hour, all guns were to concentrate their fire against the forward edges of the enemy's defenses. Before the artillery softened up the foe, bomber aircraft were to launch concerted strikes against men and matériel. Prior to jump-off by the ground units, the air force would also raid artillery sites and troop concentrations and, by 9:30 A.M. on X-day, be ready to attack Japanese reserves and prevent their intervention. Fighter planes should escort the bombers, cover the ground units, conduct reconnaissance, and hit enemy reinforcements. According to Russian sources, the Soviet air force outnumbered the Japanese in 2 out of 3 categories: fighters, 376 (311?) to 252; light bombers, 181 to 144. In heavy bombers, the Russians say that they were outnumbered, 23 to 54.[51]

These were the main ground and air forces that the First Army Group had in hand by 20 August. "Zhukov could have had no illusions about [his] assignment," asserts Erickson. "Failure was out of the question. To win and win decisively, even spectacularly, would alone suffice."[52] Committed by "proletarian and internationalist duty," the Russians were finally ready to destroy the "aggressors" who had invaded what was claimed to be the territory of the Mongolian People's Republic.[53]

Notes

Notes

For full forms of all numbered citations, see the Bibliography (in vol. 2), pp. 1181-1238.

PREFACE

1. Claude A. Buss, *War and Diplomacy in Eastern Asia* (New York: Macmillan, 1941), pp. 483-84. For an early postwar reexamination, weak on the Japanese side, see Tinch [945].
2. James R. Young, "The Struggle Inside Japan," *Vital Speeches*, 1 Mar. 1941.
3. See Paul S. Dull and Michael T. Umemura, *The Tokyo Trials: A Functional Index to the Proceedings of the International Military Tribunal for the Far East* (Ann Arbor: University of Michigan Press, 1957), pp. 90-91.
4. Ben B. Blakeney, Chief Defense Counsel, IMTFE, Opening Statement (draft), 1947 (Blakeney Collection); also Blakeney and Furness interviews.
5. Also see Coox, *Anatomy* [679], pp. xx-xxi.
6. Coox, "Soviet Armor" [694]. For another early treatment of the Kwantung Army, see Coox, "Myth" [688]. Information on BBSS from Koiwai, Toga interviews.
7. My interview was with Kitano Kenzō at my home in Hikone in Shiga prefecture.
8. JRD [965], *JSM* 11, parts 1-3. Also see my comments in the Bibliography, section II.
9. See the Bibliography, section IIA.
10. See Miura Akira's translation (Tokyo: Kenkyūsha, 1957), p. 178.
11. The reference was to the 1st (Mori) Company of the 3rd (Masano) Brigade transport unit; *Tokyo Asahi*, 2 Aug. 1966.
12. *Tokyo Asahi*, 4 Apr. 1969. See the Bibliography, section II. Also Suzuki Yoshiyasu interview.
13. Sumi interview and correspondence, and publications [49] and [50], [541] through [543]. Also see Mita [406].
14. *Nomonhan* [40], vol. 1, p. 18; vol. 3, p. 81; vol. 4, p. 27; vol. 5, p. 35.
15. Tamada Yoshio, *Nomonhan no shinsō: sensha rentaichō no shuki* [The Truth About Nomonhan: Notes of a Tank Regiment Commander], ed. Kadokawa Kōtarō (Tokyo: Hara Shobō, 1981), p. 6.
16. Examples include *Shōwa shi no tennō* between 1972 and 1975 [535], Gomikawa, *Nomonhan*, in 1975 [212], and Onda in 1977 [473]. Among the most recent publications is K. Itō, *Shizukana*, in 1983 [308].
17. Reprints include Tsuji [585].
18. BBSS, *SS* [180], vol. 27.
19. C. Satō [43]; Niiya, Mitsui Shunji interviews; Tanibayashi Hiroshi correspondence. Also see *Mainichi Shinbun*, 12 Aug. 1981; and the Bibliography, section II. Notes from Major Kanaizuka's diary of 1939 [22] also appeared in *Goyū* magazine in 1979 [51].
20. Drea [715].
21. Ienaga Saburō, *Taiheiyō sensō* [The Pacific War] (Tokyo: Iwanami Shoten, 1968); trans. Frank Baldwin as *The Pacific War: World War II and the Japanese, 1931-1945* (New York: Pantheon Books, 1978).

CHAPTER 1

1. For the text of the Portsmouth Treaty, see Carnegie Endowment [663], pp. 70-75. For the supplementary Russo-Japanese and Sino-Japanese accords of 1905, see pp. 77, 80. C. W. Young devoted an entire book to the international legal status of the Kwantung Leased Territory: [1011], vol. 2. Also see *GSS* [203], vol. 11, p. 276; *Manshū mondai* [373], pp. 267-71; Kurihara, *Tai-Man-Mō* [355], pp. 9-10.

2. GSS [203], vol. 11, pp. 103-18; *Manshū kenkoku* [372], pp. 82-90; *Manshū mondai* [373], pp. 341-42; Matsumoto Toyozō [385], pp. 1-23, 70; Takemori [559], pp. 21-34; Shimada Toshihiko, *Kantōgun* [515], pp. 2, 5-6, 12-15, and "Shōwa" [517], pp. 18-19; K. Nakamura, *Manshū* [421], p. 65; Andō [155], pp. 30-38, 41-42, 77-91; Sumiya [544], p. 385; J. Young [1012], pp. 3-4.

3. GSS [203], vol. 7, pp. 104-5; League of Nations, *Manchuria* (hereafter cited as Lytton *Report*) [824], pp. 24-26; U.S. Dept. of Commerce [970], pp. 15-18.

4. Y. Matsuoka [860], pp. 70, 82, 185; GSS [203], vol. 11, pp. 104-5. The SMR's role is eulogized by Kinney [800].

5. SMR, *Fifth Report* [928], p. 152; BBSS, *SS* [179], vol. 8, pp. 91, 129-74; BBSS, *SS* [180], vol. 27, pp. 49-53, 57-60; *TSM* [549], vol. 4, p. 74; *Manshū mondai* [373], pp. 658-740; Shimada Toshihiko, *Kantōgun* [515], pp. 8, 16-17, 21; S. Hayashi, *Kōgun* [756], pp. 1-2, 192-93.

6. BBSS, *SS* [180], vol. 27, p. 13; *Manshū mondai* [373], pp. 282-83, 296-332; Shimada Toshihiko, *Kantōgun* [515], pp. 5-11, and *Manshū* [516], pp. 181-82; Kurihara, *Tai-Man-Mō* [355], pp. 38-39.

7. An excellent dissection of the tangle of railway rights will be found in C. W. Young [1011], vol. 3, pp. 74, 288-89, n. 37-38. Authentic Japanese military materials are provided in BBSS, *SS* [180], vol. 27. Also see Shimada Toshihiko, *Kantōgun* [515], pp. 2-7; *Manshūkoku gensei* [375], 1941, p. 230; Yoshihashi [1010], pp. 130-31; GSS [203], vol. 11, pp. 158, 289-90; Andō [155], pp. 15, 77-84; K. Nakamura, *Manshū* [421], pp. 64-65; *Manshū mondai* [373], pp. 284-96; Gaimushō [194], vol. 1, pp. 210-11.

8. BBSS, *SS* [180], vol. 27, pp. 13-15; C. W. Young [1011], vol. 3, pp. 287-88; Jones, *Manchuria* [784], pp. 14-15; *Manshūkoku gensei* [375], 1941, p. 231; JRD [961], *JM* 77, chart 1, p. 4; Andō [155], pp. 90-91; *Manshū mondai* [373], pp. 333-41; Shimada Toshihiko, *Kantōgun* [515], pp. 11-15, *Manshū* [516], pp. 184-86, and "Shōwa" [517], pp. 18-19; *TSM* [549], vol. 1, p. 190; Kurihara, *Tai-Man-Mō* [355], pp. 38-43, 240-84; BBSS, *SS* [180], vol. 27, p. 13.

9. Kurihara, *Tai-Man-Mō* [355], pp. 115-25, 146, 341-59; Shimada Toshihiko, *Kantōgun* [515], pp. 24-31; BBSS, *SS* [179], vol. 8, pp. 202-7.

10. Kurihara, *Tai-Man-Mō* [355], pp. 43-57, 239-74; Shimada Toshihiko, *Kantōgun* [515], pp. 12-14, 23-24, 34-36.

11. Shimada Toshihiko, *Manshū* [516], pp. 187-88, and *Kantōgun* [515], pp. 37-39; Kurihara, *Tai-Man-Mō* [355], p. 58; *Manshū mondai* [373], pp. 333-41.

12. C. W. Young [1011], vol. 3, pp. 190-91 (July 1931); BBSS, *SS* [180], vol. 27, pp. 13, 15; *Manshūkoku gensei* [375], 1941, p. 230; JRD [961], *JM* 77, p. 3; Shimada Toshihiko, *Kantōgun* [515], pp. 39-40, and *Manshū* [516], p. 189; Kurihara, *Tai-Man-Mō* [355], p. 59.

13. BBSS, *SS* [180], vol. 27, p. 14.

14. *TSM* [549], vol. 1, pp. 168-80 and chaps. 1-3; BBSS, *SS* [179], vol. 8, pp. 210-14, 224-34; Shimada Toshihiko, *Kantōgun* [515], pp. 36-37, and "Shōwa" [517], p. 20; Nomoto [454], pp. 27-33; Hora, *Dai-ichiji* [256], p. 258; A. Takeuchi [560], pp. 163-202; Katakura, "Ansatsu" [325], pp. 203-47; GSS [203], vol. 7, chap. 9; Matsushita, *Nihon gunji shi zatsuwa* [396], p. 89.

15. BBSS, *SS* [179], vol. 8, pp. 219-23; BBSS, *SS* [180], vol. 27, pp. 53-54; S. Hayashi, *Kōgun* [756], pp. 2-3; JRD [960], *JSM* 1, pp. 15-18.

16. BBSS, *SS* [179], vol. 8, pp. 244-59, 301-2; BBSS, *SS* [180], vol. 27, pp. 54-56, 63-66; JRD [960], *JSM* 1, pp. 24-28; Andō [155], pp. 128-32; Rekishigaku Kenkyūkai [482], vol. 1, pp. 70-72; *TSM* [549], vol. 4, p. 74; S. Hayashi, *Kōgun* [756], pp. 3, 193.

17. Shimada Toshihiko, *Kantōgun* [515], pp. 15-16.

18. *Ibid.*, pp. 27, 29-30.

19. Yamaguchi [613], pp. 26-27; *Manshū mondai* [373], pp. 752-75; Kurihara, *Tai-Man-Mō* [355], pp. 94, 103, 139-59; Shimada Toshihiko, *Kantōgun* [515], pp. 31-34.

20. Sagara [495], p. 97; Kurihara, *Tai-Man-Mō* [355], pp. 163-89; BBSS, *SS* [179], vol. 8, p. 262; Shimada Toshihiko, *Kantōgun* [515], p. 40.

21. Sagara [495], p. 97; Kurihara, *Tai-Man-Mō* [355], pp. 193-224; BBSS, *SS* [179], vol. 8, p. 263; Shimada Toshihiko, *Kantōgun* [515], pp. 40-43.

22. Matsui had been promoted major general in May 1925; since there was no IJA rank of brigadier general, a full colonel was promoted directly to major general.

23. BBSS, *SS* [179], vol. 8, pp. 262-64; Shimada Toshihiko, *Kantōgun* [515], pp. 43-46; Sagara [495], pp. 100-108.

24. BBSS, *SS* [179], vol. 8, pp. 274-86; *TSM* [549], vol. 1, pp. 305-9; Matsumoto Seichō [382], vol. 3, pp. 7-8; 70; Shinmyō, *Shōwa seiji* [524], pp. 32-68, and *Shōwa shi* [525], pp. 33-44; K. Nakamura, *Manshū* [421], pp. 57-63, 79-93; *Matsuoka* [392], pp. 292-98; Yamaguchi [613], pp. 39-42; Tsuda [584], p. 288; Rekishigaku Kenkyūkai [482], vol. 1, pp. 76-78; Shimada Toshihiko, *Manshū* [516], pp. 59-176; Hayashi Kyūjirō [239], pp. 9-18; Yamamoto [614], pp. 24-31; Takamiya, *Gunkoku* [533], pp. 36-43; Banba [177], pp. 185-94, 197, 201-2, 210-12; *Shō* [526], vol. 8, pp. 12-46; *Dokyumento Shōwa shi* [188], vol. 1, pp. 226-52, 254-56; *Nihon no rekishi* [438], vol. 24, pp. 148-56; *Shidehara* [511], pp. 354-58; *Minami* [401], pp. 149-64; Shigemitsu, *Gaikō* [512], pp. 57-71; Sagara [495], pp. 109-38.

25. Kōmoto [352], pp. 194-201; Andō [155], pp. 124-42; Takemori [559], pp. 63-81; Nagamatsu [419], pp. 34-41; Usui, "Chō" [603], pp. 26-33; Murobushi [417], pp. 101-6; Togawa, "Chō" [574], pp. 53-62; Shimamine [519], pp. 151-58; Shimada Toshihiko, *Kantōgun* [515], pp. 47-48; Liang [832], pp. 114-21; Yoshihashi [1010], pp. 41-51; *Shō* [526], pp. 58-65; N. Kojima, *Manshū teikoku* [350], vol. 1, p. 257.

26. Shinmyō, *Shōwa seiji* [524], p. 101; Ugaki, *Shōrai* [594], p. 317; Yoshihashi [1010], p. 50.

27. Sagara [495], chaps. 6, 7; Hayashi Kyūjirō, *Manshū* [239], pp. 18-27; Shimada Toshihiko, *Kantōgun* [515], pp. 48, 68, 70, 74; Shinmyō, *Shōwa seiji* [524], p. 44; *Shō* [526], pp. 65-66; Akisada [152], pp. 63-70. In his surprisingly terse account of the assassination, McCormack [863], p. 248, accepts Muraoka's complicity and Kōmoto's "improvement" of the plot.

28. Sasaki [499], pp. 192-93. Sasaki was writing in 1939.

29. Shinmyō, *Shōwa seiji* [524], pp. 62, 65-68; *TSM* [549], vol. 1, p. 309; A. Takeuchi [560], pp. 170-71; Sagara [495], p. 181.

CHAPTER 2

1. Imaoka, Banba interviews; Coox, *Tiger* [697], chap. 3; Banba [177], pp. 110-19; Katakura, *Senjin* [329], pp. 6-7; K. Nakamura, "Manshū" [422], part 1, p. 82; *Ichiokunin* [264], vol. 1, pp. 1, 18; Shidehara [510], pp. 166-68; *Nihon no rekishi* [438], vol. 23, pp. 81-109, 282-337, 448-50, vol. 24, pp. 295-98; M. Nakano [426], p. 34; Ōtani, *Rakujitsu* [476], p. 14; *Minami* [401], pp. 196-99.

2. Ugaki [593], vol. 2, pp. 803-4, 822; BBSS, *SS* [179], vol. 8, pp. 248-50, 265-68; Koiso [347], pp. 454-65, 493-500; *Minami* [401], pp. 182-89; Jōhō, ed., *Rikugunshō* [312], pp. 295-310; *Nihon no rekishi* [438], vol. 23, pp. 338-60, vol. 24, pp. 277-83; Tateno [573], vol. 1, pp. 25-32; Takamiya, *Gunkoku* [553], pp. 85-89; Ōtani, *Rakujitsu* [476], pp. 14-15. For official data on ordinary and extraordinary IJA and IJN expenditures, see *Japan-Manchoukuo Year Book, 1937* [781], pp. 115-16.

3. M. Maruyama [858], pp. 14, 39-40, 44-50, 53-54; *Nihon no rekishi* [438], vol. 24, pp. 163-238, 295, 297; Awaya [174], pp. 2-56; Rekishigaku Kenkyūkai [482], vol. 1, pp. 64-70, 93-99, 112-16; *Minami* [401], pp. 189-94; Yamamoto [614], pp. 19-23, 33-37; Yamamura [1009], pp. 182-211; Banba [177], pp. 126-27.

4. Ōtani, *Rakujitsu* [476], pp. 15-16, 41; *Nihon no rekishi* [438], vol. 23, p. 312. In 1921 the court-martial regulations were improved, in 1919 conscripts were authorized family leaves of as much as a fortnight, in 1920 warrant officers were made eligible for commissions, and in 1919 graduates of civilian universities in science or engineering, or of medical or agricultural colleges, could become commissioned officers. See *Japan-Manchoukuo Year Book, 1937* [781], pp. 115, 118.

5. Kawabe [332], pp. 119-21; Yamamoto [614], pp. 51-114; Yatsugi, *Seihen* [621], vol. 1, pp. 13-38; Mori [412], pp. 58-64; M. Nakano [426], pp. 15-16, 29-33, 45; Matsushita, *Nihon gunsei* [397], pp. 78-80; Banba [177], pp. 127-29; *Nihon no rekishi* [438], vol. 24, pp. 92, 295.

6. *Nihon no rekishi* [438], vol. 10; Coox, *Tiger* [697], p. 40; Ishida Ichirō, "Zen Buddhism and Muromachi Art," trans. Delmer M. Brown, *Journal of Asian Studies*, Aug. 1963, vol. 22,

no. 4, p. 427; Joseph M. Goedertier, *A Dictionary of Japanese History* (New York and Tokyo: Walker/Weatherhill, 1968), p. 55.

7. M. Maruyama [858], pp. 93n, 109-15; Tanaka Ryūkichi, *Nihon* [567], pp. 30-31; S. Hayashi, *Kōgun* [756], pp. 5-6; Kawabe [332], p. 121; Coox, *Tiger* [697], pp. 40-54; Imai, *Shōwa* [279], pp. 101-4; K. Nakamura, *Manshū* [421], pp. 8-9.

8. K. Satō, *Tōjō* [504], pp. 35-36, and *Daitōa* [502], pp. 36-37.

9. Nishiura, Imaoka interviews; N. Kojima, *Manshū teikoku* [350], vol. 1, pp. 21-24; Rekishigaku Kenkyūkai [482], vol. 1, pp. 118-21; *Matsuoka* [392], pp. 307-17; Tsuda [584], pp. 508-15.

10. *Matsuoka* [392], pp. 363-64; GSS [203], vol. 11, pp. 188-89; Rekishigaku Kenkyūkai [482], vol. 1, p. 119; SMR, *Fifth Report* [928], pp. 151-52.

11. Bix [644], pp. 427-43; Sada [494], pp. 157-94; GSS [203], vol. 7, pp. 119-21, 128-31, 140-42; Banba [177], pp. 200-206; NGS [431], vol. 18, pp. 21-35; Hayashi Kyūjirō [239], pp. 177-80; N. Kojima, *Manshū teikoku* [350], vol. 1, pp. 52-55; *Matsuoka* [392], pp. 155-59, 171-211, 254-76, 285-92; Andō [155], pp. 92-122, 161-72; K. Nakamura, *Manshū* [421], pp. 64-73; *Manshū kenkoku* [372], pp. 82-98. For a postwar exploration by American economists, see "Foreign Influence in Northeast China: A Case Study of the Liaotung Peninsula, 1906-42," by Ramon H. Myers and Thomas R. Ulie, *Journal of Asian Studies*, Feb. 1972, vol. 31, no. 2, pp. 329-50.

12. Penlington [891], pp. 8-10 (citing Baron Sakatani), 16-18.

13. K. K. Kawakami, "Manchuria Again," *The Nineteenth Century and After*, Nov. 1931, vol. 110, no. 657, p. 542. Also see Penlington [891], pp. 263-64.

14. Yoshizawa Kenkichi at Geneva (13 Oct. 1931), cited by Penlington [891], pp. 206-7.

15. Zumoto [1018], chap. 9; Honjō [255], pp. 150-51; Gaimushō [194], vol. 1, pp. 231-35; TSM [549], vol. 1, pp. 327-52; GSS [203], vol. 11, pp. 239-74; Yamaguchi [613], pp. 46-53; K. Nakamura, *Manshū* [421], pp. 110-11; N. Kojima, *Manshū teikoku* [350], vol. 1, pp. 24-27, 157-60, 176-77; Katakura, *Senjin* [329], pp. 2-6; *Matsuoka* [392], pp. 125-27, 245-48; Imamura, *Shiki* [282], vol. 1, p. 210; Shidehara [510], pp. 168-69; *Minami* [401], pp. 234-39; Takamiya, *Gunkoku* [553], pp. 104-6.

16. Katakura says the idea was his. (Interview.) Also see Katakura, *Senjin* [329], pp. 16-21; TSM [549], vol. 1, p. 358; BBSS, SS [179], vol. 8, p. 307; N. Kojima, *Manshū teikoku* [350], vol. 1, pp. 107-22, 174-77; K. Nakamura, *Shōwa* [423], pp. 147-48, citing Imai Takeo interview; *Nihon no rekishi* [438], vol. 24, pp. 326-28; Mori [412], pp. 80-82; Imai, *Shōwa* [279], pp. 25-26; Shimada Toshihiko, *Kantōgun* [515], pp. 96-98; Hayashi Kyūjirō [239], pp. 107-15; *Minami* [401], pp. 231-32; *Shō* [526], vol. 8, pp. 210-19.

17. T. Takeuchi [939], pp. 346-47; M. Nakano [426], pp. 103-5; Shōda [527], vol. 1, pp. 120-21; Mori [412], pp. 82-85; N. Kojima, *Manshū teikoku* [350], vol. 1, pp. 146, 150-51, 157, 169-75; Toynbee [948], 1931, p. 437.

18. In the Foreign Office archives in Tokyo (hereafter cited as Gaikō Shiryōkan, Manchurian Incident File), in 1979 I discovered a very detailed compendium describing the anti-Japanese movement: "Summary of Political and Economic Relations Between Japan and China" (Osaka: Chamber of Commerce and Industry, 1931). "The anti-Japanese movement," asserts this summary, "is purposely conducted by the Kuomintang . . . and is not a boycott, but may be called a war without resorting [to] arms against Japan." Also see TSM [549], vol. 1, pp. 353-58, 422; K. Nakamura, *Manshū* [421], pp. 32-34; T. Itō et al. [310], p. 177; N. Kojima, *Manshū teikoku* [350], vol. 1, pp. 87-96, 107-22; *Manshū kenkoku* [372], pp. 240-42; Yamaguchi [613], pp. 120-21; *Manshū jihen* [367], pp. 56-68; Shimada Toshihiko, *Kantōgun* [515], pp. 82-83, 93, and *Manshū* [516], pp. 240-41; NGS [431], vol. 18, pp. 80-82; Penlington [891], pp. 137-52; Egler [717], pp. 3-4.

19. S. Hayashi, *Kōgun* [756], p. 3; Yamaguchi [613], pp. 68-70, 120; GSS [203], vol. 7, pp. 139-44, 169-79, *ibid.*, vol. 11, pp. 284-85; TSM [549], vol. 1, pp. 359-61; Takemori [559], p. 86; N. Kojima, *Manshū teikoku* [350], vol. 1, pp. 30-38, 58, 71-72, 87-90; Aoe [157], pp. 137-39; M. Nakano [426], p. 106.

20. Giga, Imaoka, Katakura interviews; Yamaguchi [613], pp. 80-82.

21. S. Hayashi, *Kōgun* [756], p. 3; N. Satō, *Kaiko* [506], p. 242; N. Kojima, *Manshū teikoku* [350], vol. 1, pp. 39-40; Shimada Toshihiko, *Kantōgun* [515], p. 89; *Shō* [526], vol. 8, pp. 128-38; Tang [940], pp. 210, 218-34.

22. A. Takeuchi [560], pp. 191-92; Shimada Toshihiko, *Manshū* [516], pp. 261-62; Hsu [768], pp. 640-43.

23. Yamamoto [614], pp. 37-48; Shigemitsu, *Gaikō* [512], pp. 82-84, 91-92; K. Nakamura, *Manshū* [421], pp. 50-53, 74-79; Banba [177], pp. 194-96, 207-9, 210-11, 218-19, 223-25; *Shō* [526], vol. 8, pp. 76-96; *Nihon no rekishi* [438], vol. 24, pp. 137-38, 142-48; Shimada Toshihiko, *Manshū* [516], pp. 24-58. Less than a month before the outbreak of the Manchurian Incident, the Japanese government announced on 21 August that the Emperor had donated ¥100,000 for Yangtze flood victims' relief. A large Japanese national relief fund was planned, with the blessing of the ministers of finance and foreign affairs, as well as of leading Japanese businessmen. Toynbee [948], *1931*, pp. 397-98.

24. According to Japanese sources, Chinese collaborationists included important men in Manchuria such as Chao Chi-po, Yu Chung-han, Cheng Haibo-hsu, Chang Hai-ping, and Yin Ju-king.

25. *Ishiwara* [303], vol. 1, pp. 40-45, 52-57, 70-73; Ogata Sadako [886], p. 41; Yokoyama [623], p. 152; *TSM* [549], vol. 1, pp. 362-63; Narusawa [428], p. 35; K. Nakamura, *Manshū* [421], p. 100; Takemori [559], pp. 86-99; Sagara [495], p. 277; Imai, *Shōwa* [279], p. 27; Banba [177], pp. 228-29; Awaya [174], p. 75; Shimada Toshihiko, *Kantōgun* [515], p. 75, and *Manshū* [516], p. 232.

26. *TSM* [549], vol. 1, p. 425; Yokoyama [623], p. 152; N. Kojima, *Manshū teikoku* [350], vol. 1, pp. 67-71, 93-94, 123-24, 134, 152-53; Tateno [573], vol. 1, p. 87; A. Takeuchi [560], pp. 190-91; K. Nakamura, *Manshū* [421], pp. 100-101, 120-21; Shimada Toshihiko, *Manshū* [516], pp. 238-40; Katakura interview. For Kwantung Army staff roster, see GSS [203], vol. 11, pp. 291-92.

27. GSS [203], vol. 7, p. 457, vol. 11, p. 184; M. Nakano [426], pp. 101-2; N. Kojima, *Manshū teikoku* [350], vol. 1, pp. 92-96, 153-54; Tateno [573], vol. 1, p. 88; Awaya [174], pp. 76-77.

28. K. Nakamura, *Manshū* [421], pp. 31, 32, 100, 103; Awaya [174], p. 76; BBSS, SS [179], vol. 8, pp. 306-8; *TSM* [549], vol. 1, pp. 352-58; Tsuda [584], pp. 425-31; N. Kojima, *Manshū teikoku* [350], vol. 1, pp. 79-82.

29. I. Hata, *Gun* [230], pp. 18-40; Katakura, "Ansatsu" [325], pp. 208-12; *TSM* [549], vol. 1, pp. 379-81; K. Nakamura, *Manshū* [421], pp. 12-15; Aoki [158], vol. 1, pp. 105-41; Koiso [347], pp. 489-522; M. Nakano [426], pp. 24-34, 47-80; Tateno [573], vol. 1, pp. 79-84; Mori [412], pp. 115-17; Sagara [495], pp. 263-76.

30. M. Nakano [426], pp. 107-10; Hanaya [218], p. 43.

31. N. Kojima, *Manshū teikoku* [350], vol. 1, p. 124; Takamiya, *Gunkoku* [553], p. 96; Minami [401], pp. 214-16; Miyamura [408], pp. 162, 189; GSS [203], vol. 7, p. 464, citing Kanda Masatane.

32. Lytton, "Diary" [844], 23 Apr. 1932. Also see Hanaya [218], p. 44: *TSM* [549], vol. 1, p. 428; *Minami* [401], p. 216; Takamiya, *Gunkoku* [553], p. 96; Awaya [174], p. 78. Also Katakura interview.

33. Katakura, interview and *Senjin* [329], pp. 23-24; *TSM* [549], vol. 1, pp. 428-29; K. Nakamura, *Manshū* [421], pp. 34-36; N. Kojima, *Manshū teikoku* [350], vol. 1, pp. 124-27, 179-80.

34. Katakura interview. For Honjō's specific instructions to IGU commanders, 13 Sept. 1931, see GSS [203], vol. 11, pp. 296-97; Honjō [255], Appendix, pp. 348-49. On 15 September, Ishiwara told the Lytton Commission, Honjō inspected exercises by the 29th Regiment designed to "determine in case of emergency what should take place in [an] open mart in Mukden." In his critique, the general stressed that it was necessary to employ the forces to best advantage to attack the walled city as well as the North Barracks in order to "dispose of both Chinese groups." 26 Apr. 1932, Mukden; Gaikō Shiryōkan, Manchurian Incident File, IV/27. For Honjō's directions to 2nd Division commander Tamon on 18 September, see Honjō [255],

Appendix, pp. 349-51. One significant point of recommended improvement was street fighting. Also see *GSS* [203], vol. 11, pp. 297, 305; N. Kojima, *Manshū teikoku* [350], vol. 1, p. 179; Shimada Toshihiko, *Kantōgun* [515], p. 102, and *Manshū* [516], p. 253.

35. Katakura interview; Imai, *Shōwa* [279], p. 30; K. Nakamura, *Manshū* [421], p. 100; Sagara [495], p. 279; BBSS, *SS* [179], vol. 8, p. 307.

36. Katakura interview; K. Nakamura, *Manshū* [421], p. 101; Imai, *Shōwa* [279], p. 35. Ishiwara was reportedly of the opinion that Dohihara would leak information to the Chinese. N. Kojima, *Manshū teikoku* [350], vol. 1, pp. 153, 256. For some of Dohihara's more sensational press conferences, see T. Takeuchi [939]. pp. 348-49.

37. Katakura interview; K. Nakamura, *Manshū* [421], pp. 100-103; Awaya [174], p. 79. Also see Koiso [347], pp. 531-32; Hanaya [218], p. 43; N. Kojima, *Manshū teikoku* [350], vol. 1, pp. 152-54; K. Nakamura, "Manshū" [422], part 1, p. 86; *TSM* [549], vol. 1, p. 425.

38. *GSS* [203], vol. 11, pp. 289-95, 903-4; BBSS, *SS* [180], vol. 27, pp. 14-15; BBSS, *SS* [181], vol. 53, pp. 6-7; N. Kojima, *Manshū teikoku* [350], vol. 1, pp. 102-6; 156; K. Nakamura, *Manshū* [421], pp. 121-22; Imai, *Shōwa* [279], p. 30; Aoki [158], vol. 1, p. 168; M. Nakano [426], p. 121; Yamaguchi [613], p. 79; Shimada Toshihiko, *Kantōgun* [515], pp. 100-101, and *Manshū* [516], pp. 260, 262-63; Awaya [174], p. 80; GSDF/CGSC [489], pp. 5-7; Koiso [347], pp. 526-30; *Itagaki* [252], p. 32; Katakura interview. Chinese sources estimate Kwantung Army strength at higher levels than stated in my text; they do not seem to understand the difference between peacetime and wartime IJA authorizations for tables of organization and equipment. See Liang [832], p. 18.

39. Zumoto [1018], pp. 16-17; BBSS, *SS* [180], vol. 27, p. 108; BBSS, *SS* [181], vol. 53, pp. 4-5; *GSS* [203], vol. 11, p. 280; JRD [955], *JSM* 2, p. 69; GSDF/CGSC [489], pp. 8, 78; Liang [832], pp. 18-19; Yamaguchi [613], pp. 78-79. The Chinese aerial inventory at Mukden included new French Potez and Caudron bombers, Dewoitine fighters, and Puss Moth liaison planes as well as Japanese Type 88 scouts. When the Kwantung Army seized the Chinese installation, it reported capturing several dozen aircraft; BBSS, *SS* [183], vol. 87, p. 87.

40. *GSS* [203], vol. 11, p. 290; N. Kojima, *Manshū teikoku* [350], vol. 1, pp. 67-71, 109-10, 156, 178; Katakura interview.

41. Ishiwara's testimony before Lytton Commission (26 Apr. 1932, Mukden), Gaikō Shiryōkan, Manchurian Incident File, IV/27; Takemori [559], pp. 89-90; Shimada Toshihiko, *Kantōgun* [515], pp. 81-82; K. Nakamura, *Manshū* [421], p. 102; *Manshū jihen to Mantetsu* [370], pp. 2-3, 12-19; Katakura interview.

42. Katakura interview; *GSS* [203], vol. 11, pp. 291-95; *TSM* [549], vol. 1, p. 424; Takemori [559], pp. 90-91; N. Kojima, *Manshū teikoku* [350], vol. 1, pp. 102-7; Yoshihashi [1010], pp. 133-34. Despite the supposed secrecy surrounding the IJA howitzer episode, Ishiwara was entirely frank in discussing it with the Lytton Commission (30 Apr. 1932, Mukden), Gaikō Shiryōkan, Manchurian Incident File, IV/41.

43. Hanaya [218], p. 43; Imai, *Shōwa* [279], p. 34; M. Nakano [426], p. 108; Yokoyama [623], p. 152; *GSS* [203], vol. 7, p. 457, citing Kanda Masatane; N. Kojima, *Manshū teikoku* [350], vol. 1, pp. 96, 154; K. Nakamura, *Manshū* [421], pp. 101-2; Katakura interview.

44. *TSM* [549], vol. 1, p. 419; Minami [401], pp. 216-24; T. Takeuchi [939], pp. 344-46; Honjō [255], Appendix, pp. 338-40, 347; Ogata Sadako [886], pp. 56-57; Hayashi Kyūjirō [239], pp. 104-5; K. Nakamura, *Manshū* [421], pp. 104-6; M. Nakano [426], pp. 88-89, 119-20; N. Kojima, *Manshū teikoku* [350], vol. 1, pp. 182-83; Tateno [573], vol. 1, pp. 90-91; Awaya [174], pp. 81, 91-92; *GSS* [203], vol. 7, pp. 149-50; Takamiya, *Gunkoku* [553], pp. 97-104; Shimada Toshihiko, *Kantōgun* [515], pp. 94-95; *Shidehara* [511], pp. 366-69, 371-75; NGS [431], pp. 75-79.

45. Kurihara, *Tennō* [356], p. 58, says the Kwantung Army was pinpointed. The army as a whole is mentioned by Baron Harada Kumao [225], vol. 2, pp. 52-53. Also see *TSM* [549], vol. 1, pp. 416-17; NGS [431], pp. 84-85.

46. Katakura interview; *TSM* [549], vol. 1, p. 434; Minami [401], pp. 255-57; M. Nakano [426], p. 120; N. Kojima, *Manshū teikoku* [350], vol. 1, pp. 183-86; K. Nakamura, *Manshū* [421], p. 105; Imamura, *Kaisōroku* [280], vol. 2, p. 197. For reevaluations of Tatekawa's role, see I. Hata, "Jinbutsu" [231], pp. 234-49; and F. Tsunoda [587], p. 146.

47. Shigemitsu, *Gaikō* [512], pp. 104-5; M. Nakano [426], p. 121; Katakura interview.

48. Yokoyama [623], p. 153; Katakura interview. Tatekawa's implication in the early part of the plot is detailed in M. Nakano [426], pp. 119-20, 124-25, recounting Tatekawa's loan to Hashimoto of the private code in use between him and Itagaki. Tatekawa's first calligraphy on the night of 18 September spoke of one heavy-artillery shell's opening up of Manchuria and Mongolia. His cover-up claimed that he had been awakened from his dreams by the gunfire, a fact which supposedly caused him shame for his lack of foresight. See F. Tsunoda [587], pp. 145-46; *GSS* [203], vol. 7, p. 184, citing Katakura diary; *TSM* [549], vol. 1, pp. 418-19; N. Kojima, *Manshū teikoku* [350], vol. 1, pp. 188-98, 204, 206-7.

49. M. Nakano [426], pp. 121-25, 134-38, 143-45, 151-86; Tateno [573], vol. 1, p. 103; K. Nakamura, *Manshū* [421], pp. 15-17; N. Kojima, *Manshū teikoku* [350], vol. 2, pp. 16-19; Imamura, *Kaisōroku* [280], vol. 2, pp. 203-19.

CHAPTER 3

1. Lytton *Report* [824], pp. 69-70, quoting testimony of Gen. Wang I-cheh; Rappaport [900], citing George H. Blakeslee to Stanley K. Hornbeck, 14 Sept. 1932. That the Chinese would not resist was supposedly known to the Kwantung Army through broken codes; Liang [832], p. 18. I am indebted to my colleague, Prof. Paochin Chu, for screening Chinese-language materials such as the Kuomintang Central Committee's historical documents and Wellington Koo's memorandum to the League of Nations. Also see *Shō* [526], vol. 9, pp. 13-20; N. Kojima, *Manshū teikoku* [350], vol. 1, pp. 166-68, 222-24, 228-30, 234-37, 240-41; Aoki [158], vol. 1, pp. 145-47; Mori [412], p. 89.

2. Awaya [174], p. 83, citing Hanaya Tadashi; Shimada Toshihiko, *Kantōgun* [515], pp. 104-5; Aoki [158], vol. 1, pp. 147-48; Mori [412], pp. 86-88; Imai, *Shōwa* [279], p. 32; N. Kojima, *Manshū teikoku* [350], vol. 1, pp. 204, 206, 208, 211; Storry, "Mukden" [937], p. 5.

3. Penlington [891], pp. 5-6; Zumoto [1018], pp. 15-16; Lytton *Report* [824], pp. 67-68, citing testimony by General Honjō, Colonel Hirata, Lieutenant Colonel Shimamoto, etc.; *Itagaki* [252], pp. 36, 38; Awaya [174], pp. 83-84, citing Hanaya; Aoki [158], vol. 1, pp. 148-50, 169; Mori [412], pp. 88-89; N. Kojima, *Manshū teikoku* [350], vol. 1, pp. 242-43; *Shō* [526], vol. 9, p. 38.

4. Kawakami, *Manchoukuo* [790], pp. 59-60.

5. Mori [412], pp. 86-88, citing Colonel Shimamoto; Kawakami, *Japan* [789], p. 37.

6. *Dokyumento Shōwa shi* [188], vol. 1, p. 79; M. Nakano [426], p. 124; Shimada Toshihiko, *Kantōgun* [515], p. 105. According to a colorful account by consul Morishima Morito, Imada went out personally on a handcar with a railwayman and forced him to set off the charge; Takemori [559], pp. 98-102. For a summary of testimony regarding IJA instigation of the railway incident, see Liang [832], pp. 12-15. Despite the postwar revelations, many questions remain unanswered concerning the events on the night of 18 September. Even staff officer Katakura, for example, wonders if a (second?) explosive charge had had to be set off on the SMR track *after* the Mukden-bound express train passed the site. (Interview.) I share the original skepticism of Lord Lytton and his colleagues, who would say no more than that "an explosion undoubtedly occurred *on or near* the railroad." Lytton *Report* [824], p. 71 (italics added). See note 11 below.

7. Tateno [573], vol. 1, p. 99. Liang [832], pp. 12-13, seeks to prove that the Japanese fired first.

8. Katakura interview.

9. Zumoto [1018], photo 1.

10. Katakura does not remember discussing the matter with Lieutenant Kawamoto, but he did hear confidentially about the indicated possibilities; Katakura interview. Also see Mori [412], p. 17.

11. Hayashi Kyūjirō [239], pp. 118-19. Hayashi immediately notified Shidehara of his information and his powerful suspicions of Kwantung Army complicity; Gaimushō [196], vol. 2, pp. 180-81. For a reexamination of the problem of the Tokyo level of response, see Conroy and Takemoto [678], pp. 42-46.

12. Katakura interview; *GSS* [203], vol. 11, pp. 297, 305, 307-8; N. Kojima, *Manshū teikoku* [350], vol. 1, pp. 238-41, 256; GSDF/CGSC [489], pp. 13-14; Aoki [158], vol. 1, p. 169.

13. AGS deputy chief Ninomiya received first word from Colonel Dohihara at 1:07 A.M. on the 19th. Honjō's report arrived afterward. BBSS, *SS* [179], vol. 8, p. 312. Also see Yokoyama [623], pp. 153-56; Honjō [255], pp. 22-23; *GSS* [203], vol. 11, pp. 306-7; *Itagaki* [252], pp. 33-34; Aoki [158], vol. 1, pp. 151-52; Miyamura [408], p. 176.

14. BBSS, *SS* [179], vol. 8, pp. 217, 319; Yokoyama [623], p. 158; *GSS* [203], vol. 11, p. 307; *Itagaki* [252], pp. 34-36, 41; Miyamura [408], p. 180.

15. Katakura interview; Yokoyama [623], pp. 150-51, 156-62; N. Kojima, *Manshū teikoku* [350], vol. 1, pp. 252-58; GSDF/CGSC [489], p. 11.

16. Katakura interview; Yokoyama [623], pp. 163-67; *GSS* [203], vol. 7, pp. 187-89, vol. 11, pp. 314-16, 527-28; Honjō [255], p. 23; Zumoto [1018], pp. 28-29; *Itagaki* [252], p. 49; N. Kojima, *Manshū teikoku* [350], vol. 1, p. 259.

17. Katakura interview; Yokoyama [623], pp. 167-69; *TSM* [549], vol. 2, pp. 39-49; *GSS* [203], vol. 7, pp. 189-91, ibid., vol. 11, pp. 318-23; *Itagaki* [252], pp. 48-50; N. Kojima, *Manshū teikoku* [350], vol. 1, pp. 265-68; Yamaguchi [613], pp. 91-92.

18. Katakura interview; *GSS* [203], vol. 11, pp. 318-23; *Itagaki* [252], p. 50; N. Kojima, *Manshū teikoku* [350], vol. 1, pp. 259-60; Honjō [255], Appendix, pp. 356-57.

19. *GSS* [203], vol. 7, pp. 192-93; Katakura interview; Penlington [891], pp. 44, 251, 257.

20. Katakura interview; Yokoyama [623], p. 221; N. Kojima, *Manshū teikoku* [350], vol. 1, pp. 272-73; Miyamura [408], pp. 182-88.

21. Zumoto [1018], p. 22; *Kindai no sensō* [336], vol. 4, pp. 265-66; *TSM* [549], vol. 2, pp. 6-7; N. Kojima, *Manshū teikoku* [350], vol. 1, pp. 245-46, 252, 271-73. General Hayashi's message about air reinforcements reached Tokyo at about 8 A.M.; BBSS, *SS* [179], vol. 8, p. 313; *GSS* [203], vol. 11, pp. 308-12. Katakura knew about the first arrival of reconnaissance planes. (Interview.) Also see BBSS, *SS* [183], vol. 87, p. 87.

22. Kamura's report that his brigade was starting to advance at 1 P.M. reached the AGS chief at 2:40 P.M. General Hayashi's message followed. See BBSS, *SS* [179], vol. 8, p. 315; *GSS* [203], vol. 11, pp. 317-19; Imamura, *Shiki* [282], vol. 1, pp. 190-92; Honjō [255], p. 23; N. Kojima, *Manshū teikoku* [350], vol. 1, pp. 246, 270, 274-76; *TSM* [549], vol. 2, pp. 9-10, 17; Miyamura [408], pp. 212-13. Zumoto [1018], p. 22, gives the same timing as noted in our text for Kamura's crossing into Manchuria (1:20 P.M.), but attributes the movement to the initiative of the commander of the forces at Sinuiju because of the "pressing situation." Col. Furujō Tanehide said the action was taken at the discretion of the Korea Army chief of staff; Penlington [891], p. 155.

23. *TSM* [549], vol. 2, pp. 6-24; *GSS* [203], vol. 7, pp. 428-35; *Minami* [401], pp. 257-63; *Kindai no sensō* [336], vol. 4, pp. 266-76; *Dokyumento Shōwa shi* [188], vol. 1, pp. 95-96; N. Kojima, *Manshū teikoku* [350], vol. 1, pp. 247-51, 276-83; Aoki [158], vol. 1, pp. 155-58; Koiso [347], pp. 533-37; BBSS, *SS* [179], vol. 8, p. 316; Conroy and Takemoto [678], pp. 43-44.

24. Japanese terminology is from my Katakura interview. One of General Hayashi's staff officers, Lt. Col. Kanda Masatane, played a key role in the whole affair, having been softened up beforehand in Tokyo by Hashimoto Kingorō and his Cherry Society colleagues. Maj. Gen. Kodama Tomoo, the Korea Army chief of staff, displeased the conspirators by his caution and resistance. See M. Nakano [426], pp. 90-91, 132; *GSS* [203], vol. 7, pp. 458, 464 (citing Kanda), 184 (citing Katakura); Miyamura [408], p. 188, citing Kanda; Yoshihashi [1010], p. 178, n. 16, citing Matsumura Shūitsu; *Kindai no sensō* [336], vol. 4, p. 273; *TSM* [549], vol. 2, p. 24; *Shō* [526], vol. 9, p. 46; Toyoshima [582], pp. 52-58; Yamaguchi [613], pp. 92-93.

CHAPTER 4

1. Hsu [768], pp. 646-47. On the Kuomintang's policy of nonresistance, see W. Willoughby, *Sino-Japanese* [1004], citing Sao-ke Alfred Sze.

2. A particularly detailed account will be found in GSDF/CGSC [489], pp. 18-50. Also see BBSS, *SS* [179], vol. 8, pp. 324-25; BBSS, *SS* [181], vol. 53, pp. 22-27; *TSM* [549], vol. 2, pp. 49-64, 85-89; Honjō [255], Appendix, pp. 391-98; *GSS* [203], vol. 7, pp. 193, 205,

211-12, 244-46, *ibid.*, vol. 11, pp. 345-50, 362-64, 367-83, 389-94; Gaimushō [194], vol. 1, pp. 77, 94, 98-99, 244-45, 252-55; N. Kojima, *Manshū teikoku* [350], vol. 2, pp. 14-15; *NGS* [431], vol. 18, pp. 172, 191-98, 230-56; Aoki [158], vol. 1, p. 178; Yokoyama [623], pp. 170-76; *Minami* [401], pp. 301-2; Penlington [891], pp. 45, 47-48, 50-53; Zumoto [1018], pp. 33-43.

3. BBSS, *SS* [179], vol. 8, p. 320; *TSM* [549], vol. 2, pp. 62-63.

4. Katakura, interview and *Senjin* [329], p. 78; *GSS* [203], vol. 7, pp. 246-47, 257, citing Katakura; Yokoyama [623], pp. 176-77; Yamaguchi [613], p. 177.

5. Kawabe [332], pp. 75-76.

6. GSDF/CGSC [489], pp. 52-193; *GSS* [203], vol. 7, pp. 258-76, *ibid.*, vol. 11, pp. 377-400, 651-61; BBSS, *SS* [179], vol. 8, pp. 319-21; BBSS, *SS* [181], vol. 53, pp. 33-38; *TSM* [549], vol. 2, pp. 65-84; Zumoto [1018], pp. 48-62; Honjō [255], Appendix, p. 387; N. Kojima, *Manshū teikoku* [350], vol. 2, pp. 65-80; *Minami* [401], pp. 300-301; *Matsuoka* [392], pp. 391-92.

7. Toynbee [948], *1931*, p. 453. The Chinese government reminded the League of Nations on 6 December that it did not recognize the Japanese claim of rights to station troops in the "so-called railway zone"; Penlington [891], p. 237. Statements issued in Honjō's name had already caused misapprehension abroad; see note 29 below. Honjō's own discomfiture is even suggested in public documentation. On 13 November the AGS chief was reported to have received an urgent wire from Honjō "requesting that he be given power to act on his own initiative under certain circumstances"; Penlington [891], p. 53, citing Nippon Denpō telegram. After consulting with Honjō, a High Command representative—Lt. Gen. Tsukushi Kumashichi—had recommended strong support for the Kwantung Army in his report to the AGS on 12 November; *GSS* [203], vol. 11, pp. 386-87.

8. Pu Yi [899], vol. 1, p. 229, called the Tientsin riots a "Dohihara masterpiece." Also see *GSS* [203], vol. 11, pp. 384, 417, *ibid.*, vol. 7, pp. 258-62, citing Katakura; *TSM* [549], vol. 2, pp. 89-96; K. Nakamura, *Manshū* [421], p. 159; N. Kojima, *Manshū teikoku* [350], vol. 2, pp. 43-45; BBSS, *SS* [179], vol. 8, pp. 323-24; Honjō [255], Appendix, p. 380; Gaimushō [194], vol. 1, pp. 687-88; *Minami* [401], p. 302; Aoki [158], vol. 1, pp. 218-21; Shimada Toshihiko, *Kantōgun* [515], pp. 113-14; Zumoto [1018], pp. 65-68; Penlington [891], pp. 127-36, 160-62.

9. Katakura, *Senjin* [329], p. 94, *GSS* [203], vol. 7, pp. 271, 273-75, 282, citing Katakura, *ibid.*, vol. 11, pp. 410, 646-68, 690-714; Yokoyama [623], pp. 183-86; K. Nakamura, *Manshū* [421], p. 173; *TSM* [549], vol. 1, pp. 65-84; N. Kojima, *Manshū teikoku* [350], vol. 2, pp. 60-66, 80-83; *Itagaki* [252], pp. 61-62; Gaimushō [194], vol. 1, pp. 616-22. Zumoto refers to Ma's "dilly-dallying with the Japanese army on the spot"; [1018], p. 51. Ma struck Akimoto as "more like a rikishaman . . . cunning, sickly, vapid" than as "the Napoleon of North Manchuria"; [632], pp. 302-8.

10. Lytton *Report* [824], p. 3.

11. *TSM* [549], vol. 2, pp. 102-3; *Shidehara* [511], pp. 491-92; BBSS, *SS* [179], vol. 8, p. 324; *Minami* [401], pp. 308-20; Yokoyama [623], pp. 202-3; Imamura, *Kaisōroku* [280], vol. 2, p. 53; Wakatsuki [606], pp. 383-87; *NGS* [431], vol. 18, p. 304; Rekishigaku Kenkyūkai [482], vol. 1, pp. 139-40; Togawa, *Shōwa* [576], pp. 102-3.

12. *GSS* [203], vol. 11, pp. 408-9, 443, 454-56, 461; Imamura, *Shiki* [282], vol. 1, pp. 201-5; Yamaguchi [613], pp. 173-74; Zumoto [1018], p. 319, citing Araki. Zumoto sees a "coincidental" connection between Ma's belligerence at Tsitsihar and the decision by Tokyo to send the first of the reinforcing brigades to Manchuria (11 November); [1018], p. 57.

13. *GSS* [203], vol. 7, pp. 278-81, citing Katakura; BBSS, *SS* [179], vol. 8, pp. 323-24; Aoki [158], vol. 1, p. 221; *Minami* [401], pp. 302-3; Imamura, *Kaisōroku* [280], vol. 2, pp. 250-51; Toynbee [948], *1931*, pp. 455-57.

14. Zumoto [1018], pp. 71-79; BBSS, *SS* [179], vol. 8, pp. 324-25; BBSS, *SS* [181], vol. 53, pp. 38-41; *TSM* [549], vol. 2, pp. 85-111; *GSS* [203], vol. 7, pp. 282-86, 302, 322-23, 328-31, *ibid.*, vol. 11, pp. 419-73; N. Kojima, *Manshū teikoku* [350], vol. 2, pp. 58-64, 87-101; Gaimushō [194], vol. 1, pp. 815-16; Aoki [158], vol. 1, pp. 239-40. For a Chinese Communist view of Chiang Kai-shek's policy toward Manchuria, see Shih [918], p. 15; for a Chinese Nationalist defense of Chiang, see Kuo [810].

15. *TSM* [549], vol. 2, pp. 361-69; *GSS* [203], vol. 11, pp. 265-96; *NGS* [431], vol. 18, pp. 193-98, 274-89; Matsuoka [392], pp. 392-94; T. Yabe [610], vol. 1, p. 197; *Minami* [401], pp. 303-7; Uchiyama [591], pp. 160-61; Toynbee [948], *1931*, pp. 448, 455.

16. Zumoto [1018], p. 100.

17. *Ibid.*, pp. 323-24, citing Araki interview with journalist Hugh Byas, 16 Jan. 1932.

18. BBSS, *SS* [179], vol. 8, pp. 326-27; BBSS, *SS* [181], vol. 53, pp. 42-46; *GSS* [203], vol. 11, pp. 318-23, 494-519; Honjō [255], Appendix, pp. 407-11; *TSM* [549], vol. 2, pp. 111-16; Yokoyama [623], pp. 208-10; *Matsuoka* [392], pp. 390-91; Aoki [158], vol. 1, pp. 248-51; Zumoto [1018], pp. 83-100; Lytton *Report* [824], pp. 100-102.

19. According to Chinese sources, their military casualties were 4,274 killed and 1,770 wounded; civilian losses were 6,080 killed, over 2,000 wounded, 10,040 missing, and 160,000 families driven from their homes. Toynbee [948], *1932*, p. 514.

20. Tanaka Ryūkichi, "Shanhai" [568], pp. 181-83, and *Haiin* [566], pp. 22, 24; *TSM* [549], vol. 2, pp. 116-49; K. Nakamura, *Manshū* [421], pp. 162-70, and "Manshū" [422], pp. 103-6; *GSS* [203], vol. 7, pp. 373-75, 467-72; Ishii [302], pp. 182-83; Shigemitsu, *Kaisōroku* [512], pp. 111-38, and *Shōwa* [513], vol. 1, p. 63; BBSS, *SS* [179], vol. 8, pp. 327-32; N. Kojima, *Manshū teikoku* [350], vol. 2, p. 116; Rekishigaku Kenkyūkai [482], vol. 1, pp. 140-44; *Matsuoka* [392], pp. 401-9, 416-18; Aoki [158], vol. 1, pp. 252-316; Zumoto [1018], pp. 105-85; Lytton *Report* [824], chap. 5. The connection between the incidents at Mukden and Shanghai was more than hinted at by Araki in the Diet on 22 March 1932; T. Takeuchi [939], p. 375.

21. Lytton *Report* [824], pp. 111-12.

22. For one of many such foreign evaluations at the time, see Lippmann [834], chap. 11. Diplomatic repercussions on the Powers and the League are detailed in Toynbee [948], *1932*, pp. 515-82.

23. *GSS* [203], vol. 11, pp. 520, 901-2; BBSS, *SS* [179], vol. 8, pp. 332-45; Lytton *Report* [824], pp. 103-4; Toynbee [948], *1932*, pp. 434-39.

24. Pu Yi [899], vol. 1, pp. 225-27; *TSM* [549], vol. 2, pp. 174-76; *GSS* [203], vol. 11, pp. 415-18; Koiso [347], pp. 544-45; Mori [412], pp. 103-6; N. Hoshino [261], pp. 33-34; K. Nakamura, *Manshū* [421], pp. 158-60; N. Kojima, *Manshū teikoku* [350], vol. 2, pp. 28-42, 45-54; Shimada Toshihiko, *Kantōgun* [515], p. 113; W. Smith [926], pp. 188-90; Wong [1007]. For the imaginative Japanese cover story issued on 21 November concerning Pu Yi's supposed request for Japanese "protection," see Penlington [891], pp. 55-56. Nationalist historian Kuo [810] still describes Pu Yi's relocation as a "kidnapping."

25. Yokoyama [623], p. 213; *GSS* [203], vol. 7, pp. 383-84, *ibid.*, vol. 11, pp. 479-88; Lytton *Report* [824], pp. 88-93; Aoki [158], vol. 2, pp. 3-76; N. Kojima, *Manshū teikoku* [350], vol. 2, pp. 111-25; Penlington [891], pp. 252-60; *Japan-Manchoukuo Year Book, 1937* [781], p. 674; Honjō [255], Appendix, p. 411.

26. Lytton *Report* [824], pp. 93-95; *Japan-Manchoukuo Year Book, 1937* [781], pp. 675-77.

27. Pu Yi [899], vol. 1, pp. 233-40; N. Kojima, *Manshū teikoku* [350], vol. 2, pp. 129-33.

28. Lytton *Report* [824], p. 126.

29. T. Yabe [610], pp. 196-97. The official text of Honjō's proclamation can be found in Penlington [891], pp. 67-69. Also see Toynbee [948], *1931*, p. 448. War Minister Minami expressed open regret that Honjō "had not shown more care in the wording of his proclamation," but said it was justified by the situation confronting the Kwantung Army; Penlington [891], p. 42.

30. Yokoyama [623], pp. 189-94; *TSM* [549], vol. 2, pp. 29-34, 152-55; Honjō [255], Appendix, pp. 366, 370-82, 398-403; *GSS* [203], vol. 7, pp. 195-203, 206-7, 210, 247-48, citing Katakura, *ibid.*, vol. 11, pp. 413-14; N. Kojima, *Manshū teikoku* [350], vol. 2, pp. 10-12, 55-56; Imamura, *Shiki* [282], vol. 1, pp. 193-200; Ogata Sadako [886], p. 188. Tanaka Ryūkichi implicated Capt. Chō Isamu in the planted story of Kwantung Army secession; IMTFE, *Transcript* [777], 6 July 1946, p. 2017. Hashimoto Kingorō connected Col. Kōmoto Daisaku with Ishiwara's dramatics; M. Nakano [426], pp. 163-65.

31. Katakura interview; Imamura, *Shiki* [282], vol. 1, pp. 201-4; M. Nakano [426], p. 174; Honjō [255], Appendix, pp. 370-72; *GSS* [203], vol. 7, pp. 227, 231-32, 239-41, citing

Katakura, *ibid.*, vol. 11, p. 337; N. Kojima, *Manshū teikoku* [350], vol. 2, pp. 21-22, 26-28; *Itagaki* [252], pp. 83-86; *TSM* [549], vol. 2, pp. 163-65.

32. Pu Yi [899], vol. 1, pp. 240-47; N. Kojima, *Manshū teikoku* [350], vol. 2, pp. 126-28; Ogata Sadako [886], p. 121; Yokoyama [623], pp. 213-15.

33. Katakura interview; *GSS* [203], vol. 7, pp. 396-426, citing Katakura, *ibid.*, vol. 11, pp. 524-26; *TSM* [549], vol. 2, pp. 174-80, 377; N. Kojima, *Manshū teikoku* [350], vol. 2, pp. 133-41; *Japan-Manchoukuo Year Book, 1937* [781], pp. 677-78; Yokoyama [623], pp. 215-16; N. Hoshino [261], p. 41; Lytton *Report* [824], pp. 8, 121, 123-24; Honjō [255], Appendix, pp. 412-14.

34. Lytton *Report* [824], pp. 7-8, 90-91, 121-26, 182; *GSS* [203], vol. 11, pp. 817-33; Honjō [255], pp. 99-102, and Appendix, pp. 415-21; Mori [412], pp. 129-49; Rappaport [900], pp. 179-82, citing Blakeslee; W. Willoughby [1004], pp. 24-28.

35. Pu Yi [899], vol. 2, pp. 268-73; N. Kojima, *Manshū teikoku* [350], vol. 2, pp. 151-52, 158.

36. Privileged Kwantung Army officer source. Since the United States did not belong to the League, McCoy was technically designated a member, not a representative, of the Lytton Commission. In addition to the Earl of Lytton and Generals McCoy and Claudel, the commission included Count Aldrovandi of Italy and Dr. Heinrich Schnee of Germany.

37. Blakeslee's comments, cited in Rappaport [900], pp. 207, 211-12, 214. For Claudel's cautious private position on the Lytton Commission's findings, which he regarded as favoring China over Japan, see *DDF* [727], vol. 1, pp. 6-7 (9 July 1932), pp. 259-61 (3 Sept. 1932).

38. Privileged Kwantung Army officer source. In 1934 an American missionary told a Japanese diplomat that Jehol, then under Kwantung Army control, "compared well with any part of the United States so far as order and security were concerned." H. Saitō [908], p. 73.

39. Privileged Kwantung Army officer source. According to Akimoto, a Kwantung Army general (Honjō?) told him in 1932 that the League's "ignorance of the elementary facts . . . , not to say the historical background, is as abysmal as is their prejudice, I had almost said jealousy, against us. Some of the League Councillors . . . know no more about Far Eastern affairs than the primary schoolboy of Japan, and yet they would sit in judgment on Japan, breathing fire and brimstone upon her head!" The general said the League was plaguing Japan with "pettifogging argument and pinpricking policy"; [632], pp. 91-93. Also see Togawa, *Shōwa* [576], p. 122.

40. *DDF* [727], vol. 1, pp. 7-9, 15, 16. The French may have been referring to an IJN captain, Kobayashi Sōnosuke, who was attached to the Japanese delegation at Geneva during one tour from December 1931 to August 1933. Captain Kobayashi was posted to France and Switzerland for a total of about six years during his career.

41. Uchiyama [591], p. 165; Miwa [407], pp. 99-100.

42. Ogata Sadako [886], pp. 158-63; T. Takeuchi [939], pp. 382-91; Rappaport [900], p. 167.

43. T. Takeuchi [939], p. 417; Togawa, *Shōwa* [576], pp. 118-19; *GSS* [203], vol. 11, pp. 549-56, 877-86; N. Kojima, *Manshū teikoku* [350], vol. 2, p. 182; *NGS* [431], vol. 18, p. 234.

44. Pu Yi [899], vol. 2, pp. 262-66; Honjō [255], Appendix, p. 424. The Japanese foreign ministry cited a precedent for the combination of all diplomatic and military powers in Mutō's hands: the case of the "similar envoy" dispatched to Admiral Kolchak's government in Omsk in 1917.

45. *GSS* [203], vol. 7, pp. 494-508; N. Kojima, *Manshū teikoku* [350], vol. 2, pp. 176-79; *NGS* [431], vol. 18, pp. 338-55; *Japan-Manchoukuo Year Book, 1937* [781], pp. 678-79; T. Takeuchi [939], pp. 391-92.

46. BBSS, *SS* [180], vol. 27, pp. 102-5; *GSS* [203], vol. 7, pp. 505-6. Supplementary agreements on railways, harbors, airlines, advisers, etc. will be found in *GSS* [203], vol. 7, pp. 499-505.

47. The Japanese delegation to the League of Nations published an English-language tract titled *Japan's Case in the Sino-Japanese Dispute* (Geneva, 1933); see pp. 6, 38, 48, 49, 62-64.

48. Miwa [407], pp. 100-101, citing Uchiyama Masakuma. Also see Rappaport [900], pp. 173-74; *Matsuoka* [392], pp. 428, 434-35, 441-42, 460-66, 480-95; *GSS* [203], vol. 11, pp. 540-41.

49. In New York, in March 1933, Matsuoka sought to clarify his tactless remarks.

50. *Minami* [401], pp. 293-94; N. Satō, *Kaiko* [506], pp. 279-86; *TSM* [549], vol. 1, pp. 166-70, *ibid.*, vol. 2, p. 382; Miwa [407], pp. 99-108; *Matsuoka* [392], pp. 440-92; Uchiyama [591], pp. 155-73; Aoki [158], vol. 2, chap. 2; T. Takeuchi [939], pp. 412-21; Togawa, *Shōwa* [576], p. 126; *NGS* [431], vol. 18, pp. 371-72; *GSS* [203], vol. 11, pp. 877-87, citing Tsuchihashi Yūitsu, a lieutenant colonel sent to Geneva in 1932 to "assist and watch" Matsuoka. Also see Stimson [935], and S. Smith [925].

51. R. K. Hall [751], pp. 100-102, citing an official ministry of education teachers' manual. For relevant documents, including the text of the imperial rescript of 27 March, see W. Willoughby, *Sino-Japanese* [1004], chap. 26; M. Hudson [771]; and Wheeler-Bennett [1001], *1932*.

52. Ogata Sadako [886], p. 173.

53. Yokoyama [623], p. 230.

54. Mutō, promoted marshal in May 1933, died in July.

55. Pu Yi [899], vol. 2, pp. 266, 273-76; Honjō [255], pp. 188-89; N. Hoshino [261], pp. 153-54, 179-80; N. Kojima, *Manshū teikoku* [350], vol. 2, pp. 194-209; *Japan-Manchoukuo Year Book, 1937* [781], pp. 679-80.

56. Gunther [748], p. 147.

CHAPTER 5

1. Matsushita, *Nihon gunji shi zatsuwa* [396], p. 90.

2. Katakura interview; Honjō [255], pp. 146-52; *GSS* [203], vol. 11, p. 851.

3. The author heard Katakura make this assertion over NHK Educational TV, Channel 4, Tokyo, 29 March 1964, when Katakura and Satō Naotake appeared on a retrospective program dealing with the Manchurian Incident. Katakura was in good historical company; Arnold Toynbee wrote in 1932 that "the movement which came to the surface in this sudden and violent fashion [at Mukden in 1931] was really a resolution of hidden, pent-up forces which had long been gathering momentum in the depths of the Japanese people's national life." [948], *1931*, p. 399.

4. Kawakami, *Japan* [789], p. 36. Toynbee likened the Mukden Incident to other recent convulsions that led to violent reversals of established national policy—e.g., the Wall Street Crash of October 1929, the German Nazis' sudden gains in the September 1930 general election, the British Labour Party debacle of October 1931; [948], *1931*, p. 399.

5. M. Maruyama [858], pp. 107-8; Coox, *Tiger* [697], chap. 3.

6. K. Satō, *Tōjō* [504], p. 31; S. Hayashi, *Kōgun* [756], pp. 5-6, 195.

7. Imaoka, Katakura interviews; Yokoyama [623], p. 221; Tsuji [585], p. 103; I. Hata, *Gun* [230], p. 81.

8. Yokoyama [623], p. 222.

9. Honjō [255], pp. 146-49; *GSS* [203], vol. 11, pp. 851-54.

10. *GSS* [203], vol. 7, p. 214.

11. *Ibid.*; Penlington [891], p. 49. Kawagishi conveyed the imperial messages from Mukden to Kirin, Changchun, etc.

12. Katakura interview; Yokoyama [623], pp. 206-7. Also see *GSS* [203], vol. 11, p. 473; Zumoto [1018], pp. 78-79. The empress sent bandages and dressings to the troops in November 1931; Penlington [891], p. 56.

13. BBSS, *SS* [179], vol. 8, p. 314.

14. Kawabe [332], p. 79.

15. K. Satō, *Tōjō* [504], p. 35.

16. *TSM* [549], vol. 2, pp. 156-58; *GSS* [203], vol. 11, pp. 328-30.

17. *TSM* [549], vol. 2, pp. 158-63; *GSS* [203], vol. 11, pp. 333-36. Elder statesman Saionji was disappointed with Uchida.

18. *TSM* [549], vol. 2, p. 161. But see Hayashi's retrospective criticisms; [239], pp. 138-40.

19. Privileged IJA officer source; Katakura interview; Honjō [255]; Y. Matsuoka, *Building Up* [860], pp. 96, 225-27; Penlington [891], p. 59.

20. K. Satō, *Daitōa* [502], p. 17; *Matsuoka* [392], pp. 446-47; Mori [412], p. 137. N. Satō, *Kaiko* [506], pp. 267-74, refers in particular to the eloquence of Chinese representatives at the League—Wellington Koo, Sao-ke Alfred Sze, and W. W. Yen.

21. Toynbee [948], *1931*, p. 506, citing an authoritative neutral observer. Also see French chargé Lens' report from Tokyo on 23 Sept. 1932 in *DDF* [727], vol. 1, p. 381.

22. Privileged IJA officer source; Katakura interview; Honjō [255]; Penlington [891], pp. 31, 45, 56, 63-65.

23. On the ambiguities of the British positions vis-à-vis Japan and the League of Nations, see Kusuyama [362], pp. 23-25.

24. Wilson [1005], p. 280.

25. Rappaport [900], p. 220, citing Blakeslee.

26. Araki interview with Frazier Hunt (INS), 2 June 1932, in Zumoto [1018], p. 334; Col. Furujō Tanehide in Penlington [891], pp. 164-65.

27. M. Maruyama [858], p. 10; W. Willoughby, *Sino-Japanese* [1004], p. 489; Araki interview with journalist Hugh Byas, 16 Jan. 1932, in Zumoto [1018], pp. 314-15.

28. Ōtani, *Rakujitsu* [476], pp. 161-76. Also see Coox, *Tiger* [697], pp. 53-54; Ogata Sadako [886], pp. 189-91.

29. Sumi interview.

30. Lockwood [837], p. 39, n. 1.

31. I. Hata, *Nitchū* [233], p. 120.

32. K. Satō, *Tōjō* [504], p. 34.

33. S. Hayashi, *Kōgun* [756], p. 6. For IJA meddling in politics, see Coox, *Tiger* [697], pp. 34-35, 46, 48; Yoshihashi [1010], pp. 238-39. For antecedents of Japanese military fascism, see M. Maruyama [858], pp. 26-34.

34. Matsushita, *Nihon gunsei* [397], pp. 88-90; Yoshihashi [1010], pp. 233-34.

CHAPTER 6

1. From Japanese paeans of the time, I have chosen the word "marvel" used by Roy Hidemichi Akagi, *Japan's Foreign Relations, 1542-1936: A Short History* (Tokyo: Hokuseidō, 1936), p. 530.

2. Penlington [891], p. 264.

3. Kawakami, *Manchoukuo* [790], p. vi.

4. Gunther [748], p. 123.

5. *Japan-Manchoukuo Year Book*, *1940* [782A], pp. 620-21. For Ishiwara Kanji's views around 1935 concerning the establishment of a consolidated Japan-Manchukuo national munitions base, see *Ishiwara shiryō* [303], vol. 1, p. 434 (Ishiwara-Prince Takeda interview, 1939).

6. Bix [644], pp. 431-32, 435, 437-40; Gunther [748], pp. 123-25; *Nihon no rekishi* [438], vol. 22, pp. 385-86, vol. 23, p. 212. SMR data on Japanese investments in Manchuria as of March 1931 can be found in *Japan-Manchoukuo Year Book, 1937* [781], p. 667.

7. Established *zaibatsu* such as the house of Mitsubishi would not be attracted to unstable, insecure Manchuria in the early period anyway. Those who came would be new industrial capitalists. (Katakura interview.) The Japanese middle class had long been enthusiastic about Manchuria. For Tōjō's private views on "mercenary capitalism" and its exclusion from Manchukuo, to the displeasure of "liberal economists," see K. Satō, *Daitōa* [502], p. 108 (War Minister Tōjō-Satō conversation, 1941). Also see *Manshū kenkoku* [372], pp. 134-46.

8. Bix [644], p. 435.

9. Yokoyama [623], p. 304; *GSS* [203], vol. 11, pp. 828-29, 843-50, 907-11; Pu Yi [899], vol. 2, pp. 261-62; Katakura interview. Egler [717] includes a discussion of Kwantung Army use of paramilitary pacification teams (*senbu han*) provided by Kyōwa Kai's predecessor Kyōwa Tō. The Concordia Society's statement derives from a pamphlet, "Concordia's New Leadership Plans" (7 May 1936), cited by Bisson, *Japan* [642], p. 379. The Kwantung Army's interest in immigration projects is treated briefly by Jones, *Manchuria* [784], chap. 5. Itagaki's early activity is cited in M. Matsumoto, ed. [381], p. 113.

10. Kawakami, *Manchoukuo* [790], p. 149.

11. Privileged Kwantung Army officer source.

12. Pu Yi [899], vol. 2, pp. 258-61; N. Hoshino [261], p. 41; Lytton *Report* [805], p. 99; Kawakami, *Manchoukuo* [790], pp. 146-52. Of 5,700 Manchukuo administrators as of 1936, Japanese numbered 3,250, according to the official tabulation. The following Japanese could be found in leading Manchukuo government posts: privy council, three; state council, including general affairs board, four; central bank of Manchukuo, the president and two directors. Of 14 governors of provinces, Chientao was headed by a Japanese. But there were two Anglo-Saxon advisers or counselors to Manchukuo: Arthur H. F. Edwardes and George Bronson Rea. *Japan-Manchoukuo Year Book, 1937* [781], pp. 637, 692.

13. Hsu [768], pp. 648-49; W. Smith [926], pp. 190-94.

14. Cited by Toynbee [948], *1932*, p. 456, n. 4.

15. Bix [644], p. 434, n. 25.

16. Toynbee [948], *1931*, pp. 446-47.

17. See *Japan-Manchoukuo Year Book, 1937* [781], pp. 727-28, *1940* [782A], p. 696 (gives peak number as 210,000 men in Sept. 1932); Kondō [804], pp. 80-103; R. Watanabe [608]; JRD [955], *JSM* 2, p. 73; BBSS, *SS* [179], vol. 8, pp. 128-29.

18. Nishiura, Imaoka interviews.

19. *Japan-Manchoukuo Year Book, 1937* [781], pp. 725, 729, *1940* [782A], p. 637. Tsuji Masanobu vividly describes the difficult life of Kwantung Army military advisers and of low- and mid-ranking IJA officers in the Manchukuo army; [585], p. 23. Also see BBSS, *SS* [179], vol. 8, p. 118; GSS [202], vol. 7, pp. 590-92, vol. 11, p. 947.

20. BBSS, *SS* [179], vol. 8, pp. 118-30; Sasaki [499], pp. 223-51; Nishiura [447], pp. 135-36.

21. BBSS, *SS* [179], vol. 8, p. 341; Kondō [804], p. 97; Gunther [748], pp. 131-33; *Japan-Manchoukuo Year Book, 1937* [781], pp. 727-37, *1940* [782A], pp. 636-37; JRD [960], *JSM* 1, p. 131. Tsuji tells of belated Kwantung Army measures to improve the lot of Manchukuo army border garrison units; [585], pp. 27-28, 31.

22. JRD [955], *JSM* 2, pp. 75-78; GSS [202], vol. 7, pp. 511-84; I. Hata, *Nitchū* [233], pp. 6-7; Imoto [285], pp. 50-51; Dohihara [187], p. 271; TSM [549], vol. 3, pp. 16-50. For the economic attractions to Japan of the five provinces of North China, see Hall [750], pp. 54-55.

23. Kahn [785], pp. 8-10; BBSS, *SS* [179], vol. 8, p. 423.

24. The IJA China Garrison Army (Chūtongun, commonly called Tenshingun or the Tientsin Army) had been established in 1912. Its current strength was about 2,000.

25. I. Hata, *Nitchū* [233], pp. 13-31; Imoto [285], p. 52; Dohihara [187], pp. 272-73; Jōhō, ed., *Umezu* [313], pp. 179-89; TSM [549], vol. 3, pp. 98-112; GSS [202], vol. 8, pp. 68-72, 77-101. General Ho, a graduate of the IJA military academy, visited Japan on occasion after the war. Once asked by old China hand Gen. Okamura Yasuji (Neiji) about his agreement with Umezu, Ho reportedly "just laughed." Privileged Japanese source.

26. *Kindai no sensō* [336], vol. 5, pp. 49-51; I. Hata, *Nitchū* [233], pp. 32-36; Imoto [285], p. 52; Dohihara [187], pp. 273-75; TSM [549], vol. 3, pp. 112-20; GSS [202], vol. 8, pp. 73-76; Kahn [785], pp. 10-14.

27. Kahn [785], pp. 44-45.

28. K. Satō, *Daitōa* [502], pp. 107-8.

29. Majima [365]; Minami [401], pp. 405-7; Coox, *Tojo* [696], p. 29.

30. Fu Tso-i's name reappeared under ideologically interesting circumstances in April 1975 when the Outer Mongolian news agency's Russian-language paper carried an article castigating Mao Tse-tung for releasing "enemies of the Chinese people" for his own ends. As far back as 1949, according to the MPR propagandists, Chairman Mao had elevated Fu Tso-i to the status of a national hero, although the former Kuomintang general had been "the bloody butcher of the people of Inner Mongolia." *Far Eastern Economic Review*, 30 May 1975, p. 30. Actually, Fu had been made a hero by the Chinese Communists because he surrendered Peking to them without resistance in 1949.

31. Tsuji [585], p. 35; Tanaka Ryūkichi, "Shanhai" [568], pp. 183-86; H. Satō [501], chap. 3; Mori [412], p. 141; Tateno [573], vol. 2, pp. 198, 205-7; Imamura, *Kaisōroku* [280], vol. 3, pp. 75-76; Ayabe Kitsuju in K. Nakamura [423], pp. 205-6; I. Hata, *Nitchū* [233], pp. 105-25;

Kindai no sensō [336], vol. 5, pp. 56-59; *TSM* [549], vol. 3, pp. 232-36, 370; T. Imai, *Shōwa* [279], pp. 88-100. From the large literature on the Sian Incident, see Chiang Kai-shek [671], pp. 72-79.

CHAPTER 7

1. I. Hata, *Reality* [755], pp. 1-3; Shishikura [48].
2. Erickson, *Soviet* [722], pp. 335-36; Toynbee [948], *1932*, p. 437; JRD [960], *JSM* 1, p. 33; JRD [968], *JSM* 13, pp. 46-47; Shishikura [48].
3. Imaoka, "Nihon" [12], p. 28; Shishikura [48]; Erickson, *Soviet* [722], p. 336; *TSM* [549], vol. 4, pp. 75-76; Inada, "Fūun no So-Man" [290], pp. 229-30.
4. Shishikura [48]; Imaoka, "Man-So-Mō" [11], pp. 31-34.
5. Ayabe interview; Imaoka, "Man-So-Mō" [11], pp. 34-38.
6. Hattori, *Daitōa* [235], vol. 1, p. 31; *Japan-Manchoukuo Year Book, 1937* [781], p. 729; Shishikura [48].
7. JRD [960], *JSM* 1, p. 35, n. 6; JRD [968], *JSM* 13, pp. 46-47; Shishikura [48].
8. Shishikura [48]; JRD [958], *JSM* 10, pp. 30-32; Imaoka, "Nihon" [12], pp. 29-30. Tsuji describes his reconnaissance flight over the Voroshilov area from Mutanchiang in May 1938; [585], pp. 1-13.
9. Toynbee [948], *1932*, p. 439, *1933*, pp. 529-30; *Japan-Manchoukuo Year Book, 1937* [781], p. 715; Liddell Hart, ed. [833], pp. 172-73; Shishikura [48]; *TSM* [549], vol. 4, chap. 2.
10. Shishikura [48]. For "Sanroku Kurabu" (The '36 Club) and the Crisis of 1936, see Crowley, "Japanese Army" [702], p. 315; Storry, *Patriots* [936], p. 316.
11. Dodd and Dodd, eds. [712], p. 63; Close [674], p. 11.
12. I. Hata, *Reality* [755], pp. 5-12; Toynbee [948], *1933*, p. 529.
13. Kawabe [332], p. 94. Attaché Kasahara Yukio's aggressive report of March 1931 fell into Soviet hands, as did Kwantung Army commander Hishikari's telegrams of September 1933. I. Hata, *Reality* [755], pp. 68-69.
14. Close [674], p. 217; Shishikura [48]; Fleisher [724], p. 233.
15. Imaoka, "Nihon" [12], pp. 31-32; Shishikura [48]; JRD [960], *JSM* 1, p. 33, JRD [968], *JSM* 13, pp. 46-47; Erickson, *Soviet* [722], p. 338; Kōtani, Shimanuki interviews.
16. Nyūmura interview.
17. I. Hata, *Reality* [755], pp. 21-22; Shishikura [48]; Hattori, *Daitōa* [235], vol. 1, p. 32; Kōtani interview. Soviet data bear out projections for military production improvements between 1930 and 1937; see statistics in *TSM* [549], vol. 4, pp. 267, 389.
18. Yabe interview; BBSS, *SS* [180], vol. 27, pp. 94-96.
19. Chapman [669], pp. 68-69; I. Hata, *Reality* [755], pp. 64-65; JRD [958], *JSM* 10, pp. 37-38; Nishiura [447], pp. 45-46; Arao, Shimanuki interviews.
20. Doi, Asada, Shimanuki, Imaoka interviews; I. Hata, *Reality* [755], p. 65; Tsuji [585], pp. 32-33. Diplomatic courier route 1: Tokyo to London (Apr., June, Aug., Nov., Feb., March) via Tokyo-Vladivostok-Moscow-Warsaw-Berlin-Budapest-Bucharest-Paris-London-Berlin-Stockholm-Helsinki-Moscow-Tokyo. Route 2: Tokyo to Berlin (May, July, Sept., Oct., Dec., Jan.) via Tokyo-Vladivostok-Moscow-Warsaw-Berlin-Moscow-Vladivostok-Tokyo. Gaimushō [80], pp. 242-44.
21. JRD [958], *JSM* 10, chap. 1.
22. Suzuki Yasushi, Imaoka, Suemori, Shimanuki, Nyūmura interviews; Tsuji [585], pp. 1-2, 31-34; JRD [958], *JSM* 10, pp. 16, 70, 78, 87; *FRUS* [974], *1938*, vol. 3, p. 445 (Harbin, 17 Feb. 1938).
23. Ayabe interview; *Japan-Manchoukuo Year Book, 1940* [782A], p. 638.
24. Ayabe interview. "Manchurian Incident" expenses of the Japanese army were officially stated to be (in ¥1,000 units): 1932—48,485; 1933—185,989; 1934—168,059; 1935—141,569; 1936—168,892; 1937—188,511; 1938—252,058; 1939—144,117 (estimate; particularly suspect); 1940—369,123 (estimate). *Japan-Manchoukuo Year Book, 1940* [782A], p. 635.
25. Official materials bear out Ayabe's recollections; Manchukuo government national de-

fense appropriations to the Japanese armed forces amounted to the following (in units of M¥1,000): year ending 31 March 1936—9,540; 1937—24,500; 1938—19,500; 1939 (estimate)—19,500. *Japan-Manchoukuo Year Book, 1940* [782A], p. 635. Also see JRD [960], JSM 1, p. 191; K. Nakamura, *Shōwa* [423], pp. 202-4, citing Ayabe; BBSS, *SS* [180], vol. 27, pp. 200-235; Nishiura [447], pp. 47-51.

26. In one day, on 31 Aug. 1935, the SMR converted the 240 km. of broad-gauge track (1.524 m. or five feet) on the old CER between Hsinking and Harbin to standard gauge (1.435 m. or four feet 8.5 inches). Standardization of other sections was postponed. SMR, *Fifth Report* [908], pp. 63-65.

27. *Japan-Manchoukuo Year Book, 1937* [781], pp. 788-93, *1940* [782A], pp. 701-3, 834-44. Around 1937 the Korea Army commander, Gen. Koiso Kuniaki, was also working to improve rail connections from Hunchun in southeastern Manchuria, through an area rich in coal and forests; Koiso [347], p. 640.

28. *Nihon no rekishi* [438], vol. 24, p. 384; Hattori, *Daitōa* [235], vol. 1, p. 33; Borton [649], pp. 415-16; *Japan-Manchoukuo Year Book, 1937* [781], pp. 775-76, 798-99, *1940*, pp. 768-93, 685; Ayabe interview. Soviet reactions to the Japanese improvements in Manchukuo are summarized in *TSM* [549], vol. 4, pp. 275-76.

29. Between 1931 and 1936, the adjacent Korea Army possessed another 30,500 men, increased to 35,700 in 1937. But even including naval forces and elements of three divisions, committed at Shanghai in 1932, total Japanese strength came only to about 150,000 or 0.4% of the entire Japanese male population of 33,796,000 in 1933, less than the commitment during the Siberian Expedition. Matsushita, *Zatsuwa* [396], pp. 89-90. Kwantung Army and Korea Army manpower figures from 1st Repatriation Bureau document, Feb. 1947; IMTFE Def. Doc. 1328. Kwantung Army order-of-battle data from JRD [961], *JM* 77, pp. 6, 11; [960], JSM 1, p. 34; [952], JSM 4, pp. 2-4, 62; BBSS, *SS* [180], vol. 27, pp. 156-99.

30. Imaoka, "Nihon" [12], p. 34; Shishikura [48]; *Gunji nenkan* [214], 1942, pp. 1044, 1055; IMTFE, *Transcript* [777], 4 June 1947, p. 23551, 20 May 1947, p. 22593 (Hashimoto Gun); Hattori, *Daitōa* [235], vol. 1, pp. 32-33, 43-44; *TSM* [549], vol. 4, p. 276; JRD [960], JSM 1, pp. 40-41, 51; BBSS, *SS* [180], vol. 27, pp. 162, 165.

31. H. Hata [228], pp. 352, 268; Mutō Teiichi, *Tokyo Asahi*, 19 July 1938 (A.M. ed.), p. 3.

32. Davies [708], pp. 183-84 (1 Apr. 1938); Dept. of State [978], *Soviet Union*, p. 547.

33. *Ishiwara shiryō* [303], vol. 1, p. 434; IMTFE, *Transcript* [777], 8 Oct. 1947, pp. 30297-99, 30302-4 (Itagaki), 20 May 1947, pp. 22582-83 (Hashimoto); Kido, "Diary" [797], 2 Feb. 1936, p. 138; Arao, Inada, Imaoka, Hashimoto, S. Hata interviews.

34. Inada, Imaoka, Shimanuki, Arao interviews; *FRUS* [974], 1937, vol. 3, pp. 564-65 (1 Oct. 1937); Mutō Teiichi, *Tokyo Asahi*, 19 July 1938 (A.M. ed.), p. 3; Toynbee [948], 1937, vol. 1, p. 150. Other IJA intelligence experts who visited the USSR with some preconceptions of Soviet power came home with the opposite evaluation—that the Red Army was *not* comparatively weaker than its Japanese counterpart. Imaoka interview; BBSS, *SS* [180], vol. 27, pp. 92-94.

35. Arao, Inada, Imaoka, Doi interviews.

36. Giga interview.

37. *Tokyo Asahi*, 2 Aug. 1938 (P.M. ed.), p. 2 (Kawamura). The Japanese consul general in Vladivostok also sent an excellent corrective account to the foreign ministry, through secret channels, on 18 Feb. 1938; Nishi interview.

38. Tanaka Ryūkichi, *Haiin* [566], pp. 55-57.

39. Imaoka, Sumi, Tsuchiya, Iwasaki interviews.

40. Imaoka interview. Also see *Ishiwara shiryō* [303], vol. 1, p. 434.

41. Hattori, *Daitōa* [235], vol. 1, p. 33; IMTFE, *Transcript* [777], 6 July 1946, p. 2044 (Tanaka Ryūkichi); Kawabe [332], pp. 75-76; JRD [965], *JSM* 11, part 1, pp. 85-86.

42. Cited by H. J. Timperley, "Collective Security in the Far East," in *Proceedings of the Institute of World Affairs*, University of Southern California, 1939, p. 157.

43. *Ishiwara shiryō* [303], vol. 1, p. 434; BBSS, *SS* [179], vol. 8, p. 221; S. Matsumura [388], p. 73; Nishiura, Imaoka, Inada, Shimanuki interviews.

44. BBSS, *SS* [180], vol. 27, chap. 7; JRD [960], *JSM* 1, chap. 2; Imaoka, interview and "Nihon" [12], p. 24.

45. Imaoka, interview and "Nihon" [12], pp. 16-20.

46. Tsuji [585], pp. 8-12 (May 1938). In 1936 the IJA attaché in Washington revealed to a U.S. army colleague that Japanese officers had crossed into Siberian territory and "discovered that the Russians had a triple row of staggered pillboxes, each bunker one kilometer from the others in the row, and the rows a kilometer apart." Extending along the entire frontier, the bunkers protruded two or three meters above the earth. The Japanese army was interested in imaginative ways of destroying the pillboxes; Mashbir [859], pp. 49-50. In 1937 the Kwantung Army also experimented fruitlessly with ultra-short-wave detection of Soviet underground installations opposite the Tungning sector; JRD [958], *JSM* 10, p. 46.

47. Inada, Imaoka interviews.

48. JRD [960], *JSM* 1, chap. 5.

49. JRD [960], *JSM* 1, pp. 99-101; *TSM* [549], vol. 4, p. 76.

50. JRD [960], *JSM* 1, chap. 6; *TSM* [549], vol. 4, p. 77; Imaoka interview.

CHAPTER 8

1. Gaimushō [76], *Man-So*, p. 8; *Shōwa jūnen* [529], pp. 20-21; *Shōwa jūichinen* [528], p. 8; S. Matsumura [388], p. 164; B. Nakamura [420], p. 14; JRD [965], *JSM* 11, part 1, pp. 13-22; Miura, Sasai interviews.

2. Imaoka, "Man-So-Mō" [11], pp. 5-14; Shimada Toshihiko, *Kantōgun* [501], pp. 125-26.

3. S. Matsumura [388], p. 164; B. Nakamura [420], p. 14.

4. JRD [965], *JSM* 11, part 1, pp. 44-54; BBSS, *SS* [180], vol. 27, p. 310.

5. IMTFE, *Transcript* [777], 15 Oct. 1946, p. 7747.

6. Kōtani interview; *TSM* [549], vol. 4, p. 75.

7. For Kwantung Army figures: JRD [965], *JSM* 11, part 1, pp. 54-55; BBSS, *SS* [180], vol. 27, p. 310. Foreign ministry data are found in H. Satō [501], chap. 6; *TSM* [549], vol. 4, p. 77; Shimada Toshihiko, *Kantōgun* [515], p. 126.

8. BBSS, *SS* [180], vol. 27, p. 314; JRD [965], *JSM* 11, part 1, pp. 55-56.

9. Kwantung Army announcement, 13 Oct. 1935: *Japan-Manchoukuo Year Book, 1937* [781], p. 713.

10. Manchukuo government statement, 21 Feb. 1936: *Japan-Manchoukuo Year Book, 1937* [781], pp. 714-15. The Soviet plane reportedly crash-landed on 12 Jan. 1936.

11. *Shōwa jūichinen* [528], pp. 13-18; *TSM* [549], vol. 4, p. 79: BBSS, *SS* [180], vol. 27, pp. 314-15; JRD [965], *JSM* 11, part 1, pp. 56-67; *Japan-Manchoukuo Year Book, 1937* [781], pp. 713-15; B. Nakamura [420], pp. 137-38; Imaoka, "Man-So-Mō" [11], pp. 15-16, 41-42; Takumi interview. Tsuji describes another Manchukuo army mutiny that occurred on the Amur in the winter of 1938; [585], pp. 25-26. Also see *FRUS* [974], *1938*, vol. 3, p. 444 (Harbin, 17 Feb. 1938).

12. *Shōwa jūichinen* [528], pp. 29-31; BBSS, *SS* [180], vol. 27, p. 315; JRD [965], *JSM* 11, part 1, pp. 57-58.

13. *Shōwa jūichinen* [528], pp. 13-14; B. Nakamura [420], p. 137.

14. Imaoka, "Man-So-Mō" [11], pp. 14-15; *Shōwa jūnen* [529], pp. 21, 31-33; B. Nakamura [420], pp. 137-50.

15. *Shōwa jūnen* [529], pp. 28-31; Imaoka, "Man-So-Mō" [11], pp. 15-16.

16. Imaoka, "Man-So-Mō" [11], pp. 16-18; B. Nakamura [420], pp. 156-58, 181-91; *Shōwa jūichinen* [528], pp. 19-27, 30-31; *Chūō-Kōron*, Aug. 1938, pp. 127-28; JRD [965], *JSM* 11, part 1, pp. 84-85.

17. IMTFE, *Transcript* [777], 21 May 1947, pp. 22833-35 (Litvinov diary, 4 Aug. 1938); Imaoka, "Man-So-Mō" [11], pp. 18-19; *Chūō-Kōron*, Aug. 1938, p. 128. Arita's presentation to the Diet on 21 Jan. 1937 can be found in condensed form in *Vital Speeches of the Day*, 1 Feb. 1937, no. 8, pp. 245-47.

18. Kawabe [332], p. 116; Imaoka interview.

19. Katakura interview.

20. For a summary of the "pinprick" incidents of 1937, see Moore [874], p. 81; BBSS, *SS* [180], vol. 27, p. 310.

21. Gaimushō [81], *Shōwa 13-nendo*, p. 77; Def. Doc. 1680 (excerpt from Gaimushō records, 1941), IMTFE, *Transcript* [777], 3 June 1947, p. 23480; B. Nakamura [420], pp. 108-10; *Chūō-Kōron*, Aug. 1938, pp. 123-24; JRD [965], *JSM* 11, part 1, pp. 42-43; *TSM* [549], vol. 4, p. 77; BBSS, *SS* [180], vol. 27, pp. 310-11. Soviet displeasure with the basis for the Japanese charges will be found in General Vasiliev's summation, IMTFE, *Transcript* [777], 17 Feb. 1948, pp. 39827-28.

22. Materials from Soviet frontier guard records for 1932-45 (dated 20 Feb. 1946) will be found in Pros. Doc. 1953, IMTFE, *Transcript* [777], 2 June 1947, p. 23414. Also see *Transcript*, 15 Oct. 1946, pp. 7744-47. It is my opinion that the Soviet data equate individuals with separate incidents, a fact that would tend to exaggerate the arithmetical tally of episodes of alleged frontier violation.

23. Major Tereshkin under examination by General Tadevosyan; IMTFE, *Transcript* [777], 15 Oct. 1946, p. 7771.

24. Miura interview; Gaimushō [81], *Shōwa 13-nendo*, p. 62. Miura was the author of this foreign ministry report.

25. Kōtani interview.

26. Some weeks later, at a Soviet reception, Budennyi espied Kōtani. "Captain," he said, "you are a very smart fellow. I understand you but not that colonel of yours." They clinked glasses, emptied the contents, and then the marshal kissed Kōtani on both cheeks. (Kōtani interview.)

27. Tass communiqué, 26 Apr. 1936.

28. I am grateful to John Erickson for supplying the text of Schulenburg's message: Deutsche Botschaft/Moscau, Tgb. Mo. A/881, 27 Apr. 1936.

29. Miura interview; Gaimushō [81], *Shōwa 13-nendo*, pp. 61-63.

CHAPTER 9

1. BBSS, *SS* [179], vol. 8, p. 432; Yokoyama [623], pp. 289-90; Akisada [152], p. 230; Tatamiya [572], p. 84; Koiso [347], pp. 634-36; Kawabe [332], p. 138; Imoto [285], p. 85.

2. GSS [205], vol. 9, pp. 3-4; BBSS, *SS* [179], vol. 8, pp. 429-30, 437-40; Yokoyama [623], pp. 287-89; Akisada [152], pp. 231-37; K. Satō [504], pp. 72-76; Jōhō, ed. [311], pp. 96-100, 102-11; I. Hata, *Nitchū* [233], pp. 144-46; Kawabe [332], pp. 134-38; *Ishiwara shiryō* [303], vol. 1, pp. 438-39; *TSM* [549], vol. 4, pp. 11-16; Imoto [285], pp. 81-84, 88-94.

3. Yatsugi Kazuo, a correspondent who had known Tōjō for years, frankly told him at Kwantung Army headquarters in 1937 that Japanese-built Hsinking was a worse city than Chinese-built Harbin; *Shōwa* [622], vol. 1, p. 328. For the Ishiwara-Tōjō feud, see Ōtani, *Shōwa* [478], pp. 426-33; Aritake, *Shōwa* [171], pp. 174-75; Yokoyama [623], pp. 308-9; S. Matsumura [388], p. 161; Akisada [152], p. 230.

4. Mori [412], p. 75.

5. Gayn [736], pp. 189-90.

6. BBSS, *SS* [179], vol. 8, pp. 463-64; GSS [205], vol. 9, pp. 107-15, vol. 12, pp. 465-73 (Maj. Gen. Nishimura Toshio), 545-46 (Lt. Gen. Kōzuki Kiyoshi–Prince Takeda interview, 1940?); Akisada [152], pp. 237-41; Tsuchiya [583], p. 185; Umemoto, *Riku-kai* [599], p. 186; "Aa! Kantōgun no saigo" [Ah, the End of the Kwantung Army], *Sandei Nippon*, Apr. 1959, pp. 10-11; Tatamiya [572], p. 84; *TSM* [549], vol. 4, pp. 27-28; Imoto [285], pp. 132-33, 145; *Kindai no sensō* [336], vol. 5, pp. 88-89. Kasahara served as Kwantung Army deputy chief of staff only between August and September 1937, at which time Ishiwara was given the post.

7. See Thiel [942], pp. 225-31; *Japan-Manchoukuo Year Book, 1937* [781], pp. 714-15.

8. Imaoka, "Man-So-Mō" [11], pp. 27-30, "Kanchatsu-tō" [9], p. 2; *Shōwa jūninen* [530], pp. 46-47; BBSS, *SS* [180], vol. 27, pp. 329-31; Higai [244], p. 197; *Manshūkoku gensei* [375], 1938, p. 10.

9. Shigemitsu, *Shōwa* [513], vol. 1, p. 201; BBSS, *SS* [180], vol. 27, p. 331; *TSM* [549], vol. 4, p. 374; Higai [244], pp. 196-97; H. Satō [501], chap. 6; *Manshūkoku gensei* [375], 1938, p. 10; Tokyo 12 Channeru [579], vol. 2, pp. 194-96 (1st Lt. Ishikawa Gunji). But as early as

February 1937, Manchurians and Japanese may have landed on the river islands. Soviet sources assert that, on 31 May, Manchukuoan patrol boats attempted to enter the northern channel to put men ashore on the islets. Moore [874], pp. 81-82; Shimada Toshihiko, *Kantōgun* [515], p. 127.

10. BBSS, *SS* [180], vol. 27, p. 332; Imaoka, "Kanchatsu-tō" [9], pp. 1, 3; *Shōwa jūninen* [530], pp. 43-45; Higai [244], pp. 197-98; Gaimushō [201], *Nisso*, p. 371. JRD [965], *JSM* 11, part 1, pp. 65-67, contains an unsatisfactory account of the incident.

11. Higai [244], pp. 198-99; Imaoka, "Kanchatsu-tō" [9], p. 5.

12. Katakura interview; Tsuji [585], p. 36; Imaoka, "Kanchatsu-tō" [9], pp. 4-6, 9; BBSS, *SS* [180], vol. 27, p. 333.

13. The 3rd Infantry Battalion was commanded by Maj. Ōsawa Kanjirō. His superior, sector chief Mihara, had been assigned by the 49th Regiment commander, Col. Takeuchi Hiroshi.

14. Higai [244], pp. 119, 122-23, 196, 199-201; Imaoka, "Kanchatsu-tō" [9], p. 6.

15. BBSS, *SS* [180], vol. 27, p. 333; Imaoka, "Kanchatsu-tō" [9], p. 4; *TSM* [549], vol. 4, pp. 80, 373.

16. *Shōwa jūninen* [530], p. 45; BBSS, *SS* [180], vol. 27, p. 334; *TSM* [549], vol. 4, pp. 80, 373; Inada, I. Hata interviews.

17. *TSM* [549], vol. 4, pp. 80, 373; *Shōwa jūninen* [530], p. 50.

18. Imaoka, "Kanchatsu-tō" [9], pp. 6-8; *TSM* [549], vol. 4, p. 373; BBSS, *SS* [180], vol. 27, pp. 334-35; Higai [244], pp. 201-2.

19. The IJA infantrymen, who had originally withdrawn to a village 500 meters from the riverbank, raced back to the shoreline once the fighting was imminent. The infantry cannon crews reported firing at a maximum range of 800-1,000 meters. Higai [244], pp. 202-4; Tokyo 12 Channeru [579], vol. 2, pp. 196-98 (PFC Yugawa Kinsaku); *Shōwa jūninen* [530], pp. 48-50; Imaoka, "Kanchatsu-tō" [9], pp. 9-10; *TSM* [549], vol. 4, p. 80; BBSS, *SS* [180], vol. 27, p. 334.

20. *Shōwa jūninen* [530], pp. 49-50; Tokyo 12 Channeru [579], vol. 2, p. 199 (PFC Yugawa).

21. Higai [244], p. 204.

22. I. Hata interview.

23. Higai [244], p. 204.

24. Sumi interview.

25. Tokyo 12 Channeru [579], vol. 2, pp. 198-99 (PFC Yugawa).

26. Cited in *Shōwa jūninen* [530], p. 49.

27. Higai [244], p. 202.

28. Imaoka, "Kanchatsu-tō" [9], pp. 10-12.

29. GSS [205], vol. 12, pp. 499-500 (Maj. Gen. Nishimura Toshio).

30. Shigemitsu, *Shōwa* [513], vol. 1, p. 201; *Shōwa jūninen* [530], pp. 48, 50-52; BBSS, *SS* [180], vol. 27, p. 334; Imaoka, "Kanchatsu-tō" [9], pp. 13-14; *TSM* [549], vol. 4, pp. 80-81, 394; Gaimushō [201], *Nisso*, p. 372; Davies [708], p. 101 (1 July 1937). For the diplomatic record, see Slusser and Triska, eds. [924], p. 116, citing *Izvestiia*, 3 July 1937; Degras, ed. [710], vol. 3, p. 243.

31. *Shōwa jūninen* [530], pp. 52-53; Higai [244], p. 207; *TSM* [549], vol. 4, p. 309; *Manshūkoku gensei* [375], 1941, p. 586.

32. *Shōwa jūninen* [530], p. 53; Gaimushō [201], *Nisso*, pp. 372-73.

33. *TSM* [549], vol. 4, p. 374; Imaoka, "Kanchatsu-tō" [9], p. 15; BBSS, *SS* [180], vol. 27, p. 335; *Shōwa jūninen* [530], p. 45; Moore [874], p. 83; Imaoka, Sumi, Ayabe, I. Hata interviews.

34. *Shōwa jūninen* [530], p. 50; *TSM* [549], vol. 4, pp. 308-9; B. Nakamura [420], p. 234. Also see Beloff, *Foreign Policy* [637], vol. 2, pp. 177-78; Moore [874], p. 80; Toynbee [948], *1937*, vol. 1, pp. 149-50.

35. *TSM* [549], vol. 4, p. 394; Joseph E. Davies, statement, Jan. 1947, uncatalogued IMTFE defense document (Blakeney Collection); Davies [708], pp. 101-3 (1 July 1937).

36. For Hirota's Diet address of 27 July 1937, see *Vital Speeches of the Day*, 1 Aug. 1937, vol. 3, no. 20, p. 640.

37. Sumi interview.

38. The Russian gunboat was of 25-26 tons, whereas the USS *Panay*, a shoal-draft river gun-

boat sunk in December, displaced 450 tons. Manchukuoan gunboats varied in displacement from 15-20 tons to the two newest of 290 tons launched in 1935. *Shōwa jūninen* [530], p. 53; Samuel Eliot Morison, *The Rising Sun in the Pacific, 1931–April 1942* (Boston: Little, Brown, 1948), p. 16, n. 2; *Japan-Manchoukuo Year Book, 1939* [782], p. 668.

39. Kōtani interview; *Shōwa jūninen* [530], pp. 48-49; Davies [708], p. 102 (1 July 1937).

40. Ōmae, I. Hata interviews. In June 1933 the Manchukuo navy was organized officially, combining new gunboats with five craft dating as far back as 1897. By 1935 the riverine fleet had been built up to 15 vessels. *Japan-Manchoukuo Year Book, 1939* [782], p. 668.

41. Katakura interview.

42. Ayabe, Kōtani, Sumi, I. Hata interviews.

43. Matsuoka, Sumi, Imaoka interviews; Higai [244], p. 203.

44. *GSS* [205], vol. 12, pp. 499-500 (Maj. Gen. Nishimura Toshio); Tsuji [585], p. 35; I. Hata, Sumi interviews.

45. Wu was consul general in Blagoveshchensk in June 1937. Wu [1008], p. 272; Wei [996], p. 135. Also see Pratt [896], pp. 46, 243.

46. Postwar Japanese scholarship has suspected Communist culpability for the outbreak of the Marco Polo Bridge Incident. In this view, the Soviets may have been responsible for provoking an affray on the Amur designed to distract the Kwantung Army at a crucial time. Imaoka, "Kanchatsu-tō" [9], p. 19; Kōtani, Inada, Sumi, Imaoka, I. Hata interviews. Building in part on the pathbreaking researches of I. Hata and Uno Shigeaki, Kimitada I. Miwa prepared "Brief Notes on the Chinese Communists' Role in the Spread of the Marco Polo Bridge Incident into a Full-scale War," *Monumenta Nipponica*, vol. 18 (1963), no. 1-4, pp. 313-28. Also see S. Hayashi, *Kōgun* [756], pp. 9, 196.

47. Imaoka, "Kanchatsu-tō" [9], p. 18; Tsuji [585], p. 37; *TSM* [549], vol. 4, p. 80.

48. Iwakuro, Katakura, Ayabe interviews; Imaoka, "Kanchatsu-tō" [9], pp. 8-9, 17; Tsuji [585], pp. 36-37; BBSS, *SS* [180], vol. 27, p. 336.

49. Inada, Ayabe, I. Hata interviews; BBSS, *SS* [180], vol. 27, p. 336; Tsuji [585], pp. 36-37.

50. "Aa! Kantōgun no saigo," p. 10 (see note 6).

CHAPTER 10

1. Dept. of State [978], *Soviet Union*, p. 188 (28 July 1937). Also see [978], p. 556 (6 June 1938).

2. Kōtani interview; *TSM* [549], vol. 4, pp. 76, 373, citing Col. Hattori Takushirō.

3. Dept. of State [978], *Soviet Union*, pp. 587-88 (9 July 1938), citing *Leningradskaya Pravda*, 24 June 1938; Degras, ed. [710], vol. 3, pp. 293-94, citing *Journal de Moscou*, 5 July 1938. Also see Degras, ed. [710], vol. 3, pp. 308-9, citing Molotov speech (9 Nov. 1938); *FRUS* [974], *1938*, vol. 3, pp. 485-86 (10 Nov. 1938), citing *Pravda* and *Izvestiia*, 7 Nov. 1938 (Voroshilov and Frinovski); Stalin [931], p. 758 (10 March 1939). Maj. Gen. Kuzma Y. Grebennik, in 1938 a colonel commanding the Soviet border guard unit in the Posyet Bay area, told the postwar Tokyo tribunal of the instructions he had received to defend the state frontier "constantly, day and night, on the whole length of the border line. . . . each meter of the Soviet state border line is constantly guarded." IMTFE, *Transcript* [777], 27 Jan. 1948, p. 38305.

4. See Coox, *Anatomy* [679]. Also see Chōsengun, *Chōkohō* [92]; 75th Inf. Regt., *Sentō shōhō* [92B]; Inada, "Kantōgun" [292], "Soren" [293], and "Fūun no So-Man" [290]. For the view toward the Maritime Province, see Coox, "Changkufeng" [680].

5. Ōgoshi, Inada interviews; *GSS* [205], vol. 10, p. xxxii; AGS [139], *Chōkohō* [Changkufeng] chronology, 7 July 1938.

6. Iwasaki, Tsuchiya, Inada interviews.

7. Chōsengun, *Chōkohō* [92], p. 2; 75th Inf. Regt., *Jinchū bidan* [Field Exploit Accounts] (Seoul, 1939), p. 23; Koiso [347], pp. 641-42; Gaimushō [81], *Shōwa 13-nendo*, p. 65; B. Nakamura [420], pp. 254-74; *Manshūkoku gensei* [375], 1939, p. 12; Akaishizawa [150], p. 319; Shigemitsu, *Gaikō* [512], p. 215.

8. Koiso [347], p. 643; T. Saitō, Sasai, Iwasaki, Arao, K. Satō interviews. Also see Coox, "Qualities" [690].

9. Tsuchiya, Iwasaki, Ōgoshi, Kōtani, Sasai, Katakura interviews; Imaoka, "Chōkohō" [8], p. 33.

10. Chōsengun, *Chōkohō* [92], p. 2; *TSM* [549], vol. 4, p. 83.

11. Inada, I. Hata, Hashimoto, S. Hata, Katakura, Imaoka, Kōtani, Shimanuki interviews; *TSM* [549], vol. 4, pp. 43-45, 248-49, 292-94, 368; BBSS, *SS* [179], vol. 8, pp. 550-52; Harada [225], vol. 6, p. 248.

12. See Coox, "Lyushkov" [685], pp. 405-20.

13. Inada interview; BBSS, *SS* [180], vol. 27, pp. 341-43.

14. Hashimoto, Iwakuro, Iwasaki, Kōtani, Katō, Sugai, Arao, Tsuchiya, Imaoka, I. Hata interviews.

15. Kusaka, Inada interviews; *GSS* [205], vol. 12, pp. 502-3 (Maj. Gen. Nishimura Toshio).

16. The Throne sanctioned IGHQ Army Order No. 154 on 16 July. Chōsengun, *Chōkohō* [92], p. 4; Iwasaki, Imaoka, Inada, Tsuchiya, Arao, Kōtani interviews; Imaoka, "Chōkohō" [8], pp. 29-30; BBSS, *SS* [180], vol. 27, pp. 346-49; *GSS* [205], vol. 12, p. 502.

17. Ōgoshi, Inada, Kōtani, Sasai, Iwasaki, T. Saitō, Tsuchiya interviews; Tsuji [585], pp. 38-39.

18. Katakura interview; N. Hoshino [261], pp. 278-79.

19. Mori [412], p. 75.

20. Sumi, Hashimoto, Kōtani, Ōgoshi, Katakura interviews; Imaoka, "Chōkohō" [8], pp. 34-35.

21. Harada [225], vol. 7, p. 55 (26 July 1938).

22. *Ibid.*, p. 56.

23. B. Nakamura [420], pp. 40, 275; Shigemitsu, *Shōwa* [513], vol. 1, p. 202; IMTFE, *Transcript* [777], 15 Oct. 1946, pp. 7806-7; 30 Oct. 1947, pp. 32106-9; 31 Oct. 1947, p. 32172; 26 Jan. 1948, pp. 38291-92; 27 Jan. 1948, pp. 38320-21; 8 March 1948, pp. 42746-47; Gaimushō [81], *Shōwa 13-nendo*, p. 67.

24. B. Nakamura [420], pp. 256, 282-84; *Tokyo Asahi*, 21 July 1938 (A.M. ed.), pp. 2, 3; (P.M. ed.), p. 1; 22 July (A.M. ed.), p. 2; IMTFE, *Transcript* [777], 26 Jan. 1948, p. 38293; 27 Jan. 1948, pp. 38327-32; Gaimushō [81], *Shōwa 13-nendo*, p. 67.

25. Chōsengun, *Chōkohō* [92], pp. 5-13.

26. K. Satō, Iwasaki, T. Saitō, Tsuchiya, Sasai, Kōtani, Hashimoto interviews; Chōsengun, *Chōkohō* [92], pp. 14-16; Akaishizawa [150], pp. 35-78; IMTFE, *Transcript* [777], 21 May 1947, pp. 22716-17; 22 May 1947, pp. 22751-52; 17 Feb. 1948, pp. 39846-50.

27. Chōsengun, *Chōkohō* [92], p. 17; *GSS* [205], vol. 12, p. 503; Inada, Arao, Hashimoto interviews.

28. IGHQ Army Directive No. 204 (20 July). Chōsengun, *Chōkohō* [92], pp. 14-15; *GSS* [205], vol. 12, p. 503; *TSM* [549], vol. 4, pp. 85, 375; Inada, I. Hata, Kōtani, Arao, Hashimoto, Tsuchiya interviews.

29. Sawamoto, M. Katō, Iwakuro, I. Hata, Imaoka interviews; Takamiya, *Tennō* [554], pp. 267-70; Ugaki [593], vol. 2, p. 1252 (22 July 1938); Kido, "Diary" [797], p. 204 (21 July 1938); Harada [225], vol. 7, pp. 46-54, 56; BBSS, *SS* [180], vol. 27, pp. 349-54; BBSS, *SS* [179], vol. 8, p. 557; IMTFE, *Transcript* [777], 10 Oct. 1947, pp. 30471-77, 30520-21; 9 June 1947, p. 23870; 10 June 1947, pp. 23884-92; 10 Nov. 1948, pp. 49392-93, 49797; *GSS* [205], vol. 12, p. 504; Imaoka, "Chōkohō" [8], p. 13.

30. Chōsengun, *Chōkohō* [92], pp. 25-26; *GSS* [205], vol. 12, p. 504; *TSM* [549], vol. 4, pp. 85, 375-76; Inada interview.

31. K. Satō, Tominaga, T. Saitō, Sasai, Kōtani, Arao, Iwasaki, Inada, Hashimoto interviews; Chōsengun *Chōkohō* [92], pp. 24-34; IMTFE, *Transcript* [777], 15 Oct. 1946, p. 7814; Imaoka, "Chōkohō" [8], p. 24; *TSM* [549], vol. 4, pp. 85, 376.

32. Chōsengun, *Chōkohō* [92], pp. 34-39; Gaimushō [81], *Shōwa 13-nendo*, p. 68; BBSS, *SS* [180], vol. 27, pp. 356-57; BBSS, *SS* [179], vol. 8, p. 559; *GSS* [205], vol. 4, p. 505; *JSM*, vol. 11, part 3/A, pp. 62-63; *TSM* [549], vol. 4, p. 86; Imaoka, "Chōkohō" [8], pp. 20-21; *Shōwa jūsannen* [531], p. 346; B. Nakamura [420], pp. 257-59, 290-92; IMTFE, *Transcript* [777], 10 June 1947, pp. 23892-93; 30 Oct. 1947, pp. 32072-73, 32116; 15 Oct. 1946,

pp. 7776, 7804-5, 7808-9, 7812; 30 Oct. 1947, pp. 32176-77; 26 Jan. 1948, pp. 38294-95; Akaishizawa [150], pp. 79-195, 318-24; K. Satō, T. Saitō, Tsuchiya, Sasai, Iwasaki, I. Hata, Imaoka interviews.

33. Chōsengun, *Chōkohō* [92], pp. 34-40; JRD [965], *JSM* 11, part 3/A, p. 63; Kitano, Sasai, T. Saitō, Iwasaki, Tsuchiya interviews; K. Nakamura affidavit 2, para. 17 (Blakeney Collection).

34. Chōsengun, *Chōkohō* [92], pp. 36-39, 43-44; K. Nakamura affidavit 2, para. 17 (Blakeney Collection); 75th Inf. Regt., *Sentō shōhō* [92B], 30 July 1938; IMTFE, *Transcript* [777], 3 Feb. 1948, pp. 38850-51; *TSM* [549], vol. 4, pp. 86-87, 376; Akaishizawa [150], p. 325; Imaoka, "Chōkohō" [8], pp. 21-27, 41-43; Iwasaki, Tsuchiya, Sasai, Hashimoto, Arao, Kōtani, Imaoka, Inada interviews.

35. Chōsengun, *Chōkohō* [92], pp. 36, 40, 43; 75th Inf. Regt., *Sentō shōhō* [92B], 30 July 1938; JRD [965], *JSM* 11, part 3/A, pp. 68-69; K. Satō, Murakoshi, Tezuka, Miyajima, Sakata interviews.

36. BBSS, *SS* [180], vol. 27, pp. 360-62; *TSM* [549], vol. 4, p. 87; JRD [965], *JSM* 11, part 3/A, p. 71; K. Satō, Inada, I. Hata interviews.

37. 75th Inf. Regt., *Sentō shōhō* [92B], 31 July 1938; Chōsengun, *Chōkohō* [92], pp. 41-44; Gaimushō [81], *Shōwa 13-nendo*, p. 68; *TSM* [549], vol. 4, pp. 86-87; BBSS, *SS* [180], vol. 27, pp. 362-66; GSS [205], vol. 12, pp. 505-6; JRD [959], *Japanese Night Combat*, part 1, pp. 45-46, part 3, pp. 496-97; Akaishizawa [150], pp. 137-41; K. Satō, Tezuka, Miyajima, Sakata, T. Saitō interviews.

38. *New York Times*, 2 Aug. 1938, pp. 1, 10.

39. Inada, Sawamoto, I. Hata interviews; Imaoka, "Chōkohō" [8], p. 23; BBSS, *SS* [180], vol. 27, pp. 366-68; GSS [205], vol. 12, p. 506.

40. T. Saitō interview; Imaoka, "Chōkohō" [8], p. 27.

41. 75th Inf. Regt., *Sentō shōhō* [92B]; K. Nakamura, affidavit 2, paras. 22, 28 (Blakeney Collection); Chōsengun, *Chōkohō* [92], pp. 78-82; JRD [965], *JSM* 11, part 3/A, p. 97; Akaishizawa [150], pp. 215, 327-28; Imaoka, "Chōkohō" [8], p. 45; Miyashi, Tominaga, Kitano, K. Satō, Ichimoto, Horiguchi, Tezuka, Miyajima, T. Saitō, Kōtani, Imaoka interviews.

42. Sasai, Sugai, Miyashi, Inada, Hashimoto, Iwasaki interviews; Chōsengun, *Chōkohō* [92], pp. 49-50; *TSM* [549], vol. 4, p. 377, n. 2; BBSS, *SS* [180], vol. 27, pp. 373-74, 403-4. Also see Coox, "Restraints" [691], pp. 18-26.

43. Chōsengun, *Chōkohō* [92], p. 78; K. Nakamura, affidavit 2, para. 28 (Blakeney Collection); S. Matsumura [388], p. 165; *TSM* [549], vol. 4, p. 89; JRD [965], *JSM* 11, part 3/A, p. 31; Akaishizawa [150], pp. 327-28; Imaoka, "Chōkohō" [8], p. 45; Kōtani, Sasai, Kitano interviews; Erickson, *Soviet* [722], pp. 496-98.

44. JRD [965], *JSM* 11, part 3/A, fig. 1; K. Nakamura, affidavit 2, paras. 22-24, 28 (Blakeney Collection); S. Matsumura [388], p. 165; IMTFE, *Transcript* [777], 21 May 1947, p. 22718; 22 May 1947, pp. 22747, 22758; Sugai, Inada, Kitano interviews.

45. Chōsengun, *Chōkohō* [92], p. 78; K. Nakamura, affidavit 2, paras. 23, 28 (Blakeney Collection); Akaishizawa [150], pp. 214-15, 327-28; JRD [965], *JSM* 11, part 3/A, p. 31; Imaoka, "Chōkohō" [8], p. 45; Kōtani interview; Erickson, *Soviet* [722], p. 498.

46. Tanaka Ryūkichi, *Haiin* [566], p. 53; Akaishizawa [150], pp. 327-28; Imaoka, "Chōkohō" [8], p. 45; JRD [965], *JSM* 11, part 3/A, p. 31; IMTFE, *Transcript* [777], 22 May 1947, pp. 22746-47, 22756; K. Nakamura, affidavit 2, para. 23 (Blakeney Collection); 75th Inf. Regt., *Sentō shōhō* [92B], 11 Aug. 1938; K. Satō, Kōtani, S. Morita interviews; *Tokyo Asahi*, 10 Aug. 1938 (A.M. ed.), p. 2.

47. Chōsengun, *Chōkohō* [92], pp. 79-83; 75th Inf. Regt., *Sentō shōhō* [92B], 11 Aug. 1938; JRD [965], *JSM* 11, part 3/A, table 9; K. Satō, Miyajima, T. Saitō, Murakoshi, Horiguchi, Ichimoto, Sugai, Inada, Arao, Hashimoto, S. Hata, Iwakuro, Imaoka interviews.

48. GSS [205], vol. 12, pp. 507-10; *TSM* [549], vol. 4, p. 89; Inada, Hashimoto, I. Hata interviews.

49. BBSS, *SS* [180], vol. 27, pp. 411-13; Gaimushō [81], *Shōwa 13-nendo*, pp. 60-61; Harada [225], vol. 7, p. 75; B. Nakamura [420], p. 263; *TSM* [549], vol. 4, p. 92; Iwasaki,

I. Hata interviews; *Tokyo Asahi*, 14 Aug. 1938 (P.M. ed.), p. 1; *FRUS* [974], *1938*, vol. 3, p. 482 (Moscow, 15 Aug. 1938).

50. 75th Inf. Regt., *Sentō shōhō* [92B], 11 Aug. 1938; Gaimushō, *Shōwa 13-nendo*, pp. 60-61; BBSS, *SS* [180], vol. 27, pp. 410-11; B. Nakamura [420], p. 263; Akaishizawa [150], pp. 215, 327-28; *Manshūkoku gensei* [375], 1939, p. 13; *Tokyo Asahi*, 17 Aug. 1938 (P.M. ed.), p. 1; K. Satō interview; *New York Times*, 5 Aug. 1938, p. 8; 14 Aug. 1938, p. 24; *FRUS* [974], *1938*, vol. 3, p. 482 (Moscow, 15 Aug. 1938; Peiping, 17 Aug. 1938).

51. Chōsengun, *Chōkohō* [92], pp. 85-86, 93-95; 75th Inf. Regt., *Sentō shōhō* [92B], 12 Aug. 1938; *TSM* [549], vol. 4, p. 91; *Tokyo Asahi*, 16 Aug. 1938 (A.M. ed.), p. 2; Akaishizawa [150], pp. 307-15; JRD [965], *JSM* 11, part 3/A, p. 122; Tominaga, Sumi, Iwasaki interviews.

52. Akaishizawa [150], pp. 345-46; *GSS* [205], vol. 12, p. 510; Inada interview.

53. Chōsengun, *Chōkohō* [92], pp. 70-75; *GSS* [205], vol. 12, pp. 79-81; JRD [965], *JSM* 11, part 3/A, pp. 141-42; T. Saitō, Sugai, Inada interviews.

54. Chōsengun, *Chōkohō* [92], pp. 87-88; Inada interview; BBSS, *SS* [180], vol. 27, p. 405; *GSS* [205], vol. 12, pp. 507-8.

55. Inada interview; *GSS* [205], vol. 12, p. 508; Gaimushō Jōhōbu [Intelligence Bureau], *Chōkohō jiken gaikoku shinbun ronchō shū* [The Changkufeng Incident: Foreign Press Comments], July-Aug. 1938, p. 17; Gaimushō [84], *Chōkohō*, pp. 12, 19-23; Kwantung Army communiqué, *Tokyo Asahi*, 8 Aug. 1938 (A.M. ed.), p. 2; IMTFE, *Transcript* [777], 15 Oct. 1946, p. 7817.

56. N. Morita, Sumi interviews; BBSS, *SS* [180], vol. 27, pp. 404-5; *GSS* [205], vol. 12, p. 507.

57. Harada interview.

58. Inada, Arao, Hashimoto, Kōtani, Iwasaki, Imaoka interviews; Chōsengun, *Chōkohō* [92], p. 87; JRD [965], *JSM* 11, part 3/A, pp. 47-48; *GSS* [205], vol. 12, p. 508; Tsuji [585], p. 39; S. Matsumura [388], p. 165; Imaoka, "Chōkohō" [8], pp. 16-17; IMTFE, *Transcript* [777], 20 May 1947, p. 22589.

59. *FRUS* [974], *1938*, vol. 3, p. 483 (Peiping, 17 Aug. 1938); *New York Times*, 15 Aug. 1938, pp. 1, 6.

60. Sasai, Tsuchiya, Noguchi, Tominaga interviews.

61. N. Hoshino [261], p. 279; Inada interview.

62. See Coox, "Lake Khasan" [686], pp. 51-65. Also see BBSS, *SS* [180], vol. 27, p. 416.

CHAPTER 11

1. Imaoka, "Man-So-Mō" [11], p. 43; JRD [967], *JSM* 3, part 4, chaps. 1-2; *Shōwa jūichinen* [528], p. 12; Y. Nishihara, Yano Mitsuji interviews.

2. Kunimatsu [354], pp. 209-10; *Shōwa jūichinen* [528], pp. 4-5; Imaoka, "Man-So-Mō" [11], p. 6; BBSS, *SS* [180], vol. 27, p. 317; T. Matsumura, Suzuki Yasushi, Nyūmura, Ishida, Numazaki interviews.

3. Numazaki interview; *Shōwa jūichinen* [528], p. 12.

4. Imaoka interview.

5. The *obos* served not only as border markers and landmarks but as important symbols of lamaistic worship. See Cammann [662], pp. 6, 87, 107, 119; Tanaka Katsuhiko [564], p. 107. Yano Mitsuji adds that markers erected for purposes of cattle-domain delineating tended to become "boundary" markers. (Interview.)

6. Numazaki interview. For further information on AGS "rectification" of boundaries: Y. Nishihara interview, citing information provided in 1960 by Lt. Gen. Kataoka Tadasu. Also see note 56.

7. Yano Mitsuji says that his 1938 reconnaissance trip was stimulated by a scouting report submitted to the AGS, via the Hailar OSS, by Kidera Hanei, head of the small branch post at Arshaan. Under cover of darkness, Kidera had infiltrated into MPR territory across the upstream Halha, some time earlier in the autumn of 1938. (Interview.)

8. In interviews with the author, Yano Mitsuji corrected errors of transcription in his report found in IMTFE, *Transcript* [777], 26 May 1947, Def. Doc. 1601, pp. 22997-98.

9. IMTFE, *Transcript* [777], 9 June 1947, Def. Ex. 3905, pp. 38856-57. Also Yano Mitsuji interview. I have been able to locate the highly classified Kwantung Army report based on field surveys conducted by the Hailar Military Police Unit in early Nov. 1938, and on interrogations of an unidentified officer (undoubtedly MPRA Captain Bimba) who defected from Outer Mongolia in August 1938: Kantōgun Sanbōbu [Kwantung Army Headquarters Staff Department], "Soto Mōko heiyō chishi shiryō" [Military Geography Materials on Outer Mongolia], Jan. 1939 (BBSS Archives). See chap. 12, n. 8.

10. Asada interview.

11. Suzuki Yasushi interview.

12. *TSM* [549], vol. 4, pp. 95, 378, n. 2. In May 1939 the American consul general in Mukden saw a Japanese war ministry map of 1933 in the Manchukuo foreign ministry, showing the frontier dividing Lake Buir in half and then flowing down the Halha. On a war ministry map of 1936 kept in his own office, the consul knew that the line was set around Lake Buir, rectifying the frontier to Manchukuo's advantage. But nothing is said by the consul about any Japanese tampering with the Halha boundary of the 1933 map. Langdon to Secretary of State, No. 365, 1 June 1939 (National Archives file 761.9315 Manchuria/118; NARS [980]).

13. *Shōwa jūnen* [529], p. 23. Also see *Shōwa jūichinen* [528], pp. 11-12. Satō Hiroshi speaks of a "false pseudo-border" two to four km. south of the "real" frontier between Abagaytuy and the Manchukuo-Mongolia boundary, deriving from a Sino-Russian agreement at Tsitsihar in 1919; [501], chap. 6.

14. See Doc. 2993-D (Blakeney Collection), a map reproduced by the Kwantung government general in 1911; and Doc. 751, Exhibit 719 (Blakeney Collection), a topographical map transmitted in Jan. 1938 by Kwantung Army chief of staff Tōjō to Vice Minister of War Umezu.

15. Yano Mitsuji interview.

16. Nyūmura interview.

17. Suzuki Yoshiyasu interview.

18. *Shōwa jūnen* [529], pp. 23-24.

19. Yano, "Shiryō" [61].

20. H. Satō [501], chap. 7/G; *TSM* [549], vol. 4, p. 390, n. 25, citing an understanding among the foreign, army, and navy ministers concerning anti-China policy. Also see Phillips [892], pp. 68-73; Shirendyb et al., eds. [919], p. 347.

21. *TSM* [549], vol. 4, p. 284, citing Gaimushō source.

22. Phillips [892], p. 56, citing a certain General Satō in *Manchukuo, the Mongolian Problem, and Our Continental Policy* (1931); Imaoka, "Man-So-Mō" [11], pp. 52-53; Shirendyb et al., eds. [919], pp. 347-48.

23. Yano, "Soto" [62], appendix. Also see Friters, *Outer Mongolia* [730], pp. 134-41; Kolarz [802], pp. 135-37; Tang [940], pp. 380-92; Lattimore, *Nationalism* [819], pp. 85-88; USSR, *History* [985], pp. 328-43.

24. For MPR accounts of subversion by feudal lamaist reactionary elements, see Shirendyb et al., eds. [919], pp. 323-37; USSR, *History* [985], pp. 334, 343, 347-49. When Justice William O. Douglas visited Outer Mongolia in 1961 he was told how, in the late 1930's and early 1940's, monasteries had been raided, Japanese arms found, and some lamas executed. By 1961 only two monasteries were still in operation. Douglas and Conger [714], p. 333. For a good summary of the suppression of monasticism by 1939, see Dupuy et al. [716A], p. 424.

25. Sometime in 1931, however, MPRA gunners near Buir Nor shot down a Lufthansa plane bound for Peking. *Japan-Manchoukuo Year Book, 1937* [781], p. 716, citing a Manchukuo government statement.

26. See Shirendyb et al., eds. [919], p. 349; USSR, *History* [985], p. 344; Friters, *Outer Mongolia* [730], p. 143; Dupuy et al. [716A], p. 425.

27. Imaoka, "Man-So-Mō" [11], pp. 43-44; BBSS, *SS* [180], vol. 27, pp. 317-18.

28. Some Japanese public sources claimed that Japanese-Manchukuoan units combined to wipe out MPRA forces occupying the downstream district, but even the Outer Mongol authorities were said to have endorsed the bloodless nature of their withdrawal. Choibalsan disagrees. See his account of the 24 Jan. action: *Soviet Monitor*, 25 Oct. 1946, in Friters, *Outer*

Mongolia [730], p. 294. Also see BBSS, *SS* [180], vol. 27, pp. 319-20; Higuchi Kōyō [246], vol. 1, p. 5; *Manshūkoku gensei* [375], 1936, p. 32; *Shōwa jūnen* [529], chap. 3; M. Watanabe [607], pp. 60-61; Shirendyb et al., eds. [919], p. 348.

29. *TSM* [549], vol. 4, p. 78. Choibalsan, however, charged that the Japanese now set up their own border posts inside MPR-claimed territory on 27 February; *Soviet Monitor*, 25 Oct. 1946, in Friters, *Outer Mongolia* [730], p. 294.

30. JRD [965], *JSM* 11, part 1, p. 80; *Japan-Manchoukuo Year Book, 1937* [781], pp. 711, 716; USSR, *History* [985], pp. 344-45; Shirendyb et al. [919], p. 348.

31. *Shōwa jūnen* [529], pp. 27-28; Higuchi Kōyō [246], vol. 1, p. 5; BBSS, *SS* [180], vol. 27, pp. 320-21; M. Watanabe [607], p. 61; *Manshūkoku gensei* [375], 1936, p. 32; *TSM* [549], vol. 4, p. 78; K. Saitō [496], p. 56; Matsuoka, Numazaki, Yano Mitsuji interviews.

32. Imaoka, "Man-So-Mō" [11], pp. 21-24; *Shōwa jūnen* [529], pp. 26-31; *TSM* [549], vol. 4, pp. 285-86; B. Nakamura [420], pp. 173-91; *Japan-Manchoukuo Year Book, 1937* [781], pp. 711, 716; JRD [965], *JSM* 11, part 1, pp. 80-82. Soviet orchestration of the MPR response is accepted by Harry Schwartz, *Tsars, Mandarins and Commissars* (New York: Lippincott, 1964), pp. 122-23. Also see Shirendyb et al., eds. [919], p. 348; USSR, *History* [985], p. 345; Friters, *Outer Mongolia* [730], pp. 236-37.

33. Made up of the 1st and 4th cavalry brigades, this was the Cavalry Group which was replaced in 1938 by the new 23rd Infantry Division and was transferred to China.

34. BBSS, *SS* [180], vol. 27, pp. 321-23; *TSM* [549], vol. 4, pp. 79 (citing BBSS materials), 286, 391, n. 30; JRD [965], *JSM* 11, part 1, p. 61; Imaoka, "Man-So-Mō" [11], p. 45. Also see Choibalsan's statement, *Soviet Monitor*, 25 Oct. 1946, in Friters, *Outer Mongolia* [730], p. 294.

35. Kōain Mōkyō Renrakubu [91], p. 73.

36. The tankette company consisted of two platoons: four tankettes per platoon, and one for the company commander. Two-man Type 94 tankettes were always employed by the Japanese army, until the end of the Pacific War, in the Philippines and elsewhere. Masuda interview.

37. Tass, reporting from Ulan Bator, spoke of three repulses of the Japanese between 24 and 26 March on Mongolian territory; but Japanese sources insisted there was only one patrol-size clash, on the 24th. *Shōwa jūichinen* [528], pp. 25-26. Also see BBSS, *SS* [180], vol. 27, pp. 323-25.

38. The Manchukuoan government claimed that one soldier was killed and another four were wounded by the MPRA warplanes' attack on 29 March; *Shōwa jūichinen* [528], p. 28.

39. *Shōwa jūichinen* [528], pp. 26-29; BBSS, *SS* [180], vol. 27, p. 325.

40. BBSS, *SS* [180], vol. 27, p. 325. The MPRA air ace was thought to have been wounded during the fighting at Tauran but to have got away to the base at Bain Tumen; Yano Mitsuji interview. According to an Outer Mongolian source, Japanese-Manchukuoan forces attacked Mongolian troops in the vicinity of the Azikdoron watchpoint in April. "In the first real combat by Mongolian aircraft, our air force bombed the enemy accurately and also strafed, despite bad weather." Kōain Mōkyō Renrakubu [91], p. 73.

41. Or the 37-mm. cannon of some of the Mongolian armored cars; others were equipped only with machine guns. Masuda interview.

42. BBSS, *SS* [180], vol. 27, p. 326; Masuda, Yano Mitsuji, Y. Nishihara interviews.

43. There may at least have been Russian drivers for the Mongolian armored cars, according to IJA intelligence. Yano Mitsuji thinks both slain crewmen in this case were Russian. (Interview.)

44. Yano Mitsuji, Masuda interviews.

45. My IJA interviewees insist that the smashed tankettes were dragged back by the Japanese on their wheels, but there is no reason to dispute the Mongolian claim that both tankettes were captured. Kōain Mōkyō Renrakubu [91], p. 72. For Japanese tally of IJA casualties, see BBSS, *SS* [180], vol. 27, p. 328.

46. Thirty armored cars and 96 truckloads of infantry and artillery, according to Japanese public accounts; the enemy was caught from the air after penetrating 20 km. into Manchukuoan-claimed territory. *Manshūkoku gensei* [375], 1937, p. 20.

47. *Shōwa jūichinen* [528], p. 25; BBSS, *SS* [180], vol. 27, pp. 326-27.

48. Y. Nishihara interview.

49. At least one Japanese officer had been captured on 29 March, when a Manchukuoan army truck was cut off and seized by MPRA troops; see text, above.

50. Yano Mitsuji interview; BBSS, *SS* [180], vol. 27, p. 328.

51. *Shōwa jūichinen* [528], p. 24; Masuda interview.

52. *Shōwa jūichinen* [528], p. 26. In addition to the specific citations noted earlier, the account of the Tauran Incident draws on *Shōwa jūichinen* [528], pp. 23-29; B. Nakamura [420], pp. 163-72; TSM [549], vol. 4, pp. 79, 286-87, 391, n. 32; Gaimushō [201], pp. 246-47; *Manshūkoku gensei* [375], 1937, p. 20; JRD [965], *JSM* 11, part 1, pp. 61-62. Also Yano Mitsuji, Masuda, Y. Nishihara interviews.

53. Kōtani interview.

54. MPRA *Red Star*, no. 28, 12 March 1938, translated by Yano, "Shiryō" [61]; Choibalsan statement, *Soviet Monitor*, 25 Oct. 1946, in Friters, *Outer Mongolia* [730], p. 294; Kōain Mōkyō Renrakubu [91], pp. 72-73; TSM [549], vol. 4, pp. 287, 391, n. 32.

55. B. Nakamura [420]; Y. Nishihara interview, citing information provided by Colonel Shibuya around 1960. It was disclosed publicly by the Japanese authorities that in April 1936 the former governor of the Hsingan North Province, Ling Sheng, and some others were shot "for conspiring with the USSR." *Japan-Manchoukuo Year Book, 1939* [782], p. 624.

56. Y. Nishihara interview, citing information provided in 1960 by Lt. Gen. Kataoka Tadasu. Between 1934 and 1936, Kataoka served as a Cavalry Group staff officer in the rank of lieutenant colonel.

57. USSR, *History* [985], p. 346.

58. Major Front in Yano, "Shiryō" [61] (Aug. 1938).

CHAPTER 12

1. Shirendyb et al., eds. [919], p. 350; USSR, *History* [985], pp. 345-46. Also see Rupen, *Mongolian* [905], p. 41, citing *The Soviet Union and the Path to Peace* (Moscow, 1936), p. 15; Dupuy et al. [716A], pp. 425-26; Friters, *Outer Mongolia* [730], pp. 143-44.

2. Cited by Yen Feng, *Peking Review*, 13 Dec. 1974, p. 6.

3. Y. Nishihara interview.

4. Heiyō chishi han: Military Geographical Research Subsection.

5. Yano Mitsuji interview.

6. Kolarz [802], pp. 137-38, citing also Dietrich Schaefer, *Kommunistische Propaganda in der Mongolei, Zeitschrift fuer Geopolitik*, Jan. 1939, no. 1, p. 166. The Mongol population numbered two million in Manchukuo, 1,250,000 in Inner Mongolia, one million in Sinkiang-Singhai. Imaoka, "Man-So-Mō" [11], p. 23.

7. The British correspondent was the *Times* man in Peking (4 Apr. 1938); Phillips [892], pp. 73-76.

8. All references to the Bimba documentation derive from the Japanese edition of his notes [178]. Owen Lattimore refers to a Russian-language version (*Krasnaya ruka nad Vneshnei Mongoliei*) put out by the Japanese in·occupied Shanghai around 1940 as "Japanese propaganda." See Lattimore, *Inner* [817], pp. xxxi, li, n. 27. Captain Bimba's date of flight from the MPR (Aug. 1938) pinpoints him as the officer defector whose interrogations contributed to the special intelligence report issued by the Kwantung Army in Jan. 1939. See chap. 11, n. 9.

9. The intelligence services in Manchukuo did not doubt the authenticity of the Demid-Gendun conspiracy. Kolarz sees connections between the cases of Demid and Tukhachevsky: "All the defense arrangements for Outer Mongolia had been planned in agreement between [the two marshals]. In view of the dependence of the [MPRA] on the Red Army, Marshal Demid could be nothing else than Tukhachevsky's local representative and had to share his fate." [802], p. 139.

10. IJA intelligence heard that Demid may have committed suicide when he learned that Gendun had been arrested in Moscow and that the plot had been exposed; Yano, "Shiryō" [61]. At first, the MPR government charged that Demid was a victim of Japanese assassins; three months later, in November, it alleged that Demid and Gendun were Japanese agents.

Gendun, for example, reportedly had sought out the Japanese ambassador in Moscow in an effort to betray his country. Citing *Pravda*, 29 Aug. 1937, Kolarz notes that Demid's remains were cremated in Moscow on the day of arrival; [802], pp. 138-39.

11. K. Ishida [294], pp. 182-83. Also see Shirendyb et al., eds. [919], p. 345.

12. Evidence by Soviet Army Major Front, a defector; see below and chap. 11, note 58.

13. *Tokyo Asahi*, 8 July 1938 (A.M. ed.), p. 3.

14. Yano, "Soto" [62], appendix.

15. Data on prisoners based on Yano Mitsuji's interrogation of Major Front in 1938; "Shiryō" [61]. For number of slain lamas, see Dupuy et al. [716A], p. 69.

16. For a succinct account of the rise of Choibalsan (Choibalsang), see Lattimore, *Nationalism* [819], pp. 73-74. The revisionist version is found in Shirendyb et al., eds. [919], pp. 344-46, 820-21. Also see Choibalsan et al. [185].

17. See *Japan-Manchoukuo Year Book, 1939* [782], p. 651.

18. Wu Ko-tei interview.

19. Yano, "Shiryō" [61]. Also see Kolarz [802], p. 137.

20. *Tokyo Asahi*, 8 July 1938 (A.M. ed.), p. 3 (Hsinking).

21. Maj. Front in Yano, "Shiryō" [61]. Bimba [178] had much to say about the low quality of the new MPRA officer corps developed after the purges of 1937-38.

22. Shimanuki interview.

23. USSR, *History* [985], p. 349. According to another Mongolian source, certain elements of the Soviet Army entered the MPR as early as April 1937; Shirendyb et al., eds. [919], p. 351.

24. The protocol, although stated in terms of complete equality, applied in reality only to Soviet assistance to the Mongolians. Friters, *Outer Mongolia* [730], pp. 143-44. Also see Shirendyb et al., eds. [919], p. 351. Tang is honest enough to admit the impossibility of estimating the Soviet military presence in the MPR since 1924, in the absence of authentic data from the Russian-Mongolian side; [940], p. 397.

25. *Tokyo Asahi*, 8 July 1938 (A.M. ed.), p. 3 (Hsinking).

26. Higuchi Kōyō [246], pp. 8, 16-17.

27. Interviewee Suzuki Yoshiyasu, however, cannot remember details of Soviet strength.

28. Shimanuki, Ōgoshi, Imaoka interviews. Erickson agrees that in late 1938 the 38th (Motorized) Rifle Division was shifted from Chita in the Trans-Baikal to Ude in the MPR; *Soviet* [722], p. 519.

29. Kōtani interview.

30. Map in author's possession; additional data from Yano Mitsuji interview. Yano had identified the 108th Regt. of the 36th Rifle Division, a battalion of the 36th Artillery Regt., and an armored detachment stationed at Ulan Bator from early Sept. to early Oct. 1938, as well as TB heavy bombers, in unknown numbers, 20 km. to the west. In addition Yano recorded: Bain Tumen, 603rd Rifle Regt. (6 Nov. 1938); about five km. west of Tamsag, main force of Soviet armored brigade (20 Nov.). These notes are excerpted from Yano's order-of-battle worksheets in "Shiryō" [61].

31. Imaoka, "Man-So-Mō" [11], p. 55. Additional data from Yano Mitsuji interview.

32. K. Ishida [19], p. 51. USSR, *History* [985], p. 345, gives a percentage of 34.7 for 1934; 52.5 for 1938.

33. Data as of 7 June 1938; Yano, "Shiryō" [61]. According to Outer Mongolian sources, 30 percent of the MPRA were Party members; about 50 percent, Revolutionary Youth, who provided several hundred policy-guidance personnel for political education. Kōain Mōkyō Renrakubu [91], pp. 70-72.

34. *Gaimō* [192], pp. 14, 15.

35. Maj. Front in Yano, "Shiryō" [61].

36. K. Ishida interview. Demographic data are amplified in Ishida's "An Outline of Outer Mongolia," *Contemporary Manchuria*, July 1939, vol. 3, no. 3, pp. 111, 113-14. Higuchi Kōyō spoke of a peacetime MPRA numbering some 30,000 men, but his figure of 130,000 for the maximum wartime force is preposterous; [246], vol. 1, p. 13.

37. Yano Mitsuji interview; *Gaimō* [192], pp. 17-22; Kōain Mōkyō Renrakubu [91], pp. 70-72; Imaoka, "Man-So-Mō" [11], p. 54.

38. For example, at division headquarters in Bain Tumen there were two Soviet commanders and one Soviet doctor; even in the regiments there was a Soviet adviser and one doctor. *Gaimō* [192], pp. 17-18.

39. Ishida, Suzuki Yoshiyasu, Yano Mitsuji interviews; Maj. Front in Yano, "Shiryō" [61]; Bimba [178].

40. Ten km., according to press reports; *Gaimō* [192], p. 17. Higuchi Kōyō [246], pp. 11-12, says the Russians established a deserted belt 30 km. deep to prevent Outer Mongol defections to the "paradise" of Manchukuo. Population density in the Hulun Buir area was very low to begin with—o.8 per sq. km. according to MPR data; Yano, "Soto" [62].

41. *Gaimō* [192], pp. 17, 18.

42. Kōain Mōkyō Renrakubu [91], p. 71.

43. Yano, "Shiryō" [61].

44. Wu, Yano Mitsuji interviews.

45. The Chū-Mō-gun was later placed under control of the North China Expeditionary Forces. Shimanuki interview. The seesaw effect on the regime is discerned in an American correspondent's report from Hankow; *New York Times*, 18 July 1938, p. 1.

46. T. Matsumura interview.

47. K. Ishida [301], p. 182.

48. Yano, "Shiryō" [61].

49. Bimba [178], p. 42.

50. H. Satō [501], chap. 7/G.

51. Danzan Lodana, who had been MPRA operations section chief; a favorite of Demid and a follower of Gendun.

52. Correspondence with Yabe.

53. Amar, 53 when he died, was an old revolutionary; he had once starred, together with Gendun, in concluding the Soviet-MPR mutual assistance pact; Ishida interview. Soviet Major Front, however, was unimpressed by Amar: "The present MPR premier is very small-minded and incapable, and has an extreme fear of the USSR." Yano, "Shiryō" [61]. Also see Dupuy et al. [716A], p. 426.

54. Ishida [301], pp. 183-84; italics added. Also see Shirendyb et al., eds. [919], pp. 339, 809, 820.

55. Shishkin [920], pp. 569, 572. Chronology explained to me in Ishida interview. A Manchukuo foreign ministry official told an American diplomat in Hsinking on 31 May 1939 that the Nomonhan Incident was thought to be related to "Outer Mongolian policies and aspirations," not to a critical development in Soviet-Japanese relations; Langdon (Mukden) to Secretary of State, no. 365, 1 June 1939 (National Archives file 761.9315 Manchuria/118; NARS [980]).

56. Ōgoshi interview.

57. Imaoka, "Man-So-Mō" [11], pp. 45-46. There had also been a small affair near Heights 768 northeast of Manchouli on 28 June 1936, when four Japanese horsemen were seized by two Soviet cavalry platoons. *Shōwa jūichinen* [528], pp. 31-33.

58. The report [112] was transmitted on 26 Dec. 1938 (T-782, F-18732-40).

59. For details of the punishments meted out at various IJA levels, see chap. 13.

60. Imaoka interview.

61. M. Watanabe [607], p. 64.

62. Ōgoshi interview.

63. *Soviet Monitor*, 25 Oct. 1946, citing Choibalsan, in Friters, *Outer Mongolia* [730], p. 294; "On the Provocative Attack of the Japanese in the Nomongan Area in 1939," Red Army General Staff, Military History Dept. (12 Mar. 1946), IMTFE, *Transcript* [777], 16 Oct. 1946, p. 7846.

64. Imaoka, "Man-So-Mō" [11], pp. 44-47, and "Nomonhan" [13], pp. 10-11. Of the 13 incidents listed in 1939, 12 involved firefights; the episode of 17 Jan. referred to the raping of lamaist nuns by MPRA soldiers at Dongor Obo.

65. Ishida interview. While Ishida's memory extends even to the name of the captured MPRA 1st lieutenant (Dashinima), two problems of reconstruction exist: first, the matter of dating the

border affrays; second, my inability to correlate Ishida's recollections specifically with the Kwantung Army tabulation of incidents, as presented by Imaoka (see preceding note).

66. Nyūmura interview.

67. *Shōwa jūyonnen* [533], p. 435.

68. Suzuki Yoshiyasu interview. But Suzuki asserts that as of April 1939 the small border incidents had not yet been reported to Kwantung Army headquarters. For details of the new 23rd Division, see chap. 14.

69. Kōtani interview.

70. Based on affidavit and examination of Maj. A. E. Bykov, in IMTFE, *Transcript* [777], 27 Jan. 1948, pp. 38361-68, 38373.

71. Stalin [931], p. 758. Ever since the Changkufeng Incident, Soviet leaders had been warning would-be aggressors of the precise arithmetic of "massive retaliation" that awaited them. On 6 Nov. 1938, Molotov said that "we shall answer any provocative attack . . . by the aggressors, whether in the East or West, with two blows for their one, three for their one. . . . Anyone who wants to be convinced of the strength . . . of our forces is welcome to try." Degras, ed. [710], vol. 3, pp. 308-9. In 1956, however, Nikita Khrushchev was to tell the 20th Party Congress that the Russians' prewar "bragging" and "positive statements were not based in all areas on concrete facts which would actually guarantee the immunity of our borders." *The Anatomy of Terror: Khrushchev's Revelations About Stalin's Regime* (Washington, D.C.: Public Affairs Press, 1956), p. 44.

72. Y. Nishihara interview.

CHAPTER 13

1. Imaoka interview.

2. The best of the new divisions, by IJA standards, was General Ogisu's 13th Division. Its numeral, curiously, was re-created from that of a division disbanded by Ugaki when he conducted his famous retrenchment as war minister in the 1920's.

3. The first of the new triangular divisions was the 26th, sent to join the expeditionary army in Inner Mongolia. The IJA war plan of 1936 had called for conversion of all ground divisions to a triangular basis, but there were still square divisions as late as 1941. New divisions were always triangular, however. Imaoka interview.

4. BBSS, *SS* [180], vol. 27, p. 166. American military intelligence first identified the 23rd Division at Hailar only in July 1939 during the Nomonhan Incident and never refined the dating; latest data as of 30 May 1945; [984], p. 60.

5. Respectively the 18th, 5th, and 12th division districts. Western Honshu (Chūgoku) was divided administratively into Okayama, Hiroshima, Yamaguchi, Shimane, and Tottori. While interviewees say there was no single division district in the homeland supporting the organization of the 23rd Division, the 12th Depot Division may have been the sponsor; JRD [965], *JSM* 11, part 3/B, p. 197.

6. JRD [965], *JSM* 11, part 3/B, pp. 198-203. Also see *Nihon kihei 80-nen shi* [80 Years' History of Japanese Cavalry], ed. Moegi-kai (Tokyo: Hara Shobō, 1983).

7. The personnel authorities in Tokyo noted that "appropriate measures" were being taken, in consonance with division commander Komatsubara's recommendation. For Komatsubara's report, see chap. 12, n. 58.

8. Evaluations of 23rd Division quality and biographical details based on composite of interviews with Shirai, Hashimoto, Inada, Shimanuki, Suzuki Yoshiyasu, S. Hara, N. Tanaka, N. Itō, Murata, Ishida, Sumi. Also see Tsuji [585], pp. 62-63; Yonemoto [623A], pp. 25-29; BBSS, *SS* [180], vol. 27, pp. 438-40.

9. Suzuki Yoshiyasu interview.

10. Details on the inner workings of the 23rd Division are based on interviews with Murata, Suzuki Yoshiyasu, S. Hara, Onozuka, N. Tanaka (commanding general's aide), Imaoka, and Inada. Also see JRD [965], *JSM* 11, part 3/B, chap. 4; K. Saitō [496], p. 58.

11. No words were uttered by His Majesty on this occasion. Suzuki Yoshiyasu interview.

12. According to Imaoka, the Kwantung Army's 1st, 2nd, 4th, and 7th divisions were all rated as "A-type"; the 23rd, as a "B-type" division, whose quality of men and of equipment was

chronically "next best." Sumi adds that triangular divisions are fine when the number of divisions is unlimited; but when there are few divisions, the square division gives greater depth— "just like a more highly capitalized business firm." (Interview.)

13. Tsuji [585], p. 62.
14. IMTFE, *Transcript* [777], 26 May 1947, pp. 23014-16.

CHAPTER 14

1. USSR, *History* [985], pp. 346-47.
2. According to Bergamini, twenty years after the war a 76-year-old IJA ex-general let slip "that in August of 1938 he had been put in charge of devising air-to-ground communications and given detailed maps of the terrain for the Nomonhan war with Russia." Subsequent insistence by the aged general that he had meant 1939, not 1938, did not shake Bergamini's conviction that the Nomonhan Incident had been plotted by the Japanese army the year before the fighting broke out. "Strike-North elements in the Kwantung Army," Bergamini convinced himself, had become persuaded in 1939 "that Hirohito was finally fulfilling his vague promise that Japan would attack Russia when the proper opportunity arrived. Well-prepared staff plans emanating from Tokyo reassured even skeptics that the moment had come." Bergamini sees a telling connection in the fact that young Prince Higashikuni was serving as an artillery lieutenant in the fighting at Nomonhan. The prince was supposedly "under the tutelage" of two officers (Yamagata and Azuma) who "had been the last two aides-de-camp of Prince Asaka, Hirohito's limping uncle who had raped Nanking." Bergamini [640], pp. 23, 704.
3. Harada Kumao [225], vol. 7, pp. 298-99 (23 Feb. 1939). Nezu retails and embellishes the story ([430], p. 204). Also see Inada Masaji's account in *Taiheiyō sensō gen'inron* [550], p. 64.
4. Suzuki Yoshiyasu interview.
5. The full text of Operations Order No. 1488 will be found in JRD [965], *JSM* 11, part 1, pp. 99-102. Also see *ibid.*, pp. 86-87; Tsuji [585], pp. 46-47; BBSS, *SS* [180], vol. 27, pp. 423-27.
6. Based on JRD [965], *JSM* 11, part 1, pp. 87-88. Also see Tsuji [585], pp. 45-46, 48-49. For reservations expressed openly at the time by the Third Army commander, Lt. Gen. Tada Hayao (Shun) (the former AGS deputy chief), see Sawada [507A], pp. 21-22.
7. *hone o hirou*: literally, to gather the ashes after cremation; i.e., to look to a person's affairs when he is dead. See Hayashi Katsuya [238], p. 173.
8. *TSM* [549], vol. 4, part 1, p. 96; Tsunoda, introduction to *GSS* [205], vol. 10, p. xlvi.
9. Y. Nishihara, Imaoka interviews; Tsuji [585], p. 48. Tsunoda Jun identifies Arao Okikatsu and Shimamura Noriyasu as AGS Operations Section officers who personally considered the Kwantung Army guidelines to be appropriate; *GSS* [205], vol. 10, p. xlvii.
10. Inada, I. Hata interviews.
11. Katakura interview.
12. IMTFE, *Transcript* [777], 16 Oct. 1946, p. 7846; Kirk (Moscow) to Secretary of State, 17 Mar. 1939, citing press of preceding day, *FRUS* [974], *1939*, vol. 3, p. 17.
13. Suzuki Yoshiyasu interview.
14. K. Saitō [496], p. 56.
15. M. Watanabe [607], pp. 64-65; *Shōwa jūyonnen no kokusai jōsei* [533], p. 435; *Manshūkoku gensei* [375], 1941, p. 260; JRD [952], *JSM* 4, p. 70; Imaoka, "Nomonhan" [13], p. 12. For detailed discussion of the historical and linguistic derivations of the word Nomonhan, see Kitagawa [341], pp. 104-17; Higuchi Kōyō [246], vol. 1, pp. 18-23.
16. *Manshūkoku gensei* [375], 1941, p. 260; M. Watanabe [607], pp. 65-66; Imaoka, "Nomonhan" [13], pp. 12-13.
17. This officer (whose MPRA rank is given as junior lieutenant) could very well be the Outer Mongolian second lieutenant referred to by Saitō in his article cited in n. 14 above.
18. Based upon affidavit (6 Dec. 1946) and oral examination of Maj. Puntsugin Chogdan, IMTFE, *Transcript* [777], 29 Jan. 1948, pp. 38533-36, and 30 Jan. 1948, pp. 38562-72.
19. Affidavit of Maj. A. E. Bykov, who had been a senior lieutenant in 1939; IMTFE, *Transcript* [777], 27 Jan. 1948, p. 38364. The Japanese-Manchukuoan cavalry numbered more than

200, said Bykov; they fought their way 15-18 km. into Mongolian-claimed territory before being evicted.

20. Suzuki Yoshiyasu interview. Suzuki remembered Green Heights (south of the Holsten, in the Noro Heights area) as the Russians' own point of frontier delimitation, but Soviet army maps show the nearest boundary lying still another 10 km. to the northeast of Green. See JRD [965], *JSM* 11, part 3/C, p. 395, based on a map in Shishkin [920]. For Yokoi's testimony, see IMTFE, *Transcript* [777], 9 June 1947, pp. 38856-57; for Ogisu's, IMTFE, *Transcript* [777], 26 May 1947, pp. 23029-30.

21. Komatsubara [25], 17 May. Also see n. 35 below.

22. Representative sources for the Soviet-MPRA version include USSR, *Far East* [986], pp. 52-53; Red Army General Staff, History Department, "On the Provocative Attack of the Japanese in the Nomongan Area in 1939" (12 Mar. 1946), IMTFE, *Transcript* [777], 16 Oct. 1946, p. 7847; and Maj. A. E. Bykov's affidavit, IMTFE, *Transcript* [777], 27 Jan. 1948, pp. 38363-64. The Hattori version is presented in IMTFE, *Transcript* [777], 26 May 1947, pp. 23016-22; and JRD [965], *JSM* 11, part 3/B, pp. 215-17; for Tsuji account, see [585], pp. 66-67. Shimanuki (interview) agrees. A vehement Japanese critic of the Kwantung Army is Hayashi Katsuya; see his "Kaisetsu" [238], pp. 171-72. A balanced Japanese account will be found in *TSM* [549], vol. 4, pp. 95, 378. Also Imaoka, "Nomonhan" [13], pp. 12-15; Suzuki Yoshiyasu, Murata interviews.

23. JRD [965], *JSM* 11, part 3/B, pp. 217-18; Tsuji [585], pp. 67-68; *TSM* [549], vol. 4, p. 95.

24. Langdon (Mukden) to Secretary of State, no. 365, 1 June 1939 (National Archives file 761.9315 Manchuria/118; NARS [980]); *New York Times*, 1 June 1939; Capt. E. H. F. Svensson, Jr., Military Attaché, Tokyo, Report No. 9900, 21 Sept. 1939, G-2 Reports/6920 (National Archives G-2 M/A file; NARS [980]). When the U.S. Department of State published the records, 16 years later, it released no reports on the Nomonhan affair prior to 26 July, as "they were lacking in detailed, authentic information." The cable of the 26th from Chargé Dooman to the Secretary of State noted the kind of information reported by Capt. Svensson. See *FRUS* [974], *1939*, vol. 3, p. 46.

25. Manchukuoan army soldiers in Hailar numbered less than 1,900; their advanced forces in the border zone did not exceed 300 men. See Tsuji [585], p. 65.

26. Komatsubara Hq., Radio Message No. 194-1-5, transmitted from Hailar, 2 P.M., 13 May 1939; received at Hsinking, 2:25 P.M. See GSS [205], vol. 10, p. 108; JRD [965], *JSM* 11, part 3/B, pp. 215-16; Tsuji [585], pp. 66-67. Discussion of the air force problem derives from interviews with K. Matsumura, Giga, Miyoshi, Murata, Suzuki Yoshiyasu, and Imaoka. Murata and Imaoka think the sequence of events was coincidental, as more than the Matsumura unit was involved in the Kwantung Army's decision. Also see chap. 15, n. 12.

27. Kwantung Army, Operations Order No. 1496, 5 P.M., 13 May; recipients to include AGS chief. GSS [205], vol. 10, p. 108; JRD [965], *JSM* 11, part 3/B, pp. 217-19. The light bombers were actually Type 94 reconnaissance planes; JRD [952], *JSM* 4, p. 65, n. 2.

28. Imaoka, "Nomonhan" [13], pp. 17-18, and interview.

29. Interview with Hara Seiroku (Zenshirō after the Second World War). He remained with the 23rd Division from May through early August, when he returned to the Kwantung Army.

30. Tsuji, [585], pp. 75-77.

31. Murata, N. Itō, Suemori, and Inada interviews.

32. Inada, interview and writings.

33. AGS Message No. 323, AGS deputy, transmitted 12:15 A.M., 14 May; received 1:50 A.M.: GSS [205], vol. 10, p. 108.

34. Tsuji [585], pp. 78-79; JRD [965], *JSM* 11, part 3/B, pp. 220-21; BBSS, *SS* [180], vol. 27, pp. 441-43; BBSS, *SS* [181], vol. 53, p. 192.

35. Komatsubara [25], 16-17 May. From these entries we also learn when Azuma returned to headquarters. But Komatsubara now admitted that the original information on incursion by 700 MPRA soldiers was in error; hostile parties numbered between 30 and 50 men in general. Intelligence concerning enemy retreat on the night of 14 May was doubtful. As for air intrusions, reports of 100 to 150 enemy planes were exaggerated.

36. Based on affidavit (6 Dec. 1946) and oral examination of Maj. Puntsugin Chogdan, IMTFE, *Transcript* [777], 29 Jan. 1948, pp. 38534-36, and 30 Jan. 1948, pp. 38568-73; affidavit and examination of A. E. Bykov, 27 Jan. 1948, pp. 38364-65; memorandum of Red Army General Staff, Military History Dept. (12 Mar. 1946), presented on 16 Oct. 1946, pp. 7846-47.

37. In interviews, fighter group commander Matsumura stated that he never heard about the light bombers attacking across the Halha, and General Giga added that "of course" border crossing was prohibited by him.

CHAPTER 15

1. Imaoka, "Nomonhan" [13], pp. 18-19; BBSS, *SS* [180], vol. 27, pp. 442-43.

2. 23rd Division, Operations Order No. A-35, 4 P.M., 21 May: 64th Inf. Regt. [114], pp. 168-72; BBSS, *SS* [180], vol. 27, pp. 443-44; *SSNT* [535], vol. 25, p. 254. In addition to his IJA forces, Yamagata was to maintain contact with about 450 Manchukuoan troops in the area. (See Table 15.1.) Azuma actually possessed only one Type 92 heavy armored car (*jūsōkōsha*) in the underequipped tankette company. BBSS, *SS* [180], vol. 27, p. 444; *SSNT* [535], vol. 25, p. 269. Also see note 93 below.

3. Imaoka, "Nomonhan" [13], pp. 19-20; BBSS, *SS* [180], vol. 27, pp. 443-44; M. Watanabe [607], pp. 66-67.

4. Notes of 2nd Lt. Oshiumi Nōsuke, a 1st Machine Gun Co. platoon leader in the 64th Inf. Regt. [BBSS Archives].

5. Ouchi's opinion was requested. Kwantung Army, Operations Message No. 777, 21 May, prepared by Hattori: *GSS* [205], vol. 10, pp. 108-9; BBSS, *SS* [180], vol. 27, p. 445.

6. Kwantung Army, Operations Message No. 242, 21 May, Ōuchi to Komatsubara: *GSS* [205], vol. 10, p. 109; BBSS, *SS* [180], vol. 27, pp. 445-46; JRD [965], *JSM* 11, part 3/B, pp. 223-24.

7. Y. Nishihara interview.

8. Tsuji [585], p. 82; S. Hara interview. Also see para. 1 of Kwantung Army, Operations Message No. 254, 24 May; *GSS* [205], vol. 10, p. 110.

9. K. Matsumura interview; BBSS, *SS* [181], vol. 53, pp. 194-96; [180], vol. 27, pp. 462-63; Yoshimitsu [627], pp. 147-48; Higuchi Kōyō [246], vol. 1, pp. 5-6. In Washington, D.C., First Secretary Kase delivered a thin informational memorandum to the State Department on 24 June dealing with the Nomonhan Incident. (National Archives file 761.9315 Manchuria/104; NARS [980].)

10. Affidavit of MPRA Maj. Puntsugin Chogdan, IMTFE, *Transcript* [777], 29 Jan. 1948, p. 38536.

11. Kwantung Army, Operations Message No. 242, 21 May, Ōuchi to Komatsubara, para. 3: *GSS* [205], vol. 10, p. 109; BBSS, *SS* [180], vol. 27, pp. 443, 446.

12. 23rd Div., Operations Order No. A-40, 12 M., 24 May: BBSS, *SS* [180], vol. 27, p. 445; 64th Inf. Regt. [114], pp. 173-75.

13. BBSS, *SS* [180], vol. 27, p. 446.

14. Kwantung Army, Operations Message No. 249, 9:40 P.M., 23 May, to AGS chief from Ueda, prepared by Tsuji: *GSS* [205], vol. 10, p. 109; BBSS, *SS* [180], vol. 27, p. 447. Also see Tsuji [585], pp. 82-83.

15. Kwantung Army, Operations Message No. 254, 24 May, Kwantung Army Operations Section chief to AGS 2nd Section chief, draft prepared by Tsuji; *GSS* [205], vol. 10, p. 110.

16. AGS Message No. 491, from AGS deputy to Kwantung Army chief of staff, transmitted 11 A.M., 24 May, received 12:55 P.M.: *GSS* [205], vol. 10, p. 110; BBSS, *SS* [180], vol. 27, p. 447.

17. BBSS, *SS* [180], vol. 27, p. 447.

18. BBSS, *SS* [181], vol. 53, pp. 198-99; [180], vol. 27, p. 463; Komatsubara [25], 27, 28 May; Kira interview.

19. 23rd Div., Operations Order No. A-46, transmitted 6 P.M., 26 May (Hailar), received 6 P.M., 27 May (Kanchuerhmiao): 64th Inf. Regt. [114], pp. 176-77; BBSS, *SS* [180], vol. 27, p. 448.

20. Yamagata Detachment, Operations Order No. 14, 9 A.M., 27 May (Kanchuerhmiao):

64th Inf. Regt. [114], pp. 65-77; BBSS, *SS* [180], vol. 27, pp. 448-50. For Azuma's operations order issued at 11 P.M. on 26 May at Amukulang, see 23rd Div. Recon. Regt. [122], p. 4. Also see JRD [965], *JSM* 11, part 3/B, p. 227; [952], *JSM* 4, p. 70.

21. 64th Inf. Regt. [114], p. 68; BBSS, *SS* [180], vol. 27, p. 449.

22. Y. Nishihara interview; Tsuji [585], pp. 84-85. K. Saitō [496], p. 57, includes an attractive vignette of Azuma's farewell.

23. BBSS, *SS* [180], vol. 27, pp. 447, 449-50.

24. The columns were able to move 12 km. without headlights during the night of 27/28 May because the moon was bright. Truck-borne troops needed grenades and antitank mines to cope with armor, and grenade launchers for use against enemy forces dug in behind clay or mud walls. See transport regiment commander Midorikawa's report to division commander; Komatsubara [25], 6 June. One of Azuma's motorized platoons was delayed by traction problems on 27/28 May; 23rd Div. Recon. Regt. [122], p. 7.

25. The reconstruction of the events of the Azuma operation is derived mainly from 23rd Div. Recon. Regt. [122] and 64th Inf. Regt. [114]. Also see Komatsubara diary entries [25] for 28-31 May and 9 June, the last containing the best account by an individual—Major Okamoto; Nomonhan-kai, *Nomonhan* [40], various vols.; BBSS, *SS* [180], vol. 27, pp. 451-54; Imaoka, "Nomonhan" [13]; *SSNT* [535], vol. 25, pp. 255-98; Higuchi Kōyō [246], vol. 1, pp. 38-44, 47-48; K. Saitō [496], p. 58. Also interviews with Y. Nishihara and Imaoka. In general, only supplementary details are cited individually in the next notes.

26. 64th Inf. Regt. [114], p. 94.

27. Satō Ryōhei in *Nomonhan* [40], vol. 2, pp. 31-33.

28. BBSS, *SS* [180], vol. 27, p. 454, citing Komatsubara [25]; *SSNT* [535], vol. 25, pp. 287-88 (Onizuka Hatsuyoshi).

29. *SSNT* [535], vol. 25, pp. 288-89 (R. Satō).

30. *Ibid.*, pp. 291, 305 (Tabata Kihachirō, Furukawa Tsuneshi).

31. 23rd Div. Recon. Regt. [122]; BBSS, *SS* [180], vol. 27, p. 454.

32. *SSNT* [535], vol. 25, p. 293 (R. Satō).

33. *Ibid.*, p. 295 (Onizuka).

34. *Ibid.*, p. 297.

35. 23rd Div. Recon. Regt. [122]; 64th Inf. Regt. [114], pp. 125-26; R. Satō in *Nomonhan* [40], vol. 3, pp. 60-62; *SSNT* [535], vol. 25, pp. 296-97 (Tabata, Onizuka). For Azuma's poignant three last testaments of 24 May—addressed to his men, to General Komatsubara, and to his wife Seiko and three daughters—see *Nomonhan* [40], vol. 1, p. 21; and *SSNT* [535], vol. 25, pp. 298-99 (Onizuka). Komatsubara recorded his copy in his diary entry [25] for 3 June. Also see BBSS, *SS* [180], vol. 27, p. 454.

36. *SSNT* [535], vol. 25, pp. 296-97 (Tabata, Onizuka); 64th Inf. Regt. [114], p. 126. Also see R. Satō in *Nomonhan* [40], vol. 4, pp. 84-87.

37. Sources for reconstruction of the Yamagata detachment's infantry combat operations include 64th Inf. Regt. [114]; Komatsubara [25]; Tsuji [585]; Nomonhan-kai, *Nomonhan* [40], various volumes; interviews with Murata, N. Itō, Y. Nishihara, and Imaoka; BBSS, *SS* [180], vol. 27, pp. 455-61; Imaoka, "Nomonhan" [13]; *SSNT* [535], vol. 25, pp. 255-66, 280-82. In general, only supplementary details are cited individually in the next notes.

38. 64th Inf. Regt. [114], pp. 95-96.

39. See Makiyama Shigenobu in *Nomonhan* [40], vol. 2, pp. 37-39; *SSNT* [535], vol. 25, pp. 254-56, 260-61, 263-64.

40. BBSS, *SS* [180], vol. 27, p. 458, citing Shimanuki Takeharu.

41. 64th Inf. Regt. [114], pp. 85-89.

42. 64th Inf. Regt. [114], pp. 89, 94-95; R. Satō in *Nomonhan* [40], vol. 2, pp. 31-33; *SSNT* [535], vol. 25, pp. 266-67 (R. Satō).

43. 64th Inf. Regt. [114], pp. 90-91.

44. I have attempted to reconcile the recollections of N. Itō (interview) with after-action annals of the IJA infantry (64th Inf. Regt. [114], p. 88). The hour is taken from the infantry records; Itō thought the episode took place before noon.

45. 64th Inf. Regt. [114], pp. 104-8.

46. *Ibid.*, pp. 108-10.

47. Information on the Yuya, Takahashi, and Nakano teams is derived from 64th Inf. Regt. [114], pp. 110-14; Oshiumi notes [BBSS Archives]; BBSS, *SS* [180], vol. 27, p. 459; Komatsubara [25], 9 June, citing Major Okamoto. Apparently blurring the actions of the Yuya and Nakano teams, Higuchi Kōyō writes that two or three men survived, after wondrous adventures, from the officer and eight men originally aboard an ammunition truck burned by the Japanese themselves; [246], vol. 1, pp. 31-37.

48. Information on the IJA secondary maneuvers is derived from 64th Inf. Regt. [114], pp. 99-103; BBSS, *SS* [180], vol. 27, p. 458.

49. Yamagata Detachment Order, 5 A.M., 28 May, at a point about 1,000 meters northwest of Heights 737; 64th Inf. Regt. [114], pp. 82-84.

50. BBSS, *SS* [180], vol. 27, p. 457; *SSNT* [535], vol. 25, pp. 264-65.

51. 23rd Div., Operations Order No. 48, 8 P.M., 28 May, received by radio, in gist, at 12:30 A.M., 29 May, as Komatsubara Hq. Message No. 257, and received in full, by communications tube, after 10 A.M., 29 May: 64th Inf. Regt. [114], pp. 178-82; BBSS, *SS* [180], vol. 27, p. 460. Also see Komatsubara [25], 28-29 May; Kwantung Army, Operations Message No. 264, from chief of staff to AGS deputy, 11:40 A.M., 29 May, prepared by Tsuji, in *GSS* [205], vol. 10, p. 110.

52. 64th Inf. Regt. [114], pp. 114-16.

53. *Ibid.*, pp. 118-20.

54. *Ibid.*, p. 120. For firsthand information on the detachment's signal problems, see *SSNT* [535], vol. 25, p. 265 (Furukawa).

55. Oshiumi notes [BBSS Archives].

56. Komatsubara [25], 30 May; Kwantung Army, Operations Message No. 264, from chief of staff to AGS deputy, 11:40 A.M., 29 May, prepared by Tsuji, in *GSS* [205], vol. 10, p. 110. Tsuji says ([585], p. 91) that in two days the enemy suffered 100 casualties and lost five armored cars and about 10 light tanks.

57. Komatsubara Hq. Message No. 270, received between 6:30 and 7 P.M., 29 May: 64th Inf. Regt. [114], pp. 122-23; Komatsubara [25], 30 May; BBSS, *SS* [180], vol. 27, p. 460. Also see Komatsubara Hq. Message No. 274, transmitted 10 P.M., 29 May, received 4 A.M., 30 May, regarding dispatch of elements of 71st Inf. Regt. from Hailar; 64th Inf. Regt. [114], p. 185.

58. 64th Inf. Regt. [114], pp. 122-23, 127.

59. Oshiumi notes [BBSS Archives]. Also see BBSS, *SS* [180], vol. 27, p. 459.

60. *SSNT* [535], vol. 25, p. 295 (Onizuka).

61. 64th Inf. Regt. [114], p. 123.

62. Murata interview.

63. N. Itō, Murata interviews.

64. Furukawa Tsuneshi in *Nomonhan* [40], vol. 11, pp. 28-29; *SSNT* [535], vol. 25, pp. 302-4 (Furukawa).

65. BBSS, *SS* [180], vol. 27, pp. 460-61; Komatsubara [25].

66. The preceding account of the events of 29/30 May incorporates and attempts to reconcile information from the following versions: Tsuji [585], pp. 84-91; Makiyama in *Nomonhan* [40], vol. 3, pp. 44-46; *SSNT* [535], vol. 25, pp. 306-7 (Makiyama); JRD [965], JSM 11, part 3/B, pp. 228-31; Komatsubara [25]. Also N. Itō, Murata interviews; BBSS, *SS* [180], vol. 27, p. 461; K. Saitō [496], pp. 54-55.

67. 64th Inf. Regt. [114], pp. 124-25.

68. BBSS, *SS* [180], vol. 27, p. 459; Komatsubara [25].

69. 64th Inf. Regt. [114], pp. 127-33. At 6 A.M. on 31 May, Yamagata learned from Komatsubara Hq. Message No. 293 that among the truck companies due to reach the battlefront that day were ten trucks containing soft drinks and sweets. *Ibid.*, p. 188.

70. Komatsubara Hq. Message No. 273, received 5:10 A.M., 30 May; 64th Inf. Regt. [114], p. 187.

71. Yamagata Detachment, Operations Order No. 17, 7 P.M., 30 May; 64th Inf. Regt. [114], pp. 138-39.

72. *SSNT* [535], vol. 25, p. 310. Also see BBSS, *SS* [180], vol. 27, p. 460.

73. 64th Inf. Regt. [114], pp. 140-41.

74. Gist of 23rd Division order delivered orally by Murata at 9:40 A.M., 31 May: 64th Inf. Regt. [114], pp. 143, 183-84; BBSS, *SS* [180], vol. 27, p. 461.

75. 64th Inf. Regt. [114], pp. 143, 148. Higuchi Kōyō mentions IJAF attacks on enemy artillery positions on the Halha shore; [246], vol. 1, p. 49.

76. Yamagata Detachment, Operations Order No. 18, 3 A.M., 31 May; 64th Inf. Regt. [114], pp. 144-47.

77. BBSS, *SS* [180], vol. 27, p. 461; 64th Inf. Regt. [114], p. 153. For Yamagata Detachment, Operations Order No. 19, 4 P.M., 31 May, see 64th Inf. Regt. [114], pp. 148-52. Also see Tsuji [585], p. 92; JRD [965], *JSM* 11, part 3/B, p. 231.

78. 64th Inf. Regt. [114], pp. 144, 154; Oshiumi notes [BBSS Archives].

79. BBSS, *SS* [180], vol. 27, p. 461; 64th Inf. Regt. [114], pp. 154, 189; *SSNT* [535], vol. 25, p. 312.

80. Komatsubara [25], 1-3, 8 June; BBSS, *SS* [180], vol. 27, p. 461.

81. Kwantung Army, Operations Message No. 264, from chief of staff to AGS deputy, 11:40 A.M., 29 May, prepared by Tsuji; Operations Message No. 901, from chief of staff to AGS deputy and vice minister of war, 30 May, drafted by Hattori: *GSS* [205], vol. 10, pp. 110-11. Supplemented by Komatsubara [25], 30 May. Also see JRD [965], *JSM* 11, part 3/B, p. 227; [952], *JSM* 4, p. 70; *SSNT* [535], vol. 25, p. 316.

82. Komatsubara [25], 29 May. Also see BBSS, *SS* [180], vol. 27, p. 460.

83. AGS Message No. 547, from AGS deputy to Kwantung Army chief of staff, dispatched 4:50 P.M., 30 May, received 10:35 P.M.; *GSS* [205], vol. 10, p. 111. Also see BBSS, *SS* [180], vol. 27, p. 467; Tsuji [585], p. 94.

84. The Kwantung Army's comment on the High Command's tacit acceptance of the border guidelines is found in Kantōgun [99], reproduced in *GSS* [205], vol. 10, pp. 72-73.

85. Kwantung Army, Operations Message No. 258, from chief of staff to AGS deputy, 2:25 P.M., 31 May, prepared by Hattori: BBSS, *SS* [180], vol. 27, p. 467; *GSS* [205], vol. 10, pp. 111-12.

86. The breakdown of IJAF claims for 28 May was six of nine I-15 and I-16 fighters downed in one encounter; 36 of "several dozen" I-15's and I-16's in another. K. Matsumura, Kira interviews; BBSS, *SS* [180], vol. 27, p. 463; [181], vol. 53, p. 199. Komatsubara's diary entry for 28 May [25] records the loss of one friendly plane; this was admitted to the press in a Kwantung Army communiqué and in Tokyo on 29 May. See Merrell (Mukden) to Secretary of State, no. 168, 31 May (National Archives file 761.9315 Manchuria/117; NARS [980]); and *New York Times*, 30 May. The admission is not repeated in official IJAF documentation; JRD [952], *JSM* 4, p. 70. The standard Japanese version is Yoshimitsu [627], pp. 148-49. News in the Russian capital was fragmentary and indirect; "Soviet quarters declined to confirm the reports" of fighting. *New York Times*, 30 May. From the U.S. embassy in Moscow, Grummon advised Washington of the Tass information from *Pravda*, 26 June, No. 338 (National Archives file 761.9315 Manchuria/105; NARS [980]).

87. BBSS, *SS* [180], vol. 27, pp. 462-64; Komatsubara [25], 31 May; "Nomonhan Incident," *The Manchuria Daily News* (Dairen), June 1939, pp. 6-9; Yoshimitsu [627], pp. 149-50; Higuchi Kōyō [246], vol. 1, pp. 24-25, 29; JRD [952], *JSM* 4, p. 70. One of the Soviet victims was a stray, shot down by a Japanese air patrol, probably on the 31st.

88. Komatsubara [25], 17, 18 June; K. Matsumura, Kira interviews. In his diary entry for 17 June, Komatsubara recorded details of the performance of Soviet I-15B biplane and I-16 monoplane fighters in combat against IJAF Type 95 (Kawasaki Ki-10) biplane and Type 97 (Nakajima Ki-27b) monoplane pursuit planes. Technical data from *Kiroku . . . sentoki* [339]; Francillon [728], pp. 86-89, 196-203; Green [744], pp. 66-69. Also see chap. 16, n. 4, below.

89. Kwantung Army, Operations Message No. 901, from chief of staff to AGS deputy and vice minister of war, 30 May; prepared by Hattori; *GSS* [205], vol. 10, pp. 110-11.

90. JRD [965], *JSM* 11, part 3/B, pp. 242-43.

91. Another 15 men were slightly wounded.

92. Komatsubara [25], 31 May, 8 June.

93. AGS Intelligence Report No. 14, 6 June [141]. As mentioned below, the Russians say they knocked out two Japanese armored vehicles. Probably surmising that the IJA reconnaissance regiment was at full strength—which it was not—Tsuji cites about 10 Japanese light armored vehicles (*keisōkōsha*) destroyed; [585], p. 91. For my figure of one IJA heavy armored car, see note 2 above.

94. AGS Intelligence Reports No. 11, 2 June, and No. 14, 6 June [141]. Tsuji [585], p. 91, gives differing figures; see note 56 above.

95. Murata, Suzuki Yoshiyasu interviews.

96. Oshiumi notes [BBSS Archives].

97. Nomura [455], pp. 57-78. Also see note 24 above.

98. Oshiumi notes [BBSS Archives].

99. Each of Azuma's subordinate officers who died in action with him—one warrant and seven commissioned officers—also received a one-rank posthumous promotion, according to the field diary of the 23rd Reconnaissance Regiment's depot unit (*rusu nisshi*) for 12 June–6 Oct. 1939 [BBSS Archives].

100. Oshiumi notes [BBSS Archives].

101. Suzuki Yoshiyasu, Murata, N. Itō, Y. Nishihara, Inada interviews; Tsuji [585], p. 92; JRD [965], *JSM* 11, part 3/B, p. 232.

102. Imaoka, "Nomonhan" [13], pp. 21-22; Tsuji [585], pp. 90, 92; JRD [965], *JSM* 11, part 3/B, pp. 231-32; Saitō Kōzō [496], p. 55; Murata, N. Itō, Suzuki Yoshiyasu, Y. Nishihara interviews.

103. Based on Imaoka's notes of the visit to the Kwantung Army, 4-9 June.

104. N. Itō, Suzuki Yoshiyasu, S. Hara, Shimanuki, Matsuoka, Y. Nishihara interviews; BBSS, *SS* [180], vol. 27, pp. 443, 447; Komatsubara [25], 9 June. Komatsubara also knew, as of 31 May, particulars of the MPRA 6th Cavalry (Tamsag) Division.

105. The following section is based on the affidavit and examination of Major Bykov, IMTFE, *Transcript* [777], 27 Jan. 1948, pp. 38365-68, 38370-74, 38381; the affidavit and examination of Maj. Puntsugin Chogdan, 30 Jan. 1948, pp. 38568-70; Grummon (Moscow) to Secretary of State, no. 338, 26 June 1939, citing Tass communiqué in *Pravda* (Blakeney Collection); Shishkin [920], pp. 573-78; JRD [965], *JSM* 11, part 3/B, pp. 237-39; USSR, *History* [985], p. 349. After the incident, Higuchi Kōyō estimated Soviet strength at 1,000 men and Outer Mongolian at another 1,000; [246], vol. 1, p. 24.

106. AGS Intelligence Report No. 13, 5 June [141].

107. See Coox, *Anatomy* [679], pp. 91-92, 204, 214, 261, 303. Also see note 86 above.

108. Maj. Frank B. Hayne, Acting Military Attaché, Moscow, Report No. 1548, 26 July. Also see Capt. R. B. Pape, Assistant Military Attaché, Tokyo, Report No. 9831, 3 July, G-2 Reports/6920; NARS [980].

109. Grummon (Moscow) to Secretary of State, no. 338, 26 June (National Archives file 761.9315 Manchuria/101); Merrell (Harbin) to Secretary of State, no. 168, 31 May (761.9315 Manchuria/117); NARS [980].

110. Langdon (Mukden) to Johnson (Peking), no. 372, 16 June (National Archives file 761.9315 Manchuria/119); NARS [980]. A transcript of D'Alton's often-ridiculous radio broadcast is found in "Nomonhan Incident," *The Manchuria Daily News* (Dairen), June 1939, pp. 19-24.

111. Hashimoto, N. Itō, Shimanuki, Katakura interviews; Kantōgun [99], in GSS [205], vol. 10, pp. 73-74. Also see Sawada [507A], pp. 22, 135, 148-49; BBSS, *SS* [180], vol. 27, p. 467.

112. Tsuji [585], p. 78. On the 25th anniversary of the outbreak of the Nomonhan Incident, I heard Shimanuki Takeharu say the identical thing during a retrospective television broadcast; NHK Educational TV, Channel 4, Tokyo, 11 May 1964.

CHAPTER 16

1. Cited in Erickson, *Soviet* [722], p. 517. Also see Grummon (Moscow) to Secretary of State, no. 282, 20; 1 June 1939 (National Archives file 861.00 SS/20; NARS [980]). Molotov had used similar language, "I must warn you that there is a limit to all patience," when he

lodged a protest with the Japanese ambassador in Moscow on 19 May; cited in USSR, *Far East* [986], p. 53.

2. Zhukov, *Memoirs* [1017], pp. 147-49.

3. Shishkin [920], pp. 576-78; Zhukov, *Memoirs* [1017], p. 149.

4. The Polikarpov I-16, a single-seat monoplane, was the world's first low-wing interceptor with a retractable undercarriage when it was accepted ca. 1935. Details of the improved model will be found in USSR, *Air Force* [990], pp. 8, 10, 392; and Green [744], pp. 161-65. Japanese pilots called the stubby, green-camouflaged I-16 "*abu*" (horsefly). The new Polikarpov I-153 was a biplane with a unique gull-type upper wing; hence its Russian nickname, "Chaika." Green [744], pp. 157-60, and USSR, *Air Force* [990], p. 392.

5. The "General Douglas" of the Spanish Civil War, Smushkevich became chief of the Red Air Force in Sept. 1939, after much-esteemed service in the Nomonhan Incident. Erickson calls him "a man who was essentially nothing more than an aviation brigade commander, although very brave. . . ." *Soviet* [722], p. 501. For Zhukov's accolades, see chap. 41 below.

6. AGS Intelligence Report No. 10, 1 June; No. 11, 2 June; No. 12, [3?] June; No. 13, 5 June; No. 14, 6 June; No. 15, 7 June; No. 17, 20 June [141].

7. Murata, Shimanuki, I. Hata interviews.

8. Kwantung Army, Operations Message No. 258, 2:35 P.M., 31 May, to AGS deputy from Kwantung Army chief of staff, prepared by Hattori; GSS [205], vol. 10, p. 111. Also see JRD [965], *JSM* 11, part 3/B, pp. 243-44; Tsuji [585], pp. 94-95. This message was in reply to AGS Message No. 547 of 30 May (see chap. 15, n. 83).

9. JRD [965], *JSM* 11, part 3/B, pp. 244-45, 247; Tsuji [585], p. 95; N. Itō interview. At the war games in Hsinking on 4-7 June, Terada stated that the Kwantung Army lacked (1) anti-fortification matériel such as flamethrowers, (2) small river ferry boats, (3) bridging equipment, (4) swamp-crossing matériel, (5) road-building equipment. Imaoka interview.

10. Testimony of Hashimoto Gun, AGS Operations Bureau chief, IMTFE, *Transcript* [777], 20 May 1947, pp. 22576-77, 22595-96; BBSS, *SS* [180], vol. 27, pp. 465-67.

11. The Manchukuoan forces would be made aware of the meaning of the concept of "sallying when a good opportunity arose"; Komatsubara [25], 11 June.

12. Imaoka, interview and "Nomonhan" [13], pp. 26-27; K. Matsumura interview. After the map exercises, Imaoka and the prince studied industrial installations in South Manchuria.

13. Morris of UP, cited in Lockhart to Secretary of State, Harbin via Peking, no. 16, 14 July (National Archives file 761.9315 Manchuria/124; NARS [980]); A. H. Steele of the *Chicago Daily News*, cited in Lockhart, No. 352, 17 July (761.9315 Manchuria/126; NARS [980]).

14. AGS Intelligence Report No. 17, 20 June [141].

15. The following enemy forces were involved: 300 cavalrymen, 34 armored cars and tanks (Buir, 17 June); 1,000 men, 50 tanks, and over 10 field guns (Buir, 19 June); 200 troops, five tanks, and six machine guns (Halhamiao, 19 June). Komatsubara [25], 18 June; AGS Intelligence Report No. 18, 21 June [141]. Information on reorganization and improvement of MPRA from AGS Report No. 19, 22 June [141].

16. Zhukov, *Memoirs* [1017], p. 150; AGS Intelligence Report No. 17, 20 June, and No. 18, 21 June [141]; Komatsubara [25], 18, 19 June; BBSS, *SS* [180], vol. 27, p. 468; K. Matsumura interview. Among many Japanese public sources, see Kwantung Army communiqué, 23 June, *Shōwa jūyonnen* [533], p. 440. Higuchi Kōyō retails two rumors: (1) In the raids on Amukulang, an I-16 fighter bore Japanese red-ball markings. [246], vol. 1, p. 51. (Also see chap. 18, n. 1 below.) (2) During the heavy bombing of the Chiangchunmiao vicinity on 24 (?) June, enemy planes "even inhumanely employed gas." *Ibid.*, pp. 51, 52.

17. Murata, Giga interviews.

18. Kantōgun [99], in GSS [205], vol. 10, p. 74; Tsuji [585], p. 96; JRD [965], *JSM* 11, part 3/B, p. 247.

19. Imaoka, interview and "Nomonhan" [13], pp. 28-31.

20. Kantōgun [99], in GSS [205], vol. 10, pp. 74-75; Tsuji [585], pp. 97-99; JRD [965], *JSM* 11, part 3/B, pp. 247-49.

21. Ambassador Craigie says the British possessed information that the Japanese AGS had

laid plans "for a single-handed war with Great Britain and that a powerful faction in the Army favoured war at that time on an issue in which American sympathies were not directly engaged." [699], p. 73.

22. I. Hata, Y. Nishihara, Inada interviews; Kantōgun [99], in GSS [205], p. 75; Tsuji [585], pp. 98-99; JRD [952], JSM 4, p. 66; JRD [965], JSM 11, part 3/B, pp. 248-50; BBSS, SS [180], vol. 27, p. 469; BBSS, SS [181], vol. 53, p. 208. Lt. Gen. Higuchi Kiichirō, AGS 2nd Bureau chief in 1938, is convinced, from having read a piece by Wang Ching-wei in *Chūka Nippō* for 22 July 1939, that the Russians had a long-standing commitment to assist Chiang Kai-shek and the Kuomintang regime by diverting Japanese military attention. This was as true of the Nomonhan as of the Changkufeng affair, writes Higuchi; [245], pp. 383-86.

23. BBSS, SS [180], vol. 27, pp. 469-70; BBSS, SS [181], vol. 53, p. 208; Kantōgun [99], in GSS [205], vol. 10, pp. 75, 112; Tsuji [585], pp. 100-101; JRD [965], JSM 11, part 3/B, pp. 250-54.

24. Tsuji [585], p. 101; Imaoka, "Nomonhan" [13], p. 37; JRD [965], JSM 11, part 3/B, pp. 254-56; Kantōgun [99], in GSS [205], pp. 75-76; BBSS, SS [180], vol. 27, pp. 470-71; BBSS, SS [181], vol. 53, p. 209.

25. Kwantung Army, Operations Order No. 1530, 9:40 P.M., 19 June, was prepared by Tsuji; GSS [205], vol. 10, pp. 113-15. Also see Tsuji [585], pp. 101-2; Kantōgun [99], in GSS [205], vol. 10, p. 76; BBSS, SS [180], vol. 27, pp. 470-71; BBSS, SS [181], vol. 53, p. 209; JRD [965], JSM 11, part 3/B, pp. 255-57.

26. Kwantung Army, Operations Order No. 1532, 2 P.M., 20 June; GSS [205], p. 116; Kantōgun [99], in GSS [205], vol. 10, pp. 76-77; BBSS, SS [180], vol. 27, pp. 471-75; BBSS, SS [181], vol. 53, p. 209; JRD [965], JSM 11, part 3/B, pp. 257-61; Noguchi, S. Hara, Y. Nishihara, Imaoka interviews. Initial instructions were wired to the units; officer couriers hand-carried the orders by air to Hailar. Noguchi stresses Tsuji's origination of the idea of using a mechanized detachment.

27. Tsuji [585], pp. 103, 105-6.

28. Kōtani interview. Also see chap. 17, n. 9.

29. Kantōgun [99], in GSS [205], vol. 10, pp. 92-93; AGS Intelligence Report No. 18, 21 June [141]; JRD [965], JSM 11, part 3/B, p. 262; I. Hata, Y. Nishihara, Imaoka, Takei interviews; Imaoka, "Nomonhan" [13], pp. 34-35; Tsuji [585], pp. 104-5.

30. Kantōgun [99], in GSS [205], vol. 10, p. 92; Yabe interview. Nationalist sources in Chungking insisted that the IJA command in China was seeking reinforcements from the Kwantung Army because of allegedly serious Japanese reverses in northern Hupeh. In this strained view, the Kwantung Army was fomenting or at least exaggerating the Nomonhan border trouble as an excuse for not releasing troops to the China theater; Durdin (Chungking), 31 May, in *New York Times*, 1 June 1939.

31. S. Hara, N. Itō, Y. Nishihara interviews.

32. Sumi, "Nihon" [542], pp. 11-19; JRD [965], JSM 11, part 3/B, pp. 308-9. But Sumi admitted that his regiment was reinforced with rapid-fire guns sufficient to equip another two regiments, since antitank combat was anticipated. (Interview.)

33. Kobayashi [24], 28 June; Komatsubara [25], 27 June; S. Hara interview.

34. N. Itō, S. Hara, N. Nishikawa, T. Hamada, Suzuki Yoshiyasu, Sumi, H. Tanaka interviews; Komatsubara [25], 1 July; Kobayashi [24], 27 June; Tsuji [585], pp. 105-6; 1st Bn., 64th Inf. Regt. [116], 28 June; 7th (Kimura) Co., 26th Inf. Regt. [105], 23-28 June; Sumi, *Jissen* [541], p. 5. On the third day of march, the 26th Regt. supplemented the 23rd Division's tasteless food caches by buying and slaughtering two small cows. (Sumi interview.) As noted in chap. 18, n. 1, the standard daily march rate of an IJA infantry division was 32 km. (Imaoka interview.)

35. Imaoka, "Nomonhan" [13], pp. 32-35; JRD [965], JSM 11, part 3/B, pp. 254, 261, 262.

CHAPTER 17

1. Shishkin [920], p. 579; Zhukov, *Memoirs* [1017], p. 150; Tass communiqué transmitted by Grummon (Moscow) to Secretary of State, no. 338, 26 June 1939 (National Archives file 761.9315 Manchuria/101; NARS [980]).

2. AGS Intelligence Report No. 20, 23 June, and No. 22, 25 June [141]; JRD [965], JSM 11,

part 3/B, pp. 263-64; Tsuji [585], p. 107; K. Matsumura, interview and writings; Kira, interview and writings; G. Nishihara interview. JRD [952], *JSM* 4, p. 70, provided the IJAF casualty data and the statistic of seven Japanese plane losses. Most other Japanese accounts mention no more than four IJAF planes lost; see Yoshimitsu [627], p. 152. Perhaps three Japanese planes crash-landed behind friendly lines; M. Watanabe [607], p. 70, mentions a master sergeant who walked back to base from his stricken plane.

3. Kira, G. Nishihara interviews. Higuchi Kōyō claims that fleeing enemy planes were so confused, they collided with each other and even fired at each other; [246], vol. 1, p. 52.

4. Although the indefatigable Tsuji says that he too reconnoitered Tamsag in a headquarters scout plane, he does not claim to have sighted any aircraft—only vehicle marks and presumable fuel storage facilities; [585], pp. 108-9.

5. Giga, Miyoshi interviews; *GSS* [205], vol. 10, pp. 82-83, 124; BBSS, *SS* [180], vol. 27, pp. 478-82; JRD [965], *JSM* 11, part 3/B, pp. 264-66; JRD [952], *JSM* 4, pp. 67, 70; Tsuji [585], pp. 107, 109; Imaoka, "Nomonhan" [13], pp. 41-43.

6. Tsuji [585], pp. 109-10; Kantōgun [99], in *GSS* [205], vol. 10, pp. 83, 124; Imaoka, "Nomonhan" [13], p. 60; JRD [965], *JSM* 11, part 3/B, pp. 266-67; Miyoshi, I. Hata interviews.

7. Shortly before the Nomonhan Incident, Katakura had occasion to scold Tsuji very sharply for being a "narrow-minded operations type." (Interview.) Also Iwakuro, Inada, Miyoshi interviews. The 2nd (1950) edition of Tsuji's *Nomonhan* [585], p. 111, carries the charge that Katakura "blabbed" to Iwakuro, as does Hattori's secret operational diary of 1939; Kantōgun [99], in *GSS* [205], vol. 10, p. 84. Hattori's record attributed the source of the Iwakuro story to Lt. Col. Arao Okikatsu at the end of August.

8. Iwakuro, Imaoka, Y. Nishihara, I. Hata interviews; Imaoka, "Nomonhan" [13], pp. 38-39.

9. Nishiura [447], pp. 87-88; Iwakuro, Nishiura interviews; Imaoka, interview and writings; Kantōgun [99], in *GSS* [205], vol. 10, pp. 92, 139; M. Itō, *Gunbatsu* [308A], vol. 3, pp. 148-49; Nezu [430], p. 205; JRD [965], *JSM* 11, part 3/B, pp. 319, 323. Orders to mobilize the artillery regiments in Chiba prefecture were issued on 26 June, after imperial approval was obtained on the 24th.

10. Miyashi interview.

11. AGS Radio Message No. 797, from AGS deputy to Kwantung Army chief of staff, dispatched 3:35 P.M., received 5:50 P.M., 24 June; *GSS* [205], vol. 10, pp. 84, 124. JRD [965], *JSM* 11, part 3/B, p. 267, gives the message number as 768. Also Tsuji [585], p. 111; Miyashi, Hashimoto, Inada interviews.

12. AGS Intelligence Report No. 22, 25 June; No. 23, 26 June; No. 24, 27 June; and No. 25, 28 June [141]. Miyoshi himself went on reconnaissance flights every other day. (Interview.)

13. AGS Intelligence Report No. 21, 24 June; No. 23, 26 June; No. 24, 27 June; and No. 25, 28 June [141]. JRD [952], *JSM* 4, p. 70, indicates that four IJAF aircraft and one pilot were lost on 23 June. Also see Yoshimitsu [627], pp. 152-53.

14. Shishkin [920], p. 579; Tass communiqué, transmitted by Grummon (Moscow) to Secretary of State, no. 338, 26 June (National Archives file 761.9315 Manchuria/102; NARS [980]); Zhukov, *Memoirs* [1017], p. 150. It is not clear what Zhukov means by saying that, after the defeat of the Japanese air force on 22 and 24 June, "the Japanese command began to withdraw its planes in a very haphazard manner."

15. AGS Intelligence Report No. 24, 27 June [141].

16. Miyashi interview.

17. Maintaining daily touch with a captain in Hailar, AGS Lieutenant Colonel Saitō was to phone Tokyo twice a day; notes of a telephone call between Saitō and Major Kōtani of AGS 5th Section, 3:44 P.M., 24 June [141].

18. Kwantung Army, Operations Message No. 333, from chief of 1st Section (Operations) to 2nd Air Division chief of staff, 7:30 [A.M.], 25 June; Kantōgun [99], in *GSS* [205], vol. 10, pp. 84, 124; JRD [965], *JSM* 11, part 3/B, p. 268; Tsuji [585], p. 111.

19. Inada, I. Hata, Y. Nishihara interviews; Imaoka, interview and "Nomonhan" [13], pp. 42-43.

20. Yoshimitsu [627], pp. 153-54; JRD [952], *JSM* 4, p. 70.

21. Shishkin [920], p. 579; Zhukov, *Memoirs* [1017], p. 150. The Tass communiqué was re-

ported from Moscow to the Secretary of State by Grummon in No. 343, 27 June (National Archives file 761.9315; Manchuria/102; NARS [980]). Two additional items deserve mention: (1) Maj. V. M. Zabaluyev, 70th Air Group commander, bailed out of his I-16 about 30 km. behind the Japanese lines on 26 June. He was rescued by his deputy, Maj. S. I. Gritsevets, who took him aboard his I-16 and escaped under Japanese ground fire. (2) A Japanese lieutenant from the 24th Air Group shot down one of three Tupolev SB-2 bombers which made their debut on 26 June. Sekigawa [915], no. 5, p. 250; Zhukov, *Memoirs* [1017], p. 163.

22. There is an unexpected discrepancy between survivors' estimates and the Kwantung Army data recorded by Tsuji [585], pp. 113-14, and JRD [965], *JSM* 11, part 3/B, pp. 271-73; the latter sources refer to 20 Fiat bombers, 27 Type 97 bombers, 10 light bombers, and about 80 fighters. One set of official records will be found in the more recent BBSS, *SS* [180], vol. 27, p. 484, which gives respective figures of 12 Fiat, 12 Type 97 bombers, six light bombers, 77 fighters, total 107; plus 12 scouts. The light bombers are listed as belonging to the 10th Air Group, but my interviewee Ishikawa uses the designation of 16th. The official IJAF record cites slightly different numbers: 12-9-9-74, total 104; BBSS, *SS* [181], vol. 53, p. 229; apparently used by Sekigawa [915], no. 5, p. 250. Interviewee Matsumura remembers a force of only 9-9-0-78, total 96, including no light bombers. My other interviewees were Shimono, U. Harada, Mikami.

23. After the war, Matsumura was told by an IJA repatriate from Siberia that 11th Air Group Leader Noguchi Yujirō had been seized by the Russians in 1945 and incarcerated as a "war criminal" for his alleged role in the Tamsag raid, although old Colonel Noguchi had not actually participated in it. At war's end, he was the Air Force School commandant in Manchuria. Noguchi died in detention.

24. Giga thinks it was during this raid that his operations officer, Lt. Col. Shimanuki Tadamasa, disappeared in a reconnaissance plane. (Interview.) As noted elsewhere, Shimanuki was actually lost on 3 July.

25. Tsuji [585], pp. 112-18; *SSNT* [535], vol. 26, pp. 98-100. The 1st Squadron commander in the 12th Heavy Bomber Group, to which Tsuji intimated he attached himself, does not think the Kwantung Army staff officer flew with his unit. Capt. Ōura Yoshikuma in *SSNT* [535], vol. 26, pp. 106-7.

26. K. Matsumura, Shimono, Mikami, U. Harada interviews; *SSNT* [535], vol. 26, pp. 104-5. For official data on the IJAF reconnaissance flights of 26 June, see BBSS, *SS* [181], vol. 53, p. 226.

27. K. Matsumura, Mikami, U. Harada, Ishikawa, Kira interviews; Tsuji [585], p. 117; *SSNT* [535], vol. 26, pp. 105, 108-15.

28. K. Matsumura, Kira interviews; Tsuji [585], p. 114.

29. K. Matsumura, Mikami, Kira, Miyashi interviews; Sekigawa [915], no. 5, p. 250; Yoshimitsu [627], p. 154; *SSNT* [535], vol. 26, p. 114. JRD [965], *JSM* 11, part 3/B, p. 274, states erroneously that plans for attacking Bain Tumen (as well as Madat) were suspended on the night of 27 June.

30. AGS Intelligence Report No. 24, 27 June [141].

31. These are the final, official figures from BBSS, *SS* [180], vol. 27, p. 484; BBSS, *SS* [181], vol. 53, pp. 233-34. Other Japanese tabulations range from 111 to, most often, 124. See Tsuji [585], p. 117; Yoshimitsu [627], p. 155; JRD [965], *JSM* 11, part 3/B, p. 273; JRD [952], *JSM* 4, p. 70; Sekigawa [915], no. 5, p. 250; Miyashi, K. Matsumura, Kira interviews. Capt. R. B. Pape, the U.S. assistant military attaché in Tokyo, summarized Japanese press accounts of the Tamsag raid and earlier air fighting in Report No. 9831, 3 July 1939, G-2 Reports/6920 (National Archives G-2 M/A file; NARS [980]). Some Japanese sources, either ignorant of the raids on MPR air bases or suppressing information on their existence, convey the impression that all the actions of 27 June were air-to-air. See Higuchi Kōyō [246], vol. 1, pp. 53-54. Even the classified AGS Intelligence Report No. 24 (see the preceding note) states that Tamsag was raided only after the IJAF strike force engaged some 200 enemy planes in a 30-minute battle over Lake Buir. For the same version, see M. Watanabe [607], pp. 71-72; *Shōwa jūyonnen* [533], p. 441.

32. Mikami claims the crew remained with the plane till it was repaired and recovered; but Sekigawa writes of a Type 97 heavy bomber which made an emergency landing near Tamsag

and was captured by enemy ground forces after the crew had been saved by another bomber which landed next to it. Capt. Uno Jūrō, Mikami's plane commander and 1st Squadron leader, confirms that the six men aboard the stricken aircraft were picked up by Lieutenant Sawairi's bomber. But enemy tanks were approaching and there was no time to burn the abandoned IJAF bomber. Mikami, Shimono interviews; Sekigawa [915], no. 5, p. 250; *SSNT* [535], vol. 26, p. 110. At least one scout plane did disappear, from the 1st Reconnaissance Squadron, 15th Air Group, according to Capt. Aoki Hideo, the squadron commander. *SSNT* [535], vol. 26, p. 104.

33. There are many small discrepancies among Japanese sources. Six IJAF planes may have been lost (JRD [952], *JSM* 4, p. 70) or seven lost and six returned crippled (Shimanuki interview; JRD [965], *JSM* 11, part 3/B, p. 274). Also Tsuji [585], p. 118; AGS Intelligence Report No. 24, 27 June, and Report No. 25, 28 June [141]; M. Watanabe [607], p. 74; Miyashi, Mikami, Shimono, K. Matsumura, Imaoka interviews.

34. There was no victory celebration, says Mikami, but he remembers having a drink that day with Wing Commander Shimono, who had been concerned because Mikami's plane was missing for a while. Mikami interview.

35. Kira, K. Matsumura, G. Nishihara, Giga interviews; Tsuji [585], p. 118; Higuchi Kōyō [246], vol. 1, pp. 53-54.

36. Shimono, K. Matsumura, Miyashi, Hanamoto, Morishita interviews.

37. Shishkin [920], p. 579; Grummon (Moscow) to Secretary of State, No. 338, 26 June 1939 (National Archives file 761.9315 Manchuria/101; NARS [980]). Nezu, confused by the geography, thinks that Tamsag lies east of the Russian Urals and that the raid was thus a direct challenge to the USSR; [430], p. 205.

38. AGS Intelligence Report No. 26, 29 June [141]. Vorozheikin identifies the 70th Air Regt. as attacked by 60 IJAF fighters, and the 22nd Air Regt. by 30 fighters; he admits that Bain Tumen was bombed. [184], p. 43.

39. Zhukov, *Memoirs* [1017], pp. 150-51.

40. Inada, Arao, I. Hata, Y. Nishihara interviews; Tsuji [585], p. 112. Also see "Haragei," *The East*, June 1974, vol. 10, no. 5, pp. 36-37.

41. Imaoka, "Nomonhan" [13], p. 45.

42. Itō, *Gunbatsu* [308A], vol. 3, p. 150. S. Hata interview, citing his diary entries for 22, 24, 29 June 1939; Inada, interviews and writings.

43. Inada, interviews and writings; Kōtani, Hashimoto, Arao interviews; JRD [965], *JSM* 11, part 3/B, pp. 268-69.

44. AGS Message No. 797, 27 June, transmitted 4:55 P.M., received 6:30 P.M., from AGS deputy to Kwantung Army chief of staff, by order of AGS chief; Kantōgun [99], in *GSS* [205], vol. 10, pp. 84, 125; JRD [965], *JSM* 11, part 3/B, p. 270; Tsuji [585], pp. 119-20.

45. Kwantung Army Message No. 339, 28 June, in reply to AGS Message No. 797, from Kwantung Army chief of staff to AGS deputy; Kantōgun [99], in *GSS* [205], vol. 10, pp. 84, 125; JRD [965], *JSM* 11, part 3/B, pp. 270-71; Tsuji [585], pp. 120-21.

46. Inada interview. Also see *SSNT* [535], vol. 26, pp. 126-30.

47. S. Hata interview, citing his diary entry for 29 June 1939. On the 30th, Hata learned from the AGS deputy that Kan'in had only mentioned to the Emperor that the army was "carefully considering" the matter of punishing the Kwantung Army commander; the deputy, however, knew what was afoot. S. Hata's diary entry for 30 June.

48. AGS Message No. 825, IGHQ Army Order No. 320, 29 June, transmitted 7:15 P.M., received 7:30 P.M., from AGS chief to Kwantung Army commander; Kantōgun [99], in *GSS* [205], vol. 10, pp. 84, 125; JRD [965], *JSM* 11, part 3/B, p. 275; Tsuji [585], p. 121.

49. AGS Message No. 826, IGHQ Army Directive No. 491, transmitted 7:15 P.M., received 7:30 P.M., 29 June, from AGS chief to Kwantung Army commander; Kantōgun [99], in *GSS* [205], vol. 10, pp. 84, 125-26; JRD [965], *JSM* 11, part 3/B, p. 275; Tsuji [585], p. 122.

50. AGS Message No. 827, transmitted 8:25 P.M., received 10:30 P.M., 29 June, from AGS deputy to Kwantung Army chief of staff; Kantōgun [99], in *GSS* [205], vol. 10, pp. 84, 126; Tsuji [585], pp. 122-23. JRD [965], *JSM* 11, part 3/B, pp. 276-77 is unreliable here.

51. Inada, Hashimoto interviews. Surprisingly, Hashimoto erred on this point in his affidavit of 1947; IMTFE, *Transcript* [777], 20 May 1947, pp. 22597-98.

52. Tsuji [585], pp. 121, 123.

53. With respect to Tsuji's famous temper, Katakura says he personally saw Tsuji knock down staff officer Shimoyama Takuma during one of their "awful fights"; Katakura interview. Other information from S. Hara, I. Hata, Miyashi, Y. Nishihara, Imaoka, Sugita interviews.

54. Inada, interviews and writings; I. Hata interview; Imaoka, "Nomonhan" [13], p. 45.

CHAPTER 18

1. On the afternoon of 22 June, three I-16's with "pink *hinomaru* markings" flew over the Kanchuerhmiao road, 40 km. southwest of Hailar, and observed IJA ground movements from as low as 700 meters, until chased away by Japanese planes. 1st Bn., 64th Inf. Regt. [116], 22 June. A Japanese infantry division was to move ordinarily at eight *ri* (20 miles or 32 km.) per day. Imaoka interview. Sumi's 26th Regiment marched at the rate of 7-12 *ri* a day for six days (132 miles or 210 km. total distance). Sumi, interview and *Jissen* [541], p. 5. Also see BBSS, *SS* [180], vol. 27, p. 490; and chap. 16, n. 34 above.

2. Kobayashi [24], 22, 23, 24 June 1939; Komatsubara [25], 23, 24, 27 June; AGS Intelligence Report No. 22, 25 June, and No. 24, 27 June [141]; Tsuji [585], p. 124; BBSS, *SS* [180], vol. 27, pp. 490-91; Maeda, H. Tanaka interviews; Nomura [455], p. 76.

3. AGS Intelligence Report No. 24, 27 June [141]. As early as 22 June, Komatsubara [25] recorded Harbin OSS intelligence (as of the preceding day) that Tarasov had recommended to Yakovlev that pressure be exerted on the Ardan [?] River area in order to check Japanese movement south to the Halha River line from Hailar.

4. Kwantung Army, Operations Order No. 12, 3 P.M., 25 June: GSS [205], vol. 10, pp. 117-18; Komatsubara [25], 26 June; Tsuji [585], pp. 124-25, 127; JRD [965], *JSM* 11, part 3/B, pp. 279-80; BBSS, *SS* [180], vol. 27, pp. 491-94; I. Saitō, S. Hara interviews. (Hara says he was merely an observer.) On 29 June, at about 9 P.M., an IJA officer patrol skirmished with an enemy force, including three tanks, some 20 km. southeast of Nomotsorin. One Japanese officer and one soldier were killed. According to another report, about 20 enemy tanks and armored cars were operating in the area. AGS Intelligence Report No. 28, 2 July [141].

5. I. Saitō, Onozuka interviews.

6. Onozuka interview. Also see Engineer 1st Lt. Jin Torao's presentation concerning Engineer Master Sergeant Asakura's feats; 23rd Div., *Bukō bidan* [113], sec. 4.

7. Kobayashi [24], 28 June. The MPRA cavalry soldier could not have known much. Kusaba says he was a young man forcibly conscripted from the Ulan Bator (Kulun) district some 10 days earlier. JRD [965], *JSM* 11, part 3/C, p. 496, citing Kusaba, *Noro kōchi* [358].

8. Garthoff, *Soviet* [735], p. 272; AGS Intelligence Report No. 22, 25 June, and No. 23, 26 June [141]; I. Saitō interview.

9. According to 4th Tank Regt. maps [134]. Also see chaps. 20, 21 below.

10. Kwantung Army intelligence coverage by 29 June encompassed the sector between the Halha-Holsten confluence and a point 30 km. upstream: AGS Intelligence Report No. 28, 2 July [141]; Suzuki Yoshiyasu, I. Saitō, Sumi interviews. Also see Tsuji [585], pp. 126-27; JRD [965], *JSM* 11, part 3/B, pp. 281-85. The 23rd Division scheduled river-crossing training exercises on 30 June; each subordinate unit was to send an officer to observe them. 1st Bn., 64th Inf. Regt. [116], 29 June.

11. Kobayashi [24], learned this information on 29 June from an unspecified regiment commander. Also see Yasuoka Detachment, Operations Order No. 14, 11 P.M., 29 June, Handagai; 4th Tank Regt. [134].

12. Komatsubara [25], 28 June; Kobayashi [24], 30 June; S. Hara interview. Although the division intelligence officer does not remember where the information originated, he does not think it came from the Kwantung Army's OSS. Suzuki Yoshiyasu interview. Also see BBSS, *SS* [180], vol. 27, p. 497.

13. JRD [965], *JSM* 11, part 3/B, pp. 286-89; Tsuji [585], pp. 128-29; BBSS, *SS* [180], vol. 27, pp. 494-501; Gomikawa, *Nomonhan* [212], pp. 40-41. A copy of the order will be found in the instructions issued by the 2nd Bn., 26th Inf. Regt., 10 A.M., 30 June; 7th Co. [105], 30 June. As will be noted, the 23rd Division originally called for the Yasuoka detachment

to strike southward along the right bank of the Halha on 2 July—before the division went into action across the river at dawn on the 3rd. BBSS, *SS* [180], vol. 27, p. 497.

14. S. Hara interview.

15. Kobayashi's leadership drew high praise from all who observed him in action, even from Tsuji. Account based on Kobayashi [24], 30 June; Komatsubara [25] 1 July; Tsuji [585], pp. 129-32; Yonemoto [623A], pp. 27-30; JRD [965], *JSM* 11, part 3/C, pp. 497-98, citing Kusaba, *Noro kōchi* [358].

16. Sumi, interview and *Jissen* [541], p. 15.

17. 72nd Inf. Regt. [121], 1, 2 July; K. Kobayashi [343], pp. 20-22; Komatsubara [25], 2, 3 July; Nishikawa interview. Also see *SSNT* [535], vol. 27, p. 7.

18. Shishkin [920], pp. 581, 583-84; JRD [965], *JSM* 11 part 3/B, p. 313.

19. Tsuji [585], pp. 127-28. Errors mar JRD [965], *JSM* 11, part 3/B, pp. 285-86. I accept Col. Saitō Isamu's dating of his last-minute final recommendation to Komatsubara of the precise crossing site. (Interview.) Also see *SSNT* [535], vol. 27, p. 8. The skillful Soviet camouflage of tank revetments is lauded in BBSS, *SS* [180], vol. 27, p. 495.

20. According to Tsuji [585], pp. 131-32, and JRD [965], *JSM* 11, part 3/B, p. 290, Fui Heights itself was occupied without a fight on 1/2 July. Also see JRD [965], *JSM* 11, part 3/C, p. 498, citing Kusaba, *Noro kōchi* [358].

21. 23rd Division, Operations Order No. 109, 5 P.M., 2 July, Fui Heights; Y. Nishihara, Sumi interviews. Also see the exchange between staff officers S. Hara and N. Itō, n. 14 above. For commentary on the unexplained reversal of regimental precedence in crossing the river, whereby the 71st Infantry became the first across on the left wing, and the 72nd Infantry followed and became the right wing, see *SSNT* [535], vol. 27, p. 8. As for the thinking regarding dawn vs. night action, see BBSS, *SS* [180], vol. 27, p. 497; e.g., enemy air interference was not expected, and direction-finding in the dark would have posed a problem.

22. The day had been showery and the night misty and moonless, I. Saitō recalls. Sumi says that visibility was 10 meters. Dramatic references to a lightning storm are found in 72nd Inf. Regt. [121] and in Mita [406], p. 62, citing a field medical unit. Gomikawa is troubled by the discrepancy too; *Nomonhan* [212], pp. 63-64. A survivor of the Ioki unit assured him that there was a fierce lightning storm on the right bank en route to the river; [212], p. 64.

23. Zhukov, *Memoirs* [1017], p. 151. Also see Vorozkeikin [184], p. 43.

24. Shishkin [920], p. 583. In addition, Shishkin thinks the Japanese crossing began at about 2 A.M.

25. According to *Shōsen reishū* [485], no. 11, Sumi's 1st Battalion had almost finished crossing the river by 10 A.M. For Colonel Tazaka's account of his 4th Motor Regiment's hauling of the 26th Infantry from Chiangchunmiao as far as Lake Odon, see *SSNT* [535], vol. 26, p. 237.

26. I. Saitō, Nishikawa, T. Hamada, Onozuka, Sumi, H. Tanaka, Imaoka. Y. Nishihara interviews; BBSS, *SS* [180], vol. 27, pp. 510-12; Komatsubara [25], 3 July; Tsuji [585], pp. 132-34; 71st Inf. Regt. [119], and 72nd Inf. Regt. [121]; Mita [406], p. 61; Gomikawa, *Nomonhan* [212], pp. 41-42; *SSNT* [535], vol. 26, pp. 242-43, and vol. 27, pp. 17-21, 24, 27. There were actually 32 complete pontoons. Usually a 120-30-meter-wide river could be spanned in 1.5 to 2 hours, but here about four hours were needed because the matériel was jumbled up when unloaded and components for the pontoon sets had to be located in the dark. *SSNT* [535], vol. 26, pp. 243-44. Colonel Tazaka's 1st Company hauled the rowing gear; the 2nd Company carried the bridging matériel—40 trucks per company. The trucks actually drove down the cliff at the riverbank to deliver the materials to the engineers; one truck platoon got stuck in the mud of the stream. Regarding the "miracle" of the unopposed river-crossing operation, Tazaka was relieved to hear a pheasant twitter at the riverbank—evidence that no enemy was there. *SSNT* [535], vol. 26, p. 240. JRD [965], *JSM* 11, part 3/B, p. 293, contains errors regarding the bridging and rowing operations. For an authoritative treatment of engineer river-crossing equipment at Nomonhan, see Takahashi Noboru, "Nihon rikugun no senshayō toka kizai" [Japanese Army's Tank River-Crossing Matériel], *Panzer*, Oct. 1979, no. 52, p. 86.

CHAPTER 19

1. In what is probably a reference to the same prisoner, Tsuji tells of using his saber to poke a prostrate Soviet first lieutenant, leading him along with a cord, trying out his Russian for the first time, eventually getting to like the captive, and untying him to serve as a "temporary orderly." The Russian officer was supposedly terrified by the sight of the Japanese troops knocking out Soviet tanks; Tsuji gave him half a cigarette. Tsuji [585], pp. 138-40. One wonders if the prisoner was brought back alive. Nishikawa tells of three enemy stragglers, soldiers or noncoms, captured on the left bank. "What to do with them? They posed a real problem, for they needed precious food and water." Nishikawa says they were "dragged along" and not executed. (Interview.)

2. Captain Kusaba (7th Battery commander, 13th FA Regt.), in 23rd Inf. Div. [113], sec. 2; JRD [965], JSM 11, part 3/C, pp. 499-503, citing Kusaba, *Noro kōchi* [358]; *Bidanroku* [451], pp. 443-44; 71st Inf. Regt. [119]; Gomikawa, *Nomonhan* [212], p. 45; Tsuji [585], pp. 134-36; BBSS, SS [180], vol. 27, p. 512; Onozuka, H. Tanaka interviews.

3. Shishkin [920], p. 584. The MPRA cavalry regiment, according to this source, ran into IJA engineer troops. Also see Zhukov, *Memoirs* [1017], p. 151, regarding the MPRA 6th Cavalry Division being driven northwest from the area of Hara Heights.

4. Hamada interview; Kusaba, in 23rd Div. [113], sec. 2. Also see JRD [965], JSM 11, part 3/B, pp. 295, 313. AGS intelligence heard that the Okamoto and Sakai regiments had pushed eight km. south of the crossing by about 8 A.M. on 3 July. AGS Intelligence Report No. 29, 3 July [141].

5. Zhukov, *Memoirs* [1017], p. 153; Shishkin [920], pp. 585-86. For 11 P.M. read 11 A.M. in the Shishkin translation, p. 585.

6. For Soviet comments, see Zhukov, *Memoirs* [1017], p. 152; Shishkin [920], pp. 571-72.

7. Shishkin [920], pp. 584-86; JRD [965], JSM 11, part 3/C, pp. 295, 313; Zhukov, *Memoirs* [1017], pp. 151-52; Vorozheikin [184], pp. 43-44. But see chap. 26, n. 27. The Japanese had only 12 regimental guns, 18 antitank (rapid-fire) guns, eight field pieces, and four 12-cm. howitzers, for a total of 42 pieces. BBSS, SS [180], vol. 27, p. 515. For IJA personnel strength, see chap. 20, n. 11.

8. Shishkin [920], p. 586; JRD [965], JSM 11, part 3/C, pp. 295, 313.

9. Soldier Nakamura's diary, in Zhukov, *Memoirs* [1017], p. 153.

10. 72nd Inf. Regt. [121], 3 July; Komatsubara [25], 3 July; Kobayashi [24], 3 July; Yamanaka [615], pp. 270-73; Gomikawa, *Nomonhan* [212], pp. 45-46; SSNT [535], vol. 27, p. 49; BBSS, SS [180], vol. 27, p. 512; Nishikawa, T. Hamada, Tsuchiya, Sumi interviews. Also see JRD [965], JSM 11, part 3/B, pp. 293-97, 313.

11. See n. 14 below.

12. Nishiura, Murata, Sumi interviews. A portion of my interview information of 1960 is found in the transcript of a talk by Nishiura at Tokyo University in 1968; SSNT [535], vol. 27, pp. 187-88. Okano's revelation is contained in Onda [473], vol. 1, p. 216. As for the *anpan* mines, Sumi calls them "absurd." He did not think much of them when, as an infantry captain, he saw a demonstration. Now, told to use *anpan* as a colonel commanding a regiment in combat, he did not esteem them any more highly. (Interview.)

13. The 71st Inf. Regt. combat diary [119], however, notes that truck-borne rapid-fire guns did enter action on 3 July. PFC Okano (see n. 12 above) explains that the men of his truck unit installed guns facing rearward. These motorized weapons could move well ahead of friendly foot soldiers but, seeming to be "mere trucks," they decoyed and lulled enemy armor. "It was a good feeling to smash the tanks," Okano remembers. Onda [473], vol. 1, p. 217.

14. Negami told me that he saw the color guard unit on the right bank. But Tsuji, in his harangue of Sumi (see chap. 20, n. 6), accused the colonel of leaving the colors to the rear at Chiangchunmiao. According to some sources, the 7th Division commander, Lt. Gen. Sonobe Waichirō, did specifically advise Sumi not to risk the colors across the river. See Gomikawa, *Nomonhan* [212], pp. 58-61; SSNT [535], vol. 27, pp. 178-81; *Nomonhan* [40], vol. 7, pp. 20-21; Mita [406], pp. 145-46. Supporting Sumi's statement to me is the testimony of a warrant officer, the command team chief of the 1st Battalion's 3rd Company; SSNT [535], vol. 27, p. 158.

15. Sumi heard nothing further about his pullback. Sumi, interviews, correspondence, and writings; AGS Intelligence Report No. 31, 5 July [141]; Negami, Maeda, Tsunashima, Suzuki Yoshiyasu interviews; *Shōsen reishū* [485], no. 11; Nomura [455], pp. 59-61; Mita [406], pp. 77, 86, 143-44.

16. Tsuji says that Hashimoto conveyed a very poor impression by allegedly leaving the battlefield for Tokyo without seeing the hard-fighting Komatsubara. [585], p. 150. Hashimoto insisted that he could not make contact with Komatsubara's combat headquarters across the Halha, but his detractors wrongly accused him of declining to fly to the divisional command post because "the front lines were no place to go," and they denounced him as "a disgrace to the name of *samurai*." Sawada [507A], p. 151. Though, as will be seen in chap. 20, Hashimoto did meet both Komatsubara and Yano on 4 July, Komatsubara—"with a disgusted look"—told Sawada in early September that he had sent a sedan for Hashimoto, "but he did not show up at the front, for some unknown reason." [507A], p. 24. It is apparent that Hashimoto's critics blamed him for not accompanying the IJA attack forces well into Outer Mongolian territory. Also see chap. 37, n. 47.

17. 64th Inf. Regt., Operations Order No. 22, 11:10 P.M., 30 June, 4 km. east of Chiang-chunmiao, para. 4: 1st Bn., 64th Inf. Regt. [116]; 23rd Division, Operations Order No. 109, 5 P.M., 2 July, para. 6: BBSS, *SS* [180], vol. 27, p. 503; Jin Torao in 23rd Div. [113], sec. 4; I. Saitō interview. It was the 10th Inf. Co. which shot down a friendly scout plane with heavy machine gun fire defending the bridge. *SSNT* [535], vol. 27, p. 29.

18. 71st Inf. Regt. [119], and 72nd Inf. Regt. [121], 3 July; JRD [965] *JSM* 11, part 3/B, pp. 298-99; Tsuji [585], pp. 131, 142-45; Gomikawa, *Nomonhan* [212], p. 52; Suzuki Yoshiyasu, N. Tanaka, Murata, Y. Nishihara, T. Hamada interviews. My combat interviewees never dwelt upon possible international complications underlying the Kwantung Army staff officers' decision to withdraw. Suzuki Yoshiyasu, however, has been heard to suggest that since the crossing of the Halha frontier ran counter to imperial intentions and did not have IGHQ sanction, the Kwantung Army—particularly chief of staff Yano, who was on the scene—must have been very concerned about a possible catastrophe befalling an IJA infantry division inside Outer Mongolia. See *SSNT* [535], vol. 27, pp. 109-10.

19. AGS Intelligence Reports No. 31, 5 July, and No. 32, 6 July [141].

20. 71st Inf. Regt. [119], and 72nd Inf. Regt. [121], 3 July. The Okamoto detachment operations order cited is no. 59.

21. Imaoka, "Nomonhan" [13], p. 53.

22. JRD [965], *JSM* 11, part 3/B, p. 254. Also see BBSS, *SS* [180], vol. 27, pp. 469-71.

CHAPTER 20

1. 23rd Division, Operations Order No. 111. Kobayashi's Infantry Corps Operations Order No. 15 was received by the 72nd Inf. Regt. at 5:20 P.M.

2. Okamoto Detachment, Operations Order No. 59.

3. 71st Inf. Regt. [119] and 72nd Inf. Regt. [121], 3 July; T. Hamada, Nishikawa interviews.

4. S. Hara, Suzuki Yoshiyasu, Hashimoto, Onozuka interviews; Tsuji [585], p. 147; Nomura [455], pp. 61-62. Some think that Ōuchi was killed by a shell fragment; others, that machine gun bullets felled him. Tsuji does not seem to have known about Hashimoto's getting to see Komatsubara and Yano. See n. 16, chap. 19. Suzuki Yoshiyasu identifies Gondō as the senior staff officer-designate for the Sixth Army, and adds that Gondō's eyes healed satisfactorily.

5. The sequence of regimental pullbacks is cleverly tidied up in JRD [965], *JSM* 11, part 3/B, p. 300, where it is stated that the 26th Regiment was ordered by Komatsubara, from the beginning, to cover the withdrawal of the entire Kobayashi task force. This version is repeated by Tsuji [585], p. 144.

6. Sumi, interviews and writings. Gomikawa refers to Tsuji's partial backdown; *Nomonhan* [212], pp. 56-57. But Tsuji's full and original version is found in the 1950 edition of *Nomonhan* [212], pp. 148-49, and in a 1967 reprint. During an interview, Sumi showed me a snapshot of him standing by a foxhole on the left shore that day of 3 July, holding the famous beer bottle filled with Halha River water.

7. For the Adachi battalion to this point: Sumi, interviews and writings; N. Tanaka, Negami,

Maeda, Tsunashima interviews; Mita [406], pp. 55-56; *SSNT* [535], vol. 27, pp. 98-100, 148-50, 152-58; Nomura [455], p. 61.

8. Onda [473], vol. 1, pp. 230-31, citing 1st Bn., 71st Inf. Regt., combat diary 5 July, and artillery Sgt. Ueda Mori's notes for 11 July recording information received that day from 1st Lt. Kaneyasu Isao, 3rd Bn. aide, 71st Inf. Regt. The *kesshitai* was apparently destroyed.

9. Zhukov, *Memoirs* [1017], p. 153; Shishkin [920], p. 587.

10. Sumi, interviews and writings; I. Saitō, Negami, Maeda, Tsunashima, Nishikawa interviews; Nomura [455], pp. 62-63; Mita [406], pp. 95, 101-2, 125, 145; *SSNT* [535], vol. 27, pp. 92-98, 161-71; Gomikawa [212], pp. 58-61. Tsuji asserts that the 26th Regiment had finally extricated about 100 casualties from the Adachi battalion, and that he only recrossed the bridge after confirming that the last man in the regiment had come out. He then mounted Komatsubara's abandoned horse. [585], p. 149. For Tsuji's imaginative version of the bridge-blowing, see [585], pp. 149-50.

11. According to one set of IJA data: 71st Inf. Regt.—47 KIA, 108 WIA; 72nd Inf. Regt.—48 KIA, 101 WIA; 26th Inf. Regt.—114 KIA, 242 WIA (many of whom died), 11 MIA; other units: unavailable. *SSNT* [535], vol. 27, p. 172. For 26th Inf. Regt., see Mita [406], p. 125; supplemented by Sumi interview. Also see BBSS, *SS* [180], vol. 27, p. 515. From Tokyo, the U.S. military attaché's office reported that a Japanese casualty list released on 5 July included 27 men killed from a Hokkaido division. Since the location of their death was confusingly given as "north Manchuria," the assistant attaché concluded that "this is the first and only indication . . . that fighting with the Soviets may not be limited to the Nomonhan area." Capt. E. H. F. Svensson, Jr., Military Attaché, Tokyo, Report No. 9843, 18 July 1939, G-2 Reports/6920 (National Archives G-2 M/A file; NARS [980]).

12. Tsuji [585], pp. 155-56.

13. The 72nd Inf. Regt.'s statistics seem particularly suspect. The "bloated" IJA claims have been likened to the notorious IGHQ victory communiqués of the Pacific War. *SSNT* [535], vol. 27, p. 173.

14. See chap. 19, n. 7.

15. Gomikawa, *Nomonhan* [212], pp. 45, 52.

16. I. Saitō, Sumi, Nishikawa, Imaoka, Y. Nishihara interviews; and *SSNT* [535], vol. 27, pp. 31-32.

17. Y. Nishihara interview; Gomikawa, *Nomonhan* [212], pp. 52-53. In an impetuous attack launched before dawn on 21 August 1942, Col. Ichiki Kiyonao hurled about 900 newly landed soldiers against strong U.S. Marine positions across the Ilu (Tenaru) River on Guadalcanal. Scarcely more than 100 Japanese survived the 12 hours of savage fighting that ensued. Ichiki burned the regimental colors and committed suicide. BBSS, *SS*, vol. 28, *Minami Taiheiyō rikugun sakusen* (2) [Army Operations in the South Pacific] (1969), pp. 9-10.

18. Suzuki Yoshiyasu interview; Tsuji [585], p. 156.

19. Sumi, "Nomonhan" [543], p. 58, and interview.

20. Onozuka, T. Hamada, Nishikawa, S. Hara interviews.

21. BBSS, *SS* [180], vol. 27, pp. 515, 545; *SSNT* [535], vol. 27, pp. 27-32, 151-52, 172-86; Gomikawa, *Nomonhan* [212], pp. 52-53; Tsuji [585], p. 150; Nomura [455], pp. 60-61; Sumi, interviews and writings; I. Saitō, Imaoka interviews. Lt. Col. Murasawa Kazuo, a Kwantung Army operations staff officer, refers to German-made 15-cm. Rheinmetall guns with a fantastic range of 25,000 meters, double the range of IJA 15-cm. artillery. JRD [965], *JSM* 11, part 3/C, p. 306. The problem of IJA air support is treated in chap. 27 below.

22. Zhukov, *Memoirs* [1017], p. 154; Shishkin [920], pp. 587-88. The Soviet-MPRA command admitted that a small portion of the left shore of the Halha River was occupied by the Japanese until 5 July, but claimed that the IJA infantry were supported by no less than 60 tanks which presumably attacked only cavalry units. See chap. 23, n. 13 below.

CHAPTER 21

1. The independent 5th Tank Regiment, at Mutanchiang, came under the Third Army. It had Type 97 medium tanks.

2. It had also been decided to form the 11th Tank Regiment at Kungchuling by March 1940.

3. Data on tables of equipment depict the numbers at Nomonhan, not Kungchuling; manpower figures reflect maximum levels. 4th Tank Regt. [134]; Kadokawa, *Teikoku* [316], p. 147; Tamada, Noguchi, Ogata, Z. Tomioka, Irie interviews. Somewhat differing data will be found in JRD [965], *JSM* 11, part 3/B, p. 260, n. 5; Gomikawa, *Nomonhan* [212], pp. 61-63. Tamada's *danretsu* company possessed 7 six-wheeled sedans, 13 of the regiment's 44 six-wheeled trucks, 7 motorcycles with sidecars, 6 repair trucks, and 1 kitchen truck. Yoshimaru also had a *danretsu* company and about the same number of miscellaneous vehicles (63) as Tamada's 65. The 3rd Regiment had 10 army civilians (*gunzoku*) serving as mechanics and interpreters; the 4th Regiment, 21.

4. Tank and tankette specifications are given in Hara and Takeuchi [223], pp. 14-15, 24-26, 36-39, 42-44. Belly and top armor was considerably thinner than side armor: 8 mm. belly plating on medium tanks, 4 mm. on tankettes; 10 mm. topside on mediums, 6 mm. on tankettes.

5. Yasuoka said that he had enough young company-grade officers but lacked field-grade officers to staff the new units. Imaoka interview, citing his notes on the inspection at Kungchuling, 9 A.M.–4 P.M., 9 June 1939. Also Tamada, Ogata, Noguchi interviews; and *Chichibunomiya* [184A], pp. 775-77.

6. Biographical sketches based on Tamada, Noguchi, Ogata, Takeshita, Masuda, Z. Tomioka interviews. A number of sources thought Yoshimaru was still only a lieutenant colonel when he fought at Nomonhan. His official curriculum vitae, however, confirms his promotion to colonel as of 9 March 1939. Effective the day he was slain at Nomonhan (3 July), he was promoted major general. Of Yoshimaru's 20 officers, only one was a reservist; of Tamada's 25 officers, eight were reservists. IJA armor possessed more noncoms, the "key to good tank units," than did the usual army unit. The well-trained noncoms served as drivers or tank commanders but not as platoon leaders, even in emergency at Nomonhan. Z. Tomioka interview.

7. Noguchi's dating indicates that Tsuji et al. were already seriously considering a trans-riverine offensive before the Russians and Outer Mongolians stepped up their air and ground action on 18-19 June. (Interview.) This is borne out by Konuma Haruo's memorandum [26] to the effect that enemy forces, especially aircraft, had become active in the Nomonhan area since 15 June.

8. Noguchi interview; BBSS, *SS* [180], vol. 27, pp. 472-74, 490 (Kwantung Army, Operations Order No. 1530, 9:40 P.M., 19 June; No. 1532, 2 P.M., 20 June; 23rd Division, Operations Order No. 76); *SSNT* [535], vol. 26, pp. 73-74, vol. 27, p. 318. Varying data will be found in JRD [965], *JSM* 11, part 3/B, pp. 257-61. For the important air force dimension of the Kwantung Army orders, see chap. 17 above.

9. Imaoka suggests that credit be shared with the railway movement officer, Colonel Kawamura. Lieutenant Irie's critique, excerpted below, is drawn from his unpublished notes [18].

10. One reason for the absence of improved roads was the Kwantung Army's desire to prevent enemy movement into the area. Noguchi, Masuda, Nyūmura interviews. For a graphic depiction of about 35 soldiers struggling to pull one truck from the mire (Yasuoka detachment, near Arshaan), see *Ichiokunin*, vol. 2 [265], p. 221. Also see 2nd Bn., 28th Inf. Regt. [110]; and *SSNT* [535], vol. 26, pp. 149-50. Tomioka Zenzō remembers difficulty with a wooden bridge over the Arshaan River. There was concern that it could not support medium tanks; the latter had to be nursed across slowly. (Interview.)

11. According to data provided by Hara and Takeuchi ([223], pp. 15, 20, 26, 37, 39, 44) on tank fording depth capability: Type 94 tankette—0.6 m.; Type 97 tankette—0.8 m.; Type 95 light, Type 89, and Type 97 medium tank—1.0 m.

12. Along the full 46 km. of the Halha River, there may eventually have been eight or nine Soviet bridges, including three or four north of the Holsten confluence. Two additional bridges spanned the Holsten near the confluence. See *SSNT* [535], vol. 27, p. 249.

13. The Type 94 tankette had a fuel storage capacity of 88 liters and a consumption of 8 liters per hour; the Type 97 tankette a capacity of 59 liters (main tank) and 32 liters (auxiliary tank), and a consumption of 7 liters per hour; the Type 95 light tank a capacity of 107 liters (main tank) and 30 liters (auxiliary tank); the Type 89 (*Kō*) medium tank a capacity of 220 liters; the Type 89 (*Otsu*) medium tank a capacity of 100 liters (main) and 70 liters (auxiliary); the Type

97 medium tank a capacity of 120 liters in each of two main tanks and 6 liters auxiliary, and an oil consumption of 3.5 liters per hour. Hara and Takeuchi [223], pp. 15, 20, 26, 37, 39, 44.

14. Noguchi interview. According to Suzuki Yoshiyasu, 2,000 to 3,000 coolies were brought in from Tsitsihar. (Interview.)

15. Irie provides a plausible alternative explanation for the use of horses for reconnaissance: tank silhouettes are big and easy to detect by the enemy on an open plain. It is also difficult to study terrain from armored vehicles. For Japanese tankers engaged in a mounted patrol, it was only logical to rely upon Manchukuoan cavalry expertise. (Interview.) Tamada also stresses the need to conceal the arrival of IJA tank forces at the front. (Interview.) Tankettes were 1.6-1.92 m. wide, 1.63-1.81 m. high, 3.37-3.64 m. long; Type 95 light tanks 2 m. wide, 2.5 m. high, 4.5 m. long; Type 89 medium tanks 2.15 m. wide, 2.58 m. high, 5.88 m. long; Type 97 medium tanks 2.33 m. wide, 2.22 m. high, 5.52 m. long. Hara and Takeuchi [223], pp. 14-16, 19-20, 24-26, 36-39, 42-45.

16. Naturally, Tamada wanted to pursue the matter, but the returned noncom was transferred to Korea and no further checking was possible. (Interview.) Z. Tomioka adds that Tamaki's company, conducting forced reconnaissance in search of Shinoda, drove off enemy truck-borne scouts, who fled after some firing, without casualties. (Interview.) Irie thinks that the truck-borne infantry (or light armor) ambushed Shinoda. (Interview.) Takeshita heard only that his military academy classmate Shinoda had been killed in action. (Interview.) Also see *SSNT* [535], vol. 26, pp. 152-55.

17. Kwantung Army, Operations Order No. 12, 3 P.M., 25 June: BBSS, SS [180], vol. 27, pp. 491-92; JRD [965], JSM 11, part 3/C, pp. 279-80; SSNT [535], vol. 27, p. 140.

18. Sumi interview. The colonel does not know why his regiment "wasted" about five days in Chiangchunmiao, but admittedly logistics were a problem for the 23rd Division. He showed me a photo of himself unhappily awaiting orders in the hamlet while his regiment was receiving supplies. Sumi was missing crucial installments of his favorite novel serialized in the *Asahi* newspaper (*Miyamoto Musashi* by Yoshikawa Eiji). Instead of the 250 trucks he insisted that he needed for his 1,460 men, the division could only spare him 194, commandeered by a local transportation firm and driven by Japanese civilians, but under the military control of the transport regiment. The new mission of the 26th Inf. Regt. is described in chaps. 18-20 above. The transport regiment commander, Colonel Tazaka, spent the night of 1/2 July at Chiangchunmiao, arranging to load the 26th Infantry for departure aboard trucks early in the morning. *SSNT* [535], vol. 26, p. 237.

19. Yasuoka Detachment, Operations Order No. 13, 6 P.M., 29 June, Handagai; Tamada Tank Unit, Operations Orders Nos. 25 and 26, 8 and 9 P.M., 29 June, Handagai: 4th Tank Regt. [134]. Also see *SSNT* [535], vol. 27, p. 158.

20. Yasuoka Detachment, Operations Order No. 14, 11 P.M., 29 June, Handagai; Tamada Tank Operations Order No. 27, 11:30 P.M., 29 June.

21. See chap. 18 above. Also see BBSS, SS [180], vol. 27, p. 495.

22. Nyūmura interviews; also Kōtani interview. Another version is recorded in Komatsubara's diary [25]. On 29 June, he transcribed the Harbin OSS intelligence report of Yakovlev's recommendation as follows: "Repair and supply of motor vehicles are difficult. Since it is dangerous to concentrate wheeled units on an all-out battlefield, it would be better to pull [them] back gradually to Tamsag, while launching a counterattack . . . short distance." However, prodding messages, repeating the information of an alleged enemy pullback, continued to arrive at Yasuoka detachment headquarters. Komatsubara admitted, in his entry for 28 June, that the division had been told by the Kwantung Army to launch the offensive as soon as possible, once the main body had completed preparations; "we would lose the opportunity if we waited for the Yasuoka Detachment to finish its entire preparations." Grigorenko has revealed that Front Group commander Shtern compelled Army Group commander Zhukov to terminate his inefficient use of provisional detachments and to return them to their parent units and customary commands. Conducted at night, the Soviet regrouping took a week. Though "the Japanese did not know what was going on, they got nervous" and fired heavily on the Russians during the regrouping process. Grigorenko gives no dates for this activity, but it seems to have taken place soon after his arrival from Moscow at Front Group headquarters around 22 June; [746A],

pp. 106-7. Perhaps it was the regrouping that caused the Japanese to surmise that the Russians were retreating.

23. BT stands for *Bystrokhodnyi Tank* (high-speed tank). The BT-7 model, equipped with one 45-mm. gun and one machine gun and weighing 13.8 tons, saw action at Nomonhan. Erickson, *Soviet* [722], p. 771.

24. Noguchi has also said it was a replacement tank (substituting for one left behind at Handagai) that was lost by Kitamura. (Interview.) The acting commander of the 2nd Tank Company, 1st Lt. Itō Yoshihisa, was ordered to salvage the burned-out Japanese tank. Due to neglect of regimental orders to the supply company's repair platoon under 1st Lieutenant Yagi, the latter lagged far behind the Kitamura company. To tow the knocked-out vehicle, another Type 95 tank had to be used, but it overheated badly on the way. 4th Tank Regt. [134]. On 1 July, en route to Lake Dorot, the Tamada unit concealed Kitamura's tank and cremated his corpse and that of the slain crewman. *SSNT* [535], vol. 26, p. 172.

25. According to the 4th Tank Regt. [134], 10 rifles, 15 overcoats, 9 gas masks, and documents were captured in this action. My interview data are complemented by *SSNT* [535], vol. 26, pp. 161-63. Also see Iida et al. [269], p. 154. Maj. Harada Kazuo reveals that on 30 June, when elements of the Tamada regiment, in support of Kitamura, turned the enemy's right flank and were swinging back, the IJA tanks were mistaken for hostile armor by friendly forces. From Kitamura's and other experience, Harada also warned how dangerous the enemy could be when "driven to bay." [224], pp. 43-44.

26. Maj. A. E. Bykov, it will be recalled, was in command of the first Soviet troops to fight at Nomonhan in May; i.e., from the 11th Tank Brigade (Undurhan). IMTFE, *Transcript* [777], 27 Jan. 1948, p. 38361.

27. 4th Tank Regt. [134]; Nyūmura, Irie interviews. The records lack specific identifying data on the nationality of the enemy, but Nyūmura confirms that all prisoners taken in the Nomonhan fighting and interrogated by IJA combat intelligence were Russian.

28. 23rd Division, Operations Order No. 105: BBSS, *SS* [180], vol. 27, pp. 493, 495-98; JRD [965], *JSM* 11, part 3/B, pp. 286-88. The 1st Bn. of the 64th Inf. Regt. issued its own order at 11:10 P.M. on 30 June. *SSNT* [535], vol. 26, pp. 179-81; vol. 27, pp. 160, 164-65. The timing of the Yasuoka offensive is described with confusion in JRD [965], *JSM* 11, part 3/B, p. 289. My citation of Yasuoka's intentions is drawn from 4th Tank Regt. [134]. The division's original notion was to unleash the Yasuoka detachment a day before Kobayashi crossed the river, to mask the primary offensive and pin the enemy on the right bank; i.e., the main body of the armored force was to approach Fui Heights on 1 July and begin attacking Soviet units on the right shore on 2 July, moving southward along the Halha. After the delay in the detachment's displacement forward, the plan had to be modified, reluctantly. BBSS, *SS* [180], vol. 27, p. 497. Also see chap. 18 above.

29. 2nd Bn., 28th Inf. Regt. [110]; 4th Tank Regt. [134]. Also see *SSNT* [535], vol. 26, pp. 167, 179-81.

30. Still concerned over the fate of the late Captain Kitamura's wrecked tank, Tamada assigned one armored platoon and one supply platoon to continue salvage work. (Interview.) In the 3rd Tank Regiment, platoon leader Irie noted [18] that his 2nd Company commander, always in the lead during the advance, was exhausted physically and psychologically by his sense of responsibility.

31. Yasuoka Detachment, Operations Order No. 19, 12:30 A.M., followed by Tamada Tank Operations Order No. 36, 1:30 A.M., 2 July, Chiangchunmiao, calling for preparations to be completed by 3:50 A.M. The Northern Garrison Force had also been attached to Yasuoka. Actions of the Yamagata regiment on 1-2 July are described in *SSNT* [535], vol. 26, pp. 255, 269-71. A night operation on 1/2 July, probably ordered on Yamagata's initiative, proved abortive when his 2nd Battalion made no contact with the enemy by 3 A.M. on the 2nd.

32. 2nd Bn., 28th Inf. Regt. [110]; and *SSNT* [535], vol. 26, p. 182.

33. Relevant orders include Yasuoka Detachment, Operations Order No. 21, 2 P.M., 2 July, Lake Hozui; Tamada Tank Unit, Operations Order No. 36-3, 3:20 P.M., 2 July, 1,500 meters northeast of Heights 739.

34. Yasuoka Detachment, Operations Order No. 22, 3:40 P.M., 2 July, Lake Manzute.

For 23rd Division, Operations Order No. 109, 5 P.M., 2 July, see BBSS, *SS* [180], vol. 27, pp. 502-3. Staff officer Itō brought the order, with the added information about an enemy withdrawal from the right bank. *SSNT* [535], vol. 26, pp. 254-57; Gomikawa, *Nomonhan* [212], p. 61. Also see BBSS, *SS* [180], vol. 27, p. 497.

35. Tamada Tank Unit, Operations Order No. 37, 5:30 P.M., 2 July, Lake Manzute; and Tamada, Noguchi, Irie interviews. Yoshimaru's Operations Order No. 21 added stipulations for possible use of a smoke screen on the right flank, and for further coordination with the infantry and artillery. *SSNT* [535], vol. 26, pp. 265-66. Irie [18] says he was at a loss regarding the contents of the deployment orders.

36. Noguchi, Ida, Sugahara, Fukushima interviews; *SSNT* [535], vol. 26, pp. 251, 258-59, 263.

37. Tamada, Nyūmura, Y. Nishihara interviews; 4th Tank Regt. [134]; 2nd Bn., 28th Inf. Regt. [110]. Nyūmura remembers that Yasuoka was unenthusiastic about "wasting" an infantry company on intelligence collection. As early as 22 June, Yamagata was ordering his regiment to try to capture prisoners (especially officers) and belongings; 1st Bn., 64th Inf. Regt. [116]. Air reconnaissance was downgraded to maximize surprise. BBSS, *SS* [180], vol. 27, p. 497. Regarding IJA cartography, also see chap. 24, n. 21, below.

38. Takeshita, Irie, Noguchi interviews; Wakabayashi Itsuo (No. 3 tank commander in Koga platoon), *Nomonhan* [40], vol. 9, p. 173. The Tamada regiment adorned its tanks only with *hinomaru* for unit commanders. (Z. Tomioka interview.) The fact that the red-ball flags mounted on Japanese armor could not be discerned at a distance of 1,000 meters caused problems of identification by friendly forces, especially when the tanks appeared from an unexpected direction. See Harada Kazuo [224], p. 44.

39. Ogata interview; Sunouchi Seiichi in *SSNT* [535], vol. 26, p. 275. Irie [18] had warned his platoon that the matter of last words should not be treated lightly; "consider your family's feelings."

40. This is the version found in 4th Tank Regt. [134]. But the 3rd Tank Regiment's combat diary asserts that the Yoshimaru unit got under way on schedule at 6 P.M., ten minutes before Tamada's regiment says it began its own advance. See *SSNT* [535], vol. 26, pp. 271, 278. According to Tamada, the Yasuoka detachment's order was issued behind schedule, at 6:15 P.M., which was why his leaving at 6:10 was "early." (Interview.)

CHAPTER 22

1. Satō Ryōhei, 4th Co., 64th Inf. Regt., in *SSNT* [535], vol. 26, p. 270.

2. Yasuoka detachment [133]; Tamada, Noguchi interviews; Gomikawa, *Nomonhan* [212], p. 62; *SSNT* [535], vol. 26, pp. 255, 269-70, 306.

3. Yasuoka detachment [133]; and *SSNT* [535], vol. 26, pp. 309-11.

4. *SSNT* [535], vol. 26, p. 269. According to the Yasuoka detachment [133], the Yamagata regiment took Heights 731 by a night attack.

5. Yasuoka detachment [133]; *SSNT* [535], vol. 26, pp. 258-62, 265, 303, 307.

6. Noguchi, Takeshita, Irie interviews; *SSNT* [535], vol. 26, pp. 329, 279.

7. Irie [18] and interview; Tamada, Noguchi, Takeshita interviews; Gomikawa, *Nomonhan* [212], p. 63.

8. There seems also to have been Soviet medium artillery but the gunners may not have had time to fire before being overrun by the Japanese tanks. As for the antitank guns, Irie notes that the Russians mounted them on tanks and armored cars whereas the Japanese used men or horses to drag counterpart weapons. (Interview.)

9. 2nd Lts. Shimizu Saburō and Koga Yasuo (platoon leaders) and Warrant Officer Tomoda. See *Nomonhan* [40], vol. 7, p. 67. Wakabayashi Itsuo says that five trucks and three guns were captured. [40], vol. 9, p. 173. On the subject of capturing enemy equipment, Irie wrote in his notes [18]: "Don't be too heroic."

10. Wakabayashi in *Nomonhan* [40], vol. 9, pp. 172-73. Also see [40], vol. 7, p. 67.

11. *SSNT* [535], vol. 26, pp. 284-85.

12. Major Kinomoto's dead subordinates were 1st Lt. Inoue Naomichi and 2nd Lt. Tazaka Masaharu.

13. Irie interview. Also see Gomikawa, *Nomonhan* [212], p. 62; *SSNT* [535], vol. 26, pp. 271-72, 280-85, 325; *Nomonhan* [40], vol. 7, p. 67.

14. The lost patrol was conducted by Lt. Col. Takazawa Hideki and 1st Lt. Okumura Masaru. Noguchi interview; and *SSNT* [535], vol. 26, p. 302.

15. Ogata, Noguchi, Tamada interviews. Also see *SSNT* [535], vol. 26, pp. 286, 287, 302.

16. Tamada, Z. Tomioka interviews; 4th Tank Regt. [134]; *SSNT* [535], vol. 26, pp. 273-76, 287; Gomikawa, *Nomonhan* [212], p. 62.

17. I am relying on the gist of the variations of the *kunji* provided me by Tamada and Ogata or transcribed in 4th Tank Regt. [134]. Also see *Nomonhan* [40], vol. 8, p. 101 (Tamada); and *SSNT* [535], vol. 26, pp. 288-89.

18. Tamada Tank Unit, Operations Order No. 38, 9 P.M. [*sic*], 2 July, at a dip on the southeast side of Heights 757 [later found to be 3 km. southeast of Lake Iringin Chagan]. The forward supply unit was directed to return to the location of the main *danretsu* company. I have melded supplementary notes from 4th Tank Regt. [134] with the text of Order No. 38.

19. Ogata, to whom I am indebted for this précis regarding the atmosphere in the 4th Regiment on the eve of the night attack, admits that the feeling that the outcome of battle lies in the laps of the gods is always the same in combat. (Interview.)

20. My treatment of the night attack is based on the 4th Tank Regt. [134]; Tamada, Ogata, Z. Tomioka, Masuda interviews; *SSNT* [535], vol. 26, pp. 287-98. For a signal officer's discussion of communication problems at regimental level, see the comments of 1st Lt. Ueda Tadanori of the 71st Inf. Regt., in Onda [473], vol. 1, pp. 182-83. Ueda mentions intercepting Soviet radio messages employed in tank commanding, in which respect the Japanese were "ten years behind." The front-line IJA infantry regiments, lacking time to expend on coding and decoding, preferred to use field telephones, although the single-line links were vulnerable to enemy fire.

21. In 1560, Imagawa Yoshimoto was on his way from the Shizuoka area to seize the key city of Kyoto when he was met by the forces of Oda Nobunaga at Okehazama in Owari (Aichi). Oda took advantage of the sudden darkness, thunder and lightning, and torrential rains to surprise and kill Imagawa. Imaoka interview. Ogata, typically low-key, calls the action of 2 July "something like the battle of Okehazama." (Interview.) Also see Gomikawa, *Nomonhan* [212], pp. 63-64.

22. *SSNT* [535], vol. 26, p. 273; and Z. Tomioka interview.

23. The wounded gunner must have staggered far to his left because, according to 4th Tank Regt. [134], it was 1st Co. commander Matsumoto who picked him up.

24. Tamada, Ogata, Z. Tomioka interviews; *SSNT* [535], vol. 26, pp. 293-95, 297-98.

25. Identifiable interview with Tamada. Also see 4th Tank Regt. [134]; and *SSNT* [535], vol. 26, pp. 295-96, vol. 27, p. 338. A copy of the Soviet photograph will be found in JRD [965], *JSM* 11, part 3/C, p. 479.

26. In's 4th Co. (medium) sustained one killed and one wounded; the 2nd Co. (Itō's lost tank), the lieutenant and his two crewmen wounded; Tamaki's 3rd Co., four men wounded. The eighth wounded man came from the supply unit. 4th Tank Regt. [134].

27. I have combined data on benzine and fuel oil consumption; omitted gear and mobile oil liter use, as well as grease poundage. 4th Tank Regt. [134].

28. Ogata, Irie, Tamada interviews; 4th Tank Regt. [134]; Yasuoka detachment [133].

29. Shishkin [920], pp. 583-84. Also see chaps. 18 and 19 above; and Vorozheikin [184], pp. 43-44.

CHAPTER 23

1. For artillery activity, Irie and Noguchi interviews; and *SSNT* [535], vol. 26, pp. 303-6. I am convinced that Noguchi confuses the day of Ise's deployment forward, since Komatsubara's diary [25] reports the artillery colonel's main force only joined Yasuoka on 5 July.

2. 2nd Bn., 28th Inf. Regt. [110]; Irie, Noguchi interviews; and *SSNT* [535], vol. 26, p. 309, citing 3rd Tank Regt. combat report.

3. Yabuuchi thinks the infantry-engineer force may have captured and used some enemy light machine guns. Yamagata's operations order of 11:30 A.M. was No. 30. *SSNT* [535], vol. 26, pp. 306-7, 310-11, 330-31.

4. Gomikawa, *Nomonhan* [235], pp. 65-66; Noguchi interview.

5. Patrols were conducted by Maj. Harada Kazuo, Capt. Higuchi Yoichi, and Lieutenant Irie, who was also to take a platoon and search for abandoned IJA vehicles. *SSNT* [535], vol. 26, pp. 307-8, citing 3rd Tank Regt. combat report.

6. The Yoshimaru regiment's Operations Order No. 24 of 11 A.M. was issued at the laager south of Heights 731. 3nd Tank Regt. combat report, cited in *SSNT* [535], vol. 26, p. 311.

7. But IJA infantry had encountered pesky Russian wire—"fine low strands [that] resembled piano-wire traps"—at Changkufeng hill in July of the preceding year. See Coox, *Anatomy* [679], pp. 141-42.

8. For piano wire: Irie, Takeshita, Ogata, Masuda interviews; *JRD* [965], *JSM* 11, part 3/B, p. 304; Tsuji [585], pp. 151-52; Gomikawa, *Nomonhan* [212], p. 65; and *SSNT* [535], vol. 26, pp. 315-18, 320. Z. Tomioka says that only the 3rd Regiment, not his 4th Regiment, encountered piano wire. He adds that the wire was really intended for use in pianos and was made in Japan and exported to the USSR. Tomioka had never heard of a combat application before Nomonhan. (Interview.) Battery commander Kusaba denied rumors that the piano wire was electrified. JRD [965], JSM 11, part 3/C, p. 514, citing Kusaba, *Noro kōchi* [358]. For a description of piano wire by a captured Soviet tank company commander, see Hōson [263], p. 104: the wire, studied in maneuvers, was sent from the Moscow Tank School. One strand could catch a light tank; three strands, even a medium machine. Piano wire was invisible at 50 meters, and could be missed sight of at even closer range. Once discerned, it looked like "paper ribbon."

9. Irie, Takeshita interviews; 3rd Tank Regt. combat report, cited in *SSNT* [535], vol. 26, pp. 321-24, 333.

10. Irie interview; and 3rd Tank Regt. combat report, cited in *SSNT* [535], vol. 26, pp. 325, 327-29.

11. *SSNT* [535], vol. 26, pp. 325-26. Irie also remembers seeing a vehicle, perhaps a tankette, with a dead man in the driver's seat, speeding across the battlefield. (Interview.)

12. Yasuoka detachment [133]; Irie, Takeshita, Noguchi interviews; and 3rd Tank Regt. combat report, cited in *SSNT* [535], vol. 26, pp. 320-25, 329-30, vol. 27, p. 190. Also see Rikugun, *Shōsen* [485], no. 29. According to a postwar summary, only 11 of 33 officers in the 3rd Tank Regt. survived; *Maru*, Sept. 1961, p. 155. Tsuji kills off Tamada in *Nomonhan* [585], p. 151. The error is parroted in JRD [965], JSM 11, part 3/B, p. 304. Both also say the Japanese lost about 30 light and 10 medium tanks in two days of fighting. Tsuji [585], p. 152; JRD [965], JSM 11, part 3/B, p. 305.

13. Shishkin [920], p. 583. On 5 July, Tass cited a joint Soviet-MPRA communiqué to the effect that, in three days, artillery had knocked out 50 of about 100 Japanese tanks, plus eight guns; IJA-Manchukuoan casualties were estimated at 800. The Soviet side admitted 100 men killed and 200 wounded, and 25 tanks and armored cars knocked out. AGS Intelligence Report No. 32, 6 July 1939 [141]. Summary also reported by Grummon from Moscow to U.S. Dept. of State, no. 369, 6 July 1939 (National Archives file 761.9315 Manchuria/118; NARS [980]).

14. Plus 743 artillery shells and 10 rolls of piano wire. 3rd Tank Regt. combat report, cited in *SSNT* [535], vol. 26, p. 330. Also see JRD [965], JSM 11, part 3/B, p. 305; and Tsuji [585], p. 152, both of which claim the Russians lost at least 60-70 tanks destroyed and a large number of infantry.

15. Gomikawa, *Nomonhan* [212], p. 66. Also see p. 63.

16. Tamada's Operations Order No. 39-2 of 10:10 A.M. was issued at a point judged to be two km. southeast of Heights 735. Again there were troubles with location. The regiment had thought it was moving west by southwest; the true direction was later found to be south by southwest. 4th Tank Regt. [134]; Tamada interview.

17. Yasuoka Detachment, Operations Order No. 23, 3 P.M., 3 July, at Heights 738. Around 5 P.M., 2nd Lieutenant Tashiro returned from patrol and reported no enemy in the Heights 755 area, and still no sign of Itō's burned tank. 4th Tank Regt. [134]; Tamada interview.

18. Tamada Tank Unit, Operations Order No. 39-3, 6:30 P.M., 3 July, at Heights 738. 4th Tank Regt. [134].

19. 2nd Bn., 28th Inf. Regt. [110].

20. Yamagata's regimental order was issued at 8:40 P.M., 3 July, at a point two km. southwest of Heights 731. 64th Inf. Regt. combat report, cited in *SSNT* [535], vol. 26, pp. 330, 332-34.

21. 4th Tank Regt. [134]; Yasuoka detachment [133]; Tamada, Noguchi interviews; and *SSNT* [535], vol. 26, pp. 334, 337-38.

22. Yasuoka Detachment, Operations Order No. 24, 9 P.M., 3 July, on heights northeast of Hill 738. 4th Tank Regt. [134].

23. Tamada Tank Unit, Operations Order No. 44-1, 6 P.M., 4 July, on high ground east of the confluence. 4th Tank Regt. [134].

24. The 4th Tank Regiment's records for 4 July [134] indicate two light tanks lost by the 1st Company, and one medium tank by the 4th Company. Also Tamada interview.

25. One Soviet tank is listed as captured on 4 July.

26. At 9 P.M. on 3 July, Yasuoka observed that the division had advanced to a point 6 km. north of the confluence. But as of 6 P.M. on 4 July, Tamada understood that "the front line of the Komatsubara unit was to have progressed near Hara [Heights] by now." Tamada Tank Unit, Operations Order No. 41-1 [134].

27. Tamada Tank Unit, Operations Order No. 44, 8 A.M., 5 July, two km. southeast of Heights 738 [134].

28. The 4th Tank Regiment's records for 5 July [134] show two light tanks lost by the 2nd Company.

29. Yasuoka Detachment, Operations Order No. 26, noon, 5 July, at Heights 738. Restructuring of the detachment and details of the proposed attack are outlined in Operations Order No. 27, 9 P.M., as is the twilight timing for the offensive. 4th Tank Regt. [134].

30. The Tanaka battery of the 12th Antiaircraft Artillery Regiment claimed to have shot down three aircraft, expending 81 rounds in the process. Yasuoka detachment [133]; 4th Tank Regt. [134].

31. Tomioka never recovered more than half of his vision. Glasses allowed him to see, after the two months of blindness, but his eyeballs remain scarred, and they pain him in the summer. He stayed in the army, becoming a captain by war's end and surviving Iwo Jima, from which he was evacuated with paratyphus aboard the last plane before the U.S. landings; he even lived through the atomic bombing of Hiroshima, about 12 km. from ground zero, where he was one of only 270 survivors of a 530-man army unit. (Interviews.)

32. Yasuoka Detachment, Operations Order No. 29, noon, 6 July. 4th Tank Regt. [134]. For the actions of the Yamagata infantry regiment's 3rd Battalion, specifically the 10th Company, see *SSNT* [535], vol. 27, pp. 206-8.

33. Tamada interview; and Yasuoka detachment [133].

34. Tamada Tank Unit, Operations Order No. 49, 4 P.M., 6 July, on south side of Heights 755; and Supplementary Order No. 49-2. 4th Tank Regt. [134].

35. Details of the tactical adjustments are contained in Yasuoka detachment, Operations Order, Supplement A, 9 P.M., 6 July; and Tamada Tank Unit, Operations Order No. 50, 9:20 P.M. 4th Tank Regt. [134].

36. 4th Regt. HQ, 1 killed; 1st Co., 2 killed, 3 wounded; 2nd Co., 4 wounded, 3rd Co., 7 killed, 2 officers (Tamaki, Tomioka) and 5 men wounded; 4th Co., 1 officer (Shiragata) and 7 men killed, 10 men wounded. In the "retired" 3rd Regt., the casualties were 1 killed and 1 wounded. 4th Tank Regt. [134]; BBSS, *SS* [180], vol. 27, p. 532.

37. Yasuoka detachment [133]; and *SSNT* [535], vol. 27, pp. 252, 262.

38. Noguchi, Irie, Tamada interviews; and Yasuoka detachment [133]. Kurusu wrote a letter about this episode to his old 3rd Regiment commander, Col. Yamaji Hideo, now an intendance school instructor. *SSNT* [535], vol. 27, p. 270. This source claims that Kurusu had 14 tanks in action, which seems high, although an IJA training document later said that there were 18 tanks and 10 tankettes left in the regiment. Additional details: the 2nd Co. counterattacked at 3:05 P.M. at 2,000 meters; the 1st Co. at 3:08 P.M. at 1,500 meters. Of 9 or 10 BT tanks, only two got away, damaged. The Japanese tanks fired 181 armor-piercing shells, and (contrary to Kurusu's comments) the Russian tanks did not get off a round. Rikugun, *Shōsen* [485], no. 30.

As for the replacements who came with Kurusu, a Captain Hamada took over the 1st Company, temporarily commanded by 1st Lieutenant Takeshita after the death of Captain Miyatake. (Takeshita interview.) Later Colonel Ikoma would assume command of the 3rd Regiment.

CHAPTER 24

1. The Kwantung Army chief of staff was the issuing authority; Tsuji was the drafting officer. Kwantung Army, 1st Section, Wire No. 382, 2:10 P.M., 9 July. Kantōgun [99], in GSS [205], vol. 10, pp. 77-78, 118. For the text of Kwantung Army Operations Order No. 50-A, see JRD [965], JSM 11, part 3/B, p. 316; BBSS, SS [180], vol. 27, pp. 547-48; Tsuji [585], pp. 154-55.

2. Kantōgun [99], in GSS [205], vol. 10, p. 78. Today, Noguchi does not recall detecting anything out of the ordinary in Yasuoka's reaction to the order. After all, IJA commanders were not supposed to reveal emotions. But Noguchi is not sure of the acuity of his observations in early July, when he fell ill. (Interview; also see n. 19.) That Yasuoka did indeed "blow his stack," as described in the following text, is confirmed by Komatsubara's diary entry for 10 July [25], lodging the criticism that it was highly inappropriate for a general officer to have "vented his displeasure in front of subordinates."

3. Yasuoka Detachment Wire No. 82 of the 9th elicited Kwantung Army 1st Section Wire No. 394, 2:10 P.M., 10 July, drafting officer Tsuji for the army chief of staff, addressed to 23rd Division chief of staff, for delivery to Yasuoka. Kantōgun [99], in GSS [205], vol. 10, pp. 78, 119. Also Masuda, Tamada, Ogata interviews. A number of other sources incorrectly date Wire No. 394 on 13 July. Y. Nishihara reminded me that there really was leeway in IJA orders bearing upon the timing of deactivation: if the situation allowed, the unit could be dissolved as of the time of the order, but if the recipient was still in action, one could wait until the combat calmed down. The second reading was entirely acceptable in the "traditional way" of IJA interpretation, since orders to a general were not "laws" as such. (Interview.)

4. Kwantung Army, 1st Section, Wire No. 384, Operations Order No. 51, 5:45 P.M., 10 July, Tsuji for the army chief of staff. Kantōgun [99], in GSS [205], vol. 10, pp. 78, 119.

5. See JRD [965], JSM 11, part 3/B, pp. 316-17.

6. See n. 5. Also see Kantōgun [99], in GSS [205], vol. 10, p. 118; SSNT [535], vol. 27, p. 328; BBSS, SS [180], vol. 27, p. 549.

7. Yasuoka's "adjusted" outlook was learned from Noguchi by the Kwantung Army at the time; Kantōgun [99], in GSS [205], vol. 10, p. 78. Information on the pullback order was derived from Yasuoka detachment [133].

8. Takeshita, Tamada interviews; BBSS, SS [180], vol. 27, pp. 540-41; Komatsubara [25], 15 July.

9. Tamada thinks that he made his recommendation to Yasuoka on 18 July. (Interview.) But Komatsubara's diary [25] indicates that it was 17 July when the division commander visited Yasuoka as well as Ioki and the Manchukuoan unit.

10. Staff officer Shimanuki Takeharu hand-carried the Kwantung Army order of 24 July to Komatsubara at 2 P.M. on the 25th. 23rd Division Operations Order No. 148 was issued at 5:30 P.M. that day; para. 6 applies to the Yasuoka detachment. SSNT [535], vol. 28, pp. 262-64. BBSS, SS [180], vol. 27, p. 551, states that the Kwantung Army's (formal?) order was issued on the night of 25 July. Tamada believes that the detachment had already been released from divisional command, but Komatsubara's diary entry for 25 July [25] gainsays the colonel's recollection.

11. A depot or cadre division (rusu shidan) was responsible for the training and equipping of recruits and the dispatch of supplies and replacements to the field division that had been raised in the divisional district of the homeland or Korea where the "parent" depot division was permanently based.

12. Irie, Tamada interviews.

13. Yasuoka detachment [133]; Masuda interview. I have attempted to reconcile varying casualty charts. Iida et al., for example, say that only 11 of 33 officers survived in the Yoshimaru regiment; [270], p. 155.

14. Two tankettes were also wrecked, one was repaired later, and four were fixed on the spot, from a total of 19 engaged. In the repairable category, some tanks broke down repeatedly: one

Type 97, three times; four Type 89 (*Otsu*) tanks, twice; and one *Otsu*, three times. A repairable breakdown was defined as immobilization requiring more than one day to fix. Iida et al. [270], p. 155; Yasuoka detachment [133]. Irie thinks that regimental aide Koga was lost in a second Type 97 tank. (Interview.)

15. Noguchi correspondence. Also Masuda, Tamada, Irie, Noguchi, Ogata interviews.

16. Yasuoka detachment [133]; Ogata interview. Some categories are lower than only the 3rd Regiment's claims for 2-3 July. Also see Tsuji [585], p. 152. The Tamada regiment captured two tanks (one on 4 July, the other on the 6th), a truck, three machine guns, an antitank weapon with 242 shells, and one prisoner (all on 6 July). 4th Tank Regt. [134]. I have omitted minor categories—small arms, light machine guns, gas masks, etc. For IJA propaganda on the eve of the Pacific War concerning the prowess at Nomonhan of Japanese tanks, however few, see G. Mishima et al. [402]. Conversely, Hayashi Katsuya downgrades IJA claims. [238], p. 185.

17. Noguchi, Ogata, Masuda, Irie, Tamada, Imaoka interviews; JRD [965], *JSM* 11, part 3/B, p. 315; Imaoka, "Nomonhan" [13], pp. 55-56.

18. Tamada, Noguchi, Irie interviews; and anonymous introduction to Noguchi's "Nomonhan no kuhai" [448], p. 71.

19. According to Noguchi, Nakamura "fled" without telling him, after the 23rd Division had reassembled on the right shore. But the episode was not really so "secret" at the time: the Yasuoka detachment's diary entry for 3 July [133] notes that Lt. Col. Takazawa had been wounded and Major Noguchi was ill, so Major Nakamura filled in. Also see Irie [18].

20. "Nihon no sensha" [439], p. 90. My discussion draws heavily on Imaoka, "Nomonhan" [13], pp. 54-55. Also see Gomikawa, *Nomonhan* [212], p. 66. In a postwar interrogation, Terada Masao—a lieutenant general by war's end—said that a major reason for the Japanese defeat at Nomonhan was "the poor quality of the Japanese armored corps." JRD [957], *Interrogations*, vol. 2, p. 493 (16 Sept. 1947).

21. The Japanese army customarily used 1:25,000 or 1:50,000 maps. But in Manchukuo, the scale was 1:100,000. Y. Nishihara interview.

22. 4th Tank Regt. [134]; Tamada, Irie interviews. Also see Gomikawa, *Nomonhan* [212], p. 62.

23. Rikugun, *Shōsen* [485], no. 31; Ogata interview.

24. Privileged 3rd Tank Regiment officer sources.

25. 4th Tank Regt. [134]; Tamada interview.

26. 4th Tank Regt. [134]; Tamada interview.

27. Noguchi, interview and [449]; BBSS, *SS* [180], vol. 27, p. 257; Rikugun, *Shōsen* [485], no. 31.

28. Privileged IJA officer sources.

29. Noguchi, interview and [449]. Noguchi does not pretend to be acquainted with Yoshimaru's thinking just before the colonel's death; Yamagata would have known best. But Noguchi was well acquainted with Yoshimaru's tactical views from the days of serving under him in the Chiba regiment.

30. Capt. Takata Kiyomi, cited by Onda, [473], vol. 1, pp. 166-67. For data on IJA armor plating, see chap. 21.

31. Takeshita interview.

32. See chap. 21, n. 4.

33. When Imaoka inspected the units in Kungchuling in early June he found that the 3rd Regiment lacked spare parts for its new Type 97 medium tanks but that there were enough parts to sustain the Type 89 *Otsu* tanks for six months of emergency use. As for the 4th Regiment, apart from the ancient Type 89 *Kō* tanks, Imaoka thinks that a little over half of the Type 95 light vehicles were of an old type. (Interview.)

34. Harada Kazuo [224], pp. 44-45; Tamada, Takeshita, Noguchi, Z. Tomioka, Irie interviews.

35. 4th Tank Regt. [134]; Irie [18].

36. Only on the eve of Nomonhan had Yoshimaru's 3rd Regiment started to convert from two to three companies with four platoons each. Tamada's 4th Regiment was made up of six companies, but the 5th and 6th (equipped with tankettes) had been sent to China. During Imaoka's

visit to Kungchuling in early June, Tamada told him that he wanted three more tanks per company for training purposes. The existing organization allowed ten for combat, only three for wartime training. As a result, combat tanks had to be diverted to training. Yoshimaru agreed with Tamada. (Imaoka interview.)

37. Tamada, Noguchi, Irie, Masuda, Takeshita, Z. Tomioka, Ogata interviews; 4th Tank Regt. [134]. Also see Kobayashi [24], 19 July; Gomikawa, *Nomonhan* [212], p. 63; SSNT [535], vol. 26, pp. 147, 276, 317-18, 325.

38. Erickson, *Soviet* [722], p. 521. Or, as the Japanese put it: "We missed by a hair. It was a pity (*oshii*)."

39. Hayashi Katsuya gives a figure of 70 IJA tanks and 75 armored cars [tankettes]. [238], pp. 182, 185. An MPRA source cites even higher figures: 156 tanks and armored cars. Sasaki [910], p. 218. The Tass communiqué of 5 July refers to three or four IJA tank regiments; see chap. 23, n. 13. For Zhukov's remarks to Stalin, see *Memoirs* [1017], p. 169.

40. "Officers and men, and commanders of army units wholeheartedly congratulated their neighbors and friends on a victory gained." Zhukov, *Memoirs* [1017], p. 154. Also see JRD [965], JSM 11, part 3/B, pp. 312-13; Shishkin [920], pp. 583, 588; BBSS, *SS* [180], vol. 27, pp. 497, 516. Colonel Icks' account is poor. For example, he says a Japanese armored regiment approximated the size of a Soviet tank brigade, with about 100 tanks. [774], p. 93.

CHAPTER 25

1. AGS 5th Section data as of 4 July. AGS Intelligence Report No. 32, 6 July [141].

2. 23rd Division, Operations Order No. 112. BBSS, *SS* [180], vol. 27, p. 526; SSNT [535], vol. 27, pp. 191-92.

3. BBSS, *SS* [180], vol. 27, p. 533; Yasuoka detachment [133]. On 4 July, the detachment incurred 22 casualties.

4. Tamada interview; Yasuoka detachment [133]; SSNT [535], vol. 27, pp. 193, 196.

5. Regarding air actions, see chap. 23. Casualties of the Tamada regiment and especially of the Kajikawa battalion are detailed elsewhere. In his diary entry for 5 July [25], Komatsubara wrote that, under air attack, vehicles should not stop (the worst procedure) or proceed, but should reverse course or zigzag.

6. Yasuoka Detachment, Operations Orders Nos. 26 and 27. Yasuoka detachment [133]; BBSS, *SS* [180], vol. 27, p. 531; SSNT [535], vol. 27, pp. 203-4, 211.

7. Tamada interview; SSNT [535], vol. 27, pp. 196-97.

8. On 4 July, the battalion found eight enemy corpses, took one prisoner, destroyed a rapid-fire gun, and captured one light machine gun, other small arms, and three trucks and two motorcycles, which broke down after use. 2nd Bn., 28th Inf. Regt. [110].

9. *Ibid.*; and Takashima, *Barushagaru* [555], pp. 44-61, 64-73. Kajikawa's casualty data are from Yasuoka detachment [133]. No mention is made of the actual performance of the neighboring 8th Infantry Company of the 64th Regiment.

10. Casualties on 6 July, apart from the tank regiments and the Kajikawa battalion: Yasuoka detachment headquarters, 1 killed; 1st Independent FA Regt., 6 killed, 7 wounded; engineers, 4 killed, 1 wounded. Yasuoka detachment [133].

11. It had been thought that Yamagata's regiment was near Heights 733, but the aerial reconnaissance indicated that the heights was occupied by the enemy. Yasuoka Detachment, Operations Order No. 29: Komatsubara [25], 6 July; Yasuoka detachment [133]; SSNT [535], vol. 27, pp. 212, 214-15.

12. 23rd Division, Operations Order No. 116, 6 July: Komatsubara [25], 6, 7 July; 4th Tank Regt. [134]; Yasuoka detachment [133]; BBSS, *SS* [180], vol. 27, pp. 533-35. The 1,000 Manchukuoan horsemen northeast of Heights 755 possessed only two mountain guns to fend off tanks. SSNT [535], vol. 27, p. 218, citing 3rd Bn., 13th FA Regt., combat report, 5 July.

13. JRD [959], parts 1-2; BBSS, *SS* [180], vol. 27, p. 533. Also see Coox, *Anatomy* [679], p. 130. For wartime propaganda about alleged Russian timidity in night fighting at close quarters, see Maj. Nishikawa Masayuki in Yamanaka [615], p. 275. Now Nishikawa tells me that the Russians *were* willing to fight at night. (Interview.)

14. 23rd Division, Operations Order No. 117, 8 A.M., 7 July: BBSS, *SS* [180], vol. 27, p. 536. Also see Mita [406], p. 160.

15. Komatsubara [25], 7 July; Yasuoka detachment [133]; Kobayashi diary, 7 July, cited in *SSNT* [535], vol. 27, p. 231. Infantry records speak of a projected 9 P.M. jump-off, with no mention of the 30-minute artillery supporting fire. See 72nd Inf. Regt. [121].

16. 64th Inf. Regt. combat record, cited in *SSNT* [535], vol. 27, p. 244. Kobayashi was relieved to see a signal flare go up on Yamagata's front at 1:30 A.M. On Sakai's sector, no flare appeared till 3:45 A.M. Kobayashi diary, 7 July, cited in *SSNT* [535], vol. 27, p. 245.

17. Based on Nishikawa interview; 72nd Inf. Regt. [121]; BBSS, *SS* [180], p. 537. But Yasuoka's information, at least at the outset, was quite different: total Left Wing Unit casualties amounted to five officers and an unstated number of men killed; merely one officer and 18 men had been wounded. Main losses inflicted on the enemy included 150 abandoned corpses, five captured artillery pieces, and two vehicles. Yasuoka detachment [133]. As of 11 July, the AGS 5th Section learned that the Yamagata regiment had captured three 15-cm. howitzers and two mountain guns, all in usable condition, southwest of Heights 733. AGS Intelligence Report No. 35, 11 July [141]. Also see General Kobayashi [343]; *SSNT* [535], vol. 27, pp. 233-40, including evidence by the 1st Battalion aide, 1st Lt. Nomura Haruyoshi. The Japanese figures for the wounded are transposed, however, in [535], vol. 27, p. 247.

18. Yasuoka Detachment, Operations Order No. 32, 5 A.M., 8 July: Yasuoka detachment [133]; Komatsubara [25], 7 July; *SSNT* [535], vol. 27, p. 246.

19. Shishkin [920], pp. 588-89. Shishkin dates the IJA attack as 6 July. Zhukov merely says that at this stage the Japanese confined their actions to "battle reconnaissance." *Memoirs* [1017], p. 154. For a partial Russian listing of the Heroes of the Soviet Union from the Nomonhan fighting, see *Nomonhan* [452], p. 19. Remizov Heights is best equated with Barunishi (Heights 733).

20. AGS Intelligence Report No. 33, 7 July [141]; 71st Inf. Regt. [119]; Onda [473], vol. 1, pp. 197-99. The orders were 23rd Division Operations Order No. 116, 6 July; and Okamoto Detachment, Operations Order No. 63, 10:20 A.M., 6 July, issued on north side of Heights 752.

21. Onozuka interview; 71st Inf. Rgt. [119]; *SSNT* [535], vol. 27, p. 221.

22. The Okamoto detachment's problem of orientation was complicated by the fact that there were two Heights 749 (Yoku Heights) and two Heights 753 (Imi Heights), and that Nigesorimot was to be identified by one pine tree whereas two pines grew on Heights 758. The discrepancies in location are well described in Onda [473], vol. 1, p. 201. Also see 71st Inf. Regt. [119]; and *SSNT* [535], vol. 27, p. 222.

23. Yasuoka Detachment, Operations Order No. 33, 9:30 A.M., 8 July: Kobayashi [24], 8 July; Yasuoka detachment [133]; 72nd Inf. Regt. [121].

24. Yasuoka Detachment, Operations Order No. 34, 6:50 P.M., 8 July: Yasuoka detachment [133]; and *SSNT* [535], vol. 27, p. 245.

25. 2nd Bn., 28th Inf. Regt. [110]; Mita [406], p. 180; Takashima, *Barushagaru* [555], pp. 77-78; Sumi interview.

26. 72nd Inf. Regt. [121]; Mita [406], p. 207; *SSNT* [535], vol. 27, pp. 253, 260-64, 282-84. Also I. Saitō, Numazaki, Sumi interviews.

27. The Yasuoka detachment operations order was delivered at 6 P.M.; the Kobayashi Infantry Corps, Operations Order No. 26, at 8:40 P.M. Sakai issued 72nd Inf. Regt. Operations Order No. 24 at 7 P.M., at his command post 3 km. southeast of Heights 733. 72nd Inf. Regt. [121]; Nishikawa interview; *SSNT* [535], vol. 27, pp. 253-55.

28. 1st Bn., 64th Inf. Regt. combat report, cited in *SSNT* [535], vol. 27, p. 257.

29. Komatsubara [25], 8 July; Yasuoka detachment [133]; 5th Co., 64th Inf. Regt., combat report, cited in *SSNT* [535], vol. 27, p. 257; PFC Tanabe Chikato (10th Co.), diary cited in [535], vol. 27, p. 258.

30. Negami interview; Sumi, *Jissen* [541], pp. 53-57; BBSS, *SS* [180], vol. 27, pp. 536-37; *SSNT* [535], vol. 27, pp. 267-68.

31. Okamoto Unit, Operations Order No. 65, 1:25 P.M., 8 July, at Heights 758 (later found to be 1 km. west of Nigesorimot): 71st Inf. Regt. [119].

32. In one of the hill-clearing actions by the 3rd Battalion, says Captain Onozuka, the Japanese easily ousted one squad of Russians. He called this particular elevation Fumi Heights (Heights 723?). Manchukuoan forces were about two kilometers to his company's left. Onozuka interview. Also see Onda [473], vol. 1, p. 203; 71st Inf. Regt. [119].

33. Komatsubara [25], 9 July.

34. *SSNT* [535], vol. 27, pp. 538-39.

35. Yasuoka Detachment, Operations Order No. 35, 1:40 P.M., 9 July: Yasuoka detachment [133]; BBSS, *SS* [180], vol. 27, p. 539.

36. Komatsubara [25], 9 July. For Uchiyama's new artillery command, see chap. 27.

37. 2nd Bn., 28th Inf. Regt. [110]; Yasuoka detachment [133]; Sumi interview; Mita [406], p. 160.

38. Sumi, interview and *Jissen* [541], pp. 67-71; Mita [406], p. 184; 2nd Bn., 28th Inf. Regt. [110]; *SSNT* [535], vol. 27, pp. 268, 278. An exciting account of events on 9/10 July is told by Superior Pvt. Shinomiya Sakae (1st Plat., 2nd Co., 1st Bn., 26th Inf. Regt.): *SSNT* [535], vol. 27, pp. 278-86. On the morning of the 10th, the only two survivors of the Hachida platoon made it to the Hinomaru positions of the Kajikawa battalion. "Several dozen over 100" badly wounded men were lying side by side in the trenches. Mita [406], p. 189, citing PFC Sakata.

39. 64th Inf. Regt., Operations Order No. 41: Someya notes, cited in *Nomonhan* [40], vol. 4, p. 82; *SSNT* [535], vol. 27, p. 274.

40. Yasuoka Detachment, Operations Order No. 35, 1:40 P.M., 9 July; Kobayashi Infantry Corps, Operations Order No. 29, 6 P.M.; 72nd Inf. Regt., Operations Order No. 25, 8:20 P.M., on a dune 3 km. south of Heights 733: 72nd Inf. Regt. [121].

41. 23rd Division, Operations Order No. 116, 5 P.M., 6 July. 1st Lt. Amiya's 1st Platoon of the 1st Engineer Company did the job. BBSS, *SS* [180], vol. 27, pp. 533-36; *SSNT* [535], vol. 27, pp. 261-62.

42. 71st Inf. Regt. (Nagano Detachment), Operations Order No. 66, 10:20 P.M., 8 July; No. 67, 2 P.M., 9 July: 71st Inf. Regt. [119]; Onda [473], vol. 1, pp. 211, 218-25, citing a 2nd Machine Gun Co. platoon leader, 2nd Lt. Kishi Akimasa.

43. Yasuoka detachment [133]; and Kobayashi diary, 10 July, cited in *SSNT* [535], vol. 27, p. 289.

44. For the restructuring of Komatsubara's command: Kobayashi Infantry Corps, Operations Order No. 31, 1:15 P.M., 10 July. For the "mop-up" order: 23rd Division, Operations Order No. 127, 7 P.M., 10 July. See *SSNT* [535], vol. 27, p. 287.

45. 2nd Bn., 28th Inf. Regt. [110].

46. Sumi, *Jissen* [541], p. 71; and *SSNT* [535], vol. 27, p. 287.

47. Someya notes, cited in *Nomonhan* [40], vol. 4, p. 82; and *SSNT* [535], vol. 27, p. 290.

48. 72nd Inf. Regt., Operations Order No. 26, 3 P.M., 10 July; No. 27, 5 P.M., 10 July, on a dune 4 km. southeast of the confluence: 72nd Inf. Regt. [121].

49. 23rd Division, Operations Order No. 123; Nagano Detachment, Operations Order No. 68, 9 A.M., 10 July: 71st Inf. Regt. [119].

50. Komatsubara [25], 11 July; 2nd Bn., 28th Inf. Regt. [110]; Takashima, *Barushagaru* [555], pp. 79-82. For additional evidence of the joy of the IJA infantry at news of the forthcoming Japanese heavy-artillery offensive, see 72nd Inf. Regt. [121], 11 July. Obviously referring to the same artillery disaster that befell the Japanese on the 11th, Kusaba wrote that at 6:30 P.M. a 15-cm. shell hit the rear wagon lanes, killing 5 and wounding 12. JRD [965], *JSM* 11, part 3/C, p. 511, citing Kusaba, *Noro kōchi* [358].

51. Sumi, *Jissen* [541], p. 71; Mita [406], p. 198; Komatsubara [25], 11 July.

52. Probably 1st Lt. Nomura Norio, a 7th Division transport company commander, is referring to this action when he describes the destruction of a trench in which one of two teams totaling 12-13 Japanese soldiers had been huddling under fire with explosives intended for bridge demolition that night. After the detonation, Nomura (who had just left the shelter of the trench) could see only an arm and scattered bits of flesh. [455], p. 63.

53. Kobayashi Inf. Corps, Operations Order No. 33, 11:30 A.M., 11 July; 64th Inf. Regt., Operations Order No. 45, 3 P.M., 11 July, 1.5 km. east of Heights 733: Kobayashi diary, 11 July, cited in *SSNT* [535], vol. 27, pp. 290-97; *Nomonhan* [40], vol. 4, pp. 79-80, citing Makiyama.

54. 72nd Inf. Regt. [121]. Kobayashi had been thinking in terms of an advance of 1,500 meters. *SSNT* [535], vol. 27, p. 290. For Hayama's patrol, see 1st Lieutenant Moriyama's eulogy in 23rd Division [113], no. 4.

55. Battery commander Kusaba gives instances of IJA soldiers who risked their lives to prevent their gas masks from falling into enemy hands. JRD [965], *JSM* 11, part 3/C, pp. 510-12, citing *Noro kōchi* [358].

56. A number of questions remain unanswered regarding the dates, locations, and intentions involved in Captain Nishimura's actions. I have sought to reconcile the varying information found in 71st Inf. Regt. [119] and in Onda [473], vol. 1, pp. 219-21, 224-25, 230.

CHAPTER 26

1. Komatsubara [25], 12 July; *SSNT* [535], vol. 27, pp. 298-99, citing Kobayashi diary.

2. *Nomonhan* [40], vol. 4, pp. 80-81 (Makiyama); *SSNT* [535], vol. 27, p. 297.

3. *SSNT* [535], vol. 27, pp. 292-95.

4. *Nomonhan* [40], vol. 4, p. 81 (Makiyama).

5. Komatsubara [25], 12, 15 July.

6. Kobayashi Inf. Group, Operations Order No. 35, 12 July. Kobayashi diary, 12 July, cited in *SSNT* [535], vol. 27, p. 299.

7. 64th Inf. Regt., Operations Order No. 46, 10 P.M., 12 July, cited in *SSNT* [535], vol. 27, p. 297.

8. *SSNT* [535], vol. 27, p. 299; and Komatsubara [25], 14 July.

9. Komatsubara [25], 13, 14 July; and *SSNT* [535], vol. 27, pp. 301, 302, 305.

10. 72nd Inf. Regt., Operations Order No. 30, 6 P.M., 12 July. 72nd Inf. Regt. [121]; and *SSNT* [535], vol. 27, p. 300. Hayama's latest patrols took place in the early morning and at midday on the 13th.

11. Mita [406], pp. 198-202.

12. 2nd Bn., 28th Inf. Regt. [110].

13. Nagano Unit, Operations Order No. 70, 7:40 A.M., 12 July; revised 12:45 P.M.; 23rd Division, Operations Order No. 132, received 7:20 P.M.; Nagano Unit, Operations Order No. 72, midnight, 12 July. 71st Inf. Regt. [119]; Onda [473], vol. 1, p. 226.

14. Sumi, interview and *Jissen* [541], pp. 72-77; Mita [406], pp. 204-5, 208.

15. 2nd Bn., 28th Inf. Regt. [110]; Takashima, *Barushagaru* [555], pp. 65, 83-97.

16. 72nd Inf. Regt. [121]; 23rd Inf. Div. [113] (Moriyama). As noted in chap. 13, all three infantry regiments had been officially incorporated into the 23rd Division exactly one year earlier.

17. 71st Inf. Regt., Operations Order No. 74, 8 P.M., 13 July, No. 75, 6 P.M., 14 July. Onozuka interview; 71st Inf. Regt. [119]; Onda [473], vol. 1, pp. 238-42; *SSNT* [535], vol. 27, pp. 310-16.

18. Komatsubara [25], 13, 14 July. AGS data, as of 15 July, for the period since the 1st: abandoned corpses (found mostly with the knocked-out armor)—at least 1,500; prisoners (battalion commander and below)—about 40; tanks and armored cars knocked out—at least 300; captured—more than 10 armored vehicles, 3 15-cm. howitzers, 2 12-cm. howitzers, 6 mountain guns, many antitank weapons, etc. AGS Intelligence Report No. 38, 15 July [141]. A remarkably similar unclassified summary was issued by the Kwantung Army on 11 July. See M. Watanabe [607], pp. 97-98.

19. Komatsubara [25], 13 July.

20. I am indebted to T. Hamada, Imaoka, and Y. Nishihara for contributing to the analysis presented here.

21. T. Hamada interview. Also see JRD [965], *JSM* 11, part 3/C, p. 528, citing Kusaba, *Noro kōchi* [358].

22. According to Superior Pvt. Satō Shin, 2nd MG Co., 64th Inf. Regt., and his company commander, Capt. Funakura Eishirō; in *SSNT* [535], vol. 27, pp. 305-7. Also Noguchi interview.

23. Also 250 horses killed, 270 injured, and 70 missing. The armor losses included 14 medium and 16 light tanks plus three tankettes. Komatsubara [25], 13, 14 July. AGS 5th Section

data on Japanese casualties, as of 15 July, totaled "about 2,000." AGS Intelligence Report No. 38 [141].

24. Privileged IJA officer sources.

25. Y. Nishihara interview. Also see *SSNT* [535], vol. 27, p. 316.

26. Shishkin [920], pp. 589-90. Zhukov speaks highly of Yakovlev, identifies him as a Hero of the Soviet Union, but does not mention his death. *Memoirs* [1017], pp. 164, 240. For a Russian listing of Heroes of the Soviet Union from the Nomonhan Incident, including Yakovlev, see chap. 25, n. 19.

27. See *Voenno istoricheskii zhurnal*, no. 8 (1979), pp. 47-49. Précis by Michael Parrish. But, as we saw in chap. 19, Zhukov indicated that by 3 July the 57th Corps had already become the First Army Group. *Memoirs* [1017], p. 151. (The translation says 15 July, but the surrounding text refers to events of 3 July.)

CHAPTER 27

1. Ellen T. Fowler (d. 1929), *The Wisdom of Folly*, stanza 3. But, as General Westmoreland points out, "A commander clearly is the bellwether of his command and must display confidence and resolution. Even the slightest pessimism on his part can quickly pervade the ranks." William C. Westmoreland, *A Soldier Reports* (New York: Doubleday, 1976), p. 26.

2. BBSS, *SS* [180], vol. 27, p. 544; BBSS, *SS* [181], vol. 53, p. 250.

3. Y. Nishihara interview; JRD [965], *JSM* 11, part 3/B, p. 305; BBSS, *SS* [180], vol. 27, p. 552.

4. Hashimoto, Murata interviews. Hashimoto admits to a natural bias, since his own basic branch was artillery.

5. Nishikawa interview. Also see S. Hayashi, *Kantōgun* [242], pp. 162-63.

6. Inada interview; BBSS, *SS* [180], vol. 27, p. 545; *SSNT* [535], vol. 28, pp. 9-11.

7. Mishima, T. Hayashi, M. Tsuchiya, Ida (Iwata) interviews; JRD [965], *JSM* 11, part 3/B, p. 324, citing communication to me from Maj. Gen. Hata Yūzaburō, 30 Aug. 1956. *Okyū hahei* mobilization did not apply to rear units. 1st Lt. Prince Higashikuni (49th military academy class; d. 1969) was 1st Battery commander in the 1st Artillery Battalion. M. Tsuchiya interview; *SSNT* [535], vol. 28, p. 274; *Nomonhan* [40], vol. 3, pp. 22-23. Mishima had been 116th Division chief of staff during the Yangtze operations, 1938-39. (Interview.)

8. JRD [965], *JSM* 11, part 3/B, p. 319.

9. JRD [965], *JSM* 11, part 3/B, pp. 321, 323, 326, citing communication to me from Capt. Tsutsui Yoshio, survey company commander, 6 Sept. 1956. The JRD monograph, which was checked at the time by my consultant Captain Ida, calls the Someya unit a provisional heavy artillery battalion. Ida continued this usage in a later interview. Also see *SSNT* [535], vol. 28, pp. 95, 108-10, referring to a Muleng regiment. Hata Yūzaburō [5] termed Someya's force the Muleng heavy artillery unit; he identified the heavy siege artillery (*kōjōjūhō*) battery as consisting of Type 45 cannon. Siege artillery possessed no brigade organization.

10. Mishima interview; 23rd Division, Operations Order No. 141, 2 P.M., 17 July, and Artillery Corps, Operations Order No. 13, 19 July: BBSS, *SS* [180], vol. 27, pp. 565-66. Major General Uchiyama was two military academy classes senior to Major General Hata.

11. Y. Hata, "Nikki" [5]; and *SSNT* [535], vol. 28, pp. 25-26, citing Hata's "Nomonhan jiken senshi" [Nomonhan Incident Military History]. But when Hata and Ida visited the Muleng unit on 11 July, it was found that Someya had misidentified his location on the map. Ida interview.

12. Y. Hata, "Nikki" [5]; Ida, Mishima, T. Hayashi, M. Tsuchiya interviews. For information on Takatsukasa, see *SSNT* [535], vol. 28, pp. 28-29.

13. 23rd Division, Operations Order No. 123, morning, 10 July. Y. Hata, "Nikki" [5]; BBSS, *SS* [180], vol. 27, p. 552.

14. The 23rd Division employed the term *sōkōgeki* or "total offensive" to describe the forthcoming artillery offensive. BBSS, *SS* [180], vol. 27, p. 557.

15. BBSS, *SS* [180], vol. 27, p. 553; Komatsubara [25], 11 July.

16. Cited by M. Watanabe [607], pp. 96-97.

17. 23rd Division, Operations Order No. 132, 3 P.M., 12 July; BBSS, *SS* [180], vol. 27, p. 554.

18. Komatsubara [25], 12 July.

19. *SSNT* [535], vol. 28, pp. 111-14. On 18 July, Hata assigned Major Matsutomo's 1st FA Battalion (which belonged to the Nagano detachment but had now been transferred to the 1st Artillery Group) to the command of Takatsukasa, since he had established his CP south of the Holsten too. Y. Hata, "Nikki" [5].

20. Mishima, T. Hayashi interviews.

21. *SSNT* [535], vol. 28, pp. 108-9.

22. Mishima, Ida, T. Hayashi, M. Tsuchiya interviews; BBSS, *SS* [180], vol. 27, pp. 560, 562.

23. The figure for the 15-cm. howitzer *kisū* is firm, but there are variations in the other categories, depending on the scale of operations, etc. Ida, Y. Nishihara, Mishima, T. Hayashi interviews; BBSS, *SS* [180], vol. 27, p. 561; JRD [965], *JSM* 11, part 3/B, p. 353, n. 4.

24. Also Type 38 field gun, 12,000 rounds; 12-cm. howitzer (Type 38), 3,600; Type 90 field gun, 4,000. Y. Hata, "Nikki" [5]; Ida interview; BBSS, *SS* [180], vol. 27, p. 561. Mishima says his regiment was the best-off of all the artillery units, with about 12 *kisū*. (Interview.) As of 23 July, the 1st Battalion's 1st Battery had (and would fire) 550 rounds (515 common, 35 shrapnel); the 2nd Battery, 800 (720 common, 80 shrapnel). M. Tsuchiya interview.

25. Ida interview; and *SSNT* [535], vol. 28, pp. 245-46.

26. 23rd Division, Operations Order No. 141, 2 P.M., 19 July; Uchiyama Artillery Corps, Operations Order No. 13, 19 July. BBSS, *SS* [180], vol. 27, pp. 564-68; *SSNT* [535], vol. 28, pp. 117-18, citing Hata. A separate clause of the operations orders applied to Lt. Col. Yamaoka Shigemitsu's 10th Field Antiaircraft Artillery Regiment.

27. M. Tsuchiya interview.

28. Y. Hata, "Nikki" [5], 20 July.

29. *Ibid.*, 21 July.

30. 7th Co., 26th Inf. Regt. [105], 22 July; Y. Hata, "Nikki" [5], 22 July; Ida, Mishima, Sumi interviews; *SSNT* [535], vol. 28, pp. 122-23, citing Hata. Onozuka notes that heavy artillery cannot fire from sand mounts, and that the construction of concrete bases took days. (Interview.)

31. Y. Hata, "Nikki" [5], 23 July; Mishima, M. Tsuchiya, Ida, T. Hayashi interviews; *Nomonhan* [40], vol. 4, pp. 56-57, citing T. Hayashi; BBSS, *SS* [180], vol. 27, p. 568; *SSNT* [535], vol. 28, pp. 135-37.

32. *SSNT* [535], vol. 28, pp. 141-52, citing 2nd Bn. combat report, and interview with Sakuma, among others. The battalion's expenditure of 937 shells included 676 common, 238 pointed, and 23 shrapnel rounds.

33. *SSNT* [535], vol. 28, pp. 138-40.

34. Privileged IJA officer source. Field artillery specifications are from Fuji Artillery School data, corrected by Sgt. H. Tanaka in an interview.

35. The various 2nd Artillery Group orders are found in 1st Bn., 13th FA Regt. [124].

36. 3rd Bn., 13th FA Regt. [125]; H. Tanaka interview.

37. JRD [965], *JSM* 11, part 3/C, p. 517, citing Kusaba, *Noro kōchi* [358]; *SSNT* [535], vol. 28, p. 175.

38. *SSNT* [535], vol. 28, pp. 118, 174. But T. Hayashi, computing the 2nd Battalion's expenditure at four *kisū* per gun, thinks his unit alone fired the 1,280 rounds on 23 July. (Interview.)

39. Shimanuki interview; and *SSNT* [535], vol. 28, p. 161.

40. Y. Hata, "Nikki" [5], 23 July; Komatsubara [25], 23 July; *SSNT* [535], vol. 28, pp. 154-55, 128-29, citing Hata; BBSS, *SS* [180], vol. 27, p. 562. Ida thinks that IJA aerial coordination was stopped after enemy planes inflicted severe losses on scouting aircraft. He remembers two or three cases of air force cooperation with the artillery in connection with the 23 July offensive. (Interview.)

41. 23rd Division, Operations Order No. 146, 4:20 P.M., 23 July; 1st Artillery Group, Operations Order No. 17, 6 P.M., 23 July; 13th FA Regt./2nd Artillery Group, Operations Order No. 83, 8 P.M., 23 July; 3rd Bn., 13th FA Regt., Operations Order No. 36, 9:20 P.M., 23

July. Komatsubara [25], 24 July; 1st Bn., 13th FA Regt. [124]; BBSS, *SS* [180], vol. 27, pp. 569-70; *SSNT* [535], vol. 28, p. 218.

42. Y. Hata, "Nikki" [5], 23, 24 July; and *SSNT* [535], vol. 28, pp. 219-23, 236, citing Hata.

43. According to an alternative version, the 15-cm. howitzer and 10-cm. howitzer battalions did not get started with the relocation until afternoon on 24 July, began the move around sunset, and entered the new positions in the early hours of 25 July. BBSS, *SS* [180], vol. 27, p. 570. But the Hata diary entry for 24 July [5] notes the movement forward and participation in the infantry-support role that day. Interviews with Mishima and T. Hayashi reinforce my presentation. Also see *SSNT* [535], vol. 28, pp. 229-37.

44. *SSNT* [535], vol. 28, pp. 224, 238-40, citing Hata.

45. *SSNT* [535], vol. 28, pp. 226-28, 241-43, citing Hata.

46. M. Tsuchiya interview. Y. Hata, "Nikki" [5], 24 July, cites the 1.5 *kisū* figure; but Komatsubara's diary entry of the same date [25] speaks of four *kisū*.

47. Komatsubara [25], 24 July; Y. Hata, "Nikki" [5], 24 July.

48. Mishima, H. Tanaka interviews; Komatsubara [25], 24 July; JRD [965], *JSM* 11, part 3/C, p. 522, citing Kusaba, *Noro kōchi* [358].

49. 13th FA Regt./2nd Artillery Group, Operations Order No. 84, 8 P.M., 24 July, on high ground 1.5 km. east of Heights 738. 1st Bn., 13th FA Regt./2nd Artillery Group [124].

50. T. Hayashi, M. Tsuchiya, Mishima interviews; *SSNT* [535], vol. 28, pp. 247-50.

51. 3rd Bn., 13th FA Regt. [125].

52. BBSS, *SS* [180], vol. 27, pp. 570-73; Komatsubara diary, 25 July; Y. Hata, "Nikki" [5], 24, 25 July; JRD [965], *JSM* 11, part 3/B, pp. 321, 323; *Nomonhan* [40], vol. 4, p. 72, citing Itō Noboru; Kusaba, *Noro kōchi* [358]; JRD [965], *JSM* 11, part 3/C, p. 523; *SSNT* [535], vol. 28, pp. 253-55. For more extensive treatment, see Sumi, *Jissen* [541], pp. 91-100. Also T. Hayashi, M. Tsuchiya, Mishima, Sumi interviews.

53. Representative data are available for two IJA artillery battalions. Major Seki's 3rd Bn., 13th FA Regt., fired a total of 6,295 rounds between 9 July and 25 July: 7th Battery (75-mm. guns), 2,234 common and pointed shells, 592 shrapnel, total 2,826 rounds; 8th Battery (75-mm. guns), 1,377 common and pointed shells, 266 shrapnel, total 1,643 rounds; and 9th Battery (12-cm. howitzers), 1,826 armor-piercing rounds only. (3rd Bn., 13th FA Regt. [125], 25 July.) Major Umeda's two 15-cm. howitzer batteries of the 1st Bn., 1st Heavy Artillery Regt., fired 2,680 rounds in the first three days of the artillery offensive: 1,235 common shells, 115 shrapnel, total 1,350 rounds on 23 July; 589 common shells, 69 shrapnel, total 658 rounds on 24 July; and 527 common shells, 145 shrapnel, total 672 rounds on 25 July. (M. Tsuchiya interview.)

54. Y. Hata, "Nikki" [5], 25 July; BBSS, *SS* [180], vol. 27, pp. 572-73.

55. Y. Hata, "Nikki" [5], 25 July.

CHAPTER 28

1. An early-18th-century "spiritual training" text, in 11 volumes, prepared for use by the Nabeshima warrior clan in Saga province. A translation will be found in *Traditions* magazine, no. 6 (1978), p. 60.

2. BBSS, *SS* [180], vol. 27, p. 554. Also see chap. 26.

3. Shishkin [920]; JRD [965], *JSM* 11, part 3/C, pp. 590-91. Zhukov [1017] refers frequently to the fast-rising Fedyuninsky.

4. Konuma [26]; 71st Inf. Regt. [119]; 72nd Inf. Regt. [121]; Onda [473], vol. 1, p. 282; *SSNT* [535], vol. 28, pp. 209-10 (re: 71st Inf. Regt.).

5. Kanaizuka interview.

6. Komatsubara [25], 14 July; Onda [473], vol. 1, p. 269.

7. On the third or fourth day, when the battalion received a barrel of pickled plums (*umeboshi*), Sergeant Tanaka drank a tall glass of the "awful, sour" juice. It cured his dysentery. (Interview.) Also Onozuka interview. From the large literature on the epidemic, see Takashima, *Barushagaru* [555], pp. 99-100; and *SSNT* [535], vol. 28, p. 191 (re: 64th Inf. Regt.).

8. 23rd Division, Operations Order No. 141, 2 P.M., 19 July. BBSS, *SS* [180], vol. 27, pp. 564-65.

9. Nishikawa, T. Hamada interviews; 72nd Inf. Regt. [121]; 3rd Bn., 13th FA Regt. [125]; Nomura Haruyoshi in *Nomonhan* [40], vol. 3, p. 52, and vol. 5, pp. 125-27; *SSNT* [535], vol. 28, pp. 178-85.

10. Kanaizuka, interview and [22]; Someya Hatsuo in *Nomonhan* [40], vol. 5, pp. 117-19; *SSNT* [535], vol. 28, pp. 186-90, 203, 194-95. The 64th Regiment's reserve 2nd Battalion had jumped off after receiving orders at 10:30 P.M., accompanied by the regimental headquarters and the colors. The attack did not develop as intended, and the force was obliged to pull back at 3:40 A.M. *SSNT* [535], vol. 28, p. 203, citing combat report of 5th Co., 2nd Bn., 64th Inf. Regt.

11. A term used in the Second World War to describe enormous air bombardment in support of ground operations, designed to demoralize enemy units and smash positions and communications. Carpet bombing was employed to facilitate the Allied breakout from the Normandy beachhead in July 1944.

12. In an interview, Hikime said he set out at about 11 P.M. on moonless 22 July and got back around 5 A.M., just before the artillery offensive. But the 7th Company's combat report for 22 and 23 July [105] notes that Major Kawai ordered a patrol to scout the battalion's advance route at 4 A.M. on the 23rd, and that Hikime left for the Halha shore at 7:30 A.M., returning at 9:40 A.M. Hikime's version is convincing, although he does not mention a patrol after daylight.

13. The fragment remains embedded behind Hikime's ear to this day. He was a sight to behold, he says. At the hospital in Hailar, he looked in a mirror and and saw his "purple swollen tongue hanging in a twisted and smashed face." He remained in hospitals until Oct. 1940, from Hailar, Harbin, and Dairen to Osaka, Tokyo, and Asahigawa. Hikime interview; Sumi, interview and *Jissen* [541], pp. 82-85; 7th Co., 2nd Bn., 26th Inf. Regt. [105], 22-23 July.

14. *Shita o kande shinu*: death by biting off one's tongue. This method of suicide through self-induced hemorrhage is resorted to when a weapon or other means of self-destruction is not available.

15. 7th Co., 2nd Bn., 26th Inf. Regt. [105], 23-24 July; Hikime, Maeda interviews; Sumi, interview and *Jissen* [541], pp. 78-81. The late jump-off by the infantry, behind schedule because friendly artillery fire was not very effective, is documented in 2nd Bn., 28th Inf. Regt. [110], 23 July. The slain machine gun company commander was 1st Lt. Yamamoto Miki, the only military academy graduate in the company. In support of the 3rd Battalion, Tsunashima's regimental-gun battery fired about 40 rounds on 23 July, 10 per gun. There was one area bombardment by all four guns, aimed in the same direction and firing at the same time, but targets could not be confirmed. On two occasions, platoon-scale firing was ordered. Tsunashima interview.

16. 71st Inf. Regt. [119]; Onozuka interview; Onda [473], vol. 1, pp. 280-83; *SSNT* [535], vol. 28, p. 208.

17. Komatsubara [25], 23 July; and *SSNT* [535], vol. 28, p. 185, citing Kobayashi diary, 23 July.

18. *SSNT* [535], vol. 28, p. 202, citing Kobayashi diary, 24 July.

19. 7th Co., 2nd Bn., 26th Inf. Regt. [105], 24 July. Also see Takashima, *Barushagaru* [555], pp. 105-7.

20. Kanaizuka, interview and [22], 24 July. Also see *SSNT* [535], vol. 28, p. 203, citing 1st Bn. combat report.

21. Nishikawa interview; 72nd Inf. Regt. [121]; *Nomonhan* [40], vol. 3, p. 52; *SSNT* [535], vol. 28, pp. 204-6.

22. Nagano [Higashi] Detachment, Operations Order No. 82, 9 P.M., 24 July. 71st Inf. Regt. [119]; Onozuka interview; Onda [473], vol. 1, pp. 283-89; *Nomonhan* [40], vol. 6, pp. 130-31; *SSNT* [535], vol. 28, pp. 209, 214. Where there were discrepancies, I have relied in general on the regimental record.

23. S. Hamada interview; Komatsubara [25], 24, 25 July; *SSNT* [535], vol. 28, pp. 259-60, citing Kobayashi diary, 25 July.

24. Komatsubara [25], 25 July; and *SSNT* [535], vol. 28, p. 260, citing Kobayashi diary, 24 July.

25. When the division headquarters moved to its new location at 4 P.M. on 24 July, Kajikawa sent one and a half companies to guard the site. 2nd Bn., 28th Inf. Regt. [110], 24 July. Also see

7th Co., 2nd Bn., 26th Inf. Regt. [105], 25 July; and *SSNT* [535], vol. 28, pp. 259-61, citing Kobayashi diary, 25 July.

26. Kanaizuka, interview and [22], 25 July.

27. 72nd Inf. Regt. [121].

28. Nagano Detachment, Operations Order No. 83, 12 P.M., 25 July, 2 km. north of Heights 742. 71st Inf. Regt. [119]; Suzuki Yoshiyasu interview.

29. The figure for downed aircraft is credited to ground fire. BBSS, *SS* [180], vol. 27, p. 574. For artillery corps' claims, see Table 27.2.

30. Kantōgun [99], in *GSS* [205], vol. 10, p. 86; Y. Hata, "Nikki" [5].

31. Ida interview; Komatsubara [25], 24 July; BBSS, *SS* [180], vol. 27, p. 561; *SSNT* [535], vol. 28, pp. 269-70. The 23rd Division's original logistical plan of 23 June called for one *kaisenbun* of ammunition, 15 days' supply in this case, which probably amounted to one *kisū* per day. Imaoka explained IJA ammunition problems to me in detail. (Interviews and "Nomonhan" [13], pp. 68-69.)

32. Shimanuki, N. Itō interviews.

33. Fuji Artillery School data; BBSS, *SS* [180], vol. 27, pp. 562-63; JRD [969], *JSM* 7, pp. 140-41; Ida, T. Hayashi, Mishima interviews.

34. Ida interview; BBSS, *SS* [180], vol. 27, pp. 559-60; S. Hayashi, *Kōgun* [756], pp. 2-3. Komatsubara noted problems with cracks in gun mounts. Komatsubara [25], 29 July.

35. Komatsubara [25], 31 July.

36. BBSS, *SS* [180], vol. 27, pp. 562, 574.

37. Colonel Takatsukasa in *SSNT* [535], vol. 28, pp. 168-69. Also Mishima interview. Kusaba wrote that in August the Russian batteries began using cast-iron shells which exploded into large fragments, probably because of their enormous expenditure of rounds and the consequent shortage of ammunition. JRD [965], *JSM* 11, part 3/C, p. 522, citing Kusaba, *Noro kōchi* [358].

38. BBSS, *SS* [180], vol. 27, pp. 573-74; *SSNT* [535], vol. 28, pp. 191 (re: 64th Inf. Regt.), 196, 210 (re: 71st Inf. Regt.).

39. Shishkin [920], pp. 590-92.

CHAPTER 29

1. Kobayashi [24], 25 July; Komatsubara [25], 24-26 July; BBSS, *SS* [180], vol. 27, pp. 571, 576; *SSNT* [535], vol. 28, pp. 259-62, 272-73; Murata interview. One sustained battle (*kaisen*) was estimated to last one month, with the most severe expenditure occurring in 4-5 days of combat. One *kaisenbun* generally amounted to more than ten *kisū* (ammunition allocations) per category of artillery. Imaoka, Y. Nishihara interviews. At the time, the Kwantung Army had available from operational stock, only one *kaisenbun* for 3.5 divisions, and one *kaisenbun* for two heavy artillery brigades, according to Kwantung Army logistics staff Maj. Ashikawa Haruo. *SSNT* [535], vol. 18, p. 26.

2. See chap. 24.

3. Shimanuki interview; Kantōgun [99], in *GSS* [205], vol. 10, p. 86; Komatsubara [25], 26 July; BBSS, *SS* [180], vol. 27, pp. 573-86; JRD [965], *JSM* 11, part 3/B, pp. 351, 356.

4. Komatsubara [25], 26 July; BBSS, *SS* [180], vol. 27, p. 576.

5. 23rd Division, Operations Order No. 148, 5:30 P.M., 25 July, on dune 3 km. east of Kikugata Heights. *SSNT* [535], vol. 28, pp. 263-64. The Infantry Corps' operations order was No. 49, issued at 9:20 P.M., according to 72nd Inf. Regt. [121]. 13th FA Regt./2nd Artillery Group, Operations Order No. 85, 10 P.M., 25 July, in 1st Bn., 13th FA Regt. [124].

6. 7th Co., 2nd Bn., 26th Inf. Regt. [105], 25, 26 July.

7. 72nd Inf. Regt. [121].

8. Kanaizuka, interview and [22]; 71st Inf. Regt. [119].

9. Y. Hata, "Nikki" [5], 25-26 July; 13th FA Regt./2nd Artillery Group, Operations Order No. 86, 9:20 P.M., 26 July, in 1st Bn., 13th FA Regt. [124].

10. Nagano Detachment, Operations Order No. 85, 3 P.M., 26 July; No. 86, 6 P.M., 27 July; No. 87, 1 A.M., 28 July; No. 88, 2:15 P.M., 28 July; No. 89, 3:30 P.M., 29 July. 71st Inf. Regt. [119]; Onozuka interview; Komatsubara [25], 28 July; BBSS, *SS* [180], vol. 27, pp. 586-87;

SSNT [535], vol. 28, pp. 282-86; Onda [473], vol. 1, pp. 294-304, vol. 2, pp. 8-14. To replace Kajikawa's battalion in divisional reserve, Komatsubara drew upon Sumi for two companies and Ioki for one.

11. Tsuchiya interview; 13th FA Regt./2nd Artillery Group, Operations Order No. 87, 7 P.M., 27 July, in 1st Bn., 13th FA Regt. [124]; Kobayashi [24], 29 July; *SSNT* [535], vol. 28, p. 280.

12. Y. Hata, "Nikki" [5], 28 July.

13. Komatsubara [25], 29 July; Y. Hata, "Nikki" [5], 29, 30, 31 July; 13th FA Regt., Operations Order No. 89, 10 A.M., 30 July, in 1st Bn., 13th FA Regt. [124]; *SSNT* [535], vol. 28, pp. 280, 303-4, citing Kobayashi, and pp. 307-8, citing Hata; BBSS, *SS* [180], vol. 27, p. 586. For brief discussion of Uchiyama's apparently routine transfer, see *SSNT* [535], vol. 28, pp. 308-9. Uchiyama, in fact, was soon promoted lieutenant general (Oct. 1939), and took command of the 13th Division (Sept. 1940) and the Third Army (Aug. 1942).

14. Kantōgun [99], in *GSS* [40], vol. 10, pp. 81-82, 122-23; Mishima, M. Tsuchiya interviews. (Tsuchiya replaced Higashikuni as battery commander.) Also see *SSNT* [535], vol. 28, pp. 274-76; Tsuji [585], pp. 173-74. Tsuji, however, assigns the prince to the wrong regiment. For Higashikuni's recollections, see *Nomonhan* [40], vol. 3, pp. 22-26.

15. 7th Co., 2nd Bn., 26th Inf. Regt. [105], 26 July.

16. *Ibid.*; and Kanaizuka [22], 27 July; 3rd Bn., 13th FA Regt. [125], 27 July; Takashima, *Barushagaru* [555], pp. 116-17.

17. I. Saitō interview.

18. Numazaki interview.

19. Mishima interview.

20. Sumi, Negami interviews; Komatsubara [25], 27 July. As early as 30 June, Komatsubara evinced worry about the operability of trucks when the winter season came, especially at night, in the absence of antifreeze. The 4th Motor Regiment commander, Col. Tazaka Sen'ichi, reassured Komatsubara that his men would keep the fuel warm somehow. *SSNT* [535], vol. 26, pp. 236-37.

21. Exclusive of air force casualties, the Japanese had lost 1,377 killed (including 96 officers), 3,044 wounded (115 officers), 36 missing (3 officers), and 828 ill (4 officers). BBSS, *SS* [180], vol. 27, p. 582; Komatsubara [25], 27 July.

22. Komatsubara [25], 29 July; Kanaizuka [22], 27 July.

23. 7th Co., 2nd Bn., 26th Inf. Regt. [105], 31 July; 72nd Inf. Regt. [121], 27 July.

24. BBSS, *SS* [180], vol. 27, p. 586, citing Komatsubara and Kobayashi diaries; Komatsubara [25], 3 Aug. (re: Nogi); 3rd Bn., 13th FA Regt. [125], 27 July.

25. Kantōgun [99], in *GSS* [205], vol. 10, pp. 80-81; Tsuji [585], pp. 164-67; Hashimoto, Inada interviews.

26. Kantōgun [99], in *GSS* [205], vol. 10, p. 87.

27. BBSS, *SS* [180], vol. 27, p. 589; Kantōgun [99], in *GSS* [205], vol. 10, p. 87. The matter of IJA acquisition of know-how during the earlier river-crossing operation is misapprehended in JRD [965], *JSM* 11, part 3/B, p. 351.

28. Kantōgun [99], in *GSS* [205], vol. 10, pp. 87-88.

29. BBSS, *SS* [180], vol. 27, p. 589; Kantōgun [99], in *GSS* [205], vol. 10, pp. 88, 129-30. Differing numbers will be found in JRD [965], *JSM* 11, part 3/B, pp. 352-54. The plan also devoted considerable attention to the east Manchurian and Korean fronts.

30. Kantōgun [99], in *GSS* [205], vol. 10, pp. 88-89. Also see BBSS, *SS* [180], vol. 27, p. 591; JRD [965], *JSM* 11, part 3/B, p. 356. An attempt to reconcile problems in the text of the Kwantung Army's operational diary is made in *SSNT* [535], vol. 28, pp. 304-6.

31. Kwantung Army, Operations Sec., Wire No. 1670, 12 Aug. A mere first lieutenant from the General Affairs Subsection was sent to Tokyo to deliver the guidelines to the AGS. BBSS, *SS* [180], vol. 27, pp. 591-92; Kantōgun [99], in *GSS* [205], vol. 10, pp. 89, 130-31; JRD [965], *JSM* 11, part 3/B, pp. 356-59. The 3rd IGU would construct winter facilities for its units in Hsingan Province. The Sixth Army's purview is already stipulated in the policy guidelines. For example, its main body was to be returned to original locations (Hailar) before the onset of deepest winter.

32. IGHQ Army Order No. 334, 4 Aug.: JRD [965], *JSM* 11, part 3/C, p. 373; and *SSNT* [535], vol. 28, p. 320.

33. S. Hamada, interview and [2]; Kantōgun [99], in *GSS* [205], vol. 10, p. 89; I. Hata, Shimanuki interviews; JRD [965], *JSM* 11, part 3/B, p. 177.

34. S. Hamada, interview and [2].

35. Suzuki Yasushi interview. Adds Kwantung Army intelligence officer Suzuki: "The operations people weren't stupid, but they were trapped by circumstances."

36. Nyūmura interview. For detailed examination of the effects of winter in Manchuria on men and equipment, see JRD [969], *JSM* 7.

37. Doi's report originally left Moscow on 12 July, but was not retransmitted from Tokyo until the night of 1 August. Kantōgun [99], in *GSS* [205], vol. 10, pp. 131-32; JRD [965], *JSM* 11, part 3/B, pp. 359-61.

38. Nyūmura, Doi, Kōtani, Arao, Inada interviews; Kantōgun [99], in *GSS* [205], vol. 10, p. 89.

39. S. Hamada, interview and [2]; JRD [965], *JSM* 11, part 3/C, pp. 519-21, citing Kusaba, *Noro kōchi* [358].

40. Zhukov, *Memoirs* [1017], p. 154. Shishkin says the Japanese decided to call a halt to their offensive operations and to dig in along the dunes 5-6 km. east of the Halha. While setting up a "solid defensive system," the Japanese were allegedly preparing simultaneously for new offensive operations designed to eliminate the Soviet bridgehead, once and for all; [920], p. 592.

41. Imaoka, interviews and "Nomonhan" [13], pp. 69-72; BBSS, *SS* [180], vol. 27, p. 586; *SSNT* [535], vol. 28, p. 270; Nyūmura interview.

CHAPTER 30

1. Attributed to Shtern, August 1939, by Vorozheikin [184], p. 94.

2. See Coox, *Anatomy* [679], pp. 293-95.

3. Kantōgun [99], in *GSS* [205], vol. 10, pp. 79, 84-85; JRD [965], *JSM* 11, part 3/B, pp. 327-38; Tsuji [585], pp. 159-62; BBSS, *SS* [180], vol. 27, pp. 577-78. According to AGS intelligence, one Soviet plane of an unknown type dropped four bombs near the bridge at about 3:20 A.M. on 16 July. The bombs fell 500 meters from the target, destroying two houses and wounding seven people, one severely. AGS Intelligence Report No. 39, 17 July [141]. For follow-up intelligence, see Report No. 42, 20 July [141].

4. Kantōgun [99], in *GSS* [205], vol. 10, p. 86; JRD [965], *JSM* 11, part 3/B, pp. 347-48; Tsuji [585], p. 175. AGS intelligence reported on 27 July that, according to information of second-class reliability, the chief of Red Army logistics headquarters arrived at Chita to discuss supply problems with all of the Far Eastern units. AGS Intelligence Report No. 48, 27 July [141].

5. Zhukov, *Memoirs* [1017], p. 156.

6. This subject is addressed in detail in BBSS, *SS* [180], vol. 27, pp. 628-29.

7. Nyūmura, Doi, S. Hamada interviews; BBSS, *SS* [180], vol. 27, p. 626. From prisoner interrogation, IJA intelligence learned of 60-70-car trains made up of horse wagons, kitchen cars, and flatcars carrying guns, tanks, and trucks. Telephones were used aboard the trains. The soldiers ate canned food supplemented by water and tea at stations. Doors were kept tightly shut, and water for the horses was delivered at the platform. When the trains stopped, local guards were deployed. AGS Intelligence Report No. 46, 25 July [141]. Probably because of interference by military traffic, the international train for Chita left Manchouli 20 hours behind schedule and arrived 14 hours late. Report No. 48, 27 July [141].

8. Komatsubara [25], 28 July.

9. Machine gunner Dovcin from the MPRA 6th Cavalry Division's 15th Regiment is credited with shooting down an IJAF plane with his light machine gun. Four Japanese crewmen were killed, the one high-ranking officer captured. See Major S. Zamsranzav's account of the 6th Cav. Div. (1965), cited by Sasaki [910], p. 223. The Russian disclosures are contained in USSR [992], vol. 2, p. 138.

10. The IJAF scout plane, however, carried only Shimanuki Tadamasa and the pilot, Capt. Ikoma Masayuki. On the other hand, 1st Lt. Sawairi Hideo was piloting a Type 97 heavy

bomber hit on 3 July, at an altitude of 3,000-4,000 meters, by an antiaircraft shell which blew the machine gunner out of the plane and killed the other five airmen aboard. Was Dovcin claiming the bomber (since it carried more than two men) or the scout plane (since a high-ranking officer with documents was aboard)? When Miyashi became assistant military attaché in Moscow in 1940, he visited the Nomonhan display in the Red Army museum, but if the Russians had captured materials from Shimanuki Tadamasa, they did not display them. Miyashi, Nishiura, Shimanuki Takeharu, K. Matsumura interviews. One month after Shimanuki Tadamasa disappeared, the Kwantung Army press section announced that he and Ikoma had "died heroic deaths while plunging with their burning plane against the heights on the west side of the Halha-Holsten junction zone, after having sustained concentrated antiaircraft fire over the area while directing combat from a headquarters plane." Watanabe [607], p. 109. A squadron commander says that IJAF scout planes, despite their supposed height and speed advantages, used "childish and clumsy" tactics in practice. Morishita interview.

11. Nyūmura interview.

12. Sixth Army Wire No. 7, to Kwantung Army commander, 12:20 A.M., 14 August: Kantōgun [99], in GSS [205], vol. 10, p. 132; JRD [965], JSM 11, part 3/C, pp. 373-74. Also S. Hamada interview; BBSS, SS [180], vol. 27, p. 626, citing Col. Isomura Takesuke, Kwantung Army intelligence senior staff officer; Komatsubara [25], 15 Aug.

13. Komatsubara [25], 3 August. Also see Takashima, *Barushagaru* [555], p. 145.

14. Shishkin [920], p. 599.

15. The weak Manchukuoan cavalry screen had been pounded from the ground and air on 30-31 July, and the remnants had retreated to the area of the IJA artillery positions, leaving the 71st Regiment's far left flank exposed. 71st Inf. Regt. [119].

16. 71st Inf. Regt. [119]; Onda [473], vol. 2, pp. 28-30, 33-34, 38; Takashima, *Barushagaru* [555], pp. 154-60; 2nd Bn., 28th Inf. Regt. [110], 7-8, 13 Aug.

17. 72nd Inf. Regt. [121]; Komatsubara [25], 8 August; Kobayashi diary, 7-8 August, cited in SSNT [535], vol. 29, pp. 10-11; Captain Tashiro's notes (12th Co., 64th Inf. Regt.), 7-8 Aug., cited in *Nomonhan* [40], vol. 10, pp. 77-78.

18. See Coox, *Anatomy* [679], chaps. 19-20. Also see Takashima, *Barushagaru* [555], p. 154; 2nd Bn., 28th Inf. Regt. [110], 6 Aug.; Captain Tashiro's notes, 6 Aug., cited in *Nomonhan* [40], vol. 10, p. 77.

19. I use these dates, based on Soviet and IJA combat records, although for some reason the Kwantung Army Operations Section dated the Russian counterattack as "about 9-10 August." Kantōgun [99], in GSS [205], vol. 10, p. 89; repeated in JRD [965], JSM 11, part 3/C, p. 374.

20. Kantōgun [99], in GSS [205], vol. 10, p. 89. A slightly different interpretation is found in JRD [965], JSM 11, part 3/C, p. 374; and Tsuji [585], p. 182. For Kwantung Army guidelines issued on 12 August, see chap. 29. Also Nyūmura interview.

21. 71st Inf. Regt. [119]. Misrecognition of targets continued to trouble the Japanese, and on 15/16 August the 1st Battalion launched a new night attack to seize the "real" Heights 744, from which the Halha but not the Higashi-watashi crossing could be observed easily. *Ibid.*

22. Zhukov, *Memoirs* [1017], p. 154, identifies the IJA objective as the Bolshiye Peske ("Great Sands") hills.

23. Asada interview; Komatsubara [25], 6, 7, 16 Aug. The restructuring of one line company of the 64th Inf. Regt. is detailed by the 12th Co. commander in *Nomonhan* [40], vol. 10, p. 76.

24. S. Hamada, Shimanuki, Imaoka, Murata, N. Morita interviews; Tsuji [585], pp. 180-81. Ogisu's admonition (*kunji*) of 15 Aug. is found in Komatsubara's diary entry for that date [15]. In Hailar, on the eve of 15 Aug., Ogisu hosted a sumptuous barbecue at Komatsubara's official residence for 100 high-ranking officers and personages; Yonaga Hyōe, ed., *Hikō dai-24 sentai kūchū sentō senshi* [A Military History of the 24th Air Group's Aerial Combat] (Tokyo, 1979), p. 78.

25. 71st Inf. Regt. [119]. On the basis of very heavy Soviet truck movements across the Halha and of the gradual increase in artillery fire, Takashima deduced on 17 August that the enemy had "some large-scale intention." On the 18th, the lieutenant noted that the foe had been building up strength in the sector south of Noro Heights for the past two or three days. The Kajikawa battalion's 6th Company night-attacked and cleared three dunes on 18/19 Au-

gust. IJA casualties (mostly from hand grenades) numbered 1 platoon leader and 6 men killed, 3 officers (including 2 platoon leaders) and 22 men wounded. Soviet losses exceeded 80 killed, from a strength of 200-300 men; 5 machine guns, and 10 rifles were captured. Takashima, *Barushagaru* [555], pp. 166, 170-71; 2nd Bn., 28th Inf. Regt. [110], 17-18 Aug.

26. Suzuki Yoshiyasu interview.

27. Suzuki Yasushi interview. For H. Hata, see BBSS, *SS* [180], vol. 27, p. 627.

28. Kantōgun [99], in *GSS* [205], vol. 10, p. 89. Also see Tsuji [585], pp. 181-82.

29. S. Hayashi, *Kantōgun* [242], p. 175; Asada, Imaoka, Suemori, Hashimoto, Kōtani, Inada interviews. A wealth of raw data on Soviet order of battle, movements, and instructions will be found in the AGS 5th Section's intelligence reports [141].

30. Shishkin refers to 216 guns of 76-mm. or larger caliber; JRD [965], *JSM* 11, part 3/C, p. 394. Kuzmin gives a figure of 266; Erickson, *Soviet* [722], p. 806.

31. The "combat factor" is expressed as a multiple of the ordinary (peacetime) issue to the Soviet forces.

32. For logistical purposes, the Russians used not only motor trucks and tankers but also prime movers ordinarily intended to tow artillery pieces. Nevertheless, the need for motor vehicles to haul troops left the Soviet command, by its own estimate, 526 trucks and more than 100 tankers short. Zhukov, *Memoirs* [1017], p. 155; Shishkin [920], pp. 593, 595; Erickson, *Soviet* [722], p. 533.

33. Suemori, Asada, Nyūmura, Imaoka, Shimanuki, Kōtani, I. Hata interviews. Also see Vorozheikin [184], p. 85.

34. On 9/10 August, the 12th Co. of the 64th Inf. Regt. detected strange sniping from the rear of the Japanese positions, but an IJA patrol found nothing. Captain Tashiro's notes, 10 Aug., cited in *Nomonhan* [40], vol. 10, p. 79.

35. The 82nd Rifle Div. and 36th Motorized Rifle Div. (2 regiments each), the 5th Machine Gun Brigade, and the 8th and 6th MPRA cavalry divisions.

36. Nyūmura interview, supplemented by Nishikawa interview.

37. Komatsubara [25], 19 August. Occasional Soviet night bombings began as early as 7 July. Lacking searchlights and night fighters, the Japanese could not repulse them. Loss of sleep began to affect airmen in particular. BBSS, *SS* [180], vol. 27, p. 574. Also see K. Matsumura, *Gekitsui* [386], pp. 124-25; Irie, *Horonbairu* [298], pp. 136-40.

38. Shishkin [920], p. 631.

39. 72nd Inf. Regt. [121], 17 Aug.

40. Y. Hata, "Nikki" [5]; Mishima interview; M. Tsuchiya notes. Also see *SSNT* [535], vol. 29, pp. 13, 21-22, citing 2nd Bn., 7th Heavy FA Regt., combat report that on 18 August "enemy artillery in the river valley responded with about ten times as many shells once our artillery opened fire."

41. 72nd Inf. Regt. [121], 18, 19 Aug. Also see chap. 31.

42. Notes of Ishikawa (1st Co. commander), cited in *SSNT* [535], vol. 29, p. 29. For comments on suspicious Soviet activity on the 64th Regt. front, see *Nomonhan* [40], vol. 10, pp. 81-82. For 71st Regiment: Onozuka interview.

43. Oizumi commanded the 3rd Squadron, 15th Air Group. See *SSNT* [535], vol. 29, pp. 25-26. For Soviet bridging activities on the eve of the offensive, see GSDF/CGSC [73], p. 84.

44. The Russians' "secret weapon" proved to be bigger and better armor, not gas, remarked Suzuki Yasushi in an interview.

45. 7th Co., 26th Inf. Regt. [105], 19 Aug.; 3rd Bn., 64th Inf. Regt. [117], 19 Aug. The 12th Co., 64th Inf. Regt., took gas-warfare countermeasures as early as 5 August, according to Captain Tashiro's notes of that date; *Nomonhan* [40], vol. 10, p. 77.

46. 2nd Bn. intelligence report, received by 7th Co., 26th Inf. Regt. [105], 5 Aug.

47. See *Nomonhan* [40], vol. 10, pp. 81-82.

48. Regarding Soviet numbered-unit nomenclature, "tank brigade" is self-explanatory, but I have used "armored brigade" instead of "mechanized brigade" or "armored car brigade"; and "rifle division" instead of "infantry division."

49. Zhukov's reserves also included two machine gun battalions and two border garrison units.

50. See n. 30 above. Zhukov also had 16 batteries (96 guns) of antiaircraft artillery covering First Army Group headquarters in the Hamardaba area. See GSDF/CGSC [73], pp. 74-75.

51. The Soviet air force included three fighter regiments (the 22nd, 56th, and 70th), two bomber regiments (the 38th and 150th), and one heavy bomber regiment made up of TB-3 aircraft. There was also one MPRA air regiment. GSDF/CGSC [73], p. 68. My summary of Zhukov's entire order-of-battle and operational planning is based on Shishkin [920], pp. 592-607; JRD [965], *JSM* 11, part 3/B, p. 189, part 3/C, p. 394; Zhukov. *Memoirs* [1017], pp. 154-59; Erickson, *Soviet* [722], pp. 533-34, 806, citing Kuzmin; S. Hayashi, *Kantōgun* [242], pp. 171-72. GSDF/CGSC [73], pp. 65-90, includes data on engineer and bridging units.

52. Erickson, *Soviet* [722], p. 522.

53. Zhukov, *Memoirs* [1017], p. 159. Vorozheikin states that the Japanese were not planning their own offensive on 24 August but were expecting the Soviet assault on that date. [184], p. 85.

Nomonhan

VOLUME TWO

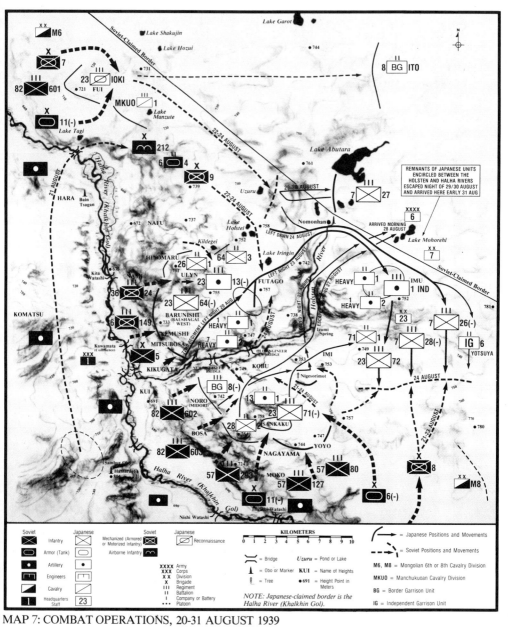

MAP 7: COMBAT OPERATIONS, 20-31 AUGUST 1939

The Road to Disaster

In two respects, Russian and Japanese sources are in rare agreement: that the weather on 20 August was fine, and that the Soviet offensive erupted with stunning intensity. Action commenced at 5:45 A.M., when Russian artillery pounded antiaircraft and machine-gun sites, as well as lobbing smoke shells on targets to be hit by the air force. Simultaneously, more than 150 bombers in 9-plane flights, accompanied by hundreds of fighters, struck both the forward edges of the Japanese lines and antiaircraft batteries, artillery emplacements, and reserves to the rear. It was the first bomber-fighter offensive in Soviet air force history.

At 8:15 A.M., concentrated artillery barrages began, with guns of every caliber firing "to the limit of their technical possibilities." Aircraft returned to the area at 8:30. By telephone and radio the coded command was transmitted that the general offensive was to get under way in 15 minutes. At 8:45, red rockets signaled the attack while the planes were hitting the enemy defenses again. Under cover of the artillery's storm of fire, infantry and armor launched their assaults at 9 A.M. Masked by early-morning mist, the troops had been able to occupy their jump-off locations in secrecy, and even to close with the Japanese directly in some places. The defenders were battered "morally and physically." IJA artillery communications lines, observation posts, and gun sites were smashed. Antiaircraft units had exposed their positions and had been silenced. Fires blazed everywhere. For 75 to 90 minutes, the Japanese artillery could not even respond.

Potapov's Southern Force made the main effort and the greatest progress during 20 August. On the easternmost wing, the 8th MPRA Cavalry Division routed Manchukuoan horsemen and reached the frontier claimed by Outer Mongolia. From south and southeast of Noro Heights, the 57th Rifle Division sent forward the 293rd Regiment on the left and 127th Regiment on the right. The latter penetrated northeastward toward Heights 757, while the former eliminated covering elements, pressed to the IJA defenses, and tried repeatedly to overcome the forward edge of the main positions, without success. To the right of the 127th Regiment, in the second wave, the 80th Regiment advanced against the Heights 780-791 sector, known to the Russians as Great Sands, and reached the fringe of it by 7 P.M. Minor IJA forces were left within the four-kilometer gap created between the 80th and 127th regiments. In the absence of the 6th Tank Brigade, which was still crossing the Halha, the 8th Armored Brigade constituted the far right flank of the Southern Force, to the east of the 80th Rifle Regiment. Negotiating difficult dunes, by the end of the day the 8th Armored pushed to the region 3-4 kilometers southwest of Nomonhan; reconnaissance elements reached the border claimed by the MPR to the southeast. Thus, on 20 August, the 57th Division and the right-wing units managed to advance about 12 kilometers to the nearest objectives.

Bisected by the Holsten, Zhukov's Central Force launched the 82nd Rifle Division on the south or Noro Heights side of the river. The 602nd Regiment attacked from the direction of Kui Heights on the west toward Heights 742, the 603rd Regiment (deployed to the left of the adjacent 57th Division) from the southwest toward Heights 754. Encountering stubborn Japanese resistance, the 82nd Division fought hard but could advance its flanks only 500 to 1,500 meters by the end of the day and failed to take the objectives at either heights.[1]

Against the din of Russian planes and artillery fire (real or feigned) on the night of 19/20 August, a Japanese gunner and two of his comrades in the 7th Heavy Field Artillery Regiment had a last little sake party at their emplacement. Savoring rare dried squid as a snack, the three soldiers drank and sang until midnight. But when 70 bombers and fighters thundered overhead at 6:30 A.M., the gunner felt that his end was at hand. Black smoke billowed up from the wagon lines, and the gun lines were strafed. Soviet armor moved toward the regiment's flank, encirclement obviously in mind. By evening, the tanks were only 1,000 meters away. One of the Japanese batteries moved forward while the second veered against the endangered flank, prepared for decisive combat, and interfered with the enemy's rear. It was not possible to do much digging of auxiliary shelters that night because of hostile fire, and the battery could not reply. The gunner survived the day, amazed that his gun site had somehow not taken a direct hit.[2]

On the Japanese left wing south of the Holsten, only Major Sugitachi's 1st Battalion of the 71st Infantry was in the line, occupying Heights 744, in the sector attacked by the Soviet 57th Division. Smaller IJA regimental elements held high ground on Sugitachi's left—Heights 747 and 757, below the location of the main body of the 71st Regiment around Nigesorimot. Overall Russian attacking strength on this front was estimated at 1,350 infantrymen and 200 tanks and armored cars, backed by 200 trucks. East of the Higashi-watashi crossing on the Halha, the enemy had built bridges at four points. Soviet fighters and bombers were "running wild," says Captain Onozuka of the 71st Regiment's 3rd Battalion. "It was a veritable circus overhead, and we suffered from rage and frustration."

The Japanese were hit especially hard on the Heights 744-747-757 sector from 9 A.M., and reinforcements had to be sent up by the regiment. At

Heights 747, the situation grew critical by 2:30 P.M., causing Colonel Morita, the new regimental commander, to rush the main body of the 3rd Battalion to defend that hill. The battalion encountered 20 tanks and 300 infantry who had penetrated into the gap between elevations and broken through the IJA lines. Fighting raged all day, but the fire of Takatsukasa's 10-cm. guns was helpful to the infantry; and the enemy, who at 6 P.M. appeared to have secured Heights 747, pulled back at 8:30, leaving pickets ahead. After being directed by the 23rd Division to hold Heights 744 and 747, the 71st Regiment withdrew the troops from Heights 757 (Futagoyama) on the farthest left flank. The regimental main force, ordered to advance three kilometers south of Nigesorimot to Hyōtan ("Gourd-Shaped") Heights, redeployed that night in confusion.[3]

Colonel Hasebe's detachment from the 8th Border Garrison Unit defended the zone to the right of the 71st Regiment, between Noro and the Holsten—the objective of the Soviet 82nd Division. IJA combat maps indicate 1,500 men and 50-60 tanks massed opposite Hasebe. Major Kajikawa's 2nd Battalion of the 28th Infantry held Hasebe's left flank, facing west-southwest. On this sector, Soviet planes struck the gun sites at 6:30 A.M., tanks attacked the battalion's main positions at 7 A.M., and artillery commenced bombardment at 7:30, using eight field guns, four 15-cm. howitzers, and two 15-cm. cannon. Visibility became so poor and the air so "stuffy" that Lieutenant Takashima felt like donning a gas mask. At 9 A.M., 150 Soviet troops approached to 200 meters and deployed, hurling grenades. Japanese machine guns and grenade launchers checked the enemy at 100 meters. Small attacks by 20-30 Soviet riflemen, launched after artillery preparation, were repulsed on both flanks between noon and 1:20 P.M., but enemy armor grew very active. Clearly intending to circle Kajikawa's left wing, a dozen Russian tanks penetrated to Heights 754 and interfered with the line units' contact with the battalion rear. From midday, the Japanese experienced great difficulty obtaining supplies of ammunition, food, and water.

Around 5 P.M., four Soviet tanks came particularly close to one infantry company's lines. Takashima could see the black shadows of Japanese close-quarter attack teams dashing near the armor. One tank was stopped by grenades, and the other machines withdrew. Several hours later, the three tanks tried to approach their crippled comrade, which was still burning, but they were driven off by grenade launchers. Machine guns and grenade launchers also repelled 100 riflemen.

Kajikawa, who was still not sure that the Russians had launched more than a "routine" attack, sent out scouts to reconnoiter hostile movements. The major was actually thinking that, if the enemy forces were going to retreat, he would press after them, on his own initiative, and drive to the

Halha. His patrols soon disabused him of that notion: the Russians not only showed no signs of withdrawal but also were massing larger formations than in the daytime and were apparently getting ready to attack. After contacting higher headquarters, Kajikawa learned that the Soviet general offensive had indeed begun. The Russians, he heard, had moved up 2,000 men, 300 trucks, and 400-500 tanks south of the Holsten. Elements of the 71st Regiment had been observed retreating toward Nigesorimot, under attack. Although their action had "of course been taken according to division orders," the enemy could now be expected to hit the exposed left flank of the Kajikawa battalion even heavier and harder with artillery. There was no way to cope with such an offensive, so the battalion must cling to its positions to the last man.[4]

The center of this sector, to the right of Kajikawa, was held by Lt. Col. Sugitani Yoshio's 1st Battalion of the Hasebe detachment. Between 6 and 7 A.M., 130 Russian bombers and fighters attacked in overwhelming strength. The battalion resisted with all of its firepower, shooting down one plane in front of the positions and another behind Soviet lines. Enemy artillery opened fire at about 7:20 A.M., when the air raids let up. The Soviet gun sites were at about the same locations, but the numbers of weapons had increased. Barrages especially hit the areas of the battalion headquarters and the first-aid station. Shortly after 9 A.M., the Soviet bombardment diminished while about 20 Japanese planes bombed enemy batteries, but the fire resumed at 9:30, once the raid ended.

At 10:30 A.M., under artillery cover, Russian infantry began to attack on this sector, crawling in the open or using trenches dug beforehand. 1st Lt. Takumi Sōtarō's right-flank 1st Company was hit by gunfire from the front and from Sambur Obo, behind and to the side. The heaviest barrages were directed against 1st Lt. Yatani Itsuo's 2nd Company in the middle, from 15-cm. howitzers emplaced at the confluence and from field artillery at three sites on the right shore. On Sugitani's left flank, 1st Lt. Yoshida Yonetoshi's 3rd Company received mortar and field-gun fire from the right bank and 15-cm. howitzer bombardment from near Sambur Obo. The Japanese stayed under cover until the enemy infantrymen came within 200 or 300 meters and then rained heavy-weapons fire on them. Yatani's 2nd Company bore the brunt of the attack, but the Japanese were not impressed by the Russians' fighting spirit. "The enemy was unable to lay a finger on our positions" and pulled back to a line 200 meters away by 2 P.M. When the Soviets attempted a new assault at 3 P.M., one Japanese platoon reported cutting down about half of the 100-man force.

Eighteen Russian machine-gun emplacements were confirmed, from a total that must have exceeded 30. Infantry-support weapons numbered eight regimental guns and 12 mortars, aided by seven or eight tanks deployed behind crestlines 700 to 1,300 meters away, firing hull-down, mainly against machine guns. Soviet optical equipment must have been excellent, for as soon as an IJA machine-gun crew took position, the enemy brought down immediate and accurate fire. Russian artillery included between 12 and 24 of the 15-cm. howitzers and between 8 and 16 field guns. Unlike IJA batteries, which unleashed concentrated barrages of short duration, Soviet artillery fired continuously for hours—sometimes as long as 10 hours—using an immense number of shells.

Sugitani estimated that two Russian infantry companies attacked his right-flank company, that one and a half or two battalions attacked his center company, and that one or one and a half battalions attacked his left company. (The Soviet troops wore blackish-green uniforms and presumably came from newly committed units.) On 20 August, according to Sugitani's claims, the Russians lost 370 men: 70 on the right, 200 in the center, and 100 on the left, where grenades were employed more than machine guns. Japanese casualties numbered only eight killed and six wounded.[5]

Less is known concerning Maj. Miyazaki Tadao's 2nd Battalion of the Hasebe force, stationed on the right flank by the Holsten. According to one infantryman, the Soviet planes blackened the sky when they thundered in after dawn. Japanese troops were not supposed to shoot at aircraft, since the Type 38 rifle would be useless and firing would only expose the positions; but the men could not restrain themselves. After the air raids, the Russians opened up with artillery, then sent tanks forward, and finally committed infantry. The pattern was unchanging and, on 20 August, particularly severe.[6]

Far to the north, the two MPRA cavalry regiments with supporting elements of the Soviet Northern Force had easily routed the opposing Manchukuoan cavalry flanking Fui Heights: ahead of the Lake Manzute–Heights 739 area, to the left of Lieutenant Colonel Ioki, the Manchukuoan 2nd Cavalry Regiment had been attacked and smashed by tanks, armored cars, and 1,000 infantry and horsemen, assisted by artillery; to the right of Ioki, over 10 kilometers away from the 2nd Regiment, the Manchukuoan 8th Cavalry Regiment was encircled and routed at Honjinganga by 40-50 tanks and armored cars and by 1,300 cavalry and riflemen.[7] Thus from the outset Ioki was obliged to fight alone.

Against the bastion at Fui Heights, the Russians sent the 601st Rifle Regiment frontally, elements of the 11th Tank Brigade around the left flank, and the 7th Armored Brigade around the right. These units penetrated to the main defenses, but although the Northern Force committed its main strength, the Japanese threw back every assault on the 20th.[8]

The prowess of Lieutenant Colonel Ioki's reinforced cavalry reconnaissance unit at Fui is all the more remarkable when one remembers that the heights was little more than a "raised pancake," as Colonel Sumi has described it, and that the garrison facing the Soviet brigades never exceeded 800 men. The core of that garrison was two cavalry squadrons (one mounted, armed with carbines; one motorized, with tankettes), an engineer company, four rapid-fire guns, a couple of heavy machine guns, and two mountain guns. In addition, two infantry companies (1st Lt. Kawabata Shinjirō's 6th since early July, and 1st Lt. Sata Naotada's 9th since August 13) had been attached from the 26th Regiment, with a battery of infantry guns.

Even the unit designations are misleading, however, since various elements were already understrength. For example, the mounted cavalry squadron had two and a half of its usual four platoons—only 80 men. But since the Fui sector was deemed to be of secondary importance, the little squadron was allocated a front of 300 meters plus reserve positions to defend. The men had been working hard to dig trenches and build shelters for the heavy weapons. At the front, bunkers had been constructed of logs, with loopholes.

There is evidence, however, that Komatsubara, concerned from the start about the weakness of the Fui sector, had been considering replacing the Ioki reconnaissance unit with an infantry force. Ioki heard about this from a Kwantung Army staff officer who had visited the division just before the August offensive, and who encouraged the Fui garrison to strengthen its defenses and check a Soviet attack until such time as the IJA infantry replacements took over. The Russians preempted implementation of any such plan by Komatsubara, who later became too involved with the main threat from the south to devote much attention to the north.

From about 5 A.M. on 20 August, helpless Fui was bombarded all day by dozens of Soviet pieces. Smoke blanketed the area and reduced visibility to a couple of meters. Earth and sky throbbed, reminding one officer of the incessant pounding of drums by Nichiren-sect Buddhists. One battery commander counted three incoming rounds every second, reverberating like "the gongs of hell." At the rate of 100 shrapnel fragments per shell, a captain computed, this would come to some 18,000 shards exploding per minute, multiplied by the 1,000 rounds undoubtedly stocked per Russian gun. The scream of fragments seemed to be "knifing out one's guts." Men fell one after another, weapons were smashed, trenches collapsed, and the defenses were holed like a honeycomb. A bearded field-artillery gunner could be seen praying for the successful impact of each of his few shells. To protect the horses, Japanese cavalrymen tethered them in a 70-meter-wide pit dug before the battle. But 80 percent of the horses were killed on the 20th; the rest stampeded or were injured. Although the sight was grisly, the horse soldiers were relieved to a certain extent because there was neither water for the animals nor time to attend to them.

Flushed by their easy success over the Manchukuoan elements at Honjinganga, the Russians steadily encircled the troops defending Fui Heights. Battle maps show an estimated 700 Soviet infantry in front, and 50 tanks swinging around the right and the left. Soon a desperate crisis developed among the Japanese concerning drinking water. Ioki had no water of his own but depended entirely on division trucks to haul in supplies daily. Now the vehicles could not get through. Against such an emergency, the Japanese had dug 10 wells, four or five meters deep, from which a bare trickle of water could be drawn with mess tins. Every well was smashed by the bombardments of the 20th. The soldiers were driven to distraction by the blistering heat of the day in their open defenses, while fighting without letup.

At about 8 P.M. the Soviet bombardment stopped, as though a light switch had been flicked off. A Japanese company commander stood up to observe and was surprised to discern enemy troops and tanks only 30-40 meters away. One of his forward platoons flushed out 50 or 60 infantrymen by hurling hand grenades, but the Russian tanks, responding with flame, burned Japanese positions and soldiers alike. Shouting and throwing grenades, the Soviet soldiers charged forward, accompanied by the tanks, and drove back the survivors of the IJA platoon. One tank bogged in a trench and was captured, but the crewmen killed themselves rather than be taken prisoner, thereby earning the reverence of the Japanese. Near 8 P.M., the tanks began to pull back, to the visible discomfiture of the Russian foot troops. Only then did the Japanese company commander lead a counterattack that ousted the infantrymen and retook the abandoned position. Half a platoon had been lost in the fight for this sector of Ioki's front. The Japanese spent the night burying the dead, ministering to the wounded, trying to rebuild the wrecked defenses, and preparing for new combat on the 21st. In the absence of water, the men used towels to wipe up night dew and then chewed on the cloth to wet their parched throats.[9]

The strongest part of the Japanese line was held by the three infantry regiments north of the Holsten. Here, Zhukov employed the 36th Motorized Rifle Division, on the left half of his Central Force. The 5th Machine-Gun Brigade, on the Russian right, and the 149th Rifle Regiment, in the middle, sought to pin down Sakai's 72nd and Yamagata's 64th regiments, respectively. On Zhukov's left, against elements of Sumi's 26th Regiment, the 36th Division launched the 24th Motorized Infantry Regiment, reinforced by the tank battalion organic to the 57th Rifle Division.[10] These latter forces advanced successfully, destroyed front-line fire points, and reached the main defenses toward the end of the day. With darkness at hand, the 24th Regiment was compelled to hold up and dig in, under powerful Japanese fire.[11]

The Japanese line unit nearest to Fui Heights, on the right wing of Kobayashi's center corps, was Major Ikuta's 1st Battalion of the 26th Infantry, under direct control of the division. At 7 A.M. on 20 August, some 200 Soviet troops and 20 tanks penetrated the 1st Battalion's lines, and fierce fighting ensued. The 2nd Battalion of Maj. Kamimura (Uemura) Minao, in reserve, tried to send a three-man unit to contact Ikuta around noon, but the severity of Russian fire is indicated by the fact that the patrol had hardly advanced 200 meters when it was annihilated by artillery fire. That night, at 11 P.M., the 1st Company of the Ikuta battalion attempted a desperate charge but lost 65 of 85 men. A despondent, badly wounded command-team soldier wrote: "To be killed is all that remains. . . . I'll become a light machine gunner and fight to the end. We few in the right-wing lines are completely surrounded. The enemy is using automatic weapons." [12]

The 23rd Division, having determined by mid-morning that the fulcrum of the Soviet general offensive lay below the Holsten, was already planning to transfer the main strength southward, including the rest of the 26th Regiment. But the deterioration of the situation on the northern flank at Fui Heights was becoming apparent. Komatsubara decided by evening to shift Sumi's reserve companies to the north instead, near Heights 752, to cover the endangered right wing of the division.[13] Russian sources have the facts straight but err in concluding that Komatsubara and his staff thought the main Soviet offensive effort was being launched against the Japanese right wing at Fui.[14]

On the center of the Japanese front north of the Holsten, from about 6 A.M. on 20 August, the 64th Regiment was struck by waves of planes and by artillery fire from numerous guns across the Halha. From a total force of several hundred aircraft, 20 bombers "blindly" attacked positions to the rear while 50 fighters peeled off repeatedly to strafe the lines in the face of heavy ground fire. A soldier remembers firing 100 shots against planes swarming like mosquitoes or dragonflies—in such profusion that collisions seemed unavoidable and shooting-down easy. Shimmering aircraft were visible on high, and the Soviet star insignia could be clearly seen at low altitude.

On the 3rd Battalion's left-hand sector, 800 Soviet infantrymen attacked three times starting at 7 A.M., blasting away at communication trenches and shelters with machine guns and machine cannon from a line of willows across a dip 150-200 meters away. The newer Japanese soldiers tended to stay under cover instead of emerging to observe under the continuing rain of artillery and mortar shells. At some points, Russian troops in groups of 50 or 60 approached within 30 meters of the defenses, especially against the 2nd Battalion on the right. Grenade duels raged "like rain." Large enemy forces came up from the south, until by evening contact with the front lines became difficult. On 20 August, the 3rd Battalion lost 12 men killed (including one officer) and 20 wounded, from an organic and attached strength of 27 officers and 671 men.[15]

Deployed on the Japanese left flank above the Holsten, Sakai's 72nd Regiment experienced the "increasingly rampant" activity of the Soviet air force from dawn on 20 August, after undergoing some bombings during the preceding night. At 7 A.M., fighters machine-gunned the positions; two hours later, Russian artillery hammered the front lines and gun sites to the rear. As the barrages increased in intensity, Soviet infantrymen attacked: 350 against the regiment's right, 300 against the left. About 150 planes made bombing and strafing runs several times. Japanese heavy weapons and artillery neutralized fire emanating from tanks emplaced in hull-down positions. Having learned that new Russian units were assaulting the Japanese outer wings, too, Sakai concluded that the enemy had indeed launched a general offensive. Nishikawa, the 1st Battalion commander, felt that it was merely an intensification, "on a larger scale," of the recent fighting. Two problem areas worried the major, however. First, he was apprehensive about the gap between his battalion and the adjoining Yamagata regiment on the right—an invitation to the enemy. Although General Kobayashi had agreed with his recommendation, on the scene, that Yamagata be asked to seal the gap, the 64th Infantry had not been able to move up very much, and Nishikawa's battalion remained vulnerable from the flank. Second, Nishikawa judged the Japanese positions to be weak and "strung out." Since they lacked depth, it would prove fatal if they were ever penetrated.[16]

It was not difficult for the Japanese local command, based on the central front above the Holsten, to discern the unfurling of the Soviet offensive. "Countless numbers" of enemy planes dominated the skies from early morning, noted Kobayashi and Komatsubara; five distinct strafing runs and six bombing raids had been counted by the afternoon, all across the front. Apparently a new air brigade had been committed, employing excellent, entirely different planes. According to intelligence, noted artillery commander Hata, the enemy air force intended to pound the Japanese artillery and force it to withdraw. The physical effects were minor, Hata added, but the psychological impact was apparent. Operating from high altitudes, bombers often struck blindly, but friendly aircraft were outnumbered and outperformed.

According to Giga's air division records, enemy fighters attacked in formations as large as several dozen planes, especially between 6:40 and 9:40 A.M. and between noon and 12:50 P.M. Heavy bombing was conducted 10 times at the front and at Arshaan between 6:40 A.M. and 6:30 P.M. by flights of as many as 20 bombers. Defending fighters and bombers did their best to contest the issue on 20 August.[17] The greatest success was claimed by the 12th Fighter Wing, covering the Japanese bombers. During a 30-minute air battle from 9:50 A.M. over the confluence, the Japanese fighter pilots reported shooting down 32 confirmed and 9 probables among a formation of

60 to 70 I-16 fighters, at the remarkable cost of only one IJAF plane (which crash-landed). In addition, the wing's 64th Fighter Group shot down two of 10 SB bombers in the early morning and may have downed four fighters. Using 36 50-kilogram bombs, the six light bombers of the 10th Group raided the hidden Soviet airstrip across the Halha at 9:30 A.M. and hit 12 of 17 I-16 fighters. Around 9:30 A.M., too, the 61st Heavy Bomber Group sent 11 Type 97 aircraft carrying 77 100-kilogram bombs against bridgehead positions near the confluence and reported considerable results, in the face of severe antiaircraft fire. (Usually, 40 Soviet antiaircraft guns of about 75-mm. caliber were in action at one time, aiming salvo fire to an altitude of 7,000-8,000 feet.) On the far left flank, in the late afternoon, the light bombers of the 10th Group attacked 15 tanks and 10 artillery pieces, and the 16th Light Bomber Group hammered 10 tanks and 30 vehicles and also raided another 62 armored vehicles. But near 5:30 P.M., 20 Soviet fighters covered by another 40 caught the 64th Fighter Group on the ground and, in 10 minutes, burned or damaged 15-18 planes, at a cost of only one.[18]

It was a bitter pill to swallow but—certainly in the eyes of the hard-pressed IJA ground forces—the Russians had wrested air supremacy from the Japanese at Nomonhan. Yet Japanese fighter unit commanders vigorously deny that they lost control of the skies. The 24th Air Group commander, Maj. Yuzuhara Hidemi, says that to the very end of August his fighters flew an average of four sorties per day, on patrol and escort duty.[19]

> If a small number of us went out, the enemy would attack. They preferred to wait until our flying time was up and we were returning or were about to return to base. Then they would dive from high altitude, fire blindly whether they scored hits or not, and rush home, without persisting in do-or-die tactics as we would have done. But if we sortied with the whole wing of four groups, as we often did, the foe stayed away from us. So we used the wing to retain air control and encourage the ground forces.

Yuzuhara's wounded predecessor, Lt. Col. Matsumura Kōjirō, agrees entirely.[20]

> At the time of the large-scale Russian attacks, we committed every plane we had. While we were out in force, flying our four daily one-hour sorties, the enemy did not challenge us. Instead, they resorted to effective guerrilla tactics—catching bombers alone, always seeking weak points, employing small forces, and avoiding pitched battles. We did not counterattack [the guerrilla planes]; it was not worth it, since we were conserving our aircraft. Thus friendly ground forces may have felt that the Russians controlled the air, but that was not really true.

So far as artillery was concerned on 20 August, Komatsubara observed that the barrages went on all day without letup along the entire front. Russian ammunition expenditure must have reached several thousand rounds. Three new 10-cm. cannon batteries had appeared, presumably 12 pieces. To support the Soviet offensive, Kobayashi and Komatsubara heard, the Russians had built four bridges overnight: two in the Fui Heights area and two to the far southeast at Higashi- and Minami-watashi. Ground assaults had been launched against every Japanese defensive sector. In the Fui district, the Russians had committed new armor, artillery, and elements of a rifle division in addition to the MPRA cavalry, or on the order of 1,000 men, 50 tanks and 100 armored cars, and 8-10 mountain guns, plus 200 Mongol horsemen. Manchukuoan forces had been driven back. South of the positions at Fui, Sumi's Ikuta battalion had been fighting off 1,400-1,500 enemy troops. Below the Holsten, Colonel Morita's regimental front had been attacked by a force including 1,200 infantry, 50-60 tanks, and 200 trucks that had crossed on the new Higashi- and Minami-watashi bridges.[21]

Komatsubara, as we saw, was apprehensive from the outset about the threat developing on both Japanese flanks, especially on the left where Colonel Morita possessed only seven companies to defend a broad front that was being sliced up, unit by unit. How best to employ the seven infantry battalions north of the Holsten? Among those consulted was Colonel Kanaoka, the senior staff officer of Hata's corps, who was asked for the artillery's standpoint. Undoubtedly reflecting Major General Hata's thinking, Kanaoka recommended that reserves be committed to break through on one front and redress the situation "slowly but steadily." Komatsubara decided fairly quickly to suspend the fortification program and to concentrate the division's main body (20 companies) south of the Holsten after sunset, with a counteroffensive in mind. Nevertheless, considering Ioki's deepening crisis at Fui, by evening the division had had to subtract Sumi's reserve units (5 companies) and shift them northward. This meant that the main redeployments would affect the regiments of Yamagata and Sakai. The former's 64th Infantry, almost alone, would now have to defend the entire front north of the Holsten. The eight companies of the 72nd Regiment, in turn, were to leave their old positions and join Japanese forces, under Kobayashi's group command, below the Holsten.[22]

At 1 P.M. on the 20th, Yamagata notified 1st Battalion commander Akai (now a lieutenant colonel) that he was to leave the reserve and take over the 72nd Regiment's front, and that he was to be ready to move by 8:30 P.M. The 2nd Battalion would have to spread out and occupy the positions previously held by Yamagata's own regiment, and the 3rd Battalion would enter regimental reserve, leaving one company to cover the gap between the battalions. Officially ordered at 4 P.M. to prepare to redeploy, Sakai was visited within the hour by Akai, and the two officers worked out details. Sakai's order of 5 P.M. called for the changeover to be effected by midnight and included injunctions to leave behind noncritical items such as blankets and wicker footlockers, to carry as many Molotov cocktails and antitank mines as possible, and to be especially cautious about concealing the movement. Although the replacement battalion arrived behind schedule, the transition proceeded quietly and effectively when it finally started after 11 P.M., despite the darkness and unfamiliar terrain. By 3 A.M. the changeover was completed.

The Sixth Army chief of staff, Maj. Gen. Fujimoto Tetsukuma, had rushed to the front in the meantime, and it soon became apparent that serious strategic differences existed between the Sixth Army and the 23rd Division about the best method of coping with the Soviet offensive. For the moment, it was decided to observe the battle situation and hold the 72nd Infantry north of Shin-Kōheibashi (New Engineer Bridge) at the upstream Holsten, instead of inserting it into Colonel Morita's 71st Infantry zone immediately. Morita, having been told that his force was to retain its positions and form the core of tomorrow's offensive (centering on the 3rd Battalion at Heights 747), was advised by a phone call from the division at 8 P.M. that the transfer of Sakai's regiment south of the Holsten was being suspended temporarily and that the main body of the 71st Regiment should pull back toward Nigesorimot. New word did not reach the 3rd Battalion, however, that it was to hold Heights 747, and by dawn the battalion had fallen back to a point east of Heights 741.[23]

Not until 9 A.M. on 21 August did the Kwantung Army learn officially from the 23rd Division about the Soviet attacks that had commenced over 24 hours earlier. Hostile activities had intensified suddenly since the morning of the 20th, reported the division, and an offensive was in full swing along almost the whole front. Against the Manchukuoan elements screening the Honjinganga sector to the north, the enemy had massed 1,000 cavalrymen and infantry, 50 tanks, and more than 10 artillery pieces, and had begun to attack at noon. The main forces had meanwhile crossed the river and approached a lake 16 kilometers west of Chiangchunmiao.[24]

From the first sketchy report, the Kwantung Army understood that the small Manchukuoan cavalry unit on the division's extreme right wing had been overpowered and driven eastward. The enemy's intention seemed to be an advance on Chiangchunmiao around the outer flank. Such an interpretation was gainsaid, however, by a short message received from the Sixth Army at 6 P.M. on the 21st. At present, the enemy's main objective appeared to be the sector south of the Holsten. Hostile forward units that had appeared on the 23rd Division's front included at least two rifle divisions plus mechanized formations.[25] This later intelligence indicated that Komatsubara's division, whose right flank had been breached first, was in real difficulty, now that the foe was emphasizing the other wing on the south.

Although such a major effort at double envelopment meant that the Russians' general offensive was truly under way, the Kwantung Army found a number of reasons for optimism at this stage: information transmitted by the Sixth Army and the 23rd Division, starting on the 20th, conveyed the impression that the enemy's offensive had taken place "at the expected time and in the anticipated manner." The division's defenses had already been reinforced and were fairly strong. New Manchukuoan forces had been moved up recently to cover the southern flank. Maj. Gen. Morita Norimasa's 14th Infantry Brigade from the 7th Division was being concentrated in the Chiangchunmiao area and could be committed to combat promptly. Lastly, the Sixth Army had completed its organization, was gradually becoming familiar with battlefield conditions, and could be expected to direct combat operations effectively.[26] With regard to these chimerical rationalizations, it should be noted specifically that the defenses were not sufficiently advanced, the Manchukuoan troops were unreliable (as we shall soon see), and General Morita's command was not really of brigade strength.

On 21 August, the Russians continued their drive designed to smash Japanese resistance below the Holsten. Potapov sent his 8th Armored Brigade northward on his right wing, together with the 6th Tank Brigade, now that it was available. These powerful units detoured the Japanese left flank, traversed difficult terrain, and occupied the Heights 780-791 (Great Sands) area by the end of the 21st. This meant that, in only two days, mechanized forces had intercepted any eastward escape by the Japanese south of the Holsten. Meanwhile, the reconnaissance battalion of the Soviet 57th Division was sent to plug the four-kilometer gap that had developed between the 80th and 127th Rifle regiments of the division, to the left of the armor.

In a related development during 21 August, there was a serious rebellion among Manchukuoan troops screening the easternmost flank of the Japanese in the zone of the 8th MPRA Cavalry Division north of the Minamiwatashi crossing. The so-called Sekiran or Shihlan detachment of the Manchukuoan army, with a total strength of 3,000 cavalrymen and infantry, had been moved from Tsitsihar after another Manchukuoan unit (the Kōan or Hsingan detachment) was badly mauled at the beginning of August. That the poorly equipped and ill-trained Manchurians were assigned a front-line (albeit defensive) mission stemmed both from the Kwantung Army's shortage of manpower and overrating of their client creation, and from the chronic underestimation of the enemy, the Outer Mongols in particular. The new force came under enemy attack from the 19th. On the night of 21 August, the attached Japanese officers at the exposed camp of one of the Manchukuoan infantry regiments had assembled separately to discuss a planned withdrawal to detachment headquarters next morning. In the absence of the Japanese, the Manchurian camp chief unfurled his plot, which led to the killing of five of the Japanese officers and the flight of 250-300 Bargut and Manchu soldiers across the upstream Halha to the sanctuary of Outer Mongolia. The surviving Japanese officers saved what was left of the unit and made it back to the detachment command post with the Manchukuoan group commander.[27]

On 22 August, Potapov's infantry forces drove a deep wedge into the Japanese main line of resistance, wiped out tactical reserves, and occupied a number of gun sites. Soviet tactics entailed moving swiftly, splitting enemy lines into a number of unconnected points, sealing them off, and eliminating them piecemeal (exactly as battalion commander Nishikawa, among other IJA officers, had feared). Artillery and flamethrowing tanks played a major role in the assaults against knots of resistance, which had to be subdued frontally. The Russians moved up guns of every caliber, including 152-mm., and blasted the strongpoints at short range, firing over open sights. Flamethrowers burned out bunkers and deep shelters, and infantry made the kill with grenades and bayonets. Elements of the 57th Division encircled particularly formidable knots at two points about five kilometers south of the Holsten and exterminated the defenders with the help of flamethrower tanks. By the end of 23 August, Potapov had broken the whole IJA defensive network. Only one pocket, in the Heights 757 sector, was still held by the Japanese. In the meantime, the 8th Armored Brigade advanced to the district southeast of Nomonhan on the boundary claimed by the MPR, occupied positions facing northeast, and cut off any route of escape by IJA forces below the Holsten.

Zhukov's Central Force continued to make negligible progress. The 82nd Rifle Division encountered stubborn resistance in the attack against the Heights 742 area on the Hasebe front, and the 36th Division against Heights 733, known to the Japanese as Barunishi (West Balshagal), above the Holsten. But it was on the Northern Force's front that a surprisingly climactic struggle raged. There, as Zhukov admitted, Ioki's little garrison put up "more obstinate resistance than we thought it could," and Fui Heights could not be taken on either 21 August or 22 August. Zhukov was critical of Shevnikov's tactics: "Instead of pinning the Japanese on the heights with a portion of his forces and continuing to drive swiftly southward with his main strength, the Northern Force commander kept up a series of unsuccessful assaults." Time and men were being consumed, and the tempo of strategic encirclement was being slowed. To "rectify" matters and regain momentum, Zhukov was obliged to buttress the artillery and commit sizable armor from reserve. Reinforced by a tank battalion from the 6th Brigade, the new 9th Armored Brigade was to sweep north along the Halha from Hamardaba, swing around Fui from the east (losing no time at that heights), and press southeastward toward Nomonhan, destroying the logistics base at Uzuru pond and cutting off the enemy's escape route. Shevnikov was replaced on the 21st by Colonel Alekseenko (Olekseyenko).

Ioki's men, however, fought on fiercely. According to the Russians, the elevation was defended by strong fortifications on all sides, with barbed wire overlaying deep bunkers connected by trenches dug at wide intervals. Since every Russian assault was repulsed by the Japanese defenders, Zhukov next sent up the 212th Airborne Brigade, his last major reserves. The Japanese would still not give up, and it was necessary to force them "from every cranny" in close-quarter fighting. Only toward the end of 23 August were the reinforced Soviet attack units able to break the back of the main resistance. When the battle finally ended, the Russians counted the corpses of more than 600 Japanese officers and men strewn in the bunkers and trenches.[28]

Komatsubara, who had transferred Sumi's reserves a bit northward to Heights 752 on 20 August, next day ordered them moved farther north toward Heights 739, west of Uzuru and halfway to Fui. Some Manchukuoan troops were supposed to be still located in the area. But in practice, Sumi had the equivalent of only about two infantry companies available, and the maneuver was obviously intended mostly to screen the open right wing of the 23rd Division rather than directly to lift the pressure from still-isolated Fui. From a distance of approximately six kilometers, Sumi observed dense black clouds billowing over the area, which was surrounded by the enemy. Then the red darts of flamethrowers could be discerned, "spitting like the tongues of snakes." Although Ioki was his old friend, Sumi was even more worried about the fate of his own troops deployed at Fui, and indeed one of the officers he lost there was 2nd Lieutenant Yamanaka, his former courier, now an infantry-gun platoon leader. It was a very painful and helpless situation; "all we could do was worry."

On the afternoon of the 21st, a liaison officer, Capt. Oshiumi Minsuke (Tamisuke), came from the division and reported to Sumi that he was going to Fui to inspect the situation. The colonel told him that daytime movement was impossible and that he should wait until sunset. Oshiumi responded that the atmosphere in division headquarters was so unbearable, he would rather be killed than return. So Sumi reluctantly assigned him an escort squad, and the captain set forth for Fui Heights. Around midnight, one surviving soldier returned, wounded.

In the evening, Sumi had been ordered to send ammunition and food to Fui, using a "do-or-die" unit (*kesshitai*). The colonel muttered bitterly to himself, "All of us out here are really *kesshitai*!" Only Kokubu's old 10th Company still approached full strength. Although Sumi was hesitant about releasing that many of his few men on such a dangerous mission, he directed acting 3rd Battalion commander Kokubu to take the troops, load the goods aboard trucks, and depart in the twilight. Kokubu made it back with his company after the foray in darkness to Fui Heights, having suffered remarkably few casualties.

Sumi was also ordered on the 21st to launch a night attack against Heights 739. How to do this with little more than the equivalent of one composite company? Major Kamimura, the new 2nd Battalion commander, volunteered to lead the force, in Sumi's stead. Later the division countermanded the order, but it was too late for Sumi to notify the assault force. Kamimura succeeded in taking Heights 739 by 4 A.M. on the 22nd without encountering resistance, and sent scouts 3,500 meters forward to reconnoiter the Fui direction. At midday on the 22nd, the Japanese repulsed 200 infantry and 10 tanks, and in the evening drove the enemy from high ground to the east. In the early hours of the 23rd, the IJA forces returned to Heights 752, apparently on Kamimura's own initiative—a decision that pleased Sumi. Close-quarter squads drove off 20 Soviet tanks at 8 A.M. The threat of Soviet detouring around the Japanese right rear disturbed Sumi, in view of the IJA attrition and lack of counterstrength. "It is just a matter of time," the colonel thought, "but we must defend our colors to the last." As a first step, he began to destroy those documents in his knapsack that had no direct bearing on the current combat—his diary, old orders, maps.[29]

The actions by Sumi's men exerted little or no beneficial effect upon the "island" at Fui, although Komatsubara was fairly optimistic about the situation as of 21 August. The construction of defensive works, the division commander heard, had progressed well and casualties in the positions were "not too bad," although the battalion was encircled by 1,000 troops and 70 or 80 tanks.[30] Conditions on the spot were far worse than Komatsubara imagined. Ioki's survivors were becoming exhausted, lacked water, and were short of food and ammunition. As the hours and days went by, field pieces, infantry guns, rapid-fire weapons, and machine guns were smashed by enemy barrages. Tanks, estimated by the defenders to number 200 eventually, constricted the vise until "not even an ant could have crawled out." The fewer the IJA troops, the more aggressive the Russians became, operating freely within the defenses and sending up "hellish" flamethrowing tanks.

From the night of 22 August, trucks supplying ammunition, food, or water could no longer get through to Fui. Telephone lines to division headquarters were severed, and at 4 P.M. on the 23rd the vital wireless apparatus was destroyed. Soviet pressure was particularly strong at the rear of the defenses, where strongpoints were steadily overrun. By the 23rd, the Russians were posting red flags all over the rear half of the positions.[31] Ioki ordered his units to charge repeatedly. Armed only with rifles, bayonets, and grenades, the men fought it out with the foe. From the Japanese standpoint, however, it was like "holding a candle to the wind," and the situation could not be retrieved. At dawn on the 24th, Soviet forces penetrated toward Ioki's tent, and catastrophe seemed near by 7 A.M. Ioki reluctantly pulled back his command post. The Russians machine-gunned and hurled grenades into the engineer trench where seriously wounded Japanese soldiers were sitting or lying, trying in vain to fend off the enemy with puny pistols. A last counterattack by the tankette company was shattered. Casualties had been frightful on both sides. Ioki's 2nd Company, for example, was down to four or five men. By now, little more than 200 able-bodied officers and men were left, and many of these hunkered down and did not even fire on enemy troops any longer, lest close-range counterfire be drawn from tanks and flamethrowers.

On the afternoon of the 24th, Ioki assembled his last commanders to discuss the fate of the unit. Although they were entirely cut off from higher headquarters, division orders, said Ioki, required defending the positions to the last man. His subordinates, however, argued that any further attempt to retain Fui would be both hopeless and meaningless. A half-day more was left, at most. It was better to get out for the time being, obtain water, food, ammunition, and reinforcements of men and equipment, and then reconquer Fui. Oppressed by his sense of responsibility, Ioki tried to shoot himself. A battery commander restrained him and beseeched him to authorize a pullout. It was an impossible situation for Ioki, whose choices were limited to death on Fui Heights or death afterward, since even if the pullback were successful he would be guilty of a so-called "retreat" without orders. As one soldier said later, "It was easy to die but hard to live on the battlefield."

Ioki was particularly pained by the hunger and thirst afflicting his men. Deciding to try to save the remnants so they could live to fight another day, Ioki finally gave in and at 4 P.M. issued the fateful instructions to disengage from doomed Fui Heights. The unit was to "break through the present urgent situation and thus facilitate the battle of the divisional main force." Breakout action was to commence, at 10 or 11 P.M. that night, with an attack on the Soviet cordon. Thereupon the Japanese should head toward Nomonhan, in the general direction of Lake Manzute, about eight kilometers to the southeast.

Waiting for night to fall, the soldiers assembled in what was left of the trenches. Those wounded men who were ambulatory were told to accompany their comrades, but those who felt that they could not make it were given hand grenades, with the implication that they should kill themselves rather than be taken prisoner. After five days with little or no food and water, the troops were listless and drained of energy. Most dozed when they could, clutching the belt of the man who was to precede them out. "If you let go of the belt, it would be the end of you, and you would be left behind." A small bag of rice and an impossibly hard dried fish (*katsuobushi*) were passed along, with instructions to nibble a little and send them on.

The pullback inevitably began behind schedule, partly because the moon was too bright. Not until 2–2:30 A.M., when the moon was down, did Ioki and the lead unit, the 6th Infantry Company from Sumi's regiment, finally emerge from the trenches. Trying to help the wounded and guarding them, the able-bodied troops followed quietly behind in four or five columns, led by commanders waving cloth signals. It was stop-and-go, stop-and-go, stumbling along the telephone line, traversing piano wire, and bearing upon the Big Dipper. The 1st Reconnaissance Company brought up the rear. After advancing three or four kilometers, at 3:30 A.M. the advance units ran into enemy sentries, who resisted but were cut down. The Japanese moved faster, for tanks could be heard and searchlights seen. In the confusion, the troops became lost and veered north, but haste was imperative as early dawn approached. The dismounted horse soldiers found the going particularly difficult once they got through the grass, for the soles of their shoes lacked hobnails, and it was impossible to run in the sandy soil. Soldiers wearing rubber-soled *jikatabi* field sneakers did better.

Eventually Ioki and his survivors got away. Darkness and surprise had helped, and Soviet attention was largely diverted to the decisive battles raging to the south by now, after organized IJA resistance at Fui was deemed broken by 23/24 August. At 5:30 A.M. on the 25th, the Japanese deployed in dispersed formation when enemy armor was observed reconnoitering. There was a special scare around 10:30 A.M.: near Lake Garot, about 15 kilometers east-northeast of Fui, a cavalry patrol appeared on a crestline nearby; fortunately for the Japanese, the horsemen proved to be not Outer Mongolians but Manchukuoan troops—from the remnant that had been driven back on the first day of the Soviet offensive. "All of us were mightily relieved," says a Japanese soldier. "It was as if we had met the Buddha in hell [*jigoku ni hotoke*]." Several trucks arrived soon afterward to pick up the wounded. The rest of the men marched on, tantalized by a mirage of water, and reached Manchukuo army district headquarters, west of Obone, by 2 P.M. Clasping a rice ball in one hand and a canteen of water in the other, the exhausted Japanese soldiers slept the sleep of the dead. After a while, stragglers turned up, unannounced and unappreciated—a medical second lieutenant and noncoms from the cavalry headquarters, presumably the party that had taken wounded men to the division command post on the 22nd, never returned to Fui, and finally left for Obone on their own.

On 26 August, Lt. Col. Ioki Eiichi's tattered little command reached the

Chiangchunmiao area and momentary safety, after the epic defense of Fui Heights for five bloody days.[32]

While Fui was being reduced, the Soviet 9th Armored Brigade bypassed the heights from the east and on 22 August attacked the IJA base near Uzuru pond (Lake Uzur Nur, in Russian usage). Located a half-dozen kilometers northwest of Nomonhan, Uzuru was a rare freshwater pool, still the advance logistical site for ammunition resupply and for a field hospital. Russian sources, ignoring the existence of medical facilities, record the destruction of motorized elements, the burning of fuel and ammunition stocks, and the elimination of a defending battery. The smashing of the logistical center seriously disorganized the Japanese-Manchukuoan supply system.[33]

Japanese survivors mainly recall the Russian tanks' attack of the 22nd against the field hospital, an octagonal tent, 10 meters high, with the Red Cross flag flying on the top. Of course, the many patients were unarmed, and the medical soldiers had nothing more than pistols for defense. When the Japanese saw that the armor was heading in their direction, the ambulatory ones sought to escape, hoisting some of the invalids on their shoulders. A soldier hospitalized because of a 15-cm.-shell-fragment wound in the thigh remembers limping toward Uzuru pond, hip-deep in muddy water. Those who tried to run in the opposite direction were pursued and trampled by the Soviet tanks, which also ran over the tent and the helpless patients trapped inside. When the storm had passed and the survivors assembled at the location of the hospital, they were sickened by the gore of the scene. By the time Lt. Col. Yotsuya Iwao's newly arrived 6th IGU Battalion and two rapid-fire guns reached the Uzuru area from Nomonhan on the night of the 22nd with the mission of engaging the Soviet tanks, the enemy was gone. At daybreak, Yotsuya and his detachment encountered the appalling devastation wrought at the Uzuru base, particularly the incineration of the field hospital and the grisly aftermath.[34]

After overrunning Uzuru, the reinforced 9th Armored Brigade[35] reached Nomonhan next day, thereby blocking the eastward escape route of IJA forces in the north. On the 24th, the 9th Brigade closed the ring by making contact with elements of the 8th Armored Brigade coming up from the Southern Force. The first stage of the offensive was over.

Aviation had played an important part in the success of the Soviet-MPRA ground forces. On one day alone—21 August—Russian bombers had sortied 256 times, striking targets at Uzuru pond, Nomonhan, Chiangchunmiao, and Kanchuerhmiao, and the rail line somewhere near Arshaan. In all, more than 86,000 kilograms of bombs were dropped.[36]

The Kwantung Army air force made one major effort, at this stage, to strike at the roots of Russian air power by launching a new attack against the bases in Outer Mongolia. For three weeks after the small but ominous Soviet raid on Fulaerhchi on 16 July, mentioned earlier, the Kwantung Army—having raised the hackles of the AGS by its arbitrary action against Tamsag at the end of June—had been arguing with the High Command for permission to be unleashed to mount an air offensive of its own against the "extension" of the battleground east of Tamsag. Instead, General Isogai had been ordered to Tokyo and had been lectured against countenancing retaliation. The High Command warned the Kwantung Army that air strikes against the Tamsag complex would be ill-advised and might be less effective than promised. Worst of all, the scope of the Nomonhan hostilities might be enlarged as the result of enemy counteraction. Even if Soviet behavior proved "almost intolerable from the standpoint of the honor of Manchukuo," Japan could not afford to be dragged into a war with the USSR because of a mere border dispute. The Kwantung Army should "grin and bear it," the Nomonhan affair should be settled promptly, and attention should be devoted to the long-range buildup of Manchukuo's defenses.

Such homilies and "insults" drove the Kwantung Army staff to fury. Tsuji and his colleagues spoke angrily of having to wage a two-front war, against the Soviet-MPRA side on the one hand and against the Japanese IGHQ on the other. Whereas the Russian High Command was prodding local chiefs to initiate aggressive action, the Japanese High Command was preventing its subordinates from taking forceful measures. Should the senior officers of the Japanese army be instructing their best field army to endure humiliation? What would become of Manchukuo if Hsinking were bombed? What would the impact be upon the great Japanese Empire? The atmosphere between Hsinking and Tokyo was poisoned for the rest of the Nomonhan war. Insult was added to injury when Colonel Inada sent two "lowly" staff officers[37] from the AGS to observe the situation at the end of July and beginning of August. These officers recommended to Tokyo exactly what the Kwantung Army brass had been requesting all along—and the High Command then accepted *their* evaluation. It was a case of real *gekokujō*, fumed Tsuji—an expert on the subject of insubordination—when Tokyo esteemed a young major's views more highly than those of the venerable Kwantung Army commander. There was danger that the validity of imperial orders emanating from Tokyo would come to be questioned.

Finally, an imperial order approving the Kwantung Army's air thrust was forthcoming on 7 August, followed by cautionary AGS directives. Lieutenant Colonel Miyashi hand-carried the Kwantung Army's resulting order next day to General Giga at Hailar, with injunctions to hold the information close. IGHQ was also demanding that exact figures not be released concerning results of the air strike and that the impression should be conveyed that Japanese air operations were always defensive.[38]

While the argument raged between Hsinking and Tokyo, the Japanese air force—like the ground units—played down or simply did not detect the substantive evidence of the Russians' offensive preparations. There seems to have been excessive reliance on visual observation because aerial cameras were "frankly troublesome to operate." An IJAF light-bomber flight leader was never able to identify friendly forces on the ground, and he only knew the general region where 23rd Division headquarters was located; since the command post was on the move, he could not pinpoint it. There were no longer any Japanese tanks in the area, so the nationality of armor was easy enough to establish once it could be discerned, but stationary or silent tanks were difficult to unmask. One never saw all of the enemy mechanized forces at once anyhow. Even when the August offensive broke, it did not strike one IJAF bomber pilot as of the "real" and overpowering scale of assault he encountered later in the Philippines and elsewhere during the Pacific War— although the use of 400 armored vehicles certainly betokened a general offensive in 1939. Another Japanese air officer, a fighter squadron commander, remembers the case of higher headquarters refusing to accept an experienced reconnaissance squadron commander's report of sighting "an enormous number" of enemy tanks. The scout pilot "blew his stack," but his information was deemed to be exaggerated and unreliable, and it was not conveyed to the ground forces—to their detriment—although air intelligence had tabulated 2,000 vehicles in the battle area, even by the end of July.[39]

Giga was elated about the authorization to strike targets in Outer Mongolia again. His wing commanders had even been wiring direct recommendations to higher headquarters in this vein. Unfortunately for the Kwantung Army air force, however, the 2nd Air Division had become exhausted physically and psychologically by mid-August, as the result of excessive wear and tear on men and machines. IGHQ permission for the aerial offensive should have been granted in July, the airmen complained. The Japanese were still winning in the air, in terms of absolute numbers of planes downed, but the ratio of kills to friendly aircraft and airmen lost was deteriorating steadily, although IJAF numbers were increasing.

There are various ways of expressing the downward trend. In July, for example, 481 hostile planes were claimed to have been shot down at a cost of 41, for a loss rate of almost 1:12. But in the first 20 days of August, 134 planes were downed at a cost of 23, for a ratio half as favorable. A Soviet air force officer, A. B. Vorozheikin, says that Soviet-to-Japanese plane-loss ratios were more than 4:1 in May, but 1:3 in June, 1:4 in July, and 1:10 in August.[40] Yet whereas the Russians were committing many fresh and blooded pilots and better planes and were improving their tactics, the Japanese—distracted by the war in China—were employing the identical pilots and aircraft, or were bringing in green replacements after having drawn heavily upon experienced personnel reserves from the homeland. As for IJAF replacement aircraft, almost all of the new production of Type 97 fighters and scout planes was sent directly to Nomonhan.[41]

The quality and quantity of Japanese crews were being eroded by the unending daily combat and multiple sorties—a maximum of six and a half hours per day. Problems included adverse flying conditions and maintenance and rotational difficulties. On an individual level, loss of appetite, stomach trouble, blackouts, and lack of sleep owing to hostile nighttime harassment were reported. An air staff officer remembers the drawn faces, glazed eyes, and hollow cheeks of Japanese aviators. Scout pilots, he learned from a military physician, were having difficulty with their respiratory systems.

Attrition took a mounting toll. Since June, 44 Japanese airmen had been killed and 17 wounded, for a total of 61 casualties. By the time of the August offensive, another eight had been killed and seven wounded. The death of Col. Abe Katsumi, 15th Air Group commander, who was caught on the ground at his airbase near Chiangchunmiao by several dozen Soviet air force marauders on 2 August, was particularly painful, for Abe had been a senior staff officer at Kwantung Army headquarters and great things were expected of him professionally. Another group, the 24th Fighter, had achieved such a formidable combat reputation that Soviet pilots reportedly avoided tangling with it when they discovered its rudder markings. On 4 August, Lt. Col. Matsumura Kōjirō, the very able commander of the group, who had been in action since May, was shot down and severely wounded in a clash against Soviet aces with Spanish Civil War experience, their underwings painted distinctively violet. His plane flipped over after crashing, the tail pinned him down, his flight suit was set aflame, and he lost all the fingers on his right hand. A fellow pilot landed nearby under enemy fire, dragged the husky, delirious colonel into his own one-seater fighter, and managed to fly back to base, hugging the ground at 75 meters.[42] Many other excellent IJAF personnel had also been killed or wounded since the Nomonhan fighting erupted, including about 80 percent of the fighter squadron commanders.[43]

Given the present rate of manpower consumption, according to the air force Personnel Section, it would not be possible to fight on until winter. At the outset, 70 percent of the IJAF pilots had 1,000 or more hours of flying time, and some had 2,000. The loss of even one pilot, says Giga, represented a painful blow to the Japanese air force. When Giga asked for replacements from Air Inspector General Tōjō Hideki, he was told that a dozen officers and noncoms were being sent from the Akeno flight school, so he should "take the offensive" with them. "I knew the 'contents of the wallet,'" Giga remarks, "so I couldn't really complain." The brand-new pilots from the air schools in Japan were not well-regarded by the surviving veterans at Nomonhan, who thought of them as mere "chauffeurs," technically proficient but lacking experience, confidence, familiarity with the area, and "fight." [44]

The order of 7 August had given Giga leeway to determine the exact date of the Japanese aerial offensive. For the causes described above, centering on human fatigue and material maintenance as well as a spell of bad flying weather in mid-August, it was decided to defer the attack for a while. Anyhow, says Giga, the raid was not going to be made because of any specific enemy concentration; "it just had to be done sometime soon," for reasons in general. In other words, the offensive against Tamsag would have been needed even without the provocation at Fulaerhchi in July. On 18 August, Giga was finally able to direct all wing commanders to get ready for "Operation S." Next day, the weather began to improve, and intelligence was received of 700 enemy vehicles operating between Tamsag and the battlefront. Giga called for the air offensive to be launched anytime from 21 August. Intelligence on the hostile situation was still needed, and this was forthcoming by the evening of the 20th, on the day the Soviet-MPR side also took advantage of the improved weather to mount their own general offensive. Combining scout and combat reports, Giga's air division concluded that hostile air strength in the Tamsag area amounted to at least 80-90 fighters and 30-40 heavier aircraft—about the same numbers the Japanese could commit to the total air offensive. One short thrust operation ought to be able to regain control of the skies, after which enemy ground forces would be attacked. The assault was set for dawn on 21 August.

For the raid, the Japanese massed two air wings of eight groups totaling 145 planes: 88 fighters, 24 light and 12 heavy bombers, and 21 scouts. A light-bomber pilot from the 16th Group remembers arising at 2:30 A.M. on the 21st, getting ready for the sortie under the stars, and taking off with his six-plane squadron at 4:20 A.M. Escorted by over 50 of the fighters, the bombers flew in two tiers across the Halha, heading for the Tamsag airfield complex approximately 60 kilometers southwest of the Higashi-watashi crossing. At 6 A.M. the ground was still dark, and only the outline of an airstrip could be seen east of Tamsag, but the first squadron dropped its bombs, observed smoke rising, and headed for home, encountering antiaircraft barrages near Higashi-watashi. The second of the bomber squadrons, which reported catching 16 large aircraft on the ground, encountered 20 I-16 fighters after completing its bombing run and starting back. Both squadrons landed safely between 6:40 and 6:50 A.M., although the second had taken a number of hits. The third squadron did not locate its target but bombed 40-50 enemy tanks near the river on the way back and reported knocking out five or six. From the 10th Group, the six participating light bombers detected 10 SB bombers on the airfield northeast of Tamsag, attacked six, and claimed to have burned two. The escorting 12th Fighter Wing met no airborne enemy planes. A fighter squadron commander recalls that the skies were covered with IJAF planes—so many that it looked like an air show, not a battle. Indeed, by their very numbers, the Japanese air groups seemed to have "scared off" enemy resistance for the moment.

Scout planes reconnoitered the target zone at 7 A.M. and reported several dozen enemy aircraft still parked in the Tamsag area. A second IJAF wave attacked again at 11 A.M. The six light bombers from the 10th Group went after the airstrip north of Tamsag but, finding no planes (only six dummy aircraft), attacked ground facilities and 50 trucks, of which only one was seen to be burning. One bomber squadron from the 16th Group struck eight large planes on the southern airstrip, smashing five of them. A second squadron from this group, intercepted by a dozen fighters, turned to attack a ground installation 10 kilometers southeast of Lake Buir on the way back, shooting down three fighters but losing one bomber in the process. The 61st Group, with a dozen heavy bombers, caught eight fighters at the south Tamsag base and claimed two. On the way home, these bombers were attacked by four I-16 and three I-15 fighters, and shot down two of the latter. As for the 12th Fighter Wing escort, this time they clashed with 50-60 enemy aircraft in the Tamsag area, shooting down 27 fighters and an SB bomber, at a cost of three fighters.[45]

In the afternoon of 21 August, around 4 P.M., Japanese airmen rendered support to friendly forces by bombing large enemy armored and motorized formations near endangered Fui Heights. Air battles ensued, in the course of which the 16th Light Bomber Group shot down six of 30 I-16 fighters, at a cost of one man killed and two wounded, while the escorting 11th Fighter Group downed 11 of a mixed force of 40 or 50 I-15's and I-16's. Toward evening, the Japanese sent flights against Soviet aircraft on the left side of the Halha. At 6:50 P.M. the 10th Group's one light-bomber squadron caught 10 enemy fighters about to take off from a concealed airstrip west of Hara Heights and bombed three planes as well as a number of trucks. Japanese fighter squadrons engaged approximately 50 Russian fighters and shot down nine, losing one of their own planes from the 64th Group.

Despite the IJAF effort to neutralize Soviet air power, Giga's staff had to admit that more than 50 enemy bombers and 180 fighters were still in action by the end of 21 August. Therefore follow-up strikes were scheduled for the next day, first against the Tamsag complex at 9:30 A.M., and then against forward targets in the Lake Buir district between 1 and 2 P.M. The raids proved fruitless, as the Russians had vacated the airfields. In the strike against Tamsag, however, the 61st Heavy Bomber Group was attacked by 30 I-16's. Six of the fighters were downed, but one Japanese bomber crashed, killing the entire crew of five. The 12th Wing ran into 30 fighters but bagged only three because the enemy did not choose to stay and fight. One IJAF fighter from the 1st Group was lost to antiaircraft fire.

While the Japanese air offensive on the 22nd was in progress, accomplishing little, reports arrived concerning the enemy buildup and the straits of friendly ground units. At 7 A.M., a scout plane had sighted 1,000 vehicles massed in the Tamsag region, suggesting the scale of Soviet reinforcements. Around 1 P.M., the 15th Air Group, attached to the 23rd Division, advised Giga's headquarters that swarms of Russian armored vehicles had been penetrating the right wing since morning and were endangering the Fui Heights and Uzuru areas in particular. Giga decided to suspend the unproductive aerial offensive operations and commit all available aircraft to the assistance of the ground units. The 16th Light Bomber Group, which had been on standby, attacked targets in the Uzuru sector four times after 1:30 P.M. The rest of the 9th Wing sent its bomber groups against both Uzuru and Fui, escorted by the fighter wing. Soviet machine cannon shot down a scout plane from the 10th Group that had been reconnoitering tank formations. Capt. Motomura Kōji, a fighter squadron commander of the 11th Group, was lost when he single-handedly took on 30 I-16's that had been attacking ground forces north of 23rd Division headquarters.[46]

The numbers of Soviet planes eliminated during the Japanese air strikes of 21-22 August have been variously estimated. According to information reaching the Kwantung Army at the time, about the same totals of enemy aircraft were destroyed on 21 August as in the first raid against Tamsag in June—namely, 97 planes of all types. On the 22nd, another 12 Russian aircraft were smashed, for a grand total of 109 in two days. Air staff officer Miyoshi asserts, however, that the enemy *had* won aerial supremacy by now, that the IJAF strike force could only sortie and return, that the claims could not be confirmed, and that considerably fewer than 90 planes must have been destroyed on the first day. Nevertheless, drawing on IJAF documentation, the latest official Japanese tabulation lists 50 Soviet fighters and 27 bombers "caught" by bomber aircraft, and 60 fighters and one bomber shot down for sure in air combat.[47]

By all Japanese accounts, IJAF losses on 21-22 August were the most severe since the outbreak of the Nomonhan fighting. The Kwantung Army heard that eight Japanese planes were lost on the first day, and six on the second. Casualty figures vary a bit. According to one authoritative Japanese source, seven airmen were killed and four were wounded on the 21st, and six were killed and none wounded on the 22nd, for a total of 17 casualties.

The official postwar history lists IJAF manpower losses on the first day alone as four killed (or missing) and three wounded in fighter units; three killed and two wounded in light bombers; one killed and one wounded in a scout plane (plus two killed in another reconnaissance aircraft operating near Fui Heights). The battle accounts for 22 August add seven killed and one wounded, which would make a grand total of 22-24.[48]

Although the Kwantung Army had been worried about the question of air control since 20 August, the results of the latest Tamsag raids seemed excellent. Nevertheless, the casualties were considered grievous from the point of view of air strength, and it was clear that the Japanese airmen were becoming exhausted. The Kwantung Army operations staff officers felt that it would be critical for the Japanese army as a whole if the air force lost aerial supremacy, quite apart from the situation on the ground. It was suggested that the air division be allowed to rest for several days. Miyoshi retorted that it was entirely impossible for the air force to ease up at a time when the ground units were conducting a decisive struggle. The airmen, he insisted, must cooperate with the ground troops, regardless of the toll in the skies. Miyoshi's emotional view prevailed, but although enemy aerial actions seemed to be somewhat weaker after the offensive against Tamsag, the Soviet air force was still able to exploit its superior numbers, drawing upon strength in European Russia and Siberia (except the "taboo" Maritime Province front). Organized in small formations now, Russian planes penetrated the overtaxed Japanese air defenses to strike at friendly ground forces. "Our aerial counteractions seemed to have become rather difficult," the Kwantung Army's understated diary noted.[49]

IJAF staff officers had not favored more than a one-time strike against the Tamsag air bases in August. If there was to be a follow-up, it should be launched elsewhere, varying the intensity, time, and location, since the initial assault would have alerted the foe. In fact, the Russians did put up much stiffer resistance during the second strike. The 2nd Air Division judged that the enemy had massed unexpectedly large forces during the period of bad weather before 20 August, and it was obvious that a massive ground and air offensive was intended. Giga admits that the August raids, though a success, were not as decisive as the thrust in June. The secret of the initial operation, he explains, had been surprise, for the Russians had until then felt free to concentrate all of their forces. Afterward they became apprehensive and alert, dispersing their planes and thus presenting far less attractive targets. The 61st Group commander, Col. Mikami Kisō, remarks upon the improved enemy airborne patrols and antiaircraft batteries, which destroyed one of his heavy bombers and caused his squadrons to strike fast and make only one pass. Mikami, not a pilot himself, could see his planes' bombs hitting the ground, but he could not discern fires as such. Did IJAF morale soar after the air thrust in August? It may have been good news, but the colonel does not remember such a reaction specifically—"we were conducting sorties all the time anyhow." Maj. Gen. Shimono Ikkaku, commanding the 9th Bomber Wing, agrees that the enemy was very active during the August raid, counterattacking quickly and putting many planes into the air. Antiaircraft fire forced the bombers to fly at 2,000-3,000 meters.

Critics have remarked about the slim preparations for the August raid, once the weather had cleared on 19 August and the Russians had launched their all-out drive on the 20th. Apart from the 15 scout planes attached to the 23rd Division, the 124 bombers and fighters that took part in the latest Tamsag raids had the support of only six reconnaissance aircraft—four of which belonged to Giga's headquarters and two of which flew with the small 10th Light Bomber Group.[50] Much operational effort was consequently expended against empty air bases, and strikes were repeated with diminishing returns and increasing losses. Not only did the Soviet air force at Nomonhan emerge essentially unhurt, but the mighty ground offensive was not appreciably slowed.

32

Desperate Remedies

That Japanese higher headquarters were taken off-balance by the Russian offensive is demonstrated by the fact that Sixth Army commander Ogisu admits he was still at Hailar on 20 August. Word reached him there, by air, that Soviet-MPRA forces, mainly armor, had penetrated along seven routes of advance. Although in his report to the Kwantung Army on 23 August Ogisu claimed he had been on the battlefield since the 20th directing operations, the Sixth Army's combat headquarters was not moved up to Lake Mohorehi until the date of the general's message, 23 August.[1] Meanwhile, as we saw, Chief of Staff Fujimoto had hurried to 23rd Division headquarters, where he and Komatsubara differed greatly in their views from the outset on 21 August.

The Sixth Army had taken two appropriate actions: to shift Major General Morita's 14th Infantry Brigade to Chiangchunmiao, instead of using it for the now-defunct program of position construction at Handagai; and to form and move up another composite infantry battalion from an Independent Garrison Unit. It was the Sixth Army's intention to mount a counter-offensive in the area most favorable to the Japanese; remaining on the defensive would mean surrendering the initiative to the enemy and allowing him to operate freely in the border area, which would be unbearable to the Sixth Army. The zone south of the Holsten was particularly accessible to support by IJA units deployed in the Handagai region. On this, the whole Sixth Army staff was in agreement.

Such an approach was certainly acceptable to higher and lower headquarters. A problem arose, however, from the Sixth Army's solution to the matter of finding the strength for the counteroffensive. Judging from intelligence that powerful Soviet-MPRA units had pushed northward after traversing the Halha at the Minami-watashi crossing, far below the confluence, the Sixth Army proposed to encircle the enemy formations south of the Holsten, strike them from the rear, and destroy them. This would require a massive shift of IJA emphasis below the Holsten, which would be accomplished by contracting the existing front greatly and leaving only a holding force along the lines—namely, Yamagata's and Hasebe's detachments and one or two field artillery battalions. The remainder of the Japanese strength—at least 10 infantry battalions—should be concentrated in the offensive area. At most, only the Morita brigade (centering on one infantry regiment and one artillery battalion) should be added to the 23rd Division; the possible employment of the entire 7th Division was regarded by the Sixth Army as lying beyond its purview.[2]

It goes without saying that all Japanese commanders despised passive actions. As Komatsubara wrote on 21 August, "There is no worse pain than standing on the defensive." But only pessimistic information was being received: enemy tanks were penetrating gaps between positions, attacking artillery emplacements, commanding the river crossings, and burning food caches. Movement and communications had been severed, friendly forces were dispersed, and concentration could not be achieved. Worries about envelopment and shortages of ammunition, etc., preyed on Komatsubara's mind and, as he noted, were "shortening his life."

Although Ioki was still holding out, Fui Heights was surrounded. Below Fui, the Ikuta battalion was being battered by two enemy infantry battalions and by four field guns, four mortars, and a couple of tanks that had come in close. A daylight counterattack by Ikuta had led to severe Japanese casualties, from company commanders down. Many of the IJA heavy weapons had been knocked out. Despite the dispatch of a company of reinforcements, Ikuta's night attack made no progress in the face of at least 30 machine guns, and the Japanese had to pull back to reserve positions. South of the Holsten, in the critical Heights 744-747 sector, Colonel Morita's three battalions had been hit by a total of 1,400 infantry and 120 tanks.[3]

As the Soviet offensive unfolded, Komatsubara originally intended to draw the enemy's Southern Force in the direction of Colonel Morita's detachment, which had performed a "tactical adjustment" by pulling back toward Nigesorimot. Then Colonels Morita and Sakai would combine to strike the Russians' right flank. By the 21st, however, the loose but large-scale Soviet circle seemed to be constricting gradually, on the wings in particular. Although, as artillery General Hata observed, the division was still thinking of breaking through on the left wing and successful antitank combat was reported that afternoon from south of the Holsten, the crisis at Fui Heights was diverting attention, as shown by the redeployment northward of Sumi's reserves and of Type 90 field artillery. Hata dreaded heavy losses among his batteries during daylight movement. Although the cost proved light, it was barely possible to advance one battery before nightfall.[4]

By now, Komatsubara and Fujimoto were no nearer to a meeting of the minds. Well aware of the limitations of his division, Komatsubara wanted to maintain the present lines, relying on the units belonging to Sumi and Yamagata on the right, and Hasebe and Colonel Morita on the left, plus sizable artillery. Instead of Fujimoto's proposed transfer southward of at least 10 infantry battalions, the division commander was thinking in terms of committing only five for the offensive below the Holsten, i.e. the Sakai regiment and the one IGU battalion. Sixth Army staff officer Hamada suggests the following reasons for Komatsubara's stance.[5]

> The 23rd Division's defenses had already been split widely. If strength were subtracted from such a wide frontage, those positions left behind in the right-bank area of the Holsten would be endangered. They would soon be penetrated by the enemy driving into the spaces between them, separating them from each other, cutting them off, and annihilating them one by one. Of course, the present positions of the division could not be called very strong, being partially completed installations. Therefore, they should be [merely] defended, the Sixth Army using them as its base until, with the added strength of the 7th Division, it went over to the offensive against the enemy's outer wing. The keys were timing and the degree of reinforcement.

In the Sixth Army's view, however, employment of the 23rd Division's positions as the base and commitment of only the Morita brigade to an offensive against one wing of the enemy would produce insufficient strength to achieve immediate combat results. Therefore the power of the 23rd Division had to be transferred to the decisive battleground south of the Holsten.

On the evening of 21 August, Komatsubara called in Hata, recounted the continuing differences of opinion between the Sixth Army and the 23rd Division concerning the proposed offensive and troop relocations, and asked for the artillery corps commander's frank views. After Hata endorsed the division commander's approach, Komatsubara made up his mind to proceed with his own plan. Meanwhile, to cope with the Soviet armored irruption from the northwest, which was harassing the Uzuru area, a field artillery battery should be sent; another battery should be displaced southward to the main front below the Holsten.[6]

The disagreements, however, were by no means reconciled yet. Quite apart from the problems between the Sixth Army and the division— reflected in differences between chiefs and staff officers, too—a minority opinion seems to have existed even among front-line commanders. Yamagata, for example, recommended against retaining his 64th Regiment on the north side of the Holsten. It would be a "waste," he argued. Why not leave only his 3rd Battalion on the right shore, in the Heights 731 sector, where the 26th Regiment's Ikuta battalion was mauled?[7]

Early on the morning of the 22nd, Hata was called in once more by Komatsubara and was asked to reason with Fujimoto, from the standpoint of an artilleryman. Fujimoto could agree with Hata about the basic employment of the artillery and the deploying of some gun sites for defensive purposes on the left side of the Holsten. Nevertheless, Fujimoto insisted that everyone must comprehend fully the intention of the Sixth Army commander. Although impelled by thinking that seemed unrealistic to Hata and "did not jibe with the actual condition of the troops," Fujimoto clung to his opinions and sought the artillery corps commander's "concrete implementation" of the Sixth Army's scheme.

Precious time was passing, and the battle situation was continuing to deteriorate on both Japanese wings. It was already 11 A.M. on the 22nd, and the artillery corps commander felt the urgency of swift action lest irreparable harm be caused by useless controversy. Therefore Hata decided to abandon what he thought was the wiser plan and to accept the Sixth Army's notion, for the sake of speedy execution. If the artillery could only endure the disadvantages of antiartillery combat, the deployment to the left shore of the Holsten would be bettered. For these reasons, Hata recommended to the division commander that he give in to Fujimoto. The problem of deployment lines, however, widened the gap between Komatsubara and the Sixth Army chief of staff. Based on their preconceptions, both generals went beyond their previous arguments to invoke such matters as responsibility and personal honor. The discussion grew quite heated, and Hata, mediating, sought to point out weaknesses in the argumentation. Finally, it was agreed that the Sixth Army would issue clear orders and the division would conduct preparations in accordance with the army's intention. The Japanese were still going to counterattack the enemy's right rear below the Holsten. Hata went off to direct the withdrawal of 10-cm. and 15-cm. cannon units from the right to the left side of the Holsten.[8]

At 5:30 P.M. on the 22nd, the order directing preparations for the counteroffensive was issued by the 23rd Division.[9] Since enemy armor in the south had already posed a serious threat to the New Engineer Bridge since 21 August, Hasebe was to defend the span from high ground south of the Holsten. To cover the movements of the division, Sumi's reserves in the north should withdraw their advance elements from the Heights 739 district after sunset and prepare to guard the zone between Uzuru and Heights 752. From the operational order, it is clear that IJA forces were to concentrate in the Lake Mohorehi sector, southeast of Abutara. Although jump-off time was not yet stipulated, Hata was directed to redeploy field and heavy artillery batteries after sunset on the 23rd and to be ready to go into action by dawn on the 24th.

Komatsubara had foreseen some of the difficulties of shifting forces across considerable distances and on short notice in the midst of the furious Soviet offensive. But even he was not acquainted with the full details of his units' dispersion and disintegration. Not only were the defenses at Fui Heights about to fall, but Russian forces had also penetrated deeply into the gaps between Colonel Morita's right flank and the Hasebe detachment since the 21st. Waves of Soviet tanks repeatedly circled exposed positions and smashed them; the unit defending Heights 744 had been annihilated, and Morita had already come close to losing classified documents at regimental headquarters. Disengagement had become nearly impossible by the 22nd, and the Japanese were learning "how hard it is to recapture a place after it has been taken by the foe." Close-range pressure increased all along Morita's front, and a reconnaissance platoon sent toward the Old Engineer Bridge disappeared. The colonel came to the conclusion that it would be better, under the circumstances, to retain his main force where it was in the south. He would try to cover Hasebe's left flank, rather than shuffle what was left of his fatigued battalions, now suffering from a shortage of food, water, and ammunition, and nearly bereft of heavy weapons.[10]

The division commander's evaluation of his regiments' capabilities was not any better in the case of Sumi's 26th Infantry. On the night of 22 August, the colonel was called to the small tent of Komatsubara. The only other person present was Chief of Staff Okamoto, who remained standing throughout the candlelight conference and never uttered a word. Subject to a few subjective embellishments after the fact, the following dialogue and bracketed commentary represent Sumi's vivid recollections.[11]

> *Komatsubara:* I have one more favor to ask of you. I plan to shift my forces back, to execute a sweeping detour across the Holsten, to reassemble south of Mohorehi with the division's main body, and, using the regiment's area as the base, to attack the enemy from the other side of the Holsten. Therefore the Sumi unit should pull back too, detour widely, serve as the left flank of the division, cross the Holsten, march along the river, and assault the foe from my extreme left.
>
> *Sumi:* [Whenever the division commander thought up a new plan, he depended on my "almighty" regiment to accomplish the impossible.] No, sir, it can't be done. My unit is a regiment in name only. I have only about two companies and a battalion commander with me.
>
> *Komatsubara:* Why is that?
>
> *Sumi:* Ikuta's battalion is under direct control of the division at Heights 731. Two companies and an infantry-gun platoon were sent to reinforce Ioki at Fui Heights. One company was detached to defend the field hospital near Uzuru pond, and still another is performing communication duties for the division. My "regiment" thus amounts to less than a battalion under my own command.
>
> *Komatsubara:* I knew only about the detaching of the Ikuta battalion, not about the others.
>
> *Sumi:* Whether you knew about it or not, I was following division orders. So what you propose cannot be done. In fact, I cannot hold my present positions more than two or three days. If I pull out now, it will be easy for the enemy to penetrate and attack the main area. The latter would be disrupted and could not be used as the base you mentioned. [I felt that Komatsubara's plan was suitable for a "picnic," not combat.] I am thinking of fighting and dying where I am located. Please let me do so.
>
> *Komatsubara:* I understand your thinking. I shall conduct further study. You may return.

Whatever Komatsubara may have thought of the outspoken Sumi and his views, and although he was constrained by Sixth Army orders, the division commander did modify the offensive deployment a bit by 23 August. Lt. Col. Yotsuya's understrength 6th IGU Battalion, which had only arrived at the front on the 21st and had been immediately sent to the area of the doomed field hospital at Uzuru, was now to take over the far left wing of the Japanese counteroffensive. Although Sumi would not be allowed to stay on the right side of the Holsten, he was assigned to the brigade belonging to his parent 7th Division, still located on the left flank of the main attack effort.[12]

Komatsubara issued his full-fledged assault order at 2 P.M. on 23 August.[13] Soviet forces, he began, were continuing their offensive against both wings, with the main body apparently operating south of the Holsten. The Japanese were going to launch a counteroffensive striking deeply toward the enemy's right rear. Splitting the hostile lines centered on Heights 780, the attacking units would sweep the foe west-southwestward, trapping and annihilating him. Jump-off time was to be announced separately, but a dawn attack was envisioned, so preparations should still be completed by 6 A.M. The 23rd Division command post would leave Nomonhan at 9 P.M. on the 23rd and proceed to its destination, Heights 752, about seven kilometers south of Lake Mohorehi.

At the old positions north and south of the Holsten, IJA garrisons were to remain on the defensive: the now-mythical Ioki force at Fui Heights; Sumi's Ikuta battalion and Yamagata's 64th Regiment on the Barunishi sector, with supporting field and heavy artillery; and the two battalions of the Hasebe detachment, reinforced by the Kajikawa battalion and some artillery, in the Noro Heights area south of the Holsten but well to the west of the Japanese offensive formations. Under his direct control, Komatsubara intended to commit a Right Wing Unit consisting of Kobayashi's infantry group headquarters, the 71st Infantry Regiment (less one and a half battalions), the 72nd Infantry Regiment (less one battalion), a field-artillery battery and three rapid-fire guns, and one engineer platoon; and a Left Wing Unit consisting of Morita's 14th Infantry Brigade headquarters, the 28th Infantry Regiment (less one battalion), the 26th Infantry Regiment (less one and a half battalions), three rapid-fire gun batteries and most of one heavy artillery battalion, and one engineer platoon.

To the left of General Morita's Left Wing Unit, Lieutenant Colonel Yotsuya was to deploy his IGU battalion, one battery from the 7th Heavy Artillery, two rapid-fire guns, and an engineer company. The transfer across the Holsten should now be covered by the 71st Regiment, based on high ground south of the Old Engineer Bridge. In reserve, Komatsubara planned to retain one battalion from the 71st Regiment and four heavy machine guns. A com-

TABLE 3 2. I

Japanese Defensive and Offensive Deployment, 20–31 Aug. 1939

23rd Inf. Div. Lt. Gen. Komatsubara Michitarō

Right [north] shore of Holsten River

Left [south] shore of Holsten River

Defensive Unit

- Recon. Unit Lt. Col. Ioki Eiichi
  - 23rd Recon. Unit — Fui Heights
- Yamagata Detachment Col. Yamagata Takemitsu
  - 26th Inf. Regt., 1st Bn. — Heights 731
  - 64th Inf. Regt. — Heights 733, Kildegei pond
- Artillery Unit
  - 13th Field Arty. Regt., 2nd Bn. — Heights 733, Kildegei pond
  - 13th Field Arty. Regt., 3rd Bn.; 1st Heavy Field Arty. Regt., 1st Bn.; 7th Heavy Field Arty. Regt., 2nd Bn.; Muleng Regt., 1 battery — Heights 755
- Hasebe Detachment Col. Hasebe Riei
  - 2 BGU bns.; 28th Inf. Regt., 2nd Bn. — Noro Heights
  - 13th FA Regt., 1st Bn.
- Morita Unit Col. Morita Tōru
  - 71st Inf. Regt. [− 1st Bn.] — Heights 754, 744, 747, Sankaku

Offensive Unit

- Right Wing Unit Maj. Gen. Kobayashi Kōichi
  - 71st Inf. Regt., 1st Bn.; 72nd Inf. Regt.
- Left Wing Unit Maj. Gen. Morita Norimasa
  - 26th Inf. Regt. [− 1st Bn.]; 28th Inf. Regt. [− 2nd Bn.] — Heights 749, 752, 780
- Left-flank Unit Col. Yotsuya Iwao
  - 6th IGU Bn.
- Artillery Corps Maj. Gen. Hata Yūzaburō
  - 1st Ind. Field Arty. Regt.; 1st Heavy Field Arty. Regt., 2nd Bn.; 7th Heavy Field Arty. Regt., 1st Bn.; Muleng Regt., 1 battery

posite detachment commanded by Col. Itō Takeo, with one battalion each of infantry and artillery, had also been formed from the 8th BGU. The Sixth Army took direct control of this detachment as a reserve for defense of the Mohorehi district against Soviet armor. (For the IJA deployments, see Table 32.1.)

A number of noteworthy features characterized the 23rd Division's offensive plan. Most importantly, the deployments represented a rearrangement of tired and lacerated existing units instead of the insertion of fresh new forces—with the exception of General Morita's brigade headquarters and the two infantry battalions from the 28th Regiment. Additionally, the anchor at Fui Heights was in effect being written off, and the positions along the Barunishi line would also be isolated by thinning out the defensive screen on the northern end of the Japanese front. Vulnerable heavy artillery batteries would be placed at risk, too, by leaving them behind Yamagata's endangered unit. In fact, every IJA higher headquarters was eventually concentrated around Lake Mohorehi—that of the 23rd Division, the Kobayashi infantry group, and Hata's artillery corps. Finally, on the morning of 23 August, about 20 personnel also arrived to set up the advance post of the Sixth Army. These commands were obsessed by the forthcoming counteroffensive and paid little attention to the holding sectors. Supposedly under the direct control of Komatsubara, the local defense commanders—Ioki, Yamagata, and Hasebe—had to fight separately, usually out of touch with the division, against overwhelming enemy forces.

Of all the senior commanders in the field, Hata tried perhaps the hardest to unify the artillery's fragmented chain of command on 22 August. Since he would be operating near Mohorehi, and since the wounded Colonel Mishima of the 1st Heavy Field Artillery Regiment would not be returning from the hospital, Hata directed Colonel Takatsukasa of the 7th Artillery to take command of Someya's Muleng unit as well as his own regiment. At the same time, the 13th Field Artillery Regiment commander, Colonel Ise, was also to control elements of the 1st Regiment plus some improvised field- and mountain-gun batteries. The reallocation of commands made it necessary for Takatsukasa to transfer his regimental headquarters above the Holsten on 22/23 August—an action that not only was taken too late but also had unhappy results, since Takatsukasa, by his own admission, was entirely unfamiliar with the terrain on the north shore. "I was in trouble," says Takatsukasa, "but nevertheless we forced ourselves onto Major Kondō's 2nd Battalion headquarters. . . . At first, I was like a hanger-on, but the situation did not allow that for long." [14]

The Sixth Army had been wrestling with the idea of requesting the dispatch of the rest of the 7th Infantry Division. General Ueda, it will be recalled, had asked his staff to consider deploying the division as far as Hailar, but the decision had been reached to send up only a brigade headquarters and another infantry regiment. Even after the Sixth Army learned of the Russians' vigorous assaults of 20 August, there was still hesitation, says Hamada. No new Soviet units were reported in action yet, only the fact of attacks. What if it proved to be merely a replay of the mini-offensive of 9-10 August? If the Sixth Army overreacted, it would "lose face."

Only after collating the flow of reports emanating from the front each night was it finally concluded that the attacks of the 20th represented "the real thing." It was the Sixth Army's understanding that only if the Russians launched a full-scale offensive would the Kwantung Army commit the 7th Division to Hailar, because the High Command in Tokyo was very nervous about the matter. Hsinking was told on 21 August about the enemy's large forces and presumable difficulties with logistics, but Hamada is not sure that he ever dispatched the portion of the telegram dealing with the vital question of sending up reinforcements. Indeed, he remembers tearing up several drafts on 22 August, attesting to the difficulty experienced by Ogisu and Fujimoto in dealing with the problem. Despite the negative evidence, says Hamada, "I would still like to believe that the telegram *was* sent out. But if, after having decided by 21 August to request the dispatch of the 7th Division, we did not actually transmit the message, then the fault does lie with the Sixth Army." [15]

The Sixth Army had correctly sensed the fact that the Kwantung Army felt pressure exerted by the High Command to localize and terminate the fighting at Nomonhan. This was especially true with regard to the introduction or redeployment of strategic-size units (*senryaku heidan*).[16] Nevertheless, on the basis of reports coming in from the battlefront, the Kwantung Army decided to commit the balance of Lt. Gen. Kunisaki Noboru's elite 7th Division—over 5,000 men. Deputy Chief of Staff Yano, who had just gone forward with Major Tsuji, was advised on 23 August that the 7th Division, less elements already attached to the Sixth Army, was being concentrated at Hailar with its river-crossing matériel. The Kwantung Army would command the division directly. In addition, to help cope with enemy armor, a total of eight antitank-gun batteries (32 pieces) from the Third and Fourth armies would be attached to the 7th Division. The 29th IGU Battalion from the Tsitsihar command was being sent to Handagai, under Sixth Army control.[17]

In view of the Sixth Army's hesitations mentioned by Hamada, it is significant that the Kwantung Army reached its decision on 23 August before receiving any plea from Ogisu. The reason given for the Kwantung Army's prompt action was "anticipation of attacks by enemy forces larger than had been expected." Indeed, nothing but upbeat messages were arriving in Hsinking from the Sixth Army commander. On the very day that the Kwan-

tung Army staff ordered the advance of the 7th Division, Ogisu was reporting that Soviet harassing movements in the Japanese rear, west of Lake
Abutara, were actually slight and posed no threat. Considerable damage
seemed to have been caused by artillery fire, but IJA morale was very high.
The left flank had been pulled back voluntarily, for the sake of the next operations; all other positions were holding fast. Preparations to strike the enemy on the 24th were proceeding on schedule. Ogisu sounded undaunted by
the Soviet offensive to date: though the foe obviously intended to envelop
both wings, there was no particular emphasis, and the intensity was weak.
Hostile artillery passed its peak in the afternoon of 23 August. "Kindly set
your mind at ease," Ogisu assured the Kwantung Army.[18]

"So the Sixth Army is about to swallow up the enemy?," mused Tsuji
when he heard about Ogisu's fearless message. Such optimism and such belittling of the foe must derive from the newness of the Sixth Army and its
lack of experience against the Russians, Tsuji thought, but he found the report strangely comforting.[19] Did the Sixth Army believe what it was saying?
Colonel Hamada provides the best insight.[20]

> I myself was not so optimistic, and the army commander and the chief of staff
> must have had the same inner feelings, I think. But the wording of the telegram
> came out sounding as it did. The reason for thinking hostile actions had slowed
> down one time on 23 August stemmed from our impression that the foe was fixing
> his attention on the arrival of the Morita brigade at the battlefield and was adjust-
> ing his setup accordingly. As for enemy armor's interference with our rear units,
> we had received such reports at the time, but of course we lacked the details that
> Tsuji supplied, on the basis of firsthand experience, when he arrived at Sixth
> Army headquarters. Under the circumstances, if you have to submit a wire report,
> how much should be said? With respect to the forthcoming IJA offensive, though I
> did not expect that the Sixth Army could destroy the foe completely by means of
> the army's plan of operations on the south shore of the Holsten, I did think that
> we could retain the initiative in the area by dealing a blow to the enemy. . . . We
> were fairly optimistic about the expected combat results beginning on the 24th
> because it was judged that if the battle situation on the left side of the Holsten de-
> veloped well, the defensive combat on the right shore would become favorable
> automatically.

The unrelenting Soviet offensive was in its fifth day before the IJA counterattack could be launched. But even then, the preparations were made almost overnight, the planning was slipshod, and the command's intentions
were not unified. Fujimoto had gone back to the 23rd Division command
post on the evening of 22 August to convey the Sixth Army's orders. When
the chief of staff had still not returned after noon the next day, Colonel
Hamada began to worry that he might have been intercepted by the enemy
en route or that Komatsubara was still not amenable to the shift of forces
to the south shore of the Holsten. Shortly before evening on 23 August,

Fujimoto got back. He was late, he said, because the division commander had been unwilling to accede to the Sixth Army's demand that he conduct the transfer, just as Hamada had feared. Fujimoto had had to work to persuade Komatsubara, and it was not until evening that the basic divisional order would be issued. As Hamada puts it, mixing metaphors, the Sixth Army's "sole trump card," the notion of mounting an offensive below the Holsten, had "stumbled" at the very outset. It had become highly doubtful that preparations for the Japanese offensive would be finished by 6 A.M. on the 24th as planned, in time for a concerted assault at dawn.[21]

There had been an ominous development affecting the Japanese artillery as early as 21/22 August. Although Sakai's 72nd Infantry had traversed the Old Engineer Bridge without encountering enemy armor, a liaison officer arrived from Takatsukasa's 7th Heavy Field Artillery Regiment early on the 22nd and reported that 40 or 50 tanks with infantry, deployed in a dip two kilometers from Heights 753, were surrounding the gun sites. Two infantry companies from the Sakai regiment, with antitank and heavy machine guns, were ordered to attack that night. When a rapid-fire gun battery arrived at Nigesorimot, several dozen tanks could be sighted 1,000 meters away, circling the location of the heavy artillery's wagon lines. The four Japanese antitank guns knocked out three or four of the tanks and drove off the foe. Infantrymen from the 71st Regiment, who had been hiding in foxholes, thanked the gunners for saving their lives. But the night before, they said, Soviet armor had overrun a quartermaster dump located in a dip, ripping up winter garments and food supplies. Barrels of pickled apricots were sundered, drenching the soil with red juice that looked like blood. More importantly, it was learned that the Russians had seized a 10-cm. cannon belonging to the 7th Regiment's 2nd Battery, which had been brought to the dip for repair. The mechanics could not withstand the tanks, which towed away the precious cannon. Takatsukasa was advised immediately.[22]

Hata had tried to get his artillery to displace early, but he was thinking in terms of two or three days of prior position reconnaissance starting on 23 August—time he would not be allowed. When he visited Komatsubara's command post at 1 P.M. on the 23rd, "half invited by the division chief of staff, half on [his] own," Hata found that the staff was still studying and talking. Close to sunset, the artillery corps was obliged to start the redeployment, a process that got under way around 9 P.M. Swinging wide around the upstream Holsten without crossing it, the unit proceeded laboriously southward via Nomonhan to the assembly zone. In the depth of night, across a distance of 20 kilometers, there was "much confusion" (in Hata's words) moving the corps train and 26 pieces: eight Type 90 field guns, eight 15-cm. howitzers, and eight 10-cm. and two 15-cm. cannon. Despite efforts to suppress noise, the units drew attention, and strange signal shells could be seen arching into the sky ahead of the Japanese columns. Several efforts at triangulation failed to locate the enemy spies. To leave good, sheltered positions for an unfamiliar area where a considerable number of enemy tanks were said to be operating left one lieutenant from Hayashi's 2nd Battalion of the 1st Heavy Field Artillery Regiment "rather depressed." Hayashi himself says that he was intending to move even farther to previously reconnoitered positions, but that enemy defenses were encountered in an unexpected area; he thus had to set up his new gun lines hurriedly, in the fog.

In the sister 1st Battalion, Captain Tsuchiya explains how his battery "changed hotel rooms" with the Hayashi battalion, acquiring ammunition and more spacious accommodations in the process:[23]

> My unit had been shifted back and forth across the Holsten many times, because I knew the terrain so well. One could move only during the six or seven hours of darkness. It was hard on the men and they disliked the transfers while other units were "loafing." Now, when ordered to cross again, I said, "No more, please." Hayashi's battalion went across instead, for the first time. Although the major was apprehensive about the move, I thanked him for his kindness and advised him about shallow fords on the Holsten. But fate turned against me in this case: Hayashi was lucky to leave, and I was unlucky to remain.

Not until 10 P.M. on the 23rd did Hata get to meet General Morita (who was with Tsuji) at the tent of the infantry brigade command post in the vicinity of Mohorehi. Hata took a nap and waited for his units to arrive. Near 4 A.M. he tried to pull together the artillery, but only a portion had moved up. In the mist of early morning, a battery commander from the Hayashi battalion remembers that the observation post could not be found. When there was a break in the fog, the lieutenant found none other than Hata sitting upright on the field, his arms crossed and his brows knit in thought. "I can't make out the location either," said the general. Although the lieutenant's battery deployed its gun line, the unit was still in no condition to open fire when daylight came.

It was after 6 A.M. when Hata was finally able to take control of some of the howitzer and heavy cannon formations, but the Type 90 field artillery had still not appeared. After issuing orders, Hata went to see Komatsubara and his staff on a dune east of Heights 752, around 7:30 A.M. The Japanese infantry were still deploying, and Hata sought to hasten the combat deployment of his guns, especially the field artillery battalion and the 10-cm. cannon battalion attached to the front lines. Piecemeal commitment of the artillery negated the plan to commence bombardment in unison.[24]

Relocation was no easier for the Japanese foot soldiers. Only on the night of 20 August, for instance, did the new 28th Regiment reach Chiangchunmiao, where the men were directed to write their last words (*yuigon*). Departing from the hamlet at 8:30 P.M. on the 22nd, the regiment marched south. After napping a bit and getting ready for breakfast, the unit sighted three enemy tanks. One armored vehicle was set afire by rapid-fire weapons and the other tanks turned tail. The infantry resumed the march, passing ghastly scenes of battle. When evening came, the soldiers sat down to eat a supper of cold, half-spoiled rice. Some of the troops received cider bottles, which they drank and then refilled with gasoline for use as firebombs. Throughout the night of 23/24 August the men marched on in dense fog, hardly knowing where they were. Between 4 and 5 A.M. on the 24th they finally reached a point southeast of Mohorehi, a few kilometers from the enemy. They had traversed a total distance of between 25 and 40 kilometers since leaving Chiangchunmiao. At 6:30 the weary men ate what would be the last breakfast for many.[25]

Other units were given even less time to assemble. Colonel Sumi had no illusions about the difficulties facing his 26th Regiment when the tardy transfer orders were received. He was directed to cover the division's movement to the Holsten from positions near Uzuru. Then, at 2 A.M. on the 24th, the main body of his depleted regiment was supposed to pull out, detour via Abutara, catch up with the division in the Mohorehi area by about 6 A.M., and come under General Morita's brigade command. Sumi dispatched orders that his detached companies should rejoin him—the unit at Uzuru, the other on communications duty at division headquarters. Distances would be great, the terrain complicated; it was necessary to measure intervals, compute times, scout and mark the route. The hauling of heavy weapons, ammunition, and food was of special concern, for the regiment had no horses and was entirely dependent on trucks sent by the division. Items that could not be moved were buried deep in the sand. Sumi's experiences with truck support to date had been "rather bitter." On every occasion when trucks were promised, he complains, they never came punctually. In this particular instance, the timing of the troop movement was crucial to the success of the counteroffensive, and one could not risk a foul-up in transportation or the chance of getting lost. Sumi phoned division logistics officer Itō and repeatedly asked him to be sure the trucks came on schedule. Itō promised to do his best this time.

Rushing to get going by 2 A.M., Sumi assembled as many of his men as possible by midnight, and phoned to encourage and advise Ikuta, whose battalion was being left behind at exposed Heights 731. It was their last conversation. As worried as Sumi about transportation, Itō came and waited with the colonel for the trucks to pull in; but they were no more prompt on 23/24 August than in earlier cases, not arriving until 3:30 A.M. Sumi was apprehensive about the possible appearance of enemy armor after daybreak, and he wanted his whole force to leave together. But, owing to the difficulty with the trucks, only half of the soldiers with the colonel—about 200 men—were able to proceed to the Abutara rendezvous, and another trip was necessary to bring up the second echelon. It was dawn, and Abutara was a scene of indescribable confusion. Enemy tanks could be heard firing in the rear. The Japanese troops were milling around, loading and unloading, while runners scurried to and fro.

At this unlikely juncture, a "gentle-looking, unfamiliar officer wearing a cape" arrived to report to Sumi. It was the new 2nd Battalion commander, Maj. Nakano Toshio, the replacement for Major Kamimura, who was ailing and had been asking to be transferred. The colonel, who was busy with the details of the troop movement, thought it would be dangerous to assign a brand-new officer to command a battalion on the very day it was to attack, so he asked Kamimura to carry on and attached Nakano to the command post. After conferring, the two majors recommended that Nakano take command of the 2nd Battalion immediately, since he bore an imperial order and Kamimura "wanted out." Sumi reconsidered, gave Nakano the battalion, and authorized Kamimura to leave. After all, the colonel comments, if an officer wanted to get out on the eve of an offensive, then Sumi did not want to take him along anyway. But there was no time for niceties or introductions, and Nakano had no chance to learn who his men were. So the new major entered a battlefield with which he was completely unacquainted. Sumi, who saw Nakano only one more time before he was killed on the 25th, still wonders whether he did the right thing in releasing Kamimura.

From unit records, we know that the 7th Company of Sumi's regiment, still in the Uzuru area, did not receive the battalion order (issued by Nakano already) to advance to Mohorehi until 8 A.M. on 24 August—the day of the "dawn" offensive. It was lucky for the Japanese that enemy tanks did not interfere. Sumi completed the assembly of his units around 7 A.M., ate breakfast, and took off with the main body for Mohorehi, about eight kilometers across the plain, near 8 A.M. (the 7th Company says 9 A.M.). He was supposed to have two battalions, but neither was up to strength, and few of his heavy weapons were operational. Sumi, who heard that Ogisu reported to the Kwantung Army that the Sixth Army was lacking two infantry battalions for the attack, thinks the general was referring to his two from the 26th Regiment. Lieutenant Kokubu, the acting commander of the 3rd Battalion, and Nakano, now commanding the 2nd Battalion (and the only major left in the regiment), tried to hasten the movement; Sumi wonders how many of the latter's men ever got to see their new chief alive. En route, three Soviet tanks, including a flamethrower, tried to intercept the Japanese advance but were knocked out by the few heavy weapons. It goes without saying that the forces from the 26th Regiment arrived at the front hours behind the intended time and had to be thrown into battle, in broad daylight, from the march. Sumi never even got to see his brigadier or the commander of his sister regiment, the 28th, until the day was over.[26]

While the left wing of the envisaged Japanese counterattacking corps was suffering from lack of synchronization of forces, another adverse development weakened the right wing. Komatsubara had expected to employ Colonel Morita's entire 71st Regiment on the far right, drawing one battalion for divisional reserve and leaving elements to cover the Old Engineer Bridge. This vital deployment never came to pass. The radio transmission of the division's operational order on 23 August was garbled so badly that Colonel Morita could comprehend only the gist of the offensive plan—with the help of information conveyed by staff officer Itō on the 22nd—but not the role of his regiment. Since errors in transmission or encoding were suspected, a repetition of the message was requested; but the division command post was already on the move and no reply was received. The fighting on 23 August had been too severe on Colonel Morita's front to extricate every unit. Sankaku Hill, east of Heights 758, for example, had been surrounded since 10 A.M. by 400 riflemen and 40 tanks, including flamethrowers. There was no communication with the positions there after 11 A.M. The 3rd Battalion was being chopped to pieces, losing its commander, Maj. Idei Tsuyoshi, and most of the other officers and men that day. An idea for a relief expedition had to be dropped.

Colonel Morita was concerned both about abandoning any remnants of the 3rd Battalion and about exposing the left rear of the adjoining Hasebe force to enemy irruption. Consequently, he decided to detach only Sugitachi's 1st Battalion to Kobayashi's right flank, and to retain what was left of his unit as the "keystone" of the division's offensive. Around sunset, after the sounds of battle abated in the vicinity of Sankaku, the colonel sent Captain Onozuka with a patrol to the hill, three kilometers away. When Onozuka's party got there, around 9 P.M., the elevation was heaped with Japanese and Russian dead—a "gloriously tragic" scene (*sōretsu hisan*). The red flag was flying atop the hill, which was guarded by Russian sentries and four tanks. Sankaku was entirely in enemy hands, and not one survivor could be found. From the location of the corpses collected later, it was learned that the 3rd Battalion had fought in conjunction with elements of Hasebe's men, trying to defend the left flank of the detachment.

At 10 P.M. on the 23rd, a very understrength 1st Battalion—lacking two companies and most of its heavy machine guns—left for the assembly zone of the 23rd Division south of Mohorehi, via the Old Engineer Bridge. It was to come under Kobayashi's command by 4 A.M. Colonel Morita raised division headquarters by radio at 8:30, reported his deployments, indicated uncertainty about the overall situation of friendly forces, and asked whether he was supposed to transfer the main body of his regiment too. There was no reply. In the absence of full information, Komatsubara concluded that Colonel Morita's unit had not moved as ordered.[27]

In short, as 24 August dawned, Japanese troop deployments on the spot did not match the paper plans for an offensive. Vital elements were late in arriving or did not show up. Reason would have dictated the postponement or cancellation of the attack, but the tempo of the Soviet drive had continued to be relentless, IJA initiative had to be recaptured, and, as we have seen, information on friendly as well as enemy strength was incomplete. Kwantung Army staff officer Tsuji—who had left his traveling companion, General Yano, at Hailar and had gone on to the front by plane, truck, and foot on 23 August—observed the situation at several levels, often under fire. When he got to the Sixth Army's forward headquarters, the atmosphere was sanguine. In a camouflaged tent behind a dune, the staff was working on the offensive plans. Everybody, from Fujimoto down, exuded confidence. Was it only on paper?, Tsuji wondered. At the commander's tent, Ogisu was sipping whiskey. He greeted Tsuji and suggested a toast to victory.

The mood was less outgoing at the command post tent of Maj. Gen. Morita Norimasa, the 14th Brigade commander. Morita, a "beloved senior" of Tsuji, hailed from the same native place. Known as a mobilization specialist on the General Staff, he was facing combat at Nomonhan for the first time. Studying a map by candlelight and working on his brigade order, the general told Tsuji that the 23rd Division's offensive directions had just arrived. Tsuji felt uneasy about the brigadier's learning about tomorrow's offensive so late the night before. The two men were about to partake of a "delicious" battlefront supper of boiled rice, one pickled apricot, and a few pieces of pickled radish when enemy fighters raided the area at low altitude. Dousing the candle, Tsuji and Morita jumped into an antiaircraft trench. If hostile aircraft could attack by night as well as day, Tsuji thought, it was clear that the foe had achieved aerial supremacy.

Once the raids were over, Tsuji took a nap until roused by a soldier on night duty. Past 3 A.M., the units started advancing quietly, without being detected by the enemy in the mist. When the eastern sky brightened, Komatsubara and his staff galloped up, and everyone hurried to the envisaged line of departure. It proved impossible to complete preparations by dawn on schedule, as Tsuji had feared, since the order had been issued so late. To complicate matters, a first lieutenant suddenly rushed to the headquarters and shouted that the Fui garrison had been wiped out. He had tried to haul ammunition to the heights by truck but found the bastion surrounded by enemy armor. According to a wounded soldier, every Japanese officer and man, including Ioki, had fallen. This was an inauspicious prelude to the offensive; even if true, growled Tsuji, there must be some other way of reporting. "You fool!," Tsuji shrieked at the lieutenant. "What do you mean by 'annihilation'? *You* are alive, aren't you?" Then he dragged the unfortunate young officer to a dip and made him reflect on his "thoughtless" mode of reporting. But Komatsubara and Fujimoto were depressed by the news from the right flank. Their hope was that the forthcoming offensive on the left would relieve the pressure at the other end of the front.[28]

General Morita, who had brought his brigade headquarters and two battalions of Col. Ashizuka Chōzō's 28th Regiment to Mohorehi from Chiangchunmiao on 22 August, agrees with Tsuji that the 23rd Division's offensive order was not received by him until 11 P.M. on 23 August. In the early evening, there had been two air raids. Since jumping into trenches each time was too troublesome, the general eventually had his tent moved over a shelter. By the time the division's order arrived and Morita had to develop his own, there was no more enemy interference. The division's instructions were very lengthy; if the brigadier took all the time he really needed to issue his counterpart order, he could not have finished. Therefore he completed the essentials by midnight and then concentrated on offensive preparations until 4 A.M. An hour later, shortly after enemy artillery bombardment commenced, Morita's units started to advance. The division commander was behind them, and their morale was "pretty high." But orders had gone out only to Ashizuka, for Morita had no idea where the Sumi regiment was— and neither did Ashizuka, of course.[29]

In the 72nd Regiment's sector, the Kobayashi group's offensive order was received at 7 P.M. on 23 August. Colonel Sakai called in all of his unit commanders, discussed the division's intentions, and made a speech in which he said he earnestly desired last-effort fighting by all officers and men, since tomorrow's combat would be truly decisive. Then, the chronicler noted, "We had farewell drinks of sake." Departing by midnight, the regiment advanced, with Kobayashi's headquarters, toward Mohorehi in fog that grew constantly thicker, until by dawn "you could not see a foot ahead." Elements of the Morita brigade were encountered en route. At daybreak, Komatsubara's headquarters arrived at the 72nd Regiment's location. After receiving Kobayashi's operations order at 5:30 A.M., Sakai issued his own at 8:30. It was obvious that the dawn assault was becoming a daylight offensive, for Sakai's order now called for the advance at 9:30 A.M. Indeed, Japanese sources stress how fortunate it was that the swirl of forces converging on Mohorehi was not raided by enemy tanks or long-range artillery after dark on 23 August.[30]

When they could discern what lay ahead of them south of the Holsten on 24 August, some of the men in the assault units experienced a mixture of dismay and confusion. A second lieutenant in the 72nd Infantry could see that the area in front of his 2nd Battalion was flat and undulating for several kilometers. He had only been sent to the unit from east Manchuria on the 22nd and hardly knew any of the officers and men, but he felt compelled to say something to battalion commander Kokura. "It may be presumptuous of me, sir," he told the major, "but I think we will be annihilated if we launch an offensive here." Kokura answered, "I think so too." Adds the lieutenant: "We simply did not know what our superiors had in mind." One company commander, however—a first lieutenant—had the nerve to visit higher headquarters to try to find out what was going on. He heard that the offensive could be pushed through "because we were Japanese soldiers."[31]

Thus it was that in mid-morning on 24 August, the Japanese infantry attempted an operation at which they did not excel: a frontal offensive in broad daylight, without prior scouting or artillery and aerial softening-up of the foe. Since the 71st Regiment had not been able to send the battalions needed by the Japanese right wing, Kobayashi was obliged to press the attack on that sector with only the two battalions of Sakai's 72nd Regiment. And since Sumi was still en route, General Morita had to launch his offensive on the left even later than Kobayashi, with only two battalions of Ashizuka's 28th Regiment, supported by the Yotsuya battalion on the far left. Differences between the Soviet offensive of 20 August and the IJA counterassault of the 24th are pronounced in terms of planning, scale, resources, intelligence, coordination, and execution. The last-gasp effort by Ogisu and Komatsubara was doomed from the start.

33

The Charge of Two
Light Brigades

Between 9:30 and 10 A.M. on 24 August, while the mist was clearing, the Sakai regiment jumped off, with Lieutenant Colonel Nishikawa's 1st Battalion on the left and Major Kokura's 2nd Battalion on the right.[1] To a young IJA second lieutenant, the impressive scene of the regiment advancing across the plain was unlike anything encountered in peacetime maneuvers. Between 3,000 and 4,000 meters away, Soviet positions could be discerned along a wide belt at a slight elevation above the Japanese and interspersed with low willows and scrub bushes. Soon after the drive began, the units met the fire of machine guns from the front and over 20 tanks from the right. Enemy gunfire intensified around 10:30, causing heavy casualties, including Sakai's senior regimental aide, Major Kunimoto Kyūrō, who was slain. The advance bogged down for a while. Units had become scattered, and the men were moving individually. Nishikawa's battalion aide, 1st Lt. Nomura Haruyoshi, "crawled like a rat," trying to use shrubs for cover. To his amazement, he saw the battalion commander boldly walking upright, brandishing a sword whose hilt was bound with red cloth. Nomura yelled to Nishikawa to get down, to no avail. A bullet hit the lieutenant's thigh but embedded itself in a towel in his trouser pocket.

Not until 11 or 11:30 A.M. did the lead troops get to the enemy's forward lines. Nishikawa says that one company—from his battalion—managed to seize a position, causing the Russian defenders to abandon their heavy weapons and flee. Only then did other IJA elements move up, as well as the headquarters of Kobayashi and Sakai. The battalion commander himself was hit for the first time by a machine-gun bullet that penetrated his left arm. At first the wound caused him no pain, for he had been wearing an overcoat against the morning fog. Now he could not get the coat off, and the battalion medical lieutenant was nowhere in sight (he had been badly wounded). When a medical noncom came to cut off Nishikawa's sleeve and render first aid, he found two "bean-size" holes in the elbow. After a makeshift sling had been fashioned for his useless limb, Nishikawa shifted his saber to his right hand and kept moving.

The advance, however, had amounted to merely 1,500 or 2,000 meters by midday. Battalion lines were confused and control was not possible, for all companies had been battered in getting even this far. From the skirt of a dune ahead of the enemy defenses, the Japanese tried to study the situation, but when a sergeant stood up, he was killed instantly by a sniper. Enemy fire seemed to be emanating from the direction of some scattered trees, into whose roots (it was learned later) Russian snipers had dug deep trenches.[2]

On Kokura's 2nd Battalion sector, the troops headed toward Ipponmatsu ("Lone Pine"), the first objective, about 3,000 meters away. A tense probationary officer, Morinaga Masatsugu (Seishi), who had just taken over his platoon a few days before, tried to keep the men together, but a veteran non-com, addressing nobody in particular, yelled to them to disperse. Enemy machine guns cut swaths in vegetation a foot high, and a horse towing an infantry gun was blown sky-high by a shell. The Japanese foot soldiers ran to the verge of exhaustion, encouraging each other to keep moving, while their numbers decreased one by one. When a sergeant from regimental headquarters hollered to the lead elements not to advance so blindly, leaving the colonel and the colors behind, the men held up and caught their breath. The sun beat down mercilessly, water canteens ran dry, and enemy positions could be barely discerned through the heat shimmers, the sweat, and the fatigue. Trying to coordinate his platoon's action with charges taking place to his right, Morinaga sought to observe the situation ahead, but the glint of the sun in his field glasses led a Russian sniper promptly to shoot him in the arm.

A sergeant took command of the few survivors in the platoon and led a charge against the Ipponmatsu objective. The first enemy lines were apparently overrun, but bushes effectively blocked any further view. Staying too high meant drawing accurate sniper shots. From the main works ahead emanated enormous firepower. The Japanese could see "literally nothing," and it was difficult to convey orders. Second Lt. Hiratsuka Matsunosuke found himself only 50 to 100 meters away from the enemy, but he could not locate the battalion or company commanders. On his own initiative, he ordered a charge by those who could hear him. Enemy fire rained down immediately, the attack force was pinned down, and the lieutenant's wristwatch was smashed at precisely 11:30 A.M. From midday till 7 P.M. he lay on his stomach and played dead while he clawed a hole for himself in the earth, using only his fingers and his toes. Enemy flamethrowing tanks set fire to the grass, and anybody who tried to get up and run was shot down. The direction of the wind saved the lieutenant.

The regiment struggled to retain whatever gains it had made, against stubborn counterattacks, but a new crisis erupted at 3 P.M. when Soviet riflemen and a half-dozen tanks "took clever advantage of the terrain" and smashed into the Japanese right flank. Casualties mounted, and the regimental colors were in such danger that it became necessary to bury them in the sand several times to protect them. On Kokura's 2nd Battalion front, the Russians came within grenade range and hurled their little bombs blindly. It was a brave man who dared to throw one back. Ordered to dig in, the soldiers scraped at the sandy earth with their little shovels and the last of their strength.

Enemy mortar fire from the woods, 300-400 meters away, was especially costly as the high-angle projectiles arched down. A noncom volunteered to fire a grenade launcher in response. After a dozen rounds had been collected from dead comrades, the gunner tried to pinpoint his target, which he finally silenced on the eighth or ninth shot. But several observers were lost to accomplish this task. Using tanks as shields, the Russians counterattacked closely all afternoon. Even when they pulled back at nightfall, they left snipers behind. Only five ambulatory soldiers were left in the Morinaga platoon by now; the platoon leader and acting sergeant had been killed. Leaving one man behind at Ipponmatsu, the survivors emerged from behind the hulk of a knocked-out Soviet tank and headed forward to try to do something about retrieving the dead and wounded. Nobody returned. The solitary Japanese sentry waited most of the night, in the eerie silence and the stench of blood, before leaving Ipponmatsu, hoping to rejoin the regimental colors and the company commander.[3]

In the 1st Battalion area, the scene was also one of confusion and death from midday on the 24th. Nishikawa saw an enemy Maxim machine gun and prepared to rush it. But there was fire from every direction and it became necessary to pull out and redeploy, since losses were very heavy but progress was nil. At this point, the battalion commander was wounded by a second machine-gun slug, which apparently went through the body of his orderly and hit Nishikawa's hip without penetrating, but which knocked him to the ground. Tactically, the battalion commander was frustrated by the fact that the left wing of his battalion was not being covered properly, leaving it open to outflanking by enemy tanks that were coming around the rear while he lay helpless to counter them. Another disappointment befell Nishikawa when he tried to designate the surviving senior officer—Capt. Honda Sanyō of the 3rd Company—as acting battalion commander. Honda declined, claiming that he had been wounded too and needed to be evacuated. Although Nishikawa says that Honda's wound was slight, in his stead he appointed 1st Lt. Nakao Sukeo, the 1st Company commander. In due course, every one of the company commanders in this battalion would be killed except Honda.

As for Nishikawa, he was carried out on a four-man litter after nightfall on the 24th. But the stretcher party could not find the aid station near the jump-off line, although they sighted on the Big Dipper and walked away from the enemy tanks that could be seen burning here and there. At an IJA gun site, the soldiers knew nothing and would not answer when Nishikawa asked for an officer. Therefore the team kept walking "toward Hailar." When they could not stop a passing IJA truck, Nishikawa told the stretcher-bearers to place him on the ground in front of the next truck's headlights. "Then they'll stop—maybe!" The desperate ploy worked, but the truck was loaded with wounded and the battalion commander could not be jammed into it. Eventually, covering his bleeding wounds, he somehow pushed himself into the cab, next to a blinded soldier.[4]

General Kobayashi and Colonel Sakai had been directing operations from a dune in the 2nd Battalion's sector. In mid-afternoon, the infantry could see enemy armor overrunning the trenches in which the senior officers had taken shelter. It was frustrating to the Japanese that their fire bottles no longer ignited the tanks, but the commanders somehow escaped this particular assault. Radio contact was reestablished briefly with division headquarters, and a noncom could see Kobayashi squatting in the tread marks left by the tanks and dictating a message. As the general reported on the unit's limited progress, the regrettable loss of subordinates, the fierce enemy resistance, and the need for support, the watching noncom was indelibly impressed by Kobayashi's look of pain (*chintsū*).

When the battle situation deteriorated again, Kobayashi, Sakai, the guard company commander, and the regimental colors displaced to a little rise beyond the noncom's view. There, we know from other sources, Kobayashi was hit in the thigh by a tank-shell fragment and fell to the ground, bleeding profusely. The Japanese troops on this front broke under fire. Fleeing "like a tidal wave," they never noticed or else ignored the fallen general whom they trampled with their boots until his wound became gory and filthy. A young officer, 1st Lt. Shimada Hatsuo of the 71st Regiment, saved Kobayashi's life. Shimada had returned to the battlefront from the hospital in Hailar that very morning, after being wounded in the earlier offensive on 24 July. Since he could not locate or get to his parent regiment, he willingly helped the general with communications on this important day. In the process, Shimada was shot in the abdomen by machine-gun fire. When he saw that Kobayashi was in danger of being killed by the stampeding soldiers or of being captured by the enemy, since the group headquarters had been decimated, the lieutenant tried to stanch his own wounds with one hand while grasping the general's belt with the other and inching him to safety behind the elevation. After making a tourniquet to stop Kobayashi's bleeding, Shimada staggered four kilometers to the rear to get a truck to evacuate the general and guided it back personally. Soon afterward, the lieutenant insisted on rejoining his regiment; he was killed in action six days later. As for Kobayashi, a medical officer later had to amputate his mangled leg, but the general never forgot the wounded lieutenant who had saved him from death.[5]

While worrying about the increasing casualties, the failure to advance, and the possible loss of his regimental colors (described below), Colonel Sakai himself was incapacitated by a serious wound in his right hand and had to be evacuated that night. As Nishikawa asserts, in the fighting until 24 August the 72nd Regiment had been relatively fortunate in conserving its officers, but on this day the key leaders "fell like flies." In fact, when Nishikawa arrived in the field hospital by truck on the 25th, he was stunned to see all of his living regimental comrades in the officer corps lying there, from the colonel down. "I felt as if it had truly been an annihilation," says Nishikawa.[6]

After having played dead all afternoon on the 24th, Lieutenant Hiratsuka had escaped with five or six soldiers who had responded to his yell of "*Oi!*" in the dark. On the way back, they found their 2nd Battalion commander, Major Kokura, lying with his right arm almost blown off, in the company of one critically wounded enlisted man. Kokura asked the lieutenant to report to any higher headquarters and prevent corpses and wounded from being taken by the enemy. Hiratsuka left canteens of water with the wounded enlisted man and instructed him to tend to the major. Proceeding on his mission in the darkness, the lieutenant felt his leg grabbed by many of the wounded who pleaded with him in vain not to abandon them. At the tents of the division headquarters, Hiratsuka made the first report on the fate of the Kokura battalion, but when he alluded to "annihilation" and casualties of 70 percent, a sharp exchange ensued with an unnamed staff officer (Tsuji?). The lieutenant backed down when he realized the adverse effect his report might have on the runners at the command post. At infantry group headquarters, he could not get to see Kobayashi and was finally told a closely kept secret—that the general had been seriously wounded. A considerable number of regimental survivors were reportedly assembled in a dip behind the division's command post.

After being assured that not only his battalion's casualties but also its weapons and equipment would be retrieved, Hiratsuka went back with the stretcher-bearers to find Kokura. A clever soldier had blazed a trail with paper or cloth, and they were thus able to find the major within an hour. The enlisted man had died but Kokura was still breathing. Devising a litter from rifles and a tent cover, the party took turns carrying the major to the rear. A passing convoy of a dozen trucks was too filled with casualties to take Kokura aboard, and when the lieutenant tried to argue with the unit commander, he was told that rank did not count and that it was a matter of first-come, first-served. Although Kokura told him not to try too hard,

Hiratsuka did not desist; but when he thought he had found some space on the driver's seat of a truck, it proved to be occupied by none other than the wounded Colonel Sakai. At this point, the lieutenant took the initiative of ordering the medical orderly and four soldiers to carry Kokura all the way to Hailar and not to bother to return. At the time it seemed improbable that the battalion commander could survive, but Hiratsuka was delighted to learn later that Kokura did make it to Hailar, where his mangled arm was amputated.[7]

With the ruination of the 72nd Regiment's command structure, Japanese movement on the right wing came to an end. Until midday, viewing the battle through field glasses from the division command post, Tsuji and his colleagues had been thinking that the 72nd Regiment's assault was developing well, as the men stormed the defense lines on the dunes. Under fire, Komatsubara and his headquarters group moved forward too. Tsuji was lying on the ground, observing, when he saw an officer approaching. It proved to be the division logistics officer, Itō, who had advanced with Kobayashi. "The positions have not been taken yet," said the very pale captain. "And I was shot." Apologizing for having been unable to get water to the front lines, Itō sank to the ground, his tunic soaked with blood from a chest wound. Tsuji took him to the division command post, where he was given first aid and pushed into Komatsubara's staff car. Itō explains what had happened to him that day.[8]

> The infantry group's offensive that morning had been very impressive. Watching the beautiful advance from the jump-off line, Komatsubara was convinced that the attack was succeeding, and he insisted on moving forward himself. But there was still powerful firing by machine guns and small arms, so I suggested that I scout first and that the general follow when the situation permitted. I went forward, past many dead Japanese soldiers, but I could not ascertain the precise location of friendly or enemy forces. When I finally reached a dune, the Soviet trenches were empty, and helmets and bodies were lying around. Since our forces must have overrun this position, I pushed ahead, veering left, looking for somebody.
>
> I had been in battle for two months by now, had become very lazy, and was too tired to crawl. I walked upright, as I had convinced myself psychologically that this was the best way to avoid getting shot. But when I had crossed the dune line and was going downhill, I noticed that my staff insignia had been cut. Had I been hit? My first concern was for my sword arm, so that I could cut down at least one enemy soldier. I was reassured when I tested my right arm and found that I could raise it, so I pressed forward until I bumped into an infantry platoon leader. But he didn't know where the brigade commander was, and there was no radio or other communication. The entire Japanese force was already badly dispersed into little platoons, out of touch with one another and merely clinging to their gains. When I inhaled now, I sweated and spat blood. From the front and back of the hole in my chest (which had actually been shot through by a small-arms slug), blood was oozing. I had no orderly with me, as I was always visiting weird places and no

orderly would volunteer to tag along. But I felt that I had to get back to division headquarters, 1,500-2,000 meters away, and warn them against advancing farther. By now, however, Soviet tanks—mainly flamethrowers—had poured into the gap. I saw the Kusaba field-artillery battery, towing only one gun, pull up and knock out three tanks in a flash. They could not loan me their truck, whose radiator had been hit by machine-gun fire; in fact, they'd have to pull their gun by hand now.

I stumbled on and at last ran into Tsuji, who said my face was pale blue. He sent me back to the division command post, after promising to go to the front himself and take care of matters, including my request for a "last favor"—the dispensing of water to the troops. When I got to the command post, I could neither lie nor sit. Somebody said that if I stayed hunched like that, it would affect everybody's morale and I ought to get out. Since I was "extra baggage" anyhow, I was shipped out by sedan to Hailar.

Tsuji and the division staff, pinned down by enemy fire and without cover, had been digging one-man foxholes on the slope. In the early afternoon, before the foxholes had been completed, enemy aircraft conducted low-level strafing runs. Then at 4 P.M., in an instance of mistaken identity, Japanese light bombers dropped a dozen bombs blindly around the division command post. Komatsubara lost a sedan, many trucks, and about 10 men, including a second lieutenant killed. As Komatsubara wrote in his diary, the bombing dispersed the members of his headquarters and rendered staff work difficult. An apology dropped by communication tube an hour later did little to assuage the anger of the headquarters, but the attitude softened when one of the Japanese planes was shot down by fighters and a crewman who parachuted down was surrounded by enemy armor. A direct threat to the division command post was lifted when Kusaba's battery knocked out four of a dozen tanks at a range of 300 meters—the action observed by Itō.

Toward the end of the day, as we saw, telephone contact was finally restored with the right wing, but the news was tragic: Kobayashi's group had charged into the enemy positions and had been almost annihilated by Soviet tanks. General Kobayashi had been badly wounded and was missing, Colonel Sakai had also been injured severely, and most of the battalion and company commanders were either dead or wounded. In the absence of information from General Morita's brigade, all hope had been pinned on the actions of the brave and knowledgeable Kobayashi. On hearing of his fate, Komatsubara blanched. "As long as Kobayashi lives," the division commander used to say, "we'll succeed." At this juncture, with the sun setting and the sounds of battle abating, Sixth Army Chief of Staff Fujimoto, who appeared "bewildered," announced that he was returning to his headquarters to report and asked if Tsuji would accompany him. The major declined, and Komatsubara voiced indirect astonishment at Fujimoto's departure at such a time; but the chief of staff took off anyhow.

The division officers, already visibly depressed, received another jolt when 40 or 50 Japanese soldiers appeared on the right flank, running "like mad." Tsuji leaped from his foxhole and intercepted the disgraceful rabble. A first lieutenant, his pupils dilated, gasped that the right wing had been annihilated. Tsuji shrieked at him that as long as one man was alive it was not "annihilation." Could Japanese soldiers desert their brigadier, their regiment commander, and their colors? Tsuji's "roar," says Komatsubara, "restored life" to the men whose morale was "shot" from continuous flight. After forcing some semblance of contriteness from the soldiers, Tsuji ordered them to get rid of their sacks, load their pockets with grenades, deploy in dispersed formation, and follow him back to the front, in the direction of the burning tanks.

It was still bright as Tsuji's motley party advanced along the yellow telephone lines. At a point 1,000 meters forward, movement was detected in a ditch, and a man's voice could be heard, identifying himself as "Lieutenant Harada, 48th class, bearing the regimental colors." Tsuji told the lieutenant that he was off to rescue the regiment, and that Harada should bring the colors back to division headquarters, following the phone lines. Although saddened to learn that his classmate Kunimoto Kyūrō (the senior regimental aide, recently promoted to lieutenant colonel) had been killed, Tsuji says he was relieved that the colors were safe and that the lieutenant was taking care of the problem.[9]

The matter of regimental colors was always sensitive in the Japanese army, and the 72nd Infantry's case was no exception. By late afternoon, say the records, the combat situation had deteriorated past the point of temporary expedients, and Colonel Sakai finally decided to send the colors back to safety for the time being. After a route of escape had been scouted, the 5th Company commander, 1st Lt. Harada Tasuku, personally escorted the colors to higher headquarters.[10]

Although even the irascible Tsuji was pleased with the handling of the crisis besetting Sakai's colors, 1st Battalion commander Nishikawa says the incident did not end so easily. The situation at the time was "really desperate," he remarks, but the decision caused problems later. Though the regimental annals, as we saw, state that Sakai directed the evacuation of the colors, Nishikawa thinks that the colonel had already withdrawn and that company commander Harada was acting on his own.[11]

> There was much criticism of that lieutenant of the 2nd Battalion. Why did he leave the field and personally escort the colors back? Actually, the color-bearer had been killed already, but the division commander reprimanded the company commander and assumed responsibility for the colors. Thereupon the lieutenant returned to the battlefield. Apparently he had felt nervous about the safety of the colors and insisted on accompanying them. In any case, ours was the only regiment of the 23rd Division that was able to save its colors at Nomonhan.

Crouching low, Tsuji's party continued to move forward, searching for the brigadier or the regiment commander. Tsuji's occasional shouts drew no response except enemy fire until finally, around 8 P.M., a feeble voice could be heard calling "Tsuji-*kun*," a familiar greeting to the major. It was Colonel Sakai, lying calmly behind a low tree, his right arm in a sling. Now Tsuji learned that after Sakai and Kobayashi had advanced at midday, enemy tanks had rushed at the Japanese and that the general had been severely wounded. There was a chance that he had been evacuated, because a second lieutenant had recently gone forward with a litter party. Kunimoto was dead, however. As for battle plans, said Sakai, his regiment would resume the offensive next morning if ordered, but probably annihilation would result. Tsuji knew that Komatsubara was thinking of attacking again on the right wing and even of "exploiting success" there, since the Morita brigade had not accomplished much on the left. Obviously, the reality differed from the general's expectations. In the absence of water, food, and ammunition, it would be absurd to send a nonexistent "regiment" forward on the 25th. Tsuji therefore decided to contravene Komatsubara's intention and at about 8 P.M., on his own responsibility, devised a new divisional order to Sakai: from the early morning of 25 August, the division would resume the attack on the Morita brigade front at the left; the Kobayashi force was to revert to divisional reserve, assembling at division headquarters by dawn, after having retrieved all of the dead and wounded.

He had no choice, Tsuji told the colonel, and it was not a matter of "retreating." The casualties must be extricated, and the able-bodied troops should follow the telephone line back to the assembly point. Sakai seemed relieved and said the order would be carried out. Nevertheless, the situation was so confused that it was impossible to control the battalions, since almost every commander had fallen and only one reservist captain, Hirowatari Kunimori, was left at regimental level. Tsuji agreed to help, and shared his water canteen with the parched colonel. Both battalions, says Tsuji, were somehow contacted by him and Hirowatari. In the process, Tsuji found his friend Kunimoto's corpse, still warm. He sprinkled his last drops of drinking water on the shattered face, begged forgiveness, and hurried back, weeping, along the phone wires. Too many casualties lay on the field to be carried by soldiers; trucks would be necessary. Near an enemy tank, Tsuji found the corpse of a Russian officer and removed a blood-stained map that would later be of great use to the Japanese.

On reaching the division command post around 10 P.M., Tsuji apologized to Komatsubara for having issued the order to Sakai in the general's name. Komatsubara shook his hand, however, and commended him, with tears in his eyes. For the use of the general's bodyguard, Tsuji delivered a light machine gun that he had pried from the fingers of a dead Japanese soldier on the battlefield. The division staff now revised the previous operational order, asked for volunteers from the transport unit, and dispatched trucks to the front.[12]

The retrieval and disengagement process proved to be enormously difficult. Sakai had turned over command of the regiment temporarily to Hirowatari at 9 P.M., before being evacuated by truck. Based upon the latest division order, which incorporated Tsuji's concept, the captain issued his redeployment instructions at midnight, on the dune west of Ipponmatsu. Hirowatari was known as a calm and courageous officer, but the survivors were scattered and fellow officers were very few. A company commander, 1st Lt. Nakao Sukeo, had replaced the wounded 1st Battalion commander, Nishikawa, and another (acting) company commander, 2nd Lt. Abe Masamori, was supposed to take over the 2nd Battalion from the wounded Major Kokura. But the regiment had been out of touch with the 2nd Battalion since twilight, and Captain Hirowatari had to go looking for it. He found the battalion doctor, who was in the process of evacuating battalion commander Kokura, the 8th Company commander, and other badly wounded personnel. Finally, after much effort, Hirowatari located Abe in the 6th Company area and officially ordered him to assume command of the 2nd Battalion. Actually, somebody had already reached the battalion by phone and conveyed the word to relocate, but the regiment was unhappy about this sloppy and potentially dangerous method of transmitting orders. The carnage had been particularly severe in the region of the 2nd Battalion, and Abe had to struggle to pull together the survivors and move them out with the wounded, the dead, and the abandoned weapons.

Near 11 P.M. on the 24th, when enemy artillery fire had ceased, the divisional transport unit, on standby, received the order to send trucks to the Kobayashi-Sakai front. Cargo was removed from only five of Capt. Sōma Seiji's 2nd Company trucks, which proceeded in the direction of the burning tanks. En route, wounded soldiers who pleaded for water and a lift were told to follow the tire marks to the rear until they could be picked up by the trucks on the way back. About 50 meters from enemy lines, the truckers reached the regimental command post, where they loaded the most seriously wounded men into the trucks. Kobayashi had already been evacuated, but Sakai was hobbling along, his right arm in a sling, his left hand clutching his saber and using it as a cane. Room was found for the colonel in the cab. It was impossible to pick up all the injured soldiers found along the road back. The immediate round trip took only about an hour, but daylight was nearing and it was necessary to proceed afterward all the way to the field station. Since more trucks were obviously needed, another five were released by Captain Sōma. In the first echelon of five trucks, there had been 140 wounded, three of whom died before reaching help. The ground in the field station itself was decked with rush pallets on which the wounded were strewn.

A total of 700 dead and wounded were evacuated by the morning of 25 August, together with much matériel, according to Tsuji. The figure accords precisely with the 72nd Regiment's tabulation of its losses on the 24th: 323 killed (including 31 officers); 377 wounded (including 21 officers). Against a listed strength of 1,295 who participated in the combat, the Sakai regiment's casualties on 24 August amounted to 54 percent. Among officers, 52 of 79 were killed or wounded. Weapon losses included 18 grenade launchers, 19 light and heavy machine guns, and 14 regimental and 11 rapid-fire guns. Enemy losses on the 24th were estimated at 300-350 men, 20 tanks, 30 machine guns, and 13-14 heavy weapons knocked out.

At sunrise on 25 August, those of the 72nd Infantry who could make it back on foot reached divisional headquarters. Tsuji says they were densely packed but calm and controlled. He called for dispersion and the construction of foxholes. But casualties were so grievous, according to regimental annals, that the battalions had to be reorganized on the basis of only two companies, companies were down to two squads each, and the regimental-gun battery was reduced to one platoon of two pieces. In the 1st Battalion alone, Lieutenant Nakao said later, only about 110 men remained when he replaced Nishikawa—against an original total Nishikawa recalls as exceeding 800 when the unit first left Hailar in June.[13]

On General Morita's sector of the line, to the left of Sakai, the main burden of the offensive of 24 August would fall to the two battalions of Col. Ashizuka Chōzō's 28th Infantry, in the absence of Sumi's sister regiment. By 9 A.M., the troops were making last-minute preparations—burying private belongings in the sand, lightening knapsacks, tightening helmet straps. As soon as the fog began to clear, enemy artillery opened fire, including 15-cm. howitzers whose shells were known to the Japanese soldiers as "big sake bottles" (*isshōbin*).

Near 10 A.M., General Morita ordered his demibrigade to advance in the direction of tree-studded Heights 780, well over 3,000 meters away. Large formations of enemy armor had come across the Halha since morning and heavy artillery sites on the opposite shore had been reinforced considerably, but much was expected of the elite forces of the 7th Division. Pep talks were given by company commanders, and then the units took off—Lt. Col. Hotta Fusakichi's 1st Battalion on the right flank (adjacent to Sakai's regiment), and Maj. Fujioka Yoshiichi's 3rd Battalion on the left. Between the battalions and to their rear, Ashizuka and his aide advanced with the regimental headquarters. At first, they heard what sounded like birds chirping in the grass, but it turned out to be machine-gun bullets whizzing overhead.

Since, as General Morita points out, he possessed only two-thirds of one infantry regiment to begin with, plus a trifling reserve made up of one engineer platoon, he could not operate a real brigade headquarters. The 23rd Division command post was in the area on the right anyhow, so he moved up with Ashizuka. Although the Soviet barrages were severe, Morita was well acquainted with artillery tactics. Whenever the enemy adjusted the range, the general would order an advance. This saved lives among the forward elements, but those coming behind would be hit. Like the foot soldiers, Morita ran forward all day: "I was a rather young brigade commander, at 47 or 48 years of age," says the general, "but I had to carry a full pack (gas mask, etc.) and jog a couple of thousand meters. It was tough for me to do, and I can remember how parched my mouth was."

The troops ran with a rifle in their right hand, a shovel in their left. They would dash ahead in 15-meter bounds, "hit the deck," and quickly scoop into the sandy earth, piling up soil as slim cover in front of their faces. Men fell on all sides, and the noise and smoke made the transmission of commands almost impossible. By 11 or 11:30 A.M., Fujioka's battalion, supported by the regimental guns, had done fairly well on the left, reaching a dip about 1,000 meters from the jump-off point. Ashizuka advanced his command post to this sector. On the regiment's right, however, Hotta's battalion encountered commanding fire from the dune 200 meters ahead—machine guns, artillery, and tanks.[14]

Around noon, a threat developed on the far left flank, where the Yotsuya battalion veered back under pressure, exposing Ashizuka's left rear to enemy irruption at a time when Sumi's units were just beginning their advance to the endangered area. In fact, sometime after 1 P.M. at least 15 tanks struck at this very sector, while a dozen enemy fighter planes came in at low altitude and strafed 1st Lt. Yorozu Toshio's reserve 11th Company, which was responsible for defending the regimental colors. According to the official account, one of Yorozu's platoons knocked out four tanks by close-quarter assaults and thus saved the colors. A firsthand version, however, states that the color-guard platoon became separated from the regimental headquarters behind the left lines when it was stormed by 20 tanks. Armed only with portable mines (*anpan*), the platoon could not cope with the armor and was cut to pieces defending the colors. By the end of the battle, there remained only two or three soldiers unhurt, plus a shell-shocked officer. During this crisis affecting the colors, the commander of the rapid-fire battery (attached from the 27th Regiment) had sighted the peril and rushed forward with one of his guns. The other three pieces followed shortly and formed a circle around the colors. Firing without letup, the gunners knocked out all but one of the Soviet tanks. By now, the battery had only two shells left, and had lost 5-6 men killed and 15-16 wounded, including the battery commander, who was hit in six places; nonetheless, the colors reached the regiment safely after nightfall. It is said that this gallant action later received only a "B-class" commendation because it was allegedly dishonorable for the regiment to have exposed the colors to such danger in the first place.[15]

The Soviet tanks' smashing of the Sakai regiment's lines on the afternoon of the 24th exposed Ashizuka's other wing on the right rear. Enemy fire grew more intense and more accurate. At 4 P.M., Russian armor overran Sakai's command post area, where Kobayashi was also located, and then hit the 1st Battalion from the flank and rear. From Ashizuka's headquarters, it was possible to observe Hotta's various companies visually but not Hotta's command post, and communications were severed for a while.

Losses in the Ashizuka regiment were severe on 24 August. Soon after Hotta's 1st Battalion had jumped off in the morning, the 1st Company commander, a first lieutenant, had been hurt in both eyes. The warrant officer who filled in for him was also wounded later, and two first lieutenants commanding platoons were killed. By nightfall, little more than 30 soldiers in this company were still on their feet, under three noncoms including a "demon sergeant." The 2nd Company lost its commander (a first lieutenant) slain. Casualties were especially heavy on the right flank, where a platoon struggling against tanks lost its leader, another lieutenant, to shell fragments. A second platoon, battered badly, was destroyed when it launched a last charge. On the 24th, too, the 3rd Company lost two lieutenants killed—the company commander and a platoon leader.

Pulling the units together when the fighting on 24 August was over did not progress as well as Ashizuka wanted, even after nightfall, in view of the losses. It was 2 A.M. on the 25th, for example, before the 1st Battalion could be regrouped. In the 3rd Battalion's area, a company commander could be seen walking around the battlefield, looking for the bodies of his men. In a dip 70 or 80 meters in diameter, which had been reached by IJA troops during the day, about 200 Japanese corpses were retrieved. The survivors of the 3rd Battalion assembled on the crestline, dug trenches, and waited to fight again at dawn.[16]

The situation to the left of the 28th Infantry, on the Yotsuya battalion's front, did not develop well either on 24 August. At the outset, the unit became entangled with Fujioka's adjoining battalion. Subsequently, when enemy armor attacked, Yotsuya's elements tended to converge toward and behind Fujioka, causing problems for the 28th Regiment's flank as well as for itself. Yotsuya explains that, when his force jumped off at about 9:30 A.M., the progress was stop-and-go because of the hostile artillery barrages. Soviet tanks struck from the flank, shattered the attached rapid-fire guns and the signal team, and caused severe casualties among the infantry. Although Yotsuya claims that his battalion somehow managed to reach its designated objective, battle maps show him only about halfway to Heights 791. Pulling back at night, as ordered, was not easy for Yotsuya, because his units were scattered and casualties had to be recovered on foot. One solitary truck, says Yotsuya, had been parked behind the crestline owing to insufficient gasoline. It was loaded now with wounded soldiers and ordered to proceed as far back as its remaining fuel would take it. Around midnight, Yotsuya's men got to their assembly point in the rear.[17]

The eventual arrival of elements of Sumi's 26th Regiment on the battlefield during the afternoon of 24 August was not decisive. Morita remarks that Sumi joined the brigade only after Ashizuka's regiment had penetrated the enemy positions. Even the usually voluble colonel has little to say about combat actions on the 24th. He remembers deploying Nakano's 2nd Battalion on the right, to advance nearest to Ashizuka, and Kokubu's 3rd Battalion on the left, nearest to Yotsuya. During this baptism of fire for the brand-new Nakano, the experienced battalion aide, First Lieutenant Uchida, was of great assistance. The major survived his first day unscathed, although he experienced great difficulty pulling together his forces on the night of 24/25 August. As for Sumi, he was very anxious to catch up with the front lines. But whereas Morita calls himself a young general at 47 or 48, Sumi says he was an "old colonel" at 47. So he took off all his impedimenta—to the extent of having his men carry even his saber—and ran forward over four kilometers to get to the left of the Ashizuka regiment. It was a little after 5 P.M., Sumi recalls, when he ordered his men to dig in along a 1,500-meter front and to conduct reconnaissance. He had no idea where General Morita was, and he still had not seen Ashizuka.

From the records, we know that Major Nakano had assigned battle objectives in the Ipponmatsu area at noon, and that his battalion jumped off at 12:30 P.M. Since a new commander (a second lieutenant) had temporarily taken over the 7th Company only a few hours earlier, platoon leader Koguchi Sadayuki (another second lieutenant) did his best to retain the company's momentum and bring the young officer up to date. By the time the unit had advanced 400 meters, enemy artillery and tank gun fire struck from the left front. At 3 P.M., three tanks attacked from the right. The one available Japanese antitank gun hit the treads, but of course this did not stop the tanks' cannon and machine guns from continuing to shoot. Koguchi organized two close-quarter teams, one of which, under the platoon's covering fire, approached from the dead angle, killed the crewmen, and set all three tanks ablaze. By 5 P.M. the company reached a point 300 meters from the foe, despite fierce enemy barrages. Lieutenant Koguchi was shot through the chest and killed. Fighting continued after dark. At 8 P.M. the 7th Company assembled in the area of the 2nd Battalion command post, secured positions 400 meters ahead, and was ready to conduct a night attack, if ordered, by midnight. The unit's lines were two kilometers northeast of Heights 780. Apart from the slain Koguchi, the company lost only five men wounded, from a strength of 81 when the day began.[18]

From the wooded area roughly to his left, Sumi detected an offensive stench of blood and sent out scouts to investigate. It proved to be the sector where Soviet tanks had trampled Lieutenant Colonel Yotsuya's infantry, leaving corpses that had begun to rot in the sun. Undoubtedly, thought Sumi, the Yotsuya unit was so new in combat that it had not comprehended the power of Russian armor, especially in daylight combat. When the detachment's command post was finally located, Sumi called in Yotsuya and told him that orders received south of Lake Mohorehi called for Yotsuya to join Sumi's command after the 26th Regiment had caught up with the rest of the brigade. Yotsuya replied that his own orders said he was to pull out of the lines for a while, since his casualties on the 24th had been so heavy. He was therefore preparing to withdraw after dark. Sumi reminded him that, according to IJA field service regulations (*jinchū yōmurei*), when conflicting instructions were issued simultaneously, one had to follow the more aggressive order. Yotsuya should therefore come under the 26th Infantry, lest he be criticized later for "cowardice." To this valid argument Yotsuya answered that his unit had been hurt so badly, its morale was extremely low. From that fact alone, the mood was such that he would rather proceed with the pullback process. Sumi closed the unhappy discussion by telling Yotsuya that if, after hearing why he should not withdraw, he still wanted to, then he should follow his own judgment. As we saw, Yotsuya chose to fall back.

Sumi wanted to share his regiment's combat experience with the newcomers, who were acquainted with neither the local terrain nor the enemy. The Japanese infantry, he felt strongly, should march only by night and push forward as far as they could. Soviet equipment, especially artillery and tanks, was massive and excellent, but the Russians were not very active in the hours of darkness, for their armor dreaded infantry assaults and their artillery batteries could not identify targets. By day, the Japanese should assemble, stay under cover, and defend their positions. Hence Sumi proposed to argue for night-attack operations instead of the "ridiculous daylight parades" that the "greenhorns" knew only from maneuvers and that were proving so costly.

When combat abated after twilight and the enemy began to "relax," Sumi set off across the front lines with his aide and Major Nakano, to confer with his senior colleagues in the brigade. When he found Ashizuka's command post, Japanese corpses were stacked up nearby and the atmosphere was "very blue." The 28th Infantry had been hoping to live up to its reputation for hard training at Tsitsihar by waging a successful first battle, but the casualties this day had been appalling. Ashizuka was too depressed to entertain Sumi's idea of a night attack, and the regiment was in no condition to consider it anyhow.

Sumi told Nakano to rejoin the 2nd Battalion and get to know it better. (This proved to be the second and last time he saw the major alive.) After sending his aide back to regimental headquarters, Sumi borrowed a couple of soldiers from Ashizuka and set off to find his old friend and senior (*senpai*), Morita. In a tent perched over a trench, the general and his aide were conversing by the light of a candle. Sumi was disturbed by the general's listless attitude, his "lack of pep." It was a beautiful night, lit by a nearly full moon, but the brigade commander was spending the night uselessly in a hole. He should be out studying the terrain aggressively, thought Sumi. After stating his reasons in some detail, the colonel recommended night movements and night attacks. Sumi felt that his advice fell on deaf ears. The general conveyed an impression of being "rather negative" and of not comprehending the situation.

Leaving Morita's command post with a sense of disappointment, Sumi headed back, in the direction of two twisted-pine landmarks. To his astonishment, he was fired on by a machine gun. "What do you mean, shooting at your commander?," he yelled. The firing stopped and a tall man peered at Sumi in the brightening night. It was a Russian outpost! Afraid that he had lost his whole regiment or that it had left the scene, Sumi considered charging with his two men; but he thought better of it and crept sideways. A hundred meters away, two remarkably similar twisted pines could be seen. "Is this the Sumi regiment?" the colonel called. It was, luckily for him.[19]

One does not have to look far to find the reasons for the failure of the Japanese offensive on 24 August. Though Komatsubara noted that the dense morning fog had allowed units to move to the jump-off line in complete concealment, the general had to admit that, since orders for the Morita brigade arrived late, the deployment south of Mohorehi proceeded behind schedule. According to the division commander's information, General Morita's assembly and battle preparations were only completed at 9 A.M. or so. In addition, the absence of the 71st Infantry dangerously weakened Kobayashi's group on the right wing, and left the job to Sakai alone.

From Komatsubara's diary, it is clear that the general had intended to seize the southern edge of Heights 780 as his first objective and then deploy his artillery forward. Kobayashi was to strike the west side of 780 with two infantry battalions and a field-artillery battery, while General Morita headed for the southwestern fringe with three rifle battalions and two field-artillery batteries. On the extreme left, the Yotsuya detachment, essentially one battalion, was supposed to advance to the southern slope of Heights 780. The artillery corps was to lend support. None of the objectives could be attained. The units moved ahead, generally in orderly fashion despite having to fight off tanks, until they entered the zone of dunes. Thereafter the deployments deteriorated, producing an overly broad frontage and dispersed strength. Hence the Japanese offensive south of the line of the sand-hill woods did not make progress.

Although Kobayashi and Yotsuya had made it to the edge of the woods by midday, wrote Komatsubara, they were hammered by infantry and armored counterattacks. The cooperation of friendly artillery was insufficient, and the first IJA shells were not fired until 10:30 A.M. By sunset, the forces on the right wing had suffered about 50 percent casualties. Kobayashi and Sakai had been wounded, and the 72nd Regiment finally had to be pulled back at night. General Morita's brigade had taken only a portion of the enemy line, and most of his men were not yet occupying the edge of the woods. Apart from the distressing episode of the friendly bombers' attack on Komatsubara's command post, a serious problem had been caused by the straying of the divisional signal unit into the front lines. As a consequence, the division lost its ability to communicate for a while. The most telling part of Komatsubara's private explanation for the stalling of the offensive includes the statement that orders were not conveyed effectively and that there had been insufficient preparation: "All the units lacked time to get ready psychologically or physically to carry out their orders."[20]

As for the Japanese artillery, whose minor role on 24 August has been mentioned, General Hata has stated that Soviet shelters were so excellent, it was thought either that the Russians were not deployed or that they were in the process of retreat. Prodded by Sixth Army Chief of Staff Fujimoto to press the offensive, Komatsubara had ordered his units to storm the dunes "in one stride." But when the division staff moved ahead on foot, they were pounded by artillery from the right and fired on by enemy forces hidden on the second crestline atop high ground straight ahead. Not a further step of advance was possible afterward, says Hata, who lay on his stomach, observing the battle, until 3 P.M. According to an officer in Takatsukasa's heavy artillery regiment, flanking fire in the antitank role was extremely difficult for the 10-cm. cannon batteries deployed to engage defensive works frontally. Miyao's Type 90 field-gun unit, however, was able to change position and engage the tanks rapidly with its 75-mm. pieces.

After recommending to Komatsubara that IJA artillery engage the enemy's covered batteries in the Nigesorimot area, with the help of the balloon unit, Hata went back to his observation post to direct firing. By evening, however, it was apparent that the front-line Japanese infantry had not been able to budge. Hata heard criticism that the close-support artillery had been moved back. The artillery corps' senior staff officer was called in by Komatsubara to discuss such matters as tighter cooperation between infantry and artillery, effective observation, and advancing of the gun sites. Hata was directed to exercise control of artillery attached to the 7th as well as the 23rd divisions.[21]

The pretty arrows and lines on Ogisu's and Komatsubara's maps for the battle of 24 August represented many illusions, paid for in blood on the scorching plain under a high sun. Why resume the carnage on the 25th? By nightfall of the 24th, higher headquarters knew that Kobayashi's right-wing force had been smashed. But, partly because Komatsubara's command post was behind Kobayashi, less was known about the Morita brigade's actions on the left. It was Sixth Army staff officer Hamada's understanding that General Morita's advance had been slow from the beginning, thus allowing the enemy sufficient time to cope with it. Combined resistance by Soviet armor and infantry had forced a deadlock, which in turn had obliged the Kobayashi force to try to penetrate alone, under bitterly difficult circumstances. The impression transmitted to the Kwantung Army must have been even less flattering to Morita. Hattori wrote later that the Morita brigade had not been able to attack because of enemy barrages and a shortage of water, and had had to hold up 500 meters from the Soviet positions.[22]

At 10 P.M. on 24 August, Komatsubara issued an operations order directing resumption of the offensive on the morrow. The decision-making process of course involved the Sixth Army, but after Chief of Staff Fujimoto had gone back to Ogisu's headquarters, it undoubtedly took little effort to convince the army commander. As far as General Morita's views are concerned, he does not specifically mention recommending the attack, but Komatsubara noted in his diary that the brigade commander had "conveyed his conviction that it was possible to attack and seize Heights 780 for sure" next day. Hence Komatsubara had ordered the offensive to reopen and had taken steps for the artillery corps to cooperate with the infantry, as Hata says. What was left of Sakai's and Yotsuya's units had been pulled back into reserve, and the two regiments of Morita's brigade were to advance alone on the 25th. Morita issued his order at 11 P.M. After preparatory artillery fire, Ashizuka's regiment—which had already come close to the primary Soviet defenses on the right—should strike toward Heights 780. To Ashizuka's left, Sumi's regiment was to attack the key line east of the hill. According to Tsuji's wire sent to the Kwantung Army on the night of 24/25 August, the 23rd Division had not been able to seize Heights 780 by evening of 24 August, but the offensive was being resumed at dawn next day.[23] This was another prediction that could not be met.

On the morning of 25 August, Fujioka's 3rd Infantry Battalion, on Ashizuka's left front, was taking cover in a dip while Maj. Karino Toyoichi's (Toyokazu's) 1st Artillery Battalion of the 7th Division's field artillery regiment fired round after round of softening-up bombardment against the enemy's main positions, which were shielded by barbed wire. The spirits of the infantrymen soared. Kneeling on the slope and peering through his binoculars, Fujioka was in the best of moods as he cheered on the gunners and watched the shells explode 200 meters away. But around 11 A.M., Morita thinks, the major was struck in the throat by an enemy fragment or bullet that killed him and grazed the shoulder of Karino, observing next to him. According to one account, the IJA artillery had just silenced the enemy batteries when a white flag appeared ahead. Fujioka stood up to investigate more closely and was cut down immediately. In any case, Morita says the death of Fujioka—just before the infantry attack—wrecked his troops' morale, which had been so high until then. When the men of the saddened 3rd Battalion finally jumped off after 1 P.M., little progress was made in the face of enormous firepower, and casualties were extremely heavy. The 11th Company commander (a first lieutenant) was wounded, and two platoon leaders and the command-team officer were killed. With the help of machine guns, the 10th Company reached its objective, but the company commander (a captain) was hurt and a platoon leader was slain.

Morita asserts not only that the 3rd Battalion could not advance after Fujioka's death, but that the situation in Hotta's 1st Battalion was even worse. This unit had been exhausted on the 24th; moreover, deployed next to the Sakai regiment, it had also been affected very badly by the scenes of death and retreat on that flank. After friendly artillery had stopped firing, the Soviet bombardment grew more severe than the Japanese guns had ever been able to mount. Morita says the 1st Battalion did not advance at all on the 25th. Evidence from the 1st Company bears him out. As soon as the unit tried to proceed, it was surrounded by tanks, hammered by artillery, and pinned down all day, without food or water. At 6 P.M., several dozen tanks struck from the rear, coming as close as 50 meters. A small force under a sergeant counterattacked and drove off the foe, but by 9:30 P.M. the company was forced to pull back because of heavy losses.[24]

When Sumi finally got back to his command post, it was near dawn on the 25th. After checking the deployment of his regiment, he stretched out in his trench at about 5:15 A.M., with his legs aching from the night's exertions. He was bothered by the situation on the left side, however, where Kokubu's 3rd Battalion would have to cover the entire flank, now that the

Yotsuya force had been pulled out of the line. Fortunately, Kokubu had already moved up a bit and occupied a couple of dunes necessary for the day's operations. Since more than half of the ammunition stocks had been expended, food was in short supply, and no water had been issued since the 24th, Sumi ordered his quartermaster lieutenant, Negami, to procure these vital items from the Mohorehi area as soon as possible.

The artillery barrages on 25 August were the most furious Sumi could remember. To the colonel, the crossfire over his head sounded like the thumping of a windmill. He was certainly pleased to receive friendly artillery support for the first time, but whereas the IJA guns were supposed to have opened up at 10 A.M., they did not commence firing until 1 P.M. Japanese casualties were still low at this stage because the targets of the enemy artillery seemed to be mainly the IJA gun sites. But Sumi was very unhappy about having to launch an infantry offensive in broad daylight, especially since the friendly artillery had not come close to suppressing the Soviet guns. Orders were orders, however, and the best he could do was to try to exploit the terrain intelligently. The region of Nakano's right flank was utterly flat and sloped gradually upward in the direction of the enemy. Kokubu's sector, on the left, was "fairly good," with hills and some woods. Therefore Sumi would have Kokubu's battalion advance before Nakano's.

Even so, it was Nakano's 2nd Battalion that incurred the heaviest casualties on 25 August. Soon after it attacked, Nakano was slain by shell fragments, on his second day of combat. Tank gunfire killed his aide, the lieutenant who had been so solicitous since the major's arrival. The machine-gun company commander, another lieutenant who had been hurt earlier and had returned from the hospital, was hit twice on the 25th while fighting at a distance of 300 meters from the enemy. His second wound proved fatal. Only 12 men were left in the company, whose strength had previously been whittled down to 40 or 50. A mere corporal became acting company commander, and a first lieutenant took over the whole battalion.

Nakano had issued his battalion attack order by 1 P.M., from a site 2,000 meters northeast of Heights 780. Emphasis was placed on the right flank, the sector of the 7th Company, supported by a machine-gun squad. Not until 2:30 P.M. did the company jump off, but the terrain was so open (as Sumi had said) that the unit was raked by fire from artillery, tanks, and machine guns. Casualties were heavy, including two platoon leaders, but the Japanese managed to get to a point only 50 meters from the enemy positions. Soviet riflemen started to retreat, but the tanks kept firing from the rear, as did machine guns from emplacements 100 meters away. Although the first line of defenses was penetrated, by 3 P.M. the company commander and every platoon leader had been wounded. After concentrating their grenade launchers and machine guns, the surviving Japanese rushed repeatedly against the stubborn Soviet defenders of the second line. For the initial charge, the 1st Platoon could muster only 13 men; the 3rd Platoon, four. No more hand grenades were left in the latter platoon after this attack. A last charge took the second line at 4:15, from the dead angle on the flank. The senior survivor in the company, a sergeant, pulled the men together at 6:30 P.M. and had them dig in. "In the light of the setting sun, the silent battlefield looked desolate." Around 7 P.M., 20 or 30 Russian troops counterattacked the center of the 7th Company's positions but were driven off, while several tanks attacked from the left flank. The Japanese organized demolition teams. Night fell with the enemy 100 meters away. The 7th Company had begun the day with 75 officers and men; it ended up with only 35. Apart from four men who were wounded but remained behind, the company lost 15 killed and 21 evacuated, including the acting company commander, 2nd Lt. Odaka Fumio.

Since frontal attacks against barbed-wire-screened hostile positions on the dunes failed repeatedly, says Sumi, his men had had to resort to flank assaults to get at machine-gun nests from the reverse slope. It was necessary to use this tactic often, in order to advance step by step. General Morita, Sumi adds, was situated to the right rear and could not observe the actions of the 26th Infantry. The colonel tried to hoist a Japanese flag to indicate the location of the regimental command post, but it drew enemy artillery fire and had to be lowered. When the fighting abated at sunset, the situation was confused and grave. The regiment had lost a total of 35 killed (including Major Nakano and the two other officers) and 70 wounded, of whom two were officers. But at least Negami finally made it back, bringing four drums of wonderful water and two loads of rice balls.[25]

General Hata felt that his artillery corps' fire in close support of the infantry charges achieved considerable results on 25 August, in conjunction with friendly air bombing. The front-line foot soldiers, in fact, thanked the artillery, as did the soldiers in the area of the division command post. Nevertheless, the infantrymen could seize only a corner of the enemy defenses, and no further progress was visible by evening.[26]

On the basis of his observations of the counteroffensive on 25 August, Komatsubara agreed that the artillery corps had rendered effective cooperation but concluded that the Morita brigade had "lacked zeal" to advance in close concert with the supporting fire. The troops had eventually stopped at the point of "peeling off one skin" of the enemy positions, and the offensive had simply not progressed as expected. The view of the Kwantung Army, as expressed by Hattori, was that the attack of the 25th had failed because General Morita lacked "aggressive fighting spirit," although admittedly the brigade did not possess sufficient combat strength.[27]

Even after nightfall on 25 August, Sumi had no idea of the situation elsewhere in the Japanese lines. Communication with higher headquarters depended entirely on radio, which was frequently out of action. The colonel hated to leave his unit for the second night in a row, but he felt that he must talk to Morita. From volunteers, he chose two soldiers and ran through the grass in the moonlight to the brigade command post, drawing enemy machine-gun fire en route. When he got to the general's command post, Sumi asked Morita to come to his own headquarters and observe the situation at firsthand, since the regiment's location was somewhat higher and was almost at the forwardmost positions. From the brigade, the distance was 1,200 or 1,300 meters across open terrain; by daylight, it would be impossible to evade enemy bombardment. Admittedly, reconnaissance needed the brightness of dawn, which meant that Morita would have had to stay overnight and not return until the next night. At minimum, said Sumi, an aide should be sent to the regiment. Morita did not accept the colonel's suggestion, but at least a phone line was installed between brigade and regiment, buried to the degree possible.

That the combat situation was not developing well on other sectors had become painfully apparent to Sumi when numerous stragglers from IJA units started showing up on 25 August with their individual rifles and machine guns and asked to join the 26th Infantry. From his discussion with Morita, the colonel realized that the 28th and 26th regiments were the last organized Japanese infantry units at the front, after the destruction or pullback of adjacent forces. Facing Heights 780, the Ashizuka and Sumi regiments were protruding like the "long nose of a goblin" (*tengusan*). Undoubtedly, Sumi raised the matter of the folly of daylight attacks.[28]

On 24 August, the Japanese counteroffensive had not succeeded with 5-7 infantry battalions and scant artillery cooperation. On the 25th, the attacks made little progress with four battalions and better gunfire support. To dare a third frontal offensive at the same location and again by daylight, with steadily diminishing manpower, suggests the validity of criticism that Japanese army leadership was often unimaginative, ponderous, and repetitive. Nevertheless, orders were forthcoming to resume the attack on General Morita's sector on 26 August. At first glance, it would seem that the idea originated at the Sixth Army headquarters of Ogisu and Fujimoto, who had overcome Komatsubara's original objections even before 24 August. There is evidence, however, that the Sixth Army now preferred to await the impending arrival of the rest of the 7th Division and to combine Morita's brigade with it before reopening the offensive. It is true that General Morita was still receiving his instructions directly from the 23rd Division and not from the Sixth Army, a fact that may color his identification of the source of decision-making. But it is his impression that there was some "mismatch" in the thinking of higher headquarters, and that the 23rd Division, in particular, was "pushing a bit."[29]

The atmosphere at Komatsubara's command post on 25/26 August is illuminated by Hata. First, the artillery corps commander reveals, on the 25th a familiar refrain contributed to the decision to hurl the Japanese infantry forward: information from the air force that the enemy was in retreat. Second, although the "grandiose intention of enveloping and annihilating the foe was about to collapse after only two days," Hata was convinced by the combat on 25 August that it would not be too difficult to break through the enemy positions if only the IJA foot soldiers could push forward "a little bit more." Prompt and close coordination between the infantry and artillery was indispensable, however.[30]

Komatsubara's operations order to the 14th Brigade, issued at 6 P.M. on 25 August, originally prescribed an offensive at dawn, with the infantry jumping off after artillery preparation. Hata instructed his close-support artillery units (the battery of Type 90 field guns and the battery of 15-cm. howitzers, under the command of Miyao) to make detailed arrangements with the infantry on Morita's sector. Morita issued his order at 8 P.M., calling for his front-line forces to consolidate quickly at their current locations and prepare to continue the offensive. But, probably influenced by Sumi, the brigade commander convinced Komatsubara to authorize a night operation.[31]

General Morita explains why he soon backed away from his own recommendation. The division order called for him to take the enemy's main defenses on Heights 780-791, still 2,000 meters away. Since daytime movement across such distances under fire would be very costly, there was some opinion that a night attack would be preferable. Morita reviewed the strength of the Ashizuka regiment, which was nearest to him and would bear the brunt of the offensive on the right wing. From 1,000 officers and men at the outset, Ashizuka now had only about 500, but even this number was not fully available. In practice, only 200 rifles were operational. To seize the objective by a night assault was feasible, but securing it and supplying it were the problem. Morita decided against this type of operation, and it was called off "for reasons of lack of preparation, etc."[32] The Sixth Army's official operations order, issued at 2:30 A.M. on the 26th, merely states that enemy resistance had been strong on 25 August, the 23rd Division's offensive had not developed as anticipated, reinforcements were being committed with continuation of the offensive in view, and the 23rd Division was to resume the attacks on the 26th.[33]

After breakfasting on hardtack on 26 August, another clear and hot day, the infantrymen in Hotta's 1st Battalion on the right flank of the Ashizuka regiment tried to advance against the next immediate target, Soviet positions 400 meters away. In a supporting heavy-machine-gun platoon, the master sergeant could be heard yelling at his men not to waste ammunition. Since the enemy held the usual topographical advantage, wrote one gunner, the unit could not break through the defenses and the offensive was checked.

Casualties had continued to soar in the Ashizuka regiment. By the 26th, for example, the 2nd Company had already been destroyed as a fighting force, having lost its commander and 31 men killed, plus 61 wounded. The strength of the 1st Battalion had been decreased by half. No officers were left in the 1st Company, and the two other infantry companies in the Hotta battalion had acting commanders following the death of their chiefs. Ashizuka's regimental aide, Maj. Ishida Ainosuke, was wounded on 26 August. Morita says that enemy bombardment was extremely severe on this day, from morning to night. Cannon and howitzer fire was bad enough, but the high-angle mortars were worse, since the Japanese front lines were in a depression and the mortar shells would come straight down, bounce, and cause more casualties after striking. This was how a splendid medical lieutenant in Ashizuka's regiment was slain. The trenches shook with explosions, and it was impossible for the assault troops to jump off. An entirely new combat sensation gripped Morita: drowsiness.

On the evening of 26 August, the 1st Battalion formed a 30-man team to collect corpses lying in no-man's-land. After moving up several hundred meters, the force ran into 70 or 80 men marching in their direction from the right rear. Lying prone, the Japanese called out a challenge; but instead of responding, the approaching soldiers began to deploy. A hand grenade hurtled in and wounded five or six men. Now squeaking noises could be heard—the familiar sound of Maxim water-cooled heavy machine guns being trundled on little wheels. The Japanese ambushed the enemy with rifle fire and then charged. Later, it was heard that the Russians thought they had been attacked by a battalion, from the fury of the charge. As for the retrieval mission, while the unit was pulling itself together and getting ready to proceed, it was ordered by the 1st Battalion to return.[34]

The effectiveness of artillery shells in breaking telephone and electric wires, as the result of air-blast concussion, had recently been noted by Komatsubara. On Sumi's sector, enemy bombardment cut the phone line to the brigade in 23 places on 26 August, and in 19 places on the 27th, despite many attempts to patch it.[35] Even the pine-tree landmark near the regimental command post was defoliated and then truncated by the third day of battle. Sumi tried to joke with and cheer up the troops, who had become quiet under the shellings. The casualties went on, for negligible or no gains. On the 26th, the regiment lost 18 killed and 54 wounded, including five officers, but Sumi estimates the forward progress on 25-26 August at only

150 meters at best. Clinging to the east side of Ipponmatsu, the 2nd Battalion was compelled to form a new 6th Company on the 27th, from platoons of the other companies. The old 7th Company had been reduced to 32 men by now. A second lieutenant who arrived on the evening of 26 August to serve as Kokubu's 3rd Battalion aide lasted overnight, being wounded the very next morning. "I hated to lose my key officers," Morita says, "but those youngsters had a tendency to stand instead of crouch, and enemy snipers were very accurate, even by moonlight."

Komatsubara's diary indicates that the offensive of 26 August was conducted continuously but did not advance. The Kwantung Army understood that the attack would be suspended and the advance forces withdrawn, while awaiting the arrival of the full 7th Division. On the night of the 26th, however, says General Morita, he was again ordered to attack next day—an order that he knew was impossible to carry out under the circumstances. Since he obviously could not admit this to his brigade, he merely issued instructions that present missions be continued. This could be understood to mean not to launch another offensive as such. In any case, Morita derived the feeling that, from around 27 August, the 23rd Division may have been "easing up," to the extent of being willing merely to carry on.[36]

After the drubbing they had taken since 24 August, the men of the Morita brigade dug in along the line of their farthest advance. The Russians launched a number of counterassaults in varying strength. At 4 P.M. on the 27th, after powerful bombardment, 20-30 enemy tanks and 300 infantrymen attacked on Sumi's sector, circling as close as 300 meters from the elements of Kokubu's 3rd Battalion deployed farthest on the Japanese left wing. Whenever tanks were knocked out, the Soviet infantry would flee, only to return with new armor. The Russians placed trees on their tanks, which rumbled forward at low speed. It was like a "moving forest," and the Japanese could hear but not see the tanks. One of the armored vehicles knocked out by the low-velocity regimental guns attached to Kokubu must have been a commander's tank, for the Russians sent other machines that struggled for two days to tow it away. Since only one rapid-fire and two 75-mm. regimental guns were still available, and since the latter pieces' optimum mode was indirect firing, the Japanese had the two smaller-caliber, high-angle battalion guns conducting "intimidating" fire too. As the acting battery commander, the only officer left in his unit, explains: "Battalion guns could not destroy hostile armor. In fact, we tried not to hit the targets directly with them! Our purpose was to convince the enemy that the Japanese were 'still in business.' It was a kind of 'camouflage' effort to conceal our actual weakness in firepower." In this particular action, Kokubu's infantry and the regimental guns claimed to have burned five tanks and killed 30 men. The Japanese incurred 36 casualties, however, and enemy artillery knocked out the last rapid-fire gun.[37]

On Ashizuka's front, after dusk on 27 August, another team was formed by the 1st Battalion to retrieve bodies. The party immediately collided with enemy forces, fought hand to hand, and suffered heavy casualties; but the battalion aide led a charge that drove off the foe, who left behind three Maxims, 30 rifles, and many grenades. On the night of the 28th, in Sumi's district, 400 Soviet riflemen attacked the 2nd Battalion, now temporarily commanded by 2nd Lt. Hoshino Kazuhiko. Grenade launchers threw the enemy troops into confusion at 400 meters and they retreated, two or three of them allegedly crying. The 7th Company repulsed small attacks by 30 soldiers at 6 A.M. on the 28th, and by 50 men at 8 P.M.

Huddling in their holes on 28-29 August, Morita's troops—still wearing summer garb—shivered as the chilling night winds of approaching winter began to blow in from the northern steppes. Sumi's units were devouring the delicious *nigirimeshi* rice balls prepared by Lieutenant Negami and his men, but in Ashizuka's regiment the soldiers ate only dry hardtack for about a week before rice finally arrived on the 30th.

Meanwhile, the Morita brigade had reverted to the command of its parent 7th Division, effective as soon as the latter reached the Lake Mohorehi area. On 29 August, Morita was ordered to withdraw his regiments 2,000 hard-earned meters to their original jump-off site near Heights 750. The 2nd Battalion of Sumi's regiment issued its own order at 11 P.M. and called for assembly by 1:50 A.M. Pullback certainly proceeded more easily than advance; by 3 A.M. the units had "disengaged cleverly" and reached the rendezvous without interference. But General Morita was tormented by this experience of retreating, which he had never done before. Should he strike one blow at the enemy before leaving, or should he just fall back quietly? He decided on the latter course, pulled out everything at once, and maintained combat deployment all the way, ready to reverse course and fight if necessary. When the men had fallen back, adds Sumi, they were relatively far from enemy artillery "for the first time in ages."[38]

Having dispatched Yano and Tsuji to the front promptly, the Kwantung Army was kept abreast of the outline of IJA counteroffensive operations from the outset. In the early afternoon of 24 August, it was learned from Tsuji that, by 8 A.M., the 23rd Division had massed five infantry battalions plus five field artillery, two 15-cm. howitzer, and two 10-cm. cannon batteries at Heights 752, about 10 kilometers southeast of Nomonhan, and that the forces were preparing for the offensive southward. Immediately afterward, a 23rd Division wire reported that the enemy was still attacking positions south of the Holsten, and that there was a high probability of Soviet offensive action directed against the right rear (north of the river), given the Japanese deployment. The Sixth Army had set up combat headquarters at Nomonhan.[39]

The Kwantung Army, it will be recalled, had decided on its own, as early as 23 August, to advance the other half of the 7th Division to Hailar, though retaining it under Hsinking's direct control. After evaluating the battle situation next day, Yano sent a message from Hailar to Kwantung Army commander Ueda, in mid-afternoon of the 24th, regarding the allocation of the new division. "We are inclined to deem it necessary," recommended Yano, that the main body of the 7th Division be assigned to the Sixth Army immediately upon arrival. Over an hour before Yano's wire was received, he was sent a message via the Sixth Army but originating in the Kwantung Army's Operations Section that the 7th Division—which was to reach Hailar in increments between 1 P.M. on the 25th and the night of the 26th—would be placed under Ogisu's command as soon as it arrived. This reinforcement was being dispatched for the purpose of insuring the annihilation of enemy forces. The need for a smashing blow had only been intensified by developments on the international scene—namely, the just-concluded German-Soviet nonaggression pact. Nevertheless, there had been no change in the established guidelines for dealing with the Nomonhan affair. The Kwantung Army operations staff then volunteered some strategic counsel for consideration: if a Japanese unit was shifted from the Amukulang-Saienjō (Saltern) area southeast of Kanchuerhmiao against hostile forces that had moved around the right wing of the 23rd Division toward Lake Abutara, "would they not fall prey to us?"[40]

The Kwantung Army had been expecting or hoping that the Russian assaults would slow down within a few days of their start on 20 August, as had been the case with the mini-offensive earlier in the month, because of presumable difficulties with supply. But the Soviet drive only intensified, and countermeasures were slow in the making and ineffective in the handling. Would even the commitment of the 7th Division suffice? News from Tsuji, received in the early hours of 25 August, indicated that the 23rd Division had not been able to seize Heights 780 by the preceding evening, that the offensive was to be reopened at dawn on the 25th, that resistance was unprecedentedly tenacious, and that many excellent enemy tanks had appeared. At this stage, Tsuji recommended the immediate commitment of the rapid-fire guns of the 2nd and 4th divisions.[41]

Although this may not have been much to go on, a trend was emerging. Quite properly, Operations Section chief Terada grew nervous about the battle situation and, that morning, began to argue vigorously for the immediate dispatch of two more infantry divisions—the 2nd Division from the eastern frontier at Mutanchiang and the 4th from the north at Chiamussu. But since transfers on such a scale would weaken the strategic defense of Manchuria and might seem to be an overreaction or even interference with the Sixth Army's direction of operations, Hattori and Shimanuki Takeharu recommended delaying a decision until the combat picture became clearer. In the evening, Tsuji transmitted further unencouraging information. The Morita brigade, he reported, had attacked on the Heights 780 front since morning, but enemy resistance was powerful and no breakthrough was foreseeable in the near future. Fire bottles were not working against the new enemy armor, and about half of all the IJA rapid-fire guns—the only effective weapon—had been knocked out by now. This was why, as Tsuji had already reported, quick reinforcement by antitank batteries was essential.[42]

The Kwantung Army chief of staff then sent the High Command a message drafted by Hattori reporting on the redeployment, arrival times, and reassignment of the 7th Division and the new rapid-fire batteries; on the Sixth Army's inability to take the Heights 780 objective; and on the firm retention of the 23rd Division's defensive positions against superior forces of infantry and armor. In particular, intelligence from the front was cited to the effect that the Soviet tanks seemed to be more effective than any encountered earlier, and that close-quarter firebomb attacks apparently had no effect on some of them. The provision of rapid-fire guns was imperative.[43]

Meanwhile, Hattori prepared a message, on Terada's behalf, to be sent to Tsuji. The Kwantung Army still deemed it imperative to mete out a "stunning blow" to hostile forces on the right shore of the Halha. As Tsuji undoubtedly knew, the Sixth Army was being reinforced by the main body of the 7th Division plus eight rapid-fire batteries slated to arrive at Hailar between 25 and 27 August. The Kwantung Army needed to know immediately whether Tsuji believed it necessary to dispatch further reinforcements of "divisional or other size."[44] In other words, the staff in Hsinking wanted to learn whether the 2nd Division should be committed now.

In the absence of Tsuji at the front, Sixth Army Chief of Staff Fujimoto rushed a reply to the Kwantung Army in the late afternoon of the 25th. The Sixth Army agreed entirely regarding the need to smash the foe. Additional issue of antitank weapons and ammunition was especially requested. Given the opposing ratios of strength at the front, the success of the offensive plan also seemed to require reinforcement by an elite division in addition to the 7th. The Sixth Army wished to know right away whether this request could be met, inasmuch as "it had a great bearing on the present conduct of combat operations."[45]

The Sixth Army's language about the operational impact of another reinforcing division drew the Kwantung Army's particular attention. Apparently, if the 2nd Division were committed, the 7th Division would be employed mainly to secure the positions held currently by the 23rd Division; but if no additional reinforcements were sent, the 7th Division would become crucial to the Sixth Army's offensive plan. To the whole operations staff in Hsinking, it appeared that the defensive capability of the 23rd Division had been overtaxed, which meant that the 7th Division would have to be employed to secure the positions. Consequently, it was decided to release the 2nd Division to the Sixth Army as soon as possible. The approval of General Ueda and the senior staff was obtained and Ogisu was notified. It took until 2 P.M. on 26 August to arrange the movement not only of the 2nd Division but also of a heavy artillery regiment, rapid-fire batteries, and motor units.[46]

The operations officers in the Kwantung Army were privately unhappy with the recent silence of the High Command concerning the dispatch of "strategic-size corps" from other commands to beef up the straitened forces in Manchuria. Starting in June, the central authorities had released two heavy artillery regiments and four truck companies, plus balloon, signal, and antiaircraft units. In early July, the AGS had even offered to transfer the 5th Infantry Division from China, if needed. Since that time, Japanese losses had mounted at Nomonhan and the combat situation had deteriorated, yet there had been no further mention of divisional transfers. It was the Kwantung Army's correct surmise that the High Command feared escalation of the Nomonhan conflict—"a dreadful misunderstanding," according to Hattori. That the central authorities comprehended the developing danger to Manchukuo as a whole, at least from the Kwantung Army's standpoint, became apparent when an AGS message was received in Hsinking in the late afternoon of 25 August. Consideration was being given, said the telegram, to the dispatch of reinforcements, in view of the situation at Nomonhan. The Kwantung Army was asked to report on its prospective operational plans in general and on the current status of the 7th Division in particular.[47]

The Kwantung Army was of course pleased to reply to this inquiry, and Hattori prepared the message promptly on the 25th for the chief of staff. Two remaining infantry regiments plus 7th Division headquarters would start to arrive at Hailar from Tsitsihar this very night, 25/26 August. With the strength available until now, the Sixth Army's offensive did not seem to have progressed. Though there had been no change in the Kwantung Army's concept of handling the Nomonhan affair, it was deemed vital to deal a smashing blow locally to enemy forces in the vicinity of the Halha, regardless of policies adopted in response to the present situation or the altered conditions in Europe. In this connection, the Kwantung Army had just taken steps to place all of its rapid-fire batteries (except the 11th Division's) and the 9th Heavy Field Artillery Regiment under the Sixth Army's command.

Thus far, the Kwantung Army's message had not addressed the delicate matter of strategic reinforcement. Covertly, the release of the 5th Infantry Division was very much desired at this stage; but Hattori was careful not to incorporate more than a hint of this in a clause saying that the Kwantung Army was conducting separate study of the matter of an increase in strategic corps. This ostensibly referred to the 2nd Division, which fell within Hsinking's own jurisdiction, but it was hoped that Tokyo would discern the underlying intent—to call attention to the 5th Division, which was controlled by the High Command. Specifically, the message limited itself to a request for quick reinforcement, if possible, by powerful elements of less than strategic size—namely, the 59th Air Group and its full complement of supporting units. Lastly, the Kwantung Army advised the High Command that the enemy had concentrated all available forces and was planning to win a "guaranteed" local victory, but it was not believed the foe would expand the battlefront to other sectors, with that strength.[48]

By early morning on 26 August, the Kwantung Army learned from the Sixth Army that although the defensive units were holding their positions on both sides of the Holsten, the 23rd Division's latest offensive, begun in the morning of the 25th, had not made much progress by nightfall.[49] Since the fighting in the Heights 780 area seemed to have calmed down, Tsuji had left for Sixth Army headquarters, where an unpleasant scene ensued. Ogisu showed him a Kwantung Army message indicating that not only the 7th but also the 2nd and 4th divisions were being assigned to the Sixth Army. "Tsuji-*kun*," Ogisu supposedly exulted, "how singularly fortunate I am! I performed to the hilt in the Hsuchow operation and now I have been given a new arena and another four divisions!" Tsuji was disgusted. Was Ogisu dreaming of medals and personal commendations? Did he comprehend the difficult circumstances afflicting the division commander at the front? The sight of a whiskey bottle on the general's desk did not improve Tsuji's reaction. After conferring with Yano at the headquarters in Chiangchunmiao, Tsuji went back to Hsinking, where he arrived on the evening of the 26th.

The Kwantung Army staff had been particularly worried about whether Fui Heights and the positions south of the Holsten could be secured. From Tsuji, it was learned that Ioki had "unabashedly abandoned" his bastion and retreated to safety, and that the offensive below the Holsten was a failure. "We felt dismal," wrote Hattori. This day, 26 August, saw the Kwantung Army overcome any lingering objections and reach a decision to commit the 4th Division as well as the last heavy artillery and almost every rapid-fire gun under its control in Manchuria. As Hattori puts it, since the

Kwantung Army was determined to smash the foe "at any cost," it had been decided to hurl all the strategic reserves and artillery into the fray. In other words, a calculated strategic risk was being taken: to wage a decisive campaign on the western front, at the expense of the hitherto-crucial east.[50]

The Kwantung Army, however, was becoming uncomfortable with the way the Sixth Army was deploying the 7th Division. Instead of securing the old defenses, it was being allocated to key points behind them, thus imposing an unrealistic burden on the tottering 23rd Division. "Probably the Sixth Army had no better alternative at the time," generously notes the Kwantung Army journal, "but it gave us a strange sensation at Hsinking." Directly involved in these redeployments, brigade commander Morita agrees in almost the same words: "I had a funny feeling because the new 7th Division units were not being thrown into the front but were held mainly around Sixth Army headquarters." For example, after reverting to its original affiliation from Tsitsihar days—Maj. Gen. Yoshizawa Tadao's 13th Infantry Brigade—the 26th Regiment was trucked back to Lake Mohorehi, where it became the 7th Division's reserve, northeast of the command post. The main body of the fresh 27th Regiment—two battalions—went into Sixth Army reserve.[51]

Senior staff officer Hamada, however, provides an insight into Sixth Army thinking. Ogisu and his staff judged that after reaching their initial objectives, the Russians would turn to an attack against the positions near Mohorehi, striking against the Japanese lines north and south of the Holsten. Only later was it realized that enemy forces would stop near the frontier they claimed, occupy positions, send ahead elements to the heights west of Lake Abutara, and undertake almost no aggressive action against Sixth Army defenses near Lake Mohorehi. Hamada felt impatient, wishing that the main body of the 7th Division would arrive sooner, for he was afraid that the 23rd Division could not hold out on both shores of the Holsten if nothing was done. Fujimoto tried to be reassuring. Division commander Kunisaki Noboru, he said, warranted confidence; the general might seem "as shy as a maiden at the outset, but he would be as bold as a lion in the end." "I waited on tiptoe for the 7th Division to come up," recalls Hamada, who greatly feared that the Sixth Army's defenses would crumble quickly, as the 23rd Division's had done. There was also concern about the difficulty of future operational guidance in the face of enemy interference with rear supply lines, for scarcely any countermeasures had been taken to cope with tank-infantry forces that might plunge to the vicinity of Chiangchunmiao. Although the 7th Division's last units finally did arrive "somehow" by 27 August, after encountering little enemy disturbance on the way, they were new on the battlefield and their deployments were far from complete.

Part of the pressure exerted upon the Kwantung Army and the Sixth Army stemmed from the slow realization of the disparities in strength between the opposing forces—of the enormity of the Soviet order of battle involved at Nomonhan. The Japanese, for instance, were making much of the arrival of the main body of the 7th Division, but Yoshizawa's 13th Brigade was bringing only six infantry battalions totaling about 3,600 men: 1,915 in Col. Sekine Kyūtarō's 25th Regiment, and 1,690 in Col. Sannomiya Mitsuji's (Manji's) 27th Regiment. An additional 1,235 men were coming in the three battalions of Col. Hirayama Yoshirō's 7th Field Artillery Regiment. These increments were a "drop in the bucket," for—according to the Sixth Army's intelligence as of 25 August or so—the enemy had already committed at least two rifle divisions and had achieved aerial supremacy. Against such odds, says Hamada, recent experience had demonstrated that there was no hope of succeeding in the event of resumption of the Japanese offensive, even if the whole 7th Division were put into the lines.[52]

An even grimmer estimate emerged at Kwantung Army headquarters upon Tsuji's return to Hsinking. From the well-marked map he had taken from a slain Soviet officer, it was apparent that the Russians had committed three rifle divisions, five tank brigades, and several corps artillery regiments in the front line, and had two rifle divisions and one or two tank brigades in the second line. Such forces exceeded the Intelligence Section's judgment by a factor of two, and exceeded Japanese strength by a factor of four or five. In addition, as Tsuji had been reporting from the front, lately the Soviets were employing high-speed medium tanks unlike the vehicles so easily knocked out in early July. Antitank mines were ineffective, as were fire bottles, because of nets girding the armor now. The once slow and backward Russian forces were manifesting the features of a revolutionary army, amassing tremendous strength and changing both weapons and tactics very rapidly.[53]

Building upon the latest intelligence available in Hsinking and Tokyo, the Kwantung Army eventually prepared the following analysis of total Soviet forces committed at Nomonhan: for the initial offensive on 20 August, 45,000 men and three rifle divisions, 350-500 tanks and 340 armored cars, 210 heavy guns in several artillery brigades, and at least 200 planes; by the end of the fighting, three or four rifle divisions, five mechanized brigades (430 tanks and 430 armored cars), one regiment of army general reserve artillery, several regiments of army corps artillery, and three air brigades (500-700 planes). Perhaps the most impressive estimated figure contrasted total troop strength: 100,000 to 120,000 Russian troops against 70,000 Japanese.[54]

It had been Zhukov's intention to circle the Japanese, compress them, and then smash them by a series of concentrated hammer blows, first to the south of the Holsten, then to the north. The IJA counterattack launched on 24 August in the zone southeast of Nomonhan was planned, say the Russians, to break the ring and relieve the encircled forces. Centripetal in design, it seemed to be directed mainly against the 80th Rifle Regiment of the 57th Division (and the 8th Armored Brigade), which were engaged in defending the northeast slopes of the Heights 780-791 sector (Great Sands). Resisting stubbornly, the 80th Regiment dealt heavy losses to the attackers. Next day, with air support, the Japanese tried very hard again, hitting the junction between the 80th Regiment's battalions in the line, but failing once more. From reserve, Zhukov committed the 6th Tank Brigade and a rifle regiment.[55]

On 26 August, Southern Force commander Potapov unleashed a decisive counterassault. The 6th Tank Brigade was to conduct a two-pointed blow simultaneously from behind the wings of the 80th Regiment as the Japanese attackers approached the Russian positions. IJA units (on the Ashizuka regiment's sector?) were able to check the left prong of the tank brigade with intense artillery fire. When the right wing of the Soviet tank force struck soon afterward, however, the Japanese on that front (the Sumi regiment?) were taken by surprise. Their antitank capability was smashed quickly and they lost more than two companies overrun by armor and gunfire.

During three days of fighting, the Japanese incurred grievous losses. Eventually demoralized by the armored attacks, they gave up their offensive after 26 August. Soviet infantry of the Southern and Northern forces had further contracted the circle by the end of the 26th. Japanese escape routes to the east were severed entirely by now. The approach of reserves was thwarted by the Soviet air force, whose bombers conducted 218 sorties and dropped 96,000 kilograms of bombs on targets in the Nomonhan, Uzuru pond, and Arshaan areas on 24-25 August. Striking ten times, Russian fighters downed 74 enemy planes between 24 and 27 August.[56]

In appraising the cause for the failure of the IJA offensive of 24-26 August, Japanese military analysts are particularly impressed by the Soviet troops' grasp of topographical advantages and their enthusiasm for and skill at digging in. By 21 August, Russian forces striking at the Japanese left wing had already reached Heights 780. Next day, they promptly secured the belt of high ground extending two kilometers eastward to Heights 791, paying particular heed to dispersion and cover. Had the Russians really foreseen a Japanese counterattack along this sector so early, or had they intended all along to advance only to the Heights 780-791 complex on this wing? The frontier claimed by the Soviet-MPR side seemed to be seven kilometers away, but the high-ground advantage of 40-50 meters did give the Russians a view that stretched 12 or 13 kilometers beyond Heights 780. Japanese forces did not discover the barbed wire until the night of the 24th. Hata was so impressed by Soviet concealment, he thought the enemy had either departed or else had not fully entered the positions. Emplacements were scattered in a "splashed pattern" (*kasuri*) and were camouflaged cleverly. Objectives that the Japanese fired on or charged against "disappeared" from the battleground, while a very real but "invisible" firing network was able to check the advancing troops. The Russians effectively concerted the actions of their 80th Rifle Regiment with those of their artillery and the armored brigades. Superior Soviet firepower and commanding terrain were too much for the Japanese again.[57]

The portions of the IJA operational field manual (*sakusen yōmurei*) dealing with offensive actions emphasized careful battle preparations, deployment in depth, and tactics of encirclement directed against the flank or flank-rear of the foe, preferably with powerful forces but undertaken even when resources were inferior. Although the Japanese assaults beginning on 24 August were aimed at the outermost Russian flank on the right and thus satisfied military doctrine, they took place in piecemeal fashion, without sufficient preparation, preliminary artillery softening-up, or (especially important) prior reconnaissance. Clearly, Soviet powers of resistance were woefully underestimated. Four days were consumed before the offensive even got under way—almost as though Russian activities in the interim did not matter. Against the alerted and potent combination of Soviet armor, infantry, artillery, and aviation, the Japanese employed mainly foot soldiers, in unimpressive strength, and without coordination, depth, tactical reserves, or logistical backup. The paucity of Japanese assets was accompanied by stolid or unimaginative generalship, which was why even Sixth Army officers wished that the Kwantung Army staff would lend a hand. As General Morita says, IJA adherence to orders was extremely strict, which was fine when the tempo of battle was slow, but which could lead to disaster when combat was fluid and severe.

After the IJA offensive failed on the first day and friendly elements on the right and left were pulled out, Morita's small force was asked to pick up the entire slack, an impossible assignment that the general could not decline but for which he was held responsible when he tried and failed. Morita asks military historians to consider the true battlefield strength of a given unit like his. Such an analysis would disclose that the "brigade" he was supposed to be commanding in the 24 August offensive existed only on paper from the outset. In addition, one of his two incomplete regiments, Sumi's 26th, had always belonged to another brigade and was attached only at the last moment. Problems of command and control over such a relatively weak and improvised force were exacerbated by the 50-percent casualty level that was incurred so quickly.[58] The close-quarter attack capability that the Japanese infantry so extolled by definition demanded closing with the enemy, preferably by dawn or dusk or night, in order to break his last resistance. To attempt a 4,000- or 5,000-meter cross-country attack on foot in broad daylight sounds more like the Crimea in 1854 than modern war in 1939. And is it not ironic that Russian gunners mowed down both Lord Cardigan's light cavalry brigade at Balaklava and the charging Kobayashi-Morita infantry brigades at Nomonhan?

34

The End Nears

*And how can man die better
Than facing fearful odds
For the ashes of his fathers
And the temples of his Gods?*

—Thomas B. Macaulay,
"Horatius," 27

The first phases of the Soviet offensive were concluded by 27 August, when Zhukov ordered his army corps to annihilate the last Japanese resistance south and north of the Holsten. In conjunction with the 602nd and 603rd regiments of the 82nd Rifle Division to his left, Potapov's Southern Force was to wipe out pockets remaining on the Noro Heights front. Prior to the unfurling of this decisive effort, say the Russians, a disorganized force of Japanese in battalion strength tried to break out at daybreak on the 27th. Moving east along the valley of the Holsten, these troops were hit by artillery fire and then attacked by a reconnaissance company and an infantry company from the 127th Infantry Regiment, which had taken up positions on the south shore. A portion of the Japanese were destroyed, and the remnants fled to the north bank, where they were finished off by the 9th Armored Brigade.

Another battalion-size group of Japanese, with some 75-mm. cannon and heavy machine guns, launched a new effort to escape eastward, near 11 A.M., but were wiped out by forces of the 57th Rifle Division. At 5 P.M., a large formation of IJA officers and noncoms who made a last attempt to break out of the Russian vise were shattered near the crossing on the Holsten. Thus, by the close of the 27th, the Southern Force, centering on the 57th Rifle Division but with the assistance of the neighboring 82nd Division, had essentially "extinguished the last flames of Japanese resistance" below the Holsten. All the IJA defenses in that sector had been secured by the two Soviet rifle divisions, and the 127th Rifle Regiment had crossed to the north side of the Holsten.[1]

Colonel Hasebe's mixed detachment of three infantry battalions had been struggling to defend the old positions in the key Noro Heights zone below the Holsten, along a too-broad frontage of about six kilometers. Against the Russians' 602nd Regiment of the 82nd Rifle Division, nearest to the river, Miyazaki's 2nd BGU Battalion was deployed. On the next sector to the south, the 603rd Rifle Regiment was pitted against Sugitani's 1st BGU Battalion. Hasebe's extreme wing, beyond Sugitani, was held by Kajikawa's 2nd Battalion of the 28th Regiment. Here, the Soviet attack was mounted by the 293rd Rifle Regiment of the 57th Division. The left rear of the Hasebe detachment was supposed to be covered by Colonel Morita's 71st Infantry, but that regiment had been chewed up by the Russians and, in addition, had been ordered to detach forces to support the right flank of the Japanese offensive of 24 August. Since Morita was well aware of the danger to the adjoining Hasebe detachment, he had originally limited his subtraction of forces to one battalion. When a division staff officer came to the 71st Regiment on 22 August, Morita pointed out the threat, but the visitor merely exhorted the unit and took no particular countermeasures. The thrust by the main force of the 23rd Division, he assured Morita, would carry it to the east side of Noro Heights.

The division staff officer, undoubtedly Captain Itō, also intimated to Hasebe that, in case of emergency, the detachment might pull back to the region of Heights 749, approximately four kilometers northeast of Noro, linking up with the right flank of Colonel Morita's regiment located in the vicinity of Nigesorimot. Such an emergency materialized after 23 August, by which time Soviet tanks had penetrated between Hasebe and Morita and were prowling around the area of the Holsten bridges. On the morning of the 25th, Hasebe's radio apparatus was destroyed, leaving him with no communication capability except some carrier pigeons and a wireless set belonging to the 1st Field Artillery Battalion. Thereafter the detachment commander was in the dark about the larger situation involving friendly as well as enemy forces.

It was becoming painfully clear by 25 August that the 23rd Division's offensive was not succeeding and that relief was not in sight for Hasebe's surrounded troops. At the same time that contact was lost with higher headquarters, Sugitani learned from the detachment that Kajikawa was planning a last sortie with his whole force. To Sugitani, this amounted to nothing less than an invitation to annihilation, for Kajikawa's left flank was wide open, and there was neither radio nor telephone communication between Hasebe's battalions. Indeed, the colonel had not been able to call a staff conference, and Sugitani had never met Kajikawa, the neighboring unit commander, during the course of the combat. The loss of the Kajikawa battalion, Sugitani was convinced, would bring about the collapse of his own battalion and of the whole detachment, by a kind of "domino" effect. Sugitani therefore conveyed a recommendation to Hasebe that the two exposed battalions be pulled back a bit instead and inclined to the left. Kajikawa's sally was suspended.

By 1:30 P.M. on the 25th, it was apparent that Kajikawa's unit was being destroyed where it was. From Sugitani's command post, Soviet tank forces including flamethrowers could be seen overrunning the adjacent positions, and red flags were going up. Sugitani ordered his men to form a half-moon perimeter and fight on. At 3 P.M. a detachment order arrived with word that the main positions of the Kajikawa battalion had been overrun and that Sugitani and Miyazaki were to defend their posts to the last. As expected, the waves of destruction spread from Kajikawa's to Sugitani's sector. On the 26th, one company and one platoon on Sugitani's left wing were near annihilation. With their last rounds, the one surviving battalion-gun crew tried to lay down interdicting fire.

Although the division had called for last-ditch defense of Noro Heights, Sugitani knew that the detachment was out of touch; from the sound of the artillery, he could also tell that the Japanese offensive was "hopeless." Therefore he ordered his men, including the Takashima platoon from the Kajikawa battalion, to abandon Noro and pull back to the area of his command post. Sugitani moved his headquarters northward and left a company to cover the old site. But the enemy crushed the defenders with a ferocious assault, and Sugitani was obliged to contract his half-circle lines still further.

By nightfall on the 26th, Hasebe decided that the end was near. Outnumbered and outgunned impossibly from the beginning, the detachment was now out of ammunition. Food supplies had run out three days earlier; water, two days before. Overall casualties approximated 70 percent, and individual infantry companies had been whittled down to little more than 30 men. Since not much of a fighting force was available to him any longer, the colonel burned his classified documents and, after ordering his men to put up a good fight, prepared to take the last steps.

Inasmuch as the division's offensive had failed, Hasebe concluded that no purpose would be served by staying where he was, doing nothing and allowing his men to be exterminated. It seemed better to implement the division staff officer's earlier suggestion and to head for high ground to the east, where a linkup could be made with Colonel Morita's regiment, presumably located near Heights 758. In the evening of the 26th, Hasebe issued his order, on his own, as Ioki had done. That night, the Miyazaki battalion was to proceed along the river to Heights 749, south of the New Engineer Bridge, while Sugitani's battalion headed for the dunes 1,500 meters to the southeast. Kajikawa's unit, with the field artillery battalion and other elements directly controlled by the detachment, should proceed to Kobuyama ("Lump Hill"), northeast of Heights 758, the former site of the 7th Heavy Field Artillery Regiment. Hasebe said he would accompany the Sugitani battalion.

At 11:30 P.M. on the 26th, the regimental-gun battery commander brought Sugitani the detachment order to break through enemy lines and withdraw, starting at 1 A.M. Sugitani was puzzled by a number of things. Why had it taken over four hours (he thinks) for the order to reach him? Why were the field artillery battalion, detachment headquarters, and attached units supposed to leave with Kajikawa, whereas only Hasebe was to go with Sugitani? Had the message been garbled? There was no time to investigate. A medical lieutenant who had gone to reconnoiter the displacement of the aid station closer to the Miyazaki battalion came rushing back to report that the unit had already begun to pull back. This meant that Miyazaki, although located farther from Hasebe, had received the order first and had completed the assembly by the time Sugitani heard about the redeployment. Sugitani pressed ahead with the gradual extrication of his battalion and reached the designated point by 2 or 2:30 A.M. While digging in around 3 A.M., he observed a unit moving north, 200-300 meters to the east. When a runner reported that it was the detachment headquarters, Sugitani concluded that Hasebe had finally made it, although behind schedule. Yet when dawn broke, neither Hasebe nor his headquarters nor the Kajikawa battalion was anywhere to be seen, within a zone of four square kilometers.

The distances involved were not great—perhaps four kilometers to traverse at most. But each battalion was moving separately, almost company by company, without any coordination by the detachment, and in the presence of a very powerful, heavily armed, and mobile foe on all sides. In addition, there were many wounded soldiers to carry. It is not surprising that the units lost contact with each other, missed destinations and linkups, and became scattered.

At about 6 A.M. on the 27th, 30 or 40 Japanese soldiers dashed down to Sugitani's area from the north—artillerymen attached to Hasebe's headquarters. When their unit had tried to cross New Engineer Bridge they had been caught by the enemy and had lost their guns and their horses. Sugitani judged that Kajikawa had not assembled his force at Kobuyama after all, but must have tried to head for the river. It was necessary to concentrate what was left of the detachment, so Sugitani, as the senior officer, assumed command of both his and Miyazaki's battalion. A new defensive perimeter was set up at Akahage ("Red Bald") Heights, near the river, but enemy tanks attacked and ammunition ran out by afternoon. Under the hot sun, without water and food for the second day, Sugitani pondered a way to break out and rejoin friendly forces rather than sit there and meet a useless death. Since Russian machine guns were emplaced along the Holsten, Sugitani decided to risk a direct plunge against the enemy center, with a view to reaching Nigesorimot, away from the river, and hopefully the site of some elements of the 71st Infantry.

Around 9:30 P.M. on 27 August, the Japanese retreat resumed, but Sugitani had to veer left to avoid enemy armor. He and his men forded the Holsten at the point where it bends north, penetrated hostile lines, recrossed the river, and by morning on the 28th made it to the sector of the 7th Division west of Heights 749. Orders were forthcoming from the Sixth Army to cover the zone east of Lake Mohorehi. Since Hasebe was not to be found, Sugitani was sure that the colonel was dead.[2]

The pullback of the 71st Regiment exerted particularly baleful effects on Kajikawa's battalion covering the Hasebe detachment's left wing. Kajikawa had detected the arrival of enemy reinforcements on 23 August. Trucks and tanks could be observed moving steadily from the high ground across the Halha toward the Japanese left wing. As hostile artillery fire grew heavier and IJA batteries did not reply, it became increasingly difficult to retain the positions. Soviet mortar barrages caused particularly severe losses. Supply lines had been cut completely by enemy tanks and infantry; supplies of ammunition, food, and water were running very low. Only at great peril had one drum of water been conveyed from Hasebe's headquarters. Telephone communications with the detachment had been severed by gunfire, and runners had enormous difficulty getting through. To the left of Kajikawa, the neighboring platoon had been driven back by armor and infantry, thus enabling the enemy to get behind the battalion's defenses. By now, the major noted, his surviving officers and men were terribly tired and sluggish in their reactions. Troops in the front lines fell asleep even under artillery fire. Kajikawa tried to perk them up by visiting the advance positions.

While the 23rd Division was launching its counteroffensive on the 24th, Kajikawa's positions were hit particularly hard. Soviet tanks scouted for the enemy artillery, whose barrages grew heavier and more effective. Supported by mountain pieces and machine guns, the Russians attacked at close range with grenades. In the front lines everybody, including Kajikawa, fired small arms and threw grenades, oblivious of the mounting casualties and hampered by the shortage of ammunition. During the fighting, a machine gun platoon and a platoon of infantrymen were overrun by 150 enemy soldiers aboard armored cars and by nine tanks including flamethrowers. In a saddle east and to the rear of the battalion command post, the tanks discovered and burned the unit's scant cache of supplies. One of the tanks was knocked out by hand grenades thrown into the turret. Kajikawa deployed a platoon, plus 40 men sent to him by Hasebe, in an effort to shore up the crumbling lines.

When phone connections were restored temporarily on the 24th, Hasebe told Kajikawa to hold out as long as possible. Kajikawa called in his commanders and issued his last instructions, including one to destroy classified materials in an emergency. Since the major did not want his men to be wiped out "doing nothing," he also devised the sally to which Sugitani objected, as we saw. In view of the severe casualties, it would be difficult to hold out until noon next day. Therefore Kajikawa proposed plunging through the enemy lines on the night of 24/25 August, crossing the Halha, reaching Sambur Obo, and fighting to the last man. Hasebe rejected the recommendation, arguing that it would exert a negative effect on future operations by the detachment and would not help the 23rd Division anyhow. In this extremity, Kajikawa and his commanders decided to meet their deaths at the present positions. Joining together, they recited a Chinese-style poem (*kanshi*) which tells of Saigō Takamori's plight during the civil war of 1877 when, isolated and seemingly defeated, he broke through enemy lines and made it back to Kagoshima.[3] Then the Japanese gave three *Banzai!* cheers for the Emperor.

Kajikawa's defenses deteriorated even more on the 25th, under the crossfire of enemy forces in front and tanks in the rear. Soviet artillery pounded the positions without encountering counterbattery fire, and enemy infantry closed in with machine guns and put up double the number of red flags to signal their locations to their artillerymen. Some white flags were also visible on the crestline. Almost all of Kajikawa's battalion pieces and machine guns had been destroyed or buried in debris, but his two remaining grenade launchers kept firing effectively until they began to run out of ammunition. Enemy mortar fire grew fierce around 3 P.M., blasting apart sandbags and wrecking the trenches. An hour later, tanks got behind the battalion and completed the encirclement. Although Soviet artillery ceased firing after nightfall, infantry assaults continued. By now, a total of 55 men were alive in the whole Kajikawa battalion, and of these, only 16 were ablebodied.[4] Beyond rifles, four weapons were left: one grenade launcher, and one heavy and two light machine guns.

Kajikawa decided to take what was left of his main force, penetrate hostile lines that night, team up with the 7th Company (with whom contact had been made), and fight to the end as a battalion. Shortly after departing at 10 P.M., the 5th Company ran into enemy forces, whereupon the company commander decided, on his own initiative, to detour to the right. No further report was forthcoming, and runners disappeared too. Even worse, the rest of the battalion moved away from Kajikawa, followed the 5th Company, and went astray. Left with only six men, the major moved forward, evaded 30 enemy soldiers, and finally found the site of the 7th Company. The wandering main body arrived around midnight. Contact had been lost with the Takashima platoon, which had been screening the Hasebe detachment at Noro Heights; only later was it learned that command of Takashima's unit had been assumed by one of Sugitani's companies. After completing his deployments, Kajikawa got through to Hasebe's command post at 2 A.M. on the 26th and learned that the "lost" 5th Company had arrived there around midnight. Hasebe issued an order stating that, since the enemy had penetrated deeply to the left of the headquarters and endangered the artillery and mortar sites, Kajikawa should leave the 7th Company in place and proceed to cover the artillery's front.

Fighting continued on the 26th against "only" 100 infantrymen and three or four tanks, one of which was stopped and burned. Takashima's platoon was returned by Hasebe on this day. When the lieutenant reached Kajikawa's tent at night, he was happy to see the battalion commander and 7th Company commander Saitō Seikichi vigorously working on plans by dim candlelight, although both officers had suffered head wounds. But Kajikawa realized how dim were the prospects of his exhausted force when he looked around and counted only eight officers, all lieutenants (including two doctors), left from his original corps of 28 officers.

At this point, Kajikawa issued what he expected would be his final instructions. He would share the men's fate at the present positions. Since ammunition and food were so low, hand-to-hand combat using cold steel would be necessary within strengthened positions. There were insufficient troops and weapons to cover the battalion's front of two kilometers, however, so each unit must fight on its own, without any expectation of assistance. Even the wounded, who could not be evacuated, must fight to the death. Takashima found the major's words "penetrating and uplifting."

At this very time, around 9:30 P.M., a message was received from Hasebe that unexpectedly directed a retreat—an order that left Kajikawa looking dispirited. Inasmuch as the detachment had consumed its ammunition and annihilation loomed, Hasebe intended to break out in the early hours, pull back to Heights 749 near Old Engineer Bridge, and cover the right flank of the "new crack units." The Kajikawa battalion was to assemble at detachment headquarters by midnight. After conducting whatever map study and reconnaissance were possible, Kajikawa hastened to implement Hasebe's order. When the battalion reached the detachment command post, its strength had increased to 124 men with five heavy weapons. Ordered to proceed to Kobuyama, Kajikawa was assigned the regimental gun battery, a mortar platoon, the engineer company, and the medical unit. More importantly, he was told that Hasebe himself and the detachment headquarters would accompany him. Obviously, the colonel had decided to leave with the first sizable unit and not wait to go with the Sugitani battalion as he had originally intended. When Kajikawa asked, Hasebe replied that Sugitani's situation was unknown. It seemed only logical that the colonel take command of the pullback operation, but Hasebe turned down Kajikawa's request that he do so, and the battalion commander reluctantly assumed control.

Takashima volunteered to lead a nine-man patrol that took off before 11 P.M., relying on the company commander's only map—torn, bloody, and sandy—and on the lieutenant's wrist compass captured from a Russian.

Among the patrol's unintended adventures was its entry into a dip used by the enemy as an assembly site. Takashima felt that he had no choice but to file across the dip, "fatalistically." Challenged by a sentry, he made up some Russian-sounding words like "*Kuto tan!*" and pulled his party out of danger for the moment.

At 1 A.M. on the 27th, the Hasebe-Kajikawa force moved out on foot, with the 7th Company (63 men) in the lead, followed by the 1st Field Artillery Battalion, detachment headquarters, and the attached units. The rest of Kajikawa's men brought up the rear. Because the medical team was hauling many wounded men and enemy interception was to be expected, the major devoted particular attention to the deployment of the columns. Nevertheless, despite the absence of contact with the foe, Kajikawa's point company, the following medical unit, the battalion guns and machine guns, and a field artillery battery got lost. No contact had been effected with any of these units by the time the main force got to Kobuyama at 6 A.M. Takashima's patrol dashed up to warn Kajikawa that the heights was already occupied by many "big noses," not by friendly forces.

Kajikawa recommended that he be authorized to command his own battalion in the impending combat and that Hasebe take over the rest of the units. The major then made preparations to fight, conducted reconnaissance of the situation on the left, and tried to make contact with friendly elements and the missing formations. In the midst of these activities, Hasebe disappeared to the west with his forces. As soon as Kajikawa found out, he rushed after the colonel and caught up with him at 11:30 A.M., a kilometer east of Heights 749, easily capturing a few enemy soldiers on the way.[5]

Near 2 P.M., scouts detected what seemed to be friendly troops to the left rear. Kajikawa personally waved a red-ball flag in that direction and soon saw a Japanese flag returning the signal. Runners sent out by Hasebe established the identity of the force: elements of Colonel Morita's regiment. Shortly afterward, while reconnoitering toward New Engineer Bridge, Kajikawa's men heard gunfire. Thinking at first that the Sugitani battalion might be involved, Kajikawa recommended to Hasebe that a relief force be sent, but the colonel turned down the idea. Still worried about the fate of his own lead company, Kajikawa dispatched a patrol toward the sound of the shooting, but nobody returned. Subsequently, Kajikawa learned that it was his 7th Company plus the machine gun and battalion gun units that had fought and died in the vicinity of the bridge, including three of his last eight officers.

Soviet artillery fire inflicted considerable losses on Hasebe's headquarters around 4 P.M. An hour later, the colonel issued an order calling for the detachment to set forth at 8 P.M., break through hostile tank lines upstream from the bridge, cross the Holsten, and proceed toward Nomonhan. The first destination would be a point four kilometers from the span. There would be three echelons of advance; the second echelon under Kajikawa was identified specifically, but no mention was made of Hasebe's own Miyazaki and Sugitani battalions.

Takashima says that the units were ready to move by 10 P.M. Meanwhile, he claims a Soviet truck blundered into the Japanese lines and was seized. It proved to be a supply truck containing a veritable feast of canned beef and biscuits. Resuming their difficult retreat along the left side of the Holsten valley, Hasebe's men had to penetrate an area occupied by enemy armor. Although the Japanese tried to pick a relatively weak sector, by 1:30 A.M. on 28 August they were surrounded by tanks, which steadily tightened the cordon. After conferring with Major Matsutomo of the field artillery, Kajikawa decided that each unit should organize a breakthrough team and designate a rendezvous for continuing together afterward. Kajikawa took the left-flank assignment, sent guides ahead, and, bearing on the North Star, broke through the line of armor rather easily. Even though the enemy tanks detected and pursued the Japanese, darkness prevented the armored vehicles from firing.

After Kajikawa encountered Japanese trucks carrying infantrymen of the sister 25th Regiment, there was a sense of relief, and the battalion stopped marching for a while. But Hasebe had become separated again, and it was not known at the time that he had made it across the Holsten. Utterly lost, even with his maps, Kajikawa headed northeast. En route, three men of the 1st Heavy Field Artillery Regiment appeared, but they were lost too. When day broke after 5 A.M. on the 28th, the battalion took cover in a saddle-shaped area and sent scouts ahead. No trace of the enemy was found. Kajikawa pieced things together: his battalion must have traversed the valley northeast of the Izumi bend instead of crossing the Holsten; the enemy tanks were encountered in the vicinity of Nigesorimot. Consequently, the present location must be the dune west of Heights 758, only three kilometers northwest of Lake Mohorehi.

Moving on, the Kajikawa battalion found the site of the Takatsukasa heavy artillery to the east. After taking a break there, by 10 A.M. the men reached the south side of Mohorehi, where Kajikawa assembled the force and looked in vain for Hasebe. Then the indefatigable major went to the north side of the lake to report to the Sixth Army, which returned his depleted battalion, at long last, to the command of the parent 7th Division, in a second-line capacity.

As for the 1st Field Artillery Battalion commander, Major Matsutomo reached General Hata's artillery corps headquarters on 28 August too. Matsutomo reported how he had withdrawn to the bridge area, at Hasebe's order, but had been encircled and mauled by the enemy on the 27th. Most of the surviving field pieces had had to be buried or blown up. Sixth Army headquarters, however, conducted a merciless investigation, found that Matsutomo had allegedly disengaged from battle on his own initiative, and released the major from duty immediately. Since Matsutomo had been attached to Hasebe from early August and was subject to the detachment's orders, one wonders why the major was taken to task for following the instructions given to him.[6]

Four kilometers south of the Holsten on 24 August, Colonel Morita's 71st Regiment had been working on the defenses, beating off tank attacks, and waiting for the Japanese counteroffensive forces to draw near. Gunfire was heard far to the northeast, but the sounds did not move southward as the hours wore on. Sugitachi's 1st Battalion had been detached to join the 23rd Division, leaving Colonel Morita with little more than three and a half infantry companies, five heavy weapons, and a dozen machine guns. Soviet 12-cm. howitzer and tank-gun fire was so severe that the shape of the dunes was transformed. Although annotations on Sixth Army maps indicated that the zone of Heights 744 was very difficult for tanks to traverse owing to complicated terrain, the region extending toward Old Engineer Bridge and south of Nomonhan proved to be a "parade ground" for enemy armor, and it became nearly impossible to evacuate casualties or obtain food and ammunition. Near midday on the 25th, Colonel Morita proposed to the division that his force come under Kobayashi's command, in order to join the Japanese offensive effort, but he was directed to secure his present positions. The regiment lacked intelligence on the enemy situation and on the division's intentions, despite repeated efforts on both scores.

On 26 August, Colonel Morita's men were hammered by artillery (especially by three 12-cm. howitzers emplaced near Heights 747) and assaulted by tanks loaded with riflemen. To the right, the Hasebe detachment was being battered too. Past noon, the Russians drew near the defenses of the 71st Regiment. Morita stood erect, peering through his binoculars and directing the defenders. Captain Onozuka, who was huddling in a conical *suribachi* hole a meter below, describes the uniqueness of the colonel and what happened next.[7]

> I had known the regiment commander since Toyama infantry school days, when he was the *kendō* fencing instructor for the whole Japanese army. In addition to his confidence in his fencing ability, he was a devout believer in Nichiren Buddhism and had the extravagant belief that he was immune to bullets. He gave me the feeling that I was a coward whenever he saw me crawling or crouching. "Devotees of *kendō* don't do that!," he would tell me. On 26 August, I tried to caution him against risking himself atop the trench, but of course he would not hear of it. To put it mildly, Colonel Morita was a bold man. But he was actually making himself into a target for the enemy. Maybe it was good in the sense of encouraging

the troops, but the colonel went too far. He was shot down and killed instantly by three Maxim machine-gun slugs that hit him in the head and chest.

The time was 12:40 P.M. Onozuka pulled the colonel's body down into the *suribachi*. Since it was not possible to evacuate the corpse, Onozuka had it buried for the time being.

After he learned of Morita's death, Komatsubara wrote in his diary that the 71st Regiment had lost its commander, "who is the heart of a unit's morale. . . . I have misgivings about the future of the Morita [regiment]." At 3 P.M., the 71st Regiment received a radio message expressing Komatsubara's regrets and exhorting the officers and men to rally around the radiant colors "for the sake of the nation." Lt. Col. Higashi Muneharu, who had just reached Komatsubara's headquarters from Hailar, was ordered by the division chief of staff to make his way through the enemy forces that were surrounding the regiment and rejoin it promptly.[8] The unit's mission was to cover the division's movement toward Old Engineer Bridge on the night of 27/28 August. Despite brilliant moonlight, Higashi got through to the regiment, where he tearfully shook hands with Onozuka and took command of the lacerated unit. Higashi's first order called for reinforcement of the positions, digging of antitank trenches, laying of antitank mines, conservation of ammunition, study of sniping techniques, and construction of reserve sites for the remaining heavy weapons.

By 27 August it was confirmed that the neighboring Hasebe detachment was pulling back under pressure. At 8 A.M., elements of the detachment could be seen in action at a point 1,500 meters northwest of the 71st Regiment. Within the hour, one of Hasebe's aides came and reported to Higashi that part of the detachment had been shifted to the area of Heights 749 south of New Engineer Bridge, though the main body was fighting its way back at the location in sight. The pullback had become unavoidable because of the combat situation and "other circumstances." After coordination between Higashi and the Hasebe detachment, it was understood that the latter would occupy positions around the present line and fight on there.[9] But, as we saw, Hasebe left hurriedly that morning, causing Kajikawa to pull out too.

Higashi's own defenses were rapidly becoming untenable. Grenades and gasoline were running low, rendering it "difficult to fight even at close quarters." At 8:40 A.M. on the 27th, Higashi notified his regiment that the Hasebe detachment had left during the preceding night and was now in the process of pulling back, occupying positions to the northwest. Higashi's men should defend their lines to the last, take care of their weapons, study enemy tactics and devise suitable countermeasures, and trust wholeheartedly in the power of hand-to-hand combat. With the return of the survivors of the 3rd

Battalion, who had been operating with the Hasebe unit since the loss of Sankakuyama, Higashi had 600 men—seven depleted rifle companies, nine machine guns, and five heavy weapons. Since 22 August, the regiment had lost 517 killed (including 21 officers) and 283 wounded (including 13 officers).

On the afternoon of the 27th, a message was received from the division, wishing Higashi's troops "a good fight." Higashi's afternoon order to redeploy toward the river that night contained the passwords "Loyalty" (*chūsetsu*) and "Valor" (*buyū*). The waving of red flashlights should be the method to signal the division main force. No other light was permitted, and silence must be absolute.

At 1:30 A.M. on 28 August, the 71st Regiment disengaged from a point two kilometers west of Nigesorimot without being detected and headed for Old Engineer Bridge. The soldiers carried as many of the wounded as possible, and individual infantrymen even lugged such heavy items as shells for the two remaining regimental guns. At dawn, the regiment joined the division main force near Heights 753, south of Old Engineer Bridge, and proceeded north across the river. After covering the division's movement from south of the bridge, the 1st Battalion caught up, but Major Sugitachi had been killed at about 2 A.M. Heavy-weapon fire drove off a dozen armored vehicles that attacked from the south shore of the Holsten at daybreak. Flamethrowing tanks appeared from the north after 9 A.M. From a gun site near the south bank, enemy 12-cm. howitzers fired all day. Japanese trucks had picked up casualties at the area of the bridge and had proceeded toward Nomonhan, but they were attacked by tanks en route and many of the wounded were slaughtered.[10]

After delivering his main hammer blows against Japanese forces south of the Holsten from 24 August, Zhukov intended to smash the final pocket of resistance above the river. This meant that the Central Force would push east while the other Soviet components pressed from south and north. Specifically, the 24th and 149th regiments of the 36th Motorized Rifle Division were to hit Balshagal Heights from west and southwest, together with the 5th Machine Gun Brigade. The 601st Regiment of the 82nd Rifle Division would advance from the north; the 9th Armored Brigade, from the east. Along the claimed frontier, cover would be provided by a machine gun battalion from the 11th Tank Brigade, by two motorized companies of border guards, and by the 212th Airborne Brigade. On 27 August, as part of his order to annihilate the Japanese, Zhukov directed elements of the Northern Force, in conjunction with the 36th Division, to seize initial objectives not more than 700-1,000 meters from the foot of Barunishi Heights. After three hours of intense artillery preparation, these units were to attack the enemy dug in on the heights.

Although the Russians' 127th Rifle Regiment of the 57th Division was able to cross to the north side of the Holsten by the close of 27 August, the Japanese had continued to cling to Barunishi Heights all day. The battle intensified on the 28th. With the arrival of another Soviet regiment—the 293rd Rifle Regiment of the 57th Division—on the northern shore, the encirclement was completed. Tightening the ring steadily, Russian guns and armor smashed almost all of the enemy's artillery, leaving the Japanese with only machine guns and grenade launchers in the main. On the night of 28/29 August, about 400 Japanese troops had gathered on the dunes with the intention of escaping the trap by sneaking eastward along the north side of the Holsten valley. After this force was detected, the 2nd and 3rd battalions of the 293rd Rifle Regiment caught the Japanese crossing the river and annihilated them in furious hand-to-hand fighting after they declined to surrender.

On the evening of the 28th, Zhukov issued direct orders to the 24th Motorized Rifle Regiment commander, Fedyuninsky, to exterminate enemy troops still holding Barunishi Heights and to seize the crest not later than midnight. Supported by armor, the regiment stormed the defenses, penetrating the crestline positions by 11 P.M. and breaking the back of the resistance. Throughout the night of 28/29 August, the Russians mopped up small, scattered remnants on the hill. During the next two days, the clearing process was completed north of the Holsten. Fedyuninsky's regiment of the 36th Division was given credit for finishing off the last Japanese troops holding soil claimed by Outer Mongolia, on the northern flank of the Balshagal line southwest of Nomonhan, by the morning of 31 August. The Soviet-MPRA command thereupon took steps to defend the frontier line that had at last been conquered.

During the climax of the operations between 28 and 31 August, the Soviet air force reported waging four major battles with the Japanese. In the most violent combat on the 31st, 126 Soviet fighters intercepted 27 Japanese bombers and 70 fighters flying to attack Russian ground forces and downed 22 IJAF planes. A total of four Japanese bombers and 45 fighters were claimed shot down between the 28th and the 31st.[11] As usual, even classified Japanese sources present a drastically different version of the air war. On 31 August, for example, 20 Russian planes were said to have been downed at a cost of three aircraft and four men. Indeed, during the entire period after the second Tamsag raids (23-31 August), IJAF records indicate that 108 Soviet aircraft were shot down, as opposed to 29 Japanese planes lost, and 20 airmen killed and 32 wounded.[12]

North of the Holsten, on 23/24 August, Major Kanaizuka's 3rd Battalion of the 64th Infantry had been ordered to the Heights 731 area to assist Ikuta's weakened battalion from the Sumi regiment in protecting the 23rd Division's rear against enemy irruptions from the north. The situation was changing from minute to minute, and Kanaizuka temporarily lost control of his unit. Apart from his headquarters and most of his heavy weapons, he could locate only one of his four infantry companies—the 11th, commanded by 1st Lt. Kawabata Motokichi. In practice, regiment commander Yamagata was directly ordering the movements of the companies when he could reach them; he told Kanaizuka that the remaining elements would catch up later. When the major went to Yamagata's command post to say goodbye, the colonel took out some Hakutaka sake, said "This is the end," and asked to see all of Kanaizuka's officers. When they were brought to the regimental tent, the major noted in his diary, "My heart was full, and I felt as if I were suffocating."

At 11:50 P.M., Kanaizuka mounted his horse and led his men north. Although the distance to traverse was only 6-8 kilometers, normally a two-hour movement, there had been no time to reconnoiter, and the force got lost en route. Soldiers from the 6th Field Artillery Battery tried to help, but it was difficult to locate the communication wires that led to the positions. Dreading the impending sunrise, Kanaizuka prayed that his unit would arrive in time to dig in. It was not until 4 A.M. that they reached the Ikuta district, but Kanaizuka's prayer had been answered: for the first time at Nomonhan, he encountered dense morning fog—a merciful cloak that assisted Japanese operations all along the front in the early hours of 24 August. Within an hour, the men had taken up a circle of positions in a dip 50-60 meters below the crest, on the reverse slope, drawing on old Japanese trenches dating back to May and on newer communication trenches dug by Ikuta's men as part of the wintering program.

Kanaizuka ended up holding the farthest positions on the right wing above the Holsten, northwest of Ikuta who was on Heights 731 two to five kilometers on the left, and 10 kilometers south of the doomed positions at Fui. Soviet strength in the area, as of dawn on the 24th, was estimated at several thousand infantry, a mechanized brigade, and 20 heavy guns. During the morning, Russian forces—perhaps of division strength—were observed advancing continuously from the direction of Fui, reaching a location four kilometers northeast of the Kanaizuka battalion by 10 A.M. Only a portion of the Soviet forces were committed against Kanaizuka; the main body kept moving against the right rear of the 23rd Division—100 tanks, 100 trucks or armored cars, 500 infantry, and at least 20 guns. On the morning of the 25th, 2,000 Russian infantrymen, with several dozen tanks and armored cars, were seen on the move, beyond range. At the peak of the Soviet advance, Kanaizuka's aide estimated the width of deployment at two or three kilometers, the depth at several kilometers.

On 24 August, says Kanaizuka, his unit was half-encircled; next day, it was entirely surrounded. In the early evening of the 24th, Yamagata got through to the battalion by truck. The colonel conferred with Kanaizuka, inspected the defenses, and exhorted the men before returning to his command post. Nobody in the 3rd Battalion saw him alive again.

Although the enemy's main body had bypassed Kanaizuka, two infantry companies, four guns, and some armor were being used to destroy the Japanese positions. At least once a day the Russians—all aboard trucks or tanks—would come very close and open heavy fire with their mobile artillery from various angles; but the range was so short that the shells would fly overhead. Small-arms counterfire was useless, and Kanaizuka had to save his precious battalion-gun and machine-gun ammunition for a "real emergency."

The tactics of the Russians soon became apparent: isolated Japanese positions would be mopped up, one after another, by "pillars" of fire massed against individual targets for about two days. After wiping out one strongpoint, the enemy moved to the next. Kanaizuka knew that Ikuta was doomed when he saw the ominous "cyclone" of fire appear to the left on the 26th, and he expected that his own battalion would be next. The process had begun on the 25th, when 18 Soviet armored cars and 300 soldiers had penetrated into the gap between the battalions. Clouds of smoke and sand obscured Ikuta's positions as Kanaizuka's bastion was gradually encircled by 60 armored cars, 1,000 infantry, and more than 10 heavy field pieces, operating at a range of 1,000 meters. With all of his telephone wires cut, Kanaizuka had to rely upon messengers and radio. When supply lines were severed on the 25th, the major reduced the men's rations to one bag of hardtack per day and tried to conserve ammunition.[13]

Within Ikuta's isolated defenses, the situation had indeed become untenable by 25 August, according to a surviving company commander. In the rapid-fire battery, only rifles remained. There was insufficient strength to man the lines, and broad gaps on the flanks allowed enemy infiltration from the direction of the Halha. In his last conversation with Colonel Sumi, when the regimental main body was transferring for the Japanese counteroffensive south of the Holsten, Ikuta had apparently been advised to displace closer to elements of the adjoining Yamagata force when the inevitable crisis materialized at Heights 731. Now, by evening of the 25th, with his unit beaten, the major decided to break out and contract his overextended frontage. Deploying himself and his swordsmen in the front, he planned a human-bullet charge through the cordon before dawn.

On the adjoining Kanaizuka sector, at a distance of 1,200-1,300 meters, the battalion aide could observe enemy artillery "ruining the terrain" where Ikuta was located while tanks and infantry overran the positions during the afternoon of the 25th. In desperation, the aide risked one of the two surviving rapid-fire guns, ordering the crew to ascend the emplacement, depress the barrel, and fire down at the Soviet armor. After three tanks were burned, the rest retreated, some colliding with each other in confusion. Next morning, however, 40-50 tanks and armored cars, with 1,000 infantrymen, reappeared four kilometers north of the Kanaizuka battalion and pressed south. The crew of one armored car, detected 300 meters to the east, was slashed to death, and a considerable amount of very welcome rations was seized. But there had been no contact with Ikuta's men since the 25th and, by noon next day, a forest of red flags was seen atop long poles on the lost positions. The neighboring battalion regarded the scene with sadness, indignation, and apprehension. Most of the Ikuta unit had been destroyed, but some men broke through toward Yamagata's main force, including the battalion commander, wounded in the chest by a shell fragment.[14]

The collapse of Ikuta's position at Heights 731 opened up a yawning gap of five kilometers between the Kanaizuka battalion and the nearest elements of the parent 64th Regiment to the south—a breach that the Russians were not slow to exploit. Kanaizuka's 12th Company, commanded by 1st Lt. Tashiro Masanao, had rejoined him on the 24th, but he never saw his 10th Company again. Later he learned that, assigned to defend the main artillery site in the area of Heights 755 on 25 August, the company had been surrounded next morning by forces estimated to number 60 tanks, 900 riflemen, and 12 or 13 guns. The heaviest Japanese weapons were grenade launchers, but these ran out of ammunition and could not be used. Light machine guns were knocked out, one after another. Though seven or eight tanks were reportedly stopped by close-quarter assaults, even cartridges for rifles had to be collected from the dead and wounded. By 3:30 P.M., every Japanese officer had been killed, and superior privates were commanding each of the three platoons. When all of the ammunition was gone by 6 P.M., the surviving Japanese soldiers fixed bayonets and launched a last charge. Wounded men committed suicide like *samurai* of old (*kobushi*). At nightfall, near 7 P.M., the Russians finally proceeded past the demolished unit.[15]

Striking into the zone vacated by Ikuta, 400 Soviet troops with 10 tanks and four armored cars fiercely attacked the southern flank of Kanaizuka's battalion from 5 P.M. on the 26th. Yamagata ordered Kanaizuka to pull back to the main body, but the major was afraid to dislocate his defenses in such close proximity to the enemy (whose attacks did not ease up until midnight) and radioed back to that effect. The situation did not improve on the 27th. Enemy forces, reinforced steadily, smashed many of Kanaizuka's shelters by 3 P.M., and artillery and tank fire, from 800 meters, inflicted many casualties. Soviet gunners, stripped to the waist and smoking cigarettes, could be seen manning four or five field pieces on high ground on the 12th Company's front. The Japanese tried to withstand the bombardment without responding.

Around 5 P.M., the battle reached a peak when 10 tanks and 500 infantrymen closed in. Gunfire collapsed the Japanese trenches and buried soldiers alive. A doctor at the 11th Company's site counted 400 shells exploding in five minutes. The smoke and dust made it difficult to breathe. When the Russian troops came within 80 meters, grenade combat ensued. The positions of both the 11th and the 12th companies were penetrated by tanks and infantry several times. Not until midnight did the foe pull back somewhat, probably to defend against expected Japanese night attacks.

Running short of food and ammunition, Kanaizuka put his men on half rations and directed them to try to capture Soviet food, forage, weapons, and ammunition. In this last stage of August, the battalion commander did not eat for seven days. The happiest time for the unit occurred when a probationary officer led an assault against an "armored vehicle" that proved to be a bakery truck. Although the young officer was killed in this action, the men rejoiced to take possession of so much bread.

By now, says Kanaizuka, his unit was not only isolated but also located behind the enemy. In the evening of the 27th, the major radioed Yamagata the situation of his battalion, reported that he was trying to rejoin the regiment that night, and asked about conditions in the main zone of the division. At 8 P.M. the reply came: all units were waging a difficult battle; the 3rd Battalion should displace to the regiment's site immediately; communication with the division was impossible. Kanaizuka had had no opportunity to disengage from the foe yet, and he could never have clung to the positions as long as he had already unless he had found water. Till now, digging wells even to a depth of 10 meters had proved fruitless, but this time—in one of several "miracles" experienced by Kanaizuka at Nomonhan—he saw clear water finally gush forth permanently from a well dug in the sand at 30-50 centimeters.[16]

Ever since the outbreak of the heaviest fighting at Nomonhan, Japanese batteries north of the Holsten had been facing mainly west toward the Halha or southwest toward the confluence. Ahead of them in every case, as was to be expected, were the positions of friendly infantry. The main emphasis in laying out gun sites centered on maximizing counterbattery and infantry-support effectiveness, and on minimizing damage from enemy artillery and air attack. Against tank irruptions, the batteries possessed almost no organic defensive capability and expected to depend on the infantry plus a few mountain guns.[17] The customary expectations were turned topsy-turvy when Soviet motorized and mechanized formations smashed the anchor at Fui Heights and streamed behind the northernmost Japanese infantry positions. Along the axis of Heights 731-752, the Russians struck at the exposed IJA artillery units from the north and northeast, as well as from the south across the Holsten. In other words, the Japanese rear lines became front lines. The longer the range of the IJA artillery, the farther were the heavy guns behind the infantry, thus the nearer to the onrushing enemy— and the more helpless. Even on the western side, of course, infantry cover had been enfeebled by the removal of the 72nd Regiment and reliance on little more than the overextended 64th Regiment.

Artillery corps commander Hata had given Colonel Takatsukasa control of the heavy artillery above the Holsten: the Muleng unit of three 15-cm. cannon, west of Heights 755; the 1st Battalion of the 1st Heavy Field Artillery Regiment (eight 15-cm. howitzers), west of the Muleng force; and the 2nd Battalion of Takatsukasa's own 7th Heavy Field Artillery Regiment (eight 10-cm. cannon), south of the 1st Regiment, toward the Holsten. Colonel Ise's 13th Field Artillery Regiment directly supported Yamagata's infantry: the 2nd Battalion (three batteries), north of Heights 733; the 3rd Battalion (headquarters and one battery), south of Heights 733 and five kilometers to the northeast.

For a month, before Hata moved his corps headquarters to the area of the Japanese counteroffensive of 24 August south of the Holsten, the nerve center of the artillery command had been located on the north side of Heights 755 at Gake cliff, which afforded a commanding view of most of the Balshagal area. With Hata's departure, Soviet forces moved in and seized Gake on the 24th. Unfortunately, Japanese artillery officers continued to think that friendly infantry belonging to Sumi's unit still held the area, whereas most of the 26th Regiment had displaced south of the Holsten on the 23rd. Even Hata's senior staff officer and the Muleng artillery staff remained convinced that Gake was in Japanese hands until patrols reported otherwise and came under fire from the cliff on 24 August. Thus the IJA heavy artillery encountered a serious reversal at the outset, from the standpoint of terrain.[18]

Hata had detected the unsubstantial nature of the infantry protection stipulated in the 23rd Division's operational planning and had called this to the attention of the staff officers. Admitting that a mistake had been made, the latter considered readjusting the deployments, which would have delayed the Japanese counteroffensive by one day. Sixth Army Chief of Staff Fujimoto, however, objected strenuously to any further postponement. The most that Hata could get was a promise by the division that the 64th Infantry would be directed to divert forces to screen the artillery's flank and rear. This was asking a lot of the hopelessly overburdened Yamagata regiment, and offers further evidence that the Sixth Army and the 23rd Division were preoccupied with the counteroffensive operation, to the detriment of the forces north of the Holsten. But it is unfortunate that few beyond battalion commander Kanaizuka remember that Yamagata did assign his 10th Company to cover the heavy artillery near Heights 755, and that the whole company was wiped out on 26 August, as we have seen.[19] In general, the Japanese artillery would pay the full price of higher headquarters' neglect of defensive dispositions.

The first of the Japanese artillery formations to be demolished was Lt. Col. Someya Yoshio's 15-cm.-cannon Muleng unit, deployed farthest behind the infantry. It consisted of 1st Lt. Kimura Jirō's 2nd Battery of two pieces, reinforced by one heavy gun of the 3rd Battery attached from the Port Arthur fortress. During the night of 23/24 August the atmosphere in the Muleng unit was "very unsettled," according to a noncom. When morning came, he observed the astounding sight of Soviet tanks crossing the river without benefit of any visible bridge. The enemy armor lumbered to the north of the IJA artillery's positions and assembled in the rear, "like ants clustering around sugar." It was said that these were the tanks that raided the Japanese field hospital at Uzuru pond. Friendly light bombers tried to harry the armor, with results as ineffective as "water dripping on a burning hot stone."

The Russian tanks no longer plunged straight against the defenders' positions; now they held up at a distance of 200 or 300 meters and fired. From behind the armor, enemy snipers shot at demolition soldiers trying to attack with gasoline bottles. When the Japanese were pinned down, the tanks advanced another 40 or 50 meters. Lieutenant Kimura assumed command of the guns. That night, the field of fire of the cannon was reversed to the northeast, in the direction of Nomonhan, Chiangchunmiao, and the enemy armor. Since there was insufficient ammunition, however, to "waste" 15-cm. shells on targets of a few tanks at a time, the Japanese gunners waited while the enemy cordon grew tighter, leaving gaps of only 200-250 meters at this stage. The soldiers dug communication trenches between the squads and labored to strengthen the gun sites, loading ammunition boxes with sand and piling them around the cannon.

On the 25th, the encircling ring closed to a diameter of 150 or 200 meters. Soviet tanks and infantry pinned the Japanese, who had nothing more than rifles with which to respond and who sometimes hurled back grenades which had just landed in the trenches. Though enemy armor was not pressing into the defenses yet, it was learned that the remnants of the one IJA infantry platoon (a mere 17 or 18 men under a noncom) situated ahead of the gun sites had been annihilated. Kimura decided to fire shrapnel, starting at zero elevation. Although smoke obscured the gunners' detection of the results of the bombardment, it was reported that the enemy had been struck "beautifully." Nevertheless, there was no sense of exultation, for the attention of Soviet armor had been attracted to the source of the fire. Kimura had the cannon loaded with armor-piercing shells and ordered them into action at less than 2,000 meters. Again, the results were excellent. The lieutenant reported seeing a tank turret blown off and five or six machines knocked out.

The success of the IJA 15-cm. cannon was transient and merely deferred the destruction of the unit for a short time. From dawn on 26 August, the Russians pushed forward a rifle corps supported by armor and artillery. Dozens of tanks began to overrun the Muleng unit's positions, in the face of futile little counterattacks. Lieutenant Colonel Someya had already prepared his last testament. Now he inserted the date of his impending death, asked a noncom to deliver it to artillery headquarters, and committed suicide at the observation post. His battery commanders and most of his other officers and men also met death at the gun sites this day. In fact, the 1st Regiment only heard about the annihilation from one straggler who turned up afterward. The field artillery learned the story at dawn on the 27th when two officers, a warrant officer, and five soldiers from Someya's formation appeared at the 3rd Battalion's positions. These last remnants of the unit had resisted at the strong shelters of the wagon train and had escaped at daybreak. Every one of them, including the officers, had undergone attacks by flamethrowers, and their bodies were cruelly blackened.

Someya's force, thrown together in less than a year, had gone into action with insufficient training and organization. Powerful but few, his cannon were neutralized when Gake was lost, his rear was turned, and his only defense against tanks became small arms, grenades, and bayonets.[20] This was to become the fate of every Japanese artillery battery above the Holsten.

In the sector of the 1st Battalion of the 1st Heavy Field Artillery Regiment, the supply train was forced back to the gun lines on the morning of 24 August. Trucks and sedans could be seen pulling back, one after another. It was said that enemy armor had already penetrated to the rear of the kitchen area, and that the Nomonhan-Chiangchunmiao road had been cut. Sensing that death was near, the soldiers sipped a little sake, ate the last food, and prepared to fight the tanks with Molotov cocktails. In the afternoon, the 15-cm. howitzers engaged armor operating 4,000 meters to the rear.

Daybreak came on the 25th without the expected close combat; but the atmosphere was tense, and the howitzers in the 2nd Battery were redeployed: two facing forward, two to the rear. Around 3 P.M., enemy tanks began to advance, supported by mountain guns. To the east, the ammunition stores of Someya's cannon could be seen ablaze. The 1st Battalion's howitzers continued to fire until its ammunition was hit too, causing the men to flee the heat and explosions and take refuge in communication trenches. Enemy barrages, already enormous, intensified when 15-cm. pieces entered the fray. Under a veritable rain of fire, the Japanese troops found it difficult to breathe. Soviet tanks and heavy machine guns drew closer. A 2nd Battery sergeant, Sakakibara Shigeo, remembers the indescribable smell of gunsmoke and blood that permeated the area, and the grisly sight of two half-naked corpses sprawled grotesquely in a trench under their shattered steel helmets. The wheel of the sergeant's own howitzer was deformed by an enemy shell, and it was decided to dismantle the vitals of two inoperable other pieces and bury them deeply in the earth. When another howitzer broke down on the 26th, it meant that the 2nd Battery was left with only one of its four howitzers, whereas the 1st Battery still had three. On the night of 25/26 August, the surviving pieces were displaced to the old 2nd Battalion positions nearer the Holsten, and the soldiers worked on the emplacements without sleep. Since the 2nd Battery's combat capability had been almost smashed by the 26th, Captain Tsuchiya, the 1st Battery commander, assigned men to the mixed force of surviving pieces regardless of original affiliation.

Before the Japanese howitzers could go into action, they were hammered again on the 26th. The scene was grim: shellcases and cartridges were scattered all over, and the earth of the trenches was scorched and torn. Enemy aircraft flew low, dropping leaflets warning the Japanese that they were completely encircled. Sakakibara had nibbled on one hardtack biscuit the day before; on the 26th, he shared it with two other soldiers. The men were so fatigued that they could doze under shellfire. It was a matter of surviving from day to day, at least until the division's main body broke through in a few more days. The 2nd Battery's last howitzer was aimed to the east; the other pieces faced in various directions, prepared to engage tanks or infantry or artillery.

When Captain Tsuchiya discerned armor moving in the rear, he contacted battalion headquarters and was told that those were tanks that had "lost their way, so don't worry." To Tsuchiya, however, the tanks seemed to be in the van of hostile forces coming from behind. Until now, the battery had been engaging any targets that were visible to the front—field guns, tanks, and routes of advance from across the Halha—since enemy heavy artillery emplacements were beyond range. Now Tsuchiya shifted one howitzer against the rear and engaged seven or eight tanks (without infantry) that were approaching within 2,000 meters. Whether hit directly or not, six of the tanks began to burn, and the others fled. Crewmen, on fire, could be seen rolling on the ground behind the armor. Cheered by this little victory, Tsuchiya's troops dashed toward the tanks to seize men and matériel. It was a dangerous foray and the Japanese were almost killed, but they finished off the enemy soldiers and captured some pistols. In all, Tsuchiya's battery fired 42 howitzer rounds in the antitank role in two days: 20 shells on 25 August, 22 on 26 August. His orders were to engage armor until the ammunition ran out, for it was tanks that were savaging both batteries. No ammunition was available from outside the battalion.

On the evening of the 26th, after fierce and desperate fighting, there were farewell speeches by the battery commanders and by the acting 1st Battalion commander, Capt. Yamazaki Masaki. Thanking his men for their efforts, the captain said that the unit faced annihilation next day, or on the 28th at the latest. The battle was going very well for the 23rd Division's main force, he claimed, but there was no chance of holding out till it arrived. Therefore, the 1st Battalion should prepare to die "like beautifully falling cherry blossoms." The captain's exhortation was met with "silence and resolve." Yamazaki called on the men to meet again as a unit, after death, at the Yasukuni national shrine. Thereupon the soldiers faced east toward Japan and gave three *Banzai!* cheers for the Emperor, raising their arms in the twilight. A battery commander led a last cheer for the unit, conducted in a "low but vigorous" voice. Then the men went back to their digging. Sakakibara wanted to live, but if his howitzer (No. 24) was destroyed, he intended to fight as an infantryman.

Starting at 7:30 A.M. on 27 August, enemy tanks and armored cars closed in for the kill, circling to the rear. The four remaining Japanese howitzers responded effectively, assisted (it was hoped) by whatever field artillery Ise's regiment still possessed. The 1st Battery observed about a company of infantrymen moving on the right bank of the Holsten, and there was some argument over whether it was a friendly or enemy force. Tsuchiya insisted that he could see the men wearing long raincoats, and he ordered his howitzers to fire. The foot soldiers, thinking they were being attacked from the south side of the Holsten, veered closer to the Japanese gun lines, presented even better targets, and were nearly annihilated. Tsuchiya was relieved when it was confirmed they were indeed Russians.

At 9 A.M., word had come that the 23rd Division was making excellent progress. Even if the news were true, which it was not, salvation was not near for the howitzer battalion. After hours of severe Russian artillery and tank fire, the armor plunged against the defenses at 3:10 P.M. Already wounded since morning, Sakakibara gripped his saber and a pistol taken from a badly wounded warrant officer. At 4 P.M., with the enemy 200 or 300 meters away, the sergeant was sure that he would die within the next half hour. He closed his diary, scribbled "like Arabic," with a last cheer for the Emperor.

Amid the cruel bombardment, Sakakibara saw two sandstorms whirling,

10 meters away. Yamazaki was standing on the artillery shelter, facing east, his face caked with blood, while enemy machine gunners zeroed in on him. Spitting blood, the captain inhaled deeply, gave a cheer for the Emperor, sat down, handed his pistol to his aide, and asked to be shot. When the second lieutenant could not go through with it, the badly wounded Yamazaki agreed to lead the unit till the end. Shouting orders hoarsely and constantly wiping the blood from his eyes, he directed the firing until there was no more ammunition, not even a last shell with which to blow up a howitzer (according to Sakakibara). Bowing deeply, with emotion and awe, the gunners then did the unthinkable: under orders, they deliberately smashed the key parts of the pieces—range finders and lenses so precious and so secret, the punishment for even a careless scratch in peacetime would have been the stockade or, at best, pushups for 30 minutes. To Sakakibara, it seemed unreal and bizarre. Yamazaki passed around a last canteen of water. Outside the emplacement, everyone got ready to charge the tanks, which could be heard moving up as soon as the barrages lifted. According to Tsuchiya, the wounded, assembled in a hollow, asked Yamazaki to dispatch them. Yamazaki had them hail the Emperor, then fired his pistol and "sent them to heaven."

As Sakakibara swapped his saber for an oaken club, strange thoughts went through his mind. For a moment he saw himself, at the age of seven or eight, wearing a splash-patterned kimono and holding his mother's hand, walking along a narrow path between paddy fields and going to pray at the village shrine. Death must be very near, the sergeant thought as he kept his eyes on the tanks and waited for the order to charge. The firing manual, which he had worked so hard to master, was at an end. No longer would he have to suffer with the English language or with triangulation. But what a shame it was that nobody would survive to tell the people in the homeland how splendidly the men of the howitzer battalion had died.

Amid this reverie, Sakakibara heard the captain, who had been observing the enemy through the slit in the gunshield, tell the men to be patient for a while longer, since 100 meters was too far for wounded soldiers to dash effectively against tanks under fire. Then Yamazaki asked for the date and the exact time (5:15 P.M.), undoubtedly to impress these last details on anyone who might survive. When the captain was again peering through the slit, Sakakibara heard a sharp exclamation, turned to look, and saw that his commander had just been shot through the forehead by a sniper. Blood and brains dyed Yamazaki's tunic as he collapsed and died on the stanchion of the howitzer.[21]

Maj. Umeda Kyōzō, the former 1st Battalion commander who had been in charge of the 1st Regiment since the wounding and evacuation of Colonel Mishima earlier in the month, assumed responsibility for the destruction of the unit and its howitzers. After all, since an IJA artillery regiment had no colors, its guns were its "soul." He transmitted a final radio message to corps commander Hata on the afternoon of 27 August, and then he sent back his last written words with three soldiers. He could die happily, said Umeda, knowing that the regiment had done everything it could, had fought gallantly till the last, and had upheld the honor of the Japanese artillery. It was 3 P.M. now, and about two hours of life were left. When the last ammunition had been expended, the unit would perform its last loyalty by charging into the enemy. Umeda himself would commit suicide on the covered shelter of his observation post. The Someya unit had already been annihilated on the 27th; Takatsukasa was facing the same fate. Umeda sent best regards to Mishima, and asked that the colonel be told that all his subordinates were very brave and had fought to the limit. What a difference there is, writes Gomikawa bitterly, between a Kwantung Army staff officer such as Major Tsuji and a fine front-line commander such as Major Umeda in terms of calm courage, sense of responsibility, and consciousness of duty. Yet almost no one knows about Umeda because he chose death instead of criticizing the ineptness and lack of vision of the command.[22]

As for 1st Battery commander Tsuchiya, he had gone to the observation post on the 27th and left command of the howitzers to his classmate Yamazaki. By nightfall the guns, 800 meters away, had fallen silent. Tsuchiya could not see what had happened, but with the observation post surrounded and communication impossible, he decided to get to the rear and report to headquarters. Armed only with a saber, he took his last dozen soldiers and headed through the cordon. The Russians, who were encountered often, generally thought it was a friendly patrol; whenever they found otherwise and opened fire, the Japanese would flee and fall prone. It helped when the moon clouded over and it started to rain, for the Soviet sentries were wearing rain caps that interfered with their vision even at close range. Since direction-finding was difficult, Tsuchiya moved sideways to the Holsten and waded in the river when he got to it. It took two days to get to the artillery corps headquarters, and by now the captain had only five or six men left. The staff seemed to know nothing about the situation above the Holsten. Tsuchiya reported on the fate of the artillery and the power of enemy armor. Friendly infantry, he guessed, must have been smashed by now too.[23]

During the last days of the 1st Heavy Field Artillery's 1st Battalion, the two howitzer batteries expended over 1,100 rounds. Only 376, however, were fired by the 2nd Battery, which was mauled on the 25th; the 1st Battery survived until the 27th.[24] The battalion as a whole lost about 250 men (some 80 percent of its strength) during the final fighting.[25]

Sakakibara lived to describe the end of acting battalion commander Yamazaki, who was honored after death with the one individual citation as a "war god" awarded by the Japanese army for the fighting at Nomonhan. The 1st Heavy Field Artillery Regiment received a unit citation (*kanjō*) for its "glorious ending."[26]

By 25 August, the combat situation was deteriorating in the area of the 10-cm. cannon belonging to Maj. Kondō Toranosuke's 2nd Battalion of Takatsukasa's 7th Heavy Field Artillery Regiment, deployed near Heights 742 on the north side of the Holsten valley. To the left rear of Akai's 1st Infantry Battalion of the 64th Regiment, which was holding the flank of the lines ahead, Soviet troops had penetrated and were starting to put up red flags "like a forest." Russian tanks and eight trucks loaded with soldiers moved up from the Old Engineer Bridge and conducted reconnaissance. To the east of the Japanese batteries, there was no friendly infantry, of course; yet this was the direction from which the enemy began to strike. Takatsukasa says that there was insufficient ammunition for his guns, reduced to six by the 26th, to fire both west and east, against tanks "swarming like flies." When the IJA gunners swung the cannon to one side—an arduous task— the enemy armor easily turned to the other; prompt firing could not be accomplished. It became apparent that the Russians were circling behind the batteries, gradually forming a ring.

After Akai notified the 7th Regiment that the infantry was going to redeploy on the night of 25/26 August, Takatsukasa tried to coordinate the movement with his artillery. First Lt. Ozaki Masamichi, commanding the 3rd Battery, attempted to shift his guns. Temporarily checking the Russians with shrapnel fired at less than 1,000 meters, the Japanese connected their guns to tractors and headed for Suribachiyama, a large dip nearby, where they parked the cannon and lay on the slopes. Enemy tanks blocked further movement. A gunner heard Japanese soldiers singing the national anthem or a military song, then shouting cheers for the Emperor—the prelude to suicide. The 3rd Battery faced its three pieces west, behind the Akai infantry battalion, and south toward Noro Heights. The three cannon of the 4th Battery were aimed eastward in the direction of the bridge and Gake cliff.

A 3rd Battery gunner remembers that, after his tractor was knocked out, the soldiers tried to haul out his cannon, using ropes. Many of the men, however, began to drop the lines and flee as the skies lightened. After being moved only 200 meters, the cannon proceeded no farther. The gunner was still clinging to the rope, not because of heroism induced by the artillery regulations but because he had no idea where Chiangchunmiao was located, and he felt more secure in the presence of other Japanese soldiers. At this point, the hulk of a tank appeared, with its turret moving quietly. The gunner "hit the deck," but another man—a conscript, he thinks—stood up in panic and was blown away by a direct hit. After the firing stopped, the gunner abandoned his cannon and crawled toward the camouflaged caves in the area. When he found and entered a cave, a dozen soldiers were huddling there already, including battery commander Ozaki. They stayed until the afternoon of the 28th, when Ozaki chased away a Soviet truck with carbine fire, and the men in the cave decided to get out and flee.

On the morning of the 26th, Soviet tanks and troops endangered the 4th Battery, causing Major Kondō to lead a relief force that extricated the unit and brought it back to the site of the battalion command post, with heavy losses. The Soviet cordon was being tightened continuously. With the end in sight, Takatsukasa reached the decision to destroy all classified documents such as code books and files of orders. On the 27th, battalion commander Kondō made a last speech to his men, after which the burning of papers began. According to the records, the smoke drew the attention of enemy artillery, which proceeded to knock out all the Japanese trucks and tractors. Takatsukasa has an unusual explanation: he had directed that all documents be burned (*shorui yake*), but in the din of battle, he claims, the order was misunderstood to mean that all wheels should be burned (*sharyō yake*); consequently, it was the Japanese incineration of their own tractors and trucks that drew the Soviet artillery bombardment.[27]

Without their motorized capability, the guns had to be pulled by hand, and the men were left "naked," with no more than grenades for self-defense. Takatsukasa was determined not to lose any soldiers in the shelters, for he had heard that the men of the 1st Artillery Regiment, which possessed better positions, had bunched up in their bunkers and been incinerated by flamethrower tanks. Therefore the colonel ordered his soldiers to disperse widely in the trenches and to prepare to counterattack the armor. In fact, Takatsukasa asserts, he and Lieutenant Ozaki[28] charged enemy tanks several times, repulsing the machines and then returning to the defenses.

Although the Russians did not mount a direct assault, they deployed snipers around the Japanese and picked off the defenders. At the observation post, according to a battalion clerk, Takatsukasa and Kondō were pinned down by the afternoon of the 27th. The shelter itself was little more than a trench covered with boards and camouflaged with willow branches or grass. Toward evening, when Kondō tried to get a better look, he was shot through the neck by a sniper and killed instantly. While Japanese soldiers rushed to the major and called out to him in vain, Takatsukasa could be seen looking at Kondō and holding back his tears.

By now, only one of the Japanese cannon and a few dozen shells were left. Near daybreak, Takatsukasa tried to lead his survivors to join Akai's infantry, but they were checked by the enemy. According to Takatsukasa, he pulled back signalmen who had wanted to remain behind and headed for the old *danretsu* supply/maintenance location to the rear. The records note that at 3:30 A.M. the colonel left both battery commanders and 29 men to defend the surviving gun, and took the other survivors toward the *danretsu* site.

A PFC from the annihilated howitzer regiment had escaped to the Takatsukasa unit—"from the frying pan into the fire." After the cannon regiment's vehicles had been burned deliberately, only three sedans remained. The order was given to load the cars with seriously wounded, break the enemy circle, and head for Chiangchunmiao, but there was a shortage of drivers. Realizing that a journey through tanks undoubtedly meant death, the PFC tried to conceal the fact that he was a tractor driver. He was found out, however, was scolded, and was designated to drive the leading sedan—a left-hand-drive Dodge that he had never operated before. Five wounded men were crammed into the backseat, two into the front. At first, foot soldiers escorted the car. As it proceeded in stop-and-go fashion, in bright moonlight and under tracer fire, the infantrymen disappeared. Near dawn, the driver reached the Holsten crossing, where Soviet bridge guards could be seen around a fire. Petrified, the PFC held up behind a hill and would not move until a soldier beside him warned that they would never be able to reach the road on the south side unless they got across before daybreak. The reluctant driver approached the bridge gingerly and then speeded up. Soviet sentries jumped in front of the sedan, raised their arms, and yelled. Sheerly out of habit, the driver honked the horn, whereupon the Russians cleared a path and saluted him! He drove across the bridge at full speed and kept on racing to his destination. To this day, he has no idea what happened to the other two ambulance sedans behind him.[29]

General Hata had already learned from a survivor on 27 August about the destruction of the Someya unit on the preceding afternoon, and about the desperate situation on the north bank of the Holsten. Messages had also been received from the Takatsukasa regiment on the night of the 26th, and from the howitzer unit on the morning of the 27th. Although the Sixth Army would not believe it, by the 28th Hata was convinced that his heavy artillery above the Holsten had been annihilated. That day, the picture grew even clearer to the artillery corps commander—causing him intense pain—when two second lieutenants got through to his headquarters, one from Takatsukasa's regiment and the other from the howitzer regiment.

Nevertheless, Hata was stunned when Takatsukasa himself turned up at artillery corps headquarters with two officers and the "main body" on the morning of 29 August. The colonel reported on the disastrous battle situation, including the death of battalion commander Kondō, and pleaded for a "comeback." Hata, however, had never authorized Takatsukasa to abandon his guns and his positions and retreat to the Sixth Army area while his officers and men were left behind to die alone. Although most of the pieces had reportedly been destroyed by enemy fire and the regiment had been nearly annihilated, guns were as important to the artillery as regimental colors were to the infantry. Therefore Takatsukasa's unauthorized action generated a "bad atmosphere" in corps headquarters, exacerbating the situation created by Ioki's retreat. Hata noted that the Japanese forces seemed to have fallen into utter confusion by the 29th, with many dispirited soldiers having fled in small numbers, one after another. Rejecting Takatsukasa's entreaty, the general reprimanded him for bringing "the greatest possible disgrace" to the artillery and ordered him to enter house arrest to the rear. As for Takatsukasa, he says that he has forgotten the details of his withdrawal but that he never once felt that he had done anything wrong—except for the mixup about the burning of the wheels.[30]

Along the 64th Infantry's sector, based on Heights 733 above the Holsten, most of Ise's 13th Field Artillery Regiment rendered close support. While the Japanese counteroffensive was unfurling without success below the river, Soviet movements southward from Fui Heights grew more pronounced. On 23 August, the 12th Battery learned that the ammunition dump at Uzuru pond had been destroyed by enemy tanks. Liaison to the rear had been severed, and there was no way to obtain supplies. "The situation seems unfavorable for us," wrote the battery chronicler. "We are being encircled completely."

From an observation post set up to the rear, on the 24th, the 5th Battery commander, 1st Lt. Tokonami Shigeji, detected many columns marching in depth, apparently a rifle division, pulling wheeled Maxim machine guns with ropes and accompanied even by a canine corps. With the loss of commanding Gake cliff, the Japanese artillery had become vulnerable to bombardment from the rear. The arc of fire of the field guns was consequently reversed from the Halha direction. In the evening, several dozen Soviet tanks plus infantry were observed to have crossed the Halha and penetrated to a distance of 5,000 meters from the rearmost Japanese positions. Since there were no friendly forces to screen the supply/maintenance unit, it was pulled back to the gun lines. A hundred horses were assembled in a dip.

Ise's 3rd Battalion commander, Major Seki, had sought to coordinate his actions with those of the heavy artillery. On the night of 24/25 August, he briefed all of his platoon leaders, none of whom was acquainted with the situation. Since no steps had been taken to fire against enemy forces detouring from the rear, Seki warned them to redeploy at least one piece per battery by dawn, ready to fire in the opposite direction.

Around 11 P.M. on the 24th, Soviet loudspeakers could be heard blaring music and an appeal (in Japanese) to surrender. Russian forces, it was said, had cut off the IJA rear in the Nomonhan area. "You fellows won't get any more food or ammunition," warned the broadcast. "Stop your useless resistance, lay down your arms, and give up." The Japanese artillerymen enjoyed the music, ignored the propaganda, and kept working on their shelters and gun emplacements.

When the morning fog lifted on the 25th, Major Morikawa's 2nd Battalion saw a dozen enemy tanks advancing against the infantry positions 1,000 meters to the left front of the gun line. After the 5th Battery had got off only one round—and missed—remarkably accurate Soviet 15-cm. howitzer counterfire (probably preranged from the 24th) smashed the Japanese positions, knocking out four guns, slaying two gunners, burying Lieutenant Tokonami in rubble, and killing most of the nearby horses.

The 3rd Battalion observed 100 Soviet tanks and armored cars plus at least 1,000 troops on the high ground across the Halha on the 25th. Russian heavy artillery inflicted heavy losses, although the IJA field batteries tried to interdict the forces driving south from Fui and Uzuru. One Japanese air strike was made against the enemy gun sites, but no further raids by friendly planes were seen.

The Japanese batteries reported their plight but were ordered to defend their locations and not to withdraw. With the loss of Ikuta's infantry positions at Heights 731 and the approach of enemy tanks and troops as close as 100 meters, the situation was deemed critical by evening and orders were given to dispose of classified documents. Thunderous firing could be heard from the area of the heavy artillery positions, which were under attack by armor. Resolved to share the fate of their guns, the field artillery officers exhorted their men to prepare to counterattack the enemy with cold steel. When 3rd Battalion commander Seki informed Ise's headquarters about his situation, he was told that an infantry company was coming to help; but it was never seen, even that night, and if it was the 10th Company of the Yamagata regiment, it was destroyed next day.

In the 5th Battery, there was some sake left; each man took one sip and passed along the bottle. By evening, Soviet infantry—undoubtedly realizing that the Japanese artillery had been crippled—came down from the high ground ahead, accompanied by two or three armored cars, and drew as close as 300 meters. Armed with nothing more than carbines, the Japanese artillery soldiers held their fire. After dark on the 25th, the battalion sent orders to redeploy closer to the infantry regiment. The men cannibalized the four wrecked guns, put together one operational field piece, dragged it by muscle power, and buried the useless artillery. Rations were low; in the 6th Battery there was only one bag of kaoliang forage for 75 horses.

By 26 August, Colonel Ise had concentrated the remaining field guns of six batteries around Yamagata's infantry command post. One of the 3rd Battalion's two batteries, made up of old Type 38 field guns captured from Chang

Hsüeh-liang's army at the time of the Manchurian Incident, had been put out of action and now had to be deactivated. The colonel issued detailed instructions for the organization of rifle platoons and demolition teams, leaving only a minimum of personnel at the gun sites. Ammunition should be conserved for antitank firing, except in emergency cases of direct support of the infantry.

The 5th Battery commander remembers being visited by Ise on the 26th and being encouraged to take good care of the one surviving field piece. Nevertheless, the gun's recoil brake had been damaged the day before and the barrel would not retract properly when one shell was fired against armor approaching the infantry on the afternoon of the 26th. Since manual operation was ineffective, the gun crew was obliged to stop trying to fire. There were some rounds left, however, so the artillerymen pondered ways to detonate them with fuzes and shellcases. Clinging to the dip, the soldiers saw tanks approaching the trenches, with crewmen peering from open hatches. The Japanese hurled gasoline bottles, which sputtered on impact but would not ignite as they had in July. Several men were killed by 15-cm. howitzer fire, including an observation-post sergeant, Tanaka Atsuichi, whose touching last words—hastily scribbled as he lay dying in the arms of his commander—warranted showing to the Emperor, as did Major Umeda's testament.[31]

> Battery commander, sir: I greatly regret dying today, hit by a shell fragment. The Soviet army does not deserve to be feared, so please fight on till the last. I am very glad to become a falling petal on the borders. I will continue to defend the frontier here forever. Please don't release this news to the homeland until the war is over. Long live the Emperor!

On the evening of the 26th, the 15-cm. howitzer regiment sent the observation section chief and two battery commanders to confer with Seki's neighboring 3rd Battalion. The latter recommended that the heavy artillery move its observation post and train as close to the field artillery as possible, in view of the enemy's obvious intention to surround the Japanese gradually. But the observation chief unwisely insisted that the 23rd Division's approach was at hand, and that hostile forces on the flank and at the rear were small and would not encircle and charge the defenders.

By 27 August, Ise had at most nine operational guns with which to strive to cope with enemy armored forces striking from behind the Yamagata regiment. In the words of the 6th Battery annalist: "The grassy field around our positions had become pocked with craters, numberless fragments were strewn across the scorched sand, and it was difficult to walk across the area. The face of the hill had truly been transformed." All day on the 27th, the Russians coordinated their barrages from every direction: from the north and east, from the heights across the Halha to the west, and from the

Hasebe district to the south—a fact that augured ill for Japanese forces below the Holsten. There were two particularly fierce artillery bombardments in the morning, and three in the afternoon. Almost every Japanese horse was killed in the course of them. "It was horrible," note the IJA records. "We saw a shell hit a horse and explode it into the sky. Loose horses were roaming around the area, stopping here and there. One soldier could be seen among the animals, caressing them and stopping them from stampeding."

The last 12-cm. howitzer of the 9th Battery was smashed by enemy fire at 5:40 P.M. on 27 August. At last the Russians, who had been trying to move north along the Holsten valley since the 21st, were able to break through. Striking first with 100 troops and several tanks, the enemy advanced against the IJA heavy artillery's observation post between 6 and 7 P.M. Observing the combat through binoculars, in frustration, men in the 3rd Battalion could see the desperate struggle and the heartrending scene of wounded men being stabbed with bayonets. At twilight, about 300 Soviet soldiers plus tanks, which had been surrounding the 9th Battery near the river, cut across the Japanese rear and made contact with Russian forces at the Holsten, while hostile artillery occupied the dip behind. As the IJA batteries lost their guns, they formed demolition squads and little rifle platoons (one with a captured Maxim) to defend the regimental headquarters site and the observation posts.

Near midnight on the 27th, the 3rd Battalion sent a young officer to Akai's 1st Infantry Battalion of Yamagata's regiment to request reinforcements to defend the area behind the artillery observation posts. At 12:30 A.M., the officer returned with word that the infantry could not spare a soldier because of the huge frontage that had to be covered. Moreover, complained the infantry, when they had been hammered by enemy batteries the 3rd Battalion had not helped. To iron out this misunderstanding and to coordinate final resistance by the infantry and the artillery, Seki wanted to visit Akai, but it was impossible to get through by now.

The 3rd Battalion had lost phone contact with the regimental command post several times on the 27th, but by signalmen's herculean efforts that night it became possible for Seki to report to Ise. Morale was high, but there was insufficient ammunition, and the infantry had rejected the plea for assistance. It was nearly impossible to retain the observation-post dune with artillerymen only. Although the 3rd Battalion was entirely encircled, Seki wanted to facilitate the 23rd Division's rescue effort by exploiting weaknesses in the enemy's defenses and breaking through to the Holsten bridge area. Ise replied that he had only five pieces: two in the 6th Battery and three in the 8th Battery. But the division's main body was almost there, "so fight hard for one more day, despite great difficulties." Seki then sent his observation-post chief to Ise's headquarters with an urgent request for the transfer

of one gun from the 8th Battery. By now, however, the Russians had penetrated between the 3rd Battalion and the 8th Battery, and daybreak was
near; so no gun could be released to Seki.

The Russians circled both Japanese flanks and the rear on 28 August, generally at a distance of 300 meters but sometimes as close as 150 meters from
the outposts, observation sites, and wagon train. To the right and rear, hostile artillery took position 800 meters behind the lines of their infantry. Red
flags could be seen in many locations. Contact between Seki's observation
post and Akai's headquarters, about 700 meters away, remained severed
after 26 August. There may have been only 100 Soviet soldiers in the gap,
but they had emplaced a line of Maxim machine guns that dominated the
zone. Enemy trucks and troops were moving constantly on the plain across
the Holsten, and the Russians' main body of artillery on the left side of the
Halha had apparently displaced forward to Sambur Obo; three batteries of
15-cm. howitzers were already near the edge of the heights.

Soviet bombardments were intense from dawn on the 28th. "The enemy
made light of us," wrote the 6th Battery chronicler, "since we had no more
guns." At 11 A.M., Russian tanks and troops attacked the left flank and rear
of the 64th Infantry, from both sides of the Holsten. An hour later, hostile
rifle units approached the 3rd Battalion's rear from the district east of
Heights 755. The 8th Battery's train was driven back in confusion to the
battalion's observation post. Near 1 P.M., enemy barrages grew very severe,
and 500 infantrymen plus five tanks struck from the rear. The armor came
as close as a few dozen meters and pounded the trenches while the foot
troops hurled grenades. One improvised IJA rifle platoon, under two second
lieutenants, was wiped out at the outset. A new Soviet assault, launched
against the left rear of the observation post, was met by desperate resistance.
According to the 6th Battery, morale remained good. Even the wounded
picked up weapons and fought back. Those without small arms took sabers
from the dead or tied bayonets to willow limbs.

Past 2 P.M. on the 28th, a radio message was received by the 3rd Battalion
to the effect that elements of the division's relief unit had reached Ise's headquarters. Seki immediately tried to break through to the regiment but took
heavy casualties. The 9th Battery commander, 1st Lt. Yoshioka Hisao, and
36 men were killed. Soviet tank forces could be seen "very violently surrounding" Ise's command post at about 2:30. Giving up his effort to penetrate the circle, Seki decided to hold on to Jūgan Heights. At this point,
a regimental observation post lieutenant, who had been trying to make
contact with Komatsubara, advised Seki that the division had reportedly
crossed the Holsten that morning, was pressing toward Heights 755, and
near noon had apparently driven off enemy forces advancing south. The artillerymen's hopes soared despite the tank attacks and the concentrated

bombardment by field and heavy batteries (especially 15-cm. howitzers) they were forced to endure between 3 P.M. and twilight. Smoke blanketed the whole area, "making us feel as if we would choke to death, even inside our shelters." The main body of the enemy from the north ripped into the 2nd Infantry Battalion of the Yamagata regiment and caused it enormous losses, as was learned from one soldier who escaped. By twilight, the Russians got within 50 meters of Seki's lines. The major tried to contact Ise and the 8th Battery, but every runner was cut down by Soviet snipers.

The 6th Battery managed to restore two of its guns to a usable state by 6 P.M. and turned them against an enemy tank and infantry force that was attacking Ise's headquarters. Results were good but the last ammunition was expended. At 6:30, the pieces were rendered inoperable by gunfire. By the night of 28/29 August, there were only three Japanese field guns left (in the 8th Battery) on the entire north shore of the Holsten.

Battered and isolated to the southeast, Seki was faced with a serious decision about the fate of the remnants of his battalion. At 11 P.M., he learned from a regimental messenger that the 9th Battery, with some infantry, was still in action 500 meters east of Mitsubosa Heights, and that Akai's 1st Infantry Battalion was apparently going to try to break through to the Holsten bridge this night and make contact with the division relief force in that vicinity. Concerned about the helplessness of his defenses, especially if he could not rejoin the regiment, Seki decided to move his men to the 9th Battery's location. At midnight, the force reached its destination, a dip about 300 meters south of Akai's infantry. Soon after Seki got to the site east of Mitsubosa Heights, the Russians laid down heavy fire, after which their infantry, shouting loudly, launched a charge. The attackers stopped at point-blank range and did not penetrate the defenses of the Japanese, who drove them off. Soviet loudspeakers broadcast propaganda, followed by dance music, "designed to break our soldiers' fighting spirit," say the IJA records. "Although almost all of the men ignored it, there were some who felt uneasy."

In the meantime, Seki finally went off to conciliate infantry battalion commander Akai. Seki expressed regret that, owing to his combat involvement elsewhere on the 27th and hampered by the shortage of ammunition, his batteries had been unable to provide the requested close-support firing. Akai "seemed to understand a bit but maintained a reserved and aloof attitude." According to the infantry commander, his battalion was not going to rejoin Yamagata as originally ordered, but would continue to resist where it was. The status of the division relief force was entirely unknown. Seki also learned, supposedly for the first time, about the very costly combat of the 2nd Infantry Battalion against enemy tanks on the evening of the 28th. There was no information concerning the progress of elements of the 1st Infantry Battalion, which had intended to break through to the Holsten.

Seki weighed this information carefully. It was apparent that the fighting strength of the Ise regiment, of Sumi's Ikuta rifle battalion (supported by the 8th Battery), and of the 2nd Infantry Battalion of the 64th Regiment had been smashed. Once the Russians resumed their attacks after dawn on 29 August, it would become extremely difficult for Seki to hold his positions till the end without relief—particularly in concert with Akai's infantry, which had not sent even one soldier when the field artillery battalion was facing a crisis on the 28th. Of course, the 3rd Battalion headquarters and its 9th Battery had sustained many casualties, but a sizable number of able-bodied soldiers were still available. If only new guns could be obtained, it would be possible to participate in combat promptly and to resume the role of artillerymen once more. After trying to contact Ise on Akai's command-post radio without success, Seki regretfully decided at 1 A.M. on the 29th to lead his force alone through the cordon, via Heights 755, in four quiet columns, and then charge through to join the division rescue unit near the Holsten bridge. Monitored by the battalion aide, the wounded—moving at the rear—should "act lively" and keep up.

Seki's decision is formalized by the Ise unit's records, which assert that, at 2:30 A.M. on the 29th, the regiment issued an order calling for a "night attack" toward Nomonhan by the field artillery, in conjunction with the Yamagata regiment, starting at 3 A.M. The 3rd Battalion, less the 7th Battery, should contact the infantry nearby and proceed toward Nomonhan. Taking a guard squad and two infantry guides, the 8th Battery commander, Capt. Imoto Kazuichi, was specifically designated to contact Seki and deliver the order. Imoto never found Seki by the time the major set forth. Nevertheless, according to the battalion aide, 1st Lt. Ishibashi Kumazō, the colonel had imparted some important information to him on the evening of the 27th, when (he says) he had made it to regimental headquarters. Prospects were bleak and would undoubtedly get worse. Ishibashi must be ready to accept the fact that a pullback was unlikely. Communications would probably be broken entirely at the end, so it might become necessary to act on one's own (*dokudan senkō*). The aide got back to the battalion and conveyed the colonel's remarks to Seki.

The elements of Seki's 3rd Battalion set out at 2:10 A.M., once clouds had masked the moon. There were only 10 cavalry carbines; the rest of the men carried makeshift bayonet-spears. Taking advantage of trenches, the troops penetrated the Soviet outposts, staying low in the face of enemy gun sites on the plain 500 meters northeast of Gake cliff, where red flags flew. "Three hundred meters from the enemy's muzzles," note the records, "we escaped the jaws of death." At 2:40, three enemy tanks or armored cars were encountered on the route, 2,000 meters south of Jūgan Heights. Seki ordered his men to restrain themselves from attacking first, since the sole objective was to disengage; if the armor took action, of course close-quarter assaults must be launched. The troops squatted and waited for what seemed like ages but may have been only a few minutes. Shortly, the armored vehicles moved away. Since Russian 15-cm. howitzers were emplaced atop Heights 755, the Japanese veered toward the Holsten, passing through an enemy bivouac area near the hill and threading their way between tanks deployed 200 meters apart. When Seki's men reached the bridge around 5:40 A.M., enemy tanks could be seen scattered across the river but there was no sign of the 23rd Division, which caused the Japanese to feel "quite uneasy."

Seki decided to proceed north along the right bank of the Holsten en route to Nomonhan. At a range of 600 meters, the Japanese met heavy-weapons and small-arms fire from across the stream. Aide Ishibashi yelled to the troops to deploy and to head for the logistics base at Nomonhan. Some of the men fired back at the enemy, but most now split into two parties: one dashed north along the valley; the other (including Ishibashi) climbed onto the slope facing the river and became separated from Seki. Several enemy tanks advanced from the heights on the right shore, and armored cars pursued swiftly from the left side. In close-quarter fighting, the attackers were repulsed, but losses were heavy and Seki himself was hit in the right leg. At 11:30 A.M., more enemy tanks appeared on the high ground on the right shore. This time, the demolition squads were supported effectively by Miyao's Type 90 field artillery firing from the direction of Nomonhan.

Maj. Seki Takeshi reached Nomonhan by 2 P.M. on the 29th and reported to General Hata. He brought with him the last of his battalion headquarters, the 9th Battery, and the 7th Battery train—about 100 men to start with, plus another 400 soldiers, mainly infantry, picked up along the way. The major had no idea of Ise's fate yet. As for Imoto, who had tried to contact Seki during the night, it is said that the captain got to Nomonhan without encountering any enemy soldiers.[32] But the fact that there was a regimental order to evacuate his positions got Seki "off the hook."

The fate of the Japanese heavy and field artillery north of the Holsten was sealed when Soviet mechanized units outflanked the river line and penetrated deeply to the rear. Never overpowering against the enemy to the west and south, the IJA batteries now had to divide their coverage to embrace the north and east as well. At first, Ise's field artillery claimed impressive results in the period of 22-24 August: 30 Soviet guns destroyed and 114 neutralized, 53 tanks knocked out, 513 armored vehicles driven off, many troops and automatic weapons eliminated.[33] But the situation became hopeless after Fui Heights fell and enemy formations drove past Uzuru pond, in concert with units striking from below the Holsten. Not only did the Japanese gunners desperately need friendly infantry assistance (which Yamagata could not do much to provide), but recriminations erupted between the separated rifle and artillery forces. At the same time that the batteries were losing their pieces, they ran low on shells. By the end of August, Hata said his biggest problem was ammunition. Precious stocks were lost when Russian armor raided the Uzuru area. After the hard-pressed howitzer regiment asked him for ammunition, he had to contact the Sixth Army, from whom he received a cool reception. The last significant mention of resupply to the field artillery, for example, is found on 25 August, when a noncom from Seki's battalion made it back from Nomonhan with a truck carrying 400 shells.[34]

Most of the Japanese batteries were forced to defend their own gun sites and were knocked out by barrages before they could engage the enemy effectively. Gunners without guns were reduced to the role of trying to resist armor with spears and a few carbines. Many fought and died on the spot, in combat or by suicide; others fled. Cut off from higher headquarters, still others withdrew in fairly orderly fashion, although commanders who could not justify their pullback were punished to varying degree, regardless of rank. The spirit of the braver gunners is illustrated by battalion commander Umeda and observation post Sergeant Tanaka, whose powerful last testaments, penned shortly before death, were chosen by the Kwantung Army for presentation to the Emperor. Nevertheless, the annihilation of Japanese artillery units above the Holsten illustrates the obsolescence of First World War tactics against modern blitzkrieg.

35

Debacle

When you die on the battlefield, you should make sure that your corpse faces the enemy camp.

—*Hagakure*, 163

Sixth Army headquarters never thought seriously of quitting the Nomonhan battlefield, even when the Soviet offensive was in full swing and its own counteraction had failed. Such a course would have been intolerable, says senior staff officer Hamada, because it would have caused the enemy to become flushed with victory, would have furnished grist for propaganda, and would have exerted an extremely adverse influence not only on the guidance of the Manchurian populace but also on the conduct of the war in China.[1] On the night of 25/26 August, General Ogisu issued an operations order that indicated his thinking: the counteroffensive south of the Holsten would be resumed with new crack units, the 7th and 2nd infantry divisions. Emphasis was placed on the Heights 749-752 line below Lake Mohorehi, for the area northeast of the Holsten was deemed to be "comparatively rich in topographical undulations."[2]

As for the 23rd Division, it was supposed to "continue the offensive." Dispersed and already hurt very badly, however, Komatsubara's division was certainly in no condition to conduct or to "continue" any offensive in the literal sense, as the command should have known. Yamagata was reportedly holding fast as of 25 August, but contact with him was lost next day, and word was received of the crisis besetting the artillery north of the Holsten. On the 26th, too, Komatsubara was shaken by the news of the death in action of Colonel Morita of the 71st Regiment. To shore up the situation south of the river, Komatsubara devised a plan for an expedition that night, with as many men as possible, originally to relieve the Hasebe detachment. Although division officer Murata won the Sixth Army staff's assent to relief of the defenses, Ogisu rejected the idea. One uncharitable explanation is that the Sixth Army did not want to release any covering forces from the area around its headquarters until the main body of the 7th Division arrived (it was expected shortly). A more favorable explanation is that Ogisu, realizing that the 23rd Division had been ground down, did not want to engender false hopes by letting it try to mount a night attack to relieve the endangered defense forces on either shore.[3]

Ogisu rethought his insensitive instructions and, on the night of 26/27 August, issued a new operations order calling for the 23rd Division merely to secure the positions on both sides of the Holsten, and for the 7th Division to continue the offensive. Undoubtedly, the Sixth Army staff was affected by what it had observed of the 23rd Division in combat on the 26th. Not only was there a scare about Soviet armor, which appeared on the high ground west of Abutara and threatened the Japanese rear, but from a firing trench at the combat headquarters near Mohorehi, Hamada could hear the explosions and see the clouds of dust caused by artillery and air bombardments north of the Holsten. After dark, the sparkle of flares could be observed, followed by the fire of mortar shells—"one merging flame flashing in the night sky."[4] As Hamada says:

> Empty-handed, the defensive units could only resist penetration of their positions, but they had almost no means to cope with tank guns, heavy-weapon and mortar shells, air bombing, and strafing. The only thing they could do was to hide and wait for time to pass. It wrung my heart, imagining our soldiers in those positions. I have no words to express my irritation, anger, and helplessness. All I could do was pray for their good fortune in combat, with the deepest of regret.

If there was any idea of saving the 23rd Division from destruction, time was fast running out. Peering from his trench, Hamada thought several times about pulling back the defensive units on both banks of the Holsten and of consolidating the battle lines. On the 27th, the colonel was standing with the Kwantung Army deputy chief of staff, Yano, watching the bursts of dust kicked up by enemy shells. "General Yano did not say a word," Hamada recalls, "and I did not have the strength to do so." His silence of late August 1939 never ceased to torment Hamada.[5]

> The capability for resistance by the 23rd Division's position-defense units had almost reached the breaking point, I was thinking. In particular, how could the Sixth Army avail itself of the sacrifice by those units' desperate fighting and annihilation, just to earn a little bit of time? Already Lieutenant Colonel Ioki had abandoned the defenses at Fui Heights. If the same situation were to develop in the defensive units on both sides of the Holsten, where should the responsibility lie? My suffering and mental anguish were repeated, again and again, at the time, but I could not bring myself to voice my thoughts. First, I was afraid that some might criticize me for lack of courage. Second, if I judged that the 23rd Division could not hold the positions, I felt as if that was an insult to the division. I had a terrific urge to express my opinion, and the words rose to my lips, but I did not because I felt it would desecrate the division commander's feelings. Lastly, there was danger to the retention of the Tako-no-atama ("Octopus Head") positions[6] if the enemy should attack by taking advantage of the 23rd Division's pullout. As I think back calmly about my estimate of the situation at that time, I think that the decision should have been reached to withdraw and assemble the 23rd Division's defensive units under cover of the 7th Division, which had just arrived on 27 August, and that the whole Sixth Army should then have been combined to face the

enemy. I regret that I, though senior staff officer, did not recommend this. I was shackled by narrow views that blocked broad judgment. It was a great failure on my part. I think it stemmed from my lack of grounding as a military officer.

The language of Ogisu's two successive orders to Komatsubara may have contained little change of substance from the Sixth Army's standpoint. After all, the army's intention was merely to retain base points on both shores of the Holsten while waiting for the arrival of fresh divisions with which to unleash a new offensive—a notion in apparent keeping with the Kwantung Army's own thinking. Nevertheless, in Komatsubara's view, time had run out for his division by 27 August, when the so-called "anchors" had fallen or were falling, and both Fui and Noro Heights were lost. Elements of the 64th Infantry were clinging to the foothold on the north bank, but more than 65 percent of the regiment had been destroyed, and the losses of artillery in the Balshagal sector had reached 70 or 75 percent. Komatsubara therefore decided that the moment had come to collect the final scraps of his division and set forth on a one-way journey to bring "relief" to Yamagata, starting on the night of 27/28 August. In the true sense, this meant joining the last of his original infantry colonels and meeting death with him and all the survivors of the 23rd Division. When Komatsubara told his divisional engineer commander about his intention to conduct a "last charge" across the Holsten, Lieutenant Colonel Saitō "of course agreed with the division commander's firm resolve." The other engineer regiment commander, Numazaki, who had just been transferred to defend the Sixth Army's own sector, saw Komatsubara at the time of his fateful decision. To Numazaki, the general looked depressed and the headquarters staff officers seemed sorry that they could not comfort the division commander. "Still, they all had definitely made up their minds to attack and rescue their comrades, and not return alive from their desperate, indeed hopeless undertaking."[7]

At 1 P.M. on the 27th, Komatsubara issued his operational order.[8] That night, at 9 P.M., the relief force should start for New Engineer Bridge, in the following sequence: first, the 71st Infantry Regiment (a total of 400-500 men); second, the division and infantry group headquarters (47 men); third, the remaining elements of the 72nd Infantry Regiment under Captain Hirowatari (300-340 men); fourth, the Yotsuya battalion of the 6th IGU (200-300 men); fifth, the division engineers (200-300 men); and last, the division signal unit (50 men). A field artillery battery was also supposed to accompany the relief column.

Even the preceding estimates of manpower strength, totaling 1,200-1,500 troops at best—hardly more than the numerical equivalent of one regiment—are undoubtedly excessive. Hirowatari says the 72nd Regiment possessed nowhere near two battalions, and had the actual strength of two line companies. From the 71st Regiment, only Maj. Sugitachi Kamenojō's 1st Battalion was with Komatsubara. Lieutenant Colonel Higashi was bringing what was left of the two other battalions from the Nigesorimot sector, in an effort to rendezvous near the Holsten. As Onozuka explains, since the infantry companies were depleted, company organization was at an end. The battalion became the lowest echelon of de facto regimental organization, and the number of missing (apart from dead and wounded) was so great that even battalion commanders could only control about 70 or 80 men now.

Division intelligence officer Suzuki judges the relief force's whole strength at 900 men; engineer Lieutenant Colonel Saitō and the infantry corps aide, 2nd Lt. Murai Masakatsu, put it at 600-700; Capt. Hanada Shunji of the 71st Regiment calls it 500. The large number of walking wounded surely reduced the figure for effectives. There was no firepower heavier than machine guns. Suzuki thinks it was too difficult to bring regimental guns without horses. As for staff, Komatsubara had only Suzuki and Chief of Staff Okamoto (apart from Saitō), since Murata (Operations) and Itō (Logistics) had been wounded and evacuated.[9]

The tenor of Komatsubara's outlook is reflected in his exhortation to all his unit commanders prior to departure.[10]

> The division has been ordered to secure the positions on both shores of the Holsten River.
> Although the front-line units are securing their present locations, under attack by enemy infantry, tanks, and artillery, the situation is extremely dangerous.
> The division is going to establish a defensive system by making contact with those [front-line] units. The mission, which is important and difficult, can only be accomplished with a do-or-die spirit, and if the entire unit is imbued with one heart.
> I am prepared to die. All of you should share my resolve and carry out this mission with a sublime spirit of sacrifice.

As he listened to Komatsubara's words, Suzuki thought of many things. It was well known that Yamagata's relatively small force had been trying to defend a broad front against great odds, but it was not certain that the regiment was still alive. Nonetheless, the division must endeavor to break through to Yamagata and secure the positions vital to the Sixth Army's planned offensive. Suzuki was reminded of an episode during the early part of the Manchurian Incident when one Japanese platoon had been ringed by 1,000 bandits, and the regiment commander had had to lead a rescue column. There was nothing more painful or difficult than such a mission, the colonel had said, especially after time had been lost. Now, before the movement to the Holsten, the feelings of Suzuki (and of everybody from Komatsubara down, he thinks) were both "tragic and painful."[11] As for Captain Hirowatari, it was his understanding that the Komatsubara force was setting out to occupy and defend the old positions of the 72nd Regiment above the Holsten. Only later did he learn that the "rescue" of the Yamagata detachment was involved.[12]

Although Komatsubara's intended night attack of 26 August had been countermanded by Ogisu, no such cancellation was forthcoming on the 27th. But when the Sixth Army learned of the division commander's resolve, according to Hamada, "all of us, including the army commander, were perplexed." Komatsubara's feelings, however, were admittedly very understandable and worthy of respect. As Hamada asserts:[13]

> The division commander himself was directing the battle, after having lost brigade commander Kobayashi, whom he had depended upon and trusted the most, like "both of his arms." [Komatsubara] could not merely sit by and watch the desperate fighting by the position-defense units, so he had decided to try to deal one [last] blow to the enemy, employing the combined strength of the 23rd Division. For his place of death, he selected the site of his old command post.

Disturbed by Komatsubara's decision, Ogisu hoped that the division commander would be more prudent, "from the larger standpoint." Komatsubara admitted in his diary that, by proceeding with his plan, annihilation was to be expected; this must have been behind the Sixth Army's private recommendation to 23rd Division Chief of Staff Okamoto to be cautious, since the destruction of the division (and its commander) would cause an "international problem." Although this counsel was not made directly to Komatsubara and no countervailing order was issued, Ogisu did direct his own chief of staff, Fujimoto, to rush to the front to try to dissuade the division commander from risking his life across the Holsten with his depleted force.

On the verge of Komatsubara's departure, around 9 P.M. on the 27th, Fujimoto arrived. A two- or two-and-a-half-hour private conversation ensued between the two generals, mainly in Komatsubara's sedan, out of earshot of the staff. From Komatsubara's notes, the highlights of the discussion are apparent. Fujimoto conveyed Ogisu's order that Komatsubara report to army headquarters immediately, but asserted that he did not know the reason for the order. Ogisu was acquainted with the night-advance plan. In reply to the question whether the movement should be implemented or suspended, Fujimoto said it could proceed. To Komatsubara, however, the advance could not be made if he was being called back "for some unknown reason"; so he had ordered the movement to continue. When Fujimoto argued that the operation could be entrusted to somebody else, Komatsubara retorted: "What is the division commander supposed to do then?"[14]

Komatsubara very rarely stood up to the pressure or disputed the counsel of higher headquarters. Now, however, he considered his honor and that of the 23rd Division at stake, and Fujimoto eventually had to give up and return to the Sixth Army. Suzuki says that when the division commander joined the march at about 11:30 P.M. on the 27th, he was very calm and no different from his usual self.[15]

Both Komatsubara and Ogisu have been criticized for the handling of the desperate night movement of 27/28 August. If the Sixth Army commander was not willing to let Komatsubara and his division seek death, he should have forthrightly ordered cancellation, as he had done the day before. Instead, Ogisu seems to have been willing to let the remnants of the 23rd Division proceed (now that the 7th Division was on the scene), but unwilling to lose Komatsubara himself. Some have said that Ogisu's approach was dictated by considerations of "obstinacy, 'face,' and friendship." Others suggest that the Sixth Army suffered from a lack of wisdom, discernment, and command ability, and that no better could have been expected of the inept but cocky Kwantung Army. Fearful of enemy forays, Ogisu and the rattled Sixth Army officers were trying to convince themselves of the feasibility of their thinking while at the same time covertly apologizing to Komatsubara for the impending loss of his division and pinning their hopes on the proposed new offensive by fresh forces. To Captain Hanada, in the forefront of the relief operation, the behavior of the Sixth Army was strange. If there was any sincere desire to save the lives of the men of the 23rd Division, which had fought hard and well, the army should not have allowed the last sortie, regardless of the rationale. It seems to Hanada as though the 23rd Division was no longer wanted.[16]

With regard to Komatsubara's own responsibility, Hanada retains similarly negative thoughts. It was reckless, he says, for the division commander to have scraped together the survivors of beaten and exhausted units and to have plunged into enemy-infested territory, deliberately courting isolation and the equivalent of suicide. Whatever the validity of such an action in theory, retention of the positions north of the Holsten was out of the question with such a small and feebly armed force. The concept was unworthy of a general officer's leadership. If the expedition stemmed from Komatsubara's desire for a journey of death, Hanada remarks, "there was neither the necessity nor the justification for him to have taken his subordinates along as companions."[17] Engineer Numazaki sums up the projected operation as follows: "Everybody at the 23rd Division must have known that they were 'pushing things' and that the attack was unsuitable. But if the action was at all useful, the Sixth Army ought to have reinforced it to insure success."[18]

Late in taking off, no doubt because of the long discussion between Fujimoto and Komatsubara, the men of the relief force—near the limit of their physical endurance—started trudging slowly and carefully toward the river between 11 and 11:30 P.M. on 27 August. The 72nd Regiment says it could not take off until midnight because the trucks arrived late. General Hata saw Komatsubara off on his "last journey" in the moonlight, wishing him the best of luck. Having conducted some reconnaissance in the afternoon, Major Sugitachi's battalion led the force from the area on the north side of Heights 749, heading straight for Old Engineer Bridge, the more easterly of the two Japanese spans over the Holsten. By the light of a nearly full moon, Hanada's 3rd Company—dispersed and moving stop-and-go—spearheaded the advance, directed by Sugitachi. Between 1 and 1:30 A.M., the vanguard encountered heavy machine gun and tank fire near Izumi spring at the bend in the Holsten. After overrunning Soviet positions on the high ground northwest of Heights 753 at 1:40 A.M., the Japanese pressed against a second line. In the melee that followed, near 2 A.M., Sugitachi was shot down; he was already dead when Suzuki (his military academy classmate) ran up to try to help. Sugitachi was the third of this battalion's commanders to fall at Nomonhan. His aide, a first lieutenant, was killed at the same time as Sugitachi. Suzuki pressed the advance force to keep going after Sugitachi's death, and Hirowatari's 2nd Company of the 72nd Infantry was rushed up to strike the Russians' left flank because (according to that regiment) "matters had not developed as intended."

Around 2 A.M., noted Komatsubara, the Japanese finally broke through the Russian lines near the Izumi bend, knocking out one antitank gun and two or three heavy machine guns in the process. By 3:30 the force reached Old Engineer Bridge. Lieutenant Murai remembers encountering trenches, covered with tents, two or three times during the advance. The holes were easy to spot, for dim lamplight seeped from them. Cautiously lifting the edge of the tent covers and peering inside, Murai could detect three or four Russian soldiers sound asleep inside in each case. Since the intention of the Japanese was to get across the river as soon as possible, without complications that could be avoided, Murai did the sleeping Russians no harm, quietly tucking down the edges and moving on.[19]

Before dawn on the 28th, Higashi's main portion of the 71st Regiment, which had disengaged from the Nigesorimot district, ran into the 1st Battalion south of Heights 753, below Old Engineer Bridge. Although the meeting was accidental, the timing of the rendezvous represented one of the few coordinated actions by the Japanese during the whole Nomonhan war. The men of the regiment thanked each other for their hard fighting and prayed for the souls of their dead, from Colonel Morita down. A soldier recalls shivering during the march in the cold of the late-August night, even though winter uniforms had been issued the night before. Higashi's "main force" was certainly not large—about 300 men (primarily from the 2nd Battalion, plus a few from the smashed 3rd) with an actual strength of three companies, to add to the two companies of the 1st Battalion. The regiment possessed only nine heavy machine guns, two regimental guns, and four battalion guns.[20]

Higashi had his men occupy positions north of Old Engineer Bridge, and had the 1st Battalion cover Komatsubara's movement from the south shore (led by elements of the 72nd Regiment now) to the dunes northeast of New Engineer Bridge, which was accomplished by 5 or 6 A.M. A dozen enemy tanks started firing from the south side at dawn but were driven off by the 71st Regiment's few heavy weapons. Past 9 A.M., flamethrowing tanks attacked on the north bank. Four kilometers downstream, on the right bank near New Engineer Bridge, the Yotsuya unit reported knocking out five tanks. Radio communication with the Sixth Army was not possible, there were no telephone lines, and neither the ammunition nor the food trucks could get through. The 10 trucks of 2nd Lt. Hamada Shōji's transport platoon, at the tail end of the relief force, had been assaulted by 100 Russian soldiers at about 6 A.M., two kilometers southeast of the old bridge. Employing his one grenade launcher, the platoon leader tried to drive off the enemy with his 17 men, but the Japanese were cut off and overrun shortly by a force of 30 or 40 tanks. All of the trucks were burned, Hamada was killed, and only four IJA soldiers got out alive.[21]

Kusaba's 7th Field Artillery Battery of three guns also could not break through the Russian cordon, although the captain had hoped to smash hostile armor by antitank and point-blank firing, at which the Japanese gunners excelled. Since horses were not available, Kusaba had borrowed five trucks; it took more than four hours even to reach the jump-off point because of terrain and liaison problems. When the battery caught up with the relief column and started the advance, rain fell for a while. The desert track became difficult for the heavily laden trucks, and the battery lost contact with the main force after 20 or 30 minutes. Kusaba's lead truck bogged down, under fire, and the men took cover. Organizing teams of rifle scouts, the captain carefully pushed across the crestline with his trucks and guns. At 400 meters, he engaged three tanks and knocked them out with a captured antitank gun, and then fired shrapnel to mow down 40-50 attacking enemy soldiers at a distance of 100 meters. Seven more tanks had apparently been abandoned on low ground ahead. Deploying one field piece and the captured antitank gun, 2nd Lt. Hashimoto Eiichi destroyed the tanks in succession, at 30 meters, his first shot blowing up an attached ammunition vehicle. IJA signalmen wiped out all 11 Soviet soldiers, probably the crewmen, who were flushed from a trench. But a three-man Japanese artillery patrol, under a lieutenant, was annihilated while scouting what proved to be a large enemy formation.

At daybreak on the 28th, Kusaba's battery detected Soviet artillerymen, in full view on a crestline, loading and aiming two pieces. With five or six rounds the Japanese gunners destroyed the hostile pieces, and then a team of signalmen charged forward and wiped out the Russian gun crews. While observing through field glasses, Kusaba was hit in the chest by a sniper firing from less than 20 meters away. The captain was evacuated to Mohorehi with two of his mortally wounded subordinates. At the time, Komatsubara had the correct impression that Kusaba's battery—which he never saw—had been compelled to pull back. Suzuki remembers the unmanageable truck problems of the field artillery. General Hata prettifies the matter by stating that, once Kusaba had been wounded and the ammunition had been used up, the unit returned to artillery corps headquarters "after obtaining the division commander's permission."[22]

Komatsubara's men remained pinned down in dips near New Engineer Bridge all day on the 28th, sustaining intense fire from artillery to the south and armor on both sides of the river. After noon, groups of as many as a dozen tanks launched a series of attacks. Since daylight movement was impossible, at 3:30 P.M. Komatsubara issued an operations order calling for the force to prepare to proceed that night to the location of the Yamagata regiment, hardly more than three kilometers to the west. The proposed action was designed to "lure" the enemy into that area and thus to facilitate the Sixth Army's offensive plans. Special attention should be paid to anti-tank defense and to conservation of ammunition.[23]

The absence of contact with higher headquarters was a source of continuing distress to Komatsubara, and "do-or-die" messengers were the only possible solution. Three officers were selected, to represent the last of the 23rd Division and of both infantry regiments: Capt. Kuroda Yoshio, a division aide; young probationary officer Niwa Hiroshi from the 72nd Regiment; and wounded old Captain Onozuka from the 71st Regiment. In the evening, Chief of Staff Okamoto, the former commander of the 71st, called in Onozuka to see Komatsubara and him, and to discuss his mission: as the ranking officer to have lived through the entire fighting and thus to know the "whole story," Onozuka was to render the final report. Komatsubara added that the division would meet its end by the Holsten. Since there would be no survivors, it was imperative to relate the division's deeds, past and present. In addition, the Sixth Army must be given the division's new radio frequency, because the Russians had captured a unit's code books and had easily broken the system.

Onozuka turned his post over to Captain Miki, and asked Lieutenant

Colonel Higashi if he had any last request. Higashi said that there was nothing really special; his only son should be told to take care of matters. In Hailar, the commander had left two wicker footlockers, containing little of value. Would Onozuka please try to deliver them to the family? "I am going to die now," stated Higashi calmly, "but there is nothing to worry about." Having penned his last testament and clipped a lock of hair, he gave them to Onozuka to convey to his kin. The captain was much moved by Higashi's splendid (*kirei*) attitude, the "embodiment of military virtue."

His arm in a sling, Onozuka took off in the twilight with one soldier on the difficult 15-kilometer journey. Enemy tanks were on all sides, and the machine gun fire was so severe that it was necessary to crawl. Relying on his compass and his instincts for direction, Onozuka encountered numerous Soviet sentry outposts, which he tried to sidestep. When engines were heard, he and the soldier hid in the grass. Near daybreak, Onozuka could discern many trucks of uncertain nationality and many tents, which seemed "somewhat Japanese." It proved to be Sixth Army headquarters. Onozuka was greeted by name by Ogisu, who had known him since regimental days. The general told him to eat before reporting, whereupon Onozuka wolfed down breakfast, for he had had no food for two days. Then he reported in detail, as Komatsubara's "proxy."[24]

On 28 August a patrol reported to Hirowatari (commanding the 72nd Infantry) that, along the proposed route of advance, several enemy tanks were operating at a distance of 1,000 meters, and that friendly infantrymen were retreating in two's and three's. Around 11 P.M., the captain led the advance by the Komatsubara force through the drizzling, moonless night. The division commander noted that the wounded slowed the march of the main body, and that snipers were encountered near the old IJA artillery supply dump. When the Japanese passed the wrecked positions of their 15-cm. howitzer and 10-cm. cannon regiments, wrote Komatsubara, "the appalling carnage was painful even to look at, and we could well imagine how difficult the struggle of the heavy artillery must have been." A headquarters sergeant was shocked to see a huge hole in the barrel of an IJA heavy artillery piece, and an overturned tractor—one of the most modern items of equipment in the army at that time. Many Japanese corpses lay in the trenches, as if asleep. To add insult to injury, between 1 and 2 A.M. Komatsubara heard Soviet loudspeakers blaring music from their positions, "as if to celebrate and savor their victory." Saitō thinks the choral folk songs were intended to cheer the Russians' own troops, not to wage psychological warfare, although they caused an eerie sensation among the Japanese.[25]

According to Hirowatari, by 1:30 A.M. his men learned that Soviet security was extremely tight, in the form of a chain of guard lines, near the old rations dump of the Sakai regiment. Tanks and trucks were coming and going constantly to the south, toward New Engineer Bridge, causing Hirowatari to veer north and west through enemy positions. As the Japanese neared their destination, they encountered stiff resistance by machine guns and antitank weapons at 3 A.M. There was also a fierce firefight an hour later at the former command post of the Kobayashi group, but the positions were reconquered by about 4 A.M.[26]

Higashi's 71st Regiment, with the main force, reported a comparatively easy time getting through to its objective three kilometers south of Heights 733. An accompanying engineer company was especially helpful because of its knowledge of the terrain. Engineer Saitō thinks that he encountered Soviet sentry fire only twice that night, but the Japanese did not respond and pressed forward. A machine gunner, soaked through and utterly exhausted from hunger and lack of sleep, recalls how the wounded, even the seriously hurt, had to keep moving with their units. The command team was carrying such a soldier on a stretcher made from two rifles and a tent cover. Every time it was necessary to break through enemy resistance, the litter was placed on the ground; it was then picked up again once it was safe to resume the advance. By 3 A.M., Higashi's men had overcome the last light resistance, after which they sought to deploy and dig in promptly, for the formations were jumbled and the confusion was great. The records say that the construction of trenches was being completed by 6 A.M., when concentrated enemy bombardment commenced. But the machine gunner admits the defenses were not ready. "It was a matter of the overwhelming difference in material strength," he remarks.[27]

But what of the Yamagata detachment, which Komatsubara was intending to relieve? Around the former Kobayashi unit command post there was no sign of Colonel Yamagata or of the artillery regiment commander, Ise. Staff officer Suzuki conferred with Komatsubara and Hirowatari, and then moved ahead with some soldiers to reconnoiter. Suddenly, around 3:40, the challenge of a Japanese sentry could be heard. Somebody in the van answered, "We have come, as you can see, so rest easy." "Thank you very much," said the guard, lowering his bayoneted rifle and sobbing at the welcome sight of the column of advancing troops. Suzuki, in turn, was overjoyed at encountering friendly forces—Lieutenant Colonel Akai's 1st Battalion of the 64th Regiment, closest to the Holsten. Akai sent his aide to contact the approaching troops, since the units had not been identified amid the tumult and confusion. The aide ran into Suzuki and brought him to Akai's command post.

Suzuki's pleasure was short-lived. To his chagrin, Akai said he was going to follow his regimental orders and leave to catch up with Yamagata and the colors. This made no sense to the major, and he said as much: the division commander himself had broken through with a rescue force to help secure Yamagata's key points as the basis for the Sixth Army's forthcoming operations; clearly, the battalion commander should stay put, or, as Suzuki more graciously phrased it, the major "would like to trouble [Akai] to loan his soldiers to the division one more time." But Akai was Yamagata's subordinate, not Suzuki's, and he chose to take his official orders from his own regiment.[28]

It seems that at 11 P.M. Akai had been ordered to rejoin the regimental colors. Twenty minutes later, the order was rescinded and the battalion was directed to attack Jūgan Heights immediately—a feint (*yōdō*) operation. Then, around 3:30 A.M.,[29] Akai received new instructions by radio from Yamagata: the regiment was falling back to Nomonhan, and Akai should take his surviving troops, break through the enemy cordon, and also proceed to Nomonhan to join the parent regiment.

The battalion commander promptly reported the arrival of the division relief force to Yamagata, but the regiment, already on the move, had shut down its radio receiver, and communication was no longer possible. Disappointed and astonished, Suzuki took leave of Akai, studied the area, and pondered ways of deploying the slender relief force, since there was no choice but to retain this corner of Balshagal, now that Komatsubara had come so far. When the division commander and the main body came up shortly, Suzuki made his recommendations for defending these final positions of the 23rd Division, after which a linkup should be made with Yamagata. The relief troops moved in without interference, and then the search began for the 64th Regiment's headquarters. Short-range patrols were dispatched in every direction, but only enemy forces were detected. There was no trace of Yamagata or Ise.

As for the problem of Akai, Komatsubara sent Major Morinaga, an officer attached to division headquarters, to reason with him. Akai indicated that he was concerned about the fate of the colors accompanying his regiment's main body, which had withdrawn, and that he would follow them unless he received a special order from the division commander. According to Komatsubara's diary entry for the 29th, he got through to Akai that night and heard from him that the battalion was encircled but that it had been directed by the regiment commander to pull out. "Since the battalion was maintaining the positions for the other companies," noted Komatsubara, "I ordered that those positions be secured if possible." Evidently this permissive, oral injunction still did not represent the official "special order" that Akai had spoken of, for he left the positions and took his battalion toward Nomonhan on the night of 29/30 August.

Some suggest that Komatsubara did not press Akai more strongly because

The 72nd Inf. Regt. northeast of Kikugata Hgts., 15 July 1939
(courtesy of BBSS)

Wounded Col. Nagano Eiji being evacuated from Noro Hgts.
area, 24 July 1939 (Nomonhan-kai)

IJA machinegunners and infantry on the defensive (courtesy of BBSS)

IJA troops at rest, fending off mosquitoes with head nets, June 1939 (author's collection)

Manchukuoan Army field artillery unit (*Nomonhan bidanroku*)

MPRA cavalry unit (author's collection)

Improvised IJA observation post (author's
collection)

IJA close-quarter teams attack Soviet armor, ca. 3 July 1939 (painting
by Fujita)

Gasoline bottles vs. Soviet armor
(drawing by 2nd Lt. K. Yoneimoto)

An IJA rapid-fire gun in action (drawing
by 2nd Lt. K. Yoneimoto)

Col. Yoshimaru Kiyotake (3rd from left, facing camera), Col. Tamada
Yoshio (4th from left, studying document), Lt. Gen. Yasuoka Masaomi
(2nd from right), early July 1939, just before the death of Yoshimaru
(courtesy of U. Masuda)

Type 89 Kō tank in use by Yoshimaru Regt. Marking: "Aikoku [Patriotism] 7 (Fukuoka)" (courtesy of U. Masuda)

IJA tankers (courtesy of BBSS)

Type 89 tank being guided across the Arshaan River bridge en route to Handagai, June 1939 (courtesy of Z. Tomioka)

The tank in which Col. Yoshimaru Kiyotake was killed, 3 July 1939 (courtesy of U. Masuda)

ımada Regt.'s night attack in the rain, 2-3 July 1939 (painting by Sergeant Fukada)

IJA armor advancing to the front, June 1939 (*Nomonhan bidanroku*)

Knocked-out Soviet armor, 24 July 1939 (author's collection)

IJA rapid-fire guns, Chiangchunmiao ordnance depot, Sept. 1939 (courtesy of Y. Imaoka)

IJA field artillery piece (foreground) and 15-cm. cannon (background), Chiangchunmiao ordnance depot, Sept. 1939 (courtesy of Y. Imaoka)

Captured Soviet artillery, 24 July 1939 (author's collection)

Captured Soviet Maxim heavy machine gun, July 1939 (courtesy of U. Masuda)

Soviet colors captured by the 72nd Inf. Regt., 24 July 1939 (author's collection)

At an IJA airbase on the open plain, 24 July 1939 (author's collection)

Master Sergeant Nishihara rescuing Lt. Col. Matsumura Kōjirō
(painting by Fukazawa Kiyoshi)

[A Type 97 fighter attacking
oviet I-16 (painting by Fukazawa
iyoshi)

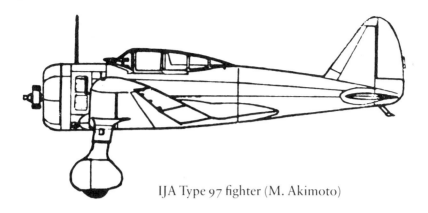

IJA Type 97 fighter (M. Akimoto)

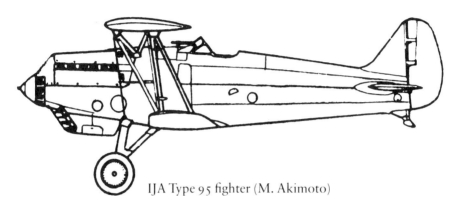

IJA Type 95 fighter (M. Akimoto)

Wreckage of Soviet aircraft (courtesy of BBSS)

Soviet I-16 ("Abu") fighter (M. Akimoto)

An IJA tank captured by Soviet forces, 3 July 1939 (Shishkin)

Soviet I-15 fighter (M. Akimoto)

Struggling to get from Arshaan to Handagai, 26 June 1939 (courtesy of BBSS)

Fighting near the Halha River crossing site, 3 July 1939 (courtesy of BBSS)

An IJA water-purification unit at work, 14 Sept. 1939 (courtesy of BBSS)

he regarded his fundamental mission as completed. Others think that the division commander simply had no clear-cut operational policy, and that finding a place to die honorably was more on his mind than securing base points above the Holsten. Why compel Akai to stay behind when Yamagata, the ostensible raison d'être of the relief expedition, had already left? It was also difficult to argue with an officer who wanted to protect his regimental colors. But perhaps the best reason for Akai's obduracy is revealed by a soldier from the 64th Infantry: "it was a manifestation of the regiment's silent resentment toward the division."[30]

Colonel Yamagata and the 2nd Battalion of his 64th Regiment had been desperately defending the Heights 733 (Remizov) sector against elements of a Soviet armored brigade, three infantry regiments, and a machine gun brigade, converging from the west, southwest, and east. Supporting Japanese field and heavy artillery batteries were systematically annihilated, as we saw, and the time of crisis came for Yamagata by 28-29 August, when Zhukov gave direct orders to his 24th Motorized Infantry Regiment, supported by armor, to smash the last Japanese resistance. Not only did Yamagata lose telephone communication with the 23rd Division from the morning of 23 August, but he was bereft of radio contact from the afternoon of the 28th. The colonel knew, however, that Komatsubara was bringing a relief force on 27/28 August, and he expected that the division would reach him by the 28th.

When a second night fell without the appearance of the reinforcements, Yamagata had to reevaluate his deteriorated situation. The positions on the right flank had been penetrated, and the 2nd Battalion was near annihilation, with less than 150 effectives (or 25 percent of the original strength). Enemy tanks and infantry were as close as 30 meters at some points. To the rear, the high ground had been occupied by the Russians since the preceding night and draped with red flags. The main armament of the defenders was reduced to infantry rifles and grenades, and engineer explosives; the 2nd Battalion had lost its remaining rapid-fire gun on 26 August. Resupply was utterly impossible, and the collapse of the last defenses seemed inevitable once day broke on the 29th—especially since Komatsubara appeared to have been unable to break through. "We felt cornered," says a battery commander.

Yamagata took some preliminary steps. He ordered Akai's 1st Battalion to launch the diversion at Jūgan Heights, and Ise's field artillery to construct gun emplacements to cope with the attacks expected on the 29th. But, after conferring with Ise, Yamagata decided on the transfer (*tenshin*) of the whole detachment toward Nomonhan to join the main forces, starting at 3 A.M.

Still hoping that Komatsubara would arrive, the colonel deferred issuing the order as long as he possibly could—until about 2 A.M. on the 29th. Akai's 1st Battalion to the south and Kanaizuka's 3rd Battalion to the north were notified as promptly as possible but, in the event, neither battalion was able to disengage that night.

At 2:30 A.M., Ise issued his own operations order to the remnants of his field artillery. Before setting out at 3, the units should bury the corpses and dispose of the destroyed weapons, get ready to carry the seriously wounded, and prepare Molotov cocktails. Since all the guns had been knocked out by now, and all the horses had been killed, noted the 2nd Battalion, the artillerymen dismantled key parts of their pieces and buried them. The slightly wounded were directed to walk alone, and litters were devised for the severely injured. In the battalion headquarters, only a few men were still unwounded.[31]

Around 3 A.M., Yamagata left Heights 733 with his headquarters, the 2nd Infantry Battalion, and the 9th Company, plus the survivors of Sumi's Ikuta battalion, two engineer platoons, and Ise's field artillery (Morikawa's 2nd Battalion and 8th Battery). The force headed south, in order to proceed along the valley above the Holsten and, hopefully, to meet Komatsubara's troops. Perhaps enemy action in that direction also seemed somewhat less formidable than to the north and east of Heights 733. The effect, however, was to enter the jaws of Zhukov's Central and Southern forces. In addition, Yamagata's timing was unfortunate: 3 A.M. had become too early or too late to leave. If the colonel could only have abandoned the idea of "changing direction" that night, Komatsubara would have reached his positions by daybreak, with results that could hardly have been worse than proved to be the case on the 29th. Alternatively, if Yamagata could have set out by midnight, his detachment might have made satisfactory progress toward Nomonhan before the sun rose. Instead, the colonel and his men were caught en route in broad daylight, and missed running into the relief force by less than an hour at best, or by a couple of hours at worst.[32]

Not until 4:30 A.M. did the field artillery units start their advance, well behind the infantry. Shortly before 5 they had already been detected by the enemy, who sent up pistol flares. On the right flank, nearest the Holsten, the 8th Field Artillery Battery came under attack by tanks that declined to come closer than 50 meters but that swept the area with withering machine-gun fire. "There was no way to resist," remarks the acting battery commander, 1st Lt. Ōmura Seitarō, "and the withdrawing units fell into confusion." Since it was thought that friendly forces were deployed at the river line and that matters had been progressing favorably on the opposite bank, the battery pressed toward the Holsten. Across the river, artillery and soldiers could be seen. When Ōmura had a soldier wave the Japanese flag in that direction, it only drew fire. Ahead lay New Engineer Bridge, but again the Russians opened fire there, forcing the Japanese to climb the higher ground above the stream. Ōmura yelled to his men (about 35, all told, at that point) to stop bunching up around him. At the old logistics site on the heights, drawing on the beer bottles and gasoline lying around, the lieutenant ordered his soldiers to prepare Molotov cocktails for use against the tanks pressing from the rear. From the hilltop, Ōmura now could see the Izumi bend below, and Japanese troops crossing the Holsten. Thus encouraged, he led his men down to the swampy ford. Halfway across, the battery was saved from the pursuing tanks by friendly artillery fire, probably Miyao's motorized Type 90 guns deployed toward Nomonhan.[33]

Matters did not develop as well to the left of the 8th Battery, where Soviet armor detected and hammered Major Morikawa's 2nd Field Artillery Battalion, from front and left, after 5 A.M. Within the hour, the number of tanks had increased to several dozen. Pinned down by fire and pursued by tanks 500-600 meters to the rear, the battalion lost precious time. Daylight had come by the time the men reached the cliffs at the Holsten. By now, Yamagata's main force was 2,000 or 3,000 meters ahead. From the left bank, the battalion incurred the fire of tanks, artillery, and a dozen heavy machine guns, directed against the right flank. As had occurred in the 8th Battery, Morikawa's force tried to wave off what were thought to be friendly troops on the opposite shore—an illusion soon demolished by the distinctive firing of water-cooled Maxim machine guns.

The withdrawal, previously orderly and quiet, broke down now, around 6:30 A.M. Many casualties were incurred, including the deaths of battalion commander Morikawa and the 6th Battery commander, 1st Lt. Kusaba Hiroshi. Surviving officers, such as the 5th Battery commander, 1st Lt. Tokonami Shigeji, remembering Major Morikawa's injunction to "get to Nomonhan with as many men as possible, no matter what," dashed down the gentle slopes, 30 meters to the Holsten, and pushed forward with their soldiers along the valley. These scattered remnants, too, were saved by the antitank firing of Miyao's field artillery located on the south shore. Few men appeared, however, at the 7th Heavy Field Artillery Regiment's gun line around 9 A.M.; a larger number proceeded toward Nomonhan by another route, north of the Holsten. At 11 A.M., the survivors of the battalion were collected near the field hospital at Nomonhan. After the wounded were committed to medical care, the 2nd Battalion was left with only 16 effectives.[34]

Seki's 3rd Battalion, which, as we saw, had set out on its own at about 2 A.M., reached the Holsten bridge at 5:40 A.M., encountered armor on both sides of the river, split up under fire, received support from Miyao's field artillery after 11:30 A.M., and made it to Nomonhan by 2 P.M. on the 29th.[35] It is strange that Seki encountered neither Yamagata nor any other friendly forces in the valley of the Holsten, although he was in the area at about the same time that Yamagata and Ise were trying to fight their way toward Nomonhan.

At the tail end of the infantry, the 50 engineers in 1st Lt. Amiya Kiichi's company had a relatively better experience, largely because they were carrying 25 packs of high explosive. The individual demolition charges were somewhat excessive, Amiya notes, but he wanted them to be effective, and "two kilograms each could blow up any kind of tank." Originally, the company's prospects did not look promising, as the men followed the trail of dead Japanese soldiers heaped along the route toward the river. When enemy tanks intercepted the column and further slowed Amiya, it became impossible to catch up with Yamagata's main force, and annihilation seemed imminent. But the engineers used their demolition charges to blow up a couple of tanks, causing the rest of the enemy armor to leave them alone and seek "easier pickings" among the Japanese infantry. After daybreak, a friendly spotter plane circled overhead several times, after which a few Japanese artillery pieces—presumably Miyao's again—laid down supporting fire, drove off the enemy armor, and allowed Amiya's men to cross the Holsten rather easily.[36]

It was the Japanese infantry, in the van of Yamagata's force, who were particularly ripped apart by Russian gunfire after dawn on the 29th. For instance, after spearheading the movement on the right flank, Maj. Ikuta Junzō (already wounded during the breakout from Hinomaru Heights on 26 August) was encircled, with what was left of his battalion, by Soviet armor near Old Engineer Bridge. His most potent firepower reduced to two heavy machine guns without tripods, Ikuta decided on a last attack toward the river. After the recitation of the Meiji Emperor's Precepts to Soldiers and Sailors, Ikuta led three *Banzai!* cheers for the Emperor. Then the men charged, trying to shield the wounded from the armor. Ikuta was killed, and the tanks trampled the wounded on their stretchers, in a hellish scene. Only 30 or 35 soldiers, under a second lieutenant, made it across the Holsten. The last of an entire battalion, they were delighted when they ran into elements of Sekine's 25th Infantry of the 7th Division. But an officer of that regiment heaped abuse on the tattered men and threatened to "kill the cowards himself."[37]

Gethsemane came for Colonels Yamagata and Ise on 29 August near New Engineer Bridge, south of Heights 747. They had somehow missed both Komatsubara's relief force, which was heading for their old positions, and Seki's 3rd Field Artillery Battalion, which had already left for Nomonhan. Yamagata's 64th Regiment headquarters team had started out behind and between the 2nd Infantry Battalion on the left and Sumi's Ikuta battalion on the right, but cohesion was lost once the desperate firefight began by the river at daybreak. The acting color-bearer, 2nd Lt. Koyama Hidehisa, had wrapped the regimental flag around his waist and was carrying the standard when, around 8:30 A.M., he was struck and killed by an artillery shell. The upper half of the pole was smashed and the imperial-chrysanthemum ornament was apparently damaged. Capt. Tachikawa Tsuneki, the infantry aide, took over from Koyama until he was hit in the right arm and incapacitated by artillery fire. Yamagata himself then tried to move the pennon to a safer place, but the bombardment was fierce, Russian tanks were closing round, and the color guards were falling like flies. None of the Japanese infantry was able (or willing?) to rally to their colonel in this last extremity, and he ended up trapped and isolated in an old IJA trench near the bridge with only Ise, Tachikawa, engineer Sgt. Misumi Jūkichi, and one soldier.

With survival or escape highly improbable in broad daylight, Yamagata saw no alternative to the burning of the regimental colors—his first concern—and then suicide. After the five survivors faced east and shouted "*Tennō Heika Banzai!*" three times, gasoline (saved for antitank use) was poured over the colors and ignited. Outliving the colors or being captured alive was unthinkable for the officers. They had already written their last testaments on the 28th (and, unfortunately, given them to the now-slain Koyama). Yamagata turned over his sword to Misumi and asked him to try to get it out safely. At 4:20 P.M., in a covered shelter, the two colonels shot themselves with their pistols, one between the eyes, the other through the temple. Tachikawa also killed himself, but Misumi, although wounded in the face by a shell fragment, managed to escape with the soldier and report to the Sixth Army concerning the fate of Yamagata, Ise, and the colors. Apparently Misumi and his comrade had buried some of the unburned cloth and the bottom of the standard under the unmarked body of Yamagata, to hide them from the enemy, but the status of the imperial crest could not be confirmed at the time. Indeed, though the Sixth Army headquarters staff mourned the death of the two regiment commanders, there was enormous concern whether, on such short notice, the 64th Regiment's colors had been entirely destroyed and thus kept from falling into enemy hands.[38]

The northernmost Japanese force surviving above the Holsten—Kanaizuka's 3rd Infantry Battalion of the Yamagata regiment—was still unable to disengage and rejoin the parent unit on 28 August. Kanaizuka's battle maps show 150 Russian troops closing in on his northeast sector, with some armor and artillery behind, between noon and 3 P.M. From the northwest, 100 troops approached, losing one armored car to machine-gun fire. Between 4 and 9 P.M., the Russians emphasized the southeast front, throwing in 200 men on the high ground, supported by four heavy guns to the rear and more than 10 tanks to the front, three of which were stopped. Under intense fire from east and west, the Japanese positions were caved in and casualties mounted. Checked momentarily on the southeast, the Russians resumed the pressure from the southwest direction with another 200 men, flanked to the east by tanks, between 9 and 10 P.M..

Meanwhile, at 6 P.M. on the 28th, Yamagata got through to Kanaizuka by radio and ordered him to rejoin the regiment, since the 3rd Battalion was isolated and the situation would only deteriorate with the passage of time. At 8 P.M., Kanaizuka consulted his main subordinates—the machine-gun company and two infantry company commanders, plus the battalion aide and a medical lieutenant. Opinion was split. Some of the officers wanted to try to break out of the encirclement, avoiding useless death and coming under the regimental colors. The others wanted to stay with the wounded—avoiding dispersion, confusion, and more losses en route—and to fight to the end where they were, pinning down enemy forces in the process. Kanaizuka thanked the officers, said nothing more, but shortly transmitted a message to the regimental command post indicating that he had selected the second option. The battalion's escape had already become extremely difficult, Kanaizuka radioed Yamagata, and a return to the main force, leaving behind the wounded, was unconscionable. Instead of risking a blot on IJA honor during an unpredictable pullback, the battalion would prefer to stay and defend the current positions. Would the regiment commander kindly understand and approve? In addition, information was desired concerning the circumstances of the regiment and the division.

Kanaizuka received no reply, but at 3:30 A.M. on the 29th, a contradictory new order crackled in on the radio, piecemeal, from Yamagata's headquarters: the regiment was proceeding toward Nomonhan from 3 A.M.; it would conduct a desperate defense of the present positions; "good luck" to the battalion. Kanaizuka derived a "funny feeling" from the message. How could the regiment move and still cling? Sensing that this was Yamagata's farewell, as indeed it was, Kanaizuka worked for up to an hour to decipher the garbled message and tried repeatedly to get through to the regimental command post using his less-than-effective, crank-operated radio transmitter. Enemy bombardment began at 4 A.M.; the radio was smashed; and contact with the regiment could never again be reestablished.

Daytime movement was out of the question, so Kanaizuka bent every effort to merely holding out. Since there was a tendency for young Japanese officers to launch a ferocious last charge when the battle situation grew critical, the battalion commander tried to make the rounds of his companies and platoons, even under fire, to restrain them from conducting "premature" sorties or other suicidal actions. The appearance of Kanaizuka in the trenches did much to cheer up the troops and assuage their feelings of isolation and doom. Indeed, Kanaizuka always sought to study and compose his face in a mirror, well knowing the effect that a commander's countenance might exert on his men.[39] But the realities were grim by the morning of the 29th: more than 20 Soviet tanks started crossfire, at first from 500 meters, and heavy and field artillery pounded the positions, masking them with dust and smoke. When the shells exploded, sand cascaded into the trenches, burying officers and men to the waist until they were dug out, dead or alive. "We were being destroyed gradually," says Kanaizuka. Pressure built up from all directions.

Between 3:30 and 4 P.M., 20 Soviet tanks and 600-650 riflemen moved against the defenses—six tanks and 150 men from the southwest, another six tanks and 300 men from the northwest, eight tanks and 200 men from the north and northeast. "As soon as they learned that we didn't have anti-tank strength," Kanaizuka remarks, "they got in close and penetrated our positions after severe firing." The Russian troops charged several times, blowing bugles and hurling grenades once they came within range, less than 50 meters away. Flamethrowing tanks, which usually operated with great caution, now moved closer than ever and burned many Japanese soldiers to death. From his so-called command post in a depression, the battalion commander, his aide, and the men fought back for five intense hours. Kanaizuka remembers how his soldiers would come with helmets outstretched, ask that they be filled with grenades, and then reenter combat. Fortunately, there still were enough grenades to go around.

To Kanaizuka, it was the Russians' two-day "cyclone of death," and annihilation was therefore near. He did not mind being killed, he says, but he prayed that his men would be spared, as he deliberately got to his feet in the firing trench and sought death. Another "miracle" occurred at this stage: the systematic enemy artillery barrages, each time, skipped the point where he was standing. This seemed to be a divine signal that more was expected of him—to save the soldiers personally—so he gave thanks and prepared his next decision. The aide, 1st Lt. Machida Michio, had noticed what the battalion commander was trying to do when Kanaizuka took off his helmet, said to take care of matters if something happened to him, and stuck his head above the shelter. Machida dragged him down and pleaded with him not to act carelessly when the lives of 300 men depended on the commander.

Around 11 P.M. on the 29th, the battle abated. By now, Kanaizuka had taken stock of the situation, had again conferred with his officers, and had decided to try to break out and join the 64th Infantry. Although there was no way of knowing the situation of the regimental main force, Yamagata's men seemed to have been engaged in heavy fighting. During the morning of the 29th, the smoke and sounds of gunfire could be detected moving gradually eastward, toward Nomonhan or at least away from the old command post. By noon, visual observation revealed no friendly forces to the south any longer. Kanaizuka realized that his battalion, encircled in enemy territory, was the last surviving Japanese unit above the Holsten. Originally, it had been thought that the battalion needed only to hold out for two to three days, or four to five at most, while the division's offensive broke through on the left wing south of the Holsten. The combat situation of the division's main forces, however, had apparently not developed at all as intended, and it was possible that they had run into extreme difficulties too. Under the circumstances, it seemed meaningless for one battalion to fight on in isolation, without relief and without supplies.

One more day of combat such as had occurred on 29 August would mean annihilation for Kanaizuka's unit, pinned helplessly in crumbling defenses under a tightening cone of fire. Food and ammunition were running out. Only two heavy machine guns and a few grenade launchers were left—no rapid-fire guns and no field pieces. The plight of the wounded was especially pitiable. In the absence of surgical equipment and medicines, wounded soldiers were catching pneumonia, weakening, and dying needlessly. Kanaizuka's officers felt that, since the battalion was "done for" at its present location, it made sense to escape and die with the regimental colors. Then, too, Kanaizuka had been ordered every day, most recently on 28/29 August, to rejoin Yamagata's main force. In his diary, the battalion commander wrote: "Should we just stay [here] and fall victim to enemy artillery shells? No! We must break through the enemy encirclement, even if we have to carry the wounded on our backs, and we must get under the colors in order to conduct the last offensive."

At 10 P.M. on the 29th, after much reflection, Kanaizuka issued his own operations order. Enemy strength in the area seemed to total several thousand infantry, several mechanized brigades, and several dozen artillery pieces. The main Soviet force was attacking the right rear of the 23rd Division, and a portion was engaging the Kanaizuka battalion defending the "Ro" positions. Though the location of the 23rd Division's main body was unknown, apparently the 64th Regiment's headquarters had moved to Nomonhan in the morning, leaving the main force at the old defenses. After assembling in a hollow at 1 A.M., the 3rd Battalion would break through the cordon and try to reach those positions. Units should deploy assault forces of a dozen men each to the front, and similar covering elements to the rear and 50 meters from the flanks. The men should dress lightly, and bury the corpses and damaged weapons completely, first dismantling the ruined mountain guns and antitank pieces. Passwords were *Yama* ("mountain") and *Kawa* ("river").

Kanaizuka made a number of additional points to his subordinates, stressing that every last soldier was to be apprised of them: since it was vital to conceal the intention to break out, complete silence must be maintained and antinoise measures devised; bayonets were to be fixed, but rifles were not to be loaded; if taken prisoner, personnel should commit suicide; no one was to run. The direction of the Holsten and of Nomonhan must be fixed clearly by all—a problem that Kanaizuka had been grappling with daily. Since no cairns or other landmarks were visible, direction-finding would have to be based on the stars, with a second lieutenant taking a squad in the lead.

The operation proceeded behind schedule. Unit commanders had been alerted by the battalion aide to confer with Kanaizuka, but they had been delayed until the worst of the fighting eased up at night on the 29th. In addition, the many preparations took considerable time, such as the disassembly and burial of heavy weapons, and the interment of the dead. To prevent bayonets from gleaming in the moonlight, the soldiers attached grass to them. Ammunition was inventoried and distributed in the painfully small amounts available: about 10 rifle cartridges per man; one hand grenade for three soldiers; two or three antitank charges per company. Kanaizuka was determined to extricate every man who breathed, but carrying them posed a problem, for there were only two stretchers for the 10 most grievously wounded. Using staves, paired rifles, twine, and mats, the soldiers improvised straw basket-litters.

Tactically, it was decided to divert the enemy by laying down grenade-launcher fire against the southern front, in order to escape to the northeast, where the cordon seemed to be relatively thinner. The lead elements set forth in dazzling moonlight between 1:30 and 2 A.M., but the point squad leader became pinned down and Kanaizuka himself led the march out. He started with a total of fewer than 300 men, including the wounded, in bunched-up files about 100 meters long, veering south-southwest toward the Holsten after the breakout. When charges occurred, the wounded were to be placed on the ground beforehand and retrieved afterward. In practice, says the aide, it was necessary to carry the badly wounded all the time and therefore to restrain the able-bodied soldiers from running or firing; for, if the wounded were once set down, they could not have been located and picked up again.

At the outset, in the moonlight, Kanaizuka espied Soviet sentries. "If you stumble around or are timid," he thought, "they would suspect something. The thing to do is to push straight ahead, unafraid. After all, the USSR is made up of many races." So Kanaizuka called out something in Russian—"Hello, friends"—which drew no reply, and the Japanese got through without incident, in silence. But after encountering the enemy, Kanaizuka broke up the overly long formation into four columns, with noncoms at the rear. Suddenly, about 30 Soviet tanks could be seen on the move. Kanaizuka "felt awful—the jig seemed up." At a distance of 200 meters, however, the armored vehicles stopped, swerved away, and passed on. After proceeding another kilometer to the south, the Japanese ran into tents, perhaps a Soviet headquarters. Kanaizuka said the same Russian words, and the men kept on walking. Evading enemy artillery sites, the Japanese finally came to the east of the old defenses of the detachment, four kilometers from the Halha, by 3 or 3:30 A.M. To Kanaizuka's surprise, nobody was in the positions and there were no flares, which would have meant the Russians had occupied the place. Nor was an error in recognition possible, for the night had been "beautiful and bright."

Despite a search, no trace of the 64th Regiment's main force could be found; so Kanaizuka continued toward the Holsten, which he reached at 4:30 A.M., near dawn. Heaps of Japanese bodies, from the Yamagata and Ise units, could be seen under the brightening sky. There were also "huge black things" on the ground. Fearing that they were tanks, Kanaizuka and the men sought cover. But then the hulks flew away: they proved to be giant vultures, as big as a man. The battalion started to take off the dog tags of the dead Japanese soldiers, but there were simply too many, and daybreak was at hand. One seriously wounded noncom from the regimental headquarters, however, was found still alive. He told the battalion aide that Yamagata had pulled back before dawn the day before, had been caught at daylight, and had been smashed by artillery and overrun by tanks. The colonel seemed to have broken through but his whereabouts was unknown.

Remembering the garbled message he had received from his headquarters on the 28th, Kanaizuka guessed that Yamagata had been trying to bring the whole regiment, not the command post alone, to Nomonhan. Many trenches were filled with Japanese dead. After weighing the situation, Kanaizuka decided to take his own battalion eastward along the Holsten valley. Twenty Soviet tanks were lined up above the shore, however, blocking passage and compelling him to turn away. The valley was 200-300 meters wide at most, and sandbars cut up the stream into narrow slivers of water. From the banks to the riverbed, the slopes descended 30 to 50 meters. When Soviet artillery opened fire at 4:30 A.M., Kanaizuka guided his troops behind the slope, lest they be mowed down in the open. To stop the men from scattering under the bombardment, the battalion commander told them to run but not to become too dispersed. He prevented casualties and broke through, says Kanaizuka, by applying the secret of battle: "Keep calm, consider the situation and the terrain, don't wander aimlessly."

Moving in stop-and-go fashion, the Japanese came under fire from artillery and machine guns on both sides of the river. Later it was learned that the withdrawal had been facilitated by friendly batteries (presumably Miyao's) firing from the direction of Nomonhan. Along the way, Kanaizuka's men found many corpses from Akai's 1st Battalion, which had set out earlier. An effort was made to carry anybody who was still alive. Between

7 and 8 A.M., Kanaizuka ran into the remnants of the Akai force above the Izumi bend on the Holsten, where willows grew, southwest of Nomonhan. Yamagata's fate was unknown to Akai too. The Japanese crossed the upstream Holsten above Heights 742 and the van reached its destination by 10 A.M., without having encountered either Yamagata or any part of Komatsubara's relief force.

On the morning of 31 August, when Kanaizuka saw Komatsubara (who had just escaped from encirclement himself), the division commander said he knew no more about the fate of Yamagata and the regimental colors than he did. Consequently, Kanaizuka and his surviving officers decided to commit suicide. At this juncture, a division staff officer brought a restraining message from Komatsubara: "Leave your lives to me for a while. We are going to launch a new offensive, and you can meet death then."

From a strength of only 372 (including 16 officers) on 24 August, Kanaizuka's battalion had incurred 129 casualties by the 30th: 72 killed (including five officers), and 57 wounded (including four officers). The battalion's survivors amounted to the equivalent of one company of able-bodied, a second company of wounded, and a third company of the sick.

Between noon and 6 P.M. on the 30th, the last of the 64th Infantry straggled through to the area north of the Nomonhan logistics base, "pursuant to the regimental order to join the division's main force" (in the words of Lieutenant Colonel Akai, now the acting regiment commander). By evening, the number of survivors in the regiment totaled a mere 659, many of them wounded, all exhausted and tattered. (New winter uniforms had to be issued on the 31st.) Firepower had been reduced to four heavy machine guns. Indeed, it was rare to find a man with any weapon, or with ammunition in particular. The regiment had been so enfeebled that on 1 September it was decided to reorganize the whole unit. For the time being, the 2nd Battalion would be deactivated and the remainder incorporated into Akai's battalion. What was left of the regimental gun and machine gun companies would be assigned to one machine gun company commander, a captain.[40]

36

The Death of
the 23rd Division

Duty is weightier than a mountain,
Death is lighter than a feather.

—*Imperial Precepts to*
Soldiers and Sailors (1882)

As of 29 August, Komatsubara's forlorn hope was trapped above the Holsten, having found no friendly forces to help it or to be helped by it. Russian snipers were picking off men from the flanks, especially in the headquarters' "soup-bowl" dip. With ever-diminishing firepower, the Japanese had to form "human bullet" teams from the infantry and engineers. On the western and southern sides of the defensive perimeter, the 72nd Infantry estimated immediate enemy strength at 25 armored vehicles, 4-6 artillery pieces, 5-6 infantry mortars, 10 heavy machine guns, and 400 infantrymen. The Soviet tanks stood off at long range and shelled the helpless Japanese troops, who could do nothing more than lie low, dig trenches, and repair shelters.

On the northern flank of the defenses, the 2nd Battalion of Higashi's 71st Regiment was hammered from three directions: south, west, and north. Fighting off tank and infantry assaults, especially after 1 P.M., the Japanese incurred heavy casualties, including a number of the remaining officers. At some points, the Russians got as close as 20 or 30 meters. Eventually there were only three boxes of ammunition, about 50 clips, for the last heavy machine guns. Food was down to a day's ration of hardtack. Fearing for the safety of the colors, Higashi ordered 2nd Lt. Yukiyoshi Tsutomu, the new standard-bearer, to dismantle the colors, wrap the flag around his body, and carry only the pole. Yukiyoshi was also instructed to be ready to burn the colors in case of emergency. When the fighting eased after twilight, Higashi decided to shift his command post and the colors to the south, where his 1st Battalion was defending the area below division headquarters. The relocation was completed at about 11 P.M.[1]

Suffering from the unceasing bombardment since daybreak, Komatsubara confided to his diary that he had been "very keenly yearning for the sun to set." The general was moved by two scenes in particular: one of a Japanese engineer captain, an academy graduate who was leading a charge from the dip, being killed 50 meters away by tanks firing at point-blank range; and the other of a soldier, bloodied by his wounds, raising his rifle and shouting "*Tennō Heika banzai!*" as loudly as he could before falling dead. In mid-afternoon, Komatsubara ordered his units to take advantage of darkness to evacuate the heaps of wounded and to do something about replenishing the dwindling store of food, ammunition, and medical supplies. He intended to retain the northern perimeter next day but to pull the forward troops back to the division command post on the night of the 30th. Still out of touch with higher headquarters, he directed more runners to break through to the Sixth Army.

Late on the 29th, Komatsubara inspected the front lines. He found that the 71st Infantry was in peril; the 2nd Battalion had lost 70 men in half a day, and the 1st Battalion was trying to dig antitank ditches to stave off destruction. The 2nd Battalion of the 72nd Infantry, also driven back and barely clinging to its defenses, had lost 30 or 40 men. In all, the already small remnants of the division had suffered another 200 casualties on the 29th. Only a portion of the wounded could be extricated on the night of 29/30 August.[2]

According to Suzuki Yoshiyasu, when Chief of Staff Okamoto had asked for volunteers to go to the Sixth Army, no officer had spoken up. Komatsubara's personal aide, 1st Lt. Tanaka Naoichi, told Suzuki that he had to stay with the general, dead or alive. Okamoto elicited Komatsubara's permission and "forced" the lieutenant to leave. Suzuki remembers some of the needs that had to be reported to higher headquarters: for trucks to evacuate the seriously wounded, for antitank guns and ammunition, and for the synchronization of radio frequencies. Since Tanaka would have to crawl, he was told to carry the messages not only in his pocket but also inside his socks. Tanaka heard later that he had been designated because Komatsubara had a son of the same age and preferred to risk the lieutenant as a courier rather than to consign him to certain death at the site of the division's final command post. As he recalls, Tanaka was to bring the Sixth Army up to date on the combat situation and transmit Komatsubara's intention of accomplishing his mission and dying in the "graveyard" north of the Holsten.

In all, three lieutenants were sent out, bearing essentially the same information and intending to stick together as long as they could. One of the junior officers was 2nd Lt. Murai Masakatsu, the personal aide of the now-evacuated General Kobayashi. Komatsubara and Okamoto asked if Murai would like to take a squad of soldiers with him, but he said a noncom and two men would suffice. (Tanaka remembers bringing only one noncom when he left.) Murai received the last wills, written on signal sheets by the division commander, the chief of staff, and chief surgeon Col. Murakami Tokuji. Okamoto also turned over his wallet as a memento and enjoined the lieutenant to burn everything if he ran into enemy troops on the way. While waiting to set forth after dark, Murai heard eerie chanting emanating from the engineer positions to the rear, which proved to be prayers to the merciful Buddha. Obsessed by his own orders to break through the enemy cordon, the lieutenant was disquieted by the litany and wished that he could blot out the sound. It went on for about two hours, however, and—worst of all— attracted enemy grenade fire, which felled a number of men unnecessarily. One other incident remains in Murai's mind: when he was chomping on his last hardtack, Colonel Okamoto called down from the hole in the *suribachi* dip above the lieutenant and said that there was no food left for the division commander and him. Could Murai spare any? The lieutenant shared half of his bag.

The third of the messengers, 1st Lt. Watanabe Shūji from the Hasebe detachment, apparently drew heavy fire at the time his team jumped off in the moonlight. When Tanaka crawled over the crestline between midnight and 1 A.M., he came under brief automatic-weapons fire which, of course, he did not return. By dawn he made it through to his destination, via the swamps of the upstream Holsten, without great difficulty, for the Russians were not ordinarily active or effective at night. Breakfast at Ogisu's headquarters—hot rice and bean-paste soup—has left a greater impression on Tanaka than what he reported, since he had not eaten for two days.

Murai got through the Soviet cordon with relative ease, probably helped by Watanabe's diversion too. The team waded through knee-deep water along the Holsten shoreline, heading toward Nomonhan, but Sergeant Umemura's gangrenous leg wound was festering and he had to be carried somehow. When an octagonal tent was finally sighted in the distance at 4 A.M., the tired party was delighted, especially after a Japanese flag confirmed its nationality. Umemura asked to be put down to rest. Murai left him with the other two soldiers and headed for the headquarters tent. He never saw Umemura or the others again, although he thinks they were near enough the Japanese lines to be saved. It was about 5:30 A.M. when Murai, muddy and exhausted, reported to Ogisu, the military academy classmate of his own father. Ogisu listened receptively and then offered the lieutenant a cup of his favorite sake. Too weary to eat, Murai retired to a cot and slept the sleep of the dead till afternoon.[3]

Until the arrival of the division's runners at dawn on 30 August, the Sixth Army had been in the dark about the latest status of Komatsubara's little force. On the preceding evening, all that it had been possible to advise the Kwantung Army was that Yamagata had apparently withdrawn from his positions on the night of the 28th and that, although the 23rd Division had definitely reached the old lines north of the Holsten at the same time, contact had been lost thereafter.[4] Such depressing information, says Sixth Army operations officer Hamada, "tore at my innards." But Tsuji, who had just rotated with Kwantung Army Deputy Chief of Staff Yano at the front and had volunteered to come to Nomonhan for the fifth time, was infuriated by Ogisu's insensitivity. After noticing the silence and depression of the staff, Tsuji went to see Ogisu. The latter, according to Tsuji's sensational account, was quite drunk and startled him by saying: "Tsuji-*kun*, I hope Komatsubara dies; what do *you* think?" Tsuji claims that he screamed at Ogisu: "Is it the Sixth Army's way of commanding to ignore the 23rd Division commander and let him perish? It is only natural for the division commander to repay the victims by giving up his own life, but shouldn't the army commander try to rescue him? A commander owes this to his subordinates."[5]

General Fujimoto rushed in and dragged Tsuji from Ogisu's tent, trying to appease the apoplectic major by assuring him that Komatsubara would be rescued somehow. According to Hamada, Tsuji told Fujimoto that the loss of Komatsubara under these circumstances would mean the annihilation of the 23rd Division both in name and in fact; to avoid this, the division commander must be saved. To Hamada and Fujimoto, these points were understandable, but the problem centered on implementation. Only the new 7th Division could launch an attack, but it was unfamiliar with the battlefield, particularly the terrain above the Holsten, and it lacked antitank strength. The relief force might be trapped too and become "the biter bit." Night afforded the only hope of penetrating the Soviet guard net and tank concentrations, but direction finding, terribly difficult by day, would be even harder in darkness. In other words, it was deemed far tougher to locate and reach Komatsubara than it was for him to escape the trap.

When none of the army staff responded to Tsuji's aggressive proposal, he warned that unless some young officer organized a relief expedition, the Sixth Army would be disgraced. Still nobody, not even Colonel Hamada, spoke up. After Tsuji said he would have to lead the rescue himself, then, Hamada finally replied that the Sixth Army would handle matters and that he, Hamada, would go. Tsuji remarked that this was only proper—the most important thing a newly formed army could do under the circumstances. At this point, notes Tsuji, handsome young Lieutenant Tanaka arrived with Komatsubara's final decision and last words, scrawled in thick pencil on a communications pad. "It was like finding light on a dark night," Hamada observes. After apologizing for losing so many of his men, Komatsubara asked the Sixth Army to rest easy: he and the troops would fight in fine fashion to the last. Little was said about the combat situation, but the dire straits of the division were apparent, and "it was touching," Hamada recalls.

After what Hamada terms "serious study," Fujimoto came up with his recommendation to Ogisu: the Sixth Army should not attempt to rescue the 23rd Division by force but should launch a small-scale nighttime operation, employing the remaining elements of the division under Capt. Kuroda Yoshio, one of the divisional aides who had broken through the day before. Every effort should be made to notify Komatsubara's force to fall back and concentrate. Fujimoto obtained Ogisu's assent and then explained the plan to Tsuji. "He seemed to be very dissatisfied and uneasy," Hamada notes, "but he gave in reluctantly." According to Tsuji, he told Lieutenant Tanaka to guide staff officer Hamada to Komatsubara's last known location. Tanaka supposedly declined the Sixth Army's help—a gallant attitude, maintained with calm and deference, in sharp contrast (claims Tsuji) to the spineless but usually arrogant Sixth Army staff and their "half-drunk" commander. Certainly, as Tanaka asserts, he was anxious to help Komatsubara. The lieutenant even offered to board and guide one of the liaison planes that was being ordered to drop a message tube to the 23rd Division. He was turned down, recalls Tanaka, but he says he had no reason to speak up to Tsuji about rejecting Sixth Army assistance. Perhaps Tsuji was merely projecting his own impressions, Tanaka suggests.

The Sixth Army did try to get runners through, to arrange bomber support, and to drop message cylinders and supplies by air. The message drops, in particular, produced a feeling of "suppressed excitement" in the Sixth Army, Hamada notes; but, in fact, nothing worked, as was learned later. Army radiomen repeatedly transmitted Ogisu's message, in the clear, to "overcome all difficulties, break through the enemy, and come back." Toward the end, in desperation, only the word "Return!" was flashed to Komatsubara. But since no reply could be picked up from the division, Komatsubara's doom seemed inevitable. Enemy artillery fire and air bombardment could be seen concentrating against one sector north of the Holsten, suggesting that all of the Japanese units across the river except the divisional headquarters must have been destroyed or driven back.[6]

Tsuji sought to apprise Kwantung Army headquarters of the situation at the front. Before dawn on the 30th, he reported that the 23rd Division was supposed to assemble gradually at Chiangchunmiao. The Sixth Army had been deployed in an eight-kilometer arc around Lake Mohorehi, checking the enemy, taking control of arriving units, and planning for the next offensive. Then Tsuji, who had been instrumental in pulling out Yasuoka's armored force in July, performed a significant volte-face: he implored the Kwantung Army to send the entire 1st Tank Corps to the battleground as quickly as possible.[7] Once the divisional couriers had broken through, Tsuji reported in late morning that Komatsubara's 500 men, mainly from the 71st and 72nd regiments, were fighting their last battle in the vicinity of Yamagata's old positions. The Sixth Army was endeavoring to rescue the force. Hasebe's and Yotsuya's troops had gathered in the Nomonhan area, but the Yamagata unit was pulling back and had been unable to assemble.

Enemy forces were not yet active against the lines occupied by the 7th Division.[8] In mid-afternoon, the Kwantung Army was advised that Komatsubara and about 500 men were still holding the old defenses, that the 23rd Division was supposed to break through the enemy and pull back toward Nomonhan that night, and that the air force had engaged enemy formations and had dropped food to the Japanese troops.[9]

Komatsubara's so-called command post—in an open, conical dip hardly more than 150 meters in diameter and three meters in depth—grew almost untenable on 30 August. The Russians had brought up infantry mortars, from whose high-angle fire the defenders had no place to hide. Soviet artillery, especially 12-cm. howitzers, pounded the shelters in particular, obviously striving to smash the foundations, as Komatsubara noted. Smoke interfered with observation of positions only 100 or 150 meters away, and the stinging smell of cordite was choking. Trying to gauge the impact of the rounds, soldiers scurried through the interlacing trenches, from hole to hole in the oval, seeking safer areas. One of the division commander's orderlies was struck in the back by a shell fragment, and an aide was hit in the leg. A military policeman shielded Komatsubara with his body and saved him, but was injured in the process. Listening to the moaning of the wounded and gazing at the wretched scene, the general felt helpless; "it was like a living hell," he wrote.[10]

At 11:15 A.M., when Komatsubara heard that radio contact had been reopened with the Sixth Army, he felt "reborn." His lieutenants must have gotten through. The safety of the radio apparatus was in doubt, however, for enemy shells were exploding near it, so the general hastened to describe his situation, in the clear, to higher headquarters. Soon afterward, at 12:30, Ogisu's order was received, also in the clear: "Return tonight." Komatsubara worked out the deployment for the withdrawal and asked the Sixth Army to dispatch trucks at 11 P.M. to evacuate the severely wounded; no reply came. Enemy attacks by armor and infantry intensified around 3 P.M., but explosives for close-quarter teams were nearly depleted. At 3:45 P.M., Komatsubara issued his operations order calling for all units to withdraw toward Nomonhan that night, in accordance with instructions from the Sixth Army.

By now, the Russians had pinned down the Japanese survivors to a degree where escape was becoming impracticable. Tanks had encircled the dip, and foot soldiers hurled grenades into the Japanese defenses. To expose one's head above the crestline was to get it blown off by merciless snipers. Men could be heard calling "Mother!" as they died; others cheered for the Emperor. Trying to observe the enemy, Major Morinaga was shot down and killed. The best the Japanese could do, says Suzuki, was to draw fire by poking a helmet above the rim of the dip and then sneak a quick peek. Apart from engineers, Komatsubara had only six able-bodied headquarters officers left (including two doctors) and 70 or 80 men near him. There was almost no contact with the main front-line infantry to the north; the Yotsuya battalion, nearer the river, had been entirely out of touch since the 29th.

Komatsubara decided against trying to break out. Since a farewell report to the Sixth Army was necessary, he brought over a clerk and asked Suzuki, "What are we going to do?" Suzuki had often expressed his opinion to the general, but this time he said nothing, for he comprehended the historic importance of the moment and was beset by "indescribable emotions" now that the death of the division was at hand. Therefore the general dictated his own message. Enemy attacks were powerful and very close; disengagement had already become difficult [i.e., impossible]. Morale remained high at all levels and the troops were fighting hard. The division would gladly struggle to the last, at its present positions, for the sake of the nation.

The clerk took down the message, then tapped it out in the clear. Documents and code books were burned. Komatsubara and his staff gathered their belongings and burned them. All of the officers removed their insignia and badges; Suzuki buried his and Komatsubara's, two meters deep. When they died, the enemy would find only bodies and soldiers' uniforms, not the evidence of a division headquarters.[11]

Several witnesses remark that Komatsubara displayed a recklessness that suggested his desire to die in battle. After grenade combat erupted near the command post dip, says engineer commander Saitō, the general decided on a last charge. Saitō calmed him down, saying, "I have to charge first." Gripping his saber and proceeding to the edge of the bowl, Saitō could see that the Russians were lobbing grenades but very carefully staying out of sword range. "All we have to do," Saitō insisted, "is to try to avoid the grenades."[12] The machine gun commander, a first lieutenant who was defending the command post, observed Komatsubara standing on his shelter under fire, watching the battle. Rushing over, the lieutenant grasped Komatsubara's arm and shoved him into the shelter. "Sir," he pleaded, "you should be the last to go."[13]

During the melee in late afternoon, the division's radio apparatus was destroyed by enemy fire and the operator was killed, but not before a last, urgent order had been received from Ogisu at 4:30 P.M.: Komatsubara must overcome every obstacle, break through enemy lines, and escape to the area southeast of Nomonhan, while trying to keep his remnants intact.[14]

Komatsubara had scant opportunity at the moment to pay much attention to Ogisu's order, for night would not fall on 30 August before further tragedies befell the Japanese north of the river. The men of Higashi's 71st

Regiment had been steadily decimated by the increasing fire of artillery, snipers, and the new mortars. Since morning, the elements of the 64th Infantry on the western flank had disappeared, opening a gap between the 2nd Battalion and the 1st Battalion to the south through which Soviet armor poured. After 11 A.M., the Russians got behind the defenders and laid down crossfire at close range. Infantrymen and engineers attempted close-quarter attacks, but all fell except for a badly wounded warrant officer who crept through to Komatsubara's hollow. Around 11:30 A.M., Higashi learned that he was to send sizable forces to Nomonhan to obtain ammunition and food. The 2nd Battalion was notified by phone, but soon the wires were cut, and communication was lost thereafter.

Enemy pressure on the exposed Japanese infantry positions became unbearable, especially for soldiers who detested defensive warfare in the first place. There was a mood of futility and panic as the men tried desperately to evade the shells and grenades by fleeing from dead angle to dead angle. Most importantly, the remaining officers were making no efforts to control the confusion. A signalman remembers his feelings of shock and anger when he heard two officers, skulking in a trench, talking about "taking care of themselves." Although only a sergeant, and a draftee at that, the combative soldier regarded the officers' attitude as "awful" in battle. He took the audacious steps of ordering nearby soldiers to perform lookout duty and of proceeding with another enlisted man to report to Lieutenant Colonel Higashi directly. Higashi promptly sent his able aide, Capt. Miki Toranosuke, to restore discipline in the line.[15]

At midday on the 30th, about 20 Russian tanks struck the 1st Battalion from all directions while shouting riflemen closed to 40 meters with five armored cars loaded with grenades. Emerging from the armored vehicles, Soviet troops—with their leather jackets shining in the sun—hurled the grenades in profusion. Counterattacks checked the enemy in an hour, but the cost was great. In the 2nd Battalion sector, grenade combat was also severe. The battalion commander, Maj. Tōi Shinji (Nobuharu), and the 5th Company commander, Captain Nishimura, were wounded. By 3 P.M., Soviet armor drew closer and knocked out the last antitank weapons. Russian infantry strength was built up to 800 men, who attacked with the support of the tanks. At 4 P.M., the Japanese launched a new counterassault, which left the positions blanketed with the dead of both sides. Amid the battle, a rare runner got through from the division and brought word about the pullback scheduled that night. But the fighting was only increasing in intensity, especially behind the 71st Infantry, where the dark-green Russian tanks seemed "huge" to the lightly armed Japanese foot soldiers, and blood dyed the dunes. "All we could do now," notes the regimental chronicler, "was to fight with an iron will transcending human strength."

The plight of the Japanese troops is typified by the experience of a machine-gun squad leader who found himself isolated in a hollow. Horrified to see four nearby Russians in possession of an IJA heavy machine gun—the squad's equivalent of regimental colors—the corporal grabbed hand grenades and a bayonet and charged forward with a private armed only with a shovel. In fierce hand-to-hand fighting, the corporal bayoneted one Soviet soldier while the private flailed away at the others with his entrenching tool. The surviving Russians fled, abandoning the Japanese machine gun. Of course the encirclement was not eased by this exploit, but as the corporal says, "We would undoubtedly have been annihilated if the Russians fought like Japanese on the attack." [16]

By late afternoon, communication to the division and within the regiment was nearly severed, although it was only 150-200 meters from the 1st Battalion to Higashi's command post and 350 meters to Komatsubara's headquarters. In the absence of wire contact, Higashi twice attempted to send volunteer runners to the division. Soviet tank fire killed the messengers, including one soldier whose helmeted head was blown off by a direct hit.

Although Higashi could not make contact with Komatsubara's command post, a mere 80 meters beyond a low crest, Russian tanks could be seen closing in on the division's hollow. It was obvious that the enemy was determined to envelop and overrun the last Japanese units separately, battalion by battalion, headquarters by headquarters. Emplaced in a dip slightly under Higashi's location, the survivors of the 1st Battalion were engaging enemy troops as close as 17-18 meters away. After the acting battalion commander, Capt. Hanada Shunji, went to try to reach division headquarters (and somehow made it), the battalion command post was left with only two second lieutenants (the aide and the medical officer), no noncoms, and five or six men. Before Hanada could get back, the aide killed himself with a pistol.

Higashi had been very concerned about the fate of the 71st Regiment's colors since the crisis on 29 August, when he had relocated southward from the 2nd Battalion's vulnerable sector. For a while on the 30th, Hanada asserts, he had talked the commander out of taking the "premature" action of destroying the colors, arguing that the unit had gone through worse and that Soviet soldiers did not charge into positions as the Japanese did. Toward 5 P.M., however, when the color-guard commander was killed and the situation became desperate, Higashi saw no alternative to the burning of the regimental colors and to the death of the regiment. Survivors were not only very few and almost helpless but also drained physically and emotionally. In the words of the orderly, PFC Sonetsuji Seiichi: "We had not been eating for a week, and our faces and bodies were so misshapen that we no longer looked human."

In a fairly large bunker that had been dug into the side of the dip, the painful task of destroying the colors began.[17] The wooden pole was broken into four pieces. Sonetsuji produced the flag, the chrysanthemum seal known as the "crown" (which had been kept in 2nd Lieutenant Yukiyoshi's pocket), and three pocket cans of fuel to drench the pyre. At 5:30 P.M., the acting aide, 1st Lt. Takashina Hidemaru, ignited the cloth and then the sticks with a match. The fire kept going out, and the tassels were particularly hard to burn. It was 6:15 P.M. before the task was done. After confirming that the colors had been destroyed, Higashi praised the survivors for having done their best. Despite their hard fighting, however, there was nothing more to be done: the enemy had tightly surrounded them. Since the time to die was vital for human beings, Higashi asked everybody who could walk to follow him in a last charge for the honor of the regiment. Those who were wounded severely should "please kill themselves bravely when the enemy approached to close quarters."

As soon as the ultimate decision was reached, a sergeant recalls how "the pressure was strangely lifted." Yukiyoshi passed around his last imperial cigarettes, and Takashina led the men in reciting all of the Meiji Emperor's precepts to the armed forces. During a very temporary lull in the battle, a corporal remembers reciting loudly and "driving away all thoughts of self, leaving only feelings of loyalty and patriotism—of the desire to serve the homeland seven times over." Then the little band, now down to 17 men, gave three lusty cheers for the Emperor. It was a scene, write the annalists, whose sincerity would have "moved demons to tears." The signalmen burned classified materials and buried most of their equipment, and the officers donned soldiers' uniforms without insignia of rank. Sonetsuji was supposed to get through to the division and report the last moments of the regiment.

At about 6:40 P.M., Higashi ordered the final charge by his smattering of color guards, headquarters soldiers, signalmen, and engineers. Like a samurai of old, he brandished his sword and leaped from the trench, shouting to the enemy, "I am Lieutenant Colonel Higashi, 49 years old!" As an already-wounded sergeant says, "We knew it was impossible"; but he and his ambulatory comrades dashed toward the Russians on a hillock ahead, with the intention of storming up the slope. Those in the lead yelled "*Wah! wah!*" Behind, several of the wounded, including Lieutenant Yukiyoshi, crept in the direction of the enemy. It was truly a suicidal mission: within 10 meters of the jump-off point, Russian machine guns and grenades felled Higashi, Takashina, Yukiyoshi, and every attacking soldier. Unable to overcome his wounds and his exhaustion, a sergeant secretly wished that a grenade would finish him off.

From the 1st Battalion command post to the south, the medical officer heard the order to charge, the shouts of "*Wah! wah!*," and a flurry of exploding grenades. Stillness followed. In the lines, Captain Hanada learned from a runner, at the very time of the charge, that the regimental colors had been burned; he could also see 14 or 15 Japanese soldiers dashing forward. Since the 1st Battalion was to charge too, Hanada ordered all companies to attack with the bayonet. The officers were dressed like enlisted men and wielded bayonets. In "typical hand-to-hand fighting," Hanada says he cut down about five Russian soldiers; the rest pulled out quickly. A Japanese machine gunner, using a saber in the absence of rifles, found no Soviet troops waiting in the first positions but saw a "forest" of Maxims and bayonets deployed beyond. The enemy, he says, "quieted down" when the Japanese returned fire with captured rifles.

On Higashi's front, the lieutenant colonel's orderly, Sonetsuji, had chosen to join the charge and had been knocked down by fragments from a Russian grenade that hit him in the thigh and hand. Sonetsuji dragged himself forward through the smoke, calling for the regiment commander. Finally he heard a response and crawled to the spot where Higashi lay. Although a grenade had ripped open the commander's intestines, his mind was lucid and his words were understandable. Sonetsuji, he insisted, must go back to the division commander and report that "it was an unskillful operation but I could not do better." When Sonetsuji pleaded to stay with Higashi to the end, the officer chided him for forgetting his assignment as a runner. He told Sonetsuji to kill himself if he encountered the Russians on the way back, and he gave the soldier his pistol, which proved to be empty. Conscious to the last, Higashi warned that if a report was not made, the fate of the regimental colors would remain unknown. The commander's dying words were "Everybody did really well" and "*Tennō Heika banzai!*" Thus perished a "rare officer" and "the mother of the regiment" (in Onozuka's words). Higashi's "classical death" was later reported to the Emperor through an imperial aide who visited Manchuria.

As for Sonetsuji, he stanched his own bleeding with his leggings and crawled back first to the old command post and then to division headquarters. It took him two and a half hours to traverse less than 100 meters and get across the crestline because of his wounds and the presence of enemy forces on the way. Komatsubara had been very worried about Higashi and the colors ever since he heard intense gunfire in the area of the 71st Regiment from about 5 P.M. and learned that Soviet troops and tanks were attacking the unit at hand-to-hand range. The general directed that the division assign priority to locating the colors and burning them if Higashi had been unable to do so. It was a relief to Komatsubara when Sonetsuji got through that night and was able to verify that the colors had been burned. Sonetsuji also brought word of the final charge by Higashi and his last officers and men.[18]

By now, Komatsubara's headquarters had experienced a hell of its own. At 6 P.M., Soviet tanks and infantry charged against the command post area. A Japanese second lieutenant led a desperate counterattack by his signal platoon and met death. While Russian snipers moved onto the crestline and went to work skillfully (as Komatsubara admitted), other Soviet soldiers approached and hurled a great number of grenades with deadly effect at point-blank range. Chief of Staff Okamoto's right knee was torn to shreds. The colonel was placed on a makeshift "operating table" scooped from the earth, under a tent roof covered with grass for camouflage. In the feeble glare of a flashlight, major surgery—the amputation of Okamoto's leg—was performed on the spot, with only local anesthetic, by the division's medical chief, Colonel Murakami, assisted by medical Capt. Amano Sakae. The tourniquet caused obvious pain, but Okamoto uttered no sound during or after the operation.[19]

Komatsubara had already lost all of his organic infantry and artillery regiment commanders, as well as his favorite group commander, General Kobayashi, and every divisional staff officer except Major Suzuki. The critical wounding of Chief of Staff Okamoto was the last straw. When Komatsubara had launched the foolhardy "relief" expedition north of the Holsten, there was a certain rationale: as long as the 23rd Division, despite its limited strength, was clinging to a corner of Balshagal Heights, there was hope of coping with the Russians' powerful August offensive by unleashing the whole 7th Division south of the river. Little did Komatsubara know that Ogisu had decided, by the morning of 29 August, to concentrate the Sixth Army's forces in the vicinity of Nomonhan, in anticipation of mounting a new offensive only after several new divisions had arrived. As for the 7th Division, its Morita brigade was being pulled back, and the main body of the division was to occupy the zone south of Mohorehi as a screen for the approaching reinforcements.[20]

Despite the lack of imagination or perception on the part of the Sixth Army command, and despite Komatsubara's enforced ignorance of the latest situation, it had become evident to the division commander on 30 August that no supporting offensive was developing below the Holsten and that his own few hundred isolated effectives, dwindling steadily, were incapable of accomplishing any significant strategic mission. Retreat had seemed unthinkable until Ogisu's order of the 30th, and impossible by the time the instructions were supposed to be implemented. But by evening—at a time not unrelated to the death of Higashi, the destruction of the 71st Regiment's colors, and the crippling of Okamoto—a change of thinking crystallized in Komatsubara's mind.

By about 8 P.M., the Soviet tanks began to pull back and the battlefield grew quiet. Suzuki dared to stand up on his shelter and look around. Flares were floating in the distance but no enemy soldiers were visible nearby. Although the encirclement had certainly not ended, the Russians seemed to have disengaged for the night to resupply and gas up their forces for the fighting on the morrow. Suzuki advised Komatsubara that he did not think the battle would resume right away; in other words, a merciful breathing spell could be expected.

Since Okamoto was out of action, the division commander shared his thoughts with Suzuki. Although the general had transmitted the earlier message concerning a fight to the finish where they stood, he had been pondering the matter of the Sixth Army's repeated orders to get out. Quite possibly conditions had changed during the period since the expedition had set forth on the night of the 27th; i.e., the Sixth Army might no longer require an anchor north of the Holsten. An army order ordinarily carried greater weight than other considerations. It seemed best for the remainder of the 23rd Division to revert to Ogisu's control now, in order to live and fight another day. What did Suzuki think? The major concurred readily, without comment. "Good," said Komatsubara, "let's carry out the army's order quickly."[21]

The major set about making the necessary preparations to handle his "first such bitter experience." Suzuki's basic idea was a disengagement by stealth instead of by force. Midnight seemed like the earliest practicable time. Komatsubara agreed. Captain Hanada, the acting 1st Battalion commander of the 71st Regiment, had already conducted useful scouting, at the division's request, around sunset. When he got back, he advised Komatsubara that enemy dispositions were markedly weak to the southeast, although it could be a trap, since the zone was susceptible to attack by both the Central and the Southern groups of the Russian forces. It was imperative to disengage quickly in order to get beyond the range of Soviet heavy artillery emplaced on the Mongolian heights and to move far to the upstream Holsten by daybreak. Hanada's 1st Battalion would gladly serve as the advance guard. Komatsubara nodded approvingly, thanked the captain, and told him to do his best.[22] In the evening, Suzuki sent out another patrol, two men under the first lieutenant commanding the machine gun company of Hasebe's unit. They reconnoitered escape routes for 300 meters and returned to report that the Russians, apparently sensing that a Japanese pullout was imminent, had deployed their forces all around the pocket.[23]

The Japanese dead could not possibly be removed, but the handling of the wounded posed a particularly cruel problem. Individual units had incurred losses of 30 to 50 percent in the three days since the 27th; nearly half of the survivors were injured to some degree. Many men had lost one or more limbs, and unnerving screams could be heard in the division command post's bowl in the darkness of 30 August. There was neither the time to locate and bring back wounded men still lying on the battlefield nor the manpower to carry all of those who had been retrieved. Certainly Komatsubara was not unmindful of the problem; he had tried to evacuate the ambulatory wounded on the 29th. Now, however, the entire dangerous pullback through a cordon of enemy troops and armor would be imperiled by delay, and there would be no second chance. The walking wounded would be encouraged to keep up with the columns, and litters for some of the others would be improvised; there were meager medical stocks that had been originally stored for wintering at the present positions. Komatsubara insisted on saving Colonel Okamoto, but when Suzuki asked about the rest of the badly wounded, Komatsubara replied, "Leave them behind." The immobilized men soon comprehended what lay in store for them—abandonment and death at best, capture at worst. Asked directly by some of them about their fate, Suzuki wept without being able to reply. It was the worst time during the Nomonhan war for both him and the division commander. They may have talked openly about revenge in another offensive, but inwardly they were suffering.[24]

A makeshift stretcher was devised for Okamoto from a portable tent tied to two pine sticks. A sergeant and two teams of four burly soldiers each were assigned to guard and to carry the colonel, who was also escorted by Captain Amano. When the stoical Okamoto was placed on the litter, the sergeant noted that his stump was bleeding profusely and that the staff officer's sash had been removed from his uniform. Suzuki sent out a sergeant to try to get some transportation from the Sixth Army, for the division commander in particular. To assist and defend the general, three noncoms were assigned.

Tactically, Suzuki was troubled by the problem of direction finding, especially since the maps had been burned. Capt. Utsui Keiji, the division's signal officer, who knew the area well, was ordered to guide the division toward Nomonhan, bearing on the North Star. Suzuki's second operational problem was contact and coordination with the forces that had been fighting in isolation all day in the positions on the perimeter north of the division command post, at Yamagata's old site. The major says that runners who were finally able to reach the supposed defensive locations found no units, causing him to think that they had either retreated already or been destroyed.

The easiest unit to contact was the nearest infantry formation—Hanada's 1st Battalion of the 71st Regiment. At the time the captain was getting ready for a second charge, a courier got through with word of the reassembly plan and told Hanada to report to division headquarters. A sergeant remembers hearing Hanada yell, "Stop the attack!" Despite all difficulties, the survivors were to hold their present locations until dark. Further orders would be forthcoming. The wounded sergeant was confused, but he took cover in a dead angle, hiding from bottle-shaped grenades lobbed from the enemy positions on high ground ahead and instinctively tossing back those that came too close. Peering at the Japanese jump-off site, he could see the corpses of his comrades who had fallen as soon as they had left the shelters. The Russians were so near that the voices of soldiers and the orders of commanders could be heard.

Hanada got back to his unit around 9:30 P.M. and reported that the division was going to escape to the Sixth Army. The survivors of the 1st Battalion should leave their positions quietly, one by one, and head for the division's command post. Apparently some men were also alive from the 71st Infantry's headquarters, for according to the regimental records, a badly wounded sergeant who had assembled injured clerks and runners and had been "desperately defending important documents" at the regimental command post did not receive Higashi's order to conduct the last charge. Crawling inch by inch through knee-high grass, Hanada's group (perhaps 110 men to begin with) traversed the difficult several hundred meters to Komatsubara's dip, while Soviet flares flooded the moonlit sky. When the painfully injured signal sergeant counted his team, there were only five unhurt and 10 wounded, including himself. The time was after 11 P.M. by now.

The scene at the division's site was depressing. In a dip "less than half the size of Hiroshima Municipal Stadium" (as perceived by a young medical officer) were jumbled the last of the division, hardly 100 men in all, the wounded outnumbering the able-bodied. Hanada knew that his shred of soldiers would have to spearhead the division's withdrawal, but when he called the roll, 2nd Lt. Ono Raizō and his medical corpsmen were missing. Thereupon Hanada took a soldier and rushed back to the area of the 1st Battalion's headquarters, where he found Ono and the surviving medics still tending to the wounded. Hanada pulled out those who could walk and left grenades for the incapacitated to kill themselves. The situation was urgent, for enemy troops were already occupying the battalion's old command post.[25]

On the northern sector, the 71st Regiment's 2nd Battalion, under its acting commander, Takada Kiyomi (now a captain), underwent a pounding until dusk on 30 August. No word ever reached him concerning Higashi's decision to launch a last charge. After nightfall, however, a runner got through, presumably from the division, with a strange order to "disband the unit" and pull back to the area of army headquarters. In the confusion of the time, Takada had no idea about the exact originator and other details of the order, but "disbandment" was unheard of and an impracticable prelude to withdrawal. What about Higashi's intention, expressed on the 29th, of fighting and dying where they stood? Although Takada insisted on keeping the survivors together, he had no choice but to pull out at midnight. Guiding a blinded probationary officer who was able to walk, the captain moved slowly toward divisional headquarters, keying his route to the Big Dipper. According to regimental records, the 2nd Battalion's disengagement supposedly proceeded "comparatively well"; but when the troops came to the division command post, there was nobody there. Takada resumed the forlorn march toward Nomonhan, although the enemy, obviously alerted, sent up flares and raked the region with machine-gun fire interlaced with tracers. When the captain finally made it to Nomonhan, his "battalion" numbered only 13 men.[26]

The other Japanese infantry elements clinging to the northern perimeter consisted of the two nominal battalions of the 72nd Regiment under Captain Hirowatari, the acting commander. Soviet strength along this front on 30 August was estimated at 500 troops, more than 20 tanks, 5-6 infantry mortars, four artillery pieces, and 30 heavy machine guns. The Russian riflemen occupied positions on high ground 200 meters away and, effectively teaming up with armor and artillery, drew very close. Grenade duels raged on every side. As the Japanese antitank capability dwindled, the enemy grew more daring. Around 1 P.M., all of the tanks moved in and hammered the IJA shelters, one after another, while the Soviet infantry mortars zeroed in from three directions. Japanese casualties mounted and, as the regimental chronicler wrote, "the situation became tragic." Only near 8 P.M., when the sun was setting, did the battle abate.

Hirowatari never received a divisional order on the 30th. That night, however, he decided to implement the instructions transmitted directly by Komatsubara the preceding midnight to pull back the 72nd Regiment to the location of the division command post on 30/31 August. As the captain understood the situation, the division would fight on at its present positions, and the 71st Regiment would handle the evacuation of the wounded to Nomonhan. During the disengagement to division headquarters, Hirowatari's units were to provide able-bodied men to protect the wounded, but since it was "necessary to economize on troop strength, the patients should walk by themselves, insofar as possible." Heavy-weapon units should carry the maximum number of rifles, and particular attention should be paid to flank and rear security.

By 10 P.M., Hirowatari had deployed his men for the pullback, in concert with Takada's battalion of the 71st Regiment. But at this time (contrary to the impression given by the 71st Infantry's chronicler), all hell broke loose: Soviet attacks became "very aggressive," and machine guns and more than 10 tanks cut off the route of escape. Completely surrounded, the Japanese could not find a chink through which to penetrate on the eastern sector. Hirowatari knew that delay would mean ultimate annihilation, so he contacted Takada again and, at 1 A.M., finally moved out, with his 1st Battalion in the lead, heading southeast and then east, under crossfire. But when

Takada's battalion started to follow, it became entangled with Hirowatari's rearmost 2nd Battalion, causing a separation from the vanguard. The snarled second echelon thereupon veered east-southeast, where more resistance was encountered.

Hirowatari pressed straight to the south, bypassing a series of enemy positions along his right flank. When he finally came to the site of Komatsubara's command post, still another disappointment waited: Soviet forces ringed the dunes on the west and south, enemy troops could be seen smoking within the old division positions, and Japanese corpses were strewn in heartrending heaps. From one severely hurt noncom who was lying in the area, it was learned that the division and all of the supporting units had retreated to Nomonhan.

Takada had said that he received orders (however bizarre) on the night of the 30th, but Hirowatari had not heard from the division, and he would not proceed immediately to Nomonhan (as Takada did) without an official order. The only defensible location would be the Old Engineer Bridge site, which had been occupied at the outset of the relief expedition on 27 August. Heading toward the Holsten, Hirowatari managed to pick up his strayed 2nd Battalion. Farther on, a signal officer conveyed the division's operational order, and Hirowatari now knew for sure that he was supposed to reach Nomonhan. On the way, trucks picked up the seriously wounded. When the 72nd Regiment finally arrived at Nomonhan around 6 A.M. on the 31st, "having overcome all kinds of difficulties," Hirowatari commanded a total of 240-50 marching men, of whom only about 150 were uninjured. The captain was pleased that almost all of the wounded had been rescued (obviously without the intended help of the 71st Infantry) and that many of the heavy weapons had been salvaged. No crisis befell the regimental colors, which Colonel Sakai had sent back to the Sixth Army for safekeeping.[27]

Suzuki's original thinking had been to extricate the division in two columns of march: division headquarters and the 71st Regiment on the left, the 72nd Regiment and the engineers on the right. But, as we have seen, the two battalions of the 72nd and the 2nd Battalion of the 71st could not be contacted in time, and they took action separately. Thus the main retreat force ended up with only the 1st Battalion of Hanada's 71st Regiment in the van, followed by division headquarters, the signal unit, and Saitō's engineers. Allowing for detours, the distances involved were about 28 kilometers to Lake Mohorehi, 40 kilometers to Chiangchunmiao. The jump-off time of midnight was met. To Lieutenant Colonel Saitō, Komatsubara seemed very calm, quiet, and still possessed of fighting spirit. Although fully aware of his responsibility, the general was not depressed.

Saitō's engineer unit moved on the right or south flank upon emerging from the hollow. Although Suzuki thinks that the engineers, pursued on that side by tanks for about two hours, were hardest hit, Saitō says that his men came under serious fire only once. At the outset, they crawled 1,500 meters; then they walked. "The Russian soldiers were so dumb," scoffs Saitō, "it was easy to evade them if we were careful and maintained silence." At the end of the march to Nomonhan, Saitō had about 125 men left, almost all wounded.[28]

Komatsubara's main column proceeded straight ahead after moving through the escape trenches dug by the engineers and climbing out of the dip into the moonlight. There were many searing moments when Japanese wounded, left behind, pleaded to be taken along. The voice of a dying signal corporal, for example, haunted his team leader long afterward, causing him to wonder whether mercy killing would have been better. Lieutenant Ono, the medical officer in Hanada's battalion, has never forgotten the agony of the many wounded and the torment of having to issue hand grenades to those who could not keep up—although there seemed to be no alternative under the circumstances.[29]

At first, however, there was no time to grieve, for the Russians on the high ground fired flares and concentrated a barrage on the breakthrough point. A machine-gun corporal in the vanguard was shot in the ankle by a heavy machine gun firing from the left. It felt like being whacked with an iron bar, but he got up and kept running. Five or six tanks appeared on the left. At the moment the corporal hit the ground and yelled a warning, he was struck in the head and blinded. When he tried to remove his helmet, the jagged edges of the perforation cut into his skull. Having expended his bandages, the corporal was tying a towel around his head when he felt a chill and passed out, "like falling into an abyss." His sergeant found him and dared to carry him all the way to safety.[30]

A signal-unit sergeant remembers peering over a hillock and discerning many tanks. Captain Utsui, the division guide, tried to reassure the troops by telling them that shells fired at night always flew high. It was therefore entirely feasible to push across the crestline and break through, man by man. The sergeant screwed up his courage and was climbing over the crest when the enemy fired flares and tracers and opened up with tank cannon and heavy machine guns. "We left our fates to the gods," says the sergeant, "and we ran and ran until our unit lost all semblance of formation." It took him a considerable time to believe that he had escaped from danger.[31]

Suzuki was aware that there had been casualties ahead and that the troops were tending to disperse, running as far as they could and then crawling like worms. But there was a big scare soon after the movement began, perhaps 80 meters from the hollow: lying on the earth and trying to determine the enemy layout, Suzuki heard the roar of armor on the move.

He put an ear to the ground and picked up the sound of 70, 80, or even more tanks. For at least 10 minutes the major held up the advance, until the armor seemed to have changed direction. He was about to signal a resumption of the march when Captain Utsui came up and admitted that he had lost his bearings. Having spent two months in the area, Suzuki felt competent to take over as guide. Using hand signals, he told the column when to stop, when to fall and wait, when to crawl, when to walk—generally in 300-meter increments. At about 1,000 meters from the dip, the enemy armor seemed to be pursuing Saitō's column on the right. Although the tanks did not come too close to the main files, the headquarters soldiers to the rear suffered many casualties from tank machine-gun fire.

Behind Komatsubara, the stretcher-bearers plodded forward carrying Okamoto. To the sergeant of the detail, the Russians seemed to be lying in wait for the column. Three of the bearers were wounded or at least forced to fall out of line, causing the sergeant to lend a hand. But although Okamoto had lost a lot of blood and said he felt cold, he never whimpered about his pain. Locking his hands behind his head, he gazed at the sky and was heard to remark, "My, but the stars are really beautiful tonight." Suzuki's rate of advance was limited by the movement of Okamoto's litter. The walking wounded did their best to limp along, supported by canes or leaning on the shoulders of able-bodied comrades from the 71st Regiment marching along the flanks. Many soldiers were shot down on the way. The unhurt men instinctively speeded up under fire and left behind those who could not keep up. Okamoto's sergeant can still remember the pathetic chorus in the dark —"Hey, take me with you," "Are you going to leave us behind here?" [32]

As for the division commander, his gait was weak and staggering. Okamoto's sergeant, moving just behind, wondered if Komatsubara had no real intention of surviving "ignobly." Indeed, Suzuki states that at one point a bodyguard rushed up and said to hurry because Komatsubara was "acting funny" and trying to draw his pistol—in other words, was preparing to commit suicide. Suzuki dashed to the general and took away his pistol, leaving him only his sword. Despite the difference in rank, the major says he had no choice, in view of the mission to get back safely to the Sixth Army. He certainly understood Komatsubara's feelings, he told him, but the division commander was the key to this operation and to future revenge, and his body simply did not belong to him right now; so "please do not act hastily." Okamoto's sergeant could see two husky corporals firmly gripping the arms of Komatsubara as they advanced, undoubtedly keeping the general from considering suicide again. [33]

Hanada, who was with Suzuki, remembers how the column threaded its way through the valley, penetrating gaps, avoiding enemy positions when possible, but ready for hand-to-hand combat at any time. Komatsubara says that the dip area had been encircled doubly and triply by Soviet tanks, machine guns, and snipers, and that the escape units passed through heavy machine gun zones of fire three times en route. The general tried in vain to make contact with the separated Yotsuya unit, sending out Captain Utsui, the divisional signal officer and erstwhile guide, with five infantrymen. Yotsuya was gone, but Utsui did encounter Hirowatari's 72nd Regiment and, as we saw, was able to confirm the division's order to head for Nomonhan.

Although the retreat had proceeded for more than three hours and the stars were beginning to grow dim, the force had not reached the bend in the upstream Holsten where it was hoped to cross. A worried Suzuki queried a second lieutenant who had been scouting ahead, but the young officer could only point in the general direction. Overhearing the discussion, Komatsubara identified the stream as the locale where the color of the grass was different. It was indeed the area north of the bend, the swampy zone near Heights 742, northeast of Old Engineer Bridge. The troops were given a rest and they drank the water gratefully. Before crossing the river near Heights 738, Komatsubara was found by a runner carrying a rather outdated Sixth Army order of 1 P.M. on the 29th. As the general already knew, his unit was to break through enemy lines and transfer toward Nomonhan, for strength was being concentrated and plans were being devised for future action. According to the Sixth Army, "our responsibility lies in the execution of this final plan. We strictly enjoin you to be cautious and to carry out this order immediately, no matter how bad the situation."[34] In addition to this courier, a warrant officer platoon leader appeared from the Holsten (in which he had remained immersed for two days and two nights) and reported to Komatsubara on the situation of the Hasebe unit.[35]

Sixth Army headquarters could not be far away; the worst was over—and none too soon, with day breaking. When a couple of very welcome army trucks were sighted to the northeast at 5 or 6 A.M., Suzuki's remaining divisional officer, Utsui (whom the major had designated to serve in his stead as Komatsubara's "aide"), escorted the general and Okamoto safely to Mohorehi. Although exhausted and famished, Komatsubara climbed aboard his truck unassisted. Suzuki stayed behind at the bend, ostensibly to "take care of" the officers and men who were arriving piecemeal, as he graciously assured the general when asking the latter to go ahead to the army command post. But Suzuki's real purpose was to straighten out stragglers. Too many of the Japanese troops were retreating with only their canteens and no weapons, or with rifles inverted. These "shabby" men made Suzuki feel miserable, on the eve of reporting to the Sixth Army with the remnants of the once-proud 23rd Division. The major remained behind for about two hours, made sure there were no more laggards, and got to Mohorehi before noon on 31 August.[36]

When Captain Onozuka, temporarily in command of the 71st Infantry,[37] took stock of the regiment on 31 August, he was hard-pressed to put together a provisional unit of four officers and 250 effectives, armed with two machine guns.[38] At most, the 1st Battalion had a fighting strength of three officers (including Hanada) and 128 soldiers. In numbers of dead alone, the battalion had lost 58 officers and men since 26 August.[39] The 3rd and 4th companies combined numbered 33 men without an officer and had to be controlled by Hanada. There were 31 men in the 1st Company, commanded by a sergeant; 33 in the 2nd Company, under a first lieutenant; 23 in the machine gun company, commanded by a corporal; and 8 in the infantry gun battery, without an officer.[40] Captain Takada's 2nd Battalion had been similarly savaged. By the time the 5th Company got to Chiangchunmiao, it possessed a total of only five or six unhurt men.[41] Takada's senior officer was a mere probationary officer in charge of the 6th Company. A master sergeant commanded the 7th Company; a superior private, the 8th Company; a warrant officer, the machine gun company.[42]

With bloodshot eyes and scraggly beards, the unhurt survivors sat on the grass in the heat of 31 August, sharing bean jelly and reliving the events of the preceding night.[43] Certainly one of the most bizarre of the experiences had been undergone by Ueda Mamoru, a sergeant in the 71st Regiment, and the little group with him. After breaking through the enemy cordon, they found themselves wandering on the plain, trying to orient themselves by the sergeant's compass. Several meters ahead and to the left, the outlines of men and of several parked aircraft could be seen. It was "like Buddha met in hell," for the Sixth Army must be near. At the top of their lungs, the Japanese yelled questions to the plane crews—How close was Nomonhan? Which air unit was this? The airmen merely stared back at the soldiers and said not a word. Then it dawned on Ueda and his men: these were Soviet planes and Soviet crews! The sergeant ordered everybody to hit the ground immediately. If attacked, they should fire at the leading edge of the aircraft. The Japanese watched and waited for a while, but the Russians seemed indifferent to their presence. Inch by inch, Ueda and his men crawled quietly away, without the slightest interference. Toward dawn, when they discerned troops and parked trucks, they were more cautious in approaching. But these were Japanese ambulance trucks, and Ueda dashed toward them, forgetting the pain in his wounded hand.[44]

The Sixth Army's "relief" expedition, despite Tsuji's ranting, amounted to no more than a few trucks, 11 supply soldiers, and 14 or 15 infantrymen "from here and there." There was no clear-cut commander, but two or three junior officers, including Komatsubara's aide Tanaka, went with the infantry. Around 4:30 P.M. on 30 August, the transport company commander, Capt. Sōma Seiji, assembled his unit and asked for volunteers to form a "do-or-die" unit (*kesshitai*) in conjunction with infantry to rescue the 23rd Division headquarters. The mission would be very dangerous, warned Sōma, as the party would have to break through the enemy encirclement, but it was an exceptional honor for a rear unit. Married men should be excluded if possible. Master Sergeant Inakura raised his hand, as did nearly all of the men, from whom ten were chosen.

Inakura organized his ten-man team, and comrades contributed such things as clean clothing, underwear, socks, and towels. The five best trucks were checked and loaded with food, ammunition, and water. At about 11 P.M., Sōma gave a short speech extolling the "glory of the quartermaster corps," after which farewell sips of water were drunk from a canteen. The infantry boarded the trucks, and the rest of the Sōma company waved goodbye. Sixth Army operations officer Hamada claims that he wanted to accompany the group but was turned down by the 23rd Division officers, who asked him to "kindly leave the matter to the division."[45] "I saw them off dolefully," asserts the colonel, "praying for their good luck." Hamada went back to his tent and lay down without talking to anybody. The hours passed, but he could not sleep.

Tanaka served as the guide for the relief party. He had never wanted to leave Komatsubara in the first place, and was more than happy to go back because of his sense of obligation—his duty to protect the division commander—and his knowledge of the terrain. When the team came to enemy outposts, the trucks stopped and the infantry dismounted and moved ahead a bit, while a first lieutenant and Tanaka studied the situation. At that time, the sky in the direction of the division turned red and very heavy gunfire could be heard. Komatsubara's force must have begun its withdrawal. The infantry wanted to plunge forward on the trucks, but the supply troops had disappeared and there were no drivers left. It seems that Sergeant Inakura had taken nine of his men and moved off boldly on foot, on his own, assigning one enlisted man to stay with the trucks. Whatever Inakura's intention, neither he nor his nine soldiers were ever seen alive again. After the cease-fire, their corpses were recovered.

Looking for the division, the infantrymen were challenged by Russian sentries and lost time evading them. It was a source of momentary encouragement when a Japanese sergeant attached to division headquarters showed up and said that, at the time he had become separated from Komatsubara, the general had broken out of the command post positions and was all right. On the basis of his own escape from the trap the night before, Tanaka believed that Komatsubara could make it out too. Among the stragglers encountered were some soldiers who could drive trucks, so the infantrymen rode back to army headquarters, without having encountered the division or the lost truckers. Tanaka says that the main objective of the rescue unit with which he went was not successful because of the timing, and that Komatsubara was already resting at Sixth Army headquarters when he got back.[46] Obviously, somebody had picked up Komatsubara and Okamoto.

In the early morning, Captain Kuroda came to Hamada's tent and reported on the encounter with the noncom from division headquarters who knew that Komatsubara was safely on his way. The relief party had returned and soldiers had already been deployed in front of the Sixth Army's lines to meet the division commander. Hamada remembers the sense of relief and pleasure that he and the rest of the staff felt, "from the bottom of our hearts," when the good news was received. Finally, according to Komatsubara's diary, the division commander arrived at army headquarters at Mohorehi around 8 A.M.: "The army commander was touched. We embraced each other and wept." Still devoid of his insignia, Komatsubara seemed drained of emotion. To Ogisu (whose own face was supposedly flushed from whiskey, jeers Tsuji), Komatsubara said: "I am very sorry that I have lost so many of my men. I thought that I ought to have died, but since I was ordered to return, I broke through the tight encirclement and came back. Now I'll do my best to rebuild the division and restore its reputation." Hamada says he cannot remember the details of the general's remarks because tears clouded his eyes, but "I could feel what he was thinking way down deep, and that awoke vibrations in my own heart."

A division headquarters tent was set up in the area of the Sixth Army. When Tanaka went to see Komatsubara, tears glistened behind the general's glasses at the sight of his aide, safe. Tanaka, who had been with Komatsubara throughout the Nomonhan war, was pained by the indescribable sorrow that etched the general's appearance, reflecting the enormous strain upon him. Before the recent expedition to relieve Yamagata, there had not been much gray in Komatsubara's hair. Now it had turned entirely white.

Among the last entries in Komatsubara's combat diary is a tribute to Warrant Officer Sasaki, who had made every effort to protect him during the escape march. Hit in the chest by machine-gun fire, Sasaki had kept going until finally, near New Engineer Bridge, he had had to drop out and was not seen again. "I truly grieve for him," wrote the general.

Tsuji detected no dissatisfaction in Komatsubara's attitude—"so different from Ogisu's." Indeed, as his diary reveals, Komatsubara was lavish in his gratitude to the Sixth Army for its "great concern and kind intentions." Although unsuccessful, the army had tried to provide air drops of food, air bombing, runners, and trucks. In addition, staff officer Hamada had volunteered to accompany the party that sought to rescue him.[47] There is no hint Komatsubara knew of the story (retailed by Tsuji) that Ogisu thought he was better off dead.

The Kwantung Army had lost the entire foothold above the Holsten for which it had fought so desperately and senselessly since May. Now only thousands of dead or severely wounded Japanese soldiers lay abandoned at desolate Balshagal. There had been innumerable scenes of bravery and tenacity during the fighting, as well as of less commendable attributes. But the Sixth Army had been outgeneraled, and the 23rd Division's last sortie, however gallant, was hopeless from the start. Everybody in the higher military echelons in Manchuria was still fulminating about "battles of revenge," as we shall see, but the location of the Japanese lines as of the 31st left no doubt about the victors and the vanquished. More men would die in September, but when the artillery commander, General Hata, went to pay his respects to Komatsubara on 31 August, "the battlefield was extremely quiet and both the ground and the sky looked still."[48] This was true only because Zhukov and the Soviet-MPRA command had achieved precisely what they had set out to do—no more, no less. It had not been a matter of good or bad karma.

37

Winding Down a Small War

History to the defeated
May say alas
but cannot help or pardon.
—W. H. Auden, "Spain 1937"

Even after Komatsubara had fallen back across the Holsten with hardly more than 400 men from the debris of the 23rd Division, the Nomonhan war did not end, solely because the Japanese side did not want the fighting to close in that fashion. In the course of concentrating fresh units for still another "last offensive" in September, the Kwantung Army had been paying new attention to the Arshaan-Handagai sector southeast of Nomonhan.

From east of Mutanchiang, Lt. Gen. Yasui Tōji's 2nd Division was alerted on 25 August to board trains and move to the Nomonhan battlefront. At the same time that the main body headed straight for Hailar through Harbin, a detachment was to proceed to Arshaan via Paichengtzu. Formed from the 15th Infantry Brigade commanded by Maj. Gen. Katayama Shōtarō, Task Force Katayama consisted of the 16th Regiment (Col. Miyazaki Shigesaburō), the 30th Regiment (Col. Kashiwa Toku), and a field artillery battalion. The assignment of the task force was to reinforce the Handagai district. On reaching Arshaan on 31 August, Katayama received an urgent order from the Sixth Army (to which he was now attached) to cover the area northwest of Lake Dorot, because Komatsubara's division was in grave danger. There was no time to send liaison officers to army headquarters. The 16th Regiment was directed to move out immediately, although the men and horses ordinarily required at least a day for rest and preparation. Miyazaki ordered his units to depart from Arshaan as soon as each arrived. Stragglers must be left behind, with instructions to catch up. In three days, the regiment had made it to its destination, via Handagai—a feat that "a certain other division" took a week to accomplish, Miyazaki was proud to say. Coming up behind Miyazaki, the 30th Regiment occupied Heights 970 on 4 September, replacing Manchukuo army elements.

After studying the terrain ahead, Miyazaki decided on a night attack to clear the enemy from the Heights 997–Akiyama Heights sector near the Halha. Careful reconnaissance was conducted, including photography, and utmost attention was paid to secrecy. Upon clearance by Katayama and by the Sixth Army, the 16th Regiment was ready to launch its attack on the night of 6 September. That afternoon, however, Miyazaki was disgusted to receive countermanding instructions from the army. When, on the morning of the 8th, a Sixth Army staff officer brought new orders to Katayama authorizing the 16th Regiment's assault that night, Miyazaki privately "deplored the army's lack of policy."

Jumping off from its positions after sunset, Maj. Minamoto Shirō's 1st Battalion, supported by the regimental and rapid-fire batteries (four pieces each), was to seize the main objective, Heights 997. Akiyama Heights, about six kilometers away, was to be taken by 1st Lt. Akiyama Takejirō's 5th Company. After enemy positions had been penetrated by 11 P.M., the assault forces should dig in promptly and be prepared for counterattacks at first light. The 2nd Battalion (less the 5th Company) was to remain in reserve.

Akiyama Heights, with a garrison of only 20 or 30, was occupied easily; Miyazaki saw the signal of success at just about 11 P.M. First Lt. Oda Kanji's 2nd Company led the 1st Battalion's attack, cut to the shore of the Halha, crossed the skirt of Heights 997 on the east slope, and detoured to the right side of the enemy defenses (held by 200 or 300 men), following a path used by enemy soldiers when they went to get water. Ignoring a pen by the river that held seven or eight horses, Oda's men rushed toward the top of the hill. Although some of the Japanese stormed soldiers' tents halfway up the slope, most of the battalion plunged to the crest. The commander of the leading platoon, 2nd Lt. Sakurai Masayasu, sabered three men before being killed by a grenade.

Attacking Heights 997 from its left, 1st Lt. Ueda Yasuhiro's 3rd Company found the going easy at first, but by the time it neared the summit the enemy put up fierce resistance with heavy and light machine guns, hand grenades, and mortars. Until 3 or 4 A.M. on the 9th, says Miyazaki, it was impossible to tell who had won. The enemy fired various kinds of pyrotechnics in a series from Heights 997 toward Higashiyama and Heights 904, between 997 and Akiyama, and even toward the left shore of the Halha to warn other forces that 997, on the extreme right flank, was in peril. After the Nomonhan war, Miyazaki heard that the Kwantung Army OSS picked up enemy emergency radio signals in the clear.

In the early hours of 9 September, the Japanese atop Heights 997 could see enemy troops fleeing from their positions and assembling at Higashiyama to the rear. Thereupon Miyazaki ordered his reserve 2nd Battalion, commanded by Maj. Oyama Suketa, to clear Higashiyama promptly. Leaving a portion at its present position, the 5th Company rejoined the parent battalion and, together with the 6th Company, led the movement across the open plain toward Higashiyama. Some ten hours after Heights 997 had fallen, at midday on 9 September, enemy tanks appeared from the west of Heights 904, at the time Oyama's troops were 500 to 600 meters away from Higashi-yama. Built up from 20 to 50 tanks at first, the foe seemed bent on retaking 997. Miyazaki ordered Minamoto's 1st Battalion, as well as the regimental and rapid-fire batteries, to support the 2nd Battalion.

Shortly after 1 P.M., the enemy put in approximately 150 tanks and two battalions of infantry and cavalry, which struck the 2nd Battalion in the area of Heights 904 and the zone to the rear. Hostile planes also attacked. Within a matter of minutes, the entire region of 6,000 meters was blanketed with smoke, through which groups of tanks could be seen churning. Enemy gun-fire ignited the dry trees and grass. Many human-bullet teams went out against the armor, but they were helpless in the face of the cannon and machine-gun fire and could stop only two tanks. The regimental and rapid-fire guns, however, burned six of the armored vehicles.

Fortunately for the Japanese, the hostile tanks came no closer than 200 or 300 meters. At his command post on Honbu ("Headquarters") Heights, Miyazaki was left with only five color guards and a few runners. Although the 2nd Battalion's 5th and 7th companies had been able to dig in quickly and thus sustained relatively light losses, the 6th Company, the 2nd Machine Gun Company, and the battalion headquarters suffered very heavily because they could not finish entrenching themselves in the rocky soil. Approximately 150 officers and men were killed, including battalion commander Oyama and the machine gun company commander. By 7 P.M., the attached truck platoon had made 27 round trips carrying the wounded back and hauling ammunition forward. It had been necessary to zigzag, speed up, and circle constantly. One truck was lost to gunfire.

At 4 P.M., the 3rd Battalion under Maj. Ōhashi Ichii arrived, with the 2nd Field Artillery Battalion. Miyazaki ordered the artillery to deploy west of Honbu Heights and engage the enemy armor, and the 3rd Battalion to attack from the north side of Akiyama toward Heights 904. With two companies up and one back, the 3rd Battalion moved forward; but as soon as the first wave reached the 2nd Battalion's sector, the enemy tank units suddenly began to withdraw to the southwest. The Japanese artillery continued pursuit fire to a range of 8,000 meters, and the 3rd Battalion chased the hostile forces after they started to withdraw at about 6:30 P.M. Sunset ended the operation.

At 9 P.M. on the 9th, Miyazaki ordered the truck platoon to evacuate the 2nd Battalion's casualties to the aid station. Orientation was difficult because of the fires blazing here and there, and a dozen tanks were still in the area, so the attempt was abandoned for the time being. At 2:15 A.M. on the 10th, with the help of a guide, the truckers made it to the 2nd Battalion's sector. Before daybreak on the 10th, Miyazaki pulled back his 2nd and 3rd battalions to the jump-off site. The 1st Battalion had already assembled there. This left the truck platoon without the protection of infantry in retrieving the last wounded, ahead of the forward lines held by the 3rd Battalion.

Miyazaki, after the cease-fire, had some of his men who were stone-masons carve markers and set them in the ground where the Japanese front lines were located, "in memory of our occupation." The joint committee that later demarcated the frontier, says the colonel, recognized the 16th Regiment's night-attack lines as the Manchukuo-MPR boundary, thanks to the powerful proof afforded by the commemorative stones.[1]

The official Japanese postwar military history asserts that Miyazaki's bold night attack against an Outer Mongolian cavalry division on 8/9 September smashed the superior force "in a wink" and improved the strategic situation in the area. The Sixth Army, however, understood that after some initial success the Katayama detachment became engaged in fierce combat and that enemy forces reinforced their strength, built up their positions, and prepared for the new Japanese counteroffensive. Once the fighting "came to a standoff, we did not make progress afterward."

According to the Katayama detachment's own tally for the actions of early September, enemy casualties amounted to a large number (*tasū*), including about 70 corpses abandoned on the battlefield. Twenty enemy tanks, two armored cars, one rapid-fire piece, nine heavy machine guns, and many rifles and light machine guns were put out of action. But the price paid by Task Force Katayama, in such a relatively short battle, was heavy: 183 killed (including ten officers) and 99 wounded (including four officers). The 2nd Division's chief of staff, Col. Harada Jirō, was distressed by the unexpectedly severe losses, especially in the Miyazaki regiment's mauled 2nd Battalion. Why had the task force lost so many officers? Why were twice as many men killed as were wounded? The best explanations the staff could provide were that IJA officers did the leading in battle, and close-quarter tactics of attack against tanks had to be expensive to be effective. When Lieutenant General Yasui reviewed the data submitted to him, he merely commented that "it was a pleasure we got 20 enemy tanks."[2]

Col. Gotō Mitsuzō, commander of the 1st Infantry Regiment of the 4th Division, headed the second task force created on 20 August from three infantry battalions, a field artillery battalion, a transport company, and Lieutenant Colonel Hirayama's engineer regiment (one company and a supply platoon, totaling 117 men). Coming under control of the Sixth Army, Gotō and his force advanced toward the Nishi-Sankakuyama (Heights 1031) sector, on the extreme right wing of the hostile forces deployed on the right shore of the Halha. In the immediate area, extending to the locale 600-700 meters south of Nishi-Sankakuyama, the Russians were thought to have two infantry battalions, six or seven tanks, and about 10 artillery pieces—12-cm. howitzers and field pieces. Overall, the Soviet 57th Corps included more than three rifle divisions and several mechanized brigades.

Hirayama's engineers arrived at Handagai on 7 September. Next morning, they moved southwest toward the Arshaan River junction to repair a road and, cutting down pine trees found locally, build a bridge designed to support the Gotō unit's crossing far south of the Halha-Holsten confluence. To the east of the river, at Nishi-Sankakuyama itself, the 3rd (Fukano) IGU Battalion, with two companies and four guns, was being pressed hard by the foe. Gotō took command of the district on the 8th. Rain had been coming down for days, and on the night of the 9th it became very cold, the wind gusted, and snow fell hard. In the swampland 1,500 meters from the river, the pathway had turned to mire. Seventy riflemen and 1st Lt. Nomiyama Takeo's company from the 24th Engineers assisted Hirayama's soldiers. Some progress was made on the bridge by early afternoon on the 9th, but as the storm intensified, the river current quickened and the waters rose to two and a half meters. Pilings were washed away several times. Hirayama gave his men a respite at 2 A.M., but Gotō phoned to say that he wanted to push his 2nd Battalion across the river by 3 A.M. The weary, drenched engineers resumed work, hewing long planks from the pines and constructing a temporary eight-meter span in the middle of the crossing by 4:30 A.M. strong enough to bear foot troops.

Between 5:40 and 6:30 A.M. on 10 September, the 2nd Battalion crossed the bridge. Machine guns and other heavy weapons had to be sent by boat, and horses and wagons could not cross at all yet. The building of the span resumed at 8 A.M. All of the pilings had been sunk by 10:30, after which the engineers began to lay the surface of the bridge. Once load resistance tests had been conducted, the battalion guns, horses, and heavy equipment of the 2nd Battalion went safely across Hirayama Bridge.

At 4 P.M. on the 10th, Gotō instructed his force that Maj. Gen. Miyazawa Saishirō, the commander of the 3rd IGU, was taking command of the whole unit plus the 5th IGU Battalion and one mountain artillery battery. An offensive would be launched against the enemy in front of Nishi-Sankakuyama early next morning. Gotō's force would constitute the left wing and would attack across the river during the night. Sensha ("Tank") Heights was the objective of the 1st Battalion; the Manjū ("Bean-Jam Bun") Heights sector, of the 2nd Battalion. The rapid-fire battery and the engineers should be prepared to engage armor coming from the valley to the south; some engineers should be left to guard the bridge. For the main units, code words were *Tokyo* and *Kōfu*; for the flank units, *Chokuyu* ("Imperial Precepts") and *Gokajō* ("Five Articles on Parliamentary Government").

The Gotō detachment assembled at the bridge very late. Heavy weapons and dismantled field artillery were sent ahead first, at 10-meter intervals, after 12:30 A.M., but the main force and the unloaded heavy vehicles did not get across until 3, behind schedule. Hirayama's engineers left the bridge area at 5:15 and took up antitank positions by 7:30 A.M. Nomiyama's company guarded the span. Firing by the infantry began at 6 A.M., followed by an artillery duel. Five hours later, the rain changed to snow again, and it grew intensely cold. By 6:30 P.M., Gotō reported that his detachment had driven the enemy to the south of the Halha and would return that night. There was obviously no interference, for the field artillery did not get back to the bridge until 9:20 A.M. and did not complete the leisurely crossing until 12:30 P.M. on the 12th.

The Sixth Army was pleased with the combat performance of the Gotō detachment, which, it heard, had swept up the enemy from the south flank, across the river, in the snow. In anticipation of its use in the army's main offensive, Gotō's force was ordered into army reserve, to be replaced by the IGU troops as of midnight on 11 September. Hirayama's engineers made repairs on the bridge and on the road on both sides of the river before pulling back at 8 A.M. on the 13th.[3]

Soviet coverage of the military actions on this sector is slim. Despite Japanese expulsion from territory claimed by the Mongolian People's Republic on the right side of the Halha by the end of August, the Kwantung Army tried to encroach again in September. Drawing upon the fresh 2nd Division, on 4 September the Japanese hurled two battalions against the heights at Eris Ulyn Obo. Reserves from the Soviet Southern Force counterattacked and drove back the Japanese, who left 350 casualties on the battlefield. On the night of 8 September the Japanese tried another assault in the same region, committing four infantry companies, but they were repulsed with severe losses.[4] From the dates alone, the Russians seem to be referring to actions involving Katayama's 30th and 16th infantry regiments, respectively, and to be omitting mention of the Gotō detachment entirely.

Sixth Army headquarters was taking a calculated risk in the way it disposed of its resources. The sector near Mohorehi, which had been selected on 29 August for the forthcoming offensive, was a northward extension of the old battleground to the south. There was no reason to doubt that the Russians could unleash a second juggernaut of their own, if they desired. Nevertheless, the Sixth Army dared to deploy Kunisaki's 7th Division, screening this forward region with only four infantry battalions, six field artillery batteries, and four rapid-fire batteries. It was hoped thereby to limit the extent of the Soviet success, geographically and psychologically, as well as to buck up friendly forces by demonstrating that army headquarters was not budging. Kwantung Army Chief of Staff Yano, who was at the front when the plan was devised, did not object to it, despite the implicit strategic dangers of operating so close to the frontier claimed by the Soviet-MPR side. That the advanced Japanese positions lay just outside the controversial boundary obviously saved them from further disaster.[5]

Preoccupied with the problems of extricating the 23rd Division from the Holsten trap and of coping with a possible Soviet irruption, the Sixth Army was not able to apply itself to the full details of its own counteroffensive. Nevertheless, it happily prepared to accommodate the numerous units that the Kwantung Army was sending up by 8-9 September: the bulk of Lt. Gen. Yasui Tōji's 2nd Division and Lt. Gen. Sawada Shigeru's 4th Division;[6] half of the 1st and part of the 8th divisions; the unscathed 5th Tank Regiment; 12 rapid-fire batteries (48 pieces); a motorized mountain artillery regiment of two battalions (24 guns) plus 17 platoons (34 guns) to be employed as infantry regimental guns; two 15-cm. howitzer regiments (the 4th and the 9th); nine antiaircraft batteries; three engineer platoons (with 36 flame-throwers); 21 transport companies; and the Manchukuo Railway Bureau motor units (a grand total of 1,500 vehicles). Quantitatively, the tripled strength allocated to the Sixth Army was impressive by Japanese standards, and the infantry divisions were not green like Komatsubara's 23rd. But in practical terms, there was still a fatal inferiority in firepower vis-à-vis the Russians, especially in armor and artillery.

Although the particulars for employing all the new formations had still not been worked out, the Sixth Army had a general idea based on its understanding of Kwantung Army intentions. Operational readiness must be achieved quickly, with the objective of destroying the Soviet-MPRA forces. In view of the lack of time and transportation to prepare defensive positions and wintering facilities for coping with the approaching cold season, as soon as the objective had been achieved (by about the end of September) the field forces would be pulled back east of Handagai and Hailar (in mid-October). If necessary, forward operations would be resumed after the spring thaw of 1940.

While strong Japanese formations attacked from the area of Handagai, the main offensive would be launched in the northern Holsten sector on the right bank of the Halha. Attacking in parallel, from right to left, would be the 2nd, 4th, and 7th divisions. To cut off the enemy forces' route of supposed retreat to the left side of the Halha and to destroy them, the 2nd Division (the "key to the offensive," in Hamada's words) was to outflank the Russians and cross the river when the time was ripe, operating in concert with elements of the neighboring 4th Division.[7] Except for the increased number of divisions committed, this simplistic and self-assured battle plan reveals no fundamental difference from the thinking that underlay the unsuccessful earlier IJA offensives, when Soviet forces were far less sizable too.

Komatsubara's survivors had been assembling eight kilometers east of Chiangchunmiao between the 2nd and 4th divisions. Satō Kōtoku, the audacious colonel commanding the spearhead regiment at Changkufeng in 1938 and now a major general in charge of the Hailar-based 8th BGU's 2nd Sector unit, had arrived to replace Kobayashi as Komatsubara's infantry group commander and had brought a replacement staff. When Komatsubara learned that the 23rd Division was being omitted from the Sixth Army's attack plan, he was outraged and, according to Suzuki, almost got into a fight with the army commander. Ogisu had convened an important preliminary staff meeting on 2 September, at which he indicated that battle frontages would be allocated according to the strength of units. Therefore the 23rd Division would not be asked to participate. Komatsubara retorted that his division did possess strength and wanted to fight. When pressed about his number of effectives, Komatsubara apparently admitted that he had only 400 or so[8] but argued that, "although we may be few, what is wrong with our trying to avenge our dead comrades?" "Forced" to yield to this emotional appeal, says Suzuki, Ogisu assigned Komatsubara the "main" sector to the right of the 7th Division. Onozuka remembers that when Komatsubara raised the need for a battle of revenge (*tomurai gassen*), Ogisu replied that he would not want to impose upon the division commander after having fought such a difficult battle but would like the unit to join the Sixth Army's offensive "in the sense of guiding us." In practice, the remnants of the 23rd Division were allotted a frontage of only 300 meters, between the other divisions, but honor was saved.[9]

X-day for the projected Sixth Army offensive had to be designated soon, but logistical considerations such as transportation of forces and stockpiling of ammunition and other stores were crucial. Since 20 August, Kwantung Army logistics officer Ashikawa Haruo had been helping the Sixth Army, first at Hailar and then at Mohorehi. After an important staff meeting on 31 August, Major Ashikawa went back for a while to Hailar, where he worked with the transport chief, Maj. Gen. Morinaga Takeo, and coordinated matters with various supply dumps. Returning to Mohorehi, Ashikawa attended the meeting of unit commanders on 5 September, and next day called in all the logistics staff officers to convey the battle plan. X-day was tentatively targeted for the 9th. This time for sure, Ashikawa wanted the Japanese to demonstrate their real combat prowess.[10]

Still, all the Japanese paper plans about decisive assaults and pursuits sidestepped a number of vital old questions, most importantly the realities of breaking through powerful defenses in depth. Of course it was impossible to win, admitted Tsuji, using elementary orthodox tactics and an army with "old-fashioned" equipment against a modern enemy possessing superior strength in armor, planes, and artillery. "We would have to change our tactics," Tsuji concluded, "in order to make up for our poor matériel." Drawing upon the earlier experiences at Nomonhan, the Japanese must attack only by night, defend only by day. Specifically, the assault forces should jump off after darkness on the first day, seize the enemy's outposts, and dig in by dawn. During daylight on the second day, friendly troops should remain in their positions and prepare to conduct a night attack. The process should be repeated for four days and four nights, with advances of 500 to 1,000 meters per night. Losses would be minimized during daylight hours by taking cover in deep defenses, while friendly artillery destroyed oncoming tanks. After careful preparations on the fifth and sixth days, the Japanese should break through the enemy's main positions by a night assault on the sixth day. The Kwantung Army's tactical thinking was shared with the Sixth Army, and each line division was ordered to train accordingly.[11]

The generalized tactical outline took the attacking infantrymen only to the main positions in the darkness and did not address the methods of seizing strongpoints by "forced raiding" even if the approaches had been penetrated successfully. Unless this difficult task was accomplished by dawn, friendly troops would be caught in the open and suffer very heavy losses after first light. According to the Soviet field manual, known to the Japanese, corps defenses covered a usual breadth of 24-30 kilometers at least and 35-40 kilometers at most, with main and supporting positions both customarily 5-7 kilometers deep. By early September, the Russian troops had done their usual fine job of preparing strong defenses along the line of their claimed frontier. The width of the Soviet front was 48 kilometers; the depth, 8-11 kilometers from the forward edge to the Halha. Even applying Tsuji's optimum formula for advancing, one cannot see how the Sixth Army could have broken through Zhukov's powerful mechanized and rifle corps by the sixth day. In addition, IJA tactical thinking did not take into account such disconcerting probabilities as Soviet counterattacks and pursuit, or a possible stalemate on the open plains, without shelter and facilities, amid the long Mongolian winter.[12]

In order to hone the army's attack skills, on 4 September Ogisu directed study of every possible way to infiltrate deeply through the bridges, artillery, and tanks scattered across the broad expanse, and to raid and destroy the enemy in one swoop by night. During the period of concentration before the offensive, the units should organize two sets of infiltration and destruction teams of 3-5 men each per company. Special drills and training should be conducted in night movement, penetration, and cover, and antitank instruction should be given concerning target points particularly vulnerable to demolition by the close-quarter squads.[13]

The tone of Ogisu's outlook on the eve of the Japanese offensive is exemplified by the instructions (*kunji*) he issued to his subordinates on 5 September. Delivered orally, the text of his bombastic exhortation was apparently captured by the Russians; it became a sensational exhibit proffered to the International Military Tribunal by Soviet prosecutors after the Second World War as evidence of Japanese military criminality.[14] It was a source of regret, Ogisu evidently asserted, that the glorious mission of defending the northwest region had failed and the army had been "cast into a whirlpool of disorderly fighting on the frontier" for more than 10 days. Thanks to the brave and resolute actions of all units under Komatsubara, the chaos had diminished. The Kwantung Army commander had decided to send well-trained reinforcements stationed in Manchuria and was planning urgent measures designed to settle the conflict. It was clear that matters had gone beyond the limits of a simple border incident. Since Japan was waging a "sacred war" in China, any changes in the Nomonhan conflict exerted immense effects on the nation, in view of complicated domestic and external circumstances. The army must immediately deal a crushing blow to the enemy and annihilate his "growing insolence." In the Chiangchunmiao district, the Sixth Army was consequently making preparations for a new offensive, would "meet the coming autumn by finishing with one blow this mouse-stirring," and would "proudly show to the world the might of the select imperial troops." Endowed with a deep faith in the Emperor and with a brave and decisive spirit at every level, the army was sure of victory.

Hattori asserts that when Ogisu's assembled officers heard of the Kwantung Army's expectations, "their morale and fighting spirit soared 'sky-high.'" But did the Sixth Army commander believe his own language? It was only natural, comments Hamada, for the general to use big words and deliver resounding addresses intended to "pep up" the men. Ogisu did not expatiate privately to his senior staff officer, but from what Hamada could observe, the general "may have had confidence in our ability to wallop the Russians." Engineer Lieutenant Colonel Numazaki agrees that Ogisu exuded defiance and was full of fight, as he pored over his maps in his tent by candlelight, with his ever-present sake.[15]

The officers around the Sixth Army commander were far less sanguine. To 4th Division commander Sawada, the Sixth Army staff lacked the élan expected of a higher headquarters on the eve of a great offensive; "not one smiling face was in evidence." "I personally did not think the offensive would solve things," Hamada admits. On such a broad frontage, "a couple of divisions meant nothing—like a drop of water in a vast ocean," adds Suzuki, who reminds us that a Japanese infantry division was ordinarily supposed to cover four kilometers at most. According to the 28th Regiment commander (7th Division), the front was so wide that domination of one enemy point by friendly artillery did not matter much.[16]

When Ogisu convened the staff meeting of division commanders, Komatsubara brought along his senior officers, including the acting 71st Regiment commander, Onozuka. All too aware of the adverse terrain on the right side of the Halha, the battle-tested captain was convinced that the new IJA divisions would be wiped out just as the 23rd Division had been. Without heavy weapons, mechanized units, and long-range artillery, the Japanese troops would be so much "flesh and bullets" against the enemy's demonstrated strength. Probably the fresh units from China and eastern Manchuria did not comprehend what lay in store for them, but even the 7th Division from Hokkaido, which had had a baptism of fire as soon as it got to the front, knew better. It was not Onozuka's place to speak up, however, so he kept his apprehensions to himself.[17]

When Major General Satō reported to Komatsubara at Chiangchunmiao, the new group commander was struck by the "atmosphere of death" that permeated the division headquarters. During the same period, after Komatsubara and Suzuki had resumed tent life, the division commander seemed "terribly depressed, worried, and in bad shape," says Suzuki. "Nobody knew what he would do." Tsuji was worried too and told Suzuki to keep a close eye on the general. Komatsubara's sword was taken away and he was left with no weapons. Somebody was always watching him, even at night, while the shattered division was getting ready to take part in its battle of revenge.[18]

Ogisu's personality was certainly forceful, but the key to the Manchurian command's consistent bellicosity was the thinking of the staff in Hsinking. To try to cope with the Russians' powerful offensive of 20 August, the Kwantung Army had been rushing heavy reinforcements to the Sixth Army —indeed all the strategic reserves, artillery, and antitank units in Manchuria. After its initial cockiness, the Kwantung Army was now even willing to accept help from the Japanese forces in China. When Gen. Sugiyama Hajime (Gen), the commander of the North China Area Army, heard that the 23rd Division was almost smashed, he sent staff officer Yabe Chūta from Peking to Hsinking for the second time. On this occasion Tsuji said, "We'd like any assistance, as much as possible, and especially antitank units." Yabe, who remained at Hsinking until the end of the Nomonhan affair, arranged matters with Sugiyama's headquarters, which drew antitank strength from all of its divisions, since such a capability was unnecessary in North China. Sugiyama also alerted as many as four infantry divisions and concentrated them around Shanhaikuan by the time the cease-fire came.[19]

The Kwantung Army was expecting that the fresh forces, pulled from all directions, would stabilize and then reverse the unfavorable front-line situation by a short but decisive offensive (described earlier), once they had completed their assembly near Nomonhan during the first part of September. There were a number of reasons for the Kwantung Army's "rage," as the diplomat Shigemitsu Mamoru called it.[20] On the evening of 29 August, for example, Deputy Chief of Staff Yano returned from the front and brought Kwantung Army headquarters up to date on the desperate developments since the 27th—the mauling of the 23rd Division and Komatsubara's expedition north of the Holsten, now out of radio contact. There was immense anxiety in Hsinking concerning the safety of the regimental colors other than those of the 72nd Infantry. In particular, it was suspected that Yamagata may not have had time to destroy the imperial crest of the 64th Infantry's colors, which might therefore fall into enemy hands.[21] Additionally, an enormous number of Japanese dead and wounded had had to be left behind. A swift battle of revenge was dictated by these painful considerations as well as by the need to preserve "face" and to acquire leverage against the despised Russians and Mongolians.

A further consideration was the weather. The cruel freeze, only two months away, would presumably nullify the danger of Soviet entry into all-out war with Japan in 1939.[22] It would also compel the logistically unprepared Japanese to evacuate the forward areas by the middle of October and suspend action until 1940. In fact, as early as 26 August, IJA line units were being ordered to turn in their summer uniforms and don winter garb.[23]

With respect to the Kwantung Army's hurried offensive, it can be asked why, if such a mighty blow was imperative and feasible, was it not meted out in the first place? Why become so bold only after the entire battlefront had caved in? Even Tsuji has admitted the Kwantung Army's sin of piecemeal, late commitment of forces, "like a poor man and his money." Yet the pattern of the Japanese military seemed always the same: shoot first and then talk— the mark, Gomikawa scoffs, of a poor loser and a poor sport.[24]

The Kwantung Army, however, would have liked considerably more strength than it currently possessed or could reasonably borrow from China. Around 25 August, it will be recalled, the staff in Hsinking had carefully limited their request for assistance, when invited by Tokyo to comment, although they had a covert desire for the release of the 5th Division to them.[25] On 27 August, there came an encouraging hint when the AGS asked Hsinking to send a staff officer to Fukuoka on 1 September for a meeting of representatives from the High Command, all the forces in China, and the Kwantung Army. The subject would be the transfer of strength from the China theater to Manchuria. There was some serious thinking among Kwantung Army operations officers that it might be advisable openly to raise the matter of strategic-size reinforcements at this particular time. The idea, implying a loss of face, was distasteful to Hattori, who was going to the

Fukuoka conference. He convinced his chief, Terada, that the High Command would probably take the initiative of providing powerful reinforcement anyhow, if only the Kwantung Army sat tight for a little while and did not importune Tokyo prematurely. After it was agreed to hold up an already-drafted message to the AGS deputy until 30 August, Hattori left for Fukuoka on the 29th.[26]

At a time when the 23rd Division was being destroyed, the obsession of the Kwantung Army with "face" and prestige is disturbing. On the night of 29 August, however, an unofficial message arrived from the AGS, as Hattori had predicted, promising the Kwantung Army even more reinforcements than it had hoped for: two more 15-cm. howitzer regiments (one from IGHQ reserve), nine rapid-fire batteries of six pieces each, 16-17 antiaircraft artillery units, the 59th Air Group and airfield elements, 25 logistical truck companies (three from North China), four field hospitals and three ambulance teams, as well as various signal and transport units. But best of all from the Kwantung Army's viewpoint, the AGS was volunteering to transfer two infantry divisions, which proved to be the well-equipped 5th Division and the 14th Division (the latter from IGHQ reserve). Details would be worked out at the Fukuoka meeting. Information on the Sixth Army's offensive plan was needed urgently. Meanwhile, the AGS deputy himself was being sent to Hsinking.[27]

The General Staff's decision to reinforce the Kwantung Army stemmed from a number of complex facts. In the early phases of the Russians' August offensive, the High Command did not have a clear picture of developments at Nomonhan, about which the Sixth Army and the Kwantung Army had been doling out incomplete, misleading information. As late as 25-27 August, senior officers in Tokyo, with the probable exception of the Soviet intelligence experts, were of the impression that the Russian attacks were being handled satisfactorily or at least that no crisis loomed, although the fighting would be heavy. Indeed, it was hoped that the Sixth Army's counteroffensive starting on 24 August would pave the way to a successful solution of the whole Nomonhan affair. Since the Kwantung Army not only required reinforcement on the Nomonhan sector but also needed holes plugged on the other weakened fronts in Manchuria, the AGS was willing to provide limited assistance.[28]

Disturbing signals emanated from the Kwantung Army, however. Inada heard from Terada, his Operations Section chief counterpart in Hsinking, that the field army certainly intended to deal the Soviet forces a hammer blow, but that with winter approaching fast, activity would have to stop soon afterward. Consequently, the Kwantung Army wanted the High Command to be ready for a decisive, full-scale campaign against the Russians next spring. For the moment, the Kwantung Army would launch an offensive with what it had. Inada was disgusted with Terada, who had promised, when he left for Manchuria only in February, to prevent all-out hostilities with the USSR, not to start them. Terada was obviously becoming "Manchurianized," like his hawkish predecessors in the Kwantung Army. The AGS colonel therefore worked on the draft of an imperial curtailing order and asked General Nakajima, the AGS deputy, to fly to Hsinking with it.[29]

On 28 August, the General Staff reported to the Emperor about the managing of the Nomonhan affair in concert with the Kwantung Army's latest operational planning. The High Command was in agreement with General Ueda's view that a blow had to be dealt the aggressors, whatever the method employed. It was imperative to handle matters speedily, regardless of the outcome, by hurling three divisions against the foe in the vicinity of Nomonhan. The connection between the progress of military operations and—finally— diplomatic negotiations was stressed. In case winter came before a settlement was reached, the Kwantung Army was contemplating withdrawal of the main body at the front. Obviously reflecting the impact of Terada's unsettling communication to Inada, the AGS then assured the Emperor that it would provide appropriate guidance of the Kwantung Army's operation, taking into consideration the pullout not only of front-line units but also of the entire strength involved, "so as not to carry the affair over into the next year."[30]

It was against the preceding backdrop that on 29 August the General Staff alerted the Kwantung Army to the release of reinforcements and that on 30 August Nakajima went to Manchuria with an imperial order. Nevertheless, new developments had also been affecting the High Command's thinking. By 28-29 August, the Kwantung Army's actions revealed a "lack of smoothness," and every countermeasure was failing. It was true that the Russians gave no evidence of intending to cross the border zone they had been claiming, and most of which they had occupied, and that the Sixth Army was consolidating in the area outside the district in dispute. But the Kwantung Army, instead of easing up, was moving sizable forces of its own toward the front with a view to waging a "battle of revenge" and, as we have seen, was talking about "finishing off" the enemy next spring if necessary. Under such circumstances, the General Staff could not be sure that, either voluntarily or under provocation, the Russians would not resume their advance, driving deep into the heartland of Manchuria, as they had done against the Chinese in 1929. (According to Soviet Maj. A. E. Bykov, "after the Japanese had been defeated we did not follow them across the border, though we had a chance of going forward up to Hailar without encountering resistance.") Therefore, as Inada points out, the Japanese High Command was sending reinforcements to the Kwantung Army, not to enlarge the Nomonhan war—despite appearances—but largely as an "operational precaution" to deter the Russians and "to keep the roof from falling in" at a time when the field army was distracted and enfeebled. Significantly, too, Inada was trying to stop the Kwantung Army from committing its own 4th Division to the September offensive.[31]

The High Command, as a matter of principle, ordinarily tried to leave the direct conduct of offensive or defensive operations to the discretion of the self-confident Kwantung Army in the field. Whereas the staff officers in Tokyo now wanted to limit and close out the Nomonhan affair, they did not wish to suspend operations by trampling on the sensibilities of the Kwantung Army in general and of commander Ueda in particular. Precise and up-to-date combat information was also lacking. Carefully weighing the various factors, Inada and his associates drafted IGHQ Army Order No. 343, which was marked by gracious indirection and imprecise expression. According to the preamble, it was the High Command's intention to prepare against the Soviets and to "maintain tranquillity on the northern frontiers" with a portion of the imperial army while the main conflict in China was being resolved. The core of the AGS order is contained in two short paragraphs, the first of which called for measures to end operations promptly in the region of Nomonhan, "while taking every possible precaution to prevent expansion" of the affair. Plans were to be formulated by the Kwantung Army commander "for resisting [holding out] with minimum strength in the Nomonhan area."

The net effect of the imperial order, as Inada saw it, was gently to induce the Kwantung Army to act with prudence. From the generalized preface, it should be apparent that the High Command wanted the Nomonhan affair terminated as soon as possible, in view of larger considerations. The second paragraph could only mean that the Kwantung Army must avoid decisive battle and evacuate the controversial area, whereas the third paragraph indicated that the forces committed to carry out the preceding measures should be kept as small as possible.[32]

Tokyo's desire to suspend the combat use of the 4th Division was hidden in the usual stipulation that a detailed directive would be forthcoming from the AGS chief. Whether or not to divulge the contents of Directive No. 530 about the 4th Division was left to Nakajima, depending on what he learned about the situation from the Kwantung Army.[33]

Inada took two private steps to monitor the mission of the general, a gentle person who might be won over by the hawks at Kwantung Army headquarters. To accompany Nakajima and serve as a "watchdog," Inada handpicked Lt. Col. Takatsuki Tamotsu, one of his senior subordinates who had recently come from attaché duty in the Baltic countries to join the AGS Operations Section. Though the trip to Manchuria would be Takatsuki's initial exposure to the Kwantung Army staff in the flesh, he had the advantage, from Inada's standpoint, of being "uncorrupted." The colonel briefed him thoroughly.

Inada's second precaution was to alert Lt. Col. Arao Okikatsu, another of his senior subordinates who was going to the conference at Fukuoka, to see Nakajima as soon as he arrived at the airport there on his way back from Hsinking. Arao was to learn exactly how the conversations at Kwantung Army headquarters had proceeded, and to notify Inada immediately, using an agreed-upon code. If Nakajima's mission proved to have been a failure, Inada intended to transmit a second and more forceful imperial order, which would be readied without delay.[34]

Originally, Nakajima had been optimistic about the battle situation at Nomonhan and seems to have thought that, since the 23rd Division was presumably retaining key points, heavy Japanese forces should be concentrated as a backup for diplomatic negotiations to settle the affair. Nevertheless, by the time the deputy left Tokyo on 30 August, the 23rd Division had been nearly destroyed and the High Command had already decided that the time was at hand to conclude all offensive action at Nomonhan, including commitment of the 4th Division. In fact, the AGS Operations Section advised Nakajima directly by phone on the 30th to bear in mind the "changed situation" when he delivered the imperial order.

On the evening of 30 August, in the Kwantung Army commander's office, Nakajima conveyed Imperial Order No. 343, with Generals Ueda and Isogai standing at attention to receive such an august document. For reasons that have not been fully explained,[35] the AGS deputy never mentioned Directive No. 530, although according to Inada, withholding the 4th Division was the raison d'être for the general's trip. Kwantung Army records provide no insight. Upon receiving the imperial order, they say, Ueda and Isogai questioned the visiting officer about the separate AGS directive mentioned in the text. Nakajima supposedly replied feebly that there was no such directive because there were no special instructions.

On the basis of what Arao learned soon afterward, however, it is possible to recreate a likely scenario.[36] Nakajima arrived at Hsinking with the intention of limiting the Nomonhan affair in general but of "playing by ear" the matter of curbing the use of the 4th Division, one of the Kwantung Army's own units. In the very private discussion with Ueda and Isogai that took place when the imperial order was transmitted, the full extent of the disaster that had befallen the 23rd Division dawned on Nakajima. Admittedly, Inada had already alerted him to the "changed situation," but now Ueda asked for a powerful "last favor": to be allowed to launch an offensive of finite scope and duration designed to evict the enemy from the border zone where thousands of unburied Japanese corpses still lay on the steppes, and to salvage the remains of lost imperial colors. Certainly Nakajima could not blot out the Kwantung Army commander's fervent plea, which meant so much to any honorable commander in the field and with which he agreed wholeheartedly as an individual soldier. Ueda's passionate words thus struck a deep chord in his fellow general—the feeling that, in crisis, warriors traditionally helped each other and showed compassion (*bushi wa aimi-tagai*). The staff briefings that followed only reinforced Nakajima's sympathy with and respect for the Kwantung Army's fighting spirit and determination to hurl all available resources, including the 4th Division, into the proposed battle of revenge for the shattered 23rd Division. Indeed, the morrow might even bring the tragic news of the death of Komatsubara with the last of his men. One final consideration, as we shall see, was on the AGS deputy's mind: to improve relations between the High Command and the Kwantung Army. When he got back to Tokyo, he would explain the psychology involved.

Once the imperial order had been transmitted, without the directive, the Kwantung Army's main section chiefs were called to Ueda's office to brief Nakajima and Takatsuki, in the presence of the commander and Isogai as well as Isogai's deputy, Yano. The estimate of the situation was presented by Lt. Col. Katō Yoshihide, acting chief of the Intelligence Section. Colonel Terada followed with the operations staff's overall view plus information on current and projected actions and concentrations. A concluding presentation on logistics was given by Col. Isoya Gorō.

Since Nakajima had not raised the matter of the 4th Division, it was Takatsuki who chose to ask Terada whether the proposed offensive was feasible without using that division. Terada replied that it was not only imperative to add the 4th Division but that the commitment of even larger forces was advisable, if possible. Indeed, the Kwantung Army was anxious to put in the 5th Division too, if that division—promised by the High Command—arrived early enough. But even if the 5th Division were delayed, it was still deemed necessary to move it quickly to the Arshaan district. The Kwantung Army wanted to employ such great strength in the offensive, explained Terada, because a hammer blow was necessary, entailing the massing and display of maximum power in minimum time, followed by prompt withdrawal. It was crucial to avoid piecemeal commitment of forces, Terada insisted. Takatsuki pressed again about the possibility of conducting the operation without the 4th Division but made no dent in the Kwantung Army's thinking. "He must have finally comprehended our explanation," claim the army records. Remarking "*Sō desuka*" ["I see"], Takatsuki fell silent. General Nakajima said not a word, causing the Kwantung Army officers to deduce that their plan had been approved in toto.

After the briefing session had been completed, Isogai brought Nakajima and Takatsuki to his office, together with Yano and Terada. Ueda had directed Isogai to clear up a very important matter once and for all. Was the offensive plan in accord with the stipulation in Order No. 343 that the Kwantung Army try to hold out in the Nomonhan region with minimum strength? Nakajima assured Isogai that the clause in question referred to "strategic endurance." The General Staff, "of course, would not interfere with your mounting of a tactical offensive, within that context." To Isogai's follow-up question, whether there was any objection to the inclusion of the 4th Division in the army's attack plan, Nakajima gave a categorical "No." Visibly relieved, Isogai said, "I understand entirely."

Kwantung Army headquarters, from Ueda down, was elated, for Nakajima had confirmed that none of the assumptions of the offensive concept clashed with the provisions of the imperial order. In fact, the senior staff had been thinking that, although the details of Sixth Army planning were not yet known, it was inadvisable to operate across the Halha this time. But Nakajima had pointed at the river on the battle map and stated unequivocally that, in view of the Kwantung Army's employment of so much attack strength, operations on the left shore appeared to be imperative.

There was "pleasant talk" and a relaxed mood at the banquet Ueda gave for Nakajima and Takatsuki at his residence that night. When the festivities were over, Nakajima called Terada into another room for a frank and helpful chat. There had been differences and a lack of coordination between Terada's section and its AGS counterpart, remarked Nakajima, concerning the handling of the Nomonhan war. By this stage, however, both agencies must work closely together. If the Kwantung Army had anything to ask of Tokyo, whether large or small, it should do so without hesitation, and the High Command would strive to follow through. Terada, deeply touched, thanked the AGS deputy and promised to cooperate. On this note of mutual confidence, the conversation ended and Nakajima left for his VIP quarters. The general was as good as his word. Early next morning, Takatsuki phoned Terada and asked whether he had anything to request from the High Command, beyond what had been mentioned on the 30th. In particular, were additional weapons, parts, and equipment needed? Takatsuki would take down any requisitions and do his best to honor them when he got back to Tokyo. Terada could only think of asking for key personnel who had undergone tank training, for heavy artillery, and for antitank matériel needed in close-quarter combat.

When Nakajima and Takatsuki flew out of Hsinking on the morning of

31 August, everybody in Kwantung Army headquarters was convinced that the true situation in Manchuria had been made known and that the visiting officers' splendid spirit of cooperation boded well for the forthcoming operations.[37] The Kwantung Army set about its self-imposed tasks with redoubled vigor. In the relative lull after Komatsubara's escape on the 31st, Ueda issued his own hortatory instructions (*kunji*) of 2 September, which fed Ogisu's controversial pronouncement three days later. At a time when Japan was confronted by many difficulties internally and externally, said Ueda's statement, all officers and men must resolve upon selfless service, fortify their faith in certain victory, surmount all obstacles, fight well and bravely, smash the outrageous and arrogant Soviet-Mongolian forces, and thus enhance the power and the prestige of the imperial army at home and abroad. The forthcoming battle was completely different from the usual border dispute, in that its outcome had a vital bearing on the destiny of the nation and could well be termed the major, decisive battle between Japan and the Soviet Union.[38]

Meanwhile, from the point of view of the Kwantung Army, more good news emanated from the Fukuoka meeting of 1 September. Lieutenant Colonel Imaoka, the logistics specialist who accompanied Arao from the General Staff, remembers that the conference, lasting all day, was businesslike and smooth. It was the High Command's intention to announce the decisions reached in Tokyo about the proposed reinforcement of the Kwantung Army and to obtain the understanding of the armies in China. The senior officers of those armies felt that the Nomonhan affair was useless and should be stopped; they were not enthusiastic about reinforcing Manchuria. Hattori, in fact, heard that the officers at the conference from Central and South China (the representative from North China being absent because of an accident) had conveyed to the AGS party the following reservations of their chiefs of staff: "Although the High Command has been saying that the conduct of the China conflict was being accorded top priority in national policy, as a matter of fact isn't our strength being gradually checked in the north because of the Nomonhan affair? Kindly devote special attention to the effect [of the affair] on the China theater."

This caveat was not the same as opposing the transfer of some forces from China, however, and the AGS officers won universal agreement to Tokyo's plan. Imaoka says that preliminary negotiations had overcome any serious resistance. Arao agrees that there were no arguments at Fukuoka. Of course IGHQ was disgusted with the Kwantung Army too, he explains, but the purpose of the meeting was to limit and settle the Nomonhan affair, so the Kwantung Army had grounds for requesting reinforcements. The High Command and the armies in China had to help, whether they really wanted to or not. "We did not talk about bygones," adds Arao.

Hattori was rather quiet, and apparently won the sympathy of his colleagues by recounting some of his own experiences at the front, where in July he had had one particularly miraculous escape from artillery fire that demolished and overturned the truck on which he had been riding. To his comment that he had earned a "new lease on life" (*inochibiroi o shita*), all of the conferees agreed that he had had "the devil's own luck" (*akuun ga tsuyoi*). So far as business was concerned, Hattori briefly described the situation at Nomonhan and admitted that the 23rd Division had been chewed up. The new divisions were needed to mete out a mighty blow to the enemy; but whether the army was attacking or retreating, he insisted, reinforcement was imperative.

Imaoka recalls that it was agreed to prepare two more divisions (including the 14th) for transfer from China, following the 5th Division, but that there was no hurry. As a priority measure, many small elements would be sent from the homeland and China, such as antiaircraft and rapid-fire batteries. To transport the infantry divisions in particular, 24 independent truck companies (with about 50 trucks each) would be mobilized, including every company earmarked for wartime mobilization in Japan itself, although the 20 additional companies in Korea were not being drawn upon yet.

According to Hattori's notes, Arao expressed the personal opinion that if the Japanese withdrew their forces beyond the boundary claimed by the other side, the enemy would advance no farther. The best way, in fact, to assure localization of the controversy was simply to pull out now. Hattori answered that, regarding the policy for dealing with the Nomonhan affair, the Kwantung Army would "polish up" its plan with an open mind and not cling to preconceptions. Since much depended on the battle situation of the 23rd Division, about which Hattori had not heard anything in the last few days, he was not in a position to agree with Arao at the moment. But there was no doubt that the Kwantung Army was particularly apprehensive about the fate of the regimental colors.

As for the use of the specific divisions being transferred, namely the 5th and 14th, Takatsuki had pressed Hattori very strongly, during a short conversation at the Hakata airport in Fukuoka on 31 August, not to send the 5th Division into battle, given the High Command's policy of restraint. At the conference itself, Arao said the same thing to Hattori. In both cases, Hattori asserted that an effort would be made to avoid putting in the 5th Division, but that everything hinged upon the combat situation. The Kwantung Army had already shifted the 7th and 2nd divisions and, lastly, the 4th Division, from within its own order of battle. It was Hattori's understanding that, by arguing against commitment of the 5th Division, Takatsuki and Arao were implicitly approving the use of the 4th Division, which both AGS officers knew had received orders to move up several days earlier. In other words, they must have had no intention of entirely stopping the Sixth Army's offensive at this stage.[39]

The pleasure engendered at Kwantung Army headquarters by the visit of Nakajima on 30-31 August and by Hattori's participation in the conference at Fukuoka on 1 September was enhanced when Tsuji returned from the Nomonhan battlefront on 3 September. During the preceding week, steadily worsening news had been arriving from the field, and the headquarters staff had been pervaded by a "rather gloomy" atmosphere as a result of the reports of extremely heavy casualties, unauthorized retreats, and possible losses of regimental colors. Tsuji, however, brought tidings of the Sixth Army's offensive plan and of the very high morale of all units, who were preparing for battle with the certainty of victory. The Kwantung Army officers were greatly heartened by Tsuji's report, especially by the prospect of improving the very difficult overall situation of Japan at a time when Europe had been plunged into crisis and was on the verge of a general war.[40]

As a consequence, the Kwantung Army moved forward still more forces. From the 8th Division, a newly formed detachment made up of an infantry regiment, a field artillery battalion, and an engineer company, under direct control of the army, was ordered on 3 September to head for Hailar as a reserve. The Kwantung Army also sent the reinforced 3rd Cavalry Brigade to an area 26 kilometers southeast of Manchouli, with the intention of diverting enemy attention westward. At the same time, three air groups were transferred to the front.[41] Aggressive thoughts certainly underlay Ueda's *kunji* of 2 September. The trouble was that the Kwantung Army was not on the same wavelength as the High Command, as would soon become painfully evident.

While AGS officers Nakajima and Takatsuki were on their trip to Hsinking with Imperial Order No. 343, Inada had been working on the draft of a tough new order to be issued if necessary. Maj. Shimamura Noriyasu of Inada's Operations Section was already discussing the subject with colleagues on the General Staff. Intelligence staff officer Kōtani remembers that a very agitated Shimamura began by requesting his opinion about the situation at Nomonhan. Kōtani responded that if only the Kwantung Army pulled back to the border line claimed by the Russians, a cease-fire could be arranged. At the very least, the Sixth Army's planned offensive ought to be canceled. Twenty days of preparation were necessary, by which time the snows would have begun. Whereas the Japanese would be fighting on foot, the enemy was mechanized. No quick or decisive victory was possible, and the struggle would drag on. How would the IJA troops be able to survive the winter on broad and treeless plains? Shimamura thereupon showed Kōtani the draft of an imperial order on which he had been working that called for suspension of the offensive. If Kōtani concurred, would he kindly coordinate the document with his Intelligence Section, while Shimamura "staffed" it through the Operations Section? Kōtani tried out the plan on his colleagues, and it went through smoothly. Shimamura had the same success in the Operations Section.[42]

Inada did not want to use his trump card of a second imperial order unless he had to, but his worst fears soon materialized. As planned, Arao had intercepted Nakajima and Takatsuki at Hakata airport when they were on their way back to Tokyo.[43] Although the conversation was short, Arao realized immediately that Nakajima's dealings at Kwantung Army headquarters had had the effect of contradicting the efforts exerted simultaneously at Fukuoka to close out the Nomonhan affair. Apparently some attempt had been made to restrain the Kwantung Army but, after Ueda had made his request for a "last favor," described previously, the idea of a massive offensive was accepted. Arao rushed off a coded telegram warning Inada that there had been a "difference in opinion."[44]

Inada now knew, as he puts it, that Nakajima had been "seduced" or "converted" by the Kwantung Army's emotionalism. The colonel had no further inclination and no more time to "humor" the field army and to worry about its prestige. In the 1st Bureau's sitting room, a night meeting of the operations staff was convened. Drinking sake next door with other officers, Kōtani could hear considerable discussion. Finally the conference decided to accept the forthright stop-the-offensive plan and prepare it for the Emperor's sanction. Just as soon as Inada learned that Nakajima had flown in on 2 September from Hsinking, he had him whisked to Operations Bureau chief Hashimoto's office with no chance to talk to anybody en route.

Before Nakajima could speak about his trip, Inada and Hashimoto placed before him the draft of brand-new Imperial Order No. 349, with the bureau chief's seal of approval already on it. IGHQ, stated the document, planned to end the Nomonhan border affair voluntarily, in view of the situation. The Kwantung Army commander was to suspend offensive operations in the Nomonhan area. To prevent the occurrence of further fighting, the forces should be separated appropriately and deployed outside the disputed zone on the right shore of the Halha River, excluding Handagai and the district east. Air (offensive) operations, if required, were subject to the terms of Imperial Order No. 336 of 7 August; i.e., the Kwantung Army commander was authorized to raid enemy air bases around Tamsag inside Mongolia and in the vicinity of the battlefield to the east, if deemed necessary to support operations around Nomonhan.[45] The time for returning the main body of the operational forces to their duty stations would be transmitted at a later date.[46]

Nakajima read the order in silence, with a look of distress. Still giving the general no time to speak, Inada said: "I hope you understand. May we proceed?" Nakajima said "Yes." Thereupon Inada raised the question of delivery of the order and asked if Hashimoto would convey it to Hsinking; the bureau chief replied that a telegram would suffice.[47] Inada insisted that the message should be hand-carried. Perhaps he himself was the appropriate courier, remarked the colonel, but a fracas might ensue in that case, and "some one such as Tsuji might go after me with a sword." In addition, Inada felt that he could not absent himself from Tokyo at this particular time. When Hashimoto refused to go, Nakajima—who probably found the scene unbearable—said he would return to Hsinking. "We had forced him to 'volunteer,'" admits Inada. The colonel was both grateful and delighted, well knowing that the AGS deputy would "carry more clout" at Hsinking. It was a very difficult mission, he told Nakajima, but "if it succeeds, the nation will be saved. Please go, sir." Inada bowed deeply, for he could guess that the general was voluntarily terminating his military career.

Inada was not unaware of the basis of Nakajima's dilemma. It was only natural for a professional soldier to identify himself with comrades in battle, and to lose the objectivity and detachment required of a high staff officer. This was why Inada stayed away from the scene of a border incident while combat was going on. But now an "immutable" imperial order had to be conveyed, without circumlocution, and the AGS deputy was the person to go. Arao agrees that Nakajima probably decided to retire shortly after he returned to Tokyo, but, looking back, feels that there must have been a better way to handle the matter. After all, at the age of 64, Ueda was not only dignified and distinguished, but he was a graduate of the 10th military academy class of 1898. Although Nakajima was the AGS deputy chief, he was only a lieutenant general, seven academy classes junior to Ueda and a dozen years younger. Arao thinks that, to have dealt effectively with Ueda, an official at the level of the AGS chief or the war minister or even the prime minister should have been sent to Hsinking.[48]

On 2 September, the General Staff obtained imperial sanction for Order No. 349. It was wired to the Kwantung Army on the evening of the 3rd. Another message followed with word that Nakajima was flying to Hsinking again on 4 September.[49] To the field army, working enthusiastically on the great offensive, the news came as a total surprise, according to Tsuji and Hattori. But there probably was some advance warning, for as soon as AGS intelligence officer Kōtani was sure the imperial order was being issued, he telephoned Kwantung Army headquarters and alerted Lt. Col. Nakayama Motoo (Genpu), the training officer, who had answered the phone.[50]

Particularly vexing to the Kwantung Army was the inexplicable turnabout in IGHQ policy in only four days, for there had been no apparent change in the situation at the front since Nakajima left Hsinking the first time. The question was raised repeatedly.[51] As Inada had intended, however, there was no doubt about the High Command's intentions this time. It was true that actions taken in self-defense were not prohibited and that secondary operations to secure key points in the Handagai sector were authorized, as were offensive air sweeps in emergency. But the ground offensive envisaged by the main forces in the Nomonhan region was undeniably "off," for as the Kwantung Army noted, "obedience to the imperial will must be absolute."

The next few days at Hsinking were dominated by desperate efforts to reconcile the thrust of Imperial Order No. 349 with the overpowering need, as Kwantung Army headquarters perceived it, to clear the battlefield first—i.e., to retrieve the slain and to collect the weapons left behind by the 23rd Division on the right side of the Halha. Since the corpses and the matériel lay behind enemy lines, it was obvious that recovery could only be done by force, and Terada, Tsuji, and Murasawa worked in particular to resolve this problem.[52] To dismiss the 23rd Division's brave struggle to the extent of not even conducting battlefield salvage not only would have been heartless but also would have led to the destruction of the authority and tradition of the Kwantung Army.

Careful analysis of the imperial order's wording about "suspension of offensive operations" led to the conclusion that it was designed to stop a large-scale offensive of the sort that had been planned, but that it did not imply an imperial intention to prevent recapturing corpses and weapons by means of brief combat action. According to the Kwantung Army staff study, the enemy positions in the Nomonhan region, occupied by a considerable number of mechanized units, possessed many deficiencies. If sufficient preparations were made with a view to employing the 2nd, 4th, and 7th divisions in night attacks, the Kwantung Army was confident that the old battleground of the 23rd Division could be cleared in several nights. The 23rd Division could put together about 3,000 men to pick up and remove its own dead and weapons.[53]

The Kwantung Army operations staff's proposal, one of several under study, was approved by Isogai, Yano, and then Ueda. On the afternoon of 4 September, Tsuji drafted the text of an operational order incorporating the concept of battlefield clearance, ostensibly to suspend offensive action in keeping with the imperial order. After "consolidating" the battlefield on the right shore of the Halha, the Sixth Army commander should shift the forces at an opportune time to the general dispositions as of the period just preceding concentration for the offensive, keeping an eye on the enemy. The air force was to cooperate closely. There being "no alternative," given the need to uphold the prestige of the Kwantung Army while deferring to the imperial will, Tsuji obtained the agreement of his superiors up to Ueda. Nevertheless, there was some feeling that signals were crossed between Hsinking and Tokyo: the High Command must have derived the impression that the Kwantung Army wanted to enlarge the Nomonhan affair, since the army's prior plan had been "obviously misinterpreted." As a result, it was decided to hold up the release of the operations order so that Isogai could explain its true meaning to Nakajima, whose arrival was expected momentarily, and seek his concurrence.[54]

By dusk on 4 September, General Nakajima and Lieutenant Colonel Takatsuki were back at Kwantung Army headquarters, which they had only left on 31 August. After delivering Imperial Order No. 349, Nakajima conveyed an oral message from AGS Chief of Staff Prince Kan'in earnestly asking Ueda to exercise prudence and patience, to wait for revenge, to use discretion in handling the situation, and to keep the officers and men under tight control. In view of the acute situation in Europe, the Japanese government was going to conduct diplomatic negotiations for an overall readjustment of relations with the USSR, particularly with respect to border security, although it was not the policy to conduct cease-fire discussions as such.

Ueda then explained the Kwantung Army's heartfelt plan for battleground cleanup, but Nakajima refused to agree. The Kwantung Army commander tried to reassure the AGS deputy, asserting that he would assume personal responsibility to guarantee that the fighting would not drag out. In fact, said Ueda, he himself would proceed to the battlefield and direct operations. Would Nakajima please authorize field clearance, at even the minimum limit? To his impassioned plea, the AGS deputy still would not yield. The proposal, he insisted, ran counter to the sense of the imperial will.

After a short intermission in their personal conversation, Ueda told Nakajima that he held himself personally responsible for what had happened. Now that even the battleground clearance plan had been rejected, Ueda felt that it was impossible for him to remain at the helm of the Kwantung Army. To settle matters, would the High Command kindly designate a successor as soon as feasible? His responsibility was entire, said Ueda. No blame should be ascribed to Isogai and the other staff officers, who had conscientiously carried out the commander's intentions. Nakajima promised to transmit Ueda's desires promptly to Tokyo and added that, as a High Command officer involved in the affair, he was deeply aware of his own sense of responsibility. Ueda absolved the central authorities of blame, repeating that the responsibility was his alone.

Isogai and Yano met with Nakajima next. The Kwantung Army chief of staff pointed out the wide and unexplained disparity between the two imperial orders issued only a few days apart, and between Nakajima's attitude on his earlier visit and now. Nakajima merely repeated that it was the imperial will and gave no explanation. While Yano conferred with Ueda and Isogai, Colonel Terada and the operations staff talked with Takatsuki. They explained the Kwantung Army's position on battlefield cleanup and on the potential effects upon leadership, implying that the counsel of IGHQ staff officers who had brought the situation to such a fickle pass was not proper. But Takatsuki was too new in his post to have been involved deeply in the handling of the Nomonhan crisis and, from the Kwantung Army staff officers' standpoint, his answers were "pointless." One or two officers suggested that the frequent lack of synchronization of opinion between the High Command and the field forces really stemmed from Tokyo's lack of comprehension of conditions on the spot. How about getting the AGS deputy to go to the front next day to inspect the real situation? Takatsuki replied that it was impracticable: Nakajima and he had to go back to Tokyo immediately because of the urgency of conducting personnel matters—i.e., arranging replacements and reassignments.

At Ueda's official residence that evening, from 8 P.M. on, Isogai, Yano, and Terada tried to "get through to" Nakajima and Takatsuki. But, say the Kwantung Army records, the AGS deputy kept his head down, cupped his chin in his hand, and kept saying "It's too bad" in a low and mournful voice. Consequently, his hosts did not pursue matters too far and addressed only topics such as personnel affairs. Early next morning, Ueda invited Nakajima to his residence and said that, after careful consideration since the evening before, he had reached the conclusion that it might not be the Emperor's intention that at least battlefield cleanup not be conducted. The commander asked for reconsideration, but Nakajima stated that the imperial order expressly prohibited even that. At 8 A.M. on 5 September, the AGS deputy and Takatsuki left by air for Tokyo.[55]

Behind him in Hsinking, Nakajima left a headquarters that was disconsolate, perplexed, and disgusted. Did the suddenly inarticulate AGS deputy comprehend the Kwantung Army's anguish and devotion? In what terms would the general convey the true feelings of the field army to Tokyo? On the morning of 5 September, Ueda instructed Isogai to have the staff explore methods of conveying the complex spectrum of problems and the Kwantung Army's "honest intentions" more effectively to the High Command. Terada coordinated the brainstorming, from which the idea emerged to wire formal recommendations to Tokyo and to send Terada there to explain the details. After Ueda's approval, message after message left Hsinking.

Summing up the Kwantung Army's thinking, the first of the cables went out at about noon on the 5th, from Ueda to the AGS chief. Receipt of the imperial order was reverently acknowledged. But the 23rd Division had fought hard for 70 days, and several thousand Japanese corpses were still unrecovered. Therefore it was planned to use the Sixth Army to clear up the battlefield on the right bank of the Halha, to the degree possible, after which the forces would be withdrawn from the zone under dispute, in accordance with the imperial will. Approval of this plan was requested officially. The consequence of a denial of sanction would be not only the ruination of the moral principles that Ueda had been strictly demanding of his subordinates but also the abandonment of the souls of several thousand officers and men who had loyally given their lives for the cause and who would now become subject to shaming by the foe. Since Ueda would no longer be able to command the Kwantung Army in such an eventuality, the AGS chief should please advise the Emperor to dismiss him immediately. Soon afterward, another message was sent by Ueda to the new war minister, Gen. Hata Shunroku: the matter of dismissal had already been indicated to Nakajima directly and then requested officially of Kan'in; Hata should kindly comprehend the true contemporary situation of the Kwantung Army and take the necessary action.[56]

On behalf of Ueda, Tsuji drafted another emotional message to the AGS chief. Transmitted in mid-afternoon on 5 September, this wire reiterated the commander's belief that IJA tradition derived from a spirit of unity, transcending self-interest and binding top to bottom like fathers and sons. In the more than three years since assuming command of the Kwantung Army, Ueda had made it his guiding principle in serving the Throne loyally to enhance the special moral qualities of the imperial forces, stressing family-like unity at all levels. As for carrying out Imperial Order No. 349, it was the commander's opinion that the natural way to obey the Emperor's will was to retrieve the 23rd Division's several thousand precious corpses remaining on the battlefield; but, when asked to understand, the AGS deputy had implied that such action was also prohibited. Ueda remained firmly convinced that the Emperor would want the recovery of the bones of subordinates who had given their lives as devoted and patriotic subjects. Careful reconsideration was beseeched for the sake of upholding the dignity of the Throne and the traditions of the imperial army.[57]

At the next lower echelon in the military chain of command, from Kwantung Army Chief of Staff Isogai to AGS Deputy Chief of Staff Nakajima, Hattori promptly prepared a message reinforcing Ueda's views. Nakajima was reminded that, as the commander had explained carefully to him in person, the Kwantung Army felt strongly that there was no alternative to the plan recommended to implement the imperial order. To abandon thousands of corpses and a large number of weapons to the enemy and to do nothing about it was reprehensible at two levels: psychologically, an indelible stain would be imprinted on the brilliant tradition of the imperial forces; practically, the Kwantung Army's exercise of command would be rendered unmanageable. After thoroughly reconsidering the army's plan in terms of the actual conditions at the front, the AGS, it was hoped, would decide to approve. The Kwantung Army had great confidence in its ability to honor the imperial will to the last by conducting all possible preparations, carrying out the plan in minimal time geared to the local situation, and then disengaging swiftly. There was no need for concern about rear supply and withdrawal matters.

The Hattori draft then addressed in detail the question of dismissals below Ueda. According to Tsuji, the topic had already arisen during the staff's painful discussions with Nakajima the day before. Isogai had stated that, although Ueda spoke of sole responsibility, the command staff would find it very difficult to function under the new mandate. Although responsibility belonged to Ueda and Isogai alone, all the rest of the staff should be replaced promptly too. When Nakajima said he could not comment officially on such matters, despite personal feelings, Isogai pressed him to see the Emperor privately. It was a matter not only of settling the Nomonhan affair itself without causing more harm, Isogai insisted, but also of settling things in general. Yano added that, though it might seem all right from the overall standpoint, the Kwantung Army simply could not leave its dead behind. Of course, the commander would not be able to retain his post, but neither Yano nor the operations staff could serve a new commander under the circumstances either. Transmission of orders to units would be impossible. It was difficult to rebuild the 23rd Division, observed Terada, without reclaiming the dead. Even a platoon would want to retrieve slain men: "We must think like human beings. There's a samurai code of benevolence, isn't there?" The colonel insisted that all the officers in his 1st Section should be removed if the army's plan could not be accepted. Nakajima remarked that he understood the staff's feelings very well, that the High Command felt much the same, but that he found himself in a difficult position.

Isogai's telegram to Nakajima on 5 September indicated that, if the army's proposal was not sanctioned, he could no longer fulfill his duties as chief of staff and wanted to be replaced. Every staff officer at Kwantung Army headquarters had asked to be relieved too, especially the section chiefs and air officer Miyoshi. Isogai, however, limited his recommended "hit list" to Yano, one section chief (Terada), and the other four key operations officers only: Hattori, Kurasawa, Tsuji, and Shimanuki Takeharu. A follow-up message to the war ministry was also necessary, and Hattori drafted one from Isogai to Vice Minister of War Yamawaki Masataka. Nakajima had already been advised directly and by cable, said Isogai's communication. The recommended personnel actions were imperative, given the real situation of the Kwantung Army at present; prompt implementation was desired.[58]

The Kwantung Army was not through with its barrage of messages to

Tokyo on 5 September. In the early evening, a cable went to Nakajima from Isogai, drafted by Tsuji. Terada was being sent to explain the Kwantung Army's concept of clearing the battlefield without provoking a decisive battle. Ueda himself would assume responsibility for directing the operation so as not to violate the principle stipulated in the imperial order. Reconsideration was once more requested.[59]

Obsessed with battlefield clearance and with their own dismissals if it did not materialize, the Kwantung Army staff officers evinced relatively little interest in the news received on the night of 5 September from the war ministry to the effect that serious diplomatic negotiations with the Soviet Union were beginning, now that war had erupted in Europe.[60] On the morning of the 6th, Terada boarded the plane for Tokyo to try to "sell" the High Command on the Kwantung Army's plan. The thinking was that Nakajima, during his strange visit on the 4th, may have been voicing only his personal interpretation of the meaning of the imperial order when he said that it forbade clearing operations. There was still hope that Terada could convince the General Staff to comply with Ueda's entreaties.

Shortly before noon on 6 September, the key response was received from the AGS chief, shattering the last illusions nurtured in Hsinking. In view of the thrust of the imperial order, Prince Kan'in's message notified Ueda, the Kwantung Army's recommendations could not be accepted. Ueda's wishes would be transmitted to the Throne, however, on the 6th. "The jig is up," wrote Hattori. "We all felt grief-stricken." Terada, whose plane had been grounded by bad weather in North Korea, was notified to return to Hsinking. His mission to Tokyo no longer made sense.[61]

As promised, the General Staff had reported to the Throne on the morning of 6 September. Since it was known that the Emperor was opposed to offensive action, says Arao, and since the AGS was against it too, the details of Ueda's request were not conveyed, only his "true feelings." The Emperor sympathized fully with these sentiments and with the High Command's explanations. It was true that the abandonment of so many corpses to the enemy would have undesirable emotional effects on imperial forces. Nevertheless, an offensive at this stage not only was unpromising but also would bring new and severe losses. Risking unexpected dangers, it could ruin mobility once winter arrived. Consequently, the imperial order remained in full effect.[62]

In the afternoon of 6 September, the Kwantung Army received a "rigid and stern" message from the AGS. The recommendations had been reported to the Throne, but it was now expected that all (offensive) intentions would be abandoned and that execution of Imperial Order No. 349 would definitely commence. The final injunction contained in paragraph 3 of the cable insulted the proud Kwantung Army: "With respect to implementation, you will submit prompt reports on your actions." Tsuji says that he and his colleagues wept in fury: "Did people who wore the same uniform act this way?" A full general in charge of Japan's greatest field army was being addressed as if he were a young and inexperienced commander. In the words of Hattori's record, "We had been concerned about the future of the whole national army and made every effort to work things out with the central authorities so as to conduct battlefield clearance, but we certainly never had the slightest intention of opposing an imperial order. The hearts of the Kwantung Army staff officers were chilled by the iciness of command reflected in the cruel third paragraph of that cable. The intensity of our anguish was indescribable." Working on a reply to be sent by Ueda, Tsuji "soaked the draft with tears and smudged the ink." In the flush of fury, the words attributed to the army commander read: "The request in your cable . . . was interpreted as a lack of confidence in me. Kindly arrange to relieve me immediately."[63]

Inada explains that he customarily issued guidelines for messages that originated in the Operations Section and left the details to his staff. Recently, however, he had become provoked by the "poor losers" in Hsinking and had begun to make changes and corrections. In the case of the cable of 6 September, he had added the whole third paragraph. Admittedly, it was ungracious for a mere section chief to use such impolite language in a message addressed to an army commander, yet Inada did it deliberately. He had tried to save face for the field army by acting "too cleverly and circumspectly," but "Hattori was the real commander of the Kwantung Army and Tsuji was the chief of staff. They ran the Nomonhan affair, pushed Terada around and neutralized him." Matters had reached a "pretty pass," laments Inada, when an imperial order was required each time the High Command wanted the Kwantung Army to take action on something it did not want to do.

There had been two opportunities for Inada to cope with this problem: at the very beginning of the episode, or at the time of the 1 August routine personnel transfers (Tsuji being the main "transferee" he had in mind). But Inada thought matters were under control in May-June; and when he broached the matter of transfers to the war minister in July, Itagaki had shrugged him off. Partly, no doubt, it was thought that Inada was exaggerating a mere personality conflict. More importantly, the High Command preferred not to "make waves" that would affect the General Staff and the war ministry. Many problems, it was expected, would be solved by the early creation of the Sixth Army and the China Expeditionary Army. Meanwhile, the central authorities had hoped that the Kwantung Army would adopt a more realistic and "down-to-earth" way of handling the Nomonhan affair, especially with the Mongolian winter not far off.

Over a month was lost before the High Command finally "straightened out" the Kwantung Army. More than Tsuji's nerves were involved; Inada regrets that his own delay in cracking down caused many more Japanese casualties, since a showdown was inevitable anyhow. "There are two ways of controlling an unruly horse: to apply the whip mercilessly and drive him until he dies of exhaustion, or to control him beforehand by dashing cold water on him. . . . The only alternative now was to apply the whip mercilessly. . . . High-handed notions that the Kwantung Army was the sole master of the situation had to be wiped out completely; this was one way to make amends for the tremendous losses sustained by that army."[64]

Before the reply drafted by Tsuji on 6 September could be sent to the AGS, a gentle message was received from War Minister Hata, responding to Ueda's plea for "appropriate personnel action." "I heartily sympathize with you," Hata stated. In his opinion, implementation of the imperial order and assumption of responsibility was the way of a loyal subject. On this very day, the Emperor had sanctioned the relief of the Kwantung Army commander. By comparison with the AGS chief's "rough" message, the Kwantung Army staff felt, the war minister's wire revealed a "sensitivity to human feelings." Its warmth elicited new tears of gratitude. Asked about the matter, Hata says: "Cavalry General Ueda was a good friend of mine, two years my senior. Handling these personnel matters was very painful but it had to be done."[65]

The Kwantung Army had been "sitting on" another document, Ueda's final operations order to the Sixth Army drafted and approved in Hsinking on 5 September. Staff officer Kurasawa had been sent to the Sixth Army command post to provide unofficial explanations and guidance, but formal issuance of the order was being held up because the serious effects it might have on the front-line forces' morale and leadership were well-known, and the Kwantung Army was still praying that the High Command would relent. When the last hopes were dashed, the order was released on the afternoon of 6 September, still subject to very restricted distribution beyond the operations staff—i.e., to Sixth Army and air corps headquarters. "Offensive operations in the Nomonhan area have been suspended by imperial command," proclaimed the order. The Sixth Army was to maintain the posture it had held during the last phase of concentration in the prearranged plan, and was to watch the enemy. Subsequent actions would be directed later. The air command should continue its assigned missions.[66]

The gist of this crucial order was reported to the AGS chief on the evening of the 6th; Tsuji's phraseology about Ueda's discomfiture was not included. After all, say Hattori's notes, the war minister's gracious message had just been received, and there was no point to Ueda's asking yet again to be relieved. But the High Command was told that a staff officer had been sent to guide the Sixth Army and that, since units operating southeast of Handagai had been under attack by superior forces since 4 September, IGU elements would be reinforced, in order to secure strategic points.[67]

Ogisu responded to the Kwantung Army's order with characteristic combativeness, as if he had never heard that it was the imperial will to suspend the attack. The Sixth Army, he reported to Ueda on the night of 6 September, was completing the operational preparations in accordance with existing plans. In view of the heavy losses of life, the Sixth Army could not stand by without smashing the enemy on the right shore of the Halha. Though the settlement of the Nomonhan affair might be left to diplomacy, hostile forces must be eliminated from the right side of the river. If time was frittered away without doing anything, the enemy would only strengthen his positions further and severe cold would set in. "We believe," concluded Ogisu, "that one must strictly guard against losing the opportunity for an offensive as a result of a lapse into diplomatic trifles."[68]

On the night of 6/7 September, the Kwantung Army commander sent a poignant reply to Ogisu, assuring him that he understood his feelings very well. When he had respectfully accepted the Emperor's order, Ueda noted, he too "felt as if my innards were being torn." Nevertheless, Ogisu should kindly act prudently at this stage and continue operational preparations until further notice, while expressly forbidding the front-line forces to undertake reckless action and striving to keep up their morale.[69]

Soon after Ueda dispatched his message to Ogisu, on the morning of 7 September Kwantung Army headquarters received an information copy of a long cable sent on the 5th to the General Staff by Colonel Doi, the military attaché in Moscow, after he had received the "heartbreaking" news that Japanese offensive operations at Nomonhan were being suspended.[70] Although he felt a keen sense of responsibility for the turn of events, Doi remained convinced that, in general, the Soviet Union had no intention of warring with Japan. In Doi's hawkish view, "We must concentrate our strength even though it involves great sacrifices on the part of those concerned. While threatening the USSR with a counteroffensive, we must at the same time conduct preparations for fortifications, communications, and winter quarters. By thus exhibiting our constant readiness to counterattack, we must check the Soviets' excessively contemptuous and arrogant attitude. They will not then attempt to precipitate second or third 'Nomonhan incidents' on other fronts."

Doi's thoughts, exemplified by the preceding excerpt, coincided entirely with those of the Kwantung Army, Hattori wrote in his diary. It was hollow reassurance. On the night of 6/7 September, the war ministry sent advance notice that Ueda, Isogai, Yano, and Terada were being attached to AGS headquarters in Tokyo—i.e., were being relieved. In the case of general officers this was customarily the first step to retirement from military service. Tsuji was being assigned to the Eleventh Army in Hankow—his "funeral march," he later wrote with melodrama and a touch of paranoia.[71] The official orders were issued on 7 September. Terada, who had still not heard about the cancellation of his special mission to Tokyo, was trying to proceed through Korea by train when he finally learned the news at Seoul; he got back to Hsinking on the 8th. His new assignment proved to be the Chiba Tank School. Hattori was ordered to the Infantry School in Chiba, as head of the research section and adjunct instructor. Shimanuki Takeharu received a not unattractive transfer to the Army War College as an instructor.

The following generals were designated to assume the duties of those being purged at Kwantung Army headquarters: Lt. Gen. Umezu Yoshijirō (Kwantung Army commander); Lt. Gen. Iimura Jō (chief of staff); and Maj. Gen. Endō Saburō (deputy chief of staff). Umezu, 57, was a graduate of the 15th military academy class of 1903, had been promoted to his present rank in 1934, was a former vice minister of war (from March 1936), and most recently had served as First Army commander in China (from May 1938). His new chief of staff, Iimura, 51, was a graduate of the 21st class (1909), and came to Hsinking from a brief stint as commandant of the Army War College in Tokyo (since March 1939); he had been promoted to the rank of lieutenant general in August. Iimura's deputy, Endō, 46, was a graduate of the 26th class (1914), had most recently been posted to the Hamamatsu Flying School (since July 1939), and was a major general since August.

Replacing Terada as operations chief at Kwantung Army headquarters was Col. Arisue Yadoru, 42, a 31st class graduate (1919). Having served in Inada's AGS Operations Section since November 1937, Arisue had become an AGS section chief himself on the eve of his promotion to colonel in August 1939. Maj. Shimamura Noriyasu, who had also belonged to Inada's office, was transferred with Arisue to the Kwantung Army Operations Section. Ironically, when Terada went back to Hsinking from Seoul on 8 September, Endō and Arisue were aboard the same train.

As expected, Nakajima was relieved as AGS deputy chief, and Hashimoto as AGS Operations Bureau head.[72] Nakajima was replaced by Sawada Shigeru, 52, a graduate of the 18th class (1905), a lieutenant general since March 1938, and 4th Division commander in Manchuria since July 1938. Hashimoto's successor was Tominaga Kyōji, 47, a 25th class graduate (1913), and a major general and chief of the AGS 4th Bureau since March 1939. Inada was removed as head of the AGS Operations Section in October and was assigned to the Narashino Scientific School in November. He was replaced by Okada Jūichi, 41, a product of the 31st class (1919), the chief of the AGS General Affairs Section since March 1939 and a colonel since August.[73] The personnel relocations and retirements were a complicated and gradual process that extended until the end of 1939. "Firing" senior commanders was not customary in the Japanese army. To avoid disgracing the officer, he would usually be relegated to the anonymity of a sinecure.

Gen. Hata Shunroku, who had just replaced Itagaki as war minister on 30 August when Hiranuma gave way to Abe as prime minister, explains the procedures and the general outlook at the time of the IJA purge.[74] Cleaning up the Nomonhan affair, from the standpoint of personnel and responsibility, was his major task and one of his biggest problems as war minister. Since the AGS had been having such a difficult time with the Kwantung Army, Hata served as a kind of neutral judge to sort out the so-called quarrel, inasmuch as the war minister was responsible for personnel affairs in the whole army. "There is a Japanese saying that 'both parties to any argument should be punished [*kenka ryōseibai*],'" remarks Hata, "so I shuffled the two sides evenhandedly." The chief of staff, Kan'in, a venerable imperial prince then 74 years old who left details to the AGS deputy and assumed no responsibility, could not be removed,[75] but reshuffling occurred down to the bureau level at the AGS and down to operations officers at the Kwantung Army. General officers could not "resign" as such, so the war minister attended to their relief or retirement.

It was entirely an internal problem for the High Command, says Hata: "The army was so influential at the time that nobody else dared to speak up, especially where personnel shifts were concerned." The legislature possessed no authority whatsoever in such cases, and neither suggestions nor pressure emanated from the outside. In fact, the prime minister never uttered a word about the personnel matters, nor did the navy minister. Draft recommendations were developed by the war ministry's Personnel Bureau, then under Maj. Gen. Iinuma Mamoru, and staffed through the vice minister of war, the AGS deputy, and the inspectorate general for training.[76] When all had concurred, the recommendation would go to the Big Three for endorsement: the war minister, the AGS chief, and the inspector general. This triumvirate met at routine times of personnel rotation and on special occasions for the reassignment of senior officers, such as the Kwantung Army commander. Since the August shifts were already over, the Big Three concentrated on the Nomonhan matter. Thanks to the considerable use of prior channels, involving careful and prudent deliberation, "the general atmosphere was widely felt by all three of us, through our subordinates," Hata notes. His colleagues voiced nothing special about the recommendations, as he recalls: "Nomonhan was such a big issue, and investigated so thoroughly, we were well informed by now."[77]

After the Big Three reached agreement, Hata would bring the report to the Emperor for final approval. The general used to go to the Court almost every day to ask for imperial sanction of specific recommendations. Throughout the fighting at Nomonhan, while Hata was chief aide de camp, the monarch (who consistently opposed enlargement of the crisis) would never say something was "good" or "bad"; he merely awaited requests and then decided. Personnel problems were part of the supreme command prerogative of the Emperor, and he expressed many opinions to the war minister about them, such as "Leave this one" or "It is all right to move that one." The Japanese military's efficiency-rating system was just, and the resulting shifts were also very fair, asserts Hata. He heard of no official complaints.

At the Kwantung Army level, Ueda and Isogai were placed on the "waiting for orders" list and were allowed to retire in December 1939. Ueda saw no more military service. Active in veterans' affairs, he died in 1962 at the age of 87. Isogai, however, was recalled in January 1942 to become Governor-General of Hong Kong, a post he retained until December 1944. After the war, he was convicted of war crimes, sentenced to life imprisonment in 1947, and released in 1952. Isogai was 80 when he died in 1967.[78]

Yano was the one general officer at the apex of the Kwantung Army command who was not retired upon being relieved of his post. After banishment to the Chinhae Bay fortress in Korea in December 1939, he was promoted to lieutenant general in August 1940, when he took charge of gendarmerie forces in North China. Subsequent assignments included command of the 26th Division (June 1941), presidency of the Kungchuling school (April 1942), and duty with the inspectorate general (July 1942). Finally retired in March 1943 after 33 years of commissioned service, Yano died in 1960 at the age of 72.

AGS Generals Nakajima and Hashimoto were retired after Nomonhan in December 1939. Recalled for military-government service in July 1942, Nakajima died in prison in Djakarta in 1949 at the age of 62. Hashimoto saw no further duty; he was 77 when he died in 1963.[79]

Thus it can be seen that for four out of five AGS or Kwantung Army headquarters generals reassigned as a result of the Nomonhan war, replacement led to retirement. But even in those cases, the High Command did not air its dirty linen in public. For example, the press release concerning Ueda's relief was camouflaged artfully by entwining it with news of the activation of the China GHQ, making the reassignment sound "routine" and therefore misleading the public about the true dénouement at Nomonhan.[80]

As for field-grade staff officers, not one of the "movers and shakers" in the Operations sections at Tokyo or Hsinking was forced to retire. Assumption of responsibility generally led to little more than a slap on the wrist or brief exile to a duty station that was sometimes less than exciting. Inada, for instance, was certainly not retired from the army. After being relegated to

Narashino for less than a year, he rose steadily in rank and in importance of command. By war's end, he was a lieutenant general (since April 1945) and chief of staff of the 16th Area Army defending Kyushu against Allied invasion.[81]

Nobody in the Kwantung Army's Operations Section was retired either. Terada remained at the Chiba Tank School until he took over the 1st Tank Regiment in August 1940. A year later, he became an Army War College instructor. Promoted to major general in October 1941, he served next as deputy chief of staff of the Armored Army. At the close of the war, Terada was in command of the Armored Headquarters, a lieutenant general since March 1945.

After a brief assignment at the Chiba Infantry School, in June 1940 Hattori returned to Tokyo, first with the inspectorate general and then for a lengthy period in the AGS nerve center, Operations. In October, he became subsection chief; the following July, section chief—Inada's old post. A lieutenant colonel only since March 1939, he was promoted rapidly to colonel in August 1941. Tōjō, in his capacity as war minister, selected Hattori to be his private secretary in December 1942. Hattori resumed direction of the Operations Section in October 1943 but later had a run-in with authority that blighted his promising career. In February 1945, he was banished to China as commander of the 65th Infantry Regiment. After the war, Hattori was active in military history and security affairs, and worked closely with MacArthur's GHQ during the American Occupation of Japan. He died in 1960 at the age of 59.

Tsuji did not meet his end when he was sent to China in 1939. Promoted to lieutenant colonel in April 1940, he subsequently saw duty with the 25th Army in Malaya, directed the vital AGS Operations Subsection in March 1942, and joined the faculty of the Army War College in February 1943. After rising to colonel in August 1943, he served with four field armies. His wartime experiences included controversial episodes such as alleged atrocities in Malaya and the Philippines, and collisions with Japanese field commanders in the South Pacific comparable to his troubles with Sumi and Ogisu at Nomonhan. At the close of hostilities, Tsuji was on the staff of the 18th Area Army stationed in Thailand. Predictably, he went underground in Southeast Asia and China, and did not surface until May 1948. "Depurged" by the U.S. Occupation authorities in 1950, he entered Japanese politics, winning elections to the House of Representatives in 1952 and to the Upper House in 1959. On a strange "fact-finding" mission of his own to Southeast Asia in 1961, Tsuji disappeared in Laos at the age of 58. He was declared officially dead in 1968.

Shimanuki Takeharu was promoted to lieutenant colonel in August 1940 while at the Army War College. After serving as a staff officer with field armies in China from March 1941, he rose to colonel in August 1943, like Tsuji. Following a very brief assignment as an AGS section chief, he returned to staff posts with field armies in Manchuria and China, and with air headquarters until war's end. Shimanuki was active in military historical studies afterward, and in 1970 became the director of the Japan Defense Agency's Office of Military History. He was 76 years old when he died in 1978.[82]

The subsequent careers of the AGS and Kwantung Army operations officers purged after Nomonhan thus ranged from the distinguished to the colorful. Hayashi Saburō, a major serving as assistant military attaché in Moscow at the time, has commented incisively on the question of calling unsuccessful IJA staff officers to account:[83]

> Despite the shake-up, most of the staff officers in the 1st Section (Operations) at Kwantung Army headquarters—officers who were alleged to have been really responsible and to have exerted major influence during the Nomonhan Incident—were merely transferred to sinecures. Moreover, the transferred officers afterward obtained important posts within the High Command—unnoticed. Some of them, indeed, ended up by occupying key positions within the Operations Bureau at IGHQ itself. The shake-up, in other words, was merely for the sake of appearances. Such were the workings of military personnel administration.
>
> Commensurate rewards or punishments were not dealt out fairly within the army. When advocates of strongly positive views made mistakes, the authorities in personnel administration overlooked them. Even if punishments were meted out, it was only for form's sake. On the other hand, proponents of a prudent approach to things were apt to be treated like cowards and were often held to strict account when they erred. This system of administering military personnel affairs fostered a foolhardiness that, in turn, was to provoke successive disturbances that were quite uncalled for. It is generally acknowledged by those who held contemporaneous High Command posts that the officers responsible for the Nomonhan debacle became strong advocates for launching the Pacific War.

The situation with respect to the punishment of Japanese front-line commanders who survived the fighting at Nomonhan, as we shall see, was far more grim and merciless, and with less reason.

Stilling the Guns

The splendid new Kwantung Army commander, Umezu Yoshijirō, lost no time leaving China for Manchuria. On 6 September an AGS Operations Section officer[1] flew in to First Army headquarters at Taiyuan to brief the general on his forthcoming assignment. Unable to dally until his replacement arrived, Umezu proceeded to Peking next day to say goodbye to his superior, General Sugiyama, commander of the North China Area Army, and to pick up his own chief of staff, Lt. Gen. Iimura, who had come from Tokyo to meet him. By 7 P.M. on 8 September, Umezu and his party had already arrived by air at Hsinking, where they were met by Deputy Chief of Staff Endō, Kwantung Army senior staff members, and Manchukuo government officials. At army headquarters, outgoing staff officer Hattori delivered a secret briefing to Umezu. Using notes provided by the general, a remaining colleague of Hattori, Lieutenant Colonel Nakayama, worked up an instructional address to the army, which Umezu issued on the 9th.[2]

Umezu was seven years younger than and five academy classes junior to his distinguished predecessor Ueda. In fact, Umezu was the first lieutenant general to command the Kwantung Army, attaining that rank during the same year (1934) that Ueda became full general. But whereas Ueda's star had set, Umezu's was rising fast. A no-nonsense officer and a favorite of the Emperor, he had an army-wide reputation for unexcelled administrative ability and seemed destined to become war minister or even prime minister. To his new post as Kwantung Army commander, Umezu brought a sense of balance and responsibility, and qualities that have been described as sharp, profound, cautious, to-the-point, and precise. Indifferent to pomp, he would not tolerate the kind of prima donnas and insubordinates who had chronically infested Kwantung Army headquarters. When the commander of the newly arrived 5th Division, Lt. Gen. Imamura Hitoshi, reported to his friend Umezu in Hsinking on 10 September, an illuminating conversation took place. Imamura said he would "take no guff" from meddling and overbearing Kwantung Army staff officers who came prowling around his division. In fact, he would arrest them and ship them back to Hsinking. Umezu replied that that was fine with him. Although it might take a while to "renovate" his headquarters, there would be no repetitions of freewheeling behavior.[3]

Between the date of Umezu's arrival in Manchuria and the promulgation of a cease-fire on 16 September, some combat continued at the Nomonhan battlefront. Imperial Order No. 349 had exempted the Handagai sector from the general suspension of offensive action and, as we saw in the last chapter, elements of the Katayama and Gotō task forces had been engaged in hard fighting as late as the 11th. Another exclusion from the imperial prohibition applied to necessary air action. Ever since the outbreak of the Russians' August offensive, Japanese airmen had struggled desperately and at long odds to contest the skies and to assist the hard-pressed ground forces. Ogisu reputedly told an air liaison officer on 28 August that the air force was "the only thing the Sixth Army can depend upon."[4]

Once the Soviet-MPRA forces had conquered the disputed border zone, the secret airstrips on the high ground on the left side of the Halha—from which low-level fighter strikes had been launched—seem to have been abandoned, and no short-range enemy bases were left near the front. The Russians were apparently building up their supplies and working on positions on the right bank. Nevertheless, the tempo of air warfare remained high when the weather was good in September and the Japanese air force chose to challenge the enemy. There were two particular spurts of activity: on 1-2 September, 37 to 41 Russian planes (among them, eleven I-17 fighters) were shot down at a cost of eight Japanese aircraft and seven casualties, including two squadron commanders killed and one wounded; on 4-5 September, the Japanese lost five planes and five airmen in the process of downing 37 to 46 enemy aircraft.[5]

After 5 September, bad weather and major Japanese air force realignments combined to limit aerial activity to occasional reconnaissance and fighter patrols for almost 10 days. Giga's 2nd Air Division was fatigued, and its combat strength had been whittled down from 160 operational planes on 29 August to 141 as of 5 September, although two new groups (the 31st Light Bomber and 64th Fighter) had already come from China in July and August. Meanwhile, ever since early June there had been a routine IJA reorganization program calling for transfer of the corps-level air command headquarters from China to Manchuria around 1 August, together with several more air groups. The command's chief of staff, Col. Shimoyama Takuma, had visited Giga's division on two occasions, in June and mid-August, to discuss the projected relocation and the battlefront situation, but there had seemed to be no need to rush matters, since front-line morale was still high and strength was adequate. Within a week of the Russians' August offensive, however, Kwantung Army air staff officer Miyoshi hastened to Peking to accelerate the movement of the air command to Manchuria. The process accordingly began on 1 September, and the corps commander, Lt. Gen. Ebashi Eijirō, left Peking on the 3rd.

Giga, of course, was acquainted with the plan to build up the air force and with the fact that one air division was insufficient to defend all of Manchuria, as the experience at Nomonhan undoubtedly proved. But, says Giga, he does not really know all the reasons for creating a brand-new organizational structure above him, the highly experienced, then-senior air commander in the Kwantung Army. "As can be seen," Giga remarks, "liaison in the Japanese army was very poor in those days, especially with respect to personnel changes. Suddenly I was 'unneeded' and was told, 'Go to Mutanchiang.' You might think of asking, 'Were you happy about it?' The answer should be obvious! But I did have my private thoughts."[6] One of Ueda's last official acts as army commander, on 5 September, was to bestow a citation on Giga's air division and all of the aerial units that had fought at Nomonhan. Giga and his staff relocated their entire headquarters from Hailar to Mutanchiang, left their combat units behind, and turned their missions over to Ebashi's air command, effective at midnight on 5 September.[7] In action throughout the fighting at Nomonhan, the air division had achieved unparalleled success in air-to-air battle, but it was obliged to depart before the affair was ended or the enemy had been brought to heel. Understandably, Ueda's citation did not help much.

Incorporating Giga's operational units, Ebashi's air command deployed a final operational strength well over 50 percent larger than that of the old air division. In particular, six new fighter, one reconnaissance, and two light bomber squadrons were brought from China. At its peak, the corps possessed four wings of 34-37 squadrons with a potential strength of as many as 325 planes, mainly fighters. The Japanese air units had been looking forward to supporting the projected Sixth Army offensive with every plane available. Despite poor weather, Ebashi directed the deployment of his constantly arriving reinforcements, the construction of airfields and other facilities, the stockpiling of fuel and ammunition, and the preparation for winter. When word came that the Sixth Army's concentration was nearly finished by 10 September, the air command accelerated its own efforts and reported that its forces were ready to go by 11-12 September.[8]

Earlier it had been thought, on the basis of aerial reconnaissance and secret intelligence, that counteraction by enemy bombers would not be possible until after the Sixth Army's offensive got under way. Soviet bomber units, needing several weeks of overall maintenance, had reportedly been pulled back to the Borzya district, where there were repair facilities. The Russians seemed to "smell a rat" from the evening of 9 September, when their movement of fuel and rations to the front was intensified. Shifting of Soviet forces from the Trans-Baikal area also began. Apparently the Russians were expecting a Japanese counteroffensive.

On the 12th, Japanese reconnaissance planes observed an increased number of aircraft in the Bain Tumen area—18 heavy and 20 light planes. On the same day there were noted at least 16 large and 68 small planes in the

Tamsag–Lake Buir complex. Scouting aircraft noted 150 trucks moving south on the Borzya–Bain Tumen road, and another 50 from Bain Tumen toward the area east of Lake Buir. The Russians must be bringing their main air strength to the battlefront. IJA artillery observers reported the existence of secret enemy fighter airstrips south of Nigesorimot on the left bank of the Holsten, eight kilometers east of Noro Heights. About 60 fighters were seen taking off and landing on the afternoon of the 12th, and engine testing had been heard recently in that area. Special intelligence conveyed information that the enemy might be planning to employ paratroop forces. The weather was still generally poor, however, and there was no contact with the Soviet air force even when an entire Japanese fighter wing sortied with eight squadrons for an hour on the 12th.

The Japanese air command was of two minds about aggressive operations. Despite the Russians' buildup, they were merely securing the frontier they claimed and had undertaken no aggressive action. The number of Soviet planes observed in the Lake Buir region decreased at nightfall, suggesting that they were being deployed to advance bases only in daylight hours—an obviously defensive measure. Even on the 14th, no enemy aircraft were sighted east of Bain Tumen or south of Lake Buir.

Some air officers nonetheless felt that it would be extremely useful to launch an aerial offensive designed to increase the leverage of Japanese diplomats negotiating a cease-fire in Moscow. Aggressive action seemed likely to be all the more helpful to the Japanese cause now that general war had broken out in Europe. The imperial order did not prohibit air strikes if deemed necessary. The Soviet buildup was becoming more pronounced on the 12th, and the enemy forces might soon be able to mount preemptive operations. Two other considerations favored forceful aerial action: the new units from the China theater were very eager to tangle with the Russians and blow them out of the skies; and the weather was about to take a great turn for the better.[9]

On 13 September, Ebashi adopted the hawkish view and ordered his command to wait for the skies to clear and then to destroy enemy air units in the area of the battlefield. All of the fighter squadrons and elements of the light bomber forces were immediately deployed to forward airstrips. A total of 255 aircraft were currently operational: 158 fighters, 66 light and 13 heavy bombers, and 18 scout planes. Aerial reconnaissance sighted 15 Soviet heavy and 33 light aircraft north of Lake Buir, and confirmed the existence of the fighter airstrip east of Noro Heights.

As soon as the weather improved on the 14th, the Japanese air command was unleashed for the first time. The fighter cap assembled at 2:20 P.M., but the light bomber units were late for their rendezvous and could not continue toward the targets around Lake Buir. Only one unit, Maj. Yoshida Tadashi's

1st Group of Type 97 fighters, encountered Soviet planes airborne (seven or eight I-15 and about 20 I-16 fighters). In the ensuing dogfighting, the Japanese claimed to have shot down nine planes, of which only three were confirmed kills. From another Japanese squadron, one plane and its pilot failed to return, the apparent victim of an oxygen malfunction. By and large, the air command noted, the action of the 14th was marked by poor coordination on the part of all the groups and by unimpressive combat results. As for the Russians, they were unaggressive and seemed to be retaining their main air strength in the region of Lake Buir.[10]

The weather was fine again on 15 September. After Japanese scout planes reported sighting 57 light and four heavy aircraft in the Lake Buir district at 9:30 A.M., Ebashi sent all of his Type 97 fighters and two light bomber groups, supported by scouts, into action—as many as 200 aircraft. Striking two airfields east of Lake Buir at about 11 A.M., the Japanese bombers did not accomplish much, destroying only four or five planes, including three heavy types. Spectacular fighter battles occurred, however. For example, about 20 planes from the 59th Fighter Group of Lt. Col. Imagawa Issaku engaged some 50 enemy aircraft and shot down 11. One of the Japanese squadrons tried to pursue the Soviet planes far to the south, was ambushed, and lost six aircraft and six pilots, including squadron leader Yamamoto Mitsugu. The veteran 24th Fighter Group, temporarily commanded by Capt. Sakagawa Toshio, claimed to have shot down nine I-15's and four I-16's. The newly arrived Sakagawa was wounded but lost none of his planes in the fierce dogfights.

At 12:30 P.M., Japanese reconnaissance aircraft, scouting the target area, reported sighting 18 heavy and 64 light planes, evidence that the Russians were moving up aerial reinforcements from the rear. Nevertheless, no further air combat ensued on the 15th after the morning strike. In the fighting that day, the Japanese air command claimed 39 confirmed kills in the air, apart from the 4-5 planes destroyed on the ground. Four to eight additional Soviet aircraft may have been shot down and as many as 12 more knocked out on the ground—for in the latter case, nine planes were seen to have been strafed but not to have caught fire. The day cost the Japanese a total of nine planes. One of the pilots, wounded, was recovered when his aircraft crashed in no-man's-land, but the officers in the other eight planes were lost, including two squadron leaders. Three of the IJA light bombers were damaged in the raid. This was the last battle of the furious air war at Nomonhan. As usual, it was characterized by the success of the agile Japanese fighters and the unimpressiveness of the primitive bombers.[11]

The Russians have been somewhat more forthcoming with respect to the aerial campaign, which, they say, reached a peak of intensity after the Japanese ground forces had been destroyed. During the first half of September, according to Soviet sources, there were six air battles—an enumeration that checks with the Japanese version—on 1, 2, 4, 5, 14, and 15 September. The most severe clash occurred on 15 September, the Russians rightly assert, when the Japanese massed their entire air force in an effort to smash Soviet air bases and regain air control. In the course of the day's air battle, 120 Japanese fighters engaged 207 Soviet planes. Losses are reported, however, with the customary discrepancy in opposing claims. The Japanese lost 20 planes, say the Russians, whereas the latter lost only six. Their "defeat" on 15 September wrecked the last Japanese effort to wrest air supremacy from the Soviet air force. Indeed, according to Russian data, in September the Japanese lost about 70 planes, at a cost of 14 Soviet aircraft.[12] Japanese records dispute this claim by a wide margin, alleging that 121 Russian planes were destroyed in the same period, against 24 IJA aircraft.[13]

Ebashi's operations of 14 and 15 September implied that the Japanese air force would not tolerate an enemy air buildup threatening to the Sixth Army but that, although willing to violate MPR airspace, the Japanese would not strike more deeply into Mongolia than the Lake Buir region west of the Nomonhan battlefield. This was merely part of the signals designed by Umezu to convince the Russians that it was worth their while to negotiate seriously but that the Kwantung Army was ready, willing, and able to enter action again, e.g., by conducting limited yet aggressive ground actions in the Handagai sector and by continuing to mass large forces at the front, including new units transferred from China and elsewhere. For instance, as soon as General Imamura arrived in Manchuria from Shantung, bringing the leading elements of the 5th Division, Umezu directed him to deploy his forces for demonstration purposes at such places as Hailar, the former duty station of the 23rd Division, and Tsitsihar, vacated by the 7th Division.[14]

Though he authorized controlled countermeasures, Umezu faithfully carried out the intent of the latest imperial order. On 10 September, he advised the General Staff concerning the Kwantung Army's projected method of phasing out the Nomonhan affair. The main force of the Sixth Army would successively withdraw from its present setup, starting on 20 September, and would return to its original duty stations. Necessary strength, about one mixed brigade, would be kept west of Arshaan through the winter to guard the Handagai district and to conduct the projected construction of a railway extension. If necessary, the railroad work might be put off until the spring of 1940. The air command would continue its current mission for the time being.[15]

Deputy Chief of Staff Endō was dispatched to the front to disseminate Umezu's policy, a task he completed by 12 September. It was apparent that the forward commanders were frustrated by the suspension of offensive operations intended even to retrieve the abandoned dead, but Endō left no doubt that the policy must be obeyed. At Ogisu's commanders' conference of the 12th, Komatsubara finally learned officially that the proposed attack had been called off and that the Sixth Army was disengaging. As he understood it, the High Command had opposed the offensive concept because circumstances—namely the international scene, problems of operational preparation, and the imminence of winter—militated against a war of attrition. There was no alternative to abandoning Ueda's project, in view of the imperial order. "It is regrettable," Komatsubara noted, "but we must be patient." Sawada heard that "a huge storm is brewing at Kwantung Army headquarters."[16]

Behind the scenes, diplomatic efforts were finally under way in Moscow. From evidence already glimpsed, it is apparent that the Japanese stance was characterized by internal feuding and foot-dragging. Traditionally, the Kwantung Army expected little from diplomacy in dealing with border disputes and preferred local settlement effected exclusively by force of arms. At the outset of the Nomonhan affair, it was the field army's policy to regard the controversy as entirely between Manchukuo and Outer Mongolia. As early as 15 May, the Kwantung Army had the Manchukuoan government lodge a firm protest with the Mongolians against the alleged MPRA incursions. Molotov, however, had inserted the Russians directly into the picture by countering promptly with a protest to the Japanese. Although the latter declined to accept the Soviet-Mongolian Mutual Defense Pact as a relevant basis for one-on-one discussion, it would be impossible to justify Japan's own role without invoking the protocol with its own client state, Manchukuo. The Japanese and Manchukuoan authorities, the Kwantung Army advised the High Command on 23 May, would have to unify their opinions beforehand. Meanwhile, claims and countermeasures were under study. On 3 June the war ministry assured the staff in Hsinking that efforts would be made to guide the foreign ministry along the lines of the Kwantung Army's recommendations. During diplomatic negotiations, the border problem would undoubtedly come up, in which case it would be insisted that the Halha River was the boundary.[17] The AGS provided an aggressive explication of this message, stressing the operational leeway afforded the Kwantung Army with respect to "flexibility" and initiative.[18]

The staff in Hsinking hardly needed encouragement. Almost until the end of the Nomonhan war, they avoided calling upon national-level diplomacy to settle the crisis. It was "rather feared" that a Japanese-initiated proposal for conversations would only stiffen the attitudes of the parties concerned. The staff in Hsinking repeatedly insisted that the authorities in Tokyo eschew negotiations, lest imperial honor be denigrated. AGS General Hashimoto remembers how the Kwantung Army kept saying "Wait a bit longer," in order to develop a setup more conducive to the pushing of Japan's contentions during any parleys. Some officers on the General Staff, admits Hashimoto, shared this view.[19]

According to postwar trial evidence attributed to Premier Hiranuma, he had learned of the fighting at Nomonhan from War Minister Itagaki. Since the military, however, acted independently without reporting its actions to the civil government, Hiranuma contended, he "knew nothing" and of course could not issue orders to restrain the army. He spoke to Itagaki many times about stopping hostilities but found that their views were at variance.[20] The criticism contained in Hiranuma's testimony, the accuracy of whose transcription has been questioned, certainly cannot apply to Itagaki's attitude after mid-July. In addition, of course, Itagaki and his associates were distracted by equally important international problems—e.g., the Wang Ching-wei project, the Tientsin crisis with England, and the Tripartite Pact.

We have seen how the Nomonhan affair escalated by mutual consent, instead of simmering down fairly soon, as even the most serious border affrays had done to date. The Kwantung Army air force's deep raid of late June into Outer Mongolia, itself partially provoked by smaller Soviet aerial attacks against targets inside Manchukuo, was followed in early July by the 23rd Division's crossing of the Halha and ejection from undeniably Mongolian territory. A desperate struggle for the confluence on the right shore ensued. It was these unsettling developments that General Hashimoto (who had personally observed a part of the unedifying river-crossing operation) described to the war ministry in detail on 8 July. The increasingly alarmed central military authorities finally evinced serious interest in stopping the fighting before it got out of hand, especially after the new Soviet air raids against the Fulaerhchi area on 16 July. Speaking for the General Staff, Inada remarks that "the Nomonhan Incident was not our doing; it was the Kwantung Army's affair." But this attitude could not be maintained indefinitely, and diplomatic negotiations had to be initiated eventually.[21]

On the eve of important governmental meetings on 18 July, the first in 20 days, the High Command began to collect its thoughts. Apparently invited to comment, on 17 July the Kwantung Army commander admitted to Tokyo that, in view of the gravity of the situation, there seemed to be no other way to settle the affair than by a resort to diplomatic negotiation. Even in such a case, however, the Japanese side should adopt a tough stand, indicating an unhesitating willingness to break off diplomatic relations if necessary. Among the developments that should be taken into account by the negotiators was the fact that Kwantung Army strength had been reinforced, an obvious allusion to the buildup for the Japanese offensive on 23 July, from which so much was expected.[22]

By 18 July, the war ministry had decided to share the responsibility for crisis management in the event of emergency, since political, diplomatic, and administrative aspects were involved. At the conference of five main ministers that followed the cabinet meeting of that date, Itagaki summarized the army's position: Japan should adhere to the policy of bending every effort to preventing the Nomonhan affair from escalating into all-out war with the Soviet Union; and Ambassador Tōgō should be promptly instructed to hasten a diplomatic settlement whenever the opportunity presented itself. The other four ministers willingly endorsed Itagaki's proposals concerning the problem with the USSR, but there was a pronounced lack of support for his further request that the military alliance with Germany and Italy be consummated quickly too. The foreign and the finance ministers especially argued that the two topics were unconnected.[23]

After the Japanese government's decision on its Nomonhan policy, the foreign ministry sent instructions to Tōgō on 20 July. Though he was to avoid conveying the impression of being overeager, he must not miss any good chance to open serious talks envisaging settlement of the crisis, perhaps in the course of other conversations on the problem of fisheries, etc. Strictly de facto recognition of the Soviet-Mongolian Mutual Assistance Pact of 1936 had become unavoidable by now. According to Tōgō, he recommended that the negotiations, once started, be carried all the way to success, since their failure could lead to war, given the heavy military buildup on both sides. After exchanging many telegrams with the foreign ministry, Tōgō was entrusted with full authority to proceed.[24]

Meanwhile, on 18 July, the Kwantung Army was instructed to send Chief of Staff Isogai to Tokyo for purposes of coordination. From the High Command's viewpoint, there seemed to be insufficient agreement between the center and the field on fundamental policy. Kwantung Army staff officers, however, considered the request to be unheard of, insulting, and inappropriate, especially amid large-scale combat operations, and preferred that the High Command send an officer to the scene. A reply along these lines was drafted, but Isogai saw advantages to his conferring with the war minister and the AGS deputy. Ueda concurred, and Isogai went. Nevertheless, to counter Tokyo's apparent suspicion of *gekokujō* infecting the Kwantung Army command, it was decided that Isogai should go without staff officers, so that he could frankly convey his opinions and demonstrate to the central authorities that the Kwantung Army was of one mind, from top to bottom.

Although Isogai had wanted only highest-level conversations on 20 July, he was disturbed to find the General Staff conference room peopled by the AGS deputy, the vice minister of war, two bureau chiefs, and two section chiefs. It was too awkward for Isogai to retreat. On the basis of his presentation, Vice Minister of War Yamawaki was convinced that there was no difference between Hsinking and Tokyo with respect to basics: solution of the conflict in China as top priority; and avoidance of war with the Soviet Union. But it was apparent that there was profound disagreement regarding operations and diplomacy. The Kwantung Army wanted to be able to retaliate against Soviet air bases and to smash enemy forces on the entire right shore of the Halha, not only bringing about a Russian backdown but also rooting out sources of future border controversy. Isogai showed no sympathy for the view that Japanese forces should evacuate the zone in dispute or that the Changkufeng Incident of 1938 served as a fine model for the handling of the Nomonhan fray. He clashed verbally with Hashimoto and Inada on these matters, and he sought to reject written guidelines (prepared by the AGS and the war ministry) that Nakajima and Yamawaki "tried to shove down his throat."

The High Command's proposed essentials called for localization of the crisis and efforts to settle it by winter 1939-40 at the latest. Japanese troops should be removed from the disputed region at the earliest opportunity: if the Kwantung Army succeeded in wiping out the enemy on the right side of the Halha, if diplomatic agreement was reached while the battle operations were in progress, or if the affair was protracted until winter. Even if hostile forces entered the region in dispute after the Japanese pulled out, no retaliatory ground action should be conducted again until the situation warranted. Strict precautions must be taken to avoid the recurrence of border disputes prior to the settlement of the current controversy. Meanwhile, efforts would be made to seize the opportunity to commence diplomatic parleys as soon as possible, depending on the progress of operations, and to steer the talks toward demarcation of boundaries and the creation of demilitarized zones. Negotiations that might lead to the rupture of diplomatic relations would not be conducted. While fostering relations between Japan, Germany, and Italy, the Japanese side would seek to effect an early solution of outstanding issues with Great Britain.

Yamawaki was particularly troubled by the dissonant views on diplomatic dealings. Certain that the USSR did not intend or dare to go to war with Japan at this time, the Kwantung Army was adamant in its contention that "accepted practice" demanded the dispatch of negotiators backed by military force who would reflect a readiness to invoke its use if matters went badly at the bargaining table. Indeed, the Japanese envoys should be prepared to risk the rupture of diplomatic relations. Such views on "dealing from strength" contradicted the dovish policy of the High Command, which Yamawaki calls "apprehensive and anxious to avoid a breakoff of diplomatic relations as well as a worsening of matters by the use of force." Although it was certainly hoped that the enemy could be dislodged from the right bank of the Halha, and although efforts would be made to build up the army in Manchuria in overall terms, there was no intention of going to war with the Soviet Union as a means of settling the Nomonhan border crisis. But, to the regret of the High Command, Isogai continued to regard the proposed essentials as nothing more than a working draft at best and labeled them as such in pencil, although they had been approved by the AGS chief and were based on government policy articulated on 18 July. Indeed, as we have seen, at Kwantung Army headquarters the guidelines were treated as "so much trash" and were essentially ignored.[25]

It was around this time that Inada began to feel that if IGHQ was to recover control of the Kwantung Army, the leadership of the field army would have to be purged. The matter had already come up after the Kwantung Army's defiant air raid against Tamsag at the end of June. Reprimanded by the Emperor, the AGS deputy had had to reply that those involved at the Kwantung Army would be punished after the present stage of operations came to an end.[26]

The deteriorating relations between the headquarters were only worsened by the General Staff's dispatch of an informational message to the Kwantung Army on 28 July, after the Japanese offensive of the 23rd had bogged down, and hardly a week after Isogai got back to Hsinking from his unsatisfying trip to Tokyo. It was now confirmed that in the event the Japanese government entered into cease-fire negotiations, two conditions had been laid down: first, every effort would be made to insure that the forces of neither side would cross the Halha River; second, if the first premise could not be met, neither side should advance beyond its lines as of a prescribed time, or, alternatively, both sides should be pulled back an equal distance from those lines.[27]

The Kwantung Army felt betrayed again. It was not being asked for its opinion; it was merely told to acknowledge a decision already made in Tokyo, in keeping with the unacceptable guidelines conveyed to Isogai. Nevertheless, there had been no change in the position of the staff in Hsinking—that the entire right bank of the Halha must be secured. To conclude an armistice while the enemy was still occupying the area near the river, on the right side, would only invite a repetition of the folly of Changkufeng. Utmost precautions must be taken to prevent a very costly trap. Of course, the Kwantung Army was not opposed to a cease-fire proposed by the Soviet side, but it looked as if the Japanese High Command might readily initiate the request (although the latest message did not expressly say so) once the slightest encouragement was evinced by the Kwantung Army. Such an intimation had already come across during Isogai's visit to Tokyo.

Although the AGS communication of 28 July did not require a detailed reply, Isogai and his colleagues were too disturbed to overlook the matter. Hattori was directed to prepare a clarification of the Kwantung Army's attitude toward a cease-fire. The resulting cable of the 30th indicated that the field army was in agreement that negotiations for an armistice should be conducted if the Soviet side suggested them, but definitely must not spring from IJA High Command initiative, which would mean a Japanese concession. Enemy forces, who were already facing difficulties in operations and logistics, would be encouraged, and the affray would only be enlarged. Current local conditions supposedly pointed to the validity of this assertion. Regarding conditions for an armistice, no agreement to retract friendly lines should be authorized; as the experience at Changkufeng had demonstrated, this would imply the acceptance of Soviet contentions. To defend the international stature of Japan and of Manchukuo, while nurturing the latter, the Japanese side could not tolerate a backdown. The Kwantung Army was firmly convinced that the best policy was to maintain lines of one's own choice, and to wear down the foe through protracted operations. A practical consideration was also pointed out: according to Japanese intelligence, the Soviet attitude was extremely firm. Even if the Japanese proposed a cease-fire, the Russians could be expected to reject it. Moreover, they would exploit the fact for purposes of propaganda.[28]

The day after Isogai sent the Kwantung Army's reply to Tokyo, Major Shimamura, still attached to the AGS Operations Section, flew in to Hsinking. Asked about the "real attitude" of the High Command toward a cease-fire, Shimamura gave a very soothing reply. Negotiations were under way with the Russians concerning Japanese retention of colliery and petroleum concessions in northern Sakhalin, the major reminded his hosts. Since the Soviet side might happen to mention the Nomonhan affair, the Japanese central authorities could merely be pondering responses. But, Shimamura said, he did not think there was any Japanese intention of first raising the matter of an armistice. Appeased by the major's presentation, the Kwantung Army did not afterward pursue the matter of a cease-fire. After all, it did not regard the outcome of the fighting of late July as a Japanese setback, although the 23rd Division's progress was hardly what had been expected.

The speed, however, with which the Kwantung Army backed off from open discussion of the touchy subject of an armistice has provoked some questions about Shimamura's role on 31 July. It was certainly well known that the Sakhalin question was a continuing source of difficulty between the diplomats in Moscow, but one wonders whether the AGS major, an operations expert on Soviet affairs, was unaware of Itagaki's proposals at the conference on 18 July and of the foreign ministry's subsequent instructions to Tōgō. Shimamura's explanation to the Kwantung Army represented either deliberate distraction by a star dissembler or true ignorance on the part of an officer who had not been let into secrets with which he ought to have been acquainted.[29]

Naturally, IGHQ was not displeased with any apparent evidence of Kwantung Army quiescence. Tokyo's extreme preoccupation with matters other than the "northern problem" is illustrated by the national security plan devised by the AGS operations staff as of 1 August. Addressing a spectrum of difficulties within the time frame of autumn 1939, the document made no mention of the Soviet Union or of the Nomonhan crisis.[30] Undoubtedly, the continuing pressure exerted by Itagaki and his associates upon the Japanese government to conclude an early alliance with Germany coincides with what Ambassador Ōshima Hiroshi told German State Secretary Ernst von Weizsäcker in Berlin on the night of 21/22 August: "If Russia were relieved of anxiety in Europe, she would strengthen her East Asiatic front and put new life into the Chinese war."[31]

Though for the moment the Kwantung Army was not crossing swords directly with the High Command about a cease-fire—after the hot exchanges of July—the problem of diplomacy vis-à-vis military operations was still very much on the minds of the staff in Hsinking. In the breathing spell before the Soviet offensive of 20 August, Kwantung Army staff officer Shimanuki Takeharu drafted "Essentials for Settling the Nomonhan Incident." Dated 12 August, this document included a stipulation that diplomatic negotiations must not originate from the Japanese side. If the initiative arose from the enemy, the Kwantung Army expected to maintain complete freedom of military action on the side of the border put forward by Manchukuo-Japan, i.e., the Halha line. Meanwhile, operational preparations would be expedited against the eventuality that the present affray might develop into full-scale war with the Soviet Union by the spring of 1940. Efforts should be made to exploit gains achieved during the course of the Nomonhan fighting, in order also to encourage the Outer Mongolians to shake off the yoke of the USSR.[32]

In Moscow, attaché Doi had originally seen the urgency of finishing with the Russians quickly before winter preparations became necessary for the Kwantung Army. By 12 August, however, at the time Shimanuki was drafting his guidelines in Hsinking, Doi advised the General Staff (which sent a copy of his message to the Kwantung Army) that the construction of powerful fortifications was imperative to defend the Nomonhan border region, to thwart Soviet intentions, and to hold out indefinitely. The USSR would increase its military preparations against Japan and strive to regain the frontier claimed by Outer Mongolia. Although the Kwantung Army should be prepared to crush the expected enemy offensive, it must avoid large-scale battles of attrition. If the present tempo of combat continued, early settlement of the affair would be impossible. Nevertheless, a Japanese-initiated withdrawal, as had occurred after the fighting at Changkufeng, or a request for a cease-fire was precisely what the Russians desired. Assured that their opponents were incapable of waging war, they would exploit the weak Japanese stand and would conduct a propaganda campaign with even greater effects than before. Hattori noted that Doi's views were very close to those of the Kwantung Army.[33]

At the outset of the Soviet-Japanese controversy in May and June, attaché Doi had noted that the Russian reaction was low-key and cautious, as reflected in the controlled press. The atmosphere in Moscow changed after the Soviet forces began to do well in July, and in Doi's words, the Russians became "noisy." On the basis of the statements successively issued by Soviet authorities, it was apparent to Doi that the USSR attached importance to the political significance of the Nomonhan affair, especially from the standpoint of policies toward the Mongols and other races, as well as from considerations of domestic policy. That the Russians had not yet launched an all-out propaganda campaign about Nomonhan stemmed from the continued Japanese battle strength, the still-undecided nature of the fighting, and the possibility that the scale of warfare might expand. Nevertheless, there was no progress toward a diplomatic settlement because, according to Doi, the Soviets were "hard-nosed" and would not retreat from their adamant position.[34]

Though it is true that Molotov would not receive Tōgō again until September, both the civil and the military authorities in Tokyo believed that the Japanese ambassador was partly responsible for the delay. The head of the foreign ministry's Euro-Asiatic Bureau, Nishi Haruhiko, felt that Tōgō was "always hesitant" about proceeding until the Japanese side's bargaining position had been solidified. Nishi even sent personal messages to the embassy counselor urging the cautious Tōgō to get started. But, like the Kwantung Army, the ambassador wanted the Russians evicted from the right side of the Halha as a precondition to cease-fire parleys. In addition, Tōgō insisted that the Japanese High Command and the Kwantung Army must synchronize their views—that is, stop feuding about the need and conditions for an armistice. From the General Staff's standpoint, too, the ambassador was dragging his feet, despite foreign ministry prompting. General Hashimoto remembers that the embassy in Moscow kept saying, "Wait a while. The military situation is not favorable yet." This not only jibed with the Kwantung Army's outlook but also seemed to reflect the fine hand of attaché Doi, in the embassy at Moscow with Tōgō.[35]

From a third party's standpoint—the German—Schulenburg had reported as early as March that Russian obstinacy in dealing with Japan (starting with the fisheries negotiations) went back to 1938, and certainly to January 1939 when Hitler assured the Polish foreign minister that he had no designs on the Ukraine. Encouraged also by economic parleys with Germany, the USSR seemed to have grown secure so far as Europe was concerned and to have concluded that "she could act all the more energetically in the Far East." Nevertheless, the not unbiased Schulenburg observed, Tōgō's performance had been unimposing. There was widespread feeling in the foreign diplomatic corps in Moscow that the Japanese ambassador was conducting negotiations very badly and that Shigemitsu Mamoru, his predecessor, would have done much better. One of Tōgō's weaknesses was apparently a lack of practical suggestions.[36]

In Berlin, the energies of Ambassador Ōshima, an unswerving anticommunist, were largely devoted to the strengthening of the anti-Comintern pact and the creation of an alliance between Japan and the Axis. Although he had heard strange intimations, since spring, of an "unthinkable" German-Soviet rapprochement, he did not take them seriously. Even when, on 26 May, Ribbentrop raised the subject directly with Ōshima, the latter could not believe his ears. The Reich foreign minister had said that it was necessary, not only for Germany but also for Japan, to take some steps in Moscow immediately. Indeed, added Ribbentrop, Germany would use its influence to prevent a clash between Japan and the USSR. Staggered by these remarks, which occurred at the time the Nomonhan war was commencing, Ōshima warned the German foreign minister that the Kremlin could never be trusted. "If you talk like that, even in jest," said Ōshima, "my friendship with you will come to an end." Ribbentrop, in turn, was taken aback by the vehemence of the ambassador's response. He sought to calm Ōshima, assuring him that he understood and would not mention the subject to him again.[37] Ōshima chose to interpret the episode as a German tactic to impel the Japanese to conclude the Tripartite Pact, and he urged Tokyo in that direction, still claiming that a German-Soviet rapprochement was impossible.[38] Reflecting upon Ōshima's reaction, Weizsäcker wired Ambassador Schulenburg in Moscow that "one link in the whole chain, namely a gradual conciliation between Moscow and Tokyo, is regarded by the Japanese as distinctly problematical."[39]

During May or June, Ōshima's senior army attaché, Maj. Gen. Kawabe Torashirō, had also picked up rumors of a possible Nazi-Soviet détente. He could collect no hard facts, however, and thus made no imprint on the High Command's thinking in Tokyo. Having failed to track down the rumors, which had struck him as "fishy," Kawabe later confessed his "incompetence."[40] In Moscow, attaché Doi—by his own admission—could not fathom Russian or German intentions either.[41]

The failings of Japanese diplomatic and military intelligence in Europe in 1939 are all the more indefensible, however, because as early as 28 April Hitler's widely publicized Reichstag speech pointedly ignored Japan, undoubtedly because of the Tripartite Alliance problem. In addition, even the Polish ambassador in Berlin noted astutely that, contrary to practice, the

German press was now for the first time printing information concerning Chinese military successes against the Japanese.[42]

Although overt, circumstantial evidence did exist for experts to dissect, certainly the Germans went to great lengths to cloak their classified designs. Immediately after the Nazi-Italian military pact was signed on 22 May, Hitler told his military commanders in chief, "Secrecy is the decisive requirement for success." German decisions "must be kept secret even from Italy and Japan."[43] In Moscow, the Germans had their own problems in the face of the Russians' "unusual mistrust" and the reserved attitude of other diplomats. The deterioration in German opportunities to acquire intelligence, embassy counsellor Werner von Tippelskirch noted, was "regrettable because, in consequence of the well-known conditions here, it is in any case difficult enough to get information."[44]

The cumulative effects of the German and the Soviet counterintelligence and "disinformation" efforts were successful. Foreign Minister Arita and his civilian and military colleagues in Tokyo were no more prescient than their representatives in Berlin and Moscow. Though hints of the approaching German-Soviet accord were received from excellent sources in Poland, Italy, and England, the Japanese government perceived few of the changes in Europe and failed to comprehend their full significance.[45]

In particular, the Japanese did not detect any indicators betokening a crucial softening of the Soviet diplomatic stance toward Japan. Yet as early as 15 August, on the eve of Zhukov's offensive at Nomonhan, Foreign Commissar Molotov had told German Ambassador Schulenburg that he was interested in learning whether the Reich was prepared to influence Japan toward improvement of Soviet-Japanese relations and settlement of border conflicts. At the end of June, Molotov revealed, he had heard from the Russian embassy in Rome that Foreign Minister Ciano was asserting privately that Germany was not disinclined to exert exactly such influence on Japan. Schulenburg replied that it was safe to assume Ribbentrop was ready to "interest himself in this matter . . . since his influence upon the Japanese Government was certainly not slight." In a follow-up report to the German foreign office, Schulenburg stressed that Molotov was "unusually compliant and candid" and evinced "surprising moderation." For example, the Soviet foreign commissar did not refer to the anti-Comintern pact and no longer demanded that the Germans "suppress . . . support of Japanese aggression." Molotov limited himself to the wish for the Reich's assistance in bettering Russian relations with Japan.[46]

Ribbentrop immediately notified Schulenburg to assure Molotov that it was entirely in accord with the German position and that the Reich was prepared to exercise its influence to improve and consolidate Russian-Japanese relations. Ribbentrop was ready to go to Moscow at any time after 18 August to address the entire range of interests, most particularly the matter of a nonaggression accord.[47] Was it partly because of the prior need to have news about the impending Soviet offensive in the Far East that Molotov delayed the German timetable a bit, stressing the advisability of thorough preparations before Ribbentrop proceeded?[48]

The initiative, for the moment, lay with the Russians. After holding out for a date of 26 or 27 August for Ribbentrop's arrival, on the 21st Molotov (after Stalin's prompt intercession) agreed to Hitler's "latest date" of 23 August, since Schulenburg stressed the exceptional need for haste. The Polish crisis was very much on the minds of both parties, plus Nomonhan in the case of the Soviets. Matters soon fell neatly into place. Zhukov's ground and air offensive jumped off on schedule at dawn on 20 August, and by the 23rd the Russians had achieved their first-phase objectives—to encircle and penetrate the Japanese forward lines and to split the defensive system. When Hitler learned of the green light given to Ribbentrop by the Russians, it is said that the joyous Führer drummed his fists on the wall and exclaimed, "Now I have the world in my pocket!" By midday on 23 August, Ribbentrop was in Moscow.[49]

The first order of business was the Japan question. Ribbentrop reiterated the German position: that the Reich's friendship with Japan was not at all directed against the USSR, that this tie could contribute to an adjustment in Soviet-Japanese differences, and that Germany was prepared to work toward that objective if the Soviet government desired it. Stalin replied that, though it was true Russia wanted to improve relations with Japan, "there were limits to its patience with Japanese provocations. If Japan desired war, it could have it. The Soviet Union was not afraid of it and was prepared for it. If Japan desired peace—so much the better!" Germany's assistance would be useful but, added Stalin (mirroring the very attitude of the Japanese military), he did not want the other side to derive the impression that the initiative had been taken by the USSR. Ribbentrop agreed, stressing that his cooperation would merely mean the continuation of conversations he had been conducting for months with Ōshima in the desired direction; the Germans would take no new initiative. In the early hours of the 24th, after detailed discussion, the Russians and the Germans signed a nonaggression pact and secret protocol defining spheres of influence in eastern Europe, both documents dated 23 August. Russian music soon began to be played by German radio stations.[50]

The volte-face in Moscow took the world by surprise. No one was more confounded than the Japanese, who, as the historian Hosoya Chihiro puts it, possessed "scant experience of the complexities of power politics." The gullible Germanophile Ōshima only learned of Ribbentrop's trip on the eve of the foreign minister's departure, and he was dumbfounded. On the night of 21/22 August, State Secretary Ernst von Weizsäcker did a good job of appeasing Ōshima, who evinced "a certain uneasiness" that only increased as the conversation proceeded. The Japanese ambassador anticipated "a certain shock" in his homeland, for it was apparent that the USSR would be able to devote its energies to the Far East, and the inconsistency of the latest developments would raise questions about the anti-Comintern pact in particular. But there was no use trying to interfere with faits accomplis, admitted Ōshima. He left Weizsäcker with the assurance of his undaunted intention to work further for German-Japanese friendship. At his office in the morning, Ōshima drafted a message to Foreign Minister Arita offering to resign as ambassador. Attaché Kawabe was "spitting nails."[51]

At this crucial time, the naiveté, simple faith, and ignorance of the Japanese diplomats again became apparent. On 22 August Hitler shared his private feelings toward Japan with his top commanders:[52]

> Since autumn 1938 . . . I have found out that Japan does not go with us without conditions. . . . I have left to Japan a whole year's time to decide. The Emperor is the companion piece of the later Czars. Weak, cowardly, irresolute, he may fall before a revolution. My association with Japan was never popular. We will furthermore cause unrest in the Far East and Arabia. Let us think of ourselves as masters and consider these people at best as lacquered half-monkeys who need to feel the knout.

Although intemperately expressed, Hitler's racial views on non-Aryans should come as no surprise. Nevertheless, there has been a tendency to accept Ribbentrop's overt contentions at face value: that, as he assured the Russians repeatedly, Germany's "friendship" with Japan was a key to the remolding of Soviet-Japanese relations and the settling of border disputes. Though Ōshima and his misguided ultra-rightist associates believed the Nazi protestations and attempted to convince the Japanese government and foreign service to do so too, it is apparent from the unfurling of the Nomonhan negotiations that Nazi Germany deserves none of the mediative credit it claimed for itself. Arita, in fact, was thought to resent Berlin's invitation to place Japan "at the mercy of Germany." The foreign ministry made a particular effort to advise the American government that "the seductive arguments of the German Ambassador . . . had been rejected with scorn."[53]

The diplomatic breakthrough, from the Japanese side, occurred on 22 August, without German assistance, while Tōgō was conferring with Lozovsky, the vice commissar for foreign affairs, about the unsolved problem of the Sakhalin concessions. It was necessary, Tōgō had stressed, to solve the various pending questions. When Lozovsky replied that the USSR also desired a normalization of relations, Tōgō seized the opportunity to urge that, among other problems, it was essential to deal with the frontiers between Manchukuo and the USSR as well as between Manchukuo and Outer

Mongolia. Lozovsky assured the Japanese ambassador that the Soviet Union was willing to study any concrete Japanese proposal concerning the border problem. This represented the first open signal to the Japanese that the USSR was ready to discuss a diplomatic settlement, and on 28 August the foreign ministry directed Tōgō to forge ahead without delay.[54]

At Hsinking, as soon as news of the Soviet-German pact was received and its import became clear, operations chief Terada argued that the Kwantung Army must still mete out a hammer blow to the Russians at Nomonhan while simultaneously finding the chance to work out a settlement—the old "shoot and talk" theory in practice. Given the importance of the Kwantung Army's opinions on international affairs in terms of the High Command's decision-making, prompt and clear policy recommendations to Tokyo were imperative, says Hattori. General Ueda called in Terada (whose strategic views he shared in the main) and directed him to pull together the entire staff's outlook toward the new developments in Europe. By 27 August, a document containing the army's recommendations had been drafted, coordinated, revised, approved by Ueda, and telegraphed to the General Staff. The Intelligence Section chief, Col. Isomura Takesuke, was sent to Tokyo to explain the policy paper in detail.

While accelerating military preparations against the USSR, said the main points in the Kwantung Army document, the Japanese side should smash Soviet forces in the Nomonhan area and cause the Russians to propose a cease-fire through the intermediation of Germany and Italy. On the geopolitical level, it was recommended seriously for the first time by the staff in Hsinking that a Japanese-Soviet nonaggression pact should be concluded speedily and an anti-British military alliance formed by Japan, Germany, Italy, and the USSR in order to extirpate English influence from the Orient and thus expedite the settlement of the conflict in China. Specifically, the Kwantung Army would employ the 2nd, 7th, and 23rd divisions in battle, and move up another corps to Hailar and Manchouli if necessary to thwart Soviet intentions entirely. In connection with a Russian-initiated, Axis-mediated cease-fire, two conditions should be laid down: recognizing the Halha River as the frontier, both armies should withdraw simultaneously from the border area to original stations in general; neither side should deploy forces or construct facilities along the Halha shores.

At the same time, the Kwantung Army plan proposed, all pending Japanese-Soviet problems should be resolved and regulated, including northern Sakhalin and fisheries rights. In dealing with the USSR vis-à-vis the China theater, the Japanese should induce the Russians to stop aiding Chiang Kai-shek, in return for which the established Soviet influence in Outer Mongolia and Sinkiang would be ignored, as well as the Russian advance southward from the region of central Asia. Regardless of the success or failure of the suggested negotiations, the settlement of the China problem should be hastened. Though propounding a continental alliance including the USSR, the Kwantung Army stipulated a target date for completing all-out preparations for war against that country: five years from now. In case the strategic and diplomatic package was not adopted, the Kwantung Army intended to mobilize and reinforce the strength in Manchuria by the spring of 1940 and to smash the Russians' Far Eastern policy at an early time through Japanese efforts alone.[55]

On 28 August, the General Staff reported to the Throne about the prospects for settling the Nomonhan dispute in concert with the Kwantung Army commander's view. The High Command agreed with the necessity of first meting out a hammer blow to the aggressors, regardless of subsequent methods of dealing with the affair. Three Japanese divisions were being committed; speedy action was imperative in any event. Utmost efforts should be made to devise means of arranging a cease-fire through diplomacy. It was the view of the AGS that negotiations should be opened, closely meshed with the progress of military operations, and based upon the diplomatic guidelines reported previously. If negotiations were not completed before the advent of winter, the Kwantung Army had considered the matter of withdrawing the main operational strength from the front. The AGS intended to guide the actions with a view to pulling back all of the forces, in order to prevent prolongation of the Nomonhan dispute into 1940. It was the High Command's policy not only to allow the Kwantung Army to carry out the proposed operation but also to try to close out the affair before the worst of winter. Therefore the necessary reinforcements would be sent to Manchuria—a reference to the Fukuoka conference planned for 1 September.[56]

An aura of unreality and fantasy surrounds the paper plans of the Kwantung Army and the detached projections of the General Staff, generated at the precise time when the Japanese government was falling and the 23rd Division was being consumed.[57] Tōgō's task, difficult enough in July, was far worse a month later, when too much time had been wasted. The Hiranuma cabinet, finding its position untenable as a result of the "treacherous and unpardonable" Soviet-German nonaggression pact, had collapsed on 28 August. In his farewell statement, Hiranuma asserted that Japanese foreign policy would have to be reconstructed in view of the "extremely complex if not baffling situation" that had developed in Europe. The new government, led by retired old Gen. Abe Nobuyuki, although it called for the creation of an independent foreign policy, was weak and ineffective; it lasted only four and a half months. At this juncture, when a particularly firm hand was needed at the tiller, no foreign minister could be found for almost a month; Abe had to act concurrently in that capacity. Formulation of central policy was therefore fuzzy and direction feeble. Daily workings were left to the career bureaucracy. For a while, says Hata Ikuhiko, governmental and military estimates of the situation "lost objectivity and disarray grew."[58]

The Russians' military and diplomatic timing had been superb. By 31 August, Zhukov's forces had completed the third phase of their offensive, cleared the Japanese from the disputed border zone, and essentially won the undeclared war at Nomonhan. Next day, on 1 September, the Germans—completely reassured about the Soviet position in eastern Europe—invaded Poland. Spurned by the Russians, the British and French governments declared war on Germany. All that remained for the Soviets was to settle with the Japanese; only then could they dare to claim the spoils in Poland promised them by the Nazis. Whereas the USSR thus retained full diplomatic initiative vis-à-vis Japan, as it had throughout the Nomonhan affair, the Abe government could merely announce feebly on 4 September that the Japanese would not intervene in the European war but would concentrate on seeking a solution to the China Incident. Five days later, Abe told the press that Japan would strive to achieve its objectives by improving relations with the Soviet Union, the United States, England, and France.

Suddenly directed, by a second imperial order on 3 September, to suspend its grandiose plans, the Kwantung Army spent several days trying in vain to dissuade the High Command. Meanwhile, on 4 and 6 September, Tōgō was sent further guidelines for negotiation. Hattori and his colleagues at Kwantung Army headquarters later complained that the central authorities did not reveal their covert intention to initiate parleys with the Russians (as had been already feared in Hsinking in July) each time an imperial order was issued. Actually, the war ministry had notified the Kwantung Army on 5 September that the authorities in Tokyo had adopted the fundamental principle of taking advantage of the outbreak of the European war to commence negotiations with the Russians. General problems would be addressed, with a view to normalizing relations between the two countries, and efforts would be made to solve the Nomonhan dispute as part of border difficulties in general.[59] As we have seen, the Kwantung Army staff was too preoccupied with matters of battlefield cleanup and personnel replacement to pay much attention to the news from Tokyo about diplomatic negotiation.

Two strong messages sent from Moscow by military attaché Doi to the General Staff, and retransmitted to Hsinking for information only, were very well received at Kwantung Army headquarters. The first set of recommendations, prepared on 3 September, indicated that it had now become advantageous for Japan to try to conclude a nonaggression pact with the USSR too. Since the Second World War had already broken out, however, the Soviet Union would not necessarily agree to German arbitration. Consequently there was no alternative to proposing a mere normalization of diplomatic relations and the settlement of disputes. Such an approach should be made not now, when Japanese forces had had to withdraw, but only after a large-scale counteroffensive had been launched. It was doubtful that the Russians would accept a proposal at this stage, for they held the Japanese in contempt and were boasting that they had already forced IJA forces across the frontier. Indeed, probably the Soviet side would take advantage of a proposal to drive Japanese troops even farther away from the border. The Russians might accept a compromise suggesting IJA withdrawal from the disputed region and its temporary demilitarization pending further negotiations—after the Japanese counterattacked.

The Kwantung Army, Doi continued, must be prepared to cope with Soviet rejection of a compromise. As the colonel had suggested earlier, positions should not be held near the Halha, where a war of attrition might ensue. Modern fortifications capable of assuring complete control of the disputed zone at any time should be constructed, but the main Japanese forces should stand by outside that zone. In fact, from the political standpoint, it was desirable to build permanent fortifications beyond the Soviet-claimed boundary line. It was also necessary to construct railroads and military installations suitable for protracted quartering of large forces. Such countermeasures would not only meet Japanese requirements in case of a Soviet turndown but would also, by manifesting IJA resolve and preparedness, serve to deter such a rejection.

Doi was convinced that, even if the Russians opposed a settlement after the Japanese counteroffensive, there was no danger of all-out war because the USSR would regard hostilities as disadvantageous over such an issue, because of domestic considerations. With the outbreak of war in Europe, the Soviets had to be ready for any emergency, despite the nonaggression pact with Germany. To carry out its own plans in relation to changes in the situation, the USSR could never reduce the strength on its western borders. As before, however, the Soviet Union would not abandon its intention of restoring the Outer Mongolian frontier.

As for negotiations, Doi observed that agreement might be reached at once if Japan yielded to Soviet contentions. Such a policy was unacceptable because it would impair Japanese prestige, invite utter contempt, and result in the bolstering of Russian assistance to China. Therefore parleys must be conducted on an equal footing, after sufficient military preparations had been made. In other words, concluded Doi, Japan should know better than to underestimate Soviet national power and will to fight, or to try to force the USSR to bend through recourse to makeshift measures. To achieve the purpose of negotiations, it was imperative to exert greater efforts to perfect war preparations while intensifying policies on the home front and fostering the unity of the nation.[60]

On 7 September the Kwantung Army received a copy of another long message from Doi, prepared in Moscow on the 5th, after the colonel had learned about the suspension of the Japanese counteroffensive on which he had been counting. Now, Doi asserted, it made no sense to resume negotiations, for the Japanese would have no choice but to recognize Soviet border contentions. Once the Russians concluded that IJA forces tolerated their actions without counterattacking, the USSR could be expected to publicize its victory, exploiting the unity of the Soviet people to stimulate confidence in certain victory over Japan. Apparently the Russians would not attack across the border they claimed, but one could not discount the possibility that the Red Army—which was more elated over its operational success than had been the case at Changkufeng—would undertake aggressive actions elsewhere, especially in disputed sectors where boundaries were indistinct. On the whole, however, the Soviet Union had no intention of going to war with Japan.

It was imperative, Doi remained sure, to display a constant readiness to counterattack, if Soviet arrogance, contempt, and provocation were to be checked. The need for IJA fortifications, communications, and winter quarters was undiminished. Since the situation by now had taken the worst possible turn, great efforts should be made, as Doi had urged earlier, to step up preparations against the Soviet Union and strengthen the domestic wartime setup without delay, to prevent the outbreak of unexpected hostilities. With respect to diplomacy, although Doi had not yet talked with Tōgō about the contents of the present telegram, it was the colonel's opinion that this was not the time for normalization of ties with the USSR, which the new cabinet of Abe had been called on to accomplish. Japan should postpone matters for a while, the only immediate undertaking being an effort to maintain silence. It was important to change the attitude of carelessly underestimating the Soviets or of dealing with them high-handedly. Every effort should also be made to avoid antagonizing the Russians unless their actions became "absolutely intolerable."[61]

Doi's messages, it has been noted frequently, resembled and influenced the Kwantung Army's own views. Inevitably, Tōgō's outlook was also colored by the thinking of his resident military consultant, for, as Nishi says, the military generally did not and could not hide information from the foreign service, with the exception of "special cases."[62] In this connection, there is evidence that the Japanese army privately but urgently sought to invoke German mediation toward a cease-fire at Nomonhan, especially between the time the 23rd Division was annihilated and the Sixth Army's final offensive was canceled. One top-secret channel originated in the General Staff and extended to Ōshima. The latter may have been referring to this matter elliptically when he said to Ribbentrop, around 8 September, that the Japanese army undoubtedly approved the notion of establishing good relations with the Soviet Union and that it was therefore to be hoped that "these ideas will soon be embraced by Japanese foreign policy."[63]

More specifically, it has been said that when Ōshima spoke with Ribbentrop after his visit to Moscow, the usually enthusiastic German "broker" balked at conveying the peacemaking conditions laid down by the IJA General Staff. The Russians had assured him, Ribbentrop told the Japanese ambassador, that they had won a great victory at Nomonhan. Ōshima retorted that that could not be true. Japanese forces were winning, without a doubt, for an IJA staff officer who had passed through the Nomonhan area one or two weeks earlier, en route to Berlin, had reported that the situation was very favorable to the Japanese side, from what he had observed. Ribbentrop, unconvinced, insisted that Stalin would not lie about the matter.[64] This sounds like German interpreter Gustav Hilger's recollection of the episode in Moscow: "Stalin was quite frank about his view of Japan as a dangerous adversary. He boasted of the lesson [that] Soviet troops had dealt the Japanese during a border incident [Nomonhan] and mentioned with almost sadistic glee that twenty thousand Japanese had been killed on that occasion. 'That is the only language these Asiatics understand,' he said. 'After all, I am an Asiatic too, so I ought to know.'"[65]

A second extracurricular route to mediation explored by the Japanese military may have originated with the Kwantung Army. As Doi says, that army was in no position to admit to an overt wish to hurry the armistice agreement even if it wanted one. It may secretly have desired to "pull in its horns" but could not very well express its true feelings by now, having lost so many men and been beaten in the field. An open admission would have hurt the army's morale. There was also the matter of the relationship with the High Command, which had consistently opposed expansion of the Nomonhan crisis whereas the headquarters in Hsinking had taken the forceful initiative throughout.[66]

Therefore the Kwantung Army may have worked backstage to save face, using a secret route through the German attachés stationed in Tokyo. Eugen Ott, the German ambassador to Japan, and like Ōshima a general officer, was an affable and receptive conduit. One useful additional channel was a former Japanese naval captain, Hattori Toyohiko, who had served in Berlin as an attaché in the early Shōwa era and was working in the Tokyo office of Lufthansa in 1939. Around the beginning of September, Hattori was approached by a Japanese hotel owner from Harbin, probably an OSS agent of the Kwantung Army, with the request that he contact the German naval attaché. The latter should kindly advise the central military authorities in Berlin that the Kwantung Army wanted assistance with the arrangement of a cease-fire at Nomonhan. Hattori was pleased to cooperate.[67]

Despite these sub-rosa efforts by the Kwantung Army and by elements of the Japanese General Staff to tap the German connection, neither the foreign ministry nor Ambassador Tōgō budged, even when the Hiranuma cabinet fell. Shortly after Tōgō had finally worked out a cease-fire accord with Molotov, the American embassy in Tokyo expressed certainty (on 18 September) that the arrangement was reached without any help from Germany. The U.S. government was also advised privately by the Japanese embassy in Washington, on the 20th, that "there is no foundation whatsoever for the rumor that the agreement was consummated by the good offices of Germany."[68]

As for Tōgō, he writes that shortly before he began serious dealings with the Russians concerning Nomonhan, Schulenburg offered Germany's assistance. The Japanese ambassador declined diplomatically, pointing out that the Reich was already engaged in war and that by now he had given much thought to the settlement of the dispute himself.[69] Schulenburg's notes bear out and amplify this version. On 6 and 7 September, the German envoy had two long conversations with Tōgō about Japanese-Soviet relations. It seemed to be the Japanese ambassador's opinion that an improvement in those relations was desirable from his country's standpoint, "although Japan [had] now got rid of England and France in the Far East and [had] a free hand in China"—a statement that caused Schulenburg to crow "Another service, therefore, that we have rendered Japan." Tōgō observed that the authorities in Tokyo apparently inclined toward his view but had obviously reached no definite decision yet, for he still did not have instructions that would allow him to approach the Russians. The first step toward a rapprochement must be the settlement of incidents along the Mongolian-Manchurian border, which were "still fraught with great dangers." Tōgō had already discussed the matter of principals with Lozovsky, and negotiations were to be conducted between Japan and the USSR, not between Manchuria and the MPR only.

Schulenburg urged Tōgō to work earnestly to improve Japanese-Soviet relations and particularly to settle the border problems. Since the adjustment of differences would undoubtedly be of great benefit to both parties, the German ambassador said he was convinced that Tōgō would encounter no refusal on the part of the Russians. He was at Tōgō's disposal, added Schulenburg, if he could be useful in any way, subject to Tokyo's concurrence in the Japanese diplomat's views. "Mr. Tōgō thanked me very much for my helpful attitude [Schulenburg advised Ribbentrop] but said that at present the inclusion of a third party could only complicate the matter. He would be grateful if I would, when the occasion presented itself, draw Mr. Molotov's attention to the advantages that an improvement in Japanese-Soviet relations would entail for the Soviet Union also." Schulenburg's final bit of advice, based on personal experience, was to stress the pointlessness of discussing important political matters with any Russian except Molotov himself.[70]

Behind the diplomatic facade, Tōgō undoubtedly resented invocation of "unnecessary" mediation from those in Germany whom he held most responsible personally for his unceremonious transfer out of Berlin in 1938; namely, Ribbentrop and Ōshima. Schulenburg realized at least a portion of Tōgō's feelings when, on 13 September, the Japanese ambassador asked that his revelation of details in his dealings with Molotov be treated as privileged information, held in strict confidence, and not communicated to the Reich. Tōgō said he was afraid of "interference by Berlin . . . [that] could only be harmful." In conveying Tōgō's private caveats to Ribbentrop, Schulenburg noted that "interference by Berlin" should be read as "*by Ōshima!*"[71]

The mood in Moscow had improved during early September. Press attacks against Japan had subsided recently, and no communiqué on the Nomonhan hostilities had appeared since 1 September, at which time the content and the tone implied that the fighting was nearing an end. Relatively few anti-Japanese banners and slogans were visible during the annual parade in Red Square on 7 September in celebration of International Youth Day.[72]

Finally, on 8 September, the day after the Kwantung Army's leadership had been purged, Tōgō received the foreign ministry's final armistice plan, worked out with the High Command. To mask Japanese military weakness at the front, discussions were supposedly to be opened only as part of a general readjustment of relations. As far back as July, the AGS had been willing to consider a buffer district and mutual withdrawals in the Nomonhan area. Now greater concessions had become necessary, and Tōgō was given three realistic alternative proposals, each subject to final border demarcation: the old demilitarized-zone (DMZ) idea; recognition of existing front lines as of a cease-fire time; or, the maximum Japanese concession, acceptance of the boundary claimed by the MPR.

Tōgō began the first of four decisive conversations with Molotov on 9 September. The new Japanese cabinet, said Tōgō, wanted to solve the various issues pending between the two countries, with mutual goodwill, as the basis for a general improvement of relations. Disputed frontiers between Manchukuo and the USSR or Outer Mongolia needed to be determined. The Japanese had no objection to the creation of a commission to cope with border controversies. If the Soviet side desired, a commercial treaty could also be negotiated. In response to Molotov's inquiry about the disputes that a commission would consider, Tōgō asserted that the Nomonhan affair required priority attention. It had assumed sizable proportions, the Japanese side had recently massed large forces, and a major offensive was expected momentarily. Once such combat occurred, the adjustment of relations would become very difficult; therefore a speedy agreement was imperative. When Molotov followed with a question about the Japanese proposal for solving the Nomonhan matter in particular, Tōgō advanced his minimum plan for a DMZ as a fine short-range as well as long-range approach. But after the ambassador explained the scope of the DMZ, based on the Japanese-Manchukuoan contention, Molotov retorted that the whole district belonged to Mongolia. Tōgō suggested that the disagreement on the border could be threshed out amicably by the proposed boundary commission, stressed the urgency of a provisional agreement, and asked for a quick reply, next day if possible. The commissar would not commit himself to a time of response but reiterated the Mongolian claim to ownership of the zone in dispute.[73]

Molotov did have a reply for Tōgō on 10 September. The Soviet government, he stated, could agree to the settlement of the frontiers between Manchukuo on the one hand and the USSR and Outer Mongolia on the other, as well as to the formation of a commission to handle border disputes. The latter, however, ought to include intrusions into territorial waters off Kamchatka and Sakhalin, as well as ground disputes that might occur in future. Conclusion of a treaty of commerce was desired. Regarding the Nomonhan affair, the Russian position approximated the third plan or maximum concession of the Japanese. The USSR intended to restore the status prevailing before the dispute broke out and to solve matters by having both sides withdraw to the boundary claimed by the Mongolians. Creation of a DMZ was unreasonable because the frontier line was of long standing. Nevertheless, if the Japanese needed a small amount of MPR territory for the purpose of building a rail line near the border, the Soviet-MPR side was willing to exchange a two-kilometer strip of Mongolian soil for an equivalent piece of Manchurian land.

Tōgō replied that he would have to query Tokyo about extending the purview of the boundary commission, but that the Soviet side's idea of restoring the situation at Nomonhan accorded in general with the Japanese proposal of 9 September. Still, there was the problem of ownership of the district in contention. Mongol soldiers had begun to infiltrate the region in March or April, causing a gradual enlargement of the controversy since May. A return to the status quo ante therefore meant that the Soviet-Mongolian "invaders" would have to withdraw to the left side of the Halha in order to reflect original conditions. The Japanese plan submitted on the 9th, however, had not touched upon this issue, since it seemed better to devise a DMZ pending adjudication.

The Soviet commissar countered that redemarcation and not demarcation of borders was at issue. An exchange of contentions ensued between Molotov and Tōgō, each diplomat asserting that rapprochement was desired but that the other's arguments could not be accepted. The Japanese ambassador continued to stress the need to normalize local conditions and to ease tensions, without insisting on border delineation at this stage.[74]

The Russian foreign commissar maintained his government's hard line against the Japanese, although Hitler had been constantly pressing the USSR to occupy the agreed-upon sphere of interest in Poland and thus prevent creation of a "political vacuum." Molotov kept telling Schulenburg that the time was not ripe for Russia and that excessive haste might prove injurious. On the same day the commissar saw Tōgō for the second time, 10 September, Molotov admitted to Schulenburg that the unexpectedly swift Nazi military successes in Poland had taken the Russians entirely by surprise. The USSR had been thinking in terms of two to three weeks more to complete preparations, whereas only a few days seemed to be on the Germans' mind. Everything was being done to hasten matters.[75]

Despite having to fend off German diplomatic pressure, the Russians still gave no hint of eagerness to settle the Nomonhan affair. Tōgō was left cooling his heels for four days. At the next meeting, on 14 September, the Japanese ambassador submitted a compromise, his next fall-back position. Explaining that the Japanese proposal was in general agreement with the Soviet idea, except that it did not allude to the problem of boundaries, Tōgō suggested that the situation in the vicinity of Nomonhan and southwest of Arshaan be restored to the condition prior to 1 May. The security of the Handagai road should be assured for the Japanese-Manchukuoan side. Both parties should suspend hostile action along the lines now held. Prisoners and corpses should be exchanged, and an agreement worked out on the spot immediately between the military representatives of both sides.

Molotov would not sweep the matter of the borders under the rug. It was imperative, he insisted, that the Japanese accept the Mongolian-claimed frontier as of 1 May. Neither diplomat budged in the course of the long discussion that followed. Tōgō concluded that in the absence of agreement on the status quo ante, the only alternative was to consider ceasing fire along existing lines. Molotov would only say that his government would consider the latest Japanese proposal.[76]

Although Tōgō had the feeling that the parleys were on the verge of a breakdown, this was not at all the case. The Japanese embassy was in the dark, but on the afternoon of 14 September, Molotov called in Schulenburg and told him that the Red Army had attained a state of readiness more quickly than anticipated and would, after all, be able to take action in Poland shortly.[77] Obviously, the USSR no longer dreaded a war on two fronts. Late on the 15th, Tōgō learned that Molotov was ready to see him again. The ambassador called in his attachés, said the call was undoubtedly about the Nomonhan problem, and asked the officers to wait for him in the chancery. Hours passed, and Tōgō did not return.

At the foreign affairs commissariat, Molotov had accepted the Japanese proposal of 14 September. He suggested a cease-fire line as of 10 P.M. on the 15th, Moscow time. With respect to clarification of the Manchukuo-Mongolia frontier in the area of the recent fighting, a joint commission should be formed in two or three days, with two representatives from Japan and Manchukuo on the one side and two from the USSR and Outer Mongolia on the other. The committee should commence work as soon as it was established. Tōgō then raised such matters as preferred timing for suspending fire and retaining the lines, lead times to notify Tokyo and the forces in the field, details that should be left to the local military delegates, and the advisability of pulling back both armies one kilometer each in sectors where they were confronting each other at close quarters. To Molotov's question whether an agreement could be reached immediately or whether Tokyo had to be consulted first, Tōgō responded that the form of the basic accord could be oral instead of in writing, as in the case of the Changkufeng settlement; details could be left to the field representatives. Molotov agreed.

The ambassador then asked whether the Russians insisted on two commissions—one to deal with the present dispute, another to handle border settlement in general. Molotov pointed out that the Soviet government had avoided references to remarcation, on which it insisted, and had simply mentioned clarification. But a mixed commission was strongly desired, apart from the border committee proposed by the Japanese. When Tōgō said the only problem was the technical impossibility of forming a commission in a few days, Molotov accepted alternative wording of "as soon as possible." The commissar's last point referred to the Japanese idea of a mutual pullback of forces. Soviet military authorities had reported that the opposing armies were nowhere closer than five or six kilometers from each other, so a withdrawal was unnecessary. Tōgō withdrew his suggestion. It was agreed that the accord, reached around 2 A.M., should be made public immediately. A joint communiqué was accordingly issued at 3 A.M. on the 16th.[78] Apart from the previously mentioned stipulations regarding a local military committee, exchange of prisoners and corpses, and creation of a mixed boundary commission, the core of the announcement stated:[79]

> 1. All military action on the part of both the Japanese-Manchukuoan forces and the Soviet-Mongolian forces shall cease at 2 A.M., 16 September, Moscow time.
>
> 2. The front of [both] forces shall be restored to the status of 1 P.M., 15 September, Moscow time.
>
> 3. Representatives of both sides on the spot shall immediately take the steps necessary to implement the above agreement. . . .

When Tōgō returned to the Japanese chancery near dawn on 16 September, his attachés were waiting expectantly. The ambassador reported that the negotiations were finished and that the Russians had made some concessions. Everyone was relieved, because the Sixth Army was not ready for winter operations and because the Japanese side was overwhelmingly inferior to the Russians in quantities of armor, artillery, and aircraft. The staff toasted the cease-fire with champagne. Later, Tōgō wrote, the foreign ministry commended him for preventing the rupture of relations with the USSR.[80]

Not all Japanese observers were pleased with the dénouement. When one read between the lines of the armistice agreement, it became apparent that the cease-fire left the Japanese military forces completely outside the disputed zone, far from the Halha that had been claimed as the frontier since the outset of the Nomonhan fighting. Subsequently, both diplomats and soldiers felt that the Japanese timing had gone awry. Nishi, for example, was very unhappy with the tardiness of the Japanese negotiations, undertaken in earnest only after the front-line IJA forces had been crushed. Hashimoto agrees that perhaps it was too late to negotiate successfully when the enemy was winning and could "push you around."[81] At the time, the Privy Council showed hostility toward the alleged sellout of Japanese interests. Privy councillor Kawai Misao, a general and former AGS chief, prevailed on the vice minister of war to reassure the council by acquainting it with recent developments in China and at Nomonhan in particular.[82]

To Doi, the hair-thin balance in sequences and timing posed problems warranting suicide (*harakiri mondai*). The Japanese were consistently "a step behind" in grasping events—e.g., the consummation of the Nazi-Soviet nonaggression pact, the German attack on the Poles, and the Russian entry into eastern Poland. Soviet diplomatic methodology, meshing of foreign and military policy, and counterintelligence were unmatched. "Since even their own people don't know what is developing," asserts Doi, "it is impossible to predict the Russians' actions." For instance, says the attaché, 15 September must have been the last bargaining day for the USSR vis-à-vis Japan, yet the Soviets betrayed no weakness or impatience. Molotov was as intractable at the end of the negotiating process as at the beginning.[83]

Some authorities were convinced that the Japanese side was outmaneuvered in Moscow and compromised too easily. The Russians exuded confidence that they had won at Nomonhan and had no doubts that the Japanese had lost. Such self-assurance on the Soviet part allowed the USSR to time the entry into Poland perfectly. On the same day that he worked out the cease-fire with Tōgō, Molotov was able to tell the German ambassador that Russian action might take place as soon as the 17th or 18th. Stalin was already consulting his military chiefs and would be in a position, that night of the 16th, to designate the day and the hour. At 2 A.M. on 17 September, the Soviet leader did in fact reveal the attack time of the Red Army: 6 A.M. that morning, hardly a day after the conclusion of the Molotov-Tōgō accord.[84] A number of Japanese, including attaché Doi and War Minister Hata, are of the opinion that Tōgō would have been able to obtain better terms if only the Japanese side had dragged out the negotiations two or three more days; by then the hard-pressed Russians could have waited no longer to settle.[85]

At the time the armistice accord was worked out, however, Doi was more interested in explanations than in adventures. On 17 September, the AGS deputy received the attaché's latest evaluation, which pointed out that the USSR had withdrawn its original contention that the border line was distinct and recognizable. Instead, the Russians had proposed the immediate formation of a frontier commission charged with defining the boundaries clearly. This measure seemed to be aimed mainly at preventing conflict in the Far East, since the Soviet Union had already conducted large-scale mobilization to cope with the new situation in Europe. Clearly, in agreeing to a settlement with the Japanese, the Russians had taken into consideration the IJA military buildup and the coming of winter. The USSR was confident that border delineation would be settled easily and that further fighting would prove disadvantageous from its standpoint.[86]

Unknown to the Japanese in 1939, high-level Soviet handling of the Nomonhan crisis was assisted immensely by the brilliant espionage activities of Richard Sorge, the Red Army's master spy, who operated a ring in Tokyo from 1933 until being unmasked in October 1941. His main objectives were to monitor (1) Japanese plans to attack the USSR and (2) the state of the Japanese armed forces. As the ostensible correspondent of four important German newspapers, including the *Frankfurter Zeitung*, Sorge had become the confidant of Eugen Ott, who was the German military attaché until his elevation to ambassador in 1938. Tapping the resources of the German embassy, Sorge sought information on the Nomonhan affair and learned the real intentions of the Japanese side. Though the IJA staff officers in Tokyo seemed evasive in replying to German inquiries, they conveyed the impression that Japan was trying to settle a border dispute that was somewhat larger than usual, without any intention of enlarging it. At the outset of the incident, Sorge had expected an early compromise, but the crisis had dragged on for an unexpectedly long time. Since the Soviet authorities were concerned about all-out hostilities, Sorge investigated the danger thoroughly. Sizable Japanese reinforcements might be transferred to the battle-front from North China and Manchuria, but there was no evidence that large-scale units, the key as Sorge saw it, were being sent from Japan. Sorge said that he "stood firm on the view that Japan had no intention of waging war against the Soviet Union" because the situation in Europe and Asia militated against it, as he radioed his superiors several times during the fighting. As for the Japanese public, Sorge had the impression that they became more and more dissatisfied as the affair wore on and that their mood was generally depressed by the end. Soviet propaganda at the time of Nomonhan, however, struck Sorge as unsatisfactory, and he told his headquarters so. A reply was received that his opinion had been conveyed to the appropriate authorities and that remedial action would be taken.

Through the German army attaché in Tokyo, Sorge heard that the Kwantung Army chief of staff, Isogai, had returned to Manchuria in late July with orders from the High Command to settle the Nomonhan affair locally. Sorge's own operatives conveyed intelligence that tended to confirm his conclusions. Branko de Voukelitch, supposedly working for Agence Havas, visited the battlefront and some air bases as a guest of the Kwantung Army and reported that he did not expect war. The most important of Sorge's agents, Ozaki Hotsumi, obtained information from such sources as the Military Affairs Bureau of the war ministry that the Japanese government planned to limit the Nomonhan affray but that there was danger of escalation toward the end of the crisis, when Japanese forces were massed near the border. According to radio operator Max Klausen, Sorge reported that Nomonhan did not have much political significance and would not expand. Agent Miyagi Yotoku was of the opinion that the Japanese populace was pessimistic and did not believe the IJA propaganda in August; next month, he described the people as predominantly defeatist so far as the Nomonhan fighting had been concerned.[87]

Message after message was transmitted instantaneously to the General Staff of the Red Army by agent *Ramzai*, the code name for "a Soviet military intelligence officer in Japan."[88] Armed with authentic and up-to-date intelligence on Japanese intentions and capabilities, Molotov and his colleagues took the measure of and adroitly dealt with adversaries like Tōgō and Doi, who were operating in a near vacuum in terms of intelligence. Gut reactions were no substitute for Sorge's entrées in Japan and Manchuria.

Even before a formal armistice document was signed, the AGS Operations Section rushed word to Kwantung Army headquarters by telephone, early on 16 September, that the time to suspend military action appeared close at hand. Details would follow but, translated into Manchurian time, the cut-off hour for suspending combat was 8 A.M. Although IJA records present a neat and orderly chronology of events,[89] the conveying of timely word to the troops proved impossible. The 26th Regiment, for example, was not able to issue its restraining order until 8:40 A.M.; the 28th Regiment, until around 9 A.M.; the 27th Regiment, until 9:30 A.M. Neither the Soviet nor the Japanese side lodged any complaints about the timing, however, and the battle-front was quiet by 9 A.M. in general. The basic instructions to each IJA unit were identical: suspend all combat operations immediately, stay alert, stand by for further orders, and hold the present lines—a practical consequence of the Moscow agreement providing for post factum retention of positions as of 7 P.M. on the 15th, Manchurian time, there having been no change since then anyhow. Individual regiments provided their own elaborations: according to the 64th Regiment, even if the enemy attacked, friendly troops were not to respond without a divisional order; anybody who opened fire after 8 A.M. would be shot! The 26th Regiment said that unit movement was prohibited but that all forces should remain prepared to fight at any time. There must be no firing at Soviet military envoys; they should instead be guided in.[90]

The imperial order, released officially at 1:10 P.M. on the 16th, called for the Kwantung Army commander to suspend all hostile activity against So-viet-MPRA forces in the entire Nomonhan area, including the vicinity of Handagai this time. An accompanying directive outlined the main stipula-tions of the Tōgō-Molotov joint communiqué, to be implemented by the Kwantung Army commander as he saw fit.[91] On 16 September, too, Prince Kan'in issued a message of appreciation to the Kwantung Army. The AGS chief thanked the front-line units, which had fought well in a desolate re-gion for such a long time, extended his condolences to the dead, and ex-pressed his sympathy to the wounded.[92]

The Kwantung Army chief of staff, Iimura, promptly acknowledged re-ceipt of the imperial order, on behalf of Umezu, and reported the formation and composition of a local armistice delegation and its dispatch to the area in dispute. Iimura himself was proceeding to the front to arrange effective liaison with the Sixth Army.[93]

Ever since Nakajima's second visit to Hsinking with an imperial order, and the sacking of the Kwantung Army's leaders, senior IJA officers were aware that Ogisu's autumn offensive plan had become academic. Line units, however, knew nothing about the negotiations in Moscow or the cancella-tion of the new Japanese attack. The Katayama and Gotō detachments had seen hard fighting in September, and the air command had launched all-out raids into Mongolia on the 14th and 15th. Ground forces earmarked for offensive operations had been sending out patrols to collect information and prisoners, conducting demolition and antigas training, practicing with and repairing weapons, improving positions and camouflage, digging wells, studying aircraft recognition, allocating ammunition, and attending to the sick. Scavenger teams collected empty bottles, cans, and boxes, and useless items made of iron and copper, especially expended fuzes. New cannon came for the artillery, and new grenade launchers, heavy and light machine guns, and rapid-fire and regimental guns for the infantry. Enough replacement officers and men arrived to reorganize mauled units. As a chill gradually came in on the wind, often accompanied by rain and sometimes by snow, the troops drew winter uniforms and underclothing. Unnecessary apparel, accouterments, and classified materials were sent to the rear.

All the while, enemy reconnaissance planes flew over the Japanese positions, and IJA scouts observed myriad blinking lights and red and blue flares by night. The troops were briefed on counterintelligence precautions. For example, strangers should be challenged and efforts made to ascertain whether Outer Mongolians had infiltrated the Japanese lines wearing IJA uniforms. Green replacements were given pep talks, and officers were invited for dinner at certain unit headquarters, "everybody to bring his own food and water." General Ueda's parting exhortation of 7 September was disseminated widely. As of 15-16 September, the 27th Infantry reported that "morale is quite high and everybody is looking forward to our all-out offensive." [94]

News of the cease-fire produced varying reactions in the Sixth Army and reinforcing units. Lieutenant General Imamura, the 5th Division commander who had already reached Tsitsihar from China, was greatly relieved, for his unit would have had to storm the Russians' lines on their farthest right flank. The commander of the 4th Division, outgoing Lieutenant General Sawada, said that if the armistice had been delayed two days, his division would have been hurled into action. He felt cheated of glory but had to confess that victory was far from assured. We have already noted the private reservations entertained by officers who had survived the hell of Nomonhan. [95]

Maj. Gen. Morita Norimasa, the much-maligned commander of the 7th Division's 14th Brigade, which had been stopped in its tracks during the bloody counterattacks starting on 24 August, had been getting ready for a new assault by 9 September. That day came and went without orders to advance. When the armistice was announced on the 16th, Morita's first reaction was anger. "I had wanted this final combat to be excellent," he asserts. "Now I felt both disappointed and relieved." [96]

In the ranks, many of the hyped-up soldiers were devastated by the cease-fire announcement. Artillerymen, in particular, had been looking forward to a "battle of revenge," for they had lost many of their pieces in action and cherished the 10-cm. howitzers and improved Type 95 field guns that had been sent up in September. It was a thrill for the survivors of the 13th Field Artillery Regiment to learn that they would now be authorized to expend in one week the amount of ammunition they had consumed in three months. [97]

On the morning of 16 September, unit commanders convened their men. At one such assembly, a soldier remembers standing stiffly at attention, waiting for word of X-day, already overdue according to rumor. The commander climbed atop a gasoline drum and, tears streaming down his cheeks, told of the cease-fire instead. His men felt drained of energy; no one could speak. Despite the casualties and the losses of matériel, there had been no general feeling of defeat. Particularly enthusiastic soldiers boasted of marching to Tamsag next time. The Japanese may have lost one round but not the fight. Now the bell had been about to ring for the following round, which could have produced a comeback victory. How could one tell the bereaved families that their men had died in vain? A truck driver who had gone to Hailar to pick up artillery ammunition was astounded to see electric lights blossoming all over town that night. Women volunteers, wearing white smocks and white sleeve bands, were gaily serving tea and cookies. Instead of being glad, the trucker—like many of his comrades—was furious.[98]

The thinking now was mainly of the missing and the dead. On 20 September there would be a great memorial service south of Chiangchunmiao, presided over by the army commander. Every commander of a company or larger unit was to attend, bringing specially selected noncoms and enlisted personnel to represent their units. At 2 P.M. on the 20th, every man was to bow his head in silent prayer for one minute.[99]

Specific scenes soon brought reality home to the Japanese: a Soviet officer standing openly on a crestline, the lining of his cape a bright red; triangular green pennons springing up all along the Russians' line, indicating their vindicated claim to the frontier.[100]

The Nomonhan war was over.

39

The Price

Asuyori wa/Itsuko no hito ga
Nagamuran/Haruha kahan ni
Nokoru tsukikage.

From tomorrow on/Someone else
will gaze/At the moonbeams remaining
On the banks of the Halha.

—Lt. Gen. Komatsubara Michitarō [1]

Data on the human toll of the Nomonhan fighting vary considerably with the source. Collating the figures available to him, Zhukov notified his unit commanders that Japanese casualties had totaled between 52,000 and 55,000. Of this number, IJA dead were put at 25,000.[2] The American consul in Mukden possessed "authoritative" information, as of early November 1939, that Japanese battle casualties amounted to 30,000, exclusive of the ill.[3] A month earlier, Baron Harada heard from a former minister in the Hiranuma cabinet that the Japanese had lost 35,000 or 36,000 men out of nearly 40,000 in action at Nomonhan.[4]

Soon after the fighting had ended, at the beginning of October, the Japanese war ministry released a single figure for IJA casualties—18,000 killed, wounded, and sick—which is remarkable for the size of the admission and for the closeness to classified military records. It had been a "disastrous, bitter battle," the prefectural governors' conference was told. Correspondent Hugh Byas reported to the *New York Times* that the magnitude of the Japanese losses "had not been expected by the Japanese public." The American newspaper's headline read: "Tokyo Admits Defeat by Soviet; Calls Mongol Battle 'Disastrous.'"[5]

According to a secret collation based upon reports submitted by all unit commanders, War Minister Hata was advised, at the time he visited Manchuria on 9 December, that the total Japanese casualty statistic of 18,000 consisted of 8,000 killed, 8,800 wounded, and 1,200 sick. When the author asked Hata after the Pacific War about the 18,000 figure, he replied, "At least."[6] In September 1942, a new monument was dedicated in Hailar to the memory of personnel from the region who had died since the Mukden Incident in the various theaters. Of 10,301 deceased, 9,471 Japanese and 202 Manchurians were attributed to the Nomonhan fighting.[7]

The most authoritative data, prepared by the Sixth Army's medical bureau, indicate that the Japanese lost a total of almost 20,000 men—17,364 in battle, 2,350 ill—from a committed number that exceeded 60,000.[8] (See Table 39.1.) These Sixth Army statistics, however, contain serious gaps, which are partly corrected by a Kwantung Army classified document, itself incomplete and confusing in other respects. (See Appendix J.) Total Japanese manpower participation adds up to the much more reasonable grand total of 75,738, by incorporation of such units as the tank corps, which left the front in July (1,627 men), and the air division (3,307), as well as by identification of the strength of the Independent Garrison Unit (3,012), the 1st Infantry Division (4,980), and the antiaircraft forces (apparently 3,576). Other unit entries are cryptic, data on missing soldiers are presumably included among the dead, officer casualties are not differentiated from enlisted men, and the number of ill is not mentioned.

Inevitably, Komatsubara's 23rd Division incurred the heaviest unit casualties. According to the division's own records, of 15,975 officers and men who participated in the fighting, 30 percent were killed in action, 34 percent were wounded, four percent were missing, and eight percent were ill—a combined loss ratio of 76 percent of the divisional commitment. (See Appendix K.) Working from a slightly smaller personnel base, the Sixth Army analysts came up with an even more disastrous total loss ratio of 79 percent.[9] (See Table 39.1.) Of the individual regiments, the 71st Infantry lost 93.5 percent of its strength; the 72nd Infantry, 78.5 percent; the 64th Infantry, 69 percent; and the 13th Field Artillery, 76 percent.

Among the more important other ground units, Hasebe's detachment from the 8th BGU lost 31.8 percent of its personnel, and Hata's artillery corps lost 50 percent. Committed piecemeal, the 7th Division suffered an uneven distribution of losses. Thus Sumi's 26th Regiment, attached to Komatsubara from the outset of major operations, took 91.4 percent casualties. The 28th Infantry, which had committed Kajikawa's hard-fighting battalion from the beginning too, suffered losses amounting to 72.8 percent. But the 25th and 27th regiments incurred casualties of only 12.3 and 25.5 percent, respectively. Overall, the 7th Division lost 36 percent of its strength.[10] (See Appendix L.) Approximately 30 percent of these losses were sustained in the July fighting; 67 percent in August; and three percent in September. But whereas the ratio of killed to wounded was about 1:2 in July, it exceeded 1:1 in the debacle of August.[11] Not surprisingly, Japanese ground officer casualties were very high. Figures for the 23rd Division are shown in Appendix M. It will be noted, in particular, that the incidence of loss was 82 percent of the 17 battalion commanders and above, 72 percent of the 43 company commanders, and 78 percent of the 232 platoon leaders.

TABLE 39.1
Sixth Army Casualty Data, June-Sept. 1939

Unit	Number participating	Killed Officers	Killed Men	Wounded Officers	Wounded Men	Missing Officers	Missing Men	Total battle Officers	Total battle Men	Ill Officers	Ill Men	Grand total Officers	Grand total Men	Grand total All ranks
23rd Division	15,140	262	4,714	202	5,119	4	345	468	10,178	29	1,283	497	11,461	11,958
7th Division	10,613	65	1,043	59	1,640	2	343	126	3,025	16	311	142	3,337	3,479
8th BGU	4,579	18	642	19	577	3	95	40	1,314	4	96	44	1,410	1,454
2nd Division	10,203	11	182	3	108	0	0	14	290	4	94	18	384	402
4th Division	9,841	0	3	0	6	1	1	1	10	5	182	6	192	198
IGU	?	3	106	5	138	0	12	8	256	1	26	9	282	291
1st Division	?	0	1	0	1	0	0	0	2	0	0	0	2	2
Ota Detachment	2,326	0	0	0	0	0	0	0	0	0	29	0	29	29
Hata Artillery	2,900	29	527	18	507	8	203	55	1,267	0	158	55	1,395	1,450
Truck Unit (Kwantung Army)	2,811	0	32	0	40	0	0	0	72	0	0	0	72	72
Yamaoka Antiaircraft Unit	?	0	21	4	94	0	0	4	115	3	26	7	141	148
Water Supply	412	1	3	0	10	1	2	2	15	1	4	3	19	22
Misc.	?	1	32	5	92	0	1	6	125	2	76	8	201	209
TOTAL	58,925	390	7,306	315	8,332	19	1,002	724	16,640	65	2,285	789	18,925	19,714

SOURCE: Medical Bureau, Sixth Army, in GSDF [68], Table 5.
NOTE: The final column does not include 54 civilian casualties, 51 in the Water Supply Unit (23 killed, 16 wounded, 12 ill).

As of 25 September, some 5,500 of the total of nearly 9,000 Japanese wounded were being treated in military hospitals in Manchuria between Harbin and Dairen. At the peak of the fighting, all of the wounded could not be accommodated in hospital rooms; some had to lie on mats in hallways and yards. Forty-five years later, the wife of Maj. Suzuki Yoshiyasu retains vivid recollections of the military hospital at Hailar, where she served as a volunteer nurse: "The hospital was just jammed with wounded. I dreaded threading my way through the halls where they lay, for, according to Japanese custom, it is not proper to walk past a person's head. And the flies (for which Hailar was famous) were simply swarming over the wounded soldiers. I had no fan but, since women wore kimonos in those days, I used my sleeve to swoosh away the flies. It was a painful and pitiable scene."[12] Because of counterintelligence considerations, the patients were not returned to Japan until the end of 1939.[13] Nevertheless, in view of the numbers involved, it was not possible to conceal the scale of operations. An American correspondent reported that, in late August, Japanese casualties had been incurred at the rate of 300-400 per day, and that hospitals were "overflowing." In Mukden, on 8 September, the U.S. consul learned of seven trains carrying the ashes of Japanese soldiers killed at Nomonhan.[14]

The Kwantung Army air force suffered 230 casualties: 89 wounded and 141 listed as killed, of whom more than one-third had been lost over enemy territory. According to one IJA tabulation, 10.1 percent of the air force casualties were incurred in May and June; 26.2 percent in July; 50 percent in August; and 13.7 percent in September. Seventeen of the killed or wounded officers were of squadron commander level or above. The highest-ranking officer slain was Col. Abe Katsumi, 15th Group commander, killed on 2 August.[15]

The staggering proportion of IJA ground troops lost at Nomonhan, as a percentage of the forces engaged, is remarked upon by all Japanese military historians. Major engagements during the Russo-Japanese War of 1904-5, for example, had been known for their savagery, but IJA battle losses had amounted to merely 17 percent on two important occasions: in five days of fighting at Liaoyang, and in a week at the Shaho. Even in the course of 13 days of combat at Mukden, the Japanese casualty rate, although bad enough, had reached only 28 percent. Throughout the Russo-Japanese War as a whole, IJA losses of infantry—the highest toll—had totaled 14.4 percent. At Changkufeng in 1938, the Japanese infantry's casualties still equaled only 24.7 percent. Comparable figures for artillery troops were 4.1 percent in 1904-5 and 7.7 percent in 1938; for engineers, 4.2 and 14.7 percent, respectively—a fraction of the losses in 1939.[16]

Nomonhan also differed drastically from other combat in the Japanese experience with respect to the causes of battle death or wounding. During the Russo-Japanese War, bullets had accounted for 81 percent of the casualties in open combat—60.5 percent in the assault on Port Arthur. But at Nomonhan, small arms caused only 35.9 percent of the wounds and 37.3 percent of the deaths; by contrast, some 54 percent of the wounds and 51.2 percent of the deaths were inflicted by artillery fire. According to a medical study prepared by the Kwantung Army in October 1939, 3.7 percent of the Japanese wounds were derived from hand grenade combat; none were caused by hand-to-hand fighting. In the air force only 20 percent of those wounded in air combat made it back to base.[17]

Japanese medical officers were pleased with the negligible incidence of gas gangrene (0.8 percent), although the death rate from this cause was 50 percent. Early treatment was quite effective, and the central authorities did not have to order vaccine from England. Given the terrain, all wounds usually contained foreign matter, especially sand, but there were remarkably few instances of tetanus, to which only one death was attributed directly. Twenty cases of fatal burns, resulting from flamethrower attacks, were verified among the dead of the 23rd Division. Since evacuation of wounded men from the battlefield sometimes took as long as five hours, temporary shock may have occurred on occasion. Neuropsychiatric cases, generally of short duration, were numerous. Enemy aircraft attacking at low altitude, for example, engendered irritability and instability.[18] According to engineer Lieutenant Colonel Saitō, neurotic soldiers were always removed from combat and sent to the rear, where they were assigned such chores as tending horses or working with matériel. Moving in a kind of vacuum, these dazed men showed no violent symptoms but did not answer to their names, and had to be pushed or poked to elicit a response.[19]

With respect to data on Russian and MPRA troop losses during the Nomonhan war, Soviet sources have been both tardy and uninformative. The most explicit total figure is 9,284.[20] There is reason to believe that this statistic represents a considerable underestimate. As authorities on the Red Army have pointed out, "Zhukov never fought a battle in which he was sparing of the lives of men. Only by expenditure of life, he believed, could the military goals be achieved."[21] Zhukov was typically ruthless in pressing his counterattacks in July and the offensive in August without regard for losses.[22] Describing conversations between Russian unit commanders at Nomonhan, the historical novelist Konstantin Simonov repeatedly alludes to very heavy Soviet casualties. In short, the official Russian data do not seem to be in accord with subjective accounts of Zhukov's unpopularity stemming from his responsibility for the severe loss rate, and of the alleged dispiritedness of the Russian command after the Nomonhan campaign.[23]

For their part, the Japanese did not come up with detailed overall estimates of Soviet losses of manpower. At the time the war ministry openly placed Japanese casualties at 18,000, it was stated that the Russian-MPRA price had been "not less."[24] Subordinate IJA commands, of course, compiled their own separate tallies. For the entire period of fighting at Nomonhan, the 13th Field Artillery Regiment alone reported inflicting a "confirmed" toll of 2,842 enemy troops killed or wounded, in addition to unverified losses numbering 6,500.[25] The composite claim of 9,342 Soviet casualties caused by the Japanese field artillery almost coincides with the Russians' entire admission.

In Moscow, on the night of 15/16 September, it had been agreed by Tōgō and Molotov that details of the armistice should be worked out locally. Neither party wasted time in appointing cease-fire teams. To handle the immediate preliminaries, the Sixth Army assigned two officers—Lt. Col. Tanaka Tetsujirō (the Intelligence Section chief) and OSS Maj. Nyūmura Matsuichi —together with two civilian interpreters, an MP noncom, and several soldiers. Since Tanaka was not fluent in Russian and the interpreters were not very proficient, linguist Nyūmura handled the main dealings with the Soviet side at the outset. The major remembers the gist of Ogisu's instructions: "Your task is extremely important. The fighting must be stopped. I want no more men killed. Try to succeed in the negotiations, somehow, and do it today." Nyūmura understood what the army commander meant. At the front, both sides were emotional and hostile; so the representatives should not get into any arguments, and the armistice arrangements should proceed smoothly.

Ogisu told Nyūmura to do his best and then, to the major's delight, bestowed the braid of a staff officer upon him. A Kwantung Army medical officer, Col. Ishii Shirō, donated a bottle of Coty perfume, which he must have been saving in case he faced death as a samurai. Nyūmura dabbed on some of the perfume to show the Russians "the fineness of a Japanese officer"; the rest, he saved for his wife. Boarding vehicles, the major and his comrades headed for the center of no-man's-land where the first talks were to take place.

It was approximately 4:30 P.M. on 16 September when Nyūmura reached the rendezvous, bearing a large white flag on a long pole. A Soviet first lieutenant showed up, but he was carrying a tiny pole and a white handkerchief that was one-quarter the size of Nyūmura's streamer. The Russian called, "Welcome! Welcome!" No other officer was visible, so Nyūmura started to walk forward, watched by dozens of Soviet soldiers. After exchanging greetings, the lieutenant invited Nyūmura to enter the Russian lines, where simple wire barriers had already been erected. Nyūmura declined. It seemed to him that the Russians were staging a tableau to make it look as if the Japanese had been beaten and had surrendered. For perhaps a half-hour, the two officers argued politely about the niceties of the situation, Nyūmura insisting that, since he had walked so far, military etiquette required that the lieutenant "come out" to meet him, while the Russian kept asking him to "come in."

Behind the Soviet lieutenant, four senior officers had appeared: a colonel of infantry and three lieutenant colonels from the air force, armor, and artillery. They all looked resplendent to Nyūmura—clean, neatly pressed, and sharp—whereas he felt ashamed of his beard. Glaring at him, the Russian colonel asked if he represented General Ogisu or the Kwantung Army. Nyūmura replied that he came from Ogisu and inquired if the colonel was acquainted with the diplomatic accord reached in Moscow. The colonel said he was, adding that that was why his troops were just standing around and comporting themselves well. "Look at your men," grumbled the Russian. "They're not behaving." Nyūmura looked back and, to his chagrin, saw IJA soldiers standing on their trenches, waving Japanese flags.

All of the Russian team, however, continued to invite Nyūmura to join them at their headquarters. They had a fine car, they said, and tea and cakes were waiting. Nyūmura claimed he would need orders from Ogisu. As a Japanese soldier, he was thinking, he must not knuckle under; honor was involved. In any case, the atmosphere was amiable and Nyūmura knew that basic agreement had been reached in Moscow. The initial meeting ended with the Japanese officer's enthusiastic remarks: "The fighting has ended, anyhow. Let's talk about details tomorrow. Please come to our side then." The Russians agreed. Nyūmura saluted and went back.

The second of the preliminary conversations proceeded next day, 17 September, on schedule, and the agenda for the main delegates' conference was worked out without difficulty. In view of Nyūmura's and Tanaka's ranks, however, it seemed "a sort of insult" that the Russians sent a young lieutenant or captain as their advance man. A smiling political officer, he struck Nyūmura as a sly "wise guy."

Between 18 and 23 September the full delegations met, six days in a row. Before the first such session, each side sent a sergeant, under a white flag, to agree on the meeting site. When the two noncoms met, the IJA military policeman tried out his Russian. "Don't you think that Japanese soldiers are brave?" he asked. The Soviet sergeant answered him in Japanese: "Don't be a jerk (*bakayarō*)! We won the war!"[26]

Major General Fujimoto, the Sixth Army chief of staff, headed the Japanese delegation to the Noro Heights location where a bell-shaped tent had been set up, midway between the two armies. Fujimoto's ten subordinates included Col. Kimura Matsujirō, the 23rd Division's new chief of staff; Maj. Shimamura Noriyasu, formerly of the AGS Operations Section and now on the Kwantung Army staff; Maj. Ōgoshi Kenji, a Kwantung Army intelligence officer; and Major Nyūmura to interpret. Col. M. I. Potapov, Zhukov's deputy who had commanded the Southern Force in the August offensive, attended with eight officers. Both parties drove to the rendezvous, parked their vehicles three kilometers from the conference tent, and walked the remaining distance. From the rear, peering at the scene through binoculars, a Japanese warrant officer was disappointed: the Soviet sedans looked "beautiful," but the Japanese cars were unimpressive, a perhaps typical qualitative difference between the two sides.[27]

During the initial plenary meeting, from 4 to 7:30 P.M. on 18 September, the Japanese achieved a "frank understanding" with the Russians on basic issues. To the Japanese proposal that concrete agreement be concluded to maintain the armistice and prevent misunderstandings, the Soviet delegates voiced no objection. Precise identification of the opposing lines and the exchange of maps were the first order of business. The Russians plotted their cease-fire locations for the Japanese and promised to furnish a reply to the proposal as soon as they received the approval of the senior officer in the district. Essentially it was decided that neither army would reinforce its strength at the front or build up its forward positions.

It was much more difficult to reach agreement on the exchange of prisoners and corpses. Nyūmura recalls how Ogisu had stressed the significance of inducing the enemy to return every last Japanese corpse, even from across the Halha. When Nyūmura had asked how many bodies were involved, the general said "at least 5,000"; it was apparent that even he did not know the exact extent of the casualties. But Nyūmura found it embarrassing when Ogisu inquired about the number of Soviet corpses in IJA possession. They were ridiculously few—not because the Japanese had not slain thousands but because the IJA forces had been forced back and almost all of the enemy dead lay on the other side of the final battle lines. Nyūmura had therefore "beat around the bush" in dealing with the general's question. The problem carried over to the bargaining table. Says Nyūmura: "The enemy had won, and everybody realized it." Knowing that the Japanese had few of their corpses to swap, the Russians suggested an equal exchange. It was hard to cope with the Soviet argument, although Nyūmura had the impression that the Russians did not really mean to limit the number but intended merely to exert pressure. Finally the Russians backed down, first asking how many bodies the Japanese wanted back, and then offering to return them all. According to Fujimoto's report, the Soviet delegation proposed, "in all sincerity," that every corpse and every prisoner be exchanged within one week or so, in the truce zone midway between both forces. They would provide information on the locations of the corpses, said the Russians, and, since they had many trucks, they would deliver the bodies to the Japanese.

There was much more to the problem, however, from the point of view of the Japanese, who wanted to unearth and transport their own dead. The real reason was not only to retrieve the corpses but also to salvage critical items that had been buried or hidden at overrun regimental headquarters— e.g., footlockers (*gunyō kōri*) containing classified documents, after-action diaries, and rosters; and, most important, parts of missing unit colors. The Russians refused to allow Japanese search parties inside their lines, where they had already constructed secret new positions.

At this point, clever Major Ōgoshi whispered in Nyūmura's ear: "Let's use religion!" Thereupon the Japanese accused the Russians of atheism and stressed that Buddhism strictly required that the Japanese attend to their own dead. It was proposed that unarmed IJA soldiers be allowed to collect the bodies lying in areas controlled by the Soviet forces. According to Nyūmura, the Russians asked the Japanese to wait two hours until they could obtain an answer from their headquarters. In an hour and a half, approval was received. By agreeing that religion was important after all, Zhukov had demonstrated, says Nyūmura, that he was more of a military man than a "real Communist," and his action won the Japanese major's honest respect.[28]

The core of the local truce agreement emerged in the form of a joint communiqué released after a three-hour conference on 19 September that was marked by the full cooperation of the Soviet representatives. Both local commands recognized the Tōgō-Molotov cease-fire accord; combat action was henceforth suspended.[29] Neither front-line army was to be reinforced or to strengthen existing forward installations. As a means of certifying the cease-fire line, the two sides would exchange maps indicating their respective advance locations. The present line was established only for cease-fire purposes, however, and had no bearing on the ultimate problem of definitive frontier demarcation.

Under the supervision of representatives from all the units on both sides, corpses would be exchanged at designated midpoint locations on the Halha battlefield between 21 and 25 September. Soviet prisoners in Japanese hands were to be delivered by truck to the rendezvous in no-man's-land. The handling of Japanese prisoners in Soviet custody became the subject of considerable discussion and led to an obvious face-saving gesture by the Russians. In the words of the communiqué, the Japanese prisoners were very few and all were severely wounded, so it would be difficult to move them by truck. Consequently Soviet military aircraft would deliver them to the front, where they would be turned over to the Japanese. The exchange of prisoners would commence immediately and be concluded within one week.[30]

The remaining four local parleys were concerned essentially with the technical details of implementation. During the meeting of 20 September, however, the Russians raised the matter of several Soviet deserters and detainees taken by the Japanese in instances mainly unconnected with the Nomonhan affair. The problem was referred to the civilian diplomats.[31] Throughout the parleys, the atmosphere was genial, and the Japanese discerned no antagonism in Soviet attitude or speech. Polite and conciliatory, the Russians seemed anxious to complete the main business of the discussions on the spot, at a time when at least a million Soviet troops were involved in the invasion of eastern Poland. In fact, when the serious local talks were over, the Russians threw a lavish party replete with champagne and vodka toasts, caviar and hors d'oeuvres heaped on tables, and female-soldier dancing partners. There was even one "crasher": AGS Colonel Inada, whom Potapov would not encourage to practice his French but whom a secret-police (NKVD) general favored with small talk.[32] It was a gala finale to a four-month-long small war that had cost no fewer than 30,000 and perhaps as many as 65,000 casualties on both sides.

CLEARING THE BATTLEFIELD

The search for and retrieval of the Japanese corpses began in earnest on 22 September, but the grisly task was too big to be completed by the 25th and went on for a week, until the 28th or even the 30th at some sites. In all, 4,386 bodies were recovered. Undoubtedly there were even more to be found, particularly those who had fallen alone and those who were lying in geographically inaccessible places or in areas declared off-limits by the security-conscious, ever-watchful Russians. Free movement was never allowed. In the Heights 758 district south of Uzuru pond, where the fighting had been particularly costly for IJA heavy artillery and infantry units around 30 August, Russian troops blocked a thorough search. They deliberately guided the Japanese through low terrain to prevent observation of their positions, and they asked the searchers not to look around. Cameras and binoculars were prohibited.[33]

The Soviets were also sticklers for detail. In the 27th Infantry's sector, the first morning's activity had to be called off when a time-consuming roll call revealed 101 instead of 100 men in the search party. Using hand flags, Russian troops posted at strategic intervals strictly directed and guided IJA truck columns through gateways in the barbed wire. There often seemed to be one Soviet guard for every Japanese laborer. In the 71st Infantry's zone, the watch grew slacker after a while. At first, the Russians ringed the unarmed searchers with tanks and machine guns. The armor disappeared on the third day or so; the machine guns, on the fourth day. By the fifth day, both sides began talking in friendly fashion. The Russians gave cigarettes to the Japanese and took photographs. Battery commander Tsuchiya explains the improvement in relations in his particular clearing sector. At first, some of the Russian guards had laughed at the IJA searchers, causing a Japanese officer to protest. An NKVD major reprimanded the disrespectful soldiers, and the atmosphere improved next day. Thereafter the Soviet troops saluted whenever Japanese crews bowed to the dead or headed back after a day's work.[34]

Although there were local variations, basically the recovery teams were restricted in size and were supposed to include no officers (or not more than one per 50 or 100 men). But since officers generally knew the terrain best and were most aware of what they were looking for (including intelligence as well as bodies), a goodly number of them put on enlisted men's uniforms and went with the troops. Komatsubara heard of a devoted regiment commander who even participated. One brand-new battalion commander, disguised as a soldier, was scolded by a subordinate, who did not recognize him, for handling his entrenching tool ineptly. Similar cases occurred.

There were four main areas of search: Fui Heights on the north, the old right-wing sector in the vicinity of Uzuru, the Izumi bend in the Holsten, and the site of the left-wing unit on the south, where the battles of 24-25 August had raged. Tight discipline and stability were imperative, lest incidents flare up in the presence of the Russians. Tsuchiya says he had trouble finding unemotional men for his search teams; some of his soldiers were already too neurotic to be chosen.[35]

Until the onset of the Soviet offensive of 20 August, the Japanese line units had been able to retrieve many of their combat dead. Frequently it had been possible to hack off and tag fingers or whole hands for purposes of improvised, covert field cremation in the rear, pending the hoped-for recovery of the entire bodies.[36] When feasible, the corpses had been put in holes, sometimes in layers with tarpaulin between to retard decomposition. Victims of the latest fighting often lay where they had fallen. In places, the Russians had already collected and buried IJA bodies in mass graves, stacked up like railroad ties.

Eager to retrieve as many of their slain comrades as possible, the Japanese search teams were confronted by numbers that nearly doubled their worst expectations. Originally, it had been thought that only a total of 2,500-2,600 bodies would be found, but 500 to 600 were being picked up each day. During combat, troops were ordinarily too keyed-up to indulge in emotion, but now the sensations were unnerving. There were heartrending death scenes sometimes bordering on the supernatural, depicting self-sacrifice and devotion to comrades, flags, and units. But there were also wretched sights of gore: dismembered or shattered corpses, remains of deformed men who had been run over by tanks or incinerated by flamethrowers. Inasmuch as the bodies had been exposed to the elements for as many as five weeks, the unit doctors warned the men not to touch the rotting flesh directly—an injunction that was usually forgotten in practice. When a portion of a body was found, it was tugged from the earth, and the rest was clawed out by hand. Odors of decomposing flesh were so bad that the crews could not eat at first, even if they had wanted to. When the recovery teams got back to camp at sunset, having labored without stop, they would bathe in old oil drums, but it was impossible to expunge the pervasive smell. It took days to get used to the stench of death.[37]

Japanese medical examinations reported that the recovered corpses were decomposed to varying degree, and that there was evidence of some physical assaults—e.g., a case of decapitation. Many of the fatal wounds had been caused by shell fragments; there were also a considerable number of burns by flamethrowers. Other than that, no deaths were the result of "special new weapons."[38]

Locating and extricating slain Japanese commanders was of the highest priority. In the case of infantry regiment commanders, not only were they important in their own right but also the fate of their colors would undoubtedly be determined once they were found. Major Suzuki of the 23rd Division staff addressed this problem from the beginning. Familiar with the terrain where the 64th Infantry and 13th Field Artillery had met their ends, an artillery warrant officer put on the uniform of a PFC and joined the team that was probing the area above the Holsten. Inside a small shelter, partly buried in earth and sand, the bodies of Colonels Yamagata and Ise and of an aide were found, all suicides by pistol fire. Since the Russian overseers were particularly sensitive about the recovery of ranking officers, the search crew tried to act nonchalant as they loaded the commanders' bodies in the corner of a truck. Their work was helped by the fact that no swords, briefcases, or documents lay by the bodies; only Ise's notebook was found. The corpses were trucked back to their regiments for proper cremation.[39]

There are two sidelights to the field clearance operation. First, lost IJA ordnance and equipment were not extricated. As Tsuchiya says, "Not a scrap of iron was left on the field." Second, no Soviet corpses were found.[40] Nevertheless, the Russians made a much-appreciated gesture; they voluntarily returned the bodies of 55 Japanese air force officers and men, and of four other soldiers, retrieved from the west side of the Halha.[41]

Identification of corpses posed an often insoluble problem. The mass graves dug by the Russians were marked by a stick and an arabic number merely telling how many dead lay there. After the mangled, faceless bodies had been brought out, teams sought to match the names on their rosters with leggings, personal belongings, notebooks, uniforms, and the serial numbers on dog tags. But it was a rather rare tag that survived. Many men had taken them off because of hot weather. Others, when death was near, buried their dog tags and burned their notes and correspondence lest the enemy be able to identify the remains. Nyūmura asserts that the Russians tried to remove every I.D. tag they could lay their hands on. Japanese in Moscow later saw such dog tags on display in a Soviet museum.[42]

Some IJA commanders had unique ways of identifying their slain. A regimental gun platoon leader in the 26th Infantry used to cut off both hands of every dead man in his unit and try to erect a marker where the body lay, using a board from a breadbox or something similar. When this lieutenant left the battlefield, he took the hands with him in fuze boxes for eventual cremation and transmission of the ashes to the bereaved, and he could also say that "any corpses picked up without hands belonged to my unit."[43] In general, however, it was impossible to guarantee that the jumbled crematory urns contained the remains of the particular dead whose names were inscribed on them, contrary to what had been taught in school or was believed in the homeland. As one young officer explained, "It was quite possible that your ashes might be delivered to my family and be called my ashes."[44]

The corpses were cremated daily at Nomonhan, at four sites, for a week; smoke from the pyres blotted out the sky. At Chiangchunmiao on 2 October, Komatsubara wrote that 200-300 men had been searching for bodies and a similar number were engaged in cremation, but that the job was still incomplete. First the bodies were laid out in rows, by the hundreds, after the search crews had brought back their doleful loads for the day. Once, near sunset, a sedan flying a general's flag pulled up. The general emerged and, with tears moistening his cheeks, moved slowly among the lines of dead, saluting them as he passed. It was division commander Komatsubara.[45]

Apart from the earnest attempts to identify the slain, special efforts were made to divest them of ammunition and live grenades. The first cremation, however, demonstrated the ever-present danger. On 24 September, an officer and a noncom were killed by explosions. Afterward, participants in the rites moved away from the bodies once the funeral fires were lit. Explosions continued to occur. Sumi explains that when line units were in extremis, hand grenades were issued to every man, including the wounded. When the individual soldier was down to his last two grenades, he would hurl one and try to blow himself up with the other, to prevent the disgrace of capture alive. Often the troops were killed before they could accomplish their intentions. Left to rot for weeks in the hot sun and the chill nights, the corpses disintegrated, as we saw, and the grenades would fall into a deep body cavity, where they sometimes defied the most careful searches.[46]

At the cremation sites, rows of shallow pits were dug behind dunes. Engineers provided firewood on which the bodies were stacked on their backs, 50 cm. apart, atop crisscrossed tiers built up to chest height. A typical hole contained the remains of two officers or four men. The bodies would be doused with gasoline, soldier priests would chant Buddhist prayers, and the watching troops would bow low and clasp their hands in silent veneration. A signal to light the fires would be given and cremation would commence. The process went on for at least three or four hours but, in view of the scale of the effort and the consequent hurry, some bodies were not entirely incinerated. Generally, however, "beautiful white bones" emerged, which the troops picked up with chopsticks made from willow branches and inserted into the customary white wooden boxes. When possible, mementos such as amulets, watches, and personal effects were enclosed in the urn. But there was a great shortage of wood boxes, and cloth sacks or comfort-kit wrappings (*imonbukuro*) had to be used. Since incense was in short supply too, the men resorted to mosquito-repellent coils.[47]

The funeral ceremonies and final review for 64th Regiment commander Yamagata on 24 September were particularly moving, conducted by his successor, Col. Ōnishi Koshirō, and attended by the new division chief of staff, Col. Kimura Matsujirō. Under the stars, wild flowers were arranged in empty cans, votive offerings were placed in the altar tent, candles were lit, *sutras* were chanted, and every officer presented smoking joss sticks.[48]

The Kwantung Army commander had sent a preliminary message to AGS Chief Kan'in and War Minister Hata on 8 September, "with a sense of enormous awe," reporting that the colors of the 64th and 71st regiments had been burned on 29-30 August and that both commanders were dead.[49] Nevertheless, there was intense private worry lest the swirling battle situation had prevented complete destruction of the precious colors bestowed personally upon all infantry regiments by the Emperor. Ueda's repeated pleas for a new offensive had envisaged not only recovery of the slain but also salvation of any remnants of the flags. Komatsubara was particularly grieved by the loss of colors on the part of two of his three infantry regiments. Never in IJA history, not even in the most costly battles of the Sino-Japanese or Russo-Japanese wars, the general wrote in agony to his wife, had regiments lost their flags. The only instance he could think of was Nogi's experience at Taharazaka in the civil war of 1877. Of course the tragedies that befell Yamagata and Higashi were entirely unavoidable under the circumstances, but Komatsubara shared the Kwantung Army commander's feelings of dread at having discomfited the Emperor.[50]

Therefore, as mentioned earlier, divisional staff officer Suzuki bent every effort to investigate the whereabouts of the colors and the commanders, as soon as the cease-fire salvage operation began. On 24 September, when a party came across Yamagata's body, underneath it lay the lower half of the regimental standard and the blackened remnants of the tassels of the colors. Apparently the colonel and those around him had not been able to burn the standard completely and had had to bury what was left. Search soldiers also located and surreptitiously dug out the chrysanthemum globe, scarred by a shell fragment and embedded in the legs of 2nd Lieutenant Koyama's corpse. For the moment, the bodies were left where they were, unmarked, while the remains of the colors were collected; only then did the men come back for the officers' corpses.[51]

As for the 71st Regiment, veteran Captain Hanada was asked by Suzuki to look for its colors. Dressed as a corporal, Hanada went with the team that was working the sector of Higashi's last charge. The pennon would have to be sought inside the shelters of the regiment, but Soviet surveillance was very tight. Hanada pretended to have to go off and answer nature's call, which allowed about a half-hour to dig unnoticed. Happily for the Japanese, no trace of the colors or of the standard could be detected. Higashi had successfully accomplished his sad task.[52]

Colonel Ōnishi hand-carried the chrysanthemum crest and the burned fringes from the 64th Regiment's flag back to Tokyo and delivered them to the war ministry on 21 October. War Minister Hata never forgot the pitiful sight of the blackened shreds, which he escorted to the Palace. At the High Command level, there was much discussion whether both infantry regiments should be disbanded. Eventually, in response to "strong sentiment expressed by the field forces," it was decided to ask the Emperor to bestow new colors on the two regiments, and a special rescript was accordingly issued.[53] Although the mystique of military corporateness is universal and well understood, critics have regarded the Japanese army's fanatical devotion to colors as excessive if not bordering on the "insane."[54]

The Japanese toll at Nomonhan was worsened by the fact that IJA officers and men were never supposed to be taken alive, whatever the reason. The Imperial Precepts to Soldiers and Sailors, for example, did not even mention the problem of becoming a prisoner. When addressing the duty of loyalty, the code merely stated: "Never by failing in moral principle fall into disgrace and bring dishonor upon your name."[55] In practice, the situation was complicated by various unanticipated developments that arose during the fluid warfare in the flatlands—for instance, the disintegration of the command structure, the blundering into hostile lines on the part of disoriented or dazed soldiers, and the inability to extricate wounded men, whether unconscious or conscious but helpless. A lieutenant who was not captured explains the plight of those who were. At the time of the Japanese retreat from the right side of the Holsten, enemy tanks were "on our tail, chasing us like sparrows," without even firing. Those soldiers who still had rifles were too weak to carry them any longer. Exhausted in body and soul, the famished men tried to subsist on weeds. When they fell, they were ignored by their helpless comrades and left to their fate on the field. Some were captured, maimed, after trying to kill each other with bayonets. Others fell into enemy hands after days of dragging themselves toward friendly lines.[56]

Although suicide was not specifically stipulated as a legal option, the Japanese army certainly could draw on a range of coercions and punishments in dealing with the prisoner who survived. Still, the most overpowering sanctions derived from the moral climate of the armed forces and society, the conventions governing social interaction in the setting of "total institutions."[57] A soldier who accepted captivity was deemed to have brought eternal shame to Emperor, homeland, community, and family. Universal abandonment and rejection, engendered by military inculcation and societal psychology, were the price of ignominious survival. The prisoner was morally "dead"; he might as well be physically dead too. One's peers openly despised the "miscreant." It is said that, during the fighting at Nomonhan, the Russians used some IJA prisoners to haul water from the river and that Japanese troops who witnessed the scene sniped at the captives because of their "exposure of Japanese shame, . . . despising the cowards who would not even commit suicide."[58]

The misery that might afflict the family of a suspected prisoner is exemplified by the experience of the widow of an excellent battalion commander, Major Ikuta of the 26th Infantry. Ikuta had actually fought to the last and, after four days and four nights, had been killed on 27 August. But at her residence in Harbin, his wife was tormented into September by a rumor that the major had been captured alive, a particular disgrace for an officer. When word finally came that her husband's body had been found after the cease-fire, Mrs. Ikuta shed tears of relief.[59] In the case of one enlisted man who had been reported killed in action, his village was preparing a formal funeral in 1940. The regimental district commander, however, first notified the soldier's father to wait, and then called him in privately and said: "To tell you the truth, your son is a prisoner. But keep it to yourself and do not mention it to anybody else in the family." The soldier in question later remarked that the whole episode "caused lots of trouble for my kinfolk."[60]

In view of the anathema attaching to prisoners, it is understandable that the army often preferred to list them as killed in action, for the presumable benefit of all concerned. Estimates in various sources range from 1,000 to 4,000 Japanese POW's, the most credible figure being over 3,000.[61] On a special train from Ulan Bator to Chita in 1939, according to one returnee, there must have been several thousand IJA prisoners. A Japanese officer (who shot himself after repatriation) remarked on the train, "What a huge number!" When an assembly was convened in Chita in 1940, there were easily 500-600 Japanese prisoners in one compound, the highest-ranking being an air force colonel and an army major.[62] Early the same year, a Polish army prisoner, captured by the Russians in September 1939, was told when he passed Semipalatinsk by train en route to central Asian detention that, according to local rumor, large numbers of Japanese prisoners were or had been in camp there.[63]

Japanese military records on the taboo subject of prisoners vary from unit to unit. The Sixth Army's data depict a total of 19 officers and 1,002 men missing (see Table 39.1). But whereas the 23rd Division's missing are listed by the Sixth Army as only four officers and 345 men, the division's own tabulation showed 639 missing, most particularly in the 71st Infantry Regiment (359), the 64th Infantry (113), the 72nd Infantry (54), and the 13th Field Artillery (98). (See Appendix K.) Although the 7th Division does not distinguish between dead and missing, the Sixth Army shows two officers and 343 men in the latter category. Major Kajikawa's 2nd Battalion of the 28th Regiment provides much greater detail (see Appendix N). As for Hata's heavy artillery command, the Sixth Army reports eight officers and 203 soldiers missing in action. Captain Tsuchiya supplies data on this category for the 1st Battalion of Mishima's 1st Heavy Field Artillery Regiment: battalion headquarters, 18 men; 1st Battery, 14; 2nd Battery, 8; maintenance unit, 0; battalion total, 40 enlisted men.[64]

Whereas from the IJA standpoint the Russians had treated the matter of the corpses with "utmost sincerity," exchanging prisoners was another matter. By the terms of the local cease-fire, the Japanese expected to return the relatively few Russians they had captured, and to receive every one of their own men in Soviet custody, even though the disparity in numbers would be enormous. The Russians ignored the agreement, refused to disclose the quantity of IJA prisoners in their hands, and plainly decided to exchange captives on a one-for-one basis. Complicating the problem was the fact that a large but unknown number of Japanese replacement personnel had disappeared before they could be integrated into their assigned units. In addition, after the cease-fire, some Japanese soldiers had wandered into the Soviet lines; most were not released, despite Japanese pleas. Sixth Army Colonel Hamada regrets that he did not institute tighter traffic-control measures because he was preoccupied with the retrieval of corpses at the time.[65]

In the event, on 27 September, the Japanese turned over their 87 Soviet prisoners. It seems that the Russians waited to see how many of their men were coming back before they released a like number—88 personnel, including five Manchurians—on the 27th and 28th.[66] According to Simonov's fictionalized account, there was a rather unpleasant scene: some of the Japanese POW's misbehaved, and the Japanese also alleged that the Russians had not given them the right times or made the right arrangements; one IJA soldier, however, was carried to a transport plane supposedly shouting "Long live the Japanese and Russian proletariat!"[67]

As for the Soviet prisoners, Nyūmura escorted them from the stockade at

Harbin to the exchange point. There, marching in two lines toward their destination, the Russian POW's hurriedly left on the grass anything Japanese that had been issued to them—toothbrushes, towels, paper, and so forth. Potapov greeted the men and thanked them for their labors, whereupon they all yelled "Hurrah for Potapov!" in unison. Whereas the Japanese POW's were downcast and ashamed, the Russians were happy, elated, and proud. As they left aboard their trucks, they began singing a military song. Nyūmura is convinced that the Soviet consul in Harbin had contacted the Russian prisoners beforehand, probably through agents, and had convinced them that they would not be punished but would be rewarded for having fought well. None of the POW's chose to stay behind. Nyūmura was not impressed by the well-orchestrated performance; in the Stalinist era, hard times undoubtedly lay ahead for the repatriated Russian soldiers.[68]

Fifty of the Japanese-Manchurian POW's were wounded. Soviet medical treatment appeared to have been good, according to IJA doctors; items such as splints were even better than Japanese. Nevertheless, some of the men were on the brink of death, and three expired immediately after their return.

At first, a lenient policy was going to be applied, and the apprehensive Japanese prisoners settled down after entering hospital. The central authorities, however, decided otherwise. A special facility was established at Kirin, where strict interrogation was to be conducted. All of the medical personnel at the Hsinking branch hospital were replaced by handpicked officers and men, although patients were supposed to be treated as such. To the displeasure of the IJA doctors, military police dressed as medics carried out the "investigations." Of the 50 wounded, 29 said they had been captured while unconscious. The unhurt men had lost their way and blundered into enemy hands. A considerable number of prisoners were still incarcerated at Chita.[69]

In Moscow, Tōgō pressed for the return of all POW's, including 13 men under a Captain Katō who had entered Soviet territory by mistake after the cease-fire. On 26 October, the Russians countered with a "matching" list of 12 more individuals they wanted back, including two mail-plane crewmen who had crash-landed and been seized in Manchuria in 1937, a man lost in central China that same year, two soldiers who had deserted at the time of the Changkufeng fighting, and three men detained by the Japanese during the Nomonhan war. At a meeting on 19 November, Tōgō told Molotov that improvement in relations between their two countries was being hampered by the misunderstanding about POW exchange that had occurred during the local truce parleys. All prisoners connected with the Nomonhan affair, except deserters, should be released. Molotov said that he agreed but that, in addition to a Soviet captain and second lieutenant and a Mongolian soldier who were still in Japanese hands, there were 25 or 30 Russians who had been taken along the Manchurian borders in 1937-38. With their release, all Japanese prisoners could be returned too. To Tōgō's suggestion that the topic of detainees might be better addressed closer to the scene—perhaps at Harbin—once basic agreement on POW's was reached in Moscow, Molotov answered that separation of the two categories of prisoner made sense. The commissar implied, however, that the freeing of the three Soviet-MPRA individuals (who, he insisted, were not deserters) would lead to the release of more than 100 Japanese and Manchurian prisoners.

The diplomatic discussions seemed to be progressing when, on 1 December, Tōgō offered to arrange the swapping of the three Soviet-Mongolian military men for Captain Katō's party and the additional prisoners mentioned by Molotov. Only the place and time for the release needed to be fixed. The commissar referred the matter to his deputy, Lozovsky. At a subsequent meeting on 3 December, however, Lozovsky would not agree to the previously suggested level of exchange. The Russians had obtained reliable information, he insisted, to the effect that the Japanese in Manchuria were holding several dozen prisoners in addition to the three already identified by the Soviet side.

Next year, on 11 March 1940, Lozovsky advised Tōgō that the Russians were willing to let 40-50 Japanese prisoners go in return for the two Soviet officers, and wanted to decide on a date. Still, arrangements should be made to release detainees antedating the Nomonhan affair, in which case Moscow was the most appropriate site of negotiation. When the picture became clearer, the Russians would discuss the exchange of the remaining Japanese-Manchurian POW's. Tōgō responded that he had been awaiting detailed information on the several dozen detainees mentioned by Lozovsky in December but that, according to their own investigations, the Japanese had found they held only the two mail-plane crewmen, an air force captain, and 20 "political deserters." Could all the POW's now be released? Lozovsky did not agree. No reconciliation of the contentions was forthcoming when Tōgō visited Molotov on 17 March. Soon afterward, however, the Russians backed down completely. On 26 March, they supplied the names of 45 Japanese and Manchurian prisoners they would set free and, on 15 April, the names of another 71. The Japanese would only have to release the two Soviet officers, the MPRA soldier having died in the meantime.[70] Arita, foreign minister in the new Yonai government formed in January, laughed when he spoke with Baron Harada on 20 April: "We are getting about 110 prisoners back but we have only two to give the Russians. Such a fact cannot even be admitted to the press!"[71]

In the Chita prison camp, on 26 April, designated Japanese POW's were unexpectedly told of their impending release. Wearing the clothing on their backs and carrying a few personal belongings, they were put aboard an ancient train in the dark, bound for the border northwest of Hailar. Next day at 1 P.M., in the square in front of a station on the Russian side of the frontier, Sixth Army Chief of Staff Fujimoto and his staff, waiting with trucks, shook hands with Soviet representatives and accepted 77 Japanese prisoners (including the strayed Captain Katō) plus 39 Manchurians, one by one. A pair of Soviet POW's were released to the Russians, as agreed.[72]

For the Japanese, it was not a pleasant scene. All of the POW's kept their eyes down, avoided looking at Fujimoto's reception committee, and uttered not a word. Pale and wan, they were wearing the same dirty uniforms in which they had been captured six months earlier. Many of the men were severely wounded and could not climb aboard the trucks without the help of the Japanese military police. Fujimoto's team was particularly saddened by the appearance of the blind and of those without arms or legs, as they tried to support each other. Obviously, such helpless soldiers had even lacked the strength to commit suicide when overwhelmed on the battlefield.

The Japanese trucks bearing the POW's detoured around Manchouli and headed for a train station in the suburbs. En route, some IJA infantrymen could be seen training in the field, but their commanders ordered them to look at the ground, not at the miserable prisoners. At the station, the POW's were helped off the trucks and processed as quickly as possible; there was hardly time to transliterate each man's name from the Cyrillic letters and phonetic *kana* syllabary identifying him. Drawn up in formation, the prisoners were first addressed by Fujimoto in remarkably humane terms. The general said he was sure they had done their best before capture, and he extended his sympathy to them. Their superiors would henceforth treat them as "returned wounded soldiers," so there was no need to worry any longer or to contemplate taking rash action—i.e., committing suicide. The men must have suffered for a long time, but now they could "rest easy and sleep tight from tonight on." They would be sent to an army hospital west of Kirin, where they would be treated and nursed back to health. There were tears in the eyes of the prisoners when Fujimoto concluded by extending his thanks (*gokurō*). Military patients' white gowns replaced the shabby clothing, and the men, greatly relieved, got ready to leave for Kirin aboard a clean hospital train.

The merciful respite afforded the Japanese prisoners did not last very long. Pending receipt of the list of names from the Russians, Fujimoto had not known the identity of those who were being released, but one of his main fears was that officer personnel might be included. In fact, the POW contingent included two air force pilots, both military academy graduates: Maj. Harada Fumio, the 1st Air Group commander shot down on 29 July and presumed dead; and 1st Lt. Daitoku Naoyuki of the 11th Group.[73] The latter's face was badly burned; he had been captured while unconscious.

One wonders whether Daitoku or Harada was the Japanese "ace" who, according to Zhukov, was shot down by Senior Lt. V. G. Pakhov, a Hero of the Soviet Union, during a fierce dogfight on 29 July. Pakhov set fire to the enemy fighter plane, whose pilot escaped by parachute but tried to commit suicide when he came down in Outer Mongolian territory.[74] Captured and nursed to recovery, the Japanese aviator asked his captors to introduce him to the skillful Soviet pilot who had shot him down. On meeting Pakhov, he bowed low "in tribute to the victor."[75]

Since Fujimoto was anxious to allay Harada's and Daitoku's uneasiness and possible suicide at this initial stage, members of the reception team brought the officers wine, chocolates, and fruit. After having been kept in a dark room for more than half a year, Daitoku stretched out on the grass now and remarked upon the beauty of the sunlight. But when Harada was thanked for his efforts, the major replied that he was no longer among the living and that he had already reached a profound resolve—namely, to kill himself in due course. In the meantime, he was willing to discuss his battle experiences and captivity.

Harada and Daitoku were sent with the other prisoners to the Shintan hospital at Kirin. Military police guarded both ends of the train, and the doors to the toilets were always kept open, to reduce the possibility of suicide. Delivered to the hospital in the middle of the night, the men were placed in rooms with tightly closed windows. Most of the medical personnel were actually *kenpei* (MP's). Preliminary hearings centered on the circumstances of capture. On the eve of trial, some say, medics were seen carrying two coffins into the hospital. Even the *kenpei* guards were forbidden to go near the officers' rooms. Then the sound of pistol fire was heard. Harada and Daitoku had been driven to suicide.[76] By all accounts, Harada had been given a loaded pistol and a Japanese publication that ominously described his "heroic death in action" at Nomonhan. A *kenpei* respondent understood that the officers were issued weapons after a six-hour special hearing in closed session.[77]

Air staff officer Miyoshi, who had been talking earnestly with Harada and Daitoku, confirmed the two officers' deaths. Grieved when he heard the news in Hailar, an OSS agent who had served on the reception committee asked about the rationale. His branch chief asserted that "mockery of the gods" had been involved: to be allowed to enter the national shrine at Yasukuni as a slain war hero required imperial authorization; returning alive meant disrespect to both Throne and shrine; only death could resolve the contradiction. Arguing that it was the fault of reporting authorities and not of the returnees—a mere matter of paperwork—and that it seemed better to be listed as missing than as dead, the OSS agent was told that he had a point. Nevertheless, he should not try to judge the actions of his superiors, and he should keep his thoughts to himself.[78]

Some details of the Japanese prisoners' life at Kirin have been reconstructed from the vantage point of a *kenpei* soldier stationed at Kungchuling. Matters of POW's were handled with extreme secrecy; even in the military police unit, only superiors said anything about them. The first the *kenpei* soldier heard about the exchange of April 1940 was when a plainclothes sergeant came in wearing an infantry uniform and carrying a rifle. He was going to Manchouli to escort prisoners lost at Nomonhan. A week later, the sergeant returned but said not a word concerning his trip. Soon afterward, an MP superior private disappeared for about a month and a half. It turned out that he had been dispatched to the army hospital not far from Kirin station, in the guise of a medic, to investigate the speech and behavior of the Nomonhan POW's. Finally, the *kenpei* soldier himself was assigned to the hospital, in uniform, on police duty.

At the Shintan facility, guarded by MP's, there were 40 or 50 soldiers in a central ward, and two or three officers in private rooms. No one wore insignia—only white name patches. About seven cell-like cubicles had been improvised for men adjudged to have been particularly culpable. Those wretched inmates were all in a half-dead condition and seemed to be receiving little medical attention. Even the *kenpei* soldier protested to a medic, but in vain. Although the patients in the main ward were apparently in satisfactory shape, they were uneasy about their fates. Two military policemen, conducting round-the-clock surveillance, prevented the exchange of even small talk.[79]

Interrogation of the returned POW's revealed that their Russian captors had made some efforts at indoctrination, particularly among younger personnel. Survivors remember the attempted brainwashing, often conducted one-on-one by the Soviet political staff. There were also nightly lectures. Stress was laid on the contradictions inherent in Japanese national policy and in IJA training. Those who "saw the light" would be given Soviet citizenship, treated well, and allowed to marry. Nyūmura heard that the Russians sent 20 or 30 Japanese textile workers to the woods near a prison camp to sing popular Japanese weavers' songs in chorus, or perhaps to play phonograph recordings of those melodies. They lauded the good life in the USSR, where there were supposedly Japanese girls too. One IJA officer (Captain Katō?), who had been detained after straying across the Soviet cease-fire lines, later told Nyūmura that the Russians made particularly tempting efforts to induce him, an officer, to defect.

Recalcitrant auditors were warned that they would be executed shortly. Many of the captured Japanese soldiers, expecting death and humiliation if they were repatriated anyhow, yielded to the cajolery and the bluffs, as we shall see. One severely wounded acting corporal, however, cleverly exploited his indifference to death and his appearance of greater age than his colleagues to wheedle much better medical attention out of his Japanese-speaking interrogator, an NKVD captain drafted from a university faculty. Intellectually curious but credulous, the Soviet officer "swallowed" many of the IJA corporal's exaggerations and memorized the phony regulations that, he was told, held the Japanese army together.[80]

While in Soviet hands, some of the Japanese POW's were recruited for espionage purposes. Nyūmura asserts that most of the soldiers voluntarily reported the fact and revealed details of identification to be employed and the like. In the case of others, assigned missions were found concealed in the linings of clothing. Such returnees were prosecuted.[81]

The preponderant cause for court-martial, however, was the "crime" of capture in the first place. A few examples will illustrate the attitude of the Japanese army authorities. Air Force Master Sgt. Miyajima Shikō, a seven-year veteran flying a Type 97 fighter of the 24th Group, was shot down on 22 June and managed to ride the plane down. As soon as he emerged from his aircraft, an I-16 fighter strafed and demolished it. Miyajima wandered for four days and nights, without food or water, trying to reach friendly lines. When it drizzled one evening, he tried to suck the moisture from his uniform. At dawn of the fifth day, as he lay senseless on the ground, an Outer Mongolian patrol seized him. Ten agonizing months of captivity followed, during which Miyajima—prevented from escape or suicide—asked to be executed and, when that was denied, joined his cellmates in a hunger strike. For this defiance, Miyajima was placed in solitary confinement in an unheated cell during the depth of winter. His spirit broken, the pilot resigned himself to the grim fate he expected: death in enemy captivity or execution after repatriation.

Returned to Japanese custody in 1940, Miyajima was interrogated and then tried before a court-martial, which, despite its brevity, had the trappings of a trial: judicial and unit staff officers in attendance, cross-examination, and prosecutor's summation. The verdict was inevitable although the penalty remained to be decided. For the alleged crime of "desertion under enemy fire," the unlucky combat pilot was sentenced to two years and 10 months of imprisonment, and demotion to PFC. On 31 December 1942, after 3 ½ years in enemy or Japanese confinement since being shot down, Miyajima was released from the Kwantung Army prison in Hsinking.[82]

Another pitiable victim of the IJA system of punishment was Superior Pvt. Nakayama Hitoshi, a 22-year-old command-team soldier in a machine gun company of the 71st Infantry. Nakayama was critically wounded by Soviet tank fire on 27 August when his company was smashed north of the

Holsten. The survivors tried to drag the unconscious, hemorrhaging soldier on a tent cover for about two days. His carotid artery had been cut, however, and his condition was diagnosed as hopeless. Finally, he was abandoned in a dip, outside a tent packed with wounded men. The last thing that Nakayama, nearly blind and deaf by now, can recall was the distant words of his noncom: "Wait here. We'll come and get you later."

Nakayama regained partial consciousness. The sound of the Japanese machine guns had faded away, to be replaced by the explosions of Soviet grenades hurled at the area of the tent where, by unhappy coincidence, the groaning wounded were lying. Some were killed on the spot. One soldier managed to run away, but Nakayama could not move as the Russians came up and kicked at the corpses and the injured. When Nakayama and some others were found to be alive, Soviet troops carried them away on stretchers. Nakayama expected to be killed, even after the enemy soldiers gave him his first water in days. When a Russian pulled him up to a sitting position, the Japanese private closed his eyes and tried to visualize his family for the last time. No gunfire ensued. Eventually, Nakayama asked the guards to execute him, acting out the slitting of his throat, but they shook their heads. He then experienced the Japanese soldier's usual next sensation: the desire to kill himself. Aboard a truck, he tried to grab a pistol; this time, his hands were bound. Later a Mongolian nurse offered him a drink, which he suspected was poison. Again acting out his preference to be shot, Nakayama was surprised when the nurse laughed and drank the beverage herself. Thereafter the private was tormented by a mixture of feelings: the wish to die versus the attachment to life. In Chita, medical treatment was absent, but suicide proved impossible. Some prisoners vainly tried to bite off their tongues. The captors removed ropes and belts that could have been used by the Japanese to hang themselves.

Finally sent to Manchouli in 1940, Nakayama remembers the repeated injunctions of the Japanese escort team not to act rashly. At the outset of the interrogations, the POW's were assured that they would not be punished, thanks to the special intervention of the Emperor. Therefore they should tell the whole truth, beginning with their capture. Nakayama, of course, was not acquitted, but his court-martial sentence was relatively light. "Distinction, none; confinement, 20 days." No further penalty was exacted and, importantly, no entry was made in his service record.

During his 20 days of arrest, Nakayama was confined to the hospital, where he was obliged to perform no menial labor but sat in the darkened room every day reciting all of the imperial precepts to the armed forces. *Kenpei* guards, always watching, prevented the slightest whispering among patients. It was "a kind of hell," punctuated by suicides. Officers, in particular, were visited by colleagues who left loaded pistols behind. Whenever there was a suicide, the patients became agitated. Nakayama felt miserable that the officers, who had not surrendered willingly, were being forced to kill themselves. Was there no other way? In fact, would it not have been better for the suicides if they had stayed behind in Russia and taken out Soviet citizenship?

As a result of the bleakness of confinement, and suffering from pain, malnutrition, and pressure, Nakayama underwent a certain degree of mental disturbance. Later offered an artificial eardrum, he declined it out of fear of meeting people. When his 20-day sentence was completed, the Kwantung Army *kenpei* commander conducted "spiritual education." The matter of captivity should be concealed from everybody, including parents and kin. Prisoners must never exchange letters and must not extend acknowledgment even when they ran into each other on the street. In the event of violation, the punishments stipulated in the Military Secrets Protection Law would be invoked.[83]

Still another hapless POW was Negishi Chōsaku, an acting corporal in the 1st Heavy Field Artillery Regiment. On the night of 26/27 August the 1st Battalion, to which Negishi belonged, had fired its last few rounds at point-blank range. Colonel Mishima's temporary replacement, Major Umeda, ordered the remnants of the encircled unit to commit suicide, and he set the example by killing himself with a pistol. Negishi, already seriously wounded, had some brief moments of torment. Would his self-destruction benefit the nation? What would happen to his wife and children? A picture of the boys of Aizu, who committed suicide rather than be taken prisoner in the civil war of 1868, flashed through his mind. There were overpowering reasons to go ahead and kill himself: the achievement of his mission, the influence of patriotism, the inevitability of being overrun by enemy tanks (since he was almost helpless anyhow), the prospect of punishment even if flight were possible, and, most importantly, the fact that the unit commander had given the order to die. In any case, says Negishi, he could never have gone through with the act unless he had been somewhat deranged. The survivors proceeded dutifully, in pairs and without insignia, to a trench where they would run each other through with bayonets. Negishi did not even know the name of his partner, a replacement, but they timed their lunge together and each drove his blade straight through the throat of the other.

A befuddled Negishi came to in a Soviet aid station containing Japanese patients. His partner was gone, the bayonet had been pulled from his own throat, and a bandage covered the hole that, he learned later, had barely missed the esophagus. A Russian interpreter told the suffering Negishi, in Japanese, that he was a fool to want to die. The corporal refused to answer questions until his leg and his throat wounds were rebandaged by a nurse.

From the battlefield tents Negishi was moved to Ulan Bator for a month and then to Chita, where he spent the rest of his eight miserable months of captivity.

Once he was back in Japanese hands in 1940, Negishi expected to be tried and shot. The best he could hope for was to be allowed to stay and work in Manchukuo; he could never go home to Japan as a disgraced prisoner of war. In due course, Negishi was court-martialed; the judicial officer, he recalls, wore the white gown of the medical corps. When the proceedings were over, the hitherto stern officer relented, smiled, and praised Negishi for being a fine soldier—i.e., he had tried to commit suicide. His punishment was three days of confinement in a room containing ten other prisoners, "far better than being put in a regimental stockade." After Negishi's brief incarceration, he was transferred to a hospital at Hsinking with other so-called "special returnees." Although he was not demoted, he never received any promotions to which he was entitled.

In the hospital, Negishi underwent one further experience that illuminates the layers of Japanese army thinking at the time. Lt. Col. Kurasawa Kinzaburō, a Kwantung Army staff officer whom he had known as his instructor and as the observation platoon leader in his artillery-unit days, came to visit him. Instead of commiserating, the officer immediately shouted at Negishi for having come back alive after being taken prisoner. The corporal's account of his last moments on the battlefield, however, brought tears to the eyes of Kurasawa, who then apologized for his thoughtless tirade and commended Negishi for possessing an invincible spirit unmatched even by officers.[84]

Japanese noncommissioned or enlisted prisoners, whether or not imprisoned for lengthy periods, were not assigned to their old units—and were certainly not assigned to units in the homeland. It is said that some men were taken into the Manchukuoan army or shipped to the China theater; two ex-POW's were never placed together. Of the specific soldiers mentioned earlier, after release from the hospital the desperately wounded Superior Private Nakayama was sent to a Kwantung Army secret unit that was building bunkers on the remote east Manchurian border north of Mutanchiang —an ideal "hideaway." The status of such exiles was undefined, however; they were neither members of the garrison force itself nor attached civilian employees. Nakayama was told by the commanding general of the unit that he need not do anything but remain until his term of military obligation expired.[85]

Negishi, the corporal who had been captured with a Japanese bayonet in his throat, was asked by Lieutenant Colonel Kurasawa what he would like to do after he was discharged from the army. Because of his "disgrace" at having become a prisoner, Negishi told Kurasawa, he was thinking of remaining in Manchuria under the assumed name that he, like other POW's, had invented for his Russian and Mongolian captors. Kurasawa, however, had a practical suggestion. He would first check with the soldier's regiment and hometown. If Negishi had not been reported as killed, he could return to Japan; otherwise Kurasawa would help to find a job for him in Manchukuo. A couple of days later, Kurasawa came back and told Negishi he was in luck; he had been listed as missing, not dead. Another prisoner, released in the first exchange, had advised an officer that Negishi had been seized too but that, although critically wounded, he had received early treatment and was expected to live. A relieved Negishi decided to go back to Japan after all. His three months in the hospital in Hsinking were followed by transfer for about two years to the Sagamihara army hospital in the Tokyo area, where he remained a patient and was able to receive visitors. On 25 December 1942, Negishi finally went home, 40 months after he had been captured at Nomonhan. Too weak to undertake physical labor, he worked as a baby-sitter most of the time. A policeman came by daily to keep an eye on him. Every day, too, Negishi worshiped before a mortuary tablet that he had made for the dead of Nomonhan.[86]

Evidently, a certain number of discharged POW's were quietly allowed to go back to Japan. Around 1941, one soldier wrote a thank-you note to a Kwantung Army military policeman who had shown kindness to him during the very difficult period of detention at the Kirin hospital. The former prisoner had changed his name and opened a flower shop in Tokyo.[87]

In short, an ineradicable stigma attached to the Japanese prisoner of war. In the absence of a legal basis for condemnation, the authorities had adopted an unofficial but very real policy of forcing officer prisoners to kill themselves—and thereby clear their names—before having to face a full-scale court-martial. Other released prisoners were tried, kept from sight, and silenced, but not executed. Though wounded men got off lightly, the physically unhurt were castigated for having lacked the will to resist or to commit suicide. Judged to have deserted under fire, they were incarcerated for varying terms. Thus the IJA approach was "a handy way of somehow reconciling the conflict between law and the Japanese military's ironclad discipline."[88]

Even four decades later, only a handful of the surviving Nomonhan prisoner returnees are willing to identify themselves and discuss what befell them. Most have tried to forget the blackest time in their lives, including a period of detention in barred cages "like wild beasts," in pilot Miyajima's words. "Until the end of the Pacific War," adds an infantry POW, "I was in agony about my shameful experience, but afterward it became somewhat easier to face." Even so, it took this man a year to brace himself for an interview, over 30 years after the event.[89]

71st Inf. Regt. positions in the Noro Hgts. area, July 1939 (courtesy of BBSS)

Ise Regt. field artillery emplacement near Hgts. 733, 14 July 1939 (courtesy of BBSS)

War Minister Hata Shunroku inspecting a water-purification apparatus, 7 Sept. 1939

Col. Yamagata Takemitsu (right) with Col. Ishii Shirō (left), at Hgts. 733 (Balshagal), 22 July 1939 (courtesy of BBSS)

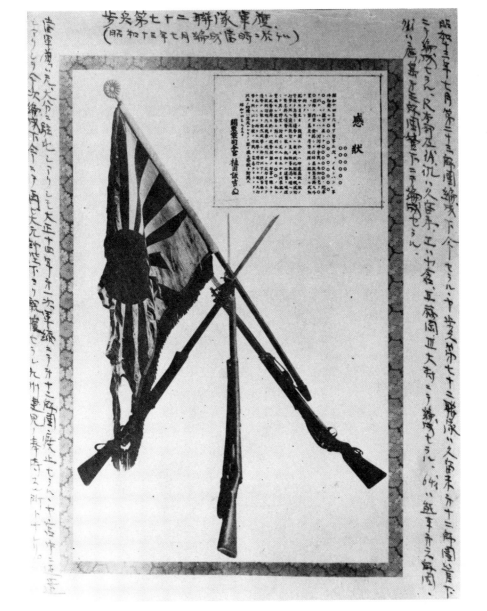

72nd Inf. Regt. colors; inset reproduces citation by General Ueda, 5 Sept. 1939 (courtesy of T. Hamada)

An IJA sergeant (left) and a Soviet sergeant (right) approach each other with white flags, Sept. 1939 (courtesy of M. Nyūmura)

Maj. Gen. Fujimoto Tetsukuma and General Potapov meet, Sept. 1939 (courtesy of M. Nyūmura)

Soviet prisoners being fed (courtesy of N. Tsunashima)

Soviet prisoners being returned, near Iringin, 27 Sept. 1939 (courtesy of BBSS)

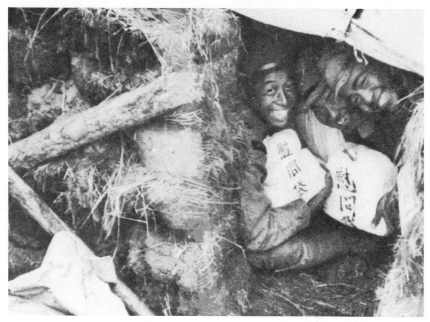

Clutching just-arrived comfort kits, IJA troops welcome news of the cease-fire, Sept. 1939 (author's collection)

After the cease-fire, a makeshift bathtub sees service, Sept. 1939 (author's collection)

An IJA unit commander reciting a eulogy, 20 Sept. 1939 (author's collection)

At prayer (drawing by 2nd Lt. K. Yoneimoto)

Funerary urns are borne to a homeward-bound train (courtesy of BBSS)

An IGHQ conference in the presence of the Emperor (author's collection)

One last category of prisoner of war remains to be considered: the men who survived in Russian or Outer Mongolian captivity but who did not return to Japan. Typically, Japanese POW's would not face a camera, identify themselves to anybody, or try to convey messages home. Often they did not speak to each other; even while allowed to do so, they limited themselves to chitchat about food and the like. A considerable number of them have been seen and talked to in the years since 1940, however, and some have gone so far as to admit they were Japanese or even Nomonhan prisoners. In 1944, for example, while Japan and the USSR were still at peace, a Kwantung Army survey team was operating slightly past Chiangchunmiao, in the direction of Nomonhan, which was of course off limits. Several men, apparently Japanese in Russian clothing, were seen working under the supervision of Soviet officers. The IJA survey party hung around the area deliberately and managed to approach and hail the suspected Japanese when their overseers were absent temporarily, but they elicited no response to repeated queries about the men's nationality. Finally, one of the exasperated workers did reply angrily in Japanese, in very low tones: "Hey, don't talk to us. We are not Japanese. The Japanese in us died at that time [of Nomonhan]. We had no choice then about living or dying. When you talk to us now, our Japanese blood is awakened and we feel homesick. So keep quiet and just go away." Thereafter the Japanese workers went about their business and never said another word to the survey team.[90]

Opportunities to meet Nomonhan-era POW's were enhanced dramatically after August 1945, when the entire Kwantung Army was marched into Soviet captivity—about 594,000 officers and men, according to the Russians. A few examples will demonstrate the quality of the postwar contacts. Around March 1946, working at a foundry in the Amurskaya suburb of Khabarovsk, IJA prisoners were excited to see a Japanese pull up in a trailer truck hauling steel plates. The driver revealed that he had been wounded critically at Nomonhan, had been picked up by the Russians, and had been nursed back to health. Afterward he had remained in the USSR, since he would have been shot for deserting under fire if he had gone back to Japan, and the effect would have harmed his family and his relatives. He became a naturalized Soviet citizen, took the name of Ivanov, married a Russian woman who worked in a hospital, and had two daughters. A considerable number of Japanese former prisoners were scattered throughout Siberia; Ivanov knew of two who lived in Khabarovsk. To the starving IJA prisoners of 1946, he brought precious bread, milk, and salted fish. But Ivanov rebuffed every effort to learn his original name or his home address. Smiling sadly, he said he must have been considered killed in action and there must be a grave in his hometown. So why trouble his family needlessly now? It would be best if he endured matters alone. After all, his life in the Soviet Union was quite comfortable, and the Russians did not evince racial prejudice.[91]

In another encounter, at a Komsomolsk bakery in 1948, an IJA prisoner met a Japanese-speaking, Mongolian-looking man. Eventually the latter admitted that he came from the Aomori district, had been drafted into the army in Manchuria, had been wounded at Nomonhan in May 1939, and had been captured while unconscious. "Under the circumstances," he could not have gone home. Originally, more than 10 Japanese ex-POW's had been with him, but the rest had dispersed and he was the only one at Komsomolsk now. He had married a Russian woman and had two children. Although he had a good job now as acting plant manager of the bakery, it was apparent that he pined for Japan. During his early phase in Russia, he used to tag migratory birds with his name and address, in the hope that they would make it to his beloved homeland. He would weep whenever the birds flew off, for they were free to go to Japan and he was not.[92]

Similar experiences have been reported from Outer Mongolia. On one occasion a Japanese enlisted prisoner, taken in Manchuria in 1945, sneaked out of camp, intent on swapping items such as soap for the much-needed food of a Mongolian family living in a tent nearby. The tent proved to be poor but clean and neat, and inhabited by a strange "family" of five or six men, all "dead soldiers" from Nomonhan. They were envious of the prisoner of 1945, who would be able to go home someday while they could not, but they refused to reveal their names or addresses in Japan. "We are no longer Japanese," they said. "We are Mongolians." As they passed around the bartered soap, with its long-remembered Japanese scent, the exiled men wept. From what their visitor heard, a considerable number of former prisoners from Nomonhan days were residing all over Ulan Bator.[93]

During a two-year period of detention as a laborer in Ulan Bator from 1945 to 1947, a new Japanese POW came to know a man who looked like a local Mongol but was an ex-prisoner from Nomonhan and who, as in the case of others, had married a Mongolian woman. Although—inevitably— he would not disclose particulars about himself, the expatriate was willing to recount some of the circumstances of his capture. Completely encircled by enemy armor, his unit had become helpless, and many of the troops were captured. Since Japanese soldiers were not allowed to accept the disgraceful lot of being taken alive, he must have been enshrined at Yasukuni among the killed in action. But whereas the POW's of 1945 were so-called "registered" or listed prisoners and could be repatriated eventually, the POW's of 1939 were "unregistered" or unlisted and thus unable to go home.[94]

We shall never know the exact number of Japanese soldiers who remained in the Soviet Union and Outer Mongolia after being seized during the

Nomonhan fighting. The Welfare Ministry, which tried to keep track of Japanese prisoners in foreign hands after the Second World War, lacks official data on the Nomonhan captives. Nevertheless, allowing for those who died of wounds or suicide or natural causes, and for those 200 men who were repatriated in 1939-40, veterans think that more than 1,000 former POW's from Nomonhan may still be residing abroad today, living proof of the fanatical and inhumane policy of the old Japanese army toward even its own unfortunate prisoners of war.[95]

40

The Punishment

Kusai mono ni futa.
Putting a lid on a bad smell.

For the Japanese army, Nomonhan was the graveyard of reputations. Typical of officers' private attitudes were Sixth Army staff officer Hamada's parting words to the author: "Others had their bright victories but it was *my* misfortune to suffer at Nomonhan!" At the time, of course, the military authorities did everything they could to conceal the debacle. Returned prisoners were rendered invisible. Even the wounded who had not been captured were "quarantined" in hospital, more strictly than if there had been a medical epidemic. Unscathed troops were secretly concentrated and secretly discharged. Every living survivor was ordered to "shut up" about Nomonhan. As for the dead, so many corpses had had to be cremated that it was necessary to send the white boxes of ashes to Japan in three shipments, lest the homeland be stunned by the numbers involved.[1]

Conversely, efforts were made to reassure and encourage the civilian populace. Troops who had marched from Chiangchunmiao to Hailar encountered an "arch of triumph" on 5-6 October and were welcomed by the Concordia Association and women's groups. Japanese, Manchurians, Mongolians, and White Russians—men, women, and children—waved flags and shouted "*Banzai!*" There was a military parade through the streets and a review at Hailar Park. On the 11th, the Sixth Army staged a grand marchpast, with such commanders as Umezu, Ogisu, and Komatsubara on the reviewing stand. Starting at noon on 14 October, the town of Hailar hosted a "victory thanksgiving" ceremony attended by the officer corps.[2]

Although the townsfolk of Hailar may have been deceived by the army's display, a 71st Regiment soldier confided to his diary: "Spent the day in the barracks. . . . It is home for me but I felt as if I were in some other unit because all the men were replacements. Few officers were left, and the old-timer soldiers were in the hospital."[3] At the other end of the chain of command, Komatsubara wrote to his wife that it was no pleasure for him to be returning to Hailar: "My heart is filled with aching and agony. What words can I find to console the families of the dead and the wounded?"[4]

✴

In connection with the restructuring of the Kwantung Army command after the defeat at Nomonhan, a number of senior officers had promptly visited Manchuria. From the war ministry's Personnel Bureau, Col. Nukada Hiroshi came to Hailar to confer with Komatsubara and Ogisu. The bureau chief, Maj. Gen. Noda Kengo, followed, as did War Minister Hata in early October. Lieutenant General Sawada closely questioned his classmate Komatsubara as well as Ogisu and senior Kwantung Army officers (Isogai, Yano, and Terada) before he left for Tokyo to become AGS deputy chief in October. In his new post, Sawada also consulted important AGS principals (Nakajima, Hashimoto, and Inada). After thorough deliberation, says Nukada, it was decided that responsibility should not be assigned to the district west of the Hsingans—that is, to the Sixth Army and the divisions located there, primarily the 23rd Division. Inasmuch as the front-line forces had fought well, the High Command and Kwantung Army headquarters should "take the rap." The subsequent purge was handled on that basis.

Admittedly, Ogisu and Komatsubara were later retired, too; but, Nukada claims, the action originated with them, because they wanted to assume responsibility for the loss of the regimental colors. Sawada, however, explains that although he would indeed have preferred to release the generals at their own request (*igan taishoku*), IJA regulations allowed such retirements only for reasons of ill health or infirmity. Since Sawada wished to convey the impression that Ogisu and Komatsubara were leaving the service voluntarily, "assuming the responsibility of samurai," their retirements were announced separately from those of Nakajima, Hashimoto, Ueda, and Isogai.[5]

Although a Japanese general could not directly resign his imperial commission, we know that by 13 September Komatsubara had already submitted a penitent request to the war minister, through Ogisu, to be allowed to retire.[6] Nevertheless, there are those who suggest it was "window dressing." According to this harsh interpretation, both Komatsubara and Ogisu really wanted to remain on active duty, which was why they allegedly sought to shift responsibility downward to the front-line commanders—a charge that we shall examine after detailing the fates of both generals.

Whatever else can be said of brash Lieutenant General Ogisu,[7] his assignment as Sixth Army commander could not have occurred at a worse time. Indeed, only the fluke of a last-minute personnel change sent him to the Sixth Army in place of Lt. Gen. Ushiroku Jun, the lucky 26th Division commander assigned to the Fourth Army instead. Ogisu arrived at Hailar from China on the eve of the Russians' August offensive, saw his combat forces smashed in 10 days, and tried to reverse the course of events by planning a big but orthodox counterattack. Even after the High Command suspended offensive operations, Ogisu pressed for aggressive action—in large part, no doubt, to try to retrieve lost colors, corpses, and guns. The general did not regard himself as beaten in battle; it was the truce that had supposedly stopped him from ultimate success. It is even said that he had had an impolitic "cease-fire celebration" party in mind.

Sawada was unimpressed by Ogisu when he spoke with the Sixth Army commander on 22 September. Ogisu, who already knew that Sawada was about to become the AGS deputy chief, hinted at his blamelessness for the Japanese defeat in August. The Sixth Army was completely surprised by the Russians, Ogisu insisted, because Kwantung Army headquarters provided no warning of the impending offensive and only stressed the need for winter preparations. The staff officers of the Kwantung Army and the Sixth Army were in direct contact with each other and exerted enormous operational influence on the 23rd Division, often ignoring Ogisu and in fact contradicting a number of his intentions. What Ogisu termed "staff officer politics" gravely affected his handling of the 24 August counteroffensive. "I feel no legal responsibility for [the outcome of] this incident," Ogisu asserted. "I feel responsible only for the Way of the Warrior [*bushidō*] and for morale." What remained, he told Sawada, was to "punish those commanders who had not done their duty."

Reviewing Ogisu's performance, the High Command discerned no major mistakes in his operational guidance and even excused his tardy appearance at the battlefront. Perhaps Ogisu continued to nurture the dream of clinging to his military career, but his perhaps-nominal offer to leave the service (mentioned by Nukada) was accepted by the central authorities. In early November 1939 he was technically attached to the General Staff and was replaced by Lt. Gen. Yasui Tōji, the 2nd Division commander. The following January, Ogisu entered retirement at the age of 55.

In the years that followed, Ogisu had hopes of becoming mayor of Sendai and then of Nagoya; neither intention materialized. With the help of Tōjō, his slightly younger classmate, Ogisu became a wartime leader in the Imperial Rule Assistance Association, the ultranationalistic and militaristic party formed in 1940. During the war, in the spring of 1942, one of Ogisu's public appearances attracted particular attention. Wearing his general's uniform, Ogisu attended the grand festival at Yasukuni Shrine, walked from seat to seat, and yelled, "Those of you who are related to my subordinates, raise your hand!" It was certainly not the behavior of a vanquished general. After the war, in 1947, Ogisu testified as a defense witness, not as a defendant, before the International Military Tribunal, and had an opportunity to deny knowledge of his grandiloquent *kunji* exhortation of early September 1939. Subsequently, in the Shibuya area of Tokyo, he owned a notions store, which he expanded into a sporting goods establishment. On 22 December 1949, ten years after Nomonhan, Ogisu died at the age of 65.[8]

From the observations of division staff officer Suzuki and of divisional aide Tanaka in particular, we learned of the grief and exhaustion that afflicted Komatsubara after the last sortie north of the Holsten in late August 1939 and the subsequent escape. The division commander impressed Sawada very favorably when the two generals chatted at length on two occasions shortly after the cease-fire—on 19 and 23 September. Unlike Ogisu, Komatsubara conveyed "the noble sense of responsibility of a samurai." The first thing he said was, "Hey, Sawada, there is a limit to men's morale." He would make no excuses for himself. Ueda—as the senior planner—had sought to take full blame, but Komatsubara felt strongly that the "practitioners"—he and Ogisu—should also assume responsibility for the failure of the campaign at Nomonhan. Though he had very much wanted to die in battle, that recourse had been explicitly denied to him; he had thought of committing suicide, but now it was too late. Reconstruction of the 23rd Division was his remaining obligation, especially since his surviving subordinates retained confidence in him. Of the highly emotional conversation of 23 September, Sawada wrote that Komatsubara wept as he spoke, and that he "gagged on his own tears" as he listened.[9]

Several personal letters, released by Mrs. Komatsubara decades after the war, provide further insight into the mental state and outlook of the division commander following the cease-fire. He was suffering from dreadful remorse, wrote the general on 24 September, as a consequence of having lost so many of his subordinates, including four slain regiment commanders—Colonels Yamagata, Morita, Ise, and Sakai. Komatsubara had wanted to die with them but, having been ordered to break out, he had had to swallow his sorrow and entrust his life to the gods for the time being. Afterward, while he had been getting ready for a battle of revenge and was resolved to die with the entire unit, the cease-fire had occurred all of a sudden. Looking in the direction of the distant Halha, the general was filled with deep emotion and heartrending sorrow for the souls of the battle dead. Although he tried, he could not keep from shedding painful tears; his mind was in agony and his heart was in pain, day and night. He profoundly deplored the fact that he had not died in combat.

A sense of enormous responsibility tormented him, Komatsubara continued. As we saw, he had already advised the Throne informally of his request to retire. In the meantime, he was very busy with such duties as the recovery and cremation of the dead, and the rebuilding of the units. Being a personal appointee of the Emperor, he must set matters straight in the aftermath of battle. Komatsubara assured his wife, however, that he would exercise the care of a loyal subject and would not act irresponsibly—an indirect allusion to his determination not to kill himself.[10]

Komatsubara's letter of 2 October to his wife was replete with the sad details of corpse retrieval and cremation. Many of the wounded survivors had lost arms or legs—a source of tears wherever he looked. In fact, admitted the general, "Recently I cry easily. Whenever I am speaking, I grow sad and my eyes fill with tears. I must have become sentimental." Soon he would go back to Hailar, leaving the battlefield reluctantly, and he would weep again upon meeting injured comrades, visiting the altars in the barracks, and extending condolences to the families of fallen officers. He could not help thinking that he would have been able to apologize by his death in battle if only the September offensive had been carried out. Nevertheless, the general could swear that he had never done anything for which he should be ashamed. He felt somewhat comforted when visitors conveyed word of what they had heard from hospitalized soldiers: that the division commander was a brave man who had always stood up fearlessly under fire. Even so, he felt the constant moral pressure of responsibility for having caused several thousand deaths. In this connection, it was an especially painful fact that some of the Japanese corpses could not be found, including those of a number of able and distinguished officers.[11] The somber tone of Komatsubara's private letters to his wife continues in the very emotional public address that he gave at the military memorial services on 3 October.[12]

One cannot doubt the reality of Komatsubara's anguish. Even Colonel Sumi, who became embittered about his own later treatment, remarked upon the general's appearance when he went to pay his respects, the day after the cease-fire. Komatsubara's eyes were bloodshot and tears were streaming down his cheeks, says Sumi, as they sipped whiskey together.[13]

Nevertheless, Komatsubara engendered some hostile reactions because of the violent efforts he made, in concert with Ogisu, to "salvage the honor" of his corps by means of obligatory retirements and even enforced suicides. In addition, Komatsubara struck some officers as astonishingly aggressive concerning his combat leadership. On the division commander's residence in Hailar, graffiti appeared after the cease-fire—e.g., "Komattarō," a play on his last and first names, meaning "Komatsubara in a jam." Crank letters also arrived. Eventually, it is said, the general had to call upon the military police for protection.[14]

Although, as mentioned earlier, Komatsubara had opted against suicide, there is no concrete evidence that he struggled to remain on active duty. Sumi, however, suggests that the High Command had been coming under fire from the National Diet for its handling of the Nomonhan war and that the beleaguered IJA heads therefore worked out a compromise of sorts: if the Diet agreed not to pursue painful questions openly, the army would see to it that those responsible—those who had handled operations—"took the rap." Consequently, the purge was carried out, from Deputy Chief of the Army General Staff Nakajima and Kwantung Army commander Ueda at the top to Komatsubara and Ogisu in the field.

Indirect support for Sumi's theory is found in the contemporary press. The *Asahi Shinbun*, for example, on 4 October praised both the military authorities for frankly admitting the 18,000 IJA casualties and the front-line troops for fighting so bravely, but also raised a cautious editorial question: Why had the imperial forces been obliged to struggle at such cost and under such unfavorable circumstances, for four long months? The Japanese resembled a bare-handed man using his fists against an armor-clad warrior.[15]

According to Sawada, the High Command investigated Komatsubara's conduct of operations throughout the Nomonhan Incident, with particular reference to the genesis of the border troubles in May, the origin of the decision to cross the Halha River in July, and the reasons for being taken by surprise by the Russians on 20 August. Komatsubara was found to have been blameless on all counts, and to have carried out the Kwantung Army commander's orders to the letter. Indeed, it was concluded that only his "calm demeanor and fine personality" had enabled Komatsubara to fight so hard and so long under such difficult conditions. But although it was personally very painful for Sawada and his colleagues to terminate the professional careers of fellow officers and old friends such as Komatsubara and Ogisu, it was necessary to "bear the pain for the sake of command and control in the imperial army and of the enforcement of military discipline."[16]

Once the immediate aftermath of Nomonhan had been taken care of, the central authorities proceeded to clean house. On 6 November, Komatsubara was replaced by his academy classmate, Lt. Gen. Inoue Masakichi, and was attached to Kwantung Army headquarters. Nominally assigned to the AGS on 1 December, he bade farewell to the staff in Hsinking, thanked aide Tanaka for all of his labors, and left for Dairen next day. By 6 December, the general's ship had docked at Kobe; it had been almost three years since he left Japan for Manchuria in March 1937. On 26 January 1940, Komatsubara was directed to await his forthcoming final orders; five days later, he was officially retired, after more than 35 years of military service.

In retirement, Komatsubara joined the prestigious National Policy Research Association (Kokusaku Kenkyūkai) and enthusiastically attended meetings. With his colleagues, he shared his knowledge of the Russians and his rich experience at Nomonhan. Although this gentle-looking man did not, at first glance, convey the impression of being a soldier who had barely survived the horrors of combat, an ineffable sense of gloom seemed to mark him. In truth, the general was dying. Found to have stomach cancer, he was admitted to the Tokyo University hospital and then to the army's medical school facility. On 6 October 1940, scarcely eight months past retirement, Komatsubara Michitarō died at the age of 54.[17]

According to the army's penal code (*rikugun keihō*), issued in 1908 and not revised until 1942, dereliction of duty occurred when a commander surrendered to the enemy, whether or not he "did his best." If he "did his best," he was liable to imprisonment of up to six months; if not, the sentence was death.[18] The operative clause, however, was susceptible to various interpretations in practice. We have seen that faultless IJA officer prisoners were forced into suicide as a result of the invoking of an "expanded interpretation" of the military regulations. Line regiment commanders usually chose to kill themselves rather than outlive the destruction of their units, their guns, or their colors. Suicide had been the voluntary choice of the following permanent or acting unit commanders when their combat situation became hopeless at the end of August: Colonel Yamagata (64th Infantry Regiment), Colonel Ise (13th Field Artillery), Lieutenant Colonel Someya (Muleng Heavy Artillery), and Major Umeda (1st Heavy Artillery). Lieutenant Colonel Higashi of the 71st Infantry Regiment deliberately met his death by leading a last charge.

Of the commanders, Yamagata Takemitsu was hounded by his superiors even after killing himself. Since contact with Komatsubara had become impossible at the time the latter had launched his last sally north of the Holsten, the colonel had decided to try to rejoin the main body but had been trapped near the river during his withdrawal. In Komatsubara's diary entry for 10 September, the general recorded his criticisms of Yamagata's handling of the pullback. First, the decision was taken too late on the night of 28/29 August, with the result that the enemy was able to conduct close pursuit by daylight. Japanese losses would not have been so severe if Yamagata had deferred the withdrawal till after sunset on the 29th. His combat situation had not deteriorated to the point that he could not have held on for one more day before trying to get out. Second, Yamagata would have gained freedom of action if only he had headed directly for Nomonhan. Instead he chose to enter the valley of the Holsten, and was thwarted by machine-gun and tank fire emanating from the south shore. Third, Yamagata lost all contact with his subordinate forces, whose pullback seemed to have degenerated into a near-rout.

Yamagata's allegedly hasty disengagement was exacerbated by the danger that all or part of the regimental colors had fallen into enemy hands. Ostensibly because the time and circumstances of Yamagata's death were uncertain, his posthumous promotion to major general was stopped, though the one-rank honor should have been awarded routinely to those killed in action honorably. Major Kanaizuka, serving in regimental headquarters, received an embarrassing inquiry from Mrs. Yamagata but found it difficult to clarify the problem. Perhaps, Kanaizuka thinks, the colonel's short temper and lack of tact in venting his blunt opinions had contributed to dislike or even hostility on the part of those above him. On one occasion in July, we do know, Yamagata had stubbornly insisted on an important point of cartographic location, and he had been proved correct. After he was dead, it apparently required the direct intervention of the war ministry to induce the unsympathetic authorities in Manchuria to reconsider the matter of Yamagata's final record. Only reluctantly did they agree to clear his name and to insure his promotion to general officer's rank. By then, search crews had found his corpse on 24 September, together with his gracious last words and the remnants of the colors.[19]

That Yamagata had killed himself after withdrawing contributed to his eventual rehabilitation. Other unit commanders who pulled back under unbearable pressure but did not voluntarily commit suicide encountered irresistible demands to "atone." A particularly tragic fate befell Lt. Col. Ioki Eiichi, the splendid commander of the little formation of scarcely 800 men—"crows thrown together"—that clung so tenaciously to isolated Fui Heights and disrupted Zhukov's timetable. When his last capability of defending the position was obliterated, Ioki intended to shoot himself. Subordinate officers convinced him otherwise, and a battery commander kept him from committing suicide.

By the time Ioki and his survivors got out on 25 August, Fui Heights had lost its original significance to the Japanese, and the battle had surged to the south. But Komatsubara, Ogisu, and the Kwantung Army regarded Ioki's desperate retreat with a mixture of disgust, pain, and fury. Ioki and his officers became the butt of insults and contempt. Supposedly the pullback from the "anchor" point had caused the large-scale envelopment and collapse of the whole Japanese right wing. When Kwantung Army Major Tsuji got back to Hsinking on 26 August, he conveyed the unsettling information that, in reporting to the division commander, Ioki had not apologized for abandoning his defenses and that, as a matter of fact, his unit had lost only about 300 men.

Tsuji's cruel data bear closer analysis. The core of Ioki's force was his own 23rd Reconnaissance Regiment. From a strength of 254 men at Fui Heights, there were 101 killed, 74 wounded, and 10 missing—a total of 185 casualties (73 percent) incurred between 20 and 25 August. Including the other elements assigned to him, Ioki had had 759 men at Fui, of whom 182 were killed, 183 were wounded, and 21 were missing, for a total of 386 casualties (51 percent).[20]

In addition, there is evidence that Ioki did explain his actions and express his regrets to his superiors, as high as Ogisu and Chief of Staff Fujimoto. Colonel Hamada asserts that the Sixth Army did not issue criticisms directly but that, in cases of unauthorized retreat, it simply could not assent. When an explanation was demanded, Ioki replied (according to Hamada) that after the lines at Fui were penetrated by enemy armor, further defense would have proved very costly. Rejoining the division's main body seemed more advisable. Admittedly, however, "the offense of abandoning a position without orders is very serious, and I respectfully await orders."

Ioki's superiors were not assuaged. On 6 September, Komatsubara wrote at length in his diary about the case. Ioki had stated that his unit had been surrounded by 100 tanks and pounded by 30,000 artillery rounds a day before the decision to escape was taken on his own initiative. All the IJA anti-tank guns had been demolished, ammunition was exhausted, and enemy riflemen had entered the positions. Komatsubara was unmoved. Ioki, he insisted, should have been able to hold out longer if only he had plugged his eastern flank by digging trenches all around. It was on the exposed eastern approaches to Ioki's perimeter that excellent enemy infantrymen made the decisive penetration, in concert with armor. But the tanks did not overrun the defenses, and enemy artillery was not almighty. Ioki simply did not launch small sallies by night against the tanks and the artillery; and he did not retain sufficient strength in reserve. Lastly, because "the commander's resolve was weak, his subordinates talked about escaping, and this engendered a climate of flight."

In his diary entry for 13 September, Komatsubara pursued the matter of Ioki's legal responsibility for retreating without orders. According to Article 43 of the IJA penal code, for a commander to take his troops and quit a defensive zone "without cause," in the presence of the enemy, was an offense punishable by death. Ioki had committed precisely such a violation by acting without permission. There were some, wrote Komatsubara, who were unacquainted with or lacked sufficient knowledge of the regulations and therefore moved troops thoughtlessly. In the case of Ioki (and of Colonel Hasebe, whose similar "crime" will be discussed shortly), to claim a lack of combat strength sufficient to retain a defensive sector owing to the destruction of guns and heavy weapons, as well as scant ammunition, "did not amount to sufficient cause." Clearly, Komatsubara did not assess Ioki's action as falling within the category of justifiable initiative. A superior officer must always grant prior authorization for a "breakout" when the circumstances were overpowering.

Komatsubara urged Ioki to assume responsibility by committing suicide. The lieutenant colonel refused at first, insisting that Fui Heights was like an isolated island, never an operationally viable key point. A heated argument ensued. Afterward, the general sent a staff officer to talk to the stubborn Ioki and "get him to comprehend the situation and be aware of the pertinent military regulations." Although the envoy was well aware of the situation at Fui and was personally sympathetic to Ioki, Komatsubara's instructions left him no choice. Every day for about a week, an hour per day, the staff officer went to Ioki's tent to "reason with him."

The division commander also resorted to a strange ploy, sending his chief medical officer, Col. Murakami Tokuji, to "work on" Ioki. "You were wounded in the leg," Ioki was told, "and your diabetes is far advanced. So your death is only a matter of time anyhow." In due course, the psychological hammering from all sides took its toll, and Ioki lost hope. He described to his classmate and already assigned successor, Lt. Col. Takahashi Hirosuke, exactly what he had tried to explain to higher headquarters: that he had been impelled by a desire to save precious lives and prevent needless slaughter after the engagement was clearly lost. He had been hoping to wage a battle of revenge when the Japanese counteroffensive got under way; "but it's all over now." In his last testament, Ioki wrote that the responsibility was entirely his; no blame should attach to his officers and men.

On the night of 16/17 September, Ioki shot himself in the temple. With his suicide, remarks Hamada, the regiment commander had "cleared himself of blame." Even after death, however, Ioki's good name was disparaged —by the Japanese, not the Russians. A sympathetic division officer tried to rewrite the after-action report to say that Ioki had been killed while trying to make contact with headquarters. This version was not accepted, for the actual circumstances were too widely condemned. Their commander disgraced, Ioki's loyal survivors were ordered to "shut up" about his fate.

Komatsubara had not relented when Sawada questioned him on 19 September. Had there been any "spiritual breakdowns" (*seishin jō no mondai*) among Komatsubara's subordinates that demanded punishment? Without elaborating, the division commander answered that Ioki had posed the only such problem, but that the case had "blown over" after Ioki's classmate and successor had convinced him to commit suicide. On 23 September, Komatsubara explained to Sawada that Ioki "had simply not understood what his responsibility was."

The Ioki affair was not quite finished. Capt. Tsuji Kiyoshi, the infantry-gun battery commander attached from the 27th Regiment, may also have been pushed into suicide. Tsuji had been among the officers who recommended withdrawal in the first place, and he had saved Ioki from an even earlier death. Because of his implication in the alleged crime of his unlucky commander, some say the captain could not be allowed to live.[21]

Forty-two years after the Ioki tragedy, many new details were disclosed by Maj. Ogi Hiroshi, who had replaced Murata as 23rd Division operations officer: (1) IGHQ and the Cavalry Inspectorate General under Lt. Gen.

Nakayama Shigeru had apparently prejudged Ioki and concluded that he must commit suicide or go before a firing squad; (2) this opinion was shared by most of the army and division commanders stationed in Manchuria, with the notable exception of the tough new commander of the Third Army, Lt. Gen. Suetaka Kamezō, who admitted that Komatsubara had "gone too far—if I had been involved, I would have saved [Ioki], even at the risk of being court-martialed myself"; (3) only two ranking officers spoke up openly in Ioki's behalf—23rd Division Chief of Staff Kimura and Major Ōgi; (4) Sixth Army Chief of Staff Fujimoto as well as General Komatsubara coldly rejected Ōgi's personal intercession and saw to it that enshrinement in Yasukuni was permanently denied to "this officer who was punishable under the army's penal code"; (5) Maj. Suzuki Yoshiyasu turned down Komatsubara's request that he officially convey orders to Ioki to commit suicide; (6) the diabetes idea was concocted by Dr. Murakami on his own; (7) Ioki irritated the "ignoramuses" at Sixth Army headquarters by stubbornly defending his battle actions; (8) Komatsubara accorded shabby treatment to Mrs. Ioki's poignant and perceptive letters; (9) Maj. Tsuji Masanobu's hasty "smear" at the Kwantung Army level helped to seal Ioki's fate.[22]

There are numerous similarities between the circumstances and the fates of Ioki and of Col. Hasebe Riei, who had been sent with two battalions from the 8th BGU in early August to reinforce the sector below the Holsten. With Kajikawa's battalion from the 28th Infantry attached to him, Hasebe possessed considerably greater strength than Ioki, but his forces were a patchwork too. Nevertheless, the Noro Heights district was of equal strategic importance as the southern anchor of the Japanese front. After the Russians' August offensive was unleashed, Potapov's Southern Force quickly smashed the Hasebe detachment. With communications severed, food, ammunition, and water very low, and casualties soaring to about 70 percent, Hasebe decided reluctantly on the night of 26/27 August to withdraw to a new line which, he had been led to believe by the division, was envisaged in case of emergency. To a Kwantung Army staff officer who ran into Hasebe during the night, the colonel conveyed a pathetic impression; his uniform was torn, his beard was scraggly, and he was leaning on a cane to support a crippled leg. Even in the darkness, the staff officer discerned "something tragic or dreadful" in Hasebe's eyes. At the end of his tether, the colonel tried to coordinate the pullback; but synchronization proved impossible and Hasebe eventually ended up in Chiangchunmiao while the rest of his scattered force made it to Sixth Army headquarters at Mohorehi by the 28th.

Unaware of the details or of Hasebe's whereabouts, Ogisu "chewed out" and sacked Lieutenant Colonel Sugitani, who had brought the remnants safely to Mohorehi, for losing the detachment commander. The edict was rescinded after investigations revealed that Hasebe was alive in Chiang-chunmiao, having apparently abandoned his battalions in flight. In his diary on 13 September, Komatsubara denounced Hasebe as well as Ioki for having inexcusably violated military regulations by quitting defenses without permission or sufficient justification. On the 14th, Hasebe's actions drew specific criticism by Komatsubara, who detected many resemblances to Ioki's mistakes. It was imperative to hold sizable elements in reserve, wrote the division commander: "I said this to Hasebe many times, but he did not listen. Those who are not strong-willed deploy many soldiers in front." Such thinking prevented both Hasebe and Ioki from launching vital night actions. It might be natural to "let down" at dark, after coming under fire all day, but that was shortsighted; "nighttime is our 'turf,' and we should exploit the enemy's weakness then" by raiding his armor. Failing to establish strong defenses in the round, Hasebe was defeated from the rear, as Ioki was beaten from the flank. And whereas Ioki listened to his underlings and retreated, Hasebe relied excessively on Colonel Morita's 71st Infantry, expected to be rescued by Komatsubara, and thus became enmeshed in the notion of withdrawing.

Hasebe was directed to return to Sixth Army headquarters, where both Ogisu and Komatsubara "suggested" that he rid himself of shame by committing suicide. No allowance was made for the fact that Hasebe had thought he was following the division's intention and evincing acceptable initiative by trying to hold up behind Noro. Death was the only way out. On 20 September, Colonel Hasebe—a gentle officer, beloved and respected by his men—killed himself, another victim of the military's unwritten law that rendered withdrawal a capital offense. Komatsubara heard that Hasebe had first taken off his soldier's tunic, saying that he did not want to stain government-issue. Clad in his undershirt, the colonel then shot himself with a captured pistol, after having donated his own weapon to a loyal subordinate.

Bitter Japanese critics have remarked upon the fact that the "executioners" of brave officers such as Hasebe and Ioki, as well as pilots Harada and Daitoku, were usually ensconced safely behind the lines, far from the combat hell endured by their victims.[24] Ignoring common sense and trading compassion for an unearthly discipline, the obstinate IJA brass threw away useful experience and extinguished promising careers that would have enriched the army as a whole. Annihilation was glorified and preferred to the extrication of men from a hopeless situation with a view to fighting another day. Higher headquarters neither allowed leeway nor took its own steps before front-line disintegration could occur. Initiative in retrograde movement was regarded as impermissible, although it would really have been "easier" in most cases to die *in situ* (since surrender was not allowed) than to try to break out of the ring of fire that Zhukov's units forged. Significantly, Japanese officers deemed culpable at division level and above were merely reassigned or pensioned off; suicide was forced only upon line commanders. Gen. Hata Shunroku, however, insists that suicide was "absolutely not ordered" by his war ministry and that, in any case, the number of commanders killed in action far exceeded those who assumed responsibility and committed suicide.[25]

To this point, we have encountered several types of circumstances that led to suicide by Japanese officers. In the voluntary cases, an officer would try to kill himself during a lost battle when capture was imminent, or during captivity when the opportunity presented itself. In the involuntary instances, an officer would be forced to commit suicide if he had been captured and released, or if he and his unit retreated without specific orders. One last category remains to be examined: the commander who killed himself voluntarily after combat for reasons of self-perceived military honor. Such an officer was Col. Sakai Mikio, who had commanded the 72nd Infantry Regiment almost until the end of the fighting at Nomonhan.

An affable but serious commander, an expert administrator considerate of his subordinates and disdainful of luxuries, Sakai had won the loyalty of his men and the adoration of his junior officers, who could always express their views frankly to him. The colonel evinced compassion and respect for the slain, the mark of an excellent, strong commander by IJA standards. Thus, when division staff officer Itō visited Sakai's headquarters one day during combat, the colonel asked him to join in prayer for the men who had fallen that day. This sensitivity left an unforgettable imprint on Itō, for in a certain other line regiment, to the disgust of the unit, the commander had ordered corpses removed from the headquarters area because they stank. Sakai forged a strong regiment from the 72nd Infantry; staff officer Suzuki says that it was the best in the 23rd Division and that Komatsubara, a harsh taskmaster, thought so too, though Sakai was the only one of his colonels who had not attended the army war college.

In the Japanese counteroffensive of 24 August, Sakai's regiment stormed forward with enthusiasm, made some progress, but was soon ripped apart by armor and superior firepower. Fifty key officers were felled, some of the troops bolted, and the colors were barely saved. Sakai and group commander Kobayashi, severely wounded, were left on the battlefield alone for hours. Kwantung Army Major Tsuji, who found Sakai, authorized a pullback, and the colonel was carried out on a stretcher that night. Although Sakai kept hoping to rejoin the battle, a doctor insisted that his wounds were more serious than he thought, and that he must be evacuated to Hailar. There, on 1 September, Tsuji visited Kobayashi and Sakai. The latter, who struck him as depressed and withdrawn, apologized for having left the battlefield because of such "trifling" wounds. Tsuji did his best to comfort the colonel.

When one of Sakai's favorite officers, Lieutenant Colonel Nishikawa (also wounded), was being reassigned to the Tsitsihar hospital, Sakai asked to be transferred there. Since the Tsitsihar facility was crammed with patients, empty regimental barracks were converted to a makeshift field hospital. After the medical director, an old colleague, arranged to have Sakai moved to the main hospital, the colonel tried to get Nishikawa to go, since he was "worse off"; but eventually Sakai agreed to the move. On 12/13 September, the night before the transfer, Nishikawa received a disturbing message from 2nd Lt. Matsunobe Yōichi, who had been in constant attendance on Sakai: the colonel had apparently reached a critical decision—i.e., to commit suicide. Nishikawa warned Matsunobe to hide Sakai's sword and pistol, and was assured that this had been done.

Usually Sakai would limp over to see his battalion commander, but since the colonel was being moved next morning, Nishikawa used crutches to visit him this time. Sakai made room on his bed for Nishikawa, and they chatted all night. Among the matters discussed were the details of the pullback and the state of mind of the colonel and his subordinates on the battlefield. Sakai reiterated that he should not have quit the front and left the colors behind— something a commander should never do. He had only intended to obtain first aid before returning to the battle. His worst mistake was to have listened to the doctor and to have allowed himself to be evacuated to the rear. When casualties began pouring into the Hailar hospital, he had felt a greater and greater sense of responsibility as the regimental commander.

On the personal level, the colonel exhorted Nishikawa to train his men well when he became a service school instructor and to apply his experience. Anti-Soviet combat operations were extremely important. At one point, Nishikawa inquired whether Sakai had reached "some grave resolve." The colonel paled and asked if Lieutenant Matsunobe had said something. Nishikawa replied that he merely suspected the fact from the regiment commander's behavior—for instance, his constant writing, even on the train. Sakai denied any such intention, and Nishikawa departed, "half relieved, half skeptical." Next morning Sakai moved to the main wing. On the 15th he told a soldier, in Matsunobe's brief absence, that he would like to clean his pistol. The man should have asked the lieutenant first but was intimidated by rank. Sneaking into a bunker at the corner of the hospital, Sakai killed himself with one pistol shot through the chin.

While Nishikawa lay in bed that morning, military police and officers appeared—an ominous sign. Sakai had killed himself, they reported, but had left a letter intended for Nishikawa's eyes only. The MP's had read the message, which they turned over to Nishikawa. Written in pencil on a military pad, the colonel's last words revealed his innermost thoughts. As he had already explained partially, his sense of fault "deserved a million deaths." He could not "keep on living this way" and had thought, many times, of committing suicide in Hailar hospital, but he had worried about the direct and indirect consequences that his death would have on the men who were so eagerly concentrating on offensive preparations. Hailar, after all, was the regimental garrison town, and the families of the bereaved would be adversely affected. Sakai had restrained himself because his suicide might cause certain matters to surface and disgrace the regiment. He had taken advantage of the chance to transfer to Tsitsihar, where the psychological price of his death would not be as great. "I have no excuse to offer," wrote the colonel, "for the fact that I stained the honor of the colors and of the unit." Nevertheless, he was extremely grateful to his subordinates for performing well, doing their brave best in combat, and achieving brilliant results that had earned universal acclaim. As a "selfish favor," the colonel asked Nishikawa to make a very special effort to prevent the fact of his death from damaging the honor of the regiment. Sakai closed with a revealing request: since he was no longer the unit commander and was apparently attached to Sixth Army headquarters, would Nishikawa kindly handle the case as "that of an individual"? The battalion commander wept as he read Sakai's personal message, especially when he noted that there was no last will for the colonel's own family.

Sakai did address a final testament to his critically wounded superior Kobayashi, expressing heartfelt regret for the great pain he must have caused the general and for "matters that could not be expiated even by my death." The colonel explained to Kobayashi, as he had to Nishikawa, about his hesitations at Hailar, lest he act "selfishly" and trouble the minds of subordinates who, for some reason, revered their "unworthy" commander. He had therefore sought to die in a place that had few connections with the regiment. Closing with profound apologies for his "truly inexcusable act," Sakai prayed for Kobayashi's recuperation and continuing activity.

Major Hamada, Sakai's aide until early August, says he had feared that the colonel would kill himself as soon as he received a letter saying, "My job is done." Undoubtedly, Sakai did not want to survive the other two infantry regiment commanders who had killed themselves in battle (Yamagata and Higashi). This was especially true because Sakai had hoped very much to resume command of the 72nd Regiment in due course. When a new colonel was appointed without consulting him, and he heard that he would most likely be assigned to the ordnance department when he recovered, Sakai must have decided to assume responsibility for what had occurred while he was still in command of the regiment.

According to the dissenting view of Colonel Sumi, Sakai probably killed himself because the army authorities blamed him for the problem of his colors, for withdrawal from the front, or for neglect of his duties as regimental commander because of a mere arm wound. Each of these factors played a role in Sakai's decision to die, but not because the army chastised him for them. From his last words to Nishikawa, from Major Tsuji's recollections, and from disclosures by Colonel Nukada of the war ministry, it is apparent that, in large part, Sakai was distressed unto death by his loss of command, regardless of the reason for it. When Nukada arrived from the Personnel Bureau in Tokyo and visited Ogisu, the Sixth Army commander complained about the carelessness with which assignments had been handled recently. For example, the 72nd Regiment commander's replacement had been designated so quickly that Sakai could not go back to his unit. Although wounded seriously, he had visited Ogisu immediately, before being hospitalized in Hailar. The colonel pleaded to be allowed to return to the battlefield, for he could not abandon his men. Ogisu had agreed in principle but said there was nothing he could do, since the orders had already been processed. Sakai should therefore proceed to the hospital, attend to his wounds, and recover quickly. His service to the nation was "just beginning." There was a terribly doleful look on the colonel's face when he left Ogisu for the last time.

Komatsubara admitted to Sawada, on 23 September, that Sakai's case was "truly unfortunate." "I had requested his replacement," the division commander explained, "as soon as I was told that his wrist had been shattered; but it proved to be an unexpectedly light injury. Colonel Sakai committed suicide because he felt a profound sense of responsibility at having been removed for such a minor wound."

The command, in short, had applied no punitive coercion against this surviving line colonel. Sakai's 72nd Regiment actually received a very rare unit citation (*kanjō*) from the Sixth Army commander for meritorious performance at Nomonhan. Sakai himself was being considered, by Ogisu and others, for eventual promotion to the command of the important IJA infantry school at Toyama. A sense of powerful responsibility, as he saw it, was the central impulse behind Sakai's death. To the colonel, as to feudal warriors of old, taking his own life "nourished the pure pursuit of honor" and was, "in itself, a moral act." [26]

For the handling of affairs at Nomonhan, no member of the Sixth Army or 23rd Division staff was chastised, apart from the commanding generals.

Maj. Gen. Fujimoto Tetsukuma, the driving force below Ogisu,[27] was left in place as Sixth Army chief of staff during the local cease-fire negotiations and for 15 months afterward, until December 1940.

The Sixth Army's advance headquarters remained at Mohorehi until 28 October. Thereafter at Hailar, Col. Hamada Sueo, the senior staff officer, worked on the reorganization of the 23rd Division and on defense plans for the region west of the Hsingans. In March 1940, when he was assigned as an instructor and research section chief at the engineer school in Matsudo, Hamada thought seriously of leaving military service. He had never really expected that the fighting at Nomonhan would turn out well, and the results were even worse than he had feared. As early as 23 July, when Hamada observed the 23rd Division's vaunted "general offensive," he had felt that "nothing could be more absurd than to be a staff officer of this [Sixth] Army." Plagued by doubts and a lack of confidence, the colonel concluded that he had "failed completely as a soldier" at Nomonhan. When the Kwantung Army's higher staff rejected his pessimistic but realistic military opinions, Hamada began to wonder if he possessed the strength to plan or to command in a "Japanese-style" war. For about two months he wrestled with the idea of resigning, but he could not bring himself to do so. Instead, Hamada stayed in the army, hoping to serve "in some way or other," such as teaching. After his engineer school tour, he served as a division staff officer and then held several technical posts involving communications, fortifications, and railways. In March 1944, he was promoted to major general.[28]

At the 23rd Division level, a third chief of staff, Col. Kimura Matsujirō, replaced the wounded Okamoto and the slain Ōuchi. The wounded group commander, Kobayashi, was replaced by Maj. Gen. Satō Kōtoku. Surviving staff officers stayed in service and duly ascended the ladder of promotion. Lt. Col. Murata Masao (Operations) was reassigned in 1940 as an instructor at the Narashino school, from which he had come to the 23rd Division in the first place. Sent to the staff of the 42nd Division at Sendai in 1943, he was lucky to escape capture by the Russians after the main body of his unit was transferred to the Kurils a month before the end of the Pacific War. Murata attained the final rank of colonel, as did Maj. Suzuki Yoshiyasu (Intelligence), his 33rd class military academy comrade. Capt. Itō Noboru (Logistics) was assigned to the Personnel Bureau of the war ministry in December 1939. He was a lieutenant colonel on the staff of the China Expeditionary Army at war's end.

No ill fate befell the technicians. The 23rd Division's engineer commander, Lt. Col. Saitō Isamu, spent most of his remaining army years in command assignments in the China theater. He was promoted to full colonel in 1940. Lt. Col. Numazaki Kyōhei remained in charge of the 24th Engineer

Regiment until March 1941, when he was given another such unit in central China. Three classes junior to Saitō, he became a full colonel in 1943.[29]

The lot of surviving infantry commanders was far different. According to Sumi, the Kwantung Army pinned the blame for the dismal outcome of the fighting at Nomonhan on the "inadequate commandship" of the front-line leaders—not on the operational planning—and as a result "decided to punish us, but without formal procedures" in most cases—as in the forced suicides of Ioki, whose command was organic to the 23rd Division, and of Hasebe, who had been attached. Although their disciplining was less cruel, a number of other line unit commanders who had fought under the 23rd Division's control were punished for allegedly poor performance. Thus Lt. Col. Yotsuya Iwao, whose composite detachment was thrown together from the 6th IGU, had been routed during the 24 August counteroffensive and, during Komatsubara's subsequent foray north of the Holsten, had lost all contact with the division and had fallen back on his own initiative. For failure to accomplish his missions, Yotsuya was suspended from duty in 1940.[30]

As for the 7th Division, Maj. Gen. Morita Norimasa's 14th Brigade and only two of his infantry battalions from the 28th Regiment had been placed under the Sixth Army on 14 August. Ten days later, deployed on the left flank of Komatsubara's counteroffensive, Morita's force jumped off with vigor but was soon stopped in its tracks with very heavy losses. The September cease-fire took place before Morita could try to redeem himself. A graduate of the 24th military academy class of 1912 and of the war college in 1920, he had had considerable administrative experience on the General Staff and in the war ministry. In addition, he had served as a staff officer at division and Korea Army level, and had seen combat in China in 1937-38 as 15th Regiment commander. Ten days at the front at Nomonhan wrecked Morita's whole career.

After displacing his entire brigade to guard the Handagai sector, Morita learned of the series of personnel decisions affecting the 7th Division in the wake of the recent fighting. The other (13th) brigade commander, Maj. Gen. Yoshizawa Tadao, who had seen even less action at Nomonhan but had not been directly involved in the 24 August attack, was being promoted to lieutenant general and given command of the 3rd Independent Mixed Brigade. Morita was neither promoted nor assigned a command. Instead, it was announced that Col. Mori Takashi, an infantry regiment commander, was being elevated to major general and given the 14th Brigade. Morita was attached to the 7th Division's depot force—a signal of his impending removal. On 1 December, his retirement became official. He had been on active duty for 27 years, was not quite 48 years old, and had been a general officer for less than a year and a half. Decades later, in the anonymity of Toyama City, Morita was able to put his misfortune behind him. "Thanks to Nomonhan," he grinned, "I am still alive today! Since I was really an excellent officer, I'd undoubtedly have died in the Pacific War. Or else I might have ended up as a war criminal!" Morita was 78 when he passed away in 1970.[31]

Nothing untoward professionally happened to Colonel Ashizuka, commanding the 28th Regiment under Morita, or to any of those other officers in the command structure of the 7th Division who arrived during the last days of the fighting at Nomonhan. Included in this category are the division commander, Lt. Gen. Kunisaki Noboru, and his staff; Colonels Sekine of the 25th Regiment and Sannomiya of the 27th; and Colonel Hirayama of the 7th Field Artillery. Only two elements of the division had been in action all of the time since June: the Ashizuka regiment's 2nd Battalion under Major Kajikawa, and the 26th Regiment commanded by Col. Sumi Shin'ichirō. Hospitalized after the cease-fire, Kajikawa died of his wounds in February 1940.[32] As for Sumi, a notice of 12 October stated that Col. Miyazaki Shūichi was coming from the First Army staff to take over the 26th Regiment. To Sumi's consternation, however, he was being nominally attached to Kwantung Army headquarters, en route to retirement. Instead of receiving the promotion to major general awarded to the two officers who were assuming command of the 13th and 14th brigades, Sumi had been singled out for punishment, although he had certainly not abandoned or pulled out his unit during combat. The only surviving infantry regiment commander who had fought under Komatsubara from the outset, Sumi never adjusted as serenely to his sacking as did Morita.

Sumi's involvement at Nomonhan had begun with high hopes and good intentions on everyone's part. Colonel Ōuchi, the 23rd Division's original chief of staff and an old friend, had joked with Sumi in June about winning the Golden Kite decoration for him. An expert on Soviet affairs, Sumi was not at all unhappy when Lt. Gen. Sonobe, then in command of the 7th Division, chose the 26th Infantry—from among his four regiments—to reinforce Komatsubara at Nomonhan. War college graduates such as Sumi were always promoted faster than others, but every colonel needed to have commanded a regiment, even briefly. Sumi, a colonel since 1937, was thinking of holding such a post for a year or so before donning the insignia of a general officer. His "beheading" or dismissal from service (*kakushu*) came from nowhere, so far as he was concerned, and was "really unusually severe"—although not as bad as some cases already described.

In late November the Kwantung Army chief of staff, Lt. Gen. Iimura, called in Sumi and showed him the war ministry telegram announcing his retirement effective 1 December. Since the colonel knew Iimura well, he blurted out tactlessly, "What on earth have I done wrong, sir?" Iimura admitted that he had no idea, since he was too new in the job to have learned the "true story" about Nomonhan, but that he would let Sumi know as soon as he found out. Seated across the office, deputy chief Endō beckoned to the colonel and said: "Sumi-*san*, I'm really sorry. There was nothing amiss about you operationally or where combat commanding was concerned. But I did hear that you spoke up to the division commander [Komatsubara] during combat."

Sumi thought back on his actions. "It was true," he admits, "that on a couple of occasions I rebuked a staff officer in front of General Komatsubara. At those times, of course, I had every intention of 'getting at' the division commander through innuendo." In a postwar article, Sumi wrote: "Though I believed that I had not failed in my command and was above reproach, it was my turn to be punished. . . . The charges against me were somewhat different from those against the others. I was accused of disobedience and of making needless operational suggestions." On 13 July, for example, Sumi had protested when, to his chagrin, division operations officer Murata reproached him for being essentially "too successful"—i.e., for arbitrarily racing toward the confluence instead of falling back as directed by Komatsubara. Then, on the verge of the IJA counteroffensive of 24 August, Sumi had objected to Komatsubara's "grandiose" notion of transferring forces (a driblet of troops in the case of the 26th Regiment) for operations south of the Holsten. In addition, during the river crossing of early July, Sumi had antagonized Major Tsuji, the influential Kwantung Army staff officer.

According to Sumi, he never received any explanation from a responsible official; but although his dissatisfaction and displeasure were intense, the situation was hopeless and there was no use harping on it or venting regrets. Nevertheless, his former 7th Division commander, Lieutenant General Sonobe, commiserated with him privately, and he heard that war ministry officers at the section-chief level—the ones who had to handle the official paperwork—sympathized with their unit-commander colleagues. It seemed unreasonable to them that front-line officers had to "take the rap"; instead, "the operations shop should have assumed full responsibility." Combat in practice could not be divorced from operational planning. When the latter was faulty, the results could not be good, no matter how hard the soldiers struggled. In other words, the greater the effort, the feebler the results. Still, Sumi thinks, the purging of the General Staff and of the Kwantung Army might have sufficed, except for the fact that the division commander had already specifically asked the authorities to take quick punitive action against a number of his subordinate commanders, in order to evade the true locus of responsibility. "Ever since the 2-26 Mutiny [of February 1936], the army handled personnel matters by a policy of 'purge and control' (*shukugun tōsei*). Thus the opinion of one's immediate superior was absolute; a personnel request emanating from the division commander was accepted by the central authorities 'as is,' for they were trying to check the turmoil in the military system."

In terms of the combat at Nomonhan, Komatsubara was Sumi's all-powerful immediate superior; hence the colonel's fate was sealed. Treating personnel affairs "incompletely and in makeshift fashion," the authorities evinced no real interest in studying and clarifying what had happened at Nomonhan. Theirs was a weakness, argues Sumi, that revealed symptoms of the eventual downfall (*makkiteki shōjō*) of the old imperial army. In his personal diary, after retirement, the colonel wrote about the high-level purge: "It is a temporary 'fake,' not a complete awakening from a long dream." He confesses that he toyed briefly with the idea of making contact with some powerful personage, perhaps Prince Higashikuni Naruhiko, to "save Japan" from the "uncontrolled bunglers," especially since the monarch was a mere figurehead.

After Nomonhan, Sumi served as managing director of the South China Research Association, but he always felt that "a dark cloud hovered over him." *Kenpei* plainclothesmen shadowed him, night and day. When he once reminisced in his native Shinshu, over tea, about his experiences at Nomonhan, his remarks were reported in detail to the central authorities through local officials. Sumi's outspoken criticism to old comrades about the army's failure to learn from Nomonhan attracted surveillance too; War Minister Hata remembers him as a "complainer." But when, during the Pacific War, Sumi was urged by the war ministry's Personnel Bureau to apply for return to active duty or for an appointment as a civil governor in the South Pacific, he stubbornly refused to do so. To submit such requests, he claimed, would have contradicted the spirit of the imperial order that had sent him into retirement. He would have to be called up, feisty Sumi insisted; but no mobilization order was ever issued by war's end. In the postwar period, Sumi ran a country inn at remote Togura spa in Nagano prefecture. Having been retired from the army at the age of 47 after 26 years of service, he proceeded to confound his detractors by living almost 40 years more. Alert, lively, and blunt, he remained loyal to his regiment and stayed in touch with survivors. Sumi welcomed the attention he occasionally received, and he continued to castigate IJA injustice and stupidity, as he saw it, to the very end. He was 85 when he died in April 1977.[33]

Even line officers below the rank of regimental commander were discharged on occasion after the Nomonhan war. One such officer was Onozuka Kichihei, who had risen from the ranks, had been decorated for heroism during the Manchurian Incident, had become a captain in 1934, and had originally commanded the 9th Company of the 71st Infantry. After the death of Lieutenant Colonel Higashi, the fourth regiment commander in two months, Onozuka—although wounded—ended up as the highest-ranking surviving officer and thus the acting commander of the last elements. As soon as Col. Shirahama Shigetō arrived, the battle-tested captain served as his assistant. For weeks he worked on the confused personnel records, night and day, at Hailar. "But someone had to assume responsibility" for the near-annihilation of the regiment and the destruction of its colors. By virtue of his seniority in terms of rank and age (46), Onozuka was that "someone." When he had finished his chores for Shirahama and had briefed a visiting imperial aide, he was discharged and sent back to Japan. At the time, says Onozuka, "I felt very bad about my retirement but, since many high-ranking officers had taken the blame, it seemed best that I do so too." Recalled by the army later, he was in Malaya when he received the Order of the Golden Kite, class B, in recognition of his performance at Nomonhan. "I felt better about it all now," Onozuka remembers. In 1943, at the age of 50, he was finally promoted to the rank of major.[34]

The vicissitudes of Captain Onozuka were not experienced by the commander of the 3rd Battalion of the 64th Regiment, Maj. Kanaizuka Yūkichi. It is true that the latter had considered committing suicide when he got back to 23rd Division headquarters on 30 August and learned that Colonel Yamagata and the colors could not be accounted for. Komatsubara, however, sent word that he should wait for the September counteroffensive, which was the proper time to die in action. When the attack was called off, no punitive action was taken against Kanaizuka or, for that matter, against the ranking officer in the 64th Infantry, Lieutenant Colonel Akai of the 1st Battalion. In the case of Kanaizuka, he remained with the regiment at Hailar, under the new commander, Col. Ōnishi Koshirō, who had taken over on 9 September. Next March, Kanaizuka was promoted to lieutenant colonel. He was given command of an IGU battalion in Harbin in December 1941 and of another battalion in the South Seas in 1943. Since he was not a war college graduate, his promotions did not at all match those of Inada Masazumi, his military academy classmate who rose from AGS colonel at the time of Nomonhan to lieutenant general at war's end. Kanaizuka, advanced to full colonel in June 1945, took command of the 220th Infantry Regiment in New Guinea. He died in 1969 at the age of 75.[35]

Among Japanese artillery units, commanders met fates as varied as those of the infantry. Col. Mishima Giichirō, commanding the 1st Heavy Field Artillery Regiment, had been hit by a shell fragment on 9 August and was evacuated to a field station (and later to Hailar) "at the suggestion of artillery corps commander Hata." The matter of "leaving the battlefield" was extremely important, however, and Mishima had the presence of mind, although wounded, to reenter the positions first and phone the 1st Battalion commander, Major Umeda, to report to him. Arriving from two kilometers away, Umeda was given the order to serve as acting regiment commander, effective immediately. Only then did the colonel enter Hata's staff car and leave for the field hospital. On 20 August, Mishima was attached to Kwantung Army headquarters but, in his case, this was not the prelude to retirement. In the hospital at Hsinking, in early September, the colonel learned from a master sergeant, who arrived in tatters, that the regiment had been destroyed. The noncom, weeping, delivered the last will of Major Umeda, who had killed himself when all was lost. Mishima wanted very much to return to the front and resume command of what was left of the regiment. The day before, however, a Kwantung Army staff officer had notified him officially that he had been relieved as commander and would be assigned to the field artillery school as soon as he had recovered. Indeed, the new regimental commander, Colonel Irie—a year his senior—arrived from Tokyo within a day.

Obliged to "hang around" in Hsinking after he became ambulatory in October, Mishima visited the sacked commanders who were awaiting retirement. On one important occasion he testified at Hailar before a tough Sixth Army investigation committee. Since his regiment had been smashed after he was evacuated, "it was lucky for me," says Mishima, "that I had taken the necessary measures prior to leaving the front." Consequently, although unable to regain command of his regiment, he was oppressed by none of the fierce internal stresses that drove Colonel Sakai to suicide. In December 1939, Mishima arrived at the field artillery school in Japan, where he was assigned to the research department. Since he was a war college graduate (class of 1925) and since his experience at Nomonhan had caused no stain on his record, Mishima rose steadily in the army. After a stint as commandant of the motor school in 1940-41, he was promoted to major general in 1941 and was given command of the artillery group of the old 23rd Division at Hailar during the critical period of preparations to fight the USSR. In 1942, Mishima took over an offshore fortress near Fukuoka; in 1944 he commanded first an artillery group protecting the Tokaido coastline and then a shipping-defense group. Promoted to lieutenant general in March 1945 at the age of 50, Mishima was in command of the 150th Division, defending southwest Korea, when the Pacific War ended.

In Mishima's regiment, no censure was meted out to Maj. Hayashi Tadaaki, the surviving 2nd Battalion commander and acting head of the regiment between the time of Umeda's death and Colonel Irie's arrival. A year after Nomonhan, in October 1940, Hayashi was assigned to the military academy, from which he had graduated in 1924. When the Pacific War ended, he was a very senior lieutenant colonel, 42 years old.

The treatment of Capt. Tsuchiya Masaichi, a mere battery commander, was radically different from that accorded to Major Hayashi. His problem, according to Tsuchiya, was that he belonged to Umeda's 1st Battalion, which waged its ill-fated defensive battle north of the Holsten in late August. "All surviving regular army officers who fought on that side of the river were discharged, but those who were deployed on the south shore, lucky ones such as Hayashi," Tsuchiya continues with a bit of exaggeration, "received the Order of the Golden Kite!" With Umeda and the other battery commander, Captain Yamazaki, already dead, and the battalion's howitzers out of action, Tsuchiya had taken a few men and left the observation post, had broken out of the encirclement, and had struggled back across the river to report to headquarters, arriving two days later. He insists that his action resulted in the salvation of a number of trapped IJA units north of the river and that the Russians made a "serious mistake" when they failed to intercept him. It is probable, however, that Tsuchiya's superiors took a dim view of his withdrawal without specific orders—although, admittedly, communication had become impossible by then.

The captain participated in the corpse-retrieval operation after the cease-fire, but he had no inkling of what lay in store for him, even when he was reassigned to a unit in Japan; "there was no court-martial, no trial, no notice, 'no nothing.'" In January 1940 he was visiting an old army friend and chatting about the severe fighting at Nomonhan, when he discerned sadness and depression on the other officer's face. "Don't you know?" his comrade asked him. Tsuchiya was being dismissed from the service. Furious and hurt, the captain rushed to the war ministry, where he was told to ask no questions and to accept this strange treatment. Even a senior acquaintance in the ministry had no idea why Tsuchiya had been sacked, since it was a "top secret" matter—an experience similar to that of Colonel Sumi. Tsuchiya never received "even a piece of paper" decreeing his retirement. Undoubtedly the official gazette (*Kanpō*) recorded it, but he never saw the entry.

To this day, Tsuchiya says he does not really know why he was retired. He heard that the cabinet had met in secret about the expense and failure at Nomonhan, and that the army had no excuse for the unexpectedly severe losses north of the Holsten. From the political standpoint, some steps had to be taken; "few of us had survived on the north shore anyhow, so we all had to take the blame." Only 27 years old at the time and a graduate of the military academy class of 1935, Tsuchiya had fought in China ever since hostilities broke out there in 1937, and had replaced Prince Higashikuni as commander of Umeda's elite 1st Battery at Nomonhan. In fact, if the campaign of 1939 had been his first combat, Tsuchiya would have committed suicide once his unit was annihilated. Instead, after two years of battle in China plus the Nomonhan experience, he wanted to "save [his] knowledge for [his] country, by living on and fighting again." The army deprived him of the chance. Three months after his discharge, he enrolled in Nihon University. During the Pacific War, Tsuchiya saw no service, although he found employment as a clerk in the secret military installation at Atami that worked on one-man bicycle boats equipped with two torpedoes each, to be used in suicide assaults against enemy shipping.[36]

From the viewpoint of the IJA artillery the darkest cloud was cast, in late August, by Col. Takatsukasa Nobuteru (Nobuhiro), commander of the 7th Heavy Field Artillery Regiment and senior artillery officer north of the Holsten. On the verge of being overwhelmed by the Russians, his unit had deliberately burned its tractors and almost all other vehicles. Although the colonel blames a misunderstanding of his instructions, the result was to leave the big 10-cm. guns virtually helpless. Losing all hope after 2nd Battalion commander Kondō was picked off by a sniper on 27 August, and anxious to save as many men as possible, Takatsukasa left behind a couple of dozen survivors to "defend" the one remaining cannon, withdrew without orders, and made it back to Sixth Army headquarters by the 29th. The colonel described the disaster that had befallen his regiment in grim detail, claiming that most of the ordnance had been destroyed by enemy fire. Hata and his staff, however, were furious with Takatsukasa for the shame he had brought upon the artillery by forsaking his guns, and the colonel was ordered to the rear under house arrest. When Komatsubara came back from his last foray across the Holsten, he too was "very displeased with Takatsukasa for abandoning the battlefield as Ioki had done." From Soviet sources, we know that the Russians captured 12 of Takatsukasa's 16 10-cm. cannon, as well as 14 tractors from unspecified IJA artillery units.[37]

After being allowed some role in the corpse-retrieval operation, Takatsukasa was suspended from duty (*teishoku*), entailing the severance of pay and allowances, and was restricted to Hsinking for a year. A baron and a man of means married to a daughter of the Mitsui family, he and his immediate kin were stripped of all titles and privileges. In his hotel in Hsinking, during the autumn of 1939, Takatsukasa played host to his more sympathetic colleagues, such as Mishima and Sumi, who sometimes came to visit. When the year was over, Takatsukasa was retired from the army. There is no doubt that, if he had been a commoner, he would have been forced to commit suicide as Ioki and Hasebe had done. Throughout the Pacific War and well into the postwar period, Takatsukasa avoided attending meetings and reunions although, he insists, he never once felt that he had done wrong at Nomonhan. More than 30 years passed before he authorized his first published interview about the battle.[38]

Maj. Gen. Uchiyama Eitarō, the overall artillery commander at the time of the July offensive, had returned to his Kwantung Army duty station at Acheng early enough to avoid attracting any blame for subsequent developments. His career progressed accordingly, and in October 1939 he was promoted to the rank of lieutenant general. In 1940, Uchiyama was given command of the 13th Division in China; in 1942, he took over the Third Army in Manchuria; and in 1944, he assumed command of the Twelfth Army in China. War's end found him in Osaka, commanding the Fifteenth Area Army, a post that he had held since April 1945.

Uchiyama's successor at Nomonhan, Maj. Gen. Hata Yūzaburō, had the misfortune of remaining in command at the front until the close, and therefore took responsibility for the behavior of Takatsukasa, his subordinate. Hata promptly advised the Sixth Army commander of his desire to be allowed to retire. After working for another three months on the last details of the Nomonhan affair and the cease-fire, he was sent back to Japan and was retired. Although this action was taken at the general's own request, it was "something like punishment," one of his staff officers admits. Hata lived another 30 years, passing away in 1970 at the age of 80.[39]

Bad karma played its part for individuals at Nomonhan, as always. But few could have been more unlucky than Col. Okamoto Tokuzō, the mild successor to the slain Ōuchi as 23rd Division chief of staff. Wounded very seriously on 30 August, Okamoto was evacuated first to Hailar and then to the Tokyo First Army Hospital, where his amputated leg was healing nicely. In 1940, however, a crazed officer patient sprang upon the helpless Okamoto and slashed him to death with a saber.[40]

Instances of avoidable attrition were numerous. Whereas Zhukov might have decorated Ioki for his defense of Fui Heights, his own command forced him to commit suicide. Nor was use made of the precious experience of Komatsubara. As for Sumi, the ousted colonel remarks that if he could have handled personnel decisions, he would have assigned himself to the infantry school as a "living lesson" from Nomonhan, rich in combat exposure to Soviet armor. "Maybe the Personnel Bureau would not have been smart enough to come up with this assignment," Sumi continues, "but they would probably have sent me, I thought, to take command of a unit on the frontier, since I was an expert on the Russians." Instead, says Sumi, he was punished and ostracized by "whitewashers and apologists" who despised his knowledge.[41]

Another example of discarded experience was Giga Tetsuji, a lieutenant general since 1938. His 2nd Air Division had fought hard and well from the outset of the Nomonhan war, but in the structural reorganization of early September, the very unhappy Giga was replaced by Ebashi before combat had ended and was shunted back to Kungchuling for reasons he never really understood. Giga had hoped, at the least, to be assigned to the advanced flying school at Akeno, but in August 1940 he was made commandant of the Hamamatsu school, where only bomber basic training was taught, thus providing him no chance to apply his battle experience. "All of us [combat commanders] who had participated at Nomonhan," remarks Giga, "were more or less evicted." In October 1941, on the eve of Japan's greatest conflict, the general was retired at the age of 56. "It showed that I was 'unnecessary,'" he remarks with ill-concealed bitterness. Although naturally disheartened, Giga said nothing at the time. He felt that, even if he had spoken up, the "braggarts" (*tengu*, or "long-nosed goblins") in Tokyo would have ignored him. They typically denigrated senior officers who, regardless of experience, supposedly lacked strength and energy. Consequently, Giga had neither the opportunity nor the inclination to become involved in wartime researches on the air force or similar subjects. He went back to farming in Fukui, says the general, adding (as have other senior respondents) that this probably "saved his neck" from postwar Allied prosecutors. The only noteworthy contribution that Giga made to the war effort was to serve as the recalled commander of the Fukui regimental district from March 1945 on. After the war, residing in Gifu, he avoided the controversy that Sumi almost sought, but he was active in veterans' affairs and revealed an excellent memory and keen intelligence even at a very advanced age. Death came to Giga in 1965 when he was 79.[42]

Nomonhan also ended the professional career of Ebashi Eijirō, the combat-tested air force lieutenant general who had succeeded Giga, two military academy classes his junior. Though Ebashi's air command, transferred from China in early September 1939, saw action at Nomonhan for scarcely ten days, the general was involuntarily retired from the service in December of the same year. "It resembled being obliged to assume responsibility for what had happened at Nomonhan, an indirect form of 'punishment' worse than Giga's fate," laments one of Ebashi's staff officers. A last disappointment lay in store. Usually an outgoing senior general was received in audience by the Emperor, but on this occasion an AGS staff officer visited Ebashi at his inn, on his return to Japan, and told him that he need only proceed to the imperial palace, sign the official register, and depart. It was a sad close to 34 years of commissioned duty. Ebashi saw no further service. He died in 1963 at the age of 77.[43]

Diverse but selective, the cruel range of coercion and punishments meted out by the Japanese army was colored by the anachronisms of feudalism and weighted against the front-line commanders at Nomonhan. Ever since the beginning of the conflict in China, the military had tended to "put down" officers who were sparing of lives and sought to apply caution and deliberateness. Such qualities were said to bespeak a "lack of courage." Since the stern code of conduct was inculcated widely and overt self-expression was suppressed mercilessly, discontent appears only in glimmers. For example, in response to the case of Hasebe, who had been driven to self-destruction, fellow officers decked the walls of their billets with poems of heart-wrenching sorrow.[44] Treating individual worth cheaply and ignoring the ultimate price to both army and nation, the military authorities squandered lives, talents, and careers. Thus did they exacerbate the already grievous human toll exacted directly during ground and air combat.

41

A Border Restored
and the Balance Tallied

There had recently been "a certain improvement" in relations between the USSR and Japan, Molotov told the Supreme Soviet on 31 October 1939. The first step was the cease-fire accord of September, ending an "absolutely unnecessary" and sometimes very bloody conflict that supposedly stemmed from the forcible Japanese attempt to appropriate Outer Mongolian territory in favor of Manchukuo. By resolutely repulsing such action, the Russians had demonstrated the value of the pacts of mutual assistance to which the USSR subscribed. When the Japanese made proposals to end the fighting, the Soviet side willingly met their wishes. It was difficult to foretell the tempo of the betterment of relations, said Molotov, for the USSR was not yet sure how far the groundwork had been prepared in Japanese circles; but the Russians welcomed Tokyo's overtures. Meanwhile, peace had been restored fully on the Mongolian-Manchurian frontier.[1]

Supporting Molotov's evaluation of the eased tension is the fact that, immediately after the truce had been arranged, the Russians announced that Konstantin Smetanin, former embassy counselor in Tokyo, was being appointed as ambassador to Japan. For over a year, since the recall of Slavoutsky, only a junior Soviet chargé d'affaires had been on duty in Tokyo, and an "ineffective" one at that, according to German Ambassador Ott. Passing through Harbin on the same day that Molotov addressed the Supreme Soviet, Smetanin was quoted in the Japanese press as saying the Nomonhan agreement indicated that the Soviet government and he were prepared to cooperate for an adjustment in relations with Japan.[2] By all accounts, the Russians did adopt a rather low posture toward Japan, in view of current preoccupation with Poland, the Baltic states, and Finland. According to Zhukov, he and his command returned from the Nomonhan front to Ulan Bator in late October.[3]

By the terms of the Nomonhan truce accord, Tōgō and Molotov had delegated the unresolved matters of border demarcation or remarcation to special negotiating teams, which were supposed to be formed without delay. In his speech of 31 October, Molotov called the formation of a mixed commission the next step in improving Soviet-Japanese relations. On the same day, in Tokyo, U.S. Ambassador Grew learned from the foreign ministry that preliminary talks were still proceeding in Moscow and that the Japanese government was "restrainedly hopeful that—contrary to the failure of the commission established after the Changkufeng Incident to accomplish anything—some progress toward a settlement of the vexed border question may come about to put an end to the costly and futile series of frontier 'incidents.'" [4]

According to Russian sources, the constitution of the frontier committee was delayed because the Japanese side balked at implementing the agreement. Therefore new negotiations had to be undertaken during the autumn. In mid-November, considerable progress was made in the Soviet capital by Tōgō, and in Tokyo by Smetanin, who conferred at length with Abe's new foreign minister, Nomura Kichisaburō, even before the presentation of ambassadorial credentials. Finally, on 19 November, Molotov and Tōgō signed a formal agreement concerning the composition, functions, and zone of operation of the mixed commission, which was to address the topic of "precise demarcation" of the borders in dispute between the Mongolian People's Republic and Manchukuo "in the area of the recent conflict." Work was to start immediately in the Siberian city of Chita; the second half of the meetings would take place in Manchuria at Harbin. [5]

The Japanese-Manchurian delegation, totaling less than 30 members, was drawn on the Japanese side from the foreign ministry, the embassy in Hsinking, and the Kwantung Army, and on the Manchukuoan side from Manchurian, Japanese, and Mongolian nationals serving in the foreign affairs bureau, the security bureau, and the armed forces. Kubota Kan'ichirō, the consul general at Harbin, headed the Japanese team; the Manchukuoan side was led by Kameyama Ichiji, the political section chief in the foreign affairs bureau in Hsinking. The Kwantung Army assigned Maj. Mishina Ryūi from the geographical survey section and, in mufti, Majors Sasai Hiroichi and Tanabe Shinshi as "special consultants." Support staff included surveyors and linguists, particularly specialists in difficult ancient Mongolian.

The Russian team was headed by the equivalent of a major general—Bogdanov, about 45, chief of staff of the Far Eastern corps. Impressive, low-key, and bespectacled, he struck the Japanese as more of a diplomat than a professional soldier. Bogdanov displayed very strong authority but seemed to be greatly influenced by a certain lieutenant colonel, undoubtedly an NKVD security officer. The Russians' chief interpreter was ineffective, although a professor from the Oriental Institute in Moscow. Whereas the Japanese delegates rather liked Bogdanov, they were unhappy with Jamsarong, the acting premier of Outer Mongolia, who resembled nothing more than a village mayor. Shabby looking and of dubious ability, he left matters entirely to Bogdanov. When Jamsarong did speak, he often said silly things.

Since the parleys were to center on boundary delimitation, both sides collected as much cartographic and supporting evidence as possible. The Japanese drew "precious and secret" documentation from all over Manchuria and from Tokyo, Peking, Nanking, Canton, and even Europe. The identification of the Halha was vital to the Japanese contentions, of course, but the ordinarily authoritative South Manchuria Railway materials proved disadvantageous in this case and had to be impounded and suppressed. In all, the Japanese brought several dozen trunks of documentation, difficult to store and to secure.

After praying at a shrine in Hsinking, in early December the Japanese-Manchukuoan committee entrained for Chita via Harbin and Manchouli, cheered on by telegrams of encouragement and by friendly crowds in Manchuria. In Chita—quiet, clean, and extremely cold and snowy at this time of year—the team members were put up in the newly painted best hotel in town, run by the municipal authorities and given over entirely to the visitors, but swarming with security men and apparently bugged. The parleys themselves were held in an attractive sanatorium located in the outskirts of the city. As a protective measure, the Japanese began to house all classified material in the Manchukuoan consulate.

The negotiators met about every third day, eight times in all, between 7 and 25 December. Use of four languages slowed the progress. Psychologically, the Japanese approached the bargaining table with the attitude of having "won" at Nomonhan; i.e., although their side had sustained considerable losses, the Russians must have suffered far more. Still, the Sixth Army's line of occupation in the Nomonhan sector was at its worst when the ceasefire occurred, deep inside Manchukuo by the Japanese contention, except in the Handagai area, where the aggressive Katayama detachment had done well in September. Though there was no doubt in the minds of the Japanese-Manchukuoan delegation that the Halha was the only boundary (reinforced by a captured Soviet army map), it would be difficult to argue against the realities of *uti possidetis*, which endowed possession with nine points of the law.

Bogdanov's initial presentation, hesitant and weak, came as a pleasant surprise to the Japanese, for the Russian-Mongolian side's boundary claim lay farther west than had been expected. The more hawkish Japanese were convinced, circumstantially, that the Soviet irresolution stemmed from a feeling of defeat at Nomonhan. After all, many rumors were still rife in Chita, the Russians' rear logistical base, about the large numbers of wounded soldiers hospitalized there prior to the arrival of the negotiators. Another consideration might be Soviet nervousness concerning their latest war—the Finnish campaign, which had just broken out on 30 November, so soon after the operations at Nomonhan and against Poland. En route to

Chita, the Japanese had seen many uncovered Russian military freight trains laden with trucks and heavy matériel, all heading west.

Whatever early advantage the Japanese hawks thought they enjoyed was vitiated, from their standpoint, by "feeble" instructions that arrived from Tokyo and Hsinking. By accepting a boundary far to the east of the Halha, the Japanese government was revealing its own attitude of having been defeated at Nomonhan. In the subcommittees at Chita, experts debated the conflicting cartography, but neither side retreated substantively and agreement could not be reached.[6] While these inconclusive conversations continued in Siberia, there were two encouraging developments at the diplomatic level in Moscow on 31 December: the Japanese finally agreed to pay the last installment on Manchukuo's 1935 purchase of the Chinese Eastern Railway, and a temporary Soviet-Japanese fisheries accord was devised for 1940.[7]

The locale of the meetings, as agreed in Moscow, was transferred to Harbin in January 1940. Headquarters for the Japanese side was Kubota's consulate; the Russians and Outer Mongolians were housed at the Yamato Hotel; and the deliberations took place at the Hotel New Harbin. Between 7 and 30 January, the delegates met another eight times. The Soviet side produced maps dating back to 1734 and 1859 in support of their claims, but the Japanese and Manchurians argued against every inaccurate or questionable point. When their opportunity came, the Russians did the same thing in reverse. In an exchange of aides-mémoires at the sixth session on 22 January, the Japanese held fast to their demands regarding the Nomonhan district but offered to yield in the area south of the Arshaan River. The Russians' plan repeated their latest contentions; no longer were they as hesitant as they had been in Chita at the beginning. Since the Japanese would not abandon their claim to the Halha line, the conference went from bad to worse. The matter of the prisoners of war became enmeshed with the frontier question and exerted indirect pressure on the Japanese. Eventually the more aggressive members came to the conclusion that the Russians—tied down in Finland and ejected from the League of Nations in mid-December —were merely probing the Japanese and were more interested in words than in actions in the Far East at this point.

During the seventh meeting, on 25 January, the Russians' attitude became "arrogant" and they intimated that they were going to break off the talks. On the same day, according to Tanabe, IJA signal intelligence intercepted radio messages transmitted from the Yamato Hotel confirming that the Russians were concerned only with "reconnoitering" their adversaries' position. Realizing that the conference was doomed unless substantive concessions were forthcoming, the Japanese and Manchurian committee members assembled to consider the impasse. Major Mishina asserted that, from the military standpoint, there was no alternative to the abandonment of discussions since the army could not accept Soviet occupation of the Nomonhan zone. The only person who dared to speak up was a young delegate, Kitagawa Shirō, who argued against a breakoff of negotiations for the reason that the Soviet claim was historically acceptable in general and did not mean Japan was either defeated or disgraced. Mishina responded courteously but emotionally, to the effect that a Japanese soldier could not agree to Russian military occupation of the bloody battlefield at Nomonhan.

The positions of the Japanese and Manchurian hawks and doves were irreconcilable. Finally the delegates adopted the recommendation of Kameyama, always a proponent of moderation, that the conference be continued and that the central authorities be queried about the possibility of dividing the Nomonhan district equally as well as giving up some territory south of the Arshaan. Approval was speedily forthcoming. On 26 and 27 January, the Japanese delegates met privately with the receptive Bogdanov and worked out a compromise in principle, to be endorsed officially on the 28th and developed in detail on the 30th. At the meeting of 28 January, however, the Soviet-Mongolian side unexpectedly reneged on the private arrangement, refused to sign it, and instead produced a document resembling an ultimatum, which closed out matters by announcing a return to the original contentions. Apparently Moscow had rejected Bogdanov's specific compromise, in order to impress the Mongolians. Since the Japanese and Manchurians recoiled too, the meeting of 30 January was the last one. The delegates, says Tanabe, filed out in silence, but the major was personally pleased with the outcome: "It had been a close call, and we almost gave in to the Russians . . . but now our dead at Nomonhan could sleep in peace."[8]

The Russians, who blame the Japanese for not recognizing the validity of the documentation they provided, suggest a deeper explanation: solution of the frontier problem was "consciously postponed" by the government in Tokyo to reassure the alarmed Americans (who were considering coming to terms) that the Japanese were not working on a rapprochement with Russia. The alleged Japanese procrastination about demarcation of the Manchurian-Mongolian boundaries is given as the Russians' reason for failing to sign a new fisheries convention. Addressing the Supreme Soviet in March 1940, Molotov said he could not express great satisfaction with respect to relations with Japan. For example, prolonged negotiations notwithstanding, "the important question of determining the frontier on the territory in the area of the military conflict of last year has remained unsettled." Linking this problem with the "quite abnormal" behavior of the Japanese authorities regarding utilization of the last CER payment and treatment of Soviet employees in Japan and Manchukuo, Molotov issued a stern warning: "It is time it was realized in Japan that under no circumstances will the Soviet

Union tolerate any infringement of her interests. Only if Soviet-Japanese relations are understood in this way can they develop satisfactorily."[9]

No explanation of Bogdanov's and Jamsarong's abrupt departure from Harbin was ever provided by the Russians. Only in 1978 did former delegate Kameyama divulge details publicly. Bogdanov had come to say goodbye and to report that his team was leaving immediately. Reflecting the anger of the Japanese-Manchurian side, Kameyama retorted that it was irresponsible to pull out on the eve of agreement. Thereupon Bogdanov revealed that his life had been threatened by White Russians. The ire of Kameyama evaporated, for he knew that the consequences of assassination would be worse than those attending the breakdown of the conference. Indeed, Kameyama is of the opinion that the White Russian terrorists were in the employ of the Kwantung Army and of Major Tsuji in particular. Though Tsuji is supposed to have been stationed in China at the time of the Harbin conference, Major Tanabe—a delegate—was his classmate, and we have already seen how displeased were both Tanabe and Major Mishina with respect to the proposed boundary settlement.[10]

In view of the presumable recalcitrance of the Russians, the Japanese government shied away from further discussion of the frontiers. But on 5 March, little more than a month after the final meeting at Harbin, Lozovsky called in Ambassador Tōgō and proposed a compromise involving Russian "compensation" in the form of two or three kilometers of land near the Handagai road on the east side of the Halha. A week later, on the 11th, Lozovsky indicated to Tōgō that the Soviet offer was of the "take it or leave it" variety. Reminding Lozovsky that the Russians had not entertained Japan's own compromise plan, the ambassador asserted that the Japanese could not accept the withdrawal of their forces from the entire district in question— i.e., could not abandon the Nomonhan sector. That such a stand provoked Molotov's displeasure is revealed in the commissar's speech before the Supreme Soviet in late March.[11]

Russia's geopolitical calculations were upset by the series of fast-moving developments that occurred in Western Europe in the spring of 1940: stunning German triumphs in Norway and Denmark, the Low Countries, and France; Italian entry into the war. It was the American government's understanding that the USSR now sought a boundary settlement with the Japanese "in order to be free to act in Europe."[12]

The resolute stance of the Soviet-Mongolian governments, Russian sources insist, compelled Japan to abandon its "unfounded claims." In Moscow on 9 June, Molotov and Tōgō signed a breakthrough agreement concerning the general shape of the frontier between the Mongolian People's Republic and Manchukuo. The cartographic basis was the Red Army's large-scale 1:200,000 plot adopted at the time of the original cease-fire in the preceding

September. Compiled between 1932 and 1934, the mapwork incorporated revisions to the Russians' earlier 1:84,000 survey whereby, most importantly, the border had been shifted east of and away from the Halha. By the terms of a follow-up agreement on 18 July, details of delimitation were left to a Manchukuoan-Mongolian boundary commission operating on the scene.[13]

In his next speech to the Supreme Soviet on 1 August, Molotov expressed pleasure with the fact that Russo-Japanese relations were beginning to assume "a somewhat more normal character." The boundary agreement was especially important because the protracted delay in settling the question had exerted an unfavorable effect on the relationships of all the parties concerned. Nevertheless, the real intentions of the new Japanese government (Konoe's second cabinet, formed in July) remained obscure and "imperialist appetites were growing." The betterment of ties with Japan was only possible if each side respected the other's interests equally and understood the need to remove "certain obstacles [that] are no longer important."[14] According to Russian sources, Molotov and his colleagues found it incomprehensible that, shortly afterward, Konoe's foreign minister, Matsuoka, chose to recall Tōgō as ambassador and replace him with Lt. Gen. Tatekawa Yoshitsugu of Manchurian Incident fame.[15]

It suited both sides, however, to proceed with the task of specific border demarcation. Six meetings were held in Chita again, between 3 and 24 August, involving the Mongolian and Manchukuoan technicians. Actual surveying on the spot began in early September. The entire arduous task was not completed until 15 May 1942, almost a year after the Soviet Union had been attacked by the Germans, and a half-year after Japan went to war with the Western powers. Without fanfare, the Soviet-Mongolian side had secured the controversial main boundary in the basin of the Holsten, which it had been demanding throughout and for which it had fought so hard. The Japanese-Manchukuoan side gained face-saving but minor adjustments of the border in the Handagai district southeast of Nomonhan.[16] It was a case of "the good old rule, the simple plan, that he shall take who has the power, and he shall keep who can." Stalin employed less elegant phraseology: attackers would always "receive a crushing repulse to teach them not to poke their pig snouts into our Soviet garden."[17]

The lopsided settlement of the frontiers is one objective way of choosing the victor at Nomonhan. In addition the Russians, as opposed to the Japanese, announced a detailed inventory of captured matériel.[18] It is in the category of artillery, a traditional favorite arm of the Russians, that the closest correlations can be made. The capture of 12 of Takatsukasa's 10-cm. cannon has already been mentioned. The Soviet command also claimed to have retrieved a dozen 15-cm. pieces that can be identified as seven of Mishima's 16 howitzers and five of Someya's six cannon. When three captured 12-cm. pieces are added (from the howitzer battalion of Ise's field artillery regiment), the total of seized heavy ordnance comes to 27. This figure resembles Sixth Army data to the effect that 28 artillery pieces were destroyed by the enemy. Among 75-mm. field guns, the Russians report capturing 50 pieces —somewhat more than the Ise regiment's own tabulation of 44 guns lost.[19]

Further evidence of Soviet pleasure with the results of the Nomonhan war is to be found in the plaudits by high officials. Choibalsan visited Zhukov's command and "cordially thanked the soldiers for what the Soviet people had done, sealing with their blood their loyalty to the commitments they had taken upon themselves." On 29 August 1939, Defense Commissar Voroshilov sent a long and fulsome telegram of congratulations to Soviet forces stationed in Mongolia. Russian units had been defending not only the MPR and the inviolability of Soviet promises, but also the territory of the USSR itself, from Lake Baikal to Vladivostok. The Japanese generals, who had sought revenge for Changkufeng, were smashed by a "doubly powerful" blow this time, meted out by "workers' and peasants' units." Captured documents, trophies, and prisoners demonstrated the destruction of two enemy divisions and the disintegration of the Hsingan line. The Soviet field army had justified the confidence of the government and the Bolshevik Party. In an order issued on 7 November, Voroshilov expressed gratitude for the heroism and excellent performance of the troops, who had covered themselves with "genuine glory."

The Soviet authorities lavished awards and decorations on deserving commanders, soldiers, and airmen, and on commissars and political instructors. Voroshilov singled out four "glorious sons of our motherland" for particular commendation: Zhukov; Group Commissar M. S. Nikishev; Front Commander G. M. Shtern; and Front Commissar Biryukov. Zhukov, in turn, has called Nikishev "a skillful leader and a highly principled Party member," who handled Military Council affairs so effectively that "even under the most unfavorable and complicated conditions we never had any disagreements."[20]

In the first round of major awards, which accompanied Voroshilov's congratulations of 29 August, the gold medal of Hero of the Soviet Union was bestowed upon 31 men. The figure eventually reached 70, including Zhukov and Shtern.[21] Other individual decorations included a minimum of 83 Orders of Lenin, 595 Red Banners, and 134 Red Stars, as well as 33 medals for bravery and 58 for merit. In addition, 25 unit citations were awarded, including the Order of Lenin (to the 36th Motorized Infantry Regiment, the 11th Tank Brigade, the 100th Air Brigade, and the 24th Motorized Infantry

Regiment) and the Order of the Red Banner (to the 57th Infantry Division, the 8th and 9th armored brigades, and the 149th Infantry Regiment).[22]

For their part, the military and Party authorities in Ulan Bator bestowed a galaxy of medals and orders, and occasionally the coveted title of Hero of the MPR, upon deserving Mongolian personnel for feats performed between May and September 1939. The 6th Cavalry Division alone won more than 300 decorations, including the Hero award to Colonel L. Dandar, the 17th Regiment commander, and to Pvt. T. Olzvoj [Olzvai], a renowned light machine gunner.[23]

Near the Halha River, the Mongolians have erected a monument to render "eternal glory to the heroic warriors of the Soviet Army and the brave men of the MPRA who fell in the battles against the Japanese invaders." At the wreath-laying ceremonies in August 1959, on the twentieth anniversary of the Nomonhan war, two particularly historic Russian personages were in attendance: I. I. Fedyuninsky, the former 24th Motorized Infantry Regiment commander, now a general of the army and chief of the Turkestan military district; and Molotov, the old foreign commissar, in virtual exile as ambassador to Mongolia. Replacing a Japanese memorial to the IJA war dead, in 1954 the Mongolians had also put up a monument in honor of Soviet tankmen—"Yakovlev's heroes" of the 11th Brigade.[24]

The Halha sector remains as underpopulated as ever; about 35,000 people dwell in the 123,000 square miles of the Dornot district. Nevertheless, a Mongolian survey has revealed that the Halha basin alone possesses 270,000 hectares of black-soil land, offering extremely attractive prospects for cattle-raising in particular. At the river battlefield there is now a large-horned beef and dairy cattle range and an experimental station growing vegetables and grain crops, fruits and berries, sunflowers and sugar beets. Nostalgic Russian soldiers have been able to revisit the bloody scenes of yesteryear. For example, a Soviet agricultural consultant who came from Chita in 1966 to visit the experimental station by the Halha had been a junior tank commander at Nomonhan. Coincidentally, his Mongolian assistant proved to have been an armored car driver in 1939 too.[25]

After the Nomonhan war, the Japanese army could not very well claim to have liberated the region east of the Halha or to have annihilated the enemy's force. Still, thousands of brave officers and men had fought to the death under difficult circumstances, and their exploits deserved recognition, partly for the intrinsic quality of their deeds and partly because of the army's devotion to *Yamato damashii*—the Japanese spirit. Like the Russians, therefore, the Japanese granted numerous awards and decorations.

Singled out for particular notice was the late Capt. Yamazaki Masaki, battery commander of the 1st Heavy Field Artillery Regiment, who received the only army-wide individual citation for merit (*kojin kanjō*) from General Ogisu on 1 October 1939, and was accorded the posthumous title of "war god" (*gunshin*). For outstanding performance in combat, the ultimate decoration was the Order of the Golden Kite (*kinshi kunshō*), emanating from the war minister on behalf of the country. Customarily the third through fifth classes went to officers below the rank of general; the fifth through seventh classes, to noncoms and enlisted personnel. Yamazaki received not only the fourth-class Order of the Golden Kite but also the same class of the Order of the Rising Sun (*kyokujitsushō*), a special honor given in both wartime and peacetime. Third-class Orders of the Golden Kite from Nomonhan went posthumously to a number of outstanding officers above the rank of captain—e.g., Majors Kajikawa of the 28th Infantry and Ikuta of the 26th. In view of the universal slowness in processing awards, some surviving recipients did not receive their decorations and citations for merit (*ronkōkōshō*) until the Pacific War was at hand or was actually under way. As for the theater of the original award, feats performed at Nomonhan were lumped together with those from the China Incident; the type of combat was termed "B" (*otsu*).[26]

Unit citations were issued by General Ueda on behalf of the Kwantung Army, by Ogisu on behalf of the Sixth Army, and by Komatsubara on behalf of the 23rd Division. The first of these came on 10 June, when Komatsubara commended the divisional reconnaissance unit that, under Lieutenant Colonel Azuma, had met the Russians at the end of May and been destroyed by them. Soon afterward, on 23 June, Ueda bestowed unit citations on Colonel Noguchi's 11th Fighter Group for its air battles in May, and on Lieutenant Colonel Matsumura's 24th Fighter Group for its combat in June. On 1 September, the Kwantung Army commander awarded a unit citation to the late 2nd Lieutenant Hayama's infantry platoon of the 72nd Regiment, which had fought without stint until annihilation in July. The only infantry regiment to receive a Kwantung Army citation was Colonel Sakai's 72nd, commended on 5 September for its performance on 3 July and 24 August. Ueda granted citations, on the same day, to units in Lieutenant General Giga's air division, including the 7th, 9th, and 12th wings, and a squadron of the 16th Group.

On 1 October, Ogisu awarded a number of unit citations: to Capt. Kusaba Sakae's 7th Battery of the Ise field artillery regiment for combat on 3 July, 23 July, and 27 August; to the 3rd Battalion of the 71st Infantry for the actions of 14 July, 23 July, and 22-23 August; and to the composite water-supply unit of the 23rd Division.[27] Lastly, on 28 October, Komatsubara issued a unit citation to Colonel Miyao's 1st Independent Field Artillery Regiment, which had operated particularly well on the left side of the Holsten in late August.[28]

A particularly impressive mode of military recognition was the personal recounting of selected exploits to an imperial aide for transmission to the Emperor. At Kwantung Army headquarters, senior officers had given general briefings on the Nomonhan fighting. But since the Emperor wanted to learn the "real, inside story," the imperial messenger proceeded to 23rd Division headquarters in Hailar, where a range of lower-ranking combat officers delivered firsthand presentations. Thus, on 16 January 1940, Captain Onozuka, the 71st Regiment aide, spoke movingly for 15 minutes about the combat performance and heroic death of Lieutenant Colonel Higashi, acting regimental commander, whose last charge was "like a scene from a movie." The gallantry of an enlisted man was recalled vividly by a company commander from the 64th Regiment, Capt. Gotō Chikashi, who eulogized an acting corporal named Sugaya. Resolved that his machine gun site should be his graveyard, Sugaya evinced a determination that was the apotheosis of the man of Yamato and that would have caused demons to weep.

Representing the 72nd Regiment, Capt. Moriyama Yasoichi, commander of the 7th Company, extolled the sense of responsibility and the martyrdom on 23 July of Lieutenant Hayama, the indomitable young officer whose platoon had won a unit citation from General Ueda. Captain Kusaba described the accomplishments of another unit that had earned a Sixth Army citation, his own 7th Battery of field artillery. In exciting detail, the captain told the imperial aide of the antitank actions of 3 July in particular, when the battery had saved Komatsubara's staff car from imminent destruction. Like his colleagues, Kusaba emphasized self-perceived attributes of the Japanese army: Yamato spirit, faith in victory, and offensive élan.[29]

42

The Lessons and
Applications of Nomonhan

After the campaign at Nomonhan was over, Russian troops entered winter quarters in Mongolia, where they surveyed their accomplishments and assessed what they had learned. During the year that followed, the Soviet army as a whole made fundamental changes in political training, including the elimination of the post of political commissar per se and the introduction of a new disciplinary code. So far as the level of military proficiency was concerned, however, Zhukov was essentially pleased with his battle-tested forces in the Far East. The best personnel were dispatched to share their skills with units that had not seen action, and with the MPRA. Results were impressive. "It was not accidental," writes Zhukov, "that the units which had fought in Mongolia . . . when moved to the Moscow area in 1941, fought the German troops so well that no praise is too high for them."

Among the highest-ranking Soviet veterans of the hostilities against the Japanese, G. M. Shtern ought to have played an important part during the approaching Russo-German crisis. Esteemed for his leadership and organizational capability, Shtern had served as principal military adviser in Spain and as chief of staff to Blyukher in the Special Far Eastern Army. At the peak of the undeclared border war with the Japanese at Changkufeng in August 1938, Shtern took personal command of the front-line 39th Rifle Corps and won the Order of Lenin. Upon Blyukher's strange ouster and eventual execution, he was given command of the offshoot 1st Special Red Banner Army on the Ussuri. A deputy to the Supreme Soviet since 1937 and a recent member of the Communist Party's Central Committee, Shtern addressed the 18th Party Congress in March 1939 as the victor of Changkufeng. With the coming of the new combat at Nomonhan, in July 1939 Shtern became the head of the "front group" that coordinated Soviet-Mongolian operations. It is said, however, that Zhukov possessed the "inside track" to Stalin, took direct orders from Moscow and, although considerably junior to Shtern, "ignored [his] polite offers of assistance." Under the circumstances, Shtern seems to have studiously avoided offending Zhukov. The latter has little more to say than that in overcoming the immense logistical difficulties on the Mongolian front, the Soviet forces were assisted greatly by the military council of the Trans-Baikal Military District and by Shtern and his personnel. As we saw, Shtern won the title of Hero of the Soviet Union for his performance in this capacity.

In November 1939, Shtern reported personally to Voroshilov about the fighting in the Far East. Early next year, with the Finnish war going very badly for the Russians, Shtern was given command of the embattled Eighth Army. The excellence of his combat direction during a difficult time is reflected in his promotion from army commander, 2nd grade, to colonel general, a new rank awarded to only four officers in the wholesale revamping announced in June 1940. Shtern then took over the powerful Far East command that had been set up at Khabarovsk. During the large-scale, army-wide field maneuvers of autumn 1940, he oversaw three days of exercises involving the forced crossing of the Amur River and two days of sharp-shooting. But in March 1941, Shtern was transferred to command of the antiaircraft forces, a post from which he was mysteriously removed a week before the German invasion in June. Together with at least one other Hero of the Soviet Union—the air force general Y. V. Smushkevich—Shtern was unaccountably executed, probably in October 1941. Thus the matter of the Red Army's possible profit from the lessons of Nomonhan is complicated by considerations that are irrelevant from the strictly military point of view. Unfair favoritism, political infighting, Stalin's paranoia, secret intrigue, and probably an element of antisemitism combined to cut down a general as capable as Shtern at the untimely age of 41. One wonders whether Shtern's professional criticism of Zhukov's position paper at the study session of December 1940 had presaged his doom.[1]

Zhukov avoided the fate that befell Shtern, Blyukher, Smushkevich, and countless other victims of Stalin's purges. In the promotions of 1940, Zhukov was elevated from corps commander to the new rank of full general, a distinction given only to five senior officers. Called to Moscow in early May of that year, Zhukov was received for the first time by Stalin personally in the presence of President Kalinin, Foreign Commissar Molotov, and other members of the Politburo. After listening carefully to Zhukov's report and asking many substantive questions, Stalin directed the general to assume command of the Kiev Military District, largest in Russia, and to apply his recent combat experience to good effect.

Among the points Zhukov made in briefing Stalin was the splendid performance of the Soviet regular troops, in particular Petrov's 36th Motorized Rifle Division, Galanin's 57th Rifle Division from the Trans-Baikal district, and the tank brigades, especially Yakovlev's 11th Brigade. The 82nd Rifle Division, raised from the Ural region, was a territorial formation and "not good at first," with poorly trained personnel and new conscripts. Zhukov stressed the indispensability of his two tank and three motorized armored brigades in surrounding and smashing the Japanese Sixth Army so quickly, although the Soviet BT-5 and BT-7 tanks were too fire-prone. The number of armored and mechanized detachments in the Red Army should be increased, Zhukov recommended. Russian artillery was far better than the Japanese, particularly with respect to accuracy. After a shaky beginning, the Soviet air force had achieved unquestioned aerial supremacy, thanks to the arrival of improved planes (Chaikas and I-16's) and of 21 experienced pilots, all Heroes of the Soviet Union, headed by Smushkevich. Generally speaking, Zhukov added, Russian troops were "greatly superior" to the Japanese. Outer Mongolian forces, trained and supported by the Russians, had fought well, as in the case of the armored battalion combat at Bain Tsagan in early July. MPRA cavalry, however, had sustained severe casualties because of being "a bit too sensitive to air raids and artillery fire."

The greatest problem, Zhukov told Stalin, had concerned material and technical supplies, which had to be hauled across distances of 650 to 700 kilometers, at great cost in gasoline. Here Zhukov indicated appreciation for the logistical assistance rendered by Shtern and his military district. One minor complaint had to do with the horrible mosquitoes of Khalkhin Gol, against which the Japanese had nets but the Russians did not. In response to specific queries by Stalin, Zhukov said that N. N. Voronov, the artillery colonel general, had provided much help in organizing supplies of ammunition and planning artillery fire, and that Col. Gen. D. G. Pavlov, the armor expert, had shared his Spanish experience with the tank forces. Marshal G. I. Kulik, the chief of the Main Artillery Administration, had not done a thing worth mentioning, however.

To Kalinin's inquiry about presumable Japanese intentions, Zhukov speculated that the immediate objective had been the seizure of Outer Mongolian territory west of the Halha, to be followed by the construction of a fortified belt along the river. The system would be designed to defend a second railroad line of strategic importance near the Trans-Baikal border, west of the Chinese Eastern Railway. Speaking for all of his troops and unit commanders and for himself personally, Zhukov remarked that the fighting at Nomonhan had "proved a very useful school of combat experience."

Once in place at Kiev, Zhukov introduced himself to the central committee secretaries of the Ukrainian Communist Party and recounted the exploits of his forces at Nomonhan. Clearly at Zhukov's behest, a number of his favorite subordinate officers in the Far Eastern battles gravitated to commands in European Russia with him. Potapov, promoted to major general of tank troops, took command of the Fifth Army at Lutsk in the Ukraine. When Kiev fell to the Germans in September 1941, he was wounded, taken prisoner, and interrogated by Guderian. Although he ended up in the

Hamelsburg concentration camp, Potapov survived the war and regained his rank. Fedyuninsky went from Nomonhan to a series of increasingly significant posts: 82nd Division commander; 15th Rifle Corps commander under Potapov; 42nd Army commander (September 1941); 54th Army commander (December 1941) on the critical Leningrad front, where he conducted the first counteroffensive operations in December 1941–January 1942; and eventually Eleventh Army commander, on the 2nd Byelorussian front, as a lieutenant general. Zhukov's old group commissar, Nikishev, was assigned to the Military Council of Potapov's Fifth Army, and died in action at the beginning of the war with Germany. Even Division Commander N. V. Feklenko, who had not impressed Zhukov as 57th Corps commander at Tamsag in June 1939, saw impressive further service in the European theater: 19th Mechanized Corps commander (and a major general) near Rovno when the German invasion began; 38th Army commander on the Dnieper front in August 1941. Brigade Commander A. M. Kushchev, Feklenko's chief of staff at Tamsag, was in on the kill at Berlin in 1945 as chief of staff of the Fifth Army.[2]

Zhukov, who had the greatest opportunity to prove himself, went the farthest professionally of any veteran of the fighting against the Japanese. During the summer and autumn of 1940, the troops of his Kiev Military District underwent intensive field maneuvers designed to implement tough new training directives that had emanated from high-level Party and governmental meetings of March and April. Zhukov's tactical games included two three-day exercises involving "aggressor" forces at the reinforced regiment level attacking reinforced battalions. In September, Marshal Timoshenko— Voroshilov's successor as defense commissar since May—inspected Zhukov's staff exercises, which addressed the mission of breaking through a fortified zone with a rifle corps and using mechanized forces to exploit the penetration.

Zhukov was obviously making his mark; he was directed to prepare a report on the nature of modern offensive operations for a highest-level military-Party conference to be held at Moscow in late December. Drawing upon his experience at Nomonhan, his paper stressed the "technical-operational revolution" whereby armor, planes, artillery, and infantry could be combined to reduce not only field fortifications but also modern multiphase defenses. Zhukov says that his presentation drew an essentially favorable response, although there were useful comments pro and con. He does not identify Shtern's criticism of his timing for insertion of armored corps into the breakthrough zone.

Another veteran of the Nomonhan fighting, air force Maj. Gen. G. P. Kravchenko, spoke up at the conference of December 1940. A "hero pilot" as a major in 1939, Kravchenko criticized a paper dealing with combat aviation in the offensive and in the struggle for air supremacy presented by Lt. Gen. P. V. Rychagov, the air force commander who had fought in Spain. Kravchenko especially disliked the decentralization of military aviation and the fractionalization of air force corps and divisions.

In the strategic war games of January 1941 that followed the main conferences in Moscow, Zhukov at one point played the commander of the Blue or German side, against Pavlov for the Red or Soviet forces. Pavlov clumsily lost that stage of the map maneuvers, to Stalin's intense annoyance during the after-action analysis. But it was the question of armor doctrine that rekindled a controversy that has an important bearing on Russian lessons drawn from the Nomonhan war. Whereas the Mongolian campaign had supposedly represented the triumph of tanks and mobile artillery operating in special combat groups, the fate of Soviet armored formations still hung in the balance. As the Russians now admit, the High Command had incorrectly assessed the experience with tanks and motorized forces in Spain. Pavlov came back with battlefield evidence purporting to demonstrate that large mechanized units should be supplanted by separate tank battalions built into infantry divisions and corps, and by tank brigades operating autonomously but available for support of infantry as needed. Convinced by Pavlov, Stalin himself took part in the meeting that endorsed the regressive decision on 21 November 1939—only three months after Zhukov's mechanized army had overrun the Japanese infantry and artillery at Nomonhan. With Voroshilov's enthusiastic agreement, the Red Army proceeded to break up the existing seven mechanized corps, whose origins went back to the early 1930's.

Professionals such as Shaposhnikov and Zhukov were unhappy about the reversal in armor doctrine. Only the brilliant performance of the panzer divisions in France in May-June 1940 prodded the Soviet decision-makers at the last minute to reconstitute mechanized corps made up of one motorized division and two tank divisions each. Nine such corps were formed hastily in 1940, and another 20 were supposed to be assembled in the spring of 1941, too late in practice to cope with the German invasion in June. Even so, as late as the war-game critique of January 1941, Marshal Kulik—a favorite of Stalin—still dared to argue for giant infantry divisions and horse-drawn transport. Against new tank chief Fedorenko's call for more and better armor, Kulik extolled the superiority of artillery. He reiterated the arguments about the Spanish experience and the need for only company- and battalion-size armored units. Zhukov has commented on the strange impression conveyed by Kulik's obsolete views. Even Stalin had to admit that the day of mechanized and motorized armies had arrived and that the government was "bringing the motor to the army." Timoshenko insisted that the military was in unanimous support of the need to mechanize. Indeed, the military district commanders were clamoring for one to three mechanized corps each. Pavlov, now in charge of the Western District, asked for three or four, and Zhukov wanted the most of all—four or five corps.

Implementing the lessons of Nomonhan was slowed as long as Kulik was in charge of the ordnance administration; he thwarted the proponents of armor in particular. Additionally, he even cut back the manufacture of anti-tank weapons and ammunition, took the excellent 76-mm. field piece out of production, and curtailed the output of antiaircraft and machine guns. In short, as Erickson points out, the Red Army's short-term measures after Nomonhan involved "a formal acceptance of the requirements of modern war but no implementation of the needs of mobility and flexibility, and an arbitrary, often contradictory order of priorities." Zhukov succeeded, however, where Kulik failed. Once the German war broke out, Kulik was disgraced as an army commander on the Leningrad front, was court-martialed, and was demoted from marshal to major general. Meanwhile, the day after Kulik's unintelligent remarks at the conference in Moscow in January 1941, Zhukov was selected by Stalin and the Politburo to replace Meretskov as chief of the General Staff. In this sense, Zhukov's experience at Nomonhan was vindicated; he always insisted that in actual combat on the steppes of Mongolia and in the forests of Karelia, the Red Army had learned lessons necessary to fight the Germans.[3]

The military application of experience acquired in combat is, of course, generally difficult to establish or to quantify. There is no evidence, for example, that the Red Army ever used the information learned at Changkufeng in 1938 in connection with the hostilities on the Mongolian border next year. As for Nomonhan itself, the Russians make the specific point that many of the valuable lessons of summer 1939 were not passed on to the Soviet forces in Finland, and that this is one of the reasons why they made such a poor showing in that campaign. It is known that revision of the Field Service Regulations (FSR) of 1936 continued throughout 1940. At the General Staff Academy that year, Sergei Shtemenko, a future general, observed that the conclusions drawn by the High Command from the Finnish war were having a pronounced effect, especially in terms of tighter discipline, upgrading of curriculum, and field training. The draft of the revised FSR did reflect Zhukov's operations at Nomonhan, on paper at least, by defining the objective of the offensive as the encirclement and annihilation of the enemy, instead of merely the "constraining" of the foe. But Marshal Biriuzov indicates that the more recent, "irrelevant" Finnish experience, the notion of gnawing against a fortified line, actually dominated Red Army thinking in

1941, to the extent that "we ceased to deal seriously with mobile combat . . . [and] we relegated to oblivion the fundamentals of combat-in-depth tactics and of combined arms maneuvers [that] had been widespread before the Finnish campaign." Marshal Yeremenko adds that it remained imperative "to overcome conservatism and to inculcate the military cadres with the idea that tanks were an independent arm and not an appendage of the infantry."

Under the circumstances, the revision of the FSR did not progress beyond the draft stage. In the summer of 1940, a special committee grappled in vain with the task of producing an acceptable version. Timoshenko finally turned the project over to the Main Commission for Manuals in late October. Marshal Budennyi directed the deliberations by several high-ranking officers, including the senior lecturer at the General Staff Academy. No definitive text had been adopted by the time the Germans attacked, which is another way of saying that the lessons of Nomonhan had not yet been assimilated. I. I. Azarov, a vice admiral, sheds light on the overshadowing of the lessons of the Far East by those of Finland: it had to be admitted, he notes, that the Soviet military was "reassured" by the victories at Changkufeng and Nomonhan, but that the Finnish campaign had proved more difficult than drills, war games, and maneuvers had led the commanding staff and political workers to expect. The facts tend to support Azarov's assertion: whereas Zhukov tore the Japanese Sixth Army to shreds in 10 days, it took the Russians three and a half months, 1,200,000 troops, and at least 200,000 casualties (including 68,000 dead) to subdue Finland, a country with a population of 3,700,000 and an army of hardly 200,000.[4]

Preparation of the new FSR was thus delayed by the difficulty of reconciling experience observed in theaters as disparate as Mongolia, Finland, and France. Nevertheless, the fighting at Nomonhan—the Russians' "first real test of war with tanks, artillery, and aircraft used on a large scale"—revealed important Soviet developments and innovations in ground and aerial equipment, ordnance, and tactics. For the first time, I-16 fighter planes, fitted with underwing rails, employed 82-mm. rockets in attacking IJA artillery sites and troop concentrations. It is also said that some Japanese aircraft were shot down by experimental RS-82 air-to-air missiles. The stubby Polikarpov I-16 low-wing monoplane, the best Russian fighter plane to date, was the battle-tested mainstay at Nomonhan. Highly maneuverable, reliable, and formidably armed, it saw combat in European Russia until 1943; some I-16's were still flying in the Spanish air force as recently as 1952. An offspring of the agile I-15 biplane, another Polikarpov design, was the much more powerful I-153 fighter-bomber (Chaika), which was equipped with retractable landing gear. The Chaika appeared in 1939 and saw battle at Nomonhan, eventually replacing the I-16.

The ingenious Soviet underwater bridges that plagued the Japanese at the Halha throughout the Nomonhan affair took the Germans by surprise a few years later. As for armor, the fast wheel-and-track, gasoline-engine BT-7M tanks, whose flammability Zhukov decried and which the Japanese incinerated easily in July, were replaced by a mass-produced version incorporating the superior V-2 diesel engine, with which the Japanese infantry and their Molotov cocktails could not cope. Lessons regarding armor plating, mobility, welding, and armament would be applied successfully by Soviet designers working on the pace-setting, fully tracked T-34 medium tank. At Nomonhan, the Russians also perfected amphibious (T-38) and flamethrowing (OT-130) armored fighting vehicles much used against the Germans.[5]

In the tactical sphere, the orchestration of the great August offensive at Nomonhan attracted much attention in the Soviet army and exerted the longest-range effects, for Zhukov and his staff had glimpsed the shape of future war. The fighting against the Japanese was particularly instructive with respect to the employment of armor operating in closest cooperation with other arms. Tanks and planes displayed enormous potential for maneuver, especially during complex actions aimed at enveloping an enemy. Thus Yakovlev's reinforced brigade was judged to have decided the whole issue in favor of the Russians and to have validated the conception of the General Staff: to concentrate armor in a single tank group of no more than two brigades per division, subordinated only to a corps or army commander, instead of dispersing tanks along the entire front below divisional level.

Zhukov's handling of operations was characterized by intensive preparations, detailed reconnaissance, a well-defined chain of command, excellent communications, and the conquest of fearful logistical obstacles. Despite his trifling overall superiority in manpower, the corps commander had skillfully achieved local and therefore decisive preponderance, catching the foe off balance in terms of timing and location. Soviet shock troops were hurled against the most vulnerable sectors of the enemy's defenses—the flanks—which were screened by the least reliable units, Manchukuoan troops and Bargut cavalry. Emphasis on striking the Japanese left or southern wing was appropriate because the line was less substantial there and the Russians' positions were advantageous. Consequently a direct thrust northward was able to hit the Japanese from the rear via the shortest axis, and to forge a ring with friendly forces pressing south.

Speed and momentum were the keys to the circling of the foe. Assisted by the air force, armor smashed Japanese reserves but did not impede the steady tightening of vises around knots of resistance. Since armored fighting vehicles could not achieve an encirclement by themselves, it proved imperative to move up motorized infantry to hold the outside of the circle and provide security against external counterattacks. At Nomonhan, this role was ably performed by infantry machine gun battalions of the mechanized brigades, by paratroopers of the 212th Airborne Brigade fighting as foot soldiers, by truck-borne frontier guards and, notably, by the 80th Regiment of the 57th Rifle Division.

Frontal assaults against IJA strongpoint elevations failed in every case, as at Fui and Noro Heights. Zhukov reportedly sacked the commander and then the chief of staff of a division that was pinned down with severe losses and unable to resume the attack—presumably against Fui. From his own staff, Zhukov sent a new commander, reinforced the unit with artillery and aircraft, and forced the offensive at very heavy cost. The most effective way to overpower the Japanese defenses was to drive wedges into the supporting network, dismember separate sectors, and seal off and then eventually destroy individual pockets of resistance. Single artillery pieces, up to 15 cm. in caliber,[6] were used to lay down precise fire and cover the advance of tanks, which were in turn followed by infantrymen operating at close quarters and throwing grenades. A number of tactical weaknesses were detected by Soviet analysts, who were more critical than the Japanese themselves. The tempo of the offensive, for instance, was said to have been slow and deliberate, and the rate of envelopment systematic and prolonged. Mortars were admittedly in short supply, and the density of artillery was insufficient.

Despite such carping, Soviet military historians agree that, in the battles on the Mongolian frontier, a new doctrine was created: the forging of an outer rim to guarantee the success of liquidation operations against a foe trapped on the inside. Subsequently, the Red Army devised even more intensive techniques to obliterate powerful defensive hedgehogs. This complicated technique of encirclement and extermination, developed by Zhukov in microcosm at Nomonhan, was eventually mastered and applied repeatedly with great success, under a multiplicity of conditions, in the course of the gigantic struggle against the Germans.[7]

Typical of Soviet public pronouncements on the quality of the Japanese army, at the time of the Nomonhan fighting, was a Tass release of mid-July 1939. In the opinion of the MPRA-Soviet command, the Japanese infantry was "fighting not badly, though it ought to fight much better," because the 23rd and 7th divisions were reputedly the best IJA divisions. That those two formations could be beaten so easily stemmed from the fact that demoralization was starting to penetrate deeply into the Japanese infantry, often causing the IJA command to launch attacks with the troops in a drunken state. Japanese air force and tank units, however, were weaker than the infantry.[8]

In answer to Stalin's inquiry during their conversation in May 1940, Zhukov asserted that Japanese troops were well trained, particularly in close-quarter combat, tightly disciplined, diligent, and tenacious, especially on the defensive. Junior commanding officers were highly trained, too, and "fanatically persistent in battle"; ordinarily they did not surrender but committed suicide when all was lost. Senior officers, however, were "not adequately trained, lacked initiative, and were apt to act according to the crammed rulebook." Japanese armament was obsolete—for example, IJA tanks, comparable to the old Soviet MS-1, were slow, feebly armed, and very limited in radius of action. Japanese artillery and troops in general were greatly inferior to the Russians; only at the outset were IJA aircraft better. Zhukov, like the Tass release (which must have quoted him or his staff), insisted that his men had engaged "the handpicked, the so-called Imperial Units of the Japanese Army." (If this claim implied an elite quality, it ought not to have been applied to the green 23rd Division—although it may represent an indirect and unintended compliment to Komatsubara's hard-fighting new formation. Units of the 7th Division that participated in the combat, however, do deserve the elite label.)

A number of similar impressions are evident from Zhukov's writings. The Japanese fought to the last man, he observes, and they evinced remarkable stoicism, as he discerned at firsthand when he interrogated a captured scout. IJA brainwashing of personnel was apparent from the unwonted fear of Soviet torture and execution of captives, and from the ideological conditioning against the Red Army. Wrongly comparing the latter to the tsarist forces they had met in 1904-5, the IJA painted the new Russians as still technically backward. Consequently, the capabilities of all the Soviet combat arms came as a shock to the Japanese. Gradually, however, says Zhukov, IJA soldiers began to comprehend "the flimsiness of the official propaganda that tried to convince them of the 'invincibility' of the Imperial Army, since it suffered incredibly heavy casualties without winning one battle in four months." Zhukov was convinced that his mighty offensive of August, which inflicted an "unheard-of defeat [on] the handpicked Japanese troops," sobered the ruling circles in Japan. As he told Stalin proudly, the Japanese could be expected to derive the "right conclusions" about the combat readiness, morale, and power of the Red Army after the experience of Nomonhan.[9]

In Japan at large, what had happened at Nomonhan was obscured by a policy of censorship that only bred suspicion and alarm. At an open Diet session in early February 1940, almost five months after the cease-fire, a member of the Seiyūkai party from Yamaguchi reminded War Minister Hata that 15,000 or 16,000 men had been slain at Nomonhan, and that the affair was therefore "etched in blood." "I need not reiterate here," the legislator added, "how much interest the Japanese people have in this incident." Another pesky Seiyūkai representative from Shizuoka charged that the statements of the war minister and the foreign minister about the Nomonhan episode were utterly at variance. The government ought to abandon the policy of secrecy and, in general, let the country know the truth. "Everything is hidden behind the doors of secretiveness," complained the Lower House member, "shutting out the people's eyes and ears." Yonai, prime minister at the time, replied feebly: "It can't be helped. Although we respect public opinion and the media, we cannot reveal secrets bearing upon the military, foreign affairs, and the economy. Please bear with us." [10]

During open budget committee hearings in late February centering on Japanese industry, a representative from Kyoto addressed a number of questions to General Hata. It was well known, observed the legislator, that the sector at Changkufeng had been mountainous and therefore appropriate for IJA tactics. Nomonhan, however, was a flat area, and the impression had been conveyed that the operations there were "not so well suited to the terrain." Viewing the Nomonhan affair as a whole, continued the representative, there seemed to have been some deficiencies in equipment; enemy tanks, for example, were apparently very good. Was Japan's present heavy industry capable of turning out armaments for use against the Russians adequate to cope with the world standard? It looked extremely difficult, yet *bushidō* had to be accompanied by weapons. As for aircraft, it was good to know that Japanese army and navy planes were excellent, but the legislator had heard that at Nomonhan, to a certain extent, the Japanese air force had had a hard time engaging the Russians' elite and up-to-date aircraft. At the outset, the Japanese pilots had been able to take on enemy planes at par despite a 1:20 ratio. As the fighting progressed, however, the figure had reportedly sunk to 1:10 and even 1:5 at the end. Would Hata kindly try to answer fully, within the limitations?

Hata replied in generalities. All he could say in an open hearing was that the fighting at Nomonhan, with its many precious victims, had provided "a very good lesson" for the Japanese military. Taking fullest advantage of the affair, the authorities had already commenced improvements for the sake of the army's future. "Please rest assured," said Hata, "that we shall not have wasted the blood that was shed on the sands of Nomonhan." The Diet member had been quite right in linking weapons with *bushidō*; "of course we do not believe that spiritual education alone can win a war." It was imperative to harmonize daily training, top-notch leadership, and the best weapons and equipment. No further details were forthcoming, for at this point the speaker of the Lower House warned the interpellators to "kindly watch their language and phraseology" when discussing incidents such as Nomonhan. [11]

The Japanese press, as we saw, welcomed the army's disclosure of casualties, but the figures revealed a seriousness of fighting that eclipsed the affairs at Kanchatzu Island and Changkufeng. Although Soviet forces were numerically superior, the scale of the enemy's mechanized corps in particular had not been known beforehand, and "we were quite shocked by the results," admitted an *Asahi* editorial writer. It was gratifying to learn that the military authorities were going to derive "living lessons" from the Nomonhan hostilities and would conduct careful studies of armament, such as the mechanization of the army—the blending of matériel with spiritual training alluded to by War Minister Hata. On the basis of Nomonhan's lessons, concluded the *Asahi* editor elliptically, "We should reprove what must be reproved and tighten what must be tightened." Perfecting the national defense structure was the way to please the Emperor and comfort the souls of those who had fallen at Nomonhan.[12]

Whether or not the Japanese army really profited from the lessons of Nomonhan will become apparent in the course of this chapter, but there can be no doubt that honest efforts were made to analyze the battle at several levels. On 4 September, for example, before the fighting was even over, the 26th Infantry Regiment ordered subordinate elements to investigate two topics and report on them to headquarters by noon next day: first, matters that needed training or improvement as the result of the combat to date; second, matters of deployment and tactics that demanded attention. On the 9th, again on merely one day's notice, the 23rd Division chief of staff, Colonel Kimura, requested all units to convey reports on their experiences. "It is one of the important responsibilities of the imperial army," stated Kimura's notice, "to collect the lessons from this incident for the benefit of future operations." The reports, submitted "as is," might be filed by units or by individuals, in which case "the more officers and noncoms involved, the better." Fifteen specific items were to be addressed: (1) operations and combat commanding; (2) antitank battle; (3) night combat; (4) countermeasures against artillery fire; (5) countermeasures against snipers; (6) defense against hand grenades, and the use of grenade launchers; (7) antiaircraft action; (8) artillery battle; (9) defense against aviation; (10) position construction; (11) communications and liaison; (12) reconnaissance, intelligence, and public relations; (13) water supply; (14) transport facilities, especially trucks; and (15) logistics.[13]

The IJA raw data eventually found their way into classified after-action reports. Typical of the flavor and substance of a line unit's summation are the 19 pages of no-nonsense lessons prepared by Major Kajikawa's 2nd Battalion of the 28th Infantry Regiment. More is said about enemy than friendly tactics and matériel, but Kajikawa's veterans did record many impressions of the strengths and weaknesses of their own combat performance. Sufficient lead time must be allowed in ordering combat movements. The practice of dispatching deep scouting patrols at night should be reconsidered;

there were many instances when contact was lost. Provision should be made for special units to guard the wounded during night actions, lest considerable losses ensue. Secrecy was vitiated by the noise of field pieces, trucks, and horses traversing steep or difficult terrain. There was a lack of cooperation among front-line IJA units. Greater flexibility was required in the use of battalion guns, which ought not to be employed against enemy heavy artillery. Friendly infantry were most anxious to see Japanese artillery concentrate on suppressing hostile guns. The foot units should attack by themselves, with their own targets. An infantry battalion, especially when operating independently, ought to possess at least two trucks to haul ammunition, food, and water, and to evacuate the wounded.

Tactically, the Kajikawa battalion suggested, Japanese troops would do best, in engaging the Russians, to start attacking from early evening, to fight through the night, and to complete action by dawn. By day, friendly forces should retain their positions, fully covered against bombardment—although this had not proved too effective against the Soviets, since they employed much artillery. It was easy for the enemy to detect and hammer the main lines of resistance. The Japanese had a tendency to cling to one location too long, a fact which facilitated the work of Russian artillerists as time went by, and caused an attitude of merely waiting to be killed. To overcome hostile automatic weapons was a simple matter for heavy machine guns, grenade launchers, and battalion guns. Against the excellent Soviet artillery, the only infantry counteraction was to storm them by night. One platoon should be sufficient to seize a gun site.

Infantry weapons were of no use against enemy planes, according to Kajikawa's commentary; it was not worth firing at them. Hostile armor was a natural target of the foot soldiers, yet infantry ordnance was not powerful enough, especially because ground cover was lacking. Portable antitank mines were satisfactory, but they were ineffective unless the tanks were moving. Molotov cocktails, though difficult to employ, were useful to a certain degree in the heat of summer, but not against diesel-fueled armor and not in winter.[14] "Sticky explosives" (*kyūchaku bakuyaku*) were fine; flamethrowers would have been even better. Rapid-fire guns might have been effective but they could not be depended upon when needed most, for enemy artillery "worked them over" just as soon as they revealed themselves by firing, and enemy armor engaged them from beyond their range. The best way to cope with tanks was to infiltrate under cover of darkness and knock them out with explosives. There had been many such opportunities for surprise attacks.

The emphasis of the Kajikawa battalion's combat from 3 July until the cease-fire is suggested by the types of ammunition it expended: heavy machine gun cartridges, 91,680; light machine gun cartridges, 52,000; rifle bullets, 38,000; grenades, 3,580; battalion gun rounds, 3,064. The sandy terrain conditions caused rifles and guns to jam easily. In particular, the 6.5-mm. Type 96 light machine gun could hardly be used because of breakdowns.

Two last problems troubled the Kajikawa unit. First, it had not been possible in practice to evacuate corpses. Instead of leaving them "as is," bodies should be buried where found. Second, something should be done to solve the problem of maintaining direction at night. Various methods had been employed without satisfactory results—flares, tracers, compass readings, guiding on the stars. Whenever a night-assault force lost its bearings, there were missing men. The whereabouts of the commander must always be known. Improved training was vital. Summing up his experience, Kajikawa judged the Japanese infantrymen to excel their Russian counterparts by a factor of 5 : 1.[15]

The main body of Ashizuka's 28th Infantry saw much less combat than did Kajikawa's detached battalion, for the regiment did not reach Lake Mohorehi until 23 August. Most of the recorded lessons derive from the experience against Soviet armor. The gasoline bottles that had once worked so well for the Japanese had become ineffective because nets now covered the vitals of the Russian tanks, which had also been painted with a fireproof compound. It was necessary to throw blazing Molotov cocktails again and again at the same spot in order to set a target afire. In view of the sandy, soft soil, portable charges had to be inserted between the treads and the bogies. After inducing the Japanese antitank weapons to give themselves away by firing on them from medium range, the enemy used his excellent artillery to finish off opposing firepower. It was imperative to wait until hostile tanks and infantry came within the range of direct fire. Dispersion and shelter were the key.

When on the offensive, said Ashizuka's survey, insufficient preparation led to severe losses, unanticipated checks, and failure of the mission in general. Maximum study and reconnaissance of the foe were demanded beforehand. Japanese infantry and artillery worked well together in late August south of the Holsten, but the great breadth of the front nullified any local preponderance. Night attacks were "the only way to go." After seizing an objective, however, one must beware of enemy assaults from flank and rear.[16]

Additional observations are to be found in the battle critique prepared by Maj. Tahara Tsuneharu's 3rd Battalion of the 27th Infantry Regiment, another relative latecomer at Nomonhan, specifically on the Uzuru sector. In the absence of trees or structures on the broad plain, direction finding was difficult by day as well as night. The movement of heavy artillery over the sandy earth posed a particular problem, although the soil absorbed enemy shell fragments. Action by scouts was limited by the long glow after sunset and before dawn. The suddenness of daybreak also exposed unit movements to enemy observers located on the higher ground. By contrast, most of the Soviet gun sites were invisible from Japanese observation posts. Lack of forest or dense vegetation impeded cover, though cross-country movement was feasible in good weather in every direction on the flatland.

Unit commanders must follow their seniors' orders, Tahara noted, if discipline was to be maintained and effective combat carried out. Against the mechanized enemy, infantrymen should retain their positions in the daytime and should advance steadily at night. Moving ahead too fast could result in the cutoff of supply lines, which was what the enemy really wanted. Systematic action when attacking positions was much to be preferred. In the event of a battle of encounter, frontal assault should be avoided. Greater care should also be exerted to locate the sources of enemy fire. The proper sequence of operation was to have heavy artillery dominate hostile guns before the infantry companies struck the enemy's flank or rear. Afterward, friendly artillery should be displaced forward to take the foe in flank and compel him to waste his counterfire. These tactics should be carefully thought out and inculcated in the troops.[17]

The preceding précis reflect the thoughts of survivors at the infantry battalion and regimental levels. Higher headquarters were interested in the larger lessons in terms of national strength and the improvement of the army as a whole—or, as one particularly candid officer put it, in "getting at the roots of the Japanese army's failure" at Nomonhan. After the cease-fire, the vice minister of war advised the AGS deputy to oversee the formation of a Nomonhan Incident Research Committee. Dealing with operations in general, a 1st Subcommittee of 22 field-grade AGS and war ministry officers was established. The topics to be addressed included strategy and tactics, staff work, organization and equipment, mobilization, defense, transport and communications, education and training, logistics and replacement, intendance and medical affairs, and Soviet military matters. Originally, border disputes and war guidance, as well as enhancement of armaments, were also supposed to be studied, but apparently word was conveyed to drop the first two very delicate subjects, and to handle the third item separately, since the national budget was involved. The topic of intelligence was assigned to a special 2nd Subcommittee of 10 experts from AGS sections and the war ministry, headed by the 5th Section chief.

Working in Manchuria (mainly at Hsinking and Hailar) with the Kwantung Army and local commands from the middle of November 1939, the teams were to complete their basic researches by the end of December and submit their findings to the Big Three leaders[18] in January 1940. Final reports (*tsūhō*) were to be disseminated to all units at division level and above. The seriousness with which the war minister regarded the committee's labors is reflected not only in his generalized reassurances to the Diet but also in a statement he made to all bureau chiefs on 6 January: lessons learned from the Nomonhan war should be implemented swiftly, and matters entailing self-reflection and improvement should be corrected with similar dispatch. Faithful compliance was required, General Hata asserted, in order to prevent recurrence of mistakes.[19]

The conduct of the investigations, by the 1st Subcommittee in particular, has been criticized by a number of officers who were called to testify, and by others who were not. Colonel Sumi, who appeared in Hsinking, derived the impression that the team members were not completely objective and entertained certain preconceptions. Since it was the same Japanese army and the same equipment that had fought in China and at Nomonhan, the investigators intimated, why did operations proceed so well in the former theater and so poorly in the latter? The combat units' unsatisfactory leadership must have accounted for the difference. By downplaying the matter of IJA matériel, which had been so inferior in quality and quantity to that of the Red Army, the subcommittee was missing the point—that the Chinese were as feebly endowed as "flies in May," whereas the Russians were incomparable "grand champions." Nevertheless, says Sumi, he could only answer questions and describe his experiences; there was no leeway to express personal opinions or to proffer advice.[20]

Since Sumi was cashiered, his disappointment with the subcommittee is understandable. But even Colonel Mishima, the wounded 1st Heavy Field Artillery Regiment commander who survived to become a general, was unhappy with the inquest when he was directed to testify before it in Hailar, under the auspices of the Sixth Army, toward the end of November. Ostensibly the investigators were seeking lessons from Nomonhan; but, like Sumi, Mishima sensed that they really constituted a "prosecution committee." Tormented by the needless loss of so much of his beloved regiment and anxious to vent his feelings, Mishima spoke up with unusual frankness during the lengthy discussion conducted by Sixth Army Chief of Staff Fujimoto. The whole Nomonhan operation, not merely isolated episodes, had been a failure, asserted the colonel. Why, he asked, try to pin the rap on low-ranking commanders? Mishima organized his presentation systematically:

1. The fatal problem concerned the vague meaning of the Nomonhan affair in general and of the operations in particular. No simpletons, IJA officers and men did not know why they were dying in a desert where the border was unclear. Since the army was in a morass in China after years of combat, it defied common sense to "make waves" or to waste even a man on the Mongolian frontier. Resolution of the China conflict would require a major war in the south, not the north. "I never found a compelling reason," stated Mishima, "for fighting at Nomonhan."

2. There had been a failure in command, a military collapse, at the top, not the bottom. Despite the limited troop strength available, operations were charac-

terized by an excessive chain of command and too much rank. The army chiefs, Mishima believed, were "way up in the clouds." Certainly the headquarters at Hsinking and Tokyo deserved censure for the defeat at Nomonhan, but the advance forces had commenced matters and therefore ought to bear their share of the blame. The trouble was that the Kwantung Army, instead of holding the aggressive front-line units in check, seemed to have been dragged along by them. In turn, the High Command failed to control the Kwantung Army.

3. The organization and equipment of Japanese forces on the spot were not appropriate for anti-Soviet combat in such a region. In particular, the use of horses was out of the question. Whereas even a slightly wounded horse was useless, motor vehicles remained in action even when hit, unless fatally damaged in their engines.

4. Mobility was crucial in vast flatlands; foot units were hopeless. Since the days were long and the nights were short at Nomonhan, deployment to new positions and supply of ammunition, etc., demanded motorization.

5. A major defect encountered in tactical training was the fact that officers, even at the war college, had been taught only the "Meckel tactics" of the German army. In other words, since the Meiji era, when Prussian Major Jakob Meckel had come to advise the Japanese military, there was no concrete analysis of the extent to which the foe could be destroyed. No methodical attention was paid, at any level, to such questions as friendly attrition rates or the time to rotate units. Meckel had stressed the need to attack the enemy's soft points, but it was left to commanders to create weaknesses by concentrating superior firepower. This was not attempted at Nomonhan. Instead, huge maneuvers were devised that looked good on paper but that only led to an accumulation of disasters. Such maneuvers were practicable when the terrain was advantageous, when friendly artillery could provide long-range cover, and when there was both mechanization and motorization. At Nomonhan, cover was absent inside the effective range of Soviet artillery.

6. Logistical failings were critical, creating a vicious circle in practice. Since the advance forces, which dragged the higher headquarters, regarded the Nomonhan crisis without profundity, the Kwantung Army made no serious studies of its own and treated logistical factors lightly.

7. The experience in China had exerted a baleful effect. It had become customary to expect the enemy to break whenever IJA forces attacked, but at Nomonhan the Japanese had run into a "brick wall." As Sumi warned, the Russians seemed to have been treated the same as the Chinese. Of course, spiritual factors should not be underestimated, but material strength was vital too.

8. Mishima's closing comment was to the effect that the spirit of *bushidō* had been misinterpreted at Nomonhan. To obtain the fullest degree of support, one should treat subordinates graciously and with compassion. "No blood flowed through the veins of command. Everything was formal and businesslike, without warmth." The warrior concept was fine, but emphasis should be placed on winning, not on recrimination, as was happening after the Nomonhan war.

Mishima did not feel that he made a dent in the subcommittee's thinking. The infantry "brass," for example, harped unendingly about the Yamato Spirit, and it was clear that the colonel was regarded as something of an "oddball." Soon after he testified at Hailar, Mishima was hustled off to the field artillery school in Japan.[21]

Another criticism that has been lodged against the members of the team is that they did not go out of their way to interview some of the most knowledgeable respondents—combat veterans still in hospital in Manchuria. Thus Lieutenant Colonel Nishikawa, the 1st Battalion commander of the 72nd Infantry Regiment, was never consulted although he was recuperating nicely from his wounds. Admittedly, regiment commander Sakai had not been able to recommend him before committing suicide; but, says Nishikawa, the subcommittee should have paid more heed to front-line troops. "It's not of much use to listen to staff officers from division and army headquarters." Even when the new 72nd Regiment commander arrived at Hailar, he talked only to company commanders from the 2nd Battalion. Nishikawa's aide was so distressed that he complained privately to the lieutenant colonel. Nevertheless, the experience of the 1st Battalion remained largely unknown to or ignored by the investigators.[22]

The Kwantung Army made some attempt to tap the experience of enlisted men, although the objectivity of the effort does not seem to have extended to topics beyond the technical, as we shall see. From the original 120 men in Capt. Miki Toranosuke's 11th Company of the 71st Infantry Regiment, the only four soldiers who emerged unscathed were ordered to report to a visiting captain for debriefing after their return to Hailar. The officer would ask many questions about the Nomonhan fighting, the men were told by their commander, who left the room after directing them to answer honestly. Two particular questions linger in the memory of Oda Daiji, then 22 and a PFC, one of the soldiers interviewed. The first inquiry concerned the kind of antitank weapons the infantrymen wanted. Oda went into great detail, criticizing the shortness of the poles attached to portable mines and the insufficient time delay after ignition, as well as the undue brevity of the gasoline bombs' flame. It had proved feasible to attach charges to armor because enemy tanks slowed down or even stopped during attacks on friendly positions during the August offensive. It had been rather easy for Japanese soldiers, as at Sankakuyama, to jump onto the back of the tanks' chassis or to trail them from the rear, although a human price naturally had to be paid for such daring.

Oda got into "hot water" when the captain asked him who he thought had won the war at Nomonhan. So far as the Miki company was concerned, replied the PFC, the Japanese had been victorious until early August. During the next phase, until 20 August, IJA forces had beaten enemy riflemen and tanks but had been defeated by artillery. After the 20th, with the increase in Soviet BT tanks, enemy armor and artillery were too much for the Japanese infantry, armed only with the Type 38 rifle. As for the Nomonhan Incident as a whole, Oda expressed the opinion that friendly forces had lost because they had not been able to drive the Russians back across the Halha boundary claimed by the Japanese, and the cease-fire occurred at the line of Soviet contention. At this point the captain warned Oda, more in a tone of counseling than of scolding, not to talk about defeat, lest the soldier face court-martial. Oda recoiled in fear, although neither the captain nor his comrades contradicted anything he had said.[23]

The thrust of the IJA investigators' deliberations is discernible in candid remarks made by the influential Col. Iwakuro Hideo at a secret meeting of war ministry section chiefs on 4 October, even before the 1st Subcommittee had been officially formed. Japanese military equipment could be made to resemble the Russians', but its capability could not be expected to exceed approximately 80 percent; there was no alternative to reliance upon spirit— a most difficult task. Of late, the Japanese army had attained a stage of historical maturity, which meant it lacked freshness and tended to "play it safe" and simply avoid making mistakes, whereas Soviet forces evinced excellent flexibility and adaptability. There were serious problems with the IJA system of "high commandship" (*tōsui*). As for armaments, Iwakuro said that he was a devotee of big guns and wanted trouble-free new weapons that would be invincible in action against the Russians. Nomonhan had taught painful lessons in showing the great discrepancy between the IJA and the Red Army with respect to tank-attack tactics and aerial fighting methods.[24]

The ultimate reports of the Nomonhan Incident Research Committee contained no surprises. Iwakuro's reference to the command problem was addressed indirectly: the fighting of the front-line corps had depended very much on the policies of higher headquarters toward the incident; such matters needed to be studied more carefully with regard to future war guidance and border-dispute handling. But the central feature of Nomonhan was the pitting of Japanese spiritual power against Soviet material strength. IJA forces had shown élan and confidence in victory, in the face of a mechanized and abundantly supplied enemy equipped with excellent planes, tanks, and artillery. Regardless of rank or branch of service, the Japanese troops had fought strongly to the end, under severe fire, and had displayed their customary spiritual strength, which was even capable of overcoming the disasters encountered in modern war. The Russians deployed a multiplicity of weapons, operated them in very close coordination, and enhanced the effectiveness of modern firepower by harmonizing it with mobility.

The greatest lessons of Nomonhan were judged to center on the need to strengthen the traditional fighting spirit while improving the capacity to wage a war of firepower, whose standard was still low in the Japanese army. There were several ways to enhance spiritual quality: by increasing and nurturing an officer corps geared to wartime, by creating a command structure at war level, and by boosting morale. As for better firepower, the army had wanted and worked on it for a long time, but the desired objectives had not been attained by 1939. Among many reasons, the most important was the fact that Japan had had no experience in Europe's Great War of 1914-18; perusal of documentation was no substitute. The experience at Nomonhan could provide the basis for a firsthand and objective comprehension of the nature of modern firepower war, and for epoch-making improvements in organization, equipment, supply, training, deployment, and techniques.

The Russians banked heavily on firepower and attrition. Arraying huge-scale armaments in great depth and breadth, they strove to consume the Japanese entirely. The only solution was to employ raiding tactics and surprise, as the First World War had foretold. This entailed the launching of operations that would take the foe entirely by surprise, dominate him with firepower, destroy his command organization before his method of attrition could ensnarl forces, and then smash him once and for all. Objective appraisal of the lessons of Nomonhan necessitated overwhelming emphasis on the tightening of cooperation between the various combat elements, perfecting the ties between mobility and logistics, and making an honest evaluation of material strength. Having yielded this concession to tangible desiderata, the report hastened to stress the equal importance of focusing on improvement of the hand-to-hand ability at which the Japanese excelled at Nomonhan, outclassing the enemy and facilitating the employment of friendly firepower.

Despite constant reaffirmations of the superiority of "mind over matter," the investigators could not avoid returning frequently to the problems of armament. It had to be admitted, for instance, that Japanese tank strength at Nomonhan had been woefully inadequate and that domestic production could not meet quantitative requirements. Communications and rear transport facilities were inadequate too, posing potential difficulties in waging modern warfare. Every effort should be made to "render such dangers utterly groundless." Combat training also had to be improved on the basis of the experience of Nomonhan. In the event that limits were imposed on the buildup of matériel, it was imperative to enhance the army's spirit by perfect coordination of training, military command (*gunrei*), and military administrative (*gunsei*) agencies.

Application of lessons required recognition of the distinctiveness of Nomonhan vis-à-vis future locales of hostilities. The recent battles had consisted of movement in a vast, deserted region, where the full brunt of Soviet mechanization could be brought to bear. Such fighting was entirely different from operations involving big rivers and mountainous terrain, where the prime concern would be attack and defense of fortifications. It was also important to note significant peculiarities: in view of the main war in China,

IJA forces at Nomonhan had had to endure piecemeal commitment and inadequate equipment and supply. By comparison with the Japanese, the Red Army was well modernized with respect to the features mentioned earlier in the report. In case of future war against the Russians, when one considered overall ratios and combinations of components, it could be expected that enemy strength in artillery, aircraft, and tanks (except armored cars) would be as good as or better than what had been encountered at Nomonhan.

It had been learned, said the analysts, that the Soviets leaned too heavily on material power. Their offensives were consequently sluggish and they lacked combat zest at close quarters. In short, the Japanese should neither underestimate nor overestimate the Russians, should detect the peculiarities of Nomonhan, and should exploit the lessons in future without fail. One topic demanded special mention: chemical warfare. Although gas had not appeared at Nomonhan, there was evidence of Soviet preparations to use it. What would have happened if the Red Army had fired gas shells against Japanese positions, instead of howitzer rounds, during the offensive in late August? What if gas shells had struck the rear, inasmuch as low-flying Russian scout planes often swept over the Japanese lines and were obviously well acquainted with the dispositions? Since IJA chemical-warfare capabilities were still very primitive, rapid improvement was vital in order to cope with the realities of modern war.[25]

Turning to strategy and tactics, the authors of the report reverted to the IJA forte, close-quarter battle, which ordinarily achieved a final decision when the enemy stood and fought. At Nomonhan, however, hostile forces were well dispersed and camouflaged, and an invisible but powerful network of firepower checked the advance of friendly troops. In fact, the latter would be dealt an annihilating blow by firepower even before there was a chance to engage in close combat, whenever the units were exposed or advanced recklessly or relied on insufficient fortification. It used to be said, during the First World War, that "artillery cultivates and infantry secures," but the idea had been largely ignored because of its presumable inapplicability to Asian battlefield conditions. Matters were different now, since the confronting enemy had adopted this very dictum.

The impressive degree of Soviet battlefield mobility enabled large-scale hostile forces to operate in a broad and desolate area 700 kilometers from the nearest railhead for two months. As soon as the Russians learned of the Japanese enveloping offensive, they broke its back by committing mechanized corps that advanced 100 km. in a day. IJA forces, suffering from inferior mobility, tried to check the superior mechanized units but were smashed, one after another. Whereas the foe was able to move freely, the Japanese were contained. Soviet artillery made a major contribution, during the confusion of combat, by linking up with tanks and infantry, thereby avoiding independent battle. The enemy's conduct of operations was facilitated by the motorization of liaison, communication, and forward supply formations. Terrain features had to be considered, of course, but the preceding factors ought not to be underestimated in the course of "calmly evaluating" Soviet armored units' ability to traverse swampland and to operate at will in the upstream reaches of both the Halha and the Holsten. It was hardly necessary to reiterate the need for mobility in order to envelop and outflank by surprise. When the enemy's mobility was superior, the impact of surprise assaults by friendly forces would not last long, and organized firepower would become decisive in the end.

Following their field manuals, the Russians employed tactics in depth, designed to pocket the Japanese by ascribing emphasis to the outer wings. Infantry units were effectively dispersed, with good cover, while tanks and armored cars fired from the flanks. When one employed unorganized fighting forces against such well-articulated strength, the possibility of "ruin" was always present. Whenever the Russians' lines were stabilized, they immediately were converted into a deep net of firepower. Improvements in armament made night combat a frequent occurrence. Most night attacks succeeded against Soviet rifle or mechanized units occupying dispersed and light positions that were not well guarded. When enemy forces were determined to retain a point, however, they put up powerful resistance. Night-attack results might be good at first, because of the element of surprise, but occupation of objectives became very difficult without resorting to tactics of forced assault. Against such attacks, the Russians used illuminating flares and a spectrum of weapons, especially grenades. At daybreak they usually conducted fierce bombardments and threw in tanks. Consequently, Japanese losses in night actions were no less than those by day. Officer casualties were particularly heavy. For example, when elements of the Katayama detachment launched a night operation, after initial success the force paid a very severe price: 43 percent overall, including 100 percent of the officers and 71 percent of the warrant officers and noncoms. To go on with such night attacks would quickly wear down fighting strength, given the nature of modern warfare.

The Russians' own night assaults relied mainly on firepower, especially grenades; only rarely did they charge into defenses. Although the Soviet offensive in August went on for days, at night the Russians usually pulled back, even when they had the Japanese surrounded. As a result, the defenders could maintain contact with other positions and even bring in supplies at the beginning. Enemy tanks ordinarily returned to the rear at night for maintenance. The Russians deployed scouts or native agents inside the Japanese lines to report on IJA movements, using signal flares by night. Enemy bomber formations flew over at low level in the darkness for several nights in succession in order to interfere with the sleep of the Japanese and thus exhaust their physical resistance. The only reason there was not even more air force interference with supply and replacement in the army rear was that both sides were trying to limit the fighting zone.

As stated repeatedly by the authors of the survey, IJA close-quarter capabilities were deemed better than those of the enemy, especially at the outset of the Nomonhan affair, but it was urgent to improve the firepower of the rifleman. The latter liked the 50-mm. heavy grenade launchers and 70-mm. Type 92 infantry guns because of their effectiveness and durability. Japanese infantry casualties had been severe, even in assaults against light positions. Enemy snipers were highly effective, not least because of the psychological dimension. Sometimes, in fact, sniping was more dreaded than machine gun fire. In every phase of the fighting, the personnel strength of units turned over completely; sometimes a regiment possessed only the strength of a battalion, and a battalion approximated a platoon. Missions should be tailored to the actual strength of a unit, and rotation should be employed when possible.

Infantrymen were effective against armor only when they retained a credible antitank capability; without it, their fear of tanks was bound to increase. Enemy flamethrowers were psychologically effective, although their radius and duration of operation were extremely limited, and they were often assigned special tasks such as the burn-off of grass. Trampling of defensive positions by armor was very dangerous when enemy forces were densely concentrated or when antitank construction was slipshod. Counterfire was the most suitable tactic to reduce the effectiveness of tank irruption, but enemy armor made it difficult for IJA infantry by engaging and knocking out antitank weapons from beyond their effective range. Close-quarter attacks by infantry, if successful, had the result of forcing tanks to avoid action at short distance. Such tactics risked the annihilation of the foot soldiers, however, when attempted in flat terrain lacking cover. Night was a proper time to attack tanks, since their self-defense capabilities were so poor in darkness that they were usually withdrawn to safety in the rear. Still, if tank crews were trained in night combat, armor could be employed in advantageous terrain even after sunset.

Subsequent sections of the 1st Subcommittee's report dealt with mechanized corps, artillery (especially problems of ammunition and mobility), aircraft by category, antiaircraft units, and engineers. Close attention was devoted to combat doctrine, reiterating the need for initiative, surprise, and combination of arms, and to types of battle: encounter, attack against positions, defense in depth, engagement of mechanized corps, encirclement, penetration. The requirement for a major engagement (*kaisen*) took up an entire chapter, with special emphasis on the need for ammunition buildup and for transport—the bane of the IJA artillery command at Nomonhan. In this connection, it was pointed out that the Japanese army tended to adhere to the notion that "operations demand, logistics follow"—a cart-before-the-horse approach. It was necessary to calculate losses and reserves of weapons and matériel—not just of manpower—in view of the fact that the Russian objective in war was attrition in general. There was a great need for backup divisions, something much discussed until now but never realized. Divisions that were to operate autonomously required a rectangular (four-regiment) structure—an obvious reference to the insufficient strength of the new, triangular 23rd Division.

Concerning organization and equipment, the recommendations centered on heightened artillery strength, especially more and better long-range ordnance and new self-propelled guns; armored corps designed for breakthrough or flank maneuver; deeper supporting elements, especially transport units; more effective air support; and signal forces. Peacetime and wartime organization should be rendered as similar as possible, an improvement particularly desirable for the Kwantung Army. Special attention should be given to antitank and antiaircraft equipment; motorization in general; road construction and repair facilities; water-supply elements attached to each unit; sanitation in mechanized and air formations; and military railway commands. The entire army's agencies dealing with training, education, and research should be reexamined and reshaped to keep pace with the envisaged developments. Further detailed studies and speedy implementation of the findings were imperative.

With respect to training and education, greater efforts must be made to teach basics to which the troops would react automatically in battle. It was a misconception to equate academic education with practical training for actual combat. At Nomonhan, a lack of appreciation for military technology had been revealed; thorough technical education was imperative. To date, artillery training had been extremely superficial and conventional, unsuited to the realities of modern warfare. Great enthusiasm and the adoption of very advanced measures were vital. Special studies, especially by officers, should be addressed to the organization, equipment, and tactics of the Red Army; the proper conception of modern war, especially of firepower and the essence of fighting strength; and the geographical configuration of potential battlefields. Such studies, drawing on the lessons of Nomonhan and preceding incidents, should stimulate research into military history and combat examples. Tactical training, maneuvers, and guidance must be renovated and toughened, and learning on the spot accelerated, for which purpose real equipment, live shells and cartridges, and actual gas should be employed, and combined forces should participate in exercises. These objectives would necessitate proper funding; suitable weapons for antiaircraft, antitank, and antigas training; matériel; maneuver zones; and firing ranges. Serious and objective inculcation of the real meaning of tactical cooperation was crucial, especially at the level of regiment, battalion, and company commanders. Arbitrary and exclusive concepts must be eliminated and errors corrected by schools and units involved in training.

Injunctions were devised in general (such as first-aid training) and for each combat arm. Thus infantry must concentrate on sniping techniques and use of heavy weapons and antitank grenades. Position-construction techniques must be enhanced, and officers' negative attitudes in this regard must be rectified. Hand-to-hand tactics must also be improved so that the infantry would possess the fullest confidence in this traditional and unique method of the imperial army. In the case of tank units, attention must be paid to command methods, firing techniques, communication and liaison, quick elimination of antitank weapons, commanders' vision devices, and movement and combat in conditions of visibility ranging from dawn to moonlight. Employing live rounds, artillerymen needed to improve fire control, particularly by battery commanders. Engineer training needed improvement in methods of reconnaissance, movement, stockpiling, and fast construction of antitank defenses, bridges, and roads by day or night and under fire. The role of the signal corps demanded close attention in every field, and the army as a whole must adjust its attitude toward communication needs, particularly when the combat situation was critical. Transport units should study night supply—a requirement imposed by anti-Soviet operations—operating off the road and in darkness without headlights, repairing and maintaining motor vehicles and roadways, and tactics of self-defense. An entire chapter was devoted to the need for closer "spiritual ties" between ground units, air force scouts, and direct-support elements, entailing identification, spotting, defense, and liaison, especially under adverse conditions of combat, weather, and terrain.[26]

The 2nd Subcommittee addressed questions of military intelligence. It soon became apparent, from analysis of the Nomonhan war, that the Kwantung Army's Operations Section had not properly used data derived from the intelligence staff but had instead conducted operations based on its own information and estimates. Admittedly, IJA intelligence officers chronically suffered from certain feelings of inferiority and were often convinced that the Operations Section was arrogant and "sold on itself." In the case of the Kwantung Army in 1939, however, the intelligence men were not professionally inferior individuals. That the section could not provide the army with strong information must therefore have derived from a very poor setup. Instead of railing at the Operations Section's attitude of self-righteousness and dogmatism as an explanation for all staff weaknesses, the subcommittee concluded, it was imperative to win the confidence of the operations officers by proving that intelligence was a reliable organization.

Many of the problems were caused by the fact that the Kwantung Army Intelligence Section had been handling collection directly, through the Harbin OSS and 10 branches. In other words, the section chief individually controlled the entire intelligence system, including radio intelligence, and was responsible for such administrative matters as finances and personnel. During a crisis, most of the energy of the chief had to be expended on functions other than intelligence per se. His three assistants were similarly preoccupied with petty administrative details that left little time for good analysis, their most important real task.

Although the experience of the special combat intelligence units (CIU's)[27] was instructive, their overall operation was not considered a success at Nomonhan. The teams, for instance, lacked organic communication facilities to transmit the results of interrogation to Hsinking. Since there had been no planning whatsoever for the activation of brand-new CIU's, no provision for supply or signal capabilities had been built into them. In addition, the Nomonhan sector lay within the jurisdiction of the Hailar OSS, not of higher headquarters at Harbin. Support from the Hailar facility was not efficient, and relations with the 23rd Division were not clear. The subcommittee looked closely into the question of the chain of command but could not locate enabling orders from Kwantung Army headquarters. Apparently the OSS chief in Harbin, Maj. Gen. Hata Hikosaburō, had set up the combat intelligence units on his own initiative, in the belief that he had the Kwantung Army's understanding. In any case, the CIU's had suffered from the odd setup, and the subcommittee recommended that, whenever teams were established in emergency, they be clearly attached to army headquarters.

OSS agents themselves were not too enthusiastic about regularizing their own functions. If the CIU structure became too systematic, it was feared, there would be an exodus from the intelligence service. A number of personnel felt that it would be better not to operate in uniform—that their military or civilian identity should be left deliberately vague. Additionally, it had been customary to draw upon the secret funds of field armies such as the Kwantung Army, not upon appropriated funds. As a result, the OSS men had enjoyed a status comparable to that of private consultants attached to armies in the field. The 2nd Subcommittee, however, recommended that the OSS apparatus be consolidated into a Kwantung Army intelligence bureau, and that the old Harbin OSS branch office become the bureau headquarters. With all of the branches reporting to the bureau, the duties of administration and intelligence were now divided. The Kwantung Army Intelligence Section was thereby freed from collection and administration, allowing it to concentrate on research and analysis of data as the basis for estimates to be submitted to the Operations Section. At the AGS level, two staff positions were created to handle intelligence collection.

Lastly, the subcommittee found that the actual handling and evaluation of intelligence had been very poor. Valuable data were received but not exploited correctly. In fact, raw information—which should always have been held closely and winnowed first by intelligence experts—was distributed directly to the gullible Operations Section. As a result, Soviet "disinformation" efforts proved successful on more than one occasion, to the chagrin of the Japanese intelligence community.[28]

For the benefit of the 1st Subcommittee and of the High Command, in late November 1939 the Kwantung Army prepared 120 copies of a lengthy report and detailed attachments, drawing mainly on direct lessons from Nomonhan. Although the subcommittee's own survey reflected many of the Kwantung Army's recommendations, a number of special findings deserve mention. Balloon units were necessary but the present equipment was useless. Attention should be paid to problems of discipline, spiritual training, and espionage encountered in military hospitals. Hospital chiefs must exercise command authority over the men who escorted and brought in wounded soldiers. The handling of regimental colors at the end of hostilities needed thorough study. Horse companies of the reconnaissance regiment should be replaced permanently by motorized companies. Indeed, there was some thinking that the search regiment itself should be abandoned in favor of a regiment of light tanks. Motor vehicles should supplant horses during flatland operations to the greatest extent possible. But horses were still needed, and the Manchurians should be encouraged to raise a better breed.

Reinforcements from Japan should be expedited, and a new national policy adopted to increase the number of reservists available in Manchuria. In connection with the latter point, the Kwantung Army might develop vocational training centers designed to retain those soldiers who retired in Manchuria, and veterans in the homeland might be encouraged to relocate there. Excellent officers were needed in quantity, and the quick replacement of unit commanders was especially important. Medical and veterinary replacement officers needed more familiarization with the army. Replacement troops must be of top-notch quality. The term of active duty should be three years; long-term volunteers should be widely accepted. Young soldiers were particularly valuable in communications, armor, and antiaircraft duties. Consideration should be given to the possible use of Manchurians as well as to the increased use of Koreans in the imperial army. Japanese subjects should be recruited for civilian employment by the army from the SMR, Manchuria Airways, and the telephone and telegraph system in Manchukuo.

For logistical and medical units, the Kwantung Army advised the 1st Subcommittee to consider such additional matters as standardization of matériel, stockpiling of spare parts, improvement of Japanese-manufactured vehicles, assurance of water-supply facilities, and training in demolition of equipment, in the use of weapons, and in self-defense. Armor plating for vehicles (including tractors) was desirable, as was the establishment of wireless communication regiments. The need for protection of secrets and tighter counterintelligence measures received elaborate attention. Troop movement was too easily exposed by the commandeering of horses and vehicles and by local purchase of foodstuffs, as well as by confinement to quarters, repair of wristwatches, and repayment of debts at such places as bars. Rail movements were given away by identification tags, by excessive use of railway phones, and by overly detailed and frequent message traffic. Conversations of officers and men at hospitals, restaurants, and train stations needed to be monitored more strictly, and personal letters must be censored in the battle zone. New procedures should be introduced with respect to ID cards, uniforms, and classified documents brought to the front. It seemed advisable to give up the common practice of identifying units by their commanders' names, and to employ numerical designators instead.

Although the Nomonhan Incident, noted the Kwantung Army, had provided "many precious lessons concerning modern warfare waged against the Soviet forces," a number of defects in IJA education and training had also been revealed. Enhanced spiritual training was crucial to smash the enemy's materialism, with stress laid upon the following features: sense of responsibility; ability to evince sound judgment in stressful combat situations; absolute obedience; elimination of "liberal, easygoing modes of thought"; heightened fighting spirit and teamwork in adversity; cooperation between officers and men; spiritual endurance; efficient handling of dead, wounded, and prisoners; fostering of soldiers' love for their weapons. Order should be simple, and reports accurate. The quality of officers needed improvement, especially since the rapid expansion of the army had caused a shortage of officers. The performance of the Japanese heavy artillery, for example, had been rendered less effective than expected, because of the inferiority (*furyō*) of the lower-ranking officers (*kakyū kanbu*). Weapons and equipment were becoming more complicated and more difficult to handle, necessitating special technical and combat training of officers as well as men. Live ammunition and real matériel should be used, marksmanship should be stressed, and better training grounds and firing ranges should be employed. The confidence of units that had served at Nomonhan should be restored by the issue of better matériel and weapons. When men retired from the army, it was extremely important that they be instructed carefully about psychological considerations that must not be allowed to affect the civilian populace.

"We were made to realize," commented the Kwantung Army analysts, "how weak we were in the techniques of modern war, military systematism, and organization." During a protracted engagement, should armor or artillery be emphasized? From the strictly tactical standpoint, both arms were of equal value; but without artillery support, tanks could not operate effectively, as Nomonhan had shown. Therefore, if the Japanese army had any spare materials and funds, they should be allocated to strengthen the artillery.

Apart from their broad conclusions, the Kwantung Army staff officers collated a wealth of technical information, a sampling of which follows. Large-scale mess trucks and salvage vehicles would be highly useful. The troops required small tools such as saws and axes. Units needed more backup uniforms. Rations should be wrapped, and the wartime staple of rice somehow supplemented with vitamins. The use of dehydrated vegetables needed to be investigated; each man should be issued doubled amounts of sugar candies; all labels must be readable even at night. Soldiers required first-aid training, at least to the extent of stanching hemorrhages.[29] Lastly, even mechanized units needed horses and camels on the plains; dogs and pigeons proved useful; and divisions should have a veterinary hospital even in peacetime.[30]

The Japanese army's technical headquarters also assembled helpful raw data on the performance and characteristics of Soviet and IJA ordnance. Among 13 very professional, objective attachments prepared by tank, artillery, and other experts, the concluding remarks of a Captain Kawakami are particularly noteworthy.[31] "By comparison with the investigations conducted in North China . . . I feel greater tension [*kinpaku*] now. The time has come to discard the mistaken ideas acquired during the China Incident. Maximum effort should be devoted to the next, improved objectives. Unless we do so, I feel very strongly that we shall come to regret it later."

In short, despite some serious attempts to analyze weaknesses and to apply the experiences of Nomonhan, the Japanese army's investigators generally did better with the technical than with the strategic and tactical challenges. Indeed, their deductions often reflected a sense of helplessness and superficiality in the face of the latest developments, and their language incorporated platitudinous allusions to the nature of firepower, maneuver, and modern war. Among the surprises admitted by the Japanese was the unexpected ability of enemy armored forces to operate without infantrymen, and the "invisible wall" of artillery bombardment that prevented the advance of friendly foot soldiers. Again and again, the IJA analysts fell back upon easy, comfortable frames of reference: spiritual élan, close-quarter antitank assaults, aerial dogfighting, night attacks, raiding, and infantry charges. The

Japanese officer, it was said, preferred and was best at the meeting engagement (*sōgūsen*), which was well suited to the terrain of Manchuria.

Reassuring note was taken of alleged Soviet weaknesses: Russian troops were short of uniforms, and their knapsacks, made of rough cotton, were little more than bags. GPU men watched the soldiers closely; those who disobeyed orders were usually shot.[32] After all, the 23rd Division had had to take on four rifle divisions and five mechanized brigades for four days in August. At Changkufeng in 1938, dug-in Japanese troops had beaten off frontal attacks by three divisions; but Nomonhan demonstrated the difficulty of resisting in isolation for seven days in a row. Since 10 consecutive days represented the outer limit of endurance, it was extremely dangerous to allow a unit to fight longer than that. The Russians only closed in for the kill when the defenders' strength was nearly depleted. Although a Japanese division was larger than its Soviet counterpart, the disproportionate factors were Russian resupply and replacement capabilities and a quantitative superiority in artillery that amounted to 2:1 by late August. On one point, there was no room for argument: the Russians had shown the effectiveness of mechanized units against rear positions.[33]

IJA investigators showed interest in Soviet antigas equipment and, as noted earlier, stressed the need for enhanced countermeasures. No special attention was devoted to the danger of bacteriological warfare, although the Japanese had publicly accused the Russians of attempting to foment epidemics during the Nomonhan affair. Manfred Boekenkamp, a German News Agency (DNB) correspondent who spent about a week at the front in July, reported personally observing nine Soviet aircraft drop strange shining objects from an altitude of more than 5,000 meters in the vicinity of the Holsten. Soon afterward, Japanese medical officers displayed "fragments of a very curious type of bomb . . . [that] looked like pieces of burnt, soft metal, which had not exploded into bits like ordinary bombs, but had . . . given way and burst like a full tin of gasoline under much pressure from within." Under the microscope, according to Boekenkamp, dysentery bacilli were detected—alleged proof that the Russians intended to poison the river from which the Japanese forces obtained their water. The seriousness with which the IJA command regarded this effort, Boekenkamp reported, was betokened by the introduction of filtration equipment and of a unit of water-wagons sent immediately from Hailar.[34]

Classified IJA records reveal very real Japanese suspicions. On 13 July, a Kwantung Army medical specialist, Col. Ishii Shirō, inspected the front-line water-supply situation on the sector of the 71st Regiment. Dr. Ishii warned the unit to avoid drawing river water because there was concern that the enemy was using it for "diabolical schemes" (*bōryaku*). AGS intelligence reported, on the same day, that there was evidence of a dysentery outbreak, that enemy bacteriological warfare was suspected, and that close watch was being maintained. The 72nd Regiment had a simpler explanation: since the heat of mid-July was intense, the water-supply section had not been able to keep up with the demand, and the troops had dug their own wells and drunk unboiled water. Consequently, cases of dysentery broke out, one after another. Sixth Army doctors discovered typhoid but no cholera among Japanese troops returning to Hailar after the cease-fire; the possibility of bacteriological warfare received no mention.[35]

At the time of the Japanese army's special concern in July, the Russian military authorities retorted angrily that "the rumors spread by the Kwantung Army headquarters about the use by Mongolian-Soviet units of toxins and bacteriological means of warfare, the headquarters of the Mongolian-Soviet forces regards . . . as an impudent lie and malicious slander."[36] From the vantage point of the IJA medical bureau in Tokyo, Lt. Col. Kinbara Setsuzō wondered if the reports of Soviet bacteriological shells were indeed no more than rumors. The Russians should have known, says Dr. Kinbara, that it was nearly impossible to disseminate a fecal infection among large groups of men by exploding bombs or shells containing dysentery bacilli. But it was known to the Japanese that the Russians had bacteriological facilities at Khabarovsk and that, even before the Nomonhan war, experiments had been conducted in the region, using diseased animals to carry anthrax to other animals and to humans. The most serious threat at Nomonhan was the possible infection of water sources if filtration was not in use. It was crucial to provide huge amounts of aseptic water, which was "more important than even ammunition." Ishii and his men did a splendid job of coping with problems of epidemic control and water supply (*bōeki kyūsui*). During the fighting, the medical bureau expended ¥2,800,000, mostly for use by the Ishii unit. Based on Chiangchunmiao, Ishii employed 50 trucks and 10,000 drums for the supply of sterilized water.[37]

After the Pacific War, several Japanese leftist writers retailed tales that at Nomonhan the Ishii unit was really engaged in spreading cholera, typhus, and plague from the upper reaches of the Halha, and that over 30 Japanese medical and civilian personnel were killed in the process. In December 1939, Ishii himself explained privately to the new Kwantung Army chief of staff, Endō, that the central authorities had directed him to undertake bacteriological warfare operations but that he had declined to do so because study of countermeasures had not been completed by that time. Endō, who agreed with Ishii, admits that it was theoretically possible to have hampered enemy pursuit at the end of the Nomonhan fighting by infecting the Halha; but Endō never heard that the Japanese actually employed bacteriological measures in 1939. In short, though the Japanese army, like the Red

Army, certainly had developed a serious interest in bacteriological warfare, no responsible IJA source accepts or authenticates the allegation that the Kwantung Army tried to poison the precious river water upon which its own forces were as dependent as the Russians and the Mongolians must have been.[38]

While still at war with China, the Japanese army dared to take on the Americans, British, and Dutch hardly two years after the cease-fire at Nomonhan. Because of insufficient time, willingness, and imagination, the fundamental lessons of 1939 had not been assimilated or heeded by 1941-42. In the case of IJA intelligence, for example, the Nakano school was only established in 1940, in an effort to supersede the unsophisticated old "newspapermen" and second-class personnel who infested the system and to lay a more scientific army-wide foundation.[39] On 31 January 1940, the Special Intelligence headquarters was set up in the Kwantung Army, along the lines of the 2nd Subcommittee's recommendations. But the experience at Nomonhan exerted no profound effect on the practitioners, and improvements were limited to reorganization and changes in structure, not in function.

Intelligence officers remained convinced that it was the ever-optimistic operations staff which had botched matters by taking their advice and warnings too lightly and by underestimating the enemy. At the highest levels of the Kwantung Army, it was claimed, even the commander and the chief of staff may have been dominated by subjective, emotional thinking. Komatsubara, according to intelligence sources, was not acquainted with the tactics of defense on a wide front in flatland terrain. If timely intelligence had reached him, the general reportedly said, he would have fought differently.[40]

Operations officers such as Tsuji insisted it was the Intelligence Section that grossly misread enemy capabilities by a factor of two. Thus Soviet rifle corps had been thought to possess only one field artillery regiment but actually contained two, and an antitank battalion supposedly was equipped with 18 of the 45-mm. pieces but really had 36. IJA tactical manuals, based upon intelligence input, as late as June 1938 were still describing Russian artillery as mostly old, heavy, slow in rate of fire, and having a range of less than 10,000 meters. The Soviet battery table of equipment was placed at three guns instead of four.[41]

With respect to armor, many Japanese officers insisted, even after Nomonhan, that the terrain of Manchuria, especially on the decisive eastern front, was not suitable for units larger than a tank regiment, although group command was necessary. Artillery Colonel Mishima tried to argue the need for super-heavy "battleship" tanks designed to overrun *tochkas*. But the opinion was widespread that small, highly mobile tanks (6-10 tons) were more practical than thickly armored and thus far heavier versions; any machine weighing more than 20 tons was called "heavy." Finally impressed by the German experience in 1940, several IJA officers did recommend building the largest tanks that could be transported aboard South Manchuria Railway trains—30-ton armored vehicles mounting 75-mm. or 100-mm. cannon. Around 1941, a few of the more lively AGS thinkers wanted to create as many as 30 tank divisions and 50 motorized infantry divisions. Despite a realization that the program of mechanization ought to be accelerated, the first two IJA tank divisions were not formed until the summer of 1942.

Like the Japanese infantry, tankers still grappled with the old problem of engaging an outnumbering enemy. At the Kungchuling tank school, Ogata always taught after Nomonhan that the Japanese must be prepared to attack despite an adverse numerical ratio of 1:100. Superb training must inculcate the vital compensation: superior fighting spirit. Training documents stressed that the experience at Nomonhan, particularly Colonel Yoshimaru's last action in early July, demonstrated that high offensive élan and appropriate tactics "more than made up for inferiority in strength in antitank battle," as was equally true of the Second World War in Europe. It was an erroneous lesson, we know, as Yoshimaru's useless death and the mauling of his 3rd Tank Regiment ought to have shown. After all, IJA armor—at its peak—was outnumbered by about 7:1 at Nomonhan, was unable to slug it out for more than a few intense days, and incurred 40 percent tank losses. Nevertheless, the Japanese army carried its notion of spiritual superiority, affecting tank crews as well as infantry, into the Pacific War. Science and technology never achieved equal billing with pride and tradition, although as Mishima baldly put it, mechanization would have been cheaper and easier in the long run.[42]

Part of the problem stemmed from the fact that the Japanese army—the Ordnance Bureau in particular—was extremely slow to adopt innovative tactics and new equipment. Yet once production finally began, one item would be turned out almost endlessly. IJA front-line forces felt the painful effects of the poor ordnance administration, but there was never speedy modification. One explanation is that intendance officers, who dealt with uniforms, boots, and other personal gear, were attached to their branch permanently and thus had time to design and test excellent matériel, whereas ordnance officers were subject to routine line assignments and therefore were rotated constantly during their careers, without getting a chance to concentrate on technical matters. Consequently, a pronounced imbalance emerged between intendance and ordnance quality. An example of the Ordnance Bureau's foot-dragging was the failure to introduce piano-wire entanglements, although Japanese tankers had recommended their employment after encountering them for the first time at Nomonhan. Since piano wire was an item for use on the defensive—abhorred by the army—there was no push for its adoption, and it did not come into use.[43]

Whereas the Red Army, despite problems with the Stalinist purges and with doctrine, forged ahead with the principle of mechanization and produced battle-tested new designs in the 1930's, a hiatus had existed in the Japanese tank branch after 1929, when the army finally accepted the Type 89 tank designed in 1925. Seven years were wasted until the Type 97 medium tank was decided on in 1936, as six years had been before the Type 95 light tank was chosen in 1935. During the deliberations on the light machine in 1935, a regiment commander had openly condemned it, saying that a puny tank with only 6 to 12 mm. of plating—scarcely sufficient to deflect machine-gun fire—was unsuitable as a main battle tank. Colonel Tamada had to take such "junk" to Nomonhan.

The difference in output of Japanese and Soviet tanks was pronounced. By 1939, the Red Army possessed approximately 17,000 armored vehicles of all kinds, and production averaged 3,000 per year. The Japanese, however, had turned out only a total of 573 tanks as late as 1940: Type 98 light, 113; Type 89 medium, 271; Type 97 medium, 25; Type 95 light, 164. With the outbreak of the Pacific War, the contest between armor and aviation for the lion's share of the Japanese army's limited budget was resolved in favor of the air force. From a modest high point of 1,024 tanks produced in 1941 and 1,165 in 1942, the output fell off to 786 in 1943, 342 in 1944, and 94 in 1945. It was a "natural" development, says Noguchi. Although a tank staff officer in Tokyo, he willingly converted tank factories into aircraft factories and "became a 'traitor' to the tank world." Talk of heavy armor and masses of independent divisions never progressed beyond the exploratory stage, despite some high hopes after Nomonhan.[44]

The Japanese army air force's ongoing problems had been intensified by the attrition of 1939. During the 30 years that the air force had been in existence, a total of only 1,700 pilots had been produced. The war ministry now laid plans to turn out that same number each year. By the time of the Pacific War, army flying schools were graduating 750 pilots annually. From a strength of 91 air squadrons in 1939 (55 of which were to be deployed in Manchuria), the High Command hoped to build the number of squadrons to 164 by 1942. A total of 1,181 military planes had been manufactured in 1936; by 1939, war plans called for production of 3,600 aircraft of all types. After Nomonhan, production rose to 4,768 in 1940 and to 5,088 by 1941. Partly affected by the success of fighters and the feebleness of bombers at Nomonhan, the Japanese ascribed increasing importance to the production of fighter planes rather than bomber aircraft.[45]

So far as ground forces were concerned, veterans of Nomonhan understood the limitations on any field artillery or reconnaissance unit based upon horses. Combat records and diaries are filled with sad accounts of horses incapacitated or killed by gunfire and bombings or by lack of water and forage. Although the 23rd Division was originally supposed to be motorized, it included 2,200 horses in its organization.[46] In late February 1940, the Ordnance Bureau chief in Japan stated that, because of the bitter experience of Nomonhan, general motorization of ground units was under way.[47]

Traditional outlooks died hard, however, and the realities of weak industrial underpinnings also intervened. Thus, at the time of the great Kantokuen mobilization in the summer of 1941 (described in the next chapter), the Kwantung Army was allocated 350,000 more men and no fewer than 370,000 horses. Of the horses, 160,000 (including 43,000 already available in Manchuria) were intended for operational use, 130,000 for backup units coming from Japan and Korea, and 80,000 for transport purposes. By contrast, the Kantokuen augmentation plan called for only 14,000 motor vehicles, including 3,700 trucks and sedans to be brought from Japan and another 2,300 commandeered in Manchuria. Significantly, exclusive of official vehicles, in all of Manchukuo there were only 9,000 motor vehicles, 50 percent of which were not expected to be able to pass military inspection. One can see why the immense scale of Soviet truck use at Nomonhan awed IJA logistical and intelligence experts. The latter spoke of the "unexpected, unpredictable" measures of which the Red Army and the Russian people were capable, and of the inconceivable pressures exerted to accomplish national objectives. Soviet forces, it was said, "attached appalling importance to military matériel. They actually limited their [troops'] provisions to black bread and rock salt, in order to make room for the transportation of ammunition, fuel, and the like."[48]

At the time, a limited number of Japanese publications and speakers indirectly admitted the setback of Nomonhan. The widely distributed soldier's handbook called it "regrettable but evident that our forces' fighting capacity [*sentō nōryoku*] was inferior to that of the Russians in the Nomonhan Incident; therein lies the reason for our 18,000 casualties." For every admission, however, there was a counterbalancing apologia: in this case the authors of the handbook hastened to add that IJA troops had defended the frontiers without stint, in the face of overwhelming enemy tank forces under the searing sun of the wastelands.[49]

Individuals who spoke up brought ire upon themselves. One example was feisty Colonel Sumi, who in January 1940, after retirement, vented his indignation during a reunion of military academy classmates. "I wondered openly," he says, "whether the army's leaders really understood the importance of modern weapons, and I suspected that they thought Japan could win a war solely by reliance on spiritual strength." Sumi argued the need for antitank and antiaircraft weapons and for superior tanks and planes. Most of his old comrades, still on active duty, did not take the retired colonel's views very seriously. Maj. Gen. Kan Haruji, the Ordnance Bureau chief, supported him, but the Personnel Bureau head, Maj. Gen. Tominaga Kyōji, did not. Tominaga could be seen whispering in the ear of the Military Affairs Bureau chief, Maj. Gen. Mutō Akira. "The latter openly attacked me," Sumi remembers. "With a menacing look he growled: 'What is the value of combat lessons from such a trifling affair as Nomonhan?'"[50]

Colonel Mishima, still in service, encountered similar resistance. At the artillery school in Japan, he strenuously opposed overreliance on élan and constantly recommended that divisional artillery consist of motorized 15-cm. howitzers to cope with the Russians. But Gen. Yamamuro Sōbu and other prominent artillery officers continued to extol horse-drawn pack guns for the divisions. Nomonhan had been a purely local, "atypical" case, they insisted. Foreseeable combat operations in East Asia would favor mountain guns that could be dismantled, loaded aboard horses, and hauled close to the infantry's front lines. The fire of heavy howitzers was comparable to "eyedrops falling from the second floor." Of the entire artillery school faculty, only Gen. Izeki Jin (later a division commander) ever came around to Mishima's view. At least one of the colonel's recommendations was implemented, however: the development of a one-ton 30-cm. howitzer shell, with a range of only 1,000 meters, designed to pulverize a *tochka* with one round. Mishima also kept harping on the need for motorization, as demonstrated at Nomonhan. In 1940, he became the head of the new motor maintenance school, which progressed beyond the training of supply-unit drivers to encompass infantrymen, cavalrymen, and artillerists.[51]

These were limited successes indeed. The Ordnance Bureau turned down the idea of issuing howitzers to infantry regiments, advising the latter to be satisfied with light and medium mortars and with infantry guns. Field or mountain artillery was quite effective against parked tanks at long range.[52] As for shortages, the thinking was still widespread—even among the artillery, which had suffered so badly from scant ammunition stocks at Nomonhan— that one must accept them as "fate" and that it represented spiritual weakness to appeal for more ammunition. Japanese artillery officers therefore recoiled from asking for more shells, with the result, as General Hata put it, that guns were lined up without ammunition like "inedible painted rice cakes." To cripple the batteries by needlessly rationing ammunition, added Hata sardonically, represented "merely womanish, trifling solicitude"; yet the most ardent conservationists were the artillerymen themselves.[53]

Against "fainthearted" critics, the response was often made that personal, not doctrinal, negligence explained many of the shortcomings in combat. "Instead of chasing after novel methods," a transport company commander,

Capt. Nomura Norio, wrote in 1941, "we should have trained harder in accordance with the Field Service Regulations." Nomura said he wrongly thought he had learned various lessons from his own experience at Nomonhan, whereas the tested solutions were readily available from the FSR, if only he had done his homework.[54]

Underlying the thinking of men such as Captain Nomura, who represented the majority of the Japanese officer corps, were two fundamental needs: to play down the enemy and to boost one's own confidence. To rate the foe highly, Prince Kan'in once explained, tended to breed defeatism and cowardice and to erode friendly forces' morale. Major Tsuji was once heard to remark that the Red Army was weaker than the Chinese. Commanders and operations officers reportedly squelched Doi, the military attaché in Moscow, when he recommended in June 1939 that the battle strength of the Russians be carefully evaluated. "Discussion of such matters is impermissible," Doi was told. When the Nomonhan research committee was reporting its findings, Lt. Col. Konuma Haruo, an expert on strategy and tactics, stressed that the Japanese army ought not to pride itself on its victories over China. Instead, it was imperative to grasp the significance of the Nomonhan conflict as an instance of modern war in general. In future, the Japanese could expect to encounter foreign armies that would be organized and equipped as well as or even better than the Russians at Nomonhan. But the AGS deputy, General Sawada, glared at Konuma and barked that he was insulting the imperial army by saying such things. It was apparent that the High Command wanted to believe that the Nomonhan affair was atypical and that the Russians had fought it with special organization and equipment.[55]

Outside the army, such an outlook incensed the ever-critical Sumi, who was freer to speak than most. Japan, the colonel felt, had just been beaten by a relatively underdeveloped country, the USSR. To take on two advanced industrial powers, the United States and Britain, so soon after Nomonhan struck Sumi as folly; the Anglo-Saxon countries were "like the Ginza," the Soviet Union "like the backwoods of Eastern Europe." Nevertheless, we know from other sources that when a Southern Army staff officer, Sugita Ichiji, tried to essay an appraisal of American military power during the Pacific War, he was promptly rebuffed by his superiors, as Doi had been in 1939.[56]

Closely intertwined with Japanese operations staffs' deliberate underestimation of adversaries was the cruel denigration of IJA commanders and staff officers whose outlooks were prudent and conservative. Many fine officers were hounded from the army for alleged cravenness, which was another way of insulting their "manhood." In one prominent instance, when General Shimizu told a class of military academy graduates to rely on their field glasses in modern battle instead of their sabers, the famed swordsman General Yamaoka "blew up" on the spot. Caution was equated with a lack of courage, and the army tended to look down at levelheaded officers who tried to win at minimum cost in lives. As we saw, a fine infantry brigade commander from the 7th Division, Maj. Gen. Morita Norimasa, was ousted from the army because of his realistic and thus unsuccessful handling of the Japanese offensive of 24 August at Nomonhan. One particularly famous case, from the China theater, concerned Lt. Gen. Sakai Kōji, a brilliant the-oretician and more promising officer than Tōjō, his classmate. The com-mander of a mechanized brigade, Sakai was retired for supposed timidity and lack of skill in combat direction. Once more, considerations of *bushidō* outweighed those of intellect.[57]

The smiting of reasonable IJA officers after Nomonhan extended to the highest level of the Kwantung Army itself—to Maj. Gen. Endō Saburō, the deputy chief of staff. A top graduate of every military school he attended, Endō had had an impressive professional career: five years' duty in the AGS Operations Section, almost four years of advanced military schooling in France, two years of service in the Kwantung Army Operations Section (all before 1934), and a two-year appointment to the faculty of the IJA war col-lege. During the China conflict, he fought as an artillery regiment com-mander, was attached to three different divisions, and participated in 12 battles. From December 1937 to July 1939, Endō was involved in military training as an AGS section chief and war college adjunct professor. A highly decorated officer and a major general from August 1939, he drew upon his earlier knowledge and what he observed of the situation in Manchuria after Nomonhan to devise two main policies: first, until the China Incident was solved, the Kwantung Army should make every effort to avoid a clash with the Russians and, by adhering to minimum strength levels, should allow the High Command to concentrate on the China theater; second, Japan ought to nurture Manchukuo and win over people at home and abroad, thus contributing to the settlement of the hostilities in China.

To achieve these objectives, Endō recommended that the mission of the Kwantung Army be changed immediately. The current planning still called for a Japanese offensive against the USSR in the event of war. This in turn necessitated a major buildup in Manchuria during peacetime—e.g., the con-struction of roads and airfields, the stockpiling of munitions, the deploy-ment of forces. Such preparations would inevitably provoke the Russians and lead to confrontations as at Changkufeng and Nomonhan, with adverse effects on the China theater. Endō believed that there was already grave danger that the USSR would commence hostilities with Japan in the near future because of IJA exhaustion in China as well as Manchukuo's insta-bility. In particular, the Russians had gained great confidence in their military prowess as a result of their recent operations at Nomonhan and in Poland. Consequently, Endō wanted to convert to a defensive strategy, whereby the Kwantung Army would engage the Soviets on Manchurian soil if war occurred. While not inciting Russian counteraction in the meantime, the Kwantung Army should build powerful positions inside Manchuria and stress troop training. Generals Umezu and Iimura approved Endō's proposals, whereupon Endō flew to Tokyo in early October 1939 to work out matters with the General Staff.

Endō was sure that he had won the central authorities' agreement in principle, but there was no progress after he got back to Hsinking. Certainly a lot of work was involved, but the Kwantung Army's Operations Section, headed by Colonel Arisue and assisted by Major Shimamura, clung to the offensive concept and sabotaged Endō's program. When the general remonstrated with the operations officers, they told him that there was no need to act hastily since there would be no war with the USSR during the current fiscal year anyhow. Shimamura continued to go to Tokyo surprisingly often on "official business." Matters deteriorated to the point that the General Staff was asked to replace both Arisue and Shimamura. It was too late. The draft of the operational plan for 1940, received on 17 November, retained the old offensive concept. Greatly disappointed, Endō felt that he could never agree to an AGS plan that called for giving up on China and for invading the Soviet Union in case of war with the Russians.

The team that brought the draft from Tokyo sought to "sell" it to the Kwantung Army's leaders. Col. Okada Jūichi, the AGS Operations Section chief, was new in his post and left details to his two assistants, Major Imaizumi (Operations) and Major Imaoka (Logistics), both of whom had spent three years in place. The visitors soon learned that Kwantung Army headquarters was very cautious, that the situation was extremely disorganized since the Nomonhan affair (about which there was no time for discussion), and that there was some thought of giving up the offensive plan, even on the critical east Manchurian front. Endō seemed to be expressing a "mostly personal" opinion that the Kwantung Army's rear preparations were not ready. Imaoka remembers explaining thoroughly to Endō that every effort would be made to rebuild the rear facilities by April 1940 and to accelerate operational preparations. Imaizumi stressed that if there was no eastern offensive, the Japanese homeland would be exposed to bombing from Siberia. It was known that the Russians had been building bases for heavy bombers in the Maritime Province since 1937—a fact that was tormenting the Japanese High Command. Endō did not seem too satisfied by the explanations, but he subsided when Umezu finally gave in, thus allowing presumable unification of the views of the Kwantung Army and of IGHQ.[58]

Once Endō's counterplan was rejected by Colonel Okada on behalf of the

High Command, the inviolable final document, approved by the Throne, was delivered to Hsinking on 16 December. Endō privately regarded the latest contingency plan as "infantile and unsuited to present circumstances." But the general's travails were far from over. Usually the annual war plan was gamed before receiving imperial sanction. This time the map maneuvers in Hsinking were scheduled for late December. When AGS Operations Bureau Chief Tominaga arrived with his staff, Endō tried to get them to play the role of the Japanese, while he directed hypothetical Soviet operations. Tominaga refused. Under Endō's supervision, the Kwantung Army's Operations Section should take the part of the Japanese while the Intelligence Section acted as the Russians. Umezu overrode Endō's objections centering on the need for impartiality, and for two days, on 22 and 23 December, the games were conducted; the Japanese side was defeated miserably. While reinforcements were still being sent from Japan and from China, they were supposedly discovered and bombed by the Soviet air force, which inflicted severe losses, even before the main body of the Kwantung Army could concentrate at the Soviet frontier. Tominaga declined to provide a critique and left Hsinking without saying anything.

Shortly afterward, Endō received his "new year's gift": the AGS General Affairs Bureau chief responsible for personnel matters, Maj. Gen. Kanda Masatane, arrived from Tokyo and requested a private meeting with Umezu, Iimura, and Endō. Could the Kwantung Army, he asked delicately, "spare" Endō during the March reassignment cycle for transfer to air force buildup duties? Endō was unenthusiastic about leaving the Kwantung Army so soon, and Umezu backed him; but it soon became apparent that Endō's successor, Maj. Gen. Hata Hikosaburō, the OSS anti-Soviet expert, had already been selected. That Endō was being punished for his heretical views (although they had been approved by his superiors) became evident when he paid his respects to the AGS deputy, Lieutenant General Sawada, in Tokyo in March 1940. "I have heard," said Sawada, "that some people in the Kwantung Army, affected by the Nomonhan Incident, have contracted 'Soviet-phobia.'" Was this true? Endō knew that Arisue and Shimamura had been working behind his back, so he merely replied that he would respond in writing and took leave of Sawada.

Disturbed about the future of Japan and of the Kwantung Army, and fully resolved to leave military service if necessary, Endō addressed a long and gracious letter to Sawada on 25 March 1940. When Sawada had asked about the accuracy of the information that there were objections to taking the offensive against the Russians, even committing the entire Japanese army, Endō realized that the deputy must have had him in mind. Without meaning to make excuses or to address matters that no longer fell within his purview, Endō wanted to reassure Sawada that he was not suffering from

"Soviet-phobia." Indeed, he had been a proponent of the concept of the offensive into the USSR ever since the Manchurian Incident, had continued to hold that view even during the China Incident, and had opposed the retreat from Changkufeng in 1938. Although involved in delivering the imperial order for the suspension of operations at Nomonhan in September 1939, Endō reminded Sawada that he had privately favored a last offensive by the Kwantung Army. In each of these cases, the Russians had had no intention of waging all-out war, and the battlefield favored a Japanese campaign of attrition.

By 1940, Endō argued, the situation had changed to the point that neither his common sense nor his conscience would allow him to envisage an offensive into Russia. The quality of the Red Army was not to be feared, but Soviet quantitative strength, fortifications, and defenses could not be ignored. From the IJA standpoint, Japan had been wearing itself out in China for three years. Officer quality had declined because of the huge casualties in the China theater and the rapid expansion of the army. The new triangular divisions were a mess. Men and units were being thrown together like a jigsaw puzzle, without historical or geographical ties. Troops came from areas as far apart as Aomori and Kagoshima, and the resulting confusion of dialects meant that they could scarcely converse intelligently with each other. In addition to weaknesses in education and training, the army suffered from insufficiency of operational matériel and of transport facilities, caused by the shortage of natural resources and of an industrial base, plus the ongoing China conflict. Under such circumstances, could one be confident of smashing through the Russian border defenses and conquering the USSR? The lessons of 1918 on the Western Front in Europe and the nature of modern war in general suggested that even if a portion of the Soviet positions could be penetrated, the price would be enormous and would cripple Japan's ability to conduct national policy. To abandon the China war for the sake of an all-out thrust into the Soviet Union would cause Japan to "fall between two stools" and to run the risk of self-destruction. It was a delusion to claim that the Russians did not have the capability of conducting full-scale war against Japan in the near future and that the contingency plan could be left unchanged. The Kwantung Army knew better. After all, it was the vanguard of the imperial forces and was directly confronting the Red Army.[59]

Although Endō was not ousted from the army, his plea to Sawada received short shrift. The meaningless old offensive plan, imposed on the Kwantung Army in the event that war broke out with the USSR, remained on the books another four years, until 1944. But there was a deeper meaning to the unseating of Endō in 1940: insubordination and arbitrary behavior by freewheeling staff officers were continuing, in the person of men such as Shimamura, a successor to Tsuji. The voluminous reports of the

Nomonhan investigation committees did not address a core problem, the lack of synchronization between the central authorities and the Kwantung Army, which had plagued the entire conduct of operations in 1939 and had engendered petulant, emotional interactions between the staffs in Tokyo and in Hsinking. Even Hattori, a close colleague of Tsuji's, had warned in the Kwantung Army's secret diary of Nomonhan that there was great need to ponder the substance and style of high-level command, "for the sake of the national military establishment and of operational guidance." [60]

43

To the Demise of the Kwantung Army

Except for a flurry of excitement in mid-1941 and again in early 1942, the forces in Manchuria were destined to play an unaccustomed secondary role in overall Japanese national security planning until the disaster that befell the nation and its armed forces in 1945. The stunning military victories of Germany in the West during the first year of the European war had contributed to a rethinking of Japan's geopolitical priorities. With Matsuoka Yōsuke as foreign minister and Tōjō Hideki as war minister, the second Konoe cabinet, formed in July 1940, sought to be on the winning side on the world scene, to exploit opportunities regarded as heaven-sent, and to carve out permanent spheres of influence for Japan in Asia. Pro-Axis elements, whose influence in the government and in the army was now paramount, were gratified by the final conclusion of the ten-year Tripartite Pact with Germany and Italy on 27 September 1940, an accord ostensibly designed to create conditions conducive to the prosperity of the three peoples. As Matsuoka later explained privately to the American ambassador in Moscow, the real premise underlying the agreement was to limit the scope of the European war and, in particular, to prevent the United States from entering it.[1]

At least temporarily, a "tilt to the south" ensued in the direction of the oil and other natural resources of the rich colonies in Southeast Asia, almost bereft of military protection after the fall of metropolitan France and Holland and the weakening of Britain. Apart from providing springboards for further advances, Japanese penetration of Southeast Asia was seen as a new means of putting pressure on Nationalist China. Indeed, the British had been induced to close the Burma Road temporarily in June 1940, and the Vichy French authorities yielded Japan a military foothold in the north in 1940 and in the south the following year.[2]

With respect to the Soviet Union, Germany's uneasy partner since the signing of the nonaggression pact during the final stage of the Nomonhan war, Japan needed quiescence in the north in order to guarantee a free hand in the south if, as seemed increasingly probable, hostilities with the ABDA powers (the Americans, British, Dutch, and Australians) were to erupt in the near future.[3] Consequently the Japanese endeavored to reassure the Russians that the Tripartite Pact was not intended to affect the existing political situation.[4] To assuage lingering Soviet doubts and to strengthen the Japanese hand, Matsuoka pursued what he called a "new diplomacy," whose centerpiece was a grand design of neutralizing the Anglo-Saxon powers by devising a "Eurasian heartland alliance" combining the interests of the Tripartite countries with those of the USSR. In particular, Matsuoka wanted Germany to act as a mediator to improve relations between Japan and Russia.[5]

Despite a whirlwind trip to Berlin, Rome, and Moscow in the spring of 1941, Matsuoka had to settle for a five-year, renewable pact of neutrality (not nonaggression) with the Russians. Signed on 13 April, the Russo-Japanese accord promised neutrality in case either party became embroiled in hostilities with one or more third powers. The Japanese bound themselves to respect the territorial integrity of Outer Mongolia in return for Russia's similar pledge regarding Manchuria.[6]

The neutrality treaty favored the short-term needs of both sides by allowing them to wage war elsewhere without distraction. For the Russians, this meant relative freedom to focus attention on their western borders, where signs of trouble with the Reich were accumulating, such as the German incursions into the Soviet zone of interest in the Balkans in March and April 1941. Postwar Russian sources, in fact, call the neutrality pact a victory for Soviet diplomacy in that it reduced the threat of a two-front war for the USSR. The Russians for their part suspected that the Japanese were purchasing time until a favorable opportunity arose for an all-out invasion of Siberia. For both sides, then, the accord was no more than a tactical scheme.[7]

Aggressive thinking vis-à-vis the Russians was not incompatible with the growing Japanese interest in Southeast Asia. Though the Japanese army still pressed for military preparedness against the Soviet Union, the neutrality treaty created "a sense of 'tranquillity in the north' that provided psychological encouragement for the policy of southern advance."[8] The pact had been in effect little more than two months when Germany invaded Russia in June. Even during this short period, it was possible to discern concrete effects of the accord. Negotiations in Moscow for a trade agreement and a fishing-rights treaty bore fruit in early June. Settlement of the long-standing issue of Japanese interests in northern Sakhalin, Matsuoka pledged, would be achieved by year's end.[9] And the old problem of border delineation, still unsettled a year and a half after the end of the fighting at Nomonhan, finally drew serious attention when negotiations between the MPR and Manchukuo got under way in May 1941 at Chita. Progress proved rapid, and a fundamental agreement was worked out by 10 June and signed on the 15th. Actual demarcation of the boundary remained to be finished—by the end of the summer, it was hoped.[10]

The most important single basis for appraising the immediate impact of the Soviet-Japanese neutrality pact, however, was the scale of military strength retained in the area of Manchuria and Siberia. The common view is that neither side adjusted its troop levels before the Germans attacked the USSR, and that, in the face of the subsequent buildup of the Kwantung Army, the Russians did not dare to divert elite forces from the Far East to the European front until after the Soviet leadership was convinced, around October, that the Japanese armed forces would strike south, not north. Nevertheless, according to IJA intelligence, the Russians began to transfer units westward, under tight security, as early as the period of February-March 1941, in response to the German buildup on the European front. Overall numerical strength in Siberia did not dip, however.[11] The extraction of Soviet forces thus preceded the neutrality agreement by a month or two, and the German invasion by several months. When Ambassador Ōshima spoke with Ribbentrop on 21 June, the day before the Wehrmacht attacked, the Nazi foreign minister remarked that the Soviet Union was concentrating forces from the Far East in European Russia. "Although he didn't mention it," reported Ōshima, "he intimated that recent Japanese-Soviet relations might have something to do with this."[12]

Throughout the late spring of 1941 the Russians and the Japanese shared a strange unwillingness to believe that Germany was on the verge of assaulting the Soviet Union. Stalin discounted to the end the many warnings and indications he received as Western provocations and tried desperately to put off facing the truth. The Japanese government, supposedly on intimate terms with the Germans, was visibly confused by the conflicting intelligence reaching it from overseas posts. Whereas Japanese sources in Germany were predicting war with increasing frequency, the Japanese embassy in Russia was steadfastly denying it. With few exceptions, the IJA High Command misjudged matters as badly as did Matsuoka and the foreign ministry. Until the beginning of June 1941 the AGS, suspecting bluff and misinformation, adhered to the opinion that there was a low probability of all-out hostilities in the near future.[13]

During the first three weeks of June, meeting after meeting was held at the highest levels in Tokyo with a view to shaping national policy and enhancing preparedness. By midmonth, army thinking was clear in one respect: in case a Russo-German war did break out, the Japanese should strengthen preparations against the USSR but intervene militarily only if the situation took a very favorable turn for Japan. This basic outlook never changed in 1941, but to hedge all bets, on 18 June the AGS Operations Section drafted a plan that called for possible action either northward or southward—the strangely worded *junbi jin taisei* or "preparatory-formation setup."[14]

Germany's onslaught against the Soviet Union on 22 June caused consternation in Tokyo. The first news came from the press. A mortified Konoe felt that the Reich had betrayed Japan a second time—the first time having been when it suddenly consummated the German-Russian nonaggression treaty in 1939. For a while the prime minister even pondered the idea of Japanese withdrawal from the Tripartite Pact. Matsuoka, however, reversed himself immediately. With an alacrity that is still the subject of controversy, the architect of the neutrality agreement of April now pressed for suspension of any Japanese movement south and insisted on military intervention against the USSR instead.[15]

Though certainly not displeased by the word that Germany had attacked Russia, the Kwantung Army was as much taken by surprise as the authorities in Tokyo. The intelligence officer on duty at headquarters that Sunday received the news from the Manchukuo national press agency. General Umezu was away inspecting border units, and the chief of staff, Lt. Gen. Yoshimoto Teiichi, was on a trip to Harbin.[16]

The initial steps taken, even before the return of the senior officers, were to alert the forces throughout Manchuria. Front-line intelligence officers were instructed to intensify surveillance of the Russians. The air force adopted strategic deployments, and fighter squadrons went on standby. Based upon all intelligence available concerning the Soviet armed forces in general and the Far Eastern armies in particular, the intelligence staff prepared an estimate of the situation. A review of order-of-battle information indicated that, on the Ussuri, Amur, and Trans-Baikal fronts, the Russians possessed 27 or 28 confirmed and two to five unverified infantry divisions, two cavalry divisions, 10-13 mechanized brigades, and 18 air brigades, including six special brigades of the strategic bomber force. In Outer Mongolia, apart from the MPRA, there were another three Soviet motorized infantry divisions, plus one cavalry, six mechanized, and two air brigades. Total Russian strength in the Far East was appraised at 700,000 men, 2,700 tanks and armored cars, and 2,800 aircraft. Generally, the Soviet armored, fortification, and air force units were considered to be at full wartime strength.[17] Against these forces, the Kwantung Army had a total of only 300,000 to 350,000 men—12 divisions (plus two backup divisions in Korea), a cavalry brigade, and 23 scattered garrison units—and fewer than 600 operational combat planes in 27 air groups.[18]

The staff in Hsinking gave some thought to the possible danger of a Russian preemptive strike against Manchuria, since Japan was the ally of Germany and Soviet forces so greatly outnumbered the Kwantung Army at the moment. As at Nomonhan in the summer of 1939, the Russians might want to smash the Japanese first and then shift their Far Eastern armies to Europe in order to avoid two-front operations. Japanese intelligence officers warned against underestimating the fighting strength of the Red Army and advised that the Kwantung Army not take precipitous action but instead keep a watchful eye on the situation for the time being. Umezu's first orders to his army reflected these prudent recommendations, though they also called for tightened combat readiness.[19]

According to the latest intelligence available to the Kwantung Army at the outset of hostilities between Germany and the USSR, the Soviet Far Eastern forces had been ordered by Moscow to take up positions along the frontier but to refrain from activities that might provoke the suspicions of the Japanese or the Manchukuoans. At the same time, however, the Russians were to continue constructing *tochka* defenses and to bring up ammunition. Soviet vigilance quickly became pronounced: by the 25th the Russians had established a complete blackout along the borders; had concentrated units of aircraft, artillery, and high-angle guns; had effected an emergency mobilization of army forces; had opened the embrasures in pillboxes; and had stepped up the construction of fortifications "on about the same scale as at the time of the Nomonhan Incident."[20]

The Soviet air force deployed bombers to the front at first, but after 26 June they were moved to the rear and replaced by fighter aircraft. Russian scout planes were penetrating Manchukuoan airspace daily, causing the Manchukuo government to complain to the Soviet consul general in Harbin, with Kwantung Army approval. As early as 24 June, however, it was reported that Russian ground units were gradually being transferred westward from the eastern Manchurian sector.[21]

In Tokyo the High Command—in frequent contact with the Kwantung Army by means of phone calls and liaison officers' visits—labored for another ten days to devise a national security policy. It was still necessary to reconcile army views with those of the navy, which traditionally espoused "defense in the north, advance in the south." In the army itself, there was no unanimity of views. The disagreement between the Go-South (*nanshin*) and the Go-North (*hokushin*) advocates was well known, but even the latter were not in accord concerning the optimum time to attack the Soviet Union. Much in vogue at the moment was the theory that Japan should wait until the persimmon ripened and fell (*jukushi shugi*).[22]

IJA operational thinking began to crystallize in late June. It seemed reasonable to expect that, by early or mid-August, Soviet military strength in the Far East would be drained by the movement westward of 50 percent of the rifle divisions (leaving 15 divisions, from 30) and some two-thirds of the supporting units, including armor (down to 900 machines) and the air force (down to 1,000 planes). This would be the ideal level at which to engage the Russians, for at the same time the Kwantung Army would have built up a 2:1 superiority. An individual Soviet Far Eastern division was evaluated at only 75 percent of the combat strength of an IJA division, because the Russians were according priority to arming and equipping their forces in Europe. The AGS was thinking of a Japanese troop basis, in the first stage, set at a total of 16 divisions: 14 in the Kwantung Army (up by two divisions) and two in the Korea Army. During the next phase, two more Japanese divisions would be transferred from North China and four from Japan. This would give the Kwantung Army a total of 22 divisions to work with and a manpower strength of 850,000 (including nondivisional forces) when and if war came with Russia.

The concentration in Manchuria at the level envisaged by the AGS planners would require an enormous mobilization and transportation effort. In addition, there was the problem of the early winter, which would hamper large-scale action in northern Manchuria and Siberia. If the Kwantung Army was to engage in hostilities in 1941, fighting would have to be finished by mid-October. Because six to eight weeks were necessary to complete the first-phase offensive into the Ussuri region, operations must get under way by the beginning of September at the latest. Sixty or 70 days, if all went well, were really necessary to finish operational preparations, including the redeployment of divisions from Japan, but about a week had been "lost" since the Russo-German war began, and Japanese national policy had still not been officially decided as June came to an end.

The AGS consequently devised a "crash" schedule, for planning purposes, that sought to shave as much time from the target dates as possible: 28 June, decide on mobilization; 5 July, issue mobilization orders; 20 July, begin concentration; 10 August, decide on hostilities; 24 August, complete readiness stance; 29 August, concentrate two divisions from North China; 5 September, concentrate four divisions from the homeland and complete combat stance; 10 September (at latest), begin combat operations; 15 October, complete the first phase of the war. It was the operational staff's strained rationalization that the decision to mobilize could be made in advance of the decision to wage war—which required the highest-level imperial conference—because the readiness stance was subsumed in the cabinet's prior approval of military preparedness against the Soviet Union. The AGS and the Kwantung Army were eager for a quick decision.[23]

Navy leaders had already accepted the "ripe persimmon" idea in principle, on condition that the concurrent notion of moving south not be weakened. But neither the navy nor the war ministry nor the Emperor was willing to accept the more hawkish planning of the AGS envisaging immediate full-scale mobilization, concentration, and expansion of the Kwantung Army with a view to "automatic" hostilities against Russia, despite German requests that Japan enter the war. One of the fears of the Japanese, articulated on 26 June by the AGS 4th Section (whose purview included air defense), was that Tokyo would be incinerated by the Russian air force based in the

Maritime Province. Even several raids by 20-30 bombers in daylight and by as few as a dozen bombers at night might have a devastating effect.[24]

The aggressive AGS view was predicated on assumptions that were quickly found not to be materializing. Though the Wehrmacht was said to have made very good progress in the first week of its offensive, German victory was not yet in sight, and the transfer of Soviet forces westward was unexpectedly slow. By 28 June, IJA intelligence reported the movement of only three infantry divisions, somewhat more than 10 air squadrons, and a mechanized corps.[25]

War Minister Tōjō, who seemed to be inclining toward the AGS concept, came up with a compromise whereby only partial mobilization would be conducted for the time being: 100,000 men were to be called up as a so-called training levy. On 1 July the first orders went out to personnel assigned to the air defense of key zones in the homeland. At the liaison conference that day, preparatory to an imperial conference, Tōjō stated that it would be necessary to put the forces in Manchuria on a war footing, in all secrecy.[26] Having been forewarned of the High Command's thinking about *junbi jin* preparations, Kwantung Army headquarters had begun to issue implementing instructions on a partial basis well before receipt of official sanction from Tokyo.[27]

The imperial conference, which had been postponed a day to 2 July because of new German urgings that Japan enter the war, easily ratified the main agenda item, "Outline of National Policies in View of the Changing Situation." Go-South proponents were heartened by the statement that Japan would not be deterred by the possibility of war with Britain and the United States, against whom military preparations would be made at the same time that "all necessary diplomatic negotiations" went on. Advocates of the Go-North policy were put off: despite the pressure from Berlin and the very belligerent comments addressed to the imperial conference by Privy Council President Hara Yoshimichi and supported by Matsuoka, it was agreed not to intervene against the Soviet Union for the time being. Military preparations against the USSR would proceed secretly in the meantime. The *junbi jin* idea had triumphed, presumably to allow a "flexible response" and to assure improved odds.

Army Chief of Staff Sugiyama explained to the conferees the specific situation affecting the Kwantung Army: of the 30 Soviet Far Eastern divisions, four had already been shifted west, but the USSR retained "an absolutely overpowering force, ready for strategic deployment." The Kwantung Army needed to be reinforced in order to defend itself, to provide the backing for diplomacy, and to be ready to undertake the offensive when the chance came. The outcome of the Russian-German war ought to become clear in

50-60 days. Until then, the Japanese would have to "mark time" in settling the China conflict and in negotiating with Britain and America.[28]

To facilitate the *junbi jin* setup, IGHQ essentially placed the entire Japanese army on a war footing. Between 3 July and 8 July a series of preliminary mobilization orders were issued, affecting fortresses, installations, and air defenses in the homeland, northern Korea, and the upper Kuril Islands. In Manchuria and Korea, all units were to be brought to full wartime strength. Nevertheless, the war ministry, viewing military priorities in the larger context, opposed the General Staff's notion of mobilizing the Kwantung Army at the 22-division level and preferred a maximum limit of 16 divisions. In the Military Affairs Bureau, Col. Sanada Jōichirō wanted no more than one infantry division plus some air, logistical, and ground units to be released to the Kwantung Army. Such a force level would have reached no more than the first plateau of AGS thinking. The Kwantung Army believed that it was impossible to engage the Russians with merely 15 or 16 divisions and that in fact it would be "rather difficult" to do so with even the 22 in the AGS plan. Concentrating masses of men, for example, did not mean that units would be at peak combat readiness after being thrown together. It would require extremely favorable conditions, from the Japanese standpoint, to reduce the risk—for example, a Soviet political upheaval or a major withdrawal of Russian forces from Siberia. The AGS Organization and Mobilization Section chief, Col. Nakayama Motoo, agreed with the Kwantung Army. Drawing on the lessons of Nomonhan, he recommended mobilization on a scale that exceeded even the requests of the Operations Section, headed since 1 July by former Kwantung Army staff officer Hattori Takushirō, whose "exile" had been very brief.

The difference between General Staff and war ministry outlooks was readily apparent to Kwantung Army visitors: AGS officers spoke of engaging the Russians when a good chance occurred, whether the persimmon was ripe or not; but the war ministry favored hostilities only when the fruit was ripe. Although, as we have seen, the Kwantung Army would have preferred being allocated even greater strength than embodied in the aggressive AGS scheme, common sense suggested restraint in requesting further reinforcements at this time. After all, the China conflict was still raging and southward operations were being prepared.

The AGS Operations Bureau chief, Maj. Gen. Tanaka Shin'ichi, had been orchestrating the hawkish anti-Soviet views in Tokyo. As early as 9 June, he almost got into a fistfight with the AGS planning team chief, Col. Arisue Yadoru, who did not favor a war in the north. As the weeks passed, Tanaka became fed up with the unending negotiations among the war ministry sections. On the evening of 5 July he went to see Tōjō privately and convinced the war minister of the rightness and viability of the General Staff's theories.

This meant, as a first step, that two infantry divisions should be dispatched shortly from the homeland to reinforce the Kwantung Army, above and beyond the plans for ground and air support units. It was apparent that the Tanaka faction's basic objective was to build the base for a 20- to 25-division offensive core in Manchuria and Korea under the guise of preparing for the strategic-readiness stance involving only 16 divisions. The retention of many units under direct IGHQ control was designed to accelerate offensive preparedness.[29] The unofficial appellation for the buildup of the Kwantung Army's readiness stance was "No. 100 setup" (*Hyaku-gō taisei*); for the offensive stance, "Nos. 101 and 102 setups." For the whole process, the code name in official use at Hsinking was the acronym *Kantokuen*, for Kwantung Army Special Maneuvers (*Kantōgun tokubetsu enshū*).[30]

On 7 July, Sugiyama went to the palace to request imperial sanction for the strengthening of the Kwantung Army (*heiryoku zōkyō*). The monarch agreed that mobilization was unavoidable but expressed some intelligent reservations. Would it not prove to be a source of difficulty that the Japanese armed forces were being dispersed into three main blocs—China, the south, and the north, lacking apparent emphasis in any particular theater? And was it not possible that the Kwantung Army might actually "do something" (commence hostilities) on its own once it had been reinforced? On this fourth anniversary of the affair at the Marco Polo Bridge where the conflict in China had begun, the Emperor was evidently worrying about the arbitrary decisions that had been made by the Kwantung Army in the past—notably the Manchurian Incident and Nomonhan. The army chief of staff could only try to reassure the sovereign by responding that he would do his very best to prevent trouble.[31]

The buildup of the Kwantung Army now progressed rapidly, accompanied by strenuous efforts to maintain secrecy. In practice, of course, it was impossible to conceal the masses of men, horses, supplies, and equipment from the sight of the populace in Japan, Korea, and Manchuria. The Soviet and Chinese espionage network on the continent and the Sorge spy ring based in Japan rather easily discerned the large-scale transportation effort.[32]

The unfolding of Kantokuen concerns essentially logistical movements and contingency planning. Although no formal order of battle was issued to the Kwantung Army for combat purposes and no central command organ was established to handle logistics, the Operations Section was increased by four or five staff officers sent from Japan, and the Logistics Section by seven or eight. Only two infantry divisions were dispatched to Manchuria (the 51st from Utsunomiya and the 57th from Hirosaki, both raised to full strength), but the numbers of "filler" troops and tactical or auxiliary units were enormous. Merely to bring the Kwantung Army's existing divisions to wartime authorization, about 180,000 men had to be shipped from the homeland, since an individual division's peacetime complement of 12,000 or 13,000 soldiers had to be expanded to 25,000. Backup service elements, ranging in size from platoons to regiments, were needed for such functions as signals, transportation, construction, ordnance, veterinary stations, field hospitals, and casualty clearing. Nondivisional combat reinforcements included artillery, antiaircraft, mortar, antitank, engineer, and chemical warfare units.

In all, over 300 independent components were mobilized in July for transfer to Manchuria and Korea—54 in the first levy, 268 in the second. By 15 July the leading elements of the manpower additions had arrived in Dairen; on 16 July the first matériel reached Pusan harbor. Concentration commenced on 22 July, two days behind the original AGS timetable. Tōjō's creation, the Kwantung Defense Command, was activated with five IGU's for the protection of the interior of Manchuria. Its first head, designated on 17 July and reporting to the Kwantung Army commander, was Lt. Gen. Yamashita Tomoyuki, newly returned from an inspection tour of Europe and now removed from potential competition with Tōjō for the post of war minister in a possible new cabinet. As of 1 August, the 51st Division was officially attached to the Kwantung Army and the 57th Division to the Third Army.[33]

To make room for the expected influx of wounded and injured men, current patients in northern and central Manchuria were moved to other hospitals in Japan, Korea, and southern Manchuria. The conditions in underdeveloped Manchuria also demanded such measures as the production and laying-in of charcoal for heating and cooking, the requisition of vehicles and horses, the organization of well-drilling units, the building or repair of airstrips, and the construction of sturdy cantonments. Special attention was paid to the expansion of lines of communication, especially the improvement of ports, feeder roads, railway trackage, coaling and watering facilities, warehouses, and loading and unloading docks.[34]

The buildup of men and matériel would have been meaningless without viable operational designs in Tokyo and Hsinking. Planning against the Russians still called for a strong offensive on the East Manchurian–Ussuri front, with the objective of achieving "a quick battle and an immediate decision" (*sokusen sokketsu*). Whether a total of 24-25 or only 20 Japanese infantry divisions were actually available when war broke out would require adjustments of detail. The core force, in any case, was the Third Army based at Mutanchiang, which would strike against Grodekovo and Poltavka, west of Voroshilov. Supporting actions would be undertaken by the following forces: on the far left flank, the Fifth Army (Tungan) would attack south of Iman; to the left of the Third Army, the new Twentieth Army (not available until organized in mid-September at Chihsi) would strike southwest of Lake

Khanka; and on the right, the Korea Army's 19th Division would penetrate the Barabash sector. In northern Manchuria, with headquarters at Sunwu, the Fourth Army was to hold at first and go over to the offensive later. The Sixth Army, still based at Hailar on the western front, would conduct holding operations throughout, using the reconstituted 23rd Division and 8th BGU.[35]

Kantokuen spawned a number of special projects. A long-range penetration force was formed to disrupt Siberian rail lines, always a primary target. For guerrilla and infiltration missions, OSS experts secretly trained small teams of White Russians and, on the western front, Bargut Mongols also, to range as far as Bain Tumen, Borzya, and perhaps Chita. The OSS officer at Hailar employed two fast, high-flying scout planes to reconnoiter Outer Mongolia and Siberia. The Kwantung Army's understaffed geographic research group, relying on "semiprofessionals," prepared updated maps covering Manchuria and Siberia as far as Lake Baikal, with good detail to Chita. In addition, the Kwantung Army was authorized a 5th Section, originally known as the Hata Agency, the brainchild of Lt. Gen. Hata Hikosaburō. This section (which remained in existence until the summer of 1943) was to handle the administration of areas to be conquered and occupied by the Kwantung Army, including the training of personnel to staff the envisaged military government.[36]

Despite the infusion of excellent and experienced officers,[37] there was considerable disorder during the Kantokuen buildup process, especially in the early stages of movement and concentration. From the operational standpoint, there was a particular problem: only the contingency plans involving the Third Army and the 19th Division were well developed.[38]

Whether or not they were convinced that hostilities against the Soviet Union were in Japan's best interest in 1941, most IJA staff and line officers did not doubt that Japanese forces could take the whole area east of Baikal, especially since the Germans were reported to be making progress in the west. The officers and the rank and file of the Kwantung Army were optimistic and enthusiastic, spurred on by rumors that the Soviet Far Eastern forces were so depleted that sergeants instead of colonels were commanding regiments.[39] The bluster of the Go-North faction was fed by rosy dispatches from the Japanese ambassadors in Germany and the USSR. On 5 July, Tatekawa reported from Moscow that morale was low among the Russian people, government, and military. The Japanese should abandon negotiations with the doomed, isolated USSR and should either deal exclusively with Germany or act entirely on their own.[40] When Yamashita's inspection team got back to Tokyo on 7 July, having traveled from Berlin via the Trans-Siberian Railway, it reported up-to-date information that the German war machine outnumbered the Soviet forces by 2:1 in infantry divisions, by

2.5:1 in overall ground strength, and by 3:1 or 4:1 in aircraft. The blitzkrieg would probably shatter the Red Army, drive the Stalin government to the east, and exert pressure on Soviet Far Eastern forces. On 15 July, AGS Intelligence Bureau chief Okamoto Kiyotomi judged that the Russians had already lost 70 percent of their air strength, 50 percent of their armor, and 25 percent of their firepower from the division artillery level upward. In Okamoto's opinion, the Soviet government had fallen into disarray and its flight from Moscow was near.[41]

Before the month of July was out, however, evidence had accumulated that Go-North advocacy was weakening at the Tokyo level. Though Tōjō had favored the reinforcement of the Kwantung Army that underlay Kantokuen, the war minister had not come down from the fence he was straddling; "flexible response" was as far as he would commit himself.[42] Brilliant but unpredictable, Matsuoka had no success in convincing the military and civilian leadership to opt for immediate war against Russia. Indeed, the foreign minister's endless urgings discomfited Konoe to the point of deciding that he must get rid of Matsuoka. On 16 July, Konoe submitted his resignation. Two days later, the prince formed his third cabinet, identical to the preceding one except that Adm. Toyoda Teijirō replaced Matsuoka as foreign minister.[43]

Obviously, the entire "persimmon" notion was based on sheer opportunism. Yet even the ordinarily hawkish AGS Operations staff was not of one mind on the subject as the date for an irreversible decision neared—10 August. Hattori asserts that his section was split evenly between the Go-North and Go-South alternatives. As the chief, Hattori took the middle ground, advocating readiness to go either way (*junbi jin*) but stipulating no preference. Between 21 July and 29 July, the AGS war diarist admitted to the difficulty of preparing solid estimates of the situation and to the fading away of Go-North sentiment in High Command circles.[44]

The input of IJA intelligence was important in reaching the ultimate decision. Despite being dazzled by German successes at the outset, the intelligence analysts did not denigrate the staying power of the Stalin regime or the quality of the Red Army.[45] Of particular interest to IJA planners was the tempo of Soviet transfers of strength to the west. In this respect, the careful studies conducted by Col. Isomura Takesuke and his AGS Russian Intelligence Section were highly regarded by Tōjō and his colleagues. As of 12 July, Isomura reported, the Soviet Far Eastern forces had not been seriously weakened. Withdrawals were estimated at only five infantry divisions, one mechanized corps, three separate tank brigades, two or three cavalry squadrons, four antiaircraft batteries, one searchlight battalion, 20 truck battalions (about 200 vehicles each), 15 fighter squadrons, and 15 bomber squadrons.

These diminutions were far fewer than the optimum the Japanese army had hoped for. The maintenance of Soviet air strength was particularly troublesome. Compounding the problem, from the IJA point of view, was the fact that the Russians were replacing the elite divisions with second-class units, so that overall manpower levels were not declining. In his other-wise positive briefing of 15 July, AGS Intelligence Bureau chief Okamoto had to admit that the only noteworthy development was the occasional ar-rival of deserters from Soviet Siberia. In some areas, a man turned up every couple of days; between June and December the total reached at least 130.[46]

According to the information available to the Kwantung Army, most of the Russian withdrawals came from the Baikal region, not from the vital sectors east of the Ussuri or north of the Amur. At the beginning of July, five Soviet troop trains headed west per day; in mid-July, two; by the end of July, none. Soviet readiness and fortification measures, pronounced on the east-ern front at first, were being extended to the northern and western sectors. Meanwhile, in the European theater, the German pace of advance seemed to slow after mid-July. Isomura's Russian Intelligence Section reached the re-luctant but important conclusion that the short, decisive war predicted by the Germans would not materialize, that subsequent developments would not favor the invaders, and that the Red Army would not give up even though Moscow might be lost by year's end.[47]

Given the continuing power of the Russian forces in Siberia, in late July the AGS was still toying with the idea of further increasing the attack strength of the Kwantung Army by transferring four more divisions from the homeland and five from China. Gen. Hata Shunroku, however, the com-mander in China, lodged an unexpectedly strenuous complaint against the proposed weakening of his forces. Hata was not alone in objecting to the more grandiose Go-North plans. One war ministry bureau chief told his subordinates, "Forget about our 'missing the bus.' The bus is not moving." General Itagaki, bound for Seoul to assume command of the Korea Army, confided to associates that he was dubious about German prospects and was worried about the fact that the objectives of the Kantokuen buildup would apparently not be attained until the end of September. The experience of Nomonhan warned against trying to fight when the Manchurian winter was at hand.[48]

The outcome might have been dramatically different had the Japanese High Command not already committed itself, as a result of the imperial conference of 2 July, to accomplishing the preliminary phase of the Go-South alternative also. In practice, this meant the occupation of southern French Indochina by the last part of July, an intention known to the U.S. government from signal intelligence intercepts as well as from the Vichy re-gime. But whereas the hard-pressed Russians remained quiescent in the north, the Americans retaliated immediately. On 26 July, invoking an "unlimited national emergency," Roosevelt issued an executive order freezing all Japanese assets in the United States and controlling all financial and trade transactions involving Japanese interests. Britain and the Dutch government-in-exile followed suit, effectively shutting down trade between Japan and the three countries. On 1 August, the Americans embargoed the export of oil. Since an invasion of Siberia would do nothing to improve Japan's fuel situation, which would soon reach a crisis, the sanctions contributed to the abandonment of the Go-North plan and the diversion of emphasis to the south. Indeed, IGHQ officers term the 26 July date critical because it narrowed Japanese options.[49]

General Tanaka did not lose hope easily. He and his supporters wanted Kantokuen to proceed, with even higher strength limits authorized for the attack mode and lightning countermeasures readied in case of a Soviet preemptive strike, which IJA hawks were hoping for. Since Tōjō's support was vital for a report to the Throne, Tanaka conferred with the war minister at the end of July. Concerning the preemptive-strike theory coupled with Japanese retaliation, Tōjō deemed it best that the Emperor be tendered no more than an estimate of the situation for the time being. The war minister favored the continuation of Kantokuen and indicated agreement with the idea of a 24-division target for the hypothetical main offensive on the eastern Manchurian front. But these were only paper plans and, significantly, Tōjō spoke of other priorities—the China war, the southern theater, and the powerful role of the navy.

The chain of command called for Sugiyama to address the Throne in connection with the Kantokuen project and AGS estimates. When he did so on 30 July, the monarch revealed uneasiness about Kantokuen. The special maneuvers, remarked the Emperor, had been exerting ill effects abroad; if the process continued, Japan's stance might be weakened gradually. As for the Russians, the shifting of their forces westward might be slowed to an undesirable extent. Shouldn't the Japanese mobilization be suspended? In an audience on 1 August, when the matter of the second stage of Kantokuen came up, the Emperor sought reassurance that war would not follow the arrival of the reinforcements. Sugiyama, of course, was convinced that the reinforcement of Manchuria was crucial, even for the readiness mode, in order to support diplomatic efforts toward the Russians and to shield the northern flank at the very time that *junbi jin* preparations went forward in the south. In accordance with the national policy decision approved on 2 July, the buildup of men and matériel was far along. Sugiyama therefore wanted the army to be allowed to proceed with Kantokuen. On the understanding that matters would not be handled carelessly, the Emperor seems to have concurred reluctantly.

During the audience on 1 August, Sugiyama found the chance to raise the matter of possible retaliatory action by the Japanese air force. He was concerned, said the chief of staff, lest the Russians team up with the Anglo-Saxon powers and attack before Japanese preparations in Manchuria were completed. The nature of aerial combat suggested the unleashing of the main body of the Japanese air force without delay in the event that the Russians did launch a preemptive air assault. Since national policy and a prior decision were involved, however, the AGS was studying the contingencies very carefully. To this part of the presentation the Emperor made no response, a fact which could be taken to mean that he was not in agreement.[50]

The Go-South option was on the verge of triumph.[51] Suddenly, in the afternoon of 2 August, Kwantung Army headquarters conveyed very disquieting information to Tokyo. According to Special Intelligence Bureau signal monitors, Soviet wireless communications had been blotted out entirely on the Amur and East Manchurian fronts since morning.[52] Although Kwantung Army intelligence reported several hours later that the blackout was apparently nothing more than a local atmospheric disturbance caused by sunspots,[53] the suggestion has been made that the first message may have been part of a scheme concocted by overzealous Kwantung Army officers, possibly acting in collusion with the Go-North hawks in Tokyo.[54] No staff officer stationed in Hsinking or Tokyo at the time has corroborated this notion of a conspiracy, and we now know that a magnetic storm did indeed occur on the morning of 2 August, but higher headquarters could not afford to treat the episode lightly. Deliberate radio silence often preceded surprise attacks, as was to be the case when the Japanese navy struck Pearl Harbor four months later.[55] On the night of 2/3 August, Umezu rushed a message to the AGS requesting prior approval of retaliation by the Kwantung Army air force, on his own initiative, in the event of large-scale preemptive air raids by the Russians. The High Command could not agree. As a stopgap measure, Sugiyama wired back instructions before dawn on the 3rd that the essential principle should be to limit counterattacks to the Manchukuoan borders.[56]

The exchanges of messages between Umezu and Sugiyama left many fundamental problems unresolved. From the Kwantung Army's standpoint, an effective aerial counterstrike demanded pursuit operations unhampered by "artificial" considerations of ground frontiers. From the vantage of Tokyo, it was true that the Emperor had just been alerted to the possibility of a Soviet preemptive strike, but penetration of Russian airspace by the Japanese would invite full-scale hostilities. Against the argument that precious time would be lost if the Kwantung Army had to await a decision at the highest level, the response could be made that it was not proper for the central authorities to abdicate responsibility by giving the field commander carte blanche, in effect, to make the choice for war before the government had reached its decision, the Emperor had sanctioned it, and IGHQ had issued the order.

The Japanese navy, its attention riveted on the high probability of fighting the Anglo-American forces in the near future, suspected army skulduggery. At one point, General Tanaka became so upset that he told IJN staff officers that the army would report to the Throne and secure an IGHQ enabling order on its own if necessary. An exchange also occurred on 4 August between Foreign Minister Toyoda, who had heard that elements of the Kwantung Army were about to attack, and General Sugiyama, who denied the rumor.

By 5 August, the army and the navy were somehow able to agree upon a mild policy statement, which was finally endorsed at a liaison conference on the 6th, after very heated discussion and the reported humiliation of the IJA chief of staff. The army's desire for advance authority to fight back in case of a serious Soviet first strike won acceptance, but only with the addition of major restraints at the insistence of the navy and civilian officials: provocation must be avoided, disputes localized, and offensive counteraction shunned. No longer was there specific mention of a decision for war; instead, the government was promptly to address the matter of Japan's response to "eventualities." Inevitably, the caution and vagueness of language vexed army circles quite as much as an initial IJA draft on 3 August had troubled the navy.[57] Imperial sanction was obtained immediately and the consequent IGHQ army order and directive went out to the Kwantung Army commander.[58]

The hair-trigger atmosphere in Tokyo and Hsinking soon dissipated. With Toyoda as foreign minister, it became apparent that the Japanese government was coming around to the view that diplomacy should take precedence over force in efforts to settle the whole array of outstanding issues between Japan and the USSR, as long as the latter strictly observed the terms of the neutrality pact and did not pose an overt threat to Japan or Manchukuo. By 1 August, the day before the blackout scare, the participants at a liaison conference in Tokyo had agreed that, although the Kantokuen preparations must be completed in order to deal with any change in the situation, the Japanese side should "guard carefully against the accidental outbreak of war." On the basis of previously agreed upon national policy, military action would not be undertaken against the Russians unless internal and external conditions developed favorably from the Japanese standpoint.[59] This policy statement is but a pale reflection of the aggressive outlook that had been so apparent at the time of the imperial conference held only one month earlier.

The self-imposed 10 August deadline was nearing for the Japanese army decision-makers, and, quite simply, time ran out for them. Though Russian and American intelligence remained apprehensive for many months about the possibility of an IJA invasion of the Maritime Province, the Japanese High Command arrived at an overall decision on 9 August. On that date the AGS finally accepted the preferences of Tōjō and the war ministry: first, to tighten the guard stance against the USSR, employing the 16 divisions stationed in Manchuria and Korea, in order to facilitate either support of diplomacy vis-à-vis Russia, response to Soviet provocation, or exploitation of an unexpected opportunity to intervene; second, to continue operations against China; and third, to accelerate preparations for war against the United States and Britain in the southern region, aiming for readiness around the end of November.[60] Despite a "clarification" to the first portion about a surviving Go-North possibility, the third clause obviously took priority. It no longer really mattered what happened in the German-Soviet war: Japan was undoubtedly heading south, once and for all.

Dissemination of the new policy was closely limited. In the war ministry, the decision not to fight the Soviet Union in 1941 was known only to Tōjō, his vice minister, and the Military Affairs Bureau head. On 12 August, Sugiyama reported to the Emperor that there was not much evidence of the weakening of the Soviet Far Eastern forces; in some areas, in fact, a partial strengthening of the Russian military posture was apparent. The so-called golden opportunity alluded to in the national policy decision of 2 July had not arrived yet.

Since the effects upon the Kwantung Army amounted to "a 180-degree turn," a high-level delegation of AGS and war ministry officers was dispatched to Hsinking on 20 August to "straighten things out." Umezu and his staff were assured that the operational preparations of Kantokuen were to proceed and that the decision of 9 August did not rule out the chance of engaging the Russians in 1942; readiness, in fact, should be targeted for the coming spring.[61] Umezu asked the delegation to tell Sugiyama that the Kwantung Army would comply carefully with the High Command's directions; he was insuring that none of his air or ground units initiated offensive or subversive action without IGHQ orders. The emergency request for advance permission to respond to Soviet air attacks was only a precautionary measure. Still, the Kwantung Army needed to be ready to cope with any eventuality arising from the rapidly changing situation. Despite the decision not to fight the Soviet Union in 1941, nobody really knew whether an opportunity might not still materialize during the year. Though it was appropriate to remain quiet against the Russians at a time when the China conflict was still under way and the situation in the south was growing tense, a heaven-sent opportunity was at hand to solve the northern problem. Indeed, it was not enough to sit and wait for an opening; every effort should be made to create and exploit one. To give up on the north and to shift to the south seemed highly unwise to Umezu. Chief of Staff Yoshimoto spoke to Tanaka in much the same vein. He was in favor of attacking on the east Manchurian sector first and then striking north before the ice melted in the spring. IGHQ, however, wanted studies to be made of a possible attack into the Ussuri region in May 1942 and against the northern zone in August, both offensives being based on a hypothetical government decision for war in March.[62]

After the Kwantung Army generals had expressed their opinions, Umezu asserted that, to avoid damaging morale, he was not immediately going to notify his subordinate commanders of the new policy. He would merely indicate that, when the time came, the Japanese government would decide whether or not there was to be war with the USSR; the monarch and prime minister of Manchukuo had already been told as much.[63]

It has been suggested that the atypical self-control exhibited by the Kwantung Army in 1941 stemmed not only from Umezu's tight governance but also from the field forces' expectation, which the commander did not openly discourage, that a new golden opportunity to thrash the Russians would arise in 1942.[64] Another explanation for the Japanese quiescence has been adduced: on 2 August, in eastern Manchuria, a tremendous chain of explosions, perhaps caused by Red saboteurs, leveled a huge Third Army ordnance and logistical dump. The date of this disaster does seem to suggest a connection with the radio communications blackout that took place on the same day, but intensive IJA investigations turned up no evidence of sabotage. The loss of ammunition and fuel reserves, some think, may have wrecked any chance for the Kwantung Army to launch an offensive in the near future. Informed sources do not agree.[65]

The "superficial" decision of 9 August to jettison decades of anti-Soviet preparations in favor of a last-minute thrust into Southeast Asia that ultimately brought ruin to Japan saddens or infuriates many former Kwantung Army staff officers. During an interview, Umezu's operations officer exploded: "It still burns me up! I don't want to talk about it. The flip-flop reveals Japan's slipshod [*darashi-ga-nai*] approach."[66] In a late August 1941 entry of the secret IGHQ war journal, we encounter the diarist's feeling of distress: "Since even Hitler could err, it is understandable for our 2nd [Intelligence] Bureau to have made a mistake too. The German forces' combat will drag out until the end of the year. I am deeply moved when I think of the changes in content that have taken place in our national policy since June. What lies in store for our empire? Dark clouds are hanging low; it is truly impossible to predict matters."[67]

Japanese determination "not to decline war" with the United States, Britain, and Holland in 1941, if negotiations did not succeed by October, was confirmed at an imperial conference on 6 September. Concerning the north, the army's position was that every effort should be made to prevent a two-front war during operations in the south, which therefore must be carried out swiftly. It was very probable that the Germans would smash the main Russian armies and seize the vital European portions of the USSR by the end of October or early November, causing the Soviet government to withdraw to the Urals or beyond; however, the Stalin regime was not expected to collapse right away. It would take time for unrest to spread to Siberia; mid-winter of 1941-42 would probably be Russia's period of greatest danger. Undoubtedly, a situation favorable to Japan would materialize sooner or later, but operations during the depth of winter would be difficult, even if a good chance did arise. Hence any Japanese thrust northward should be geared to late winter, perhaps around February 1942. Meanwhile, Sugiyama assured the conferees, there was no need to worry about the northern flank, although the Americans might team up with the Russians.[68]

By mid-September there were 710,000 soldiers in Manchuria, posing the critical new challenge of preparation for the rigors of winter. At most, before Kantokuen, the Kwantung Army had a forward strength of 240,000 to 250,000 men. To accommodate almost half a million brand-new troops where they were now, mainly near the borders, would necessitate an enormous logistical effort involving the construction of barracks and the provision of stoves, fuel, and the like in massive amounts. It was basically a problem of billeting, not of clothing or food; of winter survival, not of winter operations.[69]

Hawks in the High Command had their minds on fighting, not wintering. During a trip to Tokyo, a logistics colonel from Kwantung Army headquarters complained to the AGS about the huge winter-billeting problem. Operations chief Tanaka was infuriated. He yelled at the colonel not to say such "nonsensical things," and then slapped him.[70] Less emotional leaders comprehended that something would have to be done soon; the more exposed forces must be pulled back to livable locations before winter came. As a first step, certain units were to be withdrawn from the frontier to south Manchuria to spend the winter. After the government's determination in September to engage the ABDA powers, it was decided to transfer 88,000 men to the southern theater from the Kwantung Army, still leaving about 620,000 soldiers in Manchuria. The issuance of redeployment instructions by IGHQ had not been expected before October, and troop movements did not keep pace with the orders. Still, the most acute problems of wintering were alleviated to a degree. Kantokuen had succeeded in "killing two birds with one stone," by building up forces in both south and north—the very notion behind *junbi jin* thinking.[71]

IJA reinforcements in Manchuria totaled 463,000 men, 210,000 horses, and 23,000 motor vehicles. Maximum strength levels at one time therefore amounted to 763,000 soldiers, 253,000 horses, and 29,000 vehicles. In addition, the Korea Army was built up by 55,000 men, 16,000 horses, and 650 vehicles.[72] When the 51st Division was pulled out of Manchuria in September 1941, however, its withdrawal was not counterbalanced until the 71st Division was activated the following May, bringing the Kwantung Army's readiness stance to an estimated 80 percent of the grand target. By all accounts, ground strength was at a peak between the summer of 1942 and the first half of 1943.[73]

Although the Kwantung Army air force was to be assigned a primary role of retaliation in case the radio cutoff of early August led to hostilities, little mention has been made of an aerial buildup. The reason is that the air force had been near war footing before Kantokuen and had peaked between the end of 1940 and early 1941. In January of 1941, a number of elements had already been transferred for use in French Indochina. During the Kantokuen period, relatively few air units were sent to Manchuria from Japan. There was some small-scale reorganization and redeployment of the existing air force structure in Manchuria, but even when Kantokuen was well under way in July and August, air units were shifted from Manchuria to northern Indochina and North China. The net result was some increase in the number of supporting and logistical units in the Kwantung Army air force in 1941, but a reduction in the flight strength. Only about 500 planes (280 of which were operational) remained in Manchuria by the end of 1941, a decrease from the level of 700 serviceable aircraft during the Kantokuen period.[74]

From the Japanese point of view, it was ironic that by early or mid-October 1941 Soviet strength in the Far Eastern theater did decrease to levels that might have invited IJA intervention earlier. According to new AGS intelligence estimates, the Russians had by now transferred to the west 9-11 infantry divisions, at least 1,000 tanks, and more than 1,200 planes. This left in Siberia, by 24 October, only 19 Soviet rifle divisions, 1,200 to 1,400 tanks, and as few as 1,060 aircraft, half of which were based on the east Manchurian front.[75] Undoubtedly the Sorge spy ring's information that the Japanese had decided to strike south in 1941 played its part in the calculated risk taken by the Soviet authorities to dilute their military resources in the Far East for the benefit of the European command.

When all is said and done, the question remains whether the Kantokuen buildup would have enabled the Japanese to conquer Siberia. Despite the enhanced manpower and material strength deployed in Manchuria and Korea, there is considerable evidence to suggest that the Kwantung Army had scarcely achieved a readiness stance, much less the offensive capability desired by the AGS. Two years after the experience at Nomonhan, IJA ground divisions were still markedly inferior to Red Army divisions with respect to firepower, mobility, armor, and air support. Motorization commenced in earnest only after 1940, and mechanization on an autonomous scale did not begin until late 1942.[76]

It is true that Japanese army morale was generally high and that IJA forces could have penetrated Soviet defenses at various points. For example, against only 11 Russian divisions and four mechanized brigades stationed on the eastern front, the Kwantung Army and the Korea Army might have massed 14 or 15 divisions. In that case, as Imaoka speculates, "It may have been possible for us at least to have dealt the Russians a mighty blow, although 'annihilation in one stride' might not have been feasible." The nub of the Japanese military problem was comprehended by the staffs of the Fourth Army and the Kwantung Army after they had studied (and abandoned) the hypothesis of an attack northward before the spring thaw of 1942. Their conclusion was that the Japanese units could advance but could not be supplied and thus would encounter severe difficulty in exploiting any local successes. The scant Kwantung Army reserves would undoubtedly have been kept busy shoring up the weak sectors facing Khabarovsk and Blagoveshchensk.[77]

Once Tōjō replaced Konoe as prime minister on 18 October, any further weakening of the Soviet regime or diminution of strength in Siberia tended to be regarded as of main potential benefit to Japan's Go-South option. Sugiyama told an imperial conference on 5 November that, when war came against the United States, one could not entirely rule out the possibility that American pressure on the USSR might lead to hostilities between the Russians and the Japanese. The probability of a Soviet offensive was minimal, however, as long as the Kwantung Army was "firmly ensconced." Still, there was good reason to insure the swift conclusion of Japanese operations in the southern theater in order to allow prompt and effective response in the north if needed.[78]

By the time the Japanese leaders formally approved war against the ABDA powers, at the imperial conference of 1 December, the question of the northern problem had almost receded from view in Tokyo. Speaking for the army and the navy, NGS chief Nagano Osami merely said that, regarding the USSR, strict vigilance was being maintained in concert with diplomatic measures.[79] IGHQ promptly notified the Kwantung Army of the national policy decision and on 3 December provided the fundamental imperial order. Apart from the primary determination to wage a war of "self-defense" against the United States, Britain, and the Netherlands for the purposes of insuring self-sufficiency and creating a new order in Greater East Asia, Japan no longer intended to continue fighting in China, as had been stipulated almost four months earlier. While strategic objectives in the south were being seized, every effort must be made to avoid hostilities with the

Soviet Union. This caveat represented the first such official injunction to the Kwantung Army since the German invasion of Russia.

Umezu, of course, was to remain responsible for the defense of Manchukuo and the Kwantung Leased Territory and was to continue anti-Soviet operational preparations to cope with any changes that might occur. The broad language contained in the order of 3 December was followed by concrete restrictions that foreshadowed the limited role the Kwantung Army would play throughout the Pacific War. By contrast with the aggressive guidelines of early 1939, which had preceded and helped to bring on the Nomonhan crisis, IGHQ now told Umezu that he need not fight for border areas that were in dispute or were difficult to defend. Quarrels should be localized.[80]

Just as the Go-North advocates had felt betrayed by the dashing of their hopes on 9 August, so many army officers harbored private frustration with the policy articulated in early December. But Umezu saw to it that the Kwantung Army loyally obeyed the spirit and the letter of the imperial order of 3 December. This policy of "keeping cool" (*seihitsu kakuho*) called for conveying an impression of strength while concealing weakness, and for staying patient under provocation while refraining from stirring up the other side. Umezu restated and tightened the Kwantung Army's post-Nomonhan border defense guidelines, which established a unilateral buffer zone behind the frontiers in which all military action (including the right to shoot, except in dire self-defense) was prohibited even if enemy troops entered. In case Soviet aircraft violated the borders, only ground fire might be employed, and Japanese planes were not to counterattack (this restriction was presumably relaxed in August). Tactical movements required Umezu's explicit order, and reports of incidents were to go to higher headquarters and be accorded priority treatment. The Kwantung Army commander said he would severely punish any offenders and see to it that they were discharged. "A fire must be stopped while it is small," Umezu warned.[81]

The Russians did nothing to disturb Umezu's restraint. Once Japan attacked the ABDA countries on 7 December, Soviet forces in Siberia remained as dormant as the Kwantung Army, except for a large-scale expansion of border positions in all sectors. Stalin told British Foreign Minister Anthony Eden on 20 December that the USSR could not engage Japan in a "real war" yet: "We have to make a careful estimate of the forces involved. At present we are not ready. A considerable number of our troops were removed from the Far East to the Western front. New troops are being got ready but we shall require about four months before they are fully prepared." In any case, added Stalin, the Russians really preferred that Japan attack first, for psychological and political reasons. Very probably, Japan would strike the Soviet Union, "not just yet, but later": "If the Germans are hard pressed it is likely that they will urge the Japanese to attack us, in which case the attack may be expected about the middle of next year."[82]

Determining the extent of Soviet vulnerability in Siberia remained high on the agenda of IJA intelligence. It was believed that by the end of 1941 the Russians had mobilized at least eight new Far Eastern divisions and one brigade of infantry, plus a cavalry division, three tank brigades, and an air division. By reconciling data on Soviet replacements with the transfers west, Japanese intelligence judged that the Russian Far East now possessed 23 infantry divisions (a net drop of about seven divisions since 1940), two cavalry divisions (unchanged), 1,000 tanks (down 1,700), and 1,000 aircraft (down 1,800). Estimates of Soviet military manpower varied widely. One reckoning put the number at 600,000, another at 800,000. Whether the true figure was 100,000 more or less than the 700,000 men in 1940, IJA analysts were agreed that the Russian units had suffered a loss in overall quality and included hordes of soldiers still undergoing intensive basic training. Troop levels reportedly never dipped below 500,000, however. In addition, the Russian command structure on the Ussuri-Amur fronts was improved to the point that, by December 1941, seven army headquarters —radiating from Khabarovsk—spanned the frontiers from Outer Mongolia to the Maritime Province.[83]

For its part, the Kwantung Army in early 1942 expected to be receiving back, in a few months, much of the aviation, ground combat, and supporting strength it had "loaned" for use in the south. "Victory fever" was sweeping Japan, and IGHQ plans and estimates mirrored the general euphoria. For example, it was intended to reduce the infantry divisions in the Southern Army by half, and to release one division to Manchuria. However, the High Command also decided that the way to implement the state policy of 1 December calling for an end to the China conflict was to knock out the regime of Chiang Kai-shek once and for all. Thus even as the headquarters in Hsinking was looking forward to the return of its "loaned" units, IGHQ began planning for a decisive offensive against Chungking (Operation No. 5) that would necessitate a massive transfer of forces *from* the Kwantung Army. Specifically, the High Command was thinking of withdrawing two ground divisions, two-thirds of the motor vehicles and communication units, almost all the river-crossing equipment, and huge stocks of fuel and ammunition. The manpower decrease in Manchuria would amount to 200,000 soldiers. Called to Tokyo to discuss implementation of the project, Kwantung Army representatives objected strenuously to such weakening of their forces. The reservations soon became academic. Unexpected Japanese reverses in the Pacific theater—from the Coral Sea and Midway to Guadalcanal and New Guinea—caused grandiose Operation No. 5 to be scrapped by year's end. The fact that it was seriously considered at all suggests how secondary the once-favored Kwantung Army had become in the context of Tokyo's larger plans.[84]

IGHQ did release three air groups and more than 30 ground units from Malaya, the Philippines, and Java during 1942 for return to Manchuria. In addition, the Kwantung Army itself formed the 71st Infantry Division in May, incorporating the Hunchun Garrison Unit and a rifle regiment newly arrived from China. This brand-new division and a border guard unit became the core of the Second Army organized on 1 July at Yenchi, facing the Vladivostok front.[85] The activation of the Second Army reflected the fact that since the beginning of 1942, in the wake of Kantokuen, the staff in Hsinking had been working with the central authorities to overhaul, expand, and decentralize the entire command structure in Manchuria. The assignment of personnel was targeted for 1 July, and the revamped system scheduled to become operational by 1 August. As a first step IGHQ had, in June, ordered the redesignation of Kwantung Army headquarters as a higher-level general headquarters (GHQ), particularly because new area armies would soon be coming within its jurisdiction.[86] Umezu's title was accordingly elevated from commander to commander in chief of the Kwantung Army.

As of 1 July the Kwantung Army was authorized to organize the First Area Army at Mutanchiang, overseeing the whole east Manchurian front. Lieutenant General Yamashita, the conqueror of Singapore, was given command of this area army, and Maj. Gen. Ayabe Kitsuju was transferred from his post as deputy chief of staff of the Kwantung Army to serve as Yamashita's chief of staff. The First Area Army took control of the Third, Fifth, and Twentieth armies, the new Second Army, and the 10th Division located at Chiamussu. In parallel with Yamashita's area army, the Second Area Army was formed at Tsitsihar. Lt. Gen. Anami Korechika, brought from Central China, was given responsibility for a huge geographical area but was allocated relatively few troops—the Fourth Army in the north, and the Sixth Army and Arshaan Garrison Unit opposite Outer Mongolia in the west. At the end of June an innovative strategic concept had been realized in the Japanese army with the creation of the Mechanized Army (*Kikōgun*). The headquarters was located at Ssupingchieh, site of the tank school, which was also assigned to the new commander, Lt. Gen. Yoshida Shin. His chief of staff was Maj. Gen. Terada Masao, operations chief of the Kwantung Army during the Nomonhan fighting. The Mechanized Army included the first two IJA armored divisions organized in Manchuria, drawn from existing regiments. A tank regiment that was returned from the Philippines front and another from Malaya were also incorporated into the armored divisions.[87]

The restructuring of the Kwantung Army derived from organizational plans of long standing and was facilitated by the early Japanese successes in the Pacific War and by an improvement in budgetary allocations. Certainly the assignment of outstanding generals, promising line officers, and operations and logistical experts from Kwantung Army headquarters itself improved the combat readiness of the forward armies. Nonetheless, the realignment of the Kwantung Army's command structure cannot be directly equated with any intention to go to war with the Soviet Union in 1942. Indeed, there was some thinking in the Japanese army that Siberia might be occupied without firing a shot if Russia collapsed under German blows in the west—that is, if the wind suddenly blew the persimmon from the tree at last. A close eye was therefore kept on Wehrmacht progress toward the Baku oil fields and the Caucasus, toward Moscow and Leningrad, and toward Suez. In any event, hardheaded IJA logistics officers were convinced that a full year—until mid-1943—would be necessary to raise the capacity of the Kwantung Army to the offensive stance by bringing back and integrating units from the southern theaters and by rejuvenating the forces in Manchuria through the release of older soldiers and the rigorous training of conscripts.[88] And all this was predicated on continued successes in the south and the solution of the China conflict.

The devaluation of the northern front was also reflected in Japanese central planning in 1942. IGHQ was too preoccupied with operations in the southwest Pacific to do more than issue a supplement to the annual anti-Soviet contingency plan of 1941, adding the aggressive concept of a minor offensive on the north Manchurian front. The basic document of 1941, with supplement, accordingly remained in effect by default until 1943.[89] Obliged to abandon the notion of an offensive eastward into Siberia before the spring thaw in 1942, the Kwantung Army staff thus turned to the possibility of a northern thrust, which seemed to hold promise. By contrast to the much-studied plans for fighting on the eastern front, however, planning for a northern offensive had to start "from scratch." Much attention was devoted to the strengthening of support facilities to the rear of the line units. By and large, the Kwantung Army spent 1942 and 1943 in training and in consolidating and digesting the "overnight" buildup that had begun in the Kantokuen era.[90]

The power of the Kwantung Army was still dreaded abroad. Japanese troop landings at Kiska and Attu in Alaska in June 1942, as well as the transfer of Japanese military aircraft to Paramushiro in the northernmost Kuril chain off Kamchatka, were regarded by U.S. planners as part of Japanese preparations to attack Siberia. In mid-1943, the U.S. Joint War Plans Committee was still convinced that if the defeat of the Soviet Union was "clearly imminent" that year, the Japanese would strike at Siberia.[91]

Despite the Kwantung Army's aggressive reputation, throughout General Umezu's long tenure as its chief (from September 1939 until July 1944) he never ceased to exert tight control over his border troops.[92] Japanese restraint was matched by Russian wariness; the rebuilding and reorganization efforts by the Kwantung Army in 1942 did not go unnoticed by the Soviet side. At first the Russians reinforced their border positions and built field fortifications, especially in the Vladivostok-Voroshilov zone. At the same time, they began to improve the defenses of their air bases. New air force headquarters were established, and in May the entire Trans-Baikal Military District was restructured. After the Japanese invaded the Aleutians in 1942, the Russians strengthened their defenses on Kamchatka and in North Sakhalin.

In May 1942 the Wehrmacht, having been checked at Moscow and Leningrad, launched a new offensive, the result of which was to draw further troop transfers from the Soviet Far East in July and August: two rifle divisions each from the Ussuri, Khabarovsk, and Trans-Baikal regions. As in 1941, however, the Russians rebuilt their forces in Siberia promptly, raising approximately two infantry divisions and, either by preference or necessity, a large number of brigades (10 rifle, three tank). Additionally, 10 replacement air divisions were created. As of the end of 1942, the Japanese AGS placed Soviet Far Eastern strength as high as 750,000 men (a decrease of only 50,000 during the year) in 20 rifle divisions (down by three), 10 new infantry brigades, and two cavalry divisions (the same). The Soviets also had 1,000 combat aircraft (the same), and 800 to 1,000 tanks (perhaps a decrease of 200, if the lower figure is used).[93]

Only toward the end of 1942 did the tide begin to turn decisively for the Soviet armies in Europe; by the end of January 1943, the German Sixth Army was annihilated at Stalingrad. During the first half of 1943, IJA intelligence estimated Russian transfers from Siberia at merely one rifle and three cavalry divisions, the latter of obvious usefulness in forthcoming pursuit operations against the Germans. Once again the Soviets activated sizable replacement formations: one infantry and one cavalry division, and two air divisions. By the end of 1943, Russian Far Eastern manpower strength was probably at its lowest point—some 700,000 troops (down another 50,000 since 1942). But Japanese calculations of infantry divisions (20), cavalry divisions (two), and tanks (800 to 1,000) remained identical. The Soviet combat aircraft inventory alone may have been augmented—by 100, to 1,100.[94]

Precisely when the military situation improved for the Russians, it began to turn against the Japanese during the autumn of 1942. Operation No. 5 against Chungking had had to be abandoned, but the Kwantung Army, as the only field force not engaged in active combat, would still have to release units on demand to theaters of higher priority. Thus in February 1943, IGHQ alerted the Kwantung Army to the fact that it would have to get by, for the time being, with little air strength.[95] The "death knell" for the field army was being sounded.

The High Command subsequently tried to reassure the staff in Hsinking that there was no intention of neglecting Manchuria. Nonetheless, considerations of overall national power required that the field forces in Manchuria and China—and particularly their equipment—be held in readiness for use elsewhere.[96] IGHQ consequently instructed the Kwantung Army to draw up an operational plan requiring less strength. Significantly, during the summer and autumn of 1943, all of the Kwantung Army's offensive-minded operations officers were replaced, which suggested to the command in Hsinking that IGHQ was inclining toward an essentially static operational plan.[97] After careful study of several strategic alternatives between early October and late December, it was decided that the annual plan of 1943 (calling for offensives on two fronts, east and north) should be retained in 1944, but that a new plan would be devised for 1945, entailing an offensive only in the north and holding operations in both east and west. In the absence of any clear-cut IGHQ guidelines to the contrary, this ostensible retention of the offensive notion meant that the Kwantung Army would face enormous difficulty when it was obliged to shift to entirely defensive operations later.[98]

Although the Kwantung Army staff was allowed to believe that offensive action was still envisaged in Manchuria, the permanent removal of troops that had begun as early as July 1942 continued unabated. In October 1943 IGHQ sent orders to disband the Mechanized Army and to transfer the headquarters of the Second Army and Second Area Army to the Southern Army "north of Australia." By the close of 1943, the Kwantung Army consisted of 600,000 men (100,000 fewer than the year before) and only 250 serviceable combat aircraft.[99] The year had been largely spent in overseeing an "exodus" from Manchuria, but worse was in store for 1944, when a beleaguered IGHQ began to pull out entire divisions. By the outset of 1945, a total of 10 infantry divisions and one tank division had been removed from Manchuria, together with many supporting elements. A dozen expeditionary units were rushed to other theaters, and 25 infantry battalions were drained from the remaining divisions—the equivalent of three full divisions. The divisions that stayed behind were almost ruined by the withdrawals of men and equipment: a number of infantry companies now possessed only one or two officers, and some artillery regiments were left with no guns. Two air divisions, the bulk of the aerial strength in Manchuria, were transferred to the Philippines in mid-1944. By December of that year, not one division was left to defend Korea, and the Kwantung Army itself had only nine divisions, 12 air squadrons with 120 planes, and 460,000 men.[100]

IGHQ had expected to pull out some of the Kwantung Army's forces, but not most of the core formations. The seemingly spasmodic withdrawals not only suggested a lack of foresight on the part of the High Command but imposed added strain on the staff in Hsinking in trying to compensate for the departures and still cope with all eventualities. The removal of engineer, air-defense, and armored formations was especially painful because the Kwantung Army had never possessed enough of those units to begin with.[101] Striving to substitute quality for quantity, the staff set about concentrating on training and maneuvers and on the building of fortifications, but was impeded by the diminution in manpower, confusion in the transfer of troops, shortages of matériel and, on occasion, very bad weather.[102]

With the fall of Tōjō on 18 July 1944 and his replacement by the team of Gen. Koiso Kuniaki and Adm. Yonai Mitsumasa, the post of AGS chief went to Umezu. After nearly five years in command of the Kwantung Army, Umezu was succeeded by another senior general, Yamada Otozō, 62, who had been Inspector General of Military Training since October 1939.[103] From the outset, Yamada was buffeted by crises. B-29 bombers from China had begun to strike targets in South Manchuria on 13 July, when the iron and steel plants at Anshan were hit. The B-29's launched heavier raids on the 8th and 26th of September, prompting Yamada and his staff to recommend that Manchukuo be authorized to declare war on the United States and Britain. IGHQ rejected the idea, to avoid possible provocation of the Soviet Union.[104]

Japanese concern about the Russians was not academic, for Soviet units had been operating more aggressively along the Manchurian borders since mid-1944. On 29 July, in the Hunchun sector on the southeastern front, a small affray occurred; three days later, Japanese soldiers were fired upon and two were wounded. IGHQ promptly admonished the Kwantung Army and exhorted it to redouble efforts to acquaint all units, especially the forwardmost elements, with the policy of prudence. Although Yamada saw to it that his forces were advised, new troubles occurred on the northwestern frontier, in the Mongoshili area northeast of Manchouli, during the first ten days of August 1944. A Soviet patrol was reported to have crossed into Manchukuoan territory, set some fields ablaze, and fired a number of shots; this was followed by an overflight by Soviet aircraft. Although no escalation ensued, IGHQ was again jolted into a very stringent definition of policy designed to insure that frontier problems were not of Japanese making.[105]

The High Command also finally faced up to the need to rethink the obsolete and unworkable operational concepts still on the books. The Kwantung Army staff argued that Japan must fulfill its moral obligation to defend Manchukuo's borders, even though the frontier sectors could not be held for more than two weeks in the event of war with Russia. After weighing a number of alternatives, IGHQ on 18 September 1944 approved a Kwantung Army plan that to some extent sacrificed military for political considerations. Abandoning all of the old offensive notions for the first time, the plan called for the Kwantung Army to conduct holding operations on every front and to fight to the death, without counting on support by armor or planes. If worse came to worst, resistance should be carried out in the mountainous zone of southeast Manchuria and adjacent North Korea. By January 1945 the Kwantung Army had worked out the details of the new defensive strategy. Formations were restructured and redeployed, construction of new fortifications was begun, mobilization measures were undertaken throughout Manchuria, and the Manchukuoan army was reorganized for combat.[106]

All the while, the Russians were becoming increasingly hostile. Throughout the first half of October 1944, small incidents broke out along the Amur River boundary near Khabarovsk, eliciting Japanese recourse to diplomacy instead of force.[107] More significantly, on 6 November—the anniversary of the Bolshevik Revolution—Stalin made a speech in which he openly denounced Japan as an aggressor. Diplomat Kase Toshikazu sensed "the sharp touch of the first frost that withers the late flowers."[108] The nervous Kwantung Army picked up further ominous information during early December. In the course of a series of Russian sniping attacks on IJA troops near Hulin on the eastern frontier, intelligence learned that a Soviet garrison commander had employed the term "enemy Japan" in instructions to his men.[109]

Kwantung Army anxiety at its military impotence in Manchuria grew in proportion to the Russian buildup in Siberia. As early as October 1944 the Soviet Army was earmarking troops for movement east from Europe. Stalin and his military staff told the Western Allies that they intended to build up their Far Eastern divisions from 30 to 55 or 60 in order to mount the offensive against the Kwantung Army that had been promised as soon as Nazi Germany was subdued.[110] From late February 1945 in particular, IJA intelligence reported continuous trainloads of troops and supplies on the move eastward across the Trans-Siberian Railway. Flatcars bore tanks, aircraft, artillery, and pontoons obviously designed for river-crossing operations. On occasion the Russians even made no effort to mask the matériel with tarpaulins. The volume of eastbound military traffic increased monthly, until by May and June 1945 the Russians were using an estimated 15 trains daily. Japanese intelligence concluded that a division was being shipped east every three days, a rate of perhaps 10 divisions per month. By the end of July the Soviets were expected to have built up their Far Eastern offensive strength to a grand total of 47 divisions, 1,600,000 men, 6,500 aircraft, and 4,500 armored vehicles. Significantly, the Russian reinforcements were not equipped for cold-weather operations and would therefore have to go into action before the advent of winter.[111] Japanese apprehensions were exacerbated when, on 5 April 1945, the Russians gave Tokyo one year's notice of their intention to allow the five-year neutrality pact of 1941 to lapse, for the reason that the accord had "lost its meaning and [its] prolongation had become impossible."[112]

By now the Kwantung Army was bereft of its finest divisions—the divisions of the Kantokuen period. The oldest remaining division had been organized in the spring of 1944. Sixth Army headquarters (which had directed the last phase of the Nomonhan war from Hailar) was transferred to China in January 1945.[113] To maintain the appearance of strong field forces, IGHQ directed the Kwantung Army to increase the number of divisions and independent brigades by mobilizing the last available recruits. Col. Hayashi Saburō later explained: "We wanted to provide a . . . show of force. If the Russians only knew the weakness of our preparations in Manchuria, they were bound to attack us."[114] This philosophy greatly resembles that adopted by the Soviet Army in Siberia at the nadir of Russian fortunes.

The formation of eight divisions and four independent mixed brigades commenced in January 1945 and was pushed through within about two months. Cadres came from deactivated elements and from remnants of units dispatched elsewhere. But the Kwantung Army needed to scrape the bottom of the manpower barrel—the physically infirm, the overage, civil servants, colonists, and students—to meet three mobilization levies between May and July 1945. The draft of July brought in 250,000 men, leaving only 150,000 Japanese male civilians of military age deferred to operate key services such as communications and transportation. The result on paper was the largest Kwantung Army in history, with a total strength of 780,000 men centering on 12 brigades and 24 infantry divisions (four of which arrived from the China theater in June and July).[115] (See Map 8.)

The last Kwantung Army also was the weakest for its size. Around 1 May 1945, IGHQ ordered whatever tanks were left at the armored school in Ssupingchieh to be formed into a brigade and shipped to the homeland.[116] The air force, by August, was reduced to 230 serviceable combat planes (apart from trainers) in all of Manchuria. Of these, 175 were obsolete, leaving 55 modern fighters, bombers, and scout planes to cope with perhaps 5,000 Soviet aircraft.[117] To create the new infantry divisions, border garrison units had been reduced to one, from 14 as recently as 1944. But, worst of all, the divisions themselves were hollow despite their numbers. The chief of staff of the Third Army later evaluated the final combat effectiveness of the whole Kwantung Army at the equivalent of only eight and a half crack divisions in the Kantokuen era.[118] Overall firepower had been reduced by a half or two-thirds. Mortars, locally manufactured, were the only weapons

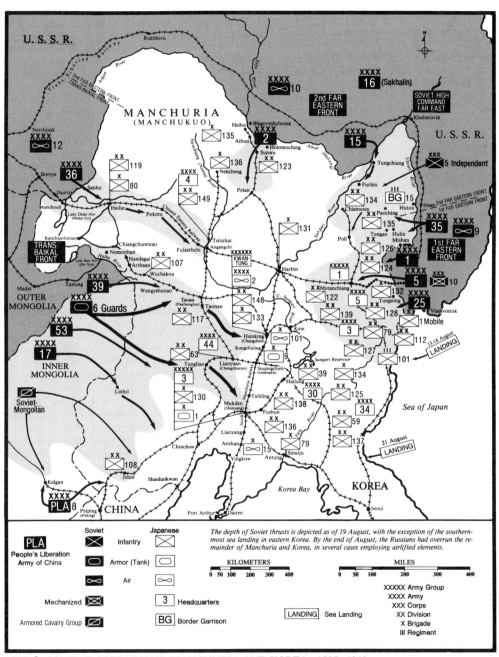

Soviet

PLA — People's Liberation Army of China

⊠ Infantry

⬭ Armor (Tank)

∞ Air

⊠ Mechanized

⬭ Armored Cavalry Group

Japanese

⊠ Infantry

▭ Armor (Tank)

∞ Air

3 Headquarters

BG Border Garrison

LANDING Sea Landing

The depth of Soviet thrusts is depicted as of 19 August, with the exception of the southern-most sea landing in eastern Korea. By the end of August, the Russians had overrun the remainder of Manchuria and Korea, in several cases employing airlifted elements.

KILOMETERS
0 50 100 200 300 400

MILES
0 50 100 200 300 400

XXXXX Army Group
XXXX Army
XXX Corps
XX Division
X Brigade
III Regiment

MAP 8: COMBAT OPERATIONS, MANCHURIA AND KOREA, AUG. 1945

available to entire artillery units; certain formations possessed obsolete relics. Border forts had been stripped of heavy weapons and ammunition, and their gun emplacements dismantled. There were acute shortages of fuel, explosives, and ammunition, for the transfers of supplies and ordnance had depleted the large stockpiles of 1941-42. Remaining air force pilots called gasoline as precious as blood. Land mines and antitank explosives were produced locally, often with powder extracted from useless heavy shells. If combat lasted three months, the Kwantung Army would have only enough ammunition for the equivalent of just over 13 divisions, apart from the needs of other tactical units. Some trainees had never fired live ammunition.[119] New defensive works were unready, their construction hampered by shortages of materials, equipment, and skilled personnel. Logistical capabilities had been sapped by the withdrawal of truck battalions, tractor companies, supply headquarters, and construction units.[120]

To compensate for material weaknesses, indoctrination stressed that one man must destroy ten enemies or one tank, employing techniques based on *tokkō* ("special attack" or suicide) tactics. When assaulting vehicles, soldiers were to use poles or satchel charges and Molotov cocktails improvised from beer or soft-drink bottles, as at Nomonhan six years earlier. Alternatively, men were to convert themselves into human bombs, strapping to their bodies a half-dozen grenades for detonation atop a tank. Some air force pilots loaded rickety trainers with antitank mines and prepared to dive into armored vehicles.[121] But fiery appeals to individual devotion could not conceal a fundamental tendency to cynicism and skepticism, if not defeatism, among the new soldiers, who now made up most of the Kwantung Army. They lacked faith in their weapons, their officers, and themselves, and they bore little resemblance to the Kwantung Army that overran Manchuria in 1931-32, that fought to the death at Nomonhan, or that was so ready to invade Siberia in 1941-42. Out of earshot of their superiors, the listless conscripts called themselves "human bullets" (*nikudan*), "victim units" (*gisei butai*), and "Manchurian orphans" (*Manshū no koji*).[122]

Time was running out. Already the staff in Hsinking had lost all realistic hope of checking the Russians along the frontiers and had recommended that a strategy of delaying operations, attrition, and guerrilla warfare be adopted instead. IGHQ officially endorsed the new operational plan on 30 May. A redoubt area, where the final stand would be made, was to be created astride the South Manchurian–North Korean border between Antu, Tunghua, and Liaoyang. By withdrawing from the regions west, north, and east of a triangle formed by the rail lines connecting Hsinking and Dairen and Hsinking and Tumen, the Kwantung Army was in effect surrendering 75 percent of its creation, Manchukuo. In fact, serious thought was given to the evacuation of Kwantung Army headquarters from Hsinking, but any sudden move, even after hostilities commenced, was rejected for security, political, and psychological reasons.[123]

With the imperial sanction of the last contingency plan for the Kwantung Army, IGHQ issued an order of battle placing that army on a wartime footing. AGS chief Umezu traveled to Seoul on 1 June and Dairen next day to confirm the new redoubt-zone strategy and the issuance of the order of battle. To Seventeenth Area Army commander Kōzuki Yoshio,[124] Kwantung Army commander Yamada, and China Expeditionary Army commander Okamura Yasuji, Umezu explained the need for coordination of strength in Manchuria, Korea, and China to cope with an invasion by Soviet forces striking from the north and by Americans landing in South Korea, Formosa, and/or coastal China. Okamura was to transfer four divisions, an army headquarters, and many support units from China to the Kwantung Army to assist with the defense of Manchuria and North Korea.[125]

The realignment of missions and the infusion of so many new ground units compelled the Kwantung Army to alter command relationships, adjust boundaries, and redeploy troops. The effect of these measures was to shift the weight of operational emphasis southward on all fronts, toward the Manchurian heartland and the redoubt region beyond. Although First Area Army headquarters was left at Mutanchiang on the eastern front, secret plans were made to displace to Tunghua when war broke out. Third Army headquarters was transferred south from Yehho to Yenchi; First Army from Tungan to Yehho. These redeployments began in late April.[126]

In May and June the Kwantung Army accelerated the restructuring process. Third Area Army headquarters at Tsitsihar was to be moved south to displace the Kwantung Defense Command at Mukden. Replacing the Third Area Army in defending most of North Manchuria would be the previously subordinate Fourth Army, relocated from Sunwu to Tsitsihar. The Kwantung Defense Command was ordered to relinquish most of its huge operational responsibility and to concentrate on coverage of the hitherto-neglected west-central provinces, including adjoining Inner Mongolia. With its headquarters transferred from Mukden to Liaoyuan, the Defense Command on 5 June was converted to a combat formation designated the Forty-fourth Army. As for Korea, it was important to face both north and south, as General Umezu had pointed out. Since the Kwantung and Korea armies needed help, China Expeditionary Army commander Okamura sent the Thirty-fourth Army headquarters to Hamhung in North Korea on 17 June and placed it under direct command of the Kwantung Army.[127]

Organizing the Manchurian redoubt posed an almost insuperable problem for the Kwantung Army, which lacked command structure, troops, weapons, and construction capability. Establishment of an army headquarters in the redoubt was of high priority, but no existing staff was available anywhere. Very late, on 30 July 1945, IGHQ finally directed the Kwantung Army to form a new headquarters—the Thirtieth Army—from its own resources, and to subordinate it to the Third Area Army.[128]

The wholesale shuffling of commands and the change in basic strategy had adverse psychological effects on military personnel as well as civilians in Manchuria. Meanwhile, indications that war with Russia was near had been accumulating. Since June, Kwantung Army watchposts had noted an increase in the number of trucks and the amount of logistical matériel being shipped east on the Trans-Siberian Railway. By late July the Russians, having apparently completed the massing of forward combat forces in Siberia, were building up their air force and antiaircraft artillery units.[129]

Japanese intelligence, however, was not of one mind on the timing of the prospective Soviet attack. Appraisals of capability, as always, clashed with those of intention, and IGHQ was generally more pessimistic than the Kwantung Army. Some IGHQ staff officers expected the invasion in late August; other analysts, in both Tokyo and Hsinking, spoke of early autumn, perhaps at the time that American forces invaded the Japanese homeland. Grasping at straws, a number of officers hoped that the Russians might honor the last year of the neutrality pact, due to expire in April 1946. One supposedly encouraging sign was the fact that the USSR had not formally joined with the United States and Britain in issuing the Potsdam Declaration of 26 July calling for Japan's unconditional surrender. Certain officers in Kwantung Army headquarters argued that the Soviet forces might not be able to complete the concentration of logistical units until after October, by which time the border sectors would be snowed in. According to this line of speculation, the Russians would not want to attack in full force before the spring thaw of 1946, though they might seize key areas in North Manchuria before the winter of 1945.[130]

On the Manchurian frontiers, Russian provocations grew in scale and aggressiveness by midsummer of 1945. In late July, for example, 300 Soviet soldiers moved into eastern Manchuria below Panchiehho and built positions for a week. On 5-6 August, south of Hutou, a hundred Russian troops crossed the Ussuri River and shot at a Japanese outpost, which did not fire back. The size of the Soviet forces involved seemed to go beyond mere probes, and Kwantung Army intelligence was sure that full-scale hostilities were imminent. The subordinate area army and army headquarters did not concur; convinced that the latest affrays were not unusual, they took no special precautions.[131]

One cannot escape the impression that as late as August 1945, the higher echelons of the Kwantung Army were living in a fool's paradise. The Japanese homeland was reeling under U.S. naval and air assaults, and almost every important urban and industrial area was in the process of being destroyed. Indeed, on 6 August, the first atomic bomb obliterated the city of Hiroshima. But in Manchuria there was still no sense of crisis. On 8 August, Lt. Gen. Iida Shōjirō and his staff left for Yenchi to attend ceremonies marking the completion of Thirtieth Army headquarters. The Fifth Army was conducting war games attended by division commanders and chiefs of staff—maneuvers that had begun on 7 August and were scheduled to last five days. Even Kwantung Army commander Yamada was unconvinced of the immediate gravity of the situation. Despite cautions by his staff, the general felt free to fly from Hsinking to Dairen on 8 August to dedicate a shrine at Port Arthur.[132]

Thus it was with a sense of disbelief that the duty officer at Hsinking received telephone calls from the First Area Army at Mutanchiang, around 1 A.M. on 9 August, reporting that the Tungning and Suifenho sectors were under attack, and that the city of Mutanchiang was being bombed. At 1:30 A.M. several planes attacked Hsinking. Some staff officers wondered if the raiders were American, from aircraft carriers or from bases in China. Though no word had yet been received from any source concerning a state of war with Russia, at 2 A.M. Kwantung Army headquarters notified subordinate units that an attack was under way on the East Manchurian front, and instructed all forces to check the enemy advance in the border area and to prepare for hostilities elsewhere. Later reports indicated that the Soviet armed forces had launched a full-scale offensive on every front. There could be no further doubt when Kwantung Army radio monitors picked up a Tass News Agency broadcast from Moscow announcing that the USSR had declared war on Japan, effective at midnight on 8 August.

Although Kwantung Army headquarters still had received no official notification of a state of war, it was imperative to lift the restrictions on operations in frontier regions and to order local commanders to put up resistance. At 6 A.M. the long-standing border guidelines were rescinded and contingency plans put into immediate effect that called for delaying action on all fronts. What was left of the Kwantung Army air force was directed to conduct reconnaissance on the eastern and western borders and to attack hostile mechanized forces, especially those reported advancing toward Taoan and Liaoyuan in the west.[133]

The Soviet authorities handled the declaration of war in an unhurried fashion. In Moscow, Foreign Commissar Molotov gave Ambassador Satō Naotake prior notice on the 8th, but the coded Japanese cable report never reached Tokyo. On 9 August the Soviet ambassador to Japan, Jacob Malik, asked to see Foreign Minister Tōgō Shigenori. Told that an interview was not possible on the 9th unless the matter was urgent, Malik answered that the next day would do. The foreign ministry and IGHQ both learned of the Soviet attack through an unofficial channel—namely, the Japanese news agency, which monitored the Tass announcement.[134] Having received the Kwantung Army's initial report, the IGHQ staff drew up an emergency order, approved by the Emperor in the early afternoon of the 9th and transmitted promptly to the army commanders in Manchuria, Korea, China, and the homeland. Effective on the morning of 10 August, the Seventeenth Area Army in Korea and its seven divisions would enter the order of battle of the Kwantung Army. The China Expeditionary Army was to defend North China against a Soviet offensive and assist the Kwantung Army.[135]

When War Minister Anami Korechika heard that the Russians had struck, he remarked that the inevitable had come at last. The AGS Operations Section chief, Maj. Gen. Amano Masakazu, felt that nothing could be done except to hope that the Kwantung Army would be able to hold out as long as possible. Adm. Suzuki Kantarō, prime minister since April, asked the chief of the Cabinet Planning Bureau, Ikeda Sumihisa, whether the Kwantung Army was capable of repulsing the Soviet army. Ikeda replied that the field army was "hopeless" and that Hsinking would fall within two weeks. Suzuki sighed and said: "Is the Kwantung Army that weak? Then it is all over."[136]

When General Yamada returned to Hsinking on the evening of 9 August, his staff summarized the situation on all fronts. In the east, the Russians had committed perhaps three infantry divisions and two or three armored brigades, striking mainly against the Tungning sector. Enemy forces totaling three infantry divisions and two armored brigades were in action on the Amur front; some Soviet units had crossed the river, but the main defenses at Heihō and Sunwu were holding. In the west, two Russian divisions and an armored brigade were pushing fast toward Hailar, which had been bombed on the morning of the 9th. Manchouli had apparently been overrun already. There were reports that two Soviet infantry divisions and an armored brigade were storming the Wuchakou sector from the direction of Nomonhan. Southwest Manchuria was still quiet.[137]

At this early point in the hostilities, serious discord appeared among high Kwantung Army commanders regarding the strategic defense of West Manchuria. Gen. Ushiroku Jun, the Third Area Army commander, who had never liked the redoubt strategy, was opposed to the use of the overcommitted Forty-fourth Army in unaccustomed raiding operations. He preferred to defend the SMR main line by deploying the core of the Forty-fourth Army to Mukden and elements to Hsinking, and counterattacking after the Russians' supply lines had been extended to the limit. On the morning of 10 August, on his own initiative, he ordered the Forty-fourth Army to withdraw to the Hsinking-Dairen line. In addition, he reversed the mission of the Thirtieth Army and transferred it north from the Tunghua redoubt to Hsinking. Faced with Ushiroku's fait accompli, the Kwantung Army reluctantly acquiesced.[138]

Meanwhile, the Russians were exerting severe new pressure in the west, from the direction of Inner Mongolia. Soviet armored units, charging far faster than anticipated, would probably reach Hsinking by the 14th or 15th. The time was at hand for the Kwantung Army to transfer its headquarters to Tunghua. On 11 August, General Yamada moved from Hsinking, leaving only a few of his staff behind. Emperor Pu Yi and his entourage were also relocated to the redoubt zone.[139]

Everywhere the frontiers were collapsing. In the west, for example, Soviet armor and cavalry units were advancing at the rate of 100 kilometers per day. From North Korea came word that a brigade of Russian troops had landed in the Najin region on 9 August, had broken through the defenses, and was now pressing south. General Yamada shuffled forces to try to delay the enemy and cope with Ushiroku's insistence on waging the decisive battle along the SMR line. To fill the vacancy left by the departed Thirtieth Army, Yamada redirected the Fourth Army from Harbin to Meihokow. The First Area Army was instructed on 10 August to withdraw from Mutanchiang to Tunhua.[140]

By concentrating on operational considerations and (with the exception of Ushiroku) reorienting its entire strategy toward North Korea, the Kwantung Army was abandoning not only its vaunted principle of "righteousness and paradise" (*ōdō rakudo*) vis-à-vis Manchukuo but also hundreds of thousands of Japanese residents and colonists. Although the Manchukuoan authorities were blamed for sloth and inefficiency in evacuation measures, a suspicious pattern of priority appeared immediately: the few evacuation trains were crammed with the families of Japanese officers and civilians attached to the army, escorted to safety by army officers. Panic engulfed towns and hamlets as word spread that the Kwantung Army was retreating on all fronts and that headquarters had "fled" Hsinking. Of course train space was in short supply, but the preferential handling of the evacuation led to very bitter recriminations, even within the Kwantung Army.[141]

The sketchy and confusing reports reaching General Yamada on 12 August suggested that the Fifth Army was engaged in desperate fighting west of Muleng on the eastern front, but that in the Amur sector to the north the Fourth Army's situation near Sunwu was essentially unchanged. In the west there was even some good news: about 50 Japanese planes, including converted trainers, had reportedly managed to slow down Soviet armored units around Linhsi and Lichuan, knocking out a total of 27 artillery pieces and 42 vehicles in the process.[142]

The rout of the Kwantung Army became apparent on 13 August. Russian troops had conquered most of Northeast Manchuria, and armored units were already shelling Mutanchiang. In North Korea enemy assault infantry had landed at Chongjin, below Najin. Soviet progress on the Amur front was relatively slow, but in the northwest the Russians had pushed beyond Hailar. On the wide-open western front, poor flying conditions had interfered with sorties by the several dozen remaining Japanese aircraft, and Soviet armor was again rumbling from Lichuan toward Taoan.[143]

Although Japanese air strikes in the west were resumed on the 14th, resulting in reported hits on 43 armored vehicles, the tactical situation was critical everywhere, and there was a large new enemy amphibious landing at Chongjin. Ushiroku's plan to defend the SMR line made less sense than ever. The stubborn Third Area Army commander was told that the Kwantung Army commander felt strongly that the larger conduct of operations was being jeopardized by the idea of waging a decisive battle in central Manchuria. "Swallowing bitter tears," Ushiroku yielded to Yamada's entreaty and began the drafting of plans to pull his area army to the Tunghua redoubt.[144]

The outcome of the fighting would not have been very different even if Ushiroku had backed down earlier, but 14 August was simply too late for the reversal to matter. Incomplete but authentic information had been received from Japan to the effect that crucial developments were taking place at the government level. Yamada flew back to Hsinking on the 14th with his chief of staff, Lt. Gen. Hata Hikosaburō, and other key officers. In the evening a telephone call came from IGHQ confirming that the Emperor would make a very important radio address at noon the next day.[145]

Heavy fighting raged in all sectors on the morning of 15 August. On the western front the Japanese air force flew 39 sorties in the Taoan area and reported hitting three planes and 135 vehicles. At noon, however, the various headquarters in Manchuria tuned in the Tokyo frequency and heard the Emperor's climactic broadcast. Reception was not uniformly good, and the language was characterized by stilted circumlocution, but it seemed that the monarch was calling for the termination of the war. This was a terribly painful turn for the listening officers, many of whom had been expecting a formal declaration of war against the USSR or at least a call for national special-attack operations to the death.

After initial dismay and grief, the Kwantung Army staff concluded that though the Japanese government had undoubtedly reached a political decision concerning termination of the war, combat operations must continue pending receipt of an imperial order. It also was decided that the Kwantung Army deputy chief of staff, Maj. Gen. Matsumura Tomokatsu, should fly to Japan for a firsthand evaluation of the situation. That evening, from Tokyo, Matsumura reported that the High Command was in a whirl and that orders had not yet been transmitted. Finally, around 11 P.M. on the 15th, an IGHQ order suspending offensive operations reached Kwantung Army headquarters. The destruction of regimental colors, portraits of the Emperor, imperial orders, and classified documents began.[146]

Battles continued on 16 August since the Russians were determined to press forward until the Japanese laid down their arms. At 6 P.M. Kwantung Army headquarters received the IGHQ order terminating all combat operations but allowing actions to be taken in self-defense before the completion of armistice negotiations. A follow-up directive explained that the Kwantung Army commander was empowered to initiate local discussions with a view to a cease-fire and the surrender of arms and equipment. Similar instructions were sent to the Japanese commands in China and Hokkaido, directing them to maintain liaison with the Kwantung Army.[147]

Although Generals Yamada and Hata were in agreement that hostilities must cease, there was still confusion, uncertainty, and diehard sentiment among a portion of the subordinate staff. For example, no specific dates for implementation of the cease-fire had been mentioned by IGHQ, and the requirements of "self-defense" might necessitate much more fighting. Consequently, on the night of the 16th a staff conference was called at Kwantung Army headquarters to consider the main alternatives: resistance to the death, combat until more favorable terms could be achieved, or immediate cessation of hostilities. The majority of the officers felt that the Kwantung Army should go on fighting, for the sake of Japan's future and military honor. Others, including the key operations officer, Col. Kusaji Teigo, believed that the army must obey the imperial will: Japan's reconstruction was beyond the purview of the staff. A long, emotional discussion followed, until the impasse was broken by General Hata. With tears in his eyes, the chief of staff asserted that loyal military men had no choice but to accept the Emperor's decree. Those who insisted that the Kwantung Army fight on would have to "cut off our heads first." After the conferees subsided into a silence broken only by muffled sobs, General Yamada ruled that the Kwantung Army would defer to the Emperor's will and devote all efforts to the ending of the war. The appropriate order was drafted at 10 P.M. and communicated to subordinate forces early on 17 August.[148]

The Russians were unhappy with the slowness of the capitulation by the Kwantung Army, although it was known that orders had gone out from Hsinking for the troops to stop fighting and that IJA envoys had been sent to a number of towns with instructions to contact the Red Army command. On the evening of the 17th, a Japanese plane flew over the positions of the Soviet Far Eastern Front and dropped two flags with a cease-fire appeal from the First Area Army. Even so, the Russians felt that the Kwantung Army's actions belied its protestations; only the Manchukuoan army, they charged, was actually surrendering on the 17th. Consequently the Soviet commander in chief, Marshal A. M. Vasilevsky, dispatched a wire to General Yamada that day, indicating that the Japanese call for a cease-fire was not the same as a surrender and alleging that Japanese troops were still counterattacking in some areas. To allow the Kwantung Army time to order all of its forces to give up, Vasilevsky was authorizing a deadline of noon on 20 August.[149]

On 17 August, General Matsumura flew back to Hsinking with word that the Japanese High Command was anxious to prevent civil disorder and to maintain military discipline and unity despite the shock and chaos of defeat. It was estimated in Tokyo that six days would be needed to disseminate details of the capitulation to all IJA forces on the Asian continent, including Manchuria. To lend further authority to the Emperor's rescript and to curb counterproductive zealotry, imperial princes were being sent as envoys to major overseas commands. At dusk on the 17th, Prince Takeda Tsuneyoshi, a lieutenant colonel who had served at Kwantung Army headquarters as recently as July, flew in to Hsinking to address the entire staff of the field army and main units stationed in the area. General Yamada assured the prince that the Kwantung Army would comply with the imperial wishes.[150] Next day, the chiefs of staff of the First, Third, and Korea-based Seventeenth area armies, and of the Second Air Army, were called to Hsinking to be briefed about the cease-fire and disarming of the troops. Based upon IGHQ instructions, the Kwantung Army also announced that all officers and men, although detained by the Soviet forces, would not be stigmatized as prisoners of war subject to court-martial on their return home—a clemency denied the men captured at Nomonhan, it will be recalled.[151]

The situation within Manchuria, however, had become nearly unmanageable. A number of high-ranking, despondent IJA officers in the field (including a division commander and his chief of staff) had committed suicide after hearing of Japan's capitulation. Some officers, refusing to fall into the hands of the Russians, simply disappeared, as in the case of a division chief of staff, a colonel, who took off with his family on 17 August and went underground. Other Japanese officers were murdered by mutinous Manchukuoan troops. In Hsinking, for example, clashes broke out on 13 August between Japanese and Manchukuoan units and lasted until 19 August.[152]

The biggest problem, however, was the continuation of resistance by surrounded or bypassed pockets of troops who had not received word of the war's end or whose commanders were either unconvinced of the authenticity of the imperial rescript or were determined to die in action. The Russians complained that on the Hutou front near the Ussuri River, a demand for unconditional surrender on 18 August was answered by Japanese gunfire, which necessitated Soviet shelling and a renewed assault. When a Russian airborne commander conferred with General Hata and his colleagues at

Harbin on 18 August, it became obvious to the Soviets that "these were generals without an army; they had lost control of their troops and could not influence the actions of the scattered and disorderly retreating units." Despite joint efforts by the Kwantung Army and the Russians to get all Japanese units to surrender, fighting continued to be reported from the Hutou sector, where the last strongpoints were wiped out only on the 22nd. Elsewhere, IJA resistance did not end until 27-30 August. According to the Russians, they were obliged to send sizable detachments to comb mountain and forest areas where small but numerous Japanese guerrilla forces were harrying logistical units and headquarters.[153]

As for the unevacuated and unprotected Japanese settlers, their time of agony had only begun. Butchered by natives no longer cowed by the Kwantung Army, brutalized by sometimes undisciplined enemy soldiers, debilitated by hunger, disease, exhaustion, and despair, those of the fleeing colonists and their families who did not kill themselves died in droves as they tried desperately to escape their fate. By some accounts, at least 200,000 Japanese civilians never made it home.[154]

The Manchukuoan regime had fallen apart, and Emperor Pu Yi (who had already abdicated) was seized by Soviet airborne troops at Mukden airport on 19 August and flown to detention in Chita. The suspicion has never been allayed that Pu Yi was caught too easily, that unidentified Kwantung Army officers viewed the puppet ruler's impending removal to Japan as a potential embarrassment to the Japanese royal family and post-surrender government.[155]

By the end of August the Soviet command was satisfied that the Kwantung Army and the Manchukuoan army had been disarmed and taken prisoner, and that Manchuria, the Liaotung Peninsula, Northeast China, South Sakhalin, the Kuril Islands, and North Korea as far as the 38th Parallel had been "liberated." The Russians' Trans-Baikal front headquarters was moved to Hsinking on 1 September and housed in the former headquarters building of the Kwantung Army.[156] Of particular interest to the Soviet authorities were the "war criminals" of the Kwantung Army—general officers (of whom a total of 148 were seized), intelligence experts, and personnel involved in the nefarious bacteriological-warfare organization known as Unit 731.[157] On 20 August all of the IJA generals in the Mukden region, directed to assemble at the airfield ostensibly to greet the incoming Russian commander, were herded aboard aircraft and transported to Siberia. On 5 September, every Japanese general in Hsinking, including army commander Yamada, was flown to captivity in Khabarovsk, as were a number of staff officers.[158]

Siberia (and to a lesser extent Outer Mongolia) was also the destination of the rank and file of the Kwantung Army, whom the Russians had no intention of releasing or promptly repatriating despite the fact that the Allied Powers' Potsdam Proclamation of 26 July 1945, to which the USSR presumably adhered following its entry into the Pacific War, stated that "the Japanese military forces, after being completely disarmed, shall be permitted to return to their homes with the opportunity to lead peaceful and productive lives."[159] Having laid down their weapons at various locations, the 600,000 prisoners were marched piecemeal to urban assembly points. Many expected to be shipped home soon, but starting in September the Russians formed labor battalions consisting of 1,000 or 1,500 prisoners each, packed them into freight cars, and sent them to about 225 camps (some as far west as the Moscow region and the Caucasus) for forced labor and indoctrination.[160] The Russians were exultant. In Marshal Zakharov's words, "Endless columns of Japanese troops with their generals at their head moved northwards, to the Soviet Union: they had dreamed of going there as conquerors, but they were going as prisoners of war."[161] Once in Siberia and Outer Mongolia, the Japanese of 1945 met compatriots from the Nomonhan era—those who had not dared to go home.

In the camps the death toll was very heavy, from malnutrition, overwork, accidents, disease, and exposure.[162] Repatriation from the USSR did not commence until December 1946; the Russians claimed that by April 1950, only 2,467 men, largely "war criminals," remained in their hands.[163] But as of October 1955, the Japanese government had the names of 16,200 detainees thought to have survived in Russia, North Korea, and Outer Mongolia. Kwantung Army commander Yamada, convicted as a war criminal, was not released until June 1956, almost eleven years after his capture. He was then 74 years old and in ill health. Two other wraiths from the past were repatriated in December of the same year: Kwantung Army chief of staff Hata, age 66; and Third Area Army commander Ushiroku, age 72.[164] As recently as 1977, however, the Japanese Welfare Ministry still could not account for 244 individuals who had once been in Soviet custody—the last of the Kwantung Army.[165]

Afterthoughts

Our survey of the Kwantung Army in general, and of the Nomonhan Incident in particular, sheds light on a number of interrelated topics: (1) the myth and the reality of the Kwantung Army itself; (2) the fate of Manchuria/Manchukuo, which the Kwantung Army coveted, shaped, and lost; (3) Nomonhan as a turning point in history; (4) connections between Nomonhan and the Pacific War; (5) a glimpse into the Soviet way of war; and (6) caveats and lessons of relevance today.

THE KWANTUNG ARMY: MYTH AND REALITY

The very name "Kwantung Army" is misleading. In Western usage, a corps consists of at least two divisions and auxiliary troops, and an army contains a variable number of corps (usually two or more) plus organic and service-support troops and trains. Yet, as we saw in Chapter 2, after more than half of its 40-year existence, on the eve of the Manchurian Incident in 1931 the Kwantung Army was made up of only one understrength infantry division and supporting elements, six battalions of the Independent Garrison Unit, and some miscellaneous units, adding up to a grand total of hardly more than 10,000 men. And after 1931, when responsibility for Manchukuo led to reinforcements that for the first time made sense of the term "Army," the same expansion of its role made "Kwantung" out of date.

These matters of terminology are more than irrelevant accidents of history. They reflect fundamental Japanese imperial policy toward the Asian continent in general and toward the former northeast provinces of the Chinese empire in particular. First, during the period after Japan's initial successful overseas war, against China in 1894-95, each of the original colonial garrisons was officially separated from the jurisdiction of the civil governors in due course and, regardless of the number of troops assigned to it, was called an army. In addition to the Kwantung Army, there was the Taiwan Army (whose strength did not amount to even one division) and the Korea Army (never more than two divisions in peacetime). Second, a sense of historical continuity and a desire to sanctify the treaty basis for Japan's presence in Manchuria caused retention of the wording "Kwantung," drawn from the leasehold of the Kwantung Territory—"the most civilized area of Manchuria," as one Japanese publicist put it. Third, independence was not envisaged for Taiwan or Korea, whereas the "empire" of Manchukuo would be endowed with its own armed forces, called the Manchurian or Manchukuoan army. Hence the old distinctive wording was retained for the Japanese garrison, the Kwantung Army.[1]

Military terminology aside, the Kwantung Army after 1931 conveyed three different images in three chronologically distinct phases. Between the Manchurian Incident and Nomonhan, the Kwantung Army was characterized by constant belligerence and occasional disobedience to central authority. From Nomonhan until 1943, the field army was increasingly strong and stable. Thereafter, until the end of the war, it was continually being weakened and was placed on the defensive.[2]

These metamorphoses are attributable to a combination of all-army and personal behavioral patterns. First, the individual Kwantung Army commanders exerted varying degrees of control. The eras of Honjō Shigeru and Ueda Kenkichi were marked by an almost feudal interplay between great lords and loyal vassals. Inada Masazumi calls Ueda "the god of all Manchuria," but he was a god who was out of touch by 1939 with the situation in Tokyo.[3] The High Command's deferential treatment of Ueda is reminiscent of the mild, sometimes ineffective handling of General of the Army Douglas MacArthur by his junior, General J. Lawton Collins, the U.S. Army chief of staff during the Korean War. Umezu Yoshijirō, however, commanded an elite, "tight ship"; and Yamada Otozō ran a collegial though harried organization. In each case the Kwantung Army commander, always a senior general, possessed enormous dominion, being located in the direct chain of command to the throne. Thus he could wield excessive troop-movement authority; on the basis of mission, he claimed the right to shift forces as he saw fit without central sanction. The Kwantung Army's unilateral decision to send air force bombers against targets inside the Mongolian People's Republic in June 1939 was an unsettling example of the evasion or defiance of the supreme command prerogative past the point of no return.[4] Similar arbitrary abuses of the power of an air force, on the part of local U.S. military authorities, took place on occasion during the American operations in Southeast Asia during the 1960's and 1970's.

Second, in the heyday of staff politics (*bakuryō seiji*), staff officers such as Ishiwara Kanji and Itagaki Seishirō, and later Tsuji Masanobu and Hattori Takushirō, exerted an influence out of proportion to their relatively modest ranks. Sir Ian Hamilton had comprehended this phenomenon as early as the Russo-Japanese War when he wrote, "The Japanese mind seems readily to lend itself to the system of one man supporting all the weight, pomp, and responsibility of a position, whilst another man works free and untrammelled in the shadow afforded by that latent power."[5] Although personnel assignments were not handled in a collusive fashion,[6] staff officers serving in Tokyo sought dispatch overseas in the knowledge that career advancement (especially the attainment of general officer rank) depended on field duty. In U.S. military parlance, one "gets one's ticket punched" in a combat theater. For IJA officers, Manchuria and China were the only active theaters prior to the outbreak of the Pacific War. The Kwantung Army was especially favored and pampered because of its critical anti-Soviet role. "In those days," remarks one Japanese author, "you were not a real officer if you did not have Kwantung Army experience."[7] Until Ueda's day in particular, an aggressive tenor held sway that equated prudence with defeatism, that denigrated diplomacy except as a last resort, and that brooked no interference by civil authority.[8]

Third, the military environment in Northeast Asia was affected by the changing equations of force between Japan and the Soviet Union. After briefly outclassing the Soviet Far Eastern setup in the late 1920's and early 1930's, the Kwantung Army lost ground, with the brief exception of the Kantokuen period. Drawing a comparison with the world of business, a Japanese critic has remarked that "the epaulets of the Kwantung Army earned it a seat at the board of directors' table, but it really represented a company of limited capitalization."[9] To Inada Masazumi, the Kwantung Army was "never much of an army. Its strength greatly exaggerated for the benefit of the Soviet Union, it was really a second- or third-class force whose organization, equipment, and supplies were never very impressive but whose staff made lots of noise." Even the strength concentrated for Kantokuen in 1941 represented the minimum necessary for all-out hostilities.[10] Yamada's army, the Kwantung Army of 1945, has been compared to a "toothless tiger" that dares not eat solid food. The commanding general and the survivors of this army suffered the ultimate ignominy—incarceration in Siberia, Outer Mongolia, or China, and, for a number, prosecution as war criminals.

THE FATE OF MANCHURIA/MANCHUKUO

A number of Kwantung Army plotters of 1928-31, Ishiwara in particular, had had a vision of Manchuria as a paradise and a treasure house—a source of raw materials, an outlet for Japan's surplus population and unemployed, and a base for the development of heavy industry—from which the "old capitalists" would be barred. "Is it too extravagant a hope to say," a Japanese civilian apologist asked in 1932, "that these half-dozen different races of Orientals now gathering in Manchukuo may be mixed and fused in due course and develop a freshly vigorous type of nation, as has been done on the North American continent?"[11] But when jingoists, opportunists, carpetbaggers, and shady characters flocked to Manchuria, much of the early idealism and patriotism foundered on greed, indifference, and arrogance. For example, gentle old Lieutenant General Hishikari Tadashi, in command of the Kwantung Army in 1933-34, provoked the resentment and contempt of his staff by showing kindness even to the lowliest Manchurian natives. He was reputedly hounded from office.[12]

Working hand in glove with the Kwantung army, the South Manchuria Railway system burgeoned into a conglomerate of vast economic and strategic dimensions. By 1938 it prided itself on directly controlling 72 subsidiaries, having built up 25 urban areas, and carrying 17,515,000 passengers per year. Its president and vice-president were appointed by the Japanese government with the sanction of the Emperor. Japanese critics, however, attacked the SMR as a "stupendous bureaucracy of parasites" whose main function seemed "to consist in spending money recklessly, especially on nonproductive enterprises connected with domestic politics."[13]

What has been termed the "blatant fiction" of Manchukuo never took healthy root under a Japanese *raj* whose proconsul was always both Kwantung Army commander and nominal ambassador to the client state. The government of Japan constantly asserted that its relations with Manchukuo were based on the principle of "one virtue and one mind." Pu Yi, in turn, assured his overlords that the alliance derived from bonds of "indivisibility." At the time of the Japanese attack on Pearl Harbor, he promised that, "In whatever circumstances we should find ourselves, we two nations shall never part from each other."[14] Yet when the bayonets of the depleted Kwantung Army were withdrawn in August 1945 and Soviet forces overran the region, the whole shaky edifice of Manchukuo toppled, leaving hardly a trace of Pu Yi's "empire." To this day, however, Japanese veterans take pride in the fact that the Kwantung Army achieved its fundamental objective for 27 years after the establishment of the Soviet Union: to prevent a communization of Manchuria similar to that which befell adjoining Outer Mongolia.

NOMONHAN AS A TURNING POINT

It is generally agreed that, despite IJA silence on the subject, the Japanese decision in 1941 to transfer strategic emphasis to the south, involving war with the United States, Britain, and the Netherlands, stemmed in part from the Kwantung Army's failure against the Russians in 1939. The Soviet historian Ponomaryov and his colleagues surmise that "the defeat inflicted by the Red Army on the Japanese troops along the Khalkhin Gol River somewhat sobered up the high-handed Japanese militarists, while the Soviet-German [Nonaggression] Treaty deprived them of the basis of their anti-Soviet designs."[15] In its overall judgment in 1948, the International Military Tribunal for the Far East (the Tokyo Trial) found that "as the door of opportunity closed in the North, the Southern gates began to open" for Japan.[16]

There is little doubt that if the Soviet Union had had to fight on two land fronts simultaneously, the Germans would have won the war on the Eastern Front. Petro Grigorenko, the Soviet general who became a dissident after the Second World War, has confirmed the Russians' own perception of the danger facing them if Japan had chosen to strike north after the Germans invaded Russia from the west. Maj. Gen. A. K. Kazakovtsev, the operations chief of the Far Eastern Front headquartered at Khabarovsk, told Grigorenko in 1941: "If the Japanese enter the war on Hitler's side . . . our cause is hopeless."[17]

NOMONHAN AND THE PACIFIC WAR

In recent years, Western writers have devoted less attention to the battle history of the more familiar Pacific War and have begun to examine the reasons why Allied intelligence, in Colonel Roy Stanley's words, "fumbled . . . a rare opportunity to size up Japan's land and air war machinery in the mid-1930's." Stanley calls the campaign in China "Japan's rehearsal for World War II [and] prelude to Pearl Harbor." Nevertheless, the U.S. soldier's guide of 1942 began inauspiciously: "To attempt an estimate of the Japanese Army is something like attempting to describe the other side of the moon, the side which is never turned toward us. . . . It is incredible that a nation could have waged ten years of war and divulged so little to the world."[18] As late as October 1944, the U.S. War Department's technical manual dealing with Japanese military forces could only conclude that "they have evinced boldness against poorly equipped troops; however, against first-class, well-equipped forces, it may be expected that they will adopt more circumspect methods."[19]

Certainly, better acquaintance with the performance of the Japanese army in China would have been beneficial to Allied intelligence analysts in 1941-42. Even more importantly, the five ignored or unknown months of fighting at Nomonhan addressed the precise desiderata of the U.S. War Department manual and could have supplied plentiful information on IJA combat experience against an adversary who was first-class, well organized—and successful. Representative deductions and commentary follow that might have been drawn with confidence in 1939 concerning IJA strengths and weaknesses, including qualitative aspects of military strength such as norms of command and leadership, morale, ethics, and martial tradition.

Unimpressive IJA Higher Leadership

Field Marshal Sir Philip Chetwode has said that "generals are always marvels if they win a battle and always fools if they lose one."[20] In assessing the Japanese army's conduct of the Nomonhan war, one cannot escape the impression that we are dealing with the type of officers whom Liddell Hart called "bow and arrow generals." Since the green 23rd Infantry Division had had no combat experience before Nomonhan, division operations officer Murata argues, "We staff people just conducted operations in a fog [*gori-muchū*]."[21] Significantly, division commander Komatsubara's career was blighted by Nomonhan, whereas after Changkufeng the year before, division commander Suetaka had reaped many rewards for his performance.[22]

The recurring follies of the Japanese army during the Second World War, from Burma to Attu, were foreshadowed exactly by the recriminatory, suicidal, and counterproductive handling of the fighting at Nomonhan. Examples include the debacles at Guadalcanal, Imphal, Saipan, and Leyte. The unsuccessful operations staff officers at Kwantung Army headquarters in 1939, as we have seen, were the equally unsuccessful operational managers clustered at IGHQ during the Pacific War.[23] Especially noticeable was the Japanese command's lack of resiliency and flexibility. At Nomonhan in early 1939 the brave IJA infantry almost made it to the Halha River confluence by a repetitive, desperate series of nightly attacks, but the operation was called off in favor of an artillery offensive, despite Komatsubara's sound reservations. Later, in Burma, the Allies were astonished by the Japanese units' same slavish devotion to one tactical plan. Yet their seemingly endless assaults would suddenly stop after "straining the defense to the breaking point." Apparently, "rugged defense baffled and upset [the Japanese commanders'] preconceived plan of campaign."[24] As the Duke of Wellington said of another, earlier enemy: "They came at us in the same old way, and we beat them in the same old way."

Postwar historian Hata Ikuhiko admits that deficient strategy rather than inferior armaments and technology explains Japanese military defeats from Nomonhan through the Pacific War.[25] Writing also after the war, General Sawada Shigeru discerned a qualitative failure in the army's leadership: "The officers who were largely responsible for our setbacks after the Great East Asia War got under way were promoted to full general, the conscientious ways of thinking that used to characterize real Japanese military men disappeared, and defeat became chronic."[26]

Piecemeal Commitment of Forces

A military maxim cautions against the reinforcement of failure. IJA operations at both Changkufeng and Nomonhan were characterized by piecemeal and disjointed commitment of strength. Nishiura Susumu, a senior staff officer in the war ministry in 1939, remembers advising his section chief, after the Azuma unit had been annihilated in late May, that the method of terminating the border affair ought to be carefully delineated beforehand, lest thoughtless escalation follow the Japanese desire for revenge.

Nishiura expressed concern that the AGS Operations staff might "commit ten soldiers when one was killed; and another 100 when those ten were wiped out." War Minister Itagaki's easy endorsement of AGS intentions from the outset thwarted any hearing for this more prudent view, and of course Nishiura's worst fears came to pass.[27]

Failure to Correct Mistakes

The Japanese army was resistant to change and slow to correct errors or make improvements. The lessons of the Changkufeng fighting had not been digested a year later. To one IJA staff officer, insufficient self-reflection was conducted by the army after Nomonhan, although the experience of 1939 was like "a god-given cruel hint of things to come . . . and resembled the Great East Asia War in microcosm." A Kwantung Army officer believes that the investigations were thorough but that, for various reasons (such as feeble industrial capacity), the army as a whole could not integrate the lessons sufficiently into the spheres of training and matériel. Thus the Japanese army entered the Pacific War "as is." As Kwantung Army deputy chief of staff in the autumn of 1939, Maj. Gen. Endō Saburō found his efforts to rethink the field army's unrealistic offensive plans sabotaged by hawks in Tokyo, and he was soon replaced because of his alleged "Soviet-phobia."[28]

Quality of Soldiery

Kwantung Army operations staff officer Shimanuki Takeharu has said that "99 percent of the front-line commanders at Nomonhan were first class." Enlisted men and noncoms developed nicely "on the job" in combat, and the new 23rd Division fought as well as the best IJA divisions in the Pacific War. Gomikawa Junpei, pondering his own disastrous military experience against the Russians in Manchuria in August 1945, when only he and three men survived from a company of 158 after merely three hours of fighting, remains amazed at the tenacity and relative success of the Japanese troops at Nomonhan six years earlier. Gomikawa is convinced that the men of the 1939 era were "tougher and stronger than those of my own time." Inada agrees that, compared with the IJA soldiers of the Pacific War, those of the Nomonhan period were better—more vigorous, lively, and able.[29]

Inexperience of Junior Officers

Undermining the strength of the ordinary soldiers, however, was considerable weakness among platoon leaders and company commanders. The latter, in particular, were too young and inexperienced—a servicewide problem. Ideally, an officer ought to have taken command of a line company no sooner than seven to eight years after his graduation from the military academy; but the expansion of the army after 1937 precluded such a leisurely process, and officers were taking over companies only four years after leaving the academy. By the last stages of the Pacific War, battalion commanders (who were already company commanders in the Nomonhan period) proved to be the weakest tactical link.[30] Allied intelligence concluded by 1944 that "the appreciation of a sudden and new situation seems to be beyond the ability of [Japanese] junior commanders."[31]

Emphasis on Spiritual Superiority

IJA operational thinking after Nomonhan remained essentially primitive, unscientific, complacent, narrow, and simplistic. Reaffirmation of faith in moral attributes and psychological factors amounted to a callous evasion of the realities of modern firepower, mechanization, and aviation. The rationale was that the quantity and quality of material possessed by Japan's enemies—and their sheer numbers—could only be offset by intangible factors such as high morale, esprit, and fearlessness in close fighting against men and armor. At Nomonhan and throughout the Pacific War, the price was paid in lives squandered in desperate *banzai* foot charges with the bayonet, though it was well known that frontal assaults had rarely succeeded since the days of the Russo-Japanese War. In a new era of dive-bombers, self-propelled artillery, and panzer divisions, the Japanese were still glorifying an anachronism, brave but naked infantry, as the "queen of battle." Indeed, there was still room for the obsolete observation balloon in IJA doctrine, despite the lessons of "balloon busters" as far back as the First World War, let alone at Nomonhan.[32]

That the stereotyped Japanese military thinking of the Nomonhan period, reminiscent of the butchery of General Nogi at Heights 203 in 1905, did not change in the years to come is illustrated by the remarks of an enlisted reservist who arrived at Truk Island in the southwest Pacific in late 1943 and was astounded by the "puerile and outmoded" nature of the defenses:

> One old gunnery-emplacement commander expressed the ludicrous but prevailing sentiment when he said that lack of equipment gave us Japanese a chance to demonstrate our superior spirit and valor. It was not weapons but outstanding bravery that counted. Though sounding like something out of a comic strip, he was completely serious. . . . Leaders totally ignorant of the scientific and mechanical excellence of the enemy and their weapons praised the waste of priceless human lives for the sake of the cause. They held up as laudatory soldiers who made human cannonballs of themselves or who dashed frantically into close conflict from which they had no hope of coming out alive.[33]

"Courage is praiseworthy," concludes the survivor from Truk, "but putting all hope of victory on it in the face of overwhelming technical superiority reveals abysmal folly." The old imperial army, of course, would have regarded these remarks as subversive—imbued with materialism and the fear of death—and would have insisted that "the battlefield is a place to die, nothing less, nothing more."[34] Allied veterans of the war against the Japanese would retort that IJA "human bullet" tactics became the "symbol of Japanese stupidity." Colonel A. J. Barker, who fought in Burma, observes that "a determined enemy can always stop a *banzai* charge and mow down his opponents even with a bolt-action rifle. With a self-loading or automatic weapon a *banzai* charge could be converted into a massacre." The U.S. 1st Marine Division had the same experience near Matanikau on Guadalcanal, where the Japanese troops evinced a "fondness for the tactically dramatic" by launching an "improvident *banzai* charge . . . at long range and without fire superiority," thereby affording the Americans "a gratuitous opportunity for annihilation by fire."[35]

Penchant for Night Attacks

Despite fallacious Allied statements concerning inferior Japanese visual acuity, IJA tactical doctrine consistently extolled the night attack as a special strength of the army, drawing on ancient military exploits. According to a famous IJA training motto, "The night is worth a million reinforcements."[36] At Nomonhan, not only the infantry but even Tamada's 4th Tank Regiment launched assault operations in the depth of night.

No-Surrender Policy

The refusal of Japanese service personnel to give up, and the need to exterminate IJA holdouts to the last man, regardless of the extremity of their combat situation or the gravity of their wounds, should have come as no surprise to the Allies in the Pacific War. Writing of the Soviet destruction of Ogisu's Sixth Army in the August 1939 offensive at Nomonhan, Grigorenko remembered that "the Japanese never surrendered or moved. . . . They never received orders to retreat from their positions."[37] We have seen how IJA officers and men sacrificed themselves for their regimental colors, artillery pieces, and armored vehicles. The Japanese command, mercilessly forbidding unauthorized withdrawal, found itself unprepared to cope with fluid circumstances entailing the disintegration and attempted flight of units that were ringed by fire, devoid of water, food, ammunition, and medical supplies, and out of contact with friendly forces or higher headquarters. The prohibition against retreat remained "carved in stone": men were expendable. To perish in action or by suicide was preferable to the ignominy of capture (whether voluntary or involuntary) or of pullout, for which the penalty would probably be execution by the Japanese army if one lived to face a court-martial. As Gomikawa says, extravagant citations masked the useless deaths of men whose lives were thrown away by inept, outclassed senior commanders.[38] IJA military doctors even wondered if it might not be better to leave wounded soldiers to be treated by the enemy under the flag of the International Red Cross, once all was lost, or even to resort to mercy killing.[39]

Abhorrence of the Defensive

IJA training manuals always stressed offensive operations and retention of the initiative. The outlook of the Japanese infantry is illustrated by a battalion commander's plea during the fighting at Changkufeng in 1938. All of his men, he begged his colonel, were "eager to sortie rather than remain passive and perish uselessly."[40] With limited strength and firepower, General Komatsubara experienced enormous difficulty defending a broad front on the open plains of Nomonhan.[41] Still, when they had to go over to the defensive, Japanese troops fought with legendary doggedness and discipline, and they dug in and camouflaged their positions with skill, as American forces learned on many an atoll in the Pacific. Nevertheless, during the middle and late stages of the Second World War, Allied intelligence concluded that in defensive situations, IJA units and their outmoded weapons operated at a disadvantage.[42]

Primitive Ground-Support Capabilities

Japanese military aircraft had sharply compartmentalized missions—air-to-air combat, top cover, reconnaissance, and bombing. No planes were designed for ground-support operations as such.[43] The air war at Nomonhan was predominantly a classic dogfighting war conducted by air-superiority fighters, presaging Japanese emphasis throughout the Pacific War. As foreign experts have observed, "Prowess in close-in high-*g* maneuvering style of combat had become something of a fetish" among Japanese army pilots.[44] Tactical bombing effectiveness and air-to-ground coordination and communications were weak at Nomonhan, as they were to be in the Second World War.[45]

Inferior Ordnance and Unimaginative Doctrine

From small arms up, IJA ordnance was generally not in the forefront of technological development. Though the Russians emphasized automatic weapons and sprayed fire, the Japanese continued to use the standard bolt-action Arisaka Type 38 rifle of 1905 design. It was barely adequate for infantry needs at Nomonhan and was not highly regarded by Allied forces in the Pacific War. In addition, IJA 6.5-mm. rifle ammunition was not usable in the 7.7-mm. heavy machine gun. Satchel-charge demolition assaults against tanks, instead of high-velocity antitank gunfire, made for great tales of heroism—and grisly casualties for the "human bullet" attackers. When

Lieutenant General Sawada took his 4th Infantry Division to the Nomonhan front in September 1939, he had to admit that it was a primitive antitank tactic to jump aboard an enemy machine and attach explosives to it.[46]

IJA heavy artillery and howitzers, the pride of the army, in practice could not cope with the range requirements forced on them by Soviet batteries emplaced on the higher ground across the Halha River. The 23 July IJA offensive, centering on heavy guns—from which so much was expected—proved to be a costly failure. Hampered by chronic ammunition shortages as well as by short reach, the Japanese artillery pieces were dominated by the Russian batteries. It seemed as if the IJA artillery, having failed to profit from European experience in the First World War, was firing "raindrops in the face of a gale." Major General Kobayashi, Komatsubara's infantry group commander, confessed in his diary that he had never felt so helpless as at Nomonhan.[47]

As for armor, the Japanese thrilled to the sight of their two tank regiments rumbling to the front at Nomonhan, but the IJA units were dealing in dozens of tanks (and hundreds of horses in the infantry and artillery), whereas the Russians worked with hundreds of tanks and left horses to the MPRA. Japanese tanks were handcrafted, beautifully polished, and hoarded; Soviet fighting vehicles were crudely finished and rather ugly, but they were expendable and highly functional. IJA tanks' primary armament was short-barreled and of low velocity. Advancing frontally and in broad daylight, Yoshimaru's medium tanks were quickly snagged in piano wire and riddled by armor-piercing antitank fire. Though the diesel power train of Japanese medium tanks represented a creditable innovation, and the speed of the flimsy Type 95 light machines was useful in essentially unopposed operations in China and Malaya, neither type of IJA tank was in the same class as the heavier, more formidably armed, and better armored tanks developed by the Allies in the Second World War, such as the Soviet T-34 medium tank, the superb descendant of models employed at Nomonhan.[48]

Low Estate of Logistics

Japanese operations officers, obsessed with battle, tended to regard logistics as a bore, in part because logisticians were cautious and deliberate by nature and not cast in the glamorous mold of the saber-wielding warrior. "Logistics follows operations," an IJA saying went; the logistical annexes of operational plans were chronically thin. At least until the Kantokuen buildup of 1941, the Kwantung Army was seriously deficient in logistical underpinning, most notably with respect to munition supply and organic motorization. As in the case of tanks, the Japanese thought in terms of dozens of trucks (including commandeered vehicles), whereas the Russians deployed hundreds and thousands in their tables of organization and equipment. The 200-km. march by the 23rd Division's infantry regiments from Hailar to Chiangchunmiao in late June 1939 attested to the stamina of the Japanese foot soldier but did not bring troops in fresh condition to the grueling battles on the plains in early July. Only Sumi's 26th Infantry, which was intended to constitute the motorized reserve, was finally put aboard scraped-together trucks near the front; but even that limited capability was soon lost, for no Japanese motorized units could get across the one feeble pontoon bridge that was thrown over the Halha for the offensive into Outer Mongolia. To Okazaki Hisahiko, a present-day foreign ministry official, the fault of IJA strategy in general lay in "solely determining how, with the troop strength available, an order could be obeyed," instead of objectively calculating the likelihood of success beforehand.[49]

Misperceptions of Reality

Not only did the typical Japanese operations officer disparage logisticians; he also distrusted intelligence "plodders" and relegated them to the distant background, except when their estimates accorded with offensive intentions.[50] Again and again at Nomonhan, from May through July 1939, the Japanese command called for pursuit and interception of a supposedly fleeing enemy. This was wishful thinking, fostered by irrelevant experience in the China theater and exacerbated by low regard for the Outer Mongolians, outdated information, and insufficient respect for what were felt to be the purge-weakened Russians. IJA illusions recall Brigadier Spears' experience with the French army in January 1917 on the Western Front in Europe: "I was told to point out to [them] . . . that visions of pursuit in open country should not be allowed to obscure the fact that the first essential to the realization of such pleasant fancies must be the capture of the first [enemy] position, and that no scheme, however bold, no method of progress in the country beyond, however well thought out, was of the least value if they failed to secure it."[51]

But the roots of Japanese misperceptions went deeper. Psychologists speak of a will to believe that leads to easy acceptance of beliefs that meet our needs, and of selective perception that enables us to see what we have a need to see and to be blind to what we do not. The Japanese army did not ignore intelligence; it tended to twist reality to fit its preconceptions and could not or would not accept evidence to the contrary. For example, when Colonel Doi, the attaché in Moscow, stopped off in Hsinking in late June 1939 and proffered words of caution, the Kwantung Army operations officers cut him short. Negative views, they insisted, must not be allowed to dampen the field army's ardent resolve to smash the Soviet-Mongolian forces once and for all.[52] We have also seen how the Kwantung Army Operations Section paid scant heed to warnings of an imminent Soviet offensive in

August 1939.[53] It was apparent that the Japanese army did not know and did not want to know about enemy capabilities. Thus the experience of Nomonhan demonstrated (and the Pacific War confirmed) that the Japanese could not visualize the ability of hostile forces to traverse great distances across difficult terrain in short periods without long stops for rest. In this sense, IJA operations officers were imposing horse-and-wagon thinking on the realities of twentieth-century mobility.

The Japanese may have "thought small" because of their geographical and historical insularity and their pleading of "poverty." Some say that they even prefer to "wrestle alone"—that is, to fight imaginary opponents (*hitorizumō*). Nevertheless, it was a grievous mistake to try to apply this mode of thought (which the Japanese called "common sense") to the presumed response of giant industrialized adversaries such as the Soviet Union and, later, the United States. Foreign ministry analyst Okazaki sees a connection between what he calls Japanese naiveté, "belittling of incoming information, and, broadly speaking, lack of strategic thinking."[54]

Disjointed Command Relationships and Lack of Central Planning

Japanese response to the Nomonhan crisis was reactive rather than measured, spasmodic rather than unified, and emotional rather than objective. Unlike Zhukov, who was told by Stalin from the outset exactly what was to be done, Ueda was left to his own devices, with the result that national policy and military strategy were never synchronized. Kwantung Army headquarters essentially "ran the show," and ostensible "stars" such as Tsuji and Hattori profoundly influenced the details of operational planning. Many promises to the High Command were broken and many important actions reported only after the fact. IGHQ failed to intervene out of respect for Ueda at first, and lost control of the situation after the arbitrary bombing raid against Tamsag in June 1939. Tokyo became disgusted with the fact that an imperial order seemed necessary every time it wanted the Kwantung Army to follow central intentions. For his part, Ueda began to complain that he was being left in the dark by Tokyo. Personality clashes worsened matters; the Kwantung Army staff felt it was at war with AGS Operations chiefs Hashimoto Gun and Inada Masazumi, with whom the best of relations ought to have obtained. "Tsuji and the Kwantung Army were too much for me," Inada later admitted.[55]

When Sawada became the AGS deputy chief of staff after Nomonhan and studied the affair from many angles, he found Kwantung Army commander Ueda ultimately responsible for such problems as the issuance of the provocative April 1939 border guidelines, the authorization of the Tamsag bombing, the indecisive handling of the reinforcement of the 23rd Division, the sloppy escalation of the frontier dispute (extending even to the unilateral invasion of the MPR), the downplaying of intelligence on the Soviet offensive of August, and the inept command and control of the Kwantung Army itself.[56] Although Ueda offered to assume full responsibility, the matter went far beyond the role of one field army commander. Not only were some of Ueda's junior staff excessively involved, but the High Command itself had to shoulder part of the blame. Many staff officers at the section chief level and below blamed IGHQ for poor guidance and control. Whereas Tokyo's handling of the Changkufeng Incident had been a success,[57] Nomonhan discomfited all concerned on the Japanese side. For example, Ueda may have issued the controversial border guidelines, but they had been allowed to pass without comment from Tokyo, and insufficient attention had been devoted to the question of localization of the Nomonhan Incident. War Minister Hata says that he had to sack officers in Tokyo as well as Hsinking because both parties were at fault. Sawada censured IGHQ for feeble direction of the Kwantung Army, resort to theoretical discussion, and feckless attempts to convince by persuasion.[58]

As for the IJA personnel procedures conducted after Nomonhan, Inada explains that "the High Command had lots of officers available in those days and could afford the luxury of transfers and retirements. During the Pacific War, there was no wholesale reshuffling for such 'minor' defeats. Nomonhan, however, was the first major Japanese reversal to date, so the personnel actions were effected on a large scale."[59] Arao Okikatsu, one of Inada's staff officers, adds: "Customarily, it was not IJA policy to replace officers for one mistake; IGHQ did not believe that it was in a position to sack officers in general. In the case of Nomonhan, personnel actions were taken at the highest level. Assisted by the personnel affairs staff, the AGS chief and the war minister and the inspector general conferred, and their recommendations were then submitted to the Emperor for sanction. But during the Pacific War, selective personnel changes were easy to make, and simple mistakes led to the replacement of individual officers."[60] To take two instances of such "punishment" in the Second World War, General Honma Masaharu was forced to retire after the Philippines campaign of 1942, and Fifteenth Army commander Mutaguchi Renya sacked all three of his division commanders in the midst of the Kohima-Imphal offensive of 1944.[61]

THE SOVIET DIMENSION

In many ways, the military performance by the Russians at Nomonhan represented an inverse image of that by the Japanese. Indeed, a number of the Japanese denigrations of the qualities of the Soviet forces—often based on outmoded appraisals and partisan preconceptions—might have been better applied to the Japanese army itself. Various insights into the Soviet approach to warfare emerge from our examination of the fighting at Nomonhan.

First, the Russians thought in terms of massive joint operations involving maneuver and teamwork by armor, infantry, artillery, and aviation, and they devised interlocking defensive belts in depth. Second, the central emphasis in Soviet operations was on firepower, whether tracked, wheeled, or airborne. This was particularly evident in artillery, which dwarfed IJA capabilities in quantity, range, and ammunition expenditure. At the front in August 1939, a Japanese correspondent saw a mere five or six IJA field artillery shots draw a tremendous counterbarrage of "drumcan" projectiles. Even a solitary Japanese soldier in the open would attract aimed Soviet artillery fire. IJA observers reported that Russian batteries often fired more rounds (120) per minute than the Japanese artillery could afford to expend in a week; one Soviet shell hit each square meter of the IJA defenses, on average.[62] Third, possessing ample firepower, the Russians greatly preferred it to the bayonet. Lacking firepower, the Japanese extolled cold steel. The difference in approach, argued the Japanese, stemmed also from alleged low Soviet morale. Some IJA soldiers at Nomonhan went so far as to gibe that the enemy had "a despicable urge to live!"[63] Fourth, at Nomonhan the Japanese lacked certain high-performance weaponry that the Russians possessed in quantity: sniper rifles with excellent optical sights; standardized, interchangeable small-arms ammunition; hand-held automatic weapons; and amphibious and flame-throwing tanks. Fifth, Soviet mobility and logistical capabilities dazzled the Japanese. From their railheads in Siberia, the Russians employed huge numbers of trucks, trailers, and tankers to convoy forward troops, fuel, weapons, supplies, and the stocks of ammunition necessary to maintain the fast tempo of their bombardments.

The experience at Nomonhan also sheds light on larger questions of high-level Soviet policy and behavior, for it is clear that Russian strategic operations were centrally planned and systematically applied at the national level. Vested in early June 1939 with almost carte blanche authorization for his ground and air buildup, Zhukov and his staff took about two and a half months to prepare the great offensive against the Japanese. The Kremlin's balancing of strategic priorities and correlation between diplomatic and military objectives on the widely separated Polish and Mongolian frontiers were deftly and quietly orchestrated, with close attention to the dictates of time as viewed from Moscow.

In the Far East until 1939, the Russians were willing to rely on client forces—the MPRA—to patrol the Mongolian borders as long as the pressure by Manchukuoan units was light and the Kwantung Army itself was not unbearably aggressive. But as soon as large-scale IJA regular forces (the Azuma and then the Yamagata detachments) made their appearance near the disputed Halha frontier, the Soviets did not hesitate to commit their "varsity team" stationed in Outer Mongolia since 1936. As the experience of Nomonhan foretold, when proxy armies cannot or will not conduct the security missions allocated to them by the USSR, the Russians themselves will intervene swiftly and powerfully—as we have seen in the postwar cases of Czechoslovakia, East Germany, Hungary, and most recently Afghanistan. Some Japanese observers discern as great a psychological as a military basis for these Soviet actions since Nomonhan—"a father's demonstration of his power to his offspring," to impress them and to keep them in line.[64]

With respect to state boundaries, the Russians of 1939 were as sensitive to the sanctity of the MPR frontier as the Russians of 1969 were to the inviolability of their Ussuri River border with the People's Republic of China in the Damansky (Chen Pao) clashes, or the Russians of 1983 were to the incursion into their airspace over Kamchatka by a Korean Air Lines passenger jet. In each case, the Soviets responded directly with sharp force to what they undoubtedly deemed to be provocations, probes, or insults.

Though willing to test an adversary's capabilities and alertness, the Soviets have shown a capacity to limit hostilities in confrontations of low intensity. For example, Russian planes hit a few targets across the North Korean border in 1938 and across the Manchukuoan frontier in 1939, but they did not retaliate against Seoul, Hsinking, Hailar, or Harbin when IJA bombers struck no farther than the Tamsag air-base complex inside Outer Mongolia on several occasions in the summer of 1939. This restraint foreshadowed the tacit rules of limited war during the Korean conflict (1950-53). In return for the U.S. Air Force's operating only against North Korea and "staying well clear of the frontiers of Manchuria and the Soviet Union," the Russians (and the Chinese Communists, whose air force they equipped) obeyed an "unspoken agreement that kept [the Americans'] South Korean and Japanese bases inviolate and . . . limited the war to the Korean peninsula."[65] Mention should also be made of the fact that, although Japanese ground forces briefly invaded the MPR at the beginning of July 1939, the Russians voluntarily stopped their own mighty offensive of August as soon as they had cleared the territory claimed by Outer Mongolia east of the Halha River. Around 13 September, Japanese troops at Chiangchunmiao, observing Soviet armor on the prowl not far away, were astonished that the tanks did not bother to come closer to the IJA lines.[66] Such self-restraint on the part of the Russians suggests that they interpret limited war to mean limited objectives.

CAVEATS AND LAST LESSONS

In all fairness, several points should be made in defense of the outlook of the Japanese army during and after the fighting at Nomonhan. First, IJA leadership was not ignorant of the need for more advanced preparation for modern war. Second, similar thinking was not unknown in other armies at the time. Third, the state of the military art was still obscure when the Second World War broke out in September 1939. Fourth, a universal continuity in doctrinal concepts and psychology exists to this day.

The Japanese army was not addicted to the mystique of the saber because it resented the advent of modern firepower, mechanization, and aviation. A have-not and outnumbered island country simply could not afford a national military establishment with assets distributed equally among competing land, sea, and air forces in support of an overextended imperial policy. As early as the 1920's, War Minister Ugaki had already struggled to invest the savings from retrenchment in a better-equipped army. Stimulated by the painful experience of 1939, the IJA study groups set up after Nomonhan recognized the importance of firepower, mobility, and matériel and the need to improve transport, signal, water-purification, and medical capabilities. But so far as combat was concerned, there seemed to be no practical way to bridge the quantitative and technological gap imposed by first-class adversaries such as the Soviet Union (a grudging admission), except by exploiting Japan's "cheapest" available commodity: men. A bright war ministry section chief, Iwakuro Hideo, told a conference on 4 October 1939 that he certainly would like the army to have "invincible" new armaments but that the facts precluded achieving parity: "Although we can fabricate equipment that resembles that of the Russians, we cannot be expected to exceed a capacity of 80 percent or so. The only method of making up for the missing 20 percent is to draw upon spiritual strength." By this, Iwakuro meant such expedients as night assaults, the martial arts of hand-to-hand fighting, and raider tactics. Hayashi Saburō explains that the idea was to "avoid cross-grip wrestling insofar as possible, because that kind of wrestling takes time and, meanwhile, the Soviets could gradually evince their latent power."[67] As Gomikawa says, "It was a logical inevitability for the Japanese, whose productive capacity was feeble and whose people were accustomed to treat life cheaply, to stake everything on infantry charges." The trouble was that the army itself was not faithful to the lessons it had learned at Nomonhan, with the result that the dictum of charging "reached the level of fanaticism," despite the fact that "being brave as a tiger had lost its meaning."[68]

Nor should it be forgotten that in 1939, when the whole "northern problem" had to be rethought, Japan was in the midst of a protracted war with China and deteriorating relations with the United States and the British Commonwealth. Almost surrounded by actual or potential enemies, the Japanese army gravitated toward what would today be called the "Israeli syndrome," built upon self-confidence, tight discipline, superb morale and training, and an ardent sense of mission, and envisaging preemptive strikes, lightning operations, and a search for quick decisions. In the case of the Japanese, however, there was a concomitant tendency to underestimate the enemy and to stress his flaws, while overestimating one's own attributes ("self-hypnosis," Gomikawa called it) and suppressing all doubts of victory. Long and irrelevant experience in China adversely affected the evolution of IJA ground and air combat doctrine and the development of state-of-the-art ordnance and equipment.

Our second point deals with certain similarities in thinking among foreign armies. The French military, Sanche de Gramont reminds us, has long been "suspicious of ideas and attached to axiomatic principles" such as the *arme blanche* (cold steel) as the perfect French weapon, "ideal for the ardent but quickly spent French temperament."

> Contempt for new weaponry [asserts de Gramont] reached astounding proportions in the years before World War II. . . . It was as if refusal to recognize the merit of new weapons might stop technology from advancing. It was the ostrich reflex, so disastrous in 1940. "Forget about armored divisions," said a member of the general staff in 1938. "There are only two bridges in France that can support the weight of an armored division." General Weygand . . . had a similar contempt for aviation: "To obtain victory one must control the terrain, and planes cannot control the terrain." [69]

Undercut by an industrial and technological base inferior to that of either the French or the Japanese, the Polish army hurled mounted lancers against German mechanized formations in September 1939.

As for confusion in the late 1930's regarding the shape of modern war, examples will be found in the history of the Royal Air Force. When the British war minister told the chiefs of staff in 1937 that the Spanish Civil War suggested the usefulness of close air support, the chief of air staff retorted that "this was a gross misuse of air power." As Williamson Murray has pointed out, "The Royal Air Force absolutely rejected close air support for the army as one of its missions. After a 1939 combined air force–army exercise, General Wavell commented that the RAF had given no thought to support for ground operations, and as a result its pilots were incapable of performing that mission." As late as May 1940, the air staff officers were trying to terminate the production of the splendid Spitfire and Hurricane fighters in favor of two-seater aircraft. [70] Across the Channel in 1940, the British 1st Armored Division's plea for close air support was met by "objections that such suggestions were impracticable and unnecessary." [71]

Our fourth point addresses the continuity in doctrinal concepts and psychology. The Japanese exaltation of spiritual factors is echoed by British, American, Chinese Communist, and North Vietnamese authorities. "In military operations, as in other things," wrote Brigadier Spears, "intangible thought will have more substance than material subjects. Mind is the reality, steel and machinery the shadows."[72] According to Eisenhower, the biggest and most powerful weapon in the world was not the atom bomb or even the fighting capability of men; it was "moral and spiritual strength." Leaders of the Chinese People's Republic would agree. Men, not atomic weapons, are the decisive factor in war, a high official asserted publicly in Peking; "it is utterly wrong to exaggerate one-sidedly the role of technology." Added one veteran Chinese military pilot: "Enemy airmen, though cunning and stubborn, are afraid of death. This is their weak point. . . . Bravery constitutes our absolute supremacy over the foe. With this spiritual atom bomb we can defeat all enemies. Our magic weapon is close-range fighting—i.e., bayonet fighting in the air."[73] The philosophy underlying the Japanese army's predilection for cold steel and close-quarter fighting finds latter-day expression in the remarks of a battle-tested North Vietnamese army captain: "We taught our troops to grab the U.S. soldiers by the belt. At a distance, the enemy had superior firepower."[74]

A number of the problems that faced the Japanese army in 1939 are not unknown to the U.S. armed forces today. In the U.S. army's up-to-date "capstone" field manual on operations, a succinct introductory paragraph (titled "Austerity") warns that the military "must expect to fight its battles at the end of a long, expensive, vulnerable line of communications. Forward deployed forces, and those reinforcements immediately available, must therefore be prepared to accomplish their missions largely with the resources on hand. They must anticipate combat against forces with ultra modern supply sources. Winning will rest predominantly with commanders of engaged forces. *The U.S. Army must prepare its units to fight outnumbered, and to win.*" The introduction concludes with the assertion that "*confidence is the cornerstone of success in battle.*" In other words, conviction in victory consists of "each soldier's belief in his own competence, his trust in that of other members of his unit, and their collective pride, cohesion, and effectiveness."[75]

During "Operation Eagle Claw," the abortive U.S. effort in April 1980 to rescue the hostages trapped in Iran, American military practitioners made mistakes not unlike those committed by the Japanese at Nomonhan. According to a report prepared for the Senate Armed Services Committee, contingency planning and intelligence were poor, training and maintenance were inadequate, and command responsibility was fragmented. The following conclusion was drawn four months later by a House Appropriations Defense Subcommittee panelist who had interviewed the commanders of the raid: "They're all over there in the Pentagon writing up reports about the lessons learned . . . but it's not yet clear to me whether they learned any."[76] After another local American military disaster—the demolition by terrorists of a U.S. Marine Corps installation in Lebanon in October 1983 with great loss of life—an ad hoc investigating commission found that the attackers' capability to destroy the American headquarters "exceeded the imagination" of Marine commanders in Beirut.[77] We applied much the same castigation to myopic operations staff officers at Kwantung Army headquarters, especially with regard to their failure to comprehend the scale of Zhukov's offensive of August 1939.

The preceding discussion has suggested the persistence of human and subjective elements in warfare despite the latest applications of science and technology to weapons systems. With particular reference to the Japanese, one wonders about the possible survival of the notion of the old "alpha factor"—the invocation of military spirit to compensate for material deficiencies. Certainly the outlook on national defense, more than forty years after the Nomonhan war, has undergone a radical transformation. Japan's practical capacity has receded to that of a minor military power stressing self-defense and mere resistance to invasion, since the current constitution renounces the nation's rights of war and of belligerency. Therefore the question of the relevance of intangible factors as a military determinant for today's Japan has come to be posed from a new angle. Inoki Masamichi, former head of the National Defense Academy, recently spoke directly to this issue: "Some observers insist that no matter how modern Japan's weapons may be, they are useless unless morale and discipline are improved. This is nonsense. It is useless to try to heighten morale by giving soldiers obsolete weapons. If they are given first-class conventional weapons, the problem of morale will solve itself, and the problem of recruitment will also be greatly relieved."[78] The IJA infantry of Nomonhan can undoubtedly be seen nodding in agreement with Inoki—the gaunt men who faced Soviet tanks, armored cars, flamethrowers, long-range artillery, and planes with little more than their ancient bolt-action rifles, satchel charges, and hastily improvised gasoline bombs.

Reference Matter

Appendix A

Japanese Cabinets
(June 1901 – Aug. 1945)

Cabinet	Prime Minister	Foreign Minister	War Minister
1st Katsura June 1901	Katsura Tarō	Sone Arasuke Komura Jutarō (Sept. 1901) Katsura Tarō (July 1905)	Kodama Gentarō Terauchi Masatake (Masaki) (March 1902)
1st Saionji Jan. 1906	Saionji Kinmochi	Katō Takaaki (Kōmei) Saionji Kinmochi (March 1906) Hayashi Tadasu (May 1906) Saionji Kinmochi (Aug. 1906)	Terauchi Masatake
2nd Katsura July 1908	Katsura Tarō	Terauchi Masatake Komura Jutarō (Aug. 1908)	Terauchi Masatake
2nd Saionji Aug. 1911	Saionji Kinmochi	Hayashi Tadasu Uchida Yasuya (Oct. 1911)	Ishimoto Shinroku Uehara Yūsaku (April 1912)
3rd Katsura Dec. 1912	Katsura Tarō	Katsura Tarō Katō Takaaki (Jan. 1913)	Kigoshi Yasutsuna
1st Yamamoto Feb. 1913	Yamamoto Gonnohyōe (Gonbei)	Makino Nobuaki (Shinken)	Kigoshi Yasutsuna Kusunose Sachihiko (June 1913)
2nd Ōkuma April 1914	Ōkuma Shigenobu	Katō Takaaki Ōkuma Shigenobu (Aug. 1915) Ishii Kikujirō (Oct. 1915)	Oka Ichinosuke Ōshima Ken'ichi (March 1916)
Terauchi Oct. 1916	Terauchi Masatake	Terauchi Masatake Motono Ichirō (Nov. 1916) Gotō Shinpei (April 1918)	Ōshima Ken'ichi
Hara Sept. 1918	Hara Takashi (Kei) Uchida Yasuya (Nov. 1921)	Uchida Yasuya	Tanaka Giichi Yamanashi Hanzō (June 1921)
Takahashi Nov. 1921	Takahashi Korekiyo	Uchida Yasuya	Yamanashi Hanzō
Katō (Tomo) June 1922	Katō Tomosaburō (Yūzaburō) Uchida Yasuya (Aug. 1923)	Uchida Yasuya	Yamanashi Hanzō

Cabinet	Prime Minister	Foreign Minister	War Minister
2nd Yamamoto Sept. 1923	Yamamoto Gonnohyōe	Yamamoto Gonnohyōe Ijūin Hikokichi (Sept. 1923)	Tanaka Giichi
Kiyoura Jan. 1924	Kiyoura Keigo	Matsui Keishirō	Ugaki Kazunari (Kazushige)
Katō (Taka) June 1924	Katō Takaaki Wakatsuki Reijirō (Jan. 1926)	Shidehara Kijūrō	Ugaki Kazunari
1st Wakatsuki Jan. 1926	Wakatsuki Reijirō	Shidehara Kijūrō	Ugaki Kazunari
Tanaka April 1927	Tanaka Giichi	Tanaka Giichi	Shirakawa Yoshinori
Hamaguchi July 1929	Hamaguchi Osachi (Yūkō) Shidehara Kijūrō (Nov. 1930) Hamaguchi Osachi (March 1931)	Shidehara Kijūrō	Ugaki Kazunari Abe Nobuyuki (June 1930) Ugaki Kazunari (Dec. 1930)
2nd Wakatsuki April 1931	Wakatsuki Reijirō	Shidehara Kijūrō	Minami Jirō
Inukai Dec. 1931	Inukai Tsuyoshi (Ki) Takahashi Korekiyo (May 1932)	Inukai Tsuyoshi Yoshizawa Kenkichi (Jan. 1932)	Araki Sadao
Saitō May 1932	Saitō Makoto	Saitō Makoto Uchida Yasuya (July 1932) Hirota Kōki (Sept. 1933)	Araki Sadao Hayashi Senjūrō (Jan. 1934)
Okada July 1934	Okada Keisuke Gotō Fumio Feb. 1936	Hirota Kōki	Hayashi Senjūrō Kawashima Yoshiyuki (Sept. 1935)
Hirota March 1936	Hirota Kōki	Hirota Kōki Arita Hachirō (April 1936)	Terauchi Hisaichi
Hayashi Feb. 1937	Hayashi Senjūrō	Hayashi Senjūrō Satō Naotake (March 1937)	Nakamura Kōtarō Sugiyama Gen (Hajime) (Feb. 1937)
1st Konoe June 1937	Konoe Fumimaro	Hirota Kōki Ugaki Kazunari (May 1938) Konoe Fumimaro (Sept. 1938) Arita Hachirō (Oct. 1938)	Sugiyama Gen Itagaki Seishirō (June 1938)
Hiranuma Jan. 1939	Hiranuma Kiichirō	Arita Hachirō	Itagaki Seishirō
Abe Aug. 1939	Abe Nobuyuki	Abe Nobuyuki Nomura Kichisaburō (Sept. 1939)	Hata Shunroku

Cabinet	Prime Minister	Foreign Minister	War Minister
Yonai Jan. 1940	Yonai Mitsumasa	Arita Hachirō	Hata Shunroku
2nd Konoe July 1940	Konoe Fumimaro	Matsuoka Yōsuke Konoe Fumimaro (March 1941)	Tōjō Hideki
3rd Konoe July 1941	Konoe Fumimaro	Toyoda Teijirō	Tōjō Hideki
Tōjō Oct. 1941	Tōjō Hideki	Tōgō Shigenori Tōjō Hideki (Sept. 1942) Tani Masayuki (Sept. 1942) Shigemitsu Mamoru (April 1943)	Tōjō Hideki
Koiso July 1944	Koiso Kuniaki	Shigemitsu Mamoru	Sugiyama Gen
Suzuki April 1945	Suzuki Kantarō	Suzuki Kantarō Tōgō Shigenori (April 1945)	Anami Korechika

Appendix B

Structure of War Ministry, Army General Staff, and Inspectorate General of Military Training, 1939

		WAR MINISTRY	
War minister	Lt. Gen.	Itagaki Seishirō	
"	Gen.	Hata Shunroku	Assumed post Aug. 1939
Vice minister	Lt. Gen.	Yamawaki Masataka	
"	Lt. Gen.	Anami Korechika	Assumed post 14 Oct. 1939
Military Affairs Bureau			
Chief	Lt. Gen.	Machijiri Kazumoto	
"	Lt. Gen.	Mutō Akira	Assumed post 30 Sept. 1939
Army Affairs Section	Col.	Iwakuro Hideo	
Military Affairs Section	Col.	Arisue Seizō	
"	Col.	Kawamura Saburō	Assumed post 1 Dec. 1939
Military Administration Section	Col.	Nakamura Aketo	

Personnel Bureau

Chief	Maj. Gen.	Iinuma Mamoru	
"	Maj. Gen.	Noda Kengo	Assumed post Oct. 1939
Appointment & Assignment Section	Col.	Nukada Hiroshi	

ARMY GENERAL STAFF

Chief of staff	Gen.	Prince Kan'in Kotohito	
Deputy chief of staff	Lt. Gen.	Nakajima Tetsuzō	
"	Lt. Gen.	Sawada Shigeru	Assumed post 2 Oct. 1939

General Affairs Bureau

Chief	Maj. Gen.	Kasahara Yukio	
"	Maj. Gen.	Kanda Masatane	Assumed post 2 Oct. 1939
General Affairs Section	Col.	Okada Jūichi	Became Operations Section chief
"	Col.	Nakagawa Tomeo	Assumed post 1 Dec. 1939
Organization & Mobilization Section	Col.	Nasu Yoshio	
Training Section	Col.	Arisue Yadoru	Became Kwantung Army staff officer
"	Col.	Koike Ryūji	Assumed post 7 Sept. 1939

1st Bureau

Chief	Maj. Gen.	Hashimoto Gun	
"	Maj. Gen.	Tominaga Kyōji	Assumed post 13 Sept. 1939
Operations Section	Col.	Inada Masazumi	
"	Col.	Okada Jūichi	Assumed post 12 Oct. 1939
Operations staff officer	Lt. Col.	Arao Okikatsu	
"	Maj.	Imoto Kumao	Transferred July 1939
"	Maj.	Imaizumi Kingo	
"	Maj.	Aoshima Ryōichi	
"	Capt.	Mizumachi Katsuki	
Air staff officer	Lt. Col.	Tanigawa Kazuo	
"	Maj.	Miyashi Minoru	Became Kwantung Army staff officer
"	Lt. Col.	Takei Seitarō	Promoted to Lt. Col. from Aug. 1939

2nd Bureau

Intelligence chief	Maj. Gen.	Higuchi Kiichirō	Promoted to Lt. Gen. from Aug. 1939, transferred Dec. 1939
"	Maj. Gen.	Tsuchihashi Yūitsu	Assumed post 1 Dec. 1939
Europe & America Section	Col.	Tatsumi Eiichi	
China Section	Col.	Imai Takeo	
"	Col.	Sonoda Seinosuke	Assumed post 18 Sept. 1939
Russia Section	Col.	Yamaoka Michitake	
Clandestine Section	Col.	Usui Shigeki	

3rd Bureau

Chief	Maj. Gen.	Watanabe Ubun	
Railway Section	Col.	Yamamoto Kiyoe	
Shipping Section	Col.	Suzuki Keiji	
Communication Section	Col.	Nakano Ryōji	

4th Bureau

Chief	Maj. Gen.	Tominaga Kyōji	Became 1st Bureau chief
Military History Section	Col.	Takashima Tatsuhiko	
Strategy & Tactics Section	Col.	Takashima Tatsuhiko	Concurrent post

INSPECTORATE GENERAL OF MILITARY TRAINING

Inspector general	Gen.	Nishio Juzō	Promoted to Gen. from Aug. 1939, transferred Sept. 1939
"	Lt. Gen.	Kawabe Shōzō	Acting IG 4 Sept.
"	Lt. Gen.	Yamada Otozō	Assumed post 14 Oct. 1939

Appendix C

Kwantung Army Command Structure, 1939

Commander	Gen.	Ueda Kenkichi	
"	Lt. Gen.	Umezu Yoshijirō	Assumed command Sept. 1939
Chief of staff	Lt. Gen.	Isogai Rensuke	
"	Lt. Gen.	Iimura Jō	Assumed post Sept. 1939
Deputy chief of staff	Maj. Gen.	Yano Otosaburō	
"	Maj. Gen.	Endō Saburō	Assumed post Sept. 1939
1st Section			
Operations chief	Col.	Terada Masao	
"	Col.	Arisue Yadoru	Assumed post Sept. 1939
Operations staff officer	Lt. Col.	Hattori Takushirō	
"	Lt. Col.	Nakayama Motoo	Assumed post Sept. 1939
"	Maj.	Tsuji Masanobu	
"	Maj.	Shimamura Noriyasu	Assumed post Sept. 1939
"	Maj.	Shimanuki Takeharu	Transferred Oct. 1939
Air staff officer	Lt. Col.	Miyoshi Yasuyuki	
"	Lt. Col.	Miyashi Minoru	Assumed post Aug. 1939
Defense staff officer	Lt. Col.	Kurasawa Kinzaburō	

Training staff officer	Lt. Col.	Nakayama Motoo	Became operations officer Sept. 1939
Organization & mobilization staff officer	Lt. Col.	Kaburagi Masataka	
"	Lt. Col.	Noguchi Kamenosuke	Attached to 1st Tank Corps June 1939
Special duty	Lt. Col.	Yamamoto Yoshirō	
Personnel subsection	Col.	Imai Hifumi	

2nd Section

Intelligence chief	Col.	Isomura Takesuke	
Intelligence staff officer	Lt. Col.	Katō Yoshihide	
"	Maj.	Ōgoshi Kenji	
"	Capt.	Ryūzaki Shōji	
Military geography	Lt. Col.	Suzuki Yasushi	

3rd Section

Logistics chief	Lt. Col.	Isoya Gorō	
Logistics staff officer	Maj.	Ashikawa Haruo	
"	Capt.	Hara Zenshirō	
Railways	Lt. Col.	Kawamura Benji	
Signal	Maj.	Takahashi Tsuruo	

4th Section

Manchukuo Affairs chief	Lt. Col.	Katakura Tadashi	
MA staff officer	Maj.	Yamada Naritoshi	
"	Maj.	Kojima Sumikatsu	
"	Maj.	Sugiyama Yasutaka	

Sixth Army

Commander	Lt. Gen.	Ogisu Ryūhei (Tatsuhei or Rippei)	Retired Jan. 1940
"	Lt. Gen.	Yasui Tōji	Assumed command 6 Nov. 1939
Chief of staff	Maj. Gen.	Fujimoto Tetsukuma	

Staff officers

Operations chief	Col.	Hamada Sueo	
Operations staff officer	Capt.	Hirai Hitoshi	
Intelligence	Lt. Col.	Tanaka Tetsujirō	
Logistics	Capt.	Iwakoshi Shinroku	

2nd Infantry Division

Commander	Lt. Gen.	Yasui Tōji	Became Sixth Army commander
"	Lt. Gen.	Yoshimoto Teiichi	Assumed command Nov. 1939
Chief of staff	Col.	Harada Jirō	

15th Infantry Brigade (Katayama Detachment)

Commander	Maj. Gen.	Katayama Shōtarō	
16th Inf. Regt.	Col.	Miyazaki Shigesaburō	
30th Inf. Regt.	Col.	Kashiwa Toku	

4th Infantry Division

Commander	Lt. Gen.	Sawada Shigeru	Became AGS deputy chief of staff Sept. 1939
"	Lt. Gen.	Yamashita Tomoyuki (Tomobumi or Hōbun)	Assumed command 23 Sept. 1939
Chief of staff	Lt. Col.	Sumi Kanshi	

7th Infantry Brigade (Koga Detachment)

Commander	Maj. Gen.	Koga Ken (Takeshi)
1st Inf. Regt.	Col.	Gotō Mitsuzō
8th Inf. Regt.	Col.	Kyō Ken'ichi

7th Infantry Division (see Appendix F)

23rd Infantry Division (see Appendix D)

3rd Independent Garrison Unit

Commander	Maj. Gen.	Miyazawa Saishirō

Appendix D

23rd Infantry Division Roster of Main Officers, Nomonhan, 1939

DIVISION HEADQUARTERS			
Commander	Lt. Gen.	Komatsubara Michitarō	Replaced 6 Nov. 1939; retired 15 Jan. 1940; died 6 Oct. 1940
"	Lt. Gen.	Inoue Masakichi	Assumed command 6 Nov. 1939
Chief of staff	Col.	Ōuchi Tsutomu	Killed 4 July 1939
"	Col.	Okamoto Tokuzō	Wounded 30 Aug. 1939; murdered in army hospital 1940
"	Col.	Kimura Matsujirō	Assumed post Sept. 1939
Attached officer	Maj.	Morinaga	Killed 30 Aug. 1939
Aide	Lt. Col.	Kamekawa Yoshio	
"	Capt.	Kuroda Yoshio	
"	1st. Lt.	Nishijima Shōhachi	
"	1st Lt.	Tanaka Naoichi	
Staff Officers			
Operations	Lt. Col.	Murata Masao	Wounded 27 Aug. 1939; returned from hospital Nov. 1939
"	Maj.	Ōgi Hiroshi	Assumed post Sept. 1939
Intelligence	Maj.	Suzuki Yoshiyasu	
Logistics	Capt.	Itō Noboru	Wounded 24 Aug. 1939
"	Maj.	Shishido Seijirō	Assumed post Sept. 1939

NOTE: The following abbreviations are used in this appendix: MG, machine gun; RF, rapid-fire (gun); P.O., Probationary Officer; W.O., Warrant Officer. Data on roster and casualties are sometimes incomplete, and given names were not always available. Ranks occasionally reflect promotion as of Aug. 1939.

Signal	Capt.	Utsui Keiji	
Medical	Col.	Murakami Tokuji	
"	Capt.	Amano Sakae	

INFANTRY GROUP HEADQUARTERS

Commander	Maj. Gen.	Kobayashi Kōichi	Wounded 24 Aug. 1939
"	Maj. Gen.	Satō Kōtoku	Assumed command Aug. 1939
Aide	Lt. Col.	Yonemoto Katsuo	Wounded 24 Aug. 1939
"	Capt.	Mori Toyohiko	
"	2nd Lt.	Murai Masakatsu	

64TH INFANTRY REGIMENT

Commander	Col.	Yamagata Takemitsu	Killed himself in battle 29 Aug. 1939
"	Col.	Ōnishi Koshirō	Assumed command 2 Sept. 1939
Attached officer	Lt. Col.	Takahata Yohei	Wounded 30 Aug. 1939
Aide	Maj.	Akai Toyosaburō	Promoted to Lt. Col., became 1st Bn. commander 21 July, acting Regt. commander 30 Aug. 1939
Color bearer	1st Lt.	Takujima Tsutomu	
"	2nd Lt.	Koyama Hidehisa	Killed 29 Aug. 1939
1st Battalion			
Commander	Maj.	Tazaka Yutaka	Killed 3 July 1939
"	Capt.	Sonoshita Zenzō	Acting bn. commander 5 July 1939, fell ill, evacuated
"	Capt.	Ōta Gunki	Acting bn. commander
"	Lt. Col.	Akai Toyosaburō	Assumed command 21 July 1939
1st Company	Capt.	Sonoshita Zenzō	Acting bn. commander
"	1st Lt.	Kira Tadao	Acting co. commander, killed 28 Aug. 1939
"	1st Lt.	Sasaki Terumasa	Acting co. commander, wounded 29 Aug. 1939
2nd Company	Capt.	Kawai Sadamu	Wounded 23 July, 26 Aug. 1939
3rd Company	Capt.	Ōta Gunki	Acting bn. commander
"	2nd Lt.	Nagai Hiroshi	Acting co. commander
"	1st Lt.	Masuda	Acting co. commander, killed 21 Aug. 1939
4th Company	1st Lt.	Someya Hatsuo	Wounded 23 July 1939
"	1st Lt.	Matsumura	Acting co. commander, killed 29 Aug. 1939
1st MG Company	Capt.	Funakura Eishirō	Wounded 13 July 1939
"	1st Lt.	Kōno Mamoru	Acting co. commander
"	Capt.	Funakura Eishirō	Returned from hospital 13 Aug., wounded 26 Aug. 1939
"	1st Lt.	Kōno Mamoru	Acting co. commander, killed 29 Aug. 1939
Bn. Gun Platoon	1st Lt.	Kōno Mamoru	Acting MG Co. commander
"	P.O.	Ikeda Tadashi	Acting platoon leader
RF Gun Battery (one platoon)	2nd Lt.	Oki Tadashi	Killed 11 July 1939
"	2nd Lt.	Kosokata Isao	Wounded 29 Aug. 1939
2nd Battalion			
Commander	Lt. Col.	Tokumaru Mitsuru	Wounded 6 July 1939
"	Maj.	Tsukui	
5th Company	1st Lt.	Itonaga Rin	

6th Company	Capt.	Mashō Kanematsu	
7th Company	1st Lt.	Mori Mineyuki	
8th Company	Capt.	Yamauchi Makitarō	
2nd MG Company	Capt.	Uchida Tadaaki	

3rd Battalion

Commander	Maj.	Fukumura Yasuhide	Wounded 9 July 1939
"	Capt.	Gotō Chikashi	Acting bn. commander
9th Company	1st Lt.	Nishimura Shinzō	
10th Company	Capt.	Gotō Chikashi	Acting bn. commander
"	1st Lt.	Kajima Yutaka	Acting co. commander
"	Capt.	Gotō Chikashi	Resumed post
11th Company	1st Lt.	Kawabata Genkichi	Killed
"	1st Lt.	Tomita Yoshimi	
12th Company	1st Lt.	Tashiro Masanao	Killed
"	1st Lt.	Kajima Yutaka	
3rd MG Company	Capt.	Yamaguchi Seiichi	
"	Capt.	Gotō Chikashi	
Bn. Gun Platoon	2nd Lt.	Nagasaka Saburō	Wounded 29 May 1939
RF Gun Battery	Capt.	Tachikawa Tsuneki	
RF Gun Platoon	2nd Lt.	Murakami Kenji	
Regt. Signal Unit	1st Lt.	Miyahara Ishizō	Wounded 29 May 1939

71ST INFANTRY REGIMENT

Commander	Col.	Okamoto Tokuzō	Became 23rd Div. chief of staff 7 July, wounded 30 Aug. 1939
"	Col.	Nagano Eiji	Assumed command 7 July, wounded 24 July 1939
"	Lt. Col.	Higashi Muneharu	Acting regt. commander 24 July 1939
"	Col.	Morita Tōru	Assumed command 9 Aug., killed 26 Aug. 1939
"	Lt. Col.	Higashi Muneharu	Acting regt. commander 27 Aug., killed 30 Aug. 1939
"	Col.	Shirahama Shigetada	Assumed command Sept. 1939
Attached officer	Lt. Col.	Higashi Muneharu	Acting regt. commander
"	Maj.	Yasuda Tsugio	Acting attached officer, killed 29 Aug. 1939
Aide	Maj.	Furukawa Akira	Killed 23 July 1939
"	Maj.	Hamada Bungo	Assumed post 23 July, wounded 24 July 1939
"	Capt.	Onozuka Kichihei	Acting aide 26 Aug. 1939
"	Capt.	Miki Toranosuke	Acting aide 28 Aug., wounded 29 Aug. 1939
"	1st Lt.	Takashina Hidemaru	Acting aide, 29 Aug., killed 30 Aug. 1939
Color bearer	1st Lt.	Kawazoe Takehiko	Became regt. aide 2 Aug. 1939
"	2nd Lt.	Yukiyoshi Tsutomu	Assumed post 2 Aug., killed 30 Aug. 1939

1st Battalion

Commander	Maj.	Fujita Kanya	Killed 3 July 1939
"	1st Lt.	Hayashi Kazuyoshi	Acting bn. commander 3 July 1939
"	Maj.	Sugitachi Kamenojō	Assumed command July, killed 28 Aug. 1939
"	Capt.	Hanada Shunji	Acting bn. commander 29 Aug. 1939

1st Company	1st Lt.	Hayashi Kazuyoshi	Acting bn. commander
"	W.O.	Senzoe Yoshimitsu	Acting co. commander 24 July 1939
"	2nd Lt.	Fukuda Michio	Acting co. commander 30 July, wounded 24 Aug. 1939
"	P.O.	Nakamura Tadashi	Acting co. commander 25 Aug., killed 28 Aug. 1939
"	Master Sgt.	Kibune Hisao	Acting co. commander, killed 31 Aug. 1939
2nd Company	1st Lt.	Kunimori Tadayoshi	Wounded 24 July 1939
"	2nd Lt.	Fukunaga Kunio	Acting co. commander
"	1st Lt.	Kunimori Tadayoshi	Resumed post 13 Aug. 1939
3rd Company	1st Lt.	Hanada Shunji	Promoted to Capt., acting bn. commander
"	P.O.	Tochimoto Nakae	Acting co. commander, killed 30 Aug. 1939
4th Company	1st Lt.	Takahashi Masami	Wounded 20 Aug. 1939
"	2nd Lt.	Kanbayashi Shōji	Acting co. commander 20 Aug., killed 23 Aug. 1939
"	Master Sgt.	Maeda Takesaburō	Acting co. commander 23 Aug., killed 30 Aug. 1939
1st MG Company	1st. Lt.	Komoto Iwao	Wounded 24 July 1939
"	2nd Lt.	Tategami Kan'ichi	Acting co. commander 24 July, wounded 31 Aug. 1939
Bn. Gun Platoon	1st Lt.	Yoshizu Fumio	Wounded 1 Aug. 1939
"	PFC	Maeda Hisashi	Acting platoon leader
"	P.O.	Kida Mitsuji	Acting platoon leader 2 Aug., killed 30 Aug. 1939
RF Gun Battery	Capt.	Haruta Ichirō	Killed 23 July 1939
"	W.O.	Maeda Gunshirō	Acting battery commander 23 July
"	1st Lt.	Ogawa Hiroshi	Acting battery commander, wounded 26 July 1939
"	2nd Lt.	Kimura Yoshio	Acting battery commander 1 Aug.
"	Master Sgt.	Hayashi Yutaka	Acting battery commander, killed 25 Aug. 1939
2nd Battalion Commander	Maj.	Baba Susumu	Wounded 28 July 1939
"	Capt.	Nishimura Taizō	Acting bn. commander 28 July 1939
"	Maj.	Tōi Shinji	Assumed command 6 Aug., wounded 30 Aug. 1939
5th Company	Capt.	Nishimura Taizō	Acting bn. commander
"	2nd Lt.	Yonei Kōichi	Acting co. commander 28 July 1939
"	Capt.	Nishimura Taizō	Returned to command 6 Aug. 1939
"	2nd Lt.	Yonei Kōichi	Acting co. commander, wounded 23 Aug. 1939
"	P.O.	Ōnuki Kichirō	Acting co. commander 23 Aug., killed 27 Aug. 1939
"	Capt.	Nishimura Taizō	Returned from Hailar 27 Aug., killed 31 Aug. 1939
6th Company	1st Lt.	Kan Yuzuru	Wounded
"	2nd Lt.	Hironaka Tadao	Acting co. commander, killed 27 July 1939

"	P.O.	Yasui Tadashi	Acting co. commander 3 Aug. 1939
"	1st Lt.	Kan Yuzuru	Returned from hospital 16 Aug., wounded 30 Aug. 1939
7th Company	1st Lt.	Imada Tsuneyoshi	Killed 24 July 1939
"	2nd Lt.	Tamaki Yukio	Acting co. commander 24 July, wounded 26 July 1939
"	P.O.	Yoshida Takashi	Acting co. commander 13 Aug. 1939
"	2nd Lt.	Natsukawa Shōgo	Acting co. commander 14 Aug., killed 26 Aug. 1939
"	P.O.	Miyayama Heihachirō	Acting co. commander 26 Aug., wounded 29 Aug. 1939
"	Sgt.	Matsumoto Fujishige	Acting co. commander
8th Company	1st Lt.	Nobeno Jiichi	
"	2nd Lt.	Tsuiki Hideo	Acting co. commander, killed 24 July 1939
"	2nd Lt.	Ueno Kōji	Acting co. commander 24 July, killed 27 July 1939
"	P.O.	Yuguchi Yasuhiro	Acting co. commander 2-14 Aug., wounded 30 Aug. 1939
"	2nd Lt.	Fujiwara Masayoshi	Acting co. commander 14 Aug., wounded 27 Aug. 1939
2nd MG Company	Capt.	Takada Kiyomi	Wounded
"	W.O.	Moriyama Tadayoshi	Acting co. commander
Bn. Gun Platoon	2nd Lt.	Nishitani Satoru	Fell ill 24 July 1939
"	Sgt.	Kaneko Hisao	Acting platoon leader 24 July 1939
"	P.O.	Kakohara Takashi	Acting platoon leader 2 Aug. 1939
3rd Battalion Commander	Maj.	Murata Mosuke	Killed 24 July 1939
"	Capt.	Onozuka Kichihei	Acting bn. commander 24 July 1939
"	Maj.	Izui Tsuyoshi	Assumed command 12 Aug., killed 23 Aug. 1939
"	Capt.	Miki Toranosuke	Acting bn. commander 23 Aug., killed 31 Aug. 1939
9th Company	Capt.	Onozuka Kichihei	Acting bn. commander
"	2nd Lt.	Fukunaga Susumu	Acting co. commander
"	P.O.	Agawa Kazutomo	Acting co. commander 1-11 Aug., killed 23 Aug. 1939
"	2nd Lt.	Hotta Naoyoshi	Acting co. commander 12 Aug., killed 23 Aug. 1939
"	P.O.	Nagai Tamaki	Acting co. commander 24 Aug., killed 25 Aug. 1939
"	Corp.	Tachibana Chikao	Acting co. commander
10th Company	1st Lt.	Fujita Hikoji	
"	1st Lt.	Hatanaka Sanjirō	
"	2nd Lt.	Sugiyama Gorō	Acting co. commander, wounded 24 July 1939
"	W.O.	Fukumoto Chikayoshi	Acting co. commander 24 July 1939
"	Master Sgt.	Takagi Tadashi	Acting co. commander, wounded 15 Aug. 1939
"	P.O.	Fujioka Yoshiichi	Acting co. commander 15 Aug., killed 22 Aug. 1939
"	2nd Lt.	Niwa Akira	Acting co. commander

11th Company	Capt.	Miki Toranosuke	Wounded 14 July 1939
"	2nd Lt.	Shimada Hatsuo	Acting co. commander 14 July, wounded 24 July 1939
"	Sgt.	Nakahara Shinzō	Acting co. commander 24 July 1939
"	P.O.	Nakayasu Masanori	Acting co. commander
"	2nd Lt.	Nakayasu Tatsugorō	Acting co. commander 14 Aug., wounded 22 Aug. 1939
"	P.O.	Nakayasu Masanori	Acting co. commander 22 Aug., killed 23 Aug. 1939
"	P.O.	Uenaka Naoichi	Acting co. commander 23 Aug., wounded 24 Aug. 1939
"	Master Sgt.	Uenaka Nobuyoshi	Acting co. commander 24 Aug., killed 25 Aug. 1939
"	Sgt.	Nakahara Shinzō	Acting co. commander 25 Aug. 1939
12th Company	1st Lt.	Kimura Takeshi	Killed 27 July 1939
"	W.O.	Furuta Yoshisuke	Acting co. commander 27 July 1939
"	2nd Lt.	Sakano Masayoshi	Acting co. commander 31 July, wounded 23 Aug. 1939
"	P.O.	Koga Masanori	Acting co. commander
"	1st Lt.	Shimada Hatsuo	Promoted to 1st Lt., returned from hospital, assumed command 29 Aug., killed 30 Aug. 1939
3rd MG Company	1st Lt.	Iwato Noboru	Killed 24 July 1939
"	2nd Lt.	Sakai Shigenobu	Acting co. commander 24 July, wounded 28 July 1939
"	2nd Lt.	Kimura Nobumasa	Acting co. commander 4 Aug., killed 23 Aug. 1939
"	Sgt.	Nakajima Shichirō	Acting co. commander 23 Aug., killed 30 Aug. 1939
Bn. Gun Platoon	2nd Lt.	Hanabusa Fukujirō	Killed 23 July 1939
"	Sgt.	Murafuji Takeo	Acting platoon leader 23 July 1939
"	P.O.	Kashitani Kōichi	Acting platoon leader 4 Aug. 1939
"	2nd Lt.	Hashimoto Kiheiji	Assumed command 13 Aug. 1939
Regt. Signal Unit	1st Lt.	Ueda Tadanori	Wounded 28 July 1939
"	2nd Lt.	Ishii Kanji	Acting unit commander 29 July, killed 30 Aug. 1939

72ND INFANTRY REGIMENT

Commander	Col.	Sakai Mikio	Wounded 24 Aug. 1939
"	Capt.	Hirowatari Kunimori	Acting regt. commander 24 Aug.
"	Col.	Nakao Koroku	Assumed command Sept. 1939
Attached officer	Lt. Col.	Noguchi Shizuo	Wounded 24 Aug. 1939
Aide	Maj.	Hamada Toshio	Transferred to 8th BGU 1 Aug. 1939
"	Maj.	Kunimoto Kyūrō	Assumed post, promoted to Lt. Col. from Aug., killed 24 Aug. 1939
Color bearer	2nd Lt.	Hirakawa Shin	Killed 24 Aug. 1939
1st Battalion			
Commander	Maj.	Nishikawa Masayuki	Promoted to Lt. Col. from Aug., wounded 24 Aug. 1939
"	1st Lt.	Nakao Sukeo	Acting bn. commander 24 Aug., killed 30 Aug. 1939

1st Company	1st Lt.	Nakao Sukeo	Acting bn. commander
"	2nd Lt.	Nemoto Hōju	Acting co. commander 24 Aug.
2nd Company	1st Lt.	Kazuki Norihisa	Killed 7 July 1939
"	1st Lt.	Morimoto Takeshi	Acting co. commander, became 8th Co. commander 29 July 1939
"	2nd Lt.	Kadota Tatsuo	Acting co. commander 29 July, killed 24 Aug. 1939
"	2nd Lt.	Ryūzu Noboru	Acting co. commander 24 Aug., killed 30 Aug. 1939
3rd Company	1st Lt.	Honda Takaharu	Promoted to Capt. from Aug.
"	1st Lt.	Kida Sanyō	Acting co. commander, wounded 24 Aug. 1939
"	Capt.	Honda Takaharu	Returned to post 30 July, wounded 24 Aug. 1939
4th Company	1st Lt.	Saitō Kyū	Killed 2 July 1939
"	2nd Lt.	Ryūzu Noboru	Acting co. commander, became acting 2nd Co. commander 24 Aug. 1939
1st MG Company	2nd Lt.	Hatano Rihachi	Acting commander, killed 24 Aug. 1939
"	Capt.	Tajiri Shigeyoshi	Resumed post 14 July, killed 24 Aug. 1939
"	W.O.	Yoshizumi Kotoku	Acting co. commander
Bn. Gun Platoon	1st Lt.	Yamashita Kiyoshi	Wounded 29 Aug. 1939
2nd Battalion			
Commander	Maj.	Kokura Keiji	Wounded 24 Aug. 1939
"	2nd Lt.	Abe Masamori	Acting co. commander 24 Aug., killed 30 Aug. 1939
5th Company	1st Lt.	Harada Tasuku	Became color guard officer
6th Company	1st Lt.	Shibao Atsushi	Killed 7 July 1939
"	1st Lt.	Yoshitsugu Seiichirō	Wounded 22 July 1939
"	2nd Lt.	Abe Masamori	Acting co. commander, acting bn. commander
"	2nd Lt.	Hiratsuka Matsunosuke	Acting co. commander
7th Company	1st Lt.	Moriyama Yasoichi	Promoted to Capt. in Aug., wounded 7 Aug. 1939
"	2nd Lt.	Soeda Yoshimi	Acting co. commander, killed 24 Aug. 1939
"	2nd Lt.	Matobe Kaoru	Acting co. commander
8th Company	1st Lt.	Ōtake Sakae	Wounded 23 July 1939
"	2nd Lt.	Morimoto Takeshi	Wounded 24 Aug. 1939
2nd MG Company	1st Lt.	Okamoto Kyūichi	Wounded 27 July 1939
"	2nd Lt.	Furukawa Masaru	Acting co. commander, wounded 7 Aug. 1939
"	1st Lt.	Kawamura Morinosuke	Killed 24 Aug. 1939
Bn. Gun Platoon	2nd Lt.	Mizoguchi Chikara	Killed 7 July 1939
"	2nd Lt.	Karube Masayuki	Killed 24 Aug. 1939
Regt. Gun Battery	1st Lt.	Noda Shōgo	Killed 24 Aug. 1939
"	2nd Lt.	Nasu Terunori	Acting battery commander, killed 30 Aug. 1939
RF Gun Battery	1st Lt.	Komiya Ryūichi	Wounded 6 July 1939
"	2nd Lt.	Ono Akira	Arrived 13 Aug. 1939

Regt. Signal Unit	1st Lt.	Matsui Shigezō	Killed 7 July 1939
"	2nd Lt.	Furukawa Yoshinori	Acting unit commander, wounded 24 Aug. 1939
"	W.O.	Kawahara Yoshizō	Acting unit commander

23RD RECON. UNIT			
Commander	Lt. Col.	Azuma Yaozō	Killed 29 May 1939
"	Lt. Col.	Ioki Eiichi	Killed himself 17 Sept. 1939
"	Lt. Col.	Takahashi Kōsuke	Assumed command Sept. 1939
Attached officer	Maj.	Okamoto Kōichi	
Aide	Capt.	Kanetake Morishige	
1st Company (horse)	Capt.	Aoyama Takashi	Killed 28 May 1939
"	Capt.	Ishikawa Yasoji	
2nd Company (motorized)	Capt.	Kōno Iwao	Killed 28 May 1939
"	1st Lt.	Ishibashi Tatsuo	

13TH FIELD ARTILLERY REGIMENT			
Commander	Col.	Ise Takahide	Killed himself 29 Aug. 1939
"	Lt. Col.	Chikamatsu Sanjirō	Acting regt. commander
"	Col.	Yoshitomi Tokuzō	Assumed command Sept. 1939
Attached officer	Lt. Col.	Chikamatsu Sanjirō	Acting regt. commander
Aide	1st Lt.	Ishibashi Kumazō	
1st Battalion			
Commander	Maj.	Matsutomo Hideo	
1st Battery	1st Lt.	Fujii Michinori	
2nd Battery	1st Lt.	Tamura Toshiji	
3rd Battery	Capt.	Ōgami Shinzō	
2nd Battalion			
Commander	Maj.	Morikawa Nobuo	Killed 29 Aug. 1939
4th Battery	1st Lt.	Hori Tagane	Killed 22 Aug. 1939
"	1st Lt.	Mori Tetsurō	Acting battery commander
5th Battery	1st Lt.	Tokonami Shigeji	Wounded 26 Aug. 1939
6th Battery	1st Lt.	Kusaba Hiroshi	Killed 29 Aug. 1939
3rd Battalion			
Commander	Maj.	Seki Takeshi	Wounded 29 Aug. 1939
7th Battery	Capt.	Kusaba Sakae	Wounded 28 Aug. 1939
8th Battery	Capt.	Imoto Kazuichi	
9th Battery	Capt.	Kai Mannosuke	Killed 23 July 1939
"	1st Lt.	Yoshioka Hisao	Acting battery commander, killed 28 Aug. 1939
12th Battery (22-26 Aug.)	1st Lt.	Egami Seitarō	

23RD SIGNAL UNIT			
Commander	Maj.	Matsui Keiji	

23RD ENGINEER REGIMENT			
Commander	Lt. Col.	Saitō Isamu	Wounded
Attached officer	Maj.	Nukata	
1st Company	Capt.	Kakoi Namiyoshi	
2nd Company	Capt.	Shimizu Yoshitake	Returned in mid-August, killed 29 Aug. 1939
"	1st Lt.	Hayase Takio	Became acting co. commander
Matériel Platoon	2nd Lt.	Akiyoshi Chiyoki	

		23RD TRANSPORT REGIMENT	
Commander	Col.	Midorikawa Chūji	
1st Company (horse)	Capt.	Mori Suematsu	
2nd Company (motorized)	Capt.	Sōma Seiji	

		23RD MEDICAL UNIT	
Commander	Lt. Col.	Hirano Hiroo	

Appendix E

Attached-Unit Roster of Main Officers, Nomonhan, 1939

		HASEBE DETACHMENT	
Commander	Col.	Hasebe Riei	8th BGU 2nd District commander, killed himself 20 Sept. 1939
1st Battalion			
Commander	Lt. Col.	Sugitani Yoshio	
1st Company	1st Lt.	Takumi Sōtarō	
2nd Company	1st Lt.	Hachiya Itsuo	
3rd Company	1st Lt.	Yoshida Yonetoshi	Killed 28 Aug. 1939
2nd Battalion			
Commander	Maj.	Miyazaki Tadao	
1st Company	Capt.	Sanemitsu Norio	As of 10 Apr. 1939
2nd Company	Capt.	Yamamoto Shigeo	As of 10 Apr. 1939
3rd Company	1st Lt.	Masubuchi Genshichirō	As of 10 Apr. 1939
Regt. Gun Unit	Capt.	Sanemitsu Norio	As of Aug. 1939
RF Gun Battery	1st Lt.	Tada Shinji	Killed 29 Aug. 1939

		6TH IGU BATTALION[1]	
Commander	Lt. Col.	Yotsuya Iwao	

		24TH ENGINEER REGIMENT	
Commander	Col.	Kawamura Shichirō	Killed 7 July 1939
"	Col.	Numazaki Kyōhei	Assumed command 1 Aug. 1939
1st Company	Capt.	Yabuuchi Retsuo	
2nd Company	1st Lt.	Nomiyama	

		4TH TRUCK REGIMENT	
Commander	Col.	Tazaka Sen'ichi	
1st Company	Capt.	Kawasaki Masahiko	
2nd Company	Capt.	Yamaguchi Hideo	

1. The 6th IGU Battalion was less one company.

Appendix F

7th Infantry Division Roster of Main Officers, Nomonhan, 1939

DIVISION HEADQUARTERS

Commander	Lt. Gen.	Kunisaki Noboru
Chief of staff	Col.	Ikeda Shunkichi
Attached officer	Lt. Col.	Matsuda Enji
Aide	1st Lt.	Nanba

Staff officers

Operations	Lt. Col.	Kaneko Moriyo
Intelligence	Maj.	Ishibashi Tadao
"	Capt.	Mugikawa
Logistics	Maj.	Sugimoto
"	Capt.	Suginoo Osao
Signal	Capt.	Yamashita Kōji

13TH INFANTRY BRIGADE HEADQUARTERS

Commander	Maj. Gen.	Yoshizawa Tadao
Aide	Maj.	Matsuda Engi

14TH INFANTRY BRIGADE HEADQUARTERS

Commander	Maj. Gen.	Morita Norimasa

25TH INFANTRY REGIMENT

Commander	Col.	Sekine Kyūtarō
Aide	Capt.	Saitō Masaichi
"	1st Lt.	Utsumi Yoshio
Color bearer	2nd Lt.	Tokuda Shigenao

1st Battalion

Commander	Maj.	Maruuchi Chūhachi	
1st Company	1st Lt.	Miura Tatsuo	
2nd Company	1st Lt.	Abe Masakatsu	
3rd Company	1st Lt.	Tsurumi Keiju	Killed 1 Sept. 1939
1st MG Company	1st Lt.	Ōmiya Ichijirō	

2nd Battalion

Commander	Maj.	Harako Masao
5th Company	Capt.	Okada Norio
6th Company	1st Lt.	Miyake Iwao
7th Company	1st Lt.	Matsumoto Masaaki
2nd MG Company	1st Lt.	Kawai Yasuo

3rd Battalion

Commander	Maj.	Yamazumi Iori	
9th Company	1st Lt.	Yokoyama Kyūhachirō	
10th Company	1st Lt.	Kataoka Yasaburō	
11th Company	1st Lt.	Tanaka Masashi	
3rd MG Company	1st Lt.	Kano Jūzō	
Regt. Gun Unit	1st Lt.	Umibe Masajiro	Attached to 26th Inf. Regt. 20 June 1939; killed 26 Aug. 1939

RF Gun Battery	2nd Lt.	Kakizaki Shōichi	Attached to 26th Inf. Regt. 20 June 1939; to Ioki Unit 13 Aug. 1939

26TH INFANTRY REGIMENT

Commander	Col.	Sumi Shin'ichirō	Replaced Oct., retired Dec. 1939
"	Col.	Miyazaki Shūichi	Assumed command Oct. 1939
Attached officer	Maj.	Ozawa Masayuki	Fell ill late July, became 2nd Bn. commander 16 Sept. 1939
Aide	Maj.	Maruyama Kōichi	Killed 3 July 1939
"	Capt.	Terajima Yoshio	
"	Capt.	Ikaga Naoomi	
"	2nd Lt.	Shinoda Kenji	Killed 3 July 1939
Color bearer	2nd Lt.	Tsurumi Hajime	Promoted to 1st Lt. from Aug., became 3rd Co. commander
"	2nd Lt.	Takahashi Eiji	
1st Battalion			
Commander	Maj.	Adachi Chikao	Killed 3 July 1939
"	Capt.	Kondō Kōjirō	Acting bn. commander
"	Maj.	Ikuta Junzō	Assumed command 13 July, killed 29 Aug. 1939
"	Maj.	Hozumi	Assumed command 16 Sept. 1939
1st Company	1st Lt.	Sakamoto Takeo	Killed 3 July 1939
"	W.O.	Noto Yohachirō	Became acting co. commander
"	2nd Lt.	Nozaki	Became co. commander 21 July 1939
2nd Company	1st Lt.	Aida Shigematsu	Killed 3 July 1939
"	W.O.	Fujii	Became acting co. commander
"	1st Lt.	Nakamori Mitsunaga	Became co. commander July, wounded 29 Aug. 1939
3rd Company	1st Lt.	Kobayashi Shirō	Wounded 3 July, returned 1 Aug., became 1st MG Co. commander
"	1st Lt.	Irahara Yoshiharu	
"	1st Lt.	Tsurumi Hajime	Became co. commander, killed 21 Aug. 1939
1st MG Company	1st Lt.	Kondō Kōjirō	Became acting bn. commander July, transferred Aug. 1939
"	2nd Lt.	Akino Eiji	Became acting co. commander July 1939
"	1st Lt.	Kobayashi Shirō	Returned from hospital, became co. commander 1 Aug., killed 25 Aug. 1939
2nd Battalion			
Commander	Maj.	Kawai Jiichi	Transferred Aug. 1939
"	Maj.	Uemura (Kamimura) Minao	Assumed command 16 Aug., transferred for illness Aug. 1939
"	Maj.	Nakano Toshio	Assumed command 24 Aug., killed 25 Aug. 1939
"	1st Lt.	Hoshino Kazuhiko	Became acting bn. commander
"	Maj.	Ozawa Masayuki	Assumed command 16 Sept. 1939
5th Company	1st Lt.	Watanabe Masao	Wounded 3 July, became 2nd MG Co. commander
"	1st Lt.	Takahashi Kazuo	Became co. commander
6th Company	1st Lt.	Kawabata Shinjirō	Attached to Ioki Unit 13 Aug. 1939
7th Company	1st Lt.	Kimura Yoshio	

2nd MG

Company	Capt.	Terajima Yoshio	Became regt. aide July 1939
"	1st Lt.	Watanabe Masao	Became co. commander, killed 25 Aug. 1939

3rd Battalion

Commander	Maj.	Kikuchi Tetsuo	Killed 3 July 1939
"	1st Lt.	Kokubu Yoshio	Acting bn. commander
"	Maj.	Hanabusa	Assumed command 16 Sept. 1939
9th Company	1st Lt.	Sata Naotada	Wounded 3 July 1939
"	2nd Lt.	Yoshida Minoru	Became acting co. commander
"	1st Lt.	Sata Naotada	Resumed command, attached to Ioki Unit 13 Aug. 1939
10th Company	1st Lt.	Kokubu Yoshio	Became acting bn. commander
"	W.O.	Fujibayashi Kishichi	Became acting co. commander, wounded 3 July 1939
"	2nd Lt.	Kudo Tomio	Became acting co. commander, killed 11 July 1939
"	1st Lt.	Kokubu Yoshio	Resumed command
11th Company	1st Lt.	Yoshizaki Suehiko	Wounded 1 Aug. 1939
3rd MG Company	1st. Lt.	Yamamoto Miki	Resumed command 21 July, wounded 23 July 1939
"	1st Lt.	Maeda Yoshinori	Acting co. commander
Regt. Gun Unit	Capt.	Ikaga Naoomi	Became regt. aide
"	1st Lt.	Togashi Tomiji	Became unit commander
RF Gun Battery	1st Lt.	Nakano Kōichi	

Attached Regimental Gun and Rapid-fire Gun Units

25th Inf. Regt., Regt. Gun Unit	1st Lt.	Umibe Masajirō	Killed 26 Aug. 1939
25th Inf. Regt., RF Gun Battery	1st Lt.	Kakizaki Shōichi	Attached to Ioki Unit 13 Aug. 1939
27th Inf. Regt., Regt. Gun Unit	Capt.	Tsuji Kiyoshi	Attached to Ioki Unit 13 Aug., died 12 Sept. 1939
27th Inf. Regt., RF Gun Battery	2nd Lt.	Kokō [Kokabu] Kōichi	

27TH INFANTRY REGIMENT

Commander	Col.	Sannomiya Mitsuji (Manji)
Attached officer	Maj.	Eguchi Tōsaku
Aide	Capt.	Sanuki Takeji
"	1st Lt.	Itō Ryūshichi
Color bearer	2nd Lt.	Nakatsugawa Shichiryō

1st Battalion

Commander	Maj.	Sakurai Kaisuke
1st Company	Capt.	Tanaka Shinjirō
2nd Company	Capt.	Kōno Sadao
3rd Company	1st Lt.	Sugawara Shōichi
1st MG Company	1st Lt.	Kuwana Kiyoshi
1st Bn. Gun Platoon	1st Lt.	Onoue Akira

2nd Battalion

Commander	Maj.	Tajima Buichirō	
5th Company	1st Lt.	Sugimoto Katsumi	
6th Company	1st Lt.	Kondō Kyūichi	
7th Company	1st Lt.	Kawamura Shirō	
2nd MG Company	1st Lt.	Koguma Kumaji	
2nd Bn. Gun Platoon	1st Lt.	Inoshita Yoshimitsu	

3rd Battalion

Commander	Maj.	Tahara Tsuneharu	Wounded 30 Aug. 1939
9th Company	1st Lt.	Nagase Genzō	Killed 29 Aug. 1939
10th Company	1st Lt.	Kasuga Yoshio	Killed 29 Aug. 1939
11th Company	1st Lt.	Takahashi Tokusaburō	
3rd MG Company	1st Lt.	Takahashi Naokichi	
3rd Bn. Gun Platoon	2nd Lt.	Kondō Takemichi	
Regt. Gun Unit	Capt.	Tsuji Kiyoshi	Attached to 26th Inf. Regt. 20 June 1939; to Ioki Unit 13 Aug., killed himself 12 Sept.
RF Gun Battery	1st Lt.	Kokō [Kokabu] Kōichi	Attached to 26th Inf. Regt. 20 June 1939

28TH INFANTRY REGIMENT

Commander	Col.	Ashizuka Chōzō	
Attached officer	Maj.	Saeki Saburō	
Aide	Maj.	Ishida Ainosuke	Wounded 26 Aug. 1939
Color bearer	1st Lt.	Tsukida Masurao	

1st Battalion

Commander	Maj.	Hotta Fusakichi	Promoted to Lt. Col. from Aug. 1939
1st Company	1st Lt.	Ōtsuka Bunkichi	Wounded 24 Aug. 1939
2nd Company	1st Lt.	Harada Toshirō	Killed 24 Aug. 1939
3rd Company	1st Lt.	Yamashita Seishichirō	Killed 24 Aug. 1939
"	1st Lt.	Tsutamori Seiichi	Became acting co. commander
1st MG Company	1st Lt.	Andō Masao	
1st Bn. Gun Platoon	1st Lt.	Ōkubo Yoshio	

2nd Battalion (attached to Yasuoka Detachment 20 June 1939)

Commander	Maj.	Kajikawa Tomiji (Tomiharu)	Wounded 25 Aug. 1939
5th Company	Capt.	Aoyanagi Kin'ichirō	Killed 5 July 1939
"	W.O.	Ōtomo Sanji	Became acting co. commander
"	1st Lt.	Sawada Tetsurō	Became co. commander, wounded
6th Company	Capt.	Tsuji Kiichi	Wounded 18 Aug. 1939
7th Company	1st Lt.	Saitō Seikichi	Killed 25 Aug. 1939
2nd MG Company	1st Lt.	Sadakaji Tetsuo	Killed 26 Aug. 1939
2nd Bn. Gun Platoon	2nd Lt.	Kijitani Tomizō	Killed

3rd Battalion

Commander	Maj.	Fujioka Yoshiichi	Killed 25 Aug. 1939
9th Company	Capt.	Takebayashi Kōichi	Killed 25 Aug. 1939

10th Company	Capt.	Soga Toshio	Wounded 25 Aug. 1939
11th Company	1st Lt.	Yorozu Toshio	Wounded 25 Aug. 1939
3rd MG Company	Capt.	Saitō Kuranosuke	
Regt. Gun Unit	Capt.	Togashi Yokichi	
RF Gun Battery	1st Lt.	Nakajima Chōichi	

7TH CAVALRY REGIMENT

| Commander | Lt. Col. | Akiyama Kyūzō | |
| " | Lt. Col. | Yamashita Hikohei | Assumed command 24 Aug. 1939 |

7TH FIELD ARTILLERY REGIMENT[1]

| Commander | Col. | Hirayama Yoshirō | |

2nd Battalion

Commander	Maj.	Ishihama Isao	Absent due to illness
"	Capt.	Shimizu Kisata	Acting bn. commander
4th Battery	1st Lt.	Inoue Masanori	
5th Battery	Capt.	Saitō Tatsuji	

3rd Battalion

Commander	Maj.	Asano Fujio	
7th Battery	1st Lt.	Muramatsu Tadataka	
8th Battery	1st Lt.	Koshizawa Saburō	

4th Battalion

Commander	Maj.	Tsuzuki Masashi	
10th Battery	1st Lt.	Matsuie Toshio	
11th Battery	1st Lt.	Sakurai Tadashi	

7TH SIGNAL UNIT

| Commander | Capt. | Yamashita Kōji | |

7TH ENGINEER REGIMENT

Commander	Lt. Col.	Yokoyama Yoshitomo	
1st Company	Capt.	Narumi Masakichi	
2nd Company	1st Lt.	Satō Hisashi	

7TH TRANSPORT REGIMENT

Commander	Lt. Col.	Honma Kōtarō	
1st Company	1st Lt.	Itakura Ken'ichi	
2nd Company	1st Lt.	Kogirima Masatake	
3rd Company	1st Lt.	Nomura Norio	

7TH DIVISION MEDICAL UNIT

| Commander | Lt. Col. | Suzuki Naozō | |

1. The 7th Field Artillery Regiment was less its 1st Battalion.

Appendix G

IJA Artillery Corps Roster of Main Officers, Nomonhan, 1939

ARTILLERY CORPS

Commander	Maj. Gen.	Uchiyama Eitarō	
Staff officer	Col.	Masai Yoshito	
Attached officer	Maj.	Tsurumi Sakuma	
Aide	Maj.	Sugano Ryō	

3RD HEAVY FIELD ARTILLERY BRIGADE

Commander	Maj. Gen.	Hata Yūzaburō	
Attached officer	Col.	Kaneoka Takashi	Arrived 29 July 1939
"	Maj.	Fukuda	
Aide	Capt.	Ishikawa Yasushi	
"	1st Lt.	Hashimoto	
"	2nd Lt.	Tazaka	
Observation	Capt.	Ida Masataka	
Signal	2nd Lt.	Nakamura	

3rd Artillery Brigade Transport Unit

Commander	Lt. Col.	Masano Kei	
1st Company	Capt.	Mori Hiroshi	
2nd Company	1st Lt.	Iida Takao	

1ST INDEPENDENT FIELD ARTILLERY REGIMENT[1]

Commander	Lt. Col.	Miyao Kan	Promoted to Col. from Aug. 1939
Attached officer	Lt. Col.	Yoshida Yutaka	
Aide	Maj.	Ōtake Kiyoji	
Repair & maintenance	Capt.	Itō Fusakichi	
1st Battery	Capt.	Abe Hayami	
3rd Battery	Capt.	Motohashi Jirō	

1ST HEAVY FIELD ARTILLERY REGIMENT

Commander	Col.	Mishima Giichirō	Wounded 9 Aug. 1939
"	Maj.	Umeda Kyōzō	Acting regt. commander, killed himself in battle 27 Aug. 1939
Observation	Capt.	Yamamoto Tatsuo	
Repair & maintenance	2nd Lt.	Aritoshi Kazuo	Killed

1st Battalion

Commander	Maj.	Umeda Kyōzō	Acting regt. commander
"	Capt.	Yamazaki Masaki	Acting bn. commander, killed 27 Aug. 1939
Observation	1st Lt.	Koike Ichirō	Killed 27 Aug. 1939
Signal	2nd Lt.	Ishii Hikoji	
1st Battery	1st Lt.	Prince Higashikuni Moriatsu	Transferred 2 Aug. 1939
"	Capt.	Tsuchiya Masaichi	Assumed command 2 Aug. 1939
2nd Battery	Capt.	Yamazaki Masaki	Acting bn. commander

2nd Battalion

Commander	Maj.	Hayashi Tadaaki	
3rd Battery	1st Lt.	Yatabe Daijirō	
4th Battery	1st Lt.	Magari Toshirō	

7TH HEAVY FIELD ARTILLERY REGIMENT

Commander	Col.	Takatsukasa Nobuhiro (Nobuteru)	
Aide	Capt.	Fujii Nobuo	Killed Aug. 1939
Observation	1st Lt.	Kurihara Shigeru	
Signal	2nd Lt.	Enomoto Takayasu	
Repair & maintenance	1st Lt.	Oka Takeo	

1st Battalion

Commander	Maj.	Sakuma Yoshio	Transferred 1 Aug. 1939
"	Maj.	Sugano Ryō	Assumed command 1 Aug. 1939
Aide	1st Lt.	Ōkubo Teizō	
Observation	2nd Lt.	Ishikawa Jirō	Acting bn. aide
"	2nd Lt.	Tsukinogi Yasushi	Acting observation officer
Signal	2nd Lt.	Koyasu Masatoshi	Killed 20 July 1939
"	2nd Lt.	Nakamura Masayoshi	Acting signal officer, killed 27 Aug. 1939
1st Battery	1st Lt.	Yamada Kanji	
2nd Battery	1st Lt.	Morimoto Fujio	

2nd Battalion

Commander	Maj.	Kondō Toranosuke	Killed 27 Aug. 1939
Aide	2nd Lt.	Yamamoto Mosuke	
Observation	2nd Lt.	Makita Rinzō	Wounded 28 Aug. 1939
Liaison	2nd Lt.	Nakamura Masayoshi	Killed 27 Aug. 1939
3rd Battery	1st Lt.	Ozaki Masamichi	
4th Battery	1st Lt.	Watanabe Hatsuya	Killed 22 Aug. 1939
"	1st Lt.	Kurihara Shigeru	Acting battery commander 22 Aug. 1939

MULENG HEAVY ARTILLERY REGIMENT

Commander	Lt. Col.	Someya Yoshio	Killed himself in battle 26 Aug. 1939
Attached officer	Maj.	Itō Masaji	
Aide	1st Lt.	Kitamura Jōzō	
1st Battery	1st Lt.	Ishii Hōshirō	Killed 26 Aug. 1939
2nd Battery	1st Lt.	Kimura Jirō	Killed 26 Aug. 1939
Matériel Park	1st Lt.	Tsuboi Matahiko	

1ST ARTILLERY INTELLIGENCE REGIMENT

Commander	Lt. Col.	Fukuda Kazuya
Aide	Maj.	Suzukawa Ken'ichi
Surveying	Capt.	Tsutsui Yoshio
Plotting	1st Lt.	Nishida Kōkichi
Sound detection	Capt.	Yoneyama Teizō

INDEPENDENT BALLOON UNIT

Commander	Lt. Col.	Kōketsu Tetsuzō
Balloon Platoon	1st Lt.	Iga

10TH ANTIAIRCRAFT ARTILLERY REGIMENT

Commander	Lt. Col.	Yamaoka Shigemitsu	
1st Battery	Capt.	Takemoto Toshichika	As of 10 Apr. 1939
2nd Battery	1st Lt.	Inoue Shinji	"

| 3rd Battery | 1st Lt. | Utsumi Seiichi | " |
| 4th Battery | Capt. | Samukawa Isao | " |

		2ND MORTAR REGIMENT	
Commander	Lt. Col.	Akashi Kenjirō	As of 10 Apr. 1939
1st Battery	1st Lt.	Shimoda Fujio	"
2nd Battery	Capt.	Toyama Hideo	"
Matériel Park	Capt.	Hayakawa Tetsuzō	"

1. The 1st Independent Field Artillery Regiment was less two batteries.

Appendix H

IJA Tank Corps Roster of Main Officers, Nomonhan, 1939

		1ST TANK CORPS	
Commander	Lt. Gen.	Yasuoka Masaomi	
Attached officer	Lt. Col.	Takazawa Hideo	
"	Maj.	Noguchi Kamenosuke	
Aide	Maj.	Masuda Umeki	
"	1st Lt.	Okumura Masaku	

		3RD TANK REGIMENT	
Commander	Lt. Col.	Yoshimaru Kiyotake	Killed 3 July 1939
Attached officer	Maj.	Harada Kazuo	Wounded 3 July 1939
"	Maj.	Kurusu Einosuke	Assumed post 8 July 1939
Aide	Capt.	Koga Ototo	Killed 3 July 1939
Gas Officer	Capt.	Higuchi Yoichi	Killed 3 July 1939
1st Company	Capt.	Miyatake Masajirō	Killed 3 July 1939
1st Platoon	1st Lt.	Sunagawa Seiji	Killed 3 July 1939
2nd Platoon	2nd Lt.	Takeshita Iwao	Acting co. commander
3rd Platoon	2nd Lt.	Shimizu Saburō	Killed 2 July 1939
4th Platoon	2nd Lt.	Koga Yasuo	Killed 2 July 1939
2nd Company	Maj.	Kinomoto Morinosuke	Killed 2 July 1939
1st Platoon	1st Lt.	Sakamoto Moriaki	Acting co. commander
2nd Platoon	1st Lt.	Irie Tachio	
3rd Platoon	2nd Lt.	Tasaka Masaharu	Killed 2 July 1939
4th Platoon	2nd Lt.	Satō Shigeo	
Matériel Park	Capt.	Yoshitake Kanji	Killed 3 July 1939
1st Platoon	Capt.	Sakano Nobuo	
2nd Platoon			
3rd Platoon	1st Lt.	Sugimoto Makoto	

		4TH TANK REGIMENT	
Commander	Col.	Tamada Yoshio	
Attached officer	Maj.	Ogata Kyūichirō	
Aide	Maj.	Miyazaki Kiyo'omi	

Liaison	Capt.	Takahashi Masaji	
"	2nd Lt.	Tashiro Sōtarō	
Signal	Capt.	Nakajima Hideo	
1st Company	Capt.	Matsumoto Takaharu	
1st Platoon	1st Lt.	Kuwabara Katsushige	Wounded
2nd Platoon	2nd Lt.	Saotome Tadahito	
2nd Company	Capt.	Kitamura Ryōichi	Killed 30 June 1939
1st Platoon	1st Lt.	Itō Yoshihisa	Acting co. commander, wounded 3 July 1939
2nd Platoon	1st Lt.	Kajiya Tsuneichi	
"	2nd Lt.	Niikura (Shinkura) Masakichi	
3rd Company	Capt.	Tamaki Sōichi	Wounded 6 July 1939
1st Platoon	1st Lt.	Shinoda Hangorō	Killed 26 June 1939
"	2nd Lt.	Hirasawa Yoshiyuki	Acting platoon leader
2nd Platoon	2nd Lt.	Tomioka Zenzō	Wounded 6 July 1939
4th Company	Capt.	In Sanji	
1st Platoon	1st Lt.	Shiragata Takurō	Killed 6 July 1939
2nd Platoon	2nd Lt.	Sunouchi Seiichi	
Matériel Park	Capt.	Kamiyama Tamotsu	
1st Platoon	1st Lt.	Yagi Susumu	
2nd Platoon	2nd Lt.	Fuchida Kumajirō	

Appendix I

IJA Air Force Roster of Main Officers, Nomonhan, 1939

		2ND AIR DIVISION[1]	
Commander	Lt. Gen.	Giga Tetsuji	
Chief of staff	Col.	Kusunoki Nobukazu (En'ichi)	
Staff officers			
Operations	Lt. Col.	Shimanuki Tadamasa	Killed 2 July 1939
"	Lt. Col.	Hanamoto Morihiko	
"	Maj.	Harada Kiyoshi	
"	Maj.	Yanase Kengo	
7th Air Wing[2]			
Commander	Maj. Gen.	Hōzōji Hisao	
1st Group[3]			
Commander	Lt. Col.	Katō Toshio	Wounded 12 July 1939
"	Lt. Col.	Makino Yasuo	Acting group commander
"	Maj.	Harada Fumio	Assumed command July, wounded 29 July, taken prisoner, committed suicide April 1940

"	Maj.	Yoshida Tadashi	Assumed command Aug. 1939
1st Squadron	Capt.	Takanashi Tatsuo	Wounded 22 July 1939
"	1st Lt.	Koizumi Shōzō	Acting sqdn. commander, killed 23 July 1939
"	Capt.	Inoue Shigetoshi	
2nd Squadron	Capt.	Yamada Keisuke	Missing 21 July 1939
"	1st Lt.	Itō Shun	Acting sqdn. commander, killed 24 July 1939
"	Capt.	Masuda Iwao	Assumed command Aug., killed 24 Aug. 1939
"	1st Lt.	Tanijima Yoshihiko	Acting sqdn. commander, killed 25 Aug. 1939

12th Group[4]

Commander	Col.	Harada Uichirō	
1st Squadron	Capt.	Ōura Hoshikuma	
2nd Squadron	Capt.	Kurihara Shigehisa	
3rd Squadron	Capt.	Sakamoto Hideo	

15th Group[5]

Commander	Col.	Abe Katsumi	Killed 2 Aug. 1939
"	Lt. Col.	Yamamoto Tatsuo	Assumed command Aug. 1939
1st Squadron[6]	Capt.	Aoki Hideo	
2nd Squadron	Capt.	Mizuzaki Kujūku	Killed 1 Sept. 1939
3rd Squadron	Capt.	Oizumi Yoshimasa	

9th Air Wing

Commander	Maj. Gen.	Shimono Ikkaku	

10th Group

Commander	Col.	Tazoe Noboru	Promoted to Maj. Gen. from Aug. 1939, transferred
"	Col.	Shirogane Jūji	Assumed command Aug. 1939
1st Squadron	Capt.	Koide Takeo	
2nd Squadron	Capt.	Jingasa Taketo	
3rd Squadron	Capt.	Okumura Masayoshi	

16th Group[7]

Commander	Lt. Col.	Ōtsuka Torao	
1st Squadron	Capt.	Hiramatsu Kenji	
2nd Squadron	1st Lt.	Toyohara Toshio	
3rd Squadron	Capt.	Namiki Yoshibumi	

31st Group[8]

Commander	Col.	Sumifuji Shōichi	
Squadron	Capt.	Inoue Jirō	Killed 31 Aug. 1939
Squadron	Capt.	Saitō	Crash-landed 31 Aug. 1939

61st Group

Commander	Col.	Mikami Kisō	
1st Squadron	Capt.	Uno Jurō	
2nd Squadron	Capt.	Muraki Hachirō	
3rd Squadron	Capt.	Ishikawa Masayasu	

12th Air Wing

Commander	Maj. Gen.	Higashi Eiji	Transferred 5 Aug. 1939
"	Col.	Matsuoka Katsuzō	Assumed command 5 Aug. 1939

11th Group[9]

Commander	Col.	Noguchi Yūjirō	Concurrently Composite Air Wing commander Sept. 1939
1st Squadron	Capt.	Shimada Kenji	Missing 15 Sept. 1939
2nd Squadron	Capt.	Motomura Kōji	Killed 22 Aug. 1939
3rd Squadron	Capt.	Fujita Takashi	Wounded 4 July 1939

4th Squadron	Capt.	Iwahashi Jōzō	
24th Group[10]			
Commander	Lt. Col.	Matsumura Kōjirō	Wounded 23 July 1939
"	Maj.	Yuzuhara Hidemi	Assumed command 18 Aug. 1939
1st Squadron	Capt.	Kani Saiji	Killed 29 July 1939
"	Capt.	Morishita Seijirō	
2nd Squadron	Capt.	Morimoto Shigenobu	Missing 22 June 1939
"	Capt.	Tashiro Shōichi	Assumed command 30 June 1939
3rd Squadron[11]	Capt.	Sakagawa Toshio	Wounded 15 Sept. 1939
64th Group[12]			
Commander	Maj.	Yokoyama Yatsuo	Wounded 25 Aug. 1939
1st Squadron	Capt.	Maruta Fumio	Wounded 1 Sept. 1939
2nd Squadron	Capt.	Anzai Shūichi	Missing 1 Sept. 1939
3rd Squadron	Capt.	Suzuki Gorō	

		AIR COMMAND[13]	
Commander	Lt. Gen.	Ebashi Eijirō	
Chief of staff	Col.	Shimoyama Takuma	
2nd Air Wing[14]			
Commander	Maj. Gen.	Sasa Makoto	
29th Group			
1st Squadron	Capt.	Adachi Seiichi	
9th Group			
Commander	Col.	Nanba Seisaku	
1st Squadron	Capt.	Tabuchi Takashi	
2nd Squadron	Capt.	Miyamoto Takeo	
33rd Group[15]			
Commander	Lt. Col.	Aoki Takezō	
1st Squadron	Capt.	Ishikawa Tadashi	
2nd Squadron	Capt.	Kawada Takeo	
3rd Squadron	Capt.	Watanabe Kei	
59th Group[16]			
Commander	Col.	Imagawa Issaku	
1st Squadron	Capt.	Yamamoto Mitsugu	Missing 15 Sept. 1939
2nd Squadron	Capt.	Yamada Kunio	
65th Group[17]			
Commander	Col.	Fujizuka Shikao	
1st Squadron	Capt.	Takahashi Ken'ichi	
2nd Squadron	Capt.	Tamura Shigeo	

1. Headquarters released 1 Sept. 1939. 2. Released 14 July 1939. 3. Transferred to 12th Wing 14 July 1939. 4. Released 14 July 1939. 5. Attached to 23rd Inf. Div. 6. Attached to 2nd Air Div. Headquarters. 7. Assigned 14 July 1939; transferred to 2nd Air Group 5 Sept. 1939. 8. Assigned 25 Aug. 1939. 9.–10. Attached to Composite Air Wing Sept. 1939. 11. From Sept. 1939. 12. Assigned 13 Aug. 1939. 13. Sept. 1939. 14. Established 1 Sept. 1939. 15. Attached 5 Sept. 1939. 16. Attached to 9th Air Wing Sept. 1939. 17. Attached to 12th Air Wing Sept. 1939.

Appendix J

Kwantung Army Casualty Data, Nomonhan, 1939

Unit	Number participated	Killed	Wounded
23rd Div.	14,137	5,224	5,561
7th Div.	10,308	1,505	1,851
[8th] BGU	4,883	779	603
2nd Div.	11,800	200	110
4th Div.	8,315	5	6
IGU	3,012	38	59
1st Div.	4,980	70	100
Ta-bi [sic] Heavy Artillery	380	96	?
3 [?] Heavy Field Artillery	2,092	256	177
3rd De [sic]	1,165	14	29
Truck Unit [Kwantung Army]	2,536	31	86
AA Hq.	2,641	16	61
AA Unit	935	7	29
Ka-ho [sic]	1,125	200	143
Mortar Unit	401	20	44
Tank Corps	1,627	77	83
Air Force	3,307	55[?]	58
Unidentified	744	?	?
Misc.	1,350	39	50
TOTAL	75,736 [75,738?]	8,629 [8,632?]	9,087 [9,050?]

SOURCE: Mita [406], p. 494. The editors note that the top-secret Kwantung Army document was put together after the cease-fire, and that the entries listed phonetically could not be deciphered and were therefore reproduced as is, together with the gaps in the original.

Appendix K

23rd Division Casualty Data, 20 June–15 Sept. 1939

Unit	Number participated	Killed	Wounded	Missing
Div. Hq.	232	26	45	6
Inf. Group Hq.	22	1	3	0
64th Inf. Regt.	4,615	1,361	1,506	113
71st Inf. Regt.	4,551[1]	1,636	1,777	359
72nd Inf. Regt.	3,014	847	1,222	54
Recon. Unit	380	120	69	9
13th FA Regt.	1,747	569	595	98
23rd Engr. Regt.	338	70	109	0
23rd Transp. Regt.	299	41	28	0
Signal Unit	180	51	38	0
Medical Unit	334	59	55	0
Field Hosp.	221	5	8	0
Veterinary Unit	42	0	0	0
TOTAL	15,975[2]	4,786	5,455	639

Unit	Total battle	Ill	Grand total	Available survivors (1 Sept.)
Div. Hq.	77	26	103	
Inf. Group Hq.	4	3	7	
64th Inf. Regt.	2,980	198	3,178	765
71st Inf. Regt.	3,772	482	4,254	332
72nd Inf. Regt.	2,123	244	2,367	251
Recon. Unit	198	53	251	145
13th FA Regt.	1,262	66	1,328	626
23rd Engr. Regt.	179	109	288	231
23rd Transp. Regt.	69	33	102	213
Signal Unit	89	32	121	
Medical Unit	114	68	182	
Field Hosp.	13	21	34	
Veterinary Unit	0	5	5	
TOTAL	10,880	1,340	12,220	

SOURCE: BBSS, SS[180], vol. 27, pp. 707-8, citing 23rd Div. Medical Section, 27 Oct. 1939.
1. Table of organization strength 3,172; replacements 1,379.
2. Table of organization strength about 13,000; JRD[965], *JSM*, 11, part 3/C, p. 461.

Appendix L

7th Division Casualty Data, 3 July–15 Sept. 1939

Unit	Number participated	Killed	Died of wounds	Wounded/ injured (recovered)
Div. Hq.	270	5	0	3
13th Brig. Hq.	75	1	0	2
25th Inf. Regt.	1,915	98	7	102
26th Inf. Regt.	1,720	598	27	756
14th Brig. Hq.	67	0	0	5
27th Inf. Regt.	1,690	211	8	184
28th Inf. Regt.	1,770	568	19	656
7th Cav. Regt.	343	0	1	2
7th FA Regt.	1,225	14	3	27
7th Engr. Regt.	368	4	2	18
7th Transp. Regt.	177	4	1	17
Signal Unit	151	0	0	0
Medical Unit	298	2	2	9
Field Hosp.	204	1	0	0
Vet. Unit	35	0	0	0
TOTAL	10,308	1,506	70	1,781

Unit	Total battle casualties	Ill	Grand total
Div. Hq.	8	2	10
13th Brig. Hq.	3	0	3
25th Inf. Regt.	207	28	235
26th Inf. Regt.	1,381	191	1,572
14th Brig. Hq.	5	2	7
27th Inf. Regt.	403	27	430
28th Inf. Regt.	1,243	46	1,289
7th Cav. Regt.	3	0	3
7th FA Regt.	44	5	49
7th Engr. Regt.	24	5	29
7th Transp. Regt.	22	6	28
Signal Unit	0	0	0
Medical Unit	13	32	45
Field Hosp.	1	1	2
Vet. Unit	0	0	0
TOTAL	3,357	346	3,703

SOURCE: 7th Div. Medical Sec. (Yoshida Yasuhiko), in *Nomonhan* [40], vol. 11, p. 121.

Appendix M

Infantry Officer Casualties, 23rd Division, Nomonhan, 1939 [1]

Category	Participated	Killed	Missing	Wounded	Unhurt
Division commander	1	0	0	0	1
Chief of staff	1	1	0	0	0
Staff officers	3	0	0	2	1
Group commander	1	0	0	1	0
Regt. commanders [2]	3	2	0	1	0
Bn. commanders	8	3	0	4	1
Co. commanders	43	11	1	19	12
Platoon leaders	232	76	15	90	51
TOTAL	292	93	16	117	66

SOURCE: BBSS, *SS*[180], vol. 27, p. 710.

1. In his diary entry for 3 Sept. 1939 [25], Komatsubara recorded higher figures for 23rd Div. officers who were missing (86) or wounded (148), and a lower number for those killed (77). His preliminary tally of officer casualties (311) was broken down as follows (KIA-MIA-WIA categories, respectively): Div. Hq.—2-0-5; Inf. Group—0-0-2; 64th Inf. Regt.—25-29-36; 71st Inf. Regt.—10-29-48; 72nd Inf. Regt.—14-10-43; 13th FA Regt.—18-15-12; 23rd Engr. Regt.—3-1-1; 23rd Transport Regt.—1-1-0; 23rd Recon. Regt.—2-1-1; Signal Unit—2-0-0.

2. The 71st Inf. Regt. had five commanders in all: Col. T. Okamoto, transferred to division, 7 July; Col. E. Nagano, wounded 24 July; Col. T. Morita, arrived 8 Aug., killed 26 Aug.; Lt. Col. M. Higashi, killed 30 Aug.; Col. S. Shirahama, assigned 16 Sept.

Appendix N

Missing in Action, 2nd Bn., 28th Inf. Regt., 7th Div., 20 June–16 Sept. 1939

Unit	Missing	Evacuated to rear but disappeared	Total missing
Battalion Hq.	1	2	3
5th Company	14	11	25
6th Company	2	16	18
7th Company	15	2	17
2nd MG Company	1	13	14
2nd Bn. Gun Platoon	14	2	16
Rapid-fire Gun Platoon	0	0	0
TOTAL	47	46	93

SOURCE: Battalion combat report [110], casualty chart. All the missing were enlisted men.

Appendix O

Kwantung Army Command Structure and Order of Battle, Sept. 1941 [1]

KWANTUNG ARMY		
Commander	Gen.	Umezu Yoshijirō
Chief of Staff	Lt. Gen.	Yoshimoto Teiichi
Deputy Chief of Staff	Maj. Gen.	Hata Hikosaburō
Deputy Chief of Staff	Maj. Gen.	Ayabe Kitsuju
10th Division Commander	Lt. Gen.	Sogō (Sogawa) Jirō
14th Division Commander	Lt. Gen.	Kita Seiichi
28th Division Commander	Lt. Gen.	Ishiguro Teizō
29th Division Commander	Lt. Gen.	Uemura Toshimichi
Third Army (established Jan. 1938)		
Commander	Lt. Gen.	Kawabe Shōzō
Chief of Staff	Maj. Gen.	Numata Takazō
9th Division Commander	Lt. Gen.	Higuchi Kiichirō
12th Division Commander	Lt. Gen.	Kasahara Yukio
Fourth Army		
Commander	Lt. Gen.	Washizu Kōhei
Chief of Staff	Maj. Gen.	Kobayashi Senzaburō
1st Division Commander	Lt. Gen.	Yokoyama Isamu
57th Division Commander	Lt. Gen.	Itō Tomotake
Fifth Army (established May 1939)		
Commander	Lt. Gen.	Hada Jūichi [2]
Chief of Staff	Maj. Gen.	Tazaka Sen'ichi
11th Division Commander	Lt. Gen.	Ushijima Mitsuru
24th Division Commander	Lt. Gen.	Nemoto Hiroshi
Sixth Army (established Aug. 1939)		
Commander	Lt. Gen.	Yasui Tōji
Chief of Staff	Maj. Gen.	Sasaki Noboru
23rd Division Commander	Lt. Gen.	Nishihara Kanji
Twentieth Army (established Sept. 1941)		
Commander	Lt. Gen.	Seki Kameji
Chief of Staff	Maj. Gen.	Nagura Kan
8th Division Commander	Lt. Gen.	Honda Masaki
25th Division Commander	Lt. Gen.	Kuwabara Shirō
Kwantung Defense Command (established July 1941)		
Commander	Lt. Gen.	Yamashita Tomoyuki (Tomobumi or Hōbun)
Chief of Staff	Maj. Gen.	Yoshioka Yasunao
Kwantung Army Air Force		
Commander	Lt. Gen.	Andō Saburō
Chief of Staff	Maj. Gen.	Shimoyama Takuma

1. Down to division level.
2. An alternate reading is Namita Shigeichi.

Appendix P

Kwantung Army Command Structure and Order of Battle, Dec. 1942[1]

KWANTUNG ARMY		
Commander	Gen.	Umezu Yoshijirō
Chief of Staff	Lt. Gen.	Kasahara Yukio
Deputy Chief of Staff	Maj. Gen.	Ikeda Sumihisa
Deputy Chief of Staff	Maj. Gen.	Hata Hikosaburō
29th Division Commander	Lt. Gen.	Uemura Toshimichi

First Area Army (established July 1942)

Commander	Lt. Gen.	Yamashita Tomoyuki
Chief of Staff	Maj. Gen.	Shidei Tsunamasa
Second Army (established July 1942)		
Commander	Lt. Gen.	Kōzuki Yoshio
Chief of Staff	Maj. Gen.	Isoya Gorō
71st Division Commander	Lt. Gen.	Tōyama Noboru
Third Army		
Commander	Lt. Gen.	Uchiyama Eitarō
Chief of Staff	Maj. Gen.	Doi Akio
9th Division Commander	Lt. Gen.	Hara Mamoru
12th Division Commander	Lt. Gen.	Numata Takazō
Fifth Army		
Commander	Lt. Gen.	Iimura Jō
Chief of Staff	Maj. Gen.	Inada Masazumi
11th Division Commander	Lt. Gen.	Takamori Takashi
24th Division Commander	Lt. Gen.	Nemoto Hiroshi
Twentieth Army		
Commander	Lt. Gen.	Seki Kameji
Chief of Staff	Col.	Nakayama Sadatake
8th Division Commander	Lt. Gen.	Yokoyama Shizuo
25th Division Commander	Lt. Gen.	Akashiba Yaezō

Second Area Army (established July 1942)

Commander	Lt. Gen.	Anami Korechika
Chief of Staff	Maj. Gen.	Watanabe Hiroshi
14th Division Commander	Lt. Gen.	Noda Kengo
Fourth Army		
Commander	Lt. Gen.	Yokoyama Isamu
Chief of Staff	Col.	Kimihira Masatake
1st Division Commander	Lt. Gen.	Nakazawa Mitsuo
57th Division Commander	Lt. Gen.	Kusumoto Sanetaka
Sixth Army		
Commander	Lt. Gen.	Kita Seiichi
Chief of Staff	Maj. Gen.	Mori Takeshi
23rd Division Commander	Lt. Gen.	Oikawa Genshichi

Mechanized Army (established July 1942)

Commander	Lt. Gen.	Yoshida Shin
Chief of Staff	Maj. Gen.	Terada Masao
1st Armored Division Commander	Lt. Gen.	Hoshino Toshimoto
2nd Armored Division Commander	Lt. Gen.	Okada Tasuku

Kwantung Defense Command

Commander	Lt. Gen.	Kusaba Tatsumi
Chief of Staff	Maj. Gen.	Tazaka Sen'ichi

Second Air Army (established June 1942)

Commander	Lt. Gen.	Suzuki Ritsudō
Chief of Staff	Maj. Gen.	Fujimoto Tetsukuma

1. Down to division level.

Appendix Q

Kwantung Army Command Structure and Order of Battle, Aug. 1945 [1]

KWANTUNG ARMY

Commander in Chief	Gen.	Yamada Otozō
Chief of Staff	Lt. Gen.	Hata Hikosaburō
Deputy Chief of Staff	Lt. Gen.	Shidei Tsunumasa [2]
Deputy Chief of Staff [3]	Maj. Gen.	Matsumura Tomokatsu

First Area Army

Commander	Gen.	Kita Seiichi
Chief of Staff	Lt. Gen.	Sakurai Ryōzō
122nd Division Commander	Lt. Gen.	Akashika Tadashi
134th Division Commander	Lt. Gen.	Izeki Jin
Third Army		
Commander	Lt. Gen.	Murakami Keisaku
Chief of Staff	Lt. Gen.	Iketani Hanjirō
79th Division Commander	Lt. Gen.	Ōta Sadamasa (Teishō)
112th Division Commander	Lt. Gen.	Nakamura Jikizō
127th Division Commander	Lt. Gen.	Koga Ryūtarō
128th Division Commander	Lt. Gen.	Mizuhara Yoshishige
132nd Independent Mixed Brigade	Maj. Gen.	Onitake Goichi
Fifth Army		
Commander	Lt. Gen.	Shimizu Noritsune

Chief of Staff	Maj. Gen.	Kawagoe Shigesada
124th Division Commander	Lt. Gen.	Shiina Masatake
126th Division Commander	Lt. Gen.	Nomizo Sukehiko
135th Division Commander	Lt. Gen.	Hitomi Yoichi

Third Area Army

Commander	Gen.	Ushiroku Jun
Chief of Staff	Lt. Gen.	Ōtsubo Kazuma
108th Division Commander	Lt. Gen.	Iwai Torajirō
136th Division Commander	Lt. Gen.	Nakayama Atsushi
79th Independent Mixed Brigade	Maj. Gen.	Okabe Tsū
130th Independent Mixed Brigade	Maj. Gen.	Kuwada Teizō
134th Independent Mixed Brigade	Maj. Gen.	Gotō Shunzō
1st Independent Tank Brigade	Maj. Gen.	Ano Yasumichi

Thirtieth Army

Commander	Lt. Gen.	Iida Shōjirō
Chief of Staff	Maj. Gen.	Katō Michio
39th Division Commander	Lt. Gen.	Sasa Shinnosuke
125th Division Commander	Lt. Gen.	Imari Tatsuo
138th Division Commander	Lt. Gen.	Yamamoto Tsutomu
148th Division Commander	Lt. Gen.	Suemitsu Motohiro

Forty-fourth Army

Commander	Lt. Gen.	Hongō Yoshio
Chief of Staff	Maj. Gen.	Obata Nobuyoshi
63rd Division Commander	Lt. Gen.	Kishikawa Ken'ichi
107th Division Commander	Lt. Gen.	Abe Kōichi
117th Division Commander	Lt. Gen.	Suzuki Hiraku
9th Independent Tank Brigade	Col.	Kita Takeki

Fourth Army

Commander	Lt. Gen.	Uemura Mikio
Chief of Staff	Maj. Gen.	Ōno Takeki
119th Division Commander	Lt. Gen.	Shiozawa Kiyonobu
123rd Division Commander	Lt. Gen.	Kitazawa Teijirō
149th Division Commander	Lt. Gen.	Sasaki Tōichi
80th Independent Mixed Brigade	Maj. Gen.	Nomura Tokie
131st Independent Mixed Brigade	Maj. Gen.	Ube Yotsuo
135th Independent Mixed Brigade	Maj. Gen.	Hamada Jūnosuke
136th Independent Mixed Brigade	Maj. Gen.	Tsuchiya Naojirō

Seventeenth Area Army[4]

Commander	Lt. Gen.	Kōzuki Yoshio
Chief of Staff	Maj. Gen.	Ihara Junjirō
120th Division Commander	Lt. Gen.	Yanagawa Shin'ichi
150th Division Commander	Lt. Gen.	Mishima Giichirō
160th Division Commander	Lt. Gen.	Yamawaki Masao
320th Division Commander	Lt. Gen.	Yasumi Kinzaburō
127th Independent Mixed Brigade	Maj. Gen.	Sakai Takeshi

Fifty-eighth Army

Commander	Lt. Gen.	Nagatsu Sahishige
Chief of Staff	Maj. Gen.	Kisaki Hisashi
96th Division Commander	Lt. Gen.	Iinuma Mamoru
111th Division Commander	Lt. Gen.	Iwasaki Tamio
121st Division Commander	Lt. Gen.	Masai Yoshito
108th Independent Mixed Brigade	Maj. Gen.	Hiraoka Tsutomu

Thirty-fourth Army

Commander	Lt. Gen.	Kushibuchi Sen'ichi
Chief of Staff	Maj. Gen.	Kawame Tarō
59th Division Commander	Lt. Gen.	Fujita Shigeru
137th Division Commander	Lt. Gen.	Akiyama Yoshimitsu
133rd Independent Mixed Brigade	Maj. Gen.	Harada Shigekichi

Second Air Army

Commander	Lt. Gen.	Harada Uichirō
Chief of Staff	Maj. Gen.	Furuya Kenzō

1. Excludes Fifth Area Army, commanded by Lt. Gen. Higuchi Kiichirō.   2. Killed in air accident on way to his new post on 18 Aug. 1945.   3. Concurrently 1st Section chief.   4. Assigned to Kwantung Army 10 Aug. 1945.

Appendix R

Soviet Command Structure and Order of Battle in the Far Eastern Theater, Aug. 1945[1]

According to Soviet sources, the three fronts employed against the Japanese—the Trans-Baikal and 1st and 2nd Far Eastern—consisted of 80 divisions (including two tank divisions), four tank and motorized corps, and 30 separate brigades. Total manpower exceeded 1,500,000 troops, supported by 26,000 field guns and mortars, more than 5,500 tanks and self-propelled guns, and over 3,800 army combat planes.[2]

Soviet High Command, Far East

Commander-in-Chief	Marshal	A. M. Vasilevsky
Chief of Staff	Col. Gen.	S. P. Ivanov
Chief of Operations	Lt. Gen.	M. M. Potapov
Chief of Intelligence (acting)	Maj. Gen.	S. M. Chuvyrin
Artillery Commander	Marshal	M. N. Chistyakov
Armored and Mechanized Forces Commander	Col. Gen.	M. D. Solomatin
Air Force Commander	Chief Marshal	A. A. Novikov
Chief of Engineers	Col. Gen.	K. S. Nazarov
Chief of Signal Corps	Col. Gen.	N. D. Psurtsev
Chief of Logistics	Col. Gen.	V. I. Vinogradov

Trans-Baikal Front

Commander	Marshal	R. Y. Malinovsky
Chief of Staff	Gen.	M. V. Zakharov
Seventeenth Army Commander	Lt. Gen.	A. I. Danilov

Thirty-sixth Army Commander	Lt. Gen.	A. A. Luchinsky
Thirty-ninth Army Commander	Col. Gen.	I. I. Lyudnikov
Fifty-third Army Commander	Col. Gen.	I. M. Managarov
Sixth Guards Tank Army Commander	Col. Gen.	A. G. Kravchenko
Twelfth Air Army Commander	Marshal	S. A. Khudyakov
Soviet-Mongolian Mechanized Cavalry Group Commander	Col. Gen.	I. A. Pliyev
Trans-Baikal Air Defense Army Commander	Maj. Gen.	P. F. Rozhkov

First Far Eastern Front

Commander	Marshal	K. A. Meretskov
Chief of Staff	Lt. Gen.	A. N. Krutikov
First Army Commander	Col. Gen.	A. P. Beloborodov
Fifth Army Commander	Col. Gen.	N. I. Krylov
Twenty-fifth Army Commander	Col. Gen.	I. M. Chistyakov
Thirty-fifth Army Commander	Lt. Gen.	N. D. Zakhavatayev
Ninth Air Army Commander	Col. Gen.	I. M. Sokolov
Primorye Air Defense Army Commander	Lt. Gen.	A. V. Gerasimov
Chuguyevka Operational Group[3]	Maj. Gen.	V. A. Zaitsev

Second Far Eastern Front

Commander	Gen.	M. A. Purkayev
Chief of Staff	Lt. Gen.	F. I. Shevchenko
Second Army Commander	Lt. Gen.	M. F. Teryokhin
Fifteenth Army Commander	Lt. Gen.	S. K. Mamonov
Sixteenth Army Commander	Maj. Gen.	L. G. Cheremisov
Tenth Air Army Commander	Col. Gen.	P. F. Zhigarev
Amur Air Defense Army Commander	Maj. Gen.	U. K. Polyakov
Kamchatka Defense Area Commander	Maj. Gen.	A. R. Gnechko

---

1. Down to army level; excludes the Military Council and Naval command structure.   2. Pospelov et al., eds. [875], p. 418. IJA intelligence believed that the Russians employed a core of 20 rifle divisions in the main offensives, from a total of 40 or 45 available divisions; second- and third-line division strength could not be estimated. The intelligence section of the Kwantung Army air force judged Soviet Far Eastern air power at 22 divisions or 5,060 planes, but actual operational strength was not confirmed; JRD[948], JSM 13, pp. 118-19, 122-27.   3. Renamed Primorye Operational Group, mid-August 1945.

Notes

CHAPTER 31

1. Vorozheikin [184], pp. 83-86; Zhukov, *Memoirs* [1017], pp. 159-60; Shishkin [920], pp. 608-10.

2. PFC Katagiri Sōsaku, 1st Battery, 1st Bn., 7th HFA Regt., diary entry, 20 Aug., cited in *SSNT* [535], vol. 29, pp. 41-42.

3. 71st Inf. Regt. [119], 20 Aug.; Onozuka interview.

4. 2nd Bn., 28th Inf. Regt. [110], 30 Aug.; Takashima, *Barushagaru* [555], pp. 175-79.

5. 1st Bn., Hasebe detachment (8th BGU), combat report, 20 Aug., cited in *SSNT* [535], vol. 29, pp. 34-36.

6. *SSNT* [535], vol. 29, p. 37.

7. The Manchukuoan command post and 1st Cavalry Regiment were located near Lake Manzute, well to the east. Shishkin [920], pp. 395, 611; *SSNT* [535], vol. 29, p. 44. The IJA officers attached to the Manchukuoan forces fought hard and took heavy casualties.

8. Shishkin [920], p. 611.

9. Report by medical 1st Lt. Tamabuchi Kahei (Recon. Unit), 20 Aug.; BBSS, *SS* [180], vol. 27, p. 657. Also see [180], pp. 683-85; notes of Captain Ishikawa, 20 Aug. cited in *SSNT* [535], vol. 29, pp. 29-32; combat reports of 1st Recon. Co. and 4th FA Battery, cited in [535], vol. 29, p. 149; Mita [406], pp. 274-75, 294-95; Master Sgt. Onizuka Hatsuyoshi in *Nomonhan* [40], vol. 9, p. 177. Also Sumi interview. The 1st Recon. Co. (mounted) was commanded by Capt. Ishikawa Yasoji, and 2nd Co. (tankettes) by 1st Lt. Ishibashi Tatsuo; the regimental gun battery (from the 27th Inf. Regt.) by Capt. Tsuji Kiyoshi; the 4th FA Battery by Capt. Hori Tagane.

10. A Soviet rifle division included one tank battalion consisting ordinarily of a reconnaissance platoon of several amphibious tanks, and three line platoons with a total of 15 light tanks. See BBSS, *SS* [180], vol. 27, pp. 159-60.

11. Shishkin [920], pp. 610-11.

12. 7th Co., 26th Inf. Regt. [105], 20 Aug.; *SSNT* [535], vol. 29, pp. 63-64, citing diary of Hirano Kazuo, 1st Co., 26th Inf. Regt. On Ikuta's front, it was so quiet on the day of 19 August that the Japanese soldiers could even sunbathe. Next morning, in the mist, a "phantom scene" appeared on the Soviet side: white flags became visible in profusion on the horizon, presumably intended for identification. Mita [406] p. 312.

13. 7th Co., 26th Inf. Regt. [105], 20 Aug.; Sumi, interview and *Jissen* [541], p. 112; *SSNT* [535], vol. 29, pp. 48-49.

14. Shishkin [920], p. 611.

15. Kanaizuka, interview and [22], 20 Aug.; 3rd Bn., 64th Inf. Regt. [117], 20 Aug.; *SSNT* [535], vol. 29, pp. 33-34, citing diary of PFC Tanobe Chikato, 10th Co. of Kanaizuka's battalion. According to [117] above, the 10th Co. lost two of the 13 killed and 10 of the 20 wounded in the 3rd Bn. on 20 August.

16. 72nd Inf. Regt. [121], 20 Aug.; Nishikawa interview.

17. At this stage of the fighting, the 12th Air Wing included the 1st Air Group (2 fighter squadrons), 11th Group (4 fighter squadrons), 24th Group (3 fighter squadrons), and 64th Group (2 fighter squadrons). The 9th Air Wing consisted of the 10th (Composite) Group (1 reconnaissance squadron and 1 light bomber squadron), 16th Group (3 light bomber squadrons), and 61st Group (3 heavy bomber squadrons). The 15th Group (with 2 of its 3 reconnaissance squadrons) was attached to the 23rd Division; the 2nd Air Division directly controlled the group's third scout squadron. IJAF front-line strength totaled 145 planes at most. BBSS, *SS* [181], vol. 53, p. 301.

18. For IJAF dimension on 20 August, see BBSS, *SS* [181], vol. 53, pp. 299-300. Also Ishikawa interview. According to one set of official IJAF data, "only" 33 Soviet planes were eliminated on 20 August, at the cost of 8 Japanese aircraft destroyed and three airmen wounded. JRD [952], *JSM* 4, p. 7.

19. Yuzuhara interview.

20. Matsumura interview. For similarly positive views (despite discouraging Soviet-MPRA recuperative powers) by a flight sergeant from the 16th Air Group, see *SSNT* [535], vol. 29, pp. 59-60. But IJAF staff officers admit that the enemy had achieved battlefield air supremacy, "more or less." Miyashi, Miyoshi interviews.

21. Kobayashi diary, 20 Aug. (final entry), cited in *SSNT* [535], vol. 29, pp. 22-23; Komatsubara [25], 20 Aug. Komatsubara understood that the Soviet 87th Division had entered action; undoubtedly the 82nd Division was meant.

22. Y. Hata, "Nikki" [5], 20 Aug.; Komatsubara [25], 20 Aug.

23. 72nd Inf. Regt. [121], and 71st Inf. Regt. [119], 20, 21 Aug.; Kanaizuka [22], 20 Aug.; and *SSNT* [535], vol. 29, p. 53, citing 1st Bn., 64th Inf. Regt., combat report, 20 Aug.

24. From 23rd Division chief of staff, to Kwantung Army chief of staff, 23rd Division Message No. 433-1-2, Secret/Urgent, transmitted 4:30 A.M., 21 Aug., received 8:55 A.M.; Kantōgun [99], in GSS [205], vol. 10, p. 132. Also see JRD [965], *JSM* 11, part 3/C, p. 375; Tsuji [585], p. 182. The lake mentioned was Garot.

25. From Sixth Army commander, to Kwantung Army commander, Sixth Army Message No. 86-1-3, Secret/Urgent, transmitted from Hailar 5:10 P.M., 21 Aug.; received 6:10 P.M.; Kantōgun [99], in GSS [205], vol. 10, p. 133. Also see Ogisu affidavit, IMTFE, *Transcript* [777], 26 May 1947, p. 23031; JRD [965], *JSM* 11, part 3/C, p. 375; Tsuji [585], p. 183.

26. Kantōgun [99], in GSS, vol. 10, pp. 90-91; JRD [965], *JSM* 11, part 3/C, pp. 379-80; Tsuji [585], pp. 183-84.

27. Shishkin [920], p. 609; *SSNT* [535], vol. 29, p. 43, citing a history of the Manchukuo army; *Nomonhan* [40], vol. 5, pp. 36-39, citing 1st Lt. Ishii Kan'ichi of the Shihlan detachment. Maj. Gen. Suzuki Kikujirō's new detachment from the 1st Military District also moved up to guard the Handagai area. For a short but useful treatment of the role of the 18,000 Manchukuoan troops who took part in the Nomonhan hostilities, see Iwasaki Yasuo, an aide at 2nd Military District headquarters, in *Nomonhan* [40], vol. 5, pp. 32-34.

28. Zhukov, *Memoirs* [1017], p. 160; Shishkin [920], pp. 610, 612-15. Shishkin misleads when he says the Japanese brought up a portion of their reserves to Fui Heights and thus thwarted the Northern Force's advance ([920], p. 614). Sumi's small elements moved only to the Heights 739 area and managed to get a few supplies through, as noted below. Even two rapid-fire guns, intended for Fui, had to be held to defend the division command post on 22/23 August, according to the notes of Pvt. Fujimoto Tsunetake (1st Recon. Co.), cited in *SSNT* [535], vol. 29, p. 149. Also see Erickson, *Soviet* [722], pp. 534-35; Mackintosh [846], p. 108.

29. 7th Co., 26th Inf. Regt. [105], 21-23 Aug.; Mita [406], pp. 290-301; Sumi, interview and *Jissen* [541], pp. 113-17, 119-21, 128-29. For further information on Major Kamimura, who fought so well despite ill health, see *Jissen* [541], pp. 109-11. Komatsubara mentions ammunition resupply of Fui, by breaking through the encirclement at night; [25], 21 Aug. The last two trucks to leave Fui, with wounded and guards, departed at 10:30 P.M. on 22 August. See the notes of Pvt. Fujimoto, cited in *SSNT* [535], vol. 29, p. 149.

30. Komatsubara [25], 21 Aug.

31. For a description of the proliferation and "metastasis" of the red signal flags posted during combat by the Russians, see BBSS, *SS* [181], vol. 53, p. 298.

32. Onizuka, in *Nomonhan* [40], vol. 9, pp. 177-78; BBSS, *SS* [180], vol. 27, pp. 685-86, 746, citing Konuma [26]; Mita [406], p. 305; *SSNT* [535], vol. 29, pp. 149-57, citing combat reports of 4th FA Battery (13th FA Regt.) and 1st Recon. Co. (23rd Recon. Regt.), and notes of Pvt. Fujimoto, 21-25 Aug. The 6th Inf. Co. led the way out, and the 1st Recon. Co. brought up the rear, insofar as there was any real organization to the breakout operation. According to the 4th Battery's reconstruction of events, it had marched 15 km. by daybreak. [535], vol. 29, p. 157. Also see BBSS, *SS* [180], vol. 27, pp. 656, 659, for excerpts from report by medical Captain Tamabuchi, 21-24 Aug.

33. Shishkin [920], p. 614.

34. Originally stationed at Fushun, Yotsuya's unit had arrived at Nomonhan from Hailar on 21 August: *Hensei shōhō kyū Yotsuya butai* [Organizational Report on the Former Yotsuya Unit], 10 Oct. 1939 (BBSS Archives); *SSNT* [535], vol. 29, p. 66, citing Yotsuya interview; and pp. 64-65, citing diary of an Ikuta battalion (26th Inf. Regt.) survivor. Also see chap. 32, n. 12. The main IJA logistical base had been relocated eastward to Lake Abutara on 11 August as the result of Soviet aerial and long-range artillery action. According to Colonel Ise, the Russians sent about 30 tanks and 300 riflemen against Uzuru on the morning of the 22nd. IJA artillery and infantry supposedly repulsed the incursion. 13th FA Regt., Operations Order No. 109, 8:30 P.M., 22 Aug.; 3rd Bn., 13th FA Regt. [125].

35. The 9th Armored Brigade was reinforced by two companies of motorized frontier guards and a machine gun battalion from the 11th Tank Brigade of the Northern Force.

36. Shishkin [920], pp. 615-16. Shishkin seems to think that the railroad extended beyond Arshaan to Kanchuerhmiao.

37. Lt. Col. Tanigawa Kazuo (AGS Air Force Section) and Maj. Shimamura Noriyasu (Operations Section).

38. Kantōgun [99], in *GSS* [205], vol. 10, pp. 84-86. IGHQ Army Order No. 336, 7 Aug.; AGS directive, AGS chief to Kwantung Army commander, Message No. 69, 7:07 A.M. [?], received 11:10 P.M., 7 Aug.; AGS directive, AGS deputy chief to Kwantung Army chief of staff, Message No. 70, 6:58 P.M., received 8:50 P.M., 7 Aug.: *GSS* [205], vol. 10, pp. 127-29. Also see JRD [965], *JSM* 11, part 3/B, pp. 339-43; Tsuji [585], pp. 157-62, 169-72; *SSNT* [535], vol. 28, p. 79; BBSS, *SS* [181], vol. 53, pp. 264-68, 276, 300; IMTFE, *Transcript* [777], 20 May 1947, p. 22598 (Hashimoto Gun); and Inada, Miyoshi, Giga, Miyashi interviews.

39. Ishikawa, Morishita interviews. Also see BBSS, *SS* [181], vol. 53, pp. 267-68, 300.

40. Vorozheikin [184], p. 111.

41. Japanese monthly production of military aircraft at the time amounted to 38 Type 97 fighters and 10 Type 97 scout planes. BBSS, *SS* [181], vol. 53, pp. 268, 289-91, 294-95; JRD [952], *JSM* 4, pp. 69-74; [965], *JSM* 11, part 3/B, p. 345; Miyashi interview.

42. For the famous Matsumura episode: Matsumura, G. Nishihara, and Kira, interviews and writings.

43. In addition to officer casualties already mentioned, the following IJAF commanders were lost prior to the August offensive: Capt. Morimoto Shigenobu (squadron commander, 24th Group), killed (?), 22 June; Lt. Col. Katō Toshio (1st Group commander), wounded, 12 July; Capt. Yamada Keisuke (squadron commander, 1st Group), killed, 21 July; Capt. Takanashi Tatsuo (squadron commander, 1st Group), wounded, 23 July; Maj. Harada Fumio (1st Group commander), killed (?), 29 July; Capt. Kani Saiji (squadron commander, 24th Group), killed, 29 July. BBSS, *SS* [181], vol. 53, pp. 276, 294-96, 355; Tsuji [585], pp. 170-71 (errs in identifying Abe's unit); Tanaka Rinpei [565], p. 159; Mita [406], p. 221; JRD [952], *JSM* 4, pp. 70-74; [965], *JSM* 11, part 3/B, pp. 341-42; Matsumura, interview and *Nomonhan* [40], vol. 7, p. 55; Morishita, Miyashi, Miyoshi, Giga, Kira, G. Nishihara, Mikami interviews.

44. Morishita, Miyashi, Giga, Matsumura interviews; BBSS, *SS* [181], vol. 53, p. 295. The average number of flying hours in Morishita's squadron was 500-800 hours. He had about 1,500 hours, the most except for the group commanders. The IJAF training minimum was 300 hours. (Interview.) Matsumura, a 17-year flying veteran by the time of Nomonhan, began with about 6,000 hours. Between May and the day he was crippled (4 Aug.), his group flew 170 sorties—well over an hour each—and fought 26 air battles. Thus the colonel must have added more than 500 flying hours at Nomonhan. (Interview.)

45. BBSS, *SS* [181], vol. 53, pp. 276, 300-302; *SSNT* [535], vol. 29, pp. 58-59; Morishita interview.

46. BBSS, *SS* [181], vol. 53, pp. 302-4.

47. Kantōgun [99], in *GSS* [205], vol. 10, p. 86; JRD [965], *JSM* 11, part 3/B, p. 344; *ibid.*, part 3/C, p. 381; [952], *JSM* 4, p. 71; Miyoshi, Shimanuki interviews.

48. BBSS, *SS* [181], vol. 53, p. 303; JRD [952], *JSM* 4, p. 71; [965], *JSM* 11, part 3/B, p. 344.

49. Kantōgun [99], in *GSS* [205], vol. 10, p. 91; JRD [965], *JSM* 11, part 3/C, p. 381. These sources are wrong in stating that Madat was also included in the IJAF air strikes.

50. Giga, Miyoshi, Miyashi, Shimono, Mikami, Imaoka interviews; BBSS, *SS* [181], vol. 53, p. 303; Kantōgun [99], in *GSS* [205], vol. 10, p. 91; JRD [965], *JSM* 11, part 3/B, p. 344; Tsuji [585], p. 172. Russian sources ignore the IJAF raids against Tamsag on 21-22 August. Instead, as noted, they stress the weight of Soviet bomber attacks, on the 21st in particular. See Shishkin [920], p. 615.

CHAPTER 32

1. For Ogisu's own recollection, see JRD [965], *JSM* 11, part 3/C, p. 379. For his report of 23 August, see *ibid.*, p. 383; and Kantōgun [99], in *GSS* [205], vol. 10, pp. 134-35.

2. S. Hamada [2]; Y. Hata, "Nikki" [5].

3. Komatsubara [25], 21 Aug. For details of the severe antitank combat by IJA infantry and artillery in Colonel Morita's sector, see 71st Inf. Regt. [119], 21 Aug.; and *SSNT* [535], vol. 29, pp. 67-71.

4. Y. Hata, "Nikki" [5], 21 Aug.

5. S. Hamada, [2] and interview. Also see Y. Hata, "Nikki" [5], 21 Aug.

6. Y. Hata, "Nikki" [5], 21-22 Aug.

7. Kanaizuka interview.

8. Y. Hata "Nikki" [5], 22 Aug.

9. 23rd Division, Operations Order No. 197, 5:30 P.M., 22 Aug., 2 km. south-southeast of Heights 752; received by 71st Inf. Regt. by radio at 6 P.M.: 71st Inf. Regt. [119], 21-22 Aug.

10. *Ibid.*

11. Adds Sumi: "Komatsubara disliked my type—one who expressed his own opinions frankly." Sumi interview, supplemented by *Jissen* [541], pp. 131-32.

12. Sumi interview. Yotsuya had brought only 3 of his 4 companies from Fushun to Mukden in July. There, his veteran three-year men were pulled out and sent to the 23rd Division as replacements; the one-year and two-year soldiers proceeded to Hailar. SSNT [535], vol. 29, p. 65, citing interview with Yotsuya.

13. 23rd Division, Operations Order No. 198, 2 P.M., 23 Aug.: JRD [965], *JSM* 11, part 3/C, pp. 384-85; Harada interview; *SSNT* [535], vol. 29, pp. 79, 85-87. Other categories of distribution included the artillery corps, the main body of the engineers, Col. Akashi Taijirō's 2nd Mortar Regiment (a chemical unit which ordinarily employed tear gas, under direct control of the Kwantung Army), field antiaircraft artillery, the attached 15th Air Group scouts, and the divisional signal unit.

14. 13th FA Regt., Operations Order No. 110, 5:30 P.M., 23 Aug., at observation post 1.5 km. east of Heights 738; 3rd Bn., 13th FA Regt. [125]. Also see *SSNT* [535], vol. 29, pp. 107-8, citing Takatsukasa interview and combat report, 2nd Bn., 7th HFA Regt., 23 Aug. Maj. Umeda Kyōzō had replaced the wounded Mishima as acting regimental commander for a while but, after the regiment headquarters displaced south, Maj. Hayashi Tadaaki replaced Umeda (one military academy class senior to him) for about two weeks, pursuant to Hata's order. T. Hayashi interview.

15. S. Hamada, interview and [2]; Imaoka interview.

16. See Kantōgun [99], in *GSS* [205], vol. 10, p. 93.

17. Kwantung Army, Operations Order No. 134 (Summary), to Kwantung Army deputy chief, from army commander, Message No. 550 (drafted by Hattori), 2:10 P.M., 23 Aug.: Kantōgun [99], in *GSS* [205], vol. 10, p. 134; JRD [965], *JSM* 11, part 3/C, p. 382; Tsuji [585], p. 185; BBSS, *SS* [180], vol. 27, p. 243. Kunisaki had replaced Lt. Gen. Sonobe Waichirō in the recent, routine command reassignments. The above-cited order also contained a clause about signal units being sent to Hailar.

18. To Kwantung Army commander, from Sixth Army commander, at Komatsubara Hq., 23rd Division Message No. 504, transmitted 6 P.M., received 8:50 P.M., 23 Aug.; Kantōgun [99], in *GSS* [205], vol. 10, pp. 134-35; S. Hamada [2]. A flawed version is found in JRD [965], *JSM* 11, part 3/C, p. 383.

19. Tsuji [585], p. 185.

20. S. Hamada, interview and [2].

21. S. Hamada, interview and [2].

22. 72nd Inf. Regt. [121], 22 Aug.; and *SSNT* [535], vol. 29, pp. 72-73. I have not found mention of the lost artillery piece elsewhere. For details of the IJA night-attack actions, which may have prevented grave danger to General Kobayashi and the 72nd Regiment, see [535], vol. 29, pp. 68-72.

23. M. Tsuchiya, T. Hayashi interviews.

24. Y. Hata, "Nikki" [5], 23 Aug.; M. Tsuchiya, T. Hayashi interviews; *SSNT* [535], vol. 29, pp. 88-90.

25. Mita [406], pp. 331-33; *SSNT* [535], vol. 29, p. 87.

26. Sumi, interview and *Jissen* [541], pp. 132-44; 7th Co., 26th Inf. Regt. [105], 23-24 Aug.; BBSS, *SS* [180], vol. 27, p. 654; Komatsubara [25], 24 Aug., regarding his operations order issued at 1 P.M. on the 23rd; N. Itō interview. Also see Sumi in *Nomonhan* [40], vol. 7, p. 23 (round table), where Kamimura is erroneously called Kawamura. Trucks for Sumi were delayed by the movement of the new Itō detachment for the Sixth Army's use. BBSS, *SS* [180], vol. 27, p. 651.

27. 71st Inf. Regt. [119], 23-24 Aug.; and *SSNT* [535], vol. 29, pp. 100-102; Komatsubara [25], 24 Aug.

28. Tsuji [585], pp. 186-91.

29. N. Morita interview.

30. Kobayashi Inf. Group, Operations Order No. 66; 72nd Inf. Regt., Operations Order No. 52, 8:30 A.M., at Heights 752: 72nd Inf. Regt. [121], 23-24 Aug. For divisional-truck supply operations in support of the infantry transfer, see Yamanaka Kiyoshi (Sōma motor company), in *Nomonhan* [40], vol. 9, pp. 132-33. Also see BBSS, *SS* [180], vol. 27, p. 649.

31. *SSNT* [535], vol. 29, pp. 127-28, citing 2nd Lt. Hiratsuka Matsunosuke.

CHAPTER 33

1. Nishikawa had received his promotion as of 1 August. (Interview.)

2. Nishikawa interview; 72nd Inf. Regt. [121], 24 Aug.; *SSNT* [535], vol. 29, pp. 121-27.

3. Serizawa Yasushi, in *Nomonhan* [40], vol. 4, pp. 104-6; *SSNT* [535], vol. 29, p. 128.

4. Nishikawa interview.

5. Col. Tazaka Sen'ichi, in *Nomonhan* [40], vol. 2, p. 53; and Serizawa, in *ibid.*, vol. 4, p. 105. Also see *SSNT* [535], vol. 29, p. 144, citing Y. Hata.

6. 72nd Inf. Regt. [121], 24 Aug.; Nishikawa interview; *SSNT* [535], vol. 29, p. 130. Nishikawa thinks that a tank ran over Sakai's foot too. (Interview.) Also see Yamanaka, in *Nomonhan* [40], vol. 9, p. 133. For a eulogy, see Kobayashi [343]. The byline notwithstanding, Nishikawa tells me that he wrote the essay in behalf of General Kobayashi. (Interview.)

7. *SSNT* [535], vol. 29, pp. 140-42 (Hiratsuka interview); and Nishikawa interview.

8. N. Itō interview; and Tsuji [585], pp. 192-93.

9. Tsuji [585], pp. 193-99; Komatsubara [25], 24 Aug.; Y. Hata, "Nikki" [5], 24 Aug.; Nishikawa interview; BBSS, *SS* [180], vol. 27, p. 653; Mita [406], p. 330.

10. 72nd Inf. Regt. [121], 24 Aug.

11. Nishikawa interview.

12. Tsuji [585], pp. 199-205; S. Hamada interview. Hirowatari's 72nd Inf. Regt., Operations Order No. 53, midnight, 24 Aug., was based on 23rd Div., Operations Order No. 199, 10 P.M., 24 Aug., at combat hq., Heights 752. See 72nd Inf. Regt. [121], 24 Aug.; and JRD [965], *JSM* 11, part 3/C, pp. 385-89.

13. 72nd Inf. Regt. [121], 24-25 Aug.; Tsuji [585], pp. 204-5; Nishikawa interview; Yamanaka, in *Nomonhan* [40], vol. 9, p. 133; BBSS, *SS* [180], vol. 27, pp. 653, 703. According to the records, 26 horses were killed and 5 injured this day, from 114 in the regiment.

14. N. Morita interview; Mita [406], pp. 335, 343-44; *SSNT* [535], vol. 29, pp. 145-46, citing 28th Inf. Regt., combat report, 24 Aug. I have attempted to reconcile Japanese figures on distances to the objectives. For the message from General Morita and the pep talk given by the 9th Company commander in the morning, see Mita [406], p. 334.

15. 28th Inf. Regt., combat report, 24 Aug., cited in *SSNT* [535], vol. 29, p. 146; and Mita [406], pp. 349-50.

16. BBSS, *SS* [180], vol. 27, p. 653; Mita [406], pp. 338, 342, 344-46; *SSNT* [535], vol. 29, p. 146, citing 28th Inf. Regt., combat report, 24 Aug.

17. BBSS, *SS* [180], vol. 27, p. 653 and pocket map (situation as of 24 Aug.); N. Morita interview; *SSNT* [535], vol. 29, p. 147, citing Yotsuya interview. The most reliable data on casualties sustained by the Yotsuya unit during the period of its participation in the Nomonhan Incident (including the Heights 780 battle) show 122 killed and 94 wounded. The force lost 186 rifles and 15 light or heavy machine guns. For the Yotsuya unit's report of 10 Oct. 1939, see chap. 31, n. 34. Also see the somewhat comparable Sixth Army data (Table 39.1) and the understated Kwantung Army entry (Appendix J).

18. 7th Co., 26th Inf. Regt. [105], 24 Aug.

19. Sumi, interview and *Jissen* [541], pp. 145-49.

20. Komatsubara [25], 24 Aug.

21. Y. Hata, "Nikki" [5], 24 Aug.; and *SSNT* [535], vol. 29, p. 129, citing interview with 2nd Lt. Tsukinoki Sei (Yasushi).

22. S. Hamada, interview and [2]; JRD [965], *JSM* 11, part 3/C, p. 386.

23. 23rd Division, Operations Order No. 199, 10 P.M., 24 Aug.; 14th Inf. Brigade, Operations Order No. 30, 11 P.M., 24 Aug.: BBSS, *SS* [180], vol. 27, pp. 654-55. Sixth Army, Battle Message No. 10-1, from Tsuji to Kwantung Army chief of staff, transmitted 1:40 A.M., 25 Aug. (Hailar), received 2:20 A.M.: Kantōgun [99], in *GSS* [205], vol. 10, p. 136. Also N. Morita interview.

24. Mita [406], pp. 334, 340-41, 343; BBSS, *SS* [180], vol. 27, p. 655; N. Morita interview. It may have been nearer 2 P.M. when Fujioka was killed, after an IJA artillery bombardment that lasted two hours.

25. Sumi, interview and *Jissen* [541], pp. 153-76; Negami interview; 7th Co., 26th Inf. Regt. [105], 25 Aug.; Mita [406], p. 458. Nakano's aide was 1st Lt. Uchida Chūgorō (wounded); the 2nd MG Co. commander was 1st Lt. Watanabe Masao (also wounded). For commentary on the fine performance of the supporting 1st Artillery Battery commanded by 1st Lt. Matsuda Heishirō, see Sumi, *Jissen* [541], pp. 186-87.

26. Y. Hata, "Nikki" [5], 25 Aug. For a short reference to the Muleng heavy artillery unit on 25 August, see *SSNT* [535], vol. 29, p. 196. For similarly brief treatment of artillery actions on 26-27 August, see [535], vol. 29, pp. 196-97.

27. Komatsubara [25], 24-25 Aug.; S. Hamada [2]; JRD [965], *JSM* 11, part 3/C, p. 389. Also see BBSS, *SS* [180], vol. 27, p. 655.

28. Sumi, interview and *Jissen* [541], pp. 176-79.

29. N. Morita, Imaoka interviews. For Zhukov's telling criticism of IJA senior leadership, expressed to Stalin and summarized in a later chapter, see Zhukov, *Memoirs* [1017], p. 169.

30. Y. Hata, "Nikki" [5], 25 Aug. The order issued by the 2nd Bn., 26th Inf. Regt., at 11 P.M. on 25 Aug. reflected the intelligence being disseminated that the enemy was retreating. 7th Co., 26th Inf. Regt. [105], 25 Aug.

31. 23rd Division, Operations Order No. 200, 6 P.M., 25 Aug.; 14th Inf. Brigade, Operations Order [number unavailable], 8 P.M., same date: BBSS, *SS* [180], vol. 27, p. 655; *SSNT* [535], vol. 29, p. 196.

32. N. Morita interview. Also see BBSS, *SS* [180], vol. 27, p. 655. Other Japanese sources have no idea why the IJA night attack was called off. See *SSNT* [535], vol. 29, p. 196.

33. Sixth Army, Operations Order No. 26, 2:30 A.M., 26 Aug., at combat hq., Lake Mohorehi: Komatsubara [25], 26 Aug. Also see BBSS, *SS* [180], vol. 27, p. 668.

34. N. Morita interview; Mita [406], pp. 342, 350-51. Mortar fire killed medical First Lieutenant Kawaji on 30 August. *Ibid.*, p. 352.

35. Komatsubara [25], 22 Aug.; Sumi interview.

36. Komatsubara [25], 26 Aug.; N. Morita interview; JRD [965], *JSM* 11, part 3/C, p. 389; S. Hamada [2].

37. 2nd Lt. Tsunashima Takeo says his regimental-gun battery engaged small formations of enemy armor on three or four occasions during the battle for Heights 780, and knocked out five tanks. (Interview.)

38. N. Morita, Negami, Maeda, Tsunashima interviews; Sumi, interview and *Jissen* [541],

pp. 179-90; 7th Co., 26th Inf. Regt. [105], 25, 27-30 Aug.; Komatsubara [25], 26 Aug.; Mita [406], pp. 351-52, 458, 461-62.

39. 23rd Division, Staff Message No. 520-1, from 23rd Division chief of staff and Tsuji, to Kwantung Army chief of staff, transmitted 9:45 A.M., 24 Aug. (Hailar), received 1:20 P.M.; 23rd Division, Staff Message No. 520-2, from 23rd Division chief of staff, to Kwantung Army chief of staff, transmitted 9:50 A.M., 24 Aug. (Komatsubara), received 1:35 P.M.: Kantōgun [99], in GSS [205], vol. 10, p. 135.

40. Abe Hq., Staff Message No. 964, from Kwantung Army deputy chief of staff, to Kwantung Army commander, transmitted 2:20 P.M., 24 Aug. (Hailar), received 2:50 P.M.; Kwantung Army, Staff (1st Sec.) Message No. 554, from Kwantung Army chief of staff (drafting officer Murasawa), to Kwantung Army deputy chief of staff, through Sixth Army chief of staff and 8th BGU commander (Hailar), transmitted 1 P.M., 24 Aug.: Kantōgun [99], in GSS [205], vol. 10, pp. 135-36.

41. Sixth Army, Combat Message No. 10-1, from Tsuji through Sixth Army commander, to Kwantung Army chief of staff, transmitted 1:40 A.M., 25 Aug. (Hailar), received 2:20 A.M.: Kantōgun [99], in GSS, vol. 10, p. 136.

42. Sixth Army, Combat Message No. 15, from Tsuji via Sixth Army chief of staff, to Kwantung Army chief of staff, transmitted 6:50 P.M., 25 Aug., received 9:10 P.M.: Kantōgun [99], in GSS [205], vol. 10, pp. 137-38.

43. Kwantung Army, Staff (1st Sec.) Message No. 558, from Kwantung Army chief of staff, drafting officer Hattori, to AGS deputy and vice minister of war, prepared 25 Aug.: Kantōgun [99], in GSS [205], vol. 10, pp. 91, 136-37. Also see BBSS, SS [180], vol. 27, p. 633.

44. Kwantung Army, Message No. 559, from 1st Sec., drafted by Hattori, to Tsuji, 25 Aug.: Kantōgun [99], in GSS [205], vol. 10, pp. 91, 137; JRD [965], JSM 11, part 3/C, p. 391.

45. Sixth Army, Combat Message No. 13, from chief of staff, to 1st Section chief, Kwantung Army, transmitted 4:25 P.M., 25 Aug., received 6:50 P.M.: Kantōgun [99], in GSS [205], vol. 10, p. 137; JRD [965], JSM 11, part 3/C, pp. 391-92.

46. Kantōgun [99], in GSS [205], vol. 10, p. 92; BBSS, SS [180], vol. 27, p. 633.

47. AGS Message No. 164, from AGS deputy, to Kwantung Army chief of staff, transmitted 12:45 P.M., 25 Aug., received 4:40 P.M.: Kantōgun [99], in GSS [205], vol. 10, pp. 92-93, 139; JRD [965], JSM 11, part 3/C, p. 399.

48. Kwantung Army, Staff (1st Sec.) Message No. 565, in reply to AGS Message No. 164, from chief of staff, drafting officer Hattori, to AGS deputy, prepared 25 Aug.: Kantōgun [99], in GSS [205], vol. 10, pp. 139-40.

49. Sixth Army, Combat Message No. 23, from chief of staff, to Kwantung Army chief of staff, transmitted 3:20 A.M., 26 Aug., received 6:20 A.M.: Kantōgun [99], in GSS [205], vol. 10, p. 138.

50. Tsuji [585], p. 205; Kantōgun [99], in GSS [205], vol. 10, p. 92; BBSS, SS [180], vol. 27, p. 633. The sequence of decisions is reversed in JRD [965], JSM 11, part 3/C, p. 393.

51. Kantōgun [99], in GSS [205], vol. 10, p. 92; N. Morita interview; 7th Co., 26th Inf. Regt. [105], 30 Aug. Also see BBSS, SS [180], vol. 27, pp. 668-70.

52. Hamada, interview and [2]. For rosters, see Mita [406], p. 12; and SSNT [535], vol. 29, p. 245.

53. Tsuji [585], pp. 183, 206-7. Also see Zhukov, *Memoirs* [1017], pp. 161-62.

54. I collated IJA information from various sources when I edited JRD [965], JSM 11, part 3/B, pp. 185-86, n. 9-11. For Soviet map data, see *ibid.*, p. 187.

55. The 1st Regiment of the 152nd Rifle Division, according to Shishkin [920], p. 618.

56. *Ibid.*, pp. 618-20.

57. Y. Hata, "Nikki" [5], 24 Aug.; and BBSS, SS [180], vol. 27, pp. 630, 649, 655; N. Morita, Sumi, Imaoka interviews.

58. N. Morita interview; JRD [956], JSM 5, pp. 55-56; BBSS, SS [180], vol. 27, pp. 650-51.

CHAPTER 34

1. Shishkin [920], pp. 620-22.

2. BBSS, SS [180], vol. 27, pp. 687-90; SSNT [535], vol. 29, pp. 177-80, 184, citing Sugitani

Yoshio; Onda, [473], vol. 2, pp. 118-20; Takashima, *Barushagaru* [555], pp. 187-97; Gomikawa, *Nomonhan* [212], pp. 261-62; *Nomonhan* [40], vol. 5, pp. 114-16, 136-42.

3. *Kogun funtō*: fighting alone and unsupported.

4. Bn. Hq., 12 men; 5th Co., 15; 6th Co., 6; 7th Co., 3; MG Co., 6; battalion-gun battery, 13; total 55, including wounded: 2nd Bn., 28th Inf. Regt. [110], 25 Aug.

5. Takashima tells the wonderful story of an unarmed IJA superior private who had gone to a dip on 27 August to defecate, ran into a Russian noncom on the crestline, jumped the soldier who was about to fire, bit him on the nose, knocked away his weapon, and tied him up with his canteen strap. *Barushagaru* [555], pp. 213-14.

6. 2nd Bn., 28th Inf. Regt. [110], 23-30 Aug.; *SSNT* [535], vol. 29, pp. 176, 180-81; Takashima, *Barushagaru* [555], pp. 184-215, and *Shunkan* [556], pp. 157-60; Mita [406], pp. 394-95; BBSS, *SS* [180], vol. 27, p. 690. For Matsutomo, see Gomikawa, *Nomonhan* [212], p. 260; Y. Hata, "Nikki" [5], 28 Aug.; *Nomonhan* [40], vol. 7, p. 118. For details on the 1st FA Regt., see Onda, [473], vol. 2, pp. 153-59. According to General Hata, a second lieutenant from the 7th FA Battery also showed up at artillery corps headquarters on 28 August.

7. Onozuka interview.

8. 1st Lt. Kawazoe Takehiko and an enlisted man could not make it through; 71st Inf. Regt. [119], 26 Aug. For their adventures, see *SSNT* [535], vol. 29, pp. 189-91, citing Kawazoe.

9. 71st Inf. Regt. [119], 27 Aug. Compare with the earlier-cited account of the Kajikawa battalion—i.e., that it had sought to conduct liaison with friendly units.

10. 71st Inf. Regt. [119], 24-28 Aug.; Komatsubara [25], 26 Aug.; Onozuka interview; Maj. Tōi Shinji (Nobuharu), 2nd Bn. commander, in *Nomonhan* [40], vol. 2, pp. 34-35; Onda [473], vol. 2, pp. 109-18; *SSNT* [535], vol. 29, p. 172.

11. Shishkin [920], pp. 617, 620-24; Zhukov, *Memoirs* [1017], pp. 160, 162. Also see Mackintosh [846], p. 108; Erickson, *Soviet* [722], p. 536.

12. JRD [952], *JSM* 4, p. 71.

13. Kanaizuka, interview and [22], 23-24 Aug.; and *SSNT* [535], vol. 29, pp. 159, 164.

14. Kanaizuka, interview and [22], 26 Aug.; Mita [406], pp. 322-23; Gomikawa, *Nomonhan* [212], p. 227; *SSNT* [535], vol. 29, pp. 164-66; *Nomonhan* [40], vol. 3, pp. 46-47. BBSS, *SS* [180], vol. 27, p. 656, kills off Major Ikuta too soon, on 25/26 August.

15. The Japanese army later used the example of the 10th Company as a model for study. See Rikugun, *Shōsen* [485], no. 14.

16. According to a story Kanaizuka told in 1942, only white poisonous water was found until the fourth day. Praying for even a mouthful of water for his wounded and sick soldiers, Kanaizuka closed his eyes, hurled his saber, and ordered his men to dig at that spot. Success ensued. Hasegawa Shin, *Naigai Times* (Tokyo), 10 Feb. 1958, p. 1. Hasegawa mistakenly called the major "Kanaizawa." My account is based on Kanaizuka, interview and [22], 26-28 Aug. Also see Gomikawa, *Nomonhan* [212], pp. 228, 272-73.

17. One mountain gun per 15-cm. cannon; and one each per 10-cm. cannon and 15-cm. howitzer battery. Y. Hata, "Nikki" [5], 24 Aug.

18. G. Nishihara interview; Y. Hata, "Nikki" [5], 24 Aug.; BBSS, *SS* [180], vol. 27, pp. 644, 664, 690; *SSNT* [535], vol. 29, pp. 200-201; 3rd Bn., 13th FA Regt. [125], 24 Aug.

19. Gomikawa, *Nomonhan* [212], p. 24.

20. 3rd Bn., 13th FA Regt. [125], 27 Aug.; *SSNT* [535], vol. 29, pp. 196-97, 201-6, 215-20; Gomikawa, *Nomonhan* [212], pp. 244, 255-56.

21. *Nomonhan* [40], vol. 9, pp. 168-71, and vol. 10, pp. 126-30; *SSNT* [535], vol. 28, pp. 199, 206-7, 220-25, 227-31; Gomikawa, *Nomonhan* [212], pp. 244-45, 258-59, 279-81; BBSS, *SS* [180], vol. 27, pp. 675-77; M. Tsuchiya, T. Hayashi, Mishima, Iwata interviews. Tsuchiya heard that Yamazaki was killed by tank fire while sighting his piece. It is also Tsuchiya's understanding that the survivors of the battalion, under a platoon leader, launched the last charge after destroying their howitzers by jamming a round into the muzzle of each barrel, wrecking the piece and killing the men in the vicinity. (Interview.) The 2nd Battalion commander, Major Hayashi, who was located south of the Holsten, is not sure whether the 1st Battalion's howitzers were destroyed by their crews or by the enemy; he thinks that tank fire was probably most responsible. (Interview.)

22. Gomikawa, *Nomonhan* [212], pp. 282-83; *SSNT* [535], vol. 29, p. 226; BBSS, *SS* [180], vol. 27, pp. 675-76. Mishima told me of his receipt of Umeda's last words in the hospital in Hsinking at the beginning of September, and how he wanted to resume command of the regiment. But his replacement, Colonel Irie, was already on the way. (Interview.) Umeda's testament was shown to the Emperor on 27 November. (Irie interview.)

23. M. Tsuchiya interview.

24. The 1st Battery fired 107 rounds on 24 August, 412 on the 25th, 124 on the 26th, and 157 on the 27th. The 2nd Battery fired 93 rounds on 24 August, 216 on the 25th, and 67 on the 26th. Data supplied by M. Tsuchiya.

25. The battalion lost 8 officers and 140 men killed: headquarters, 43 (including 3 officers); 1st Battery, 57 (1 officer); 2nd Battery, 47 (4 officers); supply and maintenance unit, 1. The wounded numbered 1 officer and 63 men: headquarters, 9; 1st Battery, 29; 2nd Battery, 22 (1 officer); supply and maintenance unit, 4. Forty men were missing: headquarters, 18; 1st Battery, 14; 2nd Battery, 8. Data supplied by M. Tsuchiya. T. Hayashi believes that about one-third of the 1st Battalion (100 men?) got out alive. (Interview.)

26. Gomikawa, *Nomonhan* [212], pp. 279-81.

27. *SSNT* [535], vol. 29, p. 223, citing interview with Takatsukasa around 1969.

28. For Ozaki's actions, see the 3rd Battery gunner's differing version, cited above.

29. *SSNT* [535], vol. 29, pp. 239-40, citing Yasaku Jirō.

30. Y. Hata, "Nikki" [5], 27-29 Aug.; *Yasen jūhōhei dai-7 rentai shi* [A History of the 7th Heavy Field Artillery Regiment] (Tokyo: Yajū Shichi Rentai-kai, 1973), pp. 244-45 (Takeda Hidezō [Shūzō], a 4th Battery soldier); Gomikawa, *Nomonhan* [212], pp. 257-58; *SSNT* [535], vol. 29, pp. 207-11, 232-39. For Gomikawa's critique, see [212], pp. 260-61.

31. Irie interview. The testaments of Tanaka and Umeda were shown to the Emperor on 27 November.

32. 3rd Bn., 13th FA Regt. [125], 25-29 Aug.; 1st Bn., 13th FA Regt. [124], 24-25 Aug.; *Nomonhan* [40], vol. 7, p. 118; *Nomonhan 90-yahō heishi no kiroku* [Type 90 Field Artillery Soldiers' Nomonhan Records], 2 vols., ed. Fukushima Kiyoshi and Sugawara Tomiya (Tokyo, 1979-80), vol. 2, pp. 114-15; *SSNT* [535], vol. 29, pp. 199-201, 212-15, 240-42, 278-80; Gomikawa, *Nomonhan* [212], pp. 259-60.

33. *Nomonhan* [40], vol. 7, p. 118.

34. Y. Hata, "Nikki" [5], 30 Aug.; 3rd Bn., 13th FA Regt. [125], 25 Aug.; BBSS, *SS* [180], vol. 27, p. 664.

CHAPTER 35

1. S. Hamada, interview and [2].

2. Sixth Army, Operations Order No. 26, 2:30 A.M., 26 Aug., Lake Mohorehi: Komatsubara [25], 26 Aug.; BBSS, *SS* [180], vol. 27, p. 668; Gomikawa, *Nomonhan* [212], p. 252; *SSNT* [535], vol. 29, p. 198; Hamada [2] and interview.

3. 23rd Division, Operations Order No. 202, 2 P.M., 26 Aug.: BBSS, *SS* [180], vol. 27, p. 668; Gomikawa, *Nomonhan* [212], pp. 252, 275; *SSNT* [535], vol. 29, pp. 198, 243, 253. The 23rd Division thought that Soviet pressure on Yamagata's front, though exerted from west, north, and east, was relatively lighter than on the other sectors. In addition, a considerable amount of ammunition and food was stored in Yamagata's area. 23rd Division, Staff Message No. 548, from division chief of staff, to Kwantung Army chief of staff, transmitted from front line, 11 P.M., 26 Aug., received 1:48 A.M., 27 Aug.; Kantōgun [99], in *GSS* [205], vol. 10, p. 138. With the break in communications from the regiment since the 26th, Komatsubara realized that Yamagata was facing a final crisis. 23rd Division, Staff Message No. 552-3, from division chief of staff, to Kwantung Army chief of staff, transmitted 1:50 P.M., 27 Aug., received 4:40 P.M.; Kantōgun [99], in *GSS* [205], vol. 10, p. 138.

4. Hamada [2]. Sixth Army, Operations Order No. 29, 26 Aug., time unavailable: BBSS, *SS* [180], vol. 27, pp. 668-69; Gomikawa, *Nomonhan* [212], p. 275.

5. Hamada, interview and [2].

6. S. Hamada asserts that the IJA positions at Tako-no-atama, located near the proposed jump-off line, received particular attention by the Sixth Army. (Interview.)

7. I. Saitō, Numazaki, Murata, Suzuki Yoshiyasu interviews.

8. 23rd Division, Operations Order No. 204, 1 P.M., 27 Aug.; Komatsubara [25], 28 Aug.; BBSS, SS [180], vol. 27, p. 696; Gomikawa, *Nomonhan* [212], p. 275; SSNT [535], vol. 29, pp. 254-55, 258, 269; Onda [473], vol. 2, p. 145. Okamoto visited and briefed the 72nd Regiment around noon. At 2 P.M., Komatsubara came, described the situation of Hasebe and Yamagata, and announced his "tragic intention." The official operations order was received at 5:30 P.M. Later, Sugitachi came to coordinate the advance. 72nd Inf. Regt. [121], 27 Aug.

9. Suzuki Yoshiyasu, S. Hamada, I. Saitō, Onozuka interviews; 71st Inf. Regt. [119]; BBSS, SS [180], vol. 27, p. 696; SSNT [535], vol. 29, p. 265; Onda [473], vol. 2, p. 145.

10. Komatsubara [25], 27 Aug. Murata apparently drafted the text of Komatsubara's exhortation before being wounded that day. (Suzuki Yoshiyasu interview.)

11. Suzuki Yoshiyasu interview; and SSNT [535], vol. 29, p. 261.

12. SSNT [535], vol. 29, p. 258, citing Hirowatari.

13. Hamada, interview and [2]. Also see BBSS, SS [180], vol. 27, p. 695.

14. Komatsubara [25], 27 August; Onda [473], vol. 2, pp. 131-32; SSNT [535], vol. 29, p. 255. Also see BBSS, SS [180], vol. 27, p. 670. At the time, Suzuki Yoshiyasu and aide N. Tanaka could only make educated guesses as to the drift of the long conversation between the two generals. (Interviews.)

15. Suzuki Yoshiyasu interview.

16. Gomikawa, *Nomonhan* [212], pp. 276-77; BBSS, SS [180], vol. 27, p. 670; Onda [473], vol. 2, pp. 208-9. Gomikawa says the 23rd Division ended up like a deserted child. [212], p. 275.

17. Onda [473], vol. 2, p. 208, citing Hanada.

18. Numazaki interview.

19. SSNT [535], vol. 29, p. 269, citing Murai; *Nomonhan* [40], vol. 8, pp. 128-30; Komatsubara [25], 28 Aug.; Y. Hata, "Nikki" [5], 27 Aug.; Suzuki Yoshiyasu and I. Saitō interviews; 71st Inf. Regt. [119] and 72nd Inf. Regt. [121], 27 Aug. Komatsubara's diary entry mentions the elimination of a tank gun; I have chosen to correct this to an antitank gun.

20. 71st Inf. Regt. [119], 28 Aug.

21. Komatsubara [25], 28 Aug.; and SSNT [535], vol. 29, pp. 265-66.

22. JRD [965], JSM 11, part 3/C, pp. 543-49, citing Kusaba, *Noro kōchi* [358]; SSNT [535], vol. 29, p. 265, citing Y. Hata; Komatsubara [25], 28 Aug.; Suzuki Yoshiyasu interview.

23. 23rd Division, Operations Order No. 205, 3:30 P.M., 28 Aug.; received by 71st Inf. Regt. at 4 P.M., by 72nd Inf. Regt. at 4:50 P.M.: 71st Inf. Regt. [119] and 72nd Inf. Regt. [121], 28 Aug.; and Onda, [473], vol. 2, pp. 146-47; BBSS, SS [180], vol. 27, p. 697; SSNT [535], vol. 29, p. 266; Suzuki interview.

24. Onozuka interview.

25. 72nd Inf. Regt. [121], 28 Aug.; Komatsubara [25], 29 Aug.; I. Saitō interview; SSNT [535], vol. 29, p. 272.

26. 72nd Inf. Regt. [121], 28 Aug.

27. 71st Inf. Regt. [119], 28 Aug.; I. Saitō interview; SSNT [535], vol. 29, p. 268.

28. Suzuki Yoshiyasu interview; and SSNT [535], vol. 29, pp. 272-74, 281, citing 1st Bn., 64th Inf. Regt., combat report, 29 Aug.

29. The 1st Battalion's records say 4:30 A.M., but I have used 3:30 because that is the time Kanaizuka's more distant 3rd Battalion recorded receipt of Yamagata's order issued at 2 A.M., and because Akai was already talking about rejoining the regimental colors when Suzuki arrived around 3:40 A.M.

30. Suzuki Yoshiyasu interview; 1st Bn., 64th Inf. Regt., combat report, 29 Aug., cited in SSNT [535], vol. 29, pp. 281-82; 3rd Bn., same regiment, [117], 29 Aug.; BBSS, SS [180], vol. 27, pp. 694-95; Gomikawa, *Nomonhan* [212], p. 293; *Nomonhan* [40], vol. 11, p. 35, citing Furukawa Tsunemi.

31. 13th FA Regt., Operations Order No. 15, 2:30 A.M., 29 Aug.: 3rd Bn., 13th FA Regt. [125], 29 Aug. The 2nd Battalion received the order at 2:45 A.M.

32. BBSS, SS [180], vol. 27, pp. 691-93; Gomikawa, *Nomonhan* [212], pp. 291-92; SSNT [535], vol. 29, pp. 169-71, 275-76, 281-82; *Nomonhan* [40], vol. 3, p. 54.

33. Fukushima and Sugawara, eds., *90-yahō*, vol. 2, pp. 114-15. *SSNT* [535], vol. 29, pp. 282-83, citing Ōmura Seitarō.

34. 6th Battery, 13th FA Regt., combat report, 29 Aug., cited in *SSNT* [535], vol. 29, p. 282; and [535], pp. 285-86, citing Tokonami Shigeji. Also see 3rd Bn., 13th FA Regt. [125], 29 Aug; Fukushima and Sugawara, eds., *90-yahō*, vol. 2, pp. 114-15.

35. 3rd Bn., 13th FA Regt. [125], 29 Aug. Fukushima and Sugawara, eds., *90-yahō*, vol. 2, pp. 114-15. Also see chap. 34.

36. Fukushima and Sugawara, eds., *90-yahō*, vol. 2, pp. 114-15. *SSNT* [535], vol. 29, p. 284, citing Amiya Kiichi.

37. Mita [406], p. 324, BBSS, *SS* [180], vol. 27, p. 656.

38. Postwar Japanese sources cite the time of 4:20 P.M. for Yamagata's death, and about 4:30 P.M. for Ise's death. But Komatsubara's preliminary report of 8 September says that, after being besieged, at 6:40 P.M. Yamagata himself burned the colors and committed suicide on the right bank of the Holsten. 23rd Division commander to Kwantung Army commander, 23rd Division Staff Message No. 967 [?], transmitted 1 A.M., 8 Sept., received 6:10 A.M.; Kantōgun [99], in *GSS* [205], vol. 10, pp. 148-49. Apparently Yamagata was trapped all day on 29 August but could not last until nightfall, only a few hours away. For the Kwantung Army's retransmission of information to the AGS and the war ministry, see [205], vol. 10, p. 149.

39. According to *Hagakure*, 107, "It is advisable to look habitually into a mirror to put one's appearance right." The warrior should strive to convey an impression of being "self-composed and firm-minded."

40. Kanaizuka, interview and [22], 28-30 Aug.; *Nomonhan* [40], vol. 3, pp. 54-55, and vol. 7, p. 118; BBSS, *SS* [180], vol. 27, pp. 692-93; *SSNT* [535], vol. 29, pp. 287-89, 166-68, 192-95; Gomikawa, *Nomonhan* [212], pp. 292-93, 273, 288-90; *Naigai Times* (Tokyo), 10 Feb. 1958, p. 1; 3rd Bn., 64th Inf. Regt. [117], 30 Aug.–3 Sept. 1939.

CHAPTER 36

1. 71st Inf. Regt. [119], 29 Aug.; Onda [473], vol. 2, p. 212, citing Capt. Takada Kiyomi.

2. 23rd Division, Operations Order No. 206, 3:40 P.M., 29 Aug., 3 km. southeast of Heights 738: Komatsubara [25], 29 Aug.; 71st Inf. Regt. [119], and 72nd Inf. Regt. [121], 29 Aug.; BBSS, *SS* [180], vol. 27, p. 698; *SSNT* [535], vol. 29, p. 297.

3. N. Tanaka, Suzuki Yoshiyasu interviews; Komatsubara [25], 29 Aug.; *SSNT* [535], vol. 29, pp. 299-306. Tanaka states that, contrary to some accounts, Lieutenant Watanabe made it through to army headquarters too. (Interview.) For such an account, see BBSS, *SS* [180], vol. 27, p. 697.

4. From Sixth Army commander, to Kwantung Army deputy chief of staff, Sixth Army Combat Staff Message No. 82, Secret/Urgent, transmitted from Hailar 6:10 P.M., 29 Aug., received 6:30 P.M.; Kantōgun [99], in *GSS* [205], vol. 10, p. 139.

5. For Gomikawa's pungent comments on this episode, see *Nomonhan* [212], p. 278. Also see n. 6, below.

6. S. Hamada, interview and [2]; Tsuji [585], pp. 207-10; N. Tanaka interview; *SSNT* [535], vol. 29, pp. 332-33. Obviously, Komatsubara's requests for evacuation of wounded and replenishment of ammunition could not be honored. BBSS, *SS* [180], vol. 27, pp. 697-98. Engineer I. Saitō remembers Tanaka as a "cute boy." (Interview.) Onozuka told me that it was thanks to *his* report on 29 August that Komatsubara was saved; that is, by being allowed to retreat honorably, according to Ogisu's order. (Interview.)

7. From Sixth Army chief of staff, to Kwantung Army chief of staff, Sixth Army Combat Message No. 92-1-2, Secret/Urgent, transmitted from Hailar 4:15 A.M., 30 Aug., received 5:10 A.M.; Kantōgun [99], in *GSS* [205], vol. 10, p. 140.

8. From Sixth Army chief of staff, to Kwantung Army chief of staff, Sixth Army Combat Message No. 97-1-2, Secret/Urgent, transmitted 10:50 A.M., 30 Aug., received 12:35 P.M.; Kantōgun [99], in *GSS* [205], vol. 10, p. 141.

9. From Sixth Army chief of staff, to Kwantung Army chief of staff, Sixth Army Combat Message No. 106-1-2, Secret/Urgent, transmitted 3:10 P.M., 30 Aug., received 5:20 P.M.; Kantōgun [99], in *GSS* [205], vol. 10, p. 141. This message also described Manchukuo army dispositions; the enemy facing them seemed to be MPRA forces with several tanks.

10. Komatsubara [25], 30 Aug.; Suzuki Yoshiyasu, I. Saitō interviews.

11. I have relied mainly on my interview with Suzuki Yoshiyasu and on Komatsubara [25], 29 Aug. Also see JRD [965], *JSM* 11, part 3/C, pp. 401-2; and *SSNT* [535], vol. 29, p. 310.

12. I. Saitō interview.

13. 1st Lt. Suzuki Heigorō, Hasebe MG Co. commander, in *Nomonhan* [40], vol. 5, p. 115. The division signal unit commander, Maj. Matsui Keiji, saw men carrying Komatsubara down into a trench. *Nomonhan* [40], vol. 2, p. 36.

14. Komatsubara [25], 29 Aug.; Suzuki Yoshiyasu, I. Saitō interviews; BBSS, *SS* [180], vol. 27, pp. 696-701; *SSNT* [535], vol. 29, p. 291, citing Sixth Army Radio Message No. 34. For 23rd Division, Operations Order No. 207, 3:45 P.M., see BBSS, *SS* [180], vol. 27, p. 698.

15. Sgt. Ueda Mamoru (Mori) in Onda [473], vol. 2, pp. 164-65.

16. Acting Corp. Mineoka Hiroshi in Onda [473], vol. 2, pp. 173-74.

17. I have attempted to reconcile the numerous discrepancies between Sonetsuji's vital account and the brief record of the 71st Inf. Regt., prepared at second-hand by my interviewee Captain Onozuka: 71st Inf. Regt. [119], 30 Aug.; Sonetsuji in Onda [473], vol. 2, pp. 177-80, and in *Nomonhan* [40], vol. 3, p. 63; and Onozuka interview.

18. Komatsubara [25], 30 Aug.; Onda [473], vol. 2, pp. 184-85, 187-88, 190, 207; Onozuka, interview and *Nomonhan* [40], vol. 5, pp. 72-73; [40], vol. 2, pp. 34-35 (Tōi); Suzuki Yoshiyasu interview. Also see BBSS, *SS* [180], vol. 27, p. 701. Komatsubara's terse preliminary report of 7 September gave the time of Higashi's death charge as 7:30 P.M. Like the regimental and other records, the division report identified already-wounded 2nd Lieutenant Yukiyoshi as the color-bearer at the end. 23rd Division chief of staff, to Kwantung Army commander, 23rd Division Staff Message No. 768, transmitted 9:50 P.M., 7 Sept., received 8:01 A.M., 8 Sept.; Kantōgun [99], in *GSS* [205], vol. 10, p. 148. The same information was retransmitted by the Kwantung Army through Hattori to the AGS chief and the war minister by telephone at 8 P.M. on 8 September. [205], vol. 10, p. 149. Also see *SSNT* [535], vol. 29, pp. 315-19.

19. Murakami Tokuji, in *Nomonhan* [40], vol. 2, p. 52. Also I. Saitō interview; BBSS, *SS* [180], vol. 27, p. 699; *SSNT* [535], vol. 29, p. 312, citing Suzuki Yoshiyasu; Gomikawa, *Nomonhan* [212], pp. 300-301. According to an earlier version, a young medical probationary officer cut off Okamoto's leg with a saber (in the absence of medical instruments), using no anesthetic. See JRD [965], *JSM* 11, part 3/C, p. 401, citing letter from Suzuki Yoshiyasu to me dated 24 Aug. 1956. Also my subsequent interview with Suzuki. In 1963 the GSDF Medical School's official history revealed that Second Lieutenant Takasaki applied the tourniquet immediately and then amputated the leg in a shelter by candlelight. [68], p. 47. For the battle itself, see Komatsubara [25], 30 Aug.; and *Nomonhan* [40], vol. 2, p. 36.

20. BBSS, *SS* [180], vol. 27, pp. 670, 698; Gomikawa, *Nomonhan* [212], p. 299; *SSNT* [535], vol. 29, p. 291.

21. In an interview, Suzuki Yoshiyasu estimated that Komatsubara's decision took place at 10 P.M., but the subsequent sequence of events suggests a time well before nightfall.

22. Hanada in Onda [473], vol. 2, p. 206; Suzuki Yoshiyasu interview.

23. 1st Lt. Suzuki Heigorō in *Nomonhan* [40], vol. 5, p. 115.

24. Suzuki Yoshiyasu interview; Komatsubara [25], 30 Aug.; BBSS, *SS* [180], vol. 27, pp. 704-5; *SSNT* [535], vol. 29, p. 322.

25. Suzuki Yoshiyasu interview; 71st Inf. Regt. [119], 30 Aug.; Onda [473], vol. 2, pp. 188-91, 207-8.

26. Onda [473], vol. 2, pp. 212-13; citing Takada; 71st Inf. Regt. [119], 30 Aug.

27. 72nd Inf. Regt. [121], 30 Aug.; BBSS, *SS* [180], vol. 27, pp. 703, 706. 1st Lt. Suzuki Heigorō, Hasebe's MG company commander, wounded on 28 August, tells a moving story of overcoming his feelings of despair for the sake of glorifying his shattered unit, of catching up with the 300 men (including engineers) under a 72nd Regiment captain (Hirowatari), and of finding 5 or 6 of his original 20 men. *Nomonhan* [40], vol. 5, p. 116.

28. I. Saitō, Suzuki Yoshiyasu interviews. When Onozuka saw Komatsubara before leaving as a courier, the day before, the general appeared to be tense but calm. He had done his best, fought to the limit, and could face the future with repose—a "fine attitude." Onozuka interview.

29. Onda [473], vol. 2, pp. 161, 191-92. Also see n. 24 above.

30. Onda [473], vol. 2, pp. 185-86, citing Kawasaki Hideo.

31. Onda [473], vol. 2, pp. 209-10, citing Ueda Mamoru (Mori).

32. Suzuki Yoshiyasu interview; Sgt. Haitani Zen'ichi in *Nomonhan* [40], vol. 2, p. 61, and in *SSNT* [535], vol. 29, p. 324.

33. Suzuki Yoshiyasu interview; and *SSNT* [535], vol. 29, pp. 323-24, 328-29.

34. Komatsubara [25], 31 Aug.; Suzuki Yoshiyasu interview; Onda [473], vol. 2, p. 36, citing Matsui; *ibid.*, p. 209, citing Hanada; *Nomonhan* [40], vol. 2, p. 60, citing 2nd Lt. Saitō Chiyokichi.

35. Onda [473], vol. 2, p. 61 (Haitani). The warrant officer was subsequently killed while taking over from a slain machine gunner.

36. Suzuki Yoshiyasu explained his thinking to me in an interview. For supplementary information, see BBSS, *SS* [180], vol. 27, p. 706; *SSNT* [535], vol. 29, pp. 328, 330.

37. Onozuka had expected to return to the 23rd Division after reporting to the Sixth Army, but Ogisu said the situation did not require it. Onozuka interview.

38. If one includes personnel who had been located at Mohorehi, such as the veterinary section, the number of effectives still amounted to only 456, according to the regimental records.

39. 1st Co., 20 dead; 2nd Co., 13; 3rd Co., 6; 4th Co., 10; MG Co. and Bn. Gun Battery, 9. Nishikawa's data, cited by his aide Nomura, in *Nomonhan* [40], vol. 9, p. 165.

40. The 1st Battalion's own records say that there was no officer in the 2nd Co. but that the 1st MG Co. had one second lieutenant and one probationary officer. Hanada himself had only two men left in battalion headquarters. I have attempted to combine the regimental and battalion data.

41. Onda [473], vol. 2, p. 192 (Ono).

42. 71st Inf. Regt. [119], 30 Aug.; 1st Bn., 71st Inf. Regt., combat report, 31 Aug., cited in Onda [473], vol. 2, pp. 211-12.

43. See *Nomonhan* [40], vol. 5, p. 116, citing 1st Lt. Suzuki Heigorō.

44. Onda [473], vol. 2, pp. 210-11, citing Ueda Mamoru (Mori).

45. Tanaka says that he did not turn down any Sixth Army officer; "but it is true that those who did not know the location of the division headquarters would be unable to find it." N. Tanaka interview.

46. N. Tanaka interview; *Nomonhan* [40], vol. 9, pp. 133-34, citing Yamanaka Kiyoshi; [40], vol. 9, p. 208, citing Sōma; Higuchi Kōyō [246], vol. 2, pp. 293-302; *SSNT* [535], vol. 29, pp. 332-33. Sōma adds that the exploits of the Inakura unit of the Midorikawa transport regiment are included in a war ballad (*biwauta*) called "Ah! Nomonhan."

47. Komatsubara [25], 31 Aug.; Hamada, interview and [2]; N. Tanaka interview; BBSS, *SS* [180], vol. 27, pp. 705-6; Tsuji [585], pp. 210-11; *SSNT* [535], vol. 29, p. 333. Hamada and Tsuji say that Komatsubara reached the army command post shortly after 2 P.M.

48. Y. Hata, "Nikki" [5], 31 Aug. For IJA praise of Komatsubara's operation north of the Holsten, which "secular tacticians might condemn as reckless," see Lieutenant Colonel Yonemoto [623A], pp. 26-27. Yonemoto had served as Major General Kobayashi's senior aide and, like the general, had been wounded on 24 August.

CHAPTER 37

1. On 7 Sept. the Kwantung Army had checked the 30th Inf. Regt.'s plan to launch a night attack against Heights 895. S. Miyazaki [411], pp. 60-65; Rikugun , *Shōsen* [485], no. 50, describing the busy truck platoon from the 2nd Transport Regiment. Where there was a conflict of dates, I have used Miyazaki's sequences. The GSDF Medical School's official history describes the activities of medical Capt. Gunma Shōji (who was wounded) at Heights 904, and of the quartermaster truck unit at Heights 944, where 60 injured men were retrieved. [68], pp. 47-48.

2. The 26th Regiment learned, on 11 September, that on the Katayama front, 20-30 of 100 enemy tanks had been knocked out. 7th Co., 26th Inf. Regt. [105]. BBSS, *SS* [180], vol. 27, pp. 715-16, 727; Hamada [2]. Also see *Nomonhan hōmen shutsudō chū dai-2 Shidan kimitsu sakusen nisshi* [2nd Div. Secret Operational Diary During the Operations in the Nomonhan Region], 26 Aug.–13 Sept. 1939, entry for 11 Sept. (BBSS Archives); JRD [965], *JSM* 11, part 3/C, p. 407; Tsuji [585], p. 216. For IJAF reports, see BBSS, *SS* [181], vol. 53, p. 337. For ex-

ample, on Katayama's front on 9 September, 200 enemy infantrymen were sighted attacking at 8 A.M. with 40 tanks, but the force was repulsed, losing 20 tanks and abandoning 75 bodies.

3. 1st Engr. Regt. [127], 8-12 Sept.; supplemented by JRD [965], JSM 11, part 3/C, pp. 407-8; Hamada [2]; Tsuji [585], p. 216. The diary of 2nd Lt. Ōki Shigeru, the 1st Infantry Regiment's doctor attached to the four rapid-fire batteries of the 1st Division, makes much reference to bad weather and poor terrain but mentions only one killed and one wounded in the 2nd MG Co. on 11 September; the enemy was driven off easily. [469], 7-13 Sept. On 13 September the 26th Regiment heard that the enemy in the Heights 1031 sector southeast of Handagai had been surrounded by the Gotō detachment and seemed to be asking Soviet higher headquarters for help. 7th Co., 26th Inf. Regt. [105]. The GSDF Medical School's official history treats the fighting in detail. [68], annex, pp. 78-87.

4. Shishkin [920], pp. 624-25.

5. BBSS, SS [180], vol. 27, p. 715.

6. On 29 August, Sawada received the official order to move the 4th Division from Sanchiang Province to the Nomonhan front. After its arrival at Arshaan on 2 September, the division came under Sixth Army command. Sawada [507A], pp. 123-30.

7. Kantōgun [99], in GSS [205], vol. 10, pp. 94-95; S. Hamada, interview and [2]; BBSS, SS [180], vol. 27, p. 716; Tsuji [585], p. 215; Gomikawa, *Nomonhan* [212], pp. 297, 311-12; SSNT [535], vol. 29, pp. 342, 349. Judging that his 4th Division lacked combat training, Lieutenant General Sawada preferred that it be employed in a flanking or rear-attack role and not in a frontal assault. [507A], pp. 125, 127-28.

8. If every unwounded survivor of the 23rd Division was counted, Suzuki Yoshiyasu claims, there were perhaps 3,000 men, all armed with rifles and lacking heavy weapons. (Interview.) Kwantung Army records agree, citing a grand total of 2,000-3,000 men as of the evening of 30 August. Kantōgun [99], in GSS [205], vol. 10, p. 94.

9. Onozuka, Suzuki Yoshiyasu interviews; SSNT [535], vol. 29, p. 348, citing Onozuka; Sawada [507A], p. 133.

10. SSNT [535], vol. 29, p. 347, citing Ashikawa; Sawada [507A], pp. 128-30.

11. Tsuji [585], pp. 217-19; S. Hamada, interview and [2]; BBSS, SS [180], vol. 27, p. 716.

12. BBSS, SS [180], vol. 27, p. 717. Also see Gomikawa, *Nomonhan* [212], p. 312.

13. For Ogisu's *kunrei* of 4 September, see Onda [473], vol. 2, p. 234; S. Hamada [2]. Also see Sawada [507A], p. 130.

14. "Proclamation of the Commanding General of the Sixth Army," 5 Sept. 1939, Prosecution Document No. 2231, Exhibit No. 766 (p. 6), IMTFE, *Transcript* [777] 16 Oct. 1946, pp. 7856-60, and 26 May 1947, pp. 23039-40. Ogisu's *kunji* was incorporated into a memorandum prepared by the Military History Department of the Red Army General Staff for submission to the IMTFE. Under direct examination by Russian prosecutors, Ogisu denied the date and authenticity of the document attributed to him. [777], 26 May 1947, pp. 23038-40. Also see JRD [965], JSM 11, part 3/C, pp. 408, 411. S. Hamada remembers hearing Ogisu's address but did not see any printed version. (Interview.)

15. S. Hamada, Numazaki interviews; JRD [965], JSM 11, part 3/C, p. 416; Kantōgun [99], in GSS [205], vol. 10, p. 96. Ogisu struck Sawada as "peppy but somewhat emaciated." [507A], p. 129.

16. Suzuki Yoshiyasu, S. Hamada interviews; 28th Inf. Regt. [107]; Sawada [507A], pp. 129, 133. Also see SSNT [535], vol. 29, pp. 347-48.

17. Onozuka interview.

18. K. Satō, Suzuki Yoshiyasu interviews.

19. Yabe interview.

20. Shigemitsu [917], pp. 172-73.

21. Kantōgun [99], in GSS [205], vol. 10, pp. 92, 139.

22. Tsuji [585], p. 217.

23. 26/27 Aug. in 71st Inf. Regt., 31 Aug. in 64th Inf. Regt. (see chap. 35), and 7 Sept. in 27th Inf. Regt. For the last-named, see 3rd Bn., 27th Inf. Regt., [106]. The battalion added that, since uniforms and accouterments were in very short supply, troops should not discard them unless specifically ordered to do so.

24. Tsuji [585], pp. 216-17; Gomikawa, *Nomonhan* [212], p. 285.

25. See chap. 33.

26. Kantōgun [99], in *GSS* [205], vol. 10, p. 93.

27. From AGS deputy, to Kwantung Army chief of staff, AGS Message No. 220, transmitted 5:05 P.M., 29 Aug., received 9:20 P.M.: Kantōgun [99], in *GSS* [205], vol. 10, p. 140; and BBSS, *SS* [180], vol. 27, p. 719.

28. Inada interview; and BBSS, *SS* [180], vol. 27, p. 719.

29. Inada interview; and *SSNT* [535], vol. 29, p. 353.

30. Gomikawa, *Nomonhan* [212], pp. 284-85. For Hashimoto Gun's recollections, see IMTFE, *Transcript* [777], 20 May 1947, pp. 22577, 22600.

31. Inada, Nyūmura interviews; BBSS, *SS* [180], vol. 27, pp. 719-20, 722; and Bykov in IMTFE, *Transcript* [777], 27 Jan. 1948, p. 38368. Bykov belonged to the Northern Force.

32. IGHQ Army Order No. 343, 30 Aug.: Kantōgun [99], in *GSS* [205], vol. 10, pp. 141-42; JRD [965], *JSM* 11, part 3/C, p. 412; BBSS, *SS* [180], vol. 27, pp. 721-22. For the High Command's philosophy of guidance (*shidō*): Inada, Hashimoto interviews; and unpublished record of Prince (Captain) Takeda's conversation with Lt. Gen. Nakajima Tetsuzō (1939), provided by a privileged source.

33. BBSS, *SS* [180], vol. 27, p. 722; Inada interview.

34. Inada, Arao interviews; and *SSNT* [535], vol. 29, pp. 355-57. The JRD monograph [965] misreads Takatsuki's name as Kozuki; *JSM* 11, part 3/C, pp. 412-15. Another possible reading would have been Kōgetsu. My IJA interviewees provided the correct rendition.

35. The sketchy materials in the Nakajima-Takeda transcript (see n. 32) shed no light on the AGS deputy's behavior on 30 August. Also see BBSS, *SS* [180], vol. 27, p. 722.

36. The key to this reconstruction is my interview with Arao. The puzzled Kwantung Army's record is found in Kantōgun [99], in *GSS* [205], vol. 10, p. 95.

37. Kantōgun [99], in *GSS* [205], vol. 10, pp. 94-96; Tsuji [585], pp. 220-23; BBSS, *SS* [180], vol. 27, pp. 720, 722; JRD [965], *JSM* 11, part 3/C, pp. 412-15. Also see Gomikawa, *Nomonhan* [212], pp. 312-15; BBSS, *SS* [181], vol. 53, pp. 331-32.

38. Kantōgun [99], in *GSS* [205], vol. 10, p. 142; JRD [965], *JSM* 11, part 3/C, p. 416. I have inverted the two paragraphs found in Ueda's *kunji*. Also see BBSS, *SS* [180], vol. 27, p. 723. For Ogisu's statement, see n. 13.

39. Hattori, Arao, Imaoka interviews; Kantōgun [99], in *GSS* [205], vol. 10, pp. 93-94.

40. Kantōgun [99], in *GSS* [205], vol. 10, p. 96; JRD [965], *JSM* 11, part 3/C, pp. 416-17.

41. BBSS, *SS* [180], vol. 27, p. 723. For air force movements, see chap. 38.

42. Kōtani interview. Kōtani undoubtedly had his facts straight but, since his remembrance of dates is imprecise, they have been omitted from this account. Hashimoto Gun stressed that tanks and artillery were in short supply. (Interview.) The Third Army commander in east Manchuria, Gen. Tada Hayao, opposed the weakening of his forces. I. Hata in Morley, ed., *Deterrent* [875], p. 171.

43. Inada interview. Hattori says that he and staff officers Arao and Matsumura met Nakajima and Takatsuki at the airport. Kantōgun [99], in *GSS* [205], vol. 10, p. 94. Imaoka adds that he and Arao "ran into" Nakajima and Takatsuki just after the conference. (Interview.) Undoubtedly, Imaoka was not aware at the time that Inada had arranged beforehand for Arao to intercept and "debrief" the AGS deputy and his associate.

44. Arao interview. Also see n. 36.

45. See chap. 29.

46. IGHQ Army Order No. 349, from AGS chief, to Kwantung Army commander: Kantōgun [99], in *GSS* [205], vol. 10, p. 142; JRD [965], *JSM* 11, part 3/C, p. 417; BBSS, *SS* [180], vol. 27, p. 723. For Hashimoto Gun's recollections, see IMTFE, *Transcript* [777], 20 May 1947, pp. 22577-78, 22600-601.

47. According to Sawada, Hashimoto's refusal to go to Hsinking stemmed from the fact that the Kwantung Army staff was known to despise him because of his allegedly aloof or craven behavior at the time of the 23rd Division's river-crossing operation in July. (See chap. 19, n. 16.) "Given the atmosphere in Hsinking," writes Sawada, "not only would Hashimoto have been unable to carry out the assignment of controlling the Kwantung Army, but an untoward

event [a physical attack on him?] might even have occurred." [507A], p. 151. Also see BBSS, *SS* [180], vol. 27, p. 723.

48. Inada, Arao interviews; and *SSNT* [535], vol. 29, pp. 357-58, citing Inada. Officially, the AGS chief decided who should go. Nakajima was even two academy classes junior to Isogai; Nukada, *Rikugunshō* [457], p. 80.

49. The order was transmitted at 3:52 P.M. on 3 September, as AGS Message No. 287, and was received at 4:40 P.M.; Kantōgun [99], in *GSS* [205], vol. 10, p. 142. For the postwar thoughts of Hashimoto Gun, interview and IMTFE, *Transcript* [777], 20 May 1947, pp. 22599-601.

50. Kōtani interview; Tsuji [585], *Nomonhan*, p. 219; JRD [965], *JSM* 11, part 3/C, p. 417.

51. On the afternoon of 4 September, the Kwantung Army sent Message No. 733 from the chief of staff to the AGS deputy; BBSS, *SS* [180], vol. 27, p. 724. Also see Kantōgun [99], in *GSS* [205], vol. 10, p. 98.

52. Hattori was on the way back from the Fukuoka meeting and Shimanuki Takeharu was on temporary duty at Sixth Army headquarters.

53. Kantōgun [99], in *GSS* [205], vol. 10, p. 97; JRD [965], *JSM* 11, part 3/C, pp. 419-20.

54. Kwantung Army, Operations Order No. 178, drafted by Tsuji on 4 Sept., not issued until 6 Sept.: Kantōgun [99], in *GSS* [205], vol. 10, p. 143; JRD [965], *JSM* 11, part 3/C, pp. 418-19.

55. Kantōgun [99], in *GSS* [205], vol. 10, pp. 97-98; Tsuji [585], pp. 223-29; JRD [965], *JSM* 11, part 3/C, pp. 421-23 (Nakajima's arrival time is given incorrectly). Also see BBSS, *SS* [180], vol. 27, p. 724, and [181], vol. 53, pp. 332-33.

56. From Kwantung Army commander, to AGS chief, Kwantung Army 1st Section, Message No. 739, drafted by Tsuji, transmitted 12:10 P.M., 5 Sept.; from Kwantung Army commander, to war minister, Kwantung Army 1st Section, Message No. 741, drafted by Hattori, transmitted 2:40 P.M., 5 Sept.: Kantōgun [99], in *GSS* [205], vol. 10, pp. 98-99, 143; Tsuji [585], pp. 229-31; JRD [965], *JSM* 11, part 3/C, pp. 423-25. Also see BBSS, *SS* [180], vol. 27, p. 725.

57. From Kwantung Army commander, to AGS chief, Kwantung Army Message No. 740, drafted by Tsuji, transmitted 4 P.M., 5 Sept.: Kantōgun [99], in *GSS* [205], vol. 10, p. 144; Tsuji [585], pp. 230-31; JRD [965], *JSM* 11, part 3/C, pp. 425-26; BBSS, *SS* [180], vol. 27, p. 725.

58. From Kwantung Army chief of staff, to AGS deputy, Kwantung Army 1st Section, Message No. 742, drafted by Hattori, transmitted 5:10 P.M., 5 Sept.; from Kwantung Army chief of staff, to vice minister of war, message number not stated, transmitted 3:20 [5:20?] P.M., 5 Sept.: Kantōgun [99], in *GSS* [205], vol. 10, pp. 99, 144-45; Tsuji [585], pp. 226-29; BBSS, *SS* [180], vol. 27, p. 725.

59. From Kwantung Army chief of staff, to AGS deputy, Kwantung Army 1st Section, Message No. 746, drafted by Tsuji, transmitted 6:45 P.M., 5 Sept.: Kantōgun [99], in *GSS* [205], vol. 10, p. 145; BBSS, *SS* [180], vol. 27, p. 725.

60. A message to this effect was received from the vice minister of war at 9:30 P.M. on 5 September: Kantōgun [99], in *GSS* [205], vol. 10, p. 145; BBSS, *SS* [180], vol. 27, p. 726. See chap. 38.

61. To Kwantung Army commander, from AGS chief, AGS message drafted 5 Sept., transmitted 9:45 A.M., 6 Sept., received 11:35 A.M.: Kantōgun [99], in *GSS* [205], vol. 10, pp. 99, 145; JRD [965], *JSM* 11, part 3/C, p. 426; BBSS, *SS* [180], vol. 27, pp. 724, 726.

62. Arao interview; and BBSS, *SS* [180], vol. 27, p. 726.

63. From AGS chief, to Kwantung Army commander, AGS Message No. 330, transmitted 1:25 P.M., 6 Sept., received 2:10 P.M.: Kantōgun [99], in *GSS* [205]; vol. 10, pp. 99, 146; JRD [965], *JSM* 11, part 3/C, p. 426; Tsuji [585], pp. 231-32; BBSS, *SS* [180], vol. 27, p. 726.

64. Inada interview; JRD [965], *JSM* 11, part 3/C, p. 430; BBSS, *SS* [180], vol. 27, p. 583, citing Inada's considerations (*kōsatsu*) dated Oct. 1939; [180], vol. 27, p. 727; *SSNT* [535], vol. 29, pp. 366-67, citing Inada.

65. From war minister to Kwantung Army commander, war ministry message, transmitted 3:55 P.M., 6 Sept., received 5:40 P.M.: Kantōgun [99], in *GSS* [205], vol. 10, pp. 99, 146; JRD [965], *JSM* 11, part 3/C, p. 427; Tsuji [585], p. 231; S. Hata interview. Tsuji incorrectly attributes the message to Itagaki.

66. Kwantung Army, Operations Order No. 178, transmitted 4 P.M., 6 Sept.: Kantōgun [99], in *GSS* [205], vol. 10, pp. 99, 147.

67. From Kwantung Army commander to AGS chief, Kwantung Army Message No. 754, drafted by Tsuji, transmitted 6:30 P.M., 6 Sept., in reply to AGS Message No. 330 [see n. 63]: Kantōgun [99], in *GSS* [205], vol. 10, pp. 99, 146-47; JRD [965], *JSM* 11, part 3/C, pp. 427-28; Tsuji [585], p. 232. Also see BBSS, *SS* [180], vol. 27, p. 727. For reinforcement of IGU elements, see beginning of this chapter.

68. From Sixth Army commander, to Kwantung Army chief of staff, Sixth Army Combat Message No. 290-1-2, transmitted 9:10 P.M., 6 Sept., received 10:45 P.M.: Kantōgun [99], in *GSS* [205], vol. 10, pp. 99, 147; JRD [965], *JSM* 11, part 3/C, p. 428; Tsuji [585], pp. 232-33.

69. From Kwantung Army commander, to Sixth Army commander, Kwantung Army Message No. 760, transmitted 3:30 A.M., 7 Sept.: Kantōgun [99], in *GSS* [205], vol. 10, pp. 99, 147; JRD [965], *JSM* 11, part 3/C, p. 429; Tsuji [585], p. 233.

70. Excerpt from Doi's message of 5 Sept. to AGS deputy, retransmitted by AGS, 5:45 P.M., 6 Sept., received 8:46 A.M., 7 Sept.: Kantōgun [99], in *GSS* [205], vol. 10, pp. 99-100, 148; JRD [965], *JSM* 11, part 3/C, pp. 448-49. For Doi's strong message prepared on 3 September, see [965], *JSM* 11, part 3/C, pp. 446-48. Also see chap. 38.

71. Tsuji [585], pp. 234-35. Nukada says that he was told by both Ogisu and war ministry Personnel Bureau chief Noda that Tsuji should be separated from the service, but that it was decided not to do so after consultation with the AGS. *Rikugunshō* [457], p. 86.

72. See Sawada [507A], pp. 151-52.

73. Kantōgun [99], in *GSS* [205], vol. 10, p. 100; JRD [965], *JSM* 11, part 3/C, p. 434; *Nihon riku-kaigun* [442]; BBSS, *SS* [180], vol. 27, p. 728; Coox, biographical appendix, in S. Hayashi, *Kōgun* [756], pp. 220-41; Hattori, Inada, Hashimoto, I. Hata interviews.

74. S. Hata interview; supplemented by Y. Nishihara interview.

75. Sawada provides details on the complexity of trying to ascribe responsibility to an imperial prince and inducing him to retire. [507A], pp. 153, 181-83. Nukada heard that Prince Kan'in did want to resign but that he was convinced to reconsider, out of concern for the possible effects domestically and externally. *Rikugunshō* [457], p. 85.

76. Iinuma was promoted lieutenant general in October 1939 and was succeeded by Maj. Gen. Noda Kengo. Hata remembers dealing with Lt. Gen. Yamada Otozō as inspector general. Nishio Juzō (Toshizō) had been replaced as inspector general on 4 September; Kawabe Masakazu filled in for about a month until Yamada took over officially in October. (S. Hata interview.)

77. AGS Deputy Chief Sawada describes the thorough investigations conducted by him and by the General Affairs Bureau chief, Maj. Gen. Kanda Masatane, and he mentions consultations with War Minister Hata and "fair-minded" Vice Minister of War Anami. [507A], pp. 152-53.

78. Toward the end of the Nomonhan Incident, there were unfounded rumors that Isogai would replace Itagaki as war minister in the Abe cabinet formed on 30 August.

79. *Nihon riku-kaigun* [442]; I. Hata, Hashimoto interviews.

80. SSNT [535], vol. 29, pp. 368-69. The escalation of the Nomonhan war had delayed the formation of the China GHQ from August until 12 September.

81. In connection with atrocities committed against Allied prisoners within the jurisdiction of the 16th Area Army in 1945, the Occupation authorities prosecuted Inada as a war criminal after the war. Found guilty and sentenced to seven years at hard labor, Inada served five years of his prison term (1946-51).

82. *Nihon riku-kaigun* [442]; Hattori, Shimanuki, Taguchi, Iwashima, I. Hata interviews.

83. S. Hayashi, *Kōgun* [756], pp. 16-17, and *Taiheiyō* [243], p. 25.

CHAPTER 38

1. The AGS officer was Maj. Shimamura Noriyasu, who himself was being transferred to Kwantung Army headquarters, as noted in chap. 37.

2. For information on Umezu, see Jōhō, ed., *Umezu* [313], pp. 365-66, citing Imaoka; pp. 370-71, citing Endō; and pp. 371-72, citing Nakayama Motoo (Genpu). Ueda had issued a moving farewell to the Kwantung Army on 7 September; a copy may be found in 7th Co., 26th

Inf. Regt. [105]. For a poignant account of division commander Imamura's last conversation with Ueda in Dairen on the morning of 10 September, see Imamura, *Shiki* [282], p. 281. For Endō's actions from Hamamatsu to Tokyo to Hsinking, see [189], pp. 172-74. Under date of 13 Sept., from Dairen, Ueda wrote a humble letter of apology to Komatsubara; [25], 17 Sept.

3. Imaoka interview; Imamura, *Shiki* [282], pp. 281-82; Nukada, *Rikugunshō* [457], p. 88; Jōhō, ed., *Umezu* [313], pp. 78-81, citing Yamawaki; pp. 82-84, citing Umezu Yoshiichi (son); and pp. 90-93, citing Uchimaru Aya (sister). When AGS Colonel Inada visited Umezu a couple of days after the September cease-fire, the new commander remarked that the Kwantung Army had apparently caused Inada a lot of trouble but that he should rest assured nothing like *gekokujō* would be permitted from now on, although border problems in Manchuria remained very difficult. *SSNT* [535], vol. 29, pp. 386-87, citing Inada.

4. BBSS, *SS* [181], vol. 53, p. 316.

5. Yoshimitsu [627], p. 165; JRD [952], *JSM* 4, p. 71; BBSS, *SS* [181], vol. 53, pp. 325-26, 337; Maruta interview. For good coverage of the preceding period, see [181], vol. 53, pp. 314-21.

6. Giga interview. Giga, at 54, was only three years younger than and four academy classes junior to new Kwantung Army commander Umezu. Both were at the rank of lieutenant general.

7. BBSS, *SS* [181], vol. 53, pp. 328-29; JRD [952], *JSM* 4, pp. 44-46; Miyoshi, Miyashi interviews. Several factual errors are contained in JRD [965], *JSM* 11, part 3/C, p. 419, n. 2. Miyoshi says he spent about a month in China at this time. (Interview.)

8. BBSS, *SS* [181], vol. 53, pp. 328-31; maintenance and supporting units are excluded. JRD [952], *JSM* 4, p. 69, contains discrepancies, but the total figure on operational planes is in agreement. Some said that Giga's division had overemphasized air-to-air fighting, wearing itself out at the expense of ground-support functions; a bigger and stronger air corps was needed by late August. (Satō Katsuo interview.)

9. BBSS, *SS* [181], vol. 53, p. 337-40.

10. BBSS, *SS* [181], vol. 53, p. 340; Yoshimitsu [627], p. 165; JRD [952], *JSM* 4, p. 71. The 27th Infantry saw 40-50 planes fighting overhead at 4 P.M. Although greatly outnumbered, the Japanese fighters drove off the enemy. 3rd Bn., 27th Inf. Regt. [106], 14 Sept.

11. BBSS, *SS* [181], vol. 53, p. 341; Yuzuhara, Matsumura interviews. There are slight numerical discrepancies between the BBSS account [181], Yoshimitsu's *Kūsenshi* [627], pp. 165-66, and JRD [952], *JSM* 4, p. 71. Sakagawa was in command of the 24th Group on 15 September because Major Yuzuhara was ill that day. (Yuzuhara interview.)

12. Shishkin [920], p. 625.

13. JRD [952], *JSM* 4, p. 71.

14. Imamura, *Shiki* [282], pp. 281-82.

15. From Kwantung Army chief of staff, to AGS deputy, Kwantung Army message, 10 Sept.: JRD [965], *JSM* 11, part 3/C, pp. 450-51; BBSS, *SS* [181], vol. 53, p. 342.

16. Komatsubara [25], 12 Sept.; Onda [473], vol. 2, pp. 234-35. For Endō's mission to the Sixth Army, see [189], pp. 174-75. Also see Sawada [507A], p. 131.

17. Kwantung Army message of 23 May, from Kwantung Army chief of staff, to AGS deputy and vice minister of war; JRD [965], *JSM* 11, part 3/C, pp. 439-40. Military Affairs Section, War Ministry, Message No. 879, from Military Affairs Bureau chief via vice minister of war, to Kwantung Army chief of staff, transmitted 8:05 P.M., 3 June, received 9:40 P.M.: Kantōgun [99], in *GSS* [205], vol. 10, pp. 121-22; excerpt in JRD [965], *JSM* 11, part 3/C, pp. 440-41. Also Hattori, Nishi, Hashimoto interviews. For statement by Director, General Affairs Board, Manchukuo Government, citing telegraphed protests to MPR on 15 May, 29 May, 18 June, and 19 June, see *Japan-Manchoukuo Year Book, 1940* [782A], p. 632. Molotov and Tōgō exchanged protests on the night of 25 May regarding the MPR-Manchukuo border clashes of 18-22 May. On 5 June, the Manchukuo government tried to lodge a direct protest with the Soviet authorities in Harbin. See *Shōwa jūyonnen* [533], pp. 436-37, 443-45; Gaimushō [201], p. 516. Also see Kutakov [812], pp. 148-49, for Molotov's protest of 19 May to Tōgō.

18. AGS Message No. 596, transmitted 7:30 P.M., 3 June, received 7:55 P.M.; Kantōgun [99], in *GSS* [205], vol. 10, p. 122.

19. Hashimoto, Hattori, Arao, Imaoka interviews.

20. Interrogation of 24 April 1946, Prosecution Doc. No. 4122, cited by General Tadevosyan; IMTFE, *Transcript* [777], 16 Oct. 1946, pp. 7854-56. Defense counsel Usami tried in vain to point out misinterpretations and omissions. *Ibid.*, pp. 7856-58.

21. Inada interview; and *Hiroku Itagaki* [252], p. 217, citing Gen. Yamawaki Masataka. Also see Nishiura [447], pp. 88-89.

22. From Kwantung Army commander, to war minister and AGS chief, Kwantung Army Staff Message No. 776, 17 July; JRD [965], *JSM* 11, part 3/C, pp. 441-42.

23. *Hiroku Itagaki* [252], p. 217 (Yamawaki); Harada Kumao [225], vol. 8, p. 24, citing phone conversation with Foreign Minister Arita, 19 July. Although Navy Minister Yonai kept quiet at the time, he later revealed that he was even more opposed to the tripartite pact than the foreign and finance ministers, when Arita spoke with him. In late September, Harada learned from Yonai that he had "chewed out" Itagaki for his early secrecy about the way things were going at Nomonhan and for consulting the five ministers' conference only after botching the affair. Itagaki had said nothing in reply. [225], vol. 8, p. 85. See *ibid.*, p. 9, for Privy Seal Yuasa's comments on the anti-Comintern positions held by the army and navy ministers and premier. Also see BBSS, *SS* [179], vol. 8, pp. 601-3; Gaimushō [201], p. 519.

24. Tōgō [577], p. 128; Gaimushō [201], p. 519; *SSNT* [535], vol. 28, p. 292, citing Gaimushō activities report, 1939.

25. Kantōgun [99], in *GSS* [205], vol. 10, pp. 79-81; *Hiroku Itagaki* [252], p. 218; BBSS, *SS* [179], vol. 8, pp. 597-98. Also see JRD [965], *JSM* 11, part 3/B, pp. 334-39. Nishiura was disappointed by Isogai's performance. [447], p. 88.

26. Inada interview; Ashida [172], p. 126. Also see *TSM* [549], vol. 4, p. 100; Morley, ed., *Deterrent* [875], pp. 165, 168, citing Hata Shunroku diary.

27. From AGS deputy, to Kwantung Army chief of staff, AGS Message No. 19 (ref.: War Ministry, Military Affairs Section, Message No. 83, n. d.), transmitted by special code 3:58 P.M., 28 July, received 6:40 P.M.: Kantōgun [99], in *GSS* [205], vol. 10, pp. 82, 123; JRD [965], *JSM* 11, part 3/C, p. 442. The foreign ministry's concrete conditions, conveyed to Tōgō, are found in [201], pp. 519-20.

28. From Kwantung Army chief of staff, to AGS deputy, Kwantung Army 1st Section Message No. 468 (ref.: AGS Message No. 19), drafted by Hattori, transmitted 2:15 P.M., 30 July: Kantōgun [99], in *GSS* [205], vol. 10, pp. 123-24; JRD [965], *JSM* 11, part 3/C, pp. 443-44.

29. Kantōgun [99], in *GSS* [205], vol. 10, p. 82; JRD [965], *JSM* 11, part 3/C, pp. 444-45; *SSNT* [535], vol. 29, pp. 290-91.

30. BBSS, *SS* [179], vol. 8, pp. 603-5.

31. Memorandum by Weizsäcker, 22 Aug.; Dept. of State, *Nazi-Soviet Relations* (hereafter *NSR*) [975], p. 70.

32. Kwantung Army Draft 1-1670, 12 Aug.: Kantōgun [99], in *GSS* [205], vol. 10, pp. 89, 130-31; JRD [965], *JSM* 11, part 3/B, pp. 356-57. After approval, the draft was hand-carried to Tokyo by a special courier.

33. From military attaché/Moscow, to AGS deputy, transmitted 10:35 P.M., 12 Aug., received 9:15 P.M., 13 Aug., retransmitted to Kwantung Army chief of staff as Message No. 138-1-5: Kantōgun [99], in *GSS* [205], vol. 10, pp. 131-32; JRD [965], *JSM* 11, part 3/B, pp. 359-61; supplemented by Doi interview; and [205], vol. 10, p. 89.

34. Doi interview; supplemented by portions of his cable of 12 August (see n. 33).

35. Nishi, Hashimoto interviews. Also see Nishi, *Kaisō* [444], pp. 91-94; *TSM* [549], vol. 4, p. 106; and Morley, ed., *Deterrent* [875], p. 173.

36. Schulenburg to Wiehl, Moscow, 1 March, referring to Schulenburg-Tōgō conversation of 28 Feb.; *DGFP* [973], D/4, p. 628. Improvement in Tōgō's negotiations was reported in Tippelskirch to Schliep, 27 March; [973], D/6, p. 140.

37. K. Suzuki [546], p. 182. There had been another important exchange between Ribbentrop, Ōshima, and the Japanese ambassador to Italy, Shiratori, on the subject of possible German-Soviet détente, during Hitler's birthday gala on 20 April. See *Arisue* [165], pp. 473-78; K. Suzuki [546], pp. 178-80; and, for Shiratori's reports of July, BBSS, *SS* [179], vol. 8, p. 601.

38. K. Suzuki [546], p. 182.

39. Weizsäcker to Schulenburg, Berlin, 27 May; *NSR* [975], p. 9.

40. Kawabe [332], pp. 163-64. In July, Usami Uzuhiko, the counselor of embassy in Berlin, had picked up cogent rumors of a nonaggression pact. The German foreign ministry called the reports "pure fabrication." Woermann, memorandum, Berlin, 19 July; *DGFP* [973], D/6, p. 943.

41. Doi interview.

42. Lipski to Beck, Berlin, 29 April; in Jozef Lipski, *Diplomat in Berlin 1933-1939*, ed. W. Jedrzejewicz (New York: Columbia University Press, 1968), p. 533. Hitler's public assertions, in the case of the Reichstag speech, jibed with his secret views. On 14 August he identified hostile, friendly, and neutral countries for the benefit of his commanders in chief. Japan was not included in the friendly category. K. Suzuki [546], p. 200.

43. From Hitler's briefing of 23 May, cited by Peter de Mendelssohn, *Design for Aggression* (New York: Harper, 1947), p. 145. The specific decision at issue here referred to the planned German attack on Poland.

44. Tippelskirch to Schliep, 27 March; *DGFP* [973], D/6, p. 139. In late August, Schulenburg commented on the great difficulty of obtaining details on Soviet military matters because of the Russians' "usual reserve and secretiveness." Schulenburg to Foreign Ministry, Moscow, 29 Aug.; *DGFP* [973], D/7, p. 408.

45. On 23 August, for example, Arita told the Polish ambassador that, although the Japanese government had been "suspicious" for some time about the German-Soviet negotiations, it had no knowledge until the 22nd that the parleys contemplated a nonaggression agreement. It was obvious to the Polish envoy that Arita "had no clear conception of the course which he would pursue." Dooman to Hull, Tokyo, 23 Aug.; *FRUS* [974] *1939*, vol. 3, p. 52. For Shiratori's comments on the Japanese government's belief that Germany was "bluffing" and that he and Ōshima "had let themselves be led around by the nose," see Counselor Johann Plessen's memorandum of conversation with Shiratori, Rome, 4 Sept.; *DGFP* [973], D/8, p. 9. For Arita's failure or unwillingness to accept the information available to him, see BBSS, *SS* [179], vol. 8, p. 602.

46. Based on a memorandum and two messages from Schulenburg to German Foreign Office, Moscow, 16 Aug.; *NSR* [975], pp. 52-57. On 26 July, Schnurre told Soviet diplomats in Berlin that the German relation with Japan "was that of well-founded friendship, which was not, however, aimed against Russia. German policy was aimed against England." Memorandum, Berlin, 27 July; [975], p. 34. A week later Ribbentrop told Astakhov, the Soviet chargé in Berlin: "German-Japanese relations [were] good and friendly; this relationship was a lasting one. As to Russian-Japanese relations, however, I had my own ideas (by which I meant a long-range *modus vivendi* between the two countries)." Ribbentrop to Schulenburg, 3 Aug.; [975], p. 38.

47. Ribbentrop to Schulenburg, 16 Aug.; *NSR* [975], p. 58.

48. Schulenburg to German Foreign Office, 18 Aug.; *NSR* [975], p. 60.

49. Hilger and Meyer [761], p. 300. For preparatory telegrams, see *NSR* [975], pp. 63-69.

50. Excellent sources include *NSR* [975], pp. 71-78; and Hilger and Meyer [761], pp. 300-304. Ribbentrop repeated Stalin's comments, at the time Gen. Terauchi Hisaichi visited Berlin on 20 September. Knoll, memorandum, Berlin, 25 Sept.; *DGFP* [973], D/8, p. 132. Also see Kawabe [332], pp. 164-65. The Russians admit that the nonaggression pact "was not a desired solution but . . . was the only way out of the dangerous situation" in the summer of 1939. USSR [987], vol. 2, p. 202.

51. Memorandum by Weizsäcker, 22 Aug.; *NSR* [975], pp. 70-71. Also see K. Suzuki [546], p. 201; Kawabe [332], p. 164; *TSM* [549], vol. 5, p. 160; Morley, ed., *Deterrent* [875], p. 192. Shiratori denigrated Ōshima's performance: ". . . as a soldier [he] had no understanding of these things [German intentions vis-à-vis the USSR]." Plessen, memorandum of conversation with Shiratori, Rome, 4 Sept.; *DGFP* [973], D/8, p. 9.

52. Dallin, *Soviet Russia* [706], citing *Nazi Conspiracy and Aggression*, vol. 7, pp. 753-54. Also see n. 42.

53. See Dooman to Hull, Tokyo, 26 and 28 Aug.; *FRUS* [974] *1939*, vol. 3, p. 56; pp. 66-67 (12 Sept.).

54. Testimony of Ōta Saburō, 3rd Secretary, Japanese embassy/Moscow (May 1938–Oct. 1940), Defense Document No. 1581, Exhibit No. 2659, IMTFE, *Transcript* [777], 27 May 1947, pp. 23093-94. Also see Gaimushō [201], pp. 513-14; *TSM* [549], vol. 4, p. 106; Morley,

ed., *Deterrent* [875], pp. 173-74; *SSNT* [535], vol. 20, p. 372, citing foreign ministry activities report, 1939. During a conversation with a German diplomat in Rome, Shiratori revealed details of Gaimushō instructions to Tōgō; Plessen, memorandum, 4 Sept.; *DGFP* [973], D/8, p. 10. There had already been one significant straw in the wind revealing the direction of Soviet policy toward Japan: Tass reported on 11 August that, after eight months of negotiations, the Japanese concessionary company in North Sakhalin had signed a collective contract in Moscow with the Soviet workers' syndicates. *Keesing's*, vol. 3, 13 August.

55. *Iken gushin* [Recommendation], 27 Aug., from Kwantung Army commander, hand-carried by 2nd Section chief Isomura; Kantōgun [99], in *GSS* [205], vol. 10, pp. 90, 133-34. Also see *SSNT* [535], vol. 29, pp. 350-51.

56. Gomikawa, *Nomonhan* [212], pp. 284-85.

57. According to Nishiura, one night in late August the AGS Operations Section officers were so preoccupied with the forthcoming Fukuoka conference that they did not bother to scrutinize the telegrams reporting the massive Russian offensive at Nomonhan. Even after Nishiura prevailed on the staff to map the situation, they optimistically concluded that the IJA forces had been presented with a golden opportunity to conduct a "reverse envelopment." "I gave up and went home," says Nishiura. [447], p. 88.

58. *TSM* [549], vol. 4, p. 109; Morley, ed., *Deterrent* [875], p. 177. Unenthusiastic Adm. Nomura Kichisaburō, who finally accepted the post of foreign minister, explained his misgivings about the Kwantung Army and his fear of all-out war with the USSR, during a conversation with Baron Harada on 17 September. Admirals Suzuki Kantarō, Okada, and Yonai helped to talk Nomura into it. Harada Kumao [225], vol. 8, p. 76 (19 Sept.). Also see *TSM* [549], vol. 5, p. 162; Morley, ed., *Deterrent* [875], p. 194; Kutakov [812], p. 55. Abe was AGS Operations Section chief Inada's father-in-law. Yatsugi, *Shōwa* [622], vol. 1, p. 86; Nishiura [447], p. 134.

59. From vice minister of war, to Kwantung Army chief of staff, Message No. 13, transmitted 7:37 P.M., 5 Sept., received 9:30 P.M.; Kantōgun [99], in *GSS* [205], vol. 10, p. 145. The matter of post factum foreign policy disclosures to the Kwantung Army is addressed in JRD [965], *JSM* 11, part 3/C, pp. 445-46.

60. From military attaché/Moscow, to AGS deputy, 3 Sept., information copy to Kwantung Army; JRD [965], *JSM* 11, part 3/C, pp. 446-48.

61. From military attaché/Moscow, to AGS deputy, 5 Sept., information copy retransmitted 5:45 P.M., 6 Sept., received by Kwantung Army 8:46 A.M., 7 Sept.: Kantōgun [99], in *GSS* [205], vol. 10, p. 148; JRD [965], *JSM* 11, part 3/C, pp. 448-50.

62. Nishi interview.

63. Ribbentrop to Ott, 9 Sept.; cited by Kutakov [812], p. 57. I. Hata tells me that he has seen the transcript of a private interview with Ōshima which attests to the secret and direct AGS-Ōshima channel. (Interview.) Still another source of pressure on Ōshima to secure German mediation emanated from Rome where, according to Shiratori, the latter had contacted Ōshima "without instruction from Tokyo" around 1 September. Plessen, memorandum, 4 Sept.; *DGFP* [973], D/8, p. 9.

64. K. Suzuki [546], p. 207. Presumably the date of this Ribbentrop-Oshima meeting was 5 September. See *TSM* [549], vol. 5, pp. 343-44; Morley, ed. *Deterrent* [875], p. 328, n. 11.

65. Hilger and Meyer [761], p. 305. Date not specified; apparently refers to Ribbentrop's second trip to Moscow in September. During that stay, according to Boyd, Ribbentrop suggested to Stalin that a joint appeal be made to Japan to collaborate with the new Soviet-German pact. Erich Kordt is the source for Stalin's reply: "'Your intentions are good, but the implementations are wrong. I know the Japanese better. They just have suffered a defeat at Nomonhan and had 20,000 killed. Now negotiations are under way to wind up the incident. They have understood my language.'" Kordt manuscript, cited by Boyd, *Extraordinary* [650], p. 140, n. 18.

66. Doi interview.

67. Hattori Toyohiko revealed this information at an IJA/Berlin "alumni" meeting in 1961. He had served in Germany between 1927 and 1929. I. Hata, interview; *TSM* [549], vol. 4, p. 382; Morley, ed., *Deterrent* [875], p. 327, n. 136. Ott advised Ribbentrop that he had held

numerous conversations with "leading personalities of the [Japanese] Foreign Ministry, the armed forces, commerce, political groups, and the press." He had found increasing appreciation of the need for a Japanese-Russian settlement. Ott to Ribbentrop, Tokyo, 16 Sept.; *DGFP* [973], D/8, p. 75.

68. Dooman to Hull, Tokyo, 18 Sept.; *FRUS 1939* [974], vol. 3, p. 71; memorandum from Japanese Embassy to Department of State, Washington, 20 Sept., *ibid.*, p. 73.

69. Tōgō [577], pp. 129-30.

70. Encl. 1 (7 Sept.) to Schulenburg's communication to Weizsäcker, 16 Sept.; *DGFP* [973], D/8, pp. 78-79. Added Schulenburg: "I hope that I have conducted myself correctly toward Mr. Tōgō. I have had no detailed instructions. . . . I have proceeded on the basis of my judgment that it is more advantageous for us if during the war Japan favors our group rather than our enemies." *Ibid.*, pp. 77-78.

71. K. Suzuki [546], p. 207; I. Hata interview; and Schulenburg to Weizsäcker, Moscow, 16 Sept., Encl. 2 (13 Sept.); *DGFP* [973], D/8, p. 79. Italics and exclamation point annotated by Schulenburg.

72. Steinhardt to Hull, Moscow, 8 Sept.; *FRUS 1939* [974], vol. 3, pp. 62-63.

73. Ōta testimony, IMTFE, *Transcript* [777], 27 May 1947, pp. 23094-95; Gaimushō [201], p. 522; *SSNT* [535], vol. 29, pp. 374-75, citing foreign ministry activities report, 1939; *TSM* [549], vol. 4, pp. 106-7; Morley, ed., *Deterrent* [875], p. 174. Also see Ponomaryov et al., eds. [894], p. 415; Kutakov [812], pp. 151-52.

74. Ōta testimony, IMTFE, *Transcript* [777], 27 May 1947, pp. 23095-97; Gaimushō [201], pp. 522-24; *SSNT* [535], vol. 29, pp. 375-77, citing foreign ministry activities report, 1939; *TSM* [549], vol. 4, p. 107; Morley, ed., *Deterrent* [875], p. 174; *Hiroku Itagaki* [252], p. 219. On 13 September, Tōgō revealed to Schulenburg, in strict confidence, details of the conversations with Molotov regarding settlement of the Lake Buir dispute. Molotov had evinced "complete good will" but demanded recognition of the MPR-claimed frontier. Japan could not agree lest she admit "she had been at fault in the conflict." A formula was being sought to "save the honor of both parties." Schulenburg to Weizsäcker, Moscow, 16 Sept., Encl. 2 (13 Sept.); *DGFP* [973], D/8, p. 79. For Tōgō's misplaced plea for confidentiality, see n. 71. Also see Ponomaryov et al., eds. [894], p. 415; Kutakov [812], p. 152.

75. From the exchanges in September, see Schulenburg to Ribbentrop, Moscow, 10 Sept.; *NSR* [975], p. 91.

76. Ōta testimony, IMTFE, *Transcript* [777], 27 May 1947, p. 23098; Gaimushō [201], pp. 524-25; *SSNT* [535], vol. 29, p. 377, citing foreign ministry activities report, 1939; *TSM* [549], vol. 4, p. 107; Morley, ed., *Deterrent* [875], p. 174. Also see Kutakov [812], p. 152.

77. Schulenburg to Ribbentrop, Moscow, 14 Sept.; *NSR* [975], p. 92.

78. Tōgō [577], pp. 128-29; Doi, Nishi interviews; Ōta testimony, IMTFE, *Transcript* [777], 27 May 1947, pp. 23098-99; Gaimushō [201], pp. 525-26; *SSNT* [535], vol. 29, pp. 377-80, citing foreign ministry activities report, 1939; *TSM* [549], vol. 4, p. 107; Morley, ed., *Deterrent* [875], pp. 174-75. At midnight on 15 September, U.S. ambassador Steinhardt reported to Washington he had just learned, on good authority, that Tōgō had held several meetings with Molotov during the past few days and that at a four-hour conference on the 15th it had been agreed to settle all outstanding issues amicably. Steinhardt to Hull, Moscow, 15 Sept.; *FRUS 1939* [974], vol. 3, p. 70.

79. For the text of the communiqué, see Gaimushō, 1st Section, Bureau of European-Asiatic Affairs, Activities Report, 1939 (Defense Document No. 1570, Exhibit No. 2661-A), IMTFE, *Transcript* [777], 28 May 1947, pp. 23141-43. Japan time equivalent was 9 A.M. on 16 Sept. for the cessation of fire; 8 P.M. on the 15th for the retention of positions. *Shōwa jūyonnen* [533], p. 454.

80. Tōgō [577], p. 129, and *Cause* [947], p. 34; Doi interview. Elsewhere, Doi has said that Tōgō reported having had to make 60 percent of the compromises; *SSNT* [535], vol. 29, p. 380. Hamada Sueo states that he had been privately counting on Tōgō to solve matters entirely; the Sixth Army's offensive plan was merely designed to cope with contingencies. (Interview.)

81. Nishi, Hashimoto interviews. Also see Onda [473], vol. 2, pp. 237-38.

82. *Hiroku Itagaki* [252], p. 220. The vice minister, from October 1939, was Lt. Gen. Anami Korechika.

83. Doi interview. For additional comments by Doi on the Soviet deceptive capability, see *SSNT* [535], vol. 29, p. 382.

84. Schulenburg to Ribbentrop, Moscow, 16, 17 Sept.; *NSR* [975], pp. 95-96. Also Y. Nishihara interview. On the same busy night of 16/17 September, Molotov called in the Polish ambassador and informed him that Soviet troops would cross the Polish frontier on the 17th. According to a Soviet army officer, the order for the advance had already been announced to the Russian troops at midday on 16 September. Col. G. I. Antonov, "The March into Poland," in Liddell Hart, ed. [833], p. 73.

85. Doi, S. Hata interviews. Heavy Russian troop movements west began right after the settlement with Japan. Nyūmura interview. On 31 August the Soviet parliament had passed a new military service law, under which the first batches of conscripts were called up immediately. Soviet sources admit there had been danger that within weeks or even days, the USSR might become involved in war on two fronts: "Nobody would come to its assistance. It was therefore the duty of the Soviet Government to deliver the country from that danger." By settling with Japan, the USSR "obtained a respite and the possibility to prepare for the inevitable clash with Nazism." USSR [987], vol. 2, p. 202.

86. From military attaché/Moscow, to AGS deputy, message received 17 Sept.; JRD [965], *JSM* 11, part 3/C, pp. 454-55.

87. For material on the Sorge ring, I have drawn mainly on the transcripts of interrogations and depositions found in *GSS* [206], parts 1-3; and on Imaoka, "Zoruge" [15]. Also see C. Willoughby [1002], pp. 104-5, 174, 192, 200, 228; and Chalmers Johnson, *An Instance of Treason: Ozaki Hotsumi and the Sorge Spy Ring* (Stanford, Calif.: Stanford University Press, 1964), pp. 105, 149-52.

88. USSR [992], vol. 2, p. 332.

89. According to JRD [965], *JSM* 11, part 3/C, pp. 451-52, at 3 A.M. on the 16th Lieutenant Colonel Arao phoned Lieutenant Colonel Nakayama the first alert; at 6 A.M. the AGS deputy (still Nakajima) went to the palace; at 6:25 A.M. the imperial order was issued; at 7 A.M. Colonel Inada phoned Colonel Arisue the news that the order had been promulgated but that the detailed directive would have to be held up for the time being; and, as of 8 A.M., Arisue reported that the front-line troops were on strict alert but ready to carry out the terms of an armistice.

90. Based on 16 Sept. combat diary entries of 64th Inf. Regt. [115]; 7th Co., 26th Inf. Regt. [105]; 3rd Bn., 27th Inf. Regt. [106]; 2nd Bn., 28th Inf. Regt. [110]. Also see Onda [473], vol. 2, pp. 245-46 (71st Inf. Regt.). In the 13th Field Artillery Regt., battery commanders were assembled at 9 A.M. to be apprised of details of the cease-fire. [473], vol. 2, p. 250.

91. Imperial Order No. 357 and IGHQ Directive No. 551: BBSS, *SS* [180], vol. 27, p. 729; JRD [965], *JSM* 11, part 3/C, pp. 452-53. Note that the imperial order is said to have been first approved at 6:25 A.M. (n. 89).

92. It took days for the prince's message to reach all units. The 7th Co., 26th Inf. Regt., received it on 20 September, according to its combat report [105] of that date.

93. JRD [965], *JSM* 11, part 3/C, p. 454.

94. Based on 1-16 Sept. combat reports of infantry units mentioned in n. 90. Also see Sawada [507A], pp. 131-33.

95. Imamura, *Shiki* [282], p. 282; Sawada [507A], pp. 133-34. Sawada credited the cease-fire to the backstage mediation of his classmate Oshima in Berlin. K. Suzuki [546], pp. 207-8. Also see chap. 37.

96. N. Morita interview.

97. Captain Tsuchiya of the 1st HFA Regt. remembers being ordered to recruit three "last attack" assault teams (*kesshitai*) whose mission would be to enter enemy positions secretly by night, destroy defenses and armor, and try to recapture IJA matériel. Only about 20 men volunteered. "Some of those who had barely survived were now living in great fear. A number had already cracked up." Tsuchiya was convinced that the IJA offensive could never have beaten the

enemy, and there were too few men to recapture and salvage the lost pieces. The *kesshitai* slept by day and trained by night, until the cease-fire. (Interview.)

98. Composite of interviews cited in Onda [473], vol. 2, pp. 239, 249-50; Mita [406], pp. 484-85; *SSNT* [535], vol. 29, pp. 385-86; *Nomonhan* [40], vol. 10, pp. 114-15. The Sixth Army's potential designation of X-day was 12 Sept., as we saw; Hamada interview. For Colonel Sumi's response to the cease-fire, see *Jissen* [541], pp. 201-2.

99. 7th Co., 26th Inf. Regt. [105], 16-18 Sept. From Hailar, the Japanese air force dispatched a 50-plane fly-by over the old battlefield. See Onda [473], vol. 2, p. 245 (71st Inf. Regt.). The 13th Field Artillery Regiment fired a funeral salute. [473], vol. 2, pp. 250-51.

100. Mita [406], p. 485; *SSNT* [535], vol. 29, p. 385.

CHAPTER 39

1. *Tanka* verse written the night before the general left the battlefront in 1939. *Nomonhan* [40], vol. 2, p. 79 (Mrs. Komatsubara Yoshie).

2. Maj. A. E. Bykov's testimony, IMTFE, *Transcript* [777], 27 Jan. 1948, p. 38370. Estimate of IJA dead from Kutakov [812], p. 151, citing *Istoriia Velikoi Otechestvennoi voiny*, vol. 1, p. 244. USSR, *History* [985], p. 350, gives a total estimate of 60,000 IJA casualties. Also see Shirendyb et al., eds. [919], p. 354. According to Shishkin, during July and August the Japanese lost 18,868 dead and 25,900 wounded; [920], p. 626. Also see *Nomonhan* [452], p. 18; Gomikawa, *Nomonhan* [212], p. 337. The Russians also reported the desertion to them of 294 Manchukuoan troops with weapons, from the 14th Inf. Regt., 1st Mixed Brigade. *Pravda*, 1 Sept. 1939, cited in USSR [992], vol. 2, p. 275.

3. Langdon (Mukden) to State Dept., 3 Nov. 1939 (National Archives file 761.93 Manchuria/246; NARS [980]).

4. Harada Kumao [225], vol. 8, p. 89 (1 Oct.). The source was Sakurauchi Yukio, who had served as agriculture minister under Hiranuma.

5. *New York Times*, 4 Oct. 1939, p. 3, citing information released by a war ministry officer on 3 Oct.; and *Asahi Shinbun*, 4 Oct. (P.M. ed.), p. 1. Also see *Japan-Manchoukuo Year Book, 1940* [782A], p. 633; Gomikawa, *Nomonhan* [212], p. 337. Almost three months later, the same figure for IJA casualties at Nomonhan—appended to the report of an IGHQ announcement of 29 Dec. concerning losses in the China theater—was buried on p. 7 of the *New York Times* of that date.

6. GSDF [68], p. 17 (also see n. 13); and S. Hata interview.

7. Mita [406], p. 488. The monument was dedicated on 10 Sept., 1942.

8. Also citing Sixth Army medical data, Imaoka lists only 5,834 dead (353 officers, 618 non-coms, 4,863 enlisted men), but more than 10,000 wounded and 3,000 missing. (Interview.)

9. The Sixth Army's base figure for 23rd Division personnel (Table 39.1) includes replacements only through August. GSDF [68], p. 17. Still other statistics are found in a Nomonhan Incident Research Committee report dated Jan. 1940. Relying on the same divisional personnel basis as the Sixth Army, this report enumerated only 5,070 killed or missing (33.5 percent), 5,348 wounded (35.3 percent), and merely 706 ill (4.7 percent), for a combined loss of 11,124 officers and men (73.5 percent). GSDF [68], chart 4; and BBSS, *SS* [180], vol. 27, p. 711. A differing figure for the 13th FA Regt. is 664 killed (obviously includes the missing) and 554 wounded. *Nomonhan* [40], vol. 7, p. 119.

10. The Sixth Army's tabulation showed 7th Division losses to be 32.8 percent. (See Table 39.1.) According to Sumi, his 26th Regiment lost 604 killed and about 1,000 wounded. At the end, some 450 men were still ambulatory, although very few were unhurt. (Interview.) Lieutenant Negami thinks the regimental casualties were nearer 800 killed and 1,600 wounded. (Interview.)

11. In July: 324 killed, 673 wounded; in August: 1,151 killed, 1,107 wounded; in September: 35 killed, 71 wounded. 7th Div. Medical Sec. (Yoshida Yasuhiko), in *Nomonhan* [40], vol. 11, p. 120. In the air force, combat accounted for 60 percent of unit casualties, of whom 88 percent were killed. The overall rate of killed to wounded was 1.9:1. Many of the injured crewmen crashed and died, of course. GSDF [68], pp. 72-73.

12. Sakazaki report of 29 Sept., in GSDF [68], p. 15. Approximately 3,500 men were hospi-

talized in the following main locations: Mukden (500 with fractures), Ryūjuton (1,500 with internal injuries), Liaoyang (1,300 for routine surgery), and Hsinking (200 for special treatment). For the hospital situation at Hailar and the rear, see Sumi, *Jissen* [541], pp. 193-94; and Mishima interview. After being wounded in early August, Colonel Mishima spent the next two months in the Hailar hospital.

13. When the war minister visited Manchuria on 9 Dec. 1939, he learned that 1,700 patients had already been repatriated. Six thousand men, including 1,100 with communicable diseases, were still hospitalized in 50 installations in Manchuria. GSDF [68], p. 17.

14. U.S. Military Attaché/Tokyo, Report No. 9883, 12 Sept., prepared by Capt. E. H. F. Svensson, Jr., G-2 Reports/6920 (National Archives G-2 M/A file; NARS [980]). The correspondent was [Relman] Morin of Associated Press, who said he had recently inspected the battle zone.

15. Basic data derived from BBSS, *SS* [181], vol. 53, pp. 345, 354-55. Appreciably lower casualty figures are found in JRD [952], *JSM* 4, pp. 70-71; namely, 64 wounded and 104 killed. It was the latter casualty toll which was incurred at the rate of 4 wounded and 13 killed in May-June; 13 wounded and 31 killed in July; 43 wounded and 41 killed in August; 4 wounded and 19 killed in September. Also see *Kaikōsha Kiji*, Dec. 1939, p. 37, citing figure of 150 air force casualties. The statistic of 55 dead, contained in Table 39.2 above, seems to be confused with the number of air force bodies returned by the Russians. Also see BBSS, *SS* [180], vol. 27, p. 618; Yonaga Hyōe, *Hikō dia-24 Sentai kūchū sentō senshi* [A Military History of the 24th Air Group's Air Battles] (Tokyo: privately printed, 1979), p. 97. A recent summary lists 116 IJAF killed (including the 55 repatriated dead), 65 missing, and only 19 wounded; Tanaka Kōji, Kōchiyama Yuzuru, and Ikuta Makoto, eds., *Nihon rikugun kōkū hiwa* [Untold Stories of the Japanese Army Air Force] (Tokyo: Hara Shobō, 1981), p. 134. As for Abe, his death and posthumous promotion to major general were disclosed publicly by the arrival of his ashes in Japan on 24 October 1939. *NYT*, same date, p. 4. In MPRA captivity during the Japanese raid of 27 June, Master Sgt. S. Miyajima was called upon to identify a dead pilot, whom he recognized as Captain Morimoto. Since there were no visible wounds, Miyajima guessed that Morimoto had killed himself. I. Hata, "Dai-niji" [229], p. 80. But on 14 July, a Tass release indicated that Morimoto had been captured. See n. 82.

16. S. Hayashi, *Kōgun* [756], p. 15; BBSS, *SS* [180], vol. 27, p. 711; Y. Nishihara interview.

17. Report of Lieutenant Colonel Baba, Kwantung Army Medical Bureau, 12 Oct. 1939, GSDF [68], p. 17; ibid., p. 72; BBSS, *SS* [180], vol. 27, p. 712. Military coroners conducted a limited number of autopsies in hospitals to the rear: 140 at Hailar, others at Harbin and Hsinking. At Tsitsihar, the emphasis was on deaths from malnutrition. Medical School instructor Hirai's report, 18 Oct. 1939; GSDF [68], p. 16. The Japanese army carefully analyzed World War I comparative data on French casualties, the closest to IJA experience at Nomonhan. Y. Nishihara interview. For air force data, see GSDF [68], pp. 72-73. For data on IJA casualties at Changkufeng, see Coox, *Anatomy*, p. 285.

18. Interview with then–Lieutenant Colonel Kinbara, M.D. Also see Lieutenant Colonel Baba's report (n. 17). Baba confirmed one case of frostbite, incurred during air evacuation at an altitude of 8,000 meters.

19. I. Saitō interview. For more information on "zombies," some of whom disappeared, see Mita [406], p. 448.

20. Shishkin [920], p. 626; S. Hayashi, *Kantōgun* [242], p. 181. According to Bykov's testimony, in IMTFE, *Transcript* [777], 27 Jan. 1948, p. 38372, the figure was 9,000-9,500. *Istoriia Velikoi Otechestvennoi voiny*, vol. 1, p. 244, cited by Kutakov [812], p. 151, merely says Soviet casualties totaled less than 10,000. A number of sources have transposed the official statistic as 9,824.

21. Harrison Salisbury, introduction to Zhukov, *Marshal* [1016], pp. 6-7.

22. Erickson, *Soviet* [722], pp. 534-35, citing Ruslanov [907], July 1956, p. 190. Also see Mackintosh [846], p. 108; and Grigorenko [746A], pp. 109-110.

23. I am grateful to Prof. John Erickson for this information. (Correspondence.) The Konstantin M. Simonov novel under discussion is *Comrades in Arms* (*Tovarishchi po orudiiu*).

24. War ministry release of 3 Oct. (see n. 5). According to a censored release in 1942, "the

combatting forces lost over 15,000 men each"; *The Orient Year Book, 1942* (Tokyo: Asia Statistics, 1942), p. 539. A Manchukuo government minister received a private letter from a Russian friend, a Red Army staff officer, to the effect that Soviet casualties at Nomonhan had been double those of the Japanese. GSDF [69], p. 205.

25. *Nomonhan* [40], vol. 7, p. 119. According to *Shōwa jūgonen Asahi nenkan* [The *Asahi* Yearbook, 1940] (Osaka, 1939), p. 214, the Russian-MPRA side left no less than 3,000 bodies on the field.

26. Nyūmura interview. One of the IJA soldiers at the first meeting sneaked the photo shown in *Nomonhan* [40], vol. 8, p. 63. Major Kanaizuka of the 64th Regt. was told by a Soviet lieutenant at the end of an armistice conversation, "See you here again next year!" (Interview.)

27. Onda [473], vol. 2, pp. 239, 241. Also see *Kaikōsha Kiji*, Oct. 1939, p. 79; *Shōwa jūyonnen* [533], pp. 454-55. The names of the Kwantung Army's original designees will be found in JRD [965], *JSM* 11, part 3/C, pp. 452, 454. Like a number of other sources, the preceding JRD monograph indicates that Fujimoto led the conversations from the start and that the main body met only twice.

28. From Sixth Army chief of staff, to AGS deputy and vice minister of war, Sixth Army message, 18 Sept.: JRD [965], *JSM* 11, part 3/C, pp. 455-56; supplemented by *Manshūkoku gensei 1940* [375], p. 262; *Shōwa jūyonnen* [533], p. 455; Inada, S. Hamada, and (especially) Nyūmura interviews.

29. Fighting had been continuing in the Handagai sector and in the air.

30. *Shōwa jūyonnen* [533], pp. 454-56; *Manshūkoku gensei 1940* [375], p. 262; *Kaikōsha Kiji*, Oct. 1939, pp. 79-80; JRD [965], *JSM* 11, part 3/C, pp. 458-59.

31. *Manshūkoku gensei 1940* [375], p. 262. Also see Gaimushō [201], p. 527.

32. Nyūmura, Inada interviews; JRD [965], *JSM* 11, part 3/C, pp. 459-60, citing Inada; and *SSNT* [535], vol. 29, pp. 388-89, citing Inada.

33. M. Tsuchiya, T. Hayashi interviews. The figure for the recovered bodies will be found in BBSS, *SS* [180], vol. 27, p. 730. It is rounded off to 4,500 by Baba (12 Oct. 1939) in GSDF [68], p. 16. For other details, see *Nomonhan* [40], vol. 9, pp. 103, 105, 196; Onda [473], vol. 2, pp. 239, 246. Relying on memory, both Nyūmura and Tsuchiya think that 5,000 to 6,000 corpses were located. (Interviews.)

34. M. Tsuchiya interview; Onda [473], vol. 2, pp. 239, 241-43; *Nomonhan* [40], vol. 9, p. 103.

35. Komatsubara letter, 2 Oct., Chiangchunmiao, in *Nomonhan* [40], vol. 2, p. 41; 7th Co., 26th Inf. Regt. [105], 20 Sept.; and Onozuka, M. Tsuchiya, T. Hayashi interviews. Also see *Nomonhan* [40], vol. 9, pp. 103, 196. The eagerness of four tattered, filthy 71st Infantry soldiers to participate in corpse recovery is vividly portrayed in *Nomonhan* [40], vol. 10, pp. 116-17. One disguised artillery officer's mustache almost "blew his cover." (T. Hayashi interview.)

36. Tsunashima, Sumi interviews; *Nomonhan* [40], vol. 5, p. 101; [40], vol. 10, p. 119; *SSNT* [535], vol. 27, pp. 307-10, citing Sumi. In Hailar on 21 June, before leaving for the front, Captain Miki of the 71st Inf. Regt. ordered his men to write last wills to be sent to kinfolk or cadre, and to enclose hair snippets and nail clippings. *Nomonhan* [40], vol. 8, p. 113.

37. Nyūmura, T. Hayashi, N. Tanaka interviews; Sumi, interview and *Jissen* [541], p. 206; *Nomonhan* [40], vol. 9, pp. 103-5; [40], vol. 10, p. 118; Onda [473], vol. 2, pp. 239-40. In the 71st Inf. Regt., the impact of lost comrades began to be felt around 22 Sept., PFC S. Satake noted in his diary entry of that date; [473], vol. 2, p. 247.

38. Hirai report, 18 Oct. 1939; GSDF [68], p. 16. Also see n. 17. A few of the dead Japanese soldiers were found with their hands and legs tied. Caught while alive, they may have resisted, been bound and shot. (T. Hayashi interview.)

39. Kanaizuka, Suzuki Yoshiyasu, Nyūmura interviews; and Onda [473], vol. 2, pp. 240, 241-42; *Nomonhan* [40], vol. 6, pp. 101-2. Location or retrieval of Higashi's remains is not mentioned. Onda [473], vol. 2, p. 243. But the heavy-artillerymen found the bodies of their Major Umeda and Captain Yamazaki, according to M. Tsuchiya and T. Hayashi. (Interviews.)

40. M. Tsuchiya interview. According to PFC S. Satake's diary entry for 21 Sept., not one

Soviet corpse lay in IJA hands as of that date. Onda [473], vol. 2, p. 247. But Sumi mentions and reproduces a photo of the return of enemy bodies in makeshift coffins, with flowers. *Jissen* [541], pp. 205-6. Nyūmura says there were 23 such bodies. (Interview.) For a photo of the marked grave dug for a Soviet fighter pilot shot down earlier, see *Nomonhan* [40], vol. 11, p. 88.

41. BBSS, *SS* [180], vol. 27, p. 730. Of IJAF aircrews which failed to return from combat, the fates of 80 percent were entirely unknown to the Japanese. GSDF [68], p. 73. In the period from June to mid-August, according to Giga's materials, five of the air groups incurred 36 missing in action (MIA) from a total of 83 casualties: 1st Group—8 MIA from 11 total casualties; 11th Group—13 MIA from 21; 24th Group—7 MIA from 9; 10th Group—2 MIA from 11; 15th Group—6 MIA from 12. BBSS, *SS* [180], vol. 27, p. 618.

42. Nyūmura, M. Tsuchiya interviews; Sumi, interview and *Jissen* [541], pp. 211-12.

43. Tsunashima interview.

44. *Nomonhan* [40], vol. 6, p. 101; Onda [473], vol. 2, p. 240. Col. S. Hamada [2] notes that the families of the deceased were to be given a detailed explanation of the circumstances of the urns and asked for their understanding.

45. *Nomonhan* [40], vol. 6, p. 130. Also Nyūmura interview; and Onda [473], vol. 2, p. 247.

46. Sumi, interview and *Jissen* [541], pp. 207-8; Onda [473], vol. 2, pp. 240, 247; *Nomonhan* [40], vol. 10, p. 121. Komatsubara noted the death of a man engaged in cremation on 1 Oct.; letter, 2 Oct., Chiangchunmiao, in *Nomonhan* [40], vol. 2, p. 40. On 21 Sept. a line company warned that six casualties had been caused the day before by careless handling of ammunition. Those engaged in corpse retrieval should beware of dud shells and live cartridges and not pick them up. 7th Co., 26th Inf. Regt. [105], 21 Sept.

47. Komatsubara letter, 2 Oct., Chiangchunmiao, in *Nomonhan* [40], vol. 2, p. 40; Sumi, interview and *Jissen* [541], p. 206; *Nomonhan* [40], vol. 9, p. 105; [40], vol. 10, p. 121; Onda [473], vol. 2, pp. 240, 247-48.

48. *Nomonhan* [40], vol. 6, pp. 101-2. After Colonel Ise's funeral, Warrant Officer Ichihara put up a simple, unmarked wooden marker in memory of his slain regimental commander; Onda [473], vol. 2, p. 242. Komatsubara alluded to the artillery regiment's mourning for Ise; letter, 2 Oct., Chiangchunmiao, in *Nomonhan* [40], vol. 2, p. 40.

49. Kwantung Army commander, to AGS chief and war minister, Kwantung Army 1st Section, Message No. 766, prepared by Hattori, transmitted 8 P.M., 8 Sept.; Kantōgun [99], in *GSS* [205], vol. 10, p. 149. *Mainichi* reporter Andō Shigenori, in Hailar, first heard a rumor that the 64th Infantry had lost its colors. He rushed to the cadre headquarters, where he was told that, surrounded by enemy armor, the regiment had *burned* the colors. (Interview.)

50. Excerpts from Komatsubara's painful letter to his wife (n.d.) can be found in *Nomonhan* [40], vol. 2, p. 79. According to Colonel Hamada who, like Ogisu and the others at Sixth Army headquarters, was very troubled by the fate of Yamagata's colors, during the Manchurian Incident an IJA cavalry regiment headquarters was annihilated and lost its colors. Afterward, a study had been made concerning how to handle colors when operating in a particularly dangerous area. S. Hamada, interview and [2].

51. Kanaizuka, Suzuki Yoshiyasu interviews; *Nomonhan* [40], vol. 3, pp. 54-55; Onda [473], vol. 2, p. 240.

52. Suzuki Yoshiyasu interview; Onda [473], vol. 2, p. 243, citing Hanada.

53. S. Hata interview; BBSS, *SS* [180], vol. 27, p. 730; *Nomonhan* [40], vol. 3, p. 55; S. Hamada, interview and [2]; Nishiura [447], p. 135.

54. See Gomikawa, *Nomonhan* [212], p. 293.

55. Authorized translation; *The Japan Year Book, 1944-45* (Tokyo: Foreign Affairs Association of Japan, 1945), p. 200.

56. *Nomonhan* [40], vol. 9, p. 102; [40], vol. 10, pp. 36-39; Onda [473], vol. 2, p. 223.

57. Japanese codes of behavior in the larger context are described by the sociologist Carr-Gregg [663A]. Also see Gomikawa, *Nomonhan* [212], pp. 330-31; Onda [473], vol. 2, p. 283 (Onda-Gomikawa colloquium); and Scribner [913], pp. 148-64.

58. Kimura Hachirō in *Bungei Shunjū*, Oct. 1961, p. 254.

59. *Nomonhan* [40], vol. 5, p. 24. Also see Onda [473], vol. 2, p. 284 (Gomikawa); and Sumi, "Ikuta" [50].

60. Onda [473], vol. 2, pp. 225-26.

61. My best source is Imaoka, citing Sixth Army medical data. (Interview.) Additional information is found in *Ichiokunin* [265], p. 227; *Nomonhan* [40], vol. 9, p. 102; Onda [473], vol. 2, p. 282.

62. Onda [473], vol. 2, p. 222; *Nomonhan* [40], vol. 10, p. 44. According to Tass, a certain Colonel Kowaro, a light-bomber detachment commander, had been shot down on 23 July, taken prisoner, and interrogated. *Izvestiya*, 27 July, cited in USSR [992], vol. 2, p. 160. No correlation is possible from IJAF records with respect to name, rank, or engagement.

63. Prof. John Erickson supplied this information. (Correspondence.)

64. M. Tsuchiya interview. In the 4th Battery of the 7th Heavy Field Artillery Regiment, over 30 men were missing. *Nomonhan* [40], vol. 9, p. 196.

65. S. Hamada, Nyūmura, Kanaizuka interviews. Onozuka of the 71st Inf. Regt. says about 70 cadet-officer replacements did not show up, so he sent death notices to the families and ward offices in Japan, rendering them legally deceased. Many turned up later, and Onozuka was blamed for the foul-up, but he simply had had no way to check their whereabouts during the fighting. (Interview.) Superior Pvt. Kanemura (Kinmura) Chūichi, serving as a driver, recounts how he and 2nd Lt. Andō Kyōji, the acting 7th HFA Regiment aide, were detained briefly when they got lost en route to meet Colonel Takatsukasa. The high point of this episode occurred when a Russian soldier said "Moskva, Tokyo, *Banzai!*" and Kanemura replied "Tokyo, Moskva, hurrah!" After hurried consultations with higher headquarters, the local Soviet commander released Andō and Kanemura and guided them to Takatsukasa. *SSNT* [535], vol. 29, pp. 390-91.

66. Including one seriously wounded officer, according to BBSS, *SS* [180], vol. 27, p. 730; including three officers (one probationary) and nine noncoms (three medics), according to GSDF [68], p. 16, citing Baba's report of 12 Oct. 1939.

67. See n. 23.

68. Nyūmura interview; Sumi, *Jissen* [541], pp. 204-5.

69. Miura's report of 27 Dec. 1939, and Baba's report of 12 Oct., in GSDF [68], pp. 16-17. According to Baba, all of the unhurt men said they had been captured while unconscious. Also see BBSS, *SS* [180], vol. 27, p. 730; Imoto [285], p. 387; Gomikawa, *Nomonhan* [212], p. 329.

70. Gaimushō [201], pp. 526-28.

71. Refers to dinner conversation of 20 April; Harada Kumao [225], vol. 8, p. 226 (2 May).

72. For numerical data on the exchange, see GSDF [68], p. 20; BBSS, *SS* [180], vol. 27, p. 730; Imoto [285], p. 387. The figure for the exchanges of Sept. 1939 is lumped together with that of April 1940 in *Ichiokunin* [265], p. 227.

73. No mention is made of the ground-force officer, Captain Katō, who had been identified in the diplomatic bargaining as a "detainee" to be released. The question is complicated by the fact that, reporting on the fighting as early as 6-12 July, the Russians had revealed that their prisoners included Capt. Katō Takeo and 12 noncoms. (Compare text, above.) *Izvestiya*, 14 July, cited in USSR [992], vol. 2, p. 138.

74. Zhukov calls the IJA pilot "Takeo," a first name. Japanese records for 29 July list the following air force officer casualties: Harada, Capt. Kani Saiji (death confirmed), and 1st Lt. Suzuki Shōichi. BBSS, *SS* [181], vol. 53, p. 355. Japanese POW's, however, often gave their captors fictitious names; see n. 86.

75. Zhukov, *Memoirs* [1017], p. 164.

76. *Nomonhan* [40], vol. 8, pp. 40-42; [40], vol. 10, pp. 46-50; I. Hata, "Dai-niji" [229], pp. 80-81; Onda [473], vol. 2, p. 224. Also see Gomikawa, *Nomonhan* [212], pp. 331-32.

77. *Nomonhan* [40], vol. 10, p. 41; Mita [406], p. 492.

78. *Nomonhan* [40], vol. 10, pp. 50-51. In IJA military police materials, mention is made of a well-known case of suicide forced by the Japanese side upon at least one junior officer prisoner repatriated by the Russians after Nomonhan. See *Nihon kenpei seishi* [An Authentic History of the Japanese Military Police], ed. Zenkoku Kenyūkai Rengōkai Hensan Iinkai (Tokyo: Kenbun Shoin, 1980).

79. Hayashi Jirō, on MP duty since April 1939; cited in Mita [406], pp. 491-92.

80. Onda [473], vol. 2, p. 223; *Nomonhan* [40], vol. 10, pp. 39-40; Nyūmura interview.

81. Nyūmura interview.

82. I. Hata, interview and "Dai-niji" [229], pp. 79-81. On 14 July 1939, Tass had listed Miadzimo [Miyajima] as an air force prisoner, together with Captain Marimoto [Morimoto], Lieutenants Amano and Mitsutomi, Sublieutenant Mitsudo, three master sergeants, and four other noncoms. Most were severely wounded. *Izvestiya*, 14 July, in USSR [992], vol. 2, p. 138. Also see n. 15.

83. Onda [473], vol. 2, pp. 216-25.

84. *Nomonhan* [40], vol. 10, pp. 35-42.

85. Onda [473], vol. 2, p. 226; Nishikawa, M. Tsuchiya, I. Hata interviews.

86. *Nomonhan* [40], vol. 10, pp. 42, 44. Carr-Gregg refers to wartime prisoners' frequent refusal to reveal their true name and rank, and their practice of assuming the identity of "famous warriors or culture heroes." [663A], p. 35.

87. Mita [406], p. 492.

88. I. Hata, interview and "Dai-niji" [229], p. 81; Onda [473], vol. 2, p. 224; *Nomonhan* [40], vol. 10, p. 50.

89. I. Hata, "Dai-niji" [229], p. 80; Onda [473], vol. 2, pp. 223, 226, 283.

90. *Nomonhan* [40], vol. 8, p. 49, citing account by T. Imano.

91. *Nomonhan* [40], vol. 7, p. 38, citing R. Ueda. Ueda was shocked to learn that there were so many IJA prisoners from the Nomonhan war; as a young conscript, he had been taught that Japanese soldiers never gave up.

92. Kadoma Tomio, "Yokuryūchi no shiki" [Four Seasons in the Detention Area], *Shūshin*, Aug. 1979, vol. 22, pp. 26-27.

93. M. Suzuki [547], p. 168.

94. *Nomonhan* [40], vol. 7, p. 40.

95. *Nomonhan* [40], vol. 9, p. 102. Also see Onda [473], vol. 2, pp. 282-84 (Gomikawa and Onda).

CHAPTER 40

1. S. Hamada, M. Tsuchiya interviews; K. Itō [308], pp. 231-33. According to *Mainichi* reporter S. Andō, the people of Saga had gone to the prefectural governor's office and asked for information about their sons who had never returned from Nomonhan. At a loss for an answer, the official had brought up the matter in the next governors' conference held at the prime minister's residence. This publicity had caused the High Command to admit the casualties and to ease up on censorship. (Interview.) Also see chap. 39, n. 5.

2. Onda [473], vol. 2, pp. 248, 251-52.

3. Onda [473], vol. 2, p. 248 (N. Satake diary, 7 Oct.).

4. Komatsubara letter, Chiangchunmiao, 24 Sept. 1939, bound for Hailar on 4 or 5 Oct.; in *Nomonhan* [40], vol. 2, p. 40.

5. Nukada, *Rikugunshō* [457], pp. 84-85; Sawada [507A], pp. 152-53.

6. See n. 4.

7. Mrs. Ogisu provided the correct reading of the general's first name—Tatsuhei—usually read as Rippei or Ryūhei. (Imaoka correspondence.)

8. Mita [406], p. 476; Gomikawa, *Nomonhan* [212], pp. 326-27; Nukada, *Rikugunshō* [457], p. 86; Sawada [507A], pp. 27, 136-37; Sumi, Imaoka, Y. Nishihara interviews.

9. Sawada [507A], pp. 134-38.

10. See n. 4. Since his revelations were so confidential, Komatsubara asked his wife to reveal them to no one except her father (a retired old general). Entirely unknown to Komatsubara, as we saw in chap. 26, Ogisu had hoped that the division commander would perish north of the Holsten at the end of August; Major Tsuji demurred strenuously and successfully. [585], p. 208.

11. See chap. 39, n. 47.

12. BBSS, *SS* [180], vol. 27, p. 728.

13. Sumi interview. Also see Nishiura [447], p. 135.

14. Mita [406], p. 476; Ogi [462], pp. 387-88, 398-99.

15. *Asahi Shinbun*, 4 Oct. 1939 (A.M. ed.), p. 3; Sumi interview. As mentioned earlier, War Minister Hata denies that the Diet could exert pressure on the army. (Interview.) Also Fukuda correspondence.

16. Sawada [507A], pp. 135, 149-50, 153.

17. BBSS, *SS* [180], vol. 27, p. 728; *Nomonhan* [40], vol. 2, p. 52 (Col. Murakami Tokuji, M.D.); [40], vol. 3, p. 75; Yonemoto [623A], pp. 26-27; N. Tanaka, Shirai, Sumi, S. Hata interviews.

18. My source is Col. Yano Muraji.

19. Kanaizuka, Suzuki Yoshiyasu, Sumi interviews; *Nomonhan* [40], vol. 3, p. 55. Mita [406], p. 477; *SSNT* [535], vol. 29, pp. 287-88.

20. Tsuji's contemporary estimate is found in Kantōgun [99], in *GSS* [205], vol. 10, p. 92. In *Nomonhan* [585], p. 191, Tsuji comes closer to the overall figure—i.e., about half of Ioki's men escaped alive.

21. BBSS, *SS* [180], vol. 27, pp. 680, 731-32; Onda [473], vol. 2, pp. 235-37; Komatsubara [25], 13 Sept.; Mita [406], pp. 305-6, 477; *SSNT* [535], vol. 29, p. 338; Gomikawa, *Nomonhan* [212], pp. 226, 240; *Nomonhan* [40], vol. 9, pp. 178-79; S. Hamada, interview and [2]; Sumi interview; JRD [965], *JSM* 11, part 3/C, p. 405, citing Sumi, "Nihon" [542]; interview with privileged IJA source; and Sawada [507A], pp. 135, 138.

22. Ōgi [462].

23. BBSS, *SS* [180], vol. 27, pp. 731-32; Mita [406], p. 477; Sumi interview; JRD [965], *JSM* 11, part 3/C, p. 405, citing Sumi, "Nihon" [542]; Onda [473], vol. 2, pp. 120, 237; *Nomonhan* [40], vol. 8, p. 64 (Kwantung Army officer Tanabe Shinshi); [40], vol. 9, p. 150; *SSNT* [535], vol. 29, pp. 179-80, 184-85 (Sugitani); S. Hamada, interview and [2]. On 23 September, Komatsubara told Sawada that Hasebe's case resembled Ioki's, but that at least Hasebe "finished the necessary paperwork and then committed suicide." [507A], p. 138.

24. See Onda [473], vol. 2, pp. 120, 237; *SSNT* [535], vol. 29, p. 338; *Nomonhan* [40], vol. 9, pp. 150-51; Gomikawa, *Nomonhan* [212], p. 240.

25. "Commanders probably took the responsibility and killed themselves because they had lost so many subordinates—almost entire regiments," S. Hata suggests. (Interview.)

26. Suzuki Yoshiyasu, N. Itō, T. Hamada, Sumi, Nishikawa interviews; *Nomonhan* [40], vol. 2, p. 75, citing Nishikawa; JRD [965], *JSM* 11, part 3/C, p. 403, citing Sumi, "Nihon" [542]; Tsuji [585], pp. 212-13; BBSS, *SS* [180], vol. 27, pp. 731-32; *SSNT* 29 [535], vol. 29, p. 370; Mita [406], p. 477; Nukada, *Rikugunshō* [457], pp. 85-86; K. Kobayashi [343], pp. 24-25; Sawada [507A], p. 138; Jack Seward, *Hara-kiri: Japanese Ritual Suicide* (Tokyo: Tuttle, 1968), p. 95. Nishikawa told me that he decided, after the war, to release Sakai's testament to the colonel's family, if he could find them. From Nishikawa's article in *Nomonhan* [40], vol. 2, p. 75, it can be seen that the document has come to rest in the archives of the GSDF at Kurume.

27. According to Nishiura, "Fujimoto seemed to have been at the center of things, both in overall terms and in the handling of [concrete] matters." [447], p. 135. In a conversation on 22 September dealing with the IJA counteroffensive of 24 August, Ogisu did not admit to Sawada that Fujimoto had operated at the battlefront and in fact had conducted the necessary commanding in Ogisu's name. [507A], p. 137.

28. S. Hamada, interview and [2].

29. Suzuki Yoshiyasu, Murata, N. Itō, I. Saitō, Numazaki interviews.

30. Mita [406], p. 477. According to Sumi, Yotsuya's pay and allowances were suspended, and then he was retired. (Interview.)

31. N. Morita interview; and 7th Co., 26th Inf. Regt. [105], 12 Oct. Sumi, who was not fond of brigadier Yoshizawa, dubbed him "Akuzawa" ("wicked Zawa"). (Interview.)

32. Suzuki Yoshiyasu supplied the information on Kajikawa's fate. (Imaoka correspondence.)

33. Sumi, interviews, correspondence, and writings; JRD [965], *JSM* 11, part 3/C, pp. 403, 435, citing Sumi, "Nihon" [542]; 7th Co., 26th Inf. Regt. [105], 12 Oct.; Mita [406], p. 478; S. Hata, Hikime, Imaoka interviews.

34. Onozuka interview.

35. Kanaizuka interview; and *Nomonhan* [40], vol. 4, p. 22.

36. Mishima, T. Hayashi, M. Tsuchiya interviews.

37. *Pravda*, 1 Sept. 1939, cited in USSR [992], vol. 2, p. 275.

38. "I don't like to talk big," says Takatsukasa; *SSNT* [535], vol. 29, pp. 234, 235. Also Sumi, Iwata, Suzuki Yoshiyasu interviews; JRD [965], *JSM* 11, part 3/C, pp. 434-35, citing Sumi,

"Nihon" [542]; Gomikawa, *Nomonhan* [212], pp. 260-61; Mita [406], p. 477; Sawada [507A], p. 135; Y. Hata, "Nikki" [5].

39. *Nomonhan* [40], vol. 6, p. 99; Gomikawa, *Nomonhan* [212], p. 260; Nishiura [447], p. 135; Iwata interview.

40. Suzuki Yoshiyasu, interviews and correspondence; JRD [965], *JSM* 11, part 3/C, p. 404; Sumi interview; Mita [406], p. 476; *Nomonhan* [40], vol. 2, p. 52 (Dr. Murakami).

41. Sumi interview.

42. Giga, Satō Katsuo interviews.

43. Satō Katsuo interview.

44. Mishima, Imaoka interviews. Also see chap. 37; and S. Hayashi, *Kōgun* [756], pp. 16-17.

CHAPTER 41

1. *Mirovoe Khoziaistvo* (1939), vol. 2, p. 3, cited by Degras, ed. [710], pp. 388-89.

2. Steinhardt to Hull, Moscow, 16 Sept. 1939, *FRUS* [974], *1939*, vol. 3, p. 71; Ott to Ribbentrop, Tokyo, 16 Sept. *DGFP* [973], vol. 8, p. 76; Grew to Hull, Tokyo, 31 Oct.; *FRUS* [974], *1939*, vol. 3, pp. 75-76.

3. Zhukov, *Memoirs* [1017], p. 166.

4. Degras, ed. [710], p. 399; *FRUS* [974], *1939*, vol. 3, p. 75. Molotov also mentioned the possibility of bilateral trade negotiations.

5. Kutakov [812], pp. 152-55; Narkomindel press release, *Izvestiya*, 20 Nov., cited by Degras, ed. [710], p. 400; Slusser and Triska, eds. [924], p. 132.

6. Seki Chōfū, in Tsuji [585], pp. 239-302. I. Hata tells me that Seki is the pen name for Tsuji's military academy classmate, Tanabe Shinshi, whom we met on the night of Hasebe's withdrawal (see chap. 40). (Interview.) Also see Kitagawa [341], pp. 142-43; BBSS, *SS* [180], vol. 27, p. 734; Gaimushō [201], pp. 533-34.

7. *Izvestiya*, 1 Jan. 1940, cited by Degras, ed. [710], pp. 415-16; Slusser and Triska, eds. [924], p. 132; Kutakov [812], pp. 157-58.

8. Gaimushō [201], pp. 533-34; Seki [S. Tanabe], in Tsuji [585], pp. 303-42; S. Tanabe, *Nomonhan* [40], vol. 4, p. 40; Kitagawa [341], pp. 143-44; BBSS, *SS* [180], vol. 27, p. 734. Also see Lockhart to Hull, Peking, 1 Feb. 1940; *FRUS* [974], *1940*, vol. 1, pp. 637-38. Lockhart reported that the conference had ended "with absolutely nothing accomplished," that Moscow denied permission for the Soviet-MPR delegation to accept an invitation to visit Hsinking, and that the Russian consul general in Peking was very discouraged about Soviet-Japanese relations and predicted new border incidents in the spring of 1940. For certain Diet members' dissatisfaction with Foreign Minister Arita's explanations, see *Kanpō* [322], 7 Feb. 1940, vol. 8, p. 103 (Fukuzawa Toyotarō), p. 111 (K. Tanaka); and 8 Feb., vol. 1, pp. 30-32, 43 (Kuboi Yoshimichi). Arita noted that procedural problems, such as disagreement on the number of members, had prevented formation of the general border commission.

9. Molotov's speech of 29 March 1940, from *Mirovoe Khoziaistvo* (1940), vol. 3, p. 5, is cited by Degras, ed. [710], p. 448. Also see Kutakov [812], pp. 157-58, 165-66; Ponomaryov et al., eds. [894], pp. 415-16.

10. Kitagawa Shirō interviewed Kameyama on 5 Sept. 1978; Kameyama authorized publication of his disclosure. [341], pp. 146-47. The Japanese consul general in Peking speculated that the Harbin conference broke down because the authorities in Moscow had suddenly stiffened their attitude after a British warship interfered with the *Asama Maru* in the East China Sea on 21 January. Nevertheless, the Japanese diplomat did not foresee new fighting at Nomonhan and predicted that the frontier problem would be addressed by a general boundary commission proposed by Tokyo. Lockhart to Hull, Peking, 2 Feb. 1940; *FRUS* [974], *1940*, vol. 1, p. 638.

11. Gaimushō [201], p. 535; Degras, ed. [710], p. 448. For Ott's attempted intercession with Smetanin on 13 March, see Kutakov [812], pp. 163-64.

12. Hull [772], vol. 1, p. 811. Chargé Smyth in Peking contributed to Hull's appraisal with a cable to this effect on 20 June. Also see Molotov's address to the Supreme Soviet, 1 Aug. 1940; Degras, ed. [710], pp. 461-62.

13. Kitagawa [341], p. 148; Gaimushō [201], p. 536; BBSS, *SS* [180], vol. 27, p. 734; Slusser and Triska, eds. [924], pp. 136-37. Also see Thurston to Hull, 10 June 1940, *FRUS 1940* [974],

vol. 1, p. 641; and Grew to Hull, Tokyo, 11 June, pp. 641-42. Grew noted that Molotov and Tōgō had merely initialed the agreement, which was then referred to the Outer Mongolian and Manchukuoan governments for their formal approval. The USSR had "been adamant about the necessity of settling this border issue before proceeding to take up other outstanding problems." Also see Thurston to Hull, 2 July; [974], *1940*, vol. 1, p. 642.

14. *Stenograficheskii Otchet*, p. 22, cited by Degras, ed. [710], pp. 467-68; Kutakov [812], p. 169.

15. Kutakov [812], p. 172; Tōgō [947], pp. 34-35. On 23 August 1940, Matsuoka told Steinhardt, who was visiting Tokyo, that he was dissatisfied with Tōgō's representation of Japan in Moscow and that many other Japanese diplomats would be recalled "because they had 'gone western' and had lost touch with the Japanese point of view." In strict confidence, Matsuoka disclosed that Tatekawa would replace Tōgō. Grew to Hull, Tokyo, 25 Aug.; *FRUS* [974], *1940*, vol. 1, p. 644.

16. S. Tanabe, *Nomonhan* [40], vol. 9, pp. 63-64; Kitagawa [341], pp. 151-55; BBSS, *SS* [180], vol. 27, p. 734; Morley, ed., *Deterrent* [875], p. 175. On 15 Oct. 1941, at Harbin, representatives of Manchukuo and the MPR signed a protocol and annex concerning the work of the border delimitation committee. On 5 May 1942, the two parties notified each other in writing that the documents had been ratified. The Manchukuoan government released this information on 15 May. Report by Grew (at sea), transmitted 19 Aug. 1942; *FRUS* [974], *1942*, vol. 1, p. 783.

17. Stalin's report to the 17th Party Congress, 26 Jan. 1934; [931], p. 595.

18. The following enumeration was prepared by the Russians as of 1 Sept. 1939 (the figures in parentheses represent a subsequent revision): rifles, 9,000 (revised to 12,000); shells—all calibers, 12,000 (revised to 42,000); cartridges, unstated number (revised to 2,000,000); machine guns, 67 heavy and 98 light (revised to 340 of both types); mine throwers, 306; tanks, 8; armored cars, 8; trucks, 68; light motor vehicles, 19. *Pravda*, 1 Sept. 1939, cited in USSR [992], vol. 2, p. 275; Shishkin [920], p. 626.

19. The Russians also recorded the capture of 14 [artillery] tractors and 67 37-mm. [battalion] guns. I have equated the Russians' designation of 105-mm. pieces with Takatsukasa's 10-cm. cannon; 122-mm. with Ise's 12-cm. howitzers; 150-mm. with Mishima's 15-cm. howitzers; and 155-mm. with Someya's 15-cm. cannon. See *Pravda*, 1 Sept. 1939, cited in USSR [992], vol. 2, p. 275. According to Sixth Army data, 20 IJA artillery pieces were destroyed by friendly forces. Miyao reported losing none of his 75-mm. field guns to the enemy.

20. Zhukov singled out a number of officers in his command for special praise: Potapov, originally his deputy, later commander of the main sector in the August offensive; Col. A. I. Leonov, the signal officer; commissars P. I. Gorokhov, R. P. Babiychuk, and V. A. Sychov; and surgeon M. N. Akhutin. In addition, Zhukov lauded the ambassador to the MPR, I. A. Ivanov, who facilitated the supply of food; and propagandists and photographers associated with the military newspaper.

21. Other well-known Heroes of the Soviet Union included I. I. Fedyuninsky and, posthumously, M. P. Yakovlev and I. M. Remizov. Among the honored pilots were Sr. Lts. V. F. Skobarikhin and V. G. Rakhov; and two-time winners Y. V. Smushkevich, whom Zhukov commended with particular warmth; S. I. Gritsevits; and G. P. Kravchenko.

22. Preceding section based on Zhukov, *Memoirs* [1017], pp. 150, 158-59, 162-66, 168; Voroshilov telegram, 29 Aug., in USSR [992], vol. 2, pp. 272-73, citing Soviet archives; and *Nomonhan* [452], pp. 18-19. Soviet awards for the Changkufeng fighting of 1938 were at least as numerous; see Coox, *Anatomy* [679], p. 361, n. 3. Fedyuninsky adds that, during the period of preparation prior to the August offensive, 1,138 men were admitted to the Communist Party and 1,280 to the Komsomol. [723], p. 47, citing data from Political Section, First Army Group. Also see Parrish's bibliographical essay in this book.

23. MPR war minister, Lt. Gen. B. Lkhamsuren, in *Krasnaya Zvezda* (Moscow), 28 Aug. 1959; and Maj. S. Zamsranzav (1965) in Sasaki [910], pp. 217-33. Zhukov mentions Olzvoj [Olzvai] as well as an MPRA armored car driver, two antiaircraft gunners, and a cavalryman; *Memoirs* [1017], p. 166. More than 690 high MPRA decorations were awarded, including a posthumous MPR Hero's medal to L. Gelegbaatar, political commissar of an artillery battery,

slain on 28 Aug. For further details, see Shirendyb et al., eds. [919], p. 355. According to Fedyuninsky, many MPRA cavalrymen received Soviet medals and orders; [723], p. 47.

24. Radio Ulan Bator, 21 Aug. 1959 (in Russian), citing a report from the Choibalsan district; Nyūmura interview, citing *Pravda*, 19 Aug. 1959, p. 4; Zhukov, *Memoirs* [1017], p. 166. Chulunbat in *Mongolia Today*, Sept.-Oct. 1966, pp. 12-13. For a photograph of an imposing monument to the Soviet army, in Ulan Bator itself, with inscriptions in Mongolian and Russian, see *Nomonhan* [40], vol. 10, p. 63.

25. J. Lodoi in *Mongolia Today*, July-Aug. 1966, pp. 19-20; Sept.-Oct. 1966, p. 13.

26. In a sample of sixteen 7th Division Golden Kites, 15 were posthumously awarded. See Mita [406], pp. 163-64. Mention of individual officers and men and their decorations can be found scattered throughout issues of *Nomonhan* magazine [40] and in *Nomonhan bidanroku* [451]. For the workings of the IJA system of awards: Imaoka, Onozuka, Takeshita, Irie interviews; Okubo [471], pp. 347-57; and *Rikugun* [486], p. 830. The Golden Kite decoration was accompanied by an annual honorarium for life: from ¥150 for Class 7 to ¥1,500 for Class 1.

27. The successive commanders of the 71st Inf. Regt.'s 3rd Bn.—Majors Murata and Izui—were killed in action. See *Bidanroku* [451]. Ueda's unit citations of 5 Sept. included an airfield battalion attached to the 15th Air Group.

28. For the two unit citations issued by Komatsubara, see *Nomonhan* [40], vol. 8, p. 89; vol. 6, p. 143; and Fukushima and Sugawara, eds., *90-yahō*, vol. 2, p. 1. The Ueda and Ogisu citations are based on *Bidanroku* [451]. For the IJAF unit citation, see *Asahi Shinbun*, 5 Oct. 1939 (A.M. ed.), p. 2.

29. 23rd Inf. Div. [113], No. 1 (Higashi), 13 pp.; No. 2 (Kusaba), 19 pp.; No. 3 (Hayama), 8 pages; No. 5 (Sugaya), 8 pp.; also Onozuka interview. Mrs. Higashi lent the text of the presentations to the BBSS archives.

CHAPTER 42

1. Parrish [889], pp. 73-75; Zhukov, *Memoirs* [1017], p. 170; Erickson, *Soviet* [722], pp. 494, 497-98, 511-12, 532-33, 742, and *Road* [721], pp. 38, 41, 55-56, 114. Also see Coox, *Anatomy* [679], p. 357. Erich Wollenberg calls Shtern a "mediocrity and careerist" who won public praise at the war college for denouncing colleagues allegedly disloyal to Stalin. [1006], pp. 258-59. Konev reportedly stalled the rehabilitation of Shtern, his superior in 1939; Chaney [667], p. 404.

2. Information on the five Soviet generals is scattered throughout Zhukov, *Memoirs* [1017]; Seaton [914]; Erickson, *Road* [721], and *Soviet* [722]. Supplementary details are from Shtemenko [922], p. 40; Pospelov et al., eds. [895], pp. 66, 97; Heinz Guderian, *Panzer Leader* (New York: Dutton, 1952), p. 225; Erickson, correspondence. For Fedyuninsky's career, see Bialer, comp. [641], pp. 240-43, 607, 631. For Potapov, see [641], p. 401 (Marshal Bagramian); Seaton [914], p. 147, n. 55.

3. Meretskov was relegated to the combat training command. Zhukov, *Memoirs* [1017], pp. 168-73, 180-89; Shtemenko [922], pp. 27-28; Pospelov et al., eds. [895], p. 44; Bialer, comp. [641], pp. 138, 139-45 (M. I. Kazakov), 146-51 (A. I. Yeremenko), 575-76; H. S. Dinerstein, *War and the Soviet Union* (New York: Praeger, 1959), p. 31; N. Galay in Liddell Hart, ed. [833], pp. 316-17; Erickson, *Soviet* [722], p. 537, *Road* [721], pp. 37-46, 50-55, 66, 194, and correspondence; Mackintosh [846], pp. 124-29, 131-33. Also see Major M. F. Vassilieff, "Soviet Armoured Principles," *Armor*, Jan.-Feb. 1956, vol. 65, no. 1, p. 24.

4. Soviet air force and navy manuals appeared in 1940, but the army's FSR were not issued until 1942-43, by which time the text hardly resembled the old draft. Bialer, comp. [641], pp. 134 (Azarov), 135-36 (N. G. Kuznetsov), 136-37 (S. S. Biriuzov), 148-49 (Yeremenko), 577; Shtemenko [922], p. 23; Erickson, correspondence and *Road* [721], p. 30; Mackintosh [846], p. 123; Kolkowicz [803], p. 62. Garder gives Soviet losses in the Finnish war as 273,000 dead, 5,648 prisoners, wounded unknown. [732], p. 104.

5. GSDF [73], p. 139; Hōson [263], pp. 211-12; Garthoff, *Soviet* [735], pp. 272, 380; H. Dorn in Liddell Hart, ed. [833], p. 373; Gunston [747], pp. 181-83; Milsom [871], pp. 41, 54-55; Crow and Icks [700], pp. 200-203; Icks [774], p. 94. Also see Mackintosh [846], p. 108; Erickson [721], pp. 32-33, 35.

6. The Soviet caliber is given as 152 mm.

7. GSDF [73], pp. 133-39; Vassilieff, "Soviet Armoured Principles," *Armor*, Jan.-Feb. 1965, vol. 65, no. 1, pp. 22-23; Shishkin [920], pp. 629-34; Moses, "Soviet" [881], p. 81; Ruslanov [907], p. 190; Erickson, *Soviet* [722], pp. 534, 536; Chaney [667], pp. 54-55; Erickson, "Marshal" [718], p. 248. In late August, according to one account, Zhukov undid the Japanese north of the Holsten by ordering his engineers to strengthen the riverbed during the night, thus enabling Soviet tank forces to traverse the Holsten. Chaney [667], p. 57, citing Lauterbach. Grigorenko, however, is extremely critical of Zhukov, whose alleged mistakes at Nomonhan "were so childish that it is embarrassing even to analyze them." According to Grigorenko, Zhukov quashed the dissemination of a comprehensive staff study of the Nomonhan fighting which "disclosed deficiencies in the preparation of enlisted men and officers"—a study which had been "warmly approved by the General Staff." Consequently, Soviet commanders were denied knowledge of "basic defects in . . . battle preparation," and the same defects appeared in the Second World War. [746A], pp. 110, 210.

8. Tass announcement, *Izvestiya*, 14 July 1939; cited in USSR [992], vol. 2, pp. 138-39.

9. Zhukov, *Memoirs* [1017], pp. 160-62, 168-70. In 1945, Zhukov told Gen. W. B. Smith, Eisenhower's chief of staff: "The Japanese are not good against armor. It took [only] about ten days to beat them" at Nomonhan. Salisbury, introduction to Zhukov [1016], p. 8.

10. The 75th Diet session convened on 23 Dec. 1939. The interpellators were Kuboi Yoshimichi and Fukuzawa Toyotarō. *Kanpō* [322], vol. 8, pp. 103-7 (7 Feb. 1940); vol. 4, p. 32 (8 Feb.).

11. Fukuda Kanjirō, a member of the Minseitō, at the budget settlement session of 28 Feb. 1940; *Kanpō* [322], vol. 2, pp. 31-33 (29 Feb.). Soviet historians have exploited Hata's statement. See Kutakov [812], p. 164, citing Soviet Archives 0146, File 1219, p. 180; Issraeljan and Kutakov [779], p. 74.

12. *Asahi Shinbun*, 4 Oct. 1939 (P.M. ed.), p. 1; 4 Oct. (A.M. ed.), p. 3.

13. 7th Co., 26th Inf. Regt. [105], 4, 11 Sept.; 64th Inf. Regt. [115], 9 Sept.

14. The Finnish army, however, achieved notable success with gasoline bottles during the winter months of 1939/40, knocking out hundreds of Soviet tanks. (Correspondence with M. Melkko, M. Palokangas, and J. Keltanen.)

15. 2nd Bn., 28th Inf. Regt. [110] (20 June–16 Sept. 1939).

16. 28th Inf. Regt. [107] (23-29 Aug. 1939).

17. 3rd Bn., 27th Inf. Regt. [106] (26 Aug.–16 Sept. 1939).

18. The Big Three consisted of the war minister, the AGS chief, and the inspector general of military training. See chap. 37.

19. GSDF [73], p. 190, citing statement by Lt. Col. Konuma Haruo; BBSS, *SS* [180], vol. 27, p. 733; Imoto [285], p. 390; JRD [958], *JSM* 10, p. 34. My copy of the final report (hereafter cited as *NJK* [137]) indicates that Chapter 5 (Border Disputes and War Guidance) is omitted in the original.

20. Sumi interview.

21. Mishima interview; details on ordnance omitted. The Kwantung Army tank expert, Major Noguchi, who had worked with General Yasuoka throughout the operations of July, was "disgusted" to be questioned for only 20 minutes by the investigation committee. (Interview.) Suzuki Yoshiyasu, examined by the investigators in Hailar, says his memory was not the best by then, and that the questions depended on who was asking them. (Interview.)

22. Nishikawa interview. N. Itō, hospitalized for half a year, was not questioned by the investigators either. (Interview.)

23. *Nomonhan* [40], vol. 10, pp. 122-24, citing Oda.

24. GSDF [68], vol. 1, p. 15. Iwakuro was the Military Service Section chief.

25. The Soviets reportedly mobilized 42 chemical warfare (CW) battalions for possible use at Nomonhan; but the Kwantung Army possessed only one CW company—part of the 2nd Mortar Regiment organized at Tsitsihar in April 1938. The unit was transferred to Hailar on 2 July 1939 and spent two or three days at the battlefront when the Russian offensive began on 20 August. Mita [406], p. 123, citing Suematsu Masao.

26. Based on *NJK* [137], parts 1-4. Also see BBSS, *SS* [180], vol. 27, p. 733; S. Hayashi,

Kantōgun [242], pp. 185-86. For combat lessons affecting ground operations, see JRD [965], *JSM* 11, part 3/C, pp. 465-82, 484-86; for air operations, pp. 487-89. For artillery and anti-aircraft operations, see JRD [969], *JSM* 7, part 1. It was found that antiaircraft guns could be employed effectively against tanks. *Ibid.*, pp. 108, 125-26; and Tsunashima interview. Imaoka stresses the signal and logistical problems. Interview and "Nomonhan" [13], pp. 96-97.

27. Combat intelligence unit: *senjō jōhōtai.*

28. The 2nd Subcommittee's report has not survived. I have drawn mainly on Kōtani's reconstruction, supplemented by Iwakuro, Nyūmura, Yano Mitsuji, Doi interviews. Also see JRD [965], *JSM*, 11 part 3/C, pp. 482-83, 489-90; [956], *JSM* 5, pp. 48-49; Y. Nishihara [446A], p. 160.

29. Komatsubara had become concerned about this problem in July. Upon visiting the field hospital, he noted that most deaths had been caused by hemorrhage, in the absence of emergency stanching. Although comrades wanted to help the wounded, the soldiers had received spiritual inculcation that assistance without specific orders would corrupt military discipline. Many died as a result. Whenever men were wounded, the general felt, their officers should promptly order medics or fellow soldiers to administer first aid. Komatsubara [25], 19 July. Also see the report by Lieutenant Colonel Baba of the Kwantung Army medical bureau, 12 Oct. 1939, in GSDF [68], vol. 1, p. 16; and Miura's excellent summary, 27 Dec. 1939, in *ibid.*, p. 19. Further medical details may be found in *ibid.*, pp. 60-61, 65.

30. Kantōgun [100], 27 Nov. 1939, 82 pp., transmitted to vice minister of war (Anami) by chief of staff (Iimura), 7 Dec. Distribution had already been made to the 1st Subcommittee; data on weapons and matériel would be sent by the end of December. Also see Lieutenant Colonel Maki's short but comprehensive commentary dated 6 April 1940; GSDF [68], vol. 1, p. 20.

31. From the report prepared by the 3rd Section, 1st Bureau, Army Technical Hq., 13-20 Sept. 1939 [94]. Captain Kawakami's 13-page report was Attachment 7.

32. Major Hiromoto, Attachment 5 [94].

33. Kantōgun [100], pp. 71-73. Also Yabe, Shimanuki, Suzuki Yoshiyasu, Numazaki, Suzuki Yasushi, N. Itō, Andō, Takei, Kōtani, Murata interviews; Imaoka, "Nomonhan" [13], pp. 87, 92; GSDF [73], pp. 177-79.

34. "Behind the Scenes at Nomonhan," in *Manchuria Daily News* [853], pp. 25-26.

35. 71st Inf. Regt. [119] and 72nd Inf. Regt. [121], 13 July; AGS Intelligence Report No. 37, 13 July [141]; GSDF [68], vol. 1, p. 60. According to a 23rd Div. intelligence summary issued at 5 P.M. on 16 July, tests of enemy aerial bombs dropped behind IJA lines on 9 July, at Lake Abutara, were definitely found to contain Types "F" and "Y" dysentery bacilli. It was believed that other enemy bombs dropped on 15 and 16 July must have contained identical contents; 1st Bn., 64th Inf. Regt., *Sentō shōhō* [Combat Report] (14-25 July 1939), Yamagata Intelligence No. 6, 17 July [BBSS Archives].

36. Tass communiqué, *Izvestiya*, 14 July; cited in USSR [992], vol. 2, p. 139.

37. Kinbara interview; and GSDF [68], vol. 1, p. 15. For information on the water-supply problem, also see [68], vol. 1, p. 63; Mita [406], p. 159; JRD [965], *JSM* 11, part 3/C, pp. 485-86. Ishii's unit was credited with overcoming a dysentery rate that had reached an overall total of one-third. Major General Endō received reports concerning the good work of Ishii's unit with respect to water purification and supply; [189], p. 163. One IJA officer remembers seeing fire engines in use for water supply at Chiangchunmiao; Toga interview.

38. Examples of pseudonymous leftist sources are Akiyama, *Tokushu* [154], p. 59; Nezu, [430], p. 198; Nara Hiroshi and Kitagami Norio (alleged physicians), "Shiroi kyotō no naka no jintai jikken no jittai" [Facts Concerning the Experiments on Humans Conducted Inside the Great White Tower], *Fujin Kōron*, March 1971, pp. 184-91; and same authors, "Kantōgun tokushu himitsu 731 butai ni yoru hijindōteki hanzai" [The Inhumane Crimes Committed by the Kwantung Army's Special Secret Unit 731], *Nitchū*, Dec. 1972, pp. 23-27. Also see Shimamura Takashi, *Sanzennin no seitai jikken: Kantōgun nazo no saikin himitsu heiki kenkyūsho* [Live Experimentation on 3,000 Human Beings: The Kwantung Army's Mysterious Secret Germ Warfare Research Institute] (Tokyo: Hara Shobō, 1967). I explored the practical range of biological warfare (BW) possibilities in interviews with Drs. Kinbara and Niiya, and with Imaoka and I. Hata. Soviet juridical interest in Japanese BW activities focuses on the

period after the Nomonhan hostilities, as can be seen from the transcripts of the postwar Khabarovsk trial of Kwantung Army personnel. But one IJA defendant, Lt. Col. Nishi Toshihide, who only arrived in Manchuria in 1943, testified that Unit 731 had used typhoid, paratyphoid, and dysentery germs to contaminate the Halha River in the area of military operations in 1939. USSR [989], p. 63. Ishii's own comments will be found in Endō's secret diary entry for 10 Dec. 1939, when the two officers conversed at Harbin and visited Ishii's "Kamo unit"; [189], pp. 162-63.

39. A small predecessor to the Nakano school had been set up in Tokyo under a lieutenant colonel in July 1938. The full-scale Nakano institution, presided over by a major general, was organized in August 1940. See Kusakabe Ichirō, *Rikugun Nakano gakkō jitsuroku* [The True Story of the Army's Nakano School] (Tokyo: Besuto Bukku, 1980), pp. 5, 49, 51, 54, 230-31. Also privileged IJA officer source.

40. Ogoshi, Iwakuro, Yano Mitsuji, Kōtani interviews. Also see S. Hayashi, *Kantōgun* [756], pp. 183-84.

41. GSDF [73], pp. 166-67. Tsuji's views were mentioned earlier [585].

42. Noguchi, Ogata, Masuda, Takeshita, Irie, Mishima interviews. The 9th Tank Regt., thrown together in Aug. 1939, joined the 3rd and 5th tank regts. in a new 1st Tank Corps under the Third Army. Two other new tank regiments, the 10th and 11th, were combined with the old 4th to form the 2nd Tank Corps under the Fifth Army, all on the east Manchurian front. (Tank corps structure as of March 1940; Kadokawa, *Teikoku* [316], p. 167.) For writings on mechanization, prepared on the eve of the Pacific War, see *Kaikōsha Kiji* [318], pp. 17-19 (by an unidentified staff officer of the Mechanized Bureau); and S. Kobayashi [344], pp. 45-49.

43. Imaoka, Z. Tomioka interviews.

44. Noguchi, Imaoka interviews; Kadokawa, *Teikoku* [316], pp. 70-71; GSDF [73], pp. 171-75. The discrepancy between Japanese production targets and actual output is illustrated by the first month's order for medium tanks under the military industrial mobilization plan around 1938: 100 tanks set for production, about five turned out. Imaoka interview.

45. Iwakuro, Imaoka interviews; Coox, "Rise" [692], pp. 79-81. Detailed air force lessons from Nomonhan will be found in the 1st Air Division's summary of 1940 [128].

46. According to one set of statistics for the period between 1 July and 16 Sept. 1939, Komatsubara had had 2,708 horses at Nomonhan, of which 2,005 were killed or injured and 325 fell ill, for a total loss of 86 percent. GSDF [68], vol. 1, p. 43.

47. GSDF [68], vol. 1, p. 19.

48. Imaoka, N. Itō interviews; GSDF [73], pp. 168-69; G. Mishima et al. [402]; JRD [965], JSM 11, part 3/C, p. 466.

49. *Rikugun* [486], p. 68. Capt. Nomura Norio set down the special conditions constraining operations at Nomonhan; [455], p. 57.

50. Sumi interview.

51. Mishima interview.

52. Gijitsu Honbu [94]. Strictly technical details of ordnance received considerable attention, and it was agreed that the new 15-cm. cannon ought to have a range of 21,000-22,000 meters.

53. GSDF [73], pp. 158-59, citing Y. Hata's recollections. Also Imaoka interview for information on the *kaisen* (combat load) factor and the constant controversy between the war ministry and AGS regarding allocations of ammunition.

54. Nomura [455], p. 78.

55. GSDF [73], p. 191. Also see Konuma [26].

56. Sumi interview; and GSDF [73], p. 191.

57. Imaoka, Mishima interviews.

58. Imaoka interview.

59. Endō [189], pp. 175-81. Soon after their trip to Hsinking, Imaizumi and Imaoka were transferred to Kwantung Army headquarters. Having disagreed with Endō, they both felt very uncomfortable, but "fortunately" the deputy left shortly after they were assigned to Manchuria. Imaoka interview. Also see Jōhō, ed., *Saigo* [313], pp. 368-70, citing Imaoka; and pp. 370-71, citing Endō.

60. Kantōgun [99], in *GSS* [205], vol. 10, pp. 100-101. For the topic of IJA commanding

in theory and practice: Hattori, Inada, Imaoka, Arao, Y. Nishihara interviews; BBSS, *SS* [180], vol. 27, pp. 582-84, 674; Imaoka, "Nomonhan" [13], pp. 80-84, 89-90; Imoto [285], pp. 388-90; M. Itō, *Gunbatsu* [308A], vol. 3, p. 153; Sawada [507A], pp. 149, 152. Also see Coox, "High Command" [683], pp. 302-12.

CHAPTER 43

1. Matsuoka-Steinhardt conversation (Moscow), Message No. 422, 8 Apr. 1941, DOD, "*Magic*" [972], vol. 1, p. A-157; Ike, trans. and ed. [775], p. 21 (liaison conference of 22 Apr. 1941); Kase [787], pp. 40-41, 44.
2. Morley, ed., *Fateful* [876], pp. 155-240.
3. Ike, trans. and ed. [775], pp. 12-13 (imperial conference of 19 Sept. 1940).
4. Kutakov [812], pp. 182, 188, citing Ōshima-Smetanin conversation at German embassy, 8 Jan. 1941.
5. TSM [549], vol. 5, pp. 252-53, 262-63; Morley, ed., *Fateful* [876], pp. 23-64; Kase [787], p. 41; Kōtani interview.
6. Tanemura [571], p. 52 (13 Apr. 1941); TSM [549], vol. 5, pp. 286-95; Morley, ed., *Fateful* [876], pp. 64-85; Kase [787], pp. 156-59; Ike, trans. and ed. [775], pp. 21-23 (liaison conference of 22 Apr. 1941); Kutakov [812], pp. 189-95; Nish [883], pp. 241-43.
7. Kutakov [812], pp. 193-94, citing Soviet archives; TSM [549], vol. 5, p. 500; Morley, ed., *Fateful* [876], p. 84, citing K. Satō, *Tōjō* [504], pp. 182-88, and AGS confidential diary, 14 and 18 Apr. 1941. Also see Tanemura [571], p. 52 (13 Apr. 1941).
8. Higashikuni [244A], pp. 42-43; TSM [549], vol. 5, p. 300; Morley, ed., *Fateful* [876], p. 84.
9. Message No. 954 (Tokyo), 7 May 1941; DOD, "*Magic*" [972], vol. 1, p. A-187.
10. Message No. 222 (Tokyo), 14 Apr. 1941; Message No. 262 (Hsinking), 20 May; Message No. 268 (Hsinking), 22 May; Message No. 230 (Tokyo), 15 June: DOD, "*Magic*" [972], vol. 1, p. A-174.
11. BBSS, *SS* [180], vol. 73, p. 61, citing Lt. Col. Asai Isamu; JRD [968], *JSM* 13, p. 43. But Col. Yabe Chūta is not sure that Siberian forces arrived in Europe as early as the Moscow campaign. (Interview.)
12. Ōshima tried to deny a connection. But he asked Matsuoka to keep him informed concerning troop movements by the Russian Far East forces. Message No. 738 (Berlin), 21 June 1941; DOD, "*Magic*" [972], vol. 2 (appendix), p. A-336.
13. Yabe, Takei, Imaoka, Doi interviews; and Arisue Seizō in JRD [957], vol. 1, p. 34 (14 July 1949). Also see Coox, "Japanese" [684], pp. 554-72; DOD, "*Magic*" [972], vol. 2 (appendix); Tanemura [571], pp. 54-55, 57, 59; Higashikuni [244A], pp. 57, 59.
14. BBSS, *SS* [180], vol. 73, pp. 7-8, 11; Hattori, *Daitōa* [235], vol. 1, pp. 134-47; Tanemura [571], pp. 59-64; Ike, trans. and ed. [775], pp. 46-56.
15. Tanemura [571], p. 64 (22 June 1941); T. Yabe [610], pp. 297-98; Mori [412], pp. 79-80; Hattori, *Daitōa* [235], vol. 1, p. 146; Kase [787], pp. 160-61; Morley, ed., *Fateful* [876], pp. 94-98; BBSS, *SS* [180], vol. 73, p. 5: Arisue Seizō in JRD [957], vol. 1, p. 43 (1949).
16. Imaoka, Kōtani interviews; BBSS, *SS* [180], vol. 73, p. 6.
17. Estimates as of end of 1940 or early 1941. I have combined Imaoka's intelligence data with AGS figures from JRD [960], *JSM* 1, p. 44, and [968], *JSM* 13, p. 47; and BBSS, *SS* [180], vol. 73, pp. 41-42. Other estimates of Soviet Far Eastern strength on the eve of the German war list 2,300 tanks and only 1,700 planes. Takei, Kōtani interviews; Hattori, *Daitōa* [235], vol. 1, p. 159. Kasahara Yukio gives figures of 30 Soviet divisions, 2,500 tanks and 2,500 planes as of spring 1941. IMTFE, *Transcript* [777], 28 May 1947, p. 23195. Also see Tanaka Shin'ichi, in [777], pp. 23305-7.
18. JRD [960], *JSM* 1, pp. 45, 82-83, 90; BBSS, *SS* [180], vol. 73, p. 41. Kase estimates Kwantung Army personnel strength at 460,000 in 1940; [787], p. 165, n. 15. Other sources give a figure of 400,000 men: S. Hayashi [756], p. 20; Ike, trans. and ed. [775], p. 76, n. 59. A higher enumeration of Kwantung Army air strength as of 20 June 1941 will be found in BBSS, *SS* [180], vol. 73, p. 31; namely, 409 fighters, 193 scout planes, 423 light and heavy bombers, 87 miscellaneous aircraft, for a total of 1,112 planes. These are paper figures; available aircraft (and pilots) were considerably less. Col. Akiyama Monjirō estimates the number of combat-

ready pilots at 800 out of perhaps 1,100 (73 percent). BBSS, *SS* [180], vol. 73, p. 32; Imaoka interview; JRD [961], *JM* 77, p. 12. Kasahara Yukio says the Kwantung Army had 800 planes in the spring of 1941. IMTFE, *Transcript* [777], 28 May 1947, p. 23195. Ushiroku Jun agreed with the figure of 600 planes (in 49 squadrons) in the Kwantung Army in 1941, p. 23266. Tanaka Shin'ichi mentioned 500 Japanese aircraft at this stage and added that two of the Kwantung Army's 12 divisions were still being organized (unrelated to the later Kantokuen buildup) with "meager strength." [777], pp. 23330, 23332.

19. BBSS, *SS* [180], vol. 73, p. 6; Imaoka interview. The 12th Division commander, Kasahara Yukio, remembered receiving a special order from Umezu to strive to prevent frontier clashes, since one could not be sure the Russians would never attack, and to strengthen backup fortifications. IMTFE, *Transcript* [777], 28 May 1947, pp. 23197-98. Also see Message No. 378 (Hsinking), 27 June 1941; DOD, "*Magic*" [972], vol. 2 (appendix), pp. A-348-49.

20. Message No. 110 (Hsinking), 24 June 1941; Message No. 117 (Hsinking), 25 June: DOD, "*Magic*" [972], vol. 2 (appendix), pp. A-347-48. Mackintosh alludes to initial panic in the Soviet Far East, with the civilian populace "frantically mobilized to be drafted into the Army to dig defences." See Liddell Hart, ed. [833], pp. 176-77.

21. Message No. 390 (Hsinking), 30 June 1941; Message No. 447 (Hsinking), 13 July: DOD, "*Magic*" [972], vol. 2 (appendix), p. A-349. Also see Higashikuni [244A], p. 61 (27 June).

22. See Coox, *Tojo* [696], pp. 76-77; Hattori, *Daitōa* [235], vol. 1, pp. 138-46; Tanemura [571], pp. 64-67.

23. BBSS, *SS* [180], vol. 73, pp. 8-9, 19-23; Morley, ed., *Fateful* [876], pp. 102-4; Ike, trans. and ed. [775], pp. 56-75; Gomikawa, *Gozen* [209], pp. 81-82; Mizumachi, Imaoka interviews. The number of divisions that the AGS considered for ultimate addition to the Kwantung Army, for offensive purposes, varied from 10 to as many as 18.

24. Gomikawa, *Gozen* [209], p. 82; BBSS, *SS* [180], vol. 73, p. 66.

25. Shimada Toshihiko, *Kantōgun* [515], pp. 159-60.

26. Ike, trans. and ed. [775], pp. 75-77; Shimada Toshihiko, *Kantōgun* [515], p. 160.

27. In Manchuria, logistical and transport considerations were always pressing. Imaoka interview.

28. For the imperial conference of 2 July, see Hattori, *Daitōa* [235], vol. 1, pp. 147-50; *Sugiyama memo* [540], vol. 1, pp. 254-61; Ike, trans. and ed. [775], pp. 77-90; Morley, ed., *Fateful* [876], pp. 99-102.

29. Tanemura [571], p. 60 (9 June 1941); Imaoka, Hattori interviews; Hattori, *Daitōa* [235], vol. 1, pp. 150-51; Morley, ed., *Fateful* [876], pp. 102-4; Shimada Toshihiko, *Kantōgun* [515], pp. 160-63; BBSS, *SS* [180], vol. 73, pp. 20-21. According to Y. Kasahara, the replenishment of Kwantung Army divisions did *not* amount to a complete mobilization—i.e., was set at only 70 to 80 percent of wartime organization. IMTFE, *Transcript* [777], 28 May 1947, p. 23000. S. Tanaka added that, under "temporary callup" measures, units were deployed on the basis of full equipment but not on a wartime footing. [777], 28 May 1947, p. 23331; 2 June 1947, p. 23362.

30. Imaoka, interview and "Kantokuen" [10], pp. 1-2. Based on IGHQ Army Order No. 506 of 11 July, the Kwantung Army stipulated the use of the term *Kantokuen*, the purposes being distinctiveness and secrecy. BBSS, *SS* [180], vol. 73, pp. 21-22; Shimada Toshihiko, *Kantōgun* [515], p. 163. The unofficial IGHQ code name for the southern operations was No. A Setup (*A-gō taisei*). Korea Army mobilization had no separate designation.

31. Imaoka interview; Tanemura [571], pp. 68-69 (7 July). Also see Shimada Toshihiko, *Kantōgun* [515], p. 162.

32. Omae, Imaoka interviews; BBSS, *SS* [180], vol. 73, pp. 12, 22-23, 34, 61; Imaoka, "Zoruge" [15]; Shimada Toshihiko, *Kantōgun* [515], p. 164; Hull [772], vol. 2, p. 1012; Grew, *Ten* [745], pp. 403-4 (Tokyo, 12 July 1941); *FRUS* [974], *1941*, vol. 4, pp. 1007-8 (Tokyo, 17 July), 1012 (Tokyo, 29 July); C. Willoughby [1002], pp. 105-6, 116, 207, 212. "In Tokyo," Sejima Ryūzō recalled, "I often saw mobilized troops passing through or leaving from the stations in profound silence." IMTFE, *Transcript* [777], 18 Oct. 1946, pp. 8101-2. Also see Tanaka Shin'ichi in [777], 2 June 1947, pp. 23363-69.

33. Imaoka provides the following mobilization schedule: first mobilization, 7 July; first day of mobilization, 13 July; completion, 17-24 July; second mobilization, 16 July; first day of mobilization, 28 July; completion, 30 July–8 August. (Interview.) Also Mizumachi, Takei, Kōtani interviews; JRD [961], *JM* 77, pp. 37-43; BBSS, *SS* [180], vol. 73, pp. 12, 23-24, 26-27, 33-34, 60; Shimada Toshihiko, *Kantōgun* [515], pp. 163-65. Y. Kasahara states that the 51st and 57th divisions had second-rate equipment. IMTFE, *Transcript* [777], 28 May 1947, p. 23199. For the purported Yamashita-Tōjō rivalry, see Coox, *Tojo* [696], p. 81.

34. BBSS, *SS* [180], vol. 73, pp. 26-27, 33-34, 46; Ishijima, Imaoka interviews.

35. JRD [960], *JSM* 1, pp. 94-98, 157; BBSS, *SS* [180], vol. 73, pp. 38-47; Imaoka, interview and "Kantokuen" [10], pp. 24-53. For a preliminary Kwantung Army plan sketched in July 1941 for a proposed attack on Khabarovsk from the Sanchiang district, or even for offensive action on the dormant western front, see BBSS, *SS* [180], vol. 73, pp. 51-52.

36. Yano Mitsuji, Arao, Ōgoshi, Suemori interviews; Kasahara Yukio in IMTFE, *Transcript* [777], 28 May 1947, pp. 23204-5; BBSS, *SS* [180], vol. 73, pp. 54, 60; JRD [958], *JSM* 10, pp. 103-5.

37. Such officers included Inada, Doi, and Ayabe. (Interviews.)

38. Imaoka, Inada, Yano Mitsuji interviews.

39. BBSS, *SS* [180], vol. 73, pp. 43-44, 46-47. Although optimistic, Doi worried about the problems which would face the Japanese west of Baikal. (Interview.) For a depressed medical view and for rumors sweeping the troops: Ishijima interview. For Kantokuen, Dr. Ishijima had been transferred to Chiamussu from Dairen–Port Arthur.

40. Morley, ed., *Fateful* [876], pp. 104-5; BBSS, *SS* [180], vol. 73, p. 63.

41. BBSS, *SS* [180], vol. 73, p. 63. Katakura says he disagreed violently with Yamashita's rosy view and argued that the Russians would succeed in "pulling off another 1812." (Interview.)

42. Ayabe, Ōgoshi, Katakura interviews; BBSS, *SS* [180], vol. 73, p. 63. Takebe Rokuzō, a Manchukuo government official, flew to Tokyo to ascertain whether Kantokuen meant war against Russia, but Tōjō "said only that it was necessary to reinforce the Kwantung Army and didn't explain the reason." IMTFE, *Transcript* [777], 28 May 1947, p. 23278. Tominaga Kyōji, however, claimed that Tōjō strongly espoused the ripe-persimmon idea to him during the Kantokuen era; [777], 18 Oct. 1946, pp. 8083-84.

43. Mori [412], pp. 81-82; Kase [787], pp. 48-49.

44. Hattori, Takayama interviews; BBSS, *SS* [180], vol. 73, pp. 63-64.

45. Circular No. 155 (Hsinking), 11 July; DOD, "*Magic*" [972], vol. 2 (appendix), p. A-353. Also see Hattori, *Daitōa* [235], vol. 1, pp. 137-38.

46. Asada, Matsuoka, Kōtani, S. Hayashi, Arao interviews; BBSS, *SS* [180], vol. 73, pp. 62-63; JRD [958], *JSM* 10, p. 56. Suemori estimates the number of Soviet deserters between June and December as 250-300. (Interview.)

47. Imaoka interview; BBSS, *SS* [180], vol. 73, p. 64.

48. Tanaka Ryūkichi, *Haiin* [566], pp. 51-52; BBSS, *SS* [180], vol. 73, p. 66; Shimada Toshihiko, *Kantōgun* [515], pp. 166-67.

49. Sejima interview; Yoshii [626], pp. 128-29, 133; Hull [772], vol. 2, pp. 1013-14; Grew, *Ten* [745], pp. 405-11 (25-26 July 1941).

50. Imaoka interview; *Sugiyama memo* [540], vol. 1, pp. 284-86; BBSS, *SS* [180], vol. 73, pp. 56-57, 65, 75; Shimada Toshihiko, *Kantōgun* [515], pp. 167-69; Hattori, *Daitōa* [235], vol. 1, pp. 152, 160.

51. BBSS, *SS* [180], vol. 73, p. 66. For Satō Kenryō's passionate efforts on 3-4 August to sway Tōjō from the Go-North option, see Coox, *Tojo* [696], pp. 76-78.

52. Kōtani interview.

53. Japanese sources call such a disturbance the "Dellinger phenomenon," after J. H. Dellinger, but Kōtani was not acquainted with the term in August 1941. (Interview.)

54. Although he was absent from Hsinking on 2 August, a Kwantung Army staff officer first suggested to me the possibility of "an insider's plot." Privileged information. At the author's instance, Dr. Sam M. Silverman, a geophysicist at Boston College, was able to locate and analyze corroborating magnetic observations of solar flare activity recorded in Japan on the specific day in question. (Interviews and correspondence.)

55. Kōtani, Matsuoka, Imaoka interviews; BBSS, *SS* [180], vol. 73, p. 57; Hattori, *Daitōa* [235], vol. 1, pp. 152, 160; Shimada Toshihiko, *Kantōgun* [515], p. 169.

56. BBSS, *SS* [180], vol. 73, p. 57; Tanemura [571], pp. 73-74 (3 Aug. 1941); Morley, ed., *Fateful* [876], p. 107; Shimada Toshihiko, *Kantōgun* [515], pp. 169-70; Ike, trans. and ed. [775], pp. 114-18. Now an AGS operations staff officer, Tsuji Masanobu pressed strategic planner Arisue Yadoru to explore immediate diplomatic contact with the Russians to dissuade them from any projected military assault on the Japanese. Hattori, *Daitōa* [235], vol. 1, pp. 152, 160-61.

57. BBSS, *SS* [180], vol. 73, p. 58; Tanemura [571], pp. 74-75 (3-6 Aug.); Imaoka interview; Morley, ed., *Fateful* [876], p. 107; Hattori, *Daitōa* [235], vol. 1, pp. 152-53, 161; Shimada Toshihiko, *Kantōgun* [515], pp. 170-71; Ike, trans. and ed. [775], pp. 115-18.

58. IGHQ Army Order No. 523 and Directive No. 918, 6 Aug.: BBSS, *SS* [180], vol. 73, pp. 58-59; Imaoka interview; Hattori, *Daitōa* [235], vol. 1, pp. 153-54, 161-62; Tanemura [571], p. 75 (6 Aug.); Shimada Toshihiko, *Kantōgun* [515], pp. 171-72; Morley, ed., *Fateful* [876], p. 107.

59. Morley, ed., *Fateful* [876], pp. 109-13; Shimada Toshihiko, *Kantōgun* [515], pp. 172-75; BBSS, *SS* [180], vol. 73, p. 66.

60. JRD [961], *JM* 77, pp. 14-15; Tanemura [571], pp. 75-76 (9 Aug.); BBSS, *SS* [180], vol. 73, pp. 66-67; Imaoka interview; Hattori, *Daitōa* [235], vol. 1, pp. 154, 162; Shimada Toshihiko, *Kantōgun* [515], p. 175.

61. Takei, Tanemura, Imaoka interviews; BBSS, *SS* [180], vol. 73, p. 67.

62. The contingency planning was based on a 24-division troop level. See BBSS, *SS* [180], vol. 73, pp. 80-81.

63. BBSS, *SS* [180], vol. 73, pp. 67-68, 76; Imaoka, Ayabe interviews.

64. Takei interview; BBSS, *SS* [180], vol. 73, pp. 76-77.

65. Sagawa Kōichi, a special intelligence agent serving with the Public Security Bureau of the Manchukuoan government, asserts that he uncovered details of the explosion in the spring of 1944. His account, summarized in JRD [958], *JSM* 10, p. 108, n. 12, was picked up by Erickson [720] in 1969 and discussed, in turn, by Berton in his introduction to Morley, ed., *Fateful* [876], pp. 12, 307. My refutation of the alleged strategic consequences of the affair is based upon details provided in interviews with Kamio and Imaoka. The latter adds that the Kwantung Army sent the Third Army an equivalent amount of replacement ammunition from its own reserves.

66. Takei interview.

67. BBSS, *SS* [180], vol. 73, p. 68, citing IGHQ diary (28 Aug. 1941).

68. Ike, trans. and ed. [775], pp. 129-63; Tōgō [947], pp. 94-97, 353-55.

69. For operational preparations lasting three months and involving 23 or 24 divisions on the offensive (including the Korea Army), the following logistical basis was decided on 16 September: 1,200,000 men, 300,000 laborers, 200,000 Japanese and 200,000 Chinese horses, 35,000 motor vehicles, and 500 tanks. Imaoka interview. Also Mizumachi, Ishijima interviews.

70. S. Hayashi interview.

71. Imaoka, interview and "Kantokuen" [10], pp. 58-64; Mizumachi interview; S. Hayashi, *Taiheiyō* [243], p. 33, and *Kōgun* [756], p. 20; Hattori, *Daitōa* [235], vol. 1, p. 194. The first withdrawal included 33,000 men, 5,800 horses, and 1,080 motor vehicles. For details of the units transferred to South China, Formosa, and northern Indochina by November, see JRD [961], *JM* 77, pp. 19-22, 43-45; and S. Tanaka in IMTFE, *Transcript* [777], 28 May 1947, pp. 23336-37.

72. Imaoka interview. For varying figures, see BBSS, *SS* [180], vol. 73, p. 27. In September 1941 the Port Arthur garrison was upgraded to regimental strength and reinforced by an anti-aircraft artillery battalion. As noted earlier, the Twentieth Army was also activated, incorporating two infantry divisions (the 8th and 25th) plus four BGU's. JRD [961], *JM* 77, p. 15. According to Red Army data, Kwantung Army strength peaked by 1 Jan. 1942 at 1,100,000 men, or 35 percent of the whole Japanese army of 3,200,000. See IMTFE, *Transcript* [777], 10 Oct. 1946, pp. 7530-33; 11 Oct. 1946, pp. 7535-38. The Russians give Korea Army strength in 1941-42 as 120,000 men; [777], p. 7587.

73. BBSS, *SS* [180], vol. 73, p. 31; Imaoka, Mizumachi interviews. The grand total of IJA units mobilized during the entire Kantokuen era may have reached 450.

74. The operational IJAF planes included 50 heavy and 100 light bombers plus 130 fighters. S. Tanaka in IMTFE, *Transcript* [777], 28 May 1947, p. 23332. Y. Kasahara cited a figure of 400 planes in the Kwantung Army at the end of 1941. [777], p. 23195. Also see BBSS, *SS* [180], vol. 73, pp. 30-32; Hattori, *Daitōa* [235], vol. 1, pp. 53-54, 158-59; JRD [961], *JM* 77, pp. 15, 19-23. Soviet military sources claim the Kwantung Army air force had a strength of 1,500 planes by 1 Jan. 1942. IMTFE, *Transcript* [777], 10 Oct. 1946, p. 7533.

75. BBSS, *SS* [180], vol. 73, pp. 19, 68-69. Citing much higher figures for Soviet strength "around November," S. Tanaka spoke of 33 rifle divisions plus four other divisions and about 1,300 tanks and 1,500 planes. IMTFE, *Transcript* [777], 28 May 1947, p. 23333.

76. Imaoka, interview and "Kantokuen" [10], pp. 58-59; BBSS, *SS* [180], vol. 73, pp. 20, 28-30, 77.

77. Mizumachi interview; Imaoka, interview and "Kantokuen" [10], pp. 59-60; BBSS, *SS* [180], vol. 73, p. 69.

78. Ike, trans. and ed. [775], pp. 226-27.

79. *Ibid.*, p. 272.

80. IGHQ Army Order No. 578: JRD [960], *JSM* 1, pp. 158-59; [961], *JM* 77, pp. 23-25. The latter monograph errs in identifying Matsumura Tomokatsu as the Kwantung Army deputy chief of staff at the time. Also see S. Tanaka in IMTFE, *Transcript* [777], 28 May 1947, pp. 23334-35, 23338.

81. Doi, Imaoka interviews; JRD [961], *JM* 77, p. 25; Shimada Toshihiko, *Kantōgun* [515], pp. 178-79; Coox, "Myth" [688], pp. 38-39. For additional information on Umezu, see Kasahara Yukio, in IMTFE, *Transcript* [777], 28 May 1947, pp. 23202-3; diplomat Hanawa Yoshiyuki, 2 June 1947, pp. 23391-94; Iimura Jō, pp. 23397-403; Yamamura Haruo, pp. 23416-19; Kōzuki Yoshio, 3 June 1947, pp. 23458-60; and Satō Naotake, p. 23582.

82. Anthony Eden, *The Reckoning: The Memoirs of Anthony Eden, Earl of Avon* (Boston: Houghton Mifflin, 1965), pp. 348-49. Also see FRUS [974], *1941*, vol. 4, pp. 730-31 (Joseph E. Davies, 7 Dec.); pp. 742-44 (Cordell Hull, 11 Dec.).

83. JRD [960], *JSM* 1, pp. 44, 170; [968], *JSM* 13, pp. 42, 47, 60-66; [961], *JM* 77, pp. 16-17. Y. Kasahara states that at the end of 1941 the Russians had only 19 rifle divisions in Siberia; his figure for Soviet aircraft is 1,100. IMTFE, *Transcript* [777], 28 May 1947, p. 23195. S. Tanaka speaks of 980 Russian army planes (80 long-range, 60 heavy, and 330 light bombers; 450 fighters; 60 assault planes) and 200 seaplanes. [777], 28 May 1947, pp. 23340-41; 2 June 1947, p. 23386. Also see Mackintosh in Liddell Hart, ed. [833], pp. 176-77.

84. Imaoka, Hattori interviews; statement by Hattori (2 May 1949), JRD [966], vol. 1, pp. 385-86; S. Tanaka, in IMTFE, *Transcript* [777], 28 May 1947, pp. 23343-45; Hattori, *Daitōa* [235], vol. 2, pp. 167-68, 175, 321.

85. JRD [961], *JM* 77, pp. 29-30, 46.

86. An IJA army approximated an American corps; an IJA area army, an American army; an IJA general army, an American army group.

87. In September, the Kwantung Army Logistics Command (Hokyū Kanbu) was also established. Information on restructuring based on Imaoka, Ayabe interviews; S. Hayashi, *Kōgun* [756], pp. 45-46; JRD [961], *JM* 77, pp. 31-32, 46-48; Hattori, *Daitōa* [235], vol. 2, p. 168.

88. Coox, *Tojo* [696], pp. 76-77; Imaoka, Yamagata interviews.

89. JRD [962], *JM* 138, pp. 13-14; [960], *JSM* 1, pp. 158-60.

90. Imaoka, interview and "Kantokuen" [10], pp. 54-57; JRD [961], *JM* 77, p. 32. At the Tokyo trial, Soviet prosecutors had much to say about the enhancement of the Kwantung Army's infrastructure.

91. Hayes [757], pp. 366-67 (2-5 May 1943). Also see *ibid.*, pp. 133-34 (14-17 June 1942), 157 (24 June), 160 (19 July), 272, 275-76 (30 Dec.), 305 (4 Jan. 1943).

92. IMTFE, *Transcript* [777], 2 June 1947, pp. 23390-93 (Hanawa Yoshiyuki), 23399-400 (Iimura Jō); 3 June 1947, pp. 23458-59 (Kōzuki Yoshio).

93. JRD [968], *JSM* 13, pp. 68-69; [961], *JM* 77, pp. 35-36. Another IJA estimate places

Soviet personnel strength in Siberia at only 500,000 by the end of 1942, a decrease of perhaps 100,000 in a year. JRD [960], *JSM* 1, p. 170.

94. JRD [968], *JSM* 13, p. 69. According to the lower IJA estimate, Soviet manpower remained at 500,000 in 1943. JRD [960], *JSM* 1, p. 170. German sources did not accept the Japanese army's high estimates. On 18 April 1943, Ribbentrop told Ōshima that the IJA figure of 800,000 troops in Siberia was exaggerated: "Our estimate is only 250,000 men, who, in addition, are second-class soldiers, since all the Siberian divisions had already been battered by the German armies last winter." German Foreign Office records, cited in IMTFE, *Transcript* [777], 18 Oct. 1946, pp. 8174-76.

95. IMTFE, *Transcript* [777], 2 June 1947, p. 23403 (J. Iimura); JRD [962], *JM* 138, pp. 15-29; [961], *JM* 77, p. 48; S. Hayashi, *Kōgun* [756], p. 171.

96. Hattori, *Daitōa* [235], vol. 2, pp. 296-99; vol. 3, pp. 31-37.

97. Matsumura Tomokatsu, Kusaji interviews.

98. JRD [962], *JM* 138, pp. 28-31, 34-37, 39-41; Matsumura Tomokatsu [389], pp. 47-49, and interview.

99. JRD [962], *JM* 138, pp. 31-34, 37-39; [961], *JM* 77, p. 48; Matsumura Tomokatsu [389], pp. 43-44; Hattori, *Daitōa* [235], vol. 3, p. 67. S. Hayashi lists a paper strength of 50 air squadrons and 500 planes at the end of 1943 (six squadrons and 60 aircraft fewer than the year before); *Kōgun* [756], p. 173.

100. JRD [961], *JM* 77, pp. 48-58; [962], *JM* 138, pp. 51-60, 63-70, 72-75, 118-19, 123-25; S. Hayashi, *Kōgun* [756], pp. 171, 173; Matsumura Tomokatsu [389], p. 44; Shimada Toshihiko, *Kantōgun* [515], p. 178.

101. JRD [962], *JM* 138, p. 39.

102. JRD [962], *JM* 138, pp. 21-23.

103. Yamada interview. Also see S. Hayashi, *Kōgun* [756], pp. 111-12, 239; Coox, *Tojo* [696], p. 143.

104. JRD [962], *JM* 138, pp. 76-82. Kwantung Army headquarters made its recommendation to Tokyo after the second B-29 raid of 8 Sept. 1944.

105. JRD [962], *JM* 138, pp. 82-89, 100-110; Shimada Toshihiko, *Kantōgun* [515], pp. 180-81. Details of the Kwantung Army's limited command authority over the Korea Army are found in JRD [962], *JM* 138, pp. 97-100, 107-8.

106. JRD [962], *JM* 138, pp. 90-96; Matsumura Tomokatsu [389], p. 52; Shimada Toshihiko, *Kantōgun* [515], p. 182.

107. JRD [962], *JM* 138, pp. 110-12.

108. Kase [787], pp. 96-97. Anti-Japanese articles had started to appear in the Russian press from around October 1944, when U.S. troops invaded the Philippines. S. Hayashi, *Kōgun* [756], p. 169.

109. JRD [962], *JM* 138, pp. 116-17.

110. Hayes [757], p. 671; DOD, "Entry" [971], p. 35.

111. T. Maeda interview; JRD [960], *JSM* 1, p. 170. According to Soviet sources, almost 136,000 railway cars were employed to haul troops and supplies to the Soviet Far East and the Trans-Baikal region. The traffic was especially heavy in June and July, when 22-30 trains each day arrived east of the Baikal. In addition to the Trans-Siberian Railway, the Russians made extensive use of inland waterways and secondary rail lines in Siberia. Zakharov, ed. [1015], p. 71.

112. Kase [787], pp. 154-55; JRD [962], *JM* 138, p. 131.

113. JRD [962], *JM* 138, pp. 120-22, 125-27.

114. S. Hayashi, interview and *Kōgun* [756], p. 171.

115. JRD [960], *JSM* 1, pp. 171-72; [962], *JM* 138, Chart 11; S. Hayashi, *Kōgun* [756], pp. 171, 173.

116. JRD [962], *JM* 138, p. 130; Coox, "Soviet Armor" [694], p. 12.

117. Harada, Gotō, Kusaji, Arinuma interviews. Also see JRD [962], *JM* 138, pp. xiv-xv.

118. Iketani [276], p. 321. Also see JRD [962], *JM* 138, p. 161; [963], *JM* 154, p. 169; S. Hayashi, *Kōgun* [756], p. 171.

119. *Hiroku Daitōa* [250], vol. 2, pp. 271-72 (G. Kitazaki); JRD [962], *JM* 138, pp. 157-59; [963], *JM* 154, pp. 55-56, 90, 92, 166, 176-78; S. Hayashi, *Kōgun* [756], p. 171; Coox, "Soviet Armor" [694], p. 14.

120. JRD [962], *JM* 138, pp. 129-30, 160; [963], *JM* 154, pp. 57-58, 91, 162.

121. JRD [962], *JM* 138, Appendix 5.

122. *Hiroku Daitōa* [250], vol. 2, p. 178 (Shiragami Yasuo); p. 231 (Nishimura Tadao). Also Nagashima interview.

123. Shimada Toshihiko, *Kantōgun* [515], pp. 183-84; JRD [962], *JM* 138, pp. 130-35, 138.

124. The Korea Army had been reorganized into the Seventeenth Area Army (with an order of battle) and the Korea Administrative Defense Command, effective 10 Feb. 1945. JRD [962], *JM* 138, pp. 107-8.

125. JRD [962], *JM* 138, pp. 141-45.

126. JRD [962], *JM* 138, pp. 134-36.

127. JRD [962], *JM* 138, pp. 136-37, 146-47, 161.

128. M. Katō interview; JRD [962], *JM* 138, pp. 137, 147-48; [964], *JM* 155, pp. 6-8; S. Hayashi, *Kōgun* [756], p. 174. The 125th Division had left Tsitsihar for Tunghua, where it arrived in June 1945.

129. Shimada Toshihiko, *Kantōgun* [515], pp. 185-86; JRD [964], *JM* 155, pp. 5-6; [963], *JM* 154, p. 2. According to Marshal Zakharov, between May and July 1945 the Soviet transfers eastward totaled approximately a million men plus "tens of thousands of field guns and mortars, tanks and vehicles [and] many tens of thousands of tons of ammunition, fuel, food and other freight." [1015], p. 73. Also see n. 111, above.

130. Shimada Toshihiko, *Kantōgun* [515], p. 187; JRD [962], *JM* 138, pp. 139-40; [963], *JM* 154, p. 2.

131. JRD [963], *JM* 154, pp. 2-3, 54-55, 174.

132. M. Katō, Yamada, Kusaji interviews; JRD [963], *JM* 154, pp. 3, 94, 180.

133. JRD [955], *JSM* 2, pp. 82-84; [963], *JM* 154, pp. 3-5.

134. Yabe interview; Tōgō [947], pp. 314, 316, 322-23; Kase [787], pp. 223-26.

135. JRD [955], *JSM* 2, pp. 84-85; [963], *JM* 154, pp. 6-8.

136. JRD [966], vol. 2, pp. 97 (Lt. Gen. Kawabe Torashirō), 427 (Matsudaira Yasumasa), 546 (Lt. Gen. Miyazaki Shūichi); vol. 1, pp. 396 (Col. Hayashi Saburō), 543 (Lt. Gen. Ikeda Sumihisa), 574 (Lt. Col. Inaba Masao); and Coox, "Myth" [688], p. 43.

137. Yamada, Kusaji interviews; JRD [963], *JM* 154, pp. 8-12; [955], *JSM* 2, p. 86.

138. Ushiroku, Kusaji, Yamada interviews; BBSS, *SS* [180], vol. 73, pp. 412-17; JRD [963], *JM* 154, pp. 10-11; [955], *JSM* 2, pp. 85-86.

139. The Kwantung Army's Civil Affairs Section remained in Hsinking to maintain liaison with Manchukuoan officials, and the Intelligence Section also stayed because communication facilities at Tunghua were not satisfactory. JRD [963], *JM* 154, pp. 12-14; [955], *JSM* 2, p. 87. Pu Yi says he won a delay of two days and thus did not leave Hsinking till late on 11 August; his train reached its destination on the 13th. [899], pp. 316-18.

140. JRD [963], *JM* 154, pp. 14-15, 17, 63.

141. Matsumura Tomokatsu [389], pp. 52, 64; Iketani [276], pp. 323-24; *Hiroku Daitōa* [250], vol. 2, pp. 277-78 (G. Kitazaki); Kamura [318A], pp. 33-36; Shimada Toshihiko, *Kantōgun* [515], p. 189; Pu Yi [899], p. 318; Allen [633], pp. 203-4; JRD [963], *JM* 154, pp. 16-17, 75-77.

142. Harada, Gotō interviews; Pu Yi [899], p. 318; JRD [963], *JM* 154, pp. 16-17. Soviet sources explain the slowdown of Col. Gen. A. G. Kravchenko's Sixth Guards Tank Army as strictly a matter of muddy roads and running out of fuel. Aerial resupply provided gasoline and ammunition on 12-13 August. Pospelov et al., eds. [895], pp. 420-21. IJA acquaintance with this episode is noted in JRD [968], *JSM* 13, pp. 33, 129-30, 132.

143. JRD [963], *JM* 154, p. 18.

144. Yamada, Ushiroku, Kusaji, Harada interviews; JRD [963], *JM* 154, pp. 18-19; [955], *JSM* 2, p. 88; Shimada Toshihiko [515], *Kantōgun*, p. 190.

145. Yamada, Kusaji interviews; JRD [963], *JM* 154, pp. 19-20; Shimada Toshihiko,

Kantōgun [515], pp. 190-91. Due to a garbled transmission from Tunghua, the Third Area Army and the Thirtieth Army ordered a cease-fire in their zones, until a correction was received.

146. Matsumura Tomokatsu, Harada interviews; JRD [963], *JM* 154, pp. 20-21; [964], *JM* 155, pp. 72-73; Zakharov, ed. [1015], p. 192.

147. JRD [963], *JM* 154, pp. 21-22; [964], *JM* 155, p. 172.

148. Yamada, Kusaji, Asada interviews; JRD [963], *JM* 154, pp. 19-20.

149. Zakharov, ed. [1015], pp. 192-93; Pospelov et al., eds. [895], p. 423.

150. Matsumura Tomokatsu, Tanemura, Kusaji interviews; JRD [963], *JM* 154, pp. 20-21.

151. JRD [964], *JM* 155, pp. 72, 114-15. Civilian conscripts were also demobilized, as were servicemen with families in Manchuria. *Ibid.*, pp. 113-14. Also see Zakharov, ed. [1015], p. 212.

152. Iketani [276], p. 324; *Hiroku Daitōa* [250], vol. 2, pp. 21 (Yamada Ichirō), 159 (Shiragami Yasuo); JRD [963], *JM* 154, pp. 71-72. In February 1946 the defiant IJA colonel emerged from hiding, secretly entered Tunghua, and tried to mount a rebellion against the Soviet occupying authorities. He was caught and executed. JRD [964], *JM* 155, pp. 72, 77.

153. Zakharov, ed. [1015], pp. 213-14. In the mountains on the western front, the 107th Division was out of touch with higher headquarters until 28 August, when an IJAF plane located it. Abe, Matsumura Tomokatsu interviews.

154. The Japanese Welfare Ministry has estimated the number of civilians who died in areas under Soviet control at 218,100: Manchuria, 179,000; North Korea, 24,000; Kurils and Sakhalin, 13,100; Siberia, 2,000. As recently as March 1977, in the same areas, about 350 Japanese were still unaccounted for. JRD [964], *JM* 155, p. 281; [963], *JM* 154, pp. 221-22; Hattori, *Daitōa* [235], vol. 4, p. 419; Kachi, Tōgasaki interviews.

155. Pu Yi [899], pp. 319-20, 323-25; Zakharov, ed. [1015], pp. 206-8; JRD [964], *JM* 155, p. 116; Hattori, *Daitōa* [235], vol. 4, p. 411. Neither Yamada nor Hata knew that Pu Yi's plane had been diverted to Mukden from its original destination of Pyongyang, and both generals were angry about the arbitrary decision taken by a thoughtless subordinate staff section chief. The latter is said to have attempted suicide. Hara Seiroku interview.

156. Zakharov, ed. [1015], p. 214; JRD [963], *JM* 154, p. 24.

157. USSR [989], pp. 5, 283, 290-91, 447; Zakharov, ed. [1015], p. 212. Also see O. Yamada [611], pp. 73-74; Matsumura Tomokatsu [389], pp. 104, 106; Shimamura, *Sanzennin* (chap. 42, n. 38, above), pp. 126-32, 139-41; *Hiroku Daitōa* [250], vol. 2, p. 643 (W. Hasegawa); S. Hayashi, *Kōgun* [756], p. 175; JRD [964], *JM* 155, p. 187.

158. Yamada, Ushiroku, Matsumura Tomokatsu, Sejima interviews; Hattori, *Daitōa* [235], vol. 4, p. 420; *Hiroku Daitōa* [250], vol. 2, pp. 623, 625 (W. Hasegawa); JRD [963], *JM* 154, pp. 24-25, 218-19, 304; [964], *JM* 155, pp. 75-76, 118, 187, 246.

159. Tōgō [947], p. 310; Kase [787], p. 209.

160. The postwar Japanese government usually estimated the original number of Kwantung Army personnel in Soviet hands at 700,000, but did not use the word "effectives." The 1st Demobilization Bureau's rough estimate of Kwantung Army losses put the dead at 21,389 out of a grand total of 713,729 officers and men in Manchuria alone; JRD [964], *JM*, 155, pp. 266-67 (data ca. 1954). The Soviet tally of casualties on both sides and of the arms and equipment seized from the Kwantung Army not only is disputed by the Japanese in many categories but also reflects variations attributable to differing Soviet reporting commands (sometimes all three fronts, usually only the Trans-Baikal and 1st Far Eastern). In addition, there are uncoordinated geographical frames of reference (sometimes North Korea and Sakhalin/Kuril Islands included with Manchuria) or undifferentiated dates of tabulation (1945, 1949, 1950). Subject to these caveats, the Soviet enumerations follow: prisoners—594,000-609,176 officers and men, including approximately 20,000 wounded; Japanese combat dead—83,737; Soviet dead—8,219, wounded 22,264, total sometimes given as nearly 32,000; captured items—aircraft 861-925, tanks 369-600 (plus 35 armored cars), artillery pieces 1,236-1,565, mortars and grenade launchers 1,340-2,139, machine guns 4,836-11,988, rifles about 300,000, vehicles 2,129-2,300, horses 13,000-17,497, ammunitions dumps 679. See Zakharov, ed. [1015], p. 223; Pospelov et al., eds. [895], p. 425; S. Hayashi, *Kōgun* [256], pp. 175-76; GHQ/FEC, Military

Intelligence Sec. compilation submitted at Allied Council Meeting, 1 Feb. 1950, *Japan Year Book, 1949-52* (Tokyo: Foreign Affairs Association of Japan, 1952), pp. 424-25.

161. Zakharov, ed. [1015], p. 221.

162. Uchiyama interview. According to Japanese Welfare Ministry data, a total of 131,600 IJA officers and men died in Soviet custody after the fighting ended: Siberia, 53,000; Manchuria, 66,400; Sakhalin/Kurils, 1,600; North Korea, 10,600. JRD [964], *JM* 155, p. 135; Hattori, *Daitōa* [235], vol. 4, p. 415.

163. Shōji interview. According to the Tass announcement of 21 April 1950, 70,880 Japanese had been released on the spot in 1945, and 510,409 had been repatriated afterward. This supposedly left 1,487 convicted or suspected war criminals, nine sick persons due to be released, and 971 men who would be turned over to the Communist Chinese. The total comes to 583,756, whereas the first *Pravda* announcement of September 1945 gave the minimum figure of 594,000. Had 10,000 men died, by explicit admission? See n. 162, above.

164. O. Yamada, interview and [611], pp. 70, 75; and Ushiroku interview. The last repatriation ship from Nakhodka, the *Kōan Maru*, docked in Maizuru on 30 Dec. 1956, carrying Generals Hata and Ushiroku and 1,200 men, two-thirds of whom had received the Soviet maximum sentence of 25 years' imprisonment. Maki, Abe, Kinoshita, Uchiyama, H. Hara interviews. Umemoto Sutezō has written a biography of Yamada: *Shōgun no shiki: saigo no Kantōgun sōshireikan: Yamada Otozō shōgun* [The Four Seasons of a General: The Last Commander in Chief of the Kwantung Army: Gen. Yamada Otozō] (Tokyo: Kōjinsha, 1983).

165. According to Welfare Ministry data as of 1 March 1977, 41 of the 1945-era Japanese might still be alive in Siberia and 203 in Sakhalin.

AFTERTHOUGHTS

1. During the combat phase of the Russo-Japanese War, the wording "Manchurian Army" was used for the Japanese field forces in Manchuria; interviews with I. Hata, Imaoka. The publicist's comment is from *Japan Year Book, 1938-39* (Tokyo: Foreign Affairs Association of Japan, 1938), p. 1,077. For the appellation "Korea Army," see Coox, *Anatomy* [679], p. 20, n. 14.

2. Sejima interview. Also see T. Matsumura [389], pp. 25-27.

3. Inada, Sumi, Y. Nishihara interviews.

4. See Sawada [507A], p. 149. Also Hashimoto, Inada, Sumi interviews.

5. Lt. Gen. Sir Ian Hamilton, *A Staff Officer's Scrap-book During the Russo-Japanese War* (London: Edward Arnold, 1907), vol. 2, p. 14.

6. Nishiura exposes weaknesses of the IJA personnel staff, whom he castigates as "personnel affairs shopkeepers," in [447], pp. 46-47.

7. *Hiroku Daitōa* [250], vol. 2, p. 164 (Nakamura Bin).

8. Coox, "High Command" [683], pp. 307-10. Also Imaoka, Hashimoto, Sumi interviews.

9. M. Itō, *Gunbatsu* [308A], vol. 3, p. 142.

10. Inada interview. Also see Nishiura [447], p. 157.

11. Akimoto [632], p. 331.

12. *Hiroku Daitōa* [250], vol. 2, p. 162 (Nakamura Bin).

13. Akimoto [632], pp. 35-38. For the Kwantung Army connection, see T. Matsumura [389], p. 26.

14. *Orient Year Book, 1942* (Tokyo: Asia Statistics, 1942), p. 539.

15. Ponomaryov et al., eds. [894], p. 415. Also S. Matsumura [388], p. 173; I. Hata interview.

16. IMTFE, *Transcript* [777], 10 Nov. 1948 (Judgment), pp. 49, 405-6.

17. Grigorenko [746A], p. 132.

18. Col. Roy M. Stanley II, USAF, *Prelude to Pearl Harbor* (New York: Scribner's, 1982), pp. vii, 1.

19. U.S. War Dept. [981], p. 85.

20. Foreword to Lt. Col. Clive Garsia, *A Key to Victory: A Study in War Planning* (London: Eyre and Spottiswoode, 1940), p. ix.

21. Murata interview.

22. S. Hayashi, *Kantōgun* [242], pp. 183-84.

23. Onda [473], vol. 2, pp. 266, 270; Umihara [601], pp. 146-47; BBSS, *SS* [180], vol. 27, pp. 673-74; S. Hayashi, *Kantōgun* [242], p. 183.

24. Capt. Peter Steyn, comp., *The History of the Assam Regiment* (Calcutta: Orient Longmans, 1959), vol. 1, pp. 65, 150.

25. I. Hata interview. For weaknesses in IJA military education, see Matsutani [399], p. 275; Onda [473], vol. 2, p. 266; Jōhō, *Rikugunshō* [312], p. 507; Umihara [601], p. 153; Gomikawa, *Nomonhan* [212], p. 339.

26. Sawada [507A], p. 137.

27. Nishiura [447], pp. 87-88. Also S. Hata interview; Imoto [285], p. 391; *SSNT* [535], vol. 29, p. 400; Onda [473], vol. 2, p. 275.

28. Endō [189], pp. 175-80; Umihara [601], p. 140; Imoto [285], pp. 390-91; K. Saitō [496], p. 65; Imaoka, "Nomonhan" [13], p. 97. Shimanuki, S. Tsuchiya, Arao interviews; Coox, *Anatomy* [679], pp. 359-61.

29. Shimanuki, Inada, N. Morita interviews; Onda [473], vol. 2, pp. 259, 279, 284 (Gomikawa).

30. Shimanuki interview.

31. Steyn, comp., *Assam*, vol. 1, p. 65.

32. Katakura, Sumi, Inada, Shimanuki, Hashimoto, N. Itō, I. Hata, Y. Nishihara, Imaoka interviews; JRD [965], *JSM* 11, part 3/C, pp. 466-69; M. Itō, *Gunbatsu* [308A], vol. 3, p. 142; Gomikawa, *Nomonhan* [212], pp. 307-10, 339-42; Onda [473], vol. 2, pp. 262-69 (Gomikawa and Onda); Horige [260], pp. 246-49; GSDF [73], p. 180; Sawada [507A], p. 131 (9 Sept. 1939); Umihara [601], pp. 141-42.

33. Hagimoto Toshio, "Sorrow and the Southern Cross," in Sōka Gakkai, comp., *Peace Is Our Duty: Accounts of What War Can Do to Man* (Tokyo: The Japan Times, 1982), pp. 165-66. Also see Tanaka Ryūkichi, *Haiin* [566], p. 54; Imaoka, "Nomonhan" [13], p. 91.

34. Nomura [455], p. 74.

35. A. J. Barker, *Japanese Army Handbook, 1939-1945* (New York: Hippocrene Books, 1979), p. 120. "Division Commander's Final Report on Guadalcanal Operation," May-July 1943, extract on file in U.S. Thirteenth Air Force records, March 1944 (Office of Air Force History Archives, Washington, D.C.).

36. JRD [959], parts 1-2; Umihara [601], p. 141.

37. Grigorenko [746A], p. 109. Also see Borojeikin [184], p. 94.

38. Gomikawa, *Nomonhan* [212], pp. 333-55; BBSS, *SS* [180], vol. 27, p. 679; K. Hayashi [238], p. 193.

39. GSDF, *Nomonhan* [68], p. 19.

40. 75th Inf. Regt. [92B], 9 Aug. 1938.

41. Ogoshi interview.

42. Barker, *Handbook*, pp. 118, 120.

43. GSDF/CGSC, *Sorengawa* [73], p. 177.

44. William Green and Gordon Swanborough, *Japanese Army Fighters*, part 2 (New York: Arco Publishing Co., 1978), p. 3.

45. GSDF/CGSC, *Sorengawa* [73], pp. 177-78.

46. Sawada [507A], p. 131. Also see Ōki Shigeru [469], pp. 98-100.

47. Umihara [601], p. 144.

48. GSDF/CGSC, *Sorengawa* [73], pp. 172-75; *SSNT* [535], vol. 29, p. 400.

49. Okazaki Hisahiko, "Strategic Lessons in Far Eastern History," *Japan Echo*, Winter 1982, vol. 9, no. 4, p. 124. Also Imaoka interview; Onda [473], vol. 2, pp. 263-64, 270-71; Umihara [601], pp. 23, 43, 65-69.

50. BBSS, *SS* [180], vol. 27, pp. 624-25; Doi interview.

51. Brig. Gen. E. L. Spears, *Prelude to Victory* (London: Jonathan Cape, 1939), pp. 91-92.

52. Doi, Ōgoshi interviews; BBSS, *SS* [180], vol. 27, pp. 625-26; GSDF/CGSC, *Sorengawa* [73], pp. 166-68, 190-91.

53. BBSS, *SS* [180], vol. 27, pp. 626-27; Ōgoshi, Nyūmura interviews.

54. Okazaki, "Strategic Lessons," p. 124. Also see Matsutani [399], p. 275; Jōhō, *Rikugunshō*

[312], p. 507; Umihara [601], pp. 21-22, 50-52; BBSS, *SS* [180], vol. 27, p. 673, S. Hayashi, *Kantōgun* [242], p. 183.

55. Inada, Doi interviews; BBSS, *SS* [180], vol. 27, p. 599.
56. Sawada [507A], pp. 148-52.
57. See Coox, "Restraints" [691].
58. S. Hata interview; Sawada [507A], p. 149.
59. Inada interview.
60. Arao interview.
61. For the Imphal-Kohima campaign, see Coox, "Maverick" [687]; for Japanese criticism of strategy, see Umihara [601], pp. 152-54.
62. Andō interview; Umihara [601], pp. 143-45. Also see GSDF/CGSC, *Sorengawa* [73], pp. 166-68, 171-73, 178-79; Gomikawa, *Nomonhan* [212], p. 340; Kōtani interview.
63. 2nd Bn., 28th Inf. Regt. [110], 16 July 1939.
64. Imaoka, Yabe interviews.
65. Matthew B. Ridgway, *The Korean War* (Garden City, N.Y.: Doubleday, 1967), p. 146; Robert F. Futrell, *The United States Air Force in Korea, 1950-1953* (New York: Duell, Sloan and Pearce, 1961), pp. 40-41, 142 n.
66. Onda [473], vol. 2, p. 245.
67. S. Hayashi, *Kantōgun* [242], pp. 185-86; GSDF, *Nomonhan* [68], pp. 15-16, 19-20, 60-61, 63, 65; Iwakuro, Ōgoshi interviews; GSDF/CGSC, *Sorengawa* [73], pp. 180, 190-91; BBSS, *SS* [180], vol. 27, p. 733; Umihara [601], p. 146.
68. Gomikawa, *Nomonhan* [212], pp. 307-10, 340.
69. Sanche de Gramont, *The French: Portrait of a People* (New York: G. P. Putnam's Sons, 1969), pp. 147-48.
70. Williamson Murray, "British and German Air Doctrine Between the Wars," *Air University Review*, Mar.-Apr. 1980, vol. 31, no. 3, pp. 44-49. In all aspects of aviation except air defense—"close air support, interdiction, airlanding operations, long-range reconnaissance, and maritime operations—the Royal Air Force had done almost nothing to anticipate the requirements of the coming war." *Ibid.*, p. 49.
71. *Ibid.*, p. 48.
72. Cited in Garsia, *Key to Victory*, p. vii.
73. New China News Agency release, in *Pacific Stars & Stripes*, 27 July 1963; *People's Daily* (Peking), in *San Diego Union*, 14 Sept. 1966, 14 Aug. 1969.
74. "Vietnam: A Television History," PBS, Nov. 1983.
75. Hq. Dept. of the Army, FM 100-5, *Operations* (1 July 1976), pp. I-2, I-5; italics in original. The parallel problem of NATO forces is discussed by Col. Daniel Gans, USAR (Ret.), "Fight Outnumbered and Win . . . Against What Odds?," in *Military Review*, Jan. 1981, part 2, pp. 24-33.
76. *San Diego Union*, 6 June 1980 (*New York Times* News Service); *Washington Star*, 16 Aug. 1980.
77. *Japan Times*, 30 Dec. 1983, citing Long Commission report.
78. Inoki Masamichi, "From Utopian Pacifism to Utopian Militarism," *Japan Echo*, Winter 1980, vol. 7, no. 4, p. 98.

Bibliography

I. INTRODUCTION

The setting for a study of the Kwantung Army in general and of the Nomonhan war in particular is extremely complex, necessitating the use of sources bearing upon diplomacy, economics, and domestic politics as well as international relations, biography, and military history. Not only are Japanese interests involved directly, but so are those of China, the Soviet Union, the client states Outer Mongolia and Manchukuo, and, at times, the League of Nations, Germany, Britain, France, and the United States. Published sources span the prewar and postwar periods and vary in ideological views and levels of reliability. They range from autobiographies and biographies to official and unofficial military accounts, journalistic exposés, novels, and scholarly histories, and they appear in a variety of media. Indeed, Japanese prewar documentary films and newsreels (such as those prepared in the Nomonhan area by Manshū Eiga) and postwar television programs and movies contain some exciting and relevant information. Though much of the secondary literature is Japanese, substantial contributions derive from English- and Russian-language sources. The reticence of the Russians is well known, but there has been considerable historiographical improvement since the death of Stalin, as is seen in the bibliography of Soviet materials compiled by Michael Parrish of Indiana University.

Complementing the secondary sources are a wide array of primary materials. Because of the factor of accessibility, these materials are mainly Japanese, although information was also culled from declassified American diplomatic and attaché messages, German, British, and French foreign office dispatches, and, to a certain degree, Soviet archival revelations. It is a source of frustration to know that in 1945 the Russians seized but have never released certain Kwantung Army files, whose main use has apparently been the provision of documentation for war crimes trials.

The materials in this bibliography are grouped as follows:

    II. Japanese Sources, Primary
        A. Interviews and Correspondence
        B. Diaries, Recollections, Reports, and Special Studies
        C. Official and Semiofficial Publications
    III. Japanese Sources, Secondary
    IV. Western Sources
    V. Selected Russian Sources

Within each section and subsection, entries are listed in alphabetical order. As a further aid to the reader grappling with the sometimes highly abbreviated short-form citations used of necessity in the Notes, beginning with section IIB a number precedes each consecutive entry to provide a sure guide from note reference to full-form citation.

To avoid considerable repetition, the 3-em dash (———) has been used to replace identical units of information from preceding entries. Where more than one dash appears, each dash represents the information contained in successive units set off by periods in the full entry. Thus entry [74], "Gaimushō [Foreign Ministry]. Chōsabu [Research Bureau]. *Shōwa 13-nendo shitsumu hōkoku* [Annual Official Report,

1938]," is followed by entry [75], "————. ————. *Shōwa 14-nendo shitsumu hōkoku* [Annual Official Report, 1939]," where the first 3-em dash replaces "Gaimushō [Foreign Ministry]" and the second "Chōsabu [Research Bureau]."

II. JAPANESE SOURCES, PRIMARY

My Japanese primary items range from once-classified after-action records, attaché reports, investigations, and histories to diaries, albums, and letters, often unearthed for me by participants or their kin. Much documentation as well as many private holdings, however, were destroyed during the Second World War or in its immediate aftermath, some by act of war, some by deliberate intent. The U.S. Strategic Bombing Survey and the International Military Tribunal for the Far East collected information of varying quality and utility, but the most sustained and systematic historical effort, prior to the establishment of the Bōeichō's own military history office, was conducted in the 1950's by the U.S. Army's Japanese Research Division. There, I and other American editors relied upon the knowledge of dozens of IJA and IJN officers to develop many monographs, originally submitted in Japanese and subsequently translated, annotated, and expanded, an example being the 13 volumes that appeared in English as Japanese Studies on Manchuria. In the 1960's, after I had left the Japanese Research Division, I personally commissioned Imaoka Yutaka, Ishida Kiyoshi, and Shishikura Jurō to prepare special studies for me in Japanese on designated topics for exclusive use in connection with the present study.

Individual IJA officers such as Hamada Sueo, Sumi Shin'ichirō, Kanaizuka Yūkichi, Onozuka Kichihei, and Yano Mitsuji contributed items saved somehow since the Nomonhan period or transcribed after the war. Other contemporary or reconstructed material was unearthed in the Bōeichō military archives or the Gaimushō vaults. When documents were prepared during the life of the old Imperial Army, I have included the ranks attained by the authors at the time; in the case of postwar military writers, I did not append their old IJA ranks to their pieces. Of particular value and interest were the 11 volumes produced for limited distribution by the Nomonhan-kai, a survivors' society I was introduced to by Suzuki Yoshiyasu in the late 1960's. Most recently I was able to obtain a copy of Lt. Satō Chōnoshin's original combat jottings and sketches, which his family only discovered in 1979.

Subsequent to the completion of the numbering system employed in this Bibliography, I came upon new primary materials at the BBSS Archives in Tokyo, plus items recently published privately or commercially, mainly in Japan, and some sources that had appeared in previous years. The appropriate Notes and the Preface contain full-form references to a number of these important items, which are accordingly not restated here. From the balance of non-coded sources—exclusive of the numerous BBSS Archives documents mentioned above—the most valuable Japanese-language publications follow in alphabetical order.

"Akeno rikugun hikōgakkō monogatari" [Stories from the Akeno Army Flying School], *Kaikō*, June 1984, pp. 22-33. Based on a roundtable meeting chaired by my respondent Maruta Fumio.

Coox, Alvin D. "Gaikokujin ga mita Nomonhan-sen no kyōkun" [Lessons of the Nomonhan Fighting as Seen by Foreigners], *Rekishi to Jinbutsu*, special edition, Nov. 1984, pp. 330-40.

Haruhagawa kaisen: sansen heishi-tachi no kaisō [The Battle of the Halha River: Recollections of (MPRA) Soldiers Who Participated], comp. Tanaka Katsuhiko. Tokyo: Kōbunsha, 1984.

Hata Shunroku. *Hata Shunroku nisshi* [The Hata Shunroku Diary], ed. Itō Takashi and Terunuma Yasutaka. Tokyo: Misuzu Shobō, 1983. Supplement 4 to the *GSS* series [202].

Hayashi Masaharu. *Manshū jihen no Kantōgun shireikan Honjō Shigeru* [Honjō Shigeru, the Kwantung Army Commander at the Time of the Manchurian Incident]. Sakai: Ōminato Shobō, 1977.

Ikuta Makoto. "Senshi koborebanashi (4): horyo mondai" [Military History Tidbits, No. 4: The Prisoner Problem], *Kanbu Gakkō Kiji*, Feb. 1973, pp. 69-78.

Kohei dai-23 Rentai kiroku: sōkatsu-hen [23rd Engineer Regiment Records: Summary Volume]. Kumamoto: n.p., 1979.

Kohei dai-24 Rentai: shirarezaru hiun no senshi [The 24th Engineer Regiment: Unknown, Tragic Military History], ed. Asari Yoshinari. Tokyo: n.p., 1982.

Komatsubara Michitarō. "Sanretsu! Komatsubara shidanchō Nomonhan jinchū nisshi" [Gruesome Tragedy! Division Commander Komatsubara's Nomonhan Combat Diary], ed. Matsuzaki Shōichi, *Rekishi to Jinbutsu*, special edition, Nov. 1984, pp. 366-410.

Kōsha senshi [A Military History of Antiaircraft], ed. Shimoshizu Kōsha Gakkō Shūshin-kai. Tokyo: Tanaka Shoten, 1978.

"Nomonhan jiken no saikentō: hishi Taiheiyō sensō" [The Nomonhan Incident Reexamined: Secret History of the Pacific War], *Rekishi to Jinbutsu*, special edition, Nov. 1984.

"Nomonhan-sen o kaiko suru" [Recollections of the Nomonhan Fighting], *ibid.*, pp. 302-15. Based on a roundtable meeting chaired by Handō Kazutoshi.

Nukada Hiroshi. *Shijo saidai no jinji: rikugun 550 man soshiki wa koshite ugoita* [The Biggest Personnel Affairs in History: How the Army System of 5,500,000 Men Worked], ed. Jōhō Yoshio. Tokyo: Fuyō Shobō, 1983.

Satō Katsuo. "Ichi kōkū bakuryō no omoide (1-3)" [Recollections of a Certain Air Staff Officer, Parts 1-3], *Kaikō*, Jan. 1984, pp. 58-68; Sept. 1984, pp. 28-34; Oct. 1984, pp. 26-32.

Sekiguchi Hiroshi et al. *Eikō hayabusa sentai: hikō dai-64 Sentai sentōroku* [The Glorious Falcon (Fighter) Group: Combat Records of the 64th Air Group]. Tokyo: Konnichi no Wadaisha, 1983.

Tanaka Kōji et al., eds. *Nihon rikugun kōkū hiwa* [Untold Stories of the Japanese Army Air Force]. Tokyo: Hara Shobō, 1981.

Umemoto Sutezō. *Zenshi Kantōgun* [A Complete History of the Kwantung Army]. Tokyo: Keizai Ōraisha, 1978.

Several English-language items also deserve mention:

Fox, Galen C. "The Nomonhan Conflict in the Tokyo International War Crimes Trial." M.A. Thesis, University of Oregon, 1965.

Lee, Chong-Sik. *Revolutionary Struggle in Manchuria: Chinese Communism and Soviet Interest, 1922-1945*. Berkeley: University of California Press, 1984.

Seki Hiroharu. "The Manchurian Incident, 1931," trans. Marius B. Jansen, in James William Morley, ed., *Japan Erupts: The London Naval Conference and the Manchurian Incident, 1928-1932*. New York: Columbia University Press, 1984. Originally published in *Taiheiyō sensō e no michi*.

Sella, Amnon. "Khalkhin-Gol: The Forgotten War," *J. Contemporary History*, 18 (1983), pp. 651-87.

Shimada Toshihiko. "The Extension of Hostilities, 1931-1932," trans. Akira Iriye,

James William Morley, ed., *Japan Erupts: The London Naval Conference and the Manchurian Incident, 1928-1932.* New York: Columbia University Press, 1984.

A. Interviews and Correspondence

To buttress the available documentation, I have devoted particular emphasis to the specialty of oral history, designed to capture information known to participants or observers and retrievable only in their lifetime. My program, which I began in Japan in 1951, achieved particular impetus between 1960 and 1964 when I tracked down survivors from one end of the country to the other. I completed my agenda during my most recent research trips to Japan in 1979 and 1983-84. The era of Nomonhan, after all, is "only" about 45 years behind us, and a lieutenant who was, say, 22 years old in 1939 is a spry man in his late sixties today. A large number of the more senior people have died since being interviewed, rendering the recorded testimony all the more precious.

Field Marshal Hata Shunroku once reminded me of the Japanese saying that defeated generals should not talk about battles; but the stricture really applies to the gratuitous volunteering of information. "I retained no records," said Hata, "and I am not a good writer anyhow. So the best approach is for historians like you to extract the facts directly from people like me." I found the marshal's advice to be well taken. After I had established my *bona fides* and my credentials in Japan, I received a positive response from nearly every potential respondent whom I approached. Two men were too advanced in years or too ill to be visited; another man had given up on life and retired to the obscurity of his farm; a younger officer simply preferred to let sleeping dogs lie. In general, however, those contacted were more than willing to invest time and energy in conversing with their American interviewer. A number indicated that they were impelled by a sense of responsibility to the souls of dead comrades and subordinates; others referred to a desire to let the truth be known for the benefit of succeeding generations. Some asserted that Japanese historians usually lack the required objectivity and, indeed, the interest to probe the military past.

Hazards of memory, of ego, and of contradiction exist, of course, but the first-hand reflective knowledge, saved from decay through careful recall, serves several important purposes: to fill lacunae, to explain motivations, and to reveal inner thinking and perceptions. Apart from their intrinsic utility and interest, interviews also convey color and personality. In this connection, I found my respondents to be a very hardy and resilient breed—lucid, forthcoming, and often painfully honest. Their central experiences, etched indelibly in their minds, took visible shape under probing, particularly when refreshed by the display of authentic documentation, maps, photos, etc. A typical session lasted between four hours and a full day. In one case, at a distant country spa, the interview proceeded into the night and resumed next morning. Sometimes I conversed with more than one veteran at a time. In many instances there were follow-up interviews, often supplemented by telephone conversations, correspondence, and the gracious loan or bequest to me of papers, albums, diaries, clippings, and photographs.

The following 204 individuals, listed alphabetically without denotation of rank or position, assisted me in various ways. Most were former IJA personnel ranging in rank from Marshal Hata to general officers and downward to field- and company-grade officers, warrant officers, noncoms, and enlisted men. Some respondents saw service in the navy, at flag level and below. Others were diplomats, legislators, bureaucrats, journalists, or educators. The women listed are the wives or widows of participants. A few unlisted individuals proffered confidential information on the condition that their identities be withheld.

Abe Kōichi
Agawa Hiroyuki
Aida Shingorō
Andō Shigenori
Arao Okikatsu
Ariga Tsutao
Arinuma Gen'ichirō
Asada Saburō
Ayabe Kitsuju
Ban Yutaka
Banba Nobuya
Doi Akio
Fujiwara Iwaichi
Fukuda Kanjirō
Fukushima Yasushi
Giga Tetsuji
Gotō Kiyotoshi
Hamada Sueo
Hamada Toshio
Hanamoto Seikō
Hara Hirokazu
Hara Seiroku (Zenshirō)
Hara Takeshi
Harada Uichirō
Hashimoto Gun
Hata Ikuhiko
Hata Shunroku
Hata Yūzaburō
Hatano Sumio
Hattori Masanori
Hattori Takushirō
Hayano Ichimi
Hayashi Saburō
Hayashi Tadaaki
Hidemura Senzō
Higashi, Mrs. Muneharu
Hikime Eizō
Horie Yoshitaka
Horiguchi Yoshio
Hosokawa Naonori
Ichimoto Yoshirō
Ida [Iwata] Masataka
Ikuta Makoto
Imaoka Yutaka
Imoto Kumao
Inaba Masao
Inada Masazumi
Inoue Tadao
Irie Tachio
Ishida Kiyoshi

Ishijima Tatsu
Ishikawa Kanshi
Itō Masanori
Itō Noboru
Itonaga Shin
Iwakuro Hideo
Iwasaki Tamio
Iwashima Hisao
Kachi Teruko
Kamio Motoo
Kanaizuka Yūkichi
Katakura Tadashi
Katō Michio
Katō Takeo
Kawasaki Torao
Kimura Toshio
Kinbara Setsuzō
Kinoshita Hideaki
Kira Katsuaki
Kitano Kenzō
Kojima Noboru
Komatsubara,
  Mrs. Michitarō
Kondō Shinji
Konishi Kenkichi
Kōno Shirō
Kōtani [Kohtani] Etsuo
Kubo Muneji
Kurihara Ken
Kusaji Teigo
Kusaka Ryūnosuke
Maeda Tadao
Maeda Yoshinori
Maki Tatsuo
Maruta Fumio
Masuda Umeki
Matsumura Kōjirō
Matsumura Tomokatsu
Matsuoka Takashi
Mikami Kisō
Mishima Giichirō
Miura Kazuichi
Miyajima Seiichi
Miyashi Minoru
Miyo Kazunari
Miyoshi Yasuyuki
Mizobe Shigemi
Mizumachi Katsuki
Mogami Sadeo
Morishita Seijirō

Morita Masayuki
Morita Norimasa
Morita Sutezō
Murakoshi Kimio
Murata Masao
Nagashima Kiyoshi
Nakagawa Keiichirō
Nakamura Masazō
Nakamura Teiji
Nakano Masao
Nakazawa Makoto
Negami Hiroshi
Niiya Kiyoshi
Nishi Haruhiko
Nishihara Gorō
Nishihara Yukio
Nishikawa Masayuki
Nishimura Kō
Nishiura Susumu
Noguchi Kamenosuke
Numazaki Kyōhei
Nyūmura Matsuichi
Odagiri Masanori
Ogata Kyūichirō
Ōgoshi Kenji
Okada Hidehiro
Okada Minoru
Ōmae [Ohmae] Toshikazu
Onozuka Kichihei
Ōtsuka Masahiro
Saitō Isamu
Saitō Miyoshi
Saitō Toshio
Sakata Hideru
Sakazaki Takayuki
Sasai Shigeo
Satō Katsuo
Satō Kōtoku
Satō, Mrs. Kōtoku
Sawamoto Rikichirō
Sejima Ryūzō
Seki Hiroharu
Shimanuki Takeharu
Shimono Ikkaku
Shirai Masatatsu
Shishikura Jurō
Shōji Tatsumi
Suemori Isamu
Sugahara Tomiya
Sugai Toshimara

Sugita Ichiji
Sumi Shin'ichirō
Suzuki Yasushi [Yasuo]
Suzuki Yoshiyasu
Suzuki, Mrs. Yoshiyasu
Taguchi Hatsuyuki
Takagi Hajime
Takahashi Tsuruo
Takai Mitsuo
Takayama Shinobu
Takei Seitarō
Takeshita Iwao
Takumi Hiroshi
Tamada Yoshio
Tanaka Hideo
Tanaka Naoichi
Tanemura Sakō
Taoka Shunji
Tatsuno Tomio

Tayui Yuzuru
Tazaki Hideyuki
Tezuka Masayoshi
Tofuku Aikichi
Toga Hiroshi
Tōgasaki, Gordon Shigeru
Tokugawa Yoshitoshi
Tominaga Kametarō
Tomioka Sadatoshi
Tomioka Zenzō
Toyama Saburō
Toyoda Kumao
Tsuchida Minoru
Tsuchiya Masaichi
Tsuchiya Sakae
Tsuge Kunio
Tsunashima Takeo
Tsutsumi Sunao
Tsuyuki Jinzō

Uchiyama Fumio
Ueda Toshio
Usami Oki'iye
Ushiroku Jun
Usui Katsumi
Utsunomiya Naokata
Watakabe Masashi
Yabe Chūta
Yamada Otozō
Yamagata Arimitsu
Yamaguchi Suteji
Yano Mitsuji
Yano Muraji
Yonaga Hyōe
Yonezawa Juntarō
Yoshimatsu Masahiro
Yuzuhara Hidemi

B. Diaries, Recollections, Reports, and Special Studies

1. Fuwa Hiroshi. "5A sakusen kosshi wa tsugi no tōri de aru" [Gist of Fifth Army Operations . . .]. 1953.
2. Hamada Sueo. "Nomonhan jiken kaisōroku" [Recollections of the Nomonhan Incident]. Ca. 1959-60.
3. Hata Ikuhiko, ed. "Shuyō gaikōkan: riku-kaigunjin ryakureki oyobi shokureki ichiran" [Major Diplomatic and Army-Navy Military Personnel: Brief Personal Histories and Position-Records Summaries]. 1961.
4. Hata Yūzaburō, Maj. Gen. "Hōheidan no sentō" [The Combat of the Artillery Corps]. Ca. 1960.
5. ———. "Nikki to kaisōroku" [Diary and Recollections]. 1939.
6. Hattori Takushirō, ed. "Manshū ni okeru Nihongun no tai-So sakusen keikaku" [Anti-Soviet Operational Plans of the Japanese Army in Manchuria]. 1953.
7. Hayashi Saburō. "Kyokutō soryō ni kanseru senryakuteki kansatsu" [Strategic Observations Concerning the Soviet Far Eastern Territory]. 1952.
8. Imaoka Yutaka. "Chōkohō jiken" [The Changkufeng Incident]. 1961.
9. ———. "Kanchatsu-tō jiken" [The Kanchatzu Island Incident]. 1961.
10. ———. "Kantokuen ni tsuite" [About the Kwantung Army Special Maneuvers]. 1962.
11. ———. "Man-So-Mō kokkyō funsō ni tsuite no gaikan" [Survey of Manchurian-Soviet-Mongolian Border Disputes]. 1961.
12. ———. "Nihon no tai-So handan" [Japanese Estimates of the Soviets]. 1962.
13. ———. "Nomonhan jiken" [The Nomonhan Incident]. 1962.
14. ———. "Shūsendoki no Kantōgun" [The Kwantung Army at War's End]. 1962.
15. ———. "Zoruge jiken ni tsuite" [About the Sorge Affair]. 1961.
16. Inaba Masao, Col. "Nomonhan jiken ni kansuru jakkan no kōsatsu" [Some Considerations on the Nomonhan Incident]. 6 Nov. 1939.
17. Inada Masazumi, Col. "Nomonhan jiken ni kansuru jakkan no kōsatsu" [Some Considerations on the Nomonhan Incident]. 17 Oct. 1939. Prepared for AGS Deputy Chief Sawada.

18. Irie Tachio. "Sensha shōtaichō to-shite no taiken: kyōkun shokan" [My Experiences as a Tank Platoon Leader: Lessons and Impressions]. Ca. 1961.

19. Ishida Kiyoshi. "Uyoku seisaku tenkan go ni okeru Mōko Jinmin Kyōwakoku kokumin keizai" [The Mongolian People's Republic's National Economy After the Switch-to-the-Right Policy]. 1962.

20. Ishiwari Heizō. "Kokkyō funsō oyobi sakusen no gaiyō: Nomonhan sen no kyōkun" [Border Disputes and Outline of Operations: Lessons of the Nomonhan Fighting]. 1953.

21. Itagaki Tōru. "Kokuryūkō no toka sakusen" [Amur River-Crossing Operations]. 1953.

22. Kanaizuka Yūkichi, Major. "Kanaizuka nikki (III/64i)" [Kanaizuka's Journal, 3rd Battalion, 64th Infantry Regiment]. 20 July–30 Aug. 1939.

23. Kobayashi, Lt. Col. "Tai-sensha yōhō (senpō) no hensen susei" [Tendency Toward Changes in Antitank Usage (Tactics)], in *Nisso senshi junbi shiryō* [Preliminary Sources for Japanese-Soviet Military History]. Ca. 1940.

24. Kobayashi Kōichi, Maj. Gen. "Nikki" [Diary]. From June 1939.

25. Komatsubara Michitarō, Lt. Gen. "Nikki" [Diary]. From May 1939.

26. Konuma Haruo, Lt. Col. "Konuma Memo." Nov. 1939–Jan. 1940.

27. Kōtani Etsuo. "Manshū ni okeru jōhō kinmu: Nomonhan jiken oyobi sono hanseiki" [Intelligence Activities in Manchuria: The Nomonhan Incident and the Period of Self-Reflection]. 1953.

28. ———. "Rekishi to tomo ni ayunda watakushi no zenhansen: Shōwa 7-nen sue kara Shōwa 20-nen made" [The First Half of My Life Paralleled History: From Late 1932 to 1945]. 1963.

29. Kubo Teizō. "Kokkyō chikujō" [Border Fortifications]. 1952.

30. Kurono Taeru, Lt. Col., GSDF. "Yūkeiteki sentōryoku (chū to ge karyoku) jō kara mita: Nomonhan jiken no ichi kyōsatsu" [A Study of the Nomonhan Incident from the Standpoint of Material Combat Strength (Medium and Light Firepower)], in *Kanbū Gakkō Kiji* [GSDF Command and General Staff College Journal], vol. 27 (1979), no. 308 (May): 67-77; no. 309 (June): 41-51; no. 310 (July): 37-53.

31. Matsumura Tomokatsu. "Ura kara mita Soren" [The USSR Seen from the Rear]. Kamakura, 1958. Preface by Gen. Yamada Otozō.

32. Matsuzaki Yō, ed. "Rekishijō yori mitaru seihoku rūto" [The Northwestern Routes Viewed Historically]. 1962.

33. Miyano Masatoshi, "Nomonhan no yakan sentō oyobi hakuhei" [Night Fighting and Hand-to-Hand Combat at Nomonhan]. 1953.

34. Mizumachi Katsuki. "Manshū ni okeru Nihongun to tai-So sakusen keikaku" [The Japanese Army in Manchuria and Anti-Soviet Operational Plans]. 1952.

35. Moriai Kojō. "Kantōgun tokushu jōhō butai ni kansuru kiroku" [Record of Kwantung Army Special Intelligence Units]. Ca. 1961.

36. Murakami Keisaku, Lt. Gen. "Nomonhan jiken ni kansuru kansatsu" [Observations Concerning the Nomonhan Incident]. 10 Oct. 1939.

37. Murasawa Kazuo. "Manshū ni okeru kakushu chikei no sakusen: Nomonhan jiken ni okeru: Haruhagawa toka sakusen" [Operations in Various Terrains in Manchuria: The Halha River-Crossing Operation During the Nomonhan Incident]. Ca. 1953.

38. Nakayama Sadatake. "Sanchi oyobi shinrin" [(Operations in) Mountains and Forests]. 1953.

39. Nihon Kunshō Kishō Kyōkai [Japan Military Decorations and Medals Soci-

ety]. "Rikugun shōkan meibo" [A Directory of Army Generals], ed. Fujinuma Kiyosuke. 1971.

Nomonhan. See Nomonhan-kai [40].

40. Nomonhan-kai [Nomonhan Society]. *Nomonhan,* ed. Uchikura Fujitsugu. 11 vols. + photo album, 1968-75.

41. Onozuka Kichihei. "Senbotsusha kakutai chōsahyō: hohei dai-71 rentai" [Research Tables of War Dead, All Units: 71st Infantry Regiment]. N.d.

42. Sakakibara Shigeo, Sgt. "Nomonhan-zakura: kaisōroku" [Nomonhan Cherry Blossoms: Recollections]. Notes of a squad leader, 1st Battery, 1st Heavy Field Artillery Regiment, 1939.

43. Satō Chōnoshin, 2nd Lt. "So-Man kokkyō Nomonhan jihen: jinchū nisshi" [Soviet-Manchurian Border Nomonhan Incident: Field Diary]. June-July 1939. Diary of an officer of the 7th Company, 71st Infantry Regiment.

44. "Senjō shinri chōsa ni motozuku shoken" [Thoughts Based on Battlefield-Psychology Investigations]. 1939. Part of "Konuma Memo."

45. Shimanuki Takeharu, Major. "Kōbakuchi" [(Operations in) Vast Wastelands]. 1953.

46. ———. "Sakusen yoheijō yori mitaru Nomonhan jiken no kyōkun" [Lessons Learned from the Nomonhan Incident with Respect to Operational Handling of Troops]. 30 Sept. 1939.

47. Shinagawa Yoshinobu. "Manshū ni okeru kikōhei no shiteki kansatsu" [A Historical Study of Tank Troops in Manchuria]. 1952.

48. Shishikura Jurō. "Nihongun no tai-So handan" [Japanese Army Estimates of the Soviets]. 1961.

49. Sumi Shin'ichirō. "Daitōa sensō to ware" [The Great East Asia War and I]. 1971.

50. ———. "Ikuta fujin no tegami ni kotau" [In Reply to Mrs. Ikuta's Letter]. 11 Jan. 1964, in response to a letter dated 31 Dec. 1963. Mimeo.

51. Tagami Shirō. "Nomonhan jiken: dai-issen daitaichō no shuki kara" [The Nomonhan Incident: From the Notes of a Front-Line Battalion Commander], in veterans' bulletin *Gōyū,* Sept. 1979. The title refers to Maj. Kanaizuka Yūkichi.

52. Tanaka Kengorō. "Dai-19 shidan no mitsurin sanchi sakusen" [19th Division Operations in Mountains and Dense Forests]. 1953.

53. ———. "Dai-20 gun no shunnan sakubatsuchi o tsūka shite okonau sentō kunren" [Combat Training Carried Out by the 20th Army in Steep and Difficult Complicated Areas]. 1953.

54. ———. "Manshū ni okeru kakushu chikei no sakusen: Kantokuen ni tomonau 20A no hensei to sakusen kōsō" [Operations in Various Terrains in Manchuria: The Organization of the 20th Army and Its Operational Thinking Involved in the Kwantung Army Special Maneuvers]. Ca. 1953.

55. Terada Masao, Col. "Nomonhan jiken ni kansuru shoken" [Views on the Nomonhan Incident]. Mid-Oct. 1939. Prepared for AGS Deputy Chief Sawada.

56. Ugaki Matsushirō and Shinagawa Yoshinobu. "Manshū ni okeru yōhei" [Utilization of Forces in Manchuria]. 1953.

57. Yamaoka Shigemitsu. "Manshū ni okeru kōshahōhei no shiteki kansatsu" [Historical Observations on Antiaircraft Troops in Manchuria]. 1952.

58. Yamashita Tomoyuki, Lt. Gen. "Yamashita shisetsudan hōkoku" [The Yamashita Inspection Team's Report]. 1 July 1941. Mimeo.

59. Yano Mitsuji, Major. "Mōko jijō ni kansuru kōwa yōshi" [Gist of Lectures Concerning Mongolia]. 21 Feb. 1942. Mimeo; Hq. Okabe Unit.

60. ———. "Nai-Gai-Mō kyōkai ni kansuru kōsatsu" [Study Concerning the Inner and Outer Mongolian Borders]. 10 Sept. 1940. Mimeo; Hq. Inner Mongolia Garrison Army.

61. ———. "Shiryō" [Data]. Ca. 1938. Handwritten; Hq. Okabe Unit.

62. ———. "Soto-Mōkō jijō" [Conditions in Outer Mongolia]. Prepared 21 Feb. 1942, Hailar; issued Aug. 1943.

63. Yoneimoto, 2nd Lt. K. Portfolio of 28 combat sketches. 1940. The artist, a platoon leader in the 5th Company, 2nd Battalion, 71st Infantry Regiment, prepared these sketches while recovering from wounds in the hospital for use in a book on Nomonhan proposed by Capt. Onozuka Kichihei. The latter, however, destroyed both his manuscript and Yoneimoto's original artwork at war's end. In 1961 Onozuka provided the present author with photographic copies of the original sketches and authorized their reproduction in this book.

C. Official and Semiofficial Publications

64. Bōeichō Rikujō Jieitai [Japan Defense Agency, Ground Self-Defense Forces (GSDF)]. Bakuryobu Dai-5 Buchō [General Staff, 5th Bureau Chief], ed. *Nomonhan jiken no hōheisen* [Artillery Combat in the Nomonhan Incident]. 1965.

65. ———. Dai-28 Futsūka Rentai [28th (GSDF) Infantry Regiment]. *Hohei dai-28 rentai gaishi* [Outline History of the 28th Infantry Regiment]. 1970.

66. ———. Eisei Gakkō [GSDF Medical School]. *Daitōa sensō rikugun eiseishi* [Great East Asia War: Army Medical History]. Vols. 1, 7-9. Ca. 1971.

67. ———. ———. *Eisei senshi: Chōkohō jiken* [Medical Military History: The Changkufeng Incident]. 1963.

68. ———. ———. *Eisei senshi: Nomonhan jiken* [Medical Military History: The Nomonhan Incident]. 1963.

69. ———. Kanbu Gakkō [GSDF Command and General Staff College]. *Nomonhan jiken shi: Dai-23 Shidan no sentō* [Nomonhan Incident History: Combat of the 23rd Division], ed. Shingō Yoshio. 1977 (revised).

70. ———. ———. *Nomonhan jiken shi: Dai-23 Shidan no sentō: fuzu fuhyō* [Nomonhan Incident History: Combat of the 23rd Division: Attached Maps and Tables]. N.d.

71. ———. ———. *Nomonhan senshi fuzu* [Military History of Nomonhan: Attached Maps]. 1960.

72. ———. Kenkyū shiryō [Research Materials]. *Mongorugawa kara mita Nomonhan jiken* [The Nomonhan Incident Viewed from the Mongolian Side]. 1978.

73. ———. *Sorengawa shiryō kara mita Nomonhan jiken: Soren no kokkyō funsō taisho* [The Nomonhan Incident Viewed from the Soviet Side: Soviet Handling of the Border Dispute]. 1978.

74. Gaimushō [Foreign Ministry]. Chōsabu [Research Bureau]. *Shōwa 13-nendo shitsumu hōkoku* [Annual Official Report, 1938]. Dec. 1938.

75. ———. ———. *Shōwa 14-nendo shitsumu hōkoku* [Annual Official Report, 1939]. Dec. 1939.

76. ———. Dai-3 Ka [3rd Section]. *Man-So tōbu kokkyō shisatsu hōkokusho* [Report of Inspection of the Manchurian-Soviet Eastern Borders]. Sept. 1938.

77. ———. Jōhōbu [Intelligence Bureau]. *Manshūkoku oyobi Shina ni okeru shinbun* [The Press in Manchukuo and China]. N.d.

78. ———. ———. *Jihenzen ni okeru kō-Nichi shiryō no kaisetsu* [Comments on Anti-Japanese Materials Prior to the China Incident]. N.d.

79. ———. ———. *Shōwa 12-nendo shitsumu hōkoku* [Annual Official Report, 1937]. Dec. 1937.

80. ———. ———. *Shōwa 13-nendo shitsumu hōkoku* [Annual Official Report, 1938]. Dec. 1938.

81. ———. Ōakyoku Dai-ikka [Euro-Asiatic Bureau, 1st Section]. *Shōwa 13-nendo shitsumu hōkoku* [Annual Official Report, 1938]. Dec. 1938.

82. ———. ———. *Shōwa 14-nendo shitsumu hōkoku* [Annual Official Report, 1939]. Dec. 1939. See in particular "Furyo kōkan ni kansuru kōshō keii" [Details of Negotiations Concerning Prisoner Exchange].

83. ———. Suisu Jōhō [Intelligence from Switzerland]. "Soren no tai-Nichisen sanka setsu ni kansuru tekigawa hōdō" [Enemy Information Concerning Rumors of Soviet Participation in the War Against Japan]. Telegrams No. 228 (6 July 1945) and No. 268 (7 Aug. 1945), from Minister Kase (Berne) to Foreign Minister Tōgō.

84. ———. Tōakyoku Dai-3 Ka [East Asia Bureau, 3rd Section]. *Chōkohō jiken to Manshūkoku* [The Changkufeng Incident and Manchukuo]. Sept. 1938.

85. Kaigun Gunreibu [Naval General Staff]. *Gikai* [The Diet]. Addresses and announcements, Jan. 1936-July 1939.

86. ———. *Kihon kokusaku kankei tsuzuri* [Files Concerning Fundamental National Policies]. 3 vols. N.d.

87. ———. *Shina jihen taigai kankei: Ei* [The China Incident: Relations Vis-à-Vis Foreign Countries: England]. Aug. 1937.

88. ———. *Shōwa 12-nen Kanchatsu jiken kankei tsuzuri* [Files Concerning the Kanchatzu Incident of 1937]. N.d.

89. ———. Dai-3 Bu [3rd Bureau]. *Soren no gunji ni tsuite no hōkoku* [Report on Military Affairs of the USSR]. No. 9, July 1945.

90. Keisatsuchō Keibibu [Police Agency Guard Bureau]. *Zoruge o chūshin to suru kokusai chōhōdan jiken* [The International Spy Ring Centering on Sorge]. June 1957.

91. Kōain Mōkyō Renrakubu [Asia Development Board, Mongolia Liaison Bureau]. *Sekishoku Mōko no zenbō* [The Complete Picture of Red Mongolia], trans. H. Katō. Sept. 1941. Based on *MPR*, issued in Russian by the Political Publications Section of the Central Committee, Soviet Communist Party; probably translated by the SMR Research Bureau.

92. Rikugun [Army]. Chōsengun Shireibu [Korea Army Headquarters]. *Chōkohō jiken no keii* [Particulars Concerning the Changkufeng Incident]. 30 Aug. 1938.

92A. ———. ———. *Kankei kakubutai ni oite tannin shōmen Sogun no dōsei ni kanshi chūi seraretashi no ken* [Cautions to All Units Regarding Soviet Forces' Activities on Assigned Sectors]. 24 Apr. 1945.

92B. ———. ———. Hohei Dai-19 Shidan [19th Infantry Division]. Hohei Dai-75 Rentai [75th Infantry Regiment]. *Chōkohō jiken sentō shōhō* [Changkufeng Incident Combat Report]. 1 Oct. 1938. Covers period 29 July–11 Aug. 1938.

93. ———. Daihon'ei Rikugunbu [IGHQ Army Department]. *Nomonhan jiken keika no gaiyō* [Outline of the Course of the Nomonhan Incident]. Nov. 1939.

94. ———. Gijitsu Honbu Dai-1 Bu, Dai-3 Ka [Army Technical Headquarters 1st Bureau, 3rd Section]. *Heiki kentōkai kiji: Nomonhan jiken* [Ordnance Investigation Conference Report, Nomonhan Incident]. 1939.

95. ———. Gunjin Iyaku Kenkyūkai [Military Medicine Research Group]. "Chōkohō jiken ni kansuru eisei kinmu no gaiyō oyobi sankō shoken narabini kaizen jikō ni tsuite" [Outline of Medical Activities, Opinions for Reference, and Matters Needing Improvement Concerning the Changkufeng Incident], *Gun'idan Zasshi*,

supplement (Aug. 1940), 327: 1001-2. Excerpt from a lecture by Maj. Inoue Kiyobumi.

96. ————. ————. "Nomonhan jiken ni okeru keiken yori etaru kyōkun" [Lessons of the Nomonhan Incident Learned Through Experience], *Gun'idan Zasshi*, supplement (Aug. 1940), 327: 998-1000. Excerpt from a lecture by Maj. Tsurugami Takashi.

97. ————. ————. "Shina jihen oyobi Nomonhan jiken ni okeru kikaika butai eisei kinmu ni tsuite" [Concerning Medical Activities in Mechanized Units During the China Incident and the Nomonhan Incident], *Gun'idan Zasshi*, supplement (Aug. 1940), 327: 1003-5. Excerpt from a lecture by Lt. Col. Ōta Haruhisa.

98. ————. Hohei Gakkō [Infantry School]. *Hohei sōten kaisei riyū setsumei sankō* [Reasons for the Revision of the Infantry Manual: Background References]. 1939.

99. ————. Kantōgun [The Kwantung Army]. Sanbobu [Headquarters]. Dai-1 Ka [1st (Operations) Section]. *Nomonhan jiken kimitsu sakusen nisshi* [Nomonhan Incident Secret Operations Diary], Vol. 1. Prepared by Hattori Takushirō after the Nomonhan Incident.

100. ————. ————. ————. Heibi Kenkyū Chōsa Iinchō [Armaments Research Committee Chairman]. *Kenkyū hōkoku: Nomonhan jiken* [Research Report Concerning the Nomonhan Incident]. 27 Nov. 1939.

101. ————. ————. ————. Sōmuka [General Affairs Section]. *Manshū jihen kimitsu seiryaku nisshi* [Secret Political Tactics Diary of the Manchurian Incident], 18 Sept.–31 Oct. 1931.

NOTE: The following sequence is used in itemizing available records from the subordinate elements of the Kwantung Army: First, the infantry divisions, commencing with their headquarters and then proceeding down the chain of command, through the organic infantry regiments and their battalions and companies, the organic reconnaissance regiments, and the divisional field artillery regiments. Second, attached ground units—provisional infantry, engineers, heavy artillery, and armor. Third, air force units.

102. ————. ————. Hohei Dai-7 Shidan [7th Infantry Division]. Shireikan [Division Commander]. *Sentō kōdō hōkoku* [Combat Action Report], 23 Aug.–16 Sept. 1939.

103. ————. ————. ————. Hohei Dai-26 Rentai [26th Infantry Regiment]. *Sentō shōhō* [Combat Report], 7 parts. 1939.

104. ————. ————. ————. ————. *Zaiman kinen: shashinchō* [Commemoration of Stationings in Manchuria: Photo Album], 1938-1940.

105. ————. ————. ————. ————. Dai-7 Chūtai [7th Company]. *Jinchū nisshi* [Field Diary], 20 June–31 July, 1 Aug.–11 Nov. 1939.

106. ————. ————. ————. Hohei Dai-27 Rentai [27th Infantry Regiment]. Dai-3 Daitai [3rd Battalion]. *Kōan Hokushō Shin Baruko sayokuki fukin Nomonhan Abutara fukin sentō shōhō* [Combat Report for the Lake Abutara Area and Nomonhan Area on the Left Flank of Shin Baruko in North Hsingan Province], 26 Aug.–16 Sept. 1939.

107. ————. ————. ————. Hohei Dai-28 Rentai [28th Infantry Regiment]. *Kōan Hokushō Shin Baruko sayokuki Horusutengawa sagan dokuritsu hyōkō 789 Kōchi fukin sentō shōhō* [Combat Report for the Area of Heights 780, An Isolated Heights on the Left Bank of the Holsten River in North Hsingan Province on the Left Flank at Shin Baruko], 23-29 Aug. 1939.

108. ——. ——. ——. *Kōdo shōhō* [Combat Action Report]. 31 July–22 Aug. 1939.

109. ——. ——. ——. *Nomonhan fukin sentō shōhō* [Combat Report for the Nomonhan Area], 30 Aug.–16 Sept. 1939.

110. ——. ——. ——. Dai-2 Daitai [2nd Battalion]. *Kōan Hokushō Shin Baruko sayokuki fukin Nomonhan fukin sentō shōhō* [Combat Report for the Nomonhan Area and the Area on the Left Flank at Shin Baruko in North Hsingan Province], 20 June–16. Sept. 1939.

111. ——. ——. ——. Yahōhei Dai-7 Rentai [7th Field Artillery Regiment]. Dai-1 Daitai [1st Battalion]. *Horusutengawa sagan 780 Kōchi fukin sentō shōhō* [Combat Report for the Heights 780 Area on the Left Bank of the Holsten River], 23-29 Aug. 1939.

112. ——. ——. Hohei Dai-23 Shidan [23rd Infantry Division]. Shidanchō [Division Commander]. *Kokkyō jiken ni kansuru tokubetsu hōkoku* [Special Report Concerning a Border Affray], 26 Dec. 1938.

113. ——. ——. ——. Shireibu [Headquarters]. *Bukō bidan* [Instances of Glorious Military Exploits]. Briefing papers prepared for presentation to the Imperial Aide, 16 Jan. 1940.

114. ——. ——. ——. Hohei Dai-64 Rentai [64th Infantry Regiment]. *Sentō shōhō: dai-ichiji Nomonhan jiken* [Combat Report: First-Phase Nomonhan Incident]. 1939.

115. ——. ——. ——. ——. *Dai-niji Nomonhan jiken jinchū nisshi an* [Draft Field Diary for Second-Phase Nomonhan Incident], 30 Aug.–6 Oct. 1939.

116. ——. ——. ——. Akai Butai Honbu [Akai Unit (1st Battalion) Headquarters]. *Gotō shitai jinchū nisshi: Nomonhan jiken jinchū nisshi shū: rokugatsu no bun* [Gotō Detachment Field Diary: Collected Field Diaries, Nomonhan Incident: June 1939].

117. ——. ——. ——. Kanaizuka Butai Honbu [Kanaizuka Unit (3rd Battalion) Headquarters]. *Nomonhan Jiken jinchū nisshi an* [Draft Field Diary, Nomonhan Incident]. Mid-August 1939.

118. ——. ——. ——. Hohei Dai-71 Rentai [71st Infantry Regiment]. *Nomonhan sentō nisshi* [Nomonhan Combat Diary], 26-31 Aug. 1939.

119. ——. ——. ——. ——. *Sentō shōhō: bassui* [Extract from Combat Report], 3 July–30 Aug. 1939.

120. ——. ——. ——. Hohei Dai-72 Rentai [72nd Infantry Regiment]. *Nomonhan jiken kinen* [In Commemoration of the Nomonhan Incident]. Album, n.d. Issued by Nakano Butai [Nakano (former Sakai) Unit].

121. ——. ——. ——. ——. *Sentō shōhō: bassui* [Extract from Combat Report]. 1939.

122. ——. ——. ——. Dai-Nijūsanshi Sōsakutai [23rd Division Reconnaissance Regiment]. *Nomonhan jiken ni okeru Azuma sōsakutai no sentō keika gaiyō* [Outline of Combat Developments Involving the Azuma Reconnaissance Regiment During the First-Phase Nomonhan Incident]. 1939.

123. ——. ——. ——. ——. *Sentō shōhō* [Combat Report]. For the second phase of the Nomonhan Incident.

124. ——. ——. ——. Yahōhei Dai-13 Rentai [13th Field Artillery Regiment]. Dai-1 Daitai [1st Battalion]. *Sentō shōhō* [Combat Report]. 1939.

125. ——. ——. ——. ——. Dai-3 Daitai [3rd Battalion]. *Jinchū nisshi dai-3 gō to dai-4 gō* [Field Diaries No. 3-4]. 1 Aug.–6 Sept., 22 Sept.–28 Oct. 1939.

126. ———. ———. Hasebe Shitai [Hasebe Detachment]. Dai-1 Daitai [1st (Sugitani) Battalion]. Dai-8 Kokkyō Shubitai Hensei [Formed from the 8th Border Garrison Unit]. *Sentō shōhō* [Combat Report]. 1939.

127. ———. ———. Kohei Dai-1 Rentai [1st Engineer Regiment]. *Dai-niji Nomonhan jiken 1079 Kōchi sentō shōhō* [Combat Report for Heights 1079 During the Second-Phase Nomonhan Incident], 8-12 Sept. 1939.

128. ———. ———. Kōkūheidan [Air Corps]. Dai-1 Hikō Shūdan [1st Air Division]. Shireibu [Headquarters]. *Kōkūheidan shireibu chōsei: Nomonhan jiken kōkū kankei chōsa iinkai gyōmu jisshi hōkoku bassui: sono 1, kyōiku rensei ni kansuru jikō* [Extract from Air Force Research Committee Reports Concerning the Nomonhan Incident as Prepared by Air Corps Headquarters: Part 1, Items Involving Education and Training]. 8 March 1940. Also see supplement, designated HOI.

129. ———. ———. ———. ———. *Kōkūheidan shireibu chōsei: Nomonhan jiken teki kōkū butai no jōkyō: sono 2* [The Nomonhan Incident and the Situation of Enemy Air Units: Part 2, as Prepared by Air Corps Headquarters]. 29 Feb. 1940.

130. ———. ———. ———. ———. Dai-9 Kōkū Chiku [9th Air District]. Shireibu [Headquarters]. *Sentō shōhō to jinchū nisshi* [Combat Report and Field Diary]. 1939.

131. ———. ———. Yasen Jūhōhei Dai-1 Rentai [1st Heavy Field Artillery Regiment]. *Jinchū nisshi* [Field Diary]. 1939.

132. ———. ———. Yasuoka Shitai [Yasuoka Detachment]. Dai-1 Senshadan [1st Tank Corps]. *Kōdō yōryō: kimitsu sakusen nisshi shiryō* [Action Essentials: Sources for the Secret Operations Diary]. 1-18 July 1939. Prepared by Maj. Noguchi Kamenosuke, July 1939.

133. ———. ———. ———. *Sentō yōkō an: bassui* [Draft Combat Outline (Excerpts)]. 1939.

134. ———. ———. ———. Sensha Dai-4 Rentai [4th Tank Regiment]. *Dai-niji Nomonhan jiken Sen-4 sentō shōhō* [Combat Report of the 4th Tank Regiment During the Second-Phase Nomonhan Incident]. June-July 1939.

135. ———. ———. ———. ———. *Dai-niji Nomonhan jiken shutsudō kinen shashinchō 1939* [Second-Phase Nomonhan Incident Participation Commemorative Photo Album, 1939]. 1939. Issued by Tamada Butai [Tamada Unit].

136. ———. Kyōto Shidan [Kyōto Division]. Shireibu [Headquarters]. *Sogun binran* [Manual on Soviet Forces]. 1941.

137. ———. Nomonhan Jiken Kenkyū Iinkai Dai-1 Kenkyū Iinkai [Nomonhan Incident Research Committee, 1st Research Subcommittee]. *Nomonhan jiken kenkyū hōkoku* [Nomonhan Incident Research Report]. 10 Jan. 1940.

138. ———. Rikugunshō [War Ministry]. *Sentō kōyō* [Combat Manual]. Tokyo, 1932; reprint ed., Ikeda Shobō, 1977.

139. ———. Sanbō Honbu [General Staff (AGS) Headquarters]. *Chōkohō jiken shi sōan: Shina jihen shi tokugō* [Draft History of the Changkufeng Incident: Special Edition of the History of the China Incident]. 2 vols. Oct. 1939.

140. ———. ———. *Chōkohō jiken shi: Shina jihen shi tokugō dai-ikkan* [The Changkufeng Incident: History of the China Incident, Special Edition, Vol. 1]. 1943.

141. ———. ———. Dai-5 Ka [5th Section]. *Nomonhan fukin kokkyō funsō jōhō hōkoku* [Nomonhan Area Border Incident Intelligence Records]. Daily intelligence reports, June-July 1939.

142. ———. ———. ———. *Sanbōchō kaidō sekijō ni okeru dai-5 kachō kōen yōshi* [Gist of the Presentation by the [AGS] 5th Section Chief at the Chiefs of Staff Conference]. 10 Oct. 1939.

143. ———. ———. Kenkyūhan [Research Section]. *Nomonhan jiken kimitsu nisshi* [Nomonhan Incident Secret Diary]. 1939.

144. ———. Shikan Gakkōchō [Commandant, Military Academy]. *Ōyō senjutsu no sankō* [A Casebook of Tactical Applications]. Dec. 1938.

NOTE: The following two items, although primary and in the Japanese language, rightly belong within the Manchukuo Government category.

145. Manshūkoku [Manchukuo]. Gunjishō Gunji Komondan [Military Affairs Ministry, Board of Consultants]. *Manshū kyōsanhi no kenkyū* [A Study of the Communist Bandits in Manchuria]. 1936.

146. ———. Manshū Teikoku Daihyobu [Imperial Manchukuo Delegation]. Man-Mō genchi kokkyō kakutei konsei iinkai [Manchukuo-Mongolia Local Border Demarcation Mixed Commission]. *Man-Mō kokkyō kakutei kinen shashinchō* [Commemorative Photo Album of Manchukuo-Mongolia Border Demarcation], 1941-42. Dec. 1942.

III. JAPANESE SOURCES, SECONDARY

NOTE: The abbreviations that follow have been used in the notes to refer to certain series:

BBSS, SS = Bōeichō Bōeikenshūsho Senshi Shitsu, *Senshi sōsho* [179]-[183]
GSS = *Gendai shi shiryō* [202]-[206]
NGS = *Nihon gaikō shi* [431]-[434]
SSNT = *Shōwa shi no tennō* [535]
TSM = *Taiheiyō sensō e no michi* [549]

147. *Aa! shōnen kōkūhei* [Ah, Young Airmen]. Tokyo: Hara Shobō, 1967.

148. "Aa! Tsuji taii" [Ah, Captain Tsuji], *Kaikōsha Kiji*, Aug. 1941, pp. 35-39.

149. Abe Genki. *Shōwa dōran no shinsō* [The Truth About the Shōwa Era Upheavals]. Tokyo: Hara Shobō, 1977.

150. Akaishizawa Kunihiko. *Chōkohō* [Changkufeng]. Tokyo: Kōa Shobō, 1941.

151. Akimoto Minoru. *Nihon no sentōki: rikugun hen* [Japanese Fighters: Army Volume]. Tokyo: Shuppan Kyōdōsha, 1961.

152. Akisada Tsuruzō. *Tōjō Hideki: sono shōgai to Nihon rikugun kōbō hishi* [Tōjō Hideki: His Life and a Secret History of the Rise and Fall of the Japanese Army]. Tokyo: Keizai Ōraisha, 1968.

153. Akiyama Hiroshi. "Saikin sen wa junbi sarete ita!" [Germ Warfare Was Prepared!], *Bungei Shunjū*, Aug. 1955, pp. 250-60.

154. ———. *Tokushu butai nanahyaku-sanjūichi* [Special Unit 731]. Tokyo: San'ichi Shobō, 1956.

155. Andō Hikotarō. *Mantetsu: Nihon teikokushugi to Chūgoku* [The South Manchuria Railway Co.: Japanese Imperialism and China]. Tokyo: Ochanomizu Shobō, 1965.

156. Andō Satoru et al. *Manshūkoku taikan* [Manchukuo Survey]. Tokyo: Shinkōsha, 1932.

157. Aoe Shunjirō. *Ishiwara Kanji*. Tokyo: Yomiuri Shinbunsha, 1973.

158. Aoki Tokuzō. *Taiheiyō sensō zenshi* [The Complete History of the Period Before the Pacific War]. Tokyo: Gakujutsu Bunken Fukyūkai, 1950-52. 6 vols.

159. Aoyama Saburō. "Kōhei chūtaichō no omoide" [Recollections of an Engineer Company Commander], *Shūshin*, Apr. 1967, pp. 90-95.

160. Araki Gorō. "Uri ni dasareta Manshūkoku" [Manchukuo for Sale], *Bungei Shunjū*, Apr. 1964, pp. 262-70.

161. Araki Sadao. "Nihon rikugun kōbō no nijūyonen" [20-some Years of the Rise and Fall of the Japanese Army], *Maru*, Oct. 1958, pp. 34-39.

162. *Araki Sadao: fūun sanjūnen* [Araki Sadao: 30 Years of Storm and Stress], ed. Aritake Shūji. Tokyo: Fuyō Shobō, 1975.

163. "Are kara nijūgonen Nomonhan jiken no nazo: hishi" [The Mystery of the Nomonhan Incident, 25 Years Later: Secret History], *Shūkan Bunshun*, 22 June 1964, pp. 32-36.

164. Arima Yoriyasu. *Shichijūnen no kaisō* [Reminiscences of 70 Years]. Tokyo: Sōgensha, 1974.

165. Arisue Seizō. *Arisue Seizō kaikoroku* [The Memoirs of Arisue Seizō]. Tokyo: Fuyō Shobō, 1974.

166. ———. *Seiji to gunji to jinji: sanbō honbu dai-ni buchō no shuki* [Politics, Military Affairs, and Personnel Affairs: Notes of the AGS 2nd Bureau Chief]. Tokyo: Fuyō Shobō, 1982.

167. Arita Hachirō. *Baka Hachi to hito wa yu* [They Call Me Foolish Hachirō]. Tokyo: Kōwadō, 1974.

168. ———. *Hito no me no chiri o miru* [Seeing Dust in the Eyes of People]. Tokyo: Kōdansha, 1948.

169. ———. "Sensō e no michi o ayunda Nihon gaikō" [Japanese Diplomacy's Path to War], *Chisei*, Special Issue 3, Dec. 1956, pp. 65-70.

170. Aritake Shūji. *Naikaku seido shichijūnen shi* [20 Years' History of the Cabinet System]. Tokyo, 1953.

171. ———. *Shōwa no saishō* [Prime Ministers of the Shōwa Era]. Tokyo: Asahi Shinbunsha, 1967.

172. Ashida Hitoshi. *Dai-niji sekai taisen gaikō shi* [Diplomatic History of World War II]. Tokyo: Jiji Tsūshinsha, 1960.

173. Ashizawa Noriyuki. *Aru sakusen sanbō no higeki* [The Tragedy of a Certain Operations Staff Officer]. Tokyo: Fuyō Shobō, 1975.

174. Awaya Kentarō. *Manshū jihen to ni-ni-roku* [The Manchurian Incident and 2-26]. Tokyo: Heibonsha, 1975. Vol. 2 of *Dokyumento Shōwa shi*.

175. Ayukawa Gisuke. "Manshū keizai shihai no 'kii pointo'" [Key Points in the Control of the Manchurian Economy], *Chisei*, Supplement 5, Dec. 1956, pp. 188-200.

176. Baba Tsunego. *Jidai to jinbutsu* [Eras and Personages]. Tokyo: Keizai Shinpōsha, 1940.

177. Banba Nobuya. *Manshū jihen e no michi* [The Road to the Manchurian Incident]. Tokyo: Chūō Kōronsha, 1972.

178. Bimba. *Soto-Mōko dasshutsuki: Binba taii no shuki* [Escape from Outer Mongolia: Captain Bimba's Notes]. Osaka: Asahi Shinbunsha, 1939.

179. Bōeichō Bōeikenshūsho Senshi Shitsu (BBSS) [Defense Agency, Institute for Defense Studies, Office of Military History]. *Senshi sōsho* [Military History Series]. Tokyo: Asagumo Shinbunsha, 1967-80. 102 vols. Vols. 8, 20, 35, 59, 63, 66, 67, 75, 81, 82: *Daihon'ei rikugunbu* (1-10) [IGHQ Army Department] (1967-75).

180. ———. Vols. 27, 73: *Kantōgun* (1-2) [The Kwantung Army], (1) *Tai-So senbi: Nomonhan jiken* [Military Preparations Against the Soviets: The Nomonhan Incident] (1969); (2) *Kantokuen: shūsendoki no tai-So sen* [Kwan-

tung Army Special Maneuvers; and Battles Against the Soviets at the End of the War] (1974).

181. ———. ———. Vol. 53: *Manshū hōmen rikugun kōkū sakusen* [Manchurian Area Army Air Operations] (1972).

182. ———. ———. Vols. 52, 78; *Rikugun kōkū no gunbi to unyō* (1-2) [Armament and Employment of the Army Air Force], (1) to the Beginning of 1938 (1971); (2) to the First Half of 1942 (1974).

183. ———. ———. Vol. 87: *Rikugun kōkūheiki no kaihatsu seisan hokyū* [The Development, Production, and Supply of Army Air Ordnance] (1975).

184. Borojeikin, A. [1st Lt. Vorozheikin]. *Nomonhan kūsenki: Soren kūsho no kaisō* [Record of the Air Fighting at Nomonhan: Reminiscences of a Soviet Air Force General], trans. K. Hayashi and T. Ōta. Tokyo: Kōbundō, 1964. (Translation based on the Russian 1961 edition.)

184A. *Chichibunomiya Yasuhito shinnō* [Prince Chichibu Yasuhito], ed. Ashizawa Noriyuki. Tokyo: Chichibunomiya o Shinobukai, 1975.

185. Choibarusan [Choibalsan] et al. *Mongoru kakumei shi* [The History of the Mongolian Revolution], trans. K. Tanaka. Tokyo: Miraisha, 1971.

186. *Dai-niji taisen sekai no sentōki* [Fighters of World War II], ed. *Kōkū Jōhō* Magazine. Tokyo: Kantōsha, 1963.

187. *Dokyumento: jiketsu to gyokusai* [Documents: Suicide and Death with Honor], ed. Yasuda Takeshi and Fukushima Jurō. Tokyo: Sōshisha, 1984.

188. *Dokyumento Shōwa shi* [Documentary History of the Shōwa Era Series]. Tokyo: Heibonsha, 1975. 5 vols.

189. Endō Saburō. *Nitchū jūgonen sensō to watakushi* [The 15-year Sino-Japanese Conflict and I]. Tokyo: Nitchū Shorin, 1974.

190. Fujiwara Akira. *Gunji shi* [Military History]. Tokyo: Keizai Shinpōsha, 1961.

191. Fukai Eigo. *Sūmitsuin jūyōgiji oboegaki* [Memoranda of Important Proceedings of the Privy Council]. Tokyo: Iwanami Shoten, 1953.

192. *Gaimō sekigun no zenbō* [The Full Aspect of the Outer Mongolian Red Army]. Tokyo: Zenrin Kyōkai, 1938.

193. Gaimushō. *Daitōa sensō shūsen ni kansuru shiryō* [Source Materials Pertaining to the Termination of the Great East Asia War] (1945).

194. ———. *Nihon gaikō bunsho: Manshū jihen* [Documents on Japanese Foreign Policy: The Manchurian Incident], vols. 1-3 (1977-78).

195. ———. *Nihon gaikō hyakunen shōshi* [A Short History of 100 Years of Japan's Foreign Policy] (1951).

196. ———. *Nihon gaikō nenpyō narabini shuyō bunsho* [Chronological Tables and Principal Documents of Japanese Diplomacy]. Tokyo: Hara Shobō, 1965-66. 2 vols.

197. ———. *Shūsen shiroku* [Historical Records of the End of the War] (1952).

198. ———. Chōsabu Dai-3 Ka [Research Bureau, 3rd Section]. "Soto-Mōko ni kansuru hōbun shiryō" [Japanese-language Materials Concerning Outer Mongolia], *Roshia Geppo*, 73 (Feb. 1940), pp. 174-87.

199. ———. Hyakunenshi Hensan Iinkai [Centennial History Editorial Committee]. *Gaimushō no hyakunen* [Foreign Ministry Centennial History]. Tokyo: Hara Shobō, 1969.

200. ———. Jōhōbu [Intelligence Bureau]. *Sekai no ugoki: kokusai jijō* [Movements in the World: The International Situation]. Tokyo: Ryōeidō, 1938-39. 2 vols.

201. ———. Ōakyoku Dai-ikka [Euro-Asiatic Bureau, 1st Section]. *Nisso kōshō shi* [A History of Japanese-Soviet Negotiations]. Tokyo: Gannandō, 1942.

202. *Gendai shi shiryō (GSS)* [Modern History Document Series]. Tokyo: Misuzu Shobō, 1962-80. 46 vols. Vol. 37: *Daihon'ei* [Imperial General Headquarters], ed. Inaba Masao (1967).

203. ———. Vols. 7, 11: *Manshū jihen* (1-2) [The Manchurian Incident], ed. Kobayashi Tatsuo and Shimada Toshihiko (1964-65).

204. ———. Vols. 31, 32, 33: *Mantetsu* (1-3) [The South Manchuria Railway Co.], ed. Itō Takeo, Ogiwara Kiwamu, and Fujii Masuo (1966-67).

205. ———. Vols. 8, 9, 10, 12, 13: *Nitchū sensō* (1-5) [The Sino-Japanese Conflict], ed. Shimada Toshihiko, Inaba Masao, Usui Katsumi, and Tsunoda Jun (1964-66).

206. ———. Vols. 1, 2, 3, 24: *Zoruge jiken* (1-4) [The Sorge Case], ed. Obi Toshito and Ishidō Kiyomoto (1962-71).

207. Gōda Mitsuru. *Kōkū senryoku: sono hatten no rekishi to senryaku senjutsu no hensen* [Air Battle Strength: The History of Its Development and the Changes in Strategy and Tactics]. Tokyo: Hara Shobō, 1979-80. 2 vols.

208. Gomi Kōsuke. "Gunki" [Colors], *Bungei Shunjū*, supplement, Sept. 1960, pp. 243-53.

209. Gomikawa Junpei. *Gozen kaigi* [The Imperial Conferences]. Tokyo: Bungei Shunjūsha, 1978.

210. ———. *Kyokō no taigi* [The Fabricated Great Cause]. Tokyo: Bungei Shunjūsha, 1973.

211. ———. "Manshū ni atta Aushuwitsu" [There Was an Auschwitz in Manchuria], *Shūkan Shinchō*, 20 Aug. 1956, pp. 90-93.

212. ———. *Nomonhan*. Tokyo: Bungei Shunjūsha, 1975.

213. Gorobin, N. [Golovin]. "Nisso kaisen seba: Kyokutō sekigun no heiryoku" [If Japan and the USSR Went to War: The Strength of the Far Eastern Red Army], trans. E. Nobushima, *Chūō Kōron*, 53 (Aug. 1938), pp. 144-53. (Based on *Contemporary Russia* (London), Apr., July 1938.)

214. *Gunji nenkan* [Armed Forces Yearbook], 1938-1942. Tokyo: Gunjin Kaikan Shuppanbu, 1939, 1943.

215. "Gunki kiseki no seikan" [Miraculous Survival of the Colors], *Maru*, special issue, 15 Dec. 1956, pp. 31-34.

216. "Gunki no eikō to junan no senshi" [Military History of the Glory and Ordeals of the Colors], *Maru*, special issue, 15 Dec. 1956, pp. 24-30.

217. Hamada Tsunejirō. "Sangoku dōmei ni odotta Matsuoka Yōsuke" [Matsuoka Yōsuke, Who Danced to the Tune of the Tripartite Alliance], *Jinbutsu Ōrai*, Feb. 1956, pp. 28-30.

218. Hanaya Tadashi. "Manshū jihen wa kōshite keikaku sareta" [This Is How the Manchurian Incident Was Plotted], *Chisei*, Supplement 5, Dec. 1956, pp. 40-50.

219. Hanbara Shigeki. *Manshū jihen gaikō shi* [Diplomatic History of the Manchurian Incident]. Tokyo: Kinkōdō, 1932.

220. Hara Keigo. *Dōran no Shōwa shi* [A History of the Shōwa Era in Upheaval]. Tokyo: Kōdansha, 1968.

221. Hara Tomio. "Mugen kidō ga egaita sekai no sensha hishi" [A Secret History of World Tanks Carved in Tread Marks], *Maru*, Sept. 1961 (tank issue), pp. 36-41.

222. ———. "Nihon sensha shi nijūnen no omoide" [Recollections of 20 Years of Japanese Tank History], *Maru*, Mar. 1959, pp. 28-35.

223. Hara Tomio and Takeuchi Akira. *Nihon no sensha* [Japanese Tanks]. Tokyo: Shuppan Kyōdōsha, 1961.

224. Harada Kazuo. "Nomonhan jiken sanka no omoide" [Recollections of Participating in the Nomonhan Incident], *Kaikōsha Kiji*, Aug. 1941, pp. 41-45.

225. Harada Kumao. *Saionji kō to seikyoku* [Prince Saionji and the Political Situation]. Tokyo: Iwanami Shoten, 1950-52. 8 vols.

226. Hasegawa Uichi. "Muteki Kantōgun no kaimetsu" [The Annihilation of the Invincible Kwantung Army], *Bungei Shunjū*, special issue, Dec. 1955, pp. 74-79.

227. Hashimoto Hiromitsu. "Eikō ni ikita Nihon yasenhō hachijūnen no ayumi" [The 80-Year Glorious Course of History of Japanese Field Artillery], *Maru*, June 1962, pp. 143-49.

228. Hata Hikosaburō. *Rinpō Roshia* [Russia, Neighboring Country]. Tokyo: Tōnan Shoin, 1937.

229. Hata Ikuhiko. "Dai-niji taisen kōkūshiwa (9): Nomonhan no horyo" [Tales from the Air History of World War II (No. 9): A Nomonhan Prisoner], *Kōkū Jōhō*, Sept. 1979, pp. 76-81.

230. ———. *Gun fashizumu undō shi* [The History of Military Fascist Movements]. Tokyo: Kawade Shobō Shinsha, 1962.

231. ———. "Jinbutsu gunzō: Shōwa no gunjintachi (18): Tatekawa Yoshitsugu" [Group Portraits: Shōwa Military Men (No. 18): Tatekawa Yoshitsugu], *Keizai Ōrai*, Sept. 1980, pp. 234-49.

232. ———. *Nihon rikugun sentōkitai* [Japanese Army Fighter Units]. Tokyo: Kantōsha, 1973.

233. ———. *Nitchū sensō shi* [A History of the Sino-Japanese Conflict]. Tokyo: Kawade Shobō Shinsha, 1961.

234. ———. *Taiheiyō kokusai kankei shi* [The History of International Relations in the Pacific]. Tokyo: Fukumura Shuppan, 1972.

234A. Hatakeyama Kiyoyuki (Seikō). *Rikugun Nakano gakkō: Nihon chōhō bōryaku senshi* [The Army Nakano School: The Military History of Japanese Espionage and Subversion]. Tokyo: Sankei Shinbun, 1967. 2 vols.

235. Hattori Takushirō. *Daitōa sensō zenshi* [The Complete History of the Great East Asia War]. Tokyo: Masu Shobō, 1953. 4 vols.

236. ———. "Nomonhan jiken no shinsō" [The True Story of the Nomonhan Incident], *Maru*, Dec. 1956, pp. 132-38.

237. ———. "Sentō sanretsuka no heitai" [Soldiers in Fierce Combat], *Bungei Shunjū*, special issue, Apr. 1956, pp. 34-41.

238. Hayashi Katsuya. "Kaisetsu: Nomonhan senshi" [Commentary on the Military History of Nomonhan], in Borojeikin, *Nomonhan kūsenki*.

239. Hayashi Kyūjirō. *Manshū jihen to Hōten sōryōji* [The Manchurian Incident and the Mukden Consul-General]. Tokyo: Hara Shobō, 1978.

240. ———, Katakura Tadashi, and Takeuchi Ayayoshi. "Manshū jihen boppatsu no hi: zadankai" [The Day the Manchurian Incident Broke Out: A Round-Table Discussion], insert accompanying *Taiheiyō sensō e no michi*, 2 (1962).

241. Hayashi Saburō. "Kantōgun nijūrokunen shi" [26 Years' History of the Kwantung Army], *Bungei Shunjū*, special edition, Sept. 1956, pp. 234-43.

242. ———. *Kantōgun to Kyokutō Sorengun: aru tai-So jōhōsanbō no oboegaki* [The Kwantung Army and the Soviet Far Eastern Army: Notes of a Certain Anti-Soviet Intelligence Staff Officer]. Tokyo: Fuyō Shobō, 1974.

243. ———. *Taiheiyō sensō rikusen gaishi* [An Outline History of the Ground Battles of the Pacific War]. Tokyo: Iwanami Shoten, 1959.

244. Higai Yoshiharu. *Senki Kōfu rentai* [Combat Records: The Kōfu Regiment]. Kofu: Sankei Shinbun, 1964.

244A. Higashikuni Naruhiko. *Ichi kōzoku no sensō nikki* [The War Diary of a Certain Member of the Royal Family]. Tokyo: Nihon Shūhōsha, 1959.

245. Higuchi Kiichirō. *Attsu Kisuka gunshireikan no kaisōroku* [Recollections of the Attu and Kiska Army Commander]. Tokyo: Fuyō Shobō, 1971.

246. Higuchi Kōyō. *Nomonhan jissenki* [Stories of the Real Fighting at Nomonhan]. Tokyo: Daitō Shuppan, 1940-41. 2 vols.

247. Higuchi Masanori, ed. *Shōwa jūgonen Asahi nenkan* [Asahi Yearbook for 1940]. Osaka: Osaka Asahi Shinbunsha, 1939.

247A. Hirai Tomoyoshi. "Soren shiryō kara mita Nomonhan jiken" [The Nomonhan Incident Viewed Through Soviet Sources], *Rekishi to Jinbutsu*, special issue, Jan. 1983, pp. 382-96.

248. Hiranuma Kiichirō. *Hiranuma Kiichirō kaisōroku* [The Hiranuma Kiichirō Memoirs]. Tokyo: Gakuyō Shobō, 1955.

249. Hiraoka Masaaki. *Ishiwara Kanji shiron* [Essays on Ishiwara Kanji]. Tokyo: Shirakawa Shoin, 1977.

250. *Hiroku Daitōa senshi* [Secret Records from the History of the Great East Asia War]. Tokyo: Fuji Shoen, 1953-54. 12 vols.

251. *Hiroku Dohihara Kenji* [The Secret Record of Dohihara Kenji]. Tokyo: Fuyō Shobō, 1972.

252. *Hiroku Itagaki Seishirō* [The Secret Record of Itagaki Seishirō]. Tokyo: Fuyō Shobō, 1972.

253. *Hiroku Nagata Tetsuzan* [The Secret Record of Nagata Tetsuzan]. Tokyo: Fuyō Shobō, 1972.

254. Hiyama Koshirō, ed. *Manshū jihen shashinshū* [Manchurian Incident Photographic Album]. Tokyo: Kaikōsha, 1934.

255. Honjō Shigeru. *Honjō nikki* [The Honjō Diary]. Tokyo: Hara Shobō, 1967.

256. Hora Tomio. *Dai-ichiji sekai taisen* [The First World War]. Tokyo: Jinbutsu Oraisha, 1966. Vol. 3 of *Kindai no senso*.

257. ———. *Kindai senshi no nazo* [Mysteries of Modern Military History]. Tokyo: Jinbutsu Ōraisha, 1967.

258. ———. "Nomonhan no shitō" [The Death Struggle at Nomonhan], *Jinbutsu Orai*, special issue, Aug. 1964, pp. 32-37.

259. Horiba Kazuo. *Shina jihen sensō shidō shi* [The History of War Direction of the China Incident]. Tokyo: Jinbutsu Ōraisha, 1967.

260. Horige Kazumaro. "Ikanishite tai-So senjutsu ga umaretaka" [How Were Anti-Soviet Tactics Born?], *Chisei*, Supplement 5, Dec. 1956, pp. 242-49.

261. Hoshino Naoki. *Mihatenu yume: Manshūkoku gaishi* [Boundless Dream: An Unofficial History of Manchukuo]. Tokyo: Daiyamondosha, 1963.

262. Hoshino Toshimoto. "Kikōbutai no kaiko to tenbō" [Recollections and Views of Mechanized Units], *Bōei to Keizai*, Spring 1955 (tank issue), pp. 45-70.

263. Hōson, Makishimu [Maxim]. *Sekigun sensha ryodan zenmetsu: sekigun Nomonhan sentōki* [The Annihilation of a Red Army Tank Brigade: Combat Account of the Red Army at Nomonhan], trans. K. Tomita. Tokyo: Shin Kōasha, 1941.

264. *Ichiokunin no Shōwa shi* [One Hundred Million People's History of the Shōwa Era Series]. Tokyo: Mainichi Shinbunsha, 1975-. Vol. 1: *Manshū jihen zengo: koritsu e no michi* [Around the Time of the Manchurian Incident: The Road to Isolation], ed. Takahara Tomiyasu (1975).

265. ———. *Nihon no senshi* [Japanese Military History Subseries]. Vol. 2: *Manshū jihen* [The Manchurian Incident], ed. Makino Kikuo (1979).

266. ———. ———. Supplement Vol. 1: *Nihon rikugun shi* [Japanese Army History], ed. Matsui Takaya (1979).

267. ———. Vol. 4: *Nitchū sensō kara dai-niji taisen e: 1937-1940* [From the Sino-Japanese Conflict to World War II: 1937-1940], ed. Makino Kikuo (1978).

268. ———. Vol. 2: *Sekaikyōkō kara Manshū jihen e: 1926-1932* [From the World Depression to the Manchurian Incident: 1926-1932], ed. Makino Kikuo (1978).

269. Iida Yoshiji et al. "Nihon senshatai tairiku kōya senjin hiroku" [The Secret Record of Japanese Tank Units' Actions in the Dust of the Vast Deserted Continent], *Maru*, Sept. 1961 (tank issue), pp. 150-55.

270. ———. "Nisso senshatai Nomonhan no kettō" [The Duel Between Japanese and Soviet Tank Units at Nomonhan], *Maru*, Sept. 1961 (tank issue), pp. 154-55.

271. Iizuka Kōji. *Nihon no guntai* [The Armed Forces of Japan]. Tokyo: Tokyo Daigaku Shuppanbu, 1951.

272. Ikeda Genji. *Tōa sen'unroku* [War Clouds in the Far East]. Tokyo: Kyōdō Shuppansha, 1952.

273. Ikeda Sumihisa. *Rikugun sōgi iinchō* [Funeral Director of the Army]. Tokyo: Nihon Shuppan, Kyōdō, 1953.

274. ———. "Soren tono sugatanaki tatakai" [The Formless War Against the Soviet Union], *Shūkan Yomiuri*, supplement, 8 Dec. 1956, pp. 34-39.

275. Ikeda Yū. *Manshū jihen* [The Manchurian Incident]. Tokyo: Fuji Shoen, 1954. Vol. 2 of *Hiroku Daitōa senshi*.

276. Iketani Hanjirō. "Hokuman kuzururu no hi" [The Days When North Manchuria Crumbled], *Chisei*, supplement, Aug. 1956, pp. 318-24.

277. Imai Jin. *Nihon gunyōki no zenbō* [The Complete Picture of Japanese Military Aircraft]. Tokyo: Kantōsha, 1960.

278. Imai Takeo. *Chūgoku to no tatakai* [The War with China]. Tokyo: Jinbutsu Ōraisha, 1966. Vol. 5 of *Kindai no sensō*.

279. ———. *Shōwa no bōryaku* [Subversion in the Shōwa Era]. Tokyo: Hara Shobō, 1967.

280. Imamura Hitoshi. *Imamura taishō kaisōroku* [The Memoirs of General Imamura]. Tokyo: Jiyū Ajiyasha, 1960. 4 vols.

281. ———. "Manshū hi o fuku koro" [When Manchuria Burst into Flame], *Chisei*, Supplement 5, Dec. 1956, pp. 60-71.

282. ———. *Shiki: ichigunjin rokujūnen no aikan* [A Private Record: 60 Years of the Joys and Sorrows of a Military Man]. Tokyo: Fuyō Shobō, 1970-71. 2 vols.

283. Imaoka Yutaka. "Daitōa sensō to Nihon no tai-So seisaku (3)" [The Great East Asia War and Japan's Policy Toward the Soviet Union (3)], *Kokubō*, Jan. 1974, pp. 116-29.

284. ———. *Ishiwara Kanji no higeki* [The Tragedy of Ishiwara Kanji]. Tokyo: Fuyō Shobō, 1981.

285. Imoto Kumao. *Sakusen nisshi de tsuzuru Shina jihen* [The China Incident, Based Upon an Operations Diary]. Tokyo: Fuyō Shobō, 1978.

286. Inaba Masao. "Bōryaku shizai seizō kōjō" [The Factory for Producing Materials for Subversion], *Shūkan Yomiuri*, supplement, 8 Dec. 1956, pp. 27-30.

287. ———. "Himitsu sen no baransu shiito" [The Balance Sheet of the Secret War], *Shūkan Yomiuri*, supplement, 8 Dec. 1956, pp. 187-90.

288. ———. "Nihon rikugun no tanjō to hensen" [The Japanese Army's Birth and Vicissitudes], *Maru*, Oct. 1958, pp. 81-83.

289. Inada Masazumi. "Daihon'ei no rekishi" [The History of Imperial General Headquarters], *Bōei to Keizai*, Sept. 1954, pp. 23-29.

290. ———. "Fūun no So-Man kokkyō" [Stormy Soviet-Manchurian Borders], in *Soren kakumei yonjūnen*.

291. ———. "Fūun Nomonhan jiken no higeki" [The Tragedy of the Stormy No-monhan Incident], *Jinbutsu Ōrai*, Feb. 1956, pp. 32-36.

292. ———. "Kantōgun to Chōkohō jiken" [The Kwantung Army and the Chang-kufeng Incident], *Maru*, Jan. 1958, pp. 46-51.

293. ———. "Soren Kyokutōgun to no taiketsu: Chōkohō-Nomonhan jiken no zenbō hiroku" [Confrontation with the Soviet Far Eastern Army: The Whole Se-cret Record of the Changkufeng and Nomonhan Incidents], *Chisei*, Supplement 5, Dec. 1956, pp. 276-98.

294. Inoue Kiyoshi. *Nihon no rekishi* [Japanese History]. Tokyo: Iwanami Shoten, 1967. 3 vols.

295. ———. *Ugaki Kazunari*. Tokyo: Asahi Shinbunsha, 1975.

296. Inoue Michio. "Nihon rikugun no hokotta shuryoku sensha sekkei no zenbō" [The Complete Picture of the Designing of the Japanese Army's Glorious Main-stay Tanks], *Maru*, Sept. 1961 (tank issue), pp. 30-36.

297. Irie Tokurō. "Haruhagawa Noro kōchi" [The Halha River and Noro Heights], insert accompanying *TSM* [549], vol. 4 (1963).

298. ———. *Horonbairu no arawashi: Nomonhan sen yonhyaku-ki gekitsuiki* [The Fierce Eagles of Hulun Buir: Stories of the Shooting Down of 400 Planes at Nomonhan]. Tokyo: Masu Shobō, 1941.

299. ———. "Kakusareta higeki: Nomonhan" [The Hidden Tragedy: Nomonhan], *Chūō Kōron*, Aug. 1964, pp. 195-201.

300. Ishida Bunshirō. *Shinbun kiroku shūsei: Shōwa dai-jiken shi* [Big Events During the Shōwa Era: A Compilation of Newspaper Articles]. Tokyo: Kinsei-sha, 1955.

301. Ishida Kiyoshi. *Mōko Jinmin Kyōwakoku* [The Mongolian People's Republic]. Tokyo: Chūō Kōronsha, 1941.

302. Ishii Itarō. *Gaikōkan no isshō* [A Diplomat's Life]. Tokyo: Yomiuri Shinbunsha, 1950.

303. *Ishiwara Kanji shiryō* [Ishiwara Kanji: Documents], ed. Tsunoda Jun. Tokyo: Hara Shobō, 1967-68. 2 vols.

304. *Ishiwara Kanji zenshū* [The Complete Works of Ishiwara Kanji]. Tokyo: Ishi-wara Kanji Kankōkai, 1977. 8 vols.

305. "Itō jun'i to Ishizuki sōchō no gōyū" [The Daring of Warrant Officer Itō and Master Sergeant Ishizuki], *Maru*, July 1958, pp. 75-77.

306. Itō Jusshi. "Manshū jihen boppatsu to Kokusai Renmei" [The Outbreak of the Manchurian Incident and the League of Nations], *Chisei*, Supplement 5, Dec. 1956, pp. 78-86.

307. Itō Keiichi. *Heitaitachi no rikugun shi* [Army History at the Soldiers' Level]. Tokyo: Banchō Shobō, 1969.

308. ———. *Shizukana Nomonhan* [Peaceful Nomonhan]. Tokyo: Kōdansha, 1983.

308A. Itō Masanori. *Gunbatsu kōbō shi* [The Rise and Fall of the Military Clique]. Tokyo: Bungei Shunjūsha, 1957-59. 3 vols.

309. ———. *Teikoku rikugun no saigo* [The End of the Imperial Army]. Tokyo: Bungei Shunjūsha, 1959-61. 5 vols.

310. Itō Takashi et al. *Gekidō no hanseiki* [A Half-Century of Upheaval]. Tokyo: Asahi Shinbunsha, 1975. Vol. 1 of *Kataritsugu Shōwa shi*.

311. Jōhō Yoshio, ed. *Gunmukyokuchō Mutō Akira kaisōroku* [The Memoirs of Military Affairs Bureau Chief Mutō Akira]. Tokyo: Fuyō Shobō, 1981.

312. ———. *Rikugunshō gunmukyoku* [The War Ministry Military Affairs Bureau]. Tokyo: Fuyō Shobō, 1979.

313. ————. *Saigo no sanbō sōchō Umezu Yoshijirō* [The Last Chief of the Army General Staff, Umezu Yoshijirō]. Tokyo: Fuyō Shobō, 1976.

313A. ————. *Tōjō Hideki.* Tokyo: Fuyō Shobō, 1974.

314. Jūkofu, Ge. Ka. [Georgi K. Zhukov]. *Jūkofu gensui kaisōroku: kakumei taisen heiwa* [Marshal Zhukov's Memoirs: Revolution, Great War, and Peace], trans. Y. Kiyokawa, S. Aiba, and T. Ōsawa. Tokyo: Asahi Shinbunsha, 1970.

315. Kadokawa Kōtarō. *Sanpachi shiki hoheijū: Nihon rikugun no shichijūgonen* [Type 38 Infantry Rifles: 75 Years of the Japanese Army]. Tokyo: Shirogane Shobō, 1975.

316. ————. *Teikoku rikugun kikō butai* [Imperial Army Tank Units]. Tokyo: Shirogane Shobō, 1974.

317. Kaikōsha Hōhei Enkakushi Kankōkai. *Hōhei enkaku shi* [A History of the Development of Artillery], vol. 5. Tokyo: Kaikōsha, 1971.

318. *Kaikōsha Kiji hachigatsugō tokugō: Nomonhan jiken kaiko* [*Kaikōsha Kiji* Special August Issue: Recollections of the Nomonhan Incident]. Tokyo: Kaikōsha, 1941.

318A. Kamura Mitsuo. *Manshūkoku kaimetsu hiki* [The Secret Record of the Destruction of Manchukuo]. Tokyo: Daigaku Shobō, 1960.

319. Kanafu Kizō. *Kokkyōron* [Border Treatise]. Tokyo: Nisshin Shoin, 1942.

320. Kanazaki Kiyoshi. "Manshū bō jūdai jiken towa" [What Was Big Incident "X" in Manchuria?], *Books*, Jan. 1961, pp. 12-16.

321. Kan'in Sumihito. *Watakushi no jijoden* [My Autobiography]. Tokyo: Jinbutsu Ōraisha, 1966.

322. *Kanpō* [Official Gazette]. Dai 75-kai Teikoku Gikai: Kizokuin Shūgiin [75th Imperial Diet: Upper/Lower Houses]. "Giji sokkiroku" [Transcripts of Proceedings], Feb. 1940.

323. Kase Shun'ichi. *Nihon gaikō no shuyakutachi* [The Main Players in Japanese Diplomacy]. Tokyo: Bungei Shunjūsha, 1974.

324. Kase Toshikazu. *Dai-niji sekai taisen hishi* [The Secret History of World War II]. Tokyo: Kadokawa Shoten, 1957.

325. Katakura Tadashi. "Ansatsu to kūdetā" [Assassinations and Coups d'Etat], in Itō Takashi et al., *Gekidō no hanseki.*

326. ————. *Katakura sanbō no shōgen: hanran to chin'atsu* [The Testimony of Staff Officer Katakura: Rebellion and Suppression]. Tokyo: Fuyō Shobō, 1981.

327. ————. "Nakamura Shintarō taii gyakusatsu no shinhannin" [The Real Criminal in the Slaughter of Capt. Nakamura Shintarō], *Jinbutsu Ōrai*, June 1956, pp. 28-32.

328. ————. "Nakamura taii jiken to Kantōgun" [The Captain Nakamura Case and the Kwantung Army], *Maru*, Jan. 1958, pp. 42-45.

329. ————. *Senjin zuiroku: Manshū jihen kara Taiheiyō sensō e* [Stray Notes from the Battlefield: From the Manchurian Incident to the Pacific War]. Tokyo: Keizai Ōraisha, 1972.

330. *Kataritsugu Shōwa shi* [Handing down the History of the Shōwa Era]. Tokyo: Asahi Shinbunsha, 1975-.

331. "Katō Katsutoshi jun'i no saigo" [The Last of Warrant Officer Katō Katsutoshi], *Maru*, July 1958, pp. 71-73.

332. Kawabe Torashirō. *Ichigayadai kara Ichigayadai e* [From Ichigaya Heights to Ichigaya Heights]. Tokyo: Jiji Tsūshinsha, 1962.

333. Kawamura Kiyoshi. *Manshū kokkyō jijō* [The Situation on the Manchurian Frontiers]. Hsinking: Manshū Jijō Annaijo, 1939.

334. Kido Kōichi. *Kido Kōichi nikki* [The Diary of Kido Kōichi]. Tokyo: Tokyo Daigaku Shuppankai, 1966. 2 vols.

335. ———. *Kido nikki* [The Kido Diary]. Tokyo: Heiwa Shobō, 1947.

336. *Kindai no sensō* [Modern War Series]. Tokyo: Jinbutsu Ōraisha, 1966. 8 vols.

337. Kinoshita Sōichi. *Nihon hyakunen no kiroku* [A Century's Record of Japan]. Tokyo: Jinbutsu Ōraisha, 1960.

338. Kira Katsuaki. "Nomonhan kūsenki" [Stories of the Nomonhan Air Fighting], *Konnichi no Wadai*, Oct. 1955, pp. 7-9.

339. *Kiroku shashinshū sen (2), Nihon no sentōki: shashin de tadoru riku-kaigun sentōki no subete* [Selected Photo Album Records No. 2, Japanese Fighters: All About Army-Navy Fighters Through Photographs], ed. *Maru* Magazine. Tokyo: Kōjinsha, 1976.

340. *Kiroku shashinshū sen (25), Nihon no sensha: yunyū kara goshiki sensha made: Nihon sensha no subete* [Selected Photo Album Records No. 25, Japanese Tanks: From Imported Tanks to Type 5 Tanks: All About Japanese Tanks], ed. *Maru* Magazine. Tokyo: Kōjinsha, 1978.

341. Kitagawa Shiro. *Nomonhan: moto Manshūkoku gaikōkan no shōgen: sensō to ningen no kiroku* [Nomonhan: The Testimony of a Former Manchukuo Diplomat: An Account of War and Men]. Tokyo: Tokuma Shoten, 1979.

342. Kobayashi Hideo. "Ishiwara Kanji to sōryokusen shisō" [Ishiwara Kanji and the Theory of Total War], *Rekishi Hyōron*, Apr. 1980, pp. 12, 49-71.

343. Kobayashi Kōichi. "Gunshin Sakai Mikio butaichō" [A War God, Unit Commander Sakai Mikio], *Kaikōsha Kiji*, Aug. 1941, pp. 20-25.

344. Kobayashi Shūjirō. "Senshasen ni sonau" [Preparing for Tank Battles], *Kaikōsha Kiji*, Aug. 1941, pp. 45-49.

345. Kodama Taizō. "Mantetsu chōsabu" [The South Manchuria Railway Co. Research Bureau], *Chūō Kōron*, Dec. 1960, pp. 188-207.

346. Kohinata Hakurō. "Himerareta Manshū jihen no dōkasen" [The Hidden Causes of the Manchurian Incident], *Jinbutsu Ōrai*, Feb. 1957, pp. 22-29.

347. Koiso Kuniaki. *Katsuzan kōsō*. Tokyo: Chūō Kōronsha, 1963. [Mount Katsu was Koiso's pen name.]

348. Kojima Kentarō. "Manshūkoku 'yoru no teiō' Amakasu taii" ["The Emperor of the Night" in Manchukuo, Captain Amakasu], *Jinbutsu Ōrai*, Feb. 1957, pp. 182-90.

349. Kojima Noboru. *Manshū jihen* [The Manchurian Incident]. Tokyo: Bungei Shunjūsha, 1974. Vol. 2 of *Tennō*.

350. ———. *Manshū teikoku* [The Empire of Manchukuo]. Tokyo: Bungei Shunjūsha, 1974. 2 vols.

351. ———. *Tennō* [The Emperor]. Tokyo: Bungei Shunjūsha, 1974-75. 5 vols.

352. Kōmoto Daisaku. "Watakushi ga Chō Sakurin o koroshita" [I Murdered Chang Tso-lin], *Bungei Shunjū*, 1954, pp. 194-201.

353. Kōtani Etsuo. "Kaisen sokushin no sekinin o kokuhaku suru: Nisso chūritsu joyaku o kian shita moto rikugun sanbō no hansei" [I Confess Responsibility for Promoting the War: Self-Reflection by a Former Army Staff Officer Who Drafted the Japanese-Soviet Neutrality Pact], *Nihon oyobi Nihonjin*, Oct. 1959, pp. 72-77.

353A. *Kumamoto heidan senshi* [The Military History of the Kumamoto Corps]. Kumamoto: Kumamoto Nichi-nichi Shinbunsha, 1965. 3 vols.

354. Kunimatsu Hisaya. *Kokkyō no hanashi* [Border Stories]. Tokyo: Kajitani Shoin, 1939.

355. Kurihara Ken. *Tai-Man-Mō seisakushi no ichimen* [An Aspect of Japanese Policy Toward Manchuria and Mongolia]. Tokyo: Hara Shobō, 1966.

356. ———. *Tennō: Shōwa shi oboegaki* [The Emperor: A Memorandum of Shōwa Era History]. Tokyo: Hara Shobō, 1970.

357. Kusaba Sakae. "Noro kōchi" [Noro Heights], *Maru*, Dec. 1956, pp. 217-48.

358. ———. *Noro kōchi: Nomonhan sensha zenmetsu senki* [Noro Heights: A Record of the Tank Annihilation Combat at Nomonhan]. Tokyo: Masu Shobō, 1941.

359. Kusaji Teigo. *Kantōgun sakusen sanbō no shōgen* [The Testimony of a Kwantung Army Staff Officer]. Tokyo: Fuyō Shobō, 1979.

360. ———. *Sono hi Kantōgun wa* [The Kwantung Army on That (Last) Day]. Tokyo: Miyakawa Shobō, 1967.

361. Kusayanagi Daizō. *Jitsuroku: Mantetsu chōsabu* [A Factual Record of the South Manchuria Railway Co. Research Bureau]. Tokyo: Asahi Shinbunsha, 1979. 2 vols.

362. Kusuyama Gitarō. "Renmei dattai to Ritton kyō no yakuwari" [The Withdrawal from the League of Nations and the Role of Lord Lytton], *Jinbutsu Ōrai*, Feb. 1956, pp. 23-25.

363. Kuzumi Teizō. "Sanbō yonka no zenman shihai" [The 4th Section Staff, Which Ruled All of Manchuria], *Bungei Shunjū*, supplement, Sept. 1956, pp. 268-74.

364. *Kyokutō gunji saiban kiroku mokuroku oyobi sakuin* [Contents and Index for the Records of the International Military Tribunal for the Far East], ed. Asahi Shinbun Chōsa Kenkyū Shitsu. Tokyo: Asahi Shinbunsha, 1953.

365. Majima Ken. *Gunbatsu antō hishi: rikugun hōkai no ichidanmen* [The Secret History of the Clandestine Maneuvers of the Military Clique: The Fallen Army in Cross Section]. Tokyo: Kyōdō Shuppansha, 1946.

366. *Manshū* [Manchuria]. Tokyo: Tōyō Keizai Shinpōsha, 1940.

367. *Manshū jihen* [The Manchurian Incident], ed. Nihon Kokusai Seiji Gakkai. Tokyo: Yūhikaku, 1970.

368. *Manshū jihen no keika* [The Course of the Manchurian Incident], ed. Nakama Teruhisa. Tokyo: Shinkōsha, 1932.

369. "Manshū jihen tenmatsuki" [The Record of the Manchurian Incident from the Beginning], *Maru*, special issue, 15 Dec. 1956, pp. 202-3.

370. *Manshū jihen to Mantetsu* [The Manchurian Incident and the South Manchuria Railway Co.]. Hsinking: Minami Manshū Tetsudō K. K., 1932.

371. *Manshū keizai nenpō* [Annual Economic Report on Manchuria]. Hsinking: Mantetsu Chōsabu, 1933-39.

372. *Manshū kenkoku no yume to genjitsu* [The Dream and the Reality of the Establishment of Manchukuo], ed. Kokusai Zenrin Kyōkai. Tokyo: Kenkōsha, 1975.

373. *Manshū mondai to kokubō hōshin: Meiji kōki ni okeru kokubō kankyō no hendō* [The Manchurian Problem and National Defense Policy: The Change in National Defense Context in the Late Meiji Era], ed. Tsunoda Jun. Tokyo: Hara Shobō, 1967.

374. *Manshū nenkan* [Manchurian Yearbook]. Hsinking: Manshū Nichi-nichi Shinbunsha, various years.

375. *Manshūkoku gensei* [The Present State of Affairs in Manchukuo], 1935-39, 1941, 1943. Hsinking: Manshūkoku Tsūshinsha, 1936-44.

376. Mantetsu [The South Manchuria Railway Co.]. Keizai Chōsakai [Economic Research Association]. *Sobieto Renpō nenkan: 1934* [USSR Yearbook: 1934]. Tokyo: Nichiro Tsūhōsha, 1934.

377. ———. Tōa Keizai Chōsakyoku [East Asia Economic Research Department].

Man-Mō seiji keizai teiyō [Handbook on the Political Economy of Manchuria and Mongolia]. Tokyo: Kaizōsha, 1932.

378. Maruyama Shizuo. *Kaeranu mittei: tai-So-Man-Mō bōryaku hishi* [A Lost Spy: The Secret History of Intrigues Toward the USSR, Manchuria, and Mongolia]. Tokyo: Heiwa Shobō, 1948.

379. Masuda Tadao. *Manshū kokkyō mondai* [Manchurian Border Problems]. Tokyo: Tōa Shinsha, 1941.

380. Masumoto Kiyoshi. *Moyuru seisōken: rikugun kōkū no monogatari* [Stratosphere Ablaze: Tales of the Army Air Force]. Tokyo: Shuppan Kyōdōsha, 1961.

381. Matsumoto Masaji, ed. *Kyōdo heidan monogatari* [Local Corps Stories]. Morioka: Iwate Nippōsha, 1953.

382. Matsumoto Seichō. *Shōwa shi hakkutsu* [Shōwa Era Historical Excavations Series], vols. 1, 3. Tokyo: Bungei Shunjūsha, 1965.

383. Matsumoto Shigeharu et al. "Gunbu ni utsuru shudōken" [The Shift in Leadership to the Military], *Asahi Jyānaru*, 25 June 1961, pp. 71-83.

384. Matsumoto Tokuaki. "Soren no tai-Nichi bōryaku shi" [A History of Soviet Subversion Against Japan], *Jinbutsu Ōrai*, Feb. 1956, pp. 161-64.

385. Matsumoto Toyozō. *Minami Manshū Tetsudō Kabushiki Kaisha sanjūnen ryakushi* [A Concise 30-Year History of the South Manchuria Railway Co.]. Dairen: Minami Manshū Tetsudō K. K., 1937.

386. Matsumura Kōjirō. *Gekitsui: Nomonhan kūchu jissenki* [Shot Down: The Factual Air Battle Record of Nomonhan]. Tokyo: Kyōgakusha, 1942. Reprinted in vol. 24 of *Taiheiyō sensō dokyumentari*.

387. ———. "Nomonhan no sora wa yaburezu" [The Skies Over Nomonhan Were Not Lost], *Maru*, Aug. 1957, pp. 40-50.

388. Matsumura Shūitsu. *Miyakezaka: gunbatsu wa ikanishite umaretaka* [The War Ministry: How Were the Militarists Born?]. Tokyo: Tōkō Shobō, 1952.

389. Matsumura Tomokatsu. *Kantōgun sanbō fukuchō no shuki* [The Notes of a Kwantung Army Deputy Chief of Staff]. Tokyo: Fuyō Shobō, 1977.

390. Matsuoka Hideo et al. "Sekkeisha ga kataru Nihon sensha no himitsu" [Japanese Tank Secrets as Revealed by the Designers], *Maru*, Sept. 1961 (tank issue), pp. 86-89.

391. Matsuoka Yōsuke. *Kōa no taigyō* [Great Enterprise: The Rise of Asia]. Tokyo: Dai'ichi Kōronsha, 1941.

392. *Matsuoka Yōsuke: sono hito to shōgai* [Matsuoka Yōsuke: As a Person and Hi- Life], ed. Matsuoka Yōsuke Denki Kankōkai. Tokyo: Kōdansha, 1974.

393. Matsushita Yoshio. *Nihon gunbatsu no kōbō* [The Rise and Fall of the Japanese Militarists]. Tokyo: Jinbutsu Ōraisha, 1967. 3 vols.

394. ———. *Nihon gunji shi jitsuwa* [True Stories from Japanese Military History]. Tokyo: Tsuchiya Shoten, 1966.

395. ———. *Nihon gunji shi sōwa* [Anecdotes from Japanese Military History]. Tokyo: Tsuchiya Shoten, 1963.

396. ———. *Nihon gunji shi zatsuwa* [Small Talk from Japanese Military History]. Tokyo: Tsuchiya Shoten, 1969.

397. ———. *Nihon gunsei to seiji* [The Japanese Military System and Politics]. Tokyo: Kuroshio Shuppan, 1960.

398. ———. *Riku-kaigun sōdō shi* [A History of Army-Navy Strife]. Tokyo: Kuroshio Shuppan, 1959.

399. Matsutani Makoto. *Daitōa sensō shūshū no shinsō* [The Truth About Controlling the Great East Asia War]. Tokyo: Fuyō Shobō, 1980.

400. Mazaki Jinzaburō. *Gunbatsu no anyaku* [Secret Maneuvers of the Military Clique]. Tokyo: Sekai Bunka, 1946.

401. *Minami Jirō*, ed. Mitarai Tatsuo. Tokyo: Minami Jirō Denki Kankōkai, 1957.

402. Mishima Giichirō et al. *Kikō gunbi o kataru* [A Discussion of Mechanized Equipment]. Tokyo: Asahi Shinbunsha, 1941.

403. Mishima Yasuo. "Kyokutō sekigun ron" [Views on the Soviet Far Eastern Red Army], *Ajiya Mondai Kōza*, 1939, pp. 175-81.

404. ———. "Nomonhan jiken to Soto-Mōko no kumon" [The Nomonhan Incident and Outer Mongolia's Agony], *Chūō Kōron*, July 1939, pp. 163-69.

405. ———, and Gotō Tomio. *Gaimō Jinmin Kyōwakoku: Soren Kyokutō no zen'ei* [The Outer Mongolian People's Republic: Spearhead of the Soviet Far East]. Tokyo: Itō Shoten, 1939.

406. Mita Masahiro. *Nomonhan no shitō: dai-nana shidan senki* [Death Struggle at Nomonhan: The 7th Division Combat Record]. Sapporo: Hokkai Times, 1965.

407. Miwa Kimitada. *Matsuoka Yōsuke: sono ningen to gaikō* [Matsuoka Yōsuke: His Character and Diplomacy]. Tokyo: Chūō Kōronsha, 1971.

408. Miyamura Saburō. *Hayashi Senjūrō, sono shōgai to shinjō* [Hayashi Senjūrō, His Life and Beliefs]. Tokyo: Hara Shobō, 1972.

409. Miyazaki Kiyotaka. *Gunpō kaigi* [Courts-Martial]. Tokyo: Fuji Shobō, 1953.

410. ———. *Kenpei* [Military Police]. Tokyo: Fuji Shobō, 1952.

411. Miyazaki Shigesaburō. "Hohei dai-jūroku rentai funsensu" [The 16th Infantry Regiment Fought Desperately], *Maru*, Jan. 1958, pp. 60-65.

412. Mori Shōzō. *Senpū nijūnen* [Twenty Turbulent Years]. Tokyo: Kōjinsha, 1968.

413. Morimatsu Toshio. *Daihon'ei* [Imperial General Headquarters]. Tokyo: Kyōikusha, 1981.

414. Morishima Gorō. *Kunō suru Soren taishikan* [The Soviet Embassy in Agony]. Tokyo: Shuppan Kyōdō, 1952.

415. Morishima Morito. *Inbō ansatsu guntō* [Intrigue, Assassination, and Sabers]. Tokyo: Iwanami Shoten, 1950.

415A. Muneta Hiroshi. *Heitai Nihon shi* [Soldiers' Japanese History]. Tokyo: Shin Jinbutsu Ōraisha, 1975. Vol. 3: *Manshū jihen, Shina jihen* [The Manchurian Incident, The China Incident].

416. Murata Kingo. "Waga rikukūgun no hatten wa naze okuretaka? Hensei to seido kara mita rikugun kōkūbutai no hensen" [Why Was Our Army Air Force's Growth Stunted? The Change in the Army Air Units from the Viewpoint of Organization and System], *Maru*, Aug. 1957, pp. 184-93.

417. Murobushi Tetsurō. *Nihon no terorisuto: ansatsu to kūdetā no rekishi* [Japanese Terrorists: The History of Assassinations and Coups d'Etat]. Tokyo: Kōbundō, 1964.

418. Mutō Akira. *Hitō kara Sugamo e* [From the Philippines to Sugamo]. Tokyo: Jitsugyō no Nihonsha, 1952.

419. Nagamatsu Asazō. "Chō Sakurin bakusatsu no zenbō" [The Complete Picture of the Bombing Murder of Chang Tso-lin], *Maru*, Jan. 1958, pp. 34-41.

420. Nakamura Bin. *Man-So kokkyō funsō shi* [A History of Manchurian-Soviet Border Disputes]. Tokyo: Kaizōsha, 1939.

421. Nakamura Kikuo. *Manshū jihen* [The Manchurian Incident]. Tokyo: Nihon Kyōbunsha, 1965.

422. ———. "Manshū jihen (1-2)" [The Manchurian Incident], *Gunji Shigaku*, Nov. 1965, pp. 79-93, and Feb. 1966, pp. 95-107.

423. ———. *Shōwa rikugun hishi* [The Untold History of the Army During the Shōwa Era]. Tokyo: Banchō Shobō, 1968.

424. Nakamura Shōgo. *Nagatachō ichibanchi* [The Prime Ministers' Official Residence]. Tokyo: Nyūsusha, 1946.

425. Nakano Gorō. "Shōwa dōran shi: ankoku no jidai" [A History of Shōwa Era Upheavals: The Time of Darkness], *Maru*, Feb. 1960, pp. 130-37.

426. Nakano Masao. *Hashimoto taisa no shuki* [Colonel Hashimoto's Notes]. Tokyo: Misuzu Shobō, 1963.

427. Nanjō Norio. "Tsuji Masanobu to iu otoko" [The Man Whose Name Is Tsuji Masanobu], *Rekishi to Jinbutsu*, supplement, Sept. 1981, pp. 355-59.

428. Narusawa Yonezō. *Ishiwara Kanji*. Tokyo: Keizai Ōraisha, 1969.

429. Naruse Kyō. *Sugiyama gensui den* [The Biography of Marshal Sugiyama]. Tokyo: Hara Shobō, 1969.

430. Nezu Masashi. *Dai Nihon teikoku no hōkai* [The Destruction of the Great Japanese Empire]. Tokyo: Shiseidō, 1961.

431. *Nihon gaikō shi (NGS)* [Japanese Diplomatic History Series]. Tokyo: Kajima Heiwa Kenkyūsho Shuppankai. Vol. 18: *Manshū jihen* [The Manchurian Incident] (1973).

432. ———. Vol. 21: *Nichi-Doku-I dōmei; Nisso chūritsu jōyaku* [The Japan-Germany-Italy Alliance; the Japan-Soviet Neutrality Pact] (1971).

433. ———. Vol. 19: *Nikka jihen* (1-2) [The Sino-Japanese Incident] (1971).

434. ———. Vol. 15: *Nisso kokkō mondai 1917-1945* [Problems of Soviet-Japanese National Relations] (1970).

435. *Nihon gendai shi* [The Modern History of Japan], ed. Soren Kagaku Akademii Tōyō Kenkyūjo [Academy of Sciences, USSR, Oriental Research Institute], trans. M. Yamamoto and K. Ono. Tokyo: Kawade Shobō Shinsha, 1959. (Translation based on the Russian 1957 edition.)

436. *Nihon gunyōki no zenbo* [The Complete Picture of Japanese Military Aircraft], ed. *Kōkū Jōhō* Magazine. Tokyo: Kantōsha, 1960.

437. *Nihon gunyōki shashin sōshū* [Japanese Military Aircraft: A Complete Photographic Album], ed. *Maru* Magazine. Tokyo: Kōjinsha, 1970.

438. *Nihon no rekishi* [Japanese History Series]. Tokyo: Chūō Kōronsha, 1965-67. 26 vols. + 5 supplements.

439. "Nihon no sensha shōshi" [A Short History of Japanese Tanks], *Bōei to Keizai*, special issue, Spring 1955, pp. 70-72, 85, 90, 93, 121.

440. *Nihon no tai-So inbō* [Japanese Plotting Against the Soviets], ed. *Shinsō* Magazine. Tokyo: Jinminsha, 1948.

441. "Nihon riku-kaigun kōkūki ichiran" [A Catalog of Japanese Army and Navy Aircraft], *Maru*, supplement, Aug. 1957, p. 98.

442. *Nihon riku-kaigun no seido soshiki jinji* [The Japanese Army-Navy System, Organization, and Personnel], ed. Nihon Kindai Shiryō Kenkyūkai. Tokyo: Tokyo Daigaku Shuppankai, 1971.

443. Nimura Toshi. *Kōkū gojūnen shi* [A 50-Year History of the Air Force]. Tokyo: Masu Shobō, 1943.

444. Nishi Haruhiko. *Kaisō no Nihon gaikō* [Recollections of Japanese Diplomacy]. Tokyo: Iwanami Shoten, 1965.

445. ———. *Watakushi no gaikō hakusho: taikenteki kokusai kankeiron* [A Diplomat's White Book: Views on International Relations in the Light of My Experience]. Tokyo: Bungei Shunjūsha, 1963.

446. "Nishihara sōchō tekijin fujichaku no sentaichō o kyūshutsu su" [Master Sergeant Nishihara Rescued His Squadron Commander Who Had Crash-landed in Enemy Positions], *Gahō Senki*, Oct. 1961, pp. 30-35.

446A. Nishihara Yukio. *Zenkiroku Harubin tokumukikan: Kantōgun jōhōbu no kiseki* [The Entire Record of the Harbin OSS: The Path of the Kwantung Army Intelligence Bureau]. Tokyo: Mainichi Shinbunsha, 1980.

447. Nishiura Susumu. *Shōwa sensō shi no shōgen* [Testimony Concerning the Military History of the Shōwa Era]. Tokyo: Hara Shobō, 1980.

448. Noguchi Kamenosuke. "Nomonhan no kuhai: niwaka jitate no kikaika heidan no sentō" [The Bitter Cup of Nomonhan: Combat of the Improvised Mechanized Group], *Bōei to Keizai*, May 1955 (tank issue), pp. 71-77.

449. ———. "Nomonhan senshasen no shinsō" [The Truth About the Nomonhan Tank Battles], *Maru*, Mar. 1959, pp. 54-58.

450. Nomi Yutaka. "Seisō kachū sekigun kaibō" [Dissection of the Red Army During the Cleanup], *Chūō Kōron*, Aug. 1938, pp. 132-43.

451. *Nomonhan bidanroku* [Collected Stories of Heroic Deeds at Nomonhan], ed. Chūrei Kenshōkai. Hsinking: Manshū Tosho, 1942.

452. *Nomonhan jiken to Doitsu no tai-So junbi* [The Nomonhan Incident and Germany's Anti-Soviet War Preparations], ed. Soren Kyōsantō Chūō Iinkai fuzoku Marukusu-Rēninshugi Kenkyūjo [Marxism-Leninism Research Institute of the Central Committee of the Soviet Communist Party], trans. T. Kawauchi. Tokyo: Kōbundō, 1963. Vol. 2 of *Dai-niji sekai taisen shi* [The History of World War II]. (Translation based on the Russian 1960 edition.)

453. "Nomonhan no oni butaichō: OO butai ko rikugun taii Nagase Genzō" [A Demon Unit Commander at Nomonhan: The Late Army Capt. Nagase Genzō of a Certain Unit], *Kaikōsha Kiji*, Aug. 1941, p. 56.

454. Nomoto Shigeyuki. "Kantōgun no tanjō to nijūyonen no senshi" [The Birth of the Kwantung Army and Its Military History of Over 20 Years], *Maru*, Jan. 1958, pp. 24-30.

455. Nomura Norio. "Nomonhan jiken sansen no omoide" [Remembrances of Participation in the Fighting During the Nomonhan Incident], *Kaikōsha Kiji*, Aug. 1941, pp. 57-78.

456. Nukada, Hiroshi. *Hiroku: Ugaki Kazunari* [A Secret Record: Ugaki Kazunari]. Tokyo: Fuyō Shobō, 1973.

457. ———. *Rikugunshō jinjikyokuchō no kaisō* [Recollections of a War Ministry Personnel Bureau Chief]. Tokyo: Fuyō Shobō, 1979.

458. Numaguchi Masataka. "Nihon no taisenshahō to wa konnamono da!" [Japanese Antitank Guns Were Like This!], *Maru*, Sept. 1961 (tank issue), pp. 48-53.

459. ———, and Takeuchi Akira. "Nihon no kahō jisōhō kōshahō no subete" [All About Japanese Artillery, Automatic Weapons, and Antiaircraft Guns], *Maru*, June 1962, pp. 150-53.

460. Ogata Shōji. "Nisso chūritsu jōyaku" [The Japanese-Soviet Neutrality Pact], *Jinbutsu Ōrai*, Feb. 1956, pp. 95-99.

461. Ogawa Shinkichi. "Kataude o ubawaru! Nomonhan no shitō" [The Death Struggle at Nomonhan Cost Me My Arm], *Jinbutsu Ōrai*, June 1956, pp. 174-78.

462. Ōgi Hiroshi. "Nomonhan jiken Ioki chūsa no jiketsu" [The Nomonhan Incident: Lt. Col. Ioki's Suicide], *Rekishi to Jinbutsu*, supplement, Sept. 1981, pp. 384-402.

463. Ōgoshi Kenji. "Nichi-Doku tai-So bōryaku no shinsō" [The True Story of Anti-Soviet Subversion by Japan and Germany], *Chisei*, Dec. 1956, pp. 207-9.

464. Ogura Masatsune. *Hiranuma Kiichirō kaisōroku* [The Hiranuma Kiichirō Memoirs]. Tokyo: Gakuyō Shobō, 1955.

465. Okada Masukichi. "Mantetsu chōsabu" [The South Manchuria Railway Co. Research Bureau], *Shūkan Yomiuri*, 18 Sept. 1970, pp. 56-59.

466. Okamoto Kōji. *Aa! Manshū* [Ah! Manchuria]. Tokyo: Keibunkan, 1963.

467. Okamura Niichi. "Nisso fukashin jōyaku to Matsuoka Yōsuke" [The Japanese-Soviet Neutrality Pact and Matsuoka Yōsuke], *Chūō Kōron*, Aug. 1964, pp. 202-10.

468. Okamura Shin'ichi. "Sekiran'un" [Cumulonimbus Clouds], *Shūshin*, Mar. 1967, pp. 113-17.

469. Oki Shigeru. *Nomonhan sansen nikki* [A Diary of Participation in the Nomonhan Fighting]. Tokyo: Kongō Shuppan, 1975.

470. Oki Shūji. *Anami Korechika den* [The Biography of Anami Korechika]. Tokyo: Kōdansha, 1970.

471. Ōkubo Kōichi. *Rikugun tokuhon* [The Army Reader]. Tokyo: Nihon Hyōronsha, 1938.

472. Okumura Yoshitarō, ed. *Aa! kōkūtai* [Ah, the Air Units]. Tokyo: Mainichi Shinbunsha, 1969.

473. Onda Shigetaka. *Nomonhan sen: ningen no kiroku* [The Nomonhan Battle: Human Records]. Tokyo: Tokuma Shoten, 1977. 2 vols.

474. Ōta Rin'ichirō. *Nihon kindai gunpuku shi* [The History of Modern Japanese Military Uniforms]. Tokyo: Yūzankaku; 1972.

475. Ōtani Keijirō. *Kōgun no hōkai: Meiji kengun kara kaitai made* [The Collapse of the Imperial Army: From the Establishment of the Meiji Army Until Dissolution]. Tokyo: Tosho Shuppansha, 1975.

476. ———. *Rakujitsu no joshō: Shōwa rikugun shi* [Prelude to Sunset: Shōwa Military History]. Tokyo: Yakumo Shoten, 1959.

477. ———. *Rikugun 80-nen* [The Army's 80 Years]. Tokyo: Tosho Shuppansha, 1978.

478.———. *Shōwa kenpei shi* [Shōwa Military Police History.] Tokyo: Misuzu Shobō, 1966.

479. Ōuchi Naomichi. *Haruhagawa: Nomonhan sentōki* [The Halha River: The Combat Story of Nomonhan]. Tokyo: Yūmunsha, 1941.

480. Ozawa Chikamitsu. *Nomonhan senki* [The Story of the Nomonhan Battle]. Tokyo: Shin Jinbutsu Ōraisha, 1974.

481. "Ōzora no yūshi retsuden" [Biographies of Air Heroes], *Maru*, July 1958, pp. 66-89.

482. Rekishigaku Kenkyūkai. *Taiheiyō sensō shi* [The History of the Pacific War], ed. Usami Seijirō et al. Tokyo: Tōyō Keizai Shinpōsha, 1953-54. 5 vols.

483. Rikugun Kikō Honbu Ichibuin [A Member of the Army Tank Headquarters]. "Nomonhan jiken no kyōkun" [Lessons of the Nomonhan Incident"], *Kaikōsha Kiji*, Aug. 1941, pp. 17-19.

484. Rikugun Kyōiku Sōkanbu [Army Directorate of Military Training]. *Kōgun shi* [A History of the Imperial Army]. Tokyo: Seibudō, 1943.

485. ———. *Shōsen reishū: Nomonhan jiken* [Selected Examples of Small Actions: The Nomonhan Incident]. Tokyo: Seibudō, 1941.

486. *Rikugun mohanhei kyōten* [Handbook for the Ideal Army Man]. Tokyo: Teikoku Gunji Kyōikusha, 1940.

487. Rikugun Sanbō Honbu [AGS]. *Daihon'ei-Seifu renraku kaigi to nikki: kaisen made no sensō shidō* [IGHQ-Government Liaison Conferences and Diary: War

Guidance Until the Opening of the War]. Tokyo: Hara Shobō, 1967. Vol. 1 of *Sugiyama memo.*

488. ———. Sensō Shidōhan [War Guidance Section]. "Daihon'ei kimitsu sensō nisshi (1)" [The IGHQ Secret War Diary], 10 Aug. 1941-7 Dec. 1942, *Rekishi to Jinbutsu,* Sept. 1971, pp. 336-73.

489. Rikujō Jieitai Kanbugakkō Rikusenshi Kenkyū Fukyūkai [Ground Self-Defense Forces Command and General Staff College (GSDF/CGSC), Military History Study and Dissemination Association]. *Manshū jihen shi* [The History of the Manchurian Incident]. Tokyo: Hara Shobō, 1967. Vol. 3 of *Rikusen shishu* [Military History Collection].

490. Rikujō Jieitai Kanbugakkō Shūshinkai [GSDF/CGSC Ethics Society]. *Dai-niji taisen no shōguntachi* [Generals and Admirals in World War II]. Tokyo: Hara Shobō, 1974. Vol. 3 of *Tōsotsu no jissai* [True Leadership Series].

491. *Riku-kaigun shōkan jinji sōran* [A Biographical Conspectus of Army Generals and Navy Admirals], ed. Toyama Misao. Tokyo: Fuyō Shobō, 1981. 2 vols.

492. *Ritton hōkokusho* [The Lytton Report]. Tokyo: Chūō Kōronsha, 1932.

493. *Roshia dai kakumei shi* [The History of the Great Russian Revolution], ed. Tomioka Sadatoshi. Tokyo: Roshia Dai Kakumei Shi Kankōkai, 1959. 12 vols.

494. Sada Kōjirō. "Shigen to keizai jijō" [Natural Resources and the Economic Situation], *Sekai Chishiki,* special issue, Feb. 1932, pp. 157-94.

495. Sagara Shunsuke. *Akai yuhi no masunogahara ni: kisai Kōmoto Daisaku no shōgai* [The Red Sun Setting on Manchurian Fields: A Life of the Genius Kōmoto Daisaku]. Tokyo: Kōjinsha, 1978.

496. Saitō Kōzō. "Nomonhan jiken hantoshi no sōkessan" [Six Months' Final Balance Sheet for the Nomonhan Incident], *Maru,* Oct. 1957, pp. 54-65.

497. Saitō Yoshie. *Azamukareta rekishi: Matsuoka to sangoku dōmei no rimen* [Distorted History: The Inside Story of Matsuoka and the Tripartite Alliance]. Tokyo: Yomiuri Shinbunsha, 1955.

498. Sakamoto Koretada. "Mongoru Jinmin Kyōwakoku no seikaku" [The Character of the Mongolian People's Republic], *Nairiku Ajiya no Kenkyū,* 1955.

499. Sasaki Tōitsu. *Aru gunjin no jiden* [The Autobiography of a Certain Military Man]. Tokyo: Futsūsha, 1963.

500. Sasamoto Shunji. *Dai-niji sekai taisen zenya, Yoroppa 1939* [On the Eve of the Second World War, Europe 1939]. Tokyo: Iwanami Shoten, 1969.

501. Satō Hiroshi. *Hoku-Shi Shiberia Mōko* [North China, Siberia, and Mongolia]. Tokyo: Sanseidō, 1938.

502. Satō Kenryō. *Daitōa sensō kaikoroku* [Recollections of the Great East Asia War]. Tokyo: Tokuma Shoten, 1966.

503. ———. *Satō Kenryō no shōgen* [The Testimony of Satō Kenryō]. Tokyo: Fuyō Shobō, 1976.

504. ———. *Tōjō Hideki to Taiheiyō sensō* [Tōjō Hideki and the Pacific War]. Tokyo: Bungei Shunjū Shinsha, 1960.

505. Satō Naotake. *Futatsu no Roshia* [The Two Russias]. Tokyo: Sekai no Nihonsha, 1948.

506. ———. *Kaiko hachijūnen* [80 Years of Recollections]. Tokyo: Jiji Tsūshinsha, 1970.

507. Satō Yasunosuke. *Nisshi kankei: Man-Mō mondai o chūshin to suru* [The Relationship Between Japan and China, Centering on Manchurian and Mongolian Problems]. Tokyo: Nihon Hyōronsha, 1931.

507A. Sawada Shigeru. *Sanbō jichō Sawada Shigeru kaisōroku* [The Memoirs of Deputy Chief of Staff Sawada Shigeru]. Tokyo: Fuyō Shobō, 1982.

508. Sejima Ryūzō. "Daihon'ei no 2000-nichi" [2,000 Days in Imperial General Headquarters], *Bungei Shunjū*, Dec. 1975, pp. 230-48.

509. Shibusawa Tadao. *Dai-niji taisen no Nihon no sensha* [Japanese Tanks in World War II]. Tokyo: Bunrindō, 1968.

510. Shidehara Kijūrō. *Gaikō gojūnen* [50 Years of Diplomacy]. Tokyo: Hara Shobō, 1974.

511. *Shidehara Kijūrō*. Tokyo: Shidehara Heiwa Zaidan, 1955.

512. Shigemitsu Mamoru. *Gaikō kaisōroku* [Diplomatic Memoirs]. Tokyo: Mainichi Shinbunsha, 1953.

513. ———. *Shōwa no dōran* [The Shōwa Era, Years of Upheaval]. Tokyo: Chūō Kōronsha, 1952. 2 vols.

514. ———. *Sugamo nikki* [Sugamo Diary]. Tokyo: Bungei Shunjūsha, 1953.

515. Shimada Toshihiko. *Kantōgun* [The Kwantung Army]. Tokyo: Chūō Kōronsha, 1965.

516. ———. *Manshū jihen* [The Manchurian Incident]. Tokyo: Jinbutsu Ōraisha, 1966. Vol. 4 of *Kindai shi no sensō*.

517. ———. "Shōwa shi o kaeta maboroshi no seiei" [The Illusory Elite Kwantung Army, Which Changed the History of the Shōwa Era], *Jinbutsu Ōrai*, Aug. 1964, pp. 18-31.

518. Shimada Toshio. "Chō Sakurin bakusatsu jiken" [The Case of the Bombing Murder of Chang Tso-lin], *Gunji Shigaku*, Aug. 1965, pp. 82-95.

519. Shimamine Seimu. "Chō Sakurin no shi" [The Death of Chang Tso-lin], *Shūkan Asahi*, supplement, March 1961, pp. 151-58.

520. Shimoda Fujio. "Sanjūgonen mae no 'Nomonhan' o shinobu: watakushi no hatsujin taikenki" [Recollections of Nomonhan 35 Years Ago: My First Battle Experience], *Shūshin*, July 1974, pp. 80-84.

521. Shinkōsha. "Manshū jihen no keika" [The Course of the Manchurian Incident], *Sekai Chishiki*, special issue, Feb. 1932.

522. Shinmyō Takeo. "Dai-niji taisen no hakkaten: Chō Sakurin bakusatsu jiken no imisuru mono" [The Ignition Point of the Second World War: The Meaning of the Chang Tso-lin Incident], *Chisei*, Special Issue 3, Dec. 1956, pp. 33-39.

523. ———. *Kaigun sensō kentō kaigi kiroku: Taiheiyō sensō kaisen no keii* [The Records of Navy War Study Conferences: Details of the Opening of the Pacific War]. Tokyo: Mainichi Shinbunsha, 1976.

524. ———. *Shōwa seiji hishi* [The Secret History of Shōwa Era Politics]. Kyoto: San'ichi Shobō, 1961.

525. ———. *Shōwa shi tsuiseki: ankoku jidai no kiroku* [In Pursuit of Shōwa Era History: Record of a Dark Period]. Tokyo: Shin Jinbutsu Ōraisha, 1970.

526. *Shō Kaiseki hiroku* [Chiang Kai-shek's Secret Records], ed. Usui Katsumi. Tokyo: Sankei Shinbunsha, 1975-77. 15 vols.

527. Shōda Tatsuo. *Jūshintachi no Shōwa shi* [Senior Statesmen's History of the Shōwa Era]. Tokyo: Bungei Shunjūsha, 1981. 2 vols.

528. *Shōwa jūichinen no kokusai jōsei* [The International Situation, 1936]. Tokyo: Nihon Kokusai Kyōkai, 1937.

529. *Shōwa jūnen no kokusai jōsei* [The International Situation, 1935]. Tokyo: NKK, 1936.

530. *Shōwa jūninen no kokusai jōsei* [The International Situation, 1937]. Tokyo: NKK, 1938.

531. *Shōwa jūsannen no kokusai jōsei* [The International Situation, 1938]. Tokyo: NKK, 1939.
532. *Shōwa jūyonnen Asahi nenkan* [The Asahi Yearbook, 1939], ed. Ōmichi Hiroo. Osaka: Osaka Asahi Shinbunsha, 1938.
533. *Shōwa jūyonnen no kokusai jōsei* [The International Situation, 1939]. Tokyo: NKK, 1941.
534. *Shōwa shi no shunkan* [Moments in Shōwa Era History], ed. Katō Hidetoshi et al. Tokyo: Asahi Shinbunsha, 1966. 2 vols.
535. *Shōwa shi no tennō* (*SSNT*) [The Emperor in the History of the Shōwa Era]. Tokyo: Yomiuri Shinbunsha, 1967-76. 30 vols.
536. *Soren kakumei yonjūnen* [40 Years of the Soviet Revolution]. Tokyo: Jiyū Ajiyasha, 1957.
537. Sugie Isamu. *Fukuoka rentai shi* [The History of the Fukuoka Regiment]. Tokyo: Akita Shoten, 1974.
538. Sugimori Hisahide. *Tsuji Masanobu*. Tokyo: Bungei Shunjūsha, 1963.
539. *Sugiyama gensui den* [The Biography of Marshal Sugiyama], ed. Sugiyama Gensui Denki Kankōkai. Tokyo: Hara Shobō, 1969.
540. *Sugiyama memo* [The Sugiyama Memorandum]. Tokyo: Hara Shobo, 1967. 2 vols.
541. Sumi Shin'ichirō. *Jissen sunteki* [Sketches of the Real Battle]. Kyoto: Sumi Butai Kinenkai, 1944.
542. ———. "Nihon no unmei kesshita hi" [The Days When Japan's Fate Was Decided], *Shūkan Yomiuri*, 7 Aug. 1955, pp. 11-19.
543. ———. "Nomonhan senshasen no sōkessan" [The Final Balance Sheet of the Nomonhan Tank Battles], *Maru*, Jan. 1958, pp. 52-59.
544. Sumiya Mikio. *Dai Nihon Teikoku no shiren* [The Great Japanese Empire on Trial]. Tokyo: Chūō Kōronsha, 1966. Vol. 22 of *Nihon no rekishi*.
545. *Sutārin dokusai to dai shukusei* [Stalin's Dictatorship and the Great Purges]. Tokyo: Roshia Dai Kakumei Shi Kankōkai, 1959. Vols. 9-10 of *Roshia dai kakumei shi*.
546. Suzuki Kenji. *Chū-Doku taishi Ōshima Hiroshi* [Ambassador to Germany Ōshima Hiroshi]. Tokyo: Fuyō Shobo, 1979.
547. Suzuki Masao. *Harunaki ninenkan: Uranbātoru shūyōjo* [Two Years Without Spring in the Ulan Bator Prison Camp]. Tokyo: Jiyū Shuppansha, 1948.
548. *Taiheiyō sensō dokyumentari* [Pacific War Documentary Series]. Tokyo: Konnichi no Wadaisha, 1968-71. 24 vols.
549. *Taiheiyō sensō e no michi* (*TSM*) [The Road to the Pacific War], ed. Nihon Kokusai Seiji Gakkai. Tokyo: Asahi Shinbunsha, 1962-63. 8 vols. + supplement.
550. *Taiheiyō sensō gen'inron* [The Origins of the Pacific War], ed. Ueda Toshio. Tokyo: Shinbun Gekkansha, 1953.
551. Takahara Tsuneharu. "Kōgun gun'i damashii" [The Spirit of the Imperial Army's Military Doctors], *Kaikōsha Kiji*, Aug. 1941, pp. 39-40.
552. Takahashi Masanori. *Kessen Manshūkoku no zenbo* [The Entire Picture of Decisive Battle in Manchukuo]. Tokyo: Shanhaidō, 1943.
553. Takamiya Tahei. *Gunkoku taiheiki* [The Military Saga of the Nation at Arms]. Tokyo: Kantōsha, 1951.
553A. ———. *Shōwa no shōsui* [Shōwa Era Commanders], Tokyo: Tosho Shuppansha, 1973.
554. ———. *Tennō heika* [The Emperor]. Tokyo: Kantōsha, 1951.
555. Takashima Masao. *Barushagaru sōgen: Nomonhan hohei nikudan senki* [The

Balshagal Plain: Battle Story of Infantry Human Bullets at Nomonhan]. Tokyo: Masu Shobō, 1942.

556. ———. *Shunkan no inochi: Nomonhan hakuhei senki* [A Moment of Life: An Account of Hand-to-Hand Fighting at Nomonhan]. Tokyo: Hara Shobō, 1970.

557. Takayama Shinobu. *Hattori Takushirō to Tsuji Masanobu*. Tokyo: Fuyō Shobō, 1980.

558. ———. *Sanbō honbu sakusenka: sakusen ronsō no jissō to hansei* [The AGS Operations Section: A True Account and Self-reflection on Operational Arguments]. Tokyo: Fuyō Shobō, 1979.

559. Takemori Kazuo. *Mantetsu kōbō shi* [The History of the Rise and Fall of the South Manchuria Railway Co.]. Tokyo: Akita Shoten, 1970.

560. Takeuchi Ayayoshi. "Manshū jihen" [The Manchurian Incident], in Itō Takashi et al., *Gekidō no hanseiki*.

561. Tamada Yoshio. "Nomonhan nijūgo shūnen: Yasuoka sensha heidan shōhei no funsen o shinobu" [The 25th Anniversary of the Nomonhan Battle: In Memory of the Hard-Fighting Officers and Men of the Yasuoka Tank Corps], *Tairiku Mondai*, Sept. 1964, pp. 47-53; Oct. 1964, pp. 47-53; Nov. 1964, pp. 60-66; Dec. 1964, pp. 68-73.

562. Tanaka Eiji. *Tōkon: Nomonhan senki* [Fighting Spirit: Combat Records of Nomonhan]. Tokyo: Yugawa Kōbunkan, 1941.

563. Tanaka Kanae. "Sajō no rakudo: Manshū kenkoku" [Paradise in the Sand: The Establishment of Manchukuo]. Mimeo of article submitted to *Chuō Kōron*, Aug. 1964.

564. Tanaka Katsuhiko. *Sōgen to kakumei: Mongoru kakumei gojūnen* [Steppes and Revolutions: 50 Years of the Mongolian Revolution]. Tokyo: Shōbunsha, 1971.

565. Tanaka Rinpei. *Tsubasa yo kumo yo senyū yo: aru sentōkinori no kiroku* [Wings, Clouds, and Comrades: The Record of a Certain Fighter Pilot]. Tokyo: Jiji Tsūshinsha, 1974.

566. Tanaka Ryūkichi. *Haiin o tsuku: gunbatsu senō no jissō* [Pointing Out the Causes of Defeat: The True Story of the Military Clique's Despotism]. Tokyo: Sansuisha, 1946.

567. ———. *Nihon gunbatsu antō shi* [A History of the Dark Conflicts Within the Japanese Military Clique]. Tokyo: Seiwadō Shoten, 1947.

568. ———. "Shanhai jihen wa kōshite okosareta" [Thus Was the Shanghai Incident Caused], *Chisei*, Supplement 5, Dec. 1956, pp. 181-86.

569. ———. "Watakushi wa Kantōgun o kokuhatsu suru" [I Accuse the Kwantung Army], *Jinbutsu Ōrai*, May 1965, pp. 42-49.

570. Tanaka Shin'ichi. *Tanaka sakusenbuchō no shōgen: taisen totsunyū no shinsō* [The Testimony of Operations Bureau Chief Tanaka: The Truth About the Charge into the Great War], ed. Matsushita Yoshio. Tokyo: Fuyō Shobō, 1978.

571. Tanemura Sakō. *Daihon'ei kimitsu nisshi* [The Top Secret IGHQ Journal]. Tokyo: Daiyamondosha, 1952.

572. Tatamiya Eitarō. *Shōwa no seijikatachi: Nihon shihaisō no uchimaku* [The Politicians of the Shōwa Era: The Inside Story of the Japanese Ruling Class]. Tokyo: Kōbundo, 1963.

573. Tateno Nobuyuki. *Shōwa gunbatsu* [The Shōwa Era Militarists]. Tokyo: Kōdansha, 1963. 2 vols.

574. Togawa Isamu. "Chō Sakurin ansatsu jiken" [The Chang Tso-lin Assassination Incident], *Shūkan Gendai*, 2 July 1961, pp. 53-61.

575. ———. "Kokusai Renmei dattai jiken: sekai no koji Nihon no higeki" [The

League of Nations Walk-out Affair: The Tragedy of Japan, "Orphan of the World"], *Shūkan Gendai*, 23 July 1961, pp. 58-62.

576. ———. *Shōwa gaikō gojūnen* [50 Years of Japanese Diplomacy]. Tokyo: Gakugei Shorin, 1973.

577. Tōgō Shigenori. *Tōgō Shigenori gaikō shuki: jidai no ichimen* [Notes on Tōgō Shigenori's Diplomacy: An Aspect of the Time]. Tokyo: Hara Shobō, 1967.

578. Tokutomi Iichirō. *Manshū kenkoku tokuhon* [A Reader on the Founding of Manchukuo]. Tokyo: Dentsū Shuppanbu, 1940.

579. Tokyo 12 Channeru. *Shōgen: watakushi no Shōwa shi* [Testimony: My History of the Shōwa Era]. Tokyo: Gakugei Shorin, 1969. 6 vols.

580. *Tokyo saiban* [The Tokyo Trials], ed. Asahi Shinbun Hōtei Kishadan. Tokyo: Tokyo Saiban Kankōkai, 1962.

581. Toriumi Yasushi. "Taigai kiki ni okeru Nihon no shinbun ronchō: Nichiro senso to Manshū jihen no bai" [Japanese Newspaper Views on External Crises: The Cases of the Russo-Japanese War and the Manchurian Incident], *Rekishi to Jinbutsu*, May 1972, pp. 22-38.

582. Toyoshima Fusatarō. "Chōsengun ekkyō shingekisu" [The Korea Army Crossed the Border and Advanced], *Chisei*, Supplement 5, Dec. 1956, pp. 52-58.

583. Tsuchiya Michio. "Mō hitori no shomin saishō" [Another Commoner Premier], *Bungei Shunjū*, Jan. 1973, pp. 184-94.

584. Tsuda Gentoku. *Manshū jihen hishi* [The Secret History of the Manchurian Incident]. Dairen: Manshū Bunka Kyōkai, 1936.

585. Tsuji Masanobu. *Nomonhan*. Tokyo: Atō Shobō, 1950.

586. Tsukushi Jirō. "Arawashi gekisenki: Nomonhan kūchūsen no tsuioku" [A Record of the Furious Fighting of the Fierce Eagles: Recollections of the Air Battles at Nomonhan], *Kaikōsha Kiji*, Aug. 1941, pp. 50-55.

587. Tsunoda Fusako. *Amakasu taii* [Captain Amakasu]. Tokyo: Chūō Kōronsha, 1979.

588. *Uchida Naoya*. Tokyo: Kajima Heiwa Kenkyūsho, 1967.

589. Uchikawa Yoshimi. *Nitchū senso* [The Sino-Japanese Conflict]. Tokyo: Heibonsha, 1975. Vol. 3 of *Dokyumento Shōwa shi*.

590. Uchikura Tōji. "Adauchi sunzen no teisen kyōtei ni naku" [Weeping Over the Cease-Fire Agreement Reached Just Before the Battle of Revenge], *Shūkan Yomiuri*, 18 Sept. 1970, pp. 66-69.

591. Uchiyama Masakuma. "Manshū jihen to Kokusai Renmei dattai" [The Manchurian Incident and the Withdrawal from the League of Nations], *Kokusai Seiji*, 1970, pp. 155-81.

592. Ugaki Kazunari. *Ugaki Kazunari nikki* [The Ugaki Kazunari Diary]. Tokyo: Asahi Shinbunsha, 1949.

593. ———. *Ugaki Kazunari nikki* [The Ugaki Kazunari Diary], ed. Tsunoda Jun. Tokyo: Misuzu Shobō, 1968-71. 3 vols.

594. ———, as told to Kamata Sawa'ichirō. *Shōrai seidan* [Tales Whispered Amid the Pines]. Tokyo: Bungei Shunjūsha, 1951.

595. Umemoto Sutezō. *Kantōgun shimatsuki* [Kwantung Army Particulars]. Tokyo: Hara Shobō, 1967.

596. ———. *Kantōgun shūsen shimatsu* [Particulars of the Kwantung Army at the End of the War]. Tokyo: Shinkokumin Shuppansha, 1974.

597. ———. *Kantōgun sōshireibu* [Kwantung Army General Headquarters]. Tokyo: Keizai Ōraisha, 1971.

598. ———. "Manshūkoku o enshutsu shita sanbōtachi" [The Staff Officers Who Directed Manchukuo], *Jinbutsu Ōrai*, Aug. 1964, pp. 38-45.

599. ———. *Riku-kai meishō hyakusen* [100 Outstanding Generals and Admirals]. Tokyo: Akita Shoten, 1971.

600. ———. *Saigo no rikugun* [The Last Army]. Tokyo: Myōgi Shuppan, 1957.

600A. ———. *Tōjō Hideki: sono Shōwa shi* [Tōjō Hideki: His Shōwa Era History]. Tokyo: Shūei Shobō, 1979.

601. Umihara Osamu. *Senshi ni manabu: asu no kokubō o kangaeru tame ni* [Learning from Military History for the Benefit of Tomorrow's National Defense Thinking]. Tokyo: Asagumo Shinbunsha, 1970.

602. Uno Hiroshi. *Asahi Shinbun ni miru Nihon no ayumi: hametsu e no gunkoku-shugi* [The Course of Japan Seen Through the *Asahi* Newspaper: Militarism Brought About Destruction]. Tokyo: Asahi Shinbunsha, 1974. 3 vols.

603. Usui Katsumi. "Chō Sakurin bakushi no shinsō" [The True Story of the Bombing Murder of Chang Tso-lin], *Chisei*, Supplement 5, Dec. 1956, pp. 26-38.

604. ———. *Nitchū sensō* [The Sino-Japanese Conflict]. Tokyo: Chūō Kōronsha, 1967.

605. Wada Kameji. *Rikugun damashii* [Army Spirit]. Tokyo: Tōsuisha, 1942.

606. Wakatsuki Reijirō. *Wakatsuki Reijirō jiden: Kōfuan kaikoroku* [The Autobiography of Wakatsuki Reijirō: Memoirs of Kōfuan (pseud.)]. Tokyo: Yomiuri Shinbunsha, 1950.

607. Watanabe Masao. "Nomonhan jiken no keika" [The Development of the Nomonhan Incident], in Bimba, *Soto-Mōko dasshutsuki.*

608. Watanabe Ryūsaku. *Bazoku: Nitchū sensō shi no sokumen* [Mounted Bandits: A Sideview of the History of the Japanese Conflict in China]. Tokyo: Chūō Kōronsha, 1964.

609. Yabe Chūta. "Soren wa honto ni tsuyoika?" [Is the USSR Really Strong?], *Tairiku Mondai*, July 1961, pp. 8-13.

610. Yabe Teiji. *Konoe Fumimaro.* Tokyo: Kobundō, 1952. 2 vols.

611. Yamada Otozō. "Sekigun ni torawarete jūichinen" [A Prisoner of the Red Army for 11 Years], *Shūkan Shinchō*, 20 Aug. 1956, pp. 70-75.

612. Yamada Seizaburō. "Manshū 'Ahen ōkoku' no seiritsu to hōkai" [The Establishment and Collapse of the "Opium Kingdom" of Manchukuo], *Chisei*, Dec. 1956, pp. 40-45.

613. Yamaguchi Shigeji. *Manshū kenkoku: Manshū jihen seishi* [The Founding of Manchukuo: The Authentic History of the Manchurian Incident]. Tokyo: Gyōsei Tsūshinsha, 1975.

614. Yamamoto Katsunosuke. *Nihon o horoboshita mono: gunbu dokusaika to sono hōkai no katei* [What Brought About Japan's Defeat: The Military Dictatorship and the Process of Its Destruction]. Tokyo: Shōkō Shoin, 1949. Foreword by Ishiwara Kanji.

615. Yamanaka Minetarō. *Tetsu ka niku ka: Nomonhansen hishi* [Iron or Flesh? The Secret History of the Nomonhan Fighting]. Tokyo: Seibundō Shinkōsha, 1940.

616. Yamazaki Kin'ichirō. *Manshū jihen no shinsō* [The True Story of the Manchurian Incident]. Wakayama: Taishō Shashin Kōgeisho, 1931.

617. Yanaibara Tadao. *Manshū mondai* [The Manchurian Problem]. Tokyo: Iwanami Shoten, 1932.

618. Yano Mitsuji. "Mōko de katsuyakushita hitobito" [People Who Played an Active Part in Mongolia], *Mongoru*, Nov. 1960, pp. 3-4.

619. ———, ed. *Mongoru no oitachi* [The Mongols' Early Days]. Tokyo: Privately printed, 1977.

620. Yasui Hisayoshi, ed. *Gyokusai senshi* [A History of Battles to the Death with Honor]. Tokyo: Gunji Kenkyūsha, 1970.

621. Yatsugi Kazuo. *Seihen Shōwa hishi: senjika no sōridaijin-tachi* [The Secret History of Changes of Government in the Shōwa Era: Wartime Prime Ministers]. Tokyo: Sankei Shuppan, 1979. 2 vols.

622. ———. *Shōwa dōran shishi* [A Personal History of the Shōwa Era Upheaval]. Tokyo: Keizai Ōraisha, 1971-73. 3 vols.

623. Yokoyama Shinpei. *Hiroku Ishiwara Kanji* [A Secret Record: Ishiwara Kanji]. Tokyo: Fuyō Shobō, 1971.

623A. Yonemoto Katsuo. "Nomonhan senjō no ryō butaichō" [A Pair of Unit Commanders on the Nomonhan Battlefield], *Kaikōsha Kiji*, Aug. 1941, pp. 25-29.

624. Yoshihara Nori. *Nihon rikugun kōheishi* [The History of the Japanese Army Engineers]. Tokyo: Kudansha, 1958.

625. ———. *Santari tetsudōhei no kiroku* [The Brilliant Record of the Railway Soldiers]. Tokyo: Zentetsukai Honbu, 1965.

626. Yoshii Hiroshi. "Doku-So fukashin jōyaku no teiketsu to Nomonhan jiken" [The Conclusion of the German-Soviet Nonaggression Pact and the Nomonhan Incident], *Hōgaku Kenkyū* (Nagoya), 1961, pp. 75-85.

627. Yoshimitsu Suemori. *Kūsenshi* [Air Battle History]. Tokyo: Daiyamondosha, 1943.

628. Yura Tetsuji, ed. *Sensha to senshasen* [Tanks and Tank Battles]. Tokyo: Daitō Shuppansha, 1944.

629. Yuzuhara Hidemi. "Nomonhan kōkūsen no sōkessan" [The Final Balance Sheet of the Nomonhan Air Battles], *Maru*, Jan. 1958, pp. 66-71.

IV. WESTERN SOURCES

630. Adachi Kinnosuke. *Manchuria: A Survey.* New York: McBride, 1925.

631. *Aireview's Seventy Fighters of World War II.* Tokyo: Kantosha, 1963.

632. Akimoto Shunkichi. *The Manchuria Scene.* Tokyo: Taisho Eibunsha, 1933.

633. Allen, Louis. *The End of the War in Asia.* London: Hart-Davis, MacGibbon, 1976.

634. Andreyev, Vladimir. "The First Days of the War," *Modern Age*, 11, no. 3 (Summer 1967), pp. 236-46.

635. Bailes, K. E. "Technology and Legitimacy: Soviet Aviation and Stalinism in the 1930's," *Technology and Culture*, 17, no. 1 (Jan. 1976), pp. 55-81.

636. Bawden, C. R. *The Modern History of Mongolia.* New York: Praeger, 1968.

637. Beloff, Max. *The Foreign Policy of Soviet Russia, 1929-1941.* London: Oxford University Press, 1947-49. Vol. 2.

638. ———. *Soviet Policy in the Far East, 1944-1951.* London: Oxford University Press, 1953.

639. Berchin, Michel, and Eliahu Ben-Horin. *The Red Army.* London: Allen and Unwin, 1943.

640. Bergamini, David. *Japan's Imperial Conspiracy.* New York: Morrow, 1971.

641. Bialer, Seweryn, comp. *Stalin and His Generals: Soviet Military Memoirs of World War II.* New York: Pegasus, 1969.

642. Bisson, T. A. *Japan in China.* New York: Macmillan, 1938.

643. ———. *Shadow Over Asia: The Rise of a Militant Japan.* New York: Foreign Policy Association, 1941.

644. Bix, Herbert P. "Japanese Imperialism and the Manchurian Economy, 1900-1931," *China Quarterly*, 51 (July-Sept. 1972), pp. 425-43.

645. Blakeney, Major Ben Bruce. "The Japanese High Command," *Military Affairs*, 9 (Summer 1945), pp. 95-113; (Fall 1945), pp. 208-18.

646. Bodley, Major R. V. C. *A Japanese Omelette: A British Writer's Impressions on the Japanese Empire*. Tokyo: Hokuseido, 1933.

647. Borg, Dorothy. *The United States and the Far Eastern Crisis of 1933-1938: From the Manchurian Incident Through the Initial Stage of the Undeclared Sino-Japanese War*. Cambridge, Mass.: Harvard University Press, 1964.

648. ———, and Okamoto Shumpei, eds. *Pearl Harbor as History: Japanese-American Relations, 1931-1941*. New York: Columbia University Press, 1973.

649. Borton, Hugh. *Japan's Modern Century: From Perry to 1970*. New York: Ronald Press, 1970. 2nd ed.

650. Boyd, Carl. *The Extraordinary Envoy: General Hiroshi Ōshima and Diplomacy in the Third Reich, 1934-1939*. Washington, D.C.: University Press of America, 1980.

651. ———. "The Role of Hiroshi Ōshima in the Preparation of the Anti-Comintern Pact," *J. Asian History*, 11, no. 1 (1977), pp. 49-71.

652. Boyle, John Hunter. *China and Japan at War, 1937-1945: The Politics of Collaboration*. Stanford, Calif.: Stanford University Press, 1972.

653. Brackman, Arnold C. *The Last Emperor: The Dramatic Story of the Emperor of China Who Became a Communist*. New York: Charles Scribner's Sons, 1975.

654. Bridges, Brian. "Mongolia in Soviet-Japanese Relations, 1933-36," in Nish, ed., *Some Aspects of Soviet-Japanese Relations in the 1930's*.

654A. Brown, William A., and Urgunge Onon, trans. and eds. *History of the Mongolian People's Republic*. Cambridge, Mass.: Harvard University Press, 1976.

655. Buck, James H., ed. *The Modern Japanese Military System*. Beverly Hills, Calif.: Sage Publications, 1975.

656. Burns, Richard Dean, and Edward M. Bennett, eds. *Diplomats in Crisis: United States–Chinese–Japanese Relations, 1919-1941*. Santa Barbara, Calif.: ABC-Clio, 1974.

657. Buss, Claude A. *War and Diplomacy in Eastern Asia*. New York: Macmillan, 1941.

658. Butow, Robert J. C. *Japan's Decision to Surrender*. Stanford, Calif.: Stanford University Press, 1954.

659. ———. *Tojo and the Coming of the War*. Princeton, N.J.: Princeton University Press, 1961.

660. Byas, Hugh. *Government by Assassination*. New York: Knopf, 1942.

661. Caidin, Martin. *The Ragged, Rugged Warriors*. New York: Dutton, 1966.

662. Cammann, Schuyler. *The Land of the Camel: Tents and Temples of Inner Mongolia*. New York: Ronald Press, 1951.

663. Carnegie Endowment for International Peace. *Manchuria: Treaties and Agreements*. Washington, D.C.: Carnegie Endowment, Division of International Law, 1921.

663A. Carr-Gregg, Charlotte. *Japanese Prisoners of War in Revolt: The Outbreaks at Featherston and Cowra during World War II*. New York: St. Martin's Press, 1978.

664. Carver, Field Marshal Sir Michael. *The War Lords: Military Commanders of the Twentieth Century*. London: Weidenfeld & Nicolson, 1976.

665. Chamberlin, W. H. *Japan Over Asia*. Boston: Little, Brown, 1937.

666. ———. "Russian Policies in the Far East," in Haring, *Japan's Prospect.*
667. Chaney, Otto Preston, Jr. *Zhukov.* Norman: University of Oklahoma Press, 1971.
668. Chang Tao-shing. *Russia, China, and the Chinese Eastern Railway.* Stanford, Calif.: Hoover Institution Press, 1972. Microfilm.
669. Chapman, John W. M. "The Polish Labyrinth and the Soviet Maze—Japan and the Floating World of Signals Intelligence, 1919-1939," in Nish, ed., *Some Aspects of Soviet-Japanese Relations in the 1930's.*
670. Cheng Tien-fong. *A History of Sino-Russian Relations.* Washington, D.C.: Public Affairs Press, 1957.
671. Chiang Chung-cheng (Chiang Kai-shek). *Soviet Russia in China: A Summing-Up at Seventy.* New York: Farrar, Straus & Cudahy, 1957.
672. Chuiko, Lt. Col. L. "The Story Told by Regimental Colours," *Soviet Military Review,* 38, no. 2 (Feb. 1968), pp. 9-11.
673. Clayberg, Anna A. "Soviet Policy Toward Japan, 1923-1941." Ph.D. dissertation, University of California, Berkeley, 1962.
674. Close, Upton (pseud. J. W. Hall). *Challenge: Behind the Face of Japan.* New York: Grosset & Dunlap, 1934.
675. Clyde, Paul Hibbert. *International Rivalries in Manchuria, 1689-1922.* Columbus: Ohio State University Press, 1928. 2nd ed.
676. Colegrove, Kenneth W. *Militarism in Japan.* Boston & New York: World Peace Foundation, 1936.
677. Collier, Basil. *Japanese Aircraft of World War II.* London: Sidgwick & Jackson, 1979.
678. Conroy, Hilary, and Takemoto Toru. "An Ounce of Prevention: A New Look at the Manchurian Incident," *Peace and Change,* 2, no. 1 (Spring 1974), pp. 42-46.
679. Coox, Alvin D. *The Anatomy of a Small War: The Soviet-Japanese Struggle for Changkufeng/Khasan, 1938.* Westport, Conn.: Greenwood Press, 1977.
680. ———. "Changkufeng and the Japanese 'Threat' to Vladivostok, 1938," *J. Asian History,* 5, no. 2 (1971), pp. 119-39.
681. ———. "Changkufeng: One Face of War," *Orient/West,* 7, no. 9 (Sept. 1962), pp. 77-88.
682. ———. "Effects of Attrition on National War Effort: The Japanese Army Experience in China, 1937-1938," *Military Affairs,* 32, no. 2 (Fall 1968), pp. 57-62.
683. ———. "High Command and Field Army: The Kwantung Army and the Nomonhan Incident, 1939," *Military Affairs,* 33, no. 2 (Oct. 1969), pp. 302-12.
684. ———. "Japanese Foreknowledge of the Soviet-German War, 1941," *Soviet Studies,* 23, no. 4 (Apr. 1972), pp. 554-72.
685. ———. "L'Affaire Lyushkov: Anatomy of a Defector," *Soviet Studies,* 19, no. 3 (Jan. 1968), pp. 405-20.
686. ———. "The Lake Khasan Affair of 1938: Overview and Lessons," *Soviet Studies,* 25, no. 1 (July 1973), pp. 51-65.
687. ———. "Maverick General of Imperial Japan" [Satō Kōtoku], *Army,* 15, no. 12 (July 1965), pp. 68-75.
688. ———. "The Myth of the Kwantung Army," *Marine Corps Gazette,* 42, no. 7 (July 1958), pp. 36-43.
689. ———. "Nomonhan, 1939," *Conflict,* no. 5 (20 June 1973), pp. 4-20 + appended war game titled "Khalkhin-Gol."
690. ———. "Qualities of Japanese Military Leadership: The Case of Suetaka Kamezō," *J. Asian History,* 2, no. 1 (1968), pp. 32-43.

691. ———. "Restraints on Air Power in Limited War: Japan vs. USSR at Changkufeng, 1938," *Aerospace Historian* 18, no. 4 (Dec. 1970), pp. 118-26.

692. ———. "The Rise and Fall of the Imperial Japanese Air Forces," *Aerospace Historian*, 27, no. 2 (June 1980), pp. 74-86.

693. ———. "Shigemitsu Mamoru: The Diplomacy of Crisis," in Burns and Bennett, *Diplomats in Crisis*, pp. 250-73.

694. ———. "Soviet Armor in Action Against the Japanese Kwantung Army, August 1945," ORO-T-38 (FEC), Sept. 1952 (Declassified). Operations Research Office, Johns Hopkins University, for Department of the Army.

695. ———. "Soviet Ousting of Japanese Consulates, 1937-38," *Orient/West*, 9, no. 5 (Sept.-Oct. 1964), pp. 48-58.

696. ———. *Tojo.* New York: Ballantine Books, 1975.

697. ———. *Year of the Tiger* [Japan domestic and external, 1937-38]. Tokyo and Philadelphia: Orient/West Press, 1964.

698. ———, and Hilary Conroy, eds. *China and Japan: Search for Balance Since World War I.* Santa Barbara, Calif.: ABC-Clio, 1978.

699. Craigie, Sir Robert. *Behind the Japanese Mask.* London: Hutchinson, 1946.

700. Crow, Duncan, and Robert J. Icks. *Encyclopedia of Tanks.* Secaucus, N.J.: Chartwell, 1975.

701. Crowley, James B. *Japan's Quest for Autonomy: National Security and Foreign Policy, 1930-1938.* Princeton, N.J.: Princeton University Press, 1966.

702. ———. "Japanese Army Factionalism in the 1930's," *J. Asian Studies*, 21, no. 3 (May 1962), pp. 309-26.

703. Culver, M. S. "Manchuria: Japan's Supply Base," *Far Eastern Survey*, 14 (1945), pp. 160-63.

704. Curtis, Monica, ed. *Documents on International Affairs, 1938.* London: Oxford University Press, 1942-43. 2 vols.

705. Dallin, David J. *The Rise of Russia in Asia.* New Haven, Conn.: Yale University Press, 1949.

706. ———. *Soviet Russia and the Far East.* New Haven, Conn.: Yale University Press, 1948.

707. ———. *Soviet Russia's Foreign Policy, 1939-42.* New Haven, Conn.: Yale University Press, 1942.

708. Davies, Joseph E. *Mission to Moscow.* New York: Simon & Schuster, 1941.

709. Deakin, F. W., and G. R. Storry. *The Case of Richard Sorge.* New York: Harper & Row, 1966.

710. Degras, Jane, ed. *Soviet Documents on Foreign Policy, 1917-1941.* London: Oxford University Press, 1951-53. 3 vols.

711. Dirksen, Herbert von. *Moscow, Tokyo, London: Twenty Years of German Foreign Policy.* Norman: University of Oklahoma Press, 1952.

712. Dodd, William E., Jr., and Martha Dodd, eds. *Ambassador Dodd's Diary, 1933-1938.* New York: Harcourt, Brace, 1941.

713. Doolin, Dennis J. *Territorial Claims in the Sino-Soviet Conflict: Documents and Analysis.* Stanford, Calif.: Hoover Institution Press, 1965.

714. Douglas, William O., and Dean Conger. "Journey to Outer Mongolia," *National Geographic Magazine*, 121, no. 3 (Mar. 1962), pp. 289-345.

715. Drea, Edward J. *Nomonhan: Japanese-Soviet Tactical Combat, 1939.* Fort Leavenworth, Kans.: Combat Studies Institute, U.S. Army Command and General Staff College, 1981.

716. Dull, Paul S. "The Assassination of Chang Tso-lin," *Far East Quarterly*, 11, no. 4 (Aug. 1952), pp. 453-63.

716A. Dupuy, Trevor N., et al. *Area Handbook for Mongolia*. Washington, D.C.: U.S. Government Printing Office, 1970.

717. Egler, David G. "Japanese Efforts at Mass Organization in Manchuria: *Kyōwa Kai* and *Minzoku Kyōwa*, 1931-1936." Manuscript.

718. Erickson, John. "Marshal Georgii Zhukov," in Carver, *The War Lords*.

719. ———. "The Red Army before June 1941," in Footman, ed., *Soviet Affairs No. 3*.

720. ———. "Reflections on Securing the Soviet Far Eastern Frontiers: 1932-1945," *Interplay*, 3, no. 2 (Aug.-Sept. 1969), pp. 54-57.

721. ———. *The Road to Stalingrad*. Vol. 1 of *Stalin's War with Germany*. New York: Harper & Row, 1975.

722. ———. *The Soviet High Command: A Military-Political History, 1918-1941*. London: Macmillan, 1962.

723. Fedyuninsky, I. "Halhin-Gol—30 Years Ago," *Soviet Military Review*, Aug. 1969, pp. 44-47.

724. Fleisher, Wilfrid. *Volcanic Isle*. Garden City, N.Y.: Doubleday, Doran, 1941.

725. Fochler-Hauke, Gustav. *Die Mandschurei*. Heidelberg, 1941.

726. Footman, David, ed. *Soviet Affairs No. 3*. London: Chatto & Windus, 1962. St. Antony's Papers No. 12.

727. France. Ministère des Affaires Étrangères. *Documents diplomatiques français, 1932-1939 (DDF)*. 1st Series (1932-35), vol. 1: 9 July–14 November 1932. Paris: Imprimerie Nationale, 1964.

728. Francillon, R. J. *Japanese Aircraft of the Pacific War*. New York: Funk & Wagnalls, 1970.

729. Friters, Gerard M. "The Development of Outer Mongolian Independence," *Pacific Affairs*, 10 (1937), pp. 315-36.

730. ———. *Outer Mongolia and Its International Position*. Baltimore, Md.: Johns Hopkins University Press, 1949.

731. ———. "The Prelude to Outer Mongolian Independence," *Pacific Affairs*, 10 (1937), pp. 168-89.

732. Garder, Michel. *A History of the Soviet Army*. New York: Praeger, 1966. Rev. ed. of *Histoire de l'Armée soviétique* (Paris, 1959), with supplementary material by John Erickson.

733. Garthoff, Raymond L. "Marshal Malinovsky's Manchurian Campaign," *Military Review*, 46 (Oct. 1966), pp. 50-61.

734. ———. "Soviet Intervention in Manchuria, 1945-1946," *Orbis*, 10, no. 2 (Summer 1966), pp. 520-47.

735. ———. *Soviet Military Doctrine*. Glencoe, Ill.: Free Press, 1953.

736. Gayn, Mark. *Japan Diary*. New York: W. Sloane Associates, 1948.

737. Germany. Auswärtiges Amt. *Documents on German Foreign Policy, 1918-45, From the Archives of the German Foreign Ministry*, Series D, 1937-45. Washington, D.C.: U.S. Government Printing Office, 1949-.

738. ———. Wehrmacht Oberkommando. *Blitzkrieg to Defeat: Hitler's War Directives, 1939-1945*, ed. H. R. Trevor-Roper. New York: Holt, Rinehart & Winston, 1965. Originally published as *Hitlers Weisungen für die Kriegsführung . . .*, ed. Walter Hubatsch (1962).

739. Gilbert, Carl L., Jr. "The Hirota Ministries: An Appraisal: Japan's Relations

with China and the U.S.S.R., 1933-1938." Ph.D. dissertation, Georgetown University, 1967.

740. Gilbert, Felix, ed. *Hitler Directs His War: The Secret Records of His Daily Military Conferences.* New York: Oxford University Press, 1950.

741. Goldman, Stuart D. "The Forgotten War: The Soviet Union and Japan, 1937-1939." Ph.D. dissertation, Georgetown University, 1970.

742. Gordon, Joseph. "The Russo-Japanese Neutrality Pact of April 1941," *Researches in the Social Sciences on Japan,* 2 (1959), pp. 119-34.

743. Gorelov, Col. G. "Rout of the Kwantung Army," *Soviet Military Review,* Aug. 1970, pp. 36-39.

744. Green, William. *Fighters.* Vol. 3 of *War Planes of the Second World War.* Garden City, N.Y.: Doubleday, 1964.

745. Grew, Joseph C. *Ten Years in Japan.* New York: Simon & Schuster, 1944.

746. ———. *Turbulent Era: A Diplomatic Record of Forty Years, 1904-1945,* ed. Walter Johnson. Cambridge, Mass.: Riverside Press, 1952. 2 vols.

746A. Grigorenko, Petro G. *Memoirs,* trans. Thomas P. Whitney. New York: W. W. Norton, 1982.

747. Gunston, Bill. *The Encyclopedia of the World's Combat Aircraft.* London: Salamander Books, 1976.

748. Gunther, John. *Inside Asia.* New York: Harper, 1942.

749. Hagerty, James Joseph. "The Soviet Share in the War with Japan." Ph.D. dissertation, Georgetown University, 1966.

750. Hall, Robert B. "Geographic Factors in Japanese Expansion," *Proceedings of the Institute of World Affairs,* University of Southern California, 1939.

751. Hall, Robert King. *Shūshin: The Ethics of a Defeated Nation.* New York: Columbia University Press, 1949.

752. Haring, Douglas G., ed. *Japan's Prospect.* Cambridge, Mass.: Harvard University Press, 1946.

753. Haslan, Jonathan. "Soviet Aid to China and Japan's Place in Moscow's Foreign Policy, 1937-1939," in Nish, ed., *Some Aspects of Soviet-Japanese Relations in the 1930's.*

754. Hata Ikuhiko. "The Japanese-Soviet Confrontation, 1935-1939," trans. Alvin D. Coox, in Morley, *Deterrent Diplomacy.*

755. ———. *Reality and Illusion: The Hidden Crisis Between Japan and the U.S.S.R., 1932-1934.* New York: Columbia University Press, 1967.

756. Hayashi Saburō, in collaboration with Alvin D. Coox. *Kōgun: The Japanese Army in the Pacific War.* Quantico, Va.: Marine Corps Association Press, 1959. Originally published as *Taiheiyō sensō rikusen gaishi.*

757. Hayes, Grace Person. *The History of the Joint Chiefs of Staff in World War II: The War Against Japan.* Annapolis, Md.: Naval Institute Press, 1982. (Declassified reprint of two-volume 1953 edition.)

758. Heald, Stephen, ed. *Documents on International Affairs, 1937.* London: Oxford University Press, 1939.

759. Hidaka Noboru, comp. *The Comintern's Intrigue in Manchoukuo.* Dairen: Manchuria Daily News, 1940.

760. ———. *Manchoukuo-Soviet Border Issues.* Dairen: Manchuria Daily News, 1938.

761. Hilger, Gustav, and Alfred G. Meyer. *The Incompatible Allies: A Memoir-History of German-Soviet Relations, 1918-1941.* New York: Macmillan, 1953.

762. Hindus, Maurice. *Russia and Japan.* Garden City, N.Y.: Doubleday, Doran, 1942.

763. Hinsley, F. H. *Hitler's Strategy.* Cambridge: Cambridge University Press, 1951.

764. Hirataka Danzō. "Khalkha River Oasis Seen as Main Cause of Manchu-Mongolian Friction," *China Weekly Review,* 90 (Sept. 1939), pp. 98-99.

765. Hishida Seiji. *Japan Among the Great Powers: A Survey of Her International Relations.* New York: Longmans, Green, 1940.

766. Historical Evaluation and Research Organization, The American University. *Area Handbook for Mongolia.* Washington, D.C.: U.S. Government Printing Office, 1970.

767. Howard, Harry Paxton. "Mongolia and the Russian-Japanese Conflict," *China Weekly Review,* 67 (Feb. 1934), pp. 442-44.

768. Hsu, Immanuel C. Y. *The Rise of Modern China.* New York: Oxford University Press, 1983. 3rd ed.

769. Hudson, G. F. *The Far East in World Politics: A Study in Recent History.* London: Oxford University Press, 1939.

770. ———, ed. *Far Eastern Affairs,* No. 1. New York: St. Martin's Press, 1957. St. Antony's Papers, No. 2.

771. Hudson, Manley O. *The Verdict of the League: China and Japan in Manchuria: The Official Documents. . . .* Boston: World Peace Foundation, 1933.

772. Hull, Cordell. *The Memoirs of Cordell Hull.* New York: Macmillan, 1948. 2 vols.

773. Humphreys, Leonard A. "The Japanese Military Tradition," in Buck, ed., *The Modern Japanese Military System.*

774. Icks, Col. Robert J. *Famous Tank Battles.* Garden City, N.Y.: Doubleday, 1972.

775. Ike Nobutaka, trans. and ed. *Japan's Decision for War: Records of the 1941 Policy Conferences.* Stanford, Calif.: Stanford University Press, 1967.

776. Iklé, Frank William. *German-Japanese Relations, 1936-1940: A Study in Totalitarian Diplomacy.* New York: Bookman Associates, 1956.

777. International Military Tribunal for the Far East (IMTFE). *Transcript of Proceedings,* 1946-1948 (mimeographed). Includes preliminary interrogations, accepted exhibits, summations, judgment, dissenting judgments, and miscellaneous documents. Rejected exhibits were made available to me in Tokyo by defense counsel, Ben Bruce Blakeney and George A. Furness; cited as Blakeney Collection and Furness Collection.

778. Ishida Kiyoshi. "An Outline of Outer Mongolia," *Contemporary Manchuria,* 3, no. 3 (July 1939), pp. 111-40.

779. Issraeljan, V., and L. Kutakov. *Diplomacy of Aggression: Berlin-Rome-Tokyo Axis, Its Rise and Fall.* Moscow: Progress Publishers, 1970.

780. James, David H. *The Rise and Fall of the Japanese Empire.* London: Allen & Unwin, 1951.

781. *The Japan-Manchoukuo Year Book, 1937: Cyclopedia of General Information and Statistics on the Empires of Japan and Manchoukuo.* Tokyo: The Japan-Manchoukuo Year Book Co., 1936.

782. *The Japan-Manchoukuo Year Book, 1939: Cyclopedia of General Information and Statistics on the Empires of Japan and Manchoukuo.* Tokyo, 1938.

782A. *The Japan-Manchoukuo Year Book, 1940: Cyclopedia of General Information and Statistics on the Empires of Japan and Manchoukuo.* Tokyo, 1939.

Japanese Research Division (JRD). See United States. Department of the Army [952]-[969].

783. Jones, F. C. *Japan's New Order in East Asia: Its Rise and Fall, 1937-45.* London: Oxford University Press, 1954.

784. ———. *Manchuria Since 1931.* London: Oxford University Press, 1949.

785. Kahn, B. Winston. *Doihara Kenji and the "North China Autonomy Movement," 1935-1936.* Tempe: Arizona State University, 1973.

786. Kajima Morinosuke. *A Brief Diplomatic History of Modern Japan.* Rutland, Vt.: Tuttle, 1965.

787. Kase Toshikazu. *Journey to the Missouri.* New Haven, Conn.: Yale University Press, 1950.

788. Kawai Tatsuo. *The Goal of Japanese Expansion.* Tokyo: Chūō Kōronsha, 1938.

789. Kawakami, K. K. *Japan Speaks on the Sino-Japanese Crisis.* New York: Macmillan, 1932.

790. ———. *Manchoukuo: Child of Conflict.* New York: Macmillan, 1933.

791. Kennan, George F. *Russia and the West Under Lenin and Stalin.* Boston: Little, Brown, 1961.

792. ———. *Soviet Foreign Policy, 1917-1941.* Princeton, N.J.: Van Nostrand, 1960.

793. Kennedy, Capt. Malcolm D. *The Estrangement of Great Britain and Japan, 1917-1935.* Manchester, Eng.: Manchester University Press, 1969.

794. ———. *The Military Side of Japanese Life.* London: Constable, 1924.

795. ———. *The Problem of Japan.* London: Nisbet, 1935.

796. ———. *Some Aspects of Japan and Her Defence Forces.* London: Kegan Paul, Trench & Trubner, 1928.

797. Kido Kōichi. "Diary," 11 July 1931 – 9 December 1945. IMTFE: IPS Doc. No. 1632 (IMT 2). Contains extracts, summaries, and full entries.

798. Kilmarx, Robert A. *A History of Soviet Air Power.* London: Faber & Faber, 1962.

799. Kim Chongham. "Konoye Fumimaro and Japanese Foreign Policy, 1937-1941." Ph.D. dissertation, Indiana University, 1956.

800. Kinney, Henry. W. *Modern Manchuria and the South Manchuria Railway Company.* Dairen: Japan Advertiser Press, 1928.

801. Kirby, E. Stuart. *The Soviet Far East.* London: Macmillan, 1971.

802. Kolarz, Walter. *The Peoples of the Soviet Far East.* New York: Praeger, 1954.

803. Kolkowicz, Roman. *The Soviet Military and the Communist Party.* Princeton, N.J.: Princeton University Press, 1967.

804. Kondo, H. "The Manchurian Bandits," *Contemporary Manchuria*, 3, no. 1 (Jan. 1939), pp. 80-103.

805. Kono Tsunekichi, Maj. Gen. *The Japanese Army.* Tokyo: Japanese Council, IPR, 1929.

806. Konoe Fumimaro. "Memoirs." IMTFE: IPS Doc. No. 3, 570, 1467, 849, 850 (IMT 3).

807. Kournakoff, Capt. Sergei N. *Russia's Fighting Forces.* New York: International Publishers, 1942.

808. Kramer, Irving I. *Japan in Manchuria.* Tokyo: Foreign Affairs Association of Japan, 1954.

809. Kuno, Yoshi S. *Japanese Expansion on the Asiatic Continent: A Study in the History of Japan with Special Reference to Her International Relations with China, Korea, and Russia.* Berkeley: University of California Press, 1937-40. 2 vols.

810. Kuo Jung-chao. "Chiang Kai-shek's Policy Toward Japan After the Mukden In-

cident, 1931-1937." Paper presented at annual conference of Asian Studies on the Pacific Coast (ASPAC), Asilomar, Calif., 16 June 1972.

811. Kurov, N. "Marshal Blucher," *Soviet Military Review*, Nov. 1969, pp. 42-43.

812. Kutakov, Leonid N. *Japanese Foreign Policy on the Eve of the Pacific War: A Soviet View*, ed. George A. Lensen. Tallahassee, Fla.: The Diplomatic Press, 1972.

813. Laffan, R. G. D., et al. *Survey of International Affairs, 1938*, ed. Veronica M. Toynbee. London: Oxford University Press, 1953. Vol. 3.

814. Langer, Robert. *Seizure of Territory: The Stimson Doctrine and Related Principles in Legal Theory and Diplomatic Practice*. Princeton, N.J.: Princeton University Press, 1947.

815. Lattimore, Eleanor. "Report on Outer Mongolia," *Far Eastern Survey*, 15 (1946), pp. 337-40.

816. Lattimore, Owen. "The Historical Setting of Inner Mongolian Nationalism," *Pacific Affairs*, 9 (1936), pp. 388-405.

817. ———. *Inner Asian Frontiers of China*. Irvington-on-Hudson, N.Y.: Capitol Publishing Co. & American Geographical Society, 1951. 2nd ed.

818. ———. "Mongolia: Filter or Floodgate?," *Geographical Magazine*, 22 (1949), pp. 212-21.

819. ———. *Nationalism and Revolution in Mongolia*. New York: Oxford University Press, 1955.

820. ———. *Nomads and Commissars: Mongolia Revisited*. New York: Oxford University Press, 1962.

821. ———. "The Outer Mongolian Horizon," *Foreign Affairs*, 24 (1946), pp. 648-60.

822. League of Nations. *Désarmement*. Vol. 9 of the 1937-38 *Annuaire Militaire: Renseignements généraux et statistiques sur les armements terrestres, navals et aériens*. Geneva, 1938.

823. ———. *Désarmement*. Vol. 9 of the 1939-40 *Annuaire Militaire*. Geneva, 1940.

824. ———. *Manchuria: Report of the Commission of Enquiry Appointed by the League of Nations*. Washington, D.C.: U.S. Government Printing Office, 1932.

825. Lee, Asher. *The Soviet Air Force*. London: Duckworth, 1961. Rev. ed.

826. Lee Chong-Sik. "The Chinese Communist Party and the Anti-Japanese Movement in Manchuria: The Initial Stage," in Coox and Conroy, eds., *China and Japan*.

827. Lensen, George Alexander. *The Damned Inheritance: The Soviet Union and the Manchurian Crises, 1924-1935*. Tallahassee, Fla.: The Diplomatic Press, 1974.

828. ———. *Japanese Diplomatic and Consular Officials in Russia: A Handbook of Japanese Representatives in Russia from 1874 to 1968. . . .* Tokyo and Tallahassee, Fla.: Sophia University in cooperation with The Diplomatic Press, 1968.

829. ———. *Japanese Recognition of the U.S.S.R.: Soviet-Japanese Relations, 1921-1930*. Tokyo and Tallahassee, Fla.: Sophia University in cooperation with The Diplomatic Press, 1970.

830. ———. *The Strange Neutrality: Soviet-Japanese Relations During the Second World War, 1941-1945*. Tallahassee, Fla.: The Diplomatic Press, 1972.

831. Lessner, Erwin. "Russia's Strategy in the Pacific," *Harper's*, 191 (July 1945), pp. 37-44.

832. Liang Chin-tung. *The Sinister Face of the Mukden Incident*. New York: St. John's University Press, 1969.

833. Liddell Hart, B. H., ed. *The Red Army.* New York: Harcourt, Brace, 1956.

834. Lippmann, Walter. *The United States in World Affairs: An Account of American Foreign Relations, 1932.* New York: Harper, 1933.

835. Litvinov, Maxim. *Notes for a Journal.* New York: Morrow, 1955.

836. Liu, F. F. *A Military History of Modern China, 1924-1949.* Princeton, N.J.: Princeton University Press, 1956.

837. Lockwood, William W. "The Political Consequences of Economic Development in Japan." Japanese Studies Seminar, Tokyo, May 1962.

838. Lory, Hillis. *Japan's Military Masters: The Army in Japanese Life.* New York: Viking, 1943.

839. Lothian, Alan. "Khalkhin-Gol 1939," *War Monthly,* 20 (Nov. 1975), pp. 11-17.

840. Lu, David. *From the Marco Polo Bridge to Pearl Harbor: A Study of Japan's Entry into World War II.* Washington, D.C.: Public Affairs Press in cooperation with Bucknell University Press, 1961.

841. Lupke, Hubertus. *Japans Russlandpolitik von 1939 bis 1941.* Frankfurt am Main: Metzner, 1962.

842. Lyons, Graham, ed. *The Russian Version of the Second World War: The History of the War as Taught to Soviet Schoolchildren.* London: Leo Cooper, 1976.

843. Lytton, The Earl of. Correspondence, 1932-1933. Typescript, Cobbold Collection, Herts., England.

844. ———. "Moukden Diary," 1932. Typescript, Cobbold Collection.

845. Lyushkoff, Gen. G. S. "The Far Eastern Red Army," *Contemporary Japan,* 8, no. 8 (Oct. 1939), pp. 1022-25. Originally published in *Kaizō,* Sept. 1939, pp. 148-63.

846. Mackintosh, J. Malcolm. *Juggernaut: A History of the Soviet Armed Forces.* London: Secker & Warburg, 1967.

847. Mammone, Gatto. "Russia, Japan, and Red Mongolia," *New International,* Sept.-Oct. 1934, pp. 88-89.

848. Manchukuo, Government of. "The Chief Executive's Proclamation, the Organic Law of Manchoukuo and Other Laws Governing Various Government Offices." Hsinking, 1932.

849. ———. *Manchoukuo: Handbook of Information.* Hsinking, 1933.

850. ———. Department of Foreign Affairs. *A General Outline of Manchoukuo.* Hsinking, 1932.

851. ———. State Council, Bureau of Information. *An Outline of the Manchoukuo Empire.* Dairen: Manchuria Daily News, 1939.

852. Manchuria Daily News. *The Comintern's Activity in Manchuria.* Hsinking: Manchuria Daily News, 1940.

853. ———. *Nomonhan Incident.* Dairen: Manchuria Daily News, 1939.

854. Mandel, William. *The Soviet Far East and Central Asia.* New York: Dial, 1944.

855. Mansvetov, Fedor S. "Inside Outer Mongolia," *Asia and the Americas,* May 1945, pp. 244-47.

856. ———. "Russia and China in Outer Mongolia," *Foreign Affairs,* 24 (Oct. 1945), pp. 143-52.

857. ———. "Strategic Mongolia," *Asia and the Americas,* April 1945, pp. 202-5.

858. Maruyama Masao. *Thought and Behaviour in Modern Japanese Politics,* ed. Ivan Morris. London: Oxford University Press, 1963.

859. Mashbir, Col. Sidney F. *I Was an American Spy.* New York: Vantage, 1953.

860. Matsuoka Yōsuke. *Building Up Manchuria.* Tokyo: Herald of Asia, 1938.

861. Maxon, Yale Candee. *Control of Japanese Foreign Policy: A Study of Civil-Military Rivalry, 1930-1945.* Berkeley: University of California Press, 1957.
862. Mayer, S. L., ed. *The Japanese War Machine.* London: Bison, 1976.
863. McCormack, Gavan. *Chang Tso-lin in Northeast China, 1911-1928: China, Japan, and the Manchurian Idea.* Stanford, Calif.: Stanford University Press, 1977.
864. McLean, Donald B., comp. and ed. *Japanese Artillery: Weapons and Tactics.* Wickenburg, Ariz.: Normount Technical Publications, 1973.
865. ———. *Japanese Infantry Weapons.* Forest Grove, Ore.: Normount Armament Co., 1966. Vol. 1.
866. ———. *Japanese Tanks, Tactics, & Antitank Weapons.* Wickenburg, Ariz.: Normount Technical Publications, 1973.
867. McSherry, James E. *Stalin, Hitler, and Europe.* Vol. 1: *The Origins of World War II, 1933-1939.* Vol. 2: *The Imbalance of Power, 1939-1941.* Cleveland: World, 1968, 1970.
868. Meskill, Johanna Menzel. *Hitler & Japan: The Hollow Alliance.* New York: Atherton, 1966.
869. Michael, Franz. "The Background for the Fight for Mongolia," *Contemporary Review,* 152 (Sept. 1937), pp. 316-24.
870. Miller, Martin. *Red Armour in Combat.* Canoga Park, Calif.: Grenadier, 1969.
871. Milsom, John. *Russian Tanks, 1900-1970.* New York: Galahad, 1970.
872. Minear, Richard H. *Victors' Justice: The Tokyo War Crimes Trial.* Princeton, N.J.: Princeton University Press, 1971.
873. Misshima [Mishima] Yasuo, and Gotō Tomio. *A Japanese View of Outer Mongolia.* New York: IPR, 1942. Originally published as *Gaimō Jinmin Kyō-wakoku.*
874. Moore, Harriet L. *Soviet Far Eastern Policy, 1931-1945.* Princeton, N.J.: Princeton University Press, 1945.
875. Morley, James William, ed. *Deterrent Diplomacy: Japan, Germany, and the USSR, 1935-1940.* New York: Columbia University Press, 1976. Originally published in *Taiheiyō sensō e no michi.*
876. ———. *The Fateful Choice: Japan's Advance into Southeast Asia, 1939-1941.* New York: Columbia University Press, 1980. Originally published in *Taiheiyō sensō e no michi.*
877. ———. *Japan's Foreign Policy, 1868-1941: A Research Guide.* New York: Columbia University Press, 1974.
878. Morton, William Fitch. *Tanaka Giichi and Japan's China Policy.* New York: St. Martin's Press, 1980.
879. Moses, Larry W. "The Battle of Nomonhan–Khalkhin Gol." M.A. thesis, Indiana University, 1966.
880. ———. "Revolutionary Mongolia Chooses a Faith: Lamaism or Leninism." Ph.D. dissertation, Indiana University, 1972.
881. ———. "Soviet-Japanese Confrontation in Outer Mongolia: The Battle of Nomonhan–Khalkhin Gol," *J. Asian History,* 1, no. 1 (1967), pp. 64-85.
882. Murphy, George G. S. *Soviet Mongolia: A Study of the Oldest Political Satellite.* Berkeley: University of California Press, 1966.
882A. Myers, LCDR Albert C., US Navy. "Khalkin Gol: Stalin's Battle to Stabilize the Soviet Far East," *Military Review,* 43, no. 4 (Apr. 1983), pp. 60-65.
883. Nish, Ian. *Japanese Foreign Policy, 1869-1942: Kasumigaseki to Miyakezaka.* London: Routledge & Kegan Paul, 1977.

884. ———, ed. *Some Aspects of Soviet-Japanese Relations in the 1930's.* London: London School of Economics and Political Science, 1982. International Studies, 1982/II.

885. Nunomura Yumiko. "The Rise and Fall of Matsuoka Yōsuke." M.A. thesis, San Diego State University, 1978.

886. Ogata, Sadako N. *Defiance in Manchuria: The Making of Japanese Foreign Policy, 1931-1932.* Berkeley: University of California Press, 1964.

887. Oka Akio. "Imperial Japan's Hypothetical Enemy: The Soviet Union, 1931-1945." M.A. thesis, San Diego State University, 1980.

888. Onon Urgunge, trans. and ed. *Mongolian Heroes of the Twentieth Century.* New York: AMS Press, 1976.

889. Parrish, Michael. "Formation and Leadership of the Soviet Mechanized Corps in 1941," *Military Affairs,* 47 (Apr. 1983), pp. 63-66.

889A. ———. "General G. M. Shtern: A Biographical Inquiry," *Soviet Jewish Affairs,* 1 (1975), pp. 73-76.

890. Peattie, Mark R. *Ishiwara Kanji and Japan's Confrontation with the West.* Princeton, N.J.: Princeton University Press, 1975.

891. Penlington, John N. *The Mukden Mandate: Acts and Aims in Manchuria.* Tokyo: Maruzen, 1932.

892. Phillips, G. D. R. *Russia, Japan and Mongolia.* London: Frederick Muller, 1942.

893. Piggott, Maj. Gen. F. S. G. *Broken Thread: An Autobiography.* Aldershot, Eng.: Gale & Polden, 1950.

894. Ponomaryov, B., A. Gromyko, and V. Khvostov, eds. *History of Soviet Foreign Policy, 1917-1945.* Moscow: Progress Publishers, 1969.

895. Pospelov, P. N., et al., eds. *Great Patriotic War of the Soviet Union, 1941-1945: A General Outline.* Moscow: Progress Publishers, 1974. Abridged translation of 1970 edition.

896. Pratt, Sir John T. *Before Pearl Harbor: A Study of the Historical Background to the War in the Pacific.* London: Caxton, 1944.

897. Prescott, J. R. V. *Boundaries and Frontiers.* London: Croom Helm, 1978.

898. Presseisen, Ernst L. *Germany and Japan: A Study in Totalitarian Diplomacy, 1933-1941.* The Hague: Nijhoff, 1958.

899. Pu Yi, Aisin-Gioro. *From Emperor to Citizen: The Autobiography of Aisin-Gioro Pu Yi.* Peking: Foreign Languages Press, 1964-65. 2 vols.

900. Rappaport, Armin. *Henry L. Stimson and Japan, 1931-33.* Chicago: University of Chicago Press, 1963.

901. Rea, George Bronson. *The Case for Manchoukuo.* New York: Appleton-Century, 1935.

902. Riess, Curt, ed. *They Were There: The Story of World War II and How It Came About, by America's Foremost Correspondents.* Garden City, N.Y.: Garden City Publishing Co., 1945.

903. Rōyama Masamichi. *Foreign Policy of Japan, 1914-1939.* Tokyo: Japanese Council, IPR, 1941.

904. Rupen, Robert A. "Mongolia in the Sino-Soviet Dispute," *China Quarterly,* 16 (Nov.-Dec. 1963), pp. 75-85.

905. ———. *The Mongolian People's Republic.* Stanford, Calif.: Hoover Institution, 1966.

906. ———. "Notes on Outer Mongolia Since 1945," *Pacific Affairs,* 28 (1955), pp. 71-79.

907. Ruslanov, P. "Marshal Zhukov," *Russian Review*, 15 (Apr. 1956), pp. 22-29; (July 1956), pp. 186-95.

908. Saitō Hirosi [Hiroshi]. *Japan's Policies and Purposes: Selections from Recent Addresses and Writings*. Boston: Marshall Jones, 1935.

909. Sapozhnikov, G., and V. B. Vorontsov. "The Soviet Union's Role in the War Against Japan," *Current Digest of the Soviet Press*, 17, no. 42 (10 Nov. 1965), pp. 15-20, 44. Trans. from *Istoria SSSR*, 4 (July-Aug. 1965), pp. 28-48.

910. Sasaki Chiyoko. *Der Nomonhan Konflikt: Das fernöstliche Vorspiel zum Zweiten Weltkrieg*. Ph.D. dissertation, Rheinischen Friedrich-Wilhelms-Universität, Bonn, 1968.

911. Schapiro, Leonard, ed. *Soviet Treaty Series: A Collection of Bilateral Agreements and Conventions, etc., Concluded Between the Soviet Union and Foreign Powers*. Washington, D.C.: Georgetown University Press, 1950-55. 2 vols.

912. Schroeder, Paul W. *The Axis Alliance and Japanese-American Relations, 1941*. Ithaca, N.Y.: Cornell University Press, 1958.

913. Scribner, Henry I., Jr. "Thought Control in Modern Japan." M.A. thesis, San Diego State University, 1979.

914. Seaton, Albert. *The Russo-German War, 1941-45*. New York: Praeger, 1971.

915. Sekigawa Eiichirō. "The Undeclared Air War," *Air Enthusiast*, 4, no. 5 (May 1973), pp. 245-50; no. 6 (June 1973), pp. 294-96; no. 7 (July 1973), pp. 26-29, 47.

916. Serebrennikov, I. I. "A Soviet Satellite, Outer Mongolia Today," *Foreign Affairs*, 9 (1931), pp. 510-15.

917. Shigemitsu Mamoru. *Japan and Her Destiny: My Struggle for Peace*, trans. Oswald White, ed. F. S. G. Piggott. London: Hutchinson, 1958.

918. Shih Li-shin. "No Repetition of the 'September 18 Incident'," *China Reconstructs* (Peking), Sept. 1971, p. 15.

919. Shirendyb Bagaryn, et al., eds. *History of the Mongolian People's Republic*, trans. from the Mongolian and annotated by William A. Brown and Urgunge Onon. Cambridge, Mass.: Harvard University Press, 1976.

920. Shishkin, Col. S. N. "Soviet Army Version of Nomonhan Incident," JRD [965], JSM 11, part 3/C, Appendix H, pp. 563-634, trans. P. Materman, abridged and ed. Alvin D. Coox. Originally published as *Khalkhin Gol*.

921. Shores, Christopher. *Fighter Aces*. London: Hamlyn, 1975.

922. Shtemenko, Gen. S. M. *The Soviet General Staff at War, 1941-1945*. Moscow: Progress Publishers, 1970.

923. Slackman, Michael. "Matsuoka and the USSR, 1940-1941." M.A. thesis, San Diego State University, 1970.

924. Slusser, Robert M., and Jan F. Triska, eds. *A Calendar of Soviet Treaties, 1917-1957*. Stanford, Calif.: Stanford University Press, 1959.

925. Smith, Sara R. *The Manchurian Crisis, 1931-1932: A Tragedy in International Relations*. New York: Columbia University Press, 1948.

926. Smith, Warren W., Jr. *Confucianism in Modern Japan: A Study of Conservatism in Japanese Intellectual History*. Tokyo: Hokuseidō, 1973.

927. South Manchuria Railway Company. *Third Report on Progress in Manchuria to 1932*. Dairen: SMR, 1932.

928. ———. *Fifth Report on Progress in Manchuria to 1936*. Dairen: SMR, 1936.

929. ———. Information & Publicity Department. "Comintern's Plottings in Manchuria," *Contemporary Manchuria*, 2, no. 3 (May 1938), pp. 146-57.

930. "The Soviet-Mongolian Campaign Against Japan, August 1945," *Central*

Asian Review, 4 (1966), pp. 306-16. Précis of Gen. I. A. Pliyev, *Cherez Gobi i Khingan* [Through the Gobi and the Hsingan] (Moscow, 1965).

931. Stalin, Joseph. *Problems of Leninism*. Moscow: Foreign Languages Publishing House, 1953.

932. Steele, A. T. *Shanghai and Manchuria, 1932: Recollections of a War Correspondent*. Tempe: Arizona State University, 1977.

933. Stein, Guenther. *Far East in Ferment*. London: Methuen, 1936.

934. Steinberg, F. "If Russia Fights Japan," *Asia*, 45 (June 1945), pp. 268-72.

935. Stimson, Henry L. *The Far Eastern Crisis: Recollections and Observations*. New York: Harper, 1936.

936. Storry, Richard. *The Double Patriots: A Study of Japanese Nationalism*. London: Chatto & Windus, 1957.

937. ———. "The Mukden Incident of September 18-19, 1931," in Hudson, ed., *Far Eastern Affairs*, No. 1.

938. ———. "Soldiers of the Showa Empire," *Pacific Affairs*, 49 (Jan. 1976), pp. 102-7.

939. Takeuchi Tatsuji. *War and Diplomacy in the Japanese Empire*. Garden City, N.Y.: Doubleday, Doran, 1935.

940. Tang, Peter S. H. *Russian and Soviet Policy in Manchuria and Outer Mongolia, 1911-1931*. Durham, N.C.: Duke University Press, 1959.

941. Tantum, W. H., IV, and E. J. Hoffschmidt. *Second World War Combat Weapons*, Vol. 2, *Japanese*. Old Greenwich, Conn.: WE, Inc., 1968.

942. Thiel, Erich. *The Soviet Far East: A Survey of Its Physical and Economic Geography*. New York: Praeger, 1957.

943. "The '39 Mongolian Border War: A Reminder to Mao," *Current Digest of the Soviet Press*, 17 Sept. 1969, pp. 3-7.

944. Tilley, Sir John. *London to Tokyo*. London: Hutchinson, n.d.

945. Tinch, Clark W. "Quasi-war Between Japan and the USSR, 1937-1939," *World Politics*, 3, no. 2 (Jan. 1951), pp. 174-99.

946. Titus, David Anson. *Palace and Politics in Prewar Japan*. New York: Columbia University Press, 1974.

947. Tōgō Shigenori. *The Cause of Japan*, trans. and ed. Tōgō Fumihiko and Ben Bruce Blakeney. New York: Simon & Schuster, 1956. Originally published as *Tōgō Shigenori gaikō shuki*.

948. Toynbee, Arnold J. *Survey of International Affairs, 1931*. London: Oxford University Press, 1932. Also *Survey* volumes for 1932, 1933, 1934, 1935 (vol. 1), 1937 (vols. 1-2), each published the year following the period covered; 1939-1946, published in 1958. For 1938 *Survey* (vol. 3), see Laffan et al. [813].

949. United Kingdom. *Documents on British Foreign Policy, 1919-1939* (*DBFP*). London: Her Majesty's Stationery Office, 1955-60.

950. ———. ———. Second Series: Vol. 8, *1929-31*, ed. Rohan Butler and J. P. T. Bury (1960).

951. ———. ———. Third Series: Vol. 8, *1938-39*, ed. E. L. Woodward and Rohan Butler (1955); Vol. 9, *1939*, ed. Woodward and Butler (1955).

United States. Department of the Army. Hq. Army Forces Far East, Military History Section, Japanese Research Division.

NOTE: The following Japanese Research Division (JRD) titles are identified by the abbreviations *JM* for Japanese Monograph and *JSM* for Japanese Studies on Manchuria.

952. *Air Operations.* JRD, *JSM* 4 (1959).

953. *Air Operations Record Against Soviet Russia.* JRD, *JM* 151 (1952).

954. *Armor Operations.* JRD, *JSM* 6 (1957).

955. *Imperial Japanese Army in Manchuria, 1894-1945,* JRD, *JSM* 2 (1959).

956. *Infantry Operations.* JRD, *JSM* 5 (1956).

957. *Interrogations of Japanese Officials.* JRD, unnumbered monograph, n.d.

958. *Japanese Intelligence Planning Against the USSR.* JRD, *JSM* 10 (1955).

959. *Japanese Night Combat.* JRD, unnumbered monograph (1955). Part 1: *Principles of Night Combat*; Part 2: *Excerpts from Japanese Training Manuals*; Part 3: *Night Combat Examples.*

960. *Japanese Operational Planning Against the USSR.* JRD, *JSM* 1 (1955).

961. *Japanese Preparations for Operations in Manchuria (Prior to 1943).* JRD, *JM* 77 (1954).

962. *Japanese Preparations for Operations in Manchuria (Jan. 43–Aug. 45).* JRD, *JM* 138 (1953).

963. *Record of Operations Against Soviet Russia, Eastern Front (August 1945).* JRD, *JM* 154 (1954).

964. *Record of Operations Against Soviet Russia on Northern and Western Fronts of Manchuria, and in Northern Korea (August 1945).* JRD, *JM* 155 (1954).

965. *Small Wars and Border Problems.* JRD, *JSM* 11 (1956). Part 1: *Small Wars and Border Problems*; Part 2: *Garrisons and Fortifications*; Part 3, Book A: *The Changkufeng Incident*; Part 3, Books B and C: *The Nomonhan Incident.*

966. *Statements of Japanese Officials.* JRD, unnumbered monograph, n.d.

967. *Strategic Study of Manchuria: Military Topography and Geography.* JRD, *JSM* 3 (1955-56). 4 parts.

968. *Study of Strategical and Tactical Peculiarities of Far Eastern Russia and Soviet Far East Forces.* JRD, *JSM* 13 (1955).

969. *Supporting Arms and Services.* JRD, *JSM* 7 (1958). Part 1: *Artillery and Anti-aircraft Artillery Operations.*

970. United States. Department of Commerce. Bureau of the Census. *The Population of Manchuria,* by Waller Wynne, Jr. Washington, D.C.: U.S. Government Printing Office, 1958.

971. ———. Department of Defense. "The Entry of the Soviet Union into the War Against Japan: Military Plans, 1941-1945." Mimeographed, 1955.

972. ———. ———. *The "Magic" Background of Pearl Harbor.* Washington, D.C.: U.S. Government Printing Office, 1978. 5 vols. + 3 appendixes. Declassified and enlarged edition of 1944 version.

973. ———. Department of State. *Documents on German Foreign Policy, 1918-1945 (DGFP).* Series D: Vol. 8, *The War Years: September 4, 1939–March 18, 1940.* Washington, D.C., 1954.

974. ———. ———. *Foreign Relations of The United States: Diplomatic Papers (FRUS).* 1938, 5 vols. (1954-55); 1939, 5 vols. (1955); 1941, 7 vols. (1956-58).

975. ———. ———. *Nazi-Soviet Relations, 1939-1941: Documents from the Archives of the German Foreign Office,* ed. R. J. Sontag and J. S. Beddie. Washington, D.C., 1948.

976. ———. ———. *Papers Relating to the Foreign Relations of the United States: Japan: 1931-1941.* Washington, D.C., 1943. 2 vols.

977. ———. ———. *Peace and War: United States Foreign Policy, 1931-1941.* Washington, D.C., 1943.

978. ———. ———. *The Soviet Union, 1933-1939.* Washington, D.C., 1952.

979. ———. Federal Broadcast and Information Service (FBIS). *Daily Reports,* Moscow and Ulan Bator monitors.

980. ———. National Archives and Records Service (NARS). Department of State File/Manchuria; War Department G-2 Reports (Military Intelligence Division), Military Attaché Reports, Tokyo and Moscow.

981. ———. War Department. *Handbook on Japanese Military Forces.* Washington, D.C., 1944. Technical Manual TM-E 30-480. Declassified.

982. ———. ———. Military Intelligence Service. *Japanese Ground and Air Forces.* Washington, D.C., 1942. MID-461. Declassified.

983. ———. ———. ———. *Disposition and Movements of Japanese Ground Forces, 1941-1945.* Washington, D.C., 1945. MID Review No. 6. Declassified.

984. ———. ———. ———. *Order of Battle of the Japanese Armed Forces.* Washington, D.C., 1945. Declassified.

985. Union of Soviet Socialist Republics (USSR). Academy of Sciences. *History of the Mongolian People's Republic.* Moscow: Nauka, 1973.

986. ———. ———. Institute of the Far East. *The Far East in the Second World War: An Outline History of International Relations and National Liberation Struggle in East and South-east Asia,* by A. M. Dubinsky. Moscow: Nauka, 1972.

987. ———. ———. Institute of History. *A Short History of the USSR.* Moscow: Progress Publishers, 1965. 2 vols.

988. ———. ———. Institute of Military History. *The Rise and Fall of the Gunbatsu: A Study in Military History,* ed. Y. M. Zhukov et al. Moscow: Progress Publishers, 1975.

989. ———. Military Tribunal of the Primorye Military Area, Khabarovsk. *Materials on the Trial of Former Servicemen of the Japanese Army Charged with Manufacturing and Employing Bacteriological Weapons.* Moscow: Foreign Languages Publishing House, 1950.

990. ———. Ministry of Defense. *The Soviet Air Force in World War II: The Official History . . .,* trans. Leland Fetzer, ed. Ray Wagner. Garden City, N.Y.: Doubleday, 1973.

991. ———. Ministry for Foreign Affairs. *Milestones of Soviet Foreign Policy, 1917-1967.* Moscow: Progress Publishers, 1967.

992. ———. ———. *Soviet Peace Efforts on the Eve of World War II (September 1938–August 1939): Documents and Records,* ed. V. M. Falin et al. Moscow: Novosti Press Agency, 1973. 2 vols.

993. Urach, Albrecht Fürst von. *Das Geheimnis Japanischer Kraft.* Berlin: Zentralverlag der NSDAP, 1944.

994. van der Wee, Herman, ed. *The Great Depression Revisited: Essays on the Economics of the Thirties.* The Hague: Nijhoff, 1972.

995. Warner, Philip. *Japanese Army of World War II.* Reading, Eng.: Osprey, 1973.

996. Wei, Henry. *China and Soviet Russia.* Princeton, N.J.: Van Nostrand, 1956.

997. Weinberg, Gerhard L. *Germany and the Soviet Union, 1939-1941.* Leiden: Brill, 1954.

998. Weland, James Edwin. "The Japanese Army in Manchuria: Covert Operations and the Roots of Kwantung Army Insubordination." Ph.D. dissertation, University of Arizona, 1977.

999. Werner, Max (pseud.). *The Military Strength of the Powers.* New York: Modern Age Books, 1939.

1000. Werth, Alexander. *Russia at War, 1941-1945.* New York: Dutton, 1964.

1001. Wheeler-Bennett, John W., ed. *Documents on International Affairs*. London: Oxford University Press. Volumes for 1929 (1930), 1932 (1933).

1002. Willoughby, Maj. Gen. Charles A. *Shanghai Conspiracy: The Sorge Spy Ring: Moscow, Shanghai, Tokyo, San Francisco, New York*. New York: Dutton, 1952.

1003. Willoughby, Westel W. *Japan's Case Examined; with Supplementary Chapters on the Far Eastern Policies of the United States, and the Significance to the World of the Conflict in the Far East*. Baltimore, Md.: Johns Hopkins University Press, 1940.

1004. ———. *The Sino-Japanese Controversy and the League of Nations*. Baltimore, Md.: Johns Hopkins University Press, 1935.

1005. Wilson, Hugh R. *Diplomat Between Wars*. New York: Longmans, Green, 1941.

1006. Wollenberg, Erich. *The Red Army: A Study of the Growth of Soviet Imperialism*, trans. C. W. Sykes. London: Secker & Warburg, 1940.

1007. Wong, William. "Henry Pu Yi and the Japanese, 1924-45: A Study in Puppetry." M.A. thesis, University of California, Berkeley, 1951.

1008. Wu, Aitchen K. *China and the Soviet Union: A Study of Sino-Soviet Relations*. New York: John Day, 1950.

1009. Yamamura Kozo. "Then Came the Great Depression: Japan's Interwar Years," in van der Wee, *The Great Depression Revisited*.

1010. Yoshihashi Takehiko. *Conspiracy at Mukden: The Rise of the Japanese Military*. New Haven, Conn.: Yale University Press, 1963.

1011. Young, C. Walter. *Japan's Jurisdiction and International Position in Manchuria*. Baltimore, Md.: Johns Hopkins University Press, 1931. Vol. 1: *Japan's Special Position in Manchuria: Its Assertion, Legal Interpretation and Present Meaning*. Vol. 2: *The International Legal Status of the Kwantung Leased Territory*. Vol. 3: *Japanese Jurisdiction in the South Manchuria Railway Areas*.

1012. Young, John. *The Research Activities of the South Manchurian Railway Company, 1907-1945: A History and Bibliography*. New York: Columbia University Press, 1966.

1013. Young, Katsu Hirai. "The Japanese Army and the Soviet Union, 1936-1941." Ph.D. dissertation, University of Washington, 1968.

1014. ———. "The Nomonhan Incident: Imperial Japan and the Soviet Union," *Monumenta Nipponica*, 22, no. 1-2 (1967), pp. 82-102.

1015. Zakharov, Marshal M. V., ed. *Finale: A Retrospective Review of Imperialist Japan's Defeat in 1945*. Moscow: Progress Publishers, 1972.

1016. Zhukov, Georgi K. *Marshal Zhukov's Greatest Battles*, trans. Theodore Shabad, ed. Harrison E. Salisbury. New York: Harper & Row, 1969.

1017. ———. *The Memoirs of Marshal Zhukov*. New York: Delacorte, 1971.

1018. Zumoto Motosada. *Sino-Japanese Entanglements, 1931-1932: A Military Record*. Tokyo: Herald Press, 1932.

V. SELECTED RUSSIAN SOURCES

Michael Parrish, Indiana University

Between 1938 and the German invasion in June 1941, the USSR was involved in three direct armed conflicts, two against the Japanese—at Lake Khasan (Changkufeng) in 1938 and at Khalkhin Gol (Nomonhan) in 1939—and a third against Finland in the winter of 1939-40.* There is no scarcity of Soviet material on Khalkhin

---

*I exclude Soviet aid to the Spanish Republic in the late 1930's and the absorption of eastern Poland and Bessarabia in 1939, since they were not wars in the real sense for the Red Army.

Gol, but we do lack a truly comprehensive study such as the book by Koltunov and Solov'ev on the battle of Kursk. In fact, in regard to Khalkhin Gol there are gaps in our knowledge of such basic facts as the Soviet formations deployed and their command personnel. Several recent publications, particularly articles in *Voenno istoricheskii zhurnal*, have given us some indications of the strength of the Soviet and Japanese forces involved. Also useful is the book *Pobeda na reke Khalkhin Gol*, published in 1981.

In 1970, drawing on archival material, Marshal M. V. Zakharov published reminiscences that shed new light on the period. As assistant chief of staff for organization and mobilization from May 1938, Zakharov was in an exceptionally good position to observe the course of the Khalkhin Gol operations. According to Zakharov, Stalin took a personal interest in the tactical aspects of the Khalkhin Gol campaign. The Soviets felt so uneasy about the situation in the Far East that they did not dissolve Zhukov's command until June 1940. Even then, they replaced it with the Red Banner Far Eastern Front based in Khabarovsk and commanded by G. M. Shtern.

In 1980, V. Odintsov and V. Ovsianikov published the first detailed Soviet study of rear area services during the campaign of 1939. Providing supplies for the 57th Corps located at Ulan Bator at the outset of the skirmishing was the responsibility of the deputy chief of staff for rear services, Major I. G. Khomus'kov. As the conflict expanded, the Russians moved up reinforcements, finally reorganized into an army group under Zhukov. The rear services became correspondingly larger and more complicated and were taken over by the Trans-Baikal Military District. Using archival resources, the authors present selected statistics underscoring the problems of supply during combat in primitive areas with less than satisfactory roads.

In 1980, too, Col. V. Starodubtsev brought out the first short study of Party political work in the Khalkhin Gol fighting. On the basis of archival data, Starodubtsev indicates feverish political activity between June and August 1939, during which time Party membership among combat forces increased by nearly 2,000, from 5,169 to 6,922. For the first time the political commissars of Zhukov's three battle groups are identified: S. I. Mel'nikov, Northern Group; V. K. Tsybenko, Southern Group; G. P. Slesarev, Central Group. The air force commissar was F. F. Vernov. Starodubtsev, however, says nothing of the role played by Mekhlis, who was present and who undoubtedly exerted great influence on Party political activity.

The leadership of the Soviet forces at Khalkhin Gol also gives rise to some troublesome questions, as do the idiosyncrasies in the chain of command. It remains a puzzle why, on 5 June 1939, KomDiv G. K. Zhukov, unknown and untested, without combat experience against the Japanese or advisory duty in Spain, was sent from the Belorussian Military District to command the 57th Rifle Corps, the main Soviet force then engaged with the Japanese. The role played by Shtern, who had survived Marshal Blyukher to become the hero at Lake Khasan the year before, is also not clear. Shtern had a full staff of his own and in the beginning was two ranks senior to Zhukov; it seems that he should have been the latter's immediate superior. Soviet sources, however, assert that Shtern commanded a "front group" (as unusual a formation designation as Zhukov's renamed 1st Army Group) and coordinated the activities of Soviet and Mongolian forces.

This strange chain of command lends force to the hints of Army General A. T. Stuchenko, in his 1968 book *Zavidnaia nasha sud'ba*, that Zhukov had direct contact with Stalin and ran his own show, and that Shtern, aware of this, kept out of Zhukov's way. Such an arrangement would have been quite in character for Stalin, from what we know of his devious ways. The fact that at the beginning of the campaign, before Zhukov's arrival, the 57th Rifle Corps received its orders directly from Moscow reinforces this interpretation.

To gain a clearer picture of the Soviet command at Khalkhin Gol we must refer to five directives of the Ministry of Defense published in the August 1979 issue of *Voenno istoricheskii zhurnal* and reprinted in *Pobeda na reke Khalkhin Gol*. Particularly interesting is Directive No. 2, in which not only the chief of staff, Shaposhnikov, but also the watchdogs Shchadenko and Mekhlis were assigned to Khalkhin Gol.

One explanation for the reluctance of Soviet writers to publish in-depth studies may be the thinking that, unlike the Great Patriotic War, the campaigns of 1938-40 were relatively secondary and local in character,* and the results, especially in the war against Finland, were far from satisfactory. Even more importantly, although the Soviets could easily marshal facts and documents demonstrating Hitler's unquestionable aggression against the USSR, they have had a much more difficult case to prove against the Japanese "imperialists" and almost no case against the Finns. An additional factor is the nature of present relations between the USSR and its former enemies—friendly with Finland and far from openly hostile with Japan.

The Russian-language entries which follow were published within the Soviet Union or the MPR during the period since Khalkhin Gol in 1939.† Unless otherwise noted, the place of publication is Moscow.

Afanas'ev, G. F. *Na strazhe rubezhei Rodiny*. Alma Ata: Kazgosizdat, 1963.
Akad'ev, A. "K voprosu o planakh napadeniia militaristskoi Iaponii na SSSR v 1939-1941 gg.," *Voenno istoricheskii zhurnal*, no. 9 (1976), pp. 93-97.
Antipov, L. *Groznye ataki*. Voenizdat, 1939.
Artilleriia iaponskikh armii. Voenizdat, 1939.
Arzhanov, F. M. *Bor'ba Kommunisticheskoi partii za obespechenie bezopasnosti dal'nevostochnykh granits Sovetskogo Soiuza (1932–avgust 1945)*. 1960.
Beliaev, Iu., and V. Moskvitin. *Za Rodinu!* Kursk: Oblizdat, 1939.
Boevoi put' Sovetskikh vooruzhennikh sil. Voenizdat, 1953, 1960.
Boevye deistviia aviatsii v Mongol'skoi Narodnoi Respublike. 1940.
Bogdanov, A. A., and V. T. Popov. *Zolotye zvezdy dal'nevostochnykh pogranichnikov*. Khabarovsk: Kn. izd., 1968.
Boi u Khalkhin-Gola: Partiino-politicheskaia rabota v boevoi obstanovke: kniga napisana uchastnikami boev. Voenizdat, 1940.
Borisenko, G. "V stepiakh Mongolii," *Voennyi vestnik*, no. 8 (1969).
Budennyi, Marshal S. M. "Zdravstvui, Mongoliia!," *Kultura i zhizn'*, no. 7 (1961), pp. 20-21.
Chimid, Ch. "Nemerknushchaia slava," *Kommunist*, no. 14 (1979).
Choibalsan, Kh. *Izbrannye stat'i i rechi*. 1961.
Dagvadorzh, P. "Druzhba, skeplennaia krov'iu," *Voennyi vestnik*, no. 9 (1969).
Dal'nevostochniki. Khabarovsk: Kn. izd., 1964, 1966.
Deistviia 1-i armgruppy v Khalkhin Gol'skoi operatsii (mai-sentiabr' 1939 g.). 1940.

*Speaking to Western reporters in Berlin on 9 June 1945, Marshal Zhukov called the Khalkhin Gol campaign "only an operation on a local scale. The battle was of interest only as a tactical battle." Limiting his comments to the Russians' 20 August offensive, Zhukov said that the fighting "lasted ten days and ended in the complete rout of the Japanese Sixth Army...." *New York Times*, 11 June 1945. ADC

† We gratefully acknowledge the bibliographical assistance rendered by John Erickson of the University of Edinburgh and John J. Stephan of the University of Hawaii, and technical help by Neil M. Heyman and Leland A. Fetzer of San Diego State University. ADC

Dokumenty i materialy po voprosam bor'by s voennymi prestupnikami i podzhiga-telyami voiny. Military-Juridical Academy, 1949.

Dragunskii, Col. Gen. D. A. *Gody v brone.* Voenizdat, 1972. 374p.

Dubinskii, A. M. *Osvoboditel'naia missiia Sovetskogo Soiuza na Dal'nem Vostoke.* Mysl', 1966.

Eidus, Kh. T. *Iaponiia ot pervoi do vtoroi mirovoi voiny.* Gospolitizdat, 1946. 245p.

Evstigneev, Maj. Gen. V. N. *Razgrom imperialisticheskoi Iaponii na Dal'nem Vostoke v 1945 godu.* Pravda, 1951. 31p.

Ezhakov, V. "Na Khalkhin-Gole," *Voennyi vestnik,* no. 8 (1969).

———. "Slavnaia pobeda na Khalkhin-Gole," *Voenno istoricheskii zhurnal,* no. 8 (1979), pp. 62-67.

Fediuninskii, Gen. I. I. "V boiakh na Khalkhin-Gole," *Voenno istoricheskii zhurnal,* no. 8 (1975), pp. 72-78.

Geroi Khalkhin-gola. Perm': Kn. izd., 1966.

Gol'dman, Iu. "Komissar s Khalkhin-Gola," *Don,* no. 6 (1976).

Gol'man, M. I., and G. I. Slesarchuk. *Sovetsko-Mongol'skie otnosheniia 1921-1956.* Nauka, 1960.

"Gritsvets, Sergei Ivanovich," *Liudi bessmertnogo podviga,* 1, pp. 246-53.

Gubel'man, M. I. (pseud.) (Iaroslavskii, E.). *Kak iaponskikh interventov vyghali s Dal'nego Vostoka.* Minsk, 1939 (in Belorussian).

Ianguzov, Z. Sh. *Boevye traditsii Dal'nevostochnikov.* Blagoveshchensk: Khabar. kn. izd., 1967.

———. *Komissary nashenskogo kraia.* Blagoveshchensk: Khabar. kn. izd., 1975.

———. *Osobaia Krasnoznamennaia Dal'nevostochnaia armiia na strazhe mira i bezopastnosti SSSR (1929-1938 gg.).* Blagoveshchensk: Khabar. kn. izd., 1970.

Ignat'ev, O., and A. Krivel'. "Tam, na Khalkhin-Gole," *Pravda,* 15 and 19 Jan. 1979.

Isaev, S. "Meropriiatiia KPSS po ukrepleniiu Dal'nevostochnykh rubezhei v 1931-1941 gg.," *Voenno istoricheskii zhurnal,* no. 9 (1981), pp. 64-69.

Istoriia Mongol'skoi Narodnoi Respubliki. Nauka, 1967.

Istoriia Velikoi Otechestvennoi voiny Sovetskogo Soiuza 1941-1945. Voenizdat, 1960. Vol. 1.

Istoriia vtoroi mirovoi voiny, 1939-1945. Voenizdat, 1973-74.

Kak my bili iaponskikh samuraev. Novosibirsk: Novosibgiz., 1939.

Kelanov, V. N. *Sovetskaia artilleriia v boiakh i operatsiiakh protiv iaponskikh voisk v raione Khalkhin-Gola.* Voenizdat, 1953.

"Khalkhin-Gol." Entries in *Bol'shaia sovetskaia entsiklopediia* (Sov. Encycl., 1957), 46, pp. 43-44; *Malaia sovetskaia entsiklopediia* (Voenizdat, 1980), 8, pp. 353-54; *Sovetskaia voennaia entsiklopediia* (Sov. Encycl., 1978), 10, pp. 10-11; *Ukrains'ka radians'ka entsiklopediia* (Kiev: Ukraine Academy of Sciences, 1964), 15, pp. 418-19.

Kiliaeva, V. "Pamiat' Khalkhin-Gola," *Sovetskaia Rossiia,* 12 May 1979.

Klevtsov, V. G. "Podvig dvukh druzhestvennykh armii na Khalkhin-Gole," *Voprosy istorii,* no. 9 (Sept. 1969), pp. 128-41.

Kolesnikov, M. "Khalkhin-Gol'skaia byl'," *Znamia,* no. 8 (1969).

Krasnoriuchenko, M. "Nad Mongoliei," *Raduga,* no. 9 (1969).

Krasnoznamennyi dal'nevostochnyi. Voenizdat, 1971.

Kuchkov, A. F. "Inzhenernoe obespechenie boevykh deistvii 57-i strelkovoi divizii na r. Khalkhin-Gol v 1939," *Sovetskie inzhenernye voiska v 1918-1940 gg.,* pp. 129-42.

Kulagin, V., and N. Iakovlev. *Podvig osoboi dal'nevostochnoi.* Mol. gvardiia, 1970.
Kutakov, L. N. *Istoriia sovetsko-iaponskikh diplomaticheskikh otnoshenii.* Izd-vo instituta mezhdunarodnykh otnoshenii, 1962.
Kuz'min, Col. N. F. *Na strazhe mirnogo truda 1921-1940 gg.* Voenizdat, 1959.
Kuznetsov, I. I. "Geroi Khalkhin-Gola," *Istoriia SSSR,* no. 1 (Jan.-Feb. 1968).
———. "Geroi Mongol'skoi Narodnoi Respubliki-uchastiki boev na Khalkhin-Gole," *Voenno istoricheskii zhurnal,* no. 8 (1977), pp. 69-73.
———. *Podvigi geroev Khalkhin-Gola.* Ulan Ude: Buriat kn. izd., 1969.
———. "Reka ispytaniia," *Baikal,* no. 4 (1969).
———. "U reke Khalkhin-Gol," *Voenno istoricheskii zhurnal,* no. 7 (1964), pp. 126-28.
Leonov, Marshal A. "Druzhba, skeplennaia v boiakh," *Kommunist vooruzhennykh sil,* no. 15 (1969).
Lin'kov, G. *Vynuzhdennye priznaniia samuraev.* Gosudarstvennoe voennoe izdatel'stvo Narkomata oborony Soiuza SSR, 1939.
Lkhagvasuren, Col. Gen. Zh. "Istoricheskaia pobeda na reke Khalkhin-Gol," *Sovrem. Mongoliia,* no. 8 (1959), pp. 10-13.
———. "40 let narodnykh voisk MNR," *Sovrem. Mongoliia,* No. 3 (1961), pp. 3-6.
———. "40 let sovmestnoi raboty," *Voenno istoricheskii zhurnal,* no. 3 (1974), pp. 63-66.
———. "Zakon druzhby—vernost'," *Krasnaia zvezda,* 28 Aug. 1959.
Malinin, I. Z. *Stranitsa boevoi slavy.* Voenizdat, 1969.
Matveev, A. "Taktika razvivalas' v boiakh," *Aviatsiia i kosmonavtika,* no. 6 (1972).
Mezhdunarodnye otnosheniia na Dal'nem Vostoke 1870-1945. Gospolitizdat, 1951. Vol. 2 (Mysl', 1973).
Mints, I. I. "Iz istorii bor'by Krasnoi Armii protiv iaponskikh zakhvatchikov na Khalkhin-Gole v 1939 g.," *Bol'shevik,* no. 15 (1945).
Mongols'kaia Narodnaia Respublika: spravochnik. Politizdat, 1976.
Netsvetailo. "Boi v raione reki Khalkhin-Gol," *Sovrem. Mongoliia,* no. 4 (1940), p. 12.
Novikov, M. V. *Pobeda na Khalkhin-Gole.* Politizdat, 1971.
———. "V nebe Khalkhin-Gola," *Voprosy istorii,* no. 3 (1974), pp. 201-4.
Obukhov, V. *Organizatsiia oborony v iaponskoi armii: Polevoi put'.* Voen. akad. mekh. i motor. Kr. Armii. im Stalina, 1940.
Odintsov, V., and V. Ovsianikov. "Nekotorye osobennosti tylvogo obespecheniia sovetsko-mongol'skikh voisk v boaikh na Khalkhin-Gole," *Voenno istoricheskii zhurnal,* no. 9 (1980), pp. 55-60.
"Organy upravleniia sovetskimi voiskami v period deistvii na Khalkhin-Gole (1939 g.)," *Voenno istoricheskii zhurnal,* no. 8 (1979), pp. 47-49.
Os'kin, G. I. *Sovetskaia armiia: detishche sovetskogo naroda.* DOSAAF, 1963.
Partiino-izdannykh v boevoi obstanovke na Khalkhin-Gole. 1940.
Partiino-politicheskaia rabota v boevoi obstanovke: sbornik dokumentov izdannykh v boevoi obstanovke na Khalkhin-Gole. 1940.
Plotnikov, G. K. *Mongol'skaia narodnaia armiia.* Voenizdat, 1971. 104p.
Pobeda na reke Khalkhin-Gol. Nauka, 1981.
Pobratimy Khalkhin-Gola, 1939-1969. Pravda, 1969, 1979.
Pogranichnye voiska SSSR, 1929-1938: sbornik dokumentov i materialov. Nauka, 1972.
Polevoi ustav iaponskoi armii. Voenizdat, 1939.
Popov, A. A. *Operatsiia na reke Khalkhin-Gol: mai-sentiabr' 1939 g.* 1943.

Prigovor Tokiiskogo Mezhdunarodnogo Tribunala. Gospolitizdat, 1950.

Raginskii, M. Iu., and S. Ia. Rozenblit. *Mezhdunarodnyi protsess glavnykh iaponskikh voennykh prestupnikov.* 1950.

Rumiantsev, N. M. *Geroi Khalkhin-Gola.* Saratov: Privolzh. kn. izd., 1964; 2nd ed., 1968.

Samurai proschitalis'. Gospolitizdat, 1939.

Savichev, T. "V boiakh na reke Khalkhin-Gol," *Voenno istoricheskii zhurnal,* no. 9 (1969), pp. 74-76.

Sbornik dokumentov o boevoi obstanovke na Khalkin-Gole. 1940.

Sevost'ianov, G. N. *Politika velikikh derzhav na Dal'nem Vostoke nakanune vtoroi mirovoi voiny.* Sotsekgiz, 1961.

———. "Sovetskii Soiuz v bor'be za bezopasnost' na Dal'nem Vostoke: iz istorii sovetsko-iaponskikh otnoshenii 1939-1941 gg.," *Novaia i noveishaia istoriia,* no. 3 (1977).

———. "Voennoe i diplomaticheskoe porazhenie Iaponii v period sobytii u reki Khalkhin-Gol," *Voprosy istorii,* no. 8 (1957), pp. 63-85.

Shelakhov, Lt. Gen. G., and G. Plotnikov. "Razgrom iaponskikh zakhvatchikov na reke Khalkhin-Gol," *Voenno istoricheskii zhurnal,* no. 8 (1969), pp. 31-41.

Shingarev, S. I. *Pod nami Khalkhin-Gol.* Voenizdat, 1979.

Shishkin, Col. S. N. *Boevye deistviia Krasnoi Armii u reki Khalkhin-Gol v 1939 g.* Voenizdat, 1946.

———. *Khalkhin-Gol.* Voenizdat, 1954. See translation in JRD [965], *JSM* 11, part 3/C.

———. *Razgrom iapono-man'chzhurskikh voisk u r. Khalkhin-Gol v 1939: kratkii operativno-takticheskii ocherk.* Voenizdat, 1945.

Simonov, K. M. *Daleko na Vostoke.* Sov. pisatel', 1969.

———. *Ot Khalkhin-Gola do Berlina.* DOSAAF, 1973.

Skobarikhin, V. "Taran nad Khalkhin-Golom," *Sovetskii patriot,* 24 Oct. 1972.

Smirnov, B. *Ot Madrida do Khalkhin-gola; zapiski letchika.* Kuibyshev, Kn. izd., 1976.

"Smushkevich, Iakov Vladimirovich," *Liudi bessmertnogo podviga,* 2, pp. 324-33.

Sodnomdarzha, Maj. Gen. Ts. "Boevoe sodruzhestvo dvukh bratskikh armii," *Voenno istoricheskii zhurnal,* no. 6 (1973), pp. 40-46.

Sokolov, B. D. "Voiska sviazi Sovetskoi Armii v boiakh u reki Khalkhin-Gol," *Trudy voennoi akademii sviazi im S. M. Budennogo,* vol. 65 (1958).

Sovetskie inzhenernye voiska v 1918-1940 gg. Voenizdat, 1959.

Sovetsko-mongol'skie otnosheniia 1921-1974: dokumenty i materialy. Mezhdunarodnye otnosheniia, 1975. Vol. 1.

Sozvezdie polkovodtsev. Blagoveshchensk: Khabar. kn. izd., 1972.

Staritsina, P. P. *Marshal Choibalsan.* Voenizdat, 1940.

———. "Marshal Choibalsan," *Kratkie soobshcheniia instituta vostokovedeniia,* no. 6 (1952).

Starodubtsev, Col. V. "Partiino-politicheskaia rabota v period boevykh deistvii na Khalkhin-Gole," *Voenno istoricheskii zhurnal,* no. 9 (1980), pp. 61-64.

Stuchenko, Gen. A. T. *Zavidnaia nasha sud'ba.* Voenizdat, 1968.

Suntsov, N. P. "Urok istorii," *Dal'nii vostok,* no. 9 (1969), pp. 126-31.

Trugov, P. I. *Opyta deistvii abtv na P. Khalkhin-Gol: mai-sentiabr' 1939.* Khabarovsk, 1940.

Tsedenbal, Iu. *Istoricheskii put' razvitiia sotsialistichekoi Mongolii.* Ulan Bator, 1976.

————. *Izbranya stat'i i rechi.* 1962.
Tsog, B. "Bezymiannykh vysot ne byvaet," *Komsomol'skaia pravda*, 15 Feb. 1979.
Tumendenberel, Ch. "Pobeda internatsional'noi druzhby," *Partiinaia zhizn'*, no. 18 (1969).
V plameni i slave: ocherki istorii Sibirskogo voennoga okruga. Novosibirsk: Zap. Sib. kn. izd., 1969.
Vasilevskii, Marshal A. M. *Delo vsei zhizni.* Politizdat, 1974.
Voronov, Chief Marshal N. N. *Na sluzhbe voennoi.* Voenizdat, 1963.
Vorotnikov, M. F. *Zapiski ad'iutanta.* Novosibirsk: Kn. izd., 1970.
Vorozheikin, Maj. Gen. A. V. *Istrebiteli.* Voenizdat, 1960.
Vstrechnyi boi; nastuplenii; oborona. Voenizdat, 1939.
Zabaikal'skii voennyi okrug. Irkutsk: Vos.-Sib. kn. izd., 1972.
Zakharov, Marshal M. V. "Nakanune vtoroi mirovoi voiny (mai 1938–sentiabr' 1939)," *Novaia i noveshaia istoriia*, no. 5 (1970), pp. 3-27.
Zdes' Rossii rubezh. Blagoveshchensk: Khabar. kn. izd., 1977.
Zhukov, E. *Istoriia Iaponii.* Sotsekgiz, 1939.
Zhukov, Marshal G. K. *Vospominaniia i razmyshleniia.* Novosti (APN), 1969; rev. ed., 1970.
Zhuravskii, A. "Boi u Khalkhin-Gola," *Tankist*, no. 2 (1958).
Zil'manovich, D. Ia. *Na orbita bol'shoi zhizni: dokumental'no-memuarnoe povestvovanie o dvazhdy Geroe Sovetskogo Soiuza Ia. V. Smushkeviche.* Vil'nius: Mintis, 1971. 285p.
"Znamenatel'naia data v istorii mongolo-sovetskoi druzhby," *Sovrem. Mongoliia*, no. 9 (1959), pp. 13-15.

Index of Names

Library of Congress Cataloging in Publication Data

Coox, Alvin D.
 Nomonhan: Japan against Russia, 1939.

 Bibliography: p.
 Includes index.
 1. Khalkhin Gol, Battle of, 1939.   1. Title
DS798.9.H33C66   1985   952.03'3   81-85447
ISBN 0-8047-1160-7 (cl: two volume set)
ISBN 0-8047-1835-0 (pbk: two volumes as one)